DOCUMENTS
ON
AMERICAN FOREIGN RELATIONS

1941–1942

THE World Peace Foundation is a non-profit organization which was founded in 1910 by Edwin Ginn, the educational publisher, for the purpose of promoting peace, justice and good-will among nations. For many years the Foundation has sought to increase public understanding of international problems by an objective presentation of the facts of international relations. This purpose is accomplished principally through its publications and by the maintenance of a Reference Service which furnishes on request information on current international problems. Recently increased attention has been focused on American foreign relations by study groups organized for the consideration of actual problems of policy.

DOCUMENTS
ON
AMERICAN FOREIGN
RELATIONS

VOL. IV
JULY 1941—JUNE 1942

EDITED BY

LELAND M. GOODRICH
Acting Director, World Peace Foundation

WITH THE COLLABORATION OF

S. SHEPARD JONES

AND

DENYS P. MYERS

32304

WORLD PEACE FOUNDATION
BOSTON
1942

Copyright, 1942, by
World Peace Foundation

FOREWORD

The war makes many enterprises cooperative which heretofore have been assigned to specific individuals. This volume represents the collaboration of a number of people.

Before going to the Department of State early in the summer both Dr. S. Shepard Jones, as Director of the World Peace Foundation, and Denys P. Myers, as Director of Research, had gathered a great deal of material for this volume, and had begun its editing. However, the principal burden of completing the collection of documents and shaping it for publication has been carried on by Leland M. Goodrich, Associate Professor of Political Science in Brown University and recently appointed Acting Director of the Foundation, who takes responsibility for the final form of the volume.

Henry M. Wriston,
Chairman, Publications Committee

November 23, 1942

CONTENTS

CONTENTS   xxiii

CONTENTS

CONTENTS

CONTENTS XXXV

CONTENTS

CONTENTS

INTRODUCTION

The year ending June 30, 1942 saw the United States become involved for a third time in a world war, participation in which we had sought to avoid. In each case we had taken refuge behind the shield of neutrality, and in each case we discovered this shield to be an inadequate instrument for the protection of our national interests. Each time it required a shorter period of time for us to make this discovery.

The outbreak of war between Great Britain and France in 1793 was the occasion for Washington's Proclamation of Neutrality of April 22, 1793 which formally initiated the American policy of neutrality toward European conflicts and represented an important contribution to the development of the international law of neutrality. After a period of nearly twenty years of almost constant conflict, the United States entered the war. Violation of American neutral rights was an important factor in bringing us into the struggle. Over a hundred years later, the United States again sought to pursue a course of neutrality when faced with a general war originating in Europe and encompassing the major part of the world outside of the Western Hemisphere. Again, the defense of American interests proved in practice to be incompatible with continued neutrality. Not only the violation of our rights as a neutral but the threat to our security implied in German domination of Europe were important factors in causing American public opinion to swing to the support of our entrance into the conflict.

When war again broke out in Europe in September 1939, following the outbreak of undeclared war in the Far East, the American people were in no mood for participation in another world conflict. The neutrality legislation of the period 1935–1937 had made clear the desire of the American people to keep out of war. The depression and recent events in Europe had deepened the disillusionment of the American people with the results of the last war. A war which we had entered with crusading zeal to make the world safe for democracy and to end all wars had seemed to many to have had quite opposite results. Democracy seemed less safe than ever and war in the years following 1931 ever more imminent. We were shocked by the excesses of the Japanese in China, the Italian Fascists in Ethiopia, and the Nazis in Germany and, after the outbreak of war, in the occupied countries of Europe, but with rather surprising facility we developed a moral callousness toward these acts of cruelty.

xlv

All in all, it is probably fair to say that when war broke out in Europe in 1939 the American people, because of their propaganda consciousness, their constant exposure to acts of cruelty and their nearness to the failures and evil consequences of the last war were more strongly resolved to avoid involvement in war than they had ever been before. And yet, within a period of a little over two and a quarter years — several months less than the period of our neutrality in World War I — the United States found itself an active belligerent. It is true of course that we were, in a sense, pushed off our increasingly precarious perch by the attack at Pearl Harbor, but from the point of view of political realism, Pearl Harbor was the natural consequence of the policy of effective aid to the victims of aggression and effective resistance to the aggressors in the carrying out of their programs of world domination, by measures short of war, which President Roosevelt had initiated and carried through with the consent of Congress and the American people. The steps in the development of this program are documented in this volume and in previous volumes of this series.

World War II is, to a greater degree than any previous war in history, both global and total. It is global in the sense that it has come to include within its scope practically all the land surface of the earth. It is total in the sense that the requirements of modern mechanized war and the methods of modern totalitarian regimes have made necessary the complete harnessing of the physical and moral resources of the people of a state for the purposes of national defense and the war effort. As the result of the total character of war, it becomes difficult in time of war or immediate threat to our security to differentiate between governmental acts that are primarily domestic in their effects and significance and those that bear primarily on our foreign relations. As the result of the global character of war, the breakdown of our foreign relations into geographic divisions becomes difficult and loses much of its value, and to omit consideration of certain matters which seem to be of primary concern to certain other countries becomes unrealistic. Finally, the close functional relation between war and national policy and the increasing recognition of the fact that decisions taken and arrangements worked out with a view to the winning of the war may largely determine the nature of the post-war order make it unrealistic to draw a hard and fast distinction between the war effort and those activities which are more directly related to normal peace-time relations with foreign countries.

Considerations such as these have dictated the inclusion in this volume of numerous documents which do not on their face appear to be related to American foreign relations. Documents explaining the broad outlines of American organization for war are included because of the light that they throw upon the requirements and practices of modern total war and because of their possible interest in connection with the development of techniques of post-war organization. A section has been devoted to India, especially the story of the Cripps mission, because of the importance to us, both from the point of view of the success of the war effort and the implementation of the principles of the Atlantic Charter, of a peaceful and forward-looking settlement of the Indian problem. Considerable space has been given to Lend-Lease operations and the development of the machinery of United Nations collaboration in the conduct of the war not only because of the importance that these things have from the point of view of national defense and the war effort but also because they point the way to methods and procedures of international cooperation in the post-war period. It is recognized, of course, that the case that has been made for the inclusion of certain documents could be made with equal semblance of validity for the inclusion of other documents that have been omitted. The only defense is that where the line of inclusion and exclusion is so vague and of necessity a matter of opinion, different views can be honestly held. Furthermore, in some instances, where perhaps if the matter were being considered without previous commitments it would be advisable to omit the document in question, it has seemed wise to include the document in order to complete or continue the documentation of a particular topic initiated in an earlier volume of the series.

Certain changes have been made in chapter headings and in the order of treatment of topics from the earlier volumes. It has seemed advisable to discard the earlier division of the volume into three Parts — *Policy, Relations with Foreign States* and *National Action.* The first is repetitious since the title of the first chapter is sufficiently explanatory and the second and third can be misleading and are not completely accurate. The entrance of the United States into war has made it advisable to change the titles of the chapters on *Neutrality* and *National Defense* to *From Neutrality to Belligerency* and *National Defense and the War Effort.* The introduction of a new chapter on *The United Nations* has also become necessary. In order to make the titles of the geographic chapters more clearly descriptive of the areas covered, even at the risk of departure from official usage, *The Far East* and *European Relations* (including the Near and Middle East) have been replaced as chapter headings by *Eastern Asia and the Pacific Area* and *Europe, Africa and Western Asia.* Certain changes have also been made in the order of chapters in order to present the material more logically. Furthermore, cross references have been extensively used to facilitate the use of the documents from different angles of approach.

The year July 1, 1941 to June 30, 1942, crowded with great events, was also productive of a correspondingly large body of documents bearing upon American foreign relations. In editing these documents, it has been necessary to make a choice between allowing the volume to assume somewhat larger page content than any of its predecessors and the omission of certain documents which would deprive the volume of the scope of its predecessors as well as discontinue the treatment of certain topics hitherto covered. It has been decided to make the first choice.

It is the hope of those who have been concerned with editing the material here presented that it will contribute not only to a better understanding of the way in which the United States came to war and the nature of the war effort, but also to the recognition of the fact that the United States is inescapably a part of the world and must assume its share of the responsibility in the building of a better world order.

Finally, speaking for Dr. Jones and Mr. Myers as well as myself, I wish to express a word of deep appreciation for the invaluable assistance of the staff of the World Peace Foundation, in particular to Miss Marie J. Carroll and Mrs. Ralph de Miranda for many hours of painstaking and thoughtful work in the preparation of this volume.

LELAND M. GOODRICH

November 23, 1942.

CHAPTER I

PRINCIPLES AND POLICY:
GENERAL STATEMENTS

(1) What Does the Future Hold? Address by the Acting Secretary of State (Welles) at the Norwegian Legation, Washington, July 22, 1941 [1]

We are met here today to join in the dedication of the new wing of the Norwegian Legation in Washington.

These ceremonies are surely symbolic of the hope and of the faith with which we meet.

Those of us who are citizens of the United States are taking part in these dedication ceremonies not only because of the welcome privilege which it affords us of rendering this tribute to our traditional friends, the heroic people of Norway, but also because we can thus best evidence our conviction that the Kingdom of Norway of the past, as we have known it, some day — and we trust that day will come soon — will once more be free and independent.

We here in the United States will always remember the superb courage with which the Norwegian people fought in the defense of their homes and of their liberties against the overwhelmingly superior strength of an invader who had treacherously taken them by surprise. We know how bravely they are still fighting with their allies on sea and land in many parts of the world.

We shall always remember the heroism of their Monarch and of their Crown Prince. And we have heard with emotion the words of that same Monarch when he said to his people only a few days ago, "Hold out. Don't lose courage. And be assured that Norway will once again be free and independent, provided that we all continue to do our duty and our utmost to reach our goal in the battle which is now being fought."

Those words seem to us to exemplify the soul of a people which will never admit defeat and which will never be cowed by alien domination.

But in a larger sense, these ceremonies constitute an act of faith in the ultimate victory of the forces of human liberty; in the triumph of civilization itself over the forces of barbarism.

[1] Department of State, *Bulletin*, V, p. 75.

I feel that there are joined with us in spirit here today, as silent witnesses, the peoples of all of the other countries which have been mercilessly overrun during these past two years. I know that they believe as we do that out of this holocaust into which the nations of the earth have been plunged by the criminal obsession of world conquest of one man and of the satellites who surround him, there can come no peace until the Hitlerite government of Germany has been finally and utterly destroyed.

For I am confident that the cause of liberty and of freedom will not go down to defeat. The determination and courage of free men and women everywhere must now be exercised to the full limit of endurance until their victory is won.

And yet, I do not doubt that millions are asking tonight — millions in England and in China — millions of enslaved peoples in Norway and in the other countries now temporarily occupied — millions in the countries which have not experienced war — yes, and millions in Germany and in Italy — are asking, What does the future hold for us after this struggle is over?

Does the end of the present carnage mean only a return to ruined homes; to the graves of slaughtered wives and children; to poverty and want; to social upheaval and economic chaos; to the same gray and empty years of confusion and bitterness, so barren in vision and in human accomplishment, which marked the decades after the termination of the last war?

It seems to me that those of us who are fortunate enough to be able to live as citizens of the free American Republics have our great responsibility in the framing of the answer to that question.

For we all of us now see clearly, if we did not before, that no matter how great our American capacity for defense may be, no matter how perfect our hemispheric system may become, our future welfare must inevitably be contingent upon the existence in the rest of the world of equally peace-minded and equally secure peoples who not only will not, but cannot, become a source of potential danger to us in the New World.

I feel it is not premature for me to suggest that the free governments of peace-loving nations everywhere should even now be considering and discussing the way in which they can best prepare for the better day which must come, when the present contest is ended in the victory of the forces of liberty and of human freedom and in the crushing defeat of those who are sacrificing mankind to their own lust for power and for loot.

At the end of the last war, a great President of the United States gave his life in the struggle to further the realization of the splendid vision which he had held up to the eyes of suffering humanity — the vision of an ordered world governed by law.

The League of Nations, as he conceived it, failed in part because of the blind selfishness of men here in the United States as well as in other parts of the world; it failed because of its utilization by certain powers primarily to advance their own political and commercial ambitions; but it failed chiefly because of the fact that it was forced to operate, by those who dominated its councils, as a means of maintaining the *status quo*. It was never enabled to operate as its chief spokesman had intended, as an elastic and impartial instrument in bringing about peaceful and equitable adjustments between nations as time and circumstance proved necessary.

Some adequate instrumentality must unquestionably be found to achieve such adjustments when the nations of the earth again undertake the task of restoring law and order to a disastrously shaken world.

But whatever the mechanism which may be devised, of two things I am unalterably convinced:

First, that the abolition of offensive armaments and the limitation and reduction of defensive armaments and of the tools which make the construction of such armaments possible, can only be undertaken through some rigid form of international supervision and control, and that without such practical and essential control no real disarmament can ever be achieved; and

Second, that no peace which may be made in the future would be valid or lasting unless it established fully and adequately the natural rights of all peoples to equal economic enjoyment. So long as any one people or any one government possesses a monopoly over natural resources or raw materials which are needed by all peoples, there can be no basis for a world order based on justice and on peace.

I cannot believe that people of good-will will not once more strive to realize the great ideal of an association of nations through which the freedom, the happiness, and the security of all peoples may be achieved.

That word, security, represents the end upon which the hearts of men and women everywhere today are set.

Whether it be security from bombing from the air, or from mass destruction; whether it be security from want, disease, and starvation; whether it be security in enjoying that inalienable right which every human being should possess of living out his life in peace and happiness, people throughout the length and breadth of the world are demanding security, and freedom from fear.

That is the objective before us all today — to try to find the means of bringing that to pass.

"Not in vain the distance beacons."

(2) *Statement of the Secretary of State (Hull), August 4, 1941* [1]

I think that no rational person needs any argument to convince him that during the weeks of my absence the most clinching demonstration has been given of what some of us for some years have insisted was being planned. That is, that there is a world movement of conquest by force, accompanied by methods of governing the conquered peoples that are rooted mainly in savagery and barbarism. That situation calls for ever-increasing preparations for our national defense and ever-increasing production of military supplies both for ourselves and for those who are resisting the would-be world conquerors. On these points there should be absolute unity among the American people, in the first place, and among the other free peoples who have not yet been conquered. With full effort and ever-increasing production and preparation for defense, whenever and wherever such defense is most effective, a successful resistance to the present world movement of invasion and destruction can be made and, in my judgment, undoubtedly will be made. I feel very strongly that with unity of purpose, maximum effort, and firm determination, the remaining free peoples of the world will win and that those who are at present the victims of the forces of barbarism can hope for the restoration of their human rights and liberties.

(3) *Radio Address by the Secretary of War (Stimson) to the Army, August 15, 1941* [2]
[Excerpt]

With the passage by Congress of a bill providing for the extension of the term of compulsory military service from 12 to 18 months, the Secretary of War, Henry L. Stimson, who had been Secretary of State from 1929–33, made a radio address to the soldiers of the Army to explain the need for the new liability to service. The first two parts of the address are given. Part three, dealing with "the vital part which you as the Army must be ready to play in that defense," is omitted.

SOLDIERS OF THE ARMY OF THE UNITED STATES:

On the request of the President, the Congress has now passed a bill which will extend the period of service for many of the men in the Army.

[1] *Ibid.*, p. 113. The statement was made by the Secretary of State at his press conference on the resumption of his duties following a month's leave.
[2] Release of War Department.

The members of the National Guard and the Officers Reserve Corps as well as the men inducted under the Selective Service Act,[1] who were all originally called for a year's training, under this bill may be retained in the Army for an additional period of not to exceed eighteen months.

I realize that this means sacrifice on your part and it is proper that I as head of the War Department should state to you the reasons why it has been found necessary.

An American Army is an intelligent Army. Its discipline is based upon cooperation. It is not an army hammered into efficiency merely by brute force. It does its work more efficiently if it knows the cause for which it is created and the reason for the sacrifices which it is asked to make.

. . . .

In my talk I shall try to describe to you briefly these points: *first*, the crisis which makes necessary America's present preparation for defense; *second*, the general principles of our national defense; and *third*, the vital part which you as the Army must be ready to play in that defense.

In the first place, the world is today facing a situation which is more dangerous to its general peace than any situation which has existed during all the years of recorded history. Three great and powerful nations, Germany, Italy, and Japan, each of them armed with the most modern and destructive weapons, have banded themselves together upon a scheme of conquest against their more peaceful neighbors.[2] Within the past seven years these three nations have successively attacked and conquered some sixteen other nations. Germany has conquered Austria, Czechoslovakia, Poland, Denmark, Norway, Holland, Belgium, Luxemburg, France, Yugoslavia, and Greece. Today she is seeking to conquer Russia. Italy has attacked Ethiopia, Albania, France, and Greece. Japan has attacked China and is now taking possession of French Indo-China.

Neither Germany, Italy, nor Japan believes in individual freedom within their own borders, nor do they believe in national independence among nations outside of their borders. Their avowed principles are the opposite of those principles of liberty and equality of rights along which the world has been continually progressing for many centuries past. They are seeking to turn back to the customs of the Dark Ages

[1] Jones and Myers, *Documents on American Foreign Relations, III, 1940–41,* p. 672 (hereinafter series cited as *Documents*, etc.).
[2] The Three-Power Pact, signed September 27, 1940, see *ibid.*, p. 304.

and they are enforcing upon the nations which have been unfortunate enough to fall under their power, systems of forced labor and subjection which substantially amount to a condition of semi-slavery.

It is hard for us to imagine the United States in such a condition of subjection. But two years ago such a contemplation would have been just as hard for the citizens of France. France had been the leader in the development of freedom in Europe ever since the French Revolution one hundred fifty years ago. Yet today France is a subject nation. German overlords pull the strings and French puppets dance. France is disarmed. France is policed by foreign secret agents. Free speech is a memory in France. French business has been taken under German direction. Frenchmen are told by foreign rulers when to go to bed and when to get up. French profits, French foodstuffs, French energy, are now going to build up the glory of the German Reich. Children will starve in France this winter and French peasants who reap good crops will live on a crust in order that the German army may be fed. France is a prison house, a thin shadow of a glorious but unprepared nation which failed to see the danger approaching it from across the Rhine. And these conditions of subjection which are now maintained in France are mild in comparison with the brutalities which are being visited upon Poland, Yugoslavia, and Russia.

Today these three Axis nations, Germany, Japan, and Italy, openly announce their intention of going further with their conquest of the world. Indeed they can hardly help themselves from going further. They have made themselves the economic slaves of the hideous system which they have established. For example, Germany with an original population of not more than seventy million is maintaining military, naval, and other armed forces of over eleven million men besides a huge civilian bureaucracy of secret police and other functionaries. Seventy-five per cent of her entire income is going into war, leaving only twenty-five per cent for all of the needs of her civilian population. She is carrying on her present conquest with the loot of past conquests and with the product of the labor of her enslaved nations. Such a system cannot remain stationary. Germany must obtain further loot by further conquests or else she will begin to slide backward into restlessness, revolt, and failure. And the presence today throughout the Western Hemisphere of German advance agents and Fifth Columnists shows only too clearly one direction in which German future efforts at conquest are likely to go.

Japan is in a similar situation in the Far East. She has an enormous and expensive army spread over Northern China. Today she is moving south for further conquests. Her union [1] with the two other Axis powers three years ago was avowedly aimed at us and our interests.

Our own hemisphere, thinly populated, rich beyond all other continents in natural resources, is an inevitable ultimate target for these marauder nations. Today Hitler holds under his domination in Europe nearly 160 million people in addition to the original 70 million of Germany itself. Adding Italy with over 40 million makes a total of over 270 million. If he succeeds in conquering Western Russia, he will have under his control 100 million more, or a total of over 370 million. The American Government which failed to take measures of protection against such a dire prospect for the future would be faithless indeed to the interests of its people.

In the second place, what are the general principles which govern our American national defense? The United States and the other twenty republics of this hemisphere have always believed in preserving their isolation as the foundation of their safety. We have had a hemisphere in which for over a century all of the governments have been republican in structure and also independent in fact. We believe in keeping up this system of independence and freedom. For that purpose the Monroe Doctrine has been the cornerstone of our foreign policy. We have recognized that the only safe way to keep America out of war was to keep war away from America. And sometimes we have found it necessary to fight in order to keep war away from our own homes and country.

With the passage of time and the invention of new methods and weapons of warfare this has become more and more difficult. The bombing airplane already has a range of several thousand miles. The development of the Fifth Column has an indefinitely longer range. Each of these hostile weapons may easily become an instrument for the invasion of this hemisphere.

When the full measure of this terrific crisis abroad burst upon us a year ago, our peace-loving country was defended by a one-ocean navy, a skeleton army, and a rudimentary air force. The navies and armies of all of the other twenty American Republics were negligible in size in comparison to the forces abroad. Our own army was smaller even than the armies of Holland or Belgium and we saw Holland and Belgium overthrown in a comparatively few days. Therefore, so far as our army and air force are concerned, we have been obliged to start practically at scratch.

[1] Anti-Comintern Pact, signed November 25, 1936, and renewed for 5-year period on November 25, 1941, see p. 199.

The past year has been spent by our Government in a steady effort to surround the United States with outposts and bastions from which it could be defended against attacks which appear so inevitable. We have commenced building a two-ocean navy, but the completion of that navy cannot be accomplished for several years. In the meanwhile we have been endeavoring with all the means in our power to stiffen the resistance of those nations which by fighting the Axis Powers were temporarily serving as a protection to us. The principal one of these nations has been Great Britain. The British fleet for many years has been protecting the security of the Atlantic while our own fleet has been in the Pacific. The continuance of this work by the British fleet depends upon the continuance of the safety and independence of the British Isles. Congress last winter enacted the Lease-Lend Act [1] chiefly for the purpose of bolstering up the sturdy resistance which Great Britain was making to the Axis Powers. Under this statute we have been able to furnish munitions and supplies to the British Isles and to harbor and repair the British fleet as well as the merchant marine which was carrying our munitions to Great Britain.

In addition to that, we have leased from Great Britain seven important Atlantic outposts to serve as bases to our defense against attacks from the direction of Europe. These bases have been in Newfoundland, in Bermuda, in the Bahamas, in Jamaica, in St. Lucia, in Trinidad, and in British Guiana. In all of these places we are establishing naval and air posts of defense. They are intended to help us keep the navies and air forces of aggressor nations far away from our shores. We are also establishing further outposts in the Atlantic at Greenland and Iceland, and a part of our Navy is patrolling the Atlantic from Greenland southward as an additional protection against hostile forces coming into our Atlantic waters.

If you take your maps, you can see how we have thus been establishing a protective line of defense running from the extreme north in Greenland to the shores of South America by which we are seeking to keep any aggressive nation from establishing air bases from which they could drop bombs upon the populous cities of our eastern seaboard.

In the Pacific we have reenforced our great naval base at Hawaii until we believe that it is now impregnable. We are also building air and naval bases in Alaska and in the Aleutian Islands to keep off attacks from the northwest where our own coast approaches to within fifty

[1] See *Documents, III, 1940–41*, p. 712–15.

miles of the Russian Siberian coast of Asia. The present attack of Germany on Russia, who has always been a peaceful neighbor of ours in the Pacific, now brings out into sharp prominence the importance of these last outposts. Japanese newspapers are already beginning to tell us the trouble we may expect to have in Alaska if Germany conquers Russia.

But the most dangerous avenue of attack against us lies in the south where are situated the friendly but almost unarmed nations of Central and South America. Germany has been pushing into North Africa and we have reason to believe that a major advance will be made by her into that continent. At Dakar, which is held by Vichy forces, now friendly with Germany, the great western bulge of the African coast narrows the South Atlantic Ocean until the distance from Dakar to the easternmost point of Brazil can be easily traversed either by air or sea. The German controlled press of Paris today is openly urging that Germany be invited by Vichy to come into Dakar. We also know that Germany and Japan with their Fifth Columnists and subversive agents have been very active in South and Central America. From our observation of what has happened in Europe, we have learned to recognize the symptoms which invariably forecast the coming of a new Axis attack. Today some of the most significant of those symptoms are occurring in South America. Any reader today of the American press can read of unrest and excitement in various South American republics which are being attributed by the governments of those republics to the machinations of foreign secret agents. If, by combining an air attack with a Fifth Column revolution, an Axis Power should succeed in making a lodgment upon the coast of South America, we should have a real task indeed; — for it would not be difficult for an enemy lodged there to get within easy bombing distance of the Panama Canal.

From this analysis of our defense you can see that what we have done has not only been absolutely essential to protect us from an ever-approaching and developing danger but that our purpose has been purely defensive. We have not been seeking any wild adventures in foreign wars; we have not been planning any expeditionary forces for the benefit of other nations. We have been simply seeking to make secure our own country and to protect it from a danger that is so real and rapidly growing that a government which did not take such steps would have been faithless to its trust.

·   ·   ·   ·   ·   ·   ·

(4) "Atlantic Charter." Message of the President (Roosevelt) to the Congress, August 21, 1941 [1]

To THE CONGRESS OF THE UNITED STATES:

Over a week ago I held several important conferences at sea with the British Prime Minister. Because of the factor of safety to British, Canadian and American ships and their personnel no prior announcement of these meetings could properly be made.

At the close, a public statement [2] by the Prime Minister and the President was made. I quote it for the information of the Congress and for the record:

"The President of the United States and the Prime Minister, Mr. Churchill, representing His Majesty's Government in the United Kingdom, have met at sea.

"They have been accompanied by officials of their two Governments, including high-ranking officers of their Military, Naval, and Air Services.

"The whole problem of the supply of munitions of war, as provided by the Lease-Lend Act, for the armed forces of the United States and for those countries actively engaged in resisting aggression has been further examined.

"Lord Beaverbrook, the Minister of Supply of the British Government, has joined in these conferences. He is going to proceed to Washington to discuss further details with appropriate officials of the United States Government. These conferences will also cover the supply problems of the Soviet Union.

"The President and the Prime Minister have had several conferences. They have considered the dangers to world civilization arising from the policies of military domination by conquest upon which the Hitlerite government of Germany and other governments associated therewith have embarked, and have made clear the stress which their countries are respectively taking for their safety in the face of these dangers.

[1] From the Office of the Secretary to the President; House Doc. No. 358, 77th Cong., 1st sess.

[2] This statement was subsequently referred to as the "Atlantic Charter." It was made public August 14, 1941. See Department of State, *Bulletin*, V, p. 125. *Development of United States Foreign Policy. Addresses and Messages of Franklin D. Roosevelt Compiled from Official Sources, Intended to Present the Chronological Development of the Foreign Policy of the United States from the Announcement of the Good Neighbor Policy in 1933, Including the War Declarations.* Washington, Government Printing Office, 1942. Senate Doc. No. 188, 77th Cong., 2d sess., p. 112.

The text without the preamble was issued in the United Kingdom as Miscellaneous No. 3 (1941), Cmd. 6321, entitled *Joint Declaration by the President of the United States of America and Mr. Winston Churchill, representing His Majesty's Government in the United Kingdom, known as the Atlantic Charter, August 14, 1941.*

For Mr. Churchill's statement on the "Atlantic Charter," see his broadcast of August 24, 1941, p. 210 below.

"They have agreed upon the following joint declaration:

"Joint declaration of the President of the United States of America and the Prime Minister, Mr. Churchill, representing His Majesty's Government in the United Kingdom, being met together, deem it right to make known certain common principles in the national policies of their respective countries on which they base their hopes for a better future for the world.

"First, their countries seek no aggrandizement, territorial or other;

"Second, they desire to see no territorial changes that do not accord with the freely expressed wishes of the peoples concerned;

"Third, they respect the right of all peoples to choose the form of government under which they will live; and they wish to see sovereign rights and self-government restored to those who have been forcibly deprived of them;

"Fourth, they will endeavor, with due respect for their existing obligations, to further the enjoyment by all States, great or small, victor or vanquished, of access, on equal terms, to the trade and to the raw materials of the world which are needed for their economic prosperity;

"Fifth, they desire to bring about the fullest collaboration between all nations in the economic field with the object of securing, for all, improved labor standards, economic advancement, and social security;

"Sixth, after the final destruction of the Nazi tyranny, they hope to see established a peace which will afford to all nations the means of dwelling in safety within their own boundaries, and which will afford assurance that all the men in all the lands may live out their lives in freedom from fear and want;

"Seventh, such a peace should enable all men to traverse the high seas and oceans without hindrance;

"Eighth, they believe that all of the nations of the world, for realistic as well as spiritual reasons, must come to the abandonment of the use of force. Since no future peace can be maintained if land, sea, or air armaments continue to be employed by nations which threaten, or may threaten, aggression outside of their frontiers, they believe, pending the establishment of a wider and permanent system of general security, that the disarmament of such nations is essential. They will likewise aid and encourage all other practicable measures which will lighten for peace-loving peoples the crushing burden of armaments.

"(Signed) FRANKLIN D. ROOSEVELT
"(Signed) WINSTON S. CHURCHILL"

The Congress and the President having heretofore determined through the Lend-Lease Act on the national policy of American aid to the democracies which East and West are waging war against dictatorships, the military and naval conversations at these meetings made clear gains in furthering the effectiveness of this aid.

Furthermore, the Prime Minister and I are arranging for conferences with the Soviet Union to aid it in its defense against the attack made by the principal aggressor of the modern world — Germany.

Finally, the declaration of principles at this time presents a goal which is worth while for our type of civilization to seek. It is so clear cut that it is difficult to oppose in any major particular without automatically admitting a willingness to accept compromise with Nazism; or to agree to a world peace which would give to Nazism domination over large numbers of conquered nations. Inevitably such a peace would be a gift to Nazism to take breath — armed breath — for a second war to extend the control over Europe and Asia to the American Hemisphere itself.

It is perhaps unnecessary for me to call attention once more to the utter lack of validity of the spoken or written word of the Nazi government.

It is also unnecessary for me to point out that the declaration of principles includes of necessity the world need for freedom of religion and freedom of information. No society of the world organized under the announced principles could survive without these freedoms which are a part of the whole freedom for which we strive.

FRANKLIN D. ROOSEVELT

(a) Comment of the Secretary of State (Hull), August 14, 1941 [1]

It is a statement of basic principles and fundamental ideas and policies that are universal in their practical application. They have heretofore been generally accepted by all civilized nations and were being strongly supported until certain countries decided to launch a universal movement to destroy the whole structure of civilized relations between nations and to establish a system of rule over peoples who would be conquered, based, as I said some days ago, largely on barbarism and savagery.[2] That interruption is still going on.

As I said, they are the basic doctrines and policies that have received the support of all civilized nations and should continue to receive their support until they are completely restored throughout the world.

[1] Department of State, Bulletin, V, p. 126.   [2] Statement of August 4, see p. 4.

(5) *Labor Day Address by the President* *(Roosevelt)*, **September 1, 1941** [1]

On this day — this American holiday — we celebrate the rights of free laboring men and women.

The preservation of these rights is now vitally important not only to us who enjoy them but to the whole future of Christian civilization.

American labor now bears a tremendous responsibility in the winning of this most brutal, most terrible of all wars.

In our factories and shops and arsenals we are building weapons on a scale great in its magnitude. To all the battle fronts of the world these weapons are being dispatched, by day and by night, over the seas and through the air. And this Nation is now devising and developing new weapons of unprecedented power toward the maintenance of democracy.

Why are we doing this? Why are we determined to devote our entire industrial effort to the prosecution of a war which has not yet actually touched our own shores?

We are not a warlike people. We have never sought glory as a nation of warriors. We are not interested in aggression. We are not interested — as the dictators are — in looting. We do not covet one square inch of the territory of any other nation.

Our vast effort and the unity of purpose which inspires that effort are due solely to our recognition of the fact that our fundamental rights — including the rights of labor — are threatened by Hitler's violent attempt to rule the world.

These rights were established by our forefathers on the field of battle. They have been defended — at great cost but with great success — on the field of battle, here on our own soil and in foreign lands and on all the seas all over the world.

There has never been a moment in our history when Americans were not ready to stand up as free men and fight for their rights.

In times of national emergency one fact is brought home to us clearly and decisively — the fact that all of our rights are interdependent.

The right of freedom of worship would mean nothing without freedom of speech. And the rights of free labor as we know them today could not survive without the rights of free enterprise.

That is the indestructible bond that is between us — all of us Americans: Interdependence of interests, privileges, opportunities, responsibilities — interdependence of rights.

[1] Broadcast from the Franklin D. Roosevelt Library, Hyde Park, N. Y., September 1, 1941, Department of State, *Bulletin*, V, p. 177.

That is what unites us — men and women of all sections, of all races, of all faiths, of all occupations, of all political beliefs. That is why we have been able to defy and frustrate the enemies who believed they could divide us and conquer us from within.

These enemies all know that we possess a strong Navy, gaining in strength. They know that that Navy, as long as the Navies of the British Empire and the Netherlands and Norway and Russia exist, can together guarantee the freedom of the seas. These enemies know that if these other Navies are destroyed, the American Navy cannot now, or in the future, maintain the freedom of the seas against all the rest of the world.

These enemies know that our Army is increasing daily in its all-round strength.

These enemies know that today the chief American fighters in the battles now raging are those engaged in American industry, employers and employees alike.

These enemies know that the course of American production in the past year has shown enormous gains and that the product of these industries is moving to the battle fronts against Hitlerism in increasing volume each day.

But these enemies also know that our American effort is not yet enough, and that unless we step up the total of our production and more greatly safeguard it on its journeys to the battlefields, these enemies will take heart in pushing their attack in old fields and new.

I give solemn warning to those who think that Hitler has been blocked and halted that they are making a very dangerous assumption. When in any war your enemy seems to be making slower progress than he did the year before, that is the very moment to strike with redoubled force — to throw more energy into the job of defeating him — to end for all time the menace of world conquest and thereby end all talk or thought of any peace founded on a compromise with evil itself.

And we know that a free labor system is the very foundation of a functioning democracy. We know that one of the first acts of the Axis dictatorships has been to wipe out all the principles and standards which labor has been able to establish for its own preservation and advancement.

Trade unionism is a forbidden philosophy under these rule-or-ruin dictators. For trade unionism demands full freedom of expression and peaceful assembly. Trade unionism has helped to give to every one who toils the position of dignity which is his due.

The present position of labor in the United States as an interdependent unit in the life of the Nation has not come about by chance. It has been an evolutionary process of a healthy democracy at work.

Hitler has not worked that way. He will not, he cannot work that way. Just as he denies all rights to individuals, he must deny all rights to groups — of labor, of business, of learning, of the church. He has abolished trade unions as ruthlessly as he has persecuted religion.

No group of Americans has realized more clearly what Nazi domination of the world means than has organized labor — what it means to their standard of living, their freedom, their lives. No group has a greater stake in the defeat of Nazism, in the preservation of the fundamental freedoms, in the continuance of democracy throughout the world.

We have already achieved much; it is imperative that we achieve infinitely more.

The singlemindedness and sacrifice with which we jointly dedicate ourselves to the production of the weapons of freedom will determine in no small part the length of the ordeal through which humanity must pass.

We cannot hesitate, we cannot equivocate in the great task before us. The defense of America's freedom must take precedence over every private aim and over every private interest.

We are engaged on a grim and perilous task. Forces of insane violence have been let loose by Hitler upon this earth. We must do our full part in conquering them. For these forces may be unleashed on this Nation as we go about our business of protecting the proper interests of our country.

The task of defeating Hitler may be long and arduous. There are a few appeasers and Nazi sympathizers who say it cannot be done. They even ask me to negotiate with Hitler — to pray for crumbs from his victorious table. They do, in fact, ask me to become the modern Benedict Arnold and betray all I hold dear — my devotion to our freedom, to our churches, to our country. This course I have rejected — I reject it again.

Instead, I know that I speak the conscience and determination of the American people when I say that we shall do everything in our power to crush Hitler and his Nazi forces.

American workers and American farmers, American businessmen and American churchmen — all of us together — have the great responsibility and the great privilege of laboring to build a democratic world on enduring foundations.

May it be said on some future Labor Day by some future President of the United States that we did our work faithfully and well.

(6) *Attack on U. S. Destroyer* Greer. *World-Wide Broadcast by the President* (*Roosevelt*), *September 11, 1941* [1]

MY FELLOW AMERICANS:

The Navy Department of the United States has reported to me that on the morning of September 4 the United States destroyer *Greer*, proceeding in full daylight towards Iceland, had reached a point southeast of Greenland. She was carrying American mail to Iceland. She was flying the American flag. Her identity as an American ship was unmistakable.

She was then and there attacked by a submarine. Germany admits that it was a German submarine. The submarine deliberately fired a torpedo at the *Greer*, followed later by another torpedo attack. In spite of what Hitler's propaganda bureau has invented, and in spite of what any American obstructionist organization may prefer to believe, I tell you the blunt fact that the German submarine fired first upon this American destroyer without warning, and with deliberate design to sink her.

Our destroyer, at the time, was in waters which the Government of the United States had declared to be waters of self-defense — surrounding outposts of American protection in the Atlantic.

In the north, outposts have been established by us in Iceland, Greenland, Labrador, and Newfoundland. Through these waters there pass many ships of many flags. They bear food and other supplies to civilians; and they bear *matériel* of war, for which the people of the United States are spending billions of dollars, and which, by congressional action, they have declared to be essential for the defense of their own land.

The United States destroyer, when attacked, was proceeding on a legitimate mission.

If the destroyer was visible to the submarine when the torpedo was fired, then the attack was a deliberate attempt by the Nazis to sink a clearly identified American warship. On the other hand, if the submarine was beneath the surface and, with the aid of its listening devices, fired in the direction of the sound of the American destroyer without even taking the trouble to learn its identity — as the official German communiqué would indicate — then the attack was even more out-

---

[1] *Ibid.*, p. 193; Senate Doc. No. 188, 77th Cong., 2d sess., p. 114. The broadcast was originally scheduled for September 8 and was postponed until the 11th by reason of the death of Sara Delano Roosevelt, mother of the President, on September 7. The broadcast from the White House was made over all networks and was transmitted in 14 languages directly and by rebroadcast or recordings.

rageous. For it indicates a policy of indiscriminate violence against any vessel sailing the seas — belligerent or non-belligerent.

This was piracy — legally and morally. It was not the first nor the last act of piracy which the Nazi Government has committed against the American flag in this war. Attack has followed attack.

A few months ago an American-flag merchant ship, the *Robin Moor*,[1] was sunk by a Nazi submarine in the middle of the South Atlantic, under circumstances violating long-established international law and every principle of humanity. The passengers and the crew were forced into open boats hundreds of miles from land, in direct violation of international agreements signed by the Government of Germany. No apology, no allegation of mistake, no offer of reparations has come from the Nazi Government.

In July 1941, an American battleship in North American waters was followed by a submarine which for a long time sought to maneuver itself into a position of attack. The periscope of the submarine was clearly seen. No British or American submarines were within hundreds of miles of this spot at the time, so the nationality of the submarine is clear.

Five days ago a United States Navy ship on patrol picked up three survivors of an American-owned ship operating under the flag of our sister Republic of Panama — the S.S. *Sessa*. On August 17, she had been first torpedoed without warning and then shelled, near Greenland, while carrying civilian supplies to Iceland. It is feared that the other members of her crew have been drowned. In view of the established presence of German submarines in this vicinity, there can be no reasonable doubt as to the identity of the attacker.

Five days ago, another United States merchant ship, the *Steel Seafarer*, was sunk by a German aircraft in the Red Sea two hundred and twenty miles south of Suez. She was bound for an Egyptian port.

Four of the vessels sunk or attacked flew the American flag and were clearly identifiable. Two of these ships were warships of the American Navy. In the fifth case, the vessel sunk clearly carried the flag of Panama.

In the face of all this, we Americans are keeping our feet on the ground. Our type of democratic civilization has outgrown the thought of feeling compelled to fight some other nation by reason of any single piratical attack on one of our ships. We are not becoming hysterical or losing our sense of proportion. Therefore, what I am thinking and saying does not relate to any isolated episode.

[1] See *Documents III, 1940–41*, p. 417.

Instead, we Americans are taking a long-range point of view in regard to certain fundamentals and to a series of events on land and on sea which must be considered as a whole — as a part of a world pattern.

It would be unworthy of a great nation to exaggerate an isolated incident or to become inflamed by some one act of violence. But it would be inexcusable folly to minimize such incidents in the face of evidence which makes it clear that the incident is not isolated but part of a general plan.

The important truth is that these acts of international lawlessness are a manifestation of a design which has been made clear to the American people for a long time. It is the Nazi design to abolish the freedom of the seas and to acquire absolute control and domination of the seas for themselves.

For with control of the seas in their own hands, the way can become clear for their next step — domination of the United States and the Western Hemisphere by force. Under Nazi control of the seas, no merchant ship of the United States or of any other American republic would be free to carry on any peaceful commerce, except by the condescending grace of this foreign and tyrannical power. The Atlantic Ocean which has been, and which should always be, a free and friendly highway for us would then become a deadly menace to the commerce of the United States, to the coasts of the United States, and to the inland cities of the United States.

The Hitler Government, in defiance of the laws of the sea and of the recognized rights of all other nations, has presumed to declare, on paper, that great areas of the seas — even including a vast expanse lying in the Western Hemisphere — are to be closed, and that no ships may enter them for any purpose, except at peril of being sunk. Actually they are sinking ships at will and without warning in widely separated areas both within and far outside of these far-flung pretended zones.

This Nazi attempt to seize control of the oceans is but a counterpart of the Nazi plots now being carried on throughout the Western Hemisphere — all designed toward the same end. For Hitler's advance guards — not only his avowed agents but also his dupes among us — have sought to make ready for him footholds and bridgeheads in the New World, to be used as soon as he has gained control of the oceans.

His intrigues, his plots, his machinations, his sabotage in this New World are all known to the Government of the United States. Conspiracy has followed conspiracy.

Last year a plot to seize the Government of Uruguay was smashed by the prompt action of that country, which was supported in full by her American neighbors. A like plot was then hatching in Argentina, and that Government has carefully and wisely blocked it at every point. More recently, an endeavor was made to subvert the Government of Bolivia. Within the past few weeks the discovery was made of secret air-landing fields in Colombia, within easy range of the Panama Canal. I could multiply instances.

To be ultimately successful in world-mastery, Hitler knows that he must get control of the seas. He must first destroy the bridge of ships which we are building across the Atlantic, over which we shall continue to roll the implements of war to help destroy him and all his works in the end. He must wipe out our patrol on sea and in the air. He must silence the British Navy.

It must be explained again and again to people who like to think of the United States Navy as an invincible protection, that this can be true only if the British Navy survives. That is simple arithmetic.

For if the world outside the Americas falls under Axis domination, the shipbuilding facilities which the Axis Powers would then possess in all of Europe, in the British Isles, and in the Far East would be much greater than all the shipbuilding facilities and potentialities of all the Americas — not only greater but two or three times greater. Even if the United States threw all its resources into such a situation, seeking to double and even redouble the size of our Navy, the Axis Powers, in control of the rest of the world, would have the manpower and the physical resources to outbuild us several times over.

It is time for all Americans of all the Americas to stop being deluded by the romantic notion that the Americas can go on living happily and peacefully in a Nazi-dominated world.

Generation after generation, America has battled for the general policy of the freedom of the seas. That policy is a very simple one — but a basic, fundamental one. It means that no nation has the right to make the broad oceans of the world, at great distances from the actual theater of land war, unsafe for the commerce of others.

That has been our policy, proved time and time again, in all our history.

Our policy has applied from time immemorial — and still applies — not merely to the Atlantic but to the Pacific and to all other oceans as well.

Unrestricted submarine warfare in 1941 constitutes a defiance — an act of aggression — against that historic American policy.

It is now clear that Hitler has begun his campaign to control the seas by ruthless force and by wiping out every vestige of international law and humanity.

His intention has been made clear. The American people can have no further illusions about it.

No tender whisperings of appeasers that Hitler is not interested in the Western Hemisphere, no soporific lullabies that a wide ocean protects us from him can long have any effect on the hard-headed, far-sighted, and realistic American people.

Because of these episodes, because of the movements and operations of German warships, and because of the clear, repeated proof that the present Government of Germany has no respect for treaties or for international law, that it has no decent attitude toward neutral nations or human life — we Americans are now face to face not with abstract theories but with cruel, relentless facts.

This attack on the *Greer* was no localized military operation in the North Atlantic. This was no mere episode in a struggle between two nations. This was one determined step towards creating a permanent world system based on force, terror, and murder.

And I am sure that even now the Nazis are waiting to see whether the United States will by silence give them the green light to go ahead on this path of destruction.

The Nazi danger to our Western World has long ceased to be a mere possibility. The danger is here now — not only from a military enemy but from an enemy of all law, all liberty, all morality, all religion.

There has now come a time when you and I must see the cold, inexorable necessity of saying to these inhuman, unrestrained seekers of world-conquest and permanent world-domination by the sword — "You seek to throw our children and our children's children into your form of terrorism and slavery. You have now attacked our own safety. You shall go no further."

Normal practices of diplomacy — note-writing — are of no possible use in dealing with international outlaws who sink our ships and kill our citizens.

One peaceful nation after another has met disaster because each refused to look the Nazi danger squarely in the eye until it actually had them by the throat.

The United States will not make that fatal mistake.

No act of violence or intimidation will keep us from maintaining intact two bulwarks of defense: first, our line of supply of *matériel* to the enemies of Hitler; and second, the freedom of our shipping on the high seas.

No matter what it takes, no matter what it costs, we will keep open the line of legitimate commerce in these defensive waters.

We have sought no shooting war with Hitler. We do not seek it now. But neither do we want peace so much that we are willing to pay for it by permitting him to attack our naval and merchant ships while they are on legitimate business.

I assume that the German leaders are not deeply concerned by what we Americans say or publish about them. We cannot bring about the downfall of Nazism by the use of long-range invective.

But when you see a rattlesnake poised to strike, you do not wait until he has struck before you crush him.

These Nazi submarines and raiders are the rattlesnakes of the Atlantic. They are a menace to the free pathways of the high seas. They are a challenge to our sovereignty. They hammer at our most precious rights when they attack ships of the American flag — symbols of our independence, our freedom, our very life.

It is clear to all Americans that the time has come when the Americas themselves must now be defended. A continuation of attacks in our own waters, or in waters which could be used for further and greater attacks on us, will inevitably weaken American ability to repel Hitlerism.

Do not let us split hairs. Let us not ask ourselves whether the Americas should begin to defend themselves after the fifth attack, or the tenth attack, or the twentieth attack.

The time for active defense is now.

Do not let us split hairs. Let us not say — "We will only defend ourselves if the torpedo succeeds in getting home, or if the crew and the passengers are drowned."

This is the time for prevention of attack.

If submarines or raiders attack in distant waters, they can attack equally well within sight of our own shores. Their very presence in any waters which America deems vital to its defense constitutes an attack.

In the waters which we deem necessary for our defense, American naval vessels and American planes will no longer wait until Axis submarines lurking under the water, or Axis raiders on the surface of the sea, strike their deadly blow — first.

Upon our naval and air patrol — now operating in large number over a vast expanse of the Atlantic Ocean — falls the duty of maintaining the American policy of freedom of the seas — now. That means, very simply and clearly, that our patrolling vessels and planes will protect all merchant ships — not only American ships but ships of any flag — engaged in commerce in our defensive waters. They will protect them from submarines; they will protect them from surface raiders.

This situation is not new. The second President of the United States,

John Adams, ordered the United States Navy to clean out European privateers and European ships of war which were infesting the Caribbean and South American waters, destroying American commerce.

The third President of the United States, Thomas Jefferson, ordered the United States Navy to end the attacks being made upon American ships by the corsairs of the nations of North Africa.

My obligation as President is historic; it is clear; it is inescapable.

It is no act of war on our part when we decide to protect the seas which are vital to American defense. The aggression is not ours. Ours is solely defense.

But let this warning be clear. From now on, if German or Italian vessels of war enter the waters the protection of which is necessary for American defense they do so at their own peril.

The orders which I have given as Commander-in-Chief to the United States Army and Navy are to carry out that policy — at once.

The sole responsibility rests upon Germany. There will be no shooting unless Germany continues to seek it.

That is my obvious duty in this crisis. That is the clear right of this sovereign Nation. That is the only step possible, if we would keep tight the wall of defense which we are pledged to maintain around this Western Hemisphere.

I have no illusions about the gravity of this step. I have not taken it hurriedly or lightly. It is the result of months and months of constant thought and anxiety and prayer. In the protection of your Nation and mine it cannot be avoided.

The American people have faced other grave crises in their history — with American courage and American resolution. They will do no less today.

They know the actualities of the attacks upon us. They know the necessities of a bold defense against these attacks. They know that the times call for clear heads and fearless hearts.

And with that inner strength that comes to a free people conscious of their duty and of the righteousness of what they do, they will — with Divine help and guidance — stand their ground against this latest assault upon their democracy, their sovereignty, and their freedom.

(7) *Arming of American-Flag Ships Engaged in Foreign Commerce.
Message of the President (Roosevelt) to the Congress, October
9, 1941* [1]

[See Chapter II, From Neutrality to Belligerency, p. 101.]

To THE CONGRESS OF THE UNITED STATES:

It is obvious to all of us that world conditions have changed violently
since the first American Neutrality Act of 1935. The Neutrality Act
of 1939 was passed at a time when the true magnitude of the Nazi
attempt to dominate the world was visualized by few persons. We heard
it said, indeed, that this new European war was not a real war, and that
the contending armies would remain behind their impregnable fortifications and never really fight. In this atmosphere the Neutrality Act
seemed reasonable. But so did the Maginot Line.

Since then — in these past two tragic years — war has spread from
continent to continent; very many nations have been conquered and
enslaved; great cities have been laid in ruins; millions of human beings
have been killed, soldiers and sailors and civilians alike. Never before
has such widespread devastation been visited upon God's earth and
God's children.

The pattern of the future — the future as Hitler seeks to shape it — is
now as clear and as ominous as the headlines of today's newspapers.

Through these years of war, we Americans have never been neutral
in thought. We have never been indifferent to the fate of Hitler's
victims. And, increasingly, we have become aware of the peril to ourselves, to our democratic traditions and institutions, to our country,
and to our hemisphere.

We have known what victory for the aggressors would mean to us.
Therefore, the American people, through the Congress, have taken
important and costly steps to give great aid to those nations actively
fighting against Nazi-Fascist domination.

We know that we could not defend ourselves in Long Island Sound
or in San Francisco Bay. That would be too late. It is the American
policy to defend ourselves wherever such defense becomes necessary
under the complex conditions of modern warfare.

Therefore, it has become necessary that this Government should not
be handicapped in carrying out the clearly announced policy of the

[1] House Doc. No. 404, 77th Cong., 1st sess., the full title of which is: *Arming of
American-Flag Ships Engaged in Foreign Commerce. Message of the President of the
United States transmitting a Recommendation for the Repeal of Section 6 of the Act of
November 4, 1939, which Prohibits the Arming of American-Flag Ships Engaged in
Foreign Commerce;* text also in Department of State, *Bulletin,* V, p. 257.

Congress and of the people. We must face the truth that the Neutrality Act requires a complete reconsideration in the light of known facts.

The revisions which I suggest do not call for a declaration of war any more than the Lend-Lease Act called for a declaration of war. This is a matter of essential defense of American rights.

In the Neutrality Act are various crippling provisions. The repeal or modification of these provisions will not leave the United States any less neutral than we are today, but will make it possible for us to defend the Americas far more successfully, and to give aid far more effectively against the tremendous forces now marching towards conquest of the world.

Under the Neutrality Act, we established certain areas as zones of combat into which no American-flag ships could proceed. Hitler proclaimed certain far larger areas as zones of combat into which any neutral ship, regardless of its flag or the nature of its cargo, could proceed only at its peril. We know now that Hitler recognizes no limitation on any zone of combat in any part of the seven seas. He has struck at our ships and at the lives of our sailors within the waters of the Western Hemisphere. Determined as he is to gain domination of the entire world, he considers the entire world his own battlefield.

Ships of the United States and of other American republics continue to be sunk, not only in the imaginary zone proclaimed by the Nazis in the North Atlantic, but also in the zoneless South Atlantic.

I recommend the repeal of section 6 of the act of November 4, 1939, which prohibits the arming of American-flag ships engaged in foreign commerce.

The practice of arming merchant ships for civilian defense is an old one. It has never been prohibited by international law. Until 1937 it had never been prohibited by any statute of the United States. Through our whole history American merchant vessels have been armed whenever it was considered necessary for their own defense.

It is an imperative need now to equip American merchant vessels with arms. We are faced not with the old type of pirates but with the modern pirates of the sea who travel beneath the surface or on the surface or in the air destroying defenseless ships without warning and without provision for the safety of the passengers and crews.

Our merchant vessels are sailing the seas on missions connected with the defense of the United States. It is not just that the crews of these vessels should be denied the means of defending their lives and their ships.

Although the arming of merchant vessels does not guarantee their safety, it most certainly adds to their safety. In the event of an attack by a raider they have a chance to keep the enemy at a distance until help comes. In the case of an attack by air, they have at least a chance to shoot down the enemy or keep the enemy at such height that it cannot make a sure hit. If it is a submarine, the armed merchant ship compels the submarine to use a torpedo while submerged — and many torpedoes thus fired miss their mark. The submarine can no longer rise to the surface within a few hundred yards and sink the merchant ship by gunfire at its leisure.

Already we take many precautions against the danger of mines — and it seems somewhat incongruous that we have authority today to "degauss" our ships as a protection against mines, whereas we have no authority to arm them in protection against aircraft or raiders or submarines.

The arming of our ships is a matter of immediate necessity and extreme urgency. It is not more important than some other crippling provisions in the present act, but anxiety for the safety of our crews and of the almost priceless goods that are within the holds of our ships leads me to recommend that you, with all speed, strike the prohibition against arming our ships from the statute books.

There are other phases of the Neutrality Act to the correction of which I hope the Congress will give earnest and early attention. One of these provisions is of major importance. I believe that it is essential to the proper defense of our country that we cease giving the definite assistance which we are now giving to the aggressors. For, in effect, we are inviting their control of the seas by keeping our ships out of the ports of our own friends.

It is time for this country to stop playing into Hitler's hands, and to unshackle our own.

A vast number of ships are sliding into the water from American ship-building ways. We are lending them to the enemies of Hitlerism and they are carrying food and supplies and munitions to belligerent ports in order to withstand Hitler's juggernaut.

Most of the vital goods authorized by the Congress are being delivered. Yet many of them are being sunk; and as we approach full production requiring the use of more ships now being built it will be increasingly necessary to deliver American goods under the American flag.

We cannot, and should not, depend on the strained resources of the exiled nations of Norway and Holland to deliver our goods, nor should we be forced to masquerade American-owned ships behind the flags of our sister republics.

I earnestly trust that the Congress will carry out the true intent of the Lend-Lease Act by making it possible for the United States to help to deliver the articles to those who are in a position effectively to use them. In other words, I ask for congressional action to implement congressional policy. Let us be consistent.

I would not go back to the earlier days when private traders could gamble with American life and property in the hope of personal gain, and thereby embroil this country in some incident in which the American public had no direct interest. But today, under the controls exercised by the Government, no ship and no cargo can leave the United States, save on an errand which has first been approved by governmental authority. And the test of that approval is whether the exportation will promote the defense of the United States.

I cannot impress too strongly upon the Congress the seriousness of the military situation that confronts all of the nations that are combating Hitler.

We would be blind to the realities if we did not recognize that Hitler is now determined to expend all the resources and all the mechanical force and manpower at his command to crush both Russia and Britain. He knows that he is racing against time. He has heard the rumblings of revolt among the enslaved peoples — including the Germans and Italians. He fears the mounting force of American aid. He knows that the days in which he may achieve total victory are numbered.

Therefore, it is our duty, as never before, to extend more and more assistance and ever more swiftly to Britain, to Russia, to all peoples and individuals fighting slavery. We must do this without fear or favor. The ultimate fate of the Western Hemisphere lies in the balance.

I say to you solemnly that if Hitler's present military plans are brought to successful fulfilment, we Americans shall be forced to fight in defense of our own homes and our own freedom in a war as costly and as devastating as that which now rages on the Russian front.

Hitler has offered a challenge which we as Americans cannot and will not tolerate.

We will not let Hitler prescribe the waters of the world on which our ships may travel. The American flag is not going to be driven from the seas either by his submarines, his airplanes, or his threats.

We cannot permit the affirmative defense of our rights to be annulled and diluted by sections of the Neutrality Act which have no realism in the light of unscrupulous ambition of madmen.

We Americans have determined our course.

We intend to maintain the security and the integrity and the honor of our country.

We intend to maintain the policy of protecting the freedom of the seas against domination by any foreign power which has become crazed with a desire to control the world. We shall do so with all our strength and all our heart and all our mind.

FRANKLIN D. ROOSEVELT

(8) *Navy and Total Defense Day Address by the President (Roosevelt), October 27, 1941* [1]

Five months ago tonight I proclaimed to the American people the existence of a state of unlimited emergency.[2]

Since then much has happened. Our Army and Navy are temporarily in Iceland in the defense of the Western Hemisphere.

Hitler has attacked shipping in areas close to the Americas throughout the Atlantic.

Many American-owned merchant ships have been sunk on the high seas. One American destroyer was attacked on September fourth. Another destroyer was attacked and hit on October seventeenth. Eleven brave and loyal men of our Navy were killed by the Nazis.

We have wished to avoid shooting. But the shooting has started. And history has recorded who fired the first shot. In the long run, however, all that will matter is who fired the last shot.

America has been attacked. The U.S.S. *Kearny* is not just a Navy ship. She belongs to every man, woman, and child in this Nation.

Illinois, Alabama, California, North Carolina, Ohio, Louisiana, Texas, Pennsylvania, Georgia, Arkansas, New York, Virginia — those are the home States of the honored dead and wounded of the *Kearny*. Hitler's torpedo was directed at every American, whether he lives on our sea-coasts or in the innermost part of the Nation, far from the seas and far from the guns and tanks of the marching hordes of would-be conquerors of the world.

The purpose of Hitler's attack was to frighten the American people off the high seas — to force us to make a trembling retreat. This is not the first time he has misjudged the American spirit. That spirit is now aroused.

[1] Delivered at a dinner at the Mayflower Hotel, Washington, and broadcast over a nation-wide hook-up, Department of State, *Bulletin*, V, p. 341; Senate Doc. No. 188, 77th Cong., 2d sess., p. 120.

[2] *Documents, III, 1940–41*, p. 754.

If our national policy were to be dominated by the fear of shooting, then all of our ships and those of our sister republics would have to be tied up in home harbors. Our Navy would have to remain respectfully — abjectly — behind any line which Hitler might decree on any ocean as his own dictated version of his own war zone.

Naturally we reject that absurd and insulting suggestion. We reject it because of our own self-interest, our own self-respect, and our own good faith. Freedom of the seas is now, as it has always been, the fundamental policy of this Government.

Hitler has often protested that his plans for conquest do not extend across the Atlantic Ocean. His submarines and raiders prove otherwise. So does the entire design of his new world order.

For example, I have in my possession a secret map made in Germany by Hitler's government — by the planners of the new world order. It is a map of South America and a part of Central America as Hitler proposes to reorganize it. Today in this area there are 14 separate countries. The geographical experts of Berlin, however, have ruthlessly obliterated all existing boundary lines and have divided South America into five vassal states, bringing the whole continent under their domination. And they have also so arranged it that the territory of one of these new puppet states includes the Republic of Panama and our great lifeline — the Panama Canal.

This map makes clear the Nazi design not only against South America but against the United States itself.

Your Government has in its possession another document made in Germany by Hitler's government. It is a detailed plan, which, for obvious reasons, the Nazis did not wish to publicize just yet, but which they are ready to impose on a dominated world — if Hitler wins. It is a plan to abolish all existing religions — Protestant, Catholic, Mohammedan, Hindu, Buddhist, and Jewish alike. The property of all churches will be seized by the Reich. The cross and all other symbols of religion are to be forbidden. The clergy are to be forever silenced under penalty of the concentration camps, where even now so many fearless men are being tortured because they placed God above Hitler.

In the place of the churches of our civilization, there is to be set up an International Nazi Church — a church which will be served by orators sent out by the Nazi government. In the place of the Bible, the words of *Mein Kampf* will be imposed and enforced as Holy Writ. And in place of the cross of Christ will be put two symbols — the swastika and the naked sword.

The God of Blood and Iron will take the place of the God of Love and Mercy.

These grim truths which I have told you of the present and future plans of Hitlerism will of course be hotly denied tomorrow in the controlled press and radio of the Axis Powers. And some Americans will continue to insist that Hitler's plans need not worry us — and that we should not concern ourselves with anything that goes on beyond rifle shot of our own shores.

The protestations of these American citizens — few in number — will, as usual, be paraded with applause through the Axis press and radio during the next few days, in an effort to convince the world that the majority of Americans are opposed to their duly chosen Government, and in reality are only waiting to jump on Hitler's bandwagon when it comes this way.

The motive of such Americans is not the point at issue. The fact is that Nazi propaganda continues in desperation to seize upon such isolated statements as proof of American disunity.

The Nazis have made up their own list of modern American heroes. It is, fortunately, a short list. I am glad that it does not contain my name.

All of us Americans, of all opinions, are faced with the choice between the kind of world we want to live in and the kind of world which Hitler and his hordes would impose upon us.

None of us wants to burrow under the ground and live in total darkness like a comfortable mole.

The forward march of Hitlerism can be stopped — and it will be stopped.

Very simply and very bluntly — we are pledged to pull our own oar in the destruction of Hitlerism.

And when we have helped to end the curse of Hitlerism we shall help to establish a new peace which will give to decent people everywhere a better chance to live and prosper in security and in freedom and in faith.

Each day that passes we are producing and providing more and more arms for the men who are fighting on actual battlefronts. That is our primary task.

And it is the Nation's will that these vital arms and supplies of all kinds shall neither be locked up in American harbors nor sent to the bottom of the sea. It is the Nation's will that America shall deliver the goods. In open defiance of that will, our ships have been sunk and our sailors have been killed.

I say that we do not propose to take this lying down.

Our determination not to take it lying down has been expressed in the orders to the American Navy to shoot on sight. Those orders stand.

Furthermore, the House of Representatives has already voted to amend part of the Neutrality Act of 1939,[1] today outmoded by force of violent circumstances. The Senate Committee on Foreign Relations has also recommended elimination of other hamstringing provisions in that act. That is the course of honesty and of realism.

Our American merchant ships must be armed to defend themselves against the rattlesnakes of the sea.

Our American merchant ships must be free to carry our American goods into the harbors of our friends.

Our American merchant ships must be protected by our American Navy.

It can never be doubted that the goods will be delivered by this Nation, whose Navy believes in the tradition of "Damn the torpedoes; full speed ahead!"

Our national will must speak from every assembly line in our vast industrial machine. Our factories and our shipyards are constantly expanding. Our output must be multiplied.

It cannot be hampered by the selfish obstruction of a small but dangerous minority of industrial managers who hold out for extra profits or for "business as usual." It cannot be hampered by the selfish obstruction of a small but dangerous minority of labor leaders who are a menace to the true cause of labor itself, as well as to the Nation as a whole.

The lines of our essential defense now cover all the seas, and to meet the extraordinary demands of today and tomorrow our Navy grows to unprecedented size. Our Navy is ready for action. Indeed, units of it in the Atlantic patrol are in action. Its officers and men need no praise from me.

Our new Army is steadily developing the strength needed to withstand the aggressors. Our soldiers of today are worthy of the proudest traditions of the United States Army. But traditions cannot shoot down dive bombers or destroy tanks. That is why we must and shall provide, for every one of our soldiers, equipment and weapons — not merely as good but better than that of any other army on earth. And we are doing that right now.

For this — and all of this — is what we mean by total national defense.

The first objective of that defense is to stop Hitler. He can be stopped and can be compelled to dig in. And that will be the beginning of his downfall, because dictatorship of the Hitler type can live only through continuing victories — increasing conquests.

The facts of 1918 are a proof that a mighty German Army and a tired

[1] See pp. 101, 112.

German people can crumble rapidly and go to pieces when they are faced with successful resistance.

Nobody who admires qualities of courage and endurance can fail to be stirred by the full-fledged resistance of the Russian people. The Russians are fighting for their own soil and their own homes. Russia needs all kinds of help — planes, tanks, guns, medical supplies, and other aids — toward the successful defense against the invaders. From the United States and from Britain she is getting great quantities of those essential supplies. But the needs of her huge army will continue — and our help and British help will have to continue!

The other day the Secretary of State of the United States was asked by a Senator to justify our giving aid to Russia. His reply was: "The answer to that depends on how anxious a person is to stop and destroy the march of Hitler in his conquest of the world. If he were anxious enough to defeat Hitler, he would not worry about who was helping to defeat him."

Upon our American production falls the colossal task of equipping our own armed forces and helping to supply the British, the Russians, and the Chinese. In the performance of that task we dare not fail. And we will not fail.

It has not been easy for us Americans to adjust ourselves to the shocking realities of a world in which the principles of common humanity and common decency are being mowed down by the firing squads of the Gestapo. We have enjoyed many of God's blessings. We have lived in a broad and abundant land, and by our industry and productivity we have made it flourish.

There are those who say that our great good fortune has betrayed us — that we are now no match for the regimented masses who have been trained in the Spartan ways of ruthless brutality. They say that we have grown fat and flabby and lazy — and that we are doomed.

But those who say that know nothing of America or of American life.

They do not know that this land is great because it is a land of endless challenge. Our country was first populated, and it has been steadily developed, by men and women in whom there burned the spirit of adventure and restlessness and individual independence which will not tolerate oppression.

Ours has been a story of vigorous challenges which have been accepted and overcome — challenges of uncharted seas, of wild forests and desert plains, of raging floods and withering drought, of foreign tyrants and domestic strife, of staggering problems — social, economic, and physical; and we have come out of them the most powerful nation — and the freest — in all of history.

Today in the face of this newest and greatest challenge, we Americans have cleared our decks and taken our battle stations. We stand ready in the defense of our Nation and the faith of our fathers to do what God has given us the power to see as our full duty.

(9) *Address by the President (Roosevelt) to the Delegates of the International Labor Conference, White House, November 6, 1941* [1]

Taking part in a conference of the ILO is not a new experience for me. It was exactly at this time of the year, in 1919, that the ILO had its first conference in Washington. Apparently someone had fallen down on the job of making the necessary physical arrangements for the conference. Finally someone picked on the then Assistant Secretary of the Navy to help. I had to find office space in the Navy Building, as well as supplies and typewriters to get the machinery organized.

In those days the ILO was still a dream. To many it was a wild dream. Who had ever heard of governments getting together to raise the standards of labor on an international plane? Wilder still was the idea that the people themselves who were directly affected — the workers and the employers of the various countries — should have a hand with government in determining these labor standards.

Now 22 years have passed. The ILO has been tried and tested. Through those extravagant years of the twenties it kept doggedly at its task of shortening the hours of labor, protecting women and children in agriculture and industry, making life more bearable for the merchant seamen, and keeping the factories and mines of the world safe and fit places for human beings to work in.

Then through the long years of depression it sought to bring about a measure of security to all workers by the establishment of unemployment and old-age insurance systems; and again to set the wheels of industry in action through the establishment of international public works, rational policies of migration of workers, and the opening of the channels of world-trade.

Now for more than two years you have weathered the vicissitudes of a world at war. Though Hitler's juggernaut has crowded your permanent staff out of its home at Geneva, here in the New World, thanks in large part to the efforts of our friend, John Winant, you have been carrying on. And when this world-struggle is over, you will be prepared to play your

[1] Department of State, *Bulletin*, V, p. 357; Conference of the International Labour Organisation, 1941, New York and Washington, D. C., *Record of Proceedings*, Montreal, 1941, p. 156.

own part in formulating those social policies upon which the permanence of peace will so much depend.

Today, you, the representatives of 33 nations, meet here in the White House for the final session of your conference. It is appropriate that I recall to you, who are in a full sense a parliament for man's justice, some words written in this house by a President who gave his life in the cause of justice. Nearly 80 years ago, Abraham Lincoln said: "The strongest bond of human sympathy, outside of the family relation, should be one uniting all working people, of all nations, and tongues, and kindreds."

The essence of our struggle is that men shall be free. There can be no real freedom for the common man without enlightened social policies. In last analysis, they are the stakes for which democracies are today fighting.

Your concern is the concern of all democratic peoples. To many of your member states, adherence to the ILO has meant great sacrifice. There is no greater evidence of the vitality of the ILO than the loyal presence here today of the representatives of the nations which suffer under the lash of the dictator. I welcome those representatives especially.

I extend the hand of courage to the delegates of those labor organizations whose leaders are today languishing in concentration camps for having dared to stand up for the ideals without which no civilization can live. Through you, delegates from these despoiled lands, the United States sends your people this message: "You have not been forgotten; you will not be forgotten."

We in the United States have so far been called upon for extremely limited sacrifices, but even in this country we are beginning to feel the pinch of war. The names may be unfamiliar to you, but the workers of Manitowoc, Wis., who used to make aluminum utensils, have had to sacrifice their jobs that we may send planes to Britain and Russia and China. Rubber workers in a hundred scattered plants have had to sacrifice their opportunities for immediate employment that there may be ships to carry planes and tanks to Liverpool and Archangel and Rangoon. Tens of thousands of automobile workers will have to be shifted to other jobs in order that the copper which might have been used in automobiles may carry its deadly message from the mills of the Connecticut Valley to Hitler. But with all this, we have not yet made any substantial sacrifices in the United States.

We have not, like the heroic people of Britain, had to withstand a deluge of death from the skies. Nor can we even grasp the full extent of the sacrifices that the people of China are making in their struggle for freedom from aggression. We have in amazement witnessed the Russians oppose the Nazi war machine for four long months — at the price of uncounted dead and a scorched earth.

Most heroic of all, however, has been the struggle of the common men and women of Europe, from Norway to Greece, against a brutal force which, however powerful, will be forever inadequate to crush the fight for freedom.

As far as we in the United States are concerned, that struggle shall not be in vain. The epic stand of Britain, of China, and of Russia receives the full support of the free peoples of the Americas. The people of this country insist upon their right to join in the common defense.

To be sure, there are still some misguided among us — thank God they are but a few — both industrialists and leaders of labor, who place personal advantage above the welfare of their Nation. There are still a few who place their little victories over one another above triumph over Hitler. There are still some who place the profits they may make from civilian orders above their obligation to the national defense. There are still some who deliberately delay defense output by using their "economic power" to force acceptance of their demands, rather than use the established machinery for the mediation of industrial disputes.

Yes, they are but few. They do not represent the great mass of American workers and employers. The American people have made an unlimited commitment that there shall be a free world. Against that commitment, no individual or group shall prevail.

The American workman does not have to be convinced that the defense of the democracies is his defense. Some of you, from the conquered countries of Europe and from China, have told this conference with the eloquence of anguish how all that you have struggled for — the social progress that you and your fellow men have achieved — is being obliterated by the barbarians.

I need not tell you that one of the first acts of the Fascist and Nazi dictators — at home and in conquered countries — was to abolish free trade unions and to take away from the common people the right of association. Labor alone did not suffer. Free associations of employers were also abolished. Collective bargaining has no place in their system; neither has collaboration of labor, industry, and government.

Nor need I tell you that the Nazi labor front is not a labor union but an instrument to keep labor in a state of permanent subjection. Labor under the Nazi system has become the slave of the military state.

To replace Nazi workers shipped to the front and to meet the gigantic needs of her total war effort, Nazi Germany has imported about two million foreign civilian laborers. They have changed the occupied countries into great slave areas for the Nazi rulers. Berlin is the principal slave market of the world.

The American worker has no illusions about the fate that awaits him and his free labor organizations if Hitler should win. He knows that his own liberty and the very safety of the people of the United States cannot be assured in a world which is three-fourths slave and one-fourth free. He knows that we must furnish arms to Britain, Russia, and China and that we must do it now — *today*.

Our place — the place of the whole Western Hemisphere — in the Nazi scheme for world-domination has been marked on the Nazi time-table. The choice we have to make is this: Shall we make our full sacri-fices now, produce to the limit, and deliver our products today and every day to the battlefronts of the entire world? Or shall we remain satisfied with our present rate of armament output, postponing the day of real sacrifice — as did the French — until it is too late?

The first is the choice of realism — realism in terms of three shifts a day; the fullest use of every vital machine every minute of every day and every night; realism in terms of staying on the job and getting things made, and entrusting industrial grievances to the established machinery of collective bargaining — the machinery set up by a free people.

The second choice is the approach of the blind and the deluded who think that perhaps we could do business with Hitler. For them there is still "plenty of time." To be sure, many of these misled individuals honestly believe that if we should later find that we can't do business with Hitler, we will roll up our sleeves later — later — later. And their tombstones would bear the legend "Too late."

In the process of working and fighting for victory, however, we must never permit ourselves to forget the goal which is beyond victory. The defeat of Hitlerism is necessary so that there may be freedom; but this war, like the last war, will produce nothing but destruction unless we prepare for the future now. We plan now for the better world we aim to build.

If that world is to be one in which peace is to prevail, there must be a more abundant life for the masses of the people of all countries. In the words of the Atlantic Charter, we "desire to bring about the fullest collab-oration between all nations in the economic field with the object of se-curing, for all, improved labor standards, economic advancement, and social security."

There are so many millions of people in this world who have never been adequately fed and clothed and housed. By undertaking to provide a decent standard of living for these millions, the free peoples of the world can furnish employment to every man and woman who seeks a job.

We are already engaged in surveying the immediate post-war require-ments of a world whose economies have been disrupted by war.

We are planning not to provide temporary remedies for the ills of a stricken world; we are planning to achieve permanent cures — to help establish a sounder life.

To attain these goals will be no easy task. Yes, their fulfillment will require "the fullest cooperation between all nations in the economic field." We have learned too well that social problems and economic problems are not separate water-tight compartments in the international any more than in the national sphere. In international, as in national affairs, economic policy can no longer be an end in itself. It is merely a means for achieving social objectives.

There must be no place in the post-war world for special privilege for either individuals or nations. Again in the words of the Atlantic Charter: "All states, great or small, victor or vanquished" must have "access, on equal terms, to the trade and to the raw materials of the world which are needed for their economic prosperity."

In the planning of such international action the ILO with its repre-sentation of labor and management, its technical knowledge and ex-perience, will be an invaluable instrument for peace. Your organization will have an essential part to play in building up a stable international system of social justice for all peoples everywhere. As part of you, the people of the United States are determined to respond fully to the oppor-tunity and challenge of this historic responsibility, so well exemplified at this historic meeting in this historic home of an ancient democracy.

(10) *Radio Address by the President (Roosevelt) to the Nation, Follow-ing a Declaration of a State of War with the Japanese Empire, December 9, 1941* [1]

[For text of Declaration, see p. 118.]

The sudden criminal attacks perpetrated by the Japanese in the Pacific provide the climax of a decade of international immorality.

Powerful and resourceful gangsters have banded together to make war upon the whole human race. Their challenge has now been flung at the United States of America. The Japanese have treacherously violated the long-standing peace between us. Many American soldiers and sailors have been killed by enemy action. American ships have been sunk; American airplanes have been destroyed.

[1] Department of State, *Bulletin*, V, p. 476; Senate Doc. No. 188, 77th Cong., 2d sess., p. 127.

The Congress and the people of the United States have accepted that challenge.

Together with other free peoples, we are now fighting to maintain our right to live among our world neighbors in freedom and in common decency, without fear of assault.

I have prepared the full record of our past relations with Japan, and it will be submitted to the Congress.[1] It begins with the visit of Commodore Perry to Japan 88 years ago. It ends with the visit of two Japanese emissaries to the Secretary of State last Sunday, an hour after Japanese forces had loosed their bombs and machine guns against our flag, our forces, and our citizens.

I can say with utmost confidence that no Americans today or a thousand years hence need feel anything but pride in our patience and our efforts through all the years toward achieving a peace in the Pacific which would be fair and honorable to every nation, large or small. And no honest person, today or a thousand years hence, will be able to suppress a sense of indignation and horror at the treachery committed by the military dictators of Japan, under the very shadow of the flag of peace borne by their special envoys in our midst.

The course that Japan has followed for the past 10 years in Asia has paralleled the course of Hitler and Mussolini in Europe and Africa. Today, it has become far more than a parallel. It is collaboration so well calculated that all the continents of the world, and all the oceans, are now considered by the Axis strategists as one gigantic battlefield.

In 1931, Japan invaded Manchukuo — without warning.

In 1935, Italy invaded Ethiopia — without warning.

In 1938, Hitler occupied Austria — without warning.

In 1939, Hitler invaded Czechoslovakia — without warning.

Later in 1939, Hitler invaded Poland — without warning.

In 1940, Hitler invaded Norway, Denmark, Holland, Belgium, and Luxemburg — without warning.

In 1940, Italy attacked France and later Greece — without warning.

In 1941, the Axis Powers attacked Yugoslavia and Greece and they dominated the Balkans — without warning.

In 1941, Hitler invaded Russia — without warning.

And now Japan has attacked Malaya and Thailand — and the United States — without warning.

It is all of one pattern.

We are now in this war. We are all in it — all the way. Every single man, woman, and child is a partner in the most tremendous under-

[1] See p. 469.

taking of our American history. We must share together the bad news and the good news, the defeats and the victories — the changing fortunes of war.

So far, the news has all been bad. We have suffered a serious set-back in Hawaii. Our forces in the Philippines, which include the brave people of that Commonwealth, are taking punishment, but are defending themselves vigorously. The reports from Guam and Wake and Midway Islands are still confused, but we must be prepared for the announcement that all these three outposts have been seized.

The casualty lists of these first few days will undoubtedly be large. I deeply feel the anxiety of all families of the men in our armed forces and the relatives of people in cities which have been bombed. I can only give them my solemn promise that they will get news just as quickly as possible.

This Government will put its trust in the stamina of the American people, and will give the facts to the public as soon as two conditions have been fulfilled: first, that the information has been definitely and officially confirmed; and, second, that the release of the information at the time it is received will not prove valuable to the enemy directly or indirectly.

Most earnestly I urge my countrymen to reject all rumors. These ugly little hints of complete disaster fly thick and fast in wartime. They have to be examined and appraised.

As an example, I can tell you frankly that until further surveys are made, I have not sufficient information to state the exact damage which has been done to our naval vessels at Pearl Harbor. Admittedly the damage is serious. But no one can say how serious until we know how much of this damage can be repaired and how quickly the necessary repairs can be made.

I cite as another example a statement made on Sunday night that a Japanese carrier had been located and sunk off the Canal Zone. And when you hear statements that are attributed to what they call "an authoritative source," you can be reasonably sure that under these war circumstances the "authoritative source" was not any person in authority.

Many rumors and reports which we now hear originate with enemy sources. For instance, today the Japanese are claiming that as a result of their one action against Hawaii they have gained naval supremacy in the Pacific. This is an old trick of propaganda which has been used innumerable times by the Nazis. The purposes of such fantastic claims are, of course, to spread fear and confusion among us, and to goad us into revealing military information which our enemies are desperately anxious to obtain.

Our Government will not be caught in this obvious trap — and neither will our people.

It must be remembered by each and every one of us that our free and rapid communication must be greatly restricted in wartime. It is not possible to receive full, speedy, accurate reports from distant areas of combat. This is particularly true where naval operations are concerned. For in these days of the marvels of radio it is often impossible for the commanders of various units to report their activities by radio, for the very simple reason that this information would become available to the enemy and would disclose their position and their plan of defense or attack.

Of necessity there will be delays in officially confirming or denying reports of operations, but we will not hide facts from the country if we know the facts and if the enemy will not be aided by their disclosure.

To all newspapers and radio stations — all those who reach the eyes and ears of the American people — I say this: you have a most grave responsibility to the Nation now and for the duration of this war.

If you feel that your Government is not disclosing enough of the truth, you have every right to say so. But — in the absence of all the facts, as revealed by official sources — you have no right to deal out unconfirmed reports in such a way as to make people believe they are gospel truth.

Every citizen, in every walk of life, shares this same responsibility. The lives of our soldiers and sailors — the whole future of this Nation — depend upon the manner in which each and every one of us fulfils his obligation to our country.

Now a word about the recent past — and the future. A year and a half has elapsed since the fall of France, when the whole world first realized the mechanized might which the Axis nations had been building for so many years. America has used that year and a half to great advantage. Knowing that the attack might reach us in all too short a time, we immediately began greatly to increase our industrial strength and our capacity to meet the demands of modern warfare.

Precious months were gained by sending vast quantities of our war material to the nations of the world still able to resist Axis aggression. Our policy rested on the fundamental truth that the defense of any country resisting Hitler or Japan was in the long run the defense of our own country. That policy has been justified. It has given us time, invaluable time, to build our American assembly lines of production.

Assembly lines are now in operation. Others are being rushed to completion. A steady stream of tanks and planes, of guns and ships, of shells and equipment — that is what these 18 months have given us.

But it is all only a beginning of what has to be done. We must be set to face a long war against crafty and powerful bandits. The attack at Pearl Harbor can be repeated at any one of many points in both oceans and along both our coast lines and against all the rest of the hemisphere.

It will not only be a long war, it will be a hard war. That is the basis on which we now lay all our plans. That is the yardstick by which we measure what we shall need and demand; money, materials, doubled and quadrupled production — ever-increasing. The production must be not only for our own Army and Navy and Air Forces. It must reinforce the other armies and navies and air forces fighting the Nazis and the war-lords of Japan throughout the Americas and the world.

I have been working today on the subject of production. Your Government has decided on two broad policies.

The first is to speed up all existing production by working on a seven-day-week basis in every war industry, including the production of essential raw materials.

The second policy, now being put into form, is to rush additions to the capacity of production by building more new plants, by adding to old plants, and by using the many smaller plants for war needs.

Over the hard road of the past months, we have at times met obstacles and difficulties, divisions and disputes, indifference and callousness. That is now all past — and, I am sure, forgotten.

The fact is that the country now has an organization in Washington built around men and women who are recognized experts in their own fields. I think the country knows that the people who are actually responsible in each and every one of these many fields are pulling together with a teamwork that has never before been excelled.

On the road ahead there lies hard work — gruelling work — day and night,[1] every hour and every minute.

I was about to add that ahead there lies sacrifice for all of us.

But it is not correct to use that word. The United States does not consider it a sacrifice to do all one can, to give one's best to our Nation, when the Nation is fighting for its existence and its future life.

It is not a sacrifice for any man, old or young, to be in the Army or the Navy of the United States. Rather is it a privilege.

It is not a sacrifice for the industrialist or the wage-earner, the farmer

[1] This policy was approved by the Senate, where S. Res. 204 was referred to the Committee on Naval Affairs, favorably reported (Senate Report No. 893, 77th Cong., 1st sess.) and agreed to December 15, 1941, as follows: "*Resolved*, That it is the sense of the Senate of the United States that all Government navy yards and all private shipyards and all other national-defense industries should take immediate steps to place themselves on a twenty-four-hour per diem work basis."

or the shopkeeper, the trainman or the doctor, to pay more taxes, to buy more bonds, to forego extra profits, to work longer or harder at the task for which he is best fitted. Rather is it a privilege.

It is not a sacrifice to do without many things to which we are accustomed if the national defense calls for doing without.

A review this morning leads me to the conclusion that at present we shall not have to curtail the normal articles of food. There is enough food for all of us and enough left over to send to those who are fighting on the same side with us.

There will be a clear and definite shortage of metals of many kinds for civilian use, for the very good reason that in our increased program we shall need for war purposes more than half of that portion of the principal metals which during the past year have gone into articles for civilian use. We shall have to give up many things entirely.

I am sure that the people in every part of the Nation are prepared in their individual living to win this war. I am sure they will cheerfully help to pay a large part of its financial cost while it goes on. I am sure they will cheerfully give up those material things they are asked to give up.

I am sure that they will retain all those great spiritual things without which we cannot win through.

I repeat that the United States can accept no result save victory, final and complete. Not only must the shame of Japanese treachery be wiped out, but the sources of international brutality, wherever they exist, must be absolutely and finally broken.

In my message to the Congress yesterday [1] I said that we "will make very certain that this form of treachery shall never endanger us again." In order to achieve that certainty, we must begin the great task that is before us by abandoning once and for all the illusion that we can ever again isolate ourselves from the rest of humanity.

In these past few years — and, most violently, in the past few days — we have learned a terrible lesson.

It is our obligation to our dead — it is our sacred obligation to their children and our children — that we must never forget what we have learned.

And what we all have learned is this:

There is no such thing as security for any nation — or any individual — in a world ruled by the principles of gangsterism.

There is no such thing as impregnable defense against powerful aggressors who sneak up in the dark and strike without warning.

[1] See p. 116.

We have learned that our ocean-girt hemisphere is not immune from severe attack — that we cannot measure our safety in terms of miles on any map.

We may acknowledge that our enemies have performed a brilliant feat of deception, perfectly timed and executed with great skill. It was a thoroughly dishonorable deed, but we must face the fact that modern warfare as conducted in the Nazi manner is a dirty business. We don't like it — we didn't want to get in it — but we are in it, and we're going to fight it with everything we've got.

I do not think any American has any doubt of our ability to administer proper punishment to the perpetrators of these crimes.

Your Government knows that for weeks Germany has been telling Japan that if Japan did not attack the United States, Japan would not share in dividing the spoils with Germany when peace came. She was promised by Germany that if she came in she would receive the complete and perpetual control of the whole of the Pacific area — and that means not only the Far East, not only all of the islands in the Pacific, but also a stranglehold on the west coast of North, Central, and South America.

We also know that Germany and Japan are conducting their military and naval operations in accordance with a joint plan. That plan considers all peoples and nations which are not helping the Axis Powers as common enemies of each and every one of the Axis Powers.

That is their simple and obvious grand strategy. That is why the American people must realize that it can be matched only with similar grand strategy. We must realize for example that Japanese successes against the United States in the Pacific are helpful to German operations in Libya; that any German success against the Caucasus is inevitably an assistance to Japan in her operations against the Dutch East Indies; that a German attack against Algiers or Morocco opens the way to a German attack against South America.

On the other side of the picture, we must learn to know that guerrilla warfare against the Germans in Serbia helps us; that a successful Russian offensive against the Germans helps us; and that British successes on land or sea in any part of the world strengthen our hands.

Remember always that Germany and Italy, regardless of any formal declaration of war, consider themselves at war with the United States at this moment just as much as they consider themselves at war with Britain and Russia. And Germany puts all the other republics of the Americas into the category of enemies. The people of the hemisphere can be honored by that.

The true goal we seek is far above and beyond the ugly field of battle.

When we resort to force, as now we must, we are determined that this force shall be directed toward ultimate good as well as against immediate evil. We Americans are not destroyers — we are builders.

We are now in the midst of a war, not for conquest, not for vengeance, but for a world in which this Nation, and all that this Nation represents, will be safe for our children. We expect to eliminate the danger from Japan, but it would serve us ill if we accomplished that and found that the rest of the world was dominated by Hitler and Mussolini.

We are going to win the war and we are going to win the peace that follows.

And in the dark hours of this day — and through dark days that may be yet to come — we will know that the vast majority of the members of the human race are on our side. Many of them are fighting with us. All of them are praying for us. For, in representing our cause, we represent theirs as well — our hope and their hope for liberty under God.

11) *One Hundred Fiftieth Anniversary of Adoption of Bill of Rights. Radio Address by the President (Roosevelt), December 15, 1941* [1]

No date in the long history of freedom means more to liberty-loving men in all liberty-loving countries than the fifteenth day of December 1791. On that day, 150 years ago, a new nation, through an elected Congress, adopted a declaration of human rights which has influenced the thinking of all mankind from one end of the world to the other.

There is not a single republic of this hemisphere which has not adopted in its fundamental law the basic principles of freedom of man and freedom of mind enacted in the American Bill of Rights.

There is not a country, large or small, on this continent which has not felt the influence of that document, directly or indirectly.

Indeed, prior to the year 1933, the essential validity of the American Bill of Rights was accepted at least in principle. Even today, with the exception of Germany, Italy, and Japan, the peoples of the world — in all probability four fifths of them — support its principles, its teachings, and its glorious results.

But, in the year 1933, there came to power in Germany a political clique which did not accept the declarations of the American bill of human rights as valid: a small clique of ambitious and unscrupulous politicians whose announced and admitted platform was precisely the destruction of the rights that instrument declared. Indeed the entire

[1] Department of State, *Bulletin*, V, p. 564; Senate Doc. No. 188, 77th Cong., 2d sess., p. 134.

program and goal of these political and moral tigers was nothing more than the overthrow, throughout the earth, of the great revolution of human liberty of which our American Bill of Rights is the mother charter.

The truths which were self-evident to Thomas Jefferson — which have been self-evident to the six generations of Americans who followed him — were to these men hateful. The rights to life, liberty, and the pursuit of happiness which seemed to Jefferson, and which seem to us, inalienable, were, to Hitler and his fellows, empty words which they proposed to cancel forever.

The propositions they advanced to take the place of Jefferson's inalienable rights were these:

That the individual human being has no rights whatever in himself and by virtue of his humanity;

That the individual human being has no right to a soul of his own, or a mind of his own, or a tongue of his own, or a trade of his own; or even to live where he pleases or to marry the woman he loves;

That his only duty is the duty of obedience, not to his God, and not to his conscience, but to Adolf Hitler; and that his only value is his value, not as a man, but as a unit of the Nazi state.

To Hitler, the ideal of the people, as we conceive it — the free, self-governing, and responsible people — is incomprehensible. The people, to Hitler, are "the masses" and the highest human idealism is, in his own words, that a man should wish to become "a dust particle" of the order "of force" which is to shape the universe.

To Hitler, the government, as we conceive it, is an impossible conception. The government to him is not the servant and the instrument of the people but their absolute master and the dictator of their every act.

To Hitler, the church, as we conceive it, is a monstrosity to be destroyed by every means at his command. The Nazi church is to be the "National Church," "absolutely and exclusively in the service of but one doctrine, race and nation."

To Hitler, the freedom of men to think as they please and speak as they please and worship as they please is, of all things imaginable, most hateful and most desperately to be feared.

The issue of our time, the issue of the war in which we are engaged, is the issue forced upon the decent, self-respecting peoples of the earth by the aggressive dogmas of this attempted revival of barbarism; this proposed return to tyranny; this effort to impose again upon the peoples of the world doctrines of absolute obedience, and of dictatorial rule, and of the suppression of truth, and of the oppression of conscience, which the free nations of the earth have long ago rejected.

What we face is nothing more nor less than an attempt to overthrow and to cancel out the great upsurge of human liberty of which the American Bill of Rights is the fundamental document: to force the peoples of the earth, and among them the peoples of this continent, to accept again the absolute authority and despotic rule from which the courage and the resolution and the sacrifices of their ancestors liberated them many, many years ago.

It is an attempt which could succeed only if those who have inherited the gift of liberty had lost the manhood to preserve it. But we Americans know that the determination of this generation of our people to preserve liberty is as fixed and certain as the determination of that earlier generation of Americans to win it.

We will not, under any threat, or in the face of any danger, surrender the guaranties of liberty our forefathers framed for us in our Bill of Rights.

We hold with all the passion of our hearts and minds to those commitments of the human spirit.

We are solemnly determined that no power or combination of powers of this earth shall shake our hold upon them.

We covenant with each other before all the world, that having taken up arms in the defense of liberty, we will not lay them down before liberty is once again secure in the world we live in. For that security we pray; for that security we act — now and evermore.

(12) *Annual Message of the President (Roosevelt) to the Congress, January 6, 1942* [1]

MR. VICE PRESIDENT, MR. SPEAKER, MEMBERS OF THE SENATE AND OF THE HOUSE OF REPRESENTATIVES:

In fulfilling my duty to report upon the state of the Union, I am proud to say to you that the spirit of the American people was never higher than it is today — the Union was never more closely knit together — this country was never more deeply determined to face the solemn tasks before it.

The response of the American people has been instantaneous. It will be sustained until our security is assured.

· Exactly one year ago today I said to this Congress: "When the dictators are ready to make war upon us, they will not wait for an act of war on our part . . . They — not we — will choose the time and the place and the method of their attack."

[1] House Doc. 501, 77th Cong., 2d sess.; Senate Doc. No. 188, 77th Cong., 2d sess., p. 136; Department of State, *Bulletin*, VI, p. 39.

We now know their choice of the time: a peaceful Sunday morning — December 7, 1941.

We know their choice of the place: an American outpost in the Pacific.

We know their choice of the method: the method of Hitler himself.

Japan's scheme of conquest goes back half a century. It was not merely a policy of seeking living room: it was a plan which included the subjugation of all the peoples in the Far East and in the islands of the Pacific, and the domination of that ocean by Japanese military and naval control of the western coasts of North, Central, and South America.

The development of this ambitious conspiracy was marked by the war against China in 1894; the subsequent occupation of Korea; the war against Russia in 1904; the illegal fortification of the mandated Pacific Islands following 1920; the seizure of Manchuria in 1931; and the invasion of China in 1937.

A similar policy of criminal conquest was adopted by Italy. The Fascists first revealed their imperial designs in Libya and Tripoli. In 1935 they seized Abyssinia. Their goal was the domination of all North Africa, Egypt, parts of France, and the entire Mediterranean world.

But the dreams of empire of the Japanese and Fascist leaders were modest in comparison with the Gargantuan aspirations of Hitler and his Nazis. Even before they came to power in 1933, their plans for conquest had been drawn. Those plans provided for ultimate domination, not of any one section of the world but of the whole earth and all the oceans on it.

With Hitler's formation of the Berlin-Rome-Tokyo alliance, all these plans of conquest became a single plan. Under this, in addition to her own schemes of conquest, Japan's role was to cut off our supply of weapons of war to Britain, Russia, and China — weapons which increasingly were speeding the day of Hitler's doom. The act of Japan at Pearl Harbor was intended to stun us — to terrify us to such an extent that we would divert our industrial and military strength to the Pacific area or even to our own continental defense.

The plan failed in its purpose. We have not been stunned. We have not been terrified or confused. This reassembling of the Seventy-seventh Congress is proof of that; for the mood of quiet, grim resolution which here prevails bodes ill for those who conspired and collaborated to murder world-peace.

That mood is stronger than any mere desire for revenge. It expresses the will of the American people to make very certain that the world will never so suffer again.

Admittedly, we have been faced with hard choices. It was bitter, for example, not to be able to relieve the heroic and historic defenders of Wake Island. It was bitter for us not to be able to land a million men and a thousand ships in the Philippine Islands.

But this adds only to our determination to see to it that the Stars and Stripes will fly again over Wake and Guam; and that the brave people of the Philippines will be rid of Japanese imperialism, and will live in freedom, security, and independence.

Powerful and offensive actions must and will be taken in proper time. The consolidation of the United Nations' total war effort against our common enemies is being achieved.

That is the purpose of conferences which have been held during the past two weeks in Washington, in Moscow, and in Chungking. That is the primary objective of the declaration of solidarity signed in Washington on January 1, 1942, by 26 nations united against the Axis Powers.[1]

Difficult choices may have to be made in the months to come. We will not shrink from such decisions. We and those united with us will make those decisions with courage and determination.

Plans have been laid here and in the other capitals for coordinated and cooperative action by all the United Nations — military action and economic action. Already we have established unified command of land, sea, and air forces in the southwestern Pacific theater of war. There will be a continuation of conferences and consultations among military staffs, so that the plans and operations of each will fit into a general strategy designed to crush the enemy. We shall not fight isolated wars — each nation going its own way. These 26 nations are united — not in spirit and determination alone but in the broad conduct of the war in all its phases.

For the first time since the Japanese and the Fascists and the Nazis started along their blood-stained course of conquest they now face the fact that superior forces are assembling against them. Gone forever are the days when the aggressors could attack and destroy their victims one by one without unity of resistance. We of the United Nations will so dispose our forces that we can strike at the common enemy wherever the greatest damage can be done.

The militarists in Berlin and Tokyo started this war. But the massed, angered forces of common humanity will finish it.

Destruction of the material and spiritual centers of civilization — this has been and still is the purpose of Hitler and his Italian and Japanese chessmen. They would wreck the power of the British Commonwealth and Russia and China and the Netherlands — and then combine all

[1] For text, see p. 203.

their forces to achieve their ultimate goal, the conquest of the United States.

They know that victory for us means victory for freedom.

They know that victory for us means victory for the institution of democracy — the ideal of the family, the simple principles of common decency and humanity.

They know that victory for us means victory for religion.

And they could not tolerate that. The world is too small to provide adequate "living room" for both Hitler and God. In proof of that, the Nazis have now announced their plan for enforcing their new German, pagan religion throughout the world — the plan by which the Holy Bible and the Cross of Mercy would be displaced by *Mein Kampf* and the swastika and the naked sword.

Our own objectives are clear; the objective of smashing the militarism imposed by warlords upon their enslaved peoples — the objective of liberating the subjugated nations — the objective of establishing and securing freedom of speech, freedom of religion, freedom from want, and freedom from fear everywhere in the world.

We shall not stop short of those objectives — nor shall we be satisfied merely to gain them and then call it a day. I know that I speak for the American people — and I have good reason to believe I speak also for all the other peoples who fight with us — when I say that this time we are determined not only to win the war but also to maintain the security of the peace which will follow.

But modern methods of warfare make it a task not only of shooting and fighting, but an even more urgent one of working and producing. Victory requires the actual weapons of war and the means of transporting them to a dozen points of combat.

It will not be sufficient for us and the other United Nations to produce a slightly superior supply of munitions to that of Germany, Japan, Italy, and the stolen industries in the countries which they have overrun.

The superiority of the United Nations in munitions and ships must be overwhelming — so overwhelming that the Axis nations can never hope to catch up with it. In order to attain this overwhelming superiority the United States must build planes and tanks and guns and ships to the utmost limit of our national capacity. We have the ability and capacity to produce arms not only for our own forces but also for the armies, navies, and air forces fighting on our side.

And our overwhelming superiority of armament must be adequate to put weapons of war at the proper time into the hands of those men in the conquered nations, who stand ready to seize the first opportunity to revolt against their German and Japanese oppressors, and against the traitors in their own ranks, known by the already infamous name of "Quislings." As we get guns to the patriots in those lands, they too will fire shots heard 'round the world.

This production of ours in the United States must be raised far above its present levels, even though it will mean the dislocation of the lives and occupations of millions of our own people. We must raise our sights all along the production-line. Let no man say it cannot be done. It must be done — and we have undertaken to do it.

I have just sent a letter of directive to the appropriate departments and agencies of our Government, ordering that immediate steps be taken:

1. To increase our production rate of airplanes so rapidly that in this year, 1942, we shall produce 60,000 planes, 10,000 more than the goal set a year and a half ago. This includes 45,000 combat planes — bombers, dive-bombers, pursuit planes. The rate of increase will be continued, so that next year, 1943, we shall produce 125,000 airplanes, including 100,000 combat planes.

2. To increase our production rate of tanks so rapidly that in this year, 1942, we shall produce 45,000 tanks; and to continue that increase so that next year, 1943, we shall produce 75,000 tanks.

3. To increase our production rate of anti-aircraft guns so rapidly that in this year, 1942, we shall produce 20,000 of them; and to continue that increase so that next year, 1943, we shall produce 35,000 anti-aircraft guns.

4. To increase our production rate of merchant ships so rapidly that in this year, 1942, we shall build 8,000,000 deadweight tons as compared with a 1941 production of 1,100,000. We shall continue that increase so that next year, 1943, we shall build 10,000,000 tons.

These figures and similar figures for a multitude of other implements of war will give the Japanese and Nazis a little idea of just what they accomplished in the attack on Pearl Harbor.

Our task is hard — our task is unprecedented — and the time is short. We must strain every existing armament-producing facility to the utmost. We must convert every available plant and tool to war production. That goes all the way from the greatest plants to the smallest — from the huge automobile industry to the village machine shop.

Production for war is based on men and women — the human hands and brains which collectively we call labor. Our workers stand ready to work long hours; to turn out more in a day's work; to keep the wheels turning and the fires burning 24 hours a day and 7 days a week. They realize well that on the speed and efficiency of their work depend the lives of their sons and their brothers on the fighting fronts.

Production for war is based on metals and raw materials — steel, copper, rubber, aluminum, zinc, tin. Greater and greater quantities of them will have to be diverted to war purposes. Civilian use of them will have to be cut further and still further — and, in many cases, completely eliminated.

War costs money. So far, we have hardly even begun to pay for it. We have devoted only 15 percent of our national income to national defense. As will appear in my budget message tomorrow, our war program for the coming fiscal year will cost 56 billion dollars or, in other words, more than one half of the estimated annual national income. This means taxes and bonds, and bonds and taxes. It means cutting luxuries and other non-essentials. In a word, it means an "all-out" war by individual effort and family effort in a united country.

Only this all-out scale of production will hasten the ultimate all-out victory. Speed will count. Lost ground can always be regained — lost time never. Speed will save lives; speed will save this Nation which is in peril; speed will save our freedom and civilization — and slowness has never been an American characteristic.

As the United States goes into its full stride, we must always be on guard against misconceptions which will arise naturally or which will be planted among us by our enemies.

We must guard against complacency. We must not underrate the enemy. He is powerful and cunning — and cruel and ruthless. He will stop at nothing which gives him a chance to kill and to destroy. He has trained his people to believe that their highest perfection is achieved by waging war. For many years he has prepared for this very conflict — planning, plotting, training, arming, fighting. We have already tasted defeat. We may suffer further setbacks. We must face the fact of a hard war, a long war, a bloody war, a costly war.

We must, on the other hand, guard against defeatism. That has been one of the chief weapons of Hitler's propaganda machine — used time and again with deadly results. It will not be used successfully on the American people.

We must guard against divisions among ourselves and among all the other United Nations. We must be particularly vigilant against racial discrimination in any of its ugly forms. Hitler will try again to breed mistrust and suspicion between one individual and another, one group and another, one race and another, one government and another. He will try to use the same technique of falsehood and rumor-mongering with which he divided France from Britain. He is trying to do this with us even now. But he will find a unity of will and purpose against him, which will persevere until the destruction of all his black designs upon the freedom and safety of the people of the world.

We cannot wage this war in a defensive spirit. As our power and our resources are fully mobilized, we shall carry the attack against the enemy — we shall hit him and hit him again wherever and whenever we can reach him.

We must keep him far from our shores, for we intend to bring this battle to him on his own home grounds.

American armed forces must be used at any place in all the world where it seems advisable to engage the forces of the enemy. In some cases these operations will be defensive, in order to protect key positions. In other cases, these operations will be offensive, in order to strike at the common enemy, with a view to his complete encirclement and eventual total defeat.

American armed forces will operate at many points in the Far East.

American armed forces will be on all the oceans — helping to guard the essential communications which are vital to the United Nations.

American land and air and sea forces will take stations in the British Isles — which constitute an essential fortress in this world struggle.

American armed forces will help to protect this hemisphere — and also bases outside this hemisphere which could be used for an attack on the Americas.

If any of our enemies, from Europe or from Asia, attempt long-range raids by "suicide" squadrons of bombing planes, they will do so only in the hope of terrorizing our people and disrupting our morale. Our people are not afraid of that. We know that we may have to pay a heavy price for freedom. We will pay this price with a will. Whatever the price, it is a thousand times worth it. No matter what our enemies in their desperation may attempt to do to us — we will say, as the people of London have said, "We can take it." And what's more, we can give it back — and we will give it back — with compound interest.

When our enemies challenged our country to stand up and fight, they challenged each and every one of us. And each and every one of us has accepted the challenge — for himself and for the Nation.

There were only some four hundred United States Marines who in the heroic and historic defense of Wake Island inflicted such great losses on the enemy. Some of those men were killed in action; and others are now prisoners of war. When the survivors of that great fight are liberated and restored to their homes, they will learn that a hundred and thirty million of their fellow citizens have been inspired to render their own full share of service and sacrifice.

Our men on the fighting fronts have already proved that Americans today are just as rugged and just as tough as any of the heroes whose exploits we celebrate on the Fourth of July.

Many people ask, "When will this war end?" There is only one answer to that. It will end just as soon as we make it end, by our combined efforts, our combined strength, our combined determination to fight through and work through until the end — the end of militarism in Germany and Italy and Japan. Most certainly we shall not settle for less.

That is the spirit in which discussions have been conducted during the visit of the British Prime Minister to Washington. Mr. Churchill and I understand each other, our motives and our purposes. Together, during the past two weeks, we have faced squarely the major military and economic problems of this greatest world war.

All in our Nation have been cheered by Mr. Churchill's visit. We have been deeply stirred by his great message to us. We wish him a safe return to his home. He is welcome in our midst, now and in days to come.

We are fighting on the same side with the British people, who fought alone for long, terrible months and withstood the enemy with fortitude and tenacity and skill.

We are fighting on the same side with the Russian people who have seen the Nazi hordes swarm up to the very gates of Moscow and who, with almost superhuman will and courage, have forced the invaders back into retreat.

We are fighting on the same side as the brave people of China who for four and a half long years have withstood bombs and starvation and have whipped the invaders time and again in spite of superior Japanese equipment and arms.

We are fighting on the same side as the indomitable Dutch.

We are fighting on the same side as all the other Governments-in-exile, whom Hitler and all his armies and all his Gestapo have not been able to conquer.

But we of the United Nations are not making all this sacrifice of human effort and human lives to return to the kind of world we had after the last world war.

We are fighting today for security, for progress, and for peace, not only for ourselves but for all men, not only for one generation but for all generations. We are fighting to cleanse the world of ancient evils, ancient ills.

Our enemies are guided by brutal cynicism, by unholy contempt for the human race. We are inspired by a faith which goes back through all the years to the first chapter of the Book of Genesis: "God created man in His own image."

We on our side are striving to be true to that divine heritage. We are fighting, as our fathers have fought, to uphold the doctrine that all men are equal in the sight of God. Those on the other side are striving to destroy this deep belief and to create a world in their own image — a world of tyranny and cruelty and serfdom.

That is the conflict that day and night now pervades our lives. No compromise can end that conflict. There never has been — there never can be — successful compromise between good and evil. Only total victory can reward the champions of tolerance and decency and freedom and faith.

FRANKLIN D. ROOSEVELT

(13) *Radio Address in Celebration of Washington's Birthday by the President (Roosevelt), February 23, 1942* [1]

Washington's Birthday is a most appropriate occasion for us to talk with each other about things as they are today and things as we know they shall be in the future.

For eight years General Washington and his Continental Army were faced continually with formidable odds and recurring defeats. Supplies and equipment were lacking. In a sense, every winter was a Valley Forge. Throughout the 13 States there existed fifth columnists — selfish men, jealous men, fearful men, who proclaimed that Washington's cause was hopeless, that he should ask for a negotiated peace.

Washington's conduct in those hard times has provided the model for all Americans ever since — a model of moral stamina. He held to his course as it had been charted in the Declaration of Independence. He and the brave men who served with him knew that no man's life or fortune was secure without freedom and free institutions.

The present great struggle has taught us increasingly that freedom of person and security of property anywhere in the world depend upon the security of the rights and obligations of liberty and justice everywhere in the world.

This war is a new kind of war. It is different from all other wars of the past, not only in its methods and weapons but also in its geography. It is warfare in terms of every continent, every island, every sea, every air-lane in the world.

---

[1] Department of State, *Bulletin*, VI, p. 183; Senate Doc. No. 188, 77th Cong., 2d sess., p. 143.

That is the reason why I have asked you to take out and spread before you the map of the whole earth and to follow with me the references which I shall make to the world-encircling battle lines of this war. Many questions will, I fear, remain unanswered, but I know you will realize I cannot cover everything in any one report to the people.

The broad oceans which have been heralded in the past as our protection from attack have become endless battlefields on which we are constantly being challenged by our enemies.

We must all understand and face the hard fact that our job now is to fight at distances which extend all the way around the globe.

We fight at these vast distances because that is where our enemies are. Until our flow of supplies gives us clear superiority we must keep on striking our enemies wherever and whenever we can meet them, even if, for a while, we have to yield ground. Actually we are taking a heavy toll of the enemy every day that goes by.

We must fight at these vast distances to protect our supply lines and our lines of communication with our allies — protect these lines from the enemies who are bending every ounce of their strength, striving against time, to cut them. The object of the Nazis and the Japanese is to separate the United States, Britain, China, and Russia, and to isolate them one from another, so that each will be surrounded and cut off from sources of supplies and reinforcements. It is the old familiar Axis policy of "divide and conquer."

There are those who still think in terms of the days of sailing ships. They advise us to pull our warships and our planes and our merchant-ships into our own home waters and concentrate solely on last-ditch defense. But let me illustrate what would happen if we followed such foolish advice.

Look at your map. Look at the vast area of China, with its millions of fighting men. Look at the vast area of Russia, with its powerful armies and proven military might. Look at the British Isles, Australia, New Zealand, the Dutch Indies, India, the Near East, and the Continent of Africa, with their resources of raw materials and of peoples determined to resist Axis domination. Look at North America, Central America, and South America.

It is obvious what would happen if all these great reservoirs of power were cut off from each other either by enemy action or by self-imposed isolation:

1. We could no longer send aid of any kind to China — to the brave people who, for nearly five years, have withstood Japanese assault, destroyed hundreds of thousands of Japanese soldiers and vast quan-

tities of Japanese war munitions. It is essential that we help China in her magnificent defense and in her inevitable counter-offensive — for that is one important element in the ultimate defeat of Japan.

2. If we lost communication with the southwest Pacific, all of that area, including Australia and New Zealand, would fall under Japanese domination. Japan could then release great numbers of ships and men to launch attacks on a large scale against the coasts of the Western Hemisphere, including Alaska. At the same time, she could immediately extend her conquests to India, and through the Indian Ocean, to Africa and the Near East.

3. If we were to stop sending munitions to the British and the Russians in the Mediterranean and Persian Gulf areas, we would help the Nazis to overrun Turkey, Syria, Iraq, Persia, Egypt and the Suez Canal, the whole coast of North Africa, and the whole coast of West Africa — putting Germany within easy striking distance of South America.

4. If, by such a fatuous policy, we ceased to protect the North Atlantic supply line to Britain and to Russia, we would help to cripple the splendid counter-offensive by Russia against the Nazis, and we would help to deprive Britain of essential food supplies and munitions.

Those Americans who believed that we could live under the illusion of isolationism wanted the American eagle to imitate the tactics of the ostrich. Now, many of those same people, afraid that we may be sticking our necks out, want our national bird to be turned into a turtle. But we prefer to retain the eagle as it is — flying high and striking hard.

I know that I speak for the mass of the American people when I say that we reject the turtle policy and will continue increasingly the policy of carrying the war to the enemy in distant lands and distant waters — as far as possible from our own home grounds.

There are four main lines of communication now being traveled by our ships: The North Atlantic, the South Atlantic, the Indian Ocean, and the South Pacific. These routes are not one-way streets — for the ships which carry our troops and munitions out-bound bring back essential raw materials which we require for our own use.

The maintenance of these vital lines is a very tough job. It is a job which requires tremendous daring, tremendous resourcefulness, and, above all, tremendous production of planes and tanks and guns and of the ships to carry them. And I speak again for the American people when I say that we can and will do that job.

The defense of the world-wide lines of communication demands relatively safe use by us of the sea and of the air along the various routes; and this, in turn, depends upon control by the United Nations of the strategic bases along those routes.

Control of the air involves the simultaneous use of two types of planes — first, the long-range heavy bombers; and, second, light bombers, dive bombers, torpedo planes, and short-range pursuit planes, which are essential to the protection of the bases and of the bombers themselves.

Heavy bombers can fly under their own power from here to the southwest Pacific, but the smaller planes cannot. Therefore, these lighter planes have to be packed in crates and sent on board cargo ships. Look at your map again, and you will see that the route is long — and at many places perilous — either across the South Atlantic around south Africa or from California to the East Indies direct. A vessel can make a round trip by either route in about four months, or only three round trips in a whole year.

In spite of the length and difficulties of this transportation, I can tell you that we already have a large number of bombers and pursuit planes, manned by American pilots, which are now in daily contact with the enemy in the southwest Pacific. And thousands of American troops are today in that area engaged in operations not only in the air but on the ground as well.

In this battle area Japan has had an obvious initial advantage. For she could fly even her short-range planes to the points of attack by using many stepping-stones open to her — bases in a multitude of Pacific islands and also bases on the China, Indo-China, Thailand, and Malay coasts. Japanese troop transports could go south from Japan and China through the narrow China Sea, which can be protected by Japanese planes throughout its whole length.

I ask you to look at your maps again, particularly at that portion of the Pacific Ocean lying west of Hawaii. Before this war even started, the Philippine Islands were already surrounded on three sides by Japanese power. On the west the Japanese were in possession of the coast of China and the coast of Indo-China, which had been yielded to them by the Vichy French. On the north are the islands of Japan themselves, reaching down almost to northern Luzon. On the east are the mandated islands, which Japan had occupied exclusively and had fortified in absolute violation of her written word.

These islands, hundreds of them, appear only as small dots on most maps, but they cover a large strategic area. Guam lies in the middle of them — a lone outpost which we never fortified.

Under the Washington Treaty of 1921 we had solemnly agreed not to add to the fortification of the Philippine Islands. We had no safe naval base there, so we could not use the islands for extensive naval operations.

Immediately after this war started, the Japanese forces moved down on either side of the Philippines to numerous points south of them — thereby completely encircling the Islands from north, south, east, and west.

It is that complete encirclement, with control of the air by Japanese land-based aircraft, which has prevented us from sending substantial reinforcements of men and material to the gallant defenders of the Philippines. For 40 years it has always been our strategy — a strategy born of necessity — that in the event of a full-scale attack on the Islands by Japan, we should fight a delaying action, attempting to retire slowly into Bataan Peninsula and Corregidor.

We knew that the war as a whole would have to be fought and won by a process of attrition against Japan itself. We knew all along that with our greater resources we could outbuild Japan and ultimately overwhelm her on sea, on land, and in the air. We knew that to obtain our objective many varieties of operations would be necessary in areas other than the Philippines.

Nothing that has occurred in the past two months has caused us to revise this basic strategy — except that the defense put up by General MacArthur has magnificently exceeded the previous estimates, and he and his men are gaining eternal glory therefor.

MacArthur's army of Filipinos and Americans, and the forces of the United Nations in China, in Burma, and in the Netherlands East Indies, are all together fulfilling the same essential task. They are making Japan pay an increasingly terrible price for her ambitious attempts to seize control of the whole Asiatic world. Every Japanese transport sunk off Java is one less transport that they can use to carry reinforcements to their army opposing General MacArthur in Luzon.

It has been said that Japanese gains in the Philippines were made possible only by the success of their surprise attack on Pearl Harbor. I tell you that this is not so.

Even if the attack had not been made, your map will show that it would have been a hopeless operation for us to send the Fleet to the Philippines through thousands of miles of ocean while all those island bases were under the sole control of the Japanese.

The consequences of the attack on Pearl Harbor — serious as they were — have been wildly exaggerated in other ways. These exaggerations come originally from Axis propagandists, but they have been repeated, I regret to say, by Americans in and out of public life.

You and I have the utmost contempt for Americans who, since Pearl Harbor, have whispered or announced "off the record" that there was no longer any Pacific Fleet — that the Fleet was all sunk or destroyed on December seventh — that more than 1,000 of our planes were destroyed on the ground. They have suggested slyly that the Government has withheld the truth about casualties — that eleven or twelve thousand men were killed at Pearl Harbor, instead of the figures as officially announced. They have even served the enemy propagandists by spreading the incredible story that shiploads of bodies of our honored American dead were about to arrive in New York harbor to be put in a common grave.

Almost every Axis broadcast directly quotes Americans who, by speech or in the press, make damnable misstatements such as these.

The American people realize that in many cases details of military operations cannot be disclosed until we are absolutely certain that the announcement will not give to the enemy military information which he does not already possess.

Your Government has unmistakable confidence in your ability to hear the worst without flinching or losing heart. You must, in turn, have complete confidence that your Government is keeping nothing from you except information that will help the enemy in his attempt to destroy us. In a democracy there is always a solemn pact of truth between government and the people, but there must also always be a full use of discretion — and that word "discretion" applies to the critics of government as well.

This is war. The American people want to know, and will be told, the general trend of how the war is going. But they do not wish to help the enemy any more than our fighting forces do, and they will pay little attention to the rumor-mongers and poison-peddlers in our midst.

To pass from the realm of rumor and poison to the field of facts: the number of our officers and men killed in the attack on Pearl Harbor on December seventh was 2,340, and the number wounded was 946. Of all the combatant ships based on Pearl Harbor — battleships, heavy cruisers, light cruisers, aircraft carriers, destroyers, and submarines — only three were permanently put out of commission.

Very many of the ships of the Pacific Fleet were not even in Pearl Harbor. Some of those that were there were hit very slightly, and others that were damaged have either rejoined the Fleet by now or are still undergoing repairs. When those repairs are completed, the ships will be more efficient fighting machines than they were before.

The report that we lost more than a thousand airplanes at Pearl Harbor is as baseless as the other weird rumors. The Japanese do not know just how many planes they destroyed that day, and I am not going to tell them. But I can say that to date — and including Pearl Harbor —

we have destroyed considerably more Japanese planes than they have destroyed of ours.

We have most certainly suffered losses — from Hitler's U-boats in the Atlantic as well as from the Japanese in the Pacific — and we shall suffer more of them before the turn of the tide. But speaking for the United States of America, let me say once and for all to the people of the world: We Americans have been compelled to yield ground, but we will regain it. We and the other United Nations are committed to the destruction of the militarism of Japan and Germany. We are daily increasing our strength. Soon we, and not our enemies, will have the offensive; we, not they, will win the final battles; and we, not they, will make the final peace.

Conquered nations in Europe know what the yoke of the Nazis is like. And the people of Korea and of Manchuria know in their flesh the harsh despotism of Japan. All of the people of Asia know that if there is to be an honorable and decent future for any of them or for us, that future depends on victory by the United Nations over the forces of Axis enslavement.

If a just and durable peace is to be attained, or even if all of us are merely to save our own skins, there is one thought for us here at home to keep uppermost — the fulfilment of our special task of production.

Germany, Italy, and Japan are very close to their maximum output of ˌplanes, guns, tanks, and ships. The United Nations are not — especially the United States of America.

Our first job then is to build up production so that the United Nations can maintain control of the seas and attain control of the air — not merely a slight superiority but an overwhelming superiority.

On January 6 of this year I set certain definite goals of production for airplanes, tanks, guns, and ships. The Axis propagandists called them fantastic. Tonight, nearly two months later, and after a careful survey of progress by Donald Nelson and others charged with responsibility for our production, I can tell you that those goals will be attained.

In every part of the country, experts in production and the men and women at work in the plants are giving loyal service. With few exceptions, labor, capital, and farming realize that this is no time either to make undue profits or to gain special advantages, one over the other.

We are calling for new plants and additions to old plants and for plant conversion to war needs. We are seeking more men and more women to run them. We are working longer hours. We are coming to realize that one extra plane or extra tank or extra gun or extra ship completed tomorrow may, in a few months, turn the tide on some distant battlefield; it may make the difference between life and death for some of our fighting men. We know now that if we lose this war it will be generations or even centuries before our conception of democracy can live again. And we can lose this war only if we slow up our effort or if we waste our ammunition sniping at each other.

Here are three high purposes for every American:

1. We shall not stop work for a single day. If any dispute arises we shall keep on working while the dispute is solved by mediation, conciliation, or arbitration — until the war is won.

2. We shall not demand special gains or special privileges or advantages for any one group or occupation.

3. We shall give up conveniences and modify the routine of our lives if our country asks us to do so. We will do it cheerfully, remembering that the common enemy seeks to destroy every home and every freedom in every part of our land.

This generation of Americans has come to realize, with a present and personal realization, that there is something larger and more important than the life of any individual or of any individual group — something for which a man will sacrifice, and gladly sacrifice, not only his pleasures, not only his goods, not only his associations with those he loves, but his life itself. In time of crisis when the future is in the balance, we come to understand, with full recognition and devotion, what this Nation is and what we owe to it.

The Axis propagandists have tried in various evil ways to destroy our determination and our morale. Failing in that, they are now trying to destroy our confidence in our own allies. They say that the British are finished — that the Russians and the Chinese are about to quit. Patriotic and sensible Americans will reject these absurdities. And instead of listening to any of this crude propaganda, they will recall some of the things that Nazis and Japanese have said and are still saying about us.

Ever since this Nation became the arsenal of democracy — ever since enactment of Lend-Lease — there has been one persistent theme through all Axis propaganda.

This theme has been that Americans are admittedly rich and that Americans have considerable industrial power — but that Americans are soft and decadent, that they cannot and will not unite and work and fight.

From Berlin, Rome, and Tokyo we have been described as a nation of weaklings — "playboys" — who would hire British soldiers or Russian soldiers or Chinese soldiers to do our fighting for us.

Let them repeat that now!

Let them tell that to General MacArthur and his men.

Let them tell that to the sailors who today are hitting hard in the far waters of the Pacific.

Let them tell that to the boys in the flying fortresses.

Let them tell that to the Marines!

The United Nations constitute an association of independent peoples of equal dignity and importance. The United Nations are dedicated to a common cause. We share equally and with equal zeal the anguish and awful sacrifices of war. In the partnership of our common enterprise we must share in a unified plan in which all of us must play our several parts, each of us being equally indispensable and dependent one on the other.

We have unified command and cooperation and comradeship.

We Americans will contribute unified production and unified acceptance of sacrifice and of effort. That means a national unity that can know no limitations of race or creed or selfish politics. The American people expect that much from themselves. And the American people will find ways and means of expressing their determination to their enemies, including the Japanese admiral who has said that he will dictate the terms of peace here in the White House.

We of the United Nations are agreed on certain broad principles in the kind of peace we seek. The Atlantic Charter applies not only to the parts of the world that border the Atlantic but to the whole world: disarmament of aggressors, self-determination of nations and peoples, and the four freedoms — freedom of speech, freedom of religion, freedom from want, and freedom from fear.

The British and the Russian people have known the full fury of Nazi onslaught. There have been times when the fate of London and Moscow was in serious doubt. But there was never the slightest question that either the British or the Russians would yield. And today all the United Nations salute the superb Russian Army as it celebrates the twenty-fourth anniversary of its first assembly.

Though their homeland was overrun, the Dutch people are still fighting stubbornly and powerfully overseas.

The great Chinese people have suffered grievous losses; Chungking has been almost wiped out of existence, yet it remains the capital of an unbeatable China.

That is the conquering spirit which prevails throughout the United Nations in this war.

The task that we Americans now face will test us to the uttermost.

Never before have we been called upon for such a prodigious effort. Never before have we had so little time in which to do so much.

"These are the times that try men's souls."

Tom Paine wrote those words on a drumhead by the light of a camp-fire. That was when Washington's little army of ragged, rugged men was retreating across New Jersey, having tasted nothing but defeat.

And General Washington ordered that these great words written by Tom Paine be read to the men of every regiment in the Continental Army, and this was the assurance given to the first American armed forces:

"The summer soldier and the sunshine patriot will, in this crisis, shrink from the service of their country; but he that stands it now, deserves the love and thanks of man and woman. Tyranny, like hell, is not easily conquered; yet we have this consolation with us, that the harder the sacrifice, the more glorious the triumph."

So spoke Americans in the year 1776.

So speak Americans today!

(14) *The Price of Free World Victory. Address by the Vice President (Wallace) before the Free World Association, New York City, May 8, 1942* [1]

We, who in a formal or an informal way represent most of the free peoples of the world, are met here tonight in the interests of the millions in all the nations who have freedom in their souls. To my mind this meeting has just one purpose — to let those millions in other countries know that here in the United States are 130 million men, women, and children who are in this war to the finish. Our American people are utterly resolved to go on until they can strike the relentless blows that will assure a complete victory, and with it win a new day for the lovers of freedom, everywhere on this earth.

This is a fight between a slave world and a free world. Just as the United States in 1862 could not remain half slave and half free, so in 1942 the world must make its decision for a complete victory one way or the other.

As we begin the final stages of this fight to the death between the free world and the slave world, it is worth while to refresh our minds about the march of freedom for the common man. The idea of freedom — the freedom that we in the United States know and love so well — is derived from the Bible with its extraordinary emphasis on the dignity of the

[1] *Congressional Record*, vol. 88, p. A1823 (daily edition, May 11, 1942); reprinted by Government Printing Office; *Free World*, June 1942, p. 9.

individual. Democracy is the only true political expression of Christianity.

The prophets of the Old Testament were the first to preach social justice. But that which was sensed by the prophets many centuries before Christ was not given complete and powerful political expression until our Nation was formed as a Federal Union a century and a half ago. Even then, the march of the common people had just begun. Most of them did not yet know how to read and write. There were no public schools to which all children could go. Men and women cannot be really free until they have plenty to eat, and time and ability to read and think and talk things over. Down the years, the people of the United States have moved steadily forward in the practice of democracy. Through universal education, they now can read and write and form opinions of their own. They have learned, and are still learning, the art of production — that is, how to make a living. They have learned, and are still learning, the art of self-government.

If we were to measure freedom by standards of nutrition, education, and self-government, we might rank the United States and certain nations of western Europe very high. But this would not be fair to other nations where education has become widespread only in the last 20 years. In many nations, a generation ago, nine out of ten of the people could not read or write. Russia, for example, was changed from an illiterate to a literate nation within one generation and, in the process, Russia's appreciation of freedom was enormously enhanced. In China, the increase during the past 30 years in the ability of the people to read and write has been matched by their increased interest in real liberty.

Everywhere, reading and writing are accompanied by industrial progress, and industrial progress sooner or later inevitably brings a strong labor movement. From a long-time and fundamental point of view, there are no backward peoples which are lacking in mechanical sense. Russians, Chinese, and the Indians both of India and the Americas all learn to read and write and operate machines just as well as your children and my children. Everywhere the common people are on the march. Thousands of them are learning to read and write, learning to think together, learning to use tools. These people are learning to think and work together in labor movements, some of which may be extreme or impractical at first, but which eventually will settle down to serve effectively the interests of the common man.

When the freedom-loving people march — when the farmers have an opportunity to buy land at reasonable prices and to sell the produce of their land through their own organizations, when workers have the opportunity to form unions and bargain through them collectively, and when the children of all the people have an opportunity to attend schools which teach them the truths of the real world in which they live — when these opportunities are open to everyone, then the world moves straight ahead.

But in countries where the ability to read and write has been recently acquired or where the people have had no long experience in governing themselves on the basis of their own thinking, it is easy for demagogues to arise and prostitute the mind of the common man to their own base ends. Such a demagogue may get financial help from some person of wealth who is unaware of what the end result will be. With this backing, the demagogue may dominate the minds of the people, and, from whatever degree of freedom they have, lead them backward into slavery. Herr Thyssen, the wealthy German steel man, little realized what he was doing when he gave Hitler enough money to enable him to play on the minds of the German people. The demagogue is the curse of the modern world, and, of all the demagogues, the worst are those financed by well-meaning wealthy men who sincerely believe that their wealth is likely to be safer if they can hire men with political "it" to change the sign posts and lure the people back into slavery of the most degraded kind. Unfortunately for the wealthy men who finance movements of this sort, as well as for the people themselves, the successful demagogue is a powerful genie who, when once let out of his bottle, refuses to obey anyone's command. As long as his spell holds, he defies God Himself, and Satan is turned loose upon the world.

Through the leaders of the Nazi revolution, Satan now is trying to lead the common man of the whole world back into slavery and darkness. For the stark truth is that the violence preached by the Nazis is the devil's own religion of darkness. So also is the doctrine that one race or one class is by heredity superior and that all other races or classes are supposed to be slaves. The belief in one Satan-inspired Fuehrer, with his Quislings, his Lavals, and his Mussolinis — his "gauleiters" in every nation in the world — is the last and ultimate darkness. Is there any hell hotter than that of being a Quisling, unless it is that of being a Laval or a Mussolini?

In a twisted sense, there is something almost great in the figure of the Supreme Devil operating through a human form, in a Hitler who has the daring to spit straight into the eye of God and man. But the Nazi system has a heroic position for only one leader. By definition only one person is allowed to retain full sovereignty over his own soul. All the rest are stooges — they are stooges who have been mentally and politically degraded, and who feel that they can get square with the world only by mentally and politically degrading other people. These stooges are really psychopathic cases. Satan has turned loose upon us the insane.

The march of freedom of the past 150 years has been a long-drawn-out people's revolution. In this Great Revolution of the people, there were the American Revolution of 1775, the French Revolution of 1792, the Latin American revolutions of the Bolivarian era, the German Revolution of 1848, and the Russian Revolution of 1918. Each spoke for the common man in terms of blood on the battlefield. Some went to excess. But the significant thing is that the people groped their way to the light. More of them learned to think and work together.

The people's revolution aims at peace and not at violence, but if the rights of the common man are attacked, it unleashes the ferocity of a she-bear who has lost a cub. When the Nazi psychologists tell their master Hitler that we in the United States may be able to produce hundreds of thousands of planes, but that we have no will to fight, they are only fooling themselves and him. The truth is that when the rights of the American people are transgressed, as those rights have been transgressed, the American people will fight with a relentless fury which will drive the ancient Teutonic gods back cowering into their caves. The Götterdämmerung has come for Odin and his crew.

The people are on the march toward even fuller freedom than the most fortunate peoples of the earth have hitherto enjoyed. No Nazi counterrevolution will stop it. The common man will smoke the Hitler stooges out into the open in the United States, in Latin America, and in India. He will destroy their influence. No Lavals, no Mussolinis will be tolerated in a Free World.

The people, in their millennial and revolutionary march toward manifesting here on earth the dignity that is in every human soul, hold as their credo the Four Freedoms enunciated by President Roosevelt in his message to Congress on January 6, 1941.[1] These Four Freedoms are the very core of the revolution for which the United Nations have taken their stand. We who live in the United States may think there is nothing very revolutionary about freedom of religion, freedom of expression, and freedom from the fear of secret police. But when we begin to think about the significance of freedom from want for the average man, then we know that the revolution of the past 150 years has not been completed, either here in the United States or in any other nation in the world. We know that this revolution cannot stop until freedom from want has actually been attained.

[1] See *Documents, III, 1940–41*, p. 33.

And now, as we move forward toward realizing the Four Freedoms of this people's revolution, I would like to speak about four duties. It is my belief that every freedom, every right, every privilege has its price, its corresponding duty without which it cannot be enjoyed. The four duties of the people's revolution, as I see them today, are these:

1. The duty to produce to the limit.
2. The duty to transport as rapidly as possible to the field of battle
3. The duty to fight with all that is in us.
4. The duty to build a peace — just, charitable, and enduring.

The fourth duty is that which inspires the other three.

We failed in our job after World War I. We did not know how to go about it to build an enduring world-wide peace. We did not have the nerve to follow through and prevent Germany from rearming. We did not insist that she "learn war no more." We did not build a peace treaty on the fundamental doctrine of the people's revolution. We did not strive wholeheartedly to create a world where there could be freedom from want for all the peoples. But by our very errors we learned much, and after this war we shall be in position to utilize our knowledge in building a world which is economically, politically, and, I hope, spiritually sound.

Modern science, which is a by-product and an essential part of the people's revolution, has made it technologically possible to see that all of the people of the world get enough to eat. Half in fun and half seriously, I said the other day to Madame Litvinoff: "The object of this war is to make sure that everybody in the world has the privilege of drinking a quart of milk a day." She replied: "Yes, even half a pint." The peace must mean a better standard of living for the common man, not merely in the United States and England but also in India, Russia, China, and Latin America — not merely in the United Nations but also in Germany and Italy and Japan.

Some have spoken of the "American Century." I say that the century on which we are entering — the century which will come out of this war — can be and must be the century of the common man. Perhaps it will be America's opportunity to suggest the freedoms and duties by which the common man must live. Everywhere the common man must learn to build his own industries with his own hands in a practical fashion. Everywhere the common man must learn to increase his productivity so that he and his children can eventually pay to the world community all that they have received. No nation will have the God-given right to exploit other nations. Older nations will have the privilege to help younger nations get started on the path to industrialization, but there must be neither military nor economic imperialism. The methods of the nineteenth century will not work in the people's century which is now about to begin. India, China, and Latin America have a tremendous stake in the people's century. As their masses learn to read and write, and as they become productive mechanics, their standard of living will double and treble. Modern science, when devoted wholeheartedly to the general welfare, has in it potentialities of which we do not yet dream.

And modern science must be released from German slavery. International cartels that serve American greed and the German will to power must go. Cartels in the peace to come must be subjected to international control for the common man, as well as being under adequate control by the respective home governments. In this way, we can prevent the Germans from again building a war machine while we sleep. With international monopoly pools under control, it will be possible for inventions to serve all the people instead of only the few.

Yes, and when the time of peace comes, the citizen will again have a duty, the supreme duty of sacrificing the lesser interests for the greater interest of the general welfare. Those who write the peace must think of the whole world. There can be no privileged peoples. We ourselves in the United States are no more a master race than the Nazis. And we cannot perpetuate economic warfare without planting the seeds of military warfare. We must use our power at the peace table to build an economic peace that is just, charitable, and enduring.

If we really believe that we are fighting for a people's peace, all the rest becomes easy. Production, yes — it will be easy to get production without either strikes or sabotage; production with the wholehearted cooperation between willing arms and keen brains; enthusiasm, zip, energy geared to the tempo of keeping at it everlastingly day after day. Hitler knows as well as those of us who sit in on the War Production Board meetings that we here in the United States are winning the battle of production. He knows that both labor and business in the United States are doing a most remarkable job and that his only hope is to crash through to a complete victory some time during the next six months.

And then there is the task of transportation to the line of battle by truck, by railroad car, by ship. We shall joyously deny ourselves so that our transportation system is improved by at least 30 per cent.

I need say little about the duty to fight. Some people declare, and Hitler believes, that the American people have grown soft in the last generation. Hitler agents continually preach in South America that we are cowards, unable to use, like the "brave" German soldiers, the weapons of modern war. It is true that American youth hates war with a holy hatred. But because of that fact and because Hitler and the German people stand as the very symbol of war, we shall fight with a tireless enthusiasm until war and the possibility of war have been removed from this planet. We shall cleanse the plague spot of Europe, which is Hitler's Germany, and with it the hell-hole of Asia — Japan.

The American people have always had guts and always will have. You know the story of Bomber Pilot Dixon and Radioman Gene Aldrich and Ordnanceman Tony Pastula — the story which Americans will be telling their children for generations to illustrate man's ability to master any fate. These men lived for 34 days on the open sea in a rubber life raft, 8 feet by 4 feet, with no food but that which they took from the sea and the air with one pocket knife and a pistol. And yet they lived it through and came at last to the beach of an island they did not know. In spite of their suffering and weakness, they stood like men, with no weapon left to protect themselves, and no shoes on their feet or clothes on their backs, and walked in military file because, they said, "if there were Japs, we didn't want to be crawling."

The American fighting men, and all the fighting men of the United Nations, will need to summon all their courage during the next few months. I am convinced that the summer and fall of 1942 will be a time of supreme crisis for us all. Hitler, like the prize fighter who realizes he is on the verge of being knocked out, is gathering all his remaining forces for one last desperate blow. There is abject fear in the heart of the madman and a growing discontent among his people as he prepares for his last all-out offensive.

We may be sure that Hitler and Japan will cooperate to do the unexpected — perhaps an attack by Japan against Alaska and our Northwest coast at a time when German transport planes will be shuttled across from Dakar to furnish leadership and stiffening to a German uprising in Latin America. In any event, the psychological and sabotage offensive in the United States and Latin America will be timed to coincide with, or anticipate by a few weeks, the height of the military offensive.

We must be especially prepared to stifle the fifth columnists in the United States who will try to sabotage not merely our war material plants but, even more important, our minds. We must be prepared for the worst kind of fifth-column work in Latin America, much of it operating through the agency of governments with which the United States at present is at peace. When I say this, I recognize that the peoples, both of Latin America and of the nations supporting the agencies through which the fifth columnists work, are overwhelmingly on the side of the democracies. We must expect the offensive against us on the military, propaganda, and sabotage fronts, both in the United States and in Latin America, to reach its apex some time during the next few months. The convulsive efforts of the dying madman will be so great that some of us may be deceived into thinking that the situation is bad at a time when it is really getting better. But in the case of most of us, the events of the next few months, disturbing though they may be, will only increase our will to bring about complete victory in this war of liberation. Prepared in spirit, we cannot be surprised. Psychological terrorism will fall flat. As we nerve ourselves for the supreme effort in this hemisphere we must not forget the sublime heroism of the oppressed in Europe and Asia, whether it be in the mountains of Yugoslavia, the factories of Czechoslovakia and France, the farms of Poland, Denmark, Holland, and Belgium, among the seamen of Norway, or in the occupied areas of China and the Dutch East Indies. Everywhere the soul of man is letting the tyrant know that slavery of the body does not end resistance.

There can be no half measures. North, South, East, West, and Middle West — the will of the American people is for complete victory.

No compromise with Satan is possible. We shall not rest until all the victims under the Nazi yoke are freed. We shall fight for a complete peace as well as a complete victory.

The people's revolution is on the march, and the devil and all his angels cannot prevail against it. They cannot prevail, for on the side of the people is the Lord.

"He giveth power to the faint; to them that have no might He increaseth strength. . . . They that wait upon the Lord shall . . . mount up with wings as eagles; they shall run, and not be weary; they shall walk and not faint."

Strong in the strength of the Lord, we who fight in the people's cause will never stop until that cause is won.

(15) *Statement of the Secretary of State (Hull), May 17, 1942* [1]

During the year that has elapsed since the last observance of Foreign Trade Week, a vast change has occurred in our country's position which as profoundly affects the work of those engaged in foreign commerce as it does the life and work of every one of our citizens.

[1] Department of State, *Bulletin*, VI, p. 478. The statement was made in connection with the celebration of National Foreign Trade Week, May 17–23, 1942.

Our country is at war. Together with more than 20 nations united with us in this great struggle, we are engaged in repelling the attacks of powerful and ruthless enemies and are marshalling our human and material resources for armed blows that will crush once and for all the forces of conquest and domination.

The greatly expanded production of our war industries is flowing in ever-increasing volume to our own heroic fighters and to all the battle-fronts of the United Nations. With unity and singleness of purpose, by doubling and redoubling our efforts, we are hastening the day of complete victory over the enemies of human freedom — the day when we can begin to build upon firm foundations a world of peace and progress.

In this all-embracing endeavor foreign trade, as all other phases of our economic activity, must serve the imperative requirements of the great task that is before us. The international movement of goods is indispensable to the winning of the war. It will be equally indispensable to the winning of the peace.

When the war is over, enduring peace and advancing prosperity will be impossible unless international trade and international economic relations in general are established on the basis of fair treatment and mutual benefit. Our war effort itself will be immensely strengthened if we make sure now that one of the principal things we are fighting for is the establishment of a new and better system of international economic relations.

The United Nations have already resolved that once victory is achieved the economic relations among nations will be based on the principles and objectives which have been tirelessly advocated by our Government on all appropriate occasions in recent years. These principles and objectives have been affirmed and incorporated in the declaration of August 14, 1941, known as the Atlantic Charter. They have been accepted as a common program by all our allies in the United Nations Declaration of January 1, 1942.[1]

Of particular interest to foreign traders is the fourth point of the Atlantic Charter which promises "to further the enjoyment by all States, great or small, victor or vanquished, of access, on equal terms, to the trade and to the raw materials of the world which are needed for their economic prosperity." This must of necessity involve the rehabilitation, on a sound basis, not only of trade relations but also of monetary, financial, and all other international economic relations.

A first step has been taken to implement the United Nations program in the economic field. In an agreement with the British Government,

[1] See p. 203.

signed on February 23, 1942,[1] it is stipulated, among other things, that in the final determination of the benefits to be provided to the United States by the United Kingdom in return for aid furnished under the Lend-Lease Act "the terms and conditions thereof shall be such as not to burden commerce between the two countries, but to promote mutually advantageous economic relations between them and the betterment of world-wide economic relations." Provision is also made for agreed action by the two Governments, open to the participation of other like-minded countries, "directed to the expansion, by appropriate international and domestic measures, of production, employment, and the xchange and consumption of goods, which are the material foundations of the liberty and welfare of all peoples; to the elimination of all forms of discriminatory treatment in international commerce, and to the reduction of tariffs and other trade barriers; and, in general, to the attainment of all the economic objectives set forth in the Joint Declaration [Atlantic Charter] . . ."

The far-reaching economic objectives of the Atlantic Charter cannot be attained by wishful thinking. We in this country must realize that their achievement will be impossible if we follow policies of narrow economic nationalism, such as our extreme and disastrous tariff policy after the last war. We must realize that our own prosperity depends fully as much on prosperous conditions in other countries as their prosperity depends on ours. We must show now by our positive acts of collaboration with other nations of like mind that we are prepared to shoulder our full share of responsibility for building a better world.

With the prospect of a better world before them, I am confident that the people of our Nation and the peoples of all the other United Nations will relentlessly pursue with unflagging zeal our common paramount objective: an early and decisive victory over our enemies.

(16) *Memorial Day Address by the Under Secretary of State (Welles), May 30, 1942* [2]

Today, as our Nation faces the gravest danger it has ever confronted since it gained its independence, the American people are once more meeting together in every State of the Union to commemorate the observance of Memorial Day.

In the elm-shaded churchyards of the New England hills, in the more newly consecrated burial places of the West, here in the quiet century-

[1] See p. 235.

[2] Delivered at the Arlington National Amphitheater. Department of State, *Bulletin*, VI, p. 485; reprinted in Department of State Publication No. 1749.

old cemeteries of the South, men and women throughout the land are now paying tribute to the memories of those who have made the ultimate sacrifice for their country and for their fellow men.

Eighty years ago our people were engaged in a fratricidal war between the States. In the fires of that devastating struggle was forged the great assurance that within the boundaries of the United States men were and would remain free. The lives of those who died in that contest were not laid down in vain.

Forty-four years ago the United States went to war to help the gallant people of Cuba free themselves from the imposition by a nation of the Old World of a brutal tyranny which could not be tolerated in a New World dedicated to the cause of liberty. Through our victory in that war there was wrought a lasting safeguard to the independence of the republics of the Western Hemisphere. Our citizens who then gave up their lives did not do so in vain.

Twenty-five years ago the United States declared war upon Germany. Our people went to war because of their knowledge that the domination of the world by German militarism would imperil the continuation of their national existence.

We won that victory. Ninety thousand of our fellow Americans died in that great holocaust in order to win that victory. They died firm in the belief that the gift of their lives which they offered their country would be utilized by their countrymen as they had been promised it would be — to insure beyond doubt the future safety of the United States through the creation of that kind of world in which a peaceful democracy such as ours could live in happiness and in security.

These ninety thousand dead, buried here on the slopes of Arlington and in the fields of France where they fell in battle, fulfilled their share of the bargain struck. Can we, the living, say as much? Can we truly say on this Memorial Day that we have done what we as a nation could have done to keep faith with them and to prevent their sacrifice from being made in vain?

The people of the United States were offered at the conclusion of the last war the realization of a great vision. They were offered the opportunity of sharing in the assumption of responsibility for the maintenance of peace in the world by participating in an international organization designed to prevent and to quell the outbreak of war. That opportunity they rejected. They rejected it in part because of the human tendency after a great upsurge of emotional idealism to seek the relapse into what was once termed "normalcy." They rejected it because of partisan politics. They rejected it because of the false propaganda, widely spread, that by our participation in a world order we would incur the danger of war rather than avoid it. They rejected it because of unenlightened selfishness.

At the dawn of the nineteenth century an English poet wrote of his own land:

> She is a fen
> Of stagnant waters: altar, sword, and pen,
> Fireside, the heroic wealth of hall and bower
> Have forfeited their ancient dower
> Of inward happiness. We are selfish men.

In 1920 and in the succeeding years we as a nation not only plumbed the depths of material selfishness but we were unbelievably blind. We were blind to what constituted our own enlightened self-interest, and we therefore refused to see that by undertaking a measure of responsibility in maintaining world order, with the immediate commitments which that might involve, we were insuring our people and our democratic ideals against the perils of an unforeseeable future, and we were safeguarding our children and our children's children against having to incur the same sacrifices as those forced upon their fathers. Who can today compare the cost in life or treasure which we might have had to contribute towards the stabilization of a world order during its formative years after 1919 with the prospective loss in lives and the lowering of living standards which will result from the supreme struggle in which we are now engaged.

During the first century of our independence our forefathers were occupying and developing a continent. The American pioneer was pushing ever westward across the Alleghenies into the fertile Ohio Valley, the Mississippi and Missouri country, the Southwest, and finally to the Pacific Coast. The shock of disaster elsewhere in the world was hardly felt; relief from recurring depressions could always be found by expanding our frontiers, by opening up new lands and new industries to supply the needs of our rapidly expanding population. Thus cushioned against the impact of events abroad, the American standard of living steadily improved and became the hope of down-trodden peoples of other lands.

Protected by two great oceans to the east and to the west, with no enemies to the north or to the south, the nineteenth century imbued into the minds of our people the belief that in their isolation from the rest of the world lay their safety.

But the oceans shrank with the development of maritime communications, and the security which we enjoyed by reason of our friendly neighbors vanished with the growth of aviation.

And even in our earlier days our industries became increasingly dependent upon raw materials imported from abroad; their products were sold increasingly in the markets of the Old World. Our urban industrial areas in the East became more and more dependent on our agricultural and mining areas in the West. All became increasingly dependent on world markets and world sources of supply.

With the close of the first World War the period of our isolation had ended. Neither from the standpoint of our physical security nor from the standpoint of our material well-being could we any more remain isolated.

But, as if by their fiat they could turn back the tides of accomplished fact, our leaders and the great majority of our people in those post-war years deliberately returned to the provincial policies and standards of an earlier day, thinking that because these had served their purpose in the past they could do so again in a new and in a changed world.

And now we are engaged in the greatest war which mankind has known. We are reaping the bitter fruit of our own folly and of our own lack of vision. We are paying dearly as well for the lack of statesmanship and for the crass errors of omission and of commission, so tragically evidenced in the policies of those other nations which have had their full share of responsibility for the conduct of human affairs during the past generation.

What can we now do to rectify the mistakes of these past two decades?

The immediate answer is self-evident. We must utterly and finally crush the evil men and the iniquitous systems which they have devised that are today menacing our existence and that of free men and women throughout the earth. There can be no compromise. There can be no respite until the victory is won. We are faced by desperate and powerful antagonists. To win the fight requires every ounce of driving energy, every resource and initiative, every sacrifice, and every instinct of devotion which each and every American citizen possesses. None of us can afford to think of ourselves; none of us can dare to do less than his full part in the common effort. Our liberty, our Christian faith, our life as a free people are at stake. Those who indulge themselves in false optimism, those who believe that the peoples who are fighting with us for our common cause should relieve us of our due share of sacrifice, those who are reluctant to give their all in this struggle for the survival on the earth of what is fine and decent must be regarded as enemies of the American people.

Now more than ever before must we keep the faith with those who lie sleeping in this hallowed ground — and with those who now at this very hour are dying for the cause and for the land they love.

And after we win the victory — and we will — what then? Will the people of the United States then make certain that those who have died that we may live as free men and women shall not have died in vain?

I believe that in such case the voice of those who are doing the fighting and the voice of those who are producing the arms with which we fight must be heard and must be heeded.

And I believe that these voices of the men who will make our victory possible will demand that justice be done inexorably and swiftly to those individuals, groups, or peoples, as the case may be, that can truly be held accountable for the stupendous catastrophe into which they have plunged the human race. But I believe they will likewise wish to make certain that no element in any nation shall be forced to atone vicariously for crimes for which it is not responsible and that no people shall be forced to look forward to endless years of want and of starvation.

I believe they will require that the victorious nations, joined with the United States, undertake forthwith during the period of the armistice the disarmament of all nations, as set forth in the Atlantic Charter, which "may threaten aggression outside of their frontiers."

I believe they will insist that the United Nations undertake the maintenance of an international police power in the years after the war to insure freedom from fear to peace-loving peoples until there is established that permanent system of general security promised by the Atlantic Charter.

Finally, I believe they will demand that the United Nations become the nucleus of a world organization of the future to determine the final terms of a just, an honest, and a durable peace to be entered into after the passing of the period of social and economic chaos which will come inevitably upon the termination of the present war and after the completion of the initial and gigantic task of relief, of reconstruction, and of rehabilitation which will confront the United Nations at the time of the armistice.

This is in very truth a people's war. It is a war which cannot be regarded as won until the fundamental rights of the peoples of the earth are secured. In no other manner can a true peace be achieved.

In the pre-war world large numbers of people were unemployed; the living standards of millions of people were pitifully low; it was a world in which nations were classified as "haves" and "have nots," with all that these words imply in terms of inequity and hatred.

The pre-war world was one in which small, vociferous, and privileged minorities in each country felt that they could not gain sufficient profits if they faced competition from abroad. Even this country with its rich natural resources, its vast economic strength, a population whose genius for efficient production enabled us to export the finest products in the world at low cost and at the same time to maintain the highest wages — a country whose competitive strength was felt in the markets of the world — even such a nation was long dominated by its minority interests who sought to destroy international trade in order to avoid facing foreign competition.

They not only sought to do so but for long years following the first World War largely succeeded in doing so. The destruction of international trade by special minority interests in this and in other countries brought ruin to their fellow citizens by destroying an essential element upon which the national prosperity in each country in large measure depended. It helped to pave the way, through the impoverishment and distress of the people, for militarism and dictatorship. Can the democracies of the world again afford to permit national policies to be dictated by self-seeking minorities of special privilege?

The problem which will confront us when the years of the post-war period are reached is not primarily one of production, for the world can readily produce what mankind requires. The problem is rather one of distribution and purchasing power, of providing the mechanism whereby what the world produces may be fairly distributed among the nations of the world, and of providing the means whereby the people of the world may obtain the world's goods and services. Your Government has already taken steps to obtain the support and active cooperation of others of the United Nations in this great task, a task which in every sense of the term is a new frontier — a frontier of limitless expanse — the frontier of human welfare.

When the war ends, with the resultant exhaustion which will then beset so many of the nations who are joined with us, only the United States will have the strength and the resources to lead the world out of the slough in which it has struggled so long, to lead the way toward a world order in which there can be freedom from want. In seeking this end we will of course respect the right of all peoples to determine for themselves the type of internal economic organization which is best suited to their circumstances. But I believe that here in our own country we will continue to find the best expression for our own and the general good under a system which will give the greatest incentive and opportunity for individual enterprise. It is in such an environment that our citizens have made this country strong and great. Given sound national policies directed toward the benefit of the majority and not of the minority and real security and equality of opportunity for all, reliance on the ngenuity, initiative, and enterprise of our citizens rather than on any form of bureaucratic management will in the future best assure the liberties and promote the material welfare of our people.

In taking thought of our future opportunities we surely must undertake to preserve the advantages we have gained in the past. I cannot believe the peoples of the United States and of the Western Hemisphere will ever relinquish the inter-American system they have built up. Based as it is on sovereign equality, on liberty, on peace, and on joint resistance to aggression, it constitutes the only example in the world today of a regional federation of free and independent peoples. It lightens the darkness of our anarchic world. It should constitute a cornerstone in the world structure of the future.

If this war is in fact a war for the liberation of peoples, it must assure the sovereign equality of peoples throughout the world as well as in the world of the Americas. Our victory must bring in its train the liberation of all peoples. Discrimination between peoples because of their race, creed, or color must be abolished. The age of imperialism is ended. The right of a people to their freedom must be recognized as the civilized world long since recognized the right of an individual to his personal freedom. The principles of the Atlantic Charter must be guaranteed to the world as a whole — in all oceans and in all continents.

And so in the fullness of God's time when the victory is won the people of the United States will once more be afforded the opportunity to play their part in the determination of the kind of world in which they will live. With courage and with vision they can yet secure the future safety of their country and of its free institutions and help the nations of the earth back into the paths of peace.

Then on some future Memorial Day the American people, as they mark the graves of those who died in battle for their country in these last two World Wars, can at last truly say: "Sleep on in quiet and in peace; the victory you made it possible for us to win has now been placed at the service of your country and of humanity; your sacrifice has not been made in vain."

(17) *United Flag Day Address by the President (Roosevelt), June 14, 1942* [1]

Today on Flag Day we celebrate the Declaration of the United Nations — that great alliance dedicated to the defeat of our foes and to the establishment of a true peace based on the freedom of man. Today

[1] Department of State, *Bulletin*, VI, p. 545.

the Republic of Mexico and the Commonwealth of the Philippine Islands join us. We welcome these valiant peoples to the company of those who fight for freedom.

The four freedoms of common humanity are as much elements of man's needs as air and sunlight, bread and salt. Deprive him of all these freedoms and he dies — deprive him of a part of them and a part of him withers. Give them to him in full and abundant measure and he will cross the threshold of a new age, the greatest age of man.

These freedoms are the rights of men of every creed and every race wherever they live. This is their heritage, long withheld. We of the United Nations have the power and the men and the will at last to assure man's heritage.

The belief in the four freedoms of common humanity — the belief in man, created free, in the image of God — is the crucial difference between ourselves and the enemies we face today. In it lies the absolute unity of our alliance, opposed to the oneness of the evil we hate. Here is our strength, the source and promise of victory.

We of the United Nations know that our faith cannot be broken by any man or any force. And we know that there are other millions who in their silent captivity share our belief.

We ask the German people, still dominated by their Nazi whip masters, whether they would rather have the mechanized hell of Hitler's "new order" or — in place of that — freedom of speech and religion, freedom from want and from fear.

We ask the Japanese people, trampled by their savage lords of slaughter, whether they would rather continue slavery and blood or — in place of them — freedom of speech and religion, freedom from want and from fear.

We ask the brave, unconquered people of the nations the Axis invaders have dishonored and despoiled whether they would rather yield to conquerors or have freedom of speech and religion, freedom from want and from fear.

We know the answer. They know the answer. We know that man, born to freedom in the image of God, will not forever suffer the oppressors' sword. The peoples of the United Nations are taking that sword from the oppressors' hands. With it they will destroy those tyrants. The brazen tyrannies pass. Man marches forward toward the light.

I am going to close by reading you a prayer that has been written for the United Nations on this Day:

"God of the free, we pledge our hearts and lives today to the cause of all free mankind.

"Grant us victory over the tyrants who would enslave all free men and nations. Grant us faith and understanding to cherish all those who fight for freedom as if they were our brothers. Grant us brotherhood in hope and union, not only for the space of this bitter war, but for the days to come which shall and must unite all the children of earth.

"Our earth is but a small star in the great universe. Yet of it we can make, if we choose, a planet unvexed by war, untroubled by hunger or fear, undivided by senseless distinctions of race, color or theory. Grant us that courage and foreseeing to begin this task today that our children and our children's children may be proud of the name of man.

"The spirit of man has awakened and the soul of man has gone forth. Grant us the wisdom and the vision to comprehend the greatness of man's spirit, that suffers and endures so hugely for a goal beyond his own brief span. Grant us honor for our dead who died in the faith, honor for our living who work and strive for the faith, redemption and security for all captive lands and peoples. Grant us patience with the deluded and pity for the betrayed. And grant us the skill and the valor that shall cleanse the world of oppression and the old base doctrine that the strong must eat the weak because they are strong.

"Yet most of all grant us brotherhood, not only for this day but for all our years — a brotherhood not of words but of acts and deeds. We are all of us children of earth; grant us that simple knowledge. If our brothers are oppressed, then we are oppressed. If they hunger, we hunger. If their freedom is taken away, our freedom is not secure. Grant us a common faith that man shall know bread and peace — that he shall know justice and righteousness, freedom and security, an equal opportunity and an equal chance to do his best, not only in our own lands, but throughout the world. And in that faith let us march, toward the clean world our hands can make. Amen."

CHAPTER II

FROM NEUTRALITY TO BELLIGERENCY

The outstanding event of the period covered by this volume from the point of view of American foreign relations was the entrance of the United States into the war as a formal belligerent. In this chapter an attempt is made to describe by the inclusion of or reference to the appropriate documents and the statement of some pertinent facts the nature of the development which culminated in declarations of war by the United States against Japan, Germany and Italy, and, more recently, other Axis associates. For reasons of a rather arbitrary nature, perhaps, having to do with the system of classification adopted, documents relating to the background of the American declaration of war against Japan are included in Chapter V on the Far East. Also, the documents on Lend-Lease operations are included in Chapter III, Defense and the War Effort, and Chapter IV, The United Nations, even though these operations undoubtedly had a direct relation to our entrance into the war.

1. APPLICATION OF THE NEUTRALITY ACT OF 1939

A. Delivery of Planes to the Near and Middle East

As the result of successful military operations in the late winter and early spring of 1941, the British succeeded in eliminating all but isolated Italian resistance in East Africa. On April 10, 1941 the President issued a proclamation [1] modifying his earlier proclamations regarding combat areas, making it possible for American vessels to enter the Red Sea and discharge cargoes at Red Sea ports. The Axis occupation of Greece and Crete, and the Axis advance in Libya, followed by the German attack on Soviet Russia in June, made the Near and Middle East an area of critical importance and raised the question in urgent form of reinforcing British and Allied forces in that area. The South Atlantic-African route was obviously the most direct route for flying American bombers and transporting by air American personnel and supplies to this area.

(1) *Announcement of the President (Roosevelt), August 18, 1941* [2]

The President announced today an important step to speed delivery of planes direct to the British forces in the Middle East.

Agreements have been concluded under which the Pan American Airways System will ferry aircraft from the United States to West Africa, and will then ferry those planes on to the Middle East.

In connection with the ferry system Pan American Airways is establishing an air transport service from West Africa to the Middle East

[1] See *Documents, III, 1940–41,* p. 654.
[2] Department of State, *Bulletin,* V, p. 147.

and plans are under way for a transport service from the United States to West Africa. Planes owned by the United States Government will be used by Pan American and they will be operated by American personnel. The route of delivery is so arranged that it will nowhere pass through the zone of actual warfare.

The transport services will supplement the ferry system by returning ferry personnel and carrying spare plane parts and items essential to effective delivery of aircraft to the Middle East. The route will also be available for general commercial use, providing direct air service from New York or Baltimore to Africa.

The ferry system and the transport services provide direct and speedy delivery of aircraft from the "arsenal of democracy" to a critical point in the front against aggression. The importance of this direct line of communication between our country and strategic outposts in Africa cannot be overestimated.

B. Interpretation of the President's Proclamation of November 4, 1939

The carrying of arms, ammunition and implements of war in American vessels to British colonial ports in Africa and the Near East and the flying of American bombers and the transportation of personnel and materials in American planes to British colonial bases in Africa and the Near East raised the question of the interpretation to be given to the term "United Kingdom" as it appeared in the President's proclamation of November 4, 1939,[1] since under the terms of section 2, par. (a) of the Neutrality Act of 1939[2] such trade with a state named in the President's proclamation as being at war was declared to be unlawful.

(1) *Definition of the Term "United Kingdom." Opinion of the Acting Attorney General (Biddle), August 29, 1941* [3]

The Honorable
    The Secretary of State.

MY DEAR MR. SECRETARY:

I have your letter of August 27 [4] requesting my opinion whether the term "United Kingdom," as used in the President's proclamation of November 4, 1939 (4 F. R. 4493), issued under the Neutrality Act of 1939, may be construed as "including only England, Wales, Scotland and Northern Ireland and as not including the overseas territories and possessions of the British Empire."

The proclamation reads in pertinent part as follows:

"Now, Therefore, I, Franklin D. Roosevelt, President of the United States of America, acting under and by virtue of the authority conferred

---

[1] See *Documents, II, 1939–40*, p. 670.   [2] *Ibid.*, p. 657.
[3] Department of State, *Bulletin*, V, p. 219.   [4] Not printed.

on me by the said joint resolution, do hereby proclaim that a state of war unhappily exists between Germany and France; Poland; and the United Kingdom, India, Australia, Canada, New Zealand and the Union of South Africa, and that it is necessary to promote the security and preserve the peace of the United States and to protect the lives of citizens of the United States."

The generally accepted meaning of "United Kingdom" is reflected in the definition set forth in Webster's *New International Dictionary of the English Language*, Second Edition, 1939. Here the term is defined as follows:

"United Kingdom, the. Great Britain and Ireland; — so called from January 1, 1801, when the Legislative Union went into operation, to 1922 when, after the establishment of the Irish Free State, the remaining portion was officially called the United Kingdom of Great Britain and Northern Ireland. By act of Parliament, 1927, the words 'United Kingdom' were omitted from the title of the king."

This definition is entirely consistent with well-established English usage. Thus, in Professor Dicey's work on *Conflict of Laws* (Second Edition, 1908) "United Kingdom" is defined as follows (at p. 68):

" 'United Kingdom' means the United Kingdom of England, Scotland, and Ireland, and the islands adjacent thereto, but does not include either the Isle of Man or the Channel Islands."

See also Keith, *The Governments of the British Empire* (1935), p. 20.

The origin of the English usage was the Union of Ireland Act, which provided that "the said Kingdoms of *Great Britain* and *Ireland* shall . . . be united into one Kingdom by the name of *The United Kingdom of Great Britain and Ireland*"; 39 & 40 G. 3, c. 67 (1800). The same meaning was also given to the term under discussion in the Interpretation Act of 1889, 52 & 53 V. c. 63, s. 18, which provided as follows:

"In this act, and in every act passed after the commencement of this act, the following expressions shall, unless the contrary intention appears, have the meanings hereby respectively assigned to them, namely —

"(1) The expression 'British Isles' shall mean the United Kingdom, the Channel Islands and the Isle of Man."

Although the foregoing provision does not directly define "United Kingdom," it points irresistibly to the conclusion that "United Kingdom" is limited to the British Isles and does not include the overseas possessions, or dependencies, or mandates of the British Empire. This is true because that provision makes "British Isles," which clearly does not include overseas possessions or dependencies, more extensive than

"United Kingdom." The definition in the Interpretation Act reflected a well-established usage which had been embodied in specific definitions of the term "United Kingdom" in previous statutes, such as An Act to Consolidate and Amend the Laws relating to Bankruptcy and Insolvency in Ireland (1857) 20 & 21 V. c. 60 s. 4; An Act to Alter Certain Duties and to Amend the Laws relating to Customs (1867), 30 & 31 V. c. 82 s. 5; An Act for Improving the Condition of Mates and Seamen and Maintaining Discipline in the Merchant Service (1850) 13 and 14 V. c. 93, s. 2.

The separation of Northern and Southern Ireland by the Government of Ireland Act of 1920, and the creation of the Irish Free State by the Irish Free State (Agreement) Act, 1922, 12 G. 5, c. 4, required, of course, a change in the definition of the term "United Kingdom." Accordingly, statutes passed shortly after these acts contained the following specific definition:

" 'United Kingdom' means Great Britain and Northern Ireland."

. . . .

In 1927, a new interpretation statute, Royal Parliamentary Titles Act, 17 G. 5, c. 4, was passed to reflect the change in political structure and provided in section 2, as follows:

"In every act passed and public documents issued after the passage of this act the expression 'United Kingdom' shall, unless the context otherwise requires, mean Great Britain and Northern Ireland."

The applicable court decisions show a uniform judicial interpretation of the term "United Kingdom" in complete harmony with the legislative definitions set forth above. See e.g., *Turnbull* v. *Solicitor of Inland Revenue*, 42 Sc. L. R. 15 (1904); *DeBeers Consolidated Mine Ltd.* v. *Howe* (1906), A. C. 455; *Tomalin* v. *S. Pearson & Son Ltd.* (1909), 2 K. B. 61.

The foregoing discussion demonstrates that the term "United Kingdom" is a term of art with a well-settled and precise meaning. No contrary purpose appearing, well-settled canons of construction require that the term as used in the proclamation should be given this meaning.

For the reasons given it is my opinion that the term "United Kingdom" as used in the proclamation of November 4, 1939, is properly to be construed as including only England, Wales, Scotland and Northern Ireland and not the overseas territories and possessions of the British Empire.

2. FREEDOM OF THE SEAS

Following the outbreak of war in Europe in September 1939, President Roosevelt on September 21 asked Congress to revise existing neutrality legislation so as to make possible the sale of arms, munitions and implements of war on a cash and carry basis. The President recommended this modification as "a return to international law" and as a step "to put this country back on the solid footing of real and traditional neutrality," [1] while at the same time reducing the likelihood "of incidents and controversies which tend to draw us into conflict." [2] At the same time, the President did not conceal his desire to give aid to the victims of aggression. Congress responded with the Neutrality Act of 1939. In his Annual Message to Congress, January 6, 1941, President Roosevelt frankly recognized the serious plight of the nations united in resistance to aggression, the increasing threat to our own security, and the approach of the time when these nations would not be able to pay for what they needed in ready cash. He therefore proposed that "we make it possible for those nations to continue to obtain war materials in the United States, fitting their orders into our own program," [3] without, however, expecting that all these materials should be paid for in dollars. The President proposed the following declaration of purpose: "Let us say to the democracies: 'We Americans are vitally concerned in your defense of freedom. We are putting forth our energies, our resources and our organizing powers to give you the strength to regain and maintain a free world. We shall send you, in ever-increasing numbers, ships, planes, tanks, guns. This is our purpose and our pledge.'" [4] This declaration of purpose Congress accepted and implemented with the Lend-Lease Act of March 11, 1941 and necessary appropriations.[5]

Axis submarine and air attacks on Atlantic shipping in the spring of 1941 threatened to nullify the program of making the United States the arsenal of democracy. Further action on the part of the United States became necessary if the goods we were providing under Lend-Lease arrangements were actually to reach their intended destinations. The first official suggestion of the nature of the action we might take came in an address by Secretary of the Navy Knox, April 24, 1941.[6] Said Secretary Knox: "Hitler cannot allow our war supplies and food to reach England — he will be defeated if they do. We cannot allow our goods to be sunk in the Atlantic — we shall be beaten if they do. We must make our promise good to give aid to Britain." [7] A month later, in an address delivered on May 27, 1941, President Roosevelt was more specific. He announced that in execution of our national policy of giving "every possible assistance to Britain and to all who, with Britain, are resisting Hitlerism," "our patrols are helping now to insure delivery of the needed supplies to Britain." Significantly, he added, "all additional measures necessary to deliver the goods will be taken." [8] To provide a broad basis in traditional national policy for this action, President Roosevelt reasserted the principle of "freedom of the seas," [9] which we were henceforth prepared to defend.

[1] *Documents, II, 1939–40*, p. 653.
[2] *Ibid.*, p. 10.
[3] *Ibid., III, 1940–41*, p. 31.
[4] *Ibid.*
[5] *Ibid.*, p. 711 *et seq.*
[6] *Ibid.*, p. 43.
[7] *Ibid.*
[8] *Ibid.*, p. 55.
[9] *Ibid.*, p. 52.

A. Sinking by Axis Powers of American or American-owned Merchant Vessels

(1) *The German Chargé d'Affaires (Thomsen) to the Under Secretary of State (Welles), June 24, 1941* [1]

The sinking by a German submarine on May 21, 1941 of an American ship, the *Robin Moor*, in the South Atlantic ocean while the vessel was en route to South Africa was regarded by the President as an open challenge to the principle of freedom of the seas. In his message to Congress, June 20, 1941, President Roosevelt said: "The sinking of this American ship by a German submarine flagrantly violated the right of United States vessels freely to navigate the seas subject only to a belligerent right accepted under international law. . . . The Government of the United States holds Germany responsible for the outrageous and indefensible sinking of the *Robin Moor*. Full reparations for the losses and damages suffered by American nationals will be expected from the German Government." [2] A copy of the message was transmitted by Under Secretary of State Welles to the German Chargé d'Affaires, June 20, 1941.[3]

MR. UNDERSECRETARY OF STATE:

In reply to your note of the 20th of this month, I have the honor to advise you that I do not find myself in a position to pass on, in accordance with your request, the text sent to me of a message to Congress from the President of the United States of America for the information of my Government.

Accept [etc.]

(2) *The Secretary of State (Hull) to the German Embassy in Washington, September 19, 1941* [4]

SIR:

Reference is made to the Department's communication of June 20, 1941 with which there was transmitted, by direction of the President of the United States, a copy of a message addressed on that date by the President to the Congress of the United States in which it was stated that the German Government would be expected to make full reparation for the losses and damages sustained by American nationals as a consequence of the unlawful sinking of the American vessel *Robin Moor* by a German submarine on May 21, 1941 in the south Atlantic Ocean.

[1] Department of State, *Bulletin*, V, p. 363.
[2] *Documents, III, 1940–41*, p. 58, 59, 417, 419.
[3] *Ibid.*, p. 419.
[4] Department of State, *Bulletin*, V, p. 364. An acknowledgment of even date from the German Embassy stated that the contents of the note had been transmitted to the German Government.

I now have to inform you that after an investigation undertaken for the purpose of ascertaining the extent of the losses and damages sustained, and with a view to effecting a prompt liquidation of the matter, the Government of the United States is prepared to accept, for appropriate distribution by it, the lump sum of $2,967,092.00, currency of the United States, in satisfaction and full settlement of all claims of the United States and its nationals against the German Government for losses and damages sustained as a consequence of the sinking, subject, however, to the condition that payment of that sum by the German Government be effected at Washington within ninety days from this date. While the sum mentioned includes an amount representing the value of property of this Government which was on board the vessel, no item of punitive damages is included.

Accept [etc.]

(3) The German Chargé d'Affaires (Thomsen) to the Secretary of State (Hull), September 26, 1941 [1]

MR. SECRETARY OF STATE:

On the 19th day of this month you sent me a new note with reference to your communication of June 20 of this year concerning the American steamer *Robin Moor*. I have the honor to reply to you herewith that the two communications made are not such as to lead to an appropriate reply by my Government. In this regard I refer to my note of June 25th [June 24] [2] of this year.

Accept [etc.]

(4) Table Showing Attacks on American Owned and/or Operated Merchant Ships, June 30–December 7, 1941

The sinking of the *Robin Moor* was followed by other attacks upon American or American-owned vessels which resulted in the President's "shoot-on-sight" order to which reference is made in his radio address of September 11, 1941 [3] and his message to Congress of October 9 [4] requesting the repeal of certain provisions of the Neutrality Act of 1939, a request to which Congress acceded by the Joint Resolution of November 17, 1941. [5]

[1] *Ibid.*
[2] See p. 85 above.
[3] See p. 22.
[4] See p. 23.
[5] See p. 112.

The essential data regarding attacks on American-owned merchant vessels is here listed:

NAME OF SHIP	REGISTRY AND CHARACTER	CARGO AND DESTINATION	CIRCUMSTANCES CONNECTED WITH ATTACK
S.S. *Sessa* [1]	Former Danish vessel acquired under authority of Public Law 101 permitting the taking over of idle foreign flagships in American waters. Under Panamanian registry	Foodstuffs, cereals, lumber, and other general cargo. En route to Iceland	Torpedoed and sunk on Aug. 17, while running darkened and under poor light conditions. 24 members of crew unreported and presumed lost
S.S. *Steel Seafarer* [2]	Under American registry and flying the American flag. American flag painted on either side	"Deck load of white cases." [3] On the Red Sea en route to Suez	Sunk by bombs dropped from airplane at between 23 : 38 and 23 : 53 Egyptian mean time, Sept. 5, 1941. Ship's side lights were burning. Visibility good. No casualties
S.S. *Montana* [4]	American-owned under Panamanian registry	Cargo of lumber. En route to Iceland	Torpedoed and sunk in latitude 63° 40' north and longitude 35° 50' west at 13 : 45 Greenwich Central time on Sept. 11. Crew saved
S.S. *Pink Star* [5]	Former Danish ship requisitioned by U. S. Maritime Commission on July 12, 1941, and placed under Panamanian registry	Sailed from New York on Sept. 3 with general cargo	Torpedoed and sunk on Sept. 19 at latitude 61° 36' north, longitude 37° 07' west, near Iceland, while in company with a Canadian-escorted convoy
S.S. *I. C. White* [6]	American-owned tanker under Panamanian registry	Sailed from Curaçao, Sept. 14, for Capetown	Torpedoed and sunk without warning on Sept. 27 at 9 : 10 P.M. E.S.T. Position was 10° 26' south, 27° 30' 30'' west. Unarmed. Painting on side not illuminated. Moonlight night but partly cloudy
S.S. *W. C. Teagle* [7]	American-owned tanker under Panamanian registry		Sunk in North Atlantic waters on Oct. 16

[1] Department of State, *Bulletin*, V, p. 199.
[2] *Ibid.*, p. 197–9.
[3] Affidavit executed by the Master, Captain Halliday, *ibid.*, p. 198.
[4] *Ibid.*, p. 200.   [5] *Ibid.*, p. 231–2.   [6] *Ibid.*, p. 264–5.
[7] *The World Almanac*, 1942, p. 111.

NAME OF SHIP	REGISTRY AND CHARACTER	CARGO AND DESTINATION	CIRCUMSTANCES CONNECTED WITH ATTACK
S.S. *Bold Venture* [1]	Former Danish ship requisitioned by the U. S. Maritime Commission and placed under Panamanian registry	Cargo of cotton, steel, copper and general. Sailed from New York on Sept. 22	Sunk on Oct. 16, 1941 at 11 : 40 ship's time, position 57° north, 24° 30′ west, south of Norway. 18 crew members missing
S.S. *Lehigh* [2]	Owned by the United States Line and flying American flag		Torpedoed and sunk near the southern end of the African bulge on Oct. 19

B. Patrolling and Convoying Operations of the U. S. Navy in the Atlantic Area

(1) *Report of the Committee on Naval Affairs on Senate Resolution 138 of Senator Wheeler (Montana), July 29, 1941* [3]

[Excerpt]

The possibility that United States naval vessels engaged in protective operations in the Atlantic might make contact with German warships and involve this country in a shooting war was a matter of concern to certain individuals who argued that successive steps of the President were manifestations of an intention to maneuver the United States into formal war. On June 30, 1941, Senator Burton K. Wheeler (Montana) introduced S. R. 138, 77th Cong., 1st sess., which quoted statements of three columnists concerning alleged incidents which had not been reported as regular news, and asked that the Committee on Naval Affairs make and report to the Senate the results of an investigation of the "charges" cited. The resolution was referred without approval to the Committee, which held hearings and on July 29, in a "preliminary report," reviewed testimony obtained from the Secretary of the Navy and Chief of Naval Operations. The resolution was ordered to be indefinitely postponed on August 11.

The resolution contained two important "resolves":

First, an investigation of the charges that American naval units are convoying or escorting ships at sea; and

Second, that American naval units are shooting or dropping depth bombs on German naval units.

The committee made detailed investigations into these two subjects, and also made inquiries of the representatives of the Navy Department before the committee on many phases of Navy policies and activities up to the present time.

In view of the limited and ex parte nature of its preliminary inquiry, the committee is of the opinion that it should make its report in the

[1] Department of State, *Bulletin*, V, p. 316.

[2] *The World Almanac*, 1942, p. 111.

[3] Senate Report No. 617, 77th Cong., 1st sess.; *Congressional Record*, vol. 87, p. 6545–8 (daily edition).

nature of questions and answers rather than pass judgment on the accuracy and inaccuracy of the statements of evidence presented in detail.

TESTIMONY

Excerpts from the hearing held on July 11, 1941, when Hon. Frank Knox, Secretary of the Navy, and Admiral H. R. Stark, Chief of Naval Operations, appeared before the committee in executive session are as follows:

THE CHAIRMAN. Secretary Knox, the first paragraph of the first "whereas" in Senate Resolution 138, which the committee has under consideration, reads as follows:

"Whereas on June 2, 1941, Joseph W. Alsop was sworn in as a Naval Reserve officer by the Secretary of the Navy, Frank Knox; and

"Whereas the said Alsop, as co-author of a syndicated newspaper column, on June 9, 1941, one week after he had taken the oath as a Naval Reserve officer, stated in that column:

"'In one case, rather more than a month ago, an encounter between German and American warcraft at sea very nearly terminated in an attack by the Germans. In another, slightly more recent, an attack on what was believed to be a German submarine was actually made by an American destroyer.'"

The committee will be pleased to have your comments on this statement.

SECRETARY KNOX. We haven't any knowledge whatever of any such incident. In fact, we are supremely confident it never occurred. I think it is a pure fabrication out of whole cloth. Not any officer of ours — and the Chief of Naval Operations will support me in this — had ever heard of such an incident, and certainly the officer commanding the American ships involved would have been in duty bound to report.

THE CHAIRMAN. The second paragraph of this first "whereas" reads as follows:

"No details of the first episode are available, but the basic facts of the second are known.

"The destroyer, the name of which cannot be ascertained, was picking up survivors from a British vessel sunk not far from the coast of Greenland. While the operation was in progress the destroyer's detecting device announced the approach of a submarine. The submarine could only have been German. It was virtually certain to use its torpedoes, as semidarkness concealed the nationality of the American ship. And the commander of the destroyer accordingly dropped three depth charges.

"Thus, although the President is waiting for the Germans to shoot first, the truth is that there has been shooting already."

SECRETARY KNOX. Now, here are the facts: One United States destroyer operating off Greenland heard the S O S of a steamer and proceeded to the location and picked up 60 of the survivors of the steamer. While engaged in this act of mercy, the operator of the listening equipment reported to the captain that he thought he heard a submerged submarine. The captain immediately turned toward the direction indicated and dropped three depth charges. In doing this, he very prudently exercised the right of self-preservation, for had there been a submarine there, his destroyer might have been sunk. There was no other evidence that a submarine was there and it is quite possible no submarine was there. The listening-equipment echo might have been received from a whale or a large fish, or a cold current, instead of a submarine — something which is frequently experienced.

Now, none of them knew whether there was a sub there or not, but the man in command did what any man would do who was on the verge of an attack by a submarine. He would do it in self-defense.

THE CHAIRMAN. The next "whereas" in Senate Resolution 138 is as follows:

"Whereas on June 23, 1941, Drew Pearson and Robert S. Allen in their syndicated newspaper column charged:

"'A group of American naval vessels has just returned from its first experience at Atlantic "patrol," or "convoying." Whatever it is called, they helped to get about 80 British merchantmen safely most of the way to the west coast of Africa. Then the British took over.

"'Three United States airplane carriers, 6 destroyers, and 3 cruisers accompanied the convoy across the Atlantic — but never within sight of the 80 British merchantmen.

"'One airplane-carrier steamed ahead of the merchantmen, another to the rear, another to the north. Each carrier was protected by two destroyers, zigzagging constantly. The carriers performed the most important part of the patrol, keeping their airplanes constantly scouring the sky.

"'Once a plane sighted a German surface raider and radioed its position to British warships, which rushed up and sank her. The battle took place so close to American vessels that they could hear the fighting, though they never saw the ships. United States radio operators picked up the distress message sent to Berlin by the Nazi vessel saying that she was sinking.

"'On another occasion an airplane-carrier detector picked up the vibrations of a submarine and signaled it to come to the surface. When there was no answer, United States destroyers immediately dropped depth charges. After that the detector picked up no more vibrations.

"'When the patrol reached its meeting place with the British, near Cape Verde Islands, off the African coast, it turned north, and shortly after this the 12 United States naval vessels headed home.'"

SECRETARY KNOX. That is a perfect piece of fabrication. There isn't a word of truth in it of any kind.

THE CHAIRMAN. That statement goes down to the statement beginning "On another occasion"?

SECRETARY KNOX. Yes; down to "On another occasion" and including that. That is completely manufactured out of whole cloth.

THE CHAIRMAN. Where did they get this information?

SECRETARY KNOX. I haven't the faintest idea. It looks to me like a pure invention.

SENATOR TYDINGS. That is worse than the other. Are you including the paragraph starting with "On another occasion"?

SECRETARY KNOX. Yes; the one about dropping depth charges. There isn't a particle of truth in it.

SENATOR BONE. Then the entire statement is utterly false?

SECRETARY KNOX. The entire statement is utterly false.

SENATOR LUCAS. Every sentence?

SECRETARY KNOX. Every single word in it, without qualification.

SENATOR BREWSTER. Nothing in it is true?

SECRETARY KNOX. Nothing whatever.

SENATOR TYDINGS. Mr. Secretary, if I may ask you two or three questions. It may be somewhat superfluous, but I would like to put it out in the clear. There was no incident where one or more airplane-carriers convoyed 80 or a lesser amount of British merchantmen across the ocean?

SECRETARY KNOX. Never.

SENATOR TYDINGS. There was no case where a battle took place at sea which we inspired or that we stood by and listened to?

SECRETARY KNOX. Nothing of that kind whatever. We do not know a single thing about it, and we would know about it if it ever happened.

ADMIRAL STARK. We never heard of it.

. . . .

ADMIRAL STARK. As regards our men-of-war going over with the British convoy and turning them over to the British authorities, there is just nothing in it at all. We have never convoyed a single merchant ship with the exception that early in the war, the American-flag steamship *Iroquois* was bringing home a large number of Americans. It all came out in the press that somebody warned — as a matter of fact, it came from the Germans, that the British were going to blow her up with a bomb. We put no credence in it, but we immediately sent ships out and escorted her from somewhere off the Grand Banks to New York. That is the only instance where we escorted a merchant ship.

THE CHAIRMAN. The other "whereas" in Senate Resolution 138 is as follows: "Whereas on June 23, 1941, Gen. Hugh S. Johnson in his syndicated column stated:

"'To an experienced eye there can be small doubt, after reading innocent but censored letters from young naval officers, that we have already sunk Nazi submarines. A submerged sub isn't so hot with the radio. A depth bomb leaves no trace. If this is an incorrect conjecture, and it can be no more than conjecture, there is little doubt that our Navy "spots" German subs and guides British ships to them.

"'It seems to be quite generally believed that the seizure of great passenger liners and recent shifts of the Navy from the Pacific (not through the Panama Canal, but around Cape Horn) are preparatory to an attack on Dakar in West Africa, or other key Atlantic positions.

"'What's the difference between that and outright war?'"

SECRETARY KNOX. There is no truth in it whatever. I do not know but what these young naval officers may have written, I am sure, but the incident never occurred. We have never sunk any submarines.

OTHER QUESTIONS AND ANSWERS RELATING TO NAVAL ACTIVITIES

. . . .

CONVOYING

THE CHAIRMAN. Admiral, it was enlightening and helpful to have you saying that naval vessels have not participated in any convoying. What distinction does the Navy make between patroling and convoying?

ADMIRAL STARK. The public uses the word "convoy" more often than it uses the word "escort." A large number of ships together would constitute a convoy, even were the Navy with it, or without the Navy, but if you put naval ships with it to protect it you escort the convoy, and I might say we have escorted no merchant ships whatever, with the single exception of the *Iroquois*.

. . . .

ATTACKS MADE UPON UNITED STATES VESSELS AND PLANES

Question. All information in the possession of the Navy relating to attacks made upon United States vessels and planes?

SECRETARY KNOX. None made; none whatever, except as attacked by the Axis vessels on ours. Is that it?

Question. All information in the possession of the Navy relating to attacks upon United States vessels and planes?

SECRETARY KNOX. None made; except the *Robin Moor*, the *Panay*, and the *Tutuila*, all of which are well known. In case the committee is not familiar with the *Tutuila* incident, she was struck by a bomb fragment during a recent bombing raid of the Japs on Chungking. The *Tutuila* was anchored in the designated spot, well clear of Chinese ships and installations.

. . . .

ATTACKS MADE BY UNITED STATES VESSELS AND PLANES

Question. All information in the possession of the Navy relating to attacks by United States Naval or Coast Guard vessels or planes on Axis vessels or planes?

SECRETARY KNOX. None made whatever, except that the *Panay* fired in self-defense when she was bombed.

SENATOR TYDINGS. That was how long ago?

SECRETARY KNOX. Two years ago.

ORDERS TO NEUTRALITY PATROL

Question. What, in general, are the orders and instructions which have heretofore been issued to commanding officers of vessels and airplanes on neutrality patrol?

SECRETARY KNOX. Of course, that is secret information.

THE CHAIRMAN. That cannot be disclosed.

ORDERS TO FIRE

Question. Are any additional steps or orders contemplated which would cause American ships of war or American personnel to fire upon the ships or personnel of any other nation?

SECRETARY KNOX. As I have already stated, I am not at liberty to discuss operating plans, contemplated or otherwise. I would not be doing my duty if I did not require the Chief of Naval Operations, as directed by law, to prepare operating plans in advance so that the Navy can be effective under all eventualities. We are not at war, and the nature of these plans is a military secret which I cannot disclose. I may add that this procedure goes on year in and year out in the Navy Department, even when times are most peaceful, and even then such matters are inherently of the greatest secrecy.

SHOOTING

Question. Does collaboration with any other country envisage shooting by American ships on the ships of other nations?

SECRETARY KNOX. That falls in the same category.

SENATOR JOHNSON. What do you mean by that, by "falls in the same category"? As what?

SECRETARY KNOX. The word is "collaboration." That necessarily would mean plans, I take it, and whatever plans we may have for a future war in collaboration with some other nation.

SENATOR JOHNSON. I think it is in the present, whether the collaboration exists now, in writing or otherwise, with any other country regarding the ships of any other nation.

SECRETARY KNOX. Again I repeat, Senator, that is secret information.

SENATOR JOHNSON. Now, has there been any change in the orders since the peaceful taking of Iceland?

SECRETARY KNOX. The only thing we have to date, sir, is contained in the message of the President on Iceland.[1] I would like to read just two paragraphs.

SENATOR JOHNSON. They are in general terms, aren't they?

SECRETARY KNOX. Yes; they are in general terms.

.   .   .   .

THE CHAIRMAN. What we are trying to do here is to break down the opinion that has been given to the public through these statements that our Navy is pursuing a course of participation, remotely or indirectly, in war. The evidence shows that is not the fact.

ADMIRAL STARK. That is right. In other words, the public has been led to believe we were shooting, working with British ships. That is not true.

SENATOR BONE. The trouble with these reports circulated by these newsmen — I know it is true in my State — when we want to get a statement clarified they will not disclose anything.

THE CHAIRMAN. And we can assure the American people that there is not an undeclared war, a hidden war, or a naval war as far as we are concerned?

SECRETARY KNOX. That is right.

.   .   .   .

(2) *U.S.S.* Greer. *Letter with Enclosures of the Chief of Naval Operations (Stark) to the Chairman of the Senate Committee on Naval Affairs (Walsh), September 20, 1941* [2]

In his radio address of September 11,[3] President Roosevelt gave a factual account of the attack upon the U.S. destroyer *Greer*. Doubt was cast on the veracity of this account by some enemies of the President's foreign policy. On September 11, 1941, Senator Gerald P. Nye (North Dakota) introduced S. Res. 164 "directing that the Committee on Naval Affairs ascertain the facts" and

---

[1] See p. 16.

[2] U. S. Congress, Senate Committee on Naval Affairs, 77th Cong., 1st sess., *Preliminary Data on S. Res. 164 . . . and S. Res. 165.*

[3] See p. 16.

Senator Bennett C. Clark (Missouri) introduced S. Res. 165 which called for a copy of the *Greer's* log for the days involved. The two resolutions were referred to the Committee on Naval Affairs. The chairman, Senator David I. Walsh (Massachusetts) transmitted S. Res. 165 to the Secretary of the Navy on September 12, suggesting that the information requested be furnished to the Committee if "not incompatible with the public interest." A letter of September 15, incorporating a series of questions prepared after consulting several members of the Committee, requested the appearance of Navy Department officials before the Committee "for the preliminary consideration of" S. Res. 164. The two letters were answered in writing and no hearings were held.

Hon. DAVID I. WALSH,

Senate Naval Affairs Committee, Washington, D. C.

DEAR SENATOR WALSH: I am again indebted to you for sending us the questions on the *Greer* incident before the hearing.

I am enclosing herewith a statement which I have drawn up and which I believe gives a good picture of what happened. I suggest it be read before the answers to the questions are read, as I think it will make the answers to the questions more readily understandable.

I have tried to present a complete and clear picture of the entire incident to you because there is nothing the Navy wishes to conceal except some purely military features. Any such omissions affect in no way whatever the complete picture. However, if they were given out they would be useful to an enemy; for instance, the distance at which the *Greer* originally picked up the submarine would be a clear indication to an enemy of the capacity of our listening gear and would be valuable information to them. The insertion of such data, I feel, would not be helpful in any way to the committee in this incident and would be harmful from the standpoint of national defense.

I want you to know that I feel you can count on our keeping the country informed of everything that we possibly can, withholding only what we feel should be withheld in the best interests of national defense.

I can think of nothing further of interest which I could give you other than what is included in my statement, together with the answers which I am also submitting to the questions.

Of course I shall be glad to appear before the committee if, after going over these, you would like to have me do so. I have endeavored, however, to make the enclosed papers so complete that it would be unnecessary to take the committee's time for further investigation.

With best wishes, as always,

STATEMENT WITH REGARD TO THE "GREER" INCIDENT, SEPTEMBER 4,
1941

On September 4, 1941, at 08 : 40 G. C. T., the U.S.S. *Greer*, while en
route to Iceland with United States mail and passengers and some
freight, was informed by a British plane of the presence of a submerged
submarine, distance about 10 miles directly ahead.

This British plane continued in the vicinity of the submarine until
10 : 52 when she departed. Prior to her departure, at 10 : 32, she dropped
four depth charges in the vicinity of the submarine.

Acting on the information from the British plane the *Greer* proceeded
to search for the submarine and at 09 : 20 she located the submarine
directly ahead by her underwater sound equipment. The *Greer* proceeded then to trail the submarine and broadcasted the submarine's
position. This action taken by the *Greer* was in accordance with her
orders, that is, to give out information but not to attack.

The *Greer* maintained this contact until about 12 : 48. During this
period (3 hours 28 minutes) the *Greer* maneuvered so as to keep the
submarine ahead.

At 12 : 40 the submarine changed course and closed the *Greer*.

The disturbance of the surface and the change in color of the water
marking the passage of the submarine was clearly distinguished by the
Greer.

At 12 : 48 an impulse bubble (indicating the discharge of a torpedo by
the submarine) was sighted close aboard the *Greer*.

At 12 : 49 a torpedo track was sighted crossing the wake of the ship
from starboard to port, distant about 100 yards astern.

At 12 : 56 the *Greer* attacked the submarine with a pattern of eight
depth charges.

At 12 : 58 a second torpedo track was sighted on the starboard bow of
the *Greer*, distant about 500 yards. The *Greer* avoided this torpedo.

At this time the *Greer* lost sound contact with the submarine.

At 13 : 00 the *Greer* started searching for the submarine and at 15 : 12
in latitude 62–43 N., longitude 27–22 W., the *Greer* made underwater
contact with a submarine. The *Greer* attacked immediately with depth
charges.

In neither of the *Greer's* attacks did she observe any results which
would indicate that the attacks on the submarine had been effective.

The *Greer* continued search until 18 : 40, at which time she again proceeded toward her destination, Iceland.

From the above it is clearly evident that the *Greer*, though continuously in contact with the submarine for 3 hours 28 minutes, did not attack the submarine although the *Greer* herself was exposed to attack.

At no time did the *Greer* sight the submarine's periscope.

The weather was good.

The commander-in-chief of the Atlantic Fleet corroborates the above report in detail and further states that the action taken by the *Greer* was correct in every particular in accordance with her existing orders.

H. R. STARK

QUESTIONS ADDRESSED TO THE SECRETARY OF THE NAVY, BY THE CHAIRMAN OF THE SENATE NAVAL AFFAIRS COMMITTEE, AND PROPOSED ANSWERS THERETO, IN CONNECTION WITH THE "GREER" INCIDENT

Question 1. Did the incident take place in an area declared to be blockaded by the German Government?

Answer. The *Greer* incident took place in an area approximately 175 miles southwest of Iceland, and directly in the path of communication between American ports and Iceland. This area was within the zone of operations announced by the German Government on March 26, 1941, as a zone within which vessels entering exposed themselves "to the danger of destruction."

Question 2. Did the *Greer* have orders from the Department to proceed through this area?

Answer. The *Greer* had orders from the commander-in-chief of the Atlantic Fleet to proceed through the area. The Navy Department had full knowledge of this.

Question 3. Were any other ships in company with, or in sight of, the *Greer* just before or at any time during the encounter? If so, (a) what were the names and nationality of these vessels, and (b) did any of these ships take part in the encounter either directly or indirectly?

Answer. A British destroyer was in sight about 5 miles distant from the *Greer* when the *Greer* made a depth bomb attack at 15 : 12. This British destroyer had arrived on the scene at 14 : 15 and had asked the *Greer* if she (the *Greer*) desired to conduct a coordinated search for the submarine. To this question, the *Greer* replied "No." The British destroyer stood through the area and disappeared to the southward.

Question 4. Were any airplanes in sight of, or in communication with, the *Greer* just before or during the encounter? If so, (a) what were the nationality of these planes, and (b) did any of these planes furnish any information to the *Greer* or take part either directly or indirectly in the encounter?

Answer. Yes. At 08 : 40, a British plane approached the U.S.S. *Greer* and signaled that a submarine had submerged about 10 miles directly ahead of the *Greer*. The plane furnished no further assistance to the *Greer*. At 10 : 32, this plane dropped four depth charges in the vicinity of the submarine and, at 10 : 52, the plane departed from the area. It should be particularly noted that this plane left the area at 10 : 52 and did not return, and that the *Greer* fired no guns or torpedoes or dropped any depth charges until 12 : 56 — some 8 minutes after the submarine fired a torpedo at the *Greer* — or, in other words, over 2 hours after the British plane had left the scene.

Question 5. Was the commanding officer of the *Greer* informed that a submarine was operating in this vicinity before his vessel was attacked or before the submarine or her periscope was seen? If so, when and from whom did he receive this information?

Answer. Yes. See answer to preceding question. The periscope of the submarine was not seen at any time by the *Greer*.

Question 6. If he had information from an outside source that there was a submarine in the vicinity, (*a*) did he change his course and speed and start a search for the submarine; (*b*) how long did he search for the submarine before he was fired upon; and (*c*) did other vessels or planes assist in this search?

Answer. As soon as information was received by the *Greer* from the British plane that a submarine was directly ahead of her, the *Greer* increased speed, started zigzagging, and commenced a search for the submarine. Five minutes after the search began, namely, at 09 : 20, the *Greer* located the submarine by her underwater sound equipment; she held this contact until 12 : 48, namely, 3 hours 28 minutes before the submarine made her attack. No assistance by either planes or ships was given to the *Greer* during this period.

Question 7. If he first learned of the presence of the submarine from his submarine detection device or from sighting it, (*a*) did he change his course to search for or head for the submarine; or (*b*) would he have been out of range of the submarine's torpedoes if he had continued on his course?

Answer. The first part of this question is answered by the answer to the preceding question. As to the second part of this question, the answer is problematical. No person can predict what the submarine's course would have been. The answer, therefore, might be "Yes" or it might be "No."

Question 8. How many torpedoes were fired at the *Greer* and at what intervals were they fired? How long was it after the submarine was sighted or first heard that the first torpedoes were fired? How near did the torpedoes come to hitting the ship?

Answer. Two torpedoes were fired at the *Greer*. The firing of the first one was indicated by the sighting of the impulse bubble at 12 : 48, just 3 hours and 28 minutes after the *Greer* first detected the submarine by means of her sound equipment. At 12 : 49 the wake of this torpedo was observed about 100 yards astern. At 12 : 58 the wake of a second torpedo was observed 500 yards distant on the starboard bow. The *Greer* avoided it, the torpedo passing about 300 yards clear of the ship.

Question 9. How many depth charges were dropped by the *Greer* and at what intervals?

Answer. U.S.S. *Greer* dropped 8 depth charges, commencing at 12 : 56; 11 depth charges were dropped, commencing at 15 : 12. All these depth charges were dropped after the first torpedo had been fired at the *Greer*.

Question 10. Has anything been seen or heard from this submarine since the last depth charges were dropped by the *Greer?*

Answer. Not by the U.S.S. *Greer,* nor has the Department any word.

Question 11. Has the Department received a copy of the log of the *Greer* from the 2d to the 5th of September, both dates inclusive?

Answer. No.

Question 12. What information in general is entered into the log?

Answer. All facts concerning the incident are entered in the log.

Question 13. Is there any reason, or reasons, why this log should not be made public? If so, what are these reasons?

Answer. It is not desirable that this log be made public for the reason that to do so would disclose confidential military information.

Question 14. Are there any reasons why the commanding officer and other officers and men of the *Greer* should not appear before the committee? If so, what are those reasons?

Answer. Yes. Testimony of such officers would be almost certain to disclose vital military secrets which would endanger other naval vessels. In addition, to establish a precedent or to have naval officers at sea feel that whenever they take action they would or might be called before a congressional investigating committee to explain and justify their action, would be prejudicial to the conduct of operations on the high seas.

Question 15. In view of the fact that the United States Navy now has orders to shoot at Axis submarines or raiders, is there any reason why the orders under which the *Greer* was operating at the time shouldn't now be made public?

Answer. Naval operation orders that in any manner do or might involve military action are considered as of the most secret nature and should not be disclosed publicly, because of the unquestioned value they would be to foreign powers.

Question 16. Have officials of the State Department taken up with the German Embassy the question of this attack upon a United States naval vessel? If so, it is requested that the committee be furnished with a copy of the official communication.

Answer. No.

Question 17. Has the German Embassy forwarded any official explanation of the attack to our Government? If so, it is requested that the committee be furnished a copy of this explanation.

Answer. No.

H. R. STARK

(a) *German Communiqué, September 6, 1941* [1]

On the fourth of September a German submarine was attacked with depth bombs and continuously pursued in the German blockade zone at a point charted at Lat. 62 degrees 31 minutes N. and Long. 27 degrees 6 minutes W. The German submarine was unable to establish the nationality of the attacking destroyer.

In justified defense against the attack, the submarine thereupon at 14 : 39 o'clock fired two torpedoes at the destroyer, both of which missed aim. The destroyer continued its pursuit and attacks with depth bombs until midnight, then abandoned them.

If official American quarters, namely the Navy Department, assert the attack was initiated by the German submarine, such charge can only have the purpose of giving the attack of an American destroyer on a German submarine which was undertaken in complete violation of neutrality a semblance of legality. This attack is evidence that President Roosevelt despite his previous assertions to the contrary has commanded American destroyers not only to report the location of German U-Boats and other German craft as violating neutrality but also to proceed to attack them.

Roosevelt there is endeavoring with all the means at his disposal to provoke incidents for the purpose of baiting the American people into the war.

The attack on the *Greer* was followed by two other incidents involving submarine (presumably German) attacks on United States warships. On the night of

[1] *New York Times*, September 7, 1941, p. 1. The authority issuing the communiqué was not specified in news dispatches, which incorporated a text handed out by the Deutsches Nachrichtenbüro. The Associated Press summary stated the encounter began at 12 : 30 P.M. and lasted 2 hours and 15 minutes.

October 16–17 the U.S.S. *Kearny* while escorting a convoy of merchant ships received distress signals from another convoy and proceeded to the aid of the attacked convoy. On sighting a merchant ship under attack, the *Kearny* dropped depth bombs. "Some time afterward three torpedo tracks were observed approaching the U.S.S. *Kearny*. One passed ahead of the ship, one astern and the third struck the U.S.S. *Kearny* on the starboard side in the vicinity of the forward fire room." [1] The ship reached port under escort.

On the night of October 30–31, the U.S.S. *Reuben James* was sunk by a torpedo while convoying in the North Atlantic west of Iceland. [2] The attack was made during complete darkness, according to reports received. [3] The news of the sinking, followed by the announcement that only 44 of the crew of approximately 120 officers and men had so far been rescued, was interpreted as "adding impetus" [4] to the drive for early revision of the Neutrality Act of 1939, repeal of certain provisions of which was under discussion in Congress at the time.

(3) *Adoption of "Shoot on Sight" Policy.   Radio Address by the President (Roosevelt), September 11, 1941* [5]

[Excerpt]

This address and the important statement of policy which it contained were apparently prompted by the attack on the *Greer*, though the charge of "international lawlessness" and "design to abolish the freedom of the seas" is supported by other instances of attacks on American vessels.

If submarines or raiders attack in distant waters, they can attack equally well within sight of our own shores. Their very presence in any waters which America deems vital to its defense constitutes an attack.

In the waters which we deem necessary for our defense American naval vessels and American planes will no longer wait until Axis submarines lurking under the water, or Axis raiders on the surface of the sea, strike their deadly blow — first.

Upon our naval and air patrol — now operating in large numbers over a vast expanse of the Atlantic Ocean — falls the duty of maintaining the American policy of freedom of the seas — now. That means, very simply and clearly, that our patrolling vessels and planes will protect all merchant ships — not only American ships but ships of any flag — engaged in commerce in our defensive waters. They will protect them from submarines; they will protect them from surface raiders.

[1] Statement of the Secretary of the Navy (Knox), October 29, 1941. *New York Times*, October 30, 1941, p. 1. For the facts on this incident see U. S. Congress, Senate, Committee on Naval Affairs, *Data on the Torpedoing of the U.S.S. Kearny* (Senate committee print, 77th Cong., 1st sess.).

[2] Press Releases of the Navy Department, October 31, 1941.

[3] *Ibid.*, November 4, 1941.

[4] *Christian Science Monitor*, November 1, 1941, p. 1.

[5] For complete text, see p. 16.

3. REVISION OF THE NEUTRALITY ACT OF 1939

By October 1941 it was widely felt that the demands of total national defense required the repeal of certain provisions of the so-called "Neutrality Act of 1939." [1] The legislation of 1935, 1937 and 1939 had been built on assumptions concerning the character of neutrality and of war which had been put forward by publicists and the Senate investigation of the munitions industry; the war which broke out in 1939, it was believed by many, corresponded less and less to those assumptions, which were being progressively belied by events and the necessary counter-action of the United States Government. Those who believed in the continuing validity of the assumptions and purposes of the neutrality legislation naturally opposed steps taken and measures proposed which would have the effect of involving this country more actively in the war. Revision of the "Neutrality Act of 1939" thus became a major contest in public opinion concerning a legislative matter of policy.

The President consulted with leading members of Congress on October 7, 1941, in order to determine to what extent a proposal should go. Proposals publicly made or introduced in Congress varied from repeal of the entire act [2] to repeal of one or more sections. Sec. 8 (Solicitation and Collection of Funds and Contributions) and sec. 12 (National Munitions Control Board) were regarded as administrative provisions useful to retain. Sec. 7 (Financial Transactions), sec. 10 (Restrictions on Use of American Ports) and sec. 11 (Submarines and Armed Merchant Vessels) were deemed to be sufficiently relaxed by the operation of the Lend-Lease Act. The provisions regarded as particularly hampering effective national defense action were sec. 2 (Commerce with States Engaged in Armed Conflict), sec. 3 (Combat Areas), and sec. 6 (Arming of American Merchant Vessels Prohibited). The question before the President was whether to ask Congress to repeal one or more of those sections immediately. The message of the President to the Congress of October 9, 1941, [3] entitled "A Recommendation for the Repeal of Section 6 of the Act," was a general statement of reasons for modification of restrictive provisions which incidentally embodied that specific recommendation.

Congressional leaders desired that speedy action should be taken. The House Committee on Foreign Affairs assigned October 13 and 14 to hearings, equally divided between proponents and opponents. Several of the minority of the Committee refused to attend. Not all persons who had applied to be heard presented themselves. [4] On October 15, the Committee reported favorably H. J. Res. 237 providing for the repeal of sec. 6 of the "Neutrality Act of 1939." [5] In order to expedite action, the Committee on Rules gave it precedence under a very special procedure by H. Res. 320, which confined general debate in Committee of the Whole House to one day and one hour, equally divided, and provided that consideration for amendment should be under the 5-minute rule; on report to the House, proceedings were without debate or amendments. The House passed H. J. Res. 237 without amendment on October 17 by a vote of 259 to 138.

The resolution was referred to the Senate Committee on Foreign Relations,

[1] *Documents, II, 1939–40*, p. 656.
[2] H. R. 5465 on July 31 and S. 1925 on September 25, 1941, proposed complete repeal of the "Neutrality Act of 1939."
[3] See p. 23.
[4] U. S. Congress, House of Representatives, Committee on Foreign Affairs, *Arming American Merchant Vessels; Hearings . . . on H. J. Res. 237.* Washington, 1941. 74 p.
[5] House Report No. 1267, 77th Cong., 1st sess.

which held hearings on October 21–24, 1941.[1] On October 25 the Committee reported H. J. Res. 237 to the Senate with amendments providing for the repeal also of secs. 2 and 3 of the Act.[2] For the next 10 days extensive debate of this forthright proposal continued in the Senate and the country, without much doubt as to the outcome. On November 7 voting took place, several amendments being defeated. A proposal by Mr. Thomas of Oklahoma to exclude sec. 3 of the 1939 Act from the repeal was voted down, 38 yeas, 50 nays. The same vote was recorded against the motion of Mr. Clark of Missouri to reject the Committee's amendment to repeal secs. 2 and 3. As a tactical maneuver Mr. Clark moved to repeal the whole Act, the motion being defeated, 11 yeas, 78 nays. The Committee amendment, to repeal secs. 2 and 3 as well as sec. 6 was passed, 50 yeas, 38 nays, and the resolution thus amended received 50 yeas to 37 nays.

The House under H. Res. 334 confined debate on the amended resolution to 8 hours, equally divided, on November 12 and 13. The House on November 13 voted to concur in the Senate amendment, 212 yeas, 194 nays.

(1) Message of the President (Roosevelt) Transmitting a Recommendation for the Repeal of Sec. 6 of the "Neutrality Act of 1939," October 9, 1941

[See p. 23.]

(2) Statement of the Secretary of State (Hull) to the House Committee on Foreign Affairs, October 13, 1941[3]

The purpose of this bill is to repeal section 6 of the Neutrality Act of 1939 prohibiting the arming of our merchant vessels engaged in foreign commerce. The provisions of this section had their origin in section 10 of the act of 1937, which had made it unlawful for American vessels engaged in commerce with a "belligerent" state to be armed. The act of 1939 broadened that provision by making it unlawful for an American vessel engaged in commerce "with any foreign state" to be armed. This makes it impossible for American merchant vessels to defend themselves on the high seas against danger from lawless forces seeking world-domination.

The neutrality acts did not remotely contemplate limiting the steps to be taken by this country in self-defense, especially were there to develop situations of serious and immediate danger to the United States and to this hemisphere. There was never any thought or intention to abandon to the slightest extent the full right of our necessary self-defense.

[1] U. S. Congress, Senate, Committee on Foreign Relations, *Modification of Neutrality Act of 1939; Hearings . . . on H. J. Res. 237.* Washington, 1941. 291 p.

[2] Senate Report No. 764, 77th Cong., 1st sess.

[3] U. S. Congress, House of Representatives, Committee on Foreign Affairs, *Arming American Merchant Vessels; Hearings . . . on H. J. Res. 237*, p. 2; Department of State, *Bulletin*, V, p. 291.

At the time when these acts were passed many people believed that reliance could be placed on established rules of warfare. One of those rules was and is that merchant vessels, while subject to the belligerent right of visit and search, should not be sunk except under certain specified conditions and limitations. We remembered then, as we do now, what had happened during the ruthless submarine warfare of the World War. We attached importance, however, to the fact that during the years that followed the World War an effort was made to reduce to binding conventional form certain rules theretofore understood to be binding on belligerents. In the London Naval Treaty of 1930, provisions were incorporated in part IV stating that the following were accepted as established rules of international law:

"(1) In their action with regard to merchant ships, submarines must conform to the rules of International Law to which surface vessels are subject.

"(2) In particular, except in the case of persistent refusal to stop on being duly summoned, or of active resistance to visit or search, a warship, whether surface vessel or submarine, may not sink or render incapable of navigation a merchant vessel without having first placed passengers, crew and ship's papers in a place of safety. For this purpose the ship's boats are not regarded as a place of safety unless the safety of the passengers and crew is assured, in the existing sea and weather conditions, by the proximity of land, or the presence of another vessel which is in a position to take them on board."

The action taken was the outgrowth of steps initiated at the Conference on the Limitation of Armament held in Washington in 1921–22. In 1936 the above-quoted rules were incorporated in a protocol concluded at London, which was signed or adhered to by 47 nations, including the United States, Great Britain, France, Germany, and Italy.

Despite this solemn commitment of the powers as to the rules which should govern submarines, the German Government is today, and has been throughout the course of the present war, sinking defenseless merchant vessels, including vessels of the United States and of other American Republics, either without warning or without allowing the passengers and crews a reasonable chance for their lives. We are, therefore, confronted with a situation where a gigantic military machine has been thrown against peaceful peoples on land and on sea in a manner unprecedented in the annals of history. Submarines, armed raiders, and high-powered bombing planes are inflicting death and destruction in a manner which would put to shame the most ruthless pirates of earlier days.

The provisions of section 6 of the Neutrality Act are not called for under international law. They were adopted by our own choice. They now serve no useful purpose. On the contrary, they are a handicap. They render our merchant vessels defenseless and make them easier prey for twentieth-century pirates.

It is our right to arm our vessels for purposes of defense. That cannot be questioned. We have, since the beginning of our independent existence, exercised this right of arming our merchant vessels whenever, for the purpose of protection, we have needed to do so. For example, in 1798 when depredations on our commerce were being committed by vessels sailing under authority of the French Republic, the Congress, after the expulsion of the French Consuls from the United States, passed, upon recommendation of President Adams, an act permitting the arming of our merchant vessels for the purpose of defense against capture as well as to "subdue and capture" any armed vessel of France. The courts of France then held that the arming of American vessels for these purposes did not render such vessels liable to condemnation when captured by French men-of-war.

In addition to what I have just said it is well known that since section 6 of the Neutrality Act was adopted entirely new conditions have developed. Section 6 must, therefore, be reconsidered in the light of these new conditions and in the light of later legislation and executive responsibilities thereunder. The new conditions have been produced by the Hitler movement of world invasion. Hitler is endeavoring to conquer the European and African and other Continents, and he therefore is desperately seeking to control the high seas. To this end he has projected his forces far out into the Atlantic with a policy of submarine lawlessness and terror. This broad movement of conquest, world-wide in its objectives, places squarely before the United States the urgent and most important question of self-defense. We cannot turn and walk away from the steadily spreading danger. Both the Congress and the Executive have recognized this change in the situation. The Congress has enacted and the Executive is carrying out a policy of aiding Great Britain and other nations whose resistance to aggression stands as the one great barrier between the aggressors and the hemisphere whose security is our security.

The theory of the neutrality legislation was that by acting within the limitations which it prescribed we could keep away from danger. But danger has come to us — has been thrust upon us — and our problem now is not that of avoiding it but of defending ourselves against a hostile movement seriously threatening us and the entire Western Hemisphere.

The blunt truth is that the world is steadily being dragged downward and backward by the mightiest movement of conquest ever attempted in all history. Armed and militant predatory forces are marching across continents and invading the seas, leaving desolation in their wake. With them rides a policy of frightfulness, pillage, murder, and calculated cruelty which fills all civilized mankind with horror and indignation. Institutions devoted to the safeguarding and promotion of human rights and welfare built up through the ages are being destroyed by methods like those used by barbarian invaders 16 centuries ago.

To many people, especially in a peace-loving country like ours, this attempt at world-conquest, now proceeding on an ever-expanding scale, appears so unusual and unprecedented that they do not at all perceive the danger to this country that this movement portends. This failure to realize and comprehend the vastness of the plan and the savagery of its unlimited objectives has been, and still is, the greatest single source of peril to those free peoples who are yet unconquered and who still possess and enjoy their priceless institutions. If the 16 nations that already have been overrun and enslaved could break their enforced silence and speak to us, they would cry out with a single voice, "Do not delay your defense until it is too late."

The Hitler government is engaged in a progressive and widening assault carried out through unrestricted attacks by submarines, surface raiders, and aircraft at widely separated points. The intent of these attacks is to intimidate this country into weakening or abandoning the legitimate defenses of the hemisphere by retreating from the seas. In defiance of the laws of the sea and the recognized rights of all nations, the Hitler government has presumed to declare on paper that great areas of the ocean are to be closed and that no ships may enter those areas for any purpose except at peril of being sunk. This pronouncement of indiscriminate sinking makes no distinction between armed and unarmed vessels, nor does the actual practice of the German Government make any such distinction. Since vessels are thus sunk whether armed or unarmed, it is manifest that a greater degree of safety would be had by arming them. Moreover, Gemany carries her policy of frightfulness, especially in the Atlantic, far outside of these paper areas.

We are confronted with a paramount problem, and we must be guided by a controlling principle. The problem is to set up as swiftly as possible the most effective means of self-defense. The principle is that the first duty of an independent nation is to safeguard its own security.

In the light of these considerations, further revision of our neutrality legislation is now imperatively required. Now, as in earlier times, necessary measures on land and sea for the defense of the United States and of the other independent nations of this hemisphere must be taken, in accordance with the wise, settled, and traditional policy of our Republic.

We are today face to face with a great emergency. We should not sit with our hands tied by these provisions of law.

If Hitler should succeed in his supreme purpose to conquer Great Britain and thus secure control of the high seas, we would suddenly find the danger at our own door.

Provisions of the Neutrality Act must not prevent our full defense. Any that stand in the way should be promptly repealed. I support the pending proposal to repeal section 6. My own judgment is that section 2 also should be repealed or modified.

(3) Statement of the Secretary of State (Hull) to the Senate Committee on Foreign Relations, October 21, 1941 [1]

The progress of events, and particularly of military and naval operations beyond and on the seas, makes it advisable and urgent that the Congress grant full authority to take certain measures which are plainly essential for the defense of the United States. It is imperative now to exercise what Elihu Root in 1914 called "the right of every sovereign state to protect itself by preventing a condition of affairs in which it will be too late to protect itself."

Such a condition of affairs now impends. Unless it is promptly dealt with, efforts at self-defense may come too late.

The paramount principle of national policy is the preservation of the safety and security of the Nation. The highest right flowing from that principle is the right of self-defense. That right must now be invoked. The key to that defense under present conditions is to prevent Hitler from gaining control of the seas.

On October 26, 1940, I said:

"Should the would-be conquerors gain control of other continents, they would next concentrate on perfecting their control of the seas, of the air over the seas, and of the world's economy; they might then be able with ships and with planes to strike at the communication lines, the commerce, and the life of this hemisphere; and ultimately we might find ourselves compelled to fight on our own soil, under our own skies, in defense of our independence and our very lives."

[1] U. S. Congress, Senate, Committee on Foreign Relations, *Modification of Neutrality Act of 1939; Hearings . . . on H. J. Res. 237*, p. 2; Department of State, *Bulletin*, V, p. 307.

In the year which has ensued, Hitler and his satellites have extended their military occupation to most of the Continent of Europe. They are already seeking control of the sea. They have attacked American vessels, contrary to all law, in widely separated areas; particularly they are now trying to sever the sea lanes which link the United States to the remaining free peoples. Hitler under his policy of intimidation and frightfulness has in effect given notice that American lives and American ships, no less than the lives and ships of other nations, will be destroyed if they are found in most of the north Atlantic Ocean. In the presence of threats and acts by an outlaw nation, there arises the right, and there is imposed the duty, of prompt and determined defense. Our ships and men are legitimately sailing the seas. The outlaw who preaches and practices indiscriminate, terroristic attack in pursuit of world-conquest is estopped to invoke any law if law-abiding nations act to defend themselves.

The conviction that the Atlantic approaches to the Western Hemisphere are under attack no longer rests on inference. The attack is continuous; there is reason to believe that it will steadily increase in strength and intensity.

When the Neutrality Act of 1939 was passed, we went far in foregoing the exercise of certain rights by our citizens in time of foreign war. This was for the purpose of avoiding incidents such as those that confronted our Government during the first World War as a result of unrestricted German-submarine warfare. But there was no waiving of our right to take the fullest measures needed for self-defense on land and sea if the tide of conquest should move in our direction.

The tide has so moved. The course of the present war has altered the picture completely. Certain provisions of the existing legislation under the changed circumstances now handicap our necessary work of self-defense and stand squarely in the way of our national safety.

The Congress has recognized the change in circumstances and has passed the Lend-Lease Act. It thereby determined that the efforts of those nations which are actively resisting aggression are important and necessary to the safety of the United States. It approved, as a necessary measure of defense, the fullest support to nations which are in the front line of resistance to a movement of world-conquest more ruthless in execution and more hideous in effects than any other such movement of all time. An indispensable part of our policy must be resolute self-defense on the high seas, and this calls especially for protection of shipping on open sea lanes.

One of the greatest mistakes that we could possibly make would be to base our policy upon an assumption that we are secure, when, if the assumption should prove erroneous, the fact of having so acted would lay us completely open to hostile invasion.

When American ships are being wantonly and unlawfully attacked with complete disregard of life and property, it is absurd to forego any legitimate measures that may be helpful toward self-defense. It is especially absurd to continue to tie our hands by a provision of law which prohibits arming our merchant vessels for their own defense.

I repeat, the highest duty of this Government is to safeguard the security of our Nation. The basic consideration is that measures and methods of defense shall be made effective when and where needed. They are now needed especially on the high seas and in those areas which must be preserved from invasion if the full tide of the movement of world-conquest is not to beat at our gates.

It would be little short of criminal negligence to proceed on the hope that some happy chance or chances will save us from a fate like that which has befallen so many other countries in the world. We cannot run away from a situation which can only be dealt with by the firm measures of a people determined and prepared to resist. It is worse than futile to read the war news from overseas and conclude that each temporary check to the would-be world-conqueror relieves us of the need to provide fully for our own national defense.

I am convinced that in the interest of our national security the passage of the pending bill to repeal section 6 of the Neutrality Act is both urgent and important. Inasmuch as section 2 is not under consideration I will offer no comment except to say that in my judgment section 2 should be repealed or modified.

(4) The Speaker of the House (Rayburn) and the Majority Leader of the House (McCormack) to the President (Roosevelt), November 12, 1941 [1]

DEAR MR. PRESIDENT:

A number of Members have asked us what effect failure on the part of the House to take favorable action on the Senate amendments [2] would have upon our position in foreign countries, and especially in Germany.

Some of these Members have stated that they hoped you would make a direct expression upon this matter.

[1] *Congressional Record*, vol. 87, p. 9116 (daily edition). The correspondence was read into the *Record* just before the House vote on November 13, 1941.

[2] The amendments added by the Senate were the present sec. 1 and the last sentence of sec. 2 of the Joint Resolution approved November 17, 1941; see p. 112.

(5) *The President (Roosevelt) to the Speaker of the House (Rayburn)
and the Majority Leader of the House (McCormack), November
13, 1941* [1]

MY DEAR MR. SPEAKER AND MR. MCCORMACK:

I had had no thought of expressing to the House my views of the
effect, in foreign countries and especially in Germany, of favorable or
unfavorable action on the Senate amendments.

But in view of your letter, I am replying as simply and clearly as I
know how.

In my message of October 9, I definitely recommended arming of
ships and removing the prohibition against sending American-flag ships
into belligerent ports. Both I regarded as of extreme importance — the
first I called of immediate importance at that time. This did not lessen
the importance of the second. Another month has gone by, and the
second I regard today as of at least equal importance with the first.

In regard to the repeal of sections 2 and 3 of the Neutrality Act, I
need only call your attention to three elements. The first concerns the
continued sinking of American-flag ships in many parts of the ocean.
The second relates to great operational advantages in making continuous voyages to any belligerent port in any part of the world; thus, in
all probability increasing the total percentage of goods — foodstuffs and
munitions — actually delivered to those nations fighting Hitlerism. The
third is the decision by the Congress and the Executive that this Nation,
for its own present and future defense, must strengthen the supply line
to all of those who are today keeping Hitlerism far from the Americas.

With all of this in mind, the world is obviously watching the course
of this legislation.

In the British Empire, in China, and in Russia — all of whom are
fighting a defensive war against invasion — the effect of failure of the
Congress to repeal sections 2 and 3 of the Neutrality Act would be definitely discouraging. I am confident that it would not destroy their
defense or morale, though it would weaken their position from the
point of view of food and munitions.

Failure to repeal these sections would, of course, cause rejoicing in
the Axis nations. Failure would bolster aggressive steps and intentions
in Germany, and in the other well-known aggressor nations under the
leadership of Hitler.

[1] *Ibid.;* Department of State, *Bulletin,* V, p. 379.

Judging by all recent experience, we could, all of us, look forward to enthusiastic applause in those three nations based on the claim that the United States is disunited as they have so often prophesied.

Our own position in the struggle against aggression would be definitely weakened, not only in Europe and in Asia, but also among our sister republics in the Americas. Foreign nations, friends and enemies, would misinterpret our own mind and purpose.

I have discussed this letter with the Secretary of State and he wholeheartedly concurs.

May I take this opportunity of mentioning that in my judgment failure of the House to take favorable action on the Senate amendments would also weaken our domestic situation? Such failure would weaken our great effort to produce all we possibly can and as rapidly as we can. Strikes and stoppages of work would become less serious in the mind of the public.

I am holding a conference tomorrow in the hope that certain essential coal mines can remain in continuous operation. This may prove successful.

But if it is not successful it is obvious that this coal must be mined in order to keep the essential steel mills at work. The Government of the United States has the backing of the overwhelming majority of the people of the United States, including the workers.

Very sincerely yours,

FRANKLIN D. ROOSEVELT

(6) *The Secretary of State (Hull) to the Speaker of the House (Rayburn) and the Majority Leader of the House (McCormack), November 13, 1941* [1]

MY DEAR MR. SPEAKER:
MY DEAR MR. McCORMACK:

In response to your request for my views on H. J. Res. 237, which provides for the repeal of sections 2, 3, and 6 of the Neutrality Act of 1939, I offer the following brief comment apart from the points covered in the President's letter to you of this date.

It is my judgment that in the light of existing conditions the passage of this bill is absolutely essential to our national defense. These conditions are completely different from those existing at the time the

[1] Department of State, *Bulletin*, V, p. 380.

Neutrality Act was passed; they present an entirely new problem of danger and of methods for dealing with it.

The Neutrality Act represented an endeavor to avoid the limited danger which might arise from the entrance of American citizens and American ships into areas of hostilities far from our own shores. The provisions of that Act did not and could not visualize the vast danger which has since arisen from a world movement of invasion under Hitler's leadership, and which is now moving steadily in the direction of this hemisphere and this country.

As a part of this movement of conquest, the greatest intermediate objective of Hitler's armed forces is to capture Great Britain and to gain control of the high seas. To this end, Hitler has projected his forces far out into the Atlantic with a policy of submarine ruthlessness. By intimidation and terror he would drive our ships from the high seas, and ships of all nations from most of the North Atlantic. Even in the waters of the Western Hemisphere he has attacked and destroyed our ships, as well as ships of other American Republics, with resulting loss of American lives.

The breadth of our self-defense must at all times equal the breadth of the dangers which threaten us. In the circumstances of today, we must be free to arm our merchant ships for their own protection; and we must be free, in the event of particular and extreme emergency, to use these ships for the carriage of supplies to nations which are resisting the world-wide movement of conquest headed in our direction. This Government would, of course, use caution in carrying out the power which it could exercise upon the passage of the bill.

To maintain our security we must pursue a resolute course in a world of danger and be prepared to meet that danger. We must take measures of defense whenever necessity arises. We cannot promote much less preserve our safety by a course of inactivity and complacency in the face of a peril which is coming toward us. Other countries and especially countries unfriendly to us will necessarily assume that this bill has been discussed and dealt with on its own merits. I hope this will be kept in mind.

The paramount duty of this Government is to preserve the safety and security of our country. I would be neglecting the responsibility of my office if I did not state the frank opinion that there is imperative need for the passage of this bill to enable our Government effectively to carry out this duty.

(7) Joint Resolution to Repeal Sections 2, 3, and 6 of the Neutrality Act of 1939, and for Other Purposes, Approved November 17, 1941, 4 : 30 P.M., E. S. T.[1]

Resolved by the Senate and House of Representatives of the United States of America in Congress assembled, That section 2 of the Neutrality Act of 1939 (relating to commerce with States engaged in armed conflict), and section 3 of such Act (relating to combat areas), are hereby repealed.

SEC. 2. Section 6 of the Neutrality Act of 1939 (relating to the arming of American vessels) is hereby repealed; and, during the unlimited national emergency proclaimed by the President on May 27, 1941, the President is authorized, through such agency as he may designate, to arm, or to permit or cause to be armed, any American vessel as defined in such Act. The provisions of section 16 of the Criminal Code [2] (relating to bonds from armed vessels on clearing) shall not apply to any such vessel.

(a) Arming of Merchant Vessels, White House Release, November 28, 1941 [3]

American merchant vessels sailing on routes between United States ports and ports of Spain, Portugal, and their adjacent island possessions will not be armed.

American merchant vessels sailing in the inter-American trade between ports of the United States and ports in Central and South America will not be armed.

American merchant vessels sailing on routes in the Pacific Ocean will not be armed under existing circumstances.

Public announcement will be made of any change of policy affecting any of these routes.

Public Law 459, 77th Cong., approved February 21, 1942, added to Sec. 7 (Financial Transactions) [4] of the Neutrality Act of 1939 a subsection (*e*) reading: "This section shall not be operative when the United States is at war."

Public Law 414, 77th Cong., approved January 26, 1942, amended Sec. 12 (National Munitions Control Board)[5] by adding to subsection (*h*) the following: "Any reports required by this section may be omitted or dispensed with in the discretion of the Secretary of State during the existence of a state of war."

[1] Public Law 294, 77th Cong., originated as H. J. Res. 237, on which hearings were held; House Report No. 1267; Senate Report No. 764.

For texts of the repealed sections, see *Documents, II, 1939–40*, p. 657–62.

[2] U. S. Code, title 18, sec. 28.

[3] Department of State, *Bulletin*, V, p. 425.

[4] See *Documents, II, 1939–40*, p. 662.

[5] *Ibid.*, p. 667.

4. AMERICAN ENTRANCE INTO THE WAR

The formal entrance of the United States into war came as the result of the surprise Japanese attack in the Hawaiian Islands, commencing on Sunday, December 7, at 1 : 25 P.M., E.S.T.[1] Partly as the result of the anomalous character of military operations in the Far East, the relation of the United States to the war then in progress was regarded primarily in terms of our relation to the European struggle, although the conclusion of the Three-Power Pact between Germany, Italy and Japan, on September 27, 1940,[2] made it clear that we could not dissociate the war in Europe from Japanese aggression in the Far East.

As a result of the Pearl Harbor attack, the entrance of the United States into the war was made to appear as the direct result of the growing stresses and strains in our relations with Japan which are covered, in so far as they fall within the period of this volume, in Chapter VI. That there was close collaboration between the Axis Powers in their acts of aggression was reasonably certain from the beginning and became crystal clear with the signing of the Three-Power Pact of September 27, 1940. While Japan's attack upon us, when negotiations were still in progress, was undoubtedly prompted primarily by the conviction of Japan's leaders that war with the United States was inevitable if Japan were to satisfy her ambitions in the Far East and should therefore be commenced under conditions most favorable to Japan, it seems reasonably clear that Japan's aggression was also part of the strategy of the Axis Powers in waging the global war in which they were engaged. As the assistance which we gave to those nations resisting Axis aggression became ever more effective, the likelihood that we would become formally involved in this war correspondingly increased.

A. War with Japan

(1) *The Japanese Attack of December 7, 1941. Extract from the Message of the President (Roosevelt) to the Congress, December 15, 1941* [3]

Following the tension resulting from the sending of Japanese forces into southern French Indo-China in July 1941, and at the suggestion of the Japanese Government,[4] conversations undertaken at an earlier date with a view to finding possible bases for the settlement of differences between the United States and Japan were resumed.[5] In the midst of these conversations new movements of Japanese armed forces into French Indo-China were reported. On November 26, definite proposals were submitted to the Japanese Ambassador by Secretary of State Hull.[6] Failure to receive a satisfactory explanation of Japanese troop movements through ordinary diplomatic channels prompted President Roosevelt to address a personal message to the Emperor of Japan, dated December 6.[7]

[1] This is the time given in the Roberts Commission Report (Sen. Doc. No. 159, 77th Cong., 2d sess.)

[2] *Documents, III, 1940–41*, p. 304–5.

[3] House Doc. No. 458, 77th Cong., 1st sess., this volume, p. 469.

[4] The Secretary of State (Hull) to the Japanese Ambassador (Nomura), October 2, 941, this volume, p. 513.

[5] *Ibid.*

[6] *Ibid.*, p. 519.

[7] *Ibid.*, p. 525.

On the afternoon of December 7, at 2 : 15 P.M., E.S.T., the Japanese Ambassador handed to the Secretary of State a reply to the American proposals of November 26. At 1 : 25 P.M. the Japanese had commenced their attack upon American naval and land forces and establishments at Pearl Harbor. For summary of past relations, as well as more immediate events, see the President's Message to Congress, December 15, 1941, p. 469.

For the record of history, it is essential in reading this part of my message always to bear in mind that the actual air and submarine attack in the Hawaiian Islands commenced on Sunday, December 7, at 1 : 20 P.M., Washington time; 7 : 50 A.M., Honolulu time of same day — Monday, December 8, 3 : 20 A.M., Tokyo time.

To my message of December 6 (9 P.M., Washington time — December 7, 11 A.M., Tokyo time) to the Emperor of Japan, invoking his cooperation with me in further effort to preserve peace, there has finally come to me on December 10 (6 : 23 A.M., Washington time — December 10, 8 : 23 P.M., Tokyo time) a reply conveyed in a telegraphic report by the American Ambassador at Tokyo dated December 8, 1 P.M. (December 7, 11 P.M., Washington time).

The Ambassador reported that at 7 o'clock on the morning of the 8th (December 7, 5 P.M., Washington time) the Japanese Minister for Foreign Affairs asked him to call at his official residence; that the Foreign Minister handed the Ambassador a memorandum dated December 8 (December 7, Washington time), the text of which had been transmitted to the Japanese Ambassador in Washington to be presented to the American Government (this was the memorandum which was delivered by the Japanese Ambassador to the Secretary of State at 2 : 20 P.M. on Sunday, December 7 (Monday, December 8, 4 : 20 A.M., Tokyo time); that the Foreign Minister had been in touch with the Emperor; and that the Emperor desired that the memorandum be regarded as the Emperor's reply to my message.

Further, the Ambassador reports, the Foreign Minister made an oral statement. Textually, the oral statement began, "His Majesty has expressed his gratefulness and appreciation for the cordial message of the President." The message further continued to the effect that, in regard to our inquiries on the subject of increase of Japanese forces in French Indo-China, His Majesty had commanded his Government to state its views to the American Government. The message concluded textually, with the statement:

Establishment of peace in the Pacific, and consequently of the world, has been the cherished desire of His Majesty for the realization of which he has hitherto made his Government to continue its earnest endeavors. His Majesty trusts that the President is fully aware of this fact.

Japan's real reply, however, made by Japan's warlords and evidently formulated many days before, took the form of the attack which had already been made without warning upon our territories at various points in the Pacific.

There is the record, for all history to read in amazement, in sorrow, in horror, and in disgust!

(2) *Rescript of the Japanese Emperor (Hirohito), December 8, 1941* [1]

According to the Associated Press account, the state of war was declared by Japan against the United States and the British Empire by Japanese Imperial Headquarters at Tokyo, 6 A.M., December 8, 1941 (4 P.M., December 7, E.S.T.), the attack on Pearl Harbor having preceded the declaration by some 3 hours.

We, by the grace of Heaven, Emperor of Japan seated on the throne of a line unbroken for ages eternal, enjoin upon ye, our loyal and brave subjects:

We hereby declare war on the United States of America and the British Empire.

Men and officers of our Army and Navy shall do their utmost in prosecuting the war, our public servants of various departments shall perform faithfully and diligently their appointed tasks and all other subjects of ours shall pursue their respective duties; the entire nation with united will shall mobilize their total strength so that nothing will miscarry in the attainment of our war aims.

To insure the stability of East Asia and to contribute to world peace is the far-sighted policy which was formulated by our great, illustrious, imperial grandsire and by our great imperial sire succeeding him and which we lay constantly to heart. To cultivate friendship among the nations and to enjoy prosperity in common with all nations has always been the guiding principle of our Empire's foreign policy.

It has been truly unavoidable and far from our wishes that our Empire has now been brought to cross swords with America and Britain. More than four years have passed since China, failing to comprehend the true intentions of our Empire and recklessly courting trouble, disturbed the peace of East Asia. Although there has been re-established a national government of China with which Japan has effected neighborly intercourse and cooperation, the regime which has survived at Chungking, relying upon American and British protection, still continues its fratricidal opposition.

[1] *The Times* (London), December 9, p. 3.

Eager for the realization of their inordinate ambition to dominate the Orient, both America and Britain, in giving support to the Chungking regime, have aggravated the disturbances in East Asia. Moreover, these two powers, inducing other countries to follow suit, increased military preparations on all sides of our Empire to challenge us. They have obstructed by every means our peaceful commerce, and finally have resorted to the direct severance of economic relations, menacing gravely the existence of our Empire.

Patiently have we waited and long have we endured in the hope that our Government might retrieve the situation in peace.

But our adversaries, showing not the least spirit of conciliation, have unduly delayed a settlement, and in the meantime they have intensified economic and political pressure to compel thereby our Empire to submission.

This trend of affairs would, if left unchecked, not only nullify our Empire's efforts of many years for the sake of stabilization of East Asia, but also endanger the very existence of our nation. The situation being such as it is, our Empire, for its existence and self-defense, has no other recourse but to appeal to arms and to crush every obstacle in its path.

Hallowed spirits of our imperial ancestors guarding us from above, we rely upon the loyalty and courage of our subjects in our confident expectation that the task bequeathed by our forefathers will be carried forward and that sources of evil will be speedily eradicated and enduring peace immutably established in East Asia, preserving thereby the glory of our Empire.

(3) War Message of the President (Roosevelt) to the Congress, December 8, 1941, 12 : 30 P.M., E.S.T.[1]

To the Congress of the United States:

Yesterday, December 7, 1941 — a date which will live in infamy — the United States of America was suddenly and deliberately attacked by naval and air forces of the Empire of Japan.

The United States was at peace with that Nation and, at the solicitation of Japan, was still in conversation with its Government and its Emperor looking toward the maintenance of peace in the Pacific. Indeed, one hour after Japanese air squadrons had commenced bombing in Oahu, the Japanese Ambassador to the United States and his col-

[1] House Doc. 453, 77th Cong., 1st sess.; Sen. Doc. 148, 77th Cong., 1st sess., p. 7; Department of State, *Bulletin*, V, p. 474.

league delivered to the Secretary of State a formal reply to a recent American message. While this reply stated that it seemed useless to continue the existing diplomatic negotiations, it contained no threat or hint of war or armed attack.

It will be recorded that the distance of Hawaii from Japan makes it obvious that the attack was deliberately planned many days or even weeks ago. During the intervening time the Japanese Government has deliberately sought to deceive the United States by false statements and expressions of hope for continued peace.

The attack yesterday on the Hawaiian Islands has caused severe damage to American naval and military forces. Very many American lives have been lost.[1] In addition American ships have been reported torpedoed on the high seas between San Francisco and Honolulu.

Yesterday the Japanese Government also launched an attack against Malaya.

Last night Japanese forces attacked Hong Kong.

Last night Japanese forces attacked Guam.

Last night Japanese forces attacked the Philippine Islands.

Last night the Japanese attacked Wake Island.

This morning the Japanese attacked Midway Island.

Japan has, therefore, undertaken a surprise offensive extending throughout the Pacific area. The facts of yesterday speak for themselves. The people of the United States have already formed their opinions and well understand the implications to the very life and safety of our Nation.

As Commander-in-Chief of the Army and Navy I have directed that all measures be taken for our defense.

Always will we remember the character of the onslaught against us.

No matter how long it may take us to overcome this premeditated invasion, the American people in their righteous might will win through to absolute victory.

I believe I interpret the will of the Congress and of the people when I assert that we will not only defend ourselves to the uttermost but will make very certain that this form of treachery shall never endanger us again.

Hostilities exist. There is no blinking at the fact that our people, our territory, and our interests are in grave danger.

---

[1] The casualties, officers and men, were: killed, 2,340; wounded, 946. The President also discussed damage to warships and airplanes without precise figures in his Washington's Birthday address, February 23, 1942, see p. 53. See also report of Roberts Commission (Sen. Doc. No. 159, 77th Cong. 2d sess.).

With confidence in our armed forces — with the unbounded determination of our people — we will gain the inevitable triumph — so help us God.

I ask that the Congress declare that since the unprovoked and dastardly attack by Japan on Sunday, December seventh, a state of war has existed between the United States and the Japanese Empire.

FRANKLIN D. ROOSEVELT

(4) **Joint Resolution Declaring that a State of War Exists between the Imperial Government of Japan and the Government and the People of the United States and Making Provisions to Prosecute the Same, Approved December 8, 1941, 4 : 10 P.M., E.S.T.**[1]

Whereas the Imperial Government of Japan has committed unprovoked acts of war against the Government and the people of the United States of America: Therefore be it

Resolved by the Senate and House of Representatives of the United States of America in Congress assembled, That the state of war between the United States and the Imperial Government of Japan which has thus been thrust upon the United States is hereby formally declared; and the President is hereby authorized and directed to employ the entire naval and military forces of the United States and the resources of the Government to carry on war against the Imperial Government of Japan; and, to bring the conflict to a successful termination, all of the resources of the country are hereby pledged by the Congress of the United States.

B. War with Germany and Italy

(1) **Declaration of War by Germany. The German Secretary of State for Foreign Affairs (Ribbentrop) to the American Chargé d'Affaires at Berlin (Morris), December 11, 1941** [2]

MR. CHARGÉ D'AFFAIRES:

The Government of the United States having violated in the most flagrant manner and in ever-increasing measure all rules of neutrality

[1] Public Law 328, 77th Cong.; originated as S. J. Res. 116, introduced by Senator Tom Connally (Chairman of the Committee on Foreign Relations) without reference to a committee; passed by the Senate, yeas 82, nays 0; taken from the Speaker's table in the House of Representatives by unanimous consent and passed without record vote; House proceedings vacated on identic H. J. Res. 254, reported from Committee on Foreign Affairs and previously passed, yeas 388, nays 1; Sen. Doc. 148; 77th Cong., 1st sess., p. 11, 17.

[2] Department of State, *Bulletin,* V, p. 481.

in favor of the adversaries of Germany and having continually been guilty of the most severe provocations toward Germany ever since the outbreak of the European war, provoked by the British declaration of war against Germany on September 3, 1939, has finally resorted to open military acts of aggression.

On September 11, 1941, the President of the United States publicly declared that he had ordered the American Navy and Air Force to shoot on sight at any German war vessel. In his speech of October 27, 1941, he once more expressly affirmed that this order was in force. Acting under this order, vessels of the American Navy, since early September 1941, have systematically attacked German naval forces. Thus, American destroyers, as for instance the *Greer*, the *Kearny* and the *Reuben James*, have opened fire on German submarines according to plan. The Secretary of the American Navy, Mr. Knox, himself confirmed that American destroyers attacked German submarines.

Furthermore, the naval forces of the United States, under order of their Government and contrary to international law have treated and seized German merchant vessels on the high seas as enemy ships.

The German Government therefore establishes the following facts:

Although Germany on her part has strictly adhered to the rules of international law in her relations with the United States during every period of the present war, the Government of the United States from initial violations of neutrality has finally proceeded to open acts of war against Germany. The Government of the United States has thereby virtually created a state of war.

The German Government, consequently, discontinues diplomatic relations with the United States of America and declares that under these circumstances brought about by President Roosevelt Germany too, as from today, considers herself as being in a state of war with the United States of America.

Accept, Mr. Chargé d'Affaires, the expression of my high consideration.

(a) *Notification by the German Chargé d'Affaires (Thomsen) to the Chief of the European Division, Department of State (Atherton), for the Secretary of State (Hull), December 11, 1941, 9 : 30 A.M., E.S.T.*[1]

The German Chargé d'Affaires, Dr. Hans Thomsen, and the First Secretary of the German Embassy, Mr. von Strempel, called at the

[1] Narrative press release, *ibid.*, p. 480.

State Department at 8 : 20 A.M. on December 11, 1941. The Secretary, otherwise engaged, directed that they be received by the Chief of the European Division of the State Department, Mr. Ray Atherton. Mr. Atherton received the German representatives at 9 : 30 A.M.

The German representatives handed to Mr. Atherton a copy of a note that was being delivered that morning, December 11, to the American Chargé d'Affaires in Berlin. Dr. Thomsen said that Germany considered herself in a state of war with the United States. He asked that the appropriate measures be taken for the departure of himself, the members of the German Embassy, and staff in this country. He reminded Mr. Atherton that the German Government had previously expressed its willingness to grant the same treatment to American press correspondents in Germany as that accorded the American official staff on a reciprocal basis and added that he assumed that the departure of other American citizens from Germany would be permitted on the same basis of German citizens desiring to leave this country. He referred to the exchange of civilians that had been arranged at the time Great Britain and Germany broke off diplomatic relations.

The German Chargé d'Affaires then stated that the Swiss Government would take over German interests in this country and that Dr. Bruggmann had already received appropriate instructions from his Government.

He then handed Mr. Atherton the note from the German Government. Mr. Atherton stated that in accepting this note from the German Chargé d'Affaires he was merely formalizing the realization that the Government and people of this country had faced since the outbreak of the war in 1939 of the threat and purposes of the German Government and the Nazi regime toward this hemisphere and our free American civilization.

(2) Notification of State of War by Italian Minister for Foreign Affairs (Ciano), December 11, 1941 [1]

The Italian Foreign Minister, Count Ciano, sent for the American Chargé d'Affaires, Mr. George Wadsworth, at Rome at 2 : 30 the afternoon of December 11, and when Mr. Wadsworth arrived at his office Count Ciano informed him that as of December 11, 1941, Italy considers itself at war with the United States.

[1] Press release, *ibid.*, p. 482.

a) Inquiry of the Italian Ambassador (Colonna) at the Department of State, December 11, 1941 [1]

The Italian Ambassador, accompanied by Signor Conti, First Secretary of the Embassy, called on the morning of December 11 at Mr. [James Clement] Dunn's [2] office at 10 : 30 to inform the Department that he was without instructions from his Government and to inquire as to his status. When he was informed that the Italian Government had notified the American Chargé d'Affaires in Rome December 11 that Italy considered itself at war with the United States the Ambassador asked that measures be taken to permit the staff of the Embassy to make their final arrangements for departure from the United States. He added that many Italian nationals in this country had requested that they be allowed to depart with the Italian diplomatic mission. He was informed that all arrangements for the departure of the Italian mission from this country and the treatment of Italian nationals would be dealt with strictly on a reciprocal basis in accordance with the treatment given by the Italian Government to the American diplomatic mission and American nationals in Italy.

The Italian Ambassador was informed that we had long expected Germany to carry out its threat against this hemisphere and the United States and that we fully anticipated that Italy would obediently follow along.

3) War Message of the President (Roosevelt) to the Congress, December 11, 1941 [3]

To the Congress of the United States:

On the morning of December eleventh, the Government of Germany, pursuing its course of world-conquest, declared war against the United States.

The long known and the long expected has thus taken place. The forces endeavoring to enslave the entire world now are moving towards this hemisphere.

Never before has there been a greater challenge to life, liberty, and civilization.

Delay invites greater danger. Rapid and united effort by all of the peoples of the world who are determined to remain free will insure a world victory of the forces of justice and of righteousness over the forces of savagery and of barbarism.

Italy also has declared war against the United States.

I therefore request the Congress to recognize a state of war between the United States and Germany, and between the United States and Italy.

FRANKLIN D. ROOSEVELT

---

[1] Narrative press release, *ibid.*

[2] Adviser on Political Relations, Department of State.

[3] House Doc. 454, 77th Cong., 1st sess.; Sen. Doc. 148, 77th Cong., 1st sess., p. 12, 0; Department of State, *Bulletin*, V, p. 475.

(4) *Joint Resolution Declaring that a State of War Exists between the Government of Germany and the Government and the People of the United States and Making Provision to Prosecute the Same Approved December 11, 1941, 3 : 05 P.M., E.S.T.*[1]

Whereas the Government of Germany has formally declared war against the Government and the people of the United States of America. Therefore be it

Resolved by the Senate and House of Representatives of the United States of America in Congress assembled, That the state of war between the United States and the Government of Germany which has thus been thrust upon the United States is hereby formally declared; and the President is hereby authorized and directed to employ the entire naval and military forces of the United States and the resources of the Government to carry on war against the Government of Germany; and, to bring the conflict to a successful termination, all of the resources of the country are hereby pledged by the Congress of the United States.

(5) *Joint Resolution Declaring that a State of War Exists between the Government of Italy and the Government and the People of the United States and Making Provision to Prosecute the Same Approved December 11, 1941, 3 : 06 P.M., E.S.T.*[2]

[The text is the same as that of the Joint Resolution declaring war against Germany, *mutatis mutandis.*]

C. War with Bulgaria, Hungary and Rumania

(1) *The Secretary General of the Rumanian Foreign Office to the United States Legation at Bucharest, December 12, 1941* [3]

The Royal Rumanian Government has the honor to communicate to the Government of the United States of America that, in conformity with the dispositions of the Tripartite Pact and respecting the obligations of solidarity contained in this pact, as a result of the state of war which has arisen between the United States of America on the one hand, and the German Reich, Italy and Japan on the other, Rumania herself is in a state of war with the United States of America.

[1] Public Law 331, 77th Cong.; originating as S. J. Res. 119, introduced by Mr. Connally from the Committee on Foreign Relations; passed Senate, yeas 88, nays 0; taken from Speaker's table by unanimous consent of the House and passed without record vote; House proceedings on H. J. Res. 256, passed, yeas 393, "present" 1, vacated Sen. Doc. 148, 77th Cong., 1st sess., p. 12, 20.

[2] Public Law 332, 77th Cong.; originating as S. J. Res. 120, by Mr. Connally from the Committee on Foreign Relations; passed Senate, yeas 90, nays 0; passed House under suspension of the rules, yeas 399, "present" 1; Sen. Doc. 148, 77th Cong., 1 sess., p. 14, 22.　　　　　　　　　[3] Department of State, *Bulletin,* V, p. 483

2) *Declarations of the Hungarian Prime Minister (Bardosy), December 11 and 13, 1941* [1]

The Hungarian Prime Minister informed the American Minister at 8 P.M. on he evening of December 11 that in view of the solidarity of the Central European states, which he compared with the solidarity of the republics of the Western Hemisphere, Hungary was obliged to break diplomatic relations with the United States. He said that this was not with the intention of declaring war on the United States.

On December 13, at 5 : 30 P.M., the American Minister was informed by the Hungarian Prime Minister that Hungary considered war to exist between Hungary and the United States.

3) *Declaration of the Bulgarian Government, December 13, 1941* [2]

The American Minister in Sofia informed the Department of State on December 13, 1941, that the Bulgarian Government had just declared in Parliament hat in accordance with Article 3 of the Tripartite Pact [3] Bulgaria was in a state of war with the United States. He added that he was expecting official notification momentarily.

4) *United States Declarations of War against Bulgaria, Hungary and Rumania, June 5, 1942*

The request of the President for declarations of war against these three states came a little less than six months after these Axis satellites had declared war on he United States. It was generally believed at the time of the President's equest that his action was linked with the American-Anglo-Soviet conferences on a second front to relieve pressure against the U.S.S.R. and on a supply agreement to succeed the one that expired June 30, 1942. It was considered a response o the urging of Premier Stalin that the United States declare war against these hree states which had been so actively supporting German military operations against the U.S.S.R.

a) *Message of the President (Roosevelt) Recommending a Declaration of War against Bulgaria, Hungary and Rumania, June 2, 1942* [4]

TO THE CONGRESS OF THE UNITED STATES OF AMERICA:

The Governments of Bulgaria, Hungary, and Rumania have declared war against the United States. I realize that the three Governments took this action not upon their own initiative or in response to the wishes of their own peoples but as the instruments of Hitler. These

---

[1] Summary given is based upon narrative press releases, December 11 and 13, *ibid.*, p. 482.

[2] Summary given is based upon narrative press release, *ibid.*, p. 483.

[3] Bulgaria had adhered on March 1, 1941.

[4] From the Office of the Secretary to the President; *ibid.*, VI, p. 509; House Doc. No. 761, 77th Cong., 2d sess.

three Governments are now engaged in military activities directed against the United Nations and are planning an extension of these activities.

Therefore, I recommend that the Congress recognize a state of war between the United States and Bulgaria, between the United States and Hungary, and between the United States and Rumania.

FRANKLIN D. ROOSEVELT

(b) Joint Resolution Declaring that a State of War Exists between the Government of Bulgaria and the Government and the People of the United States and Making Provisions to Prosecute the Same, Approved June 5, 1942 [1]

Whereas the Government of Bulgaria has formally declared war against the Government and the people of the United States of America Therefore be it

Resolved by the Senate and House of Representatives of the United States of America in Congress assembled, That the state of war between the United States and the Government of Bulgaria which has thus been thrust upon the United States is hereby formally declared; and the President is hereby authorized and directed to employ the entire naval and military forces of the United States and the resources of the Government to carry on war against the Government of Bulgaria; and, to bring the conflict to a successful termination, all of the resources of the country are hereby pledged by the Congress of the United States.

(c) Joint Resolution Declaring a State of War with Hungary, Approved June 5, 1942 [2]

[The text is the same as that of the Joint Resolution Declaring a State of War with Bulgaria, *mutatis mutandis.*]

(d) Joint Resolution Declaring a State of War with Rumania, Approved June 5, 1942 [3]

[The text is the same as that of the Joint Resolution Declaring a State of War with Bulgaria, *mutatis mutandis.*]

[1] Public Law 563, 77th Cong.; originated as H. J. Res. 319, introduced by Mr McCormack (Majority floor leader); passed by the House, after suspension of the rules, June 3, yeas 357, nays 0; passed by the Senate, June 4, yeas 73, nays 0. *Congressional Record,* vol. 88, p. 4979–81, 5045–47 (daily edition).

[2] Public Law 564, 77th Cong.; originated as H. J. Res. 320, introduced by Mr McCormack; passed by the House, after suspension of the rules, June 3, yeas 360, nays 0; passed by the Senate, June 4, yeas 73, nays 0. *Ibid.*

[3] Public Law 565, 77th Cong.; originated as H. J. Res. 321; introduced by Mr McCormack; passed by the House, after suspension of the rules, June 3, yeas 361, nays 0; passed by the Senate, June 4, yeas 73, nays 0. *Ibid.*

CHAPTER III

DEFENSE AND THE WAR EFFORT

[See *Documents, I, 1938–39*, p. 481; *II, 1939–40*, p. 730; *III, 1940–41*, p. 661.]

The nature of modern war is such that it requires a total effort of the nation either to provide for defense in time of peace or to prosecute war to a successful conclusion. In his message to Congress, July 10, 1940, President Roosevelt said: "The principal lesson of the war up to the present time is that partial defense is inadequate defense. If the United States is to have any defense, it must have total defense. We cannot defend ourselves a little here and a little there. We must be able to defend ourselves wholly and at any time." [1] Following up this line of thought, the President, in his Budget Message of January 3, 1941,[2] said: "It is safe only to prepare for total defense. Total defense means more than weapons. It means an industrial capacity stepped up to produce all the *matériel* for defense with the greatest possible speed. It means people of health and stamina, conscious of the democratic rights and responsibilities. It means an economic and social system functioning smoothly and geared to high-speed performance." Following our formal entrance into the war, the President made it clear that an all-out effort was required if victory was to be attained. In his address to the joint session of the two Houses of Congress on January 6, 1942,[3] he emphasized the need of a total national effort in the field of production, even at the cost of individual sacrifice, and warned against excessive complacency and against defeatism and internal dissension produced by enemy propaganda. In his radio address of February 23, 1942,[4] the President called attention to the global aspects of the war and stressed the necessity that the United Nations should "share in a unified plan in which all of us must play our several parts, each of us being equally indispensable and dependent on the other."

The policies and measures adopted by the United States in preparation for or in the actual prosecution of a war of such total and global proportions naturally cover a wider field both functionally and geographically than can be encompassed in any one chapter. In fact, with the United States engaged in total and global war, our relations with every part of the world and our activities in every main field of governmental operation, have largely to do, directly or indirectly, with the winning of the war. In this chapter, an attempt is made to show the unity of the defense and war effort by listing briefly some of the essential facts, by referring to some of the more important documents included in other chapters, and by listing those documents not given elsewhere which are important to an understanding of our national defense policy.

---

[1] Senate Doc. No. 188, **77**th Cong., 2d sess., p. 68.
[2] *Documents, III, 1940–41*, p. 685.   [3] See p. 45.   [4] See p. 53.

1. GOVERNMENTAL POWERS AND ORGANIZATION

(1) *"First War Powers Act, 1941," Approved December 18, 1941* [1]

[Excerpt]

In times of national emergency and of war the powers of the national government are greatly expanded within the framework of the Constitution. In particular, the Constitution and statutes provide for a very great expansion of the powers of the President. Under existing statutes, the President has certain powers in time of emergency or in a state of war which he does not have in normal times.[2] On September 8, 1939, the President proclaimed a national emergency "in connection with and to the extent necessary for the proper observance, safeguarding, and enforcing of the neutrality of the United States and the strengthening of our national defense within the limits of peace-time authorizations." [3] On May 27, 1941, the President proclaimed "an unlimited national emergency." [4] On December 8, 1941, the declaration of war against Japan became effective.[5]

To give the President "authority which is urgently needed in order to put the Government of the United States on an immediate war footing," [6] Congress enacted the "First War Powers Act." The Act was based on the experience of World War I and was intended to give to the President certain powers similar to those which President Wilson had during that war.

Title I is substantially a reenactment of the "Overman Act," approved May 20, 1918 (40 Stat. 556), which was repealed in accordance with Public Resolution No. 64 of March 3, 1921 (41 Stat. 1369).

Be it enacted by the Senate and House of Representatives of the United States of America in Congress assembled,

TITLE I — COORDINATION OF EXECUTIVE BUREAUS IN THE INTEREST OF THE MORE EFFICIENT CONCENTRATION OF THE GOVERNMENT

SECTION 1. That for the national security and defense, for the successful prosecution of the war, for the support and maintenance of the Army and Navy, for the better utilization of resources and industries, and for the more effective exercise and more efficient administration by the President of his powers as Commander-in-Chief of the Army and Navy, the President is hereby authorized to make such redistribution of functions among executive agencies as he may deem necessary, including any functions, duties, and powers hitherto by law conferred upon any executive department, commission, bureau, agency, governmental corporation, office, or officer, in such manner as in his judgment shall seem best fitted to carry out the purposes of this title, and to this end is authorized to make such regulations and to issue such orders as he may deem necessary, which regulations and orders shall be in writing and

[1] Public Law 354, 77th Cong., An Act to Expedite the Prosecution of the War Effort; originated as H. R. 6233, from the Committee on the Judiciary, December 15, 1941; House Report No. 1567.

[2] See *Congressional Record*, vol. 87, p. 4605–12 (daily edition, May 28, 1941).

[3] *Documents, II, 1939–40*, p. 647–8.   [4] *Ibid., III, 1940–41*, p. 754–5.

[5] See p. 118.   [6] House Report No. 1507, 77th Cong., 1st sess., p. 1.

hall be published in accordance with the Federal Register Act of 1935: *Provided*, That the termination of this title shall not affect any act done or any right or obligation accruing or accrued pursuant to this title and during the time that this title is in force: *Provided further*, That the authority by this title granted shall be exercised only in matters relating to the conduct of the present war: *Provided further*, That no redistribution of functions shall provide for the transfer, consolidation, or abolition of the whole or any part of the General Accounting Office or of all or any part of its functions.

SEC. 2. That in carrying out the purposes of this title the President is authorized to utilize, coordinate, or consolidate any executive or administrative commissions, bureaus, agencies, governmental corporations, offices, or officers now existing by law, to transfer any duties or powers from one existing department, commission, bureau, agency, governmental corporation, office, or officer to another, to transfer the personnel thereof or any part of it either by detail or assignment, together with the whole or any part of the records and public property belonging thereto.

SEC. 3. That for the purpose of carrying out the provisions of this title, any moneys heretofore and hereafter appropriated for the use of any executive department, commission, bureau, agency, governmental corporation, office, or officer shall be expended only for the purposes for which it was appropriated under the direction of such other agency as may be directed by the President hereunder to perform and execute said functions, except to the extent hereafter authorized by the Congress in appropriation Acts or otherwise.

SEC. 4. That should the President, in redistributing the functions among the executive agencies as provided in this title, conclude that any bureau should be abolished and it or their duties and functions conferred upon some other department or bureau or eliminated entirely, he shall report his conclusions to Congress with such recommendations as he may deem proper.

SEC. 5. That all laws or parts of laws conflicting with the provisions of this title are to the extent of such conflict suspended while this title is in force.

Upon the termination of this title all executive or administrative agencies, governmental corporations, departments, commissions, bureaus, offices, or officers shall exercise the same functions, duties, and powers as heretofore or as hereafter by law may be provided, any authorization of the President under this title to the contrary notwithstanding.

.   .   .   .

TITLE IV — TIME LIMIT AND SHORT TITLE

SEC. 401. Titles I and II of this Act shall remain in force during the continuance of the present war and for six months after the termination of the war, or until such earlier time as the Congress by concurrent resolution or the President may designate.

SEC. 402. This Act may be cited as the "First War Powers Act, 1941."

The "Second War Powers Act, 1942" [1] was approved by the President March 7, 1942. The Act is composed of 15 titles dealing with a variety of governmental activities, each of which is directly related to the prosecution of the war. For the most part the provisions of this Act are to remain in force only until December 31, 1944, "or until such earlier time as the Congress by concurrent resolution, or the President, may designate." [2]

Administrative Organization. To meet the requirements of the ever-changing situation, frequent changes in administrative organization became necessary. These changes were accomplished by executive or administrative order, directly or indirectly under the authority of constitutional or statutory provisions.

Following the proclamation of a limited emergency, the Council of National Defense, created by the Act of August 29, 1916, was called into activity and the Advisory Commission, provided for by the same act, was created. [3] By Administrative Order of May 25, 1940, the Office for Emergency Management was established in the Executive Office of the President. [4] By Executive Orders of January 7 and 11, 1941 and Administrative Order of January 7 other agencies were established in or coordinated through the Office for Emergency Management, including in particular the Office of Production Management. [6] The outbreak of war made the further reconstruction of administrative structure necessary, and by Executive Order No. 9024 of January 16, 1942 the War Production Board was established. [7]

Recognition that adequate production alone was not enough to provide for the defense of national interests led to the adoption of the Lend-Lease program to be administered originally by the Division of Defense Aid Reports within the Office for Emergency Management. [8] By Executive Order of October 28, 1941 this function was assumed by the Office of Lend-Lease Administration, [9] also within the Office for Emergency Management. Responsibility in connection with the carrying out of the shipping program necessary to provide transportation facilities for getting Lend-Lease and other goods to those engaged in resisting aggres-

[1] Public Law 507, 77th Cong.

[2] Title XV, sec. 1501.

[3] *Documents, III, 1940–41,* p. 661; *United States Government Manual,* Spring 1942 p. 59.

[4] *Documents, III, 1940–41,* p. 664.

[5] *Ibid.,* p. 667.

[6] *Ibid.,* p. 668.

[7] See p. 161; see also, *United States Government Manual,* Spring 1942, p. 83–4.

[8] Executive Order No. 8751, May 2, 1941; *Documents, III, 1940–41,* p. 731.

[9] This volume, p. 169.

sion was originally placed in the United States Maritime Commission.[1] By Executive Order of February 7, 1942,[2] there was established within the Office for Emergency Management a War Shipping Administration to which were transferred certain of the duties formerly performed by the Commission. The use of economic and financial weapons in defense of American interests was originally the responsibility of the regular departments of administration, especially the Treasury and State Departments. By Executive Order of July 30, 1941, the Economic Defense Board was established.[3] By Executive Order of December 17, 1941, the name of the Board was changed to Board of Economic Warfare.

While the importance of correct information and good civilian morale was recognized from the beginning, no official independent agency was established to deal especially with these matters until the creation by Executive Order of October 24, 1941, of the Office of Facts and Figures.[4] With the declaration of war, official censorship in the national interest became necessary·and by Executive Order of December 19, 1941, the Office of Censorship under a Director of Censorship was established.[5] To provide proper coordination of the informational activities, foreign and domestic, of different governmental agencies, the President, by Executive Order of June 13, 1942, established an Office of War Information.[6]

For further information on the evolution of governmental organization for meeting the emergency requirements of defense and the war effort, consult *United States Government Manual*, formerly prepared by the United States Information Service, Office of Government Reports, issued beginning Fall 1942, by the Bureau of Public Inquiries, Office of War Information.

2. MILITARY AND NAVAL POLICIES AND ESTABLISHMENTS

A. Financial Statistics

(1) *Appropriations and Contract Authorizations, by Appropriation Acts, for the Navy Department and War Department, Military Activities, for the Fiscal Years 1941, 1942 and 1943, as of July 2, 1942*[7]

NAVY DEPARTMENT

APPROPRIATING ACTS AND DATE APPROVED	BUREAU OF AERONAUTICS	OTHER	TOTAL
Fiscal Year 1941			
Pub. No. 588, June 11, 1940:			
Appropriations	$138,483,300	$1,135,493,820 [8]	$1,273,977,120 [8]
Contract authorizations .	125,000,000	23,741,612	148,741,612

[1] *United States Government Manual*, Spring 1942, p. 528. [2] This volume, p. 776.
[3] *Ibid.*, p. 180.   [4] *Ibid.*, p. 186.   [5] *Ibid.*   [6] *Ibid.*, p. 189.
[7] From the Executive Office of the President, Bureau of the Budget.
[8] Exclusive of $190,000 "State Marine Schools" transferred to U. S. Maritime Commission and $4,018 transferred to Post Office Department pursuant to the provisions of the Reorganization Act of 1939 and Reorganization Plan No. IV. Also, $34,000,000 "Emergency Fund for the President."

NAVY DEPARTMENT — *Continued*

APPROPRIATING ACTS AND DATE APPROVED	BUREAU OF AERONAUTICS	OTHER	TOTAL
Fiscal Year 1941 — Cont'd			
Pub. No. 667, June 26, 1940:			
Appropriations	22,885,000	536,388,170	559,273,170
Contract authorizations .	——	129,014,000	129,014,000
Pub. No. 668, June 27, 1940:			
Appropriations	——	21,900	21,900
Pub. No. 781, September 9, 1940:			
Appropriations	180,000,000	423,643,860	603,643,860
Contract authorizations .	375,000,000	127,740,000	502,740,000
Pub. No. 800, October 8, 1940:			
Appropriations	15,000,000	60,401,000	75,401,000
Contract authorizations .	——	8,500,000	8,500,000
Pub. No. 9, March 1, 1941:			
Appropriations	——	522,775	522,775
Pub. No. 13, March 17, 1941:			
Appropriations	96,382,300	584,839,302	681,221,602
Contract authorizations .	30,000,000	127,102,500	157,102,500
Pub. No. 25, April 1, 1941:			
Appropriations	——	1,543,314	1,543,314
Pub. No. 29, April 5, 1941:			
Appropriations	——	295,416,820	295,416,820
Pub. No. 150, July 3, 1941:			
Appropriations	——	59,367,556	59,367,556
Coast Guard Transferred from Treasury Dept. pursuant to E. O. 8929, November 1, 1941:			
Appropriations	——	78,709,588	78,709,588
Contract authorizations .	——	500,000	500,000
Permanent appropriation (from special receipts)	——	135,084	135,084
Total fiscal year 1941:			
Appropriations . . .	$452,750,600	$3,176,483,189	$3,629,233,789
Contract authorizations	530,000,000	416,598,112	946,598,112
Fiscal Year 1942			
Pub. No. 48, May 6, 1941:			
Appropriations	$ 434,980,400	$ 2,980,541,350	$ 3,415,521,750
Contract authorizations .	——	31,448,894	31,448,894

NAVY DEPARTMENT — *Continued*

APPROPRIATING ACTS AND DATE APPROVED	BUREAU OF AERONAUTICS	OTHER	TOTAL
Pub. No. 150, July 3, 1941:			
Appropriations	482,046,600	201,340,000	683,386,600
Coast Guard appropriations transferred from Treasury Dept. pursuant to E. O. 8929, November 1, 1941 .	——	50,721,320	50,721,320
Contract authorizations .	10,000,000	——	10,000,000
Pub. No. 247, August 25, 1941:			
Appropriations	90,000,000	1,494,795,785	1,584,795,785
Pub. No. 282, October 28, 1941:			
Appropriations	——	120,996,000	120,996,000
Coast Guard transferred from Treasury Dept. pursuant to E. O. 8929, November 1, 1941	——	27,544,585	27,544,585
Pub. No. 253, December 17, 1941:			
Appropriations . . .	309,720,000	774,230,727	1,083,950,727
Contract authorizations .	640,000,000	——	640,000,000
Pub. No. 463, February 21, 1942:			
Appropriations	——	1,425,469	1,425,469
Pub. No. 528, April 28, 1942:			
Appropriations	464,827,500	1,044,924,000	1,509,751,500
Contract authorizations .	——	25,000,000	25,000,000
Pub. No. 626, June 23. 1942:			
Appropriations	——	444,984,740	444,984,740
Contract authorizations .	150,000,000	——	150,000,000
Pub. No. 441, February 7, 1942:			
Appropriations: . . .	4,408,300,000	5,285,225,500	9,693,525,500
Pub. No. 648, July 2, 1942:			
Appropriations	——	672,622	672,622
Permanent appropriations .	——	2,058,500	2,058,500
Coast Guard:			
Transferred from Treasury Dept. pursuant to E. O. 8929, November 1, 1941:			

NAVY DEPARTMENT — *Continued*

APPROPRIATING ACTS AND DATE APPROVED	BUREAU OF AERONAUTICS	OTHER	TOTAL
Fiscal Year 1942 — Cont'd			
Coast Guard *Cont'd:*			
Appropriations	—	$ 62,193,150	$ 62,193,150
Contract authorizations .	—	6,370,000	6,370,000
Other appropriations transferred from Treasury Dept. pursuant to E. O. 8929, November 1, 1941	—	83,080	83,080
Transferred to Coast Guard pursuant to E. O. 9083, February 28, 1942, from:			
U. S. Maritime Commission:			
Construction Fund . .	—	28,000,000	28,000,000
State Marine Schools .	—	190,000	190,000
Department of Commerce:			
Bureau of Marine Inspection and Navigation	—	2,898,995	2,898,995
Total fiscal year 1942:			
Appropriations . . .	$6,189,874,500	$12,522,825,823	$18,712,700,323
Contract authorizations	$ 800,000,000	$ 62,818,894	$ 862,818,894
Fiscal Year 1943 [1]			
Pub. No. 441, Feb. 7, 1942:			
Appropriations			
Annual	$1,436,418,585	$12,608,921,389	$14,045,339,974
Permanent	—	2,551,700	2,551,700
Contract authorizations .	—	500,000,000	500,000,000
Transferred to Coast Guard pursuant to E. O. 9083, Feb. 28, 1942:			
From:			
U. S. Maritime Commission:			
State Marine Schools	—	360,417	360,417
Fiscal year 1943: [2]			
Appropriations . . .	$1,436,418,585	$12,611,833,506	$14,048,252,091
Contract authorizations	—	$ 500,000,000	$ 500,000,000

[1] Indefinite contract authorizations for construction of the expanded navy, according to estimates of the Navy Department, will call for appropriations after the fiscal year 1943 amounting to more than $10,000,000,000.

[2] Total, as of July 2, 1942.

WAR DEPARTMENT, MILITARY ACTIVITIES

APPROPRIATING ACTS AND DATE APPROVED	AIR CORPS	OTHER	TOTAL
Fiscal Year 1941			
Pub. No. 611, June 13, 1940:			
Appropriations	$ 266,278,418	$ 1,167,025,297 [1]	$ 1,433,303,715 [1]
Contract authorizations .	103,300,000	153,929,636	257,229,636
Pub. No. 667, June 26, 1940:			
Appropriations	293,456,282	527,545,765	821,002,047
Contract authorizations .	109,259,597	144,917,164	254,176,761
Pub. No. 668, June 27, 1940:			
Appropriations	—	135,000	135,000
Pub. No. 781, Sept. 9, 1940:			
Appropriations	520,802,304	1,272,570,228	1,793,372,532
Contract authorizations .	1,002,600,000	1,249,130,000	2,251,730,000
Pub. Res. No. 99, September 24, 1940:			
Appropriations	—	338,263,902	338,263,902
Pub. No. 800, Oct. 8, 1940:			
Appropriations	109,995,957	1,113,192,017 [2]	1,223,187,974 [2]
Contract authorizations .	60,000,000	90,000,000	150,000,000
Pub. No. 812, Oct. 9, 1940:			
Appropriations	—	3,400,000	3,400,000
Pub. No. 6, Feb. 13, 1941:			
Appropriations	—	175,000,000	175,000,000
Pub. No. 13, March 17, 1941:			
Appropriations	—	695,118,000	695,118,000
Pub. No. 25, April 1, 1941:			
Appropriations	—	2,800,452	2,800,452
Pub. No. 29, April 5, 1941:			
Appropriations	982,236,000	1,015,575,100	1,997,811,100
Contract authorizations .	524,025,000	1,569,428,254	2,093,453,254
Pub. No. 282, Oct. 28, 1941:			
Appropriations	—	314,236	314,236
Total, fiscal year 1941:			
Appropriations . .	$2,172,768,961	$6,310,939,997	$8,483,708,958
Contract authorizations	$1,799,184,597	$3,207,405,054	$5,006,589,651

Note: Pub. No. 23, March 27, 1941, contained an appropriation of $7,000,000,-000 and Pub. No. 474, March 5, 1942, contained an appropriation of $5,425,000,-000 for Defense Aid. The Navy Department and the War Department, Military Activities, will probably receive a large proportion of these appropriations by allocations.

[1] Exclusive of $66,000,000 "Emergency Fund for the President" and $19,607 transferred to Post Office Department pursuant to provisions of the Reorganization Act of 1939 and Reorganization Plan No. IV.

[2] Exclusive of $24,825,108 "Selective Service system."

WAR DEPARTMENT, MILITARY ACTIVITIES — *Continued*

APPROPRIATING ACTS AND DATE APPROVED	AIR CORPS	OTHER	TOTAL
Fiscal Year 1942			
Pub. No. 139, June 30, 1941:			
Appropriations	$ 4,342,253,322	$ 6,042,568,302	$10,384,821,624
Contract authorizations .	104,258,995	78,886,700	183,145,695
Pub. No. 150, July 3, 1941:			
Appropriations	——	6,500,000	6,500,000
Pub. No. 247, Aug. 25, 1941:			
Appropriations	204,007,800	4,049,949,863	4,253,957,663
Pub. No. 353, Dec. 17, 1941:			
Appropriations	779,000,000	6,597,026,583	7,376,026,583
Pub. No. 442, Jan. 30, 1942:			
Appropriations	9,041,373,090	3,484,499,384	12,525,872,474
Pub. No. 463, Feb. 21, 1942:			
Appropriations	——	793,284	793,284
Pub. No. 474, March 5, 1942:			
Appropriations	167,440,000	23,318,297,900	23,485,737,900
Pub. No. 528, March 28, 1942:			
Appropriations	8,515,861,251	8,878,816,092	17,394,677,343
Pub. No. 648, July 2, 1942:			
Appropriations	——	447,927	447,927
Total, fiscal year 1942:			
Appropriations . . .	$23,049,935,463	$52,378,899,335	$75,428,834,798
Contract authorizations	$ 104,258,995	$ 78,886,700	$ 183,145,695
Fiscal Year 1943			
Pub. No. 649, July 2, 1942:			
Appropriations	$11,317,416,790	$31,502,586,277	$42,820,003,067

B. Mobilization of Manpower

(1) *"Selective Training and Service Act of 1940." Sections as Amended, August 16 and 18, and December 20, 1941* [1]

[See *Documents, III, 1940–41*, p. 672.]

The enactment of Public Law 783, 76th Cong., September 16, 1940 (54 Stat. 885; U. S. Code, title 50, App.) established selective compulsory military training and service in the United States. This Selective Training and Service Act

[1] The Act has been amended in other respects by Public Law 87, 77th Cong., approved May 29, 1941.

of 1940 was amended on August 16 and December 20, 1941 in order to meet changing conditions.[1] The amended sections which define liability to service and training are given below.

The President on July 21, 1941 addressed a message to the Congress in which he asked authority to extend the term of service in peace-time from 12 to 18 months. The "Selective Service Extension Act of 1941," approved August 18, 1941, granted the authority, the Congress declaring in sec. 1 of the Act "that the national interest is imperiled." The authority was made effective by Executive Order No. 8862 (6 *Fed. Reg.*, p. 4319), August 22, 1941.

Registration days have been set under the legislation as follows:

1. Age 21–36, October 16, 1940 by Proclamation No. 2425 (*Documents, III, 1940–41*, p. 682) and for Hawaii, October 26, for Puerto Rico, November 20 and for Alaska, January 22, 1941, by Proclamations Nos. 2430, 2431, 2442 (6 *Fed. Reg.*, p. 3897, 4061, 4477);

2. Age 21, July 1, 1941 by Proclamation No. 2486 (6 *Fed. Reg.*, p. 2599);

3. Age 20–44, February 16, 1942 by Proclamation No. 2535 (7 *Fed. Reg.*, p. 177);

4. Age 45–64, April 27, 1942 by Proclamation No. 2541 (7 *Fed. Reg.*, p. 2181);

5. Age 18–20, June 30, 1942 by Proclamation No. 2558 (7 *Fed. Reg.*, p. 3866).

SEC. 2.[2] Except as otherwise provided in this Act, it shall be the duty of every male citizen of the United States, and of every other male person residing in the United States, who, on the day or days fixed for the first or any subsequent registration, is between the ages of eighteen and sixty-five,[3] to present himself for and submit to registration at such time or times and place or places, and in such manner and in such age group or groups, as shall be determined by rules and regulations prescribed hereunder.

SEC. 3.[4] (a) Except as otherwise provided in this Act, every male citizen of the United States, and every other male person residing in the United States, who is between the ages of twenty and forty-five [3] at the time fixed for his registration, or who attains the age of twenty after having been required to register pursuant to section 2 of this Act, shall be liable for training and service in the land or naval forces of the United States: *Provided*, That any citizen or subject of a neutral country shall be relieved from liability for training and service under this Act if, prior to his induction into the land or naval forces, he has made application to be relieved from such liability in the manner prescribed by and

---

[1] The Act has been amended in other respects by Public Law 87, 77th Cong., approved May 29, 1941.

[2] Sec. 1 of Public Law 360, 77th Cong., approved December 20, 1941, An Act to Amend the Selective Training and Service Act of 1940 by providing for the Extension of Liability for Military Service and for the Registration of the Manpower of the Nation and for Other Purposes; originated as H. R. 6215 and S. 2126; House Report No. 1508; Senate Report No. 915; House (conference) Report No. 1554.

[3] The act of 1940 read: "Twenty-one and thirty-six." The amended section applies to "every other male person" instead of to "every male alien."

[4] Sec. 2 of Public Law 360, 77th Cong.

in accordance with rules and regulations prescribed by the President, but any person who makes such application shall thereafter be debarred from becoming a citizen of the United States: *Provided further*, That no citizen or subject of any country who has been or who may hereafter be proclaimed by the President to be an alien enemy of the United States shall be inducted for training and service under this Act unless he is acceptable to the land or naval forces. The President is authorized from time to time, whether or not a state of war exists, to select and induct into the land and naval forces of the United States for training and service, in the manner provided in this Act, such number of men as in his judgment is required for such forces in the national interest: *Provided*, That within the limits of the quota determined under section 4 (*b*) for the subdivision in which he resides, any person, regardless of race or color, between the ages of eighteen and forty-five,[1] shall be afforded an opportunity to volunteer for induction into the land or naval forces of the United States for the training and service prescribed in subsection (*b*), but no person who so volunteers shall be inducted for such training and service so long as he is deferred after classification: *Provided further*, That no man shall be inducted for training and service under this Act unless and until he is acceptable to the land or naval forces for such training and service and his physical and mental fitness for such training and service has been satisfactorily determined: *Provided further*, That no men shall be inducted for such training and service until adequate provision shall have been made for such shelter, sanitary facilities, water supplies, heating and lighting arrangements, medical care, and hospital accommodations, for such men, as may be determined by the Secretary of War or the Secretary of the Navy, as the case may be, to be essential to public and personal health: *Provided further*, That except in time of war there shall not be in active training or service in the land forces of the United States at any one time under subsection (*b*) more than nine hundred thousand men inducted under the provisions of this Act. The men inducted into the land or naval forces for training and service under this Act shall be assigned to camps or units of such forces.

(*b*) Each man inducted under the provisions of subsection (*a*) shall serve for a training and service period of twelve consecutive months,[2] unless sooner discharged, except that whenever the Congress has declared that the national interest is imperiled, such twelve-month period [2] may

---

[1] Amended from "thirty-six" by sec. 9 of Public Law 360, 77th Cong., December 20, 1941.

[2] By the Service Extension Act of 1941, approved August 18, 1941 (Public Law 213, 77th Cong.), Congress declared "that the national interest is imperilled" and

be extended by the President to such time as may be necessary in the interests of national defense.

(c) Each such man, after the completion of his period of training and service under subsection (b), shall be transferred to a reserve component of the land or naval forces of the United States; and until he attains the age of forty-five, or until the expiration of a period of ten years after such transfer, or until he is discharged from such reserve component, whichever occurs first, he shall be deemed to be a member of such reserve component and shall be subject to such additional training and service as may now or hereafter be prescribed by law: *Provided*, That any man who completes at least twelve months' training and service in the land forces under subsection (b), and who thereafter serves satisfactorily in the Regular Army or in the active National Guard for a period of at least two years, shall, in time of peace, be relieved from any liability to serve in any reserve component of the land or naval forces of the United States and from further liability for the training and service under subsection (b), but nothing in this subsection shall be construed to prevent any such man, while in a reserve component of such forces, from being ordered or called to active duty in such forces.[1]

(d) With respect to the men inducted for training and service under this Act there shall be paid, allowed, and extended the same pay, allowances, pensions, disability and death compensation, and other benefits as are provided by law in the case of other enlisted men of like grades and length of service of that component of the land or naval forces to which they are assigned, and after transfer to a reserve component of the land or naval forces as provided in subsection (c) there shall be paid, allowed, and extended with respect to them the same benefits as are provided by law in like cases with respect to other members of such reserve component. Men in such training and service and men who have been so transferred to reserve components shall have an opportunity to qualify for promotion.

(e) Persons inducted into the land forces of the United States under this Act shall not be employed beyond the limits of the Western Hemi-

authorized the President to extend the period of military service under the Act for such period of time as may be necessary but not exceeding eighteen months.

By section 2 of Public Law 338, 77th Cong., approved December 13, 1941, the periods of service of all members of the Army of the United States was extended to the period of the duration of the war and the six months immediately following the termination of the war.

[1] Active service is credited against service in a reserve component by sec. 5 of the "Service Extension Act of 1941."

sphere except in the Territories and possessions of the United States, including the Philippine Islands.[1]

(f) Nothing contained in this or any other Act shall be construed as forbidding the payment of compensation by any person, firm, or corporation to persons inducted into the land or naval forces of the United States for training and service under this Act, or to members of the reserve components of such forces now or hereafter on any type of active duty, who, prior to their induction or commencement of active duty, were receiving compensation from such person, firm, or corporation.

SEC. 4. (a) The selection of men for training and service under section 3 (other than those who are voluntarily inducted pursuant to this Act) shall be made in an impartial manner, under such rules and regulations as the President may prescribe, from the men who are liable for such training and service and who at the time of selection are registered and classified but not deferred or exempted: *Provided*, That in the selection and training of men under this Act, and in the interpretation and execution of the provisions of this Act, there shall be no discrimination against any person on account of race or color: *Provided further*,[2] That in the classification of registrants within the jurisdiction of any local board, the registrants of any particular registration may be classified, in the manner prescribed by and in accordance with rules and regulations prescribed by the President, before, together with, or after the registrants of any prior registration or registrations; and in the selection for induction of persons within the jurisdiction of any local board and within any particular classification, persons who were registered at any particular registration may be selected, in the manner prescribed by and in accordance with rules and regulations prescribed by the President, before, together with, or after persons who were registered at any prior registration or registrations.

(b) Quotas of men to be inducted for training and service under this Act shall be determined for each State, Territory, and the District of Columbia, and for subdivisions thereof, on the basis of the actual

[1] This section is affected by sec. 1 of Public Law 338, 77th Cong., approved December 13, 1941, which provides -

"That the provisions of Public Resolution Numbered 96, Seventy-sixth Congress, approved August 27, 1940, as amended, and of Public, Numbered 783, Seventy-sixth Congress (the Selective Training and Service Act of 1940), as amended, insofar as they restrict the territorial use of units and members of the Army of the United States, are suspended during the existence of any war in which the United States is engaged, and during the six months immediately following the termination of any such war."

[2] Proviso added by sec. 3 of Public Law 360, 77th Cong., December 20, 1941.

number of men in the several States, Territories, and the District of Columbia, and the subdivisions thereof, who are liable for such training and service but who are not deferred after classification, except that credits shall be given in fixing such quotas for residents of such subdivisions who are in the land and naval forces of the United States on the date fixed for determining such quotas. After such quotas are fixed, credits shall be given in filling such quotas for residents of such subdivisions who subsequently become members of such forces. Until the actual numbers necessary for determining the quotas are known, the quotas may be based on estimates, and subsequent adjustments therein shall be made when such actual numbers are known. All computations under this subsection shall be made in accordance with such rules and regulations as the President may prescribe.

SEC. 5. (a) Commissioned officers, warrant officers, pay clerks, and enlisted men of the Regular Army, the Navy, the Marine Corps, the Coast Guard, the Coast and Geodetic Survey, the Public Health Service, the federally recognized active National Guard, the Officers' Reserve Corps, the Regular Army Reserve, the Enlisted Reserve Corps, the Naval Reserve, and the Marine Corps Reserve; cadets, United States Military Academy; midshipmen, United States Naval Academy; cadets, United States Coast Guard Academy; men who have been accepted for admittance (commencing with the academic year next succeeding such acceptance) to the United States Military Academy as cadets, to the United States Naval Academy as midshipmen, or to the United States Coast Guard Academy as cadets, but only during the continuance of such acceptance; cadets of the advanced course, senior division, Reserve Officers' Training Corps or Naval Reserve Officers' Training Corps; and diplomatic representatives, technical attachés of foreign embassies and legations, consuls general, consuls, vice consuls, and consular agents of foreign countries,[1] and persons in other categories to be specified by the President, residing in the United States, who are not citizens of the United States, and who have not declared their intention to become citizens of the United States, shall not be required to be registered under section 2 and shall be relieved from liability for training and service under section 3 (b).

[2] (b) In time of peace, the following persons shall be relieved from liability for training and service under section 3 (b) and from the liability

[1] The phrase "and persons in other categories to be specified by the President," added by sec. 4 of Public Law 360, 77th Cong., December 20, 1941.

[2] Sec. 5(b) (1-5) is an amendment of the original act so as to make it applicable to the sea-going forces; it was enacted by Public Law 87, 77th Cong., approved May 29, 1941.

to serve in any Reserve component of the land or naval forces imposed by this Act:

(1) Any person who shall have satisfactorily served as an officer or enlisted man for at least three consecutive years in the Regular Army, Navy, Marine Corps, or Coast Guard before or after or partially before and partially after the time fixed for registration under section 2, or any enlisted man who has been or is hereafter honorably discharged from the Regular Army or the Coast Guard for the convenience of the Government within six months prior to the completion of his regular three-year period of enlistment: [1] *Provided,* That any person who has had such prior service and who has already been inducted for service may upon application be discharged and shall not be liable for further training and service in time of peace.

(2) Any person who as a member of the active National Guard shall have satisfactorily served as an officer or enlisted man for at least one year in active Federal service in the Army of the United States, and subsequent thereto for at least two consecutive years in the Regular Army or in the active National Guard, before or after or partially before and partially after the time fixed for registration under section 2; or any person who as a member of the Naval Reserve or Marine Corps Reserve shall have satisfactorily served for at least three consecutive years on active duty before or after or partially before and partially after the time fixed for such registration; or any person who as a member of the Naval Reserve or Marine Corps Reserve shall have satisfactorily served for at least one year on active duty and for at least two consecutive years in the Regular Navy or Marine Corps or with an organized unit of the Naval Reserve or Marine Corps Reserve, before or after or partially before and partially after the time fixed for such registration.

(3) Any person who is an officer or enlisted man in the active National Guard at the time fixed for registration under section 2, and who shall have satisfactorily served therein for at least six consecutive years, before or after or partially before and partially after the time fixed for such registration.

(4) Any person who is an officer in the Officers' Reserve Corps or the eligible list at the time fixed for registration under section 2, and who shall have satisfactorily served therein on the eligible list for at least six consecutive years, before or after or partially before and partially after the time fixed for such registration.

[1] The clause from "or any enlisted man" to the proviso, added by sec. 1 of Public Law 206, approved August 16, 1941.

(5) Any person who is an officer or an enlisted man in the organized Naval Reserve or the organized Marine Corps Reserve at the time fixed for registration under section 2, and who shall have satisfactorily served therein for at least six consecutive years, before or after or partially before and partially after the time fixed for such registration or any person who is an officer or an enlisted man in the Naval Merchant Marine Reserve or Volunteer Naval Reserve or Volunteer Marine Corps Reserve at the time fixed for registration under section 2, and who shall have satisfactorily served therein for at least eight consecutive years, before or after or partially before and partially after the time fixed for such registration.

(c) (1) The Vice President of the United States, the Governors, and all other State officials chosen by the voters of the entire State,[1] of the several States and Territories, members of the legislative bodies of the United States and of the several States and Territories, judges of the courts of record of the United States and of the several States and Territories and the District of Columbia, shall, while holding such offices, be deferred from training and service under this Act in the land and naval forces of the United States.

(2) The President is authorized, under such rules and regulations as he may prescribe, to provide for the deferment from training and service under this Act in the land and naval forces of the United States, of any person holding an office (other than an office described in paragraph (1) of this subsection) under the United States or any State, Territory, or the District of Columbia, whose continued service in such office is found in accordance with section 10 (a) (2) to be necessary to the maintenance of the public health, safety, or interest.

(d) Regular or duly ordained ministers of religion, and students who are preparing for the ministry in theological or divinity schools recognized as such for more than one year prior to the date of enactment of this Act, shall be exempt from training and service (but not from registration) under this Act.

(e) (1) The President is authorized, under such rules and regulations as he may prescribe, to provide for the deferment from training and service under this Act in the land and naval forces of the United States of those men whose employment in industry, agriculture, or other occupations or employment, or whose activity in other endeavors, is found in accordance with section 10 (a) (2) to be necessary to the maintenance of the national health, safety, or interest. The President is also

[1] The clause from "and all" was added by sec. 4 of Public Law 360, approved December 20, 1941.

authorized, under such rules and regulations as he may prescribe, to provide for the deferment from training and service under this Act in the land and naval forces of the United States (1) of any or all [1] of those men in a status with respect to persons dependent upon them for support which renders their deferment advisable, and (2) of any or all [1] of those men found to be physically, mentally, or morally deficient or defective. No deferment from such training and service shall be made in the case of any individual except upon the basis of the status of such individual, and no such deferment shall be made of individuals by occupational groups or of groups of individuals in any plant or institution.[2] Rules and regulations issued pursuant to this subsection shall include provisions requiring that there be posted in a conspicuous place at the office of each local board a list setting forth the names and classifications of those men who have been classified by such local board.

[3] (2) Anything in this Act to the contrary notwithstanding, the President is authorized, under such rules and regulations as he may prescribe, to provide for the deferment, by age group, or groups, from training and service under this Act in the land and naval forces of the United States, of those men whose age or ages are such that he finds their deferment to be advisable in the national interest: *Provided*, That the President may, upon finding that it is in the national interest, terminate the deferment by age group or groups of any or all of the men so deferred.

. . . .

(2) *Executive Order No. 9139 Establishing the War Manpower Commission in the Executive Office of the President and Transferring and Coordinating Certain Functions to Facilitate the Mobilization and Utilization of Manpower, April 18, 1942* [4]

[Excerpt]

The requirements of total war have led other nations engaged as belligerents sooner or later to apply the principle of compulsory selective service to the utilization of manpower resources for all aspects of the war effort. While the United States has not as yet taken that action, the establishment of the War Manpower Commission is a significant step in the direction of the more effective utilization of manpower in the waging of total war.

1. There is established within the Office for Emergency Management of the Executive Office of the President a War Manpower Commission,

[1] Words "of any or all" inserted by sec. 5 of Public Law 360, approved December 20, 1941.

[2] This sentence and a subparagraph (2), not printed here, were added by Public Law 206, approved August 16, 1941.

[3] Sec. 6 of Public Law 360, 77th Cong., approved December 20, 1941, substituted a new subsection 5(e) (2) which appears here.   [4] 7 *Fed. Reg.*, p. 2919.

hereinafter referred to as the Commission. The Commission shall consist of the Federal Security Administrator as Chairman, and a representative of each of the following Departments and agencies: The Department of War, the Department of the Navy, the Department of Agriculture, the Department of Labor, the War Production Board, the Labor Production Division of the War Production Board, the Selective Service System, and the United States Civil Service Commission.

2. The Chairman, after consultation with the members of the Commission, shall:

    a. Formulate plans and programs and establish basic national policies to assure the most effective mobilization and maximum utilization of the Nation's manpower in the prosecution of the war; and issue such policy and operating directives as may be necessary thereto.

    b. Estimate the requirements of manpower for industry; review all other estimates of needs for military, agricultural, and civilian manpower; and direct the several departments and agencies of the Government as to the proper allocation of available manpower.

    c. Determine basic policies for, and take such other steps as are necessary to coordinate, the collection and compilation of labor market data by Federal departments and agencies.

    d. Establish policies and prescribe regulations governing all Federal programs relating to the recruitment, vocational training, and placement of workers to meet the needs of industry and agriculture.

    e. Prescribe basic policies governing the filling of the Federal Government's requirements for manpower, excluding those of the military and naval forces, and issue such operating directives as may be necessary thereto.

    f. Formulate legislative programs designed to facilitate the most effective mobilization and utilization of the manpower of the country; and, with the approval of the President, recommend such legislation as may be necessary for this purpose.

3. The following agencies shall conform to such policies, directives, regulations, and standards as the Chairman may prescribe in the execution of the powers vested in him by this Order, and shall be subject to such other coordination by the Chairman as may be necessary to enable the Chairman to discharge the responsibilities placed upon him:

    a. The Selective Service System with respect to the use and classification of manpower needed for critical industrial, agricultural and governmental employment.

    b. The Federal Security Agency with respect to employment service and defense training functions.

    c. The Work Projects Administration with respect to placement and training functions.

    d. The United States Civil Service Commission with respect to functions relating to the filling of positions in the Government service.

    e. The Railroad Retirement Board with respect to employment service activities.

    f. The Bureau of Labor Statistics of the Department of Labor.

    g. The Labor Production Division of the War Production Board

    h. The Civilian Conservation Corps.

    i. The Department of Agriculture with respect to farm labor statistics, farm labor camp programs, and other labor market activities.

    j. The Office of Defense Transportation with respect to labor supply and requirement activities.

Similarly, all other Federal Departments and agencies which perform functions relating to the recruitment or utilization of manpower shall, in discharging such functions, conform to such policies, directives, regulations, and standards as the Chairman may prescribe in the execution of the powers vested in him by this Order; and shall be subject to such other coordination by the Chairman as may be necessary to enable the Chairman to discharge the responsibilities placed upon him.

C. Requisition of Property

(1) *An Act to Authorize the President of the United States to Requisition Property Required for the Defense of the United States, Approved October 16, 1941* [1]

Requisitioning of private property during World War I was effectuated by some 17 different statutes relating to specific commodities. A general power of requisition was recommended by the War Policies Commission in its industrial mobilization plan of 1931 (House Doc. 271, 72d Cong., p. 450).

The United States Maritime Commission acquired a limited right to requisition vessels by legislation of August 7, 1939 (53 Stat. 1255; U. S. Code, title 46, sec. 1242(*a*)).

Sec. 9 of the Selective Training and Service Act, September 16, 1940, extended the President's power to take possession of industrial plants in time of war to the time of emergency and Public Law 829, 76th Cong., October 10, 1940, authorized the requisition for national defense of specific property the exportation of which had been forbidden (*Documents, III, 1940–41,* p. 744). The

[1] Public Law 274, 77th Cong.; 55 Stat. 742; originating as S. 1579 from the Committee on Military Affairs after extensive hearings; Senate Report No. 565; House Report No. 1120; House (conference) Reports Nos. 1153, 1214.

general power to requisition private property during the national emergency was first proposed without restrictions. After hearings the Senate Committee on Military Affairs reported a bill in which definition of circumstances of requisition, limitation of duration, provision for return of property to owners and reports to the Congress were stipulated. That bill passed the Senate July 21, 1941. The House revised it and agreement was reached only after conference reports of August 12 and September 25 enabled the two houses to accept a single text some three weeks later.

Be it enacted by the Senate and House of Representatives of the United States of America in Congress assembled, That whenever the President, during the national emergency declared by the President on May 27, 1941, but not later than June 30, 1943, determines that (1) the use of any military or naval equipment, supplies, or munitions, or component parts thereof, or machinery, tools, or materials necessary for the manufacture, servicing, or operation of such equipment, supplies, or munitions is needed for the defense of the United States; (2) such need is immediate and impending and such as will not admit of delay or resort to any other source of supply; and (3) all other means of obtaining the use of such property for the defense of the United States upon fair and reasonable terms have been exhausted, he is authorized to requisition such property for the defense of the United States upon the payment of fair and just compensation for such property to be determined as hereinafter provided, and to dispose of such property in such manner as he may determine is necessary for the defense of the United States. The President shall determine the amount of the fair and just compensation to be paid for any property requisitioned and taken over pursuant to this Act and the fair value of any property returned under section 2 of this Act, but each such determination shall be made as of the time it is requisitioned or returned, as the case may be, in accordance with the provision for just compensation in the fifth amendment to the Constitution of the United States.[1] If, upon any such requisition of property, the person entitled to receive the amount so determined by the President as the fair and just compensation for the property is unwilling to accept the same as full and complete compensation for such property he shall be paid 50 per centum of such amount and shall be entitled to sue the United States in the Court of Claims or in any district court of the United States in the manner provided by sections 24 (20) and 145 of the Judicial Code (U. S. C., 1934 ed., title 28, secs. 41 (20) and 250) for an additional amount which, when added to the amount so paid to him,

[1] The sentence amended by sec. 602, Title VI of the Act to Further Expedite the Prosecution of the War ("Second War Powers Act"), approved March 27, 1942, 3 P.M., Eastern War Time.

he considers to be fair and just compensation for such property. Such courts shall also have power to determine in an appropriate proceeding any questions that may arise with respect to the amount of the fair value to be paid upon the return of any property under section 2 of this Act, regardless of the amount in controversy in any such proceeding.

Nothing contained in this Act shall be construed —

(1) to authorize the requisitioning or require the registration of any firearms possessed by any individual for his personal protection or sport (and the possession of which is not prohibited or the registration of which is not required by existing law),

(2) to impair or infringe in any manner the right of any individual to keep and bear arms.[1]

SEC. 2. Wherever the President determines that property acquired under this Act and retained is no longer needed for the defense of the United States, he shall, if the original owner desires the property and pays the fair value thereof, return such property to the owner; but, in any event, property so acquired and retained shall, if the owner desires the property and pays the fair value thereof, be returned to the owner not later than December 31, 1943.

SEC. 3. The President from time to time, but not less frequently than once every six months, shall transmit to the Congress a report of operations under this Act.

SEC. 4. The President may issue such rules and regulations and require such information as may be necessary and proper to carry out the provisions of this Act, and he may exercise any power or authority conferred on him by this Act through such department, agency, board, or officer as he shall direct or appoint.

D. Naval Construction

(1) Report from the House Committee on Naval Affairs (Vinson, Chairman) on H. R. 7184 to Establish the Composition of the United States Navy, etc., June 17, 1942 [2]

[Excerpt]

The lessons of the war up to June 1942 pointed fairly conclusively to the need of re-examining the roles of aircraft and capital ships in modern war. The attack on the Italian fleet at Taranto, the cornering of the *Bismarck*, and the sinking

[1] Sec. 601, Title VI of the Act to Further Expedite the Prosecution of the War ("Second War Powers Act"), deleted the following subdivision: "(3) to authorize the requisitioning of any machinery or equipment which is in actual use in connection with any operating factory or business and which is necessary to the operation of such factory or business."

[2] House Report No. 2252, 77th Cong., 2d sess.

of the *Prince of Wales* and the *Repulse* off Singapore demonstrated the vulnerability of the capital ship to air attack. The battles of the Coral Sea and of Midway Island gave additional proof of the striking power of carrier and land-based planes. While the lessons of actual combat were pointing to the need of fuller recognition of the plane, experience with the protection of commerce against the submarine was pointing to the need of a large number of relatively small boats for convoy and patrol duties. Taking account of these lessons, the Navy Department made recommendations for new construction which were incorporated in H. R. 7184. The Report of the Committee on Naval Affairs contains an informative summary of recent authorizations for naval construction and at the same time throws light on naval construction policy.

The purpose of section 1 of the bill, as introduced, is to increase the present authorized composition of the United States Navy in underage vessels by 500,000 tons of aircraft carriers, 500,000 tons of cruisers, and 900,000 tons of destroyers and destroyer escort vessels. This section also contains a proviso which would authorize the varying by not more than 30 per cent of the amount of tonnage assigned to each of the three categories of vessels provided for, so long as the total authorized tonnage of 1,900,000 tons of combatant vessels is not exceeded.

The committee believe that it would be appropriate to analyze the recent authorization acts for the construction of combatant ships as contained in the acts of March 27, 1934 (48 Stat. 503); May 17, 1938 (52 Stat. 401); June 14, 1940 (54 Stat. 394);[1] July 19, 1940 (54 Stat. 799);[2] December 23, 1941 (Public Law 369, 77th Cong.); February 6, 1942 (Public Law 440, 77th Cong.); and May 13, 1942 (Public Law 551, 77th Cong.).[3]

The Vinson-Trammell Act of March 27, 1934, authorized the construction of sufficient vessels to raise the underage strength of combatant ships to the following figures:

	Tons
Capital ships	525,000
Aircraft carriers	135,000
Cruisers	343,770
Destroyers	190,000
Submarines	68,298
Total	1,262,068

This act also authorized the President to maintain these tonnages of underage ships by permitting the replacements of any ship becoming overage or lost as permitted by the terms of the treaties providing for

[1] *Documents, II, 1939–40,* p. 761.

[2] *Ibid.,* p. 764.

[3] For ship construction authorizations table from 1938 to May 11, 1942 see *Congressional Record,* vol. 88, p. 5565 (daily edition, June 18, 1942).

the limitations of arms. Of the tonnage authorized by this act, 915,647
tons are in service, 304,151 tons are under construction, leaving an
unused balance of 42,270 tons. This balance, because of the restrictions
of this act, is available only for the construction of 33,000 tons of aircraft
carriers and 9,270 tons of cruisers.

The act of May 17, 1938, authorized the construction of combatant
tonnages in excess of those authorized by the 1934 act as follows:

	Tons
Capital ships	135,000
Aircraft carriers	40,000
Cruisers	68,754
Destroyers	38,000
Submarines	13,658
Total	295,412

This act retained those features of the 1934 act which restricted the
use of the tonnage authorized to the specific types and amounts stated
in the act. Of this tonnage, 68,088 tons are in service, 227,324 tons are
under construction, and there is no unused balance.

The so-called 11 per cent expansion act, approved June 14, 1940,
followed the pattern of the 1938 act, except that it provided flexibility
as between the types of vessels to be constructed, it being permitted
under the act to vary not more than 20 per cent of the total tonnage
between the various categories. This act authorized tonnages as follows

	Tons
Capital ships	—
Aircraft carriers	79,500
Cruisers	66,500
Destroyers	—
Submarines	21,000
Total	167,000

Of this total authorized tonnage, 7,630 tons are in service, 159,370
tons are under construction, and there is no remaining balance.

The 70 per cent Expansion Act, approved July 19, 1940, was similar
to the 11 per cent act, except that it authorized the transfer of tonnage
between categories up to 30 per cent. The authorizations by categories
under this act were as follows:

	Tons
Capital ships	385,000
Aircraft carriers	200,000
Cruisers	420,000
Destroyers	250,000
Submarines	70,000
Total	1,325,000

Of this authorization, 17,880 tons are in service, 1,273,016 tons are under construction, and there is a balance of 34,104 tons.

The next authorization was contained in the act of December 23, 1941, and provided for the construction of 150,000 tons of combatant ships. It was unrestricted as to the categories which might be built thereunder. The total construction authorized by this act is now under construction.

The last authorization for the construction of combatant ships is contained in the act approved May 13, 1942. The bill leading up to this authorization was sponsored by this committee as the result of the realization of the important part which submarines are playing in the present war. Although the wording of the law provided for the construction of "combatant ships" it is being used solely for submarine construction. Of this authorization, 182,745 tons is under construction leaving a balance of 17,255 tons.

The Navy Department is proceeding with the construction of 350,000 tons of destroyer escort vessels under the act of February 6, 1942, which authorized the construction of 1,799 vessels of any type.

In summarizing the above authorization acts it is noted that they provide for a fleet of a maximum tonnage of 3,749,480 tons. Of this total authorization 1,009,245 tons are in service, 2,646,606 tons are under construction, and there is a balance of only 93,629 tons available.

The committee is aware that at some future date a readjustment will impend requiring the conversion of some of our combatant shipbuilding facilities to peacetime production. The committee, however, is further of the opinion that we should utilize to the fullest extent, for the time being, our entire combatant ship productivity. Every combatant ship that can possibly be constructed is urgently needed in order to bring the present war to an early and successful conclusion. In order to utilize the trained skill of the available shipbuilding industry to the maximum it is necessary to make plans in such a way that there will be no hiatus in the productive rate.

.   .   .   .

The committee is pleased to report that the Navy Department is fully alive to the major, if not decisive, role that aircraft carriers and the planes based thereon have been playing in the present war. This does not mean that other types of combatant ships have lost their long-range value, but the policy of the Navy Department in concentrating, for the present, on the construction of aircraft carriers is, in the committee's opinion, entirely sound. This will necessitate deferring the construction of certain other types of ships, the immediate need for which is not so urgent. In other words, the committee understands that the Navy Department in projecting its immediate ship construction program from time to time will be guided by the most recent war experiences in determining the types of combatant ships which require the highest priority.

Section 3 authorizes the construction of 800 small vessels such as subchasers, motor torpedo boats, and minesweepers. There have been a number of previous acts for the same purpose. Some of them covered only construction and some permitted their construction or acquisition. Of those which permitted construction, all were fully utilized in that way and no vessels were acquired under those authorizations. The acts under which vessels of the types covered by section 3 were acquired are listed below:

(a) Experimental program, enacted as a part of the 20-per cent Expansion Act of 1938, limited the cost to $15,000,000, but did not specify anything about numbers or types. Under this authority 38 craft were constructed.

(b) Under the 70-per cent act of July 19, 1940, there was authorization for the construction or acquisition and conversion of patrol, escort, and miscellaneous craft at a total cost not to exceed $50,000,000. Under this act the construction of 72 craft was undertaken.

(c) The act of January 31, 1941, authorized 400 small craft.

(d) The act of November 21, 1941, authorized 400 small craft.

(e) The act of December 17, 1941, amended the act of November 21, 1941, increasing the number of ships authorized by 400.

Thus, under the 5 enactments listed above, the Navy Department has undertaken the construction of 1,310 craft, of which 904 were patrol craft, 345 mine craft, and 61 other types.

The vital need today for vessels of the small-boat type is in the patrol-craft category. The committee has been advised that, from all indications, there will probably be no extension of the present program of mine craft. If the present indications are borne out by subsequent events the entire 800 ship authorizations contained in this section will be used for the construction of submarine chasers and torpedo boats.

· · · · · · ·

(2) An Act to Establish the Composition of the United States Navy, to Authorize the Construction of Certain Naval Vessels, and for Other Purposes, Approved July 9, 1942 [1]

Be it enacted by the Senate and House of Representatives of the United States of America in Congress assembled, That the authorized composition of the United States Navy in underage vessels, as established by the Act of March 27, 1934 (48 Stat. 503), as amended by the Acts of May 17, 1938 (52 Stat. 401), June 14, 1940 (54 Stat. 394), July 19, 1940 (54 Stat. 779), December 23, 1941 (Public Law 369, Seventy-seventh Congress, first session), and May 13, 1942 (Public Law 551, Seventy-seventh Congress, second session), is hereby further increased by one million nine hundred thousand tons of combatant ships, as follows:

(a) Aircraft carriers, five hundred thousand tons;

(b) Cruisers, five hundred thousand tons; and

(c) Destroyers and destroyer escort vessels, nine hundred thousand tons: *Provided,* That the foregoing increases in tonnages for each of the three classes of aircraft carriers, cruisers, and destroyers and destroyer escort vessels may be varied downward in the amount of 30 per centum of the total increased tonnage authorized herein, and if so varied downward, the tonnage so decreased may be used to increase the tonnage of any other class of vessel authorized above, or to increase the tonnage of submarines heretofore authorized, so long as the sum of the total increases in tonnages of these classes, including submarines as authorized herein, is not exceeded: *Provided further,* That the total authorized tonnage by classes of vessels' authorized by the Acts of May 27, 1934 (48 Stat. 503), May 17, 1938 (52 Stat. 401), and June 14, 1940 (54 Stat. 394), may be varied upward or downward in the amount of 30 per centum so long as the sum of the total increases in tonnage of these classes so authorized is not exceeded.

SEC. 2. The President of the United States is hereby authorized to construct such vessels as may be necessary to provide the total underage composition authorized in section 1 of this Act and to maintain such total increased authorized composition by constructing replacement vessels for such vessels as may be overage as defined in section 7 of the Act approved June 14, 1940 (54 Stat. 395), or as may have been or may be lost: *Provided,* That notwithstanding the provisions of any other law, parts of laws, or other provisions of this Act, the replacement vessels

---

[1] Public Law 666, 77th Cong.; originating as H. R. 7184 from Committee on Naval Affairs, June 17, 1942; House Report No. 2252; Senate Report No. 1514; passed by House of Representatives, June 18, 1942, *Congressional Record,* vol. 88, p. 5567, June 18, 1942 (daily edition); passed by Senate, June 26, 1942, *ibid.,* p. 5801.

herein authorized are not required to be of the same class as the vessels which have become overage or been lost, so long as they are either battleships, cruisers, aircraft carriers, destroyers or destroyer escort vessels, or submarines, and so long as the total authorized composition of the United States Navy in underage vessels, as herein or hereafter increased, is not exceeded.

SEC. 3. The Secretary of the Navy, with the approval of the President, is hereby authorized to undertake the construction of not to exceed eight hundred small vessels suitable for use as patrol vessels, mine vessels and the like, as he may consider best suited for the successful prosecution of the war, such vessels to be in addition to those heretofore authorized.

SEC. 4. The Secretary of the Navy is hereby authorized to acquire and convert not to exceed two hundred small vessels for coastal defense, patrol, mine sweeping, and similar purposes as he may consider necessary for the successful prosecution of the war, such vessels to be in addition to those heretofore authorized.

SEC. 5. (a) Section 5 (a) of the Act approved July 19, 1940 (54 Stat. 780), is hereby amended by striking out the words "at a total cost not to exceed $50,000,000," and inserting in lieu thereof the words "to a total number not to exceed seventy-two."

(b) Section 2 of the Act approved January 31, 1941 (55 Stat. 5), is hereby amended by striking out the words "to a total amount not exceeding $400,000,000."

SEC. 6. There is hereby authorized to be appropriated, out of any money in the Treasury of the United States not otherwise appropriated, such sums as may be necessary to effectuate the purposes of this Act.

E. Coordination of Defense Forces

(1) *Report of the Commission ("Roberts Commission") Appointed by the President of the United States (Roosevelt) to Investigate and Report the Facts Relating to the Attack Made by Japanese Armed Forces upon Pearl Harbor, Submitted January 23, 1942* [1]

[Excerpt]

The success of the Japanese attack upon American forces at Pearl Harbor created a strong reaction in the United States in view of the fact that, while the attack was without warning, it had been preceded by an extended period of diplomatic tension.[2] Furthermore, the method of surprise employed was not without precedent in Japanese history and in the current war in Europe. There was a general inclination to accuse the Army and Navy of failure to make

[1] Senate Doc. No. 159, 77th Cong., 2d sess.
[2] See headnote on p. 469.

adequate preparations and to cooperate effectively in meeting a common danger. The result was the appointment by the President, by Executive Order of December 18, 1941, of a Commission consisting of Justice Owen J. Roberts of the Supreme Court (Chairman), Rear Admiral W. H. Standley (retired), Rear Admiral J. M. Reeves (retired), Brigadier-General Frank R. McCoy (retired) and Brigadier-General Joseph T. McNarney of the Army Air Corps to investigate the facts. The duties of the Commission were defined by the Executive Order as follows: to ascertain and report the facts relating to the attack made by Japanese armed forces upon the Territory of Hawaii on December 7, 1941.

The purposes of the required inquiry and report were to provide bases for sound decisions whether any derelictions of duty or errors of judgment on the part of United States Army or Navy personnel contributed to such successes as were achieved by the enemy on the occasion mentioned; and, if so, what these derelictions or errors were, and who were responsible therefor.

Only the concluding portion of the Report is given here.

Summary of the More Important Facts

Pearl Harbor is an important outlying naval base, and its security is vital to both offensive and defensive operations. It is the Army's function to insure the security of Pearl Harbor against hostile attack, and the Navy's function to support the Army indirectly by operations at sea and directly by making available therefor such instrumentalities of the Navy as are on the vessels of the fleet when in harbor and are located or based on shore either temporarily or permanently.

Effective utilization of the military power of the Nation is essential to success in war and requires that the operations of the Army and the Navy be coordinated. Under the then existing plans the joint defense of the Hawaiian frontier was to be coordinated by mutual cooperation between the commanders concerned. Plans for the defense of the Hawaiian coastal frontier were prepared by the Commanding General, Hawaiian Department, and the Commandant of the Fourteenth Naval District, the latter acting as a subordinate of the Commander-in-Chief of the Pacific Fleet. Adherence to such a plan prepared in advance of hostilities does not suffice to relieve commanders of their responsibility to apply and adapt the plan to the situation as it develops.

Where, as here, the defense of an area is the joint responsibility of two commanders who are to coordinate their activities by mutual cooperation, the first duty of such commanders in the case of an emergency is conference and consultation with respect to the measures to be taken under the existing plans and the adaptation of those plans in whole or in part to the situation.

At about the time that Admiral Kimmel and General Short assumed their respective commands, the War and Navy Departments were in correspondence with respect to adequate defense against air raids on

Oahu and the naval base. The correspondence between the departments exhibits a deep concern respecting the probability of this form of attack. These commanders were acquainted with this correspondence. Nevertheless there has been amongst the responsible commanders and their subordinates, without exception, a conviction, which persisted up to December 7, 1941, that Japan had no intention of making any such raid. Consequently this form of attack was a complete surprise to all of the superior officers of Army and Navy stationed in the Hawaiian area. This conviction persisted notwithstanding messages containing warnings and orders, brought to the attention of both commanders over a period of weeks prior to the attack. As early as October 16 the commanders were warned of the possibility of an attack by Japan on the United States and were directed to take precautions and make preparatory dispositions in the light of this information. A significant warning message was communicated to both the local commanders on November 24. On November 27 each responsible commander was warned that hostilities were momentarily possible. The warnings indicated war, and war only.

Both of these messages contained orders. The Commanding General was ordered to undertake such reconnaissance and other measures as he deemed necessary. The Commander-in-Chief of the fleet was ordered to execute a defensive deployment in preparation for carrying out war tasks. Other significant messages followed on succeeding days. These emphasized the impending danger and the need for war readiness.

In this situation, during a period of 10 days preceding the Japanese attack, the responsible commanders held no conference directed to a discussion of the meaning of the warnings and orders sent them, and failed to collaborate and to coordinate defensive measures which should be taken pursuant to the orders received. Dispositions as a result of the messages were independently made by each commander. Neither of them informed himself of the measures and dispositions taken by the other.

The dispositions so made were inadequate to meet a surprise air attack.

Both commanders were handicapped by lack of information as to Japanese dispositions and intent. The lack of such knowledge rendered more urgent the initiation of a state of readiness for defense.

The personnel, *matériel,* and equipment were insufficient to place the forces on a war footing and maintain them on that footing for an extended period. These deficiencies did not preclude measures which would have to a great extent frustrated the attack or mitigated its severity.

A considerable number of the Army and Navy personnel were on pass or liberty December 6, for the reason that the state of alert or of readiness demanded by the emergency had not been put into effect. With immaterial exceptions Army and Navy personnel had returned from leave and liberty hours before the attack ensued, fit for duty.

Both officers and men responded immediately in the emergency and exhibited initiative, efficiency, and bravery in meeting the raid.

Based upon its findings of fact, the Commission reaches the following

CONCLUSIONS

1. Effective utilization of the military power of the Nation is essential to success in war and requires: First, the coordination of the foreign and military policies of the Nation; and, second, the coordination of the operations of the Army and Navy.

2. The Secretary of State fulfilled his obligations by keeping the War and Navy Departments in close touch with the international situation and fully advising them respecting the course and probable termination of negotiations with Japan.

3. The Secretary of War and the Secretary of the Navy fulfilled their obligations by conferring frequently with the Secretary of State and with each other and by keeping the Chief of Staff and the Chief of Naval Operations informed of the course of the negotiations with Japan and the significant implications thereof.

4. The Chief of Staff and the Chief of Naval Operations fulfilled their obligations by consulting and cooperating with each other, and with their superiors, respecting the joint defense of the Hawaiian coastal frontier; and each knew of, and concurred in, the warnings and orders sent by the other to the responsible commanders with respect to such defense.

5. The Chief of Staff of the Army fulfilled his command responsibility by issuing a direct order in connection with his warning of probable hostilities, in the following words: "Prior to hostile Japanese action you are directed to undertake such reconnaissance and other measures as you deem necessary."

6. The Chief of Naval Operations fulfilled his command responsibility by issuing a warning and by giving a direct order to the Commander-in-Chief, Pacific Fleet, in the following words:

This despatch is to be considered a war warning.

and

Execute an appropriate defensive deployment preparatory to carrying out the tasks assigned.

7. The responsible commanders in the Hawaiian area, in fulfillment of their obligation so to do, prepared plans which, if adapted to and used for the existing emergency, would have been adequate.

8. In the circumstances the responsibility of these commanders was to confer upon the question of putting into effect and adapting their joint defense plans.

9. These commanders failed to confer with respect to the warnings and orders issued on and after November 27, and to adapt and use existing plans to meet the emergency.

10. The order for alert No. 1 of the Army command in Hawaii was not adequate to meet the emergency envisaged in the warning messages.

11. The state of readiness of the naval forces on the morning of December 7 was not such as was required to meet the emergency envisaged in the warning messages.

12. Had orders issued by the Chief of Staff and the Chief of Naval Operations November 27, 1941, been complied with, the aircraft warning system of the Army should have been operating; the distant reconnaissance of the Navy, and the inshore air patrol of the Army, should have been maintained; the antiaircraft batteries of the Army and similar shore batteries of the Navy, as well as additional antiaircraft artillery located on vessels of the fleet in Pearl Harbor, should have been manned and supplied with ammunition; and a high state of readiness of aircraft should have been in effect. None of these conditions was in fact inaugurated or maintained for the reason that the responsible commanders failed to consult and cooperate as to necessary action based upon the warnings and to adopt measures enjoined by the orders given them by the chiefs of the Army and Navy commands in Washington.

13. There were deficiencies in personnel, weapons, equipment, and facilities to maintain all the defenses on a war footing for extended periods of time, but these deficiencies should not have affected the decision of the responsible commanders as to the state of readiness to be prescribed.

14. The warning message of December 7, intended to reach both commanders in the field at about 7 A.M. Hawaiian time, December 7, 1941, was but an added precaution, in view of the warning and orders previously issued. If the message had reached its destination at the time intended, it would still have been too late to be of substantial use, in view of the fact that the commanders had failed to take measures and make dispositions prior to the time of its anticipated receipt which would have been effective to warn of the attack or to meet it.

15. The failure of the officers in the War Department to observe that

General Short, neither in his reply of November 27 to the Chief of
Staff's message of that date, nor otherwise, had reported the measures
taken by him, and the transmission of two messages concerned chiefly
with sabotage which warned him not to resort to illegal methods against
sabotage or espionage, and not to take measures which would alarm the
civil population, and the failure to reply to his message of November 29
outlining in full all the actions he had taken against sabotage only, and
referring to nothing else, tended to lead General Short to believe that
what he had done met the requirements of the warnings and orders
received by him.

16. The failure of the Commanding General, Hawaiian Department,
and the Commander-in-Chief, Pacific Fleet, to confer and cooperate
with respect to the meaning of the warnings received and the measures
necessary to comply with the orders given them under date of November 27, 1941, resulted largely from a sense of security due to the opinion
prevalent in diplomatic, military, and naval circles, and in the public
press, that any immediate attack by Japan would be in the Far East.
The existence of such a view, however prevalent, did not relieve the
commanders of the responsibility for the security of the Pacific Fleet
and our most important outpost.

17. In the light of the warnings and directions to take appropriate
action, transmitted to both commanders between November 27 and
December 7, and the obligation under the system of coordination then
in effect for joint cooperative action on their part, it was a dereliction
of duty on the part of each of them not to consult and confer with the
other respecting the meaning and intent of the warnings, and the
appropriate measures of defense required by the imminence of hostilities.
The attitude of each, that he was not required to inform himself of, and
his lack of interest in, the measures undertaken by the other to carry out
the responsibility assigned to such other under the provisions of the plans
then in effect, demonstrated on the part of each a lack of appreciation
of the responsibilities vested in them and inherent in their positions as
Commander-in-Chief, Pacific Fleet, and Commanding General, Hawaiian
Department.

18. The Japanese attack was a complete surprise to the commanders,
and they failed to make suitable dispositions to meet such an attack.
Each failed properly to evaluate the seriousness of the situation. These
errors of judgment were the effective causes for the success of the attack.

19. Causes contributory to the success of the Japanese attack were:
Disregard of international law and custom relating to declaration of
war by the Japanese and the adherence by the United States to such laws
and customs.

Restrictions which prevented effective counterespionage.

Emphasis in the warning messages on the probability of aggressive Japanese action in the Far East, and on antisabotage measures.

Failure of the War Department to reply to the message relating to the antisabotage measures instituted by the Commanding General, Hawaiian Department.

Nonreceipt by the interested parties, prior to the attack, of the warning message of December 7, 1941.

20. When the attack developed on the morning of December 7, 1941, the officers and enlisted men of both services were present in sufficient number and were in fit condition to perform any duty. Except for a negligible number, the use of intoxicating liquor on the preceding evening did not affect their efficiency.

21. Subordinate commanders executed their superiors' orders without question. They were not responsible for the state of readiness prescribed.

(2) Army and Navy Reorganization and Cooperation. Joint Army and Navy War Review, May 17, 1942 [1]

[Excerpt]

A most encouraging feature since the beginning of the war has been the rapid manner in which machinery has been established for the efficient prosecution of the war. This commenced with reorganizational changes both within the Army and the Navy, progressed through closer coordination of joint operations between the Army and the Navy, and reached its peak in machinery established for close collaboration among the United Nations.[2] Both the War and the Navy Departments have been reorganized since December 7 with a view to eliminating delay and expediting administrative procedure. In the War Department, the War Department General Staff has been materially reduced in size and most of its administrative duties have been transferred to other divisions. The heads of the three major divisions of the Army, the Army Air Forces, the Ground Forces, and the Services of Supply, report directly to General George C. Marshall, the Chief of Staff, and relieve him of an enormous burden of administrative duties. Similarly, the reorganization of the Navy Department has combined the office of the Chief of Naval Operations with that of the Commander-in-Chief of the U. S. Fleet. This position of highest naval command is held by Admiral E. J. King. The Chief of Staff, U. S. Fleet, and the Vice Chief of Naval Operations, acting directly under the Commander-in-Chief, relieve him of many

[1] From the Bureau of Public Relations, War Department.
[2] See p. 239.

administrative duties and leave him free for the strategic direction of naval combat units.

On all of our far-flung battle fronts the Army and the Navy are cooperating to the closest possible degree. The principle of unity of command has been put into effect in every theater of operation. In the Southwest Pacific General MacArthur has been placed in supreme command of the land, air and sea forces of the United Nations. In the Pacific Area, military and naval forces are under the command of Admiral Nimitz, Commander-in-Chief of the Pacific Fleet. In the Panama Canal and the immediate adjacent areas, the Army has control of military and naval forces. In the Eastern Caribbean, all military and naval forces are under the Navy. In the defense of the Atlantic and Pacific coastal frontiers, the efforts of the Army and the Navy are completely unified.

With respect to collaboration among the United Nations, tremendous progress has been made as compared to the World War. Three weeks after the beginning of the present war, in conjunction with a visit of the Prime Minister of England and the leading members of the British Army, Navy and Air Forces in Washington, machinery was established that will insure complete unity of purpose on the part of the nations concentrating their efforts on the defeat of the Axis Powers. The existing machinery also permits collaboration with the members of the British Commonwealth and other powers which have dedicated their efforts towards achieving this purpose.

F. Coordination of Information

(1) *Appointment of Coordinator of Information.* **Release by the Office** *of the Secretary to the President* **(Roosevelt),** *July 11, 1941*

The President today, as Commander-in-Chief of the Armed forces, appointed William J. Donovan Coordinator of Information.

In his capacity as Coordinator, Mr. Donovan will collect and assemble information and data bearing on national security from the various departments and agencies of the Government and will analyze and collate such materials for the use of the President and such other officials as the President may designate.

Mr. Donovan's task will be to coordinate and correlate defense information, but his work is not intended to supersede or to duplicate, or to involve any direction of or interference with, the activities of the General Staff, the regular intelligence services, the Federal Bureau of Investigation, or of other existing departments and agencies.

(2) *Military Order of the President (Roosevelt) Changing the Office of Coordinator of Information into the Office of Strategic Services, June 13, 1942* [1]

By virtue of the authority vested in me as President of the United States and as Commander-in-Chief of the Army and Navy of the United States, it is ordered as follows:

1. The office of Coordinator of Information established by Order of July 11, 1941,[2] exclusive of the foreign information activities transferred to the Office of War Information by Executive Order of June 13, 1942,[3] shall hereafter be known as the Office of Strategic Services, and is hereby transferred to the jurisdiction of the United States Joint Chiefs of Staff.

2. The Office of Strategic Services shall perform the following duties:
   a. Collect and analyze such strategic information as may be required by the United States Joint Chiefs of Staff.
   b. Plan and operate such special services as may be directed by the United States Joint Chiefs of Staff.

3. At the head of the Office of Strategic Services shall be a Director of Strategic Services who shall be appointed by the President and who shall perform his duties under the direction and supervision of the United States Joint Chiefs of Staff.

4. William J. Donovan is hereby appointed as Director of Strategic Services.

5. The Order of July 11, 1941 is hereby revoked.

3. PRODUCTION, PROCUREMENT AND TRANSFER OF NECESSARY MATERIALS

Before the entrance of the United States into the war, this country was committed to serving as the "arsenal of democracy." [4] Once we entered the war the job of producing and procuring necessary materials and transporting these materials to the places where needed became even more pressing. The job of procurement and production is primarily a domestic problem, though in so far as it involves the coordination of the production facilities of the United States with those of other countries or the procurement from other countries of materials necessary to production here, it has a very definite connection with American foreign relations. The documents that are given here are those which bear more particularly on the domestic aspects of the problem though their listing seems desirable because of their fundamental place in our defense and war effort. Additional documents are given in other chapters. To the more important of these, cross reference is made.

[1] From the Office of the Secretary to the President, June 13, 1942.
[2] See p. 159.
[3] See p. 189.
[4] Address on National Security by the President (Roosevelt), December 29, 1940, *Documents, III, 1940–41,* p. 17.

A. Production

(1) *Executive Order No. 9024 Establishing the War Production Board in the Executive Office of the President and Defining its Functions and Duties, January 16, 1942* [1]

The establishment of the War Production Board on January 16, 1942 resulted in the amendment of the organization of the Office of Production Management as set up by Executive Order No. 8629, January 7, 1941 (*Documents, III, 1940–41*, p. 668) and the supersession of provisions conflicting with those of the present order Sec. 4 of Executive Order No. 9040, January 24, 1942 (7 *Fed. Reg.*, p. 527) abolished the Office of Production Management and transferred its personnel, records, property and funds. By Executive Order No. 9125, April 7, 1942 (7 *Fed. Reg.*, p. 2719), the Chairman of the War Production Board, with the advice and assistance of the members of the Board, was authorized to "perform the additional functions and duties, and exercise the additional powers, authority and discretion conferred upon the President of the United States by title III of the Second War Powers Act, 1942."

By virtue of the authority vested in me by the Constitution and statutes of the United States, as President of the United States and Commander-in-Chief of the Army and Navy, and in order to define further the functions and duties of the Office for Emergency Management with respect to the state of war declared to exist by Joint Resolutions of the Congress, approved December 8, 1941, and December 11, 1941, respectively, and for the purpose of assuring the most effective prosecution of war procurement and production, it is hereby ordered as follows:

1. There is established within the Office for Emergency Management of the Executive Office of the President a War Production Board, hereinafter referred to as the Board. The Board shall consist of a Chairman, to be appointed by the President, the Secretary of War, the Secretary of the Navy, the Federal Loan Administrator, [the Lieutenant General in charge of War Department Production and the Director of the Labor Division of the War Production Board],[2] the Administrator of the Office of Price Administration, the Chairman of the Board of Economic Warfare, and the Special Assistant to the President supervising the defense aid program.

[1] As modified by Executive Order No. 9040, January 24, 1942; 7 *Fed. Reg.*, p. 329, 527.

[2] Substituted by sec. 2 of Executive Order No. 9040 for: "the Director General and the Associate Director General of the Office of Production Management." William S. Knudsen, the Director General, was appointed by the President and confirmed by the Senate as Lieutenant General in charge of War Department Production. The Associate Director General of the Office of Production Management, Sidney Hillman, was Director of the Labor Division, which was transferred.

2.[1] The Chairman of the War Production Board,[2] with the advice and assistance of the members of the Board, shall:

  a. Exercise general direction over the war procurement and production program.

  b. Determine the policies, plans, procedures, and methods of the several Federal departments, establishments, and agencies in respect to war procurement and production, including purchasing, contracting, specifications, and construction; and including conversion, requisitioning, plant expansion, and the financing thereof; and issue such directives in respect thereto as he may deem necessary or appropriate.

  c. Perform the functions and exercise the powers vested in the Supply Priorities and Allocations Board by Executive Order No. 8875 of August 28, 1941.

  d. Supervise the Office of Production Management in the performance of its responsibilities and duties, and direct such changes in its organization as he may deem necessary.

  e. Report from time to time to the President on the progress of war procurement and production; and perform such other duties as the President may direct.

3. Federal departments, establishments, and agencies shall comply with the policies, plans, methods, and procedures in respect to war procurement and production as determined by the Chairman; and shall furnish to the Chairman such information relating to war procurement and production as he may deem necessary for the performance of his duties.

4. The Army and Navy Munitions Board shall report to the President through the Chairman of the War Production Board.

5. The Chairman may exercise the powers, authority, and discretion conferred upon him by this Order [or any other Order[3]] through such

----

[1] Amendment by sec. 1 of Executive Order No. 9040 as follows:
"1. In addition to the responsibilities and duties described in paragraph 2 . . . th Chairman . . . shall:
  a. Perform the functions and exercise the powers heretofore vested in the Office of Production Management.
  b. Perform the functions and exercise the powers vested in the Supply Prioritie and Allocations Board, by Executive Order No. 8942, of November 19, 1941.
  c. Perform the functions and exercise the powers vested in the President by Section 120 of the National Defense Act of 1916 (39 Stat. 213)."
[2] The President on January 13, 1942 announced that he would appoint Donald M. Nelson, Director of the Priorities Division, chairman of the War Production Board when it was established.
[3] Amendment by sec. 3 of Executive Order No. 9040.

fficials or agencies and in such manner as he may determine; and his
lecisions shall be final.

6. The Chairman is further authorized within the limits of such funds
s may be allocated or appropriated to the Board to employ necessary
)ersonnel and make provision for necessary supplies, facilities, and
ervices.

7. The Supply Priorities and Allocations Board, established by the
Executive Order of August 28, 1941, is hereby abolished, and its person-
el, records, and property transferred to the Board. The Executive
Orders No. 8629 of January 7, 1941,[1] No. 8875 of August 28, 1941,
No. 8891 of September 4, 1941, No. 8942 of November 19, 1941, No.
9001 of December 27, 1941, and No. 9023 of January 14, 1942, are hereby
mended accordingly, and any provisions of these or other pertinent
Executive Orders conflicting with this Order are hereby superseded.

General Administrative Order 2–45, issued on July 8, 1942, realigned the
major functions and established the principal lines of authority and responsi-
pility within the War Production Board. Divisions had been established origin
lly by General Administrative Order 2, January 6, 1942. A description of the
livisional organization set up by General Administrative Order 2 is given in
United States Government Manual, Spring 1942, p. 84. A description of the
evised organization is given in the *Manual*, Fall 1942, p. 92.

B. Procurement and Supply of Strategic and Critical Materials

[See *Documents, I, 1938–39*, p. 511; *II, 1939–40*, p. 786; *III, 1940–41*, p. 736.
For documents dealing with measures that have been taken in our relations with
oreign countries, see especially Chapter IV, The United Nations, and Chapter V,
The Western Hemisphere. Export control is covered in Chapter VIII, Trade and
Finance.]

1) *Governmental Organizations Concerned with the Purchase, Pro-
duction and Conservation of Strategic and Critical Materials* [2]

1. *Army and Navy Munitions Board.* Designated by Public Law 117 [3] as the
gency for the determination of the kind, quality, and quantities of materials
o be assigned and stored. On April 29, 1939, the Army and Navy Munitions
Board appointed a committee designated "Specifications and Storage Committee
or Strategic Materials" to study and submit recommendations. On June 15,

---

[1] Rescinded by sec. 5 of Executive Order No. 9040.
[2] Based on data contained in House Report No. 982, 77th Cong., 1st sess., supple-
nented by data contained in the *United States Government Manual* and the *Federal
Register.*
[3] *Act to Provide for the Common Defense by Acquiring Stocks of Strategic and
Critical Materials,* approved June 7, 1939; *Documents, I, 1938–39*, p. 513.

1939 the Army and Navy Munitions Board asked the Secretaries of State
Treasury, Commerce and the Interior to designate a representative to cooperate
with the Board in carrying out the provisions of the Act. By Executive Order No
9024 of January 16, 1942,[1] the Board reports to the President through the Chairman of the War Production Board.

2. *Procurement Division of the Treasury.* Charged under Public Law 117
with the responsibility for the procurement, transportation, maintenance, rota-
tion and storage of material. To effectuate the policies as set forth there was
established under the direct supervision of the Director of Procurement the
Strategic and Critical Materials Division.

3. *The Reconstruction Finance Corporation.* The R.F.C. has created the
following companies and corporations in furtherance of the purposes of the 1939
act:

a. The *Metals Reserve Company*, set up June 28, 1940, to acquire and carry a
reserve supply of critical and strategic materials in connection with the national
defense program.

b. The *Rubber Reserve Company*, created on June 28, 1940, to acquire and carry
a reserve supply of rubber in connection with the national defense program.

c. The *Defense Plant Corporation*, created on August 22, 1940, with extensive
powers in connection with the producing, processing, marketing and storing of
strategic and critical materials.

d. The *Defense Supplies Corporation*, created August 29, 1940 to acquire and
carry strategic and critical materials or supplies which may be necessary or appropriate in connection with the national defense program.

4. *Board of Economic Warfare.* Pursuant to the provisions of section 6 of the
Act of July 2, 1940 ("Export Control Act") [2] the responsibility for the adminis
tration of export control was vested in the Administrator of Export Control in
the Department of Commerce. Under the Act the President was given power to
curtail or prohibit the export of material or supplies necessary to the manufac
ture of military equipment or munitions. By Executive Order No. 8900 [3] and
Administrative Order No. 1 [4] of September 15, 1941 the powers and functions
of the Administrator were transferred to the Economic Defense Board, estab
lished by Executive Order No. 8839, July 30, 1941 (see p. 180) and renamed the
Board of Economic Warfare by Executive Order No. 8982, December 17, 1941.
By Executive Order No. 9128 of April 13, 1942, the powers and duties of the
Board were greatly expanded with the result that it has become the agency for
coordinating governmental operation in this field subject to directives from the
Chairman of the War Production Board.[6]

5. *Department of State.* In view of the importance of economic factors in the
present international situation, the Department has established a Board of
Economic Operations [7] which has the function of coordinating the formulation
and execution of policies in the economic field. The Division of Defense Ma
terials [8] which functions as a component part of the Board is responsible for
formulating and executing policies in the field of defense materials and the
maintenance of liaison with other agencies of the Government concerned with
these matters. Matters of foreign policy involved in the administration of the

[1] 7 *Fed. Reg.*, p. 329. [2] *Documents, III, 1940–41*, p. 474.
[3] 6 *Fed. Reg.*, p. 4795. [4] *Ibid.*, p. 4818. [5] *Ibid.*, p. 6530
[6] This volume, p. 182. [7] See p. 845. [8] See p. 847.

DEFENSE AND THE WAR EFFORT

Act of July 2, 1940 (export of materials necessary to national defense),[1] and the
Act of June 28, 1940,[2] as amended May 31, 1941 [3] (so far as priorities or allocations for export are concerned), are also responsibilities of the Division of Defense Materials, acting in collaboration with the Adviser on International
Economic Affairs and the affected geographical divisions, except in so far as
responsibility is vested in the American Hemisphere Exports Office.

6. *Office of Inter-American Affairs.* Established by Executive Order No. 8840,
July 30, 1941.[4] It cooperates with buying agencies of the Government in an
attempt to increase imports to this country from the other American Republics.
It works closely with the Export-Import Bank of Washington and the Department of State in carrying out a program of loans to the various American Republics. In the field of agriculture, the Office is lending its aid to the development of complementary agricultural products. In close collaboration with the
Inter-American Development Commission,[5] it is seeking to encourage the development of natural resources and industries in the other American Republics.

7. *Export-Import Bank of Washington.* By Act of September 26, 1940,[6] the
Bank was authorized to make loans to assist in the development of the resources,
the stabilization of the economies, and the orderly marketing of the products
of the countries of the Western Hemisphere.

8. *Department of Agriculture.* The following agencies have been set up within
the Department with functions related to the procurement and conservation of
strategic and critical materials:[7]

a. *Office of Agricultural War Relations.* Designed to serve as a clearing house
to bring into common focus the consideration of agricultural needs and problems
as they relate to the war program. Following the establishment of the Foods
Requirements Committee in June 1942, the Office has been reorganized and its
principal functions have been centered in the Foods Requirements Branch.

b. *Office of Foreign Agricultural Relations.* Primarily a fact-finding agency.
Maintains close liaison with the State Department, the Board of Economic
Warfare, the War and Navy Departments, and other war agencies.

c. *Commodity Credit Corporation.* Purchases foreign agricultural commodities
required by the United States and the other United Nations in addition to the
quantities that may be available in the United States.

9. The *Bureau of Mines and the Geological Survey of the Department of the
Interior.*

10. *Office of Price Administration and Civilian Supply.* Though primarily
concerned with the satisfaction of civilian needs, this office is responsible for
preventing price spiraling, hoarding and such practices and conditions as might
interfere with the production and procurement of necessary materials for defense
purposes.

11. *War Production Board.*[8] Has taken over the powers and duties formerly
belonging to the Office of Production Management. Its function thus becomes
that of advising and coordinating the activities of other Governmental agencies.

12. *War Shipping Administration.* Established by Executive Order No. 9054
of February 7, 1942 [9] and responsible for making available the necessary shipping
or the transportation of strategic and critical materials.

[1] *Documents, III, 1940–41,* p. 474.   [2] *Ibid., II, 1939–40,* p. 793.
[3] *Ibid., III, 1940–41,* p. 748.   [4] See p. 329.
[5] *Documents, III, 1940–41,* p. 112.   [6] *Ibid.,* p. 550.
[7] *United States Government Manual,* Fall 1942, p. 282.   [8] See p. 161.   [9] See p. 776.

(2) *List of Strategic and Critical Materials as of June 14, 1941. Interim Report ("Faddis Report") from the House Committee on Military Affairs, June 21, 1941* [1]

As of June 14, 1941, the Army and Navy Munitions Board approved the following definitions and lists of strategic and critical materials:

DEFINITIONS

Strategic materials.   Strategic materials are those essential to national defense, for the supply of which in war dependence must be placed in whole, or in substantial part, on sources outside the continental limits of the United States; and for which strict conservation and distribution control measures will be necessary.

Critical materials.   Critical materials are those essential to national defense, the procurement problems of which in war would be less difficult than those of strategic materials either because they have a lesser degree of essentiality or are obtainable in more adequate quantities from domestic sources; and for which some degree of conservation and distribution control will be necessary.

Strategic materials (15)

Antimony.
Chromium.
Coconut shell char.
Industrial diamonds.
Manganese, ferrograde.
Manila fiber.
Mercury.
Mica.

Nickel.
Quartz crystal.
Quinine.
Rubber.
Silk.
Tin.
Tungsten.

Critical materials (19)

Aluminum and bauxite.
Asbestos.
Cork.
Graphite.
Hides.
Copper.
Gasoline, 100 octane.
Iodine.
Kapok.
Opium.

Optical glass.
Phenol.
Nitrogen compounds.
Platinum.
Tanning materials.
Toluol.
Vanadium.
Wool.
Zinc and zinc concentrates.

The Army and Navy Munitions Board maintains a list of, and keeps under surveillance, certain additional materials which might become strategic or critical.

A revised and expanded priorities critical list was issued June 10, by the Division of Priorities, Office of Production Management. The list

[1] House Report No. 982, 77th Cong., 1st sess., p. 14–15.

ncluded approximately 40 new items and classes of items, thus expanding he total number of materials and classes of materials to over 300.

The critical list is a compilation of materials on orders for which Army nd Navy contracting officers may automatically assign preference ertificates.

On varying dates the following commodities have been placed under xport license: Abrasives, beryllium, cadmium, chlorine, copper, cotton inters, flaxseed, magnesium, molybdenum, petroleum, titanium, and ranium.

As of June 14, 1941, the accumulation in the Government stock pile f strategic materials is satisfactory to the Army and Navy Munitions 3oard, with the exception of chrome ore, industrial diamonds, man-anese, quartz crystals, rubber, tin, and tungsten. However, it is ntirely possible, in view of changing world conditions and uncertainty f shipping that the situation in regard to most of these materials may ecome progressively worse.

3) *List of Materials in Short Supply as of June 1, 1942* [1]

GROUP I

The available supply of the following materials is inadequate for war nd essential civilian uses and in many cases for war purposes alone.

METALS

lloy Iron	Copper	Tantalum
lloy Steel	Copper Scrap	Tin
luminum	Iridium	Tinplate and Terneplate
luminum Pigments	Magnesium	Tungsten
admium	Manganese, Electro	Tungsten Carbides
alcium-Silicon	Nickel	Vanadium
hromium	Nickel Scrap	Wrought Iron
obalt	Rhodium	Zinc (high grade)
olumbium		

CHEMICALS

cetone	Chlorine	Phosphates:
lkyd Resins	Cresols	Tricresyl
lumina	Diphenylamine	Triphenyl
mmonia	Methyl Methacrylate	Phthalic Anhydride and
niline	Sheets	Phthalates
nthraquinone Deriva-	Naphthalene	Polystyrene
tives	Pentarythritol	Polyvinyl Chloride
enzol	Phenol	Sodium Nitrate
utadiene	Phenol Formaldehyde	Sulphur Chlorides
hlorinated Hydrocar-	Resins and Plastics	Toluol
bon Solvents		

[1] Excerpt from War Production Board Press Release 1254, June 1, 1942.

MISCELLANEOUS PRODUCTS

Agar
Asbestos (long fiber)
Babassu Oil
Burlap
Cashew Nut Shell Oil
Chrome Pigments
Coconut Oil
Corundum
Cotton:
  Duck
  Linters
  Raw, Long Staple
Feathers and Down
  (Goose and Duck)
Graphite (Madagascar
  Flake)
Hemp:
  Agave Fiber
  Henequen
  Manila Fiber
  Cordage
  Seed
  Sisal

Jewel Bearings
Jute
Kapok
Kyanite
Lumber:
  Certain Grades Hard
  and Soft Woods
Mica, Block
Natural Resins, except
  Rosin
Nylon
Oiticica Oil
Palm Oil
Palm Kernel Oil
Pig and Hog Bristles
Quartz Crystals
Quinine
Rape Seed Oil

Rayon, High Tenacity
Rubber:
  Chlorinated
  Crude
  Latex
  Reclaimed
  Synthetic
Shearlings
Shellac
Silk:
  Raw
  Noils
  Garnetted
  Reclaimed
Sperm Oil
Teak
Tung Oil

GROUP II

Materials that are essential to the war industries but the supplies of which are not limited as those of Group I.

METALS

Aluminum Scrap
  No. 12, Remelt
Antimony
Arsenic
Bismuth
Calcium
Ferrosilicon
Iron:
  Gray
  Cast
  Malleable

Lead
Lithium
Manganese (Ferro)
Mercury
Molybdenum
Palladium
Pig Iron and Scrap
Platinum
Ruthenium

Silicon and Alloys
Steel:
  Bessemer
  Carbon
  Basic
  Scrap
Zinc (low grades)
Uranium

CHEMICALS

Alcohol:
  Ethyl
  Methyl
Atebrine (for Quinine)
Barium Carbonate

Bleaching Powder
Bromine
Butanol
Cadmium Pigments
Carbon Tetrachlorides

Citric Acid
Formaldehyde
Glycol
Halogenated Hydrocar-
  bon Refrigerants

Iodine
Lactic Acid
Lithopone
Mannitol
Methyl Methacrylate
  Powder

Phosphorus
Potassium:
  Perchlorate
  Permanganate
Sorbitol
Strontium Salts

Tetraethyl Lead
Titanium Pigments
Urea Formaldehyde
  Plastic
Vinylidine Chloride
  Plastic
Xylol

MISCELLANEOUS PRODUCTS

Albumin, Blood
Bauxite
Castor Oil
Cellophane
Cellulose Nitrate, Ace-
  tate, and Other Deriv-
  atives
Cork
Cotton Seed
Cryolite
Diamonds:
  Industrial
  Dies
Fish Liver Oils
Flax
Fluorspar
Glassine Paper

Glues, Animal and Vege-
  table
Glycerine
Hides
Lead Pigments
Leather
Linseed Oil
Magnesite
Mercury Pigments
Mica, Splittings
Molasses
Natural Gas
Parchment Paper
Pine Oil
Rayon Filament, Staple
  Fiber

Rotenone
Rutile
Steatite Talc
Tanning Materials
Vitamin "A" Products
Vulcanized Fiber
Wood Pulp
Wool
Zircon

C. Allocation and Transfer

1. LEND–LEASE

[See *Documents, III, 1940–41*, p. 711.]

The decision of the United States to become the "arsenal of democracy," to provide defense materials for the countries engaged in resisting aggression, made necessary the setting up of some machinery for determining how defense materials, available after the satisfaction of our own needs, were to be distributed among those countries eligible to receive them. The documents here given deal with the more definitely domestic aspects of the administration of the Lend-Lease program. For documents bearing more directly on arrangements made with foreign nations, see Chapter IV, The United Nations, p. 225.

1) *Lend-Lease Administration, Executive Order No. 8926, October 28, 1941* [1]

[Excerpt]

Reorganization of administrative machinery resulted in the establishment of the Lend-Lease Administration and the consequent revocation of Executive Order of May 2, 1941, establishing the Division of Defense Aid Reports.[2]

1. There shall be in the Office for Emergency Management of the Executive Office of the President an Office of Lend-Lease Adminis-

[1] 6 *Fed. Reg.*, p. 5519.   [2] *Documents, III, 1940–41*, p. 731.

tration, at the head of which shall be an Administrator, appointed by the President, who shall receive compensation at such rate as the President shall approve, and, in addition, shall be entitled to actual and necessary transportation, subsistence, and other expenses incidental to the performance of his duties.

2. Subject to such policies as the President may from time to time prescribe, the Administrator is hereby authorized and directed, pursuant to Section 9 of the Act, to exercise any power or authority conferred upon the President by that Act and by the Defense Aid Supplemental Appropriation Act, 1941, and any acts amendatory or supplemental thereto, with respect to any nation whose defense the President shall have found to be vital to the defense of the United States: *Provided* That the master agreement with each nation receiving lend-lease aid setting forth the general terms and conditions under which such nation is receiving such aid, shall continue to be negotiated by the State Department, with the advice of the Economic Defense Board and the Lend Lease Administration.

3. The Administrator shall make appropriate arrangements with the Economic Defense Board for the review and clearance of those lend-lease transactions which in the judgment of the Board affect the economic defense of the United States as defined in Executive Order No. 8839 of July 30, 1941.[1]

(2) *Mechanics of Lend-Lease.   Report of the President (Roosevelt) to Congress, on the First Year of Lend-Lease Operations, March 11, 1942* [2]
[Excerpt]

THE OFFICE OF LEND-LEASE ADMINISTRATION

The functions of the Office of Lend-Lease Administration are:

(1) To cooperate with lend-lease nations and other government agencies in formulating broad programs for lend-lease aid, and to allocate to the various procurement agencies the funds appropriated by the Congress to the President;

(2) To approve or disapprove requisitions of lend-lease nations for particular defense articles and services;

(3) To forward these requisitions to the procuring agencies and to assist in obtaining the necessary priorities;

(4) To expedite the storage and transportation of lend-lease articles ready for shipment;

---

[1] See p. 180.
[2] H. Doc. No. 661, 77th Cong., 2d. sess., p. 38–43.

(5) To assist in obtaining the proper use of lend-lease material abroad; and

(6) To keep detailed records of all lend-lease transactions.

ALLOCATION OF FUNDS

The duty of allocating funds appropriated directly to the President or the procurement of nonmilitary items (and also for the procurement f military items before the change in appropriation policy referred to bove) has been delegated by the President to the Lend-Lease Adminis-rator, and is handled in two ways.

First, allocations are made on a program basis to cover those items for hich the need can readily be foreseen. After consultation among the pplicant country, the Lend-Lease Administration, the procuring agency, nd, when appropriate, the Board of Economic Warfare, programs to over future requirements are formulated and the necessary funds llocated. In this way, a 6-month chemical or steel program can be valuated, in terms of need, funds, and supply, more quickly and more ccurately than can piecemeal and recurring requests for smaller quanti-ies of such material.

Second, the Lend-Lease Administration and the various procuring gencies agree as to the nature and amount of certain "blanket" allo-ations made to cover the cost of the many items, such as emergency nip repairs, which cannot readily be planned in advance on a program asis. These items must be handled separately, from day to day, as ritical needs arise. "Blanket" allocations are also made available to ne procurement agencies for "spot" and other rush purchases and are eplenished from time to time as needed.

APPROVAL OF REQUISITIONS

Requests for aid are presented to the Lend-Lease Administration in ne form of requisitions drawn up by the applicant country with the ssistance of the liaison officer of the Lend-Lease Administration ssigned to that country. The requisition must set forth the use to which ne requested article or service is to be put, and the reason why it is eeded. No items are approved unless the following conditions are met:

(a) The lend-lease aid requested must be for a specific use essential to the total war or defense effort of a country whose defense the President has found vital to the defense of the United States.

(b) The lend-lease aid requested must be more important to the total war effort of the United Nations than any other competing demand for the funds available.

(c) The lend-lease aid requested must be scheduled for use where it can best contribute to the total war effort.

(d) The lend-lease aid requested must be obtainable at as low a cost, in terms of lend-lease funds and of component critical materials, as is consistent with the need which it is designated to meet.

(e) The lend-lease aid requested must not be obtainable, as a practical matter, by payment therefor in American dollars or other currency available to the requisitioning country.

If the requisition contains the necessary information, and the above requirements are satisfied, the liaison officer recommends its clearance, subject to the approval of the Legal Division and of the Assistant Administrator in charge of clearance. If the material requested is in short supply in the United States, further information is requested as to the available supply, consumption, rationing restrictions, exports, and estimated requirements of the applicant country. The judgment of the Board of Economic Warfare is requested on all such long-range problems In addition to these administrative controls, each nation is impelled by its own desire to cooperate in the common effort, as well as by limited shipping facilities, to submit requisitions only for its most urgent needs.

Constant reexamination and improvement of the requisition procedure has resulted in decreasing the average elapsed time for clearance to less than 48 hours.

Forwarding to Procuring Agency and Obtaining Priorities

Upon approval, the requisition is forwarded to the appropriate procurement agency. These agencies do not, as originally, have to await the allocation of funds by the Lend-Lease Administrator for each individual requisition, since the money has already been allocated to them on a program or "blanket" basis. If for any reason the agency does not feel that it should procure a particular article — for example because it believes the article should be retained in this country — the agency notifies the Lend-Lease Administration and the matter is worked out in consultation between them. In almost all cases, however, these matters are thoroughly checked and agreed upon in advance, and the agency is prepared immediately to proceed with procuring the defense articles or services requested. If disagreement persists, the problem may be referred to the Combined Munitions Assignment Board or the Combined Raw Materials Board, depending upon the nature of the article under discussion.

Before production can begin, the necessary priorities must be obtained An important function of the Office of Lend-Lease Administration is when necessary, to present the case of the applicant country to the appropriate priorities authority, and to bring about an understanding of the urgent need for the article requested. In all cases, however, the final priorities decision is made, with due regard to the entire war production plan, by the War Production Board or the Army-Navy Munitions Board and the Joint Aircraft Committee, to which the War Production Board has delegated part of its priorities power.

Storage and Transportation

At the time it approves nonmilitary requisitions, the Lend-Lease Administrator, with the approval of the Board of Economic Warfare, authorizes the transfer and export of the defense article by the purchasing agency to the applicant country. To assure actual delivery, however, involves much more than granting the authority to transfer. As the areas of combat mushroom over the surface of the globe, the difficulties of transportation continue to multiply, until today they have become one of the principal problems confronting the United Nations.

Each procuring agency is primarily responsible for the movement of its own lend-lease articles from point of production to shipboard. The Lend-Lease Administration maintains a special staff of transportation experts to assist in assuring a steady flow of lend-lease articles to domestic and foreign ports.

All traffic in the continental United States is subject to the coordination and direction of the Office of Defense Transportation. This agency assembles comprehensive information on inland traffic conditions and the utilization of port facilities, as a basis for directive control of the flow of cargo to the loading ports. Thus intelligent decisions can be made as to whether particular lend-lease articles should be shipped immediately to tidewater or whether intermediate storage is advisable. Each procuring agency arranges for its own storage as needed. In addition, with the assistance of lend-lease funds, the War Department has constructed and now operates additional emergency storage facilities, and many more War Department storage depots are in process of construction. The Office of Defense Transportation maintains a storage division responsible for all master storage plans and is consulted with respect to all storage facilities acquired for lend-lease purposes. As information is received that ocean shipping will become available, each procuring agency arranges for shipment over the route and to the loading port determined to be most efficient by the Office of Defense Transportation and the United States War Shipping Administration, in view of the entire land and water traffic situation.

The movement of all American, British, Dominion, and exile government shipping is controlled by the United States War Shipping Administration and the British Ministry of War Transport. The activities of these two agencies and the operation of the merchant fleets of the other United Nations are coordinated by the Combined Shipping Adjustment Board. The movement of all vessels is geared to achieve the fullest and most economical use of outgoing and incoming shipping space, to assure a steady supply of strategic materials to the production centers, and to conform with the most pressing military needs of the moment. The Lend-Lease Administration assists the transportation authorities in reaching informed judgments by furnishing periodic estimates of the nature and destination of lend-lease cargoes expected to become ready for carriage at stated future intervals.

CONTROL OF USE

The governments to which aid has been rendered keep the Lend-Lease Administration informed on the use, condition, and continued need of materials transferred. Lend-lease representatives are on the ground in all of the major areas to which lend-lease supplies are being delivered

Much advisory work has been done in the distribution of lend-lease food in Great Britain. Lend-lease foods are distributed through the usual wholesale and retail channels under strict governmental supervision and price control. Where possible, each product bears a distinctive American identification symbol. Special efforts have been made to accustom the British public to many unfamiliar American foods.

Once articles are transferred to a lend-lease country, they may not be retransferred, either to private individuals or to other countries without the consent of the United States. This consent is granted only where it will further the total war effort.

An extension of this control, with special reference to exports from the United Kingdom containing lend-lease materials or materials similar to those supplied under lend-lease, was undertaken by the British Government in the so-called Eden White Paper dated September 10, 1941 Under this White Paper, reprinted in Appendix IV,[1] permission to reexport has been granted from time to time, but only after it has been established that such export would benefit the total war effort of the United Nations.

REPORTS AND RECORDS

The Lend-Lease Administration maintains a careful system of records to account for all funds appropriated by the Congress, whether to the

[1] Not reproduced here, but see this volume, p. 592.

President directly or to the various procurement agencies. Through prescribed reporting procedures, each procurement agency supplies up to date data on its progress in procuring the articles and services requested. Records are compiled on the amount of aid supplied to each United Nation, by type of article or service and by value.

Periodically, this information is summarized in reports on total lend-ease progress circulated among the interested agencies, and weekly and monthly summaries are also furnished to the President. The frequency and thoroughness of these reports have been of great assistance to those who make the day-to-day decisions so vital to the success of the entire lend-lease program.

3) *Fifth Ninety-Day Report of the President (Roosevelt) to Congress on Operations under the Lend-Lease Act, June 11, 1942* [1]

[Excerpt]

Pursuant to the requirement of sec. 5 [2] of the Lend-Lease Act of March 11, 1941, that the President shall, from time to time, "but not less frequently than once every ninety days," transmit to Congress a report on operations under the Act, President Roosevelt had, up to June 30, 1942, transmitted five reports to Congress. The first report was made June 10, 1941 (Senate Doc. No. 66, 77th Cong., 1st sess.).[3] The subsequent reports were transmitted as follows: second report, September 15, 1941 (Sen. Doc. No. 112, 77th Cong., 1st sess.); third report, December 15, 1941 (Sen. Doc. No. 149, 77th Cong., 1st sess.); fourth report, "A Report on the First Year of Lend-Lease Operations," March 11, 1942 (House Doc. No. 661, 77th Cong., 2d sess.), and fifth report, June 11, 1942 (House Doc. No. 799, 77th Cong., 2d sess.)

LEND–LEASE PROGRESS

The lend-lease program was inaugurated on March 11, 1941 as our peacetime contribution to nations aiding our defense by resisting Axis aggression. Now that we are at war, lend-lease continues as an instrument by which we strengthen our allies according to the strategic plans of the United Nations as a whole. The assistance we have rendered to date represents 12 per cent of our entire war program.

AMOUNT OF LEND-LEASE AID

Lend-lease aid for the 15-month period from March 1941 through May 1942 has totaled $4,497,000,000. The rapidly rising trend in the amount of this aid is indicated by the chart,[4] which shows the amount

[1] House Doc. No. 799, 77th Cong., 2d sess., p. 7–11.
[2] *Documents, III, 1940–41*, p. 714.
[3] For message of the President transmitting the report, see *ibid.*, p. 731.
[4] Not reproduced.

of aid provided during each month since lend-lease began. Currently aid is being provided at a rate equal to approximately $8,000,000,00(per year.

Lend-lease aid has two main divisions — the value of goods, actually shipped, awaiting shipment or in process of manufacture, and the value of various services of production and supply. Goods include military items, such as planes, tanks, guns and ammunition, as well as food medical supplies, machine tools, metals and other materials. Service include the shipping necessary to carry goods to lend-lease countries the servicing and repair of warships and merchant ships of the United Nations, new factory and shipyard facilities in the United States for production of lend-lease goods, and facilities for supply bases abroad

A breakdown of the total of $4,497,000,000 of lend-lease aid is given in Table No. 2. About 82 per cent of aid is represented by goods and 18 per cent by services.

While lend-lease aid has continued to increase each quarter, the proportion of fighting weapons included in the materials transferred to our allies has also increased. Whereas last fall munitions comprised a relatively small part of total transfers and the major portion consisted of foodstuffs and industrial materials, during recent months military items have constituted more than half of total transfers. (See chart.[1]

The proportion of our total production of guns, planes, ships and industrial materials that goes to lend-lease countries and the proportion that is furnished to our own armed forces and industries is determined by the expert military and civilian bodies in charge of our entire war program, not by the agencies charged with the immediate supervision of the lend-lease program. Every decision is aimed at putting our resources to their most effective use in fighting our common enemies

Exports of Lend-Lease Goods

Articles transferred are those which have been delivered in this country to lend-lease nations, either at points of production or at points of export Articles transferred up to May 31, 1942 amounted to $2,601 million, as shown in Table No. 2. Of this amount $2,138 million has been exported The difference between the value of articles transferred and the value of those which have actually left the United States is due to the necessity of maintaining adequate inventories of finished articles at points of export, the fact that transfers of ships are not included in the export figure, and other factors.

[1] Not reproduced.

TABLE NO. 1. ACCELERATION IN LEND-LEASE AID

[Millions of Dollars]

	QUARTER ENDED				
	May 31, 1941	Aug. 31, 1941	Nov. 30, 1941	Feb. 28, 1942	May 31, 1942
Quarterly . .	118	369	715	1,368	1,927
Cumulative .	118	487	1,202	2,570	4,497

TABLE NO. 2. TOTAL LEND-LEASE AID

[Millions of Dollars]

TYPE OF AID	TOTAL AID TO MAY 31, 1942	AID DURING QUARTER ENDED MAY 31, 1942
GOODS:		
Articles transferred	2,601	1,210
Articles awaiting transfer or use	231	136
Articles in process of manufacture	841	320
Total Goods	3,673	1,666
SERVICES:		
Servicing and repair of ships, etc., in U. S. .	157	31
Production facilities in U. S.	283	114
Rental of ships, ferrying of aircraft, etc. . .	371	107
Facilities for supply bases abroad, etc. . .	13	9
Total Services	824	261
Total Aid	4,497	1,927

Lend-lease exports have accounted for a steadily increasing part of all exports from this country, excluding "exports" shipped to our own forces fighting abroad. From March 1941 through May 1942 the value of lend-lease exports amounted to 29 per cent of the value of all exports. In May 1942 lend-lease exports were approximately 54 per cent of total exports.

In the beginning, lend-lease exports went primarily to the United Kingdom to help in the battle of Britain. As the theaters of war in Africa, the Middle East, India, and Australia became critical lend-lease aid was sent to the support of our allies fighting in those areas. With the signing of the Russian protocol last October, arms and supplies began to flow to Russia in large quantities. Transportation difficulties, climaxed by the closing of the Burma Road, have been the factor limiting the volume of aid to China, but new ways of getting help to China in substantial amounts are being developed.

LEND-LEASE COUNTRIES

As the war has spread over the world and aid to more and more countries has become essential to our own national safety, the President has added to the list of lend-lease nations now eligible for lend-lease assistance. The roll now includes the members of the British Commonwealth of Nations and 35 other countries:

Argentina	Egypt	Nicaragua
Belgium	El Salvador	Norway
Bolivia	France (Free) [1]	Panama
Brazil	Greece	Paraguay
Chile	Guatemala	Peru
China	Haiti	Poland
Colombia	Honduras	Turkey
Costa Rica	Iceland	U. S. S. R.
Cuba	Iran	Uruguay
Czechoslovakia	Iraq	Venezuela
Dominican Republic	Mexico	Yugoslavia
Ecuador	Netherlands	

British Commonwealth of Nations

(4) *Lend-Lease Appropriations and Transfer Authorizations* [2]

APPROPRIATIONS

First Lend-Lease Appropriation Act, Approved March 27,
1941 — Public Law 23, 77th Cong. . . . . $ 7,000,000,000
Second Lend-Lease Appropriation Act, Approved October 28,
1941 — Public Law 282, 77th Cong.   5,985,000,000
Third Lend-Lease Appropriation Act (5th Supplemental), Approved March 5, 1942 — Public Law 474, 77th Cong. . .   5,425,000,000

$18,410,000,000

[1] Though the Free French have not been recognized by the Government of the United States as a government representing France, the President by letter of November 11, 1941 to E. R. Stettinius, Jr., Lend-Lease Administrator, did make them eligible for lend-lease assistance. The letter follows:

"For purposes of implementing the authority conferred upon you as Lend-Lease Administrator by Executive Order No. 8926, dated October 28, 1941, and in order to enable you to arrange for Lend-Lease aid to the French Volunteer Forces (Free French) by way of retransfer from His Majesty's Government in the United Kingdom or their allies, I hereby find that the defense of any French territory under the control of the French Volunteer Forces (Free French) is vital to the defense of the United States." *The Inter-Allied Review*, No. 11, December 15, 1941, p. 13; announcement from Free French headquarters, New York City, published in *New York Times* November 25, 1941, p. 1.   [2] From the Bureau of the Budget, July 29, 1942.

TRANSFERS AUTHORIZED FROM OTHER APPROPRIATIONS

War Department — Third Supplemental, Approved December 17, 1941 — Public Law 353, 77th Cong. . . . . . $ 2,000,000,000

War Department — Fourth Supplemental, Approved January 30, 1942 — Public Law 422, 77th Cong. 4,000,000,000

War Department — Fifth Supplemental, Approved March 5, 1942 — Public Law 474, 77th Cong. 11,250,000,000

War Department — Sixth Supplemental, Approved April 28, 1942 — Public Law 528, 77th Cong. 2,220,000,000

Navy Department — Naval Appropriation Act (Ships), Approved February 7, 1942, Public Law 441, 77th Cong. . . 3,900,000,000

Navy Department — Naval Appropriation Act (Articles), Approved February 7, 1942, Public Law 441, 77th Cong. . . 2,500,000,000

Navy Department — Sixth Supplemental, Approved April 28, 1942 — Public Law 528, 77th Cong. 18,000,000

Maritime Commission — First Supplemental, Approved August 25, 1941 — Public Law 247, 77th Cong. 1,296,650,000

Maritime Commission — Fifth Supplemental (Appropriation Funds), Approved March 5, 1942 — Public Law 474, 77th Cong. 1,500,000,000

Maritime Commission — Fifth Supplemental (Contract Authorization), Approved March 5, 1942 — Public Law 474, 77th Cong. 2,350,000,000

Other Departments — Third Supplemental, Approved December 17, 1941 — Public Law 353, 77th Cong. 800,000,000

$31,834,650,000

Maximum Amount of Aid That Can Be Provided . . . $50,244,650,000

2. COMMUNICATIONS AND SHIPPING

[For documents bearing on water transportation see Shipping and Communications, Chapter IX, pp. 403 and 770.]

Materials that are produced for defense or war purposes do not accomplish their purpose until they are transported to the place or places where they are needed. Transportation may be by land, by water, or by air. Since the actual fighting has been largely outside the Western Hemisphere, the problem of transportation, except for getting materials to ports, is primarily one of providing the necessary water or air transportation facilities. The possibilities of air transportation were not under as serious consideration before June 30, 1942 as they subsequently have been.

4. ECONOMIC WARFARE

The need of ordering our international economic and financial relations in the interest of our national defense and in harmony with our major foreign policies and interests led to the establishment on July 30, 1941 of the Economic Defense Board. As originally conceived, its duties were primarily advisory, but as the international situation steadily worsened, the need of a coordinating body with real power was recognized. Executive Order No. 9128 of April 13,

1942 gave the Board, renamed by Executive Order No. 8982 of December 17, 1941 the Board of Economic Warfare, real power to determine and direct the economic warfare program of the Government.

For the powers and functions of the Board in relation to Export Control, see p. 723.

(1) Executive Order No. 8839, Establishing the Economic Defense Board, July 30, 1941 [1]

By virtue of the authority vested in me by the Constitution and statutes of the United States, by virtue of the existence of an unlimited national emergency, and for the purpose of developing and coordinating policies, plans, and programs designed to protect and strengthen the international economic relations of the United States in the interest of national defense, it is hereby ordered as follows:

1. The term "economic defense," whenever used in this Order, means the conduct, in the interest of national defense, of international economic activities including those relating to exports, imports, the acquisition and disposition of materials and commodities from foreign countries including preclusive buying, transactions in foreign exchange and foreign-owned or foreign-controlled property, international investments and extensions of credit, shipping and transportation of goods among countries, the international aspects of patents, international communications pertaining to commerce, and other foreign economic matters.

2. There is hereby established an Economic Defense Board (hereinafter referred to as the "Board"). The Board shall consist of the Vice President of the United States, who shall serve as Chairman, the Secretary of State, the Secretary of the Treasury, the Secretary of War, the Attorney General, the Secretary of the Navy, the Secretary of Agriculture, and the Secretary of Commerce. The Chairman may, with the approval of the President, appoint additional members to the Board. Each member of the Board, other than the Chairman, may designate an alternate from among the officials of his Department, subject to the continuing approval of the Chairman, and such alternate may act for such member in all matters relating to the Board.

3. In furtherance of such policies and objectives as the President may from time to time determine, the Board shall perform the following functions and duties:

a. Advise the President as to economic defense measures to be taken or functions to be performed which are essential to the effective defense of the Nation.

---

[1] 6 *Fed. Reg.*, p. 37; Department of State, *Bulletin*, V, p. 97.

b. Coordinate the policies and actions of the several departments and agencies carrying on activities relating to economic defense in order to assure unity and balance in the application of such measures.

c. Develop integrated economic defense plans and programs for coordinated action by the departments and agencies concerned and use all appropriate means to assure that such plans and programs are carried into effect by such departments and agencies.

d. Make investigations and advise the President on the relationship of economic defense (as defined in paragraph 1) measures to post-war economic reconstruction and on the steps to be taken to protect the trade position of the United States and to expedite the establishment of sound, peace-time international economic relationships.

e. Review proposed or existing legislation relating to or affecting economic defense and, with the approval of the President, recommend such additional legislation as may be necessary or desirable.

4. The administration of the various activities relating to economic defense shall remain with the several departments and agencies now charged with such duties but such administration shall conform to the policies formulated or approved by the Board.

5. In the study of problems and in the formulation of programs, it shall be the policy of the Board to collaborate with existing departments and agencies which perform functions and activities pertaining to economic defense and to utilize their services and facilities to the maximum. Such departments and agencies shall cooperate with the Board in clearing proposed policies and measures involving economic defense considerations and shall supply such information and data as the Board may require in performing its functions. The Board may arrange for the establishment of committees or groups of advisers, representing two or more departments and agencies as the case may require, to study and develop economic defense plans and programs in respect to particular commodities or services, geographical areas, types of measures that might be exercised, and other related matters.

6. To facilitate unity of action and the maximum use of existing services and facilities, each of the following departments and agencies, in addition to the departments and agencies represented on the Board, shall designate a responsible officer or officers, subject to the approval of the Chairman, to represent the department or agency in its continuing relationships with the Board: The Departments of the Post Office, the Interior, and Labor, the Federal Loan Agency, the United States Maritime Commission, the United States Tariff Commission, the Federal Trade Commission, the Board of Governors of the Federal

Reserve System, the Securities and Exchange Commission, the National Resources Planning Board, the Defense Communications Board, the Office of Production Management, the Office of Price Administration and Civilian Supply, the Office for Coordination of Commercial and Cultural Relations Between the American Republics, the Permanent Joint Board on Defense, the Administrator of Export Control, the Division of Defense Aid Reports, the Coordinator of Information, and such additional departments and agencies as the Chairman may from time to time determine. The Chairman shall provide for the systematic conduct of business with the foregoing departments and agencies.

7. The Chairman is authorized to make all necessary arrangements, with the advice and assistance of the Board, for discharging and performing the responsibilities and duties required to carry out the functions and authorities set forth in this Order, and to make final decisions when necessary to expedite the work of the Board. He is further authorized, within the limits of such funds as may be allocated to the Board by the President, to employ necessary personnel and make provision for the necessary supplies, facilities, and services. The Chairman may, with the approval of the President, appoint an executive officer.

(2) *Executive Order No. 9128, Conferring Additional Duties on the Board of Economic Warfare, April 13, 1942* [1]

[Excerpt]

The Board of Economic Warfare is authorized and directed to

1. . . . (*a*) Receive and be responsible for executing directives from the Chairman of the War Production Board as to quantities, specifications, delivery time schedules, and priorities of materials and commodities (other than arms, munitions, or weapons of war as defined in the President's Proclamation of May 1, 1937, as amended) required to be imported for the war production effort and the civilian economy; and determine the policies, plans, procedures, and methods of the several Federal departments, establishments, and agencies with respect to the procurement and production of such materials and commodities, including the financing thereof. . . .

(*b*) Direct, with the approval of the President, the creation, organization, and financing of a corporation or corporations, pursuant to . . . the Reconstruction Finance Corporation Act, as amended, the objects and purposes of which shall be: (1) To obtain from foreign sources such materials, supplies, and commodities (other than arms, munitions, or

---

[1] 7 *Fed. Reg.*, p. 2809; the excerpts here given were reprinted in the Department of State, *Bulletin*, VI, p. 337.

weapons of war . . .) as are necessary for the successful prosecution of the war, and provide for the production, delivery, sale, or other disposition thereof; and (2) to take such other action as may be deemed necessary to facilitate the war effort and strengthen the international economic relations of the United States.

(c) Advise the State Department with respect to the terms and conditions to be included in the master agreement with each nation receiving lend-lease aid . . .

(d) Provide and arrange for the receipt by the United States of reciprocal aid and benefits (other than arms, munitions, or weapons of war . . .) from the government of any country whose defense shall have been determined by the President to be vital to the defense of the United States . . . and determine the terms upon which such aid and benefits shall be received, including the authorization of other governmental agencies to receive such aid and benefits.

(e) Represent the United States Government in dealing with the economic warfare agencies of the United Nations for the purpose of relating the Government's economic warfare program and facilities to those of such nations.

2. For the purpose of carrying out its responsibilities, the Board of Economic Warfare may arrange through the Department of State to send abroad such technical, engineering, and economic representatives responsible to the Board as the Board may deem necessary.

(3) *Clarification and Interpretation of Executive Order No. 9128 of April 13, 1942, in Respect of Certain Functions of the Department of State and the Board of Economic Warfare, May 20, 1942* [1]

The scope of the duties assigned to the Board of Economic Warfare on April 13, 1942 raised the question as to whether its authority had been extended at the expense of established executive departments, particularly the Department of State which represents the President in the conduct of foreign relations.

The following will clarify certain relations and functions of the Department of State and the Board of Economic Warfare in the administration of the President's Executive Order No. 9128 regarding the Board and provide for cooperative action between them.

It is contemplated that meetings of the Board will be held at least every two weeks. An agenda for each meeting will be circulated in advance, and each member of the Board is free to raise questions upon his own initiative.

[1] From the Office of the Secretary to the President; Department of State, *Bulletin*, VI, p. 475.

In the making of decisions, the Board and its officers will continue to recognize the primary responsibility and position, under the President, of the Secretary of State in the formulation and conduct of our foreign policy and our relations with foreign nations. In matters of business judgment concerned with providing for the production and procurement of materials to be imported into this country for the war effort, including civilian supply, the Department will recognize the primary responsibility and position of the Board. In many cases a decision may involve both matters of foreign policy and business judgment in varying degrees. No clear-cut separation is here possible. Accordingly, if occasions arise in which proposed action of the Board or its officers is thought by officials of the State Department to be at variance with essential considerations of foreign policy, the Secretary of State and the Chairman of the Board will discuss such matters and reach a joint decision, in matters of sufficient importance obtaining direction from the President.

The Board will continue to recognize that it is the function of the Department of State to conduct or authorize the conduct of all negotiations with foreign governments in Washington and abroad. In negotiations relating to the production and procurement of commodities intended for import in accordance with the President's Executive Order, the State Department will recognize the necessity for the participation of representatives of the Board in order that the latter may adequately discharge its responsibilities. In short, for the effective exercise of the functions both of the Board and the Department, it is essential that from the inception of any project there be complete exchange of information, mutual consultation and mutual confidence.

In negotiations regarding lend-lease master agreements, subsidiary agreements, and arrangements for their implementation, including reciprocal aid to the United States, the Department will obtain the advice, and with respect to the importation of materials and commodities (other than arms and munitions) will obtain the participation of the Board and keep it fully informed.

Missions and individuals desired by the Board to be sent to the field shall be agreed upon by the State Department and the Board in the light of their common desire to increase to the maximum the war effort. The Board will recognize that all functions which are being or can be performed through the regular or auxiliary Foreign Services of the Department should be so performed. The persons and missions which the Board contemplates being sent to the field, other than through the services mentioned, are those needed for the specialized technical and operational functions connected with production and procurement.

'he Department of State will recognize the need for sending such per-
ons. In exceptional circumstances the Board and the State Department
ill collaborate in sending joint missions on problems arising from export
ontrol or the general economic warfare activities of this Government.

The Board will recognize that persons sent abroad, as provided above,
nall be authorized by the Secretary of State, shall assume the status
irected by the Secretary of State, and in this respect be subject to the
urisdiction of the Secretary of State. The Chief of the United States
Diplomatic Mission in a foreign country is the officer of the United States
a charge in that country under whose supervision are coordinated the
ctivities there of all the official representatives of the United States.
ll negotiations abroad with foreign governments or officials should
e conducted by or under the direction of the Chief of the Diplomatic
Iission in the manner described above applicable to negotiations in
hich the Department and the Board participate. All activities should
e fully reported to the Chief of the Diplomatic Mission and be con-
ucted under his advice and instructions. He will respect the position
f the Board's representatives in matters of technical and business
idgment and, should questions arise that cannot be settled by agree-
ent in the field, which should rarely be the case, they will be reported
rough the State Department and settled by the Secretary of State
nd the Chairman of the Board.

All communications to and from persons or missions sent abroad shall
e through the facilities of the Department of State and diplomatic
issions unless other means are agreed upon between the Board and the
epartment of State. The Department will do its utmost to provide
xpeditious means for such communications.

Both the Department of State and the Board of Economic Warfare
nd their officers recognize in the present emergency the need for speed
 action and the importance of avoiding all delay in the decision of
nportant matters.

5. PUBLIC INFORMATION AND PROPAGANDA

In a democracy, the importance of keeping the people well and accurately
formed about facts affecting the national security or, in case of war, about
e course of the war effort cannot be exaggerated.[1] Obviously there are things
at cannot be made known in time of war that can be safely publicized in time
 peace, but the danger of excessive secrecy is real. Also, the experience of World
ar I, and of this one, points to the importance, as part of the total war effort,
 intelligently planned psychological warfare having as its purpose the weak-
ing of the morale and inner unity of enemy peoples, and, in this case, the
rengthening of the resistance of the subject peoples.

[1] See radio address of the President, December 9, 1941, p. 36.

(1) *Clearing of Information.* **Executive Order No. 8922 Establishing a**
  Office of Facts and Figures in the Office for Emergency Manage
  ment, October 24, 1941 [1]

[Excerpt]

2. Subject to such policies and directions as the President may fror
time to time prescribe, the Office of Facts and Figures shall formulat
programs designed to facilitate a widespread and accurate understandin
of the status and progress of the national defense effort and of the defens
policies and activities of the Government; and advise with the severa
departments and agencies of the Government concerning the dissem:
nation of such defense information. The Office of Facts and Figures sha
rely upon the services and facilities of existing agencies of the Goverr
ment for the dissemination of information.

3. The several departments and agencies of the Government sha
make available to the Director, upon his request, such information an
data as he may deem necessary to facilitate the most coherent and con
prehensive presentation to the Nation of the facts and figures of nation:
defense.

4. There shall be in the Office of Facts and Figures an Advisory Con
mittee consisting of the Director as chairman and such representatives (
the Federal Government and other members as he may determine. Th
members of the Advisory Committee shall serve without compensatior
but shall be entitled to necessary travel, subsistence, and other expens(
incidental to the performance of their duties.

(2) *Executive Order No. 8985 Establishing the Office of Censorship an*
  Prescribing Its Functions and Duties, December 19, 1941 [2]

In a statement accompanying the Executive Order, the President pointed o*
the importance of administering such forms of censorship as might be necessai
"effectively and in harmony with the best interests of our free institutions
He stressed the necessity that military information of aid to the enemy *
withheld at the source, that such information be prevented from reaching th
enemy through the mails, radio or cable communication or other means, an*
that statutory prohibitions against the domestic publication of certain typ
of information be rigidly enforced.

By virtue of the authority vested in me by the Constitution and th
statutes of the United States, and particularly by section 303,[3] Title I.

[1] 6 *Fed. Reg.*, p. 5477. Archibald MacLeish, Librarian of Congress, was appoint*
Director of the Office.
[2] 6 *Fed. Reg.*, p. 6625.
[3] See p. 763.

of the act of December 18, 1941, Public Law 354, 77th Congress, 1st Session, and deeming that the public safety demands it, I hereby order as follows:

1. There is hereby established the Office of Censorship, at the head of which shall be a Director of Censorship. The Director of Censorship shall cause to be censored, in his absolute discretion, communications by mail, cable, radio, or other means of transmission passing between the United States and any foreign country or which may be carried by any vessel or other means of transportation touching at any port, place, or Territory of the United States and bound to or from any foreign country, in accordance with such rules and regulations as the President shall from time to time prescribe. The establishment of rules and regulations in addition to the provisions of this order shall not be a condition to the exercise of the powers herein granted or the censorship by this order directed. The scope of this order shall include all foreign countries except such as may hereafter be expressly excluded by regulation.

2. There is hereby created a Censorship Policy Board, which shall consist of the Vice-President of the United States, the Secretary of the Treasury, the Secretary of War, the Attorney General, the Postmaster General, the Secretary of the Navy, the Director of the Office of Government Reports, and the Director of the Office of Facts and Figures. The Postmaster General shall act as Chairman of the Board. The Censorship Policy Board shall advise the Director of Censorship with respect to policy and the coordination and integration of the censorship herein directed.

3. The Director of Censorship shall establish a Censorship Operating Board, which shall consist of representatives of such departments and agencies of the Government as the Director shall specify. Each representative shall be designated by the head of the department or agency which he represents. The Censorship Operating Board shall, under the supervision of the Director, perform such duties with respect to operations as the Director shall determine.

4. The Director of Censorship is authorized to take all such measures as may be necessary or expedient to administer the powers hereby conferred, and, in addition to the utilization of existing personnel of any department or agency available therefor, to employ, or authorize the employment of, such additional personnel as he may deem requisite.

5. As used in this order the term "United States" shall be construed to include the Territories and possessions of the United States, including the Philippine Islands.

(a) *Communications Ruling No. 1 Issued under the Authority Veste* *in the Office of Censorship Pursuant to the Trading with th* *Enemy Act, as Amended, and the "First War Powers Act, 1941,* *March 18, 1942* [1]

(1) By virtue of the authority vested in me by Executive Orde No. 8985 (*Fed. Reg.* Doc. 41-9600) and T.D. 50536 (*Fed. Reg.* Doc. 41 9799), the sending or transmitting out of the United States in the ordi nary course of the mail of any letter or other writing, book, or othe paper, or through any public telegraph or cable service of any telegram cablegram or wireless message of any communication is permitted, pro vided that both of the following conditions are satisfied:

(a) Such communication complies with all regulations issued by th Office of Censorship; and

(b) Such communication is not addressed to or intended for, or t be delivered, directly or indirectly, to an enemy national.

(2) Nothing contained in this Ruling shall be deemed to limit th authority of the Office of Censorship to cause to be censored in its absc lute discretion, communication by mail, cable, radio or other means c transmission passing between the United States and any foreign country All communications permitted by this Ruling shall be subject to censor ship as fully as if this Ruling had not been issued.

(3) As used in this ruling the term "United States" and the terr "person" shall have the meaning prescribed in Executive Order Nc 8389,[2] as amended, and the term "enemy national" shall have the mear ing prescribed in General Ruling No. 11,[3] issued by the Secretary of th Treasury thereunder.

(4) This Ruling may be amended or modified at any time; and th right is reserved to exclude from the operation hereof, or from the priv: leges hereby conferred, and to restrict the applicability hereof wit respect to, particular persons or communications or classes thereof.

BYRON PRICE
Director of Censorship

Acting under the authority conferred upon him, the Director of Censorshi has had prepared a series of regulations for the guidance of affected persons : follows:

U. S. Cable and Radio Censorship Regulations (Edition of February 19, 194: U. S. Radiotelephone Censorship Regulations (Edition of February 19, 194: U. S. Postal Censorship Regulations (Edition of April 13, 1942)

[1] 7 *Fed. Reg.*, p. 2168.   [2] See p. 180.   [3] See p. 767.

Code of Wartime Practices for the American Press (Edition of June 15, 1942)
    Code of Wartime Practices for American Broadcasters (Edition of June 15,
942)
    Whereas the regulations are enforceable, the codes are in the nature of guides
ɔ voluntary cooperation.

3) *Executive Order No. 9182 Consolidating Certain War Information
    Functions into an Office of War Information, June 13, 1942* [1]

[Excerpt]

The effect of this order is to consolidate into one agency the information
ınctions of the Government — domestic and foreign — except Latin America.
Vhile the actual information services of the different departments and agencies
·ill remain intact, their activities are expected to conform to directives issued
y the Director of the Office of War Information. The Director of the new
▸ffice is Mr. Elmer Davis. The information service for Latin America continues
ɔ be handled by the Coordinator of Latin American Affairs.

In recognition of the right of the American people and of all other
eoples opposing the Axis aggressors to be truthfully informed about the
ommon war effort, and by virtue of the authority vested in me by the
:onstitution, by the First War Powers Act, 1941, and as President of
he United States and Commander-in-Chief of the Army and Navy, it is
ereby ordered as follows:
    1. The following agencies, powers, and duties are transferred and
onsolidated into an Office of War Information which is hereby estab-
shed within the Office for Emergency Management in the Executive
▸ffice of the President:

  a. The Office of Facts and Figures and its powers and duties.
  b. The Office of Government Reports and its powers and duties.
  c. The powers and duties of the Coordinator of Information [2]
     relating to the gathering of public information and its dis-
     semination abroad, including, but not limited to, all powers
     and duties now assigned to the Foreign Information Service,
     Outpost, Publications, and Pictorial Branches of the Coordinator
     of Information.
  d. The powers and duties of the Division of Information of the
     Office for Emergency Management relating to the dissemination
     of general public information on the war effort, except as pro-
     vided in paragraph 10.

  2. At the head of the Office of War Information shall be a Director
ppointed by the President. The Director shall discharge and perform

[1] From the Office of the Secretary to the President; 7 *Fed. Reg.*, p. 4468.
[2] See p. 159.

his functions and duties under the direction and supervision of the President. The Director may exercise his powers, authorities, and duties through such officials or agencies and in such manner as he may determine.

3. There is established within the Office of War Information a Committee on War Information Policy consisting of the Director as Chairman, representatives of the Secretary of State, the Secretary of War, the Secretary of the Navy, the Joint Psychological Warfare Committee, and of the Coordinator of Inter-American Affairs, and such other members as the Director, with the approval of the President, may determine. The Committee on War Information Policy shall formulate basic policies and plans on war information, and shall advise with respect to the development of coordinated war information programs.

4. Consistent with the war information policies of the President and with the foreign policy of the United States, and after consultation with the Committee on War Information Policy, the Director shall perform the following functions and duties:

> a. Formulate and carry out, through the use of press, radio, motion picture, and other facilities, information programs designed to facilitate the development of an informed and intelligent understanding, at home and abroad, of the status and progress of the war effort and of the war policies, activities and aims of the Government.
>
> b. Coordinate the war informational activities of all Federal departments and agencies for the purpose of assuring an accurate and consistent flow of war information to the public and the world at large.
>
> c. Obtain, study, and analyze information concerning the war effort and advise the agencies concerned with the dissemination of such information as to the most appropriate and effective means of keeping the public adequately and accurately informed.
>
> d. Review, clear, and approve all proposed radio and motion picture programs sponsored by Federal departments and agencies; and serve as the central point of clearance and contact for the radio broadcasting and motion picture industries, respectively, in their relationships with Federal departments and agencies concerning such Government programs.

    e. Maintain liaison with the information agencies of the United Nations for the purpose of relating the Government's informational programs and facilities to those of such nations.

    f. Perform such other functions and duties relating to war information as the President may from time to time determine.

5. The Director is authorized to issue such directives concerning war information as he may deem necessary or appropriate to carry out the purposes of this Order, and such directives shall be binding upon the several Federal departments and agencies. He may establish by regulation the types and classes of informational programs and releases which shall require clearance and approval by his office prior to dissemination. The Director may require the curtailment or elimination of any Federal information service, program, or release which he deems to be wasteful or not directly related to the prosecution of the war effort.

6. The authority, functions, and duties of the Director shall not extend to the Western Hemisphere exclusive of the United States and Canada.

7. The formulation and carrying out of informational programs relating exclusively to the authorized activities of the several departments and agencies of the Government shall remain with such departments and agencies, but such informational programs shall conform to the policies formulated or approved by the Office of War Information. The several departments and agencies of the Government shall make available to the Director, upon his request, such information and data as may be necessary to the performance of his functions and duties.

8. The Director of the Office of War Information and the Director of Censorship shall collaborate in the performance of their respective functions for the purpose of facilitating the prompt and full dissemination of all available information which will not give aid to the enemy.

9. The Director of the Office of War Information and the Defense Communications Board shall collaborate in the performance of their respective functions for the purpose of facilitating the broadcast of war information to the peoples abroad.

10. The functions of the Division of Information of the Office for Emergency Management with respect to the provision of press and publication services relating to the specific activities of the constituent agencies of the Office for Emergency Management are transferred to those constituent agencies respectively, and the Division of Information is accordingly abolished.

(a) *Office of War Information Regulation 1, July 10, 1942* [1]

The organization of the Office of War Information was provided for by Staf Order No. 1, dated July 10, 1942. OWI Regulation No. 1, of the same date is important because it develops the policy which the Office intends to follo' in the handling of war information.

TO THE HEADS OF ALL EXECUTIVE DEPARTMENTS AND AGENCIES

Pursuant to Executive Order No. 9182, issued June 13, 1942, author izing the Director of War Information

(a) to formulate and carry out information programs designed t facilitate the development of an informed and intelligent under standing, at home and abroad, of the status and progress of th war effort and of the war policies, activities, and aims of th government

(b) to coordinate the war informational activities of all Federa departments and agencies

(c) to issue directives concerning war information which shall b binding upon the several Federal departments and agencies, an

(d) to establish by regulation the types and classes of informatione programs and releases which shall require clearance and approve by the Office of War Information prior to dissemination

this regulation is issued, effective Monday, July 13, 1942.

1. *War Information Policy.* The Federal Government will issue a promptly as possible all news and background information essential to clear understanding of this Nation's war effort. The what, why, wher and how will be told. The impact of the war on all phases of America life will be reported. So will the cooperative efforts of the Unite Nations. Only information which would give aid and comfort to th enemy will be withheld.

(a) With the aid of the Committee on War Information Polic and of the policy staff of the Office of War Information, the Directo of War Information will establish, and keep current, policies governin the war information activities of all Federal agencies.

(b) Within the general policies so established and in harmony wit the clearance procedures hereinafter set forth, officers of Federa Departments and agencies are directed to maintain an open-doc policy in their relations with representatives of the press, radio, an other media.

(c) War information problems requiring policy decision shall b brought promptly to the attention of the Director of War Informatio

[1] From the Office of the Director.

through his liaison representatives, in order that policies may be determined and the information issued without delay.

2. *Information Activities of Federal Departments and Agencies.* Within the framework of policies established by the Director of War Information, all Departments and agencies of the Government will continue to be responsible for and will release direct to the public information which relates exclusively to their authorized activities and which does not bear significantly upon the war information program and policies of the Government.

(*a*) After consultation between representatives of the Office of War Information and of each Federal Department or agency, this general regulation will be developed in greater detail to meet the specific problems that may arise in each such Department or agency.

(*b*) Each Department and agency shall immediately review its information program and, in the interest of economy and effective war work, discontinue all non-essential phases thereof. An enumeration of the classes and types of information thus discontinued shall be reported by each Department and agency to the Director of War Information not later than August 15, 1942.

(*c*) Each Department and agency shall designate a representative with authority to cooperate with the Office of War Information in expediting the handling of those classes of war information requiring central clearance, as enumerated in succeeding sections of this regulation.

3. *News.*

(*a*) *General.* News releases relating significantly to the war effort or dealing with activities broader than the authorized work of the initiating agency shall, where possible, be prepared by the appropriate Federal Department or agency for clearance and issuance by the News Bureau of the Office of War Information. The Chief of the News Bureau will be responsible for clearing such releases with the appropriate policy officers of OWI and with the Departments and agencies concerned. Announcements, statements, material for radio news and newsreels, news pictures, and other material which have the same purpose as a news release shall be handled in the same manner as news releases.

(*b*) *Information Involving the Armed Services.* The Office of War Information will cooperate with the War and Navy Departments in facilitating the fullest possible dissemination of information involving military and naval actions. Whether specific military information would be of aid to the enemy will be determined by the War or

Navy Department after consultation with the Director of War Information.

4. *Addresses.* In accordance with directives heretofore issued by the President, all addresses by the heads of Federal Departments and agencies and by other policy-forming officials will be cleared by the originating agency with the Chief of the Bureau of Publications and Graphics of the Office of War Information. The Chief of the Bureau will consult with the appropriate policy officers of OWI and with other governmental agencies in handling such clearance.

5. *Publications.* Most bulletins relate exclusively to the work of a single agency and do not involve war information policy; they will therefore continue to be prepared and published by the initiating Department or agency, without clearance. Publications relating significantly to the war effort, or dealing with activities broader than the authorized work of the initiating agency shall be cleared with the Chief of the Bureau of Publications and Graphics, who will be responsible for consulting appropriate Federal officials in reaching decisions.

6. *Radio.* Because radio time is limited, the Office of War Information will review and clear all proposed radio programs sponsored by Federal Departments and agencies (whether they directly bear upon war information or not), will allocate available time for such programs, and will serve as the central point of clearance and contact for the broadcasting industry in its relationships with Federal Departments and agencies concerning such government programs. Federal Departments and agencies desiring to disseminate information by radio, will make necessary arrangements through the Chief of the Radio Bureau, Office of War Information; the Chief of Bureau will be responsible for consulting the appropriate policy officers and subject-matter authorities in arranging final clearance of such programs.

7. *Motion Pictures.* The Chief of the Bureau of Motion Pictures, Office of War Information, will serve as the central point of contact between the motion picture industry and Federal officials to the end that the motion picture industry, both theatrical and non-theatrical, may make the maximum contribution to keeping the American public fully informed on vital aspects of the war. Official motion pictures of the Federal Government as a rule will be produced under the direction of the Chief of the Bureau of Motion Pictures; they may be produced by individual Departments and agencies after review, clearance, and approval of the Chief of Bureau.

8. *Posters and Other Graphics.* To reduce costs, the Office of War Information will maintain a central graphics service; proposed posters

and related graphic material relating to the war effort shall be cleared with the Chief of the Bureau of Publications and Graphics who, after clearance of the initial plans, will make the services of the central staff available for production of such graphics.

9. *Advertising.* To avoid conflict and confusion, the Advertising Division of the Bureau of Special Operations, OWI, will, whenever war information is involved, serve as a central point of contact and clearance between government Departments and agencies and all branches of the advertising industry.

10. *Foreign Language Services.* To reduce the cost involved when several Departments and agencies arrange for the translation of news, features, and other material for the use of foreign language publications and radio stations in this country and provide special services to such media, all war information proposed for dissemination to such media shall be handled through the Foreign Language Division, Bureau of Special Operations, Office of War Information.

11. *Comprehensive War Information.* As contrasted to the specialized releases and information programs of the several Departments and agencies, the Office of War Information will prepare and publish comprehensive war information.

(*a*) The office will prepare and issue press releases, radio programs, publications, posters, motion pictures, and related materials which deal with subjects broader than the activities of a single agency, and shall have access to such information as may be necessary to carry out this task.

(*b*) The office will manage coordinated information programs involving the assistance of many Departments and agencies and the use of many media.

(*c*) The office will assign to specific Departments and agencies the responsibility for preparing for OWI materials needed in comprehensive information programs.

12. *Information in the Field.* The News Bureau of the Office of War Information will maintain a restricted number of field offices, located at centers of greatest war activity and of concentrated news-dissemination facilities.

(*a*) The field services of each Federal Department or agency will be responsible for preparing and disseminating information not related significantly to the war effort. The head of each Federal Department or agency shall instruct his field employees to release in the field only such information as is within clearly defined policy and exclusively within the authorized activities of his agency.

(*b*) Releases which bear definitely upon war activities or policy or which include material broader than the authorized activities of the preparing agency shall be cleared with and issued by the nearest OWI field office.

(*c*) Radio programs relating to the war effort prepared by Federal agencies in the field for individual stations or regional or national networks shall be reviewed and cleared by the most convenient OWI field information office.

(*d*) Publications and graphics prepared and issued in the field and relating significantly to the war effort, or dealing with activities broader than the authorized work of the initiating agency shall be cleared with the nearest OWI field office.

13. *Overseas Information.* All information for official dissemination outside the continental limits of the United States (except to Central and South America) shall be handled exclusively by the Overseas Branch of the Office of War Information, whether such dissemination involves news releases, radio, short-wave radio, publications, graphics, motion pictures, or other media.

(*a*) To avoid duplication the News Bureau of the Office of War Information will gather news for the Overseas Branch as well as for the Domestic Branch of the Office, but dissemination abroad will be the responsibility of the Overseas Branch.

(*b*) All Departments and agencies shall provide the Overseas Branch with materials they believe useful for overseas use, and shall prepare material at the request of OWI.

14. *Personnel.* In view of the importance of providing all the people with information so presented that they shall be "truthfully informed about the common war effort," the Office of War Information and the Departments and agencies shall cooperate in insuring that informational work is in competent, experienced hands. As required by Executive Order 9182, the Director of War Information, after consultation with the appropriate Departments or agencies, will direct the discontinuance of the activities of persons performing unnecessary information work.

15. *OWI–OCD Cooperation.* To meet the requests of discussion groups throughout the United States for facts on all phases of the war effort, the Office of War Information will cooperate with the Office of Civilian Defense in aiding such local discussion groups to obtain special pamphlets and related materials on the war effort.

16. Despite the distinctions made in this regulation between information issued direct by the several Departments and agencies and that

issued by the Office of War Information, the appropriate media bureaus
of OWI will, at the request of Departments or agencies which lack their
own facilities, prepare and issue information materials for such Departments or agencies.

(Signed) ELMER DAVIS
Director

CHAPTER IV

THE UNITED NATIONS

1. BACKGROUND OF COLLABORATION

The seeds of United Nations collaboration, formally established by the Joint Declaration of January 1, 1942, are to be found in early relations between States engaged in war against the Axis Powers and in the relations of States then neutral to those engaged in opposition to aggression. The development of the policy and action of the United States evidenced from the beginning a determination to give substantial aid to those engaged in resisting aggression.[1] This policy received its most striking implementation in the Lend-Lease Act of March 11, 1941,[2] which provided the mechanism for United States assistance to those engaged in resisting aggression down to our entrance into the war and, after that time, was the means by which we gave economic and financial assistance to our associates in return now for more concrete and direct assistance received from them. The Act also provided the United States with the means by which we might gain acceptance of the principles of post-war reconstruction, particularly economic, which we supported.

A basis for collaboration in the acceptance by a group of nations of a set of common principles was provided by the formulation of the so-called "Atlantic Charter" by President Roosevelt and Prime Minister Churchill and the general adherence of countries at war with the Axis Powers, along with many others, to the principles here set forth.[3]

Anticipating on a somewhat extensive basis the United Nations relationship was the action of fourteen Governments engaged in war against the Axis Powers in adopting at London, June 12, 1941, resolutions pledging themselves to continue the struggle until victory was won and laying down some of the broad principles of enduring peace.[4] This was followed by the Inter-Allied Meeting at London, September 24, 1941,[5] which was in a real sense the precursor of the United Nations as now constituted.

Axis aggression against the United States, followed by declarations of war by many of the Latin American Republics and by China, engaged until then in a *de facto* armed conflict with Japan since July 7, 1937, laid the basis for formal collaboration on a world-wide basis. In view of the fact that the principles of the Atlantic Charter had been generally accepted or adhered to by the States now at war with the Axis Powers, the establishment of a treaty basis for collaboration was not difficult. By virtue of the nature of the undertakings which the United Nations assume, membership in this group is necessarily limited to states at war with one or more of the Axis Powers.

[1] See Chapter II, p. 169–79.
[2] *Documents, III, 1940–41*, p. 712.
[3] See p. 209.
[4] *Documents, III, 1940–41*, p. 444.
[5] See p. 219–22, 262.

A. The Axis Powers

(1) Agreement between the German and Japanese Governments Respecting the Communist International, Berlin, November 25, 1936 [1]

This agreement while purporting to provide for collaboration in the taking of defensive and presumably internal measures to combat Communism was generally interpreted at the time as having more aggressive purposes. It was in line with the grand strategy which the Nazis so cleverly used of weakening and dividing their prospective victims by playing up the Communist menace and making Nazi Germany appear as the only protection against the Communist peril. The success of this general strategy was not at all measured by the number of states which adhered to this agreement. As a matter of fact the number of formal adherences was small. Italy adhered on November 6, 1937. Hungary and "Manchoukuo" signed on February 24, 1939. Spain adhered on March 27, 1939. The action of the German Government in signing a Treaty of Non-Aggression with the U.S.S.R. on August 23, 1939 made it expedient to soft-pedal the anti-Comintern motif for the time being but the attack on the Soviet Union, June 22, 1941, in violation of this agreement, removed the need of any further restraint in this connection. Meanwhile, on September 27, 1940, the three principal Axis Powers had entered into a formal alliance pledging each other full political, economic and military assistance in case of attack by "a Power at present not involved in the European War or in the Chinese-Japanese conflict. [2] Furthermore, and curiously enough in view of the original anti-Communist professions of the German and Japanese Governments, the Soviet Union was excluded from the operation of the alliance, making it appear that the pact was directed particularly against the United States. The 1936 agreement, by its terms, ran for five years. When it came up for renewal, Germany and Italy were at war with the Soviet Union and Japan was on the point of attacking the United States. It now served the purposes of the Axis leaders to marshal as much support as possible for the fight against Communism, particularly since Communism and democracy were regarded by them as practically synonymous.

The Government of the German Reich and the Imperial Japanese Government, recognizing that the aim of the Communist International, known as the Comintern, is to disintegrate and subdue existing States by all the means at its command; convinced that the toleration of interference by the Communist International in the internal affairs of the nations not only endangers their internal peace and social well-being, but is also a menace to the peace of the world; desirous of cooperating in the defense against Communist subversive activities; have agreed as follows:

ARTICLE I. The High Contracting States agree to inform one another of the activities of the Communist International, to consult with one

[1] English version of *The Times* (London), reprinted from Royal Institute of International Affairs, *Documents on International Relations*, 1936, p. 297, checked to the German original, *Reichsgesetzblatt*, 1936, II, No, 4; *Nouveau recueil général de traités*, 3e série, XXXIII, p. 376.

[2] *Documents, III, 1940–41*, p. 304.

another on the necessary preventive measures, and to carry these through in close collaboration.

ARTICLE II. The High Contracting Parties will jointly invite third States whose internal peace is threatened by the subversive activities of the Communist International to adopt defensive measures in the spirit of this agreement or to take part in the present agreement.

ARTICLE III. The German as well as the Japanese text of the present agreement is to be deemed the original text. It comes into force on the day of signature and remains in force for a period of five years. Before the expiry of this period the High Contracting Parties will come to an understanding over the further method of their cooperation.

In witness whereof the undersigned, being duly and properly authorized by their respective Governments, have signed this agreement and affixed their seals.

Done in duplicate at Berlin on November 25, 1936 — that is, November 25 of the 11th year of Showa Period.

(Signed) JOACHIM VON RIBBENTROP, *Extraordinary and Plenipotentiary Ambassador of the German Reich.*

(Signed) VISCOUNT KINTOMO MUSHAKOJI, *Imperial Japanese Extraordinary and Plenipotentiary Ambassador.*

SUPPLEMENTARY PROTOCOL

On the occasion of the signing today of the agreement against the Communist International, the undersigned Plenipotentiaries have agreed as follows:

(a) The competent authorities of the two High Contracting States will work in close collaboration in matters concerning the exchange of information over the activity of the Communist International as well as investigatory and defensive measures against the Communist International.

(b) The competent authorities of the two High Contracting States will within the framework of the existing laws take severe measures against those who at home or abroad are engaged directly or indirectly in the service of the Communist International or promote its subversive activities.

(c) In order to facilitate the cooperation of the competent authorities of the two High Contracting Parties provided for in paragraph (a) a permanent committee will be set up. In this committee the further defensive measures necessary for the struggle against the subversive activities of the Communist International will be considered and discussed.

Berlin, November 25, 1936, that is, November 25 of the 11th year of he Showa period.

(Signed) VON RIBBENTROP.
(Signed) MUSHAKOJI.

2) *Protocol Prolonging the Anti-Comintern Pact, Berlin, November 25, 1941* [1]

This protocol, by its terms, was concluded between the Governments of Germany, Italy, Japan, Hungary, "Manchoukuo" and Spain. The adherents, ported to be also signatories of the protocol on November 25, 1941, were the overnments of Bulgaria, "Croatia," Denmark, Finland, Rumania, "Slovakia" nd the Wang Ching-wei regime in China.[2]

The Government of the German Reich, the Royal Italian Government nd the Imperial Japanese Government, as well as the Royal Hungarian overnment, the Imperial Government of Manchoukuo [3] and the panish Government, recognizing that international agreements made y them to ward off activity of the Communist International have proved 1emselves in the best possible manner and, in the conviction that the nited interests of their countries further demand their close cooperation ζainst a common enemy, have decided to extend the effectiveness of the ɔove-mentioned agreement and have agreed for this purpose on the llowing terms:

ARTICLE I. The pact against the Communist International, consisting the agreement and supplementary protocol of November 25, 1936, as ell as the protocol of November 6, 1937,[4] by which Italy adhered; rough the protocol of February 24, 1939,[5] by which Hungary adhered; 1d the protocol of March 27, 1939,[6] by which Spain adhered, will be rolonged for five years, reckoned from November 25, 1941.

[1] English version as transmitted from Berlin by the United Press, *New York Times*, ovember 26, 1941, p. 12, with certain technical alterations.
[2] The Quisling regime in Norway was not "invited" to sign. The Nasjonal Samling wspaper *Fritt Folk* ruefully wrote: "If Norway had been permitted to keep its ygaardsvold] government of April 9, then Norway's signature would not have been issing from this epochal agreement."
[3] The protocol of adherence, which is omitted from the enumeration in Article I, is signed February 24, 1939, *Nouveau recueil général de traités*, 3e série, XXXVII, 329.
[4] The German and Italian texts are in *Nouveau recueil général de traités*, 3e série, XXV, p. 3.
[5] *Ibid.*, XXXVII, p. 327.
[6] *Ibid.*, p. 331.

ARTICLE II. States which, on the invitation of the German Reich Government, the Royal Italian Government and the Imperial Japanese Government, as original signatories of this pact against the Communist International, adhere to this pact, will hand over their declarations of adherence in writing to the German Reich Government which, for its part, will inform the remaining contracting powers of the receipt of these declarations. The adherence enters into force on the day of receipt of the declaration of adherence by the German Reich Government.

ARTICLE III. The foregoing protocol is drawn up in the German, Italian and Japanese languages, and each text counts as an original. The protocol enters into force on the day of its signature. The high contracting powers will agree on a further form of their cooperation in good time before the expiration of the period of five years foreseen in Article I.

In witness whereof, the signers, well and truly equipped with full powers by their Governments, have signed this protocol and affixed their seals thereto.

Done in six copies, Berlin, November 25, 1941.

[Signatures lacking.]

Following the signing of the protocol by Eric Scavenius, the Danish Foreign Minister, he was branded a traitor by demonstrators in Copenhagen. A Stockholm dispatch reported that Scavenius signed the protocol without approval and against the judgment of the King and the ministry. The Germans threatened to revoke their guaranty for the internal independence of Denmark, given in August 1940, if the promise of its minister were not fulfilled, and they vetoed a intention of the Danish Government to have Scavenius resign (*New York Times*, November 27, 1941, p. 5).

(3) *Agreement between the German, Italian and Japanese Governments, December 11, 1941* [1]

The Japanese attack on the United States and Great Britain on December 7, 1941, followed by the German and Italian declarations of war on the United States, naturally called for a reaffirmation of the principle of mutual support to which the three Axis partners had committed themselves by the Three-Power Pact of September 27, 1940. The fact that Japan was at peace with Soviet Russia required that that country be omitted from the list of countries against which this agreement was directed.

[1] Reuter version, *The Times* (London), December 12, 1941, p. 4. The text of the agreement was included in the speech of Adolf Hitler to the Reichstag on December 11. Its announcement was prefaced with the following statement:

"We had always endeavored to prevent a breach with the United States, but now Italy and Germany are forced, in loyal fulfilment of their obligations under the Tripartite Agreement, to associate themselves with the struggle of Japan against America and England."

In their unshakable determination not to lay down arms until the
ommon war against the United States of America and Britain has been
rought to a successful conclusion, the German Government, the Italian
overnment, and the Japanese Government have agreed upon the
llowing provisions:

ARTICLE 1. Germany, Italy, and Japan jointly and with every means
their disposal shall proceed with the war forced upon them by the
nited States of America and Britain until victory is achieved.

ARTICLE 2. Germany, Italy, and Japan undertake not to conclude an
mistice or peace with the United States of America or Britain except
complete mutual agreement.

ARTICLE 3. After victory has been achieved Germany, Italy, and
pan will continue in closest cooperation with a view to establishing
new and just order along the lines of the Tripartite Agreement con-
uded by them on September 27, 1940.[1]

ARTICLE 4. The present agreement will come into force with its
gnature, and will remain valid as long as the Tripartite Pact of Sep-
mber 27, 1940. The High Contracting Parties will in good time before
e expiry of this term of validity enter into consultation with each
her as to the future development of their cooperation, as provided
der Article 3 of the present agreement.

B. Action taken by United Nations against Axis Powers

[Table printed at p. 204–7.]

2. BASIC PRINCIPLES OF COLLABORATION

) *Declaration by United Nations, Washington, January 1, 1942* [2]

*Joint Declaration by The United States of America, The United King-
dom of Great Britain and Northern Ireland, The Union of Soviet Socialist
Republics, China, Australia, Belgium, Canada, Costa Rica, Cuba,
Czechoslovakia, Dominican Republic, El Salvador, Greece, Guatemala,
Haiti, Honduras, India, Luxemburg, Netherlands, New Zealand, Nica-
ragua, Norway, Panama, Poland, South Africa, Yugoslavia*

The Governments signatory hereto,
Having subscribed to a common program of purposes and principles
mbodied in the Joint Declaration of the President of the United States
America and the Prime Minister of the United Kingdom of Great

[1] *Documents, III, 1940–41*, p. 304.
[2] From the Office of the Secretary to the President; Department of State, *Bulletin*,
, p. 3; Executive Agreement Series 236. The signing of the instrument extended
o January 2. On the conclusion of that ceremony the Secretary of State made the
lowing statement: (Continued on p. 208.)

	GERMANY	ITALY	JAPAN
UNITED STATES	Dec. 11, 1941, 3:05 P.M. E.S.T. Public Law 331, 77th Cong., *B. S.*,[1] V, p. 475, 560	Dec. 11, 1941, 3:06 P.M. E.S.T. Public Law 332, 77th Cong., *B. S.*, V, p. 476, 560	Dec. 8, 1941, 4:10 P.M. E.S.T. Public Law 328, 77th Cong., *B. S.*, V, p. 475, 557
UNITED KINGDOM OF GREAT BRITAIN AND NORTHERN IRELAND	Sept. 3, 1939, 11 A.M. British Command Paper 6106, Misc. No. 9 (1939); *B. S.*, V, p. 551	June 11, 1940, 4:45 P.M. Note by Italy delivered June 10, 1940.[2]	Dec. 8, 1941. Statement by Prime Minister, *B. S.*, V, p. 557
UNION OF SOVIET SOCIALIST REPUBLICS	Invasion, June 22, 1941	June 22, 1941, 5:30 A.M. *N. Y. Times*, June 23, 1941, p. 5	
CHINA	Dec. 9, 1941. *B. S.*, V, p. 506, 560	Dec. 9, 1941. *B. S.*, V, p. 506, 560	Dec. 9, 1941. Text *B. S.*, V, p. 507
AUSTRALIA	Sept. 3, 1939. Proclamation, *B. S.*, V, p. 552	June 11, 1940, 9 A.M. Notification, *B. S.*, V, p. 554	Dec. 8, 1941, 5 P.M Note, Dec. 9, 1941. *B. S.*, V, p. 559
BELGIUM	Invasion, May 10, 1940. State of war "already exists." Note, Dec. 20, 1941. *B. S.*, VI, p. 143	State of war "already exists." Note, Dec. 20, 1941, *B. S.*, VI, p. 143	State of war "already exists." Note, Dec. 20, 1941, *B. S.*, VI p. 143.
CANADA	Sept. 10, 1909. *B. S.*, V, p. 552	June 10, 1940. Proclamation, *B. S.*, V, p. 553	Dec. 7, 1941. Proclamation, *B. S.*, V, p 558
COSTA RICA	Dec. 11, 1941. *B. S.*, V, p. 491, 560	Dec. 11, 1941, *B. S.*, V, p. 491, 560	Dec. 8, 1941, 11 A.M Telegram, Dec. 9 1941, *B. S.*, V, p. 490 558
CUBA	Dec. 11, 1941. *B. S.*, V, p. 492, 560	Dec. 11, 1941. *B. S.*, V, p. 492, 560	Dec. 9, 1941. Telegram Dec. 10, 1941, *B. S.* V, p. 492, 558
CZECHOSLOVAKIA	Dec. 16, 1941. Decree *B. S.*, V, p. 543, 561	Dec. 16, 1941. Decree, *B. S.*, V, p. 543, 561	Dec. 16, 1941. Decree *B. S.*, V, p. 543, 561
DOMINICAN REPUBLIC	Dec. 11, 1941. Telegram, Dec. 12, 1941, *B. S.*, V, p. 547, 561	Dec. 11, 1941. Telegram, Dec. 12, 1941, *B. S.*, V, p. 547, 560	Dec. 8, 1941. Note *B. S.*, V, p. 492, 558
EL SALVADOR	Dec. 12, 1941. Telegram, *B. S.*, V, p. 494, 560	Dec. 12, 1941. Telegram, *B. S.*, V, p. 494, 560	Dec. 8, 1941, 1 P.M *B. S.*, V, p. 493, 558

[1] *B. S.*, Department of State, *Bulletin.*
[2] From information from Division of Research and Publication.

State of War by the United Nations

BULGARIA	HUNGARY	RUMANIA	FINLAND	THAILAND
June 5, 1942. Public Law 563, 77th Cong., *B. S.*, VI, p. 510 [Bulgarian Declaration, Dec. 13, 1941, *B. S.*, V, p. 482]	June 5, 1942. Public Law 564, 77th Cong., *B. S.*, VI, p. 510 [Hungarian Declaration, Dec. 13, 1941, 5:30 P.M. *B. S.*, V, p. 561]	June 5, 1942. Public Law 565, 77th Cong., *B. S.*, VI, p. 510 [Rumanian Declaration, Dec. 12, 1941, *B. S.*, V, p. 561]		Jan. 25, 1942. Notification by Thai Ministry of For. Affairs. Telegram, *B. S.*, VI, p. 144
Dec. 13, 1941. Note of Brit. For. Off. in telegram of Dec. 29, 1941, *B. S.*, VI, p. 144 [Bulgarian Declaration, Dec. 13, 1941, *B. S.*, V, p. 483]	Dec. 7, 1941, 1:01 A.M. Note, *B. S.*, V, p. 557	Dec. 7, 1941, 1:01 A.M. Note, *B. S.*, V, p. 557	Dec. 7, 1941, 1:01 A.M. Note, *B. S.*, V, p. 557	Jan. 25, 1942, 5 A.M. Note, Feb. 9, 1942 in files of Dept. of State [2]
Relations not "normal" [3]	June 27, 1941. Hungarian action due to "air attacks." *The Times* (London), June 28, p. 3	June 22, 1941. Order to Rumanian army. *N. Y. Times*, June 23, 1941, p. 7	June 25, 1941. Statement of Speaker of Finnish Diet, reported in dispatch from Helsinki, Jan. 29, 1942 [2]	
Proclamation, Jan. 14, 1942, *Com. Aus. Gazette*, No. 14. Jan. 6, 1942.	Dec. 8, 1941, 5 P.M. A.E.S.T. Note, *B. S.*, V, p. 557	Dec. 8, 1941, 5 P.M. Note, *B. S.*, V, p. 557	Dec. 8, 1941, 5 P.M. Note, *B. S.*, V, p. 557	
	Dec. 7, 1941. Proclamation, *B. S.*, V, p. 557	Dec. 7, 1941. Proclamation, *B. S.*, V, p. 557	Dec. 7, 1941. Proclamation, *B. S.*, V, p. 557	
Dec. 16, 1941. Decree, *B. S.*, V, p. 543, 561	Dec. 16, 1941. Decree, *B. S.*, V, p. 543, 561	Dec. 16, 1941. Decree, *B. S.*, V, p. 543, 561	Dec. 16, 1941. Decree, *B. S.*, V, p. 543, 561	Dec. 16, 1941.[4] Decree, *B. S.*, V, p. 543, 561

[3] See Note of Soviet People's Commissar for Foreign Affairs Molotov to Bulgarian Minister to Moscow, September 11, 1941 (*New York Times*, September 12, 1941, p. 10).
[4] The Department of State has no conclusive data with reference to question whether declaration of December 16, 1941 applies to Thailand (Communication from the Division of Research and Publication.)

205

	GERMANY	ITALY	JAPAN
GREECE	Invasion Apr. 6, 1941, 5:15 A.M. Notification, 6:30 A.M.	Oct. 28, 1940,[1] 5:30 A.M. Note, B. S., V, p. 554	
GUATEMALA	Dec. 11, 1941. Telegram, Dec. 12, 1941, B. S., V, p. 495, 560	Dec. 11, 1941. Telegram, Dec. 12, 1941, B. S., p. 495, 560	Dec. 8, 1941. Telegram Dec. 9, 1941, B. S., V p. 494, 558
HAITI	Dec. 12, 1941. B. S., V, p. 495, 560	Dec. 12, 1941. B. S., V, p. 495, 560	Dec. 8, 1941. B. S., V p. 495, 558
HONDURAS	Dec. 12, 1941. Telegram, Dec. 13, 1941, B. S., V, p. 548, 560	Dec. 12, 1941. Telegram, Dec. 13, 1941, B. S., V, p. 548, 560	Dec. 8, 1941, 11:25 A.M Telegram, B. S., V p. 493, 558
INDIA	Sept. 3, 1939. Proclamation,[3] B. S., V, p. 552		
LUXEMBURG	Invasion, May 10, 1940, dawn. No record of formal declaration.[4] B. S., V, p. 553		
MEXICO	May 22, 1942. Telegram, June 2, 1942, B. S., VI, p. 505	May 22, 1942. Telegram, June 2, 1942, B. S., VI, p. 505	May 22, 1942. Telegram, June 2, 1942 B. S., VI, p. 505
NETHERLANDS	May 10, 1940. Note, B. S., V, p. 553	Dec. 11, 1941. Note, Dec. 30, 1941, B. S., VI, p. 144	Dec. 8, 1941. Statement, B. S., V, p. 55
NEW ZEALAND	Sept. 3, 1939. Statement, B. S., V, p. 552	June 11, 1940, 10:30 A.M. B. S., V, p. 554	Dec. 8, 1941, 11 A.M Telegram, B. S., V p. 559
NICARAGUA	Dec. 11, 1941. B. S., V, p. 499, 560	Dec. 11, 1941. B. S., V, p. 499, 560	Dec. 8, 1941. La Gaceto Managua, Dec. 11 1941
NORWAY	Invasion, Apr. 9, 1940. No record of formal action. B. S., V, p. 552		
PANAMA	Dec. 12, 1941. B. S., V, p. 500, 560	Dec. 12, 1941. B. S., V, p. 500, 560	Dec. 10, 1941. Gacet Oficial, Dec. 10, 194
PHILIPPINES [5]			
POLAND	Invasion, Sept. 1, 1939, dawn		Dec. 11, 1941. B. S., V p. 507, 560
SOUTH AFRICA, UNION OF	Sept. 6, 1939. Proclamation, B. S., V, p. 552	June 11, 1940. Proclamation, B. S., V, p. 554	Dec. 8, 1941. Proclamation, Dec. 8, 1941[2]
YUGOSLAVIA	Attack, Apr. 6, 1941	Italian Govt. announced close collaboration with Germany. Ital. press dispatch, Apr. 6, 1941	Dec. 7, 1941. Note Jan. 19, 1942, B. S VI, p. 144

[1] B. S., Department of State, *Bulletin.*
[2] From information from Division of Research and Publication.
[3] India, though accepted as a United Nation, has no independent power to declare war. Un Sec. 11 (1) of the Government of India Act of August 2, 1935 (United Kingdom, Foreign Office, *Constitutions of all Countries*, I, p. 248) the Governor-general, responsible to His Majesty the King, discretionary powers in the conduct of external affairs. The Governor-general's proclamation of S tember 3, 1939 proclaimed "that war has broken out between His Majesty and Germany" (Departme of State, *Bulletin*, V, p. 552).

BULGARIA	HUNGARY	RUMANIA	FINLAND	THAILAND
Apr. 24, 1941. Bulgarian announcement B. S., V, p. 555				
Dec. 24, 1941, 11:30 A.M. Note, B. S., VI, p. 144	Dec. 24, 1941, 11:30 A.M. Note, B. S., VI, p. 144	Dec. 24, 1941, 11:30 A.M. Note, B. S., VI, p. 144		
	Dec. 7, 1941, 12:01 P.M. N.Z. summer time. Proclamation, Dec. 8, 1941, B. S., VI, p. 145	Dec. 7, 1941, 12:01 P.M. N.Z. summer time. Proclamation, Dec. 8, 1941, B. S., VI, p. 145	Dec. 7, 1941, 12:01 P.M. N.Z. summer time. Proclamation, Dec. 8, 1941, B. S., VI, p. 145	
Dec. 20, 1941. Telegram, B. S., V, p. 584; VI, 143	Dec. 20, 1941. Telegram in files of D. of S., B. S., V, p. 584; VI, 143	Dec. 20, 1941. Telegram in files of D. of S., B. S., V, p. 584; VI, 143		
Dec. 13, 1941. Note, Dec. 31, 1941. B. S., VI, p. 144	Dec. 8, 1941. Note, B. S., V, p. 557	Dec. 8, 1941. Note, B. S., V, p. 557	Dec. 8, 1941. Note, B. S., V, p. 557	Jan. 25, 1942, 5 A.M. Note, Feb. 13, 1942 in files of Dept. of State [2]
Apr. 6, 1941. Statement, June 5, 1941. B. S., V, p. 555	Apr. 10, 1941. Statement, June 5, 1941. B. S., V, p. 555			

[4] Luxemburg "considers itself in a state of war with the Axis Powers." Note of Sept. 8, 1942 to the Secretary of State, from the Minister of Luxemburg at Washington.

[5] Listed here since the Commonwealth Government was accepted as a United Nation because of its adherence to Declaration of United Nations on June 10, 1942 (B. S., VI, p. 547). Under the Philippine Commonwealth Independence Law (Public 127, 73d Congress), Sec. 2, (a)(11) foreign affairs remain under the direct supervision and control of the United States pending the complete withdrawal of United States sovereignty.

Britain and Northern Ireland dated August 14, 1941, known as th
Atlantic Charter,

Being convinced that complete victory over their enemies is essenti;
to defend life, liberty, independence and religious freedom, and to pr(
serve human rights and justice in their own lands as well as in oth(
lands, and that they are now engaged in a common struggle again:
savage and brutal forces seeking to subjugate the world, *Declare:*

(1) Each Government pledges itself to employ its full resource
military or economic, against those members of the Tripartite Pa(
and its adherents with which such government is at war.

(2) Each Government pledges itself to cooperate with the Govern
ments signatory hereto and not to make a separate armistice or peac
with the enemies.

The foregoing declaration may be adhered to by other nations whic
are, or which may be, rendering material assistance and contribution
in the struggle for victory over Hitlerism.

Done at WASHINGTON,
January First, 1942.

The United States of America
  by FRANKLIN D. ROOSEVELT
The United Kingdom of Great Britain
  and Northern Ireland
  by WINSTON CHURCHILL
On behalf of the Government of the
  Union of Soviet Socialist Republics
  MAXIM LITVINOFF
    Ambassador
National Government of the Republic
  of China
  TSE VUNG SOONG
    Minister for Foreign Affairs
The Commonwealth of Australia
  by R. G. CASEY

The Kingdom of Belgium
  by Cte R. V. D. STRATEN
Canada
  by LEIGHTON McCARTHY
The Republic of Costa Rica
  by LUIS FERNANDEZ
The Republic of Cuba
  by AURELIO F. CONCHESO
Czechoslovak Republic
  by V. S. HURBAN
The Dominican Republic
  by J. M. TRONCOSO
The Republic of El Salvador
  by C. A. ALFARO

"The Declaration by the United Nations joins together, in the greatest comm(
war effort in history, the purpose and will of 26 free nations, representing the ove
whelming majority of the inhabitants of all 6 continents. This is a living proof th
law-abiding and peace-loving nations can unite in using the sword when necessa
to preserve liberty and justice and the fundamental values of mankind. Against th
host we can be sure that the forces of barbaric savagery and organized wickedne
cannot and will not prevail." (Department of State, *Bulletin*, VI, p. 4.)

This Declaration was printed as Canada, *Treaty Series* 1942, No. 1, accompani(
by the following "related documents": Declaration of principles, August 14, 194
resolution of the Inter-Allied Meeting, London, September 24, 1941; the Three-Pow
Pact between Germany, Italy and Japan, September 27, 1940 (*Documents, II
1940–41*, p. 304).

'he Kingdom of Greece
  by CIMON P. DIAMANTOPOULOS
'he Republic of Guatemala
  by ENRIQUE LOPEZ-HERRARTE
a République d'Haïti
  par FERNAND DENNIS
'he Republic of Honduras
  by JULIAN R. CACERES
ıdia
  GIRJA SHANKAR BAJPAI
'he Grand Duchy of Luxemburg
  by HUGUES LE GALLAIS
'he Kingdom of the Netherlands
  A. LOUDON

Signed on behalf of the Government of
  the Dominion of New Zealand
  by FRANK LANGSTONE
The Republic of Nicaragua
  by LEON DEBAYLE
The Kingdom of Norway
  by W. MUNTHE DE MORGENSTIERNE
The Republic of Panama
  by JAEN GUARDIA
The Republic of Poland
  by JAN CIECHANOWSKI
The Union of South Africa
  by RALPH W. CLOSE
The Kingdom of Yugoslavia
  by CONSTANTIN A. FOTITCH

2) *Declaration of Principles, Known as the Atlantic Charter, by the President of the United States of America (Roosevelt) and the Prime Minister of the United Kingdom (Churchill), August 14, 1941* [1]

The Declaration of Principles was signed by President Roosevelt and Prime Iinister Churchill on August 12, 1941,[2] at the conclusion, presumably, of a three-ay conference held "somewhere in the Atlantic." Though August 12 was the ate of signature, August 14, the date of the announcement of the Declaration, the date officially given to it.

At this conference, President Roosevelt and Prime Minister Churchill were :companied by important military and civilian advisers. In addition to this :reement on the broad principles and aims guiding the actions of the two overnments, important conclusions were reached on measures to be taken for ıe aid of the Soviet Union, the policy to be pursued with respect to Japan, and :her matters of a technical nature.[3]

Joint declaration of the President of the United States of America ıd the Prime Minister, Mr. Churchill, representing His Majesty's overnment in the United Kingdom, being met together, deem it right) make known certain common principles in the national policies of ıeir respective countries on which they base their hopes for a better ıture for the world.

First, their countries seek no aggrandizement, territorial or other;
Second, they desire to see no territorial changes that do not accord ith the freely expressed wishes of the peoples concerned;
Third, they respect the right of all peoples to choose the form of govern-ent under which they will live; and they wish to see sovereign rights

[1] Executive Agreement Series 236, p. 4.
[2] Statement of Prime Minister Churchill in the House of Commons, September 9, ▪41, this volume, p. 213.
[3] United Kingdom, Parliamentary Debates, House of Commons, 5th Series, ▪l. 374, col. 67.

and self-government restored to those who have been forcibly deprive
of them;

Fourth, they will endeavor, with due respect for their existing obliga
tions, to further the enjoyment by all States, great or small, victor o
vanquished, of access, on equal terms, to the trade and to the ra
materials of the world which are needed for their economic prosperit

Fifth, they desire to bring about the fullest collaboration betwee
all nations in the economic field with the object of securing, for al
improved labor standards, economic advancement and social security

Sixth, after the final destruction of the Nazi tyranny, they hope t
see established a peace which will afford to all nations the means ‹
dwelling in safety within their own boundaries, and which will affor
assurance that all the men in all the lands may live out their lives i
freedom from fear and want;

Seventh, such a peace should enable all men to traverse the high sea
and oceans without hindrance;

Eighth, they believe that all of the nations of the world, for realisti
as well as spiritual reasons must come to the abandonment of the us
of force. Since no future peace can be maintained if land, sea or ai
armaments continue to be employed by nations which threaten, o
may threaten, aggression outside of their frontiers, they believe, pendin
the establishment of a wider and permanent system of general security
that the disarmament of such nations is essential. They will likewis
aid and encourage all other practicable measures which will lighten fo
peace-loving peoples the crushing burden of armaments.

(a) Broadcast of the Prime Minister of the United Kingdom (Churchill) London, August 24, 1941 [1]

[Excerpts]

Those portions of the speech are given in which the Prime Minister elaborate
the meaning and significance of the Atlantic meeting and declaration of prir
ciples.

The meeting was, therefore, symbolic. That is its prime importanc
It symbolizes, in a form and manner which every one can understan
in every land and in every clime, the deep underlying unities which st
and, at decisive moments, rule the English-speaking peoples throughou
the world. Would it be presumptuous for me to say that it symboliz
something even more majestic, namely, the marshalling of the goo
forces of the world against the evil forces which are now so formidab

[1] British Library of Information; also printed in the *New York Times,* August 2
1941, p. 4.

and triumphant and which have cast their cruel spell over the whole of Europe and a large part of Asia?

This was a meeting which marks forever in the pages of history the taking up by the English-speaking nations, amid all this peril, tumult and confusion, of the guidance of the fortunes of the broad toiling masses in all the continents, and our loyal effort, without any clog of selfish interest, to lead them forward out of the miseries into which they have been plunged, back to the broad high road of freedom and justice. This is the highest honor and the most glorious opportunity which could ever have come to any branch of the human race.

When one beholds how many currents of extraordinary and terrible events have flowed together to make this harmony, even the most sceptical person must have the feeling that we all have the chance to play our part and do our duty in some great design, the end of which no mortal can foresee. Awful and horrible things I have seen in these days.

．　．　．　．　．　．　．

And thus we come back to the quiet bay, somewhere in the Atlantic, where misty sunshine plays on great ships which carry the White Ensign or the Stars and Stripes.

We had the idea when we met there, the President and I, that without attempting to draw final and formal peace aims, or war aims, it was necessary to give all peoples, and especially the oppressed and conquered peoples, a simple, rough-and-ready war-time statement of the goal towards which the British Commonwealth and the United States mean to make their way, and thus make a way for others to march with them on a road which will certainly be painful and may be long.

There are, however, two distinct and marked differences in this joint declaration from the attitude adopted by the Allies during the latter part of the last war, and no one should overlook them. The United States and Great Britain do not now assume that there will never be any more war again. On the contrary, we intend to take ample precaution to prevent its renewal in any period we can foresee by effectively disarming the guilty nations while remaining suitably protected ourselves. The second difference is this: that instead of trying to ruin German trade by all kinds of additional trade barriers and hindrances, as was the mood of 1917, we have definitely adopted the view that it is not in the interests of the world and of our two countries that any large nation should be unprosperous or shut out from the means of making a decent living for itself and its people by its industry and enterprise.

These are far-reaching changes of principle upon which all countries should ponder. Above all, it was necessary to give hope and the assurance of final victory to those many scores of millions of men and women who are battling for life and freedom or who are already bent down under the Nazi yoke.

. . . .

The ordeals, therefore, of the conquered peoples will be hard. We must give them hope. We must give them the conviction that their sufferings and their resistances will not be in vain. The tunnel may be dark and long, but at the end there is light. That is the symbolism and that is the message of the Atlantic meeting.

Do not despair, brave Norwegians; your land shall be cleansed not only from the invader but from the filthy Quislings who are his tools.

Be strong in your souls, Czechs; your independence shall be restored.

Poles, the heroism of your people, standing up to cruel oppressors, the courage of your soldiers, sailors and airmen shall not be forgotten. Your country shall live again and resume its rightful part in the new organization of Europe.

Lift up your heads, gallant Frenchmen. Not all the infamies of Darlan and of Laval shall stand between you and the restoration of your birthright.

Stout-hearted Dutch, Belgians, Luxemburgers, tormented, mishandled, shamefully cast away peoples of Yugoslavia, glorious Greece, now subjected to the crowning insult of the rule of the Italian jackanapes, yield not an inch. Keep your souls clean from all contact with the Nazis. Make them feel even in their fleeting hour of brutish triumph that they are the moral outcasts of mankind. Help is coming. Mighty forces are arming in your behalf. Have faith, have hope, deliverance is sure.

There is the signal which we have flashed across the waters, and if it reaches the hearts of those to whom it is sent they will endure with fortitude and tenacity their present misfortune in the sure faith that they too, are still serving the common cause and that our efforts will not be in vain.

You will, perhaps, have noticed that the President of the United States and the British representative, in what is aptly called the Atlantic Charter, have jointly pledged their countries to the final destruction of the Nazi tyranny. That is a solemn and grave undertaking. It must be made good. It will be made good. And, of course, many practical arrangements to fulfil that purpose have been and are being organized and set in motion.

. . . .

(b) Statement of the Prime Minister of the United Kingdom (Churchill)
in the House of Commons, September 9, 1941 [1]

[Excerpt]

I have, as the House knows, hitherto consistently deprecated the
formulation of peace aims or war aims — however you put it — by His
Majesty's Government, at this stage. I deprecate it at this time, when
the end of the war is not in sight, when the conflict sways to and fro with
alternating fortunes and when conditions and associations at the end of
the war are unforeseeable. But a Joint Declaration by Great Britain and
the United States is an event of a totally different nature. Although the
principles in the Declaration, and much of the language, have long been
familiar to the British and American democracies, the fact that it is a
united Declaration sets up a milestone or monument which needs only
the stroke of victory to become a permanent part of the history of
human progress. The purpose of the Joint Declaration signed by President Roosevelt and myself on 12th August, is stated in the Preamble to
be:

"To make known certain common principles in the national policies
of our respective countries on which they base their hopes for a better
future for the world."

No words are needed to emphasize the future promise held out to the
world by such a Joint Declaration by the United States and Great Britain. I need only draw attention, for instance, to the phrase in Paragraph
5, "after the final destruction of the Nazi tyranny," to show the profound
and vital character of the solemn agreement into which we have jointly
entered. Questions have been asked, and will no doubt be asked, as to
exactly what is implied by this or that point, and explanations have
been invited. It is a wise rule that when two parties have agreed [upon]
a statement one of them shall not, thereafter, without consultation with
the other, seek to put special or strained interpretations upon this or
that passage. I propose, therefore, to speak today only in an exclusive
sense.

First, the Joint Declaration does not try to explain how the broad principles proclaimed by it are to be applied to each and every case, which
will have to be dealt with when the war comes to an end. It would not
be wise for us, at this moment, to be drawn into laborious discussions
on how it is to fit all the manifold problems with which we shall be faced

[1] United Kingdom, Parliamentary Debates, House of Commons, 5th series, vol.
374, cols. 67–9.

after the war. Secondly, the Joint Declaration does not qualify in any way the various statements of policy which have been made from time to time about the development of constitutional government in India, Burma or other parts of the British Empire. We are pledged by the Declaration of August 1940 to help India to obtain free and equal partnership in the British Commonwealth with ourselves, subject, of course, to the fulfilment of obligations arising from our long connection with India and our responsibilities to its many creeds, races and interests. Burma also is covered by our considered policy of establishing Burmese self-government and by the measures already in progress. At the Atlantic meeting, we had in mind, primarily, the restoration of the sovereignty, self-government and national life of the States and nations of Europe now under the Nazi yoke, and the principles governing any alterations in the territorial boundaries which may have to be made. So that is quite a separate problem from the progressive evolution of self-governing institutions in the regions and peoples which owe allegiance to the British Crown. We have made declarations on these matters which are complete in themselves, free from ambiguity and related to the conditions and circumstances of the territories and peoples affected. They will be found to be entirely in harmony with the high conception of freedom and justice which inspired the Joint Declaration.

(c) Address of the Ambassador of the Soviet Union (Maisky) to the Inter-Allied Meeting, London, September 24, 1941 [2]

The present conference has assembled in London at a time when Hitlerite Germany, after having enslaved and ravaged several European countries, is conducting with particular force and unprecedented brutality her predatory war against the Soviet Union.

Three months have elapsed since that day when the Panzer hordes of Nazi Germany treacherously attacked my country and invaded it territory.

For three months the Soviet people and their beloved Red Army Navy, and Air Force have been waging a heroic battle against the perfidious enemy, bearing upon their shoulders the main burden of the fight against a bloodthirsty aggressor, who threatens the social and political institutions and achievements of freedom-loving nations, who endanger the very foundations of culture and civilization.

---

[1] The British Government subsequently undertook, through the Cripps Mission to advance the realization of self-government in India, see p. 544–73.

[2] United Kingdom, Parliamentary Papers, Miscellaneous No. 3 (1941), Cmd. 631. p. 4. For Stalin's statement of November 6 on Soviet war aims, see p. 615.

In this war, imposed by Hitlerite fascism upon the democratic coun-ries, the destiny of Europe and the destiny of humanity itself for many lecades to come is being decided.

It cannot be tolerated that peaceful and freedom-loving peoples should be menaced by the Nazi yoke, and that a gang of Hitlerite marauders, armed to the teeth, pretending and proclaiming itself to be a *Herrenvolk*, a master race, should continue to demolish towns and villages, to convert flourishing lands into deserts, to exterminate thousands and hundreds of thousands of peaceful people, with the delirious idea that the Hitlerite murderers must dominate the world.

The first task of all nations and all states compelled to wage war against Hitlerite Germany and her allies is to bring about the speediest and most decisive defeat of the aggressor. For the full accomplishment of that task they must assemble and devote all their strength and resources, and determine the most effective ways and means of reaching their goal. It is the task which at the present time unites all the Governments which have sent their representatives to this conference.

Our countries face also the most important problem of laying the basis for the organization of international relations, and of constituting the post-war world in such a way as to spare our peoples and our future generations the monstrous crimes of Nazism, incompatible with human culture. The U.S.S.R. is firmly convinced that this task will be success-fully accomplished and that as a result of complete and final victory over Hitlerism there will be laid the true foundations of international coopera-tion and friendship, corresponding to the aspirations and ideals of free-dom-loving peoples.

That is what all the peoples of my country are striving for. That is what inspires the Soviet Government in all its activities and in its foreign policy. The Soviet Union has applied, and will apply, in its foreign policy the high principle of respect for the sovereign rights of peoples.

The Soviet Union was, and is, guided in its foreign policy by the prin-ciple of self-determination of nations. It is guided by the same principle which, in fact, embodies recognition of the sovereignty and the equality of nations in its dealings with various nationalities embraced within the frontiers of the Soviet Union. Indeed, this principle forms one of the pillars on which the political structure of the U.S.S.R. is built.

Accordingly, the Soviet Union defends the right of every nation to the independence and territorial integrity of its country, and its right to establish such a social order and to choose such a form of government as it deems opportune and necessary for the better promotion of its economic and cultural prosperity.

The Soviet Union, which followed that principle in all its policy an in all its relations with other nations, has consistently and with full forc denounced all violations of sovereign rights of peoples, all aggression an aggressors, all and any attempts of aggressive states to impose their wi upon other peoples and to involve them in war. The Soviet Union ha untiringly and resolutely advocated, and advocates today, the necessit of collective action against aggressors, as one of the most effective mean of bringing about the triumph of those principles, and advancing th peace and security of nations.

Striving for a radical solution of the problem of safeguarding freedon loving peoples against all the dangers they encounter from aggressor the Soviet Union has at the same time fought for complete and gener disarmament. The Soviet Union is ready to give a fitting answer to an blow from the aggressor. At the same time it has been, and still i building its foreign policy upon the desire to maintain peaceful an neighborly relations with all countries which respect the integrity an inviolability of its borders. The Soviet Union was, and is, willing t render all possible assistance to peoples becoming victims of aggressio and fighting for the independence of their native land.

In accordance with a policy inspired by the above principles, whic have been unswervingly applied by the Soviet Union, a policy whicl moreover, has been expressed in numerous acts and documents, tl Soviet Government proclaims its agreement with the fundamental prir ciples of the declaration of Mr. Roosevelt, President of the United State and of Mr. Churchill, Prime Minister of Great Britain — principl which are so important in the present international circumstances.

Considering that the practical application of these principles wi necessarily adapt itself to the circumstances, needs, and historic pecul arities of particular countries, the Soviet Government can state that consistent application of these principles will secure the most energet support on the part of the Government and peoples of the Soviet Unio

At the same time, the Soviet Government considers it imperative t declare with particular emphasis that all peoples which have recognize the necessity of smashing Hitlerite aggression and annihilating the yol of Nazism today have one main task — *to mobilize all the economic ar military resources of freedom-loving peoples, in order to attain a full ar speedy emancipation of the nations groaning under the oppression of tl Hitlerite hordes.*

Attributing great importance to the equitable use of all materi resources and foodstuffs in the post-war period, the Soviet Governmei believes that the most imperative and most pressing task of today is tl

correct allocation of all the economic resources and war supplies with a
view to an early liberation of all the European peoples now oppressed by
Hitlerite slavery.

*(d) Text of Generalissimo Chiang Kai-shek's Message to the Indian
People on the Eve of his Departure from Calcutta, Released in
Chungking on February 22, 1942* [1]

In this message to the Indian people following a visit which he and Madame
Chiang had made to India, the Generalissimo expresses the adherence of China
to the principles of the Atlantic Charter. He also develops a point of view with
regard to the meaning of these principles which has come to have special importance since the Atlantic Charter became the basis of United Nations collaboration.

During my two weeks' stay in India I had the opportunity of discussing
very frankly with the highest civil and military authorities as well as
with my Indian friends questions concerning joint plans against aggression and the objective of our common efforts. I was happy to find that
here was full sympathy and general understanding between us. My
mission is now drawing to a close. On the eve of my departure I wish
to bid farewell to all my friends in India and to thank you for the many
kindnesses showered upon Madame Chiang and myself. The briefness
of my stay has not permitted me to tell the Indian people all that I
wished to say. I avail myself of this opportunity to address to them this
farewell message. It is an expression of my high and warm regard and
of long cherished hopes for India. It comes from the depth of my heart.

Since my arrival in this country I found to my great satisfaction that
here exists among the people of India a unanimous determination to
oppose aggression.

China and India comprise one half of the world's population. Their
common frontier extends three thousand kilometers. In the two thousand years' history of their intercourse, which has been of a purely
cultural and commercial character, there has never been any armed
conflict. Indeed nowhere else can one find so long a period of uninterrupted peace between two neighboring countries. This is irrefutable
proof that our two peoples are peace-loving by nature. Today they have
not only identical interests but also the same destiny. For this reason
they are duty bound to side with anti-aggression countries and to fight
shoulder to shoulder in order to secure real peace for the whole world.

Moreover our two peoples have an outstanding virtue in common,
namely the noble spirit of self-sacrifice for the sake of justice and right-

[1] *China at War*, Vol. VIII, No. 4, April 1942, p. 59.

eousness. It is this traditional spirit which should move them towards self-negation for the salvation of mankind. It is also this spirit which prompted China to be the first to take up arms against aggression and in the present war to ally herself unhesitatingly with other anti-aggression countries, not merely for the purpose of securing her own freedom but also for the purpose of securing justice and freedom for all.

I venture to suggest to my brethren people of India at this most critical moment in the history of civilization that our two peoples should exert themselves to the utmost in the cause of freedom for all mankind, for only in a free world could the Chinese and Indian peoples obtain their freedom. Furthermore, should freedom be denied to either China or India, there could be no real international peace.

The present international situation divides the world into two camps the aggression camp and the anti-aggression camp. All those who opposed aggression by striving for the freedom of their country and of other countries should join the anti-aggression camp. There is no middle course and there is no time to wait for developments. Now is the crucial moment for the whole future of mankind. The issue before us does not concern the dispute of any one man or country, nor does it concern any specific questions now pending between one people and another. Any people therefore which joins the anti-aggression front may be said to be cooperating, not with any particular country, but with the entire front. This leads us to believe that the Pacific war is the turning point in the history of nationalism. The method, however, by which the peoples of the world could achieve their freedom might be different from what it used to be. The anti-aggression nations now expect that in this new era the people of India will voluntarily bear their full share of responsibility in the present struggle for the survival of a free world, in which India must play her part. The vast majority of world opinion is in full sympathy with India's aspirations for freedom. This sympathy is so valuable and so difficult to obtain that it cannot be appraised in terms of money or material and should therefore by all means be retained

The present struggle is one between freedom and slavery, between light and darkness, between good and evil, between resistance and aggression. Should the anti-aggression front lose the war, world civilization would suffer a setback for at least one hundred years and there would be no end of human suffering.

. . . .

In these horrible times of savagery and brute force, the people of China and their brethren people of India should for the sake of civilization and human freedom give their united support to the principles embodied in the Atlantic Charter and in the Joint Declaration of Twenty-Six Nations, and ally themselves with the anti-aggression front. I hope they will wholeheartedly join the allies, namely, China, Great Britain, America and the Soviet Union, and participate in the struggle for the survival of a free world until complete victory is achieved and the duties incident upon them in these troubled times have been fully discharged.

Lastly, I sincerely hope and I confidently believe that our ally Great Britain, without waiting for any demands on the part of the people of India, will as speedily as possible give them real political power so that they may be in a position further to develop their spiritual and material strength and thus realize that their participation in the war is not merely aid to the anti-aggression nations for securing victory but also the turning point in their struggle for India's freedom. From the objective point of view, I am of the opinion this would be the wisest policy which will redound to the credit of the British Empire.

(e) Resolution Expressing Adherence to the Principles of the Atlantic Charter Adopted by the Inter-Allied Meeting, St. James's Palace, London, September 24, 1941 [1]

The Governments of Belgium, Czechoslovakia, Greece, Luxemburg, the Netherlands, Norway, Poland, U.S.S.R., Yugoslavia, and the representatives of General de Gaulle, leader of Free Frenchmen,

Having taken note of the declaration recently drawn up by the President of the United States and the Prime Minister, Mr. Winston Churchill, on behalf of His Majesty's Government in the United Kingdom,

Now make known their adherence to the common principles of policy set forth in that declaration and their intention to cooperate to the best of their ability in giving effect to them.

f) Observations of the Acting Foreign Minister of Poland (Raczynski), at Inter-Allied Meeting, London, September 24, 1941 [2]

[Excerpt]

The Polish Government is confident that none of the illegal acts perpetrated by Germany on the territory of Poland shall be recognized by

[1] United Kingdom, Parliamentary Papers, Miscellaneous No. 3 (1941), Cmd. 6315, p. 6. The Secretary of State for Foreign Affairs of the United Kingdom, who was chairman of the meeting, made the following explanation:
"The preamble of this resolution makes no mention of His Majesty's Government in the United Kingdom or of His Majesty's Governments in Canada, the Commonwealth of Australia, New Zealand, and the Union of South Africa, for the reason that His Majesty's Government in the United Kingdom is a party to the original declaration, and that the Dominion Governments are already associated with it."
[2] *Ibid.*, p. 14.

the victorious democracies which will finally convince the German nation that aggression does not pay. In particular, the Polish population of the Western provinces, so ruthlessly transplanted, must be given a possibility of an immediate reintegration in the land of their ancestors; and the German settlers, installed in Polish homesteads, sent back to the Reich.

The Polish Government has a profound faith in the sense of justice of Great Britain as well as of the United States and is therefore persuaded that Poland — the first country to stand up to the German onslaught, staking in this struggle her territorial integrity, cannot emerge from this war with a territory reduced in strength and importance. The future frontiers of Poland should safeguard the country's security as a part of the general security of Europe; they should assure Poland's vital need of a wide access to the sea adequately protected from foreign interference, as well as her economic development in proportion to the number of her population. Poland's "Free Access to the Sea" stipulated in point 13 of President Wilson's 14 points, as a guarantee of our country's independence, should this time be made really free and secure.

The Roosevelt-Churchill declaration, as it is understood by the Polish Government, places security against another war and the achievement of economic prosperity in the forefront as the principal aims of a new democratic order. These aims are also those of Poland. The British Prime Minister gave us in his eloquent broadcast speech on August 24,[1] the assurance that Great Britain and the United States do not wish to repeat the mistake of 1918 by believing that this war was certain to be the last. It follows that prevention against aggression and the outbreak of a third world war will remain as a major problem of the postwar period. The remedial measures against a new war should be varied as were also the causes of the outbreak of the two wars. Point 8 of the joint declaration concerning the disarmament of nations guilty of aggression represents an important guarantee. It can, however, hardly remain as the sole guarantee. Experience of the last twenty years is there to prove it. It will be necessary to find other effective additional guarantees.

Both the solution of the problem of European security as well as the task of assuring prosperity of Europe is unthinkable without a close collaboration of the continent with the British Empire and the United States of America. The continental nations will assuredly see in the Roosevelt-Churchill declaration a new proof that the two democracies are determined to maintain their interest in the Continent after victory over Germany has been achieved.

[1] See p. 210.

(g) Joint Polish-Czechoslovak Declaration Made at the Inter-Allied Meeting, London, September 24, 1941 [1]

The Polish and the Czechoslovak Governments, animated by the spirit of solidarity which inspired their joint declaration of November 11, 1940, on the necessity of establishing after the war a confederation between the two countries, make the following joint declaration before the Conference of the Allies:

The Governments of the Republic of Poland and of the Republic of Czechoslovakia declare that they are determined to assist in the spirit of close and friendly collaboration in the realization of the principal aims of the Roosevelt-Churchill declaration, namely the security against a third war and the economic prosperity of the world. Moreover, remembering the experience of the Polish and Czechoslovak nations, which have suffered so much from the insatiable aggressiveness of Germany, both Governments are of the opinion that safeguards against a third German war must be sought not only in the complete preventive destruction of the means which Germany might use in the future in another attempt at the realization of her aggressive plans, but also in furnishing effective political and material guarantees, and in offering the necessary economic assistance for the reconstruction of the despoiled economies of these nations, which were, and may again become, the object of the initial aggressive acts on the part of Germany.

The two Governments are convinced that the carrying out of the Roosevelt-Churchill declaration in the spirit of justice, which does not admit the uniformity of treatment of those guilty of provoking world wars and of the victims of these wars, will lay the foundations of a new order in Europe, based upon a permanent system of general security, on general prosperity, and on social justice. The achievement of this aim will convince the nations of the continent that their sufferings during the world war of 1914–1918 and during the present war were neither unavailing nor fruitless.

[1] United Kingdom, Parliamentary Papers, Miscellaneous No. 3 (1941), Cmd. 6315, p. 16.

For a more extended declaration of the position of the Polish Government-in-Exile, see address of General Sikorski, Prime Minister, London, February 24, 1942 *The Inter-Allied-Review*, II, No. 3, March 15, 1942, p. 62). A similar declaration by Dr. Hubert Ripka, Acting Foreign Minister of Czechoslovakia, before the Czechoslovak State Council on January 7, 1942, is given *ibid*, p. 48–9.

(h) Statement of the Minister for Foreign Affairs of the Netherlands (Van Kleffens) at Inter-Allied Meeting, London, September 24, 1941 [1]

The words "with due respect for their existing obligations" appear to be in the nature of a reservation, and in their strictly legal sense these words seem natural enough. But it seems to us equally natural that, if the object expressed in this fourth point of the declaration is to be achieved, such existing obligations should not be perpetuated, even as exceptions, when it is clear that their continued operation would seriously impair or diminish the beneficial effect which is to accrue to all from the application of the general rule. In our present world, which is only the morrow of yesterday's world with its nefarious autarchic tendencies, the very opposite of the spirit expressed in the Atlantic Charter, we shall all have to do away, to some considerable extent, with measures designed to protect existing economic units. This will mean sacrifices for all, though these sacrifices will be worth the price if, as we confidently anticipate, greater national and international stability and greater prosperity is the result. Since in the economic field protection engenders protection, there should not be left in being, in our opinion, important exceptions to the general rule of free access to trade and raw materials on the basis of equal opportunities for all. Otherwise this fine principle, to which the Netherlands who has always stood for freedom of commerce professes full adhesion, would degenerate into a fine phrase. It does not seem to us out of place to state this explicitly: at the end of the last war, the same principle found solemn expression in almost identical terms, and we all know what became of it when the snowball of protection was set rolling until it became so large that it was a serious obstacle in the path of international trade.

My Government therefore takes the reservation in point 4 to mean that, just as no existing obligation is invalidated by that point *ipso facto*, so no such obligation is thereby to be perpetuated. Further I should like to place on record the view of my Government that the highly important aims enunciated in point 4 of the declaration cannot be attained if considerable exceptions thereto are left in being. For that reason we express the earnest hope that, desirous as we are to see trade barriers removed and discriminatory treatment in international commerce abolished, a serious common effort be made to that end for the ultimate benefit of all.

[1] United Kingdom, Parliamentary Papers, Miscellaneous No. 3 (1941), Cmd. 6315, p. 12.

(3) Adherences to the Declaration by United Nations

(a) Adherence of the Government of Mexico. The Minister for Foreign Affairs (Padilla) to the Secretary of State (Hull), Mexico City, June 5, 1942 [1]

[Translation]

51274. Your Excellency has undoubtedly had occasion during recent years to evaluate the international conduct observed by Mexico in the face of the constant transgressions of law committed by the powers which, having equal aims from the beginning, subsequently ended by associating themselves in their unbridled ambition for world domination, signing the Tripartite Pact. From the time when, in September 1939, an uncontainable Pan-Germanism, clothed in a singularly arbitrary dictatorial ideology, unloosed war on Europe, the Government of Mexico has given public expression to its sympathy for the cause of the democracies which are trying to prevent the world from falling under the despotism of the totalitarian states. Hence, interpreting this obvious policy of the Government of Mexico, at the Third Consultative Meeting of Ministers of Foreign Affairs of the American Republics, it, with true pleasure, signed resolution XXXV relating to the Atlantic Charter. Now that my Government — for reasons of which Your Excellency is aware — has found itself compelled, in defense of its outraged sovereignty, to declare itself to be in a state of war with Germany, Italy, and Japan, it considers that the time has arrived to give more concrete adherence to the joint program outlined by His Excellency Franklin D. Roosevelt, President of the United States of America and by His Excellency Winston Churchill, Prime Minister of the United Kingdom of Great Britain and Northern Ireland, on August 14, 1941. In taking this decision my Government does but continue the firm line of its national policy. In fact, the principles contained in the Atlantic Charter coincide with the aspirations for social justice which have invariably ruled the actions of my country in the international field; they indicate, as goals of the present conflict, objectives of such importance and nobility as to justify the greatest sacrifices; and, in brief, they constitute an ideal for the realization of which Mexico has worked from the beginning of its independent life. Accordingly, I have the honor to inform Your Excellency that in accordance with instructions which I have received from the President of the Republic Mexico formally adheres, by means of the present message, to the declaration of the United Nations dated January 1, 1942.[2]

I renew [etc.]

[1] Department of State, *Bulletin*, VI, p. 546.
[2] The ceremony of signature occurred at the White House on June 14.

(i) *The Secretary of State (Hull) to the Minister of Foreign Affairs (Padilla), June 12, 1942* [1]

I have received your telegram of June 5, 1942 stating that the principles contained in the Atlantic Charter coincide with the aspirations for social justice of the Mexican people; that these principles clearly express the directives which have invariably ruled the actions of Mexico in the international field; that the principles indicate, as goals of the present conflict, objectives of such importance and nobility as to justify the greatest sacrifices; and that accordingly Mexico formally adheres to the Declaration by United Nations of January 1, 1942.

It is indeed gratifying that Mexico has associated itself with the other United Nations which have pledged themselves to employ their full resources, military or economic, in the task of overwhelming the forces of evil that seek to dominate and enslave the world. On behalf of this Government, which is the depository for the Declaration by United Nations, I take pleasure in welcoming Mexico to the group of United Nations which are engaged in the struggle for the preservation of liberty and the democratic way of life.

Please accept [etc.]

(b) *Adherence of the Government of the Philippines. The President of the Commonwealth (Quezon) to the Secretary of State (Hull) Washington, June 10, 1942* [2]

MR. SECRETARY:

The people of the Philippines are wholeheartedly devoted to liberty and fully subscribe to the principle set forth in that great document known as the Atlantic Charter which was proclaimed by President Roosevelt and Prime Minister Churchill on August 14, 1941.

We have been battling since December 7, 1941 to preserve our country from the menace of Japanese aggression. Although a large part of our territory is overrun by Japanese military forces, our soldiers are still actively engaged in meeting and harassing the foe wherever possible. We do not intend to be cowed by the armed might of Japan. We shall continue the struggle with every means in our power.

We desire to associate ourselves with those nations which are fighting for the preservation of life and liberty against the forces of barbarism that seek world domination. Accordingly, the Commonwealth of the Philippines hereby formally adheres to the Declaration by United Nations of January 1, 1942.

I am [etc.]

[1] Department of State, *Bulletin*, VI, p. 547.
[2] *Ibid.* The ceremony of signature occurred at the White House on June 14.

(i) The Secretary of State (Hull) to the President of the Commonwealth (Quezon), Washington, June 13, 1942[1]

MY DEAR MR. PRESIDENT:

I have received your communication of June 10, 1942 stating that the people of the Philippines are wholeheartedly devoted to liberty and fully subscribe to the principles set forth in the Atlantic Charter; that they desire to associate themselves with the nations which are fighting for the preservation of life and liberty against the forces of barbarism that seek world domination; and that accordingly the Commonwealth of the Philippines formally adheres to the Declaration by United Nations of January 1, 1942.

The entire freedom-loving world admires the great courage and valor shown by the people of the Philippines during the past six months as they have gallantly fought to preserve their country from Japanese aggression. On behalf of this Government, as depository for the Declaration by United Nations, I take pleasure in welcoming into this group the Commonwealth of the Philippines.

Please accept [etc.]

(4) Statement of the Department of State, January 5, 1942[2]

In order that liberty-loving peoples silenced by military force may have an opportunity to support the principles of the Declaration by United Nations, the Government of the United States, as the depository for that Declaration, will receive statements of adherence to its principles from appropriate authorities which are not governments.

The Department of State had not, by the end of June 1942, "officially accepted" any adherences under this statement.

3. IMPLEMENTATION OF PRINCIPLES: PROSECUTION OF THE WAR AND POST-WAR RECONSTRUCTION

A. Lend-Lease

[See Chapter III for documents bearing on the more definitely national aspects of Lend-Lease, namely, administrative organization and mechanics, production and export of defense materials, and appropriations and authorizations. For text of Lend-Lease Act, approved March 11, 1941, see *Documents, III, 1940-41*, p. 712-5.]

[1] *Ibid.*
[2] *Ibid.*, p. 44.

(1) *Fifth Ninety-Day Report of the President (Roosevelt) to the Congress on Operations under the Lend-Lease Act, June 11, 1942* [1]

[Excerpt]

LEND–LEASE AND THE WAR

In the three months since the last report, the lend-lease program has been further adapted to the needs of war. The administrative machinery for fulfilling the Act of March 11, 1941, has evolved in response to the pressures and shortages of our wartime economy. That machinery now serves the United Nations in the developing processes by which they are unifying their strategy and pooling their resources.

One of the major contributions of the lend-lease program has been the resulting expansion of American munitions capacity to meet the needs of our allies and ourselves. The first lend-lease orders, together with the earlier munitions contracts of the British, French, and Netherlands Governments, helped to erect the factory facilities that have become the backbone of our armament program. Today the battle of production is on the way to being won. The pressing immediate problem is to distribute our weapons where the need is greatest, and to get them there in sufficient quantities in the shortest time. The battle of distribution is in its critical phase.

In this battle, lend-lease is the principal means through which those charged with strategic direction of the war allot American supplies to our allies. And it is becoming an element of increasing importance in the process by which our allies supply us with reciprocal aid.

LEND-LEASE AND THE UNITED NATIONS

On January 1, 1942, the United States, Great Britain, Russia, China, and 22 other nations [2] united in a declaration that "they are now engaged in a common struggle against savage and brutal forces seeking to subjugate the world." They resolved that "complete victory over their enemies is essential to defend life, liberty, independence, and religious freedom, and to preserve human rights and justice in their own lands as well as in other lands." They subscribed unanimously to the principles and purposes set forth in the Atlantic Charter. They pledged themselves

[1] House Doc. No. 799, 77th Cong., 2d sess., p. 12–23.
[2] Mexico has now become the twenty-seventh government to announce its adherence to the Declaration, the Philippines the twenty-eighth, Brazil the twenty-ninth and Ethiopia the thirtieth.

o employ their full military and economic resources in the war, and not
o make a separate peace.

The United Nations have thus declared that they are more than a
emporary military combination, and that they will wage the war
ogether for a common victory and a common program of peace aims.

To fight a common war which extends around the world, the United
Nations need a common plan for the most effective possible use of their
esources in men and materials and machines. All the battlefronts are
inked together. The United Nations are concentrating their weapons
n those battlefronts where pressure is heaviest and where military
uccess is of the greatest strategic importance. They are moving in a
oordinated way toward organizing offensives backed by their combined
esources.

Our lend-lease program is one means, and a simple one, by which the
ommon economic effort pledged in the Declaration by United Nations
nay be secured. The lend-lease principle, as it develops, is removing
he possibility that considerations of finance can interfere with the full
se of material resources. The transfers made under the Lend-Lease
Act are not commercial loans to other nations. They are contributions
f material to a common pool with which a common war is being waged.
n return, other United Nations are contributing their utmost to the
ommon fight — in men, materials and machines — and are furnishing
s with the weapons and supplies which we, rather than they, can most
ffectively use.

Considerations of transportation, supply, and strategy must determine
he countries from which war materials are to be drawn and where they
re to be sent. Some nations are able to contribute vast quantities of
nished munitions; some only the materials from which those munitions
re to be made. Some are able to give industrial and military information
vhich will expedite the war production of all the United Nations. These
ontributions, varying greatly both in character and amount, find their
ses in various parts of the world, as common plans for victory dictate.

It is for this reason that American, Canadian, and British tanks are
ound in North Africa, and American planes, based in England, fly
egularly over Germany, that British and American planes fight in
Russia and English antiaircraft guns defend our bases. This is why the
United States sends food to Great Britain while American troops on
British and Australian soil are being maintained and equipped in part
with British and Australian materials and weapons; and why the patents,
ecret processes, production know-how, and battle experience of each
United Nation are available to the armies and industries of its allies.

Control by United Nations Cooperation

Long strides have been made toward achieving the unified direction necessary to put the combined resources of the United Nations to most effective use. Combined agencies have been established by joint action of the United States and Great Britain to coordinate strategy and to map the production and distribution of munitions and raw materials. The members of these combined boards have been instructed to "confer with representatives of the Union of Soviet Socialist Republics, China and such other of the United Nations as are necessary to attain common purposes and provide for the most effective utilization of the joint resources of the United Nations." [1]

To date, the combined boards which have been created include the Combined Chiefs of Staff, the Munitions Assignments Board, the Combined Raw Materials Board, the Combined Shipping Adjustment Board, the Combined Production and Resources Board, and the Combined Food Board. These expert bodies are welding the American and British war efforts together. As part of their job, they exercise control over all lend-lease transfers. They plan for the production of materials to fill lend-lease needs, determine the quantities of finished and raw material available for immediate lend-lease transfer, fix their destination, and provide the necessary shipping. By shaping their plans to fit the needs of all United Nations, they are helping us to fight a world-wide war on a world-wide basis.

Combined Chiefs of Staff [2]

The Combined Chiefs of Staff is composed of the ranking staff officers of the various branches of the American and British armed forces. It meets in Washington to formulate the broad strategic plans to which the actions of the other combined agencies are adjusted. Production requirements, raw material allocations, munitions assignments, and ship routings are all related to its decisions.

Munitions Assignments Board [3]

With Russia and China locked in decisive struggles on their own soil, the principal United Nations in a position to export munitions are Great

---

[1] The quotation is from the joint announcement issued January 26, 1942, when the combined boards for munitions, raw materials and shipping were established. (See p. 248.)

[2] See p. 245.

[3] See p. 249.

Britain and the United States. To solve the technical and practical problems involved in distributing British and American munitions among all the United Nations, the Munitions Assignments Board was created on January 26, 1942. It has two coordinate branches, sitting in London and Washington, under the Combined Chiefs of Staff. Each branch is staffed by officers of the British and American armed forces, under the direction of a civilian chairman.

The Board operates upon the principle that the entire munition resources of Great Britain and the United States are considered as a common pool. As munitions are produced and ready for distribution in each country, the branch of the Board sitting in that country advises on their assignment to Great Britain, the United States, or one of the other United Nations in accordance with strategic needs. The American branch of the Board now assigns almost all munitions manufactured in this country and presently ready for distribution. Regardless of whether a given weapon was originally ordered for our own Army or Navy, for cash sale to another nation, or for transfer under lend-lease authority, its assignment is examined anew to meet the most urgent need existing at the time it rolls off the production lines.[1] As part of this same pooling policy, most of the munitions now being ordered are usually not earmarked in advance for particular forces. To facilitate final assignment, efforts have been made to integrate the requirements and specifications of other nations with our own, so that, where feasible, standard types of each weapon can be manufactured.

Assignments of finished munitions raise many complex strategic and technical problems. The needs of the forces of the nation producing the munitions must be appraised in terms of the uses to which those forces will be put, and weighed against the competing needs presented by the forces of other United Nations. After the basic decisions on such questions have been made in accordance with broad principles determined by the Combined Chiefs of Staff, they must be implemented by specific assignments of innumerable types of equipment. To handle this vast body of work, various groups of technical subcommittees have been organized. Thus, the branch of the Board in the United States has a special aircraft assignment committee under which there are subcommittees for aircraft, for aircraft ammunition and bombs, and for aviation petroleum products. Similar committees and subcommittees advise on assignments of land and naval items.

---

[1] Assignments to nations other than the United States are made within the limits of the authority granted by the Congress in the appropriation acts summarized in Appendix II [printed in more detail, p. 178].

Except for a substantial number of British and other dollar contracts on which deliveries are still being made with the approval of the Munitions Assignments Board, American munitions allocated to other nations are usually transferred under lend-lease authority. The actual assignments, however, are not made by the Office of Lend-Lease Administration, but by the military experts on the Munitions Assignments Board. A copy of each request for American munitions is submitted to the Lend-Lease Administration, which in appropriate cases will assist the applicant country to present its case to the Board. The Lend-Lease Administration also acts as the central recording agency for all lend-lease munitions transfers.

Combined Raw Materials Board [1]

The common war pool of the United Nations goes far beyond munitions. It also includes the raw materials from which munitions are made. Scarcities in many of these materials have been caused by military reverses which have shut off or curtailed sources of supply, by shortages of shipping space, and by the rapidly expanding requirements of war production.

To manufacture munitions, the United States must import many raw materials; Great Britain, nearly all of hers. To a considerable extent they have competing needs which must be filled from the same sources of supply. The entire war effort of the United Nations depends on the most efficient possible distribution, use, and expansion of these available raw material resources.

On January 26, 1942, the Combined Raw Materials Board was set up to achieve these results. It consists of an American member, representing the Chairman of the War Production Board, and a British member, representing the British Minister of Production. The Board allocates strategic raw materials controlled by the United States and Great Britain among the United Nations and collaborates with other countries to secure the maximum development and utilization of their raw material resources.

Complete allocations have been made on a world basis for such materials as tin, rubber, and manila fiber, of which the principal sources of supply were cut off by the war. Similar action has been taken on certain ferro-alloys, copper and other materials which have not been cut off, but which are in short supply because war requirements have outstripped available production. In addition, the Combined Board makes temporary allocations from time to time to meet urgent special

[1] See p. 248.

needs, as, for example, tin plate,for Great Britain, aluminum for the United States, and rubber for Russia.

Through the allocations made by the Board, the United States receives strategic materials under British control and provides Britain with materials under American control, while other United Nations share in the total supply on the basis of relative need in terms of the common war effort. Normal considerations of international commerce, finance, and foreign exchange are not permitted to interfere with fundamental war needs. In appropriate cases where dollars have been needed to purchase materials for the use of another United Nation, and are unavailable to it, lend-lease has been used to obtain the supplies to further the prosecution of the war.

The Combined Raw Materials Board performs other important functions. It has acted to increase the supply of strategic raw materials by recommending specific production projects in many parts of the world. It has promoted conservation of materials by changes in specifications, substitutions, and other means. Where present buying methods have been found to impede effective distribution, the Board has recommended changes. In collaboration with the Combined Shipping Adjustment Board and other agencies, it has also acted to secure more effective use of shipping and rail transport in order to speed the flow of materials and to bring strategic supplies out of war-threatened areas to safe destinations under emergency conditions.

Combined Shipping Adjustment Board [1]

The Combined Shipping Adjustment Board was created on January 26, 1942, in recognition of the principle that the shipping resources of the United States and Great Britain are a common pool, to be operated for the benefit of all the United Nations.

The Ministry of War Transport directly controls the movement of British shipping, while American vessels operate under orders from our War Shipping Administration. Norway, the Netherlands, and many other United Nations have contributed their many ships and sailors to the service of the common cause, for charter operation under Ministry of Transport or War Shipping Administration direction.

The Combined Shipping Adjustment Board integrates the work of these two agencies and the portions of the pool under their respective control. The Board has coordinate branches in London and Washington, each composed of a representative of the War Shipping Administration and a representative of the Ministry of War Transport.

[1] See p. 249.

The struggle to move materials in sufficient quantities to the places where they are most needed has assumed paramount importance. The job of the Combined Board is to see that the shipping of the United Nations is utilized in the most effective manner, by eliminating over-lapping and unnecessary duplication of services, and by exploring the possibilities of joint economies in the use of the two portions of the pool

With available cargoes in excess of available ships, loading and routing have become matters of strategic selection among conflicting needs. The ships which carry lend-lease goods are assigned by the Combined Board through the Ministry of War Transport and the War Shipping Adminis tration after appraisal of all competing needs. When American-controlled shipping is assigned to carry lend-lease cargoes, lend-lease funds are used to finance their operation, in order to prevent dollar exchange problems from impeding vital movements to the battle areas. Addi tional sums have been provided to service and supply the vessels of other United Nations which carry materials to and from our shores.

Combined Production and Resources Board [1]

One of the most recent additions to the machinery being developed for coordination of the United Nations war effort is the Combined Pro duction and Resources Board, which was established on June 9, 1942 by the United States and Great Britain.

The Combined Production and Resources Board consists of the Chairman of the War Production Board and the British Minister of Production. The Board is charged with responsibility for combining the war production programs of the United States and Great Britain in a single, integrated program which will meet the military requirement and essential civilian needs of the United Nations as a whole.

The Board will work in close collaboration with the Combined Chief of Staff and the Munitions Assignments Board in order to assure continu ous adjustment of the combined production program to munition requirements. It will keep the Combined Chiefs and Munitions Assign ments Board currently informed of all relevant factors and potentialities of war production, and they will keep the Board informed of changing military needs.

Planning for utilization of the combined resources of the two countries in such a way as to reduce demands on shipping space will be one of the Board's prime objectives.

[1] See p. 250.

Combined Food Board [1]

On the same day the Combined Production and Resources Board was established, the United States and Great Britain created a Combined Food Board "to obtain a planned and expeditious utilization of the food resources of the United Nations."

The Board will sit in Washington and be composed of the Secretary of Agriculture and the head of the British Food Mission. It will consider common problems concerning the supply, production, transportation, disposal, allocation or disposition of food and food-producing equipment throughout the world.

These are the principal agencies so far developed to carry out the principles of combined effort set forth in the Declaration by United Nations, and to govern the distribution of lend-lease aid. Additional agencies will be established to function in other fields when necessary.

LEND–LEASE AND THE PEACE

The lend-lease program has already become a prime mechanism in the combined efforts the United Nations are making to win the war. The program of lend-lease agreements is also emerging as a factor in the combined effort of the United Nations to weave a pattern for peace. Those agreements are taking shape as key instruments of national policy, the first of our concrete steps in the direction of affirmative post-war reconstruction.

The agreement with Great Britain was signed on February 23, 1942.[2] On June 2, 1942, an agreement was made with the Republic of China embodying the same terms.[3] On June 11, 1942, a similar agreement was signed with the Union of Soviet Socialist Republics.[4] The provisions of these agreements are now being offered to our other allies receiving lend-lease assistance.

These basic lend-lease agreements place the problem of the peacetime settlement in a realistic and appropriate setting. The agreements postpone final determination of the lend-lease account until "the extent of the defense aid is known and until the progress of events makes clearer the final terms and conditions and benefits which will be in the mutual interests" of the signatory nations, and which "will promote the establishment and maintenance of world peace." Final settlement has been postponed since the course of the war may further change the complexion of the issue.

[1] See p. 251.   [2] See p. 235.   [3] See p. 237.   [4] See p. 238.

We are now in the war, as we were not in March 1941 when the Lend-Lease Act was passed. We have pledged our resources without limit to win the war, and the peace which will follow it. We look forward to a period of security and liberty, in which men may freely pursue lives of their choice, and governments will achieve policies leading to full and useful production and employment. If the promise of the peace is to be fulfilled, a large volume of production and trade among nations must be restored and sustained. This trade must be solidly founded on stable exchange relationships and liberal principles of commerce. The lend-lease settlement will rest on a specific and detailed program for achieving these ends, which are, as Article VII of the agreements with Great Britain, China and Russia points out, "the material foundations of the liberty and welfare of all peoples."

Cooperative action among the United Nations is contemplated to fulfill this program for economic progress, in the many spheres where action is needed. It is hoped that plans will soon develop for a series of agreements and recommendations for legislation, in the fields of commercial policy, of money and finance, international investment and reconstruction.

Article VII of each of the basic agreements pledges that "the terms and conditions" of the final determination of the benefits to be provided the United States in return for aid furnished under the Act "shall be such as not to burden commerce between the two countries, but to promote mutually advantageous economic relations between them and the betterment of world-wide economic relations." By this provision we have affirmatively declared our intention to avoid the political and economic mistakes of international debt experience during the twenties.

A lend-lease settlement which fulfills this principle will be sound from the economic point of view. But it will have a greater merit. It will represent the only fair way to distribute the financial costs of war among the United Nations.

The real costs of the war cannot be measured, nor compared, nor paid for in money. They must and are being met in blood and toil. But the financial costs of the war can and should be met in a way which will serve the needs of lasting peace and mutual economic well-being.

All the United Nations are seeking maximum conversion to war production, in the light of their special resources. If each country devotes roughly the same fraction of its national production to the war, then the financial burden of war is distributed equally among the United Nations in accordance with their ability to pay. And although the nations richest in resources are able to make larger contributions, the

daim of war against each is relatively the same. Such a distribution of
he financial costs of war means that no nation will grow rich from the
var effort of its allies. The money costs of the war will fall according
o the rule of equality in sacrifice, as in effort.

2) *Agreements for Mutual Aid Pursuant to the Lend-Lease Act of March 11, 1941*

a) *Agreement between the United States and the United Kingdom, Signed at Washington, February 23, 1942* [1]

WHEREAS the Governments of the United States of America and the
United Kingdom of Great Britain and Northern Ireland declare that
they are engaged in a cooperative undertaking, together with every
other nation or people of like mind, to the end of laying the bases of a
just and enduring world peace securing order under law to themselves
and all nations;

AND WHEREAS the President of the United States of America has
determined, pursuant to the Act of Congress of March 11, 1941, that the
defense of the United Kingdom against aggression is vital to the defense
of the United States of America;

AND WHEREAS the United States of America has extended and is continuing to extend to the United Kingdom aid in resisting aggression;

AND WHEREAS it is expedient that the final determination of the terms
and conditions upon which the Government of the United Kingdom
receives such aid and of the benefits to be received by the United States
of America in return therefore should be deferred until the extent of the
defense aid is known and until the progress of events makes clearer the
final terms and conditions and benefits which will be in the mutual
interests of the United States of America and the United Kingdom and
will promote the establishment and maintenance of world peace;

AND WHEREAS the Governments of the United States of America and
the United Kingdom are mutually desirous of concluding now a preliminary agreement in regard to the provision of defense aid and in regard
to certain considerations which shall be taken into account in determining such terms and conditions and the making of such an agreement has
been in all respects duly authorized, and all acts, conditions and formalities which it may have been necessary to perform, fulfill or execute prior

---

[1] From the Office of the Secretary to the President; Department of State, *Bulletin*,
I, p. 190. The explanatory statement which, among other things, called particular
attention to Article VII is omitted here.

The agreement was signed by the Acting Secretary of State (Welles) and the
United Kingdom Ambassador (Halifax).

to the making of such an agreement in conformity with the laws either of the United States of America or of the United Kingdom have been performed, fulfilled or executed as required;

The undersigned, being duly authorized by their respective Government ments for that purpose, have agreed as follows:

ARTICLE I. The Government of the United States of America will continue to supply the Government of the United Kingdom with such defense articles, defense services, and defense information as the President shall authorize to be transferred or provided.

ARTICLE II. The Government of the United Kingdom will continue to contribute to the defense of the United States of America and the strengthening thereof and will provide such articles, services, facilities or information as it may be in a position to supply.

ARTICLE III. The Government of the United Kingdom will not without the consent of the President of the United States of America transfer title to, or possession of, any defense article or defense information transferred to it under the Act or permit the use thereof by anyone not an officer, employee, or agent of the Government of the United Kingdom.

ARTICLE IV. If, as a result of the transfer to the Government of the United Kingdom of any defense article or defense information, it becomes necessary for that Government to take any action or make any payment in order fully to protect any of the rights of a citizen of the United States of America who has patent rights in and to any such defense article or information, the Government of the United Kingdom will take such action or make such payment when requested to do so by the President of the United States of America.

ARTICLE V. The Government of the United Kingdom will return to the United States of America at the end of the present emergency as determined by the President, such defense articles transferred under this Agreement as shall not have been destroyed, lost or consumed and as shall be determined by the President to be useful in the defense of the United States of America or of the Western Hemisphere or to be otherwise of use to the United States of America.

ARTICLE VI. In the final determination of the benefits to be provided to the United States of America by the Government of the United Kingdom full cognizance shall be taken of all property, services, information, facilities, or other benefits or considerations provided by the Government of the United Kingdom subsequent to March 11, 1941, and accepted or acknowledged by the President on behalf of the United States of America.

ARTICLE VII. In the final determinaton of the benefits to be provided to the United States of America by the Government of the United Kingdom in return for aid furnished under the Act of Congress of March 11, 1941, the terms and conditions thereof shall be such as not to burden commerce between the two countries, but to promote mutually advantageous economic relations between them and the betterment of world-wide economic relations. To that end, they shall include provision for agreed action by the United States of America and the United Kingdom, open to participation by all other countries of like mind, directed to the expansion, by appropriate international and domestic measures, of production, employment, and the exchange and consumption of goods, which are the material foundations of the liberty and welfare of all peoples; to the elimination of all forms of discriminatory treatment in international commerce, and to the reduction of tariffs and other trade barriers; and, in general, to the attainment of all the economic objectives set forth in the Joint Declaration made on August 12, 1941, by the President of the United States of America and the Prime Minister of the United Kingdom.

At an early convenient date, conversations shall be begun between the two Governments with a view to determining, in the light of governing economic conditions, the best means of attaining the above-stated objectives by their own agreed action and of seeking the agreed action of other like-minded Governments.

ARTICLE VIII. This Agreement shall take effect as from this day's date. It shall continue in force until a date to be agreed upon by the two Governments.

Signed and sealed at Washington in duplicate this 23rd day of February, 1942.

b) *Agreement between the United States and China, Signed at Washington, June 2, 1942* [1]

"The provisions of the agreement with China are the same in all substantial respects as those of the agreement between the Governments of the United States and Great Britain signed on February 23, 1942." (Department of State Release.) [2]

The second paragraph of the preamble is new and reads as follows:

"AND WHEREAS the Governments of the United States of America and the Republic of China, as signatories of the Declaration by United Nations of January 1, 1942, have subscribed to a common program of purposes and

[1] Department of State, *Bulletin*, VI, p. 507.
[2] *Ibid.*

principles embodied in the Joint Declaration made on August 14, 1941 by th
President of the United States of America and the Prime Minister of th
United Kingdom of Great Britain and Northern Ireland, known as th
Atlantic Charter";

In Article VII the words "economic objectives identical with those set forth'
are used in place of "all the economic objectives set forth."

(c) Agreement between the United States and the Union of Sovie Socialist Republics, Signed at Washington, June 11, 1942 [1]

"The provisions of the agreement are the same in all substantial respects a
those of the agreement between the Governments of the United States and Grea
Britain signed on February 23, 1942 and the agreement between the Unite
States and China signed on June 2, 1942." [2]
The second paragraph of the preamble is similar to but not identical with th
second paragraph of the preamble of the Chinese agreement.   It reads as follows

"And whereas the Governments of the United States of America and th
Union of Soviet Socialist Republics, as signatories of the Declaration b
United Nations of January 1, 1942, have subscribed to a common prograr
of purposes and principles embodied in the Joint Declaration, known as th
Atlantic Charter, made on August 14, 1941 by the President of the Unite
States of America and the Prime Minister of the United Kingdom of Grea
Britain and Northern Ireland, the basic principles of which were adhered t
by the Government of the Union of Soviet Socialist Republics on Septembe
24, 1941";[3]

To the first paragraph of Article VII of the British agreement, *mutatis mutar
dis*, are added the following words:

". . . the basic principles of which were adhered to by the Governmer
of the Union of Soviet Socialist Republics on September 24, 1941."

(d) Agreement between the United States and Belgium, Signed Washington, June 16, 1942 [4]

"The provisions of the agreement are the same in all substantial respects a
those of the agreements between this Government and the Governments
Great Britain, China, and the Soviet Union." [5]
The preamble is the same as that of the agreement with China.
Article VII is the same, *mutatis mutandis*, as Article VII of the agreemer
with Great Britain.

[1] *Ibid.*, p. 531.
[2] *Ibid.*
[3] See p. 219.
[4] Department of State, *Bulletin*, VI, p. 551.
[5] *Ibid.*

B. Coordination of the War Effort

1. THE WASHINGTON CONFERENCES

There was set up, toward the end of World War I, a Supreme War Council which had the responsibility, subject to ratification by the Governments concerned, for over-all planning of the war effort of the Allied and Associated Powers. Thus far there has not been established any such agency for planning the war effort on a global scale. The nearest approach is the Pacific War Council in Washington which appears to have a comparable function in connection with the prosecution of the war against Japan. For the over-all planning of the European war effort, involving particularly the coordination of the activities of the United States, the United Kingdom and the Soviet Union, and the fitting together of the operations in the European and Pacific areas into the pattern of global warfare with which we are faced at the present time, reliance has been placed upon occasional conferences between political leaders or their representatives and more regularized contacts between administrative officials. The two Roosevelt-Churchill Conferences and the Roosevelt-Molotov Conference have been high points in this activity.

1) *Conference of the President of the United States (Roosevelt) and the Prime Minister of the United Kingdom (Churchill), Washington, December 22–28, 1941, January 1–[1], 1942*

The visit to Washington of the British Prime Minister was a milestone in the development of collaboration as it followed almost immediately upon the United States declarations of war against the Axis nations and thus set the pattern which was to be followed. The drafting and signing of the Joint Declaration by United Nations [2] by the representatives of 26 governments on January 1, 1942 was the principal immediate tangible result of the consultation. The consultation also prepared the way for the more complete coordination of the economic and military efforts of the two nations and their allies. During his visit the Prime Minister addressed both houses of Congress on December 26.[3]

a) *Conversations between the President (Roosevelt) and the Prime Minister of the United Kingdom (Churchill), Release of December 22, 1941* [4]

The British Prime Minister has arrived in the United States to discuss with the President all questions relevant to the concerted war effort. Mr. Churchill is accompanied by Lord Beaverbrook and a technical staff. Mr. Churchill is the guest of the President.

[1] Mr. Churchill arrived in London on January 17. It was announced that he had come by air, via Bermuda, where he stayed 20 hours, and that he had had a few days holiday in Florida before leaving the United States. (*The Bulletin of International News*, XIX, January 24, 1942, p. 71.)

[2] See p. 203.

[3] House Doc. 153, 77th Cong., 1st sess.; Department of State, *Bulletin*, V, p. 573.

[4] From the Office of the Secretary to the President; Department of State, *Bulletin*, , p. 573.

There is, of course, one primary objective in the conversations to be held during the next few days between the President and the British Prime Minister and the respective staffs of the two countries. That purpose is the defeat of Hitlerism throughout the world.

It should be remembered that many other nations are engaged today in this common task. Therefore, the present conferences in Washington should be regarded as preliminary to further conferences which will officially include Russia, China, the Netherlands, and the Dominions It is expected that there will thus be evolved an over-all unity in the conduct of the war. Other nations will be asked to participate to the best of their ability in the over-all objective.

It is probable that no further announcements will be made until the end of the present conferences, but it may be assumed that the other interested nations will be kept in close touch with this preliminary planning.

(b) Statement of the President (Roosevelt), December 27, 1941 [1]

Much has been accomplished this week through the medium of the many conferences held, in the meetings of the Supply and Production officials, in the sessions held by members of the military and naval groups and in the discussions with the chiefs of missions of all nations at war with the common enemy. Included were conferences with the Russian and Chinese Ambassadors, the Canadian Prime Minister, and the Netherlands Minister.

As a result of all of these meetings, I know tonight that the position of the United States and of all nations aligned with us has been strengthened immeasurably. We have advanced far along the road toward achievement of the ultimate objective — the crushing defeat of those forces that have attacked and made war upon us.

The conferences will continue for an indefinite period of time. It is impossible to say just now when they will terminate.

It is my purpose, as soon as it is possible, to give in so far as safety will permit — without giving information of military value to the enemy — a more detailed accounting of all that has taken place in Washington this week and of all that will take place during the remainder of the meetings.

The present over-all objective is the marshaling of all resources, military and economic, of the world-wide front opposing the Axis. Excellent progress along these lines is being made.

[1] From the Office of the Secretary to the President; Department of State, *Bulletin* V, p. 578. The statement was made after the British-American conferees had held their seventh meeting.

) Conference of the President of the United States (Roosevelt) and the Prime Minister of the United Kingdom (Churchill), June 19–26, 1942

The second conference was held at a time when the plight of the two principal ies of Great Britain and the United States was not an enviable one. Soviet ussia was being called upon to meet a general German offensive for the second me practically alone and naturally a cry was going up from that country for a cond front which would actually relieve the increasing German pressure. Ir. Molotov, the People's Commissar of Foreign Affairs of the U.S.S.R., had en in Washington about three weeks earlier for an important conference with e President during which the Russian point of view had been made known. e had stopped in London to confer with Mr. Churchill. At both capitals nportant agreements had been reached.[1] China, in spite of the fact that the nited States had been in the war for over six months, was worse off than when e entered as the result of the Japanese occupation of Burma and control of a ibstantial part of the Burma Road.

) Joint Statement of the President (Roosevelt) and the Prime Minister of the United Kingdom (Churchill), June 22, 1942 [1]

The President and the Prime Minister, assisted by high naval, military, nd air authorities, are continuing at Washington the series of conversa- ons and conferences which began on Friday last [June 19]. The object a view is the earliest maximum concentration of Allied war power upon ie enemy, and reviewing or, where necessary, further concerting all the leasures which have for sometime past been on foot to develop and istain the effort of the United Nations. It would naturally be impossible) give any account of the course of the discussions, and unofficial state- ients about them can be no more than surmise. Complete understand- ig and harmony exist between all concerned in facing the vast and grave isks which lie ahead. A number of outstanding points of detail which would have been difficult to settle by correspondence have been djusted by the technical officers after consultation with the President nd the Prime Minister.

) Release by the President (Roosevelt), June 27, 1942 [2]

The week of conferences between the President and the Prime Minister overed very fully all the major problems of the war which is conducted y the United Nations on every continent and in every sea.

We have taken full cognizance of our disadvantages as well as our dvantages. We do not underrate the task.

We have conducted our conferences with the full knowledge of the ower and resourcefulness of our enemies.

[1] Department of State, *Bulletin*, VI, p. 561.
[2] *Ibid.*

In the matter of the production of munitions of all kinds, the surve gives on the whole an optimistic picture. The previously planne monthly output has not reached the maximum but is fast approachi it on schedule.

Because of the wide extension of the war to all parts of the worl transportation of the fighting forces, together with the transportatio of munitions of war and supplies, still constitutes the major problem the United Nations.

While submarine warfare on the part of the Axis continues to tal heavy toll of cargo ships, the actual production of new tonnage is great increasing month by month. It is hoped that as a result of the ste planned at this conference the respective Navies will further reduce tl toll of merchant shipping.

The United Nations have never been in such hearty and detaile agreement on plans for winning the war as they are today.

We recognize and applaud the Russian resistance to the main attac being made by Germany, and we rejoice in the magnificent resistanc of the Chinese Army. Detailed discussions were held with our milita advisers on methods to be adopted against Japan and for the relief China.

While exact plans — for obvious reasons — cannot be disclosed, can be said that the coming operations which were discussed in detail our Washington conferences between ourselves and our respective mil tary advisers will divert German strength from the attack on Russia.

The Prime Minister and the President have met twice before: first August 1941 and again in December 1941. There is no doubt in the minds that the over-all picture is more favorable to victory than it w either in August or December of last year.

(3) *Conference of the President of the United States (Roosevelt) wit the People's Commissar of Foreign Affairs of the U.S.S.I (Molotov), May 29–June —,[1] 1942. Release from the Office the Secretary to the President, June 11, 1942* [2]

On June 11, the mutual-aid agreement between the Governments of tl United States and the U.S.S.R. was signed in Washington.[3] On June 22, on tl anniversary of the German attack upon Soviet Russia, the Secretary of Sta addressed to Mr. Molotov a message of congratulation and assurance on th successful resistance of the people of the Soviet Union.[4]

[1] Arrived in Moscow on June 13 after second visit to London.
[2] Department of State, *Bulletin*, VI, p. 531.
[3] See p. 238.
[4] Department of State, *Bulletin*, VI, p. 562.

The People's Commissar of Foreign Affairs of the Union of Soviet Socialist Republics, Mr. V. M. Molotov, following the invitation of the President of the United States of America, arrived in Washington on May 29 and was for some time the President's guest. This visit to Washington afforded an opportunity for a friendly exchange of views between the President and his advisers on the one hand and Mr. Molotov and his party on the other. Among those who participated in the conversations were: The Soviet Ambassador to the United States, Mr. Maxim Litvinoff; Mr. Harry Hopkins; the Chief of Staff, General George C. Marshall; and the Commander-in-Chief of the United States Fleet, Admiral Ernest J. King. Mr. Cordell Hull, Secretary of State, joined in subsequent conversations on non-military matters.

In the course of the conversations full understanding was reached with regard to the urgent tasks of creating a second front in Europe in 1942. In addition, the measures for increasing and speeding up the supplies of planes, tanks, and other kinds of war materials from the United States to the Soviet Union were discussed. Also discussed were the fundamental problems of cooperation of the Soviet Union and the United States in safeguarding peace and security to the freedom-loving peoples after the war. Both sides state with satisfaction the unity of their views on all these questions.

At the conclusion of the visit the President asked Mr. Molotov to inform Mr. Stalin on his behalf that he feels these conversations have been most useful in establishing a basis for fruitful and closer relations between the two Governments in the pursuit of the common objectives of the United Nations.

2. THE PACIFIC WAR COUNCIL

To advance further the purposes which President Roosevelt and Prime Minister Churchill had in mind in meeting in Washington in December 1941, so far as prosecution of the war with Japan was concerned, it was decided to establish a Pacific council. It was announced from London on February 9 that such a council, representing the British Commonwealth and the Netherlands, which would coordinate views on the war in the Pacific for transmission to the Anglo-American Chiefs of Staff in Washington, had been established. The announcement read as follows: [1]

"A Pacific Council has been set up on a ministerial plane. Australia, Great Britain, the Netherlands and New Zealand will each have representatives on the council. Other Ministers and advisers will attend as necessary."

This arrangement did not make provision for the representation of Canada and fell short of the desires of the Australian Government, which favored Washington as the seat of such a council.

[1] Communiqué from *New York Times* dispatch, February 10, 1942, p. 6.

On March 30, President Roosevelt announced through his secretary, Stephe
T. Early, that a Pacific War Council had been created, which would meet i
April with the following members: Mr. Roosevelt, representing the Unite
States; Dr. Herbert V. Evatt, the Foreign Minister of Australia; Walter Nasl
the Minister of New Zealand; Dr. T. V. Soong, the Foreign Minister of Chin.
Dr. Alexander Loudon, the Minister of the Netherlands; Hume Wrong, Cour
selor of the Canadian Legation, and Viscount Halifax, the British Ambassado

(1) Statement of the President (Roosevelt), March 30, 1942 [1]

It is imperative that all of the United Nations now actively engage
in the Pacific conflict consider together matters of policy relating to ou
joint war effort. An effective war can only be prosecuted with th
complete cooperation and understanding of all nations concerned. Th
new Council will be in intimate contact with a similar body in Londor

3. COMBINED WAR STAFFS AND UNIFIED COMMANDS

(1) Assignment of Commands in the Southwest Pacific Area. Ar nouncement of the President (Roosevelt), January 3, 1942 [2]

1. As a result of proposals put forward by the United States an
British Chiefs of Staff, and of their recommendations to President Roose
velt and to the Prime Minister, Mr.. Churchill, it is announced that, wit
the concurrence of the Netherlands Government and of the Dominio
Governments concerned, a system of unified command will be establishe
in the southwest Pacific area.

2. All the forces in this area — sea, land, and air — will operate unde
one Supreme Commander. At the suggestion of the President, in whic
all concerned have agreed, General Sir A. Wavell has been appointed t
this command.

3. Major General George H. Brett, Chief of the Air Corps of th
U. S. Army, will be appointed Deputy Supreme Commander. He
now in the Far East. Under the direction of General Wavell, Admir:
Thomas C. Hart, U. S. Navy, will assume command of all naval force
in the area. General Sir Henry Pownall will be Chief of Staff to Gener:
Wavell.

4. General Wavell will assume his command in the near future.

5. At the same time, His Excellency Generalissimo Chiang Kai-she
has accepted the Supreme Command over all land and air forces of th
United Nations which are now or may in the future be operating in th

[1] Oral announcement was made on March 20, 1942, of the 1st meeting of tl
Council and the President authorized this statement, printed in *New York Time*
March 31, 1942, p. 1.

[2] From the Office of the Secretary to the President; Department of State, *Bulleti*
VI, p. 4.

Chinese theater, including initially such portions of Indo-China and Thailand as may become available to troops of the United Nations. United States and British representatives will serve on his joint headquarters planning staff. _____

As a result of the Japanese occupation of Singapore and the Netherlands East Indies, a wedge was driven between the United Nations forces operating from Burma, India and China and the United Nations forces operating from Australia and the islands of the Pacific. The unified command of these forces seemed no longer feasible. General Wavell retained his position as Commander-in-Chief of the British forces in India.

Simultaneously with his arrival in Australia on March 17, the War Department announced that General Douglas MacArthur was to take over supreme command of the United Nations forces "in that region, including the Philippine Islands, in accordance with the request of the Australian Government." [1] According to President Roosevelt, General MacArthur was to be in command of everything, including sea and air forces, east of Singapore, in the Southwestern Pacific.[2] There still remained some uncertainty, however, as to the basis and scope of General MacArthur's authority. The situation was clarified by an announcement of April 19, 1942 from United States headquarters in Australia and a statement by Prime Minister John Curtin of Australia. The announcement from United States headquarters said that "by agreement among the Governments of Australia, the United Kingdom, the Netherlands and the United States the Southwest Pacific area has been constituted" with General MacArthur in command "by virtue of that authority." [3] In a letter to General MacArthur, Mr. Curtin said: "You have received a charter as Supreme Commander not from your own government alone, but also from the Governments of the United Kingdom, Australia, New Zealand and the Netherlands. At the request of a sovereign State you are being placed in Supreme Command of its Navy, Army and Air forces so that with those of your own great nation they may be welded into a homogeneous force and given that unified direction which is so vital for the achievement of victory." [4]

On April 21, it was announced from Washington that New Zealand was to be included in a new South Pacific command under an American naval officer receiving his orders from Admiral Chester W. Nimitz, Commander-in-Chief of the United States Pacific Fleet.[5]

2) Combined [6] Chiefs of Staff. Announcement of War Department, February 6, 1942 [7]

The "Combined Chiefs of Staff" group has been established by the United States and Great Britain to insure complete coordination of the

[1] *New York Times*, March 18, 1942, p. 1, 3.   [2] *Ibid.*
[3] *Ibid.*, April 20, 1942, p. 1, 3.   [4] *Ibid.*   [5] *Ibid.*, April 22, 1942, p. 1.
[6] The United Nations have agreed to use the term "combined" to denote collaboration between two or more of them, and to use the term "joint" to denote interservice collaboration of one nation. United Kingdom, Parliamentary Papers, *The Organization for Joint Planning*, Cmd. 6351.
[7] Release of War Department, Bureau of Public Relations, February 6, 1942; *New York Times*, February 7, 1942, p. 4.

war effort of these two nations, including the production and distributio
of their war supplies, and to provide for full British and American collal
oration with the United Nations now associated in prosecution of th
war against the Axis Powers. The Combined Chiefs of Staff, as repre
sentatives of the United States and British military and naval effor
have two principal subdivisions — one is of the United States Chiefs c
Staff. the other the British Chiefs of Staff.

United States membership of the Combined Chiefs of Staff consists o

    Admiral Harold R. Stark, Chief of Naval Operations
    General George C. Marshall, Chief of Staff, U. S. Army
    Admiral E. J. King, Commander-in-Chief, U. S. Fleet
    Lieutenant General H. H. Arnold, Chief of Army Air Forces

The British Chiefs of Staff are represented in Washington by:

    Field Marshal Sir John Dill (until recently Chief of Staff of
      the Imperial General Staff)
    Admiral Sir Charles Little
    Lieutenant General Sir Colville Wemyss
    Air Marshal A. T. Harris

They are in constant communication with Admiral Sir Dudley Poun
General Sir Alan Brooke, and Air Chief Marshal Sir Charles Portal, tl
British Chiefs of Staff in London.

Brigadier General W. B. Smith, formerly Secretary of the War Depar
ment General Staff, has been designated as United States Secretary
the Combined Chiefs of Staff and also as Secretary for the Joint Boa
and for many other boards and agencies established by the United Stat
War and Navy Departments to insure coordination and unity in maj
strategical direction and military operations. General Smith's sta
of assistants, initially about eight officers, will be selected from office
of the United States Army and United States Navy.

The British Secretary of the Combined Chiefs of Staff will be Brigadi
V. Dykes, who served for some years as the Secretary of the Committ
of Imperial Defense and War Cabinet in London. He will be assist
by officers of the British Navy, Army, and Royal Air Force.

While the action of the Combined Chiefs of Staff on broad strategic
questions will be in the form of joint recommendations to the heads
their respective governments, in minor and immediate matters relatir
to current operations they are prepared to take action without dela
The setup therefore amounts to a Combined Command Post for tl
conduct of all joint operations of the two governments in the war.
will be the control agency for planning and coordinating. In additio
it will provide a medium for adjusting such joint operations as invol

ther governments of the United Nations, such as China, the Nether-
nds East Indies, Australia, and New Zealand at the present moment.
'he representatives of these governments will participate with the
'ombined Chiefs of Staff in the consideration of matters concerning their
ational interests.

The organization described is being established in the Public Health
uilding on Constitution Avenue, directly opposite the War Department.

In addition, a most important factor in this setup will be the Munitions
ssignment Board, of which Mr. Harry Hopkins is the Chairman and
Iajor General James H. Burns the Executive, and which has its counter-
art in London, both with British and United States membership. The
roposals of these committees will be submitted to the Combined Chiefs
i Staff for their recommendation to the heads of their governments.

Mr. Hopkins' committee will also be established in the Public Health
uilding. In the same building will be representatives of the central
gency to allocate shipping and of the agency to allocate raw material.
ffices for other governments of the United Nations will be established
 the same building.

ɩ) Redesignation of War Plans Division as Operations Division and Definition of Duties. War Department Release, April 2, 1942 [1]

The War Department announces the redesignation of the War Plans
ivision of the General Staff as the Operations Division.

Major General Dwight D. Eisenhower, as Chief of Operations, heads
ɪe Division which is the controlling nerve center of the Army for all
. S. theaters of operations and overseas garrisons.

The situation of the United States in the present war presents a
ɪmewhat different problem from that of 1917–1918. With widely sep-
ʾated theaters of operations, and numerous overseas garrisons, and
ith the rapidity of movement and wide range of air units, the War
epartment is faced with the necessity not only of meeting responsi-
lities similar to those of the Department in the first World War, but
ɪo many of the problems of General Pershing's Headquarters at Chau-
ont and to a considerable extent those of General Harbord's S.O.S. at
ours, France. This situation was one of the compelling reasons for
e complete reorganization of the War Department and is responsible
r the development of an Operations Division in the General Staff.

This Division will also coordinate strategical and operational planning
ith the U. S. Navy, and with the Military Headquarters of all United

[1] War Department, Bureau of Public Relations, Press Branch.

Powers. In this connection, a further change is involved in the prese
arrangement whereby the strategical planning groups of the Army a
Navy have been merged and moved out of their respective Departmen
and set up under the U. S. Chiefs of Staff in the headquarters of t
Combined Chiefs of Staff. There they are in intimate touch with
similar planning group of British officers, — air, ground and naval, a
the representatives of the United Nations. In the same manner
Military-Naval intelligence group has been established.

4. JOINT AND COMBINED ECONOMIC BOARDS AND COMMITTEES

[See p. 436 for documents on United States–Canada Joint Committees.]

(1) *Executive Decision to Create Combined British-American Board* *January 26, 1942* [1]

To further coordination of the United Nations war effort, the Preside
and Prime Minister Churchill have set up three boards to deal wi
munition assignments, shipping adjustment, and raw materials. T
functions of these boards are outlined in the following statements.

Members of the boards will confer with representatives of the Uni
of Soviet Socialist Republics, China, and such other of the United Natio
as are necessary to attain common purposes and provide for the mo
effective utilization of the joint resources of the United Nations.

COMBINED RAW MATERIALS BOARD

A planned and expeditious utilization of the raw material resourc
of the United Nations is necessary in the prosecution of the war.
obtain such a utilization of our raw material resources in the most ef
cient and speediest possible manner, we hereby create the "Combin
Raw Materials Board."

This Board will:

(a) Be composed of a representative of the British Government a
a representative of the United States Government. The Briti
member will represent and act under the instruction of the Minist
of Supply. The Board shall have power to appoint the st
necessary to carry out its responsibilities.

[1] From the Office of the Secretary to the President; Department of State, *Bullet*
VI, p. 87. The text presented to the Parliament of the United Kingdom was entitl
United States No. 1 (1942), *Coordination of the Allied War Effort*, Cmd. 6332. T
texts here referred to as "statements" are there called "documents" and are giv
in this enumerated order: (*i*) Munitions Assignments Board; (*ii*) Combined Shippi
Adjustment Board; (*iii*) Combined Raw Materials Board.

(b) Plan the best and speediest development, expansion and use of the raw material resources, under the jurisdiction or control of the two Governments, and make the recommendations necessary to execute such plans. Such recommendations shall be carried out by all parts of the respective Governments.

(c) In collaboration with others of the United Nations work toward the best utilization of their raw material resources, and, in collaboration with the interested nation or nations, formulate plans and recommendations for the development, expansion, purchase, or other effective use of their raw materials.

MUNITIONS ASSIGNMENTS BOARD

1. The entire munition resources of Great Britain and the United States will be deemed to be in a common pool, about which the fullest information will be interchanged.

2. Committees will be formed in Washington and London under the Combined Chiefs of Staff in a manner similar to the South-West Pacific Agreement. These Committees will advise on all assignments both in quantity and priority, whether to Great Britain and the United States or other of the United Nations in accordance with strategic needs.

3. In order that these Committees may be fully apprised of the policy of their respective Governments, the President will nominate a civil Chairman who will preside over the Committee in Washington, and the Prime Minister of Great Britain will make a similar nomination in respect of the Committee in London. In each case the Committee will be assisted by a Secretariat capable of surveying every branch and keeping in touch with the work of every subcommittee as may be necessary.

4. The Civilian Chairman in Washington and London may invite representatives of the State Department, the Foreign Office or production ministries or agencies to attend meetings.

COMBINED SHIPPING ADJUSTMENT BOARD

1. In principle, the shipping resources of the two countries will be deemed to be pooled. The fullest information will be interchanged.

2. Owing to the military and physical facts of the situation around the British Isles, the entire movement of shipping now under the control of Great Britain will continue to be directed by the Ministry of War Transport.

3. Similarly, the appropriate Authority in the United States will continue to direct the movements and allocations of United States shipping, or shipping of other Powers under United States control.

4. In order to adjust and concert in one harmonious policy the work of the British Ministry of War Transport and the shipping authorities of the United States Government, there will be established forthwith in Washington a combined shipping adjustment board, consisting of a representative of the United States and a representative of the British Government, who will represent and act under the instructions of the British Minister of War Transport.

5. A similar adjustment board will be set up in London consisting of the Minister of War Transport and a representative of the United States Government.

6. In both cases the executive power will be exercised solely by the appropriate shipping agency in Washington and by the Minister of War Transport in London.

(2) *Combined Production and Resources Board. Memorandum of the President (Roosevelt) to the Chairman of the War Production Board (Nelson), Released June 9, 1942* [1]

Announcement of the creation of a Combined Production and Resources Board and a Combined Food Board was made by the President "on behalf of himself and the Prime Minister of Great Britain." [2]

In order to complete the organization needed for the most effective use of the combined resources of the United States and the United Kingdom for the prosecution of the war, there is hereby established a Combined Production and Resources Board.

1. The Board shall consist of the Chairman of the War Production Board, representing the United States, and the Minister of Production representing the United Kingdom.

2. The Board shall:

(a) Combine the production programs of the United States and the United Kingdom into a single integrated program, adjusted to the strategic requirements of the war, as indicated to the Board by the Combined Chiefs of Staff, and to all relevant production factors. In this connection, the Board shall take account of the need for maximum utilization of the productive resources available to the United States, the British Commonwealth of Nations, and the United Nations, the need to reduce demands on shipping to a minimum, and the essential needs of the civilian populations.

---

[1] Department of State, *Bulletin*, VI, p. 535.
[2] *Ibid.*

(b) In close collaboration with the Combined Chiefs of Staff, assure
the continuous adjustment of the combined production program to meet
changing military requirements.

3. To this end, the Combined Chiefs of Staff and the Combined
Munitions Assignments Board shall keep the Combined Production and
Resources Board currently informed concerning military requirements,
and the Combined Production and Resources Board shall keep the
Combined Chiefs of Staff and the Combined Munitions Assignments
Board currently informed concerning the facts and possibilities of
production.

4. To facilitate continuous operation, the members of the Board shall
each appoint a Deputy; and the Board shall form a combined staff.
The Board shall arrange for such conferences among United States and
United Kingdom personnel as it may from time to time deem necessary
or appropriate to study particular production needs; and utilize the
Joint War Production Staff in London, the Combined Raw Materials
Board, the Joint Aircraft Committee, and other existing combined or
national agencies for war production in such manner and to such extent
as it shall deem necessary.

3) *Combined Food Board. Memorandum of the President (Roosevelt)
to the Secretary of Agriculture (Wickard), Released June 9,
1942* [1]

By virtue of the authority vested in me by the Constitution and as
President of the United States, and acting jointly and in full accord with
the Prime Minister of Great Britain, I hereby authorize, on the part of
the Government of the United States, the creation of a joint Great
Britain–United States board to be known as the Combined Food Board.

In order to coordinate further the prosecution of the war effort by
obtaining a planned and expeditious utilization of the food resources
of the United Nations, there is hereby established a Combined Food
Board.

The Board will be composed of the Secretary of Agriculture and of the
Head of the British Food Mission who will represent and act under the
instruction of the Minister of Food.

The duties of the Board shall be:

To consider, investigate, enquire into, and formulate plans with regard
to any question in respect of which the Governments of the U.S.A. and
the U.K. have, or may have, a common concern, relating to the supply,

[1] *Ibid.*

production, transportation, disposal, allocation or distribution, in o:
to any part of the world, of foods, agricultural materials from which food;
are derived, and equipment and non-food materials ancillary to the
production of such foods and agricultural materials, and to make recom
mendations to the Governments of the U.S.A. and the U.K. in respec
of any such question.

To work in collaboration with others of the United Nations towar(
the best utilization of their food resources, and, in collaboration with the
interested nation or nations, to formulate plans and recommendation
for the development, expansion, purchase, or other effective use of thei
food resources.

The Board shall be entitled to receive from any Agency of the Govern
ment of the United States and any Department of the Government o
the United Kingdom, any information available to such Agency o
Department relating to any matter with regard to which the Board i
competent to make recommendations to those Governments, and ir
principle, the entire food resources of Great Britain and the Unitec
States will be deemed to be in a common pool, about which the fulles
information will be interchanged.

C. Relations between the U.S.S.R. and the United Kingdom

Following the German attack upon the Soviet Union June 22, 1941, Prim
Minister Churchill immediately announced that the British Government woul(
give all possible assistance to the people of the Soviet Union in their resistance t
Nazi aggression. This promise was made reciprocal by the treaty of July 12
1941. The unexpected strength of Russian resistance combined with the diver
sionary effect which the war on the Eastern Front had upon German bombin
operations in Great Britain contributed mightily to a more sympathetic attitud
on the part of the British people and their Government toward the Soviet Unio
and facilitated consultations and negotiations which led to the treaty of Ma;
26, 1942.

(1) *Agreement for Joint Action by His Majesty's Government in th United Kingdom and the Government of the Union of Sovie Socialist Republics in the War against Germany, July 12, 1941*

In force July 12, 1941–July 4, 1942

His Majesty's Government in the United Kingdom and the Govern
ment of the Union of Soviet Socialist Republics have concluded th
present Agreement and declare as follows: —

(1) The two Governments mutually undertake to render each othe
assistance and support of all kinds in the present war against Hitlerit
Germany.

[1] *Ibid.*, V, p. 240.

(2) They further undertake that during this war they will neither negotiate nor conclude an armistice or treaty of peace except by mutual agreement.

The present Agreement has been concluded in duplicate in the English and Russian languages.

Both texts have equal force.

Moscow,

> the twelfth of July, nineteen hundred and forty-one.

By authority of His Majesty's Government in the United Kingdom:

R. STAFFORD CRIPPS,

> *His Majesty's Ambassador Extraordinary and Plenipotentiary in*
> *the Union of Soviet Socialist Republics.*

By authority of the Government of the Union of Soviet Socialist Republics:

V. MOLOTOV,

> *The Deputy President of the Council of People's Commissars and*
> *People's Commissar for Foreign Affairs of the Union of Soviet*
> *Socialist Republics.*

a) Protocol to the Agreement for Joint Action by His Majesty's Government in the United Kingdom and the Government of the Union of Soviet Socialist Republics in the War against Germany, Concluded July 12, 1941 [1]

Upon the conclusion of the Agreement for Joint Action by His Majesty's Government in the United Kingdom and the Government of the Union of Soviet Socialist Republics in the War against Germany, the Contracting Parties have agreed that the aforesaid Agreement enters into force immediately upon signature and is not subject to ratification.

The present Protocol has been drawn up in duplicate in the English and Russian languages.

Both texts have equal force.

Moscow,

> the twelfth of July, nineteen hundred and forty-one.

[Signatures follow as given above.]

2) British-Soviet Consultation. Announcement of United Kingdom Foreign Office, December 28, 1941 [2]

In the second half of December 1941 there took place in Moscow between the President of the Council of People's Commissars, Joseph

[1] *Ibid.*   [2] *New York Times*, December 29, 1941, p. 5.

Stalin, and the People's Commissar for Foreign Affairs, V. M. Molotov on the one hand, and the British Secretary of State for Foreign Affairs Anthony Eden, on the other, an exhaustive exchange of views on questions relating to the conduct of the war and to post-war organization of peace and security in Europe.

The Soviet Ambassador in Great Britain, I. M. Maisky, and His Majesty's Ambassador in the U.S.S.R., Sir S. Cripps, were present at these conversations.

Further, some of the meetings were attended by the British Permanent Under-Secretary of State for Foreign Affairs, Sir A. Cadogan, and by the Vice Chief of the British Imperial General Staff, Lieut. Gen. Archibald Nye.

The conversations, which took place in a friendly atmosphere, showed an identity of views of both parties on all questions relating to the conduct of the war, and especially with regard to the necessity for the utter defeat of Hitlerite Germany and adoption of measures to render completely impossible any repetition of German aggression in the future

An exchange of views on questions relating to the post-war organization of peace and security provided much important and useful material which will facilitate future elaboration of concrete proposals on this subject.

Both parties are convinced that the Moscow conversations constitute a new important forward step toward closer collaboration between the U.S.S.R. and Great Britain.

(3) *Treaty of Alliance in the War against Hitlerite Germany and Her Associates in Europe and of Collaboration and Mutual Assistance Thereafter Concluded between the Union of Soviet Socialist Republics and the United Kingdom of Great Britain and Northern Ireland, Signed at London, May 26, 1942* [1]

In force July 4, 1942

His Majesty The King of Great Britain, Ireland, and the British Dominions beyond the Seas, Emperor of India, and the Presidium of the Supreme Council of the Union of Soviet Socialist Republics;

Desiring to confirm the stipulations of the Agreement between His Majesty's Government in the United Kingdom and the Government of

[1] United Kingdom, Parliamentary Papers, Russia No. 1 (1942). Cmd. 6368 London, H. M. Stationery Office, 1942. 7 p.
Ratification by Supreme Soviet of the U.S.S.R., June 19, 1942. (*Information Bulletin*, U.S.S.R.), Washington, June 20, 1942, No. 74, p. 1; on June 24, King George VI signed the instrument of ratification of the treaty (*Bulletin of International News* XIX, July 11, 1942, p. 629).

the Union of Soviet Socialist Republics for joint action in the war against Germany, signed at Moscow on the 12th July, 1941,[1] and to replace them by a formal treaty;

Desiring to contribute after the war to the maintenance of peace and to the prevention of further aggression by Germany of the States associated with her in acts of aggression in Europe;

Desiring, moreover, to give expression to their intention to collaborate closely with one another as well as with the other United Nations at the peace settlement and during the ensuing period of reconstruction on the basis of the principles enunciated in the declaration made on the 14th August, 1941 [2] by the President of the United States of America and the Prime Minister of Great Britain to which the Government of the Union of Soviet Socialist Republics has adhered;

Desiring, finally, to provide for mutual assistance in the event of an attack upon either High Contracting Party by Germany or any of the States associated with her in acts of aggression in Europe.

Have decided to conclude a treaty for that purpose and have appointed as their Plenipotentiaries: —

His Majesty The King of Great Britain, Ireland, and the British Dominions beyond the Seas, Emperor of India,

For the United Kingdom of Great Britain and Northern Ireland:

THE RIGHT HONORABLE ANTHONY EDEN, M.P., *His Majesty's Principal Secretary of State for Foreign Affairs;*

The Presidium of the Supreme Council of the Union of Soviet Socialist Republics:

M. VYACHESLAV MIKHAILOVICH MOLOTOV, *People's Commissar for Foreign Affairs,*

Who, having communicated their Full Powers, found in good and due form, have agreed as follows: —

PART I

ARTICLE I. In virtue of the alliance established between the United Kingdom and the Union of Soviet Socialist Republics the High Contracting Parties mutually undertake to afford one another military and other assistance and support of all kinds in the war against Germany and all those States which are associated with her in acts of aggression in Europe.

ARTICLE II. The High Contracting Parties undertake not to enter into any negotiations with the Hitlerite Government or any other Government in Germany that does not clearly renounce all aggressive intentions,

---

[1] See p. 252.
[2] See p. 209.

and not to negotiate or conclude except by mutual consent any armistice or peace treaty with Germany or any other State associated with her in acts of aggression in Europe.

PART II

ARTICLE III. (1) The High Contracting Parties declare their desire to unite with other like-minded States in adopting proposals for common action to preserve peace and resist aggression in the post-war period.

(2) Pending the adoption of such proposals, they will after the termination of hostilities take all the measures in their power to render impossible a repetition of aggression and violation of the peace by Germany or any of the States associated with her in acts of aggression in Europe.

ARTICLE IV. Should one of the High Contracting Parties during the post-war period become involved in hostilities with Germany or any of the States mentioned in Article III (2) in consequence of an attack by that State against that Party, the other High Contracting Party will at once give to the Contracting Party so involved in hostilities all the military and other support and assistance in his power.

This Article shall remain in force until the High Contracting Parties by mutual agreement, shall recognize that it is superseded by the adoption of the proposals contemplated in Article III (1). In default of the adoption of such proposals, it shall remain in force for a period of twenty years, and thereafter until terminated by either High Contracting Party as provided in Article VIII.

ARTICLE V. The High Contracting Parties, having regard to the interests of the security of each of them, agree to work together in close and friendly collaboration after the re-establishment of peace for the organization of security and economic prosperity in Europe. They will take into account the interests of the United Nations in these objects and they will act in accordance with the two principles of not seeking territorial aggrandizement for themselves and of non-interference in the internal affairs of other States.

ARTICLE VI. The High Contracting Parties agree to render one another all possible economic assistance after the war.

ARTICLE VII. Each High Contracting Party undertakes not to conclude any alliance and not to take part in any coalition directed against the other High Contracting Party.

ARTICLE VIII. The present Treaty is subject to ratification in the shortest possible time and the instruments of ratification shall be exchanged in Moscow as soon as possible.

It comes into force immediately on the exchange of the instruments of
ratification and shall thereupon replace the Agreement between the
Government of the Union of Soviet Socialist Republics and His Majesty's Government in the United Kingdom, signed at Moscow on the
12th July, 1941.

Part I of the present Treaty shall remain in force until the re-establishment of peace between the High Contracting Parties and Germany and
the Powers associated with her in acts of aggression in Europe.

Part II of the present Treaty shall remain in force for a period of
twenty years. Thereafter, unless twelve months' notice has been given
by either Party to terminate the Treaty at the end of the said period of
twenty years, it shall continue in force until twelve months after either
High Contracting Party shall have given notice to the other in writing
of his intention to terminate it.

IN WITNESS WHEREOF the above-named Plenipotentiaries have signed
the present Treaty and have affixed thereto their seals.

DONE in duplicate in London on the 26th day of May, 1942, in the
English and Russian languages, both texts being equally authentic.

(L.S.)   ANTHONY EDEN.   (L.S.)   V. MOLOTOV.

(a) Message from His Majesty (King George VI) to the Chairman of the Presidium of the Supreme Council of the U.S.S.R. (Kalinin), May 26, 1942

I cannot let this occasion pass without expressing to you, Mr. President, my gratification at the signature which has taken place this day of
our Treaty of Alliance.

This treaty consecrates the efforts of our two countries in the hard
and bitter struggle they are waging, and pledges them to wholehearted
cooperation and mutual support in the years that will follow our victory.

I like to believe that you, Mr. President, welcome it as sincerely as I
do myself, and that you share my confidence that its effect will be to the
benefit not only of our two countries but of all the world.

(b) Message in Reply from the Chairman of the Presidium of the Supreme Council of the U.S.S.R. (Kalinin) to His Majesty (King George VI)

I fully share the satisfaction expressed by Your Majesty at the signing of the Treaty of Alliance between our countries.

I am sure that the treaty now signed will consolidate yet further the
fighting Alliance of our countries in their stern and uncompromising

struggle against the common enemy and will ensure cordial cooperation and mutual assistance in the years following victory.

I welcome the treaty as sincerely as does Your Majesty, and express the conviction that this treaty will be of benefit not only to our two countries but to all the world.

(c) Speech by the Secretary of State for Foreign Affairs (Eden) on the Occasion of the Signature of the Treaty, May 26, 1942

On behalf of His Majesty's Government in the United Kingdom, I welcome you, M. Molotov, as Foreign Secretary of the Union of Soviet Socialist Republics.

We are met in a world at war, when our two countries are together at grips with the common enemy. Under the impact of war we have found that understanding which escaped us in the uneasy years of peace. The treaty which we have just signed engages us to continue the struggle together until the victory be won. On behalf of my colleagues I give you the pledge that there will be no wavering in this endeavor on the part of the Government or people of these islands.

Such, then, is the first chapter of our task, the overthrow of Hitler and the destruction of all that his regime stands for. But there is a second chapter also to our treaty. One day the war will end. One day the common enemy will be defeated and there will be peace again. We must see to it that this time peace endures. In the treaty which we have signed we pledge ourselves to work together for this purpose.

Never before in the history of our two countries has our association been so close, or our mutual pledge for the future so complete. This is surely a happy augury. There is nothing exclusive in our agreement. We are seeking peace and security not only for our two countries, but for all the United Nations. But understanding between us is one of the foundations of peace, not for us alone, but for the world. We have signed our treaty, and part of the work is behind us.

I would like to say now, M. Molotov, how much we have valued the statesmanship and insight which you have shown in our negotiations. I would like, too, to thank M. Maisky, your Ambassador, who has done so much in his years here to build a bridge between our two countries.

Part of the work is behind us. But the greater part yet lies ahead. There is the war to win. There is the peace to build. Neither of these tasks is for ourselves alone. You yourself, M. Molotov, are leaving our shores for the United States. Upon the cooperation of the Soviet Union, the United States of America and the British Commonwealth the future of mankind will largely depend. We thank you for your work with us here and we wish you well upon your journey.

(d) Speech by the People's Commissar for Foreign Affairs (Molotov), on the Occasion of the Signature of the Treaty, May 26, 1942

MR. CHURCHILL, GENTLEMEN:

The Treaty between the Union of Soviet Socialist Republics and Great Britain of alliance in the war against Hitlerite Germany and her accomplices in Europe, and of cooperation and mutual assistance after the war, which I have just had the honor to sign in the name of the Government of the U.S.S.R., represents an important political landmark in the development of relations between Great Britain and the Soviet Union. The treaty between us is essential not only to the peoples of the U.S.S.R. and Great Britain, but also to the peoples of other countries. Permit me to express my confidence that all peoples who have experienced the aggression of the German-Fascist Imperialists or whose freedom and honor have been threatened, and may still be threatened, by the Hitlerite band of robbers, oppressors and ravishers — all these will express their satisfaction at the conclusion of this historic treaty. Our allies all over the world will share with us the warmest feelings of satisfaction. Our treaty is indispensable in order the more quickly to ensure the destruction of Hitlerite Germany and to attain our desired aim — victory.

The present treaty also determines the common line of action of the Soviet Union and Great Britain after the war. The fact that this treaty operates for a period of twenty years, and is based on mutual military and economic assistance against possible further aggression on the part of Germany and is intended to ensure the security and economic well-being of the peoples of Europe, speaks for itself. Hitler and his accomplices in their blood-stained robbery in Europe will now feel more than ever that the united forces of their adversaries have been rallied and strengthened. So much the better for us, for our peoples, for our common cause.

This treaty signifies and contains much more than the Anglo-Soviet agreement of last year. The treaty of the 26th May, 1942, marks a new and important stage in the development of Anglo-Soviet relations on a basis of alliance and mutual military assistance against our common and irreconcilable foe, both of today and of the future, in Europe. It provides the desired basis for joint action after the war, thus greatly adding to its importance.

It is still further necessary to emphasize that what relates to the present day in this treaty is already successfully being realized and carried into effect. Such a treaty will be welcomed with great satisfaction by the masses of the Soviet Union, where, under the direction of their great Leader and Supreme Commander, J. V. Stalin, the Red Army is carrying on a heroic struggle against the German invaders, confident in the belief that the time is not far distant when our just cause will achieve full victory.

Please accept, Mr. Prime Minister Churchill and Mr. Secretary Eden to whom the present treaty owes so much, my sincere gratitude for the active part you have taken at all stages.

I express my sincere personal gratitude to His Majesty's Government for the hospitality shown to me as the representative of the Government of the U.S.S.R.

In conclusion I wish to express my firm conviction that the treaty which has been signed today well serves the cause of our victory, the cause of the great future of our two peoples.

D. Relations between the U.S.S.R. and Poland

(1) *Agreement between the Governments of Poland and the Union of Soviet Socialist Republics, London, July 30, 1941* [1]

Germany and the Soviet Union had signed a Treaty of Non-Aggression on August 23, 1939.[2] Following the successful German attack on Poland, the Soviet Government notified the Polish Ambassador on September 17 that the "Polish State and Government have virtually ceased to exist" and that "treaties concluded between the U.S.S.R. and Poland have thereby lost their value." [3] The Red Army thereupon proceeded to the occupation of a substantial part of Poland. On September 29 the Soviet Union concluded with Germany a treaty of friendship,[4] by which the territory of Poland was divided between them, and on October 10 the Soviet Union in a pact of mutual assistance with Lithuania transferred the city and district of Vilna to Lithuania, which in August 1940 became a member of the Union of Soviet Socialist Republics. On January 10 1941 a frontier treaty between Germany and the Soviet Union [6] defined the boundary between the two states. On June 22, 1941 German forces attacked the Soviet Union.

ARTICLE 1. The Government of the U.S.S.R. recognizes the Soviet-German treaties of 1939 as to territorial changes in Poland as having lost their validity. The Polish Government declares Poland is not bound by any agreement with any third power which is directed against the U.S.S.R.

---

[1] Embassy of the Union of Soviet Socialist Republics, Washington, D. C., *Information Bulletin*, No. 123, December 6, 1941, p. C.

[2] *Documents, II, 1939–40*, p. 334.

[3] *Ibid.*, p. 361.

[4] *The Bulletin of International News*, XVI, October 7, 1939, p. 1041.

[5] *Ibid.*, p. 1130.

[6] *Documents, III, 1940–41*, p. 346.

ARTICLE 2. Diplomatic relations will be restored between the two Governments upon the signing of this agreement, and an immediate exchange of Ambassadors will be arranged.

ARTICLE 3. The two Governments mutually agree to render one to another aid and support of all kinds in the present war against Hitlerite Germany.

ARTICLE 4. The Government of the U.S.S.R. expresses its consent to the formation on territory of the U.S.S.R. of a Polish Army under a commander appointed by the Polish Government in agreement with the Soviet Government, the Polish Army on territory of the U.S.S.R. being subordinated in an operational sense to the Supreme Command of the U.S.S.R., in which the Polish Army will be represented. All details as to command, organization and employment of this force will be settled in a subsequent agreement.

ARTICLE 5. This agreement will come into force immediately upon signature and without ratification. The present agreement is drawn up in two copies, in the Russian and Polish languages. Both texts have equal force.

The Soviet Government grants amnesty to all Polish citizens now detained on Soviet territory either as prisoners of war or on other sufficient grounds, as from the resumption of diplomatic relations.

(a) Communiqué of the Polish Embassy, Washington, August 16, 1941 [1]

As a result of the Polish-Soviet agreement recently signed in London by virtue of which diplomatic relations between Poland and the U.S.S.R. have been resumed, the Polish Ambassador in Washington today called officially on the Soviet Ambassador, thereby re-establishing relations between the two countries.

(2) Joint Declaration of Friendship and Mutual Aid by the Polish Premier (Sikorski) and the President of Council of People's Commissars (Stalin), Moscow, December 4, 1941 [2]

The Government of the Soviet Union and the Government of the Polish Republic, imbued with a spirit of friendly concord and fighting collaboration, declare:

1. German Hitlerite imperialism is the worst enemy of mankind — no compromise with it is possible. Both States jointly with Great Britain and other Allies and with the support of the United States of America, will wage war until complete victory and the final destruction of the German invaders.

[1] New York Times, August 17, 1941, p. 21.
[2] The Inter-Allied Review, I, No. 10, January 15, 1942, p. 19.

2. Implementing the treaty concluded July 30, 1941,[1] both Governments will render each other during the war full military assistance, and the troops of the Polish Republic located in territory of the Soviet Union will wage war against the German bandits hand in hand with the Soviet troops. In peace time their relations will be based on good neighborly collaboration, friendship, and mutual honest observance of the undertakings they have assumed.

3. After the victorious war and appropriate punishment of the Hitlerite criminals, it will be the task of the Allied States to ensure a durable and just peace. This can be achieved only through a new organization of international relations on the basis of unification of the democratic countries in a durable alliance. Respect for international law backed by the collective armed force of all the Allied States, must form the decisive factor in the creation of such an organization. Only under this condition can a Europe destroyed by the German barbarians be restored and can a guarantee be created that the disaster caused by the Hitlerites will never be repeated.

> Signed: By authorization of the Government
> of the Soviet Union — STALIN.
> For the Government of the Polish
> Republic — SIKORSKI.

4. IMPLEMENTATION OF PRINCIPLES: POST–WAR RECONSTRUCTION

A. Inter-Allied Meeting, London, September 24, 1941

Representatives of 14 Governments engaged in the war against Germany and Italy adopted a resolution of solidarity at a meeting in London, June 12, 1941 (*Documents, III, 1940–41*, p. 444–7). The same Governments and those of India, Burma and the Soviet Union met at London, September 24, 1941 [2] and adopted two resolutions, one declaring adherence to the Atlantic Charter (see p. 219) and the other providing for post-war collaboration in reprovisioning of the occupied territories.

(1) *Statement of the Secretary of State for Foreign Affairs of the United Kingdom (Eden) in Introducing a Resolution Providing for Collaboration in Meeting Post-War Needs, September 24, 1941* [3]

The second resolution which I have to put before you today deals with the practical steps which must be taken in order to provide for the

[1] See p. 269.

[2] The proceedings were printed in United Kingdom, Parliamentary Papers, Miscellaneous No. 3 (1941), *Inter-Allied Meeting Held in London at St. James's Palace on September 24, 1941; Report of Proceedings.* Cmd. 6315, and in *The Inter-Allied Review* I, No. 9, October 15, 1941.

[3] United Kingdom, Parliamentary Papers, Miscellaneous No. 3 (1941), Cmd. 6315, p. 18.

upply of necessities to the occupied territories as soon as the German
ppressors have been removed.

Speaking at the Mansion House on May 29, I observed that as long
go as August of last year the Prime Minister emphasized the importance
f building up reserves of food all over the world, so that the peoples of
Europe might have the present certainty of its speedy entry into their
ountries immediately the Nazi power was shattered. The Prime Min-
ster's statement has been developed by the Minister without Portfolio,
who has declared on more than one occasion that when we have freed the
peoples of Europe, we must be in a position to help to feed and clothe
hem and to restart the wheels of industry. Looking forward to a Europe
berated from fear and from want, I have also observed that in the
ransition from war to peace an initial pool of resources will be needed;
nd that it is the duty of all free countries to organize such a pool in good
ime and to create the channels through which, when the moment comes,
s flow to Europe may be directed.

It is to organize in good time the action required to give effect to this
olicy that His Majesty's Government in the United Kingdom has
nvited the Allied Governments and authorities to meet here today. In
his, as in so much else, we may confidently hope that the great nation
cross the Atlantic, as well as other friendly nations, will in due course
nd their cooperation. But it is our direct responsibility. I invite you
ow to consider how best to advance our common aim.

As most of the representatives here today are aware, some preliminary
ork has already been done. There is already established a Ministerial
ommittee on Export Surpluses, of which the Minister without Portfolio
Chairman, and a committee of British Government officials under the
hairmanship of Sir Frederick Leith-Ross, chief economic adviser to
is Majesty's Government in the United Kingdom. So far these
ommittees have in the main been concerned with the arrangement of
urchases, mostly within the British Empire, of commodities which, as
result of the war and of the wartime exigencies of shipping, have
ecome surplus to current demand. Such purchases have been on a
ubstantial scale and cover a fairly wide range of goods. They have been
ade primarily for the immediate purpose of stabilizing the economics
f the territories concerned, but we have been mindful also of their value
s a potential relief store for the European peoples, who are at present
eing systematically denuded of their resources by a ruthless enemy.
he two committees which I have named have therefore also started
nquiries as to probable European needs. Only a beginning has been
ade. For true estimates of such needs the Governments of the countries

concerned must of course be the authorities; so, also, it will be for then
to consider at the appropriate time how far they may wish to draw upon
any stocks which are being acquired and held by the Governments of th
British Empire. Certain of the Allied Governments have also alread;
taken action with the immediate post-war relief of their peoples in view
and have been in touch with Sir Frederick in regard to their plans. Th
Netherlands Government, following the announcement some months ag
of Her Majesty Queen Wilhelmina, has taken positive measures to buil
up a relief store for their country. The Polish and Belgian Government
have prepared preliminary memoranda on the estimated requirement
of their countries in the immediate post-war period, and the Norwegia
and Czechoslovak Governments have informed us that they are puttin;
in hand the preparation of corresponding memoranda.

His Majesty's Government welcomes this spirit of initiative sinc
we recognize that it is primarily the function of each Government an
authority to be responsible for the reprovisioning and rehabilitation o
its country. Our concern today is to agree to the first necessary steps t
insure that the initiatives severally taken shall so far as possible b
brought into accord with a common plan for the general good. Hov
shall we set about it? What practical program of action are we to devise
There are four principal features of such a program: At the outset
comprehensive survey must be made of probable requirements in th
order of their urgency, and data must be collected regarding potentiall
available supplies. A broad scheme of long distance transport must b
planned well in advance. Gradually reserve stocks must be organize
in the most convenient places. In due course the administration an
finance of their transfer to Europe and of their further distribution mus
be arranged.

The framing and coordination of estimates of probable requirement
is the first task. It is not easy to assess what may be the more and th
less urgent needs of individual countries in the unpredictable circum
stances of their release from enemy domination. But some estimate
must be made, and they can later be revised in the light of changin
circumstances. Such estimates must take account of the urgent needs i
the first weeks after the Nazi yoke is lifted from the destitute people
for whose relief supplies will have to be rushed to Europe; they mus
further take account of the probable demands of European countries fc
supplies from overseas in order to restore their economies to workin
order during a period of reorganization, which is likely to last at lea;
two years after the war. It is only if the interested governments an
authorities maintain continuous contact with one another through

central bureau that estimates can be coordinated and a practical working approach made to a survey of the needs of all on a common basis. This is the ground from which springs the proposal in the resolution for the establishment of a bureau which will report to an Inter-Allied Committee under the chairmanship of Sir Frederick.

The importance of estimates prepared by the bureau is clear when we consider the need to plan ahead the possibilities for moving goods from overseas. Shipping will be the crux of the physical problem of transfer; and a broadly unified scheme will have to be prepared if delay and congestion are to be avoided, and if no one country is to be prejudiced for lack of adequate facilities. His Majesty's Government in the United Kingdom will in this regard contribute all that is within their power. Other Allied Governments will wish, I am certain, to contribute to the extent of their shipping resources. And the ship-building yards of the United States will not, as we know, have been idle. Once again coordination is vital. Quantities of goods from particular sources must be related to quantities of tonnage and particular shipping routes; a balance must be maintained between supplies from nearer and from more distant sources as deliveries proceed. The British Ministry of War Transport has already been considering what shipping might be available. In this connection of course not much can be done until the estimates of requirements have been made. We can, however, express our common intention to arrange that our merchant fleets shall be utilized as fully as possible for the relief and reconstruction of the countries of Europe when they are liberated. This intention is expressed in the resolution before you.

It is too early, before the steps are taken which I have mentioned, to raise the large question of the organization of reserve stocks. But there will fortunately be little difficulty in most cases about the existence of the supplies required. Stocks of certain essential foodstuffs and basic materials are even now accumulating in those parts of the world not directly ravaged by war. Some, as I have said, have been acquired by the Governments of the British Commonwealth, by the Allied Governments, and by other producing countries; and large quantities remain in the hands of private producers and merchants. The yield of the season 1941–1942, added to present stores, will secure that in such cases the granaries and warehouses shall be full. In other cases the demands from the stricken countries will be so great that it will tax the resources of the world to organize sufficient supplies for relief purposes. In such cases, clearly most careful coordination of purchasing and distribution will have to be effected. These, however, are matters for subsequent consideration by the interested governments and authorities. It will be to their mutual advantage to consult with one another in maturing their plans, and a suitable organization for this purpose can be set up as and when required.

There remain, finally, complex problems of finance and administration in connection with the actual transfer of supplies for the relief and reconstruction of Europe. We can leave these problems for the present; they arise only at a later stage of our efforts. It is proposed that we shall start with first things first; namely, an agreed declaration on shipping policy, the establishment of a bureau to survey requirements, and of an Inter-Allied Committee to deal with the proposals of the bureau. By this means effective collaboration amongst ourselves will be assured.

Such collaboration alone, however, will not be enough. It is obvious that the satisfaction of the post-war needs of Europe will also depend upon the cooperation of the great primary producing countries overseas. We have therefore already approached the Governments of the Dominions and of the United States of America and informed them of our immediate plans and of our hopes. The presence here today of the Dominion representatives, and the association of the Dominion Governments with the resolution, is substantial proof that we can count upon the invaluable help of these Governments.

As regards the United States of America, I am sure that all those present will share my great satisfaction at the encouragement we have already received at this stage from the United States Government, who through their Ambassador has authorized me to make the following statement at the meeting on their behalf:

[Here follows the statement printed separately at p. 269.]

I have, of course, been very happy to give the United States Ambassador an assurance that the United States Government will be kept fully informed of the discussions at and arising out of this meeting and of the work accomplished by the bureau and the Inter-Allied Committee, and that they will be consulted before any concrete plans are decided upon. We have also previously had some contact with the United States Government in regard to the treatment of surplus production and we know that they are deeply interested in planning for the coordination of stocks and marketing of some of the most important commodities especially wheat and cotton.

The statement which they have authorized me to make on their behalf shows that they will not be unwilling at the right time to join in framing the plans for the supply of Europe's needs on a basis of cooperation. It is clear that some joint marketing arrangements will be required both from the point of view of producers and consumers. Wasteful and costly competition in acquiring stocks and the violent price movements which would result from such competition should be avoided, and nothing must be allowed to prevent a fair allocation of supplies reaching the countries which may most need them but be least able to compete for them.

I now propose to put before you, for your approval, a resolution to serve as the starting point for that concerted action without which we cannot hope to bridge the gap between war and a lasting peace. We do not propose to play the grim game of "beggar my neighbor." Our declared purpose is to insure that with freedom there will come succor, at the earliest possible moment, to the distressed peoples of Europe.

No one can know when this war will end, and we should make our preparations in good time. The measures which we take now, measures which we make known that we have taken, may bring some encouragement to the millions in Europe whose present sufferings we cannot prevent, and give them strength of heart to endure, and, where they can, to resist.

(2) Resolution Providing for Collaboration in Post-War Economic Needs, London, Adopted September 24, 1941 [1]

The Governments of the United Kingdom of Great Britain and Northern Ireland, Canada, the Commonwealth of Australia, New Zealand and the Union of South Africa, the Governments of Belgium, Czechoslovakia, Greece, Luxemburg, the Netherlands, Norway, Poland, the Union of Soviet Socialist Republics and Yugoslavia, and the representatives of General de Gaulle, leader of Free Frenchmen, agree:

1. That it is their common aim to secure that supplies of food, raw materials, and articles of prime necessity should be made available for the post-war needs of the countries liberated from Nazi oppression.

2. That while each of the Allied Governments and authorities will be primarily responsible for making provision for the economic needs of its own peoples, their respective plans should be coordinated, in a spirit of inter-allied collaboration, for the successful achievement of the common aim.

3. That they welcome the preparatory measures which have already been undertaken for this purpose and express their readiness to collabo-

[1] United Kingdom, Parliamentary Papers, Miscellaneous No. 3 (1941), Cmd. 6315, p. 17; *The Inter-Allied Review*, I, No. 9, October 15, 1941, p. 1.

rate to the fullest extent of their power in pursuing the action required.[1]

4. That accordingly, each of the Allied Governments and authorities should prepare estimates of the kinds and amounts of foodstuffs, raw materials, and articles of prime necessity required and indicate the order of priority in which it would desire supplies to be delivered.

5. That the reprovisioning of Europe will require the most efficient employment after the war of the shipping resources controlled by each Government and of allied resources as a whole, as well as of those belonging to other European countries, and that plans to this end should be worked out as soon as possible between the Allied Governments and authorities in consultation, as and when appropriate, with other Governments concerned.[2]

6. That, as a first step a bureau should be established by His Majesty's Government in the United Kingdom with which the Allied Governments and authorities would collaborate in framing estimates of their requirements and which, after collating and coordinating these estimates would present proposals to committee of allied representatives under the chairmanship of Sir Frederick Leith-Ross.

(a) *Scope of the Resolution. Concluding Remarks of the Secretary of State for Foreign Affairs of the United Kingdom (Eden) September 24, 1941* [3]

One or two points have been raised which I should like to deal with:
First, the Netherlands representative has made the point that his Government understand this resolution not to exclude action by individual Governments to help their own peoples.[4] I entirely agree and I wish to make it clear

[1] From statement of Major Arne Sunde, Norwegian Minister of Supply: "It is now perfectly clear to us that this point does not imply any responsibility of the Norwegian Government for decisions taken previously and without consultation with them. We can therefore give our assent also to point 3 of the draft resolution."

[2] From statement of Major Arne Sunde, Norwegian Minister of Supply: "The Norwegian Government attach great importance to point 5, which regards shipping We hope that in this respect we shall have the opportunity of making a considerable contribution and are therefore particularly interested in taking our share of the direction of, and the responsibility for, this part of the work." (Miscellaneous No. (1941), Cmd. 6315, p. 27.)

[3] *Ibid.*, p. 31.

[4] The Netherlands Foreign Minister (Van Kleffens) said: "The Netherlands Government gladly adopt the resolution on the understanding that nothing therein will be deemed to preclude them from carrying out, under their own responsibility, the arrangements made by them for provisional relief of the Netherlands at the end of hostilities." (*Ibid.*, p. 26.)

that our idea is that responsibility rests in the first place with the individual Governments to help their own people. But we shall also do our best to help one another.

Secondly, the Soviet representative has made certain reservations regarding Article 6 of the resolution.[1] I think that the point he raised can be fully met.

Under Article 6 it is proposed to set up not only a bureau but also a committee of inter-allied representatives. It is not intended that there should be anything sacrosanct about the bureau.

We thought that the time had come, particularly in view of the helpful statement made by the United States Government, to get down to practical work; and this would be the first task of the bureau.

But there is no reason why exchanges should not take place after this meeting between the Allied Governments concerning the composition of the bureau, or the modification and extension of its functions if these are desired. His Majesty's Government's main wish is that both the bureau and the Inter-Allied Committee shall enable the views of the Allied Governments to be fully represented, and any proposals for alteration in the machinery can readily be discussed.

I can only repeat that it is my belief that this work, much of the burden of which will fall upon Sir Frederick Leith-Ross, will be an important first step towards post-war reconstruction. This first meeting for this purpose will be followed by other meetings as and when necessary, and meanwhile a body will be set up to work for a better Europe after the war.

3) *Proffer of Cooperation by the United States. Statement of the United States Ambassador at London (Winant), September 24, 1941* [2]

The Government of the United States has been advised of the purpose of this meeting and acquainted with the terms of the draft note which has been distributed and of the draft resolution which is to be presented for consideration. It has requested my Government to state to this meeting its opinion that the undertaking is of great prospective usefulness. It understands that the present discussions will be of an explora-

---

[1] The Ambassador of the U.S.S.R. in London (Maisky) made the following formal statement:

"The Soviet Government has no objection to the principle dealt with in paragraph 5, but it considers it very important that the central bureau, which is envisaged there, should have an inter-allied character and, for this purpose, should be built on the basis of equal representation of all the Governments concerned. The Soviet Government, with this aim in view, also believes that the best way to proceed in this matter would be to submit all the questions concerning the structure, scope of activities, forms and methods of work, etc., of this bureau for preliminary consideration to the Allied Governments so that a final decision on this point can be approved of at the next Inter-Allied Conference.

"As a consequence the Soviet Government is not able to accept paragraph 6 in its present form and reserves its right to put forward at a later date certain proposals in this connection." (*Ibid.*, p. 29.)

[2] *Ibid.*, p. 22; Department of State, *Bulletin*, V, p. 235.

tory nature and states that it stands ready at the appropriate time to consider in what respects it can cooperate in accomplishing the aims in view.

It has pointed out that any plans that may be worked out are of great potential interest to the United States for various reasons. They might affect the current American defense effort. According to their substance form, and method they might also affect commercial policies and relation ships and even broader post-war arrangements. For these reasons it makes the request that it be kept fully advised regarding the course of these exploratory discussions and that it be consulted regarding any plans that might emerge therefrom.

B. Central and Eastern European Planning Board

The delegations of Czechoslovakia, Greece, Poland and Yugoslavia to the session of the International Labor Conference at New York in a resolution of November 5, 1941 declared the intention of their Governments to cooperat closely in preparing for post-war reconstruction. In furtherance of this declaration of purpose, the four delegations established on January 7, 1942, the Central and Eastern European Planning Board.

(1) *Joint Declaration by the Government, Employers' and Workers Delegations of Czechoslovakia, Greece, Yugoslavia and Poland to the International Labor Conference, New York City, November 5, 1941* [1]

The Government, Employers' and Workers' delegations of the Central European and Balkan countries represented at the International Labor Conference, having met and jointly reviewed the situation, have unanimously adopted the following declaration:

1. With feelings of indescribable sadness, we pay a tribute to our tormented peoples, to their unconquerable spirit, their courage and the magnitude of their sacrifices. We proclaim the solidarity of our countries in the common struggle for freedom.

2. We protest before the civilized world against the innumerable and unprecedented atrocities that are being daily committed by the invader and their satellites. For the sole crime of remaining loyal to their country, thousands of men, women and children are subjected to the tortures of the concentration camps or are executed. The invader respects neither the laws of God nor the rights of man. We do particularly protest against the barbarous practice of taking hostages and executing them.

[1] *The Inter-Allied Review*, I, No. 10, November 15, 1941, p. 1.

We send a fraternal greeting to the other oppressed nations of Europe. We pay tribute to the great and valiant peoples of the British Empire, of the Soviet Union, and to the great American nation. Our most sympathetic thoughts go also to the people of China.

3. We solemnly assure our peoples that the struggle for their liberation, carried on jointly with the world's great democracies, shall be continued untiringly until the day of victory.

4. In pursuing this struggle we count on the help and wholehearted support of all the free nations, and above all of their organized working people. The duration of the war depends very largely on the extent to which these nations, and especially their workers, show a spirit of sacrifice.

5. The countries of Central Europe and the Balkans reaffirm their profound devotion to the democratic principle and express their solidarity with the great democracies.

6. We express the firm conviction that the peace that will follow victory will bring to our peoples, as well as to all peoples throughout the world, enjoyment of the four freedoms defined in the Roosevelt-Churchill declaration.

We hope that the end of this war, which was forced upon us, will save hundred million inhabitants of Central Europe and of the Balkans from their present state of wretchedness by assuring them the possibility of stable employment, guaranteed by reconstruction and by the development of their industries, agriculture and that those peoples will be included within the sphere of international exchanges of goods and services. Special attention goes to the masses of the peasant population and to their social and economic standards, because it is on those elements that peace and security in that region depend. It is in this spirit that our present joint declaration has been conceived, and it is in this same spirit of frank and friendly collaboration that we conceive the part to be played by our countries in the reconstruction of a new Europe, enjoying a stable peace, with freedom and prosperity.

2) *Joint Declaration of the General Steering Committee, January 14, 1942* [1]

Our nations have suffered most during this war. The tyrannical order of Nazi Germany and satellites has tried with all possible means to enslave, politically and economically, the peoples of our states.

This war is a war of the forces of Fascism and Nazism against the

[1] *Ibid.,* II, No. 3, March 15, 1942, p. 42–3.

order and the principles of Democracy. We expect that the peace that will come will definitely do away with those forces of backwardness and darkness and secure to our nations, as well as to all the nations of the world, economic and social security and lasting international peace.

Our Allies' governments are working not only to win the war but also to win the peace. Both tasks are to be achieved in full cooperation and in harmony with all free nations.

The aims of our struggle and the outlines of our friendship were given in the Atlantic Charter, and the Joint Declaration of the Twenty-six United Nations in Washington.

To prepare a better world the International Labor Conference held in New York unanimously accepted the resolution submitted by the U.S.A. delegation, i.e., government's, employers' and workers' delegates.

According to this resolution the International Labor Office shall organize a committee for post-war reconstruction.

The four Central and Eastern European states, Czecholslovakia, Greece, Poland and Yugoslavia, in connection with the U.S.A. resolution declared at this conference, on November 5, 1941, the intention of the closest cooperation in the struggle for freedom and in preparing post-war reconstruction.

To further this aim, the four delegations established on January 7, 1942, the Central and Eastern European Planning Board.[1]

We agree on the essential need of close collaboration among people and governments of the small nations of Central and Eastern Europe while war is still being fought, and later, after peace comes back to the world. The East European region has its own problems and those must be handled and solved by mutual consent and friendly collaboration of the respective nations. Doing so they believe that the democratic world of today and tomorrow will be enriched by a new sincere effort and by a constructive experiment in the way of the building of a better order.

The cooperation of all these nations constitutes a step towards the establishment of a future world order based on mutual friendship.

It is in that spirit that the idea of the Central and Eastern European Planning Board was conceived, and it is in that spirit that its founders want to see it work for the benefit of their peoples, their part of the world, and all democratic peoples.

Furthermore, we want to stress the unshaken belief in the victory of the cause of the United Nations, which is the cause of justice, decency and respect for the rights of individuals and nations, large and small alike. We also want to give expression to the special feelings of sympathy

[1] See also *Documents and Reports* issued by the Board. (New York.)

oward the United States, Great Britain, the Soviet Union, and China, or their part in this struggle of today.

C. Polish-Czechoslovak Confederation

1) *Agreement for a Polish-Czechoslovak Confederation, London, January 23, 1942* [1]

In execution of the declaration of the Governments of Poland and Czechoslovakia of November 11, 1940, whereby both Governments decided that after the war Poland and Czechoslovakia shall form a confederation of States in that area of Europe with which the vital interests of the two countries are bound, the Governments of Poland and Czechoslovakia conducted uninterrupted negotiations on the subject of the method of bringing the above declaration to fruition. Both Governments reached agreement with regard to a number of principles of the projected Confederation, which were defined in the following declaration adopted during the current week:

The Governments of Poland and Czechoslovakia have agreed on the following points with regard to the future confederation of Poland and Czechoslovakia: —

1. The two Governments desire that the Polish-Czechoslovak Confederation should embrace other States of the European area with which the vital interests of Poland and Czechoslovakia are linked up. [2]

2. The purpose of the Confederation is to assure common policy with regard to foreign affairs; defenses; economic and financial matters; social questions; transport, posts, and telegraphs.

3. The Confederation will have a common general staff, whose task it will be to prepare the means of defense, while in the event of war a unified supreme command will be appointed.

4. The Confederation will coordinate the policy of foreign trade and custom tariffs of the States forming the Confederation with a view to the conclusion of a customs union.

MONETARY POLICY

5. The Confederation will have an agreed monetary policy. Autonomous banks of issue of the States forming the Confederation will be

[1] *The Inter-Allied Review*, II, No. 2, February 15, 1942, p. 26.

[2] According to an official communiqué issued on November 11, 1941, the Confederation "is to be a nucleus of the political and economic organization of that European region, in the security and development of which both Poland and Czechoslovakia are interested, and therefore, the Confederation is to constitute one of the indispensable elements of the new, democratic order in Europe. *Ibid.*, II, No. 1, January 15, 1942, p. 8.

maintained. It will be their task to assure that the parity established be
tween the various national currencies shall be permanently maintained

6. The Confederation will coordinate the financial policies of th
States forming the Confederation, especially with regard to taxation

7. The development and administration of railway, road, water, an
air transport, as also of the telecommunication services will be carrie
out according to a common plan. An identical tariff for postal and tele
communication services will be binding on all the territories of th
Confederation. The States in possession of sea and inland harbors wi
take into consideration the economic interests of the Confederation as
whole. Moreover, the States forming the Confederation will mutuall
support the interests of the sea and inland harbors of the States formin
the Confederation.

8. Coordination will also be applied in the realm of social policy of th
various States of the Confederation.

9. The Confederation will assure cooperation among its members i
educational and cultural matters.

10. Questions of nationality will remain within the competence of th
individual States forming the Confederation. The passenger traffi
between the various States included in the Confederation will take plac
without any restrictions, in particular without passports and visas. Th
question of free domicile and of the right to exercise any gainful occu
pation of the citizens of the individual States forming the Confederatio
over the whole territory of the Confederation will be regulated.

11. The question of the mutual recognition by the States forming th
Confederation of school and professional diplomas, of documents an
sentences of court, as well as the question of mutual legal aid, in particu
lar in the execution of court sentences, will be regulated.

12. The constitutions of the individual States included in the Con
federation will guarantee to the citizens of these States the followin
rights: — Freedom of conscience; personal freedom; freedom of learning
freedom of the spoken and written word; freedom of organization an
association; equality of all citizens before the law; free admission of a
citizens to the performance of all State functions; the independence o
the courts of law; and the control of government by representativ
national bodies elected by means of free elections.

13. Both Governments have agreed that in order to ensure the com
mon policy with regard to the above-mentioned spheres, the establish
ment of common organs of the Confederation will be necessary.

14. The States included in the Confederation will jointly defray th
costs of its maintenance.

2) *Joint Communiqué of the Czechoslovak and Polish Governments-in-Exile, London, June 12, 1942* [1]

While attaching greatest importance to the general international rganization of all democratic and peace-loving nations from a point of iew of both the security and prosperity of Europe, the Governments Poland and Czechoslavakia consider, however, the confederation of oland and Czechoslavakia to be a primary and fundamental aim of ieir foreign policy during and after the war. This, in the opinion of the vo Governments, should serve as a basis for regional organization of aat part of Europe with which the vital interests of their countries are ound. The two Governments, abiding by their common decisions of ovember 11th, 1940, and January 19th, 1942, and being desirous of beeding up preparatory work in this respect, have instructed the zechoslovak Polish Coordination Committee to convoke four mixed ommissions: economic, military, social, and cultural. It will be the ity of these commissions to study the principles and methods of economic, military, cultural and social organization of confederation.

D. Balkan Union

) *Agreement Concerning the Constitution of a Balkan Union between Greece and Yugoslavia, London, January 15, 1942* [2]

Having observed that past experience, and more particularly recent periences, which have demonstrated that a lack of close understanding tween the Balkan peoples has caused them to be exploited by the owers of aggression in their aim toward political and military penetion and domination of the peninsula, and considering that in order to sure the independence and peace of the Balkan states the fundamental inciples of their policy must be the principle of "The Balkans for the alkan peoples,"

His Majesty, the King of the Hellenes, and His Majesty, the King of ugoslavia, have decided to conclude the present Agreement concerning e Constitution of a Balkan Union and to that effect have named their enipotentiaries:

His Majesty, the King of the Hellenes, has named His Excellency, nmanuel Tsouderos, President of the Council of Ministers and Minis- r of Foreign Affairs, and His Excellency, Charalampos Simopoulos, avoy Extraordinary and Minister Plenipotentiary and Permanent ider-Secretary of State for Foreign Affairs;

[1] *Ibid.*, II, No. 6, June 15, 1942, p. 118.
[2] *Ibid.*, p. 25.

His Majesty, the King of Yugoslavia, has named His Excellency Professor Slobodan Jovanovic, President of the Council of Ministers and Minister of the Interior, and His Excellency, Momcilo Nincic, Minister of Foreign Affairs.

After receiving the communications of their plenary powers, which were found to be drawn up in good and due form, these Ministers have agreed to the following dispositions:

Chapter One: Organs of the Union

Article I.   The Organs of the Union which will meet at regular intervals are:

1. A Political Organ constituted by the Ministers for Foreign Affairs and
2. An Economic and Financial Organ constituted by two members of each government who will be competent in economic and financial matters.

Article II.   The Permanent Military Organ. This Organ, wherein the Governments will be represented by their Chiefs or by their Representatives will constitute at the side of the National General Staffs a Common General Staff of the National Armies. This Organ will comprise two bureaus, one for the Army and Aviation and the other for the Navy.

Article III.   A Permanent Bureau will comprise three sections

A. Political.

B. Economic and Financial.

C. Military.

Article IV.   The Presidents of the Councils of Ministers of the States composing the Union will meet whenever circumstances require, in order to discuss questions of a general order of interest to the Union

Article V.   Collaboration between Parliaments. The governments of the Union will facilitate regular meetings between parliamentary delegations of the States of the Union, allowing these delegations to proceed to exchanges of views and of expressions of their wishes in the form of questions of common interest which would be submitted to them by competent organs.

Chapter Two: Business of the Organs of the Union

Article VI.   (1) The task of the political organ will be:

A. To coordinate the foreign policy of the members with a view to enabling the Union to act in a uniform manner on an international plane and to proceed with preliminary consultation at all times when the vital exterior interests of the members of the Union should be menaced.

B. To prepare projects for agreements of conciliation and arbitration between the members of the Union. The political Organ will undertake the constitution of the following Organizations:

    a. A Commission charged with the elaboration of agreements of intellectual cooperation between members of the Union and with the supervision of their application.

    b. A Commission charged with the coordination of the efforts of the Organs of the members in view of the reciprocal rapprochement of public opinion in States which are members of the Union, and of the defense of their interests.

ARTICLE VII. (2) The task of the Economic and Financial Organ ill be:

A. To coordinate the policies of exterior commerce and customs tariffs with a view to the conclusion of a customs union.

B. An elaborate common economic plan for members of the Union.

C. To constitute by means of special organs all means which will permit the amelioration of communications between members of the Union (railways, roads, navigation by sea, air and river, posts and telegraph), as well as tourist development within the Union.

D. To prepare a draft of an Agreement instituting a Balkan monetary union.

ARTICLE VIII. (3) The task of the Military Organ will be to coordinate activities concerning collaboration of the international organs of the members of the Union, adoption of a common plan of defense and a common type of armament, etc. The mission of the armed forces of the Union will be to defend the European frontiers of the States of the Union.

ARTICLE IX. (4) The permanent bureau will form a secretariat of the different organs of the Union and its task will be:

A. To prepare material for the labors of the Organs of the Union.

B. To study all questions the solution of which may render more efficacious the political, economic, financial and military cooperation of the members of the Union.

C. To supervise the application of the decisions of the Organs of the Union.

CHAPTER THREE

ARTICLE X. The High Contracting Parties declare that this agreement presents the general foundations for the organization of a Balkan

Union. They consider themselves bound by the foregoing disposition from the date of exchange of the instruments of ratification, and they envisage with satisfaction the future adhesion to this agreement of other Balkan states ruled by governments freely and legally constituted.

ARTICLE XI. The present Agreement will be ratified, and the ratifications will be exchanged, as soon as this is possible.

IN WITNESS WHEREOF, the representative plenipotentiaries have hereto placed their signatures and their seals.

DONE in London in duplicate, the original in French, on the 15th day of January, one thousand nine-hundred and forty-two.

[Here follow signatures.]

CHAPTER V

THE WESTERN HEMISPHERE

1. INTER-AMERICAN RELATIONS

. Third Meeting of the Ministers of Foreign Affairs of the American
Republics, Rio de Janeiro, Brazil, January 15–28, 1942

[For the two preceding meetings see *Documents, II, 1939–40*, p. 99 and *III, 1940–
*, p. 63. The third meeting, convened on the initiative of the United States, was
e first not held at the capital of the proposing Government.]

**) *Request for Consultation by the Government of the United States
to the Governments of All American Republics, December 9, 1941*** [1]

The American Republics, at the Inter-American Conferences held in
uenos Aires, Lima, Panama, and Havana have jointly recognized that
threat to the peace, security, or territorial integrity of any American
epublic is of common concern to all.

In the Fifteenth Resolution adopted by the American Republics at the
onsultative Meeting held in Havana in July of 1940, and entitled
Reciprocal Assistance and Cooperation for the Defense of the Nations
the Americas," the American Republics declared that "any attempt
n the part of a non-American state against the integrity or inviolability
the territory, the sovereignty, or the political independence of an
merican state shall be considered as an act of aggression against the
ates which signed this declaration," and further declared that in case
ch acts of aggression are committed against an American state by a
on-American nation "the nations signatory to the present declaration
ill consult among themselves in order to agree upon the measures it
ay be advisable to take."

[1] Department of State, *Bulletin*, V, p. 484.
The proposal was made to the Governing Board of the Pan American Union on
ecember 10. The request was presented in accordance with Resolution XV (*Docu-
ents, III, 1940–41*, p. 76) adopted by the Second Meeting of the Ministers of
aggression are committed, the American Republics will consult among themselves
order to agree upon the measures it may be advisable to take and pursuant to the
ocedure for invoking a consultation established by Resolution XVII (*ibid.*, p. 77)
dopted at the same meeting.

On December 7, 1941, without warning or notice, and during the course of negotiations entered into in good faith by the Government of the United States for the purpose of maintaining peace, territory of the United States was treacherously attacked by armed forces of the Japanese Empire.

The course of events since the outbreak of war in Europe in 1939 clearly demonstrates that the fate of every free and peace-loving nation of the world hinges upon the outcome of the present struggle against the ruthless efforts of certain powers, including the Japanese Empire to dominate the entire earth by the sword.

The wave of aggression has now broken upon the shores of the New World.

In this situation that menaces the peace, the security and the future independence of the Western Hemisphere, a consultation of the Minister of Foreign Affairs appears to be of urgent desirability.

Therefore, in conformity with the procedure on consultation approved by the Second Meeting of Foreign Ministers at Havana, the Government of the United States is informing the Governing Board of the Pan American Union of its desire to hold a consultative meeting at the earliest possible moment.

In as much as the procedure agreed upon in Havana provides that the Governing Board of the Pan American Union shall not only transmit the request for consultation but, on the basis of the answer received determine the date of the meeting, prepare the agenda, and adopt all other measures advisable for the preparation of the meeting, it is hoped that each country will appropriately instruct its diplomatic representatives in Washington in the premises.

(2) *Address of the Under Secretary of State (Welles), January 15, 1942*
[Excerpt]

The Under Secretary of State was the first delegate of the United States and the chairman of the Inter-American Financial and Economic Advisory Committee. His address began with a review of events since 1936 in which he dwelt upon the "black reversion to barbarism" confronting the American Republics in the purposes of Hitler and Japan.

The security of the three hundred millions of people who inhabit the Western Hemisphere and the independence of each of the countries here represented will be determined by whether the American nations stand together in this hour of peril, or whether they stand apart one from the other.

. . . .

[1] Department of State, *Bulletin*, VI, p. 55, 59.

The United States is now in the war. Our industrial production, the greatest in the world, is fast mounting towards the maximum. During the coming year we will produce some 60,000 airplanes, including 45,000 military airplanes, some 45,000 tanks, some 300 new combatant ships, from the mightiest battleships to coastal patrol craft, and some 600 new merchant ships. We will attain a rate of 70,000 per year in the training of combat airplane pilots. We have drafted for military service all of our men between the ages of 20 and 44 years, and of this great total we will soon have an initial army of three million men fully trained and fully equipped. We will spend 50 billions of dollars, or half of our total national income, in the year thereafter in order to secure the use of every ounce of our national resources in our war effort. Every weapon that we produce will be used wherever it is determined that it may be of the most service in the common cause, whether that be here in the Western Hemisphere, on the deserts of Libya, on the steppes of Russia, or in the territory of the brave people of China.

Those of us who have joined in this holy war face a ruthless and barbarous foe. The road before us will be hard and perhaps long. We will meet unquestionably with serious reverses from time to time. But the tide has turned and will run swiftly and ever more swiftly until it ends in the flood of victory.

As each one of you knows, my Government has made no suggestion, and no request, as to the course which any of the governments of the other American Republics should pursue subsequent to the Japanese attack upon the United States, and the declaration of war upon it by the other Axis Powers.

We do not function in that way in the American family of nations.

But may I assure you from my heart today that the spontaneous declaration of war upon the enemies of mankind of nine of the other American Republics; the severance of all relations with Germany, Italy, and Japan by Mexico, Colombia, and Venezuela; and the official declarations of solidarity and support by all of the other American Republics, including our traditional and unfailing friend, in evil days as well as good, the great Republic of Brazil, whose guests we all are today, represents to my Government and to my fellow citizens a measure of support, of strength, and of spiritual encouragement which no words of mine would be adequate to express.

May I merely say that these acts of faith in our common destiny, so generously realized, will never be forgotten by the people of the United States. They have heartened us all. They have made us all, all the more anxious to be worthy, not in words but in deeds, of your confidence.

They have made us all the more desirous of showing our gratitude through the extent of the cooperative strength which we can furnish to insure the ultimate triumph of the cause to which we are dedicated.

Each one of the American governments has determined, and will continue to determine, in its own wisdom, the course which it will pursue to the best interest of its people in this world struggle. But of one thing I feel sure we are all convinced. In accordance with the obligations we have all undertaken under the provisions of our inter-American agreements and in accordance with the spirit of that continental solidarity unanimously proclaimed, those nations of the Americas which are not engaged in war will never permit their territory to be used by agents of the Axis Powers in order that these may conspire against, or prepare attacks upon, those republics which are fighting for their own liberties and for those of the entire continent.

We all of us are fully aware of the record of the activities of Axis agents in our several countries which the past two years have brought to light. We know how the Axis diplomatic representatives, taking advantage of the immunity which international custom has granted them for their legitimate functions, have been doing their utmost to poison inter-American relations; to create internal discord; and to engender domestic strife, so as to try and pave the way for subversive movements financed with funds obtained through extortion from residents in our midst, or transferred from the loot they have procured in the occupied countries of Europe. We know that their so-called consular officials have in reality been the directing heads of espionage rings in every part of this hemisphere. The full history of this record will some day be published in full detail, when the divulging of this information will no longer be of assistance to the enemy.

So long as this hemisphere remained out of the war all of our governments dealt with this ever-increasing danger in the manner which they believed most effective, exchanging intelligence one with the other, as existing agreements between them provide, whenever such exchange was mutually helpful.

But today the situation has changed. Ten of the American Republics are at war and three others have severed all relations with the Axis Powers. The continued presence of these Axis agents within the Western Hemisphere constitutes a direct danger to the national defense of the republics engaged in war. There is not a Japanese nor a German consul nor a consul of Hitler's satellite countries, in the New World at this moment who is not reporting to his superiors every time a ship leaves the ports of the country where he is stationed, for the purpose of having

hat ship sunk by an Axis submarine. There is not a diplomatic representative of the Axis Powers anywhere in the Americas who is not seeking
o get for his masters information regarding the defense preparations of
he American nations now at war; who is not conspiring against the
nternal security of every one of us; who is not doing his utmost, through
very means available to him, to hinder our capacity to insure the
ntegrity of our freedom and our independence.

Surely this danger must be of paramount concern to all of us. The
reeminent issue presented is solely that those republics engaged in war
hall not be dealt a deadly thrust by the agents of the Axis ensconced
pon the soil and enjoying the hospitality of others of the American
Republics.

The shibboleth of classic neutrality in its narrow sense can, in this
ragic modern world, no longer be the ideal of any freedom-loving people
f the Americas.

There can no longer be any real neutrality as between the powers of
vil and the forces that are struggling to preserve the rights and the
ndependence of free peoples.

It is far better for any people to strive gloriously to safeguard its
ndependence; it is far better for any people to die, if need be, in the
attle to save its liberties, than by clinging to the tattered fiction of an
lusory neutrality, to succeed only by so doing in committing suicide.

Our devotion to the common cause of defending the New World
gainst aggression does not imply necessarily engagement in war. But
 does imply, I confidently believe, the taking of all measures of cooper-
tion between us which redound to the great objective of keeping the
mericas free.

Of equal importance with measures of political solidarity, defense
operation, and the repression of subversive activity are economic
easures related to the conduct of war against the aggressor nations and
e defense of the Western Hemisphere.

All of the American Republics have already taken some form of
easures breaking off financial and commercial intercourse between
em and the non-American aggressor states and to eliminate other alien
onomic activities prejudicial to the welfare of the American Republics.

It is of the utmost importance that these measures be expanded in
der that they may prevent all business, financial, and trade transac-
ns between the Western Hemisphere and the aggressor states, and
 transactions within the Western Hemisphere which directly or
directly redound to the benefit of the aggressor nations or are in any
y inimical to the defense of the hemisphere.

The conduct of war and the defense of the hemisphere will require a
ever-increasing production of the implements of war and an ever
increasing supply of the basic and strategic materials necessary fo
their production. The spread of the war has cut off many of the mos
important sources of strategic materials, and it is essential that th
American Republics conserve their stocks of such commodities and, b
every possible means, encourage the production and the free flow withi
the hemisphere of the greatest possible quantity of these materials.

The universal character of the war is placing increasing demands upo
the merchant-shipping facilities of all of us. The increased production c
strategic materials will be of no avail unless adequate transportation ca
be provided, and it is consequently of vital importance that all of th
shipping facilities of the Americas be mobilized to this essential en

The Government of the United States is prepared to cooperate whole
heartedly with the other American Republics in handling the problem
arising out of these economic warfare measures. It stands prepared t
render financial and technical assistance, where needed, to alleviat
injury to the domestic economy of any of the American Republics whic
results from the control and curbing of alien economic activities inimic
to our common defense.

It is ready to enter into broad arrangements for the acquisition c
supplies of basic and strategic materials, and to cooperate with each c
the other American Republics in order to increase rapidly and efficientl
their production for emergency needs. Finally, it stands ready throug
the United States Maritime Commission to render every assistance i
the efficient operation of merchant vessels in accordance with the pla
of August 28, 1941, of the Inter-American Financial and Economi
Advisory Committee.[1]

My Government is also fully aware of the important role whic
imported materials and articles play in the maintenance of the economi
of your nations. On December 5, 1941, I advised the Inter-America
Financial and Economic Advisory Committee in Washington that th
United States was making every effort consistent with the defen
program to maintain a flow to the other American Republics of materia
to satisfy the minimum essential import requirements of your economie
I added that the policy of my Government was being interpreted by a
of the appropriate agencies as calling for recognition of and provision f
the essential needs of the American Republics equal to the treatme
accorded United States civilian needs.

The attack by Japan and the declarations of war by the other membe

[1] See p. 403.

f the Tripartite Pact have resulted in greater and unprecedented demands upon our production facilities. But I am able to state today, as did on the 5th of December, that the policy of the United States toward he satisfaction of your essential requirements remains firm.

On December 26, 1941, after the outbreak of war, the Board of Economic Warfare of my Government resolved unanimously:

It is the policy of the Government of the United States to aid in maintaining he economic stability of the other American Republics by recognizing and providing for their essential civilian needs on the basis of equal and proportionate consideration with our own.

Pursuant to this declaration of policy our allocation of 218,600 tons of in-plate for your needs during this year has been followed by further llocations, which I am privileged to announce today. The Office of Production Management has advised me that allocations[1] have been made to you for the next quarter in amounts adequate to meet your needs for rayon; for twenty essential agricultural and industrial chemicals, including copper sulphate, ammonium sulphate, soda ash, and caustic soda; for farm equipment; and for iron and steel products.

In addition, I am able to announce that a special mechanism has been organized within the Office of Production Management which is now facilitating the clearance of your individual priority applications.

In the light of this action, it seems appropriate to recognize that the arsenal of democracy continues mindful of its hemisphere responsibilities.

I am confident that your people will join the people of the United States, who are sharing their civilian supplies with you, in recognizing that military and other defense needs must continue to be given precedence over civilian demands.

All of these economic measures relate directly to the conduct of war, the defense of the hemisphere, and the maintenance of the economies of our several nations during the war emergency. Obviously our greatest efforts must be extended towards victory. Nevertheless, the full consummation of victory must include the building of an economic and social order in which all of our citizens may subsequently enjoy the blessings of peace.

My Government believes that we must begin now to execute plans, vital to the human defense of the hemisphere, for the improvement of health and sanitary conditions, the provision and maintenance of adequate supplies of food, milk, and water, and the effective control of insect-borne and other communicable diseases. The United States is

---

[1] See p. 389.

prepared to participate in and to encourage complementary agreement among the American Republics for dealing with these problems of healt and sanitation by provision, according to the abilities of the countrie involved, of funds, raw materials, and services.

The responsibility with which we are all charged requires that we pla for broad economic and social development, for increased production c the necessities of the world, and for their equitable distribution amon the people.

If this economic rehabilitation of the world is to take place it is indis pensable that there be a resurgence of international trade — interna tional trade, as was declared by the Second Meeting of Ministers c Foreign Affairs at Havana, "conducted with peaceful motives and base upon equality of treatment and fair and equitable practices."

I urge upon you all the imperative need for unity between us, nc only in the measures which must presently be taken in the defense of ou Western World, but also in order that the American Republics, joined a one, may prove to be the potent factor which they should be of right i the determination of the nature of the world of the future, after th victory is won.

We, the American nations, are trustees for Christian civilization. I our own relationships we have wished to show scrupulous respect for th sovereign rights of all states; we have sought to undertake only peacefu processes in the solution of controversies which may have arisen betwee us; and we have wished to follow the course of decency and of justice i our dealings with others.

When peace is restored it is to the interest of the whole world tha the American Republics present a united front and be able to speak an act with the moral authority to which, by reason of their own enlightene standards as much as by reason of their number and their power, the are entitled.

The prayer of peoples throughout the world is that when the task c peacemaking is once more undertaken it will be better done than it wa in 1919. And we cannot forget that the task this time will be infinitel more difficult than it was the last time.

In the determination of how these stupendous problems may best b solved, the united voice of the free peoples of the Americas must b heard.

The ideals which men have cherished have always throughout th course of history proved themselves to be more potent than any othe factor. Nor conquest, nor migrations; nor economic pressure, nc pestilence; nor revolt, nor assassinations have ever yet been able t riumph over the ideals which have sprung from men's hearts and men's minds.

Notwithstanding the hideous blunders of the past generation; notwithstanding the holocaust of the present moment, that great ideal of "a universal dominion of right by such a concert of free peoples as shall bring peace and safety to all nations and make the world itself at last free" still stands untarnished as the supreme objective of a suffering humanity.

That ideal will yet triumph.

We, the free peoples of the Americas, must play our full part in its realization so that we may hasten the day when we can thus insure the maintenance of a peaceful world in which we, and our children, and our children's children, can safely live.

At this time the issue is clearly drawn. There can be no peace until Hitlerism and its monstrous parasites are utterly obliterated, and until the Prussian and Japanese militarists have been taught in the only language they can understand that they will never again be afforded the opportunity of wrecking the lives of generation upon generation of men and women in every quarter of the globe.

When that time comes men of good-will must be prepared and ready to build with vision afresh upon new and lasting foundations of liberty, of morality, of justice, and, by no means least perhaps, of intelligence.

In the attainment of that great achievement the measure of our devotion will be the measure of the world's regeneration.

3) *Broadcast of the Under Secretary of State* (*Welles*), *January 24, 1942* [1]

[Excerpt]

This broadcast summarizes responsibly from the point of view of the United States Government the accomplishments of the meeting. It puts into perspective the substance of the detailed resolutions.

Yesterday the governments of 21 American Republics officially and unanimously proclaimed that they jointly recommended the severance of diplomatic relations between all of the American Republics and the Governments of Japan, Germany, and Italy because of the aggression committed by a member of the Tripartite Pact against one of the American family of nations, namely, the United States. This means that the diplomatic and consular agents of the Axis Powers within the American Republics will no longer be able to use territory within the

[1] Department of State, *Bulletin*, VI, p. 77. The address was delivered over the facilities of the National Broadcasting Company from Rio de Janeiro.

Western Hemisphere as their basis of activities against us and our allies

For the first time in the history of our hemisphere joint action of the highest political character has been taken by all of the American nations acting together without dissent and without reservation.

It is true that we have not all seen eye to eye as to the exact details of the agreement which has been reached, but the objectives which all of us had in mind have been completely attained and, what is everlastingly important, the complete unity and solidarity of the 21 American Republics has been preserved.

The economic resolutions of the meeting have reached a degree of importance and immediacy not attained by those of earlier conferences. Most significant, of course, is the resolution calling for the immediate breaking off of all commercial and financial intercourse direct or indirect with the Axis Nations and the suspension of any other commercial and financial activities prejudicial to the welfare and security of the American Republics.[1] In accordance with this resolution not only will all direct economic relations with the Axis be terminated but Axis nationals and other persons inimical to the Americas will not be permitted, through control of corporations and other enterprises or by means of the profits arising out of business activity with or within the American Republics to enter into any activities subversive to the welfare and defense of the continent.

The resolution also provides for the control, supervision, reorganization, or seizure of such enterprises in order that they may be operated under government auspices or otherwise in the interests of the economy of the particular American republic involved. Measures are also to be taken to alleviate any injuries to the economies of the American Republics which may arise out of the application of these measures of restriction and control.

The meeting has also adopted other measures of great significance to our war and defense effort. Among these is a strong resolution calling for the most complete cooperation of all the nations of the hemisphere in increasing by all possible means the production of the strategic materials essential for the conduct of the war and the defense of our country and recommending mechanisms and measures for attaining this objective. Recognizing that the production of materials is of little avail unless adequate transportation is provided, the meeting has also recommended the most rapid development of essential means of transportation with particular emphasis on the closest coordination of shipping service in order to give preference to the speedy delivery of those strategic

[1] See pp. 293, 310.

materials without which war cannot be waged, adequate defenses prepared, and the economies of our nations maintained. In accordance with this resolution the Axis merchant vessels immobilized in ports of the hemisphere which have already been acquired by the governments of the respective nations will now be placed immediately into efficient and closely coordinated service along with the merchant fleets of all of the American nations. To this end the maritime authorities of all of the republics will work closely together in scheduling and routing the vessels under their control.

In preparing these measures of economic solidarity looking towards the defense of the continent and resistance against the aggressor nations the meeting has not overlooked the necessity of assuring full consideration by the exporting nations of the minimum import requirements of commodities essential to the maintenance of the economic life of all of them. In accordance with this resolution appropriate mechanisms will be set up in each country to present accurate statements of the import requirements of each, export quotas will be determined wherever possible and in a measure consistent with exigencies of war and defense, and mechanisms for equitable distribution will be established in the importing countries. All of these measures will tie in closely with the priority and allocations procedures already established in the United States, and on its part the United States has already announced that it would give to the civilian needs of the other American Republics consideration equal and proportionate to that given to its own civilian needs.

In connection with these problems of supply of commodities essential to the maintenance of economic activity the meeting has also considered questions of fair and equitable prices both for imported and exported products. In this field it has recommended that undue price increase be avoided; that domestic price ceilings be extended to cover exports with due regard to the additional costs involved in exporting; that importing countries prevent any runaway price increases in scarce imported commodities; and that every effort be made to assure a fair relationship between the prices of exports and imports, of agricultural and mineral raw materials and manufactured products.

In addition to the financial and economic measures of control to which I have just referred, the foreign ministers of the American Republics have reached unanimous agreement on a number of other practical measures for assuring the security of the hemisphere.

All subversive activities directed by the Axis Powers or states subservient to them are brought under rigid control; telecommunications — whether by telephone, telegraph, or radio — are likewise brought under strict control in order that they may not be used by or for the benefit of the aggressor nations; nationals or companies of the Axis Powers are prevented from operating civilian or commercial aircraft; and procedures have been established for coordinating the activities of all the American Republics in all matters relating to their national security.

As all of the delegates of the 21 Governments leave the closing session of our meeting Monday I think we will all of us leave with the conviction deep in our hearts that there exists today a more practical, a more solid, and a more real Pan Americanism than has ever existed in the history of the world.

(4) Final Act and Resolutions, January 28, 1942 [1]

The meetings of Ministers of Foreign Affairs of the American Republics follow the practice of other Inter-American conferences of consolidating their decisions within a single Final Act, which imparts a unitary character to the individual conclusions. The resolutions and recommendations are here extracted from their sequence in the Final Act and the substantive ones are arranged under subject headings in order to facilitate study of related matter. Reservations are listed after the resolution to which they refer. The reservation of the Delegation of Chile, which is of general application, is appended to the text of the final paragraph of the Act.

The Governments of the American Republics, desirous that their Ministers of Foreign Affairs or their respective representatives meet for purposes of consultation, in accordance with agreements adopted at previous Inter-American conferences, designated for this purpose the representatives listed below in the order determined by lot, who met in the City of Rio de Janeiro from January 15–28, 1942:

COSTA RICA: — His Excellency ALBERTO ECHANDI, *Minister of Foreign Affairs*

COLOMBIA: — His Excellency GABRIEL TURBAY, *representative of the Minister of Foreign Affairs*

CUBA: — His Excellency AURELIO FERNÁNDEZ CONCHESO, *representative of the Minister of State*

DOMINICAN REPUBLIC: — His Excellency ARTURO DESPRADEL, *Secretary of State for Foreign Affairs*

HONDURAS: — His Excellency JULIÁN R. CÁCERES, *representative of the Minister of Foreign Affairs*

[1] Department of State, *Bulletin*, VI, p. 117–44; *Report of the Third Meeting of the Ministers of Foreign Affairs of the American Republics, Rio de Janeiro, January 15–28 1942, submitted to the Governing Board of the Pan American Union by the Director General* (Congress and Conference Series No. 36), p. 32.

EL SALVADOR: — His Excellency HECTOR DAVID CASTRO, *representative of the Minister of Foreign Affairs*

PARAGUAY: — His Excellency LUIS A. ARGAÑA, *Minister of Foreign Affairs*

URUGUAY: — His Excellency ALBERTO GUANI, *Minister of Foreign Affairs*

ARGENTINA: — His Excellency ENRIQUE RUIZ-GUIÑAZÚ, *Minister of Foreign Affairs and Worship*

CHILE: — His Excellency JUAN BAUTISTA ROSSETTI, *Minister of Foreign Affairs*

BOLIVIA: — His Excellency EDUARDO ANZA MATIENZO, *Minister of Foreign Affairs and Worship*

PANAMA: — His Excellency OCTAVIO FÁBREGA, *Minister of Foreign Affairs*

VENEZUELA: — His Excellency CARACCIOLO PARRA PEREZ, *Minister of Foreign Affairs*

ECUADOR: — His Excellency JULIO TOBAR DONOSO, *Minister of Foreign Affairs*

GUATEMALA: — His Excellency MANUEL ARROYO, *representative of the Minister of Foreign Affairs*

MEXICO: — His Excellency EZEQUIEL PADILLA, *Secretary of Foreign Affairs*

UNITED STATES OF AMERICA: — The Honorable SUMNER WELLES, *representative of the Secretary of State*

PERU: — His Excellency ALFREDO SOLF Y MURO, *Minister of Foreign Affairs*

HAITI: — His Excellency CHARLES FOMBRUN, *Secretary of State for Foreign Affairs*

NICARAGUA: — His Excellency MARIANO ARGUELLO VARGAS, *Minister of Foreign Affairs*

BRAZIL: — His Excellency OSWALDO ARANHA, *Minister of Foreign Affairs*

His Excellency Getulio Vargas, President of Brazil, delivered an address at the Inaugural Session held in the Tiradentes Palace on January 15th, under the provisional presidency of His Excellency Oswaldo Aranha, Minister of Foreign Affairs of Brazil. The response on behalf of the delegates was delivered by His Excellency Juan B. Rossetti, Minister of Foreign Affairs of Chile.

At a Plenary Session held immediately after the Inaugural Session, His Excellency Oswaldo Aranha was elected by acclamation Permanent President of the Meeting. In accordance with the Regulations, the

Government of Brazil designated His Excellency José de Paula Rodrigues Alves, Secretary General of the Meeting.

The program of the Meeting was approved by the Governing Board of the Pan American Union on December 17, 1941.

The regulations [1] had been previously formulated by the Governing Board in accordance with a resolution of the Second Meeting of Foreign Ministers.

As provided for in the regulations a Committee on Credentials was appointed, composed of His Excellency Dr. Ezequiel Padilla, Secretary of Foreign Affairs of Mexico; His Excellency Dr. Alberto Echandi Montero, Minister of Foreign Affairs of Costa Rica; and His Excellency Dr. Luis A. Argaña, Minister of Foreign Affairs of Paraguay.

In order to coordinate the texts of the conclusions in the four official languages of the Meeting, a Committee on Coordination was appointed composed of L. A. Podestá Costa (Argentina), Camillo de Oliveira (Brazil), Warren Kelchner (United States of America), and Dantes Bellegarde (Haiti).

The Meeting further agreed that there should be two committees to consider the topics included in the Agenda, each Committee to be composed of the Ministers of Foreign Affairs, or their representatives, of all the countries, with the right to appoint another member of their respective Delegations in the event they were unable to attend a session in person.

As a result of its deliberations the Third Meeting of Ministers of Foreign Affairs of the American Republics approved the following conclusions:

[Here follow the texts of 41 documents.]

IN WITNESS WHEREOF, The Ministers of Foreign Affairs of the American Republics or their personal representatives sign and seal the present Final Act.

Done in the city of Rio de Janeiro, this 28th day of January, 1942, in the English, French, Portuguese and Spanish languages. The Secretary General shall deposit the original of the Final Act in the archives of the Pan American Union through the intermediary of the Ministry of Foreign Affairs of Brazil, and shall send certified copies thereof to the Governments of the American Republics.

[1] Resolution XXXIV (Department of State, *Bulletin*, VI, p. 138) proposed a revision of the regulations to permit substitute delegates for the Ministers of Foreign Affairs to sit and vote.

Reservation of the Delegation of Chile

2. The Minister of Foreign Affairs of Chile gives his approval to these agreements insofar as they do not conflict with the provisions of the Political Constitution of Chile, declaring further that such agreements will only be valid, with respect to his country, when approved by the National Congress and ratified by its constitutional agencies.

SOLIDARITY AND RECIPROCAL DEFENSE

I. Breaking of Diplomatic Relations

I. The American Republics reaffirm their declaration to consider any act of aggression on the part of a non-American State against one of them as an act of aggression against all of them, constituting as it does an immediate threat to the liberty and independence of America.

II. The American Republics reaffirm their complete solidarity and their determination to cooperate jointly for their mutual protection until the effects of the present aggression against the Continent have disappeared.

III. The American Republics, in accordance with the procedures established by their own laws and in conformity with the position and circumstances obtaining in each country in the existing continental conflict, recommend the breaking of their diplomatic relations with Japan, Germany and Italy, since the first-mentioned State attacked and the other two declared war on an American country.

IV. Finally, the American Republics declare that, prior to the reestablishment of the relations referred to in the preceding paragraph, they will consult among themselves in order that their action may have a solidary character.

XVII. Subversive Activities

Whereas:

1. Acts of aggression of the nature contemplated in Resolution XV adopted by the Second Meeting of the Ministers of Foreign Affairs of the American Republics at Havana [1] have now taken place against the integrity and inviolability of the territory of an American Republic;

2. Acts of aggression of a non-military character, including systematic espionage, sabotage, and subversive propaganda are being committed on this Continent, inspired by and under the direction of member states of the Tripartite Pact and states subservient to them, and the fate of numbers of the formerly free nations of Europe has shown them to be

[1] *Documents, III, 1940–41*, p. 76.

both preliminary to and an integral part of a program of military aggression;

3. The American Republics are determined to maintain their integrity and solidarity, in the emergency created by aggression by non-American States, and to give the fullest cooperation in the establishment and enforcement of extraordinary measures of continental defense;

4. The Second Meeting of the Ministers of Foreign Affairs of the American Republics recommended that the necessary steps be taken to prevent the carrying on of such subversive activities in the resolutions entitled: [1]

II. Norms Concerning Diplomatic and Consular Functions.
III. Coordination of Police and Judicial Measures for the Defense of Society and Institutions of Each American State.
V. Precautionary Measures with Reference to the Issuance of Passports.
VI. Activities Directed from Abroad against Domestic Institutions
VII. Diffusion of Doctrines Tending to Place in Jeopardy the Common Inter-American Democratic Ideal or to Threaten the Security and Neutrality of the American Republics.

5. The gravity of the present emergency requires that the American states, individually and in concert, take additional and more stringent measures to protect themselves against groups and individuals that seek to weaken their defenses from within,

The Third Meeting of the Ministers of Foreign Affairs of the American Republics

Resolves:

1. To reaffirm the determination of the American Republics to prevent individuals or groups within their respective jurisdictions from engaging in activities detrimental to the individual or collective security and welfare of the American Republics as expressed in Resolutions II, III. V, VI, and VII of the Second Meeting of the Ministers of Foreign Affairs of the American Republics.

2. To recommend to the Governments of the American Republics the adoption of similar legislative measures tending to prevent or punish as crimes, acts against the democratic institutions of the States of the Continent in the same manner as attempts against the integrity, independence or sovereignty of any one of them; and that the Governments of the American Republics maintain and expand their systems of surveillance designed to prevent subversive activities of nationals of non-American countries, as individuals or groups of individuals, that

[1] See *ibid.*, p. 65–72 for the resolutions referred to.

originate in or are directed from a foreign country and are intended to
interfere with or limit the efforts of the American Republics individually
or collectively to preserve their integrity and independence, and the
integrity and solidarity of the American Continent.

3. To recommend to the American Republics that they adopt in
conformance with their constitutions and laws, regulatory provisions
that are, as far as possible, in keeping with the memorandum which is
attached to this Resolution for purposes of information.

4. To recommend, according to Resolution VII of the Havana Meeting on the subject of anti-democratic propaganda, that the Governments
of the American Republics control, within their respective national
jurisdictions, the existence of organizations directed or supported by
elements of non-American States which are now or may in the future be
at war with American countries, whose activities are harmful to American security; and proceed to terminate their existence if it is established
that they are centers of totalitarian propaganda.

5. That, to study and coordinate the measures recommended in this
Resolution, the Governing Board of the Pan American Union shall
elect, prior to March 1, 1942, a committee of seven members to be known
as "The Emergency Advisory Committee for Political Defense." [1]

6. The Governing Board of the Pan American Union, after consulting
the Governments of the American Republics, shall determine the functions of this committee, prepare the regulations which shall govern its
activities, and fix its budget of expenditures.

ATTACHMENT TO RESOLUTION XVII. MEMORANDUM ON THE REGULATION
OF SUBVERSIVE ACTIVITIES

It is recommended to the American Republics that, as far as practicable in
view of present conditions and those which may be foreseen, they take comprehensive regulatory measures, that are not in conflict with their respective constitutional provisions, and that these measures include the following, it being
recognized that many of them are already in force:

A) To control dangerous aliens by:

1. Requiring that all aliens register and periodically report in person to the
proper authorities and exercising a strict supervision over the activities and
conduct of all nationals of member states of the Tripartite Pact and states sub-

[1] The committee was set up on February 25, 1942, to consist of representatives
designated by Argentina, Brazil, Chile, Mexico, the United States, Uruguay and
Venezuela, with liaison officers from all the American Republics. The committee
established headquarters at Montevideo, holding an inaugural meeting April 15
Bulletin of the Pan American Union, LXXVI, p. 283; Department of State, *Bulletin*,
VI, p. 322).

servient to them; communicating immediately to other American Republic information that may be obtained relative to the presence of foreigners suspec with relation to the peace and security of such other Republics;

2. Establishing procedures whereby such nationals of the aforesaid states a are deemed dangerous to the country of their residence shall during their sta; therein remain in detention or be restricted in their freedom of movement;

3. Preventing such nationals from possessing, trading in or making use c aircraft, firearms, explosives, radio transmitting instruments, or other imple ments of warfare, propaganda, espionage, or sabotage;

4. Limiting internal travel and change of residence of those aliens deemee dangerous in so far as such travel may be incompatible with national security;

5. Forbidding the participation by such nationals in organizations controlle by or acting in the interest of member states of the Tripartite Pact or state subservient to them;

6. Protecting all aliens not deemed dangerous from being deprived of ade quate means of livelihood, unfairly discriminated against, or otherwise inter fered with in the conduct of their normal social and business activities.

(B) To prevent the abuse of citizenship by:

1. Exercising that redoubled vigilance which the circumstances demand i the naturalization of aliens, with particular reference to denying citizenship t those who continue in any way to retain allegiance to, or to recognize citizenshi] in the member states of the Tripartite Pact or states subservient to them;

2. Causing the status of citizenship and the inherent rights with respect there to of those citizens of non-American origin who have been granted the privileg of becoming citizens of an American state to be forfeited if, by acts detriment to the security or independence of that state or otherwise, they demonstrat allegiance to a member state of the Tripartite Pact or any state subservient t them, including the termination of the status of citizenship of such persons recog nizing or attempting to exercise dual rights of citizenship.

(C) To regulate transit across national boundaries by:

1. Exercising strict surveillance over all persons seeking to enter or depai from the country, particularly those persons engaged in the interests of membe states of the Tripartite Pact or subservient to them, or whose point of departui or destination is such a state, without prejudice, however, to the maintenanc of the most liberal practices consistent with local conditions for the granting safe refuge to those persons who, as victims of aggression, are fleeing from o] pression by foreign powers, and by cooperating fully in the exchange of inform: tion on the transit of persons from one state to another;

2. Strictly regulating and controlling the entry and departure of all persons to whom there are well-founded and sufficient grounds to believe that they a] engaged in political activities as agents or in the interest of member states of th Tripartite Pact or states subservient to them;

(D) To prevent acts of political aggression by:

1. Establishing penalties for acts designed to obstruct the war or defen: efforts of the country concerned or its cooperation with other American Repul lics in matters of mutual defense;

2. Preventing the dissemination by any agent or national of or by any political party organized in any member state of the Tripartite Pact or any state subservient to them, or by any other person or organization acting at the behest or under the direction thereof, of propaganda designed to impair the security of any of the American Republics or the relations between them, to create political or social dissension, to intimidate the nationals of any American Republic, or to influence the policies of any American state;

3. Requiring the registration with an appropriate agency of Government of or otherwise regulating any persons or organizations seeking to act in any way on behalf of, or in the political interest of, any non-American state which is not engaged at war on the side of an American Republic; or of a political party thereof, including clubs, societies and institutions, whether of a social, humanitarian, sporting, educational, technical or charitable nature, which are directed or supported by nationals of any such states; requiring the full and constant public disclosure to the people of the country in which they are carried on, of the identity and nature of all activities of such persons and organizations, and maintaining constant surveillance of all such persons and members of such organizations, whether citizens or aliens;

4. Punishing acts of sabotage, injury to and destruction of essential defense materials, factories, buildings, areas and utilities for manufacture and storage, public services, means of transportation and communication, and water front areas and facilities; punishing acts of espionage and the collection and communication of vital defense information for hostile purposes; and anticipating and forestalling acts of sabotage and espionage by measures to protect and safeguard vital documents, installations, and operations;

5. Supervising all communications to and from states subservient to or in communication with member states of the Tripartite Pact, in order to censor any information or intelligence of use to any such state in the execution of hostile designs against any of the American Republics, or in activities otherwise detrimental to the security of any or all of the American Republics.

XVIII. INTER-AMERICAN CONFERENCE ON COORDINATION OF POLICE AND JUDICIAL MEASURES

VHEREAS:

1. The Second Meeting of the Ministers of Foreign Affairs of the American Republics approved a resolution [1] providing for the convocation, by the Governing Board of the Pan American Union, of the States members thereof, to an international conference at such place and date as it would determine, to draft international conventions and recommendations deemed necessary to assure, through the action of the proper authorities in each State, and through the coordination of such action with that of other States in the Continent, the most complete and effective defense against acts of an unlawful character, as well as against any other unlawful activities likely to affect the institutions of American

[1] Resolution III, *Documents, III, 1940–41*, p. 66.

States. The resolution also stated that each State would be represented at the Conference by a jurist with plenipotentiary powers accompanied, if deemed desirable, by experts on police and judicial matters. It was likewise resolved that prior to the Conference, the Pan American Union would undertake the preparatory work by means of an inquiry among the Governments of the Continent, with regard to existing legislation as well as with respect to their opinions on the various topics which it might be thought advisable to consider:

2. In accordance with this resolution, the Governing Board of the Pan American Union, after consulting with the Government of the Argentine Republic, decided that the Conference should be held in Buenos Aires in September, 1942, the Governing Board having prepared the agenda and the regulations of the Conference, which after being submitted to the consideration of the respective Governments were approved at the meeting of November 5, 1941. Inquiries having been made of all the Governments of the Continent by the Pan American Union, and several countries having replied, the compiled material is available for use; and

3. The unjustified aggression of which the United States of America has been the victim and the war which has followed as a consequence make it necessary to hold the projected Conference because the measures for the coordination of national defense against espionage, sabotage, treason, sedition and other unlawful or subversive activities, as well as inter-American cooperation for the coordination of the systems adopted in each State for the identification and registration of persons and the recording of data for the preparation of rules and procedures concerning the communication of judicial decisions and for the fulfillment of requests for extradition, the presentation of evidence and the expulsion of foreigners, in accordance with the program approved by the Pan American Union, require its immediate execution,

The Third Meeting of the Ministers of Foreign Affairs of the American Republics

Resolves:

1. That the Inter-American Conference on the Coordination of Police and Judicial Measures shall convene in Buenos Aires next May, the date for the opening of the Conference to be determined by the Argentine Government and the corresponding invitations to be sent by it.[1]

[1] The date set by the Government of the Argentine Republic was May 27, 1942, and invitations were sent accordingly. Department of State, *Bulletin*, VI, p. 480.

2. To recommend that the Conference study the possibility of broadening the South American Police Convention, signed at Buenos Aires on February 29, 1920,[1] so that its provisions may be applicable to all the countries of the Continent, and that it incorporate in this Convention the establishment of an "Inter-American Registry of Police Records," which will permit identification in the American Republics of persons indicted or condemned for international offenses and subversive activities directed against the American Republics, individually or collectively.

3. To request the Governments of the American Republics which have not yet answered the questionnaire prepared by the Pan American Union, to do so as soon as possible.

XIX. Coordination of the Systems of Investigation

WHEREAS:

1. Ten of the American Republics are presently at war as a result of the aggression perpetrated by the Empire of Japan on December 7, 1941, against the United States of America and consequently against all the American States;

2. The evidence establishes that for the development of their activities against the safety and integrity of the American Continent the aggressors have resorted to methods of espionage, sabotage and subversive incitement which they have organized and coordinated throughout the entire Western Hemisphere, the repression of which requires an equally effective coordination on the part of the intelligence and investigation services of the American Republics,

The Third Meeting of the Ministers of Foreign Affairs of the American Republics

Resolves:

That the Governments of the American Republics shall coordinate their national intelligence and investigation services, providing adequate personnel for the inter-American interchange of information, investigations and suggestions for the prevention, repression, punishment and elimination of such activities as espionage, sabotage and subversive incitement which endanger the safety of the American Nations.

[1] League of Nations, *Treaty Series*, CXXVII, p. 433; Hudson, Manley O., *International Legislation*, I, p. 448.

XX. Reiteration of a Principle of American Law

Whereas:

1. In accordance with its historical, racial, political and juridical tradition, there is and can be no room in America for the so-called racial linguistic or religious "minorities"; and

2. In accordance with this concept, Resolutions XXVII and XXVIII approved at the Pan American Conference in Lima in 1938, confirm the principle that "residents who, according to domestic law, are considered aliens, cannot claim collectively the condition of minorities; individually however, they will continue to enjoy the rights to which they are entitled,"

The Third Meeting of the Ministers of Foreign Affairs of the American Republics

Declares:

That it reiterates the principle of American Public Law, according to which aliens residing in an American State are subject to the jurisdiction of that State, and the Governments and agencies of the countries of which such aliens are nationals cannot lawfully interfere, directly or indirectly, in domestic affairs for the purpose of controlling the status or activities of such aliens.

XXI. Continental Solidarity in Observance of Treaties

Whereas:

1. The concept of solidarity, in addition to embodying altruistic sentiments held in common, includes that of cooperation so necessary to forestall obstacles which may prejudice the maintenance of that principle, or the reestablishment of harmony when weakened or disrupted by the adoption of measures contrary to the dictates of international law and morality;

2. This solidarity must be translated into facts in order to become a living reality; since from a philosophical concept it has developed into an historic affirmation through repeated and frequent reaffirmations in international agreements freely agreed upon;

3. Respect for the pledged word in international treaties rests upon incontestable juridical principles as well as on precepts of morality in accordance with the maxim of canon law: *Pacta sunt servanda;*

4. Such agreements, whether bilateral or multilateral, must not be modified or nullified unilaterally, except as otherwise provided, as in the case of "denunciation" clearly authorized by the parties;

5. Only thus can peace, inspired by the common welfare of the peoples, be founded on an enduring basis, as proclaimed at the Meeting in Havana; and

6. All peaceful relations among peoples would be practically impossible in the absence of strict observance of all pacts solemnly celebrated which have met all the formalities provided for in the laws of the High Contracting Parties in order to render them juridically effective,

The Third Meeting of the Ministers of Foreign Affairs of the American Republics

Declares:

1. That should the Government of an American nation violate an agreement or a treaty duly perfected by two or more American Republics or should there be reason to believe that a violation which might disturb the peace or solidarity of the Americas is being contemplated, any American State may initiate the consultation contemplated in Resolution XVII [1] of Havana with the object of agreeing upon the measures to be taken.

2. That the Government desiring to initiate the consultation and propose a Meeting of the Ministers of Foreign Affairs of the American Republics, or their representatives, shall communicate with the Governing Board of the Pan American Union specifying in detail the subjects to be considered as well as the approximate date on which the meeting should take place.

RESERVATION OF THE DELEGATION OF THE REPUBLIC OF PERU [2]

5. As to Resolution XXI on Continental Solidarity in Observance of Treaties:

"The project voted upon does not refer to the defense of the American Hemisphere against dangers from without the continent and, consequently, it is outside the agenda of this Meeting, the regulations for which, approved by all the Governments, require the unanimous consent of the Ministers of Foreign Affairs of the American Republics.

"In any case, the project voted upon cannot be applied to incidents occurring in connection with conflicts or differences which the interested parties have submitted to a special jurisdiction for settlement or solution."

[1] *Documents, III, 1940–41*, p. 77.
[2] The reservation bore upon the boundary dispute between Ecuador and Peru which was in course of settlement; see p. 431.

XXII. The Good Neighbor Policy

Whereas:

1. Relations among nations, if they are to have foundations which will assure an international order under law, must be based on the essential and universal principle of justice;

2. The standard proclaimed and observed by the United States of America to the effect that its international policy must be founded on that of the "good neighbor" is a general criterion of right and a source of guidance in the relations between States; and this well-conceived policy prescribes respect for the fundamental rights of States as well as cooperation between them for the welfare of international society; and

3. This policy has been one of the elements contributing to the present solidarity of the Americas and their joint cooperation in the solution of outstanding problems of the Continent,

The Third Meeting of the Ministers of Foreign Affairs of the American Republics

Declares:

That the principle that international conduct must be inspired by the policy of the good neighbor is a norm of international law of the American Continent.

XXIII. Condemnation of Inter-American Conflicts

Whereas:

1. A state of war exists between the United States of America and the Axis Powers;

2. The other American Republics, in conformity with inter-American agreements, have declared themselves to be in solidarity with the United States of America; and

3. This consequently implies that all the countries of the hemisphere should closely unite for the defense of the Continent, which is the defense of each and all the American Republics,

The Third Meeting of the Ministers of Foreign Affairs of the American Republics

Resolves:

To appeal to the spirit of conciliation of the various Governments to settle their conflicts by recourse to the inter-American peace agreements formulated during the course of the recent Pan American conferences, or to any other juridical machinery, and to recognize the meritorious work f the countries which have lent and are lending their collaboration with view to reaching a pacific solution of the differences existing between American countries and to urge them to continue intensifying their fforts in favor of the noble cause of continental harmony and solidarity.

XXIV. Condemnation of Japanese Aggression

Whereas:

1. On December 7, 1941, the armed forces of Japan attacked, without previous warning or without a declaration of war, certain possessions of the United States of America in the Pacific Ocean;

2. These unforeseen and hostile acts were perpetrated by Japan while diplomatic conversations were in progress between the two States looking toward the pacific solution of their international differences;

3. The aforementioned nature and circumstances of these acts characterizes them as armed aggression in flagrant violation of all the standards f international law which proscribe and condemn the use of force in the solution of international controversies, and particularly those of American international law;

4. Several instruments signed by the American Republics at recent international conferences and meetings impose the unlimited duty of solidarity upon the signatory Governments for the defense of their sovereignty, independence, and territorial integrity; and

5. Resolution XV on Reciprocal Assistance and Cooperation for the Defense of the Nations of the Americas,[1] signed at the Second Meeting of the Ministers of Foreign Affairs of the American Republics, held at Havana, established the principle "That any attempt on the part of a non-American State against the integrity or inviolability of the territory, the sovereignty, or the political independence of an American State shall be considered as an act of aggression against the States which sign this declaration,"

The Third Meeting of the Ministers of Foreign Affairs of the American Republics

Resolves:

1. To make it of record that Japan by perpetrating armed aggression against the United States of America has violated the fundamental principles and standards of international law.

2. To condemn such aggression and protest against it to the civilized world and extend this condemnation and protest to the powers which have associated themselves with Japan.

[1] *Documents, III, 1940–41*, p. 76.

XXXII. Penal Colonies of Non-American Nations on American Territory

WHEREAS:

1. Certain non-American States reserve certain territories in th American Continent for the establishment of penal colonies;

2. The use of American territories for penal colonies of non-America States infringes on the fundamental principles of the Pan American idea

The Third Meeting of the Ministers of Foreign Affairs of the America Republics

Resolves:

To request the Governing Board of the Pan American Union to ap proach those States which possess territories in America used as pens colonies in order to eliminate the future use of such American territorie for this purpose.

XXXVI. Interests of Non-American Countries

The Third Meeting of the Ministers of Foreign Affairs of the America Republics

Recommends:

That no American State shall authorize another American State ● assume before its Government the representation of the interests of non-American State with which it has no diplomatic relations or which at war with nations of this hemisphere.

XXXVII. Treatment of Non-Belligerents

The Third Meeting of the Ministers of Foreign Affairs of the America Republics

Resolves:

1. That in conformity with the principles of American solidarity, th Republics of this Continent shall not consider as a belligerent ar American State which is now at war or may become involved in a sta of war with another non-American State.

2. To recommend that special facilities be granted to those countri which, in the opinion of each Government, contribute to the defense the interests of this hemisphere during this emergency.

XXXVIII. Relations with the Governments of Occupied Countries

The Third Meeting of the Ministers of Foreign Affairs of the American Republics

Recommends:

That the Governments of the American Republics continue their relations with the Governments of those occupied countries which are fighting for their national sovereignty and are not collaborating with the aggressors, and express the fervent hope that they may recover their sovereignty and independence.

XXXIX. Inter-American Defense Board [1]

Whereas:

1. In accordance with the action taken at the Conference for the Maintenance of Peace and in conformity with the Declaration of Lima, a system of coordination exists between the American Republics which fortunately responds to the spirit of sincere collaboration animating the peoples of our Continent; and

2. This system, the results of which have heretofore been satisfactory, is, from every point of view, the most effective means on the part of the Western Hemisphere for meeting the present grave emergency in a coordinated and solidary manner,

The Third Meeting of the Ministers of Foreign Affairs of the American Republics

Recommends:

The immediate meeting in Washington of a commission composed of military and naval technicians appointed by each of the Governments to study and to recommend to them the measures necessary for the defense of the Continent.

ECONOMIC AND FINANCIAL COOPERATION

XL. Production of Strategic Materials

Whereas:

1. Continental solidarity must be translated into positive and efficient action of the highest significance, which action can be no other than an

[1] The first meeting of the Board was held at the Pan American Union, Washington, March 30, when it organized with Lieutenant General S. D. Embick, U.S.A., as permanent chairman. Permanent quarters were established in the Federal Reserve Building. *Bulletin of the Pan American Union*, LXXVI, p. 335.

economic mobilization of the American Republics capable of rapidly and fully guaranteeing the supply of strategic and basic materials necessary to the defense of the hemisphere;

2. This mobilization should include all activities which will advance the desired end, and must have the preferential character which it nature and purpose require;

3. In order to ensure the smooth carrying out of the suggested plan every positive action must be taken; all existing obstacles or those which may in the future appear should be eliminated or minimized; and all contributory factors should be strengthened;

4. Commercial speculation should be prevented from taking unfair advantage of the situation;

5. Guarantees should be given for the continuance of long-term contracts and for the maintenance of prices, equitable both for the consumer and profitable to the producer, to permit the attainment and mainte nance of a fair wage level;

6. Consideration must be given to measures providing for transition to the post-war period and the resulting readjustment with a minimum of disturbance to production and commerce; taking steps to protect, at the opportune time, producers against competition from goods produced in countries with a low standard of living;

7. Credit operations should have, as far as possible, an economic character, and should take into account the real ability of the debtors to repay;

8. There should exist in each country of the Americas special organizations to formulate promptly the respective national plans for economic mobilization;

9. A Pan American organization should formulate coordinated general plans of mobilization on the basis of the national plans above indicated and

10. The Inter-American Financial and Economic Advisory Committee can efficiently carry out these functions if its authority and powers are enlarged,

The Third Meeting of the Ministers of Foreign Affairs of the American Republics

Recommends:

1. That, as a practical expression of continental solidarity, an economic mobilization of the American Republics be effected, with a view to assuring to the countries of this hemisphere, and particularly to those

var, an adequate supply of basic and strategic materials in the shortest possible time.

2. That such mobilization include mining, agricultural, industrial and commercial activities related to the supply not only of materials for strictly military use but also of products essential for civilian needs.

3. That full recognition be given to the imperative character and extreme urgency of the existing situation when formulating measures necessary to effect economic mobilization.

4. That the mobilization include measures to stimulate production and other measures designed to eliminate or minimize administrative formalities and the regulations and restrictions which impede the production and free flow of basic and strategic materials.

5. That, in addition, measures be adopted to strengthen the finances of the producing countries.

6. That the American nations take measures to prevent commercial speculation from increasing export prices of basic and strategic products above the limits fixed for the respective domestic markets.

7. That, in so far as possible, the increase of production be assured by bilateral or multilateral agreements or contracts which provide for purchases during long periods at prices which are equitable for the consumer, remunerative to the producer and which provide a fair standard of wages for the workers of the Americas, in which producers are protected against competition from products originating in areas wherein real wages are unduly low; and which make provision for the period of transition after the war and the readjustments which will follow in a manner guaranteeing the continuance of adequate production and permitting the existence of trade under conditions equitable to producers.

8. That the service of financial obligations incurred to maintain and stimulate production in each country be made conditional, in so far as possible, upon the proceeds of its exports.

9. That the American nations which do not possess appropriate agencies organize special commissions prior to April 30, 1942, to formulate national plans for economic mobilization.

10. That the said commissions provide the Inter-American Financial and Economic Advisory Committee with the necessary material so that it may formulate a coordinated general plan for economic mobilization.

11. That the Inter-American Financial and Economic Advisory Committee be further charged with preparing a list, to be periodically revised, of the basic and strategic materials considered by each country as necessary for the defense of the hemisphere; and

Resolves:

12. That, in order to enable the Inter-American Financial and Eco
nomic Advisory Committee to carry out the new duties entrusted to it
its means of operation be expanded immediately, and that it be em
powered to request the American Governments to execute the inter
American economic agreements which they have previously approved.

III. MAINTENANCE OF THE INTERNAL ECONOMY OF THE AMERICA COUNTRIES

WHEREAS:

1. The First and Second Meetings of the Ministers of Foreign Affair
of the American Republics recommended that there be established
among them, a close and sincere cooperation in order to protect thei
economic and financial structure, maintain their fiscal equilibrium, safe
guard the stability of their currencies, promote and expand their con
merce and, in addition, declared that the American nations continue t
adhere to the liberal principles of international trade, conducted wit
peaceful motives and based upon equality of treatment and fair an
equitable trade practices, and that they do everything in their power t
strengthen their economic position, to improve further the trade an
other economic relations among themselves, by devising and applyin
appropriate measures to lessen the difficulties, disadvantages and dange
arising from disturbed and dislocated world conditions;

2. The dislocations of the economy of the American nations caused b
the war demand, more than ever before, common and coordinated actio
in order that their trade may be intensified in accordance with the
mutual needs and upon the basis of the greatest possible equality;

3. The establishment of adequate facilities for commercial credit, (
the part of nations which produce raw materials, industrial machinery (
manufactured articles, is an indispensable requirement for the mai
tenance of a sound economy in the consuming countries;

4. The fixing of prices and ceilings on raw materials and foodstu
should be based upon a fair correlation, which takes into account n
only costs of production, transportation, insurance and a reasonab
profit, but also the general price level of products exported by t
country which imports such raw materials and foodstuffs;

5. The systems of priority and licenses established by some countri
with respect to the exportation of materials, which are related to the
defense requirements, have brought about consequences affecting co

nercial interchange and it is therefore necessary to recommend adequate ystems and measures to alleviate said consequences,

The Third Meeting of the Ministers of Foreign Affairs of the American Republics

Resolves:

1. To recommend to the nations which produce raw materials, industrial machinery and other articles essential for the maintenance of the domestic economies of the consuming countries that they do everything possible to supply such articles and products in quantities sufficient to prevent a scarcity thereof, which might bring about consequences detrimental to the economic life of the American peoples. The application of this recommendation is subject to the practical limitations of the existing emergency and shall not endanger the security or the defense of the exporting nations.

2. To recommend that all the nations of this continent have access, with the greatest possible degree of equality, to inter-American commerce and to the raw materials which they require for the satisfactory and prosperous development of their respective economies, provided, however, that they shall give preferential treatment to the nations at war for equal access to materials essential to their defense; and that, in agreements which may be concluded, the essential needs of other American countries be considered with a view to preventing dislocations in their domestic economies.

3. To recommend to the countries which export industrial raw materials, foodstuffs, manufactured products or industrial machinery, that they establish adequate, ample, liberal and effective systems of credit which will facilitate the acquisition of such of these products as may be required by the industry and commerce of the consumer nations to maintain their economy upon firm foundations, and that this be done in such a way as to lessen and alleviate the adverse effects upon the consumer nations of the extension of the war and the closing down of non-American markets.

4. To urge the Governments of America to adopt necessary measures to harmonize prices on the following bases:

(*a*) That sharp increases in the prices of export products shall not be permitted;

(*b*) That the distributors or processors of imported goods shall likewise not be permitted to increase unduly the prices to be paid by the consumer;

(*c*) That the maximum purchase price fixed by an American Republic for any product or article which it imports from another American Republic shall be submitted to consultation, if deemed advisable by the Governments of the interested countries;

(d) That in their price policies the American Republics endeavor to establish a fair relation between the prices of foodstuffs, raw materials and manufactured articles.

5. Finally to recommend to the American Governments the following standards for the purpose of improving their economic relations:

(a) The establishment, for the control of exports, of simple administrative systems of the greatest possible autonomy based upon rapid and efficient methods which will satisfy essential requirements promptly, especially for the maintenance of the basic industries of each country;

(b) The adoption by the governments of exporting countries of a system of allocation to each country of products and articles subject to priorities and licenses which are essential to the domestic economy of the importing countries;

(c) The appointment by exporting countries which maintain systems of priorities, licenses or allocations of representatives in the capitals of the importing countries to cooperate with the appropriate organizations of the latter in the study of questions arising in connection with the export and import of products and articles subject to allocations or special controls, so as to accelerate procedure and to diminish, as much as possible, other difficulties involved in the interchange of such products and articles. The recommendation or opinion of such representatives shall constitute, in principle, a recognition on their part of the need and desirability of such imports;

(d) The prompt exchange of statistics relating to consumer needs and to the production of raw materials, foodstuffs and manufactured products, utilizing, whenever appropriate, such organizations as the Inter-American Financial and Economic Advisory Committee of others which appropriately may facilitate and stimulate commercial interchange among the nations of the Americas.

V. Severance of Commercial and Financial Relations

WHEREAS:

1. At the Second Meeting of Ministers of Foreign Affairs of the American Republics, held at Havana in July 1940, it was declared that any attempt on the part of a non-American State against the integrity or inviolability of the territory, the sovereignty or the political independence

ence of an American State should be considered as an act of aggression against all of the American States;

2. As a result of the aggression committed against the Western Hemisphere a state of war exists between American Republics and non-American States, which affects the political and economic interests of the whole Continent and demands the adoption of measures for the defense and security of all of the American Republics;

3. All of the American Republics have already adopted measures which subject to some control the exportation or re-exportation of merchandise; most of the American Republics have instituted systems of restriction and control of financial and commercial transactions with the nations signatory to the Tripartite Pact and the territories dominated by them, and others have adopted measures to curb other alien economic activities prejudicial to their welfare; and all the American Republics have approved the recommendations of the Inter-American Financial and Economic Advisory Committee regarding the immediate placing into service of the merchant vessels of non-American registry lying immobilized in American ports,

The Third Meeting of the Ministers of Foreign Affairs of the American Republics

Recommends:

1. That the Governments of the American Republics, in a manner consistent with the usual practices and the legislation of the respective countries, adopt immediately:

(*a*) Any additional measures necessary to cut off for the duration of the present hemispheric emergency all commercial and financial intercourse, direct or indirect, between the Western Hemisphere and the nations signatory to the Tripartite Pact and the territories dominated by them;

(*b*) Measures to eliminate all other financial and commercial activities prejudicial to the welfare and security of the American Republics, measures which shall have, among others, the following purposes:

(i) To prevent, within the American Republics, all commercial and financial transactions inimical to the security of the Western Hemisphere, which are entered into directly or indirectly, by or for the benefit of the members of the Tripartite Pact, the territories dominated by them, as well as the nationals of any of them, whether real or juridical persons, it being understood that real persons may be excepted if they are resident within an American Republic and on condition that they are controlled according to the following paragraph;

(ii) To supervise and control all commercial and financial transactions within the American Republics by nationals of the states signatory to the Tripartite Pact, or of the territories dominated by them, who are resident within the American Republics, and to prevent all transactions of whatsoever nature which are inimical to the security of the Western Hemisphere.

Whenever a government of an American Republic considers it desirable and in accordance with its national interest and its own legislation, and especially if any of the aforesaid measures, when applied to concrete cases, should be prejudicial to its national economy, the properties, interests, and enterprises of such states and nationals which exist within its jurisdiction, may be placed in trust or subjected to permanent administrative intervention for purposes of control; moreover, such government of an American Republic may resort to sales to its nationals, provided that the proceeds thereof be subject to the same control and to similar regulations as those applicable to the funds of the above-mentioned aliens.

2. That the Governments of the American Republics adopt, severally or jointly, measures to counteract any adverse effects upon their respective economies which may result from the application of this recommendation. Special consideration should be given to measures to avoid the problems of partial or total unemployment which might arise in the American countries as a result of the application of the measures of control and restriction of the activities of aliens.

RESERVATION OF THE DELEGATION OF THE ARGENTINE REPUBLIC

1. As to Resolution V on the Severance of Commercial and Financial Relations:

"The Argentine Delegation requests that it be recorded in the minutes, as well as at the end of this draft resolution, that the Argentine Republic agrees with the necessity of adopting economic and financial control measures with regard to foreign and domestic activities of firms or enterprises which may, in one way another, affect the welfare of the republics of America or the solidarity or defense of the Continent. It has adopted and is prepared to adopt further measures this respect, in accordance with the present resolution, extending them, however to firms or enterprises managed or controlled by aliens or from foreign belligerent countries not in the American Continent."

VI. Conference to Standardize Procedure in Banking Operations Relating to Nationals of Aggressor Countries

The Third Meeting of the Ministers of Foreign Affairs of the American Republics

Recommends:

That the Inter-American Financial and Economic Advisory Committee convoke, when it believes it opportune, a conference of representatives of the central banks or equivalent or analogous institutions [1] of the American Republics for the purpose of drafting standards of procedure for the uniform handling of bank credits, collections, contracts of lease and consignments of merchandise, involving real or juridical persons who are nationals of a State which has committed an act of aggression against the American Continent.

VII. Development of Commercial Interchange

The Third Meeting of the Ministers of Foreign Affairs of the American Republics

Recommends:

That the Governments of the American Republics, as a means of promoting the development of commercial interchange among them, study the desirability of making an exception in the commercial agreements which they conclude with nations outside the Western Hemisphere of the treatment which they extend in commercial and customs matters to all of the other American Republics.

RESERVATION OF THE DELEGATION OF THE UNITED STATES OF AMERICA

3. As to Resolutions VII and XIV on the Development of Commercial Interchange and Commercial Facilities for the Inland Countries of America:

"The Government of the United States of America desires to have recorded in the Final Act its reservation to Resolution VII (Development of Commercial Interchange) and Resolution XIV (Commercial Facilities for the Inland Countries of the Americas), since the terms of these Resolutions are inconsistent with the traditional policy of liberal principles of international trade maintained by the United States of America and as enunciated and reaffirmed at the recent International Conferences of American States and the First and Second Meetings of the Ministers of Foreign Affairs of the American Republics."

[1] See p. 393.

VIII. Inter-American Development Commission

WHEREAS:

1. The Second Meeting of the Ministers of Foreign Affairs of th
American Republics reaffirmed Resolution XIII of the Inter-America
Financial and Economic Advisory Committee by which the Inte
American Development Commission was created, and made recon
mendations for the promotion of the economic forces of the America
nations in accordance with the program of the Inter-American Develor
ment Commission; [1]

2. The Inter-American Development Commission, in order to carr
out specific provisions of said Resolution XIII, as well as the recon
mendations of the Second Meeting of Foreign Ministers, sent fror
Washington a mission to the other twenty American Republics to estal
lish national commissions affiliated with it;

3. The work accomplished during 1941 by the Inter-American Deve.
opment Commission in creating an inter-American system of twenty
one national commissions affiliated with it and functioning with th
collaboration of their respective governments has been completel
satisfactory;

4. The time has come to stimulate, intensify and coordinate the wor
of such national commissions and of the Inter-American Developmen
Commission in Washington in order to promote, or maintain, the ecc
nomic forces of the American nations, using for this purpose to th
fullest extent possible the advantages offered by the existence of sucl
system of inter-American commissions,

The Third Meeting of the Ministers of Foreign Affairs of the America
Republics

Resolves:

1. To recommend that the Governments of the American Republic
continue to lend to the national commissions and to the Inter-American
Development Commission in Washington all the assistance and suppor
they may need to carry out the objectives for which they were created

2. To recommend that the Inter-American Financial and Economi
Advisory Committee entrust, when deemed appropriate by the Com
mittee, to the Commission such further matters and problems as th
Committee may wish to have studied, surveyed or carried out for th
benefit of inter-American economic development.

[1] Resolution XXV, section 4, *Documents, III, 1940–41*, p. 85.

3. To instruct the Inter-American Financial and Economic Advisory Committee to create, under the auspices of the Inter-American Development Commission, a permanent body of technical experts to study the natural resources of each country when so requested by its government.

IX. DEVELOPMENT OF BASIC PRODUCTION

WHEREAS:

1. The war situation has impelled certain American nations to create, in special cases, emergency industries which under normal circumstances would be considered as uneconomic or prejudicial to the economic solidarity of the Americas; and

2. It is imperative that there be avoided, in so far as is possible, the prejudicial effects on the economies of the American Republics of such action,

The Third Meeting of the Ministers of Foreign Affairs of the American Republics

Resolves:

That the nations of the Americas stimulate the development of the basic production of each of them, avoiding in so far as possible the establishment or expansion of production of substitute or synthetic commodities which is economically artificial and might displace the consumption of natural products available in other American nations, there being excepted only those industries which are indispensable for national defense provided that such defense needs cannot be effectively met with natural products.

X. INTER-AMERICAN BANK

The Third Meeting of the Ministers of Foreign Affairs of the American Republics

Recommends:

That the Governments of the American Republics which have not already adhered to the Convention for the Establishment of an Inter-American Bank [1] study the proposal in accordance with their respective situations and make their decision in the matter known, as soon as possible, to the Inter-American Financial and Economic Advisory Committee.

[1] See *Documents, II, 1939–40,* p. 147.

XI. INVESTMENT OF CAPITAL IN THE AMERICAN REPUBLICS

The Third Meeting of the Ministers of Foreign Affairs of the American Republics

Recommends:

That the Inter-American Financial and Economic Advisory Committee take steps to encourage capital investments by any of the American Republics in any one of the others, requesting the various governments to adopt the measures necessary to facilitate the flow and protection of such investments within the Continent.

XII. INTER-AMERICAN STATISTICAL INSTITUTE

The Third Meeting of the Ministers of Foreign Affairs of the American Republics

Agrees:

1. To request the American Governments to participate in and support the Inter-American Statistical Institute of Washington in order to establish, as soon as possible, a service for the interchange of statistical information and standards among the American nations; and

2. To recommend to the Pan American Union that it organize periodic meetings of representatives of the national statistical services of the American Republics for the coordination of their work.

XIII. UTILIZATION OF RAW MATERIALS

The Third Meeting of the Ministers of Foreign Affairs of the American Republics

Declares:

1. That to raise the standard of living of the people, the economic policy of the American nations must be founded upon a broad and complete utilization of their natural resources and directed toward a greater industrialization of those raw materials which present favorable and permanent economic possibilities both as to production and markets and at the same time it shall be the policy to seek to improve continental coordination through international agreements.

2. That it is the desire of the Third Meeting of the Ministers of Foreign Affairs that the Inter-American Development Commission and the respective National Commissions endeavor to put into practice the economic policy referred to in this declaration.

XIV. COMMERCIAL FACILITIES FOR THE INLAND COUNTRIES OF THE AMERICAS [1]

The Third Meeting of the Ministers of Foreign Affairs of the American Republics

Recommends:

That the American Republics study promptly the possibility of concluding a multilateral convention binding themselves not to claim, by virtue of the most-favored-nation clause, concessions and facilities which each of them may grant or may have granted to the commerce of the inland countries of the Americas in order to eliminate or minimize the disadvantages inherent in the geographical position of such countries.

XV. INTERNATIONAL STABILIZATION FUND

WHEREAS:

1. A more effective mobilization and utilization of foreign exchange resources would be of assistance in the struggle against aggression and would contribute to the realization of the economic objectives set forth at the First and Second Meetings of the Ministers of Foreign Affairs of the American Republics at Panama and Havana; and

2. The American Republics which are combined in a common effort to maintain their political and economic independence can cooperate in the creation of an organization to promote stability of foreign exchange rates, encourage the international movement of productive capital, facilitate the reduction of artificial and discriminatory barriers to the movement of goods, assist in the correction of the maldistribution of gold, strengthen monetary systems, and facilitate the maintenance of monetary policies that avoid serious inflation or deflation.

The Third Meeting of the Ministers of Foreign Affairs of the American Republics

Recommends:

1. That the Governments of the American Republics participate in a special conference of Ministers of Finance or their representatives to be called for the purpose of considering the establishment of an international stabilization fund;

[1] See the reservation of the United States attached to Resolution VII, p. 313.

2. That the conference in considering the establishment of such a fund shall formulate the plan of organization, powers and resources necessary to the proper functioning of the fund, shall determine the conditions requisite to participation in the fund, and shall propose principles to guide the fund in its operation.

XVI. Economic Collaboration

The Third Meeting of the Ministers of Foreign Affairs of the American Republics

Declares:

1. That since the best interests of the Continent require the proper utilization of the natural resources of each country, including those of the subsoil, the American Republics should endeavor, within their own economic systems, to develop such resources.

2. That in keeping with the spirit of solidarity and collaboration inspired by the doctrine of Pan Americanism, plans for cooperation should be made through the Inter-American Development Commission and its National Commissions in order to facilitate the financing of such development projects, with due regard to the economic possibilities of each country.

COMMUNICATIONS

IV. Mobilization of Transportation Facilities

Whereas:

1. The problem of increasing to the highest degree the efficiency of transportation facilities among the Republics of the Western Hemisphere is of great importance in view of the difficulties arising from the existing emergency;

2. The establishment of the greatest possible coordination of the various inland waterway, land, maritime and air services of the American Republics is indispensable for their most effective use;

3. The difficulties of transporting essential articles and materials normally exported and imported by each nation could provoke economic and social dislocation and diminish or paralyze its industrial activities, a particularly serious situation when such activities are devoted primarily to the production of articles or materials necessary for the defense of the Continent; and

4. In order properly to provide for defense and to develop inter American commerce it is indispensable to improve and expand the systems of communication among the countries of the Continent,

The Third Meeting of the Ministers of Foreign Affairs of the American Republics

Resolves:

1. To recommend to the Governments of the American Republics:

(*a*) That they adopt immediately, in so far as possible, adequate measures to expand and improve all the communications systems of importance to continental defense and to the development of commerce between the American nations;

(*b*) That they make every effort consistent with national or continental defense fully to utilize and develop their respective internal transportation facilities in order to assure the rapid delivery of those goods which are essential to the maintenance of their respective economies;

(*c*) That through their national authorities, the Inter-American Financial and Economic Advisory Committee, and all other instruments of inter-American economic cooperation which may have been established, they take every appropriate measure individually and jointly to improve and supplement inter-American communication facilities — air, maritime, land, inland waterway — related to the economy and defense of the Western Hemisphere and to the other objectives set forth in this resolution;

(*d*) That they adopt measures to insure the allocation of sufficient shipping tonnage for general trade and cooperate in creating and facilitating, by every means in their power, the maintenance of adequate maritime services, utilizing especially all the vessels that are immobilized in their ports,[1] belonging to countries at war with any American nation;

(*e*) That those with merchant fleets consider the necessity of maintaining in service sufficient vessels to guarantee maritime transportation which will permit the nations of the Continent to import and export products essential to their respective economies and that, in cooperation with the Inter-American Financial and Economic Advisory Committee, maritime organizations functioning in various American nations and the Inter-American Maritime Technical Commission, they endeavor to coordinate shipping between the American Republics so that the vessels now in continental service, without omitting or changing existing stops, may make such calls at ports of nations, which are most affected in certain regions of the hemisphere, as are necessary in order to assure them regular and suitable transportation;

[1] See *Documents, III, 1940–41,* p. 621.

320   DOCUMENTS ON AMERICAN FOREIGN RELATIONS

(*f*) That they take, in so far as possible, measures necessary to minimize expenses at ports of call, such as port dues and lighthouse charges, etc.;

(*g*) That they endeavor to expand port facilities and provide means necessary for the rapid repair of damaged vessels and for their normal maintenance;

(*h*) That they undertake to speed up internal transportation and increase the carrying capacity of railway systems, taking steps rapidly to complete routes important for continental defense which are under construction or reconstruction;

(*i*) That they study the desirability of recognizing the right of each State to full participation in international trade under a system of free access to transportation for all classes of cargo in conformity with the provisions of existing international agreements and consistent with the legislation of each country;

(*j*) That they undertake to improve and enlarge existing airports and to construct new airports equipped with necessary installations and repair shops, so as to create a system of air transportation, with terminals in the Americas, which fully meets the requirements of inter-American and domestic air services;

(*k*) That they speed up the construction of the unfinished sections of the Pan American Highway [1] and the improvement of the sections already constructed so as to provide efficient transportation in the hemisphere and permit the development of inter-American and domestic commerce, connecting centers of production with centers of consumption. To this end, there are expressly reiterated the conclusions approved in recommendation number LII of the Lima Conference of 1938 [2] and in resolution number XXIII of the Havana Meeting of 1940; [3] and

(*l*) That they give full support and render the fullest practicable measure of cooperation to the work of the Inter-American Financial and Economic Advisory Committee and of its Inter-American Maritime Technical Commission in all their problems and, particularly in the field of merchant shipping, taking joint steps necessary to enable the Governments of the American Republics to mobilize, in the fullest and most effective manner, all the ships available in the Western

[1] See p. 407.
[2] *Eighth International Conference of American States, Lima, Peru, December 9–27 1938, Report on the Results of the Conference submitted to the Governing Board of the Pan American Union by the Director General* (Congress and Conference Series No. 27) p. 71.
[3] *Documents, III, 1940–41*, p. 80.

Hemisphere, so as to give priority to the transportation of strategic and basic materials essential for the defense of the Continent and for the maintenance of the economic welfare of the American Republics.

2. To recommend to the Inter-American Financial and Economic Advisory Committee and the Inter-American Maritime Technical Commission:

(a) That they suggest to the Governments measures necessary in order, by previous agreement between administrative agencies of such Governments, aviation and shipping concerns, and public or private railway companies operating in the American Republics, to promote and improve the entire system of inter-American transportation, endeavoring to guarantee regular and coordinated mobilization and provision of means necessary for the transportation both of products which are imported and exported by each of the countries as well as for the effective and comfortable travel of their peoples;

(b) That they encourage the conclusion of agreements regarding the matters set forth in the preceding paragraph between countries that wish to enter into them, and study ways of replacing existing means of transportation should they become inadequate;

(c) That they study the possibility of allocating adequate and sufficient transportation to each country, taking into account not only tonnage but also the speed of and the facilities for loading and discharging vessels which carry essential raw materials, and that, moreover, they encourage the fixing, from time to time, of maximum freight rates;

(d) That they study a general plan of inter-American maritime transportation, taking into account the availability of vessels and the minimum requirements of each of the Republics of the Continent, so that they will all be linked, by regular and adequate services, with their principal import and export markets;

(e) That they examine the desirability of applying the "Cash and Carry System" to the transportation of commodities.

XXI. Civil and Commercial Aviation

WHEREAS:

1. The American Republics by mutual understanding have agreed to unite in a common effort to resist the attempts of any foreign power through force or subversion to destroy their individual or collective freedom;

2. The peaceful pursuit of such a course is presently threatened by the non-American countries at war with American Republics whose resort to subversive methods and force is inimical to our common integrity; and

3. It has been amply demonstrated that the operation or use of aircraft in the American Republics by nationals of non-American countries at war with American Republics and the use of airfields and aviation facilities in these Republics by such nationals constitute a serious threat to hemispheric defense,

The Third Meeting of the Ministers of Foreign Affairs of the American Republics

Resolves:

To recommend to each American Republic that in harmony with its national laws, immediate steps be taken to restrict the operation or use of civil or commercial aircraft and the use of aviation facilities to bona fide citizens and enterprises of the American Republics or to citizens or enterprises of such other countries as have shown themselves, in the judgment of the respective Governments, to be in full sympathy with the principles of the Declaration of Lima.

XL. Telecommunications

The Third Meeting of the Ministers of Foreign Affairs of the American Republics

Resolves:

1. To recommend that each American Republic adopt the necessary and immediate measures to close all radiotelephone and radiotelegraph communication between the American Republics and the aggressor States and all territories subservient to them, except in so far as official communications of the American Governments are concerned.

2. To recommend the establishment and maintenance, through a system of licenses, or other adequate means, of an effective control of the transmission and reception of messages whatever might be the telecommunication system used; and that telecommunications which might endanger the security of each American State and of the Continent in general be prohibited.

3. To recommend the adoption of immediate measures to eliminate clandestine telecommunication stations and that bilateral or multilateral agreements be concluded by the interested Governments to facilitate the fulfillment of the technical requirements of this Resolution

HUMANITARIAN AND HEALTH

XIX. Red Cross

WHEREAS:

1. The continuation and extension of hostilities have brought, and will continue to bring, great distress to millions of civilians as a result of invasion, indiscriminate bombing from the air, and other ravages of war;

2. The voluntary organizations functioning under the Convention of Geneva can cooperate in the treatment of the sick and wounded of the military forces;

3. The threat of hostilities in the Western Hemisphere requires preparation and training in first aid, nursing, disaster relief, and related activities;

4. These needs and opportunities for service domestically and internationally can best be met by taking advantage of the humanitarian services of strong Red Cross Societies;

5. It is desirable to take advantage of the valuable services which Red Cross Societies may render as consultative and cooperative agencies in social welfare problems;

6. The Second Meeting of Ministers of Foreign Affairs of the American Republics held at Havana declared that it was desirable to organize an Inter-American League of National Red Cross Societies and this organization has not yet been created;

7. In the present circumstances the existence of such a League is now even more necessary, and its work should be extended to the civilians of the American Republics suffering from the consequences of the present war;

8. The important part which women have played in the noble work of the Red Cross deserves express recognition of their special position with reference to these services.

The Third Meeting of the Ministers of Foreign Affairs of the American Republics

Resolves:

To recommend to the Governments of the American Republics:

1. That they lend all possible support toward the greatest development and strengthening of their respective Red Cross Societies.

2. That they study the desirability of using these Societies as consultative agencies.

3. That they consult among themselves as soon as possible with

regard to the available means for putting into effect Recommendatio
IV approved at the Havana Meeting.[1]

4. That, when they deem it desirable, they consider whether th
services rendered by women to the Red Cross in times of peace or wa
can be given equal weight within the framework of their respectiv
domestic legislation to those of a military nature rendered by men.

XXX. IMPROVEMENT OF HEALTH AND SANITARY CONDITIONS

WHEREAS:

1. The American Republics are now undertaking measures for th
development of certain common objectives and plans which will con
tribute to the reconstruction of world order;

2. The American Republics are now undertaking measures seekin
to conserve and develop their resources of critical and strategic material
to maintain their domestic economies and eliminate economic activitie
prejudicial to the welfare and security of the American Republics;

3. The defense of the Western Hemisphere requires the mobilizatio
of the vital forces, human and material, of the American Republics; an

4. Adequate health and sanitary measures constitute an essentia
contribution in safeguarding the defensive powers and the ability t
resist aggression of the peoples of the American Republics,

The Third Meeting of the Ministers of Foreign Affairs of the America
Republics

Resolves:

1. To recommend that the Governments of the American Republic
take individually, or by complementary agreements between two c
more of them, appropriate steps to deal with problems of public healt
and sanitation, by providing, in accordance with ability, raw material
services and funds.

2. To recommend that to these ends there be utilized the technica
aid and advice of the national health service of each country in coope
ation with the Pan American Sanitary Bureau.

XXXIII. HUMANIZATION OF WAR

The Third Meeting of the Ministers of Foreign Affairs of the America
Republics

Resolves:

To reaffirm the principles contained in Resolution VI[2] of Panam
on humanization of war, and in Resolution IX[3] of that Meeting on th

---

[1] *Documents, III, 1940–41,* p. 67.   [2] *Ibid., II, 1939–40,* p. 105.   [3] *Ibid.,* p. 10

naintenance of international activities in accordance with Christian
norality; and condemns the practice of holding prisoners as hostages
and taking reprisals on them as contrary to the principles of law and the
umanitarian sentiments which states must observe during the course
of hostilities.

POST-WAR ORGANIZATION AND LAW

XXV. Post-War Problems

WHEREAS:

1. World peace must be based on the principles of respect for law, of
ustice and of cooperation which inspire the Nations of America and
which have been expressed at Inter-American Meetings held from 1889
o date;

2. A new order of peace must be supported by economic principles
which will insure equitable and lasting international trade with equal
pportunities for all Nations;

3. Collective security must be founded not only on political institu-
ions but also on just, effective, and liberal economic systems;

4. It is indispensable to undertake the immediate study of the bases
or this new economic and political order; and

5. It is an imperative necessity for the countries of America to increase
heir productive capacity; to secure, from their international trade,
eturns which will permit them adequately to remunerate labor and
mprove the standard of living of workers; to protect and preserve the
ealth of their peoples and develop their civilization and culture,

The Third Meeting of the Ministers of Foreign Affairs of the American
Republics

Resolves:

1. To request the Governing Board of the Pan American Union to
onvoke an Inter-American Technical Economic Conference charged
ith the study of present and post-war economic problems.

2. To entrust the Inter-American Juridical Committee with the
ormulation of specific recommendations relative to the international
rganization in the juridical and political fields, and in the field of interational security.

3. To entrust the Inter-American Financial and Economic Advisory
ommittee with a similar function in the economic field, to make the
ecessary preparations for the Inter-American Technical Economic
onference, referred to in the first paragraph of this Resolution.

4. To request the Pan American Union to appoint an Executive Com mittee [1] to receive such projects as the American nations may present and to submit said projects, respectively, to the Inter-American Juridica Committee and to the Inter-American Financial and Economic Advisor, Committee.

5. To request the Pan American Union to direct this Executive Com mittee to submit the recommendations of the Inter-American Juridica Committee to the Governments of the American Republics so that th conclusions reached may be adopted at a subsequent Meeting of Min isters of Foreign Affairs.

6. To request the Pan American Union to determine, in agreemen with the Governments of the American Republics, the date and place c meeting of the Inter-American Technical Economic Conference, referre to in the first paragraph of this Resolution.

XXVI. INTER-AMERICAN JURIDICAL COMMITTEE

WHEREAS:

1. In the General Declaration of Neutrality of the American Republic signed in Panama, the Inter-American Neutrality Committee [2] wa created for the purpose of studying and formulating recommendatior with respect to the problems of neutrality; and

2. The profound alteration in the international situation in Americ demands a substantial expansion of the scope of said Committee,

The Third Meeting of the Ministers of Foreign Affairs of the America Republics

Resolves:

1. To pay tribute and to congratulate His Excellency Afranio de Mel Franco, Chairman of the Inter-American Neutrality Committee and i members: Their Excellencies Luis A. Podestá Costa, Mariano Fontecill A. Aguilar Machado, Charles G. Fenwick, Gustavo Herrera, Robert Cordoba, Manuel Francisco Jimenez Ortiz, Salvador Martinez Mercad

[1] The Governing Board of the Pan American Union on February 25, 1942, desi nated the Executive Committee as follows: Dr. Carlos Martins, Ambassador of Br zil; Dr. Gabriel Turbay, Ambassador of Colombia; Dr. Aurelio F. Concheso, Ar bassador of Cuba; Captain Colón Eloy Alfaro, Ambassador of Ecuador; and D Francisco Castillo Nájera, Ambassador of Mexico. (*Bulletin of the Pan Americ Union*, LXXVI, p. 284.)

[2] See *Documents, II, 1939-40,* p. 109; *III, 1940-41,* p. 63. For the texts of recor mendations submitted by this Committee, see *American Journal of International La* vol. 34 (1940), Supplement, p. 75, 135; vol. 35 (1941), Supplement, p. 38; and v 36 (1942), Supplement, p. 173.

Eduardo Labougle, Carlos Eduardo Stolk and Fernando Lagarde y Vigil, who have been members or are at present members of this Committee, for the valuable services they have rendered to the American Republics and in the development of international law.

2. That the Inter-American Neutrality Committee at present existing will continue to function in its present form under the name of "Inter-American Juridical Committee," will have its seat at Rio de Janeiro and may meet temporarily, if it deems it necessary, in other American capitals.

3. That the members of the Inter-American Juridical Committee will be the jurists especially appointed by their respective Governments, and that they will have no other duties than those pertaining to the Committee.

4. The Inter-American Juridical Committee, in exceptional cases, may have recourse to the services of technical experts which it considers indispensable for the most efficient performance of its duties, and the salaries of these experts will be met by the American States through the intermediary of the Pan American Union.

5. The Committee may also invite American jurists, whom they consider to be specialists on specific subjects, to take part in their deliberations on special juridical matters.

6. The Committee will have as its object:

(a) To study, in accordance with experience and the development of events, the juridical problems created for the American Republics by the world war and those which are submitted to it in accordance with the resolutions approved at the Meetings of the Ministers of Foreign Affairs or at the International Conferences of American States;

(b) To continue the studies on the subject of contraband of war and on the project of a code relative to the principles and rules of neutrality;

(c) To report on possible claims arising from the requisition or use of immobilized merchant vessels or those under the flag of a non-American enemy, or belonging to states whose territories are occupied by a non-American enemy; as well as on possible claims by any American Republic against a non-American enemy state for unlawful acts committed to the detriment of such Republic, its nationals or their property;

(d) To develop and coordinate the work of codifying international law, without prejudice to the duties entrusted to other existing organizations;

(e) To formulate recommendations with regard to the manner of solving the problems mentioned under sub-paragraph (a), transmitting

the same to the Governments through the Pan American Union, o
directly when it considers it necessary, on condition that the Unio
be duly informed.

RESERVATION OF THE DELEGATION OF THE
REPUBLIC OF PERU

6. As to Resolution XXVI on the Inter-American Juridical Committee:
"Peru votes in favor of this project with the reservation that, in accordanc
with the express purpose of this meeting, the enemy State referred to in para
graph 'c' must be a non-American State.
"Furthermore, it places on record the fact that the Third Meeting of th
Ministers of Foreign Affairs gave it this true interpretation."

XXVII. COORDINATION OF THE RESOLUTIONS OF THE MEETINGS O THE MINISTERS OF FOREIGN AFFAIRS OF THE AMERICA REPUBLICS

WHEREAS:

In view of the continual changes which characterize the present perio
of emergency, it is necessary to coordinate the resolutions, declaration
and other acts of the Meetings of the Ministers of Foreign Affairs of th
American Republics, by incorporating the changes which circumstance
require,

The Third Meeting of the Ministers of Foreign Affairs of the America
Republics

Resolves:

1. To recommend to the Governing Board of the Pan American Unio
that the agenda of future Meetings of the Ministers of Foreign Affai
of the American Republics shall always include the following topic:
"Coordination of the resolutions, declarations and other acts of prev
ous Meetings of the Ministers of Foreign Affairs."

2. To recommend to the Inter-American Juridical Committee tl
study and coordination referred to in the preceding paragraph, entrus
ing it to transmit its conclusions to the Meetings of the Ministers
Foreign Affairs through the Pan American Union.

XXVIII. AFFIRMATION OF THE TRADITIONAL THEORY OF LAW

The Third Meeting of the Ministers of Foreign Affairs of the Americ
Republics

Agrees:

To refer to the Inter-American Juridical Committee the project of t
Delegation of Bolivia entitled "Affirmation of the traditional theory
law in face of a deliberate disregard of international justice and morality

XXV. Support and Adherence to the Principles of the
"Atlantic Charter"[1]

The Third Meeting of the Ministers of Foreign Affairs of the American
Republics

Resolves:

To take note of the contents of the "Atlantic Charter" and to express
to the President of the United States of America its satisfaction with
the inclusion in that document of principles which constitute a part of
the juridical heritage of America in accordance with the Convention on
Rights and Duties of States approved at the Seventh International Conference of American States, held at Montevideo in 1933.[2]

RESERVATION OF THE DELEGATION OF GUATEMALA

4. The Representative of the Secretary of Foreign Affairs of Guatemala
agrees fully to the adherence and support of the principles of the Atlantic
Charter; and, in so far as these principles may affect the rights of Guatemala to
Belize, it makes an express declaration and reservation in the same terms as the
reservation made by Guatemala at the First Meeting of the Ministers of Foreign
Affairs of the American Republics, held at Panama,[3] which it maintains in its
entirety while bearing in mind the resolutions and Convention on this question
approved at the Second Meeting of the Ministers of Foreign Affairs of the American Republics held at Havana.[4]

B. Solidarity and Defense

ESTABLISHMENT OF THE OFFICE OF COORDINATOR OF INTER-AMERICAN
AFFAIRS

[See *Documents, III, 1940–41*, p. 109 for text of Order establishing the Office of
Coordinator of Commercial and Cultural Relations Between the American Republics,
the powers and functions of which are vested by Executive Order No. 8840 in the
newly created office of Coordinator of Inter-American Affairs.]

1) *Executive Order No. 8840 Establishing the Office of the Coordinator
of Inter-American Affairs in the Executive Office of the President
and Defining Its Functions and Duties, July 30, 1941* [5]

By virtue of the authority vested in me by the Constitution and
Statutes of the United States, and in order to define further the functions
and duties of the Office for Emergency Management with respect to the

[1] Costa Rica, Cuba, Dominican Republic, Guatemala, Haiti, Honduras, Mexico,
Nicaragua, Panama, Salvador and the United States are parties to the Atlantic
Charter by reason of being parties to the Declaration by United Nations of January
, 1942. Mexico adhered to the Declaration on June 5, 1942.
[2] *Treaties, Conventions, etc.*, 1923–1937, IV, p. 4807.
[3] *Documents, II, 1939–40*, p. 119. [4] *Ibid., III, 1940–41*, p. 79, 85.
[5] 6 *Fed. Reg.*, p. 3857; Department of State, *Bulletin*, V, p. 94.

unlimited national emergency declared by the President on May 27, 1941 and to provide for the development of commercial and cultural relation between the American Republics and thereby increasing the solidarit: of this hemisphere and furthering the spirit of cooperation between th Americas in the interest of hemisphere defense, it is hereby ordered a follows:

1. There is established within the Office for Emergency Managemen of the Executive Office of the President the Office of the Coordinator o Inter-American Affairs, at the head of which there shall be a Coordinato appointed by the President. The Coordinator shall discharge and per form his duties and responsibilities under the direction and supervisio of the President. The Coordinator shall serve as such without compen sation, but shall be entitled to actual and necessary transportation, sub sistence, and other expenses incidental to the performance of his duties

2. Subject to such policies, regulations, and directions as the Presiden may from time to time prescribe, the Office of the Coordinator of Inter American Affairs shall:

a. Serve as the center for the coordination of the cultural and com mercial relations of the Nation affecting hemisphere defense.

b. Formulate and execute programs, in cooperation with the De partment of State which, by effective use of governmental and privat facilities in such fields as the arts and sciences, education and travel, th radio, the press, and the cinema, will further the national defense an strengthen the bonds between the nations of the Western Hemisphere

c. Formulate, recommend, and execute programs in the commercia and economic fields which, by the effective use of governmental an private facilities, will further the commercial well-being of the Wester Hemisphere.

d. Assist in the coordination and carrying out of the purposes o Public Resolution No. 83 approved June 15, 1941, entitled "T authorize the Secretaries of War and of the Navy to assist the govern ments of American Republics to increase their military and nava establishments, and for other purposes."

e. Review existing laws and recommend such new legislation as ma be deemed essential to the effective realization of the basic cultura and commercial objectives of the Government's program of hemispher solidarity.

f. Exercise and perform all powers and functions now or heretofor vested in the Office for Coordination of Commercial and Cultural Re lations Between the American Republics, established by order of th Council of National Defense on August 16, 1940.

g. Keep the President informed with respect to progress made in carrying out this Order; and perform such other related duties as the President may from time to time assign or delegate to it.

3. In the study of problems and in the execution of programs, it shall e the policy of the Office of the Coordinator of Inter-American Affairs) collaborate with and to utilize the facilities of existing departments nd agencies which perform functions and activities affecting the cultural nd commercial aspects of hemisphere defense. Such departments and gencies are requested to cooperate with the Coordinator in arranging)r appropriate clearance of proposed policies and measures involving 1e commercial and cultural aspects of Inter-American affairs.

4. Within the limits of funds appropriated or allocated for purposes 1compassed by this Order, the Coordinator may contract with and :ansfer funds to existing governmental agencies and institutions and 1ay enter into contracts and agreements with individuals, educational, 1formational, commercial, scientific, and cultural institutions, associa-.ons, agencies, and industrial organizations, firms, and corporations.

5. The Coordinator is authorized and directed to take over and carry ut the provisions of any contracts heretofore entered into by the Office)r Coordination of Commercial and Cultural Relations Between the .merican Republics, established by order of the Council of National)efense on August 16, 1940. The Coordinator is further authorized to ssume any obligations or responsibilities which have heretofore been ndertaken by the said Office for and on behalf of the United States iovernment.

6. There is hereby established within the Office of the Coordinator of nter-American Affairs a Committee on Inter-American Affairs, consist-1g of the Coordinator as Chairman, one designee each from the Depart-1ents of State, Treasury, Agriculture, and Commerce, the President of he Export-Import Bank and such additional representatives from other gencies and departments as may be designated by the heads of such epartments or agencies at the request of the Coordinator of Inter-.merican Affairs. The Committee shall consider and correlate proposals 'ith respect to the commercial, cultural, educational, and scientific spects of hemisphere defense relations, and shall make recommenda-.ons to the appropriate Government departments and agencies.

7. The Coordinator may provide for the internal organization and 1anagement of the Office of the Coordinator of Inter-American Affairs. 'he Coordinator shall obtain the President's approval for the establish-1ent of the principal subdivisions of the office and the appointment of the eads thereof. The Coordinator may appoint such committees as may e required for the conduct of the activities of his office.

8. Within the limits of such funds as may be appropriated to the Co ordinator or as may be allocated to him by the President, the Coordi nator may employ necessary personnel and make provisions for necessar supplies, facilities, and services. However, the Coordinator shall use suc statistical, informational, fiscal, personnel, and other general busines services and facilities as may be made available to him through the Offic for Emergency Management.

2. PROVISIONAL ADMINISTRATION OF EUROPEAN COLONIES AND POSSES SIONS IN THE AMERICAS

(1) Convention on Provisional Administration of European Colonies an Possessions in the Americas, Signed at Havana, July 30, 1940

In force January 8, 1942

[For text of Convention, see *Documents, III, 1940–41*, p. 85.]

(a) Action Taken and Entrance into Force

Article XX stipulates that the convention "shall enter into force when two thirds of the American Republics have deposited their respective instruments of ratification." The instrument of ratification by Honduras was deposited with the Pan American Union on January 8, 1942 and, since this was the fourteenth ratification, it completed the "two-thirds" provision and brought the convention into force as of January 8, 1942. (Department of State, *Bulletin* VI, p. 72.)

	APPROVED	RATIFIED	DEPOSIT
Argentine Republic	July 24, 1941	Aug. 22, 1941	Oct. 1, 1941
Bolivia			
Brazil		Nov. 26, 1940	Jan. 14, 1941
Chile			
Colombia	Oct. 2, 1940	Sept. 17, 1941	Nov. 5, 1941
Costa Rica	Sept. 23, 1940	Oct. 10, 1940	Dec. 17, 1940
Cuba			
Dominican Republic		Nov. 7, 1940	Nov. 28, 1940
Ecuador	Sept. 25, 1941	Oct. 23, 1941	Dec. 27, 1941
Guatemala	Apr. 24, 1941	July 28, 1941	Aug. 14, 1941
Haiti		July 24, 1941	Aug. 13, 1941
Honduras	Dec. 23, 1940	Jan. 3, 1942	Jan. 8, 1942
Mexico		Feb. 19, 1942	Mar. 21, 1942
Nicaragua		Dec. 19, 1941	May 12, 1942
Panama		April 30, 1942	May 13, 1941
Paraguay			
Peru.		Mar. 6, 1941	Apr. 4, 1941
Salvador	Nov. 27, 1940	May 20, 1940	July 9, 1941
United States		Oct. 10, 1940	Oct. 24, 1940
Uruguay		Feb. 5, 1942	Mar. 26, 1942
Venezuela		Sept. 24, 1941	Oct. 22, 1941

2) *Inter-American Commission for Territorial Administration. Resolution of the Governing Board of the Pan American Union, April 6, 1942* [1]

The Act of Havana [2] created an Emergency Committee, composed of one representative from each of the American Republics. As soon as the Convention came into force, the authority and functions exercised by the Emergency Committee were to be transferred to the Inter-American Commission for Territorial Administration. The question arose as to whether the persons appointed to serve on the Emergency Committee should be considered members of the Inter-American Commission for Territorial Administration.

1. That until the respective Governments shall communicate to the Pan American Union the name of another representative, the member designated to serve on the Emergency Committee created by the Act of Havana shall be considered to be a member of the Inter-American Commission for Territorial Administration.

2. That the Governments which have ratified the Convention, but have not named a representative on the Emergency Committee or the Inter-American Commission for Territorial Administration, be urged to designate their member on the latter Commission as soon as possible.

3. That those Governments that have not yet ratified the Convention on the Provisional Administration of European Colonies and Possessions in the Americas be urged to give early consideration to such ratification.

4. That the representatives of those Governments that have not yet ratified the Convention but have appointed members on the Emergency Committee be considered as eligible to attend any meetings that may be held by the Inter-American Commission for Territorial Administration pending ratification of the Convention by their respective Governments.

5. That the Government which desires to convene the Commission, as provided for in the Convention, shall communicate this desire to the Pan American Union, indicating the city in which the meeting is to be held, and the Union shall notify the members of the Commission and shall inform all the other States, parties to the Convention.

3. MUTUAL DEFENSE AGAINST AGGRESSION

Alberto Guani, Minister of Foreign Relations of Uruguay, on June 21, 1941, transmitted to the Governments of the American Republics a memorandum in which, after reviewing Uruguay's attitude in 1917 [3] and the subsequent Declara-

[1] *Bulletin of the Pan American Union,* LXXVI, p. 406.
[2] Act of Havana Concerning Provisional Administration of European Colonies and Possessions in the Americas, signed July 30, 1940. For text, see *Documents, II, 939–40,* p. 93.
[3] The decree of June 18, 1917, ordered "that no American country which in defense of its own rights should find itself in a state of war with nations of other continents will be treated as belligerents" (Kelchner, Warren H., *Latin American Relations with the League of Nations,* p. 24).

tion of Lima of 1938 [1] and Resolution XV of Havana,[2] the "concordance of th attitudes of all the American countries" was asked for the criterion alread agreed to "that any act against a continental [*i.e.* hemisphere] state should b regarded as an aggression against all."

Each of the American Republics replied, in various affirmative forms. Mos of the replies were short and categorical. The Argentine Ministry of Foreig Relations and Education wrote June 27: "The position of the Argentin Government shows definitively its complete agreement with the Governmer of Uruguay in the appreciation of the problems related to the security an territorial integrity of the American countries to which the memorandum unde review refers." The Ministry of Foreign Relations of Chile on July 2 reviewe the scope of the commitments already taken and concluded that it "is supporte by solid arguments in not desiring any innovation in the system of collectiv defense which the American states have adopted"; this attitude was believed nc to be a departure "from the traditional line of its international policy of stric solidarity toward and with all and each of the countries of the Continent." Se Uruguay, Ministerio de relaciones exteriores, *Solaridad americana; Consulta sob el caso de un estado americano en una guerra extracontinental* (Montevide Imprenta "El Siglo ilustrado," 1941).

(1) *Memorandum Handed by the Acting Secretary of State* (*Welles*) t *the Minister of Uruguay* (*Richling*)*, July 1, 1941* [3]

The Acting Secretary of State of the United States of America desire to inform His Excellency the Minister of Foreign Affairs of the Orienta Republic of Uruguay of the gratification with which the Government c the United States has learned of the views of the Government of Urugua as communicated by Dr. Guani in his memorandum of June 21, 1941.

The Government of Uruguay has once again lighted the way toward . constructive and practical cooperation between all of the American Re publics at this moment which is more critical than any which has tran spired since the achievement of their independence.

A black night of fear and destruction and organized murder has er gulfed almost all of Europe and a great part of the rest of the worlc Aggression without comparison in history for its deliberately planne frightfulness has annihilated the independence of one country afte another. The right inherent in every man and woman to worship Go has been ruthlessly and methodically destroyed. The cultures of cer turies, the cultures from which every one of the American nations ha derived its own national inspiration have not only been temporaril blotted out but an endeavor is being made to extirpate them forever. N country anywhere, today, is secure from this unmasked lust for powe and loot which has no limit but domination of the entire world.

In view of this situation, the Government of Uruguay addresses itse

[1] *Documents, I, 1938–39*, p. 46.   [2] *Ibid., III, 1940–41*, p. 76.
[3] Department of State, *Bulletin*, V, p. 8.

the other American Republics urging positive implementation of the
policy of hemisphere solidarity already unanimously adopted by the
American nations at previous inter-American conferences.

Uruguay recalls that its great liberator Artigas, over a hundred years
ago, recognized the common interests of the peoples of the Western
Hemisphere and suggested the undertaking of an offer of reciprocal and
mutual assistance. Uruguay recollects that during the World War of
1914–1918 it adopted, long before its general acceptance in this hemisphere, the policy that any act susceptible of affecting adversely the
rights of any nation of the Americas should be considered as constituting
an offense committed against all the American nations, and should bring
about a uniform and common reaction.

Pursuant to this policy, Uruguay declared in 1917 that it would not
treat as a belligerent any American country which, in defense of its own
rights, should find itself in a state of war with nations of other continents.
Finally, Uruguay recalls that the policy of solidarity which it espoused
twenty-five years ago has now been accepted by all the other American
countries in a series of inter-American instruments and, therefore, in-
quires of the other American Republics, whether, in their judgment, the
moment is not opportune to give new content and definition to the policy
of inter-American solidarity.

The Government of the United States welcomes the opportunity
afforded by the initiative of the Government of Uruguay briefly to restate
the policies which it is presently pursuing.

In the first place, the Government of the United States has considered
it axiomatic that the security of each of the American Republics was
dependent upon the security of all. It was for this simple but basic
reason that it wholeheartedly supported at Buenos Aires, Lima, Panama,
and Havana the several agreements to make inviolate the peace, security
and territorial integrity of the Americas.

In the second place, the President of the United States has frequently
declared, the last time formally before the chiefs of mission of the other
American Republics in Washington on May 27 last, the unshakable
determination of the United States to give aid to whatever extent and
in whatever quantity may lie within its power, to countries prepared to
resist the forces of aggression. The Congress has passed legislation to
enable the transfer of equipment and supplies to such countries, and
practical assistance on a stupendous scale is now being furnished.

In pursuance of these two policies, the one of hemispheric solidarity,
the other of aid to countries resisting aggression — but both of them with
the end in view, namely, the security of the Western Hemisphere — the

Government of the United States has offered and extended cooperati
assistance of various types to the other American Republics. The ec
nomic and financial resources of the United States, the naval and air ba
facilities acquired from Great Britain and from Denmark, and milita
and naval *matériel*, have been made available to all the American R
publics on the fullest cooperative basis for the common defense of th
New World.

Equally significant of the desire and purpose of the United States
afford the greatest possible opportunity for realizing to the full the pri
ciple of hemispheric solidarity and defense, there was incorporated in th
Neutrality Act of 1939 a provision excepting, subject to certain cond
tions not here important, American states from the operation of the a
when engaged in war against a non-American state or states.

The safety of the Americas hangs in the balance today. Constructi
and far-sighted action now on the part of all the American Republi
acting together will ensure the preservation for future generations
those liberties and other blessings which our forefathers so laborious
gained.

The Government of the United States welcomes and wholehearted
supports the present initiative of the Government of Uruguay, a
earnestly hopes that it may secure the common approval of the Gover
ments of all of the American Republics.

**4. DECLARATIONS OF WAR, SEVERANCES OF DIPLOMATIC RELATIONS AN
OTHER MANIFESTATIONS OF CONTINENTAL SOLIDARITY BY THE OTH
AMERICAN REPUBLICS**

Resolution XV, Reciprocal Defense and Cooperation for the Defense of t
Nations of the Americas, signed on behalf of all the American Republics in t
Final Act of the Second Meeting of the Ministers of Foreign Affairs of t
American Republics, Havana, July 30, 1940, provided:

"That any attempt on the part of a non-American State against the integri
or inviolability of the territory, the sovereignty or the political independence
an American State shall be considered as an act of aggression against the Stat
which sign this declaration." [1]

The unilateral consideration given by the American Republics under this pr
vision to the aggression of Japan and the aggressive declarations of war l
Germany and Italy against the United States is set forth in the table given belo
The subsequent decisions of the American Republics in consequence of the pr
visions for consultation of Resolution XV were taken in the Third Meeting of t
Ministers of Foreign Affairs of the American Republics (p. 279).

The Government of the United States promptly on December 7, 1941 by te
graph informed its diplomatic missions to all American Republics of the Japane
attacks on United States territory, and the facts were at once communicated
the foreign offices. Without delay or exception, the Governments of all t
republics took affirmative action to align themselves with the United States

[1] *Documents, III, 1940–41*, p. 76.

cordance with the inter-American program of solidarity which they had
veloped. In most cases cordial fraternal messages were exchanged between the
esidents or foreign ministers of the republics and of the United States, in addi-
n to prompt notification of the formal action taken. Similar steps were taken
December 11 following the German and Italian declarations of war and the
nerican Republics, again without exception, took action identic with that
opted with respect to Japan.

) *Declarations of War, Severances of Diplomatic Relations, etc.,
by the American Republics against Axis Powers, as of June 30,
1942*

COUNTRY	DECLARATION OF WAR	SEVERANCE OF DIPLOMATIC RELATIONS	SOLIDARITY AND NON-BELLIGERENCY [1]
'gentina .			Dec. 9, 1941 *B.S.,*[2] V, p. 485–7, 545
)livia . .		Japan } Germany } Jan. 28, Italy } 1942 *B.S.,* VI, p. 90, 339	Dec. 10, 1941 *B.S.,* V, p. 487
'azil . . .		Japan } Germany } Jan. 28, Italy } 1942 *B.S.,* VI, p. 89, 339	Dec. 8, 1941 *B.S.,* V, p. 488
iile . . .		Hungary — May 2, 1942 [3]	Dec. 9, 1941 *El Mercurio,* Dec. 11, 1941
lombia .		Japan — Dec. 8, 1941 *B.S.,* VI, p. 340, 489 Germany } Dec. 19, Italy } 1941 *B.S.,* VI, p. 339, 546	Dec. 22, 1941 *Diario Oficial,* Jan. 28, 1942
)sta Rica .	Japan — Dec. 8, 1941, 11 A.M. *B.S.,* V. p. 490–91 Germany } Dec. 11, Italy } 1941 *B.S.,* V, p. 491	Hungary } May 15, Rumania } 1942 *La Gaceta,* May 22, 1942 [3]	

[1] *Non-belligerency:* characterized by a refusal on the part of the American Republics
t in a state of war to apply to the United States, and other American Republics in a
te of war, certain measures which a neutral under international law is required to
ce against all belligerents without discrimination. Acting under Resolution XV of
: Havana Conference of Foreign Ministers (1940), the Governments of the Latin
nerican Republics have refused to treat as belligerents other American Republics
gaged in war in defense of their rights.
[2] Abbreviation for Department of State, *Bulletin.*
[3] Information from Department of State, Division of Research and Publication.

Country	Declaration of War	Severance of Diplomatic Relations	Solidarity and No. Belligerency
Cuba . . .	Japan — Dec. 9, 1941 Germany } Dec. 11, Italy } 1941 *B.S.*, V, p. 491–92		
Dominican Republic .	Japan — Dec. 8, 1941 Germany } Dec. 11, Italy } 1941 *B.S.*, V, p. 492, 547		
Ecuador . .		Japan } Germany } Jan. 29, Italy } 1942 *B.S.*, VI, p. 91, 340, 493	Dec. 8, 1941 *El Telégrafo*, Dec. 1941 *B.S.*, V, p. 493
Guatemala .	Japan — Dec. 8, 1941 *B.S.*, V, p. 494 Germany } Dec. 11, Italy } 1941 *B.S.*, V, p. 495, 547		
Haiti . . .	Japan — Dec. 8, 1941 Germany } Dec. 12, Italy } 1941 *B.S.*, V, p. 495, 548 Hungary } Rumania } Dec. 24, Bulgaria } 1941 *B.S.*, VI, p. 144		
Honduras .	Japan — Dec. 8, 1941, 11 : 25 A.M. *B.S.*, V, p. 495–96 Germany } Dec. 12, Italy } 1941 *B.S.*, V, p. 548		
Mexico . .	Japan } Germany } May 22, Italy } 1942 *B.S.*, VI, p. 505. Decree issued June 1, 1942, *Diario Oficial*, June 2, 1942.	Japan — Dec. 8, 1941 Germany — Dec. 11, 1941 Italy — Dec. 11, 1941 Hungary — Dec. 19, 1941	

Country	Declaration of War	Severance of Diplomatic Relations	Solidarity and Non-Belligerency
		Bulgaria — Dec. 20, 1941 Rumania — Dec. 23, 1941 *B.S.*, VI, p. 345–97, 496–98, 548	
caragua .	Japan — Dec. 8, 1941 *La Gaceta,* Dec. 13, 1941 Germany } Dec. 11, Italy } 1941 *B.S.*, V, p. 498–99 Rumania } Hungary } Dec. 19, Bulgaria } 1941 *La Prensa,* Dec. 20, 1941		
nama . .	Japan — Dec. 10, 1941 *Gaceta Oficial,* Dec. 10, 1941 Germany } Dec. 12, Italy } 1941 *B.S.*, V, p. 500, 584		
raguay .		Japan } Germany } Jan. 25, Italy } 1942 *B.S.*, VI, p. 91, 348, 500	Dec. 10, 1941 *N. Y. Times,* Jan. 27, 1941
:u . . .		Japan } Jan. 24, Germany } 1942, Italy } 6 : 00 } P.M. *B.S.*, VI, p. 89, 348, 501, 548	
Salvador .	Japan — Dec. 8, 1941, 1 : 00 P.M. *B.S.*, V, p. 493 Germany } Dec. 13, Italy } 1941 *B.S.*, V, p. 494, 547		
iguay . .		Japan } Germany } Jan. 25, Italy } 1942	Dec. 8, 1941 *Diario Oficial,* Dec. 30, 1941

Country	Declaration of War	Severance of Diplomatic Relations	Solidarity and No: Belligerency
Venezuela .		B.S., VI, p. 90, 349, 501, 548	Extended to other Amer. Reps. at war, Dec. 18, 1941 *Diario Oficial*, Jan 5, 1942; *B.S., V,* p. 502
		Japan ⎫ Germany ⎬ Dec. 31, Italy ⎭ 1941 *Gaceta Oficial*, Jan. 1, 1942	Dec. 9, 1941 *Gaceta Oficial*, Dec 9, 1941

(2) *Action of Argentina and Chile Following Japanese Attack Upon a: German and Italian Declarations of War against the United Stat*

The refusal of the Governments of Argentina and Chile to follow the lead other South American Republics in severing diplomatic relations with Japa Germany and Italy, under the terms of Resolution I of the Rio de Janeiro Me ing of Foreign Ministers, gives special importance to the action originally tak by the Governments of these two countries following the Japanese attack Pearl Harbor and the German and Italian supporting declarations of war.

(a) *Decree of the Acting President of the Argentine Republic (Castill(December 9, 1941* [1]

The Argentine Ambassador advised the Secretary of State of the attitude his Government before the issuance of the decree of December 9. Preside Ortiz, Acting President Castillo and General Agustín P. Justo of Argentina s(cordial telegrams to the President, who replied in the same tone. The Acti President conveyed "the friendly wishes of the Argentine Government a people."

Having considered the communications received from the Embas of the United States of America, from the Embassy of Great Britain a from the Embassy of Japan stating that there exists a state of war l tween the said powers, and

Whereas:

These communications make it necessary to determine the position the Argentine Republic in this state of war, as well as the line of condt to be observed in this case without precedent since this is the first ti: that the declarations and agreements with respect to solidarity, mut(assistance and defensive cooperation of the American nations as approv

[1] Department of State, *Bulletin*, V, p. 485.

the Conference of Buenos Aires and the meetings of Lima, Panama
ıd Havana, will be applicable.

To this end it is especially fitting to invoke Declaration XV of the
ːeeting of Havana to which the Argentine Republic adhered with the
her American countries, since this case relates to an extracontinental
ːgression against the sovereignty of one of the American states and the
olation of its territory.

The Vice President of the Argentine Nation in exercise of the executive
)wer in a general Ministerial resolution decrees:

ARTICLE I. The position of the Argentine Republic in the present
ternational conflict will be governed with respect to the United States
ⅴ the Pan American obligations assumed with regard to solidarity,
ɪutual assistance and defensive cooperation.

ARTICLE II. As a consequence of this, the Argentine Republic does
ɪt consider the United States of America in the position of a belligerent
ɪuntry in this conflict.

ARTICLE III. The provisions of the decree regarding neutrality pre-
ribed by Ministerial Resolution of September 4, 1939, are made appli-
ːble to the present state of war and only with respect to Great Britain
ıd Japan.

ARTICLE IV. The Argentine Republic in due course and following the
ocedure provided by the above mentioned convention XV of Havana
ill proceed to negotiate the necessary complementary agreements.

ARTICLE V. Let this be communicated, published in the official bulletin
ıd given to the National Registry.

*) *Decree of the Acting President of the Argentine Republic* (*Castillo*),
     December 13, 1941 [1]

In view of the communications received from the Embassies of the
ɑited States of America, Germany and Italy regarding the state of war
ɪsting among these nations, considering the terms of the decree issued
ⅴ this government by a general Ministerial Resolution of the 9th instant
view of the war into which that American country has been drawn as a
ːsult of the aggression carried out against it and in accordance with the
ːclarations and agreements applicable to the case under the terms of
ɪich the Argentine position is defined within principles of continental
ɪity, the Vice President of the Argentine Nation exercising executive
)wer decrees — ARTICLE I: The position established by decree on the
h instant is hereby extended to the state of war existing between the

[1] *Ibid.*, p. 545.

United States of America and Germany and Italy in so far as it declar
that the Republic does not consider the United States of America in tʰ
situation of a belligerent country and there are hereby applied to Ge
many and Italy the provisions of the decree of neutrality issued throuʒ
a Ministerial Resolution on September 4, 1939.

(c) The Vice President of Chile (Mendez) to the President of tʰ United States (Roosevelt), December 10, 1941 [1]

The United States was assured on December 7 that the Chilean Governme
would take all precautions to protect the production and furnishing of strateʒ
materials to the United States and had taken measures to protect mines aʳ
industries belonging to United States citizens.

I have the honor to inform Your Excellency that, after a unanimoᵘ
decision by the Council of Ministers, I have proceeded to issue a decrʳ
in which it is provided that the Government of Chile will not consid
belligerent, for the effects of the application of the laws and principl
which govern neutrality, the Government of the United States and tʰ
Governments of the other American nations which have declared or mᵃ
declare themselves to be in a state of war in connection with the preseʳ
conflict.   In transmitting the foregoing to Your Excellency, I am pa
ticularly happy to forward to you the adherence of the Chilean peop
and Government on the occasion of the aggression of which your countʳ
has been the object.   Chile, in accordance with its invariable inte
national tradition, is ready to comply with the engagements which it hᵃ
contracted with respect to continental defense. Together with my wish
for the prosperity of the American people and for Your Excellency
personal happiness, I beg you to accept the assurances of my highest aʳ
most distinguished consideration.

5. USE OF FACILITIES IN PANAMA AND CUBA FOR MILITARY PURPOSʳ

Under the terms of the General Treaty of Defense and Cooperation, concludᵉ
March 2, 1936,[2] the Governments of Panama and the United States obligat
themselves to take all measures required for the effective protection of t
Panama Canal. In the light of this special obligation, the declaration made ᵇ
the Government of Panama on December 7, 1941, following the Pearl Harbᵇ
attack, is of special significance.

(1) Proclamation of the Government of Panama, December 7, 1941 [3]

The Government of the United States of America has officiaᴵ
informed the Government of Panama that the military forces of tʰ

---

[1] Department of State, Bulletin, V, p. 489. The President gratefully acknowledʒ
the message on December 11.

[2] Documents, II, 1939–40, p. 199.   [3] Department of State, Bulletin, V, p. 4⁹

nperial Government of Japan today unexpectedly attacked the military
ises of the United States situated in Hawaii and the Philippines, this
tack being in the form of an aerial bombardment which has caused an
ppreciable number of casualties and severe damage. Following this
eacherous aggression carried out while a conference was being held in
'ashington in the midst of a spirit of peace between the Diplomatic
nvoy of the Emperor of Japan and the Secretary of State of the United
ates the Government of Japan has declared that a state of war exists
etween that country and the United States of America. The Govern-
ent at Washington at the same time has been forced to declare that
ere were immediately placed in operation all the war plans prepared
y the United States to defend itself against the Government of Japan.
The critical situation thus created places the Government of Panama
the face of a state of emergency the gravity of which is of indisputable
roportions, and in the face of such facts the Executive power after
areful and detailed study of the situation and with the unanimous
pproval of the Cabinet Council has arrived at the conclusion that the
esent moment demands from the Panamanian Government a clear and
efined declaration of Panama's position in the face of this conflict and
r that reason the Government proceeds to issue this proclamation
hich has as its purpose to declare that the Republic of Panama mindful
its principles of a purely democratic nation true to its international
pligations has taken and will take all the measures which this emergency
quires in order to cooperate in the defense and the protection of the
anama Canal the security of which as well as of the Republic itself are
minently threatened by the aggressor forces of the Government of
pan.

The Panama Canal is the center of American defense and is a project
which the Panamanian nation as well as the United States has a joint
d vital interest as was clearly established in the General Treaty of
arch 2, 1936, signed by the two countries, Article X of which states
at in the event of a conflagration or of threat of aggression which would
danger the security of the Republic of Panama or the neutrality or
curity of the Panama Canal the two Governments will take such
easures of prevention and defense as they may consider necessary for
e protection of their common interests. Mindful of this situation the
overnment has proceeded to intern Japanese subjects residing on the
thmus as a precautionary measure, to forbid the exportation of gold
other funds belonging to the Government of Japan or to its subjects
ho are in Panama, to order censorship of radio and cable communi-
tions and to intensify the surveillance of all elements who constitute

or may constitute a threat against the common interests of Panama an
the United States in the security of the Panama Canal. The Goverr
ment of Panama takes this occasion to reassert once more a univers:
declaration that Panama at all times shall be on the side of the dem(
cratic principles which form the constitutional and republican foundatio
of the Panamanian nation and that it shall continue to cooperate wit
the Government of the United States in a loyal, honest, decided, an
energetic manner in this grave emergency which threatens the vit:
interests of the two countries and which also threatens the principles s
ardently defended by the American Republics as the indispensabl
foundation for their existence as sovereign and free nations.

(2) Agreement for Lease of Defense Sites between Panama and th United States, Panamá, May 18, 1942 [1]

Panama declared war on Japan, Germany and Italy immediately after tl
attack on Pearl Harbor. Following other effective measures taken for the defens
of the Panama Canal, this agreement for the lease to the United States of defen:
sites constituted a further contribution to the security of the Canal and hem
spheric defense. Pending the entry of the agreement into force, the Panamania
Government has permitted the military forces of the United States to occup
and develop these areas as gun emplacements, airplane-detector stations, boml
ing ranges, and auxiliary air fields. The largest of these is the Rio Hato air bas
situated some 80 miles to the southwest of the Canal.
At the same time announcement was made of the satisfactory settlement (
certain outstanding problems in the relations between the two countries, :
embodied in notes exchanged May 18, 1942 between the Secretary of State ar
the Panamanian Ambassador in Washington, Señor Don Ernesto Jaén Guardi
Among the various points on which agreement has been reached, those of pa
ticular significance follow: The withdrawal of the Panama Railroad Compar
from real-estate operations in the cities of Panamá and Colón by turning over '
Panama certain lots owned by the company in those cities; the delivery to tl
Government of Panama of the waterworks and sewerage systems lying whol
within territory under the jurisdiction of the Republic of Panama; and tl
liquidation of Panama's indebtedness arising out of the construction of tl
strategic Rio Hato–Chorrera Highway. It was stated by the Department th:
the agreements reached on these three points would be submitted to the Col
gress of the United States for approval.
The agreement was not in force, as of September 1, 1942.

The undersigned, Octavio Fábrega, Minister for Foreign Affairs of tl
Republic of Panama, and Edwin C. Wilson, Ambassador of the Unite
States of America, acting on behalf of our respective Governments, f(
which we are duly and legally authorized, have concluded the followir
Agreement:

[1] Ibid., VI, p. 448.

The Governments of the Republic of Panama and of the United
States of America, conscious of their joint obligation, as expressed in
the provisions of the General Treaty of Friendship and Cooperation,
concluded March 2, 1936,[1] to take all measures required for the effective
protection of the Panama Canal in which they are jointly and vitally
interested, have consulted together and have agreed as follows:

ARTICLE I. The Republic of Panama grants to the United States the
temporary use for defense purposes of the lands referred to in the
Memorandum attached to this Agreement and forming an integral part
hereof.[2] These lands shall be evacuated and the use thereof by the
United States of America shall terminate one year after the date on
which the definitive treaty of peace which brings about the end of the
present war shall have entered into effect. If within that period the two
Governments believe that, in spite of the cessation of hostilities, a state
of international insecurity continues to exist which makes vitally
necessary the continuation of the use of any of the said defense bases or
areas, the two Governments shall again enter into mutual consultation
and shall conclude the new agreement which the circumstances require.

The national authorities of the Republic of Panama shall have
adequate facilities for access to the defense sites mentioned herein.

ARTICLE II. The grant mentioned in the foregoing article shall include
the right to use the waters adjacent to the said areas of land and to
improve and deepen the entrances thereto and the anchorage in such
places as well as to perform in/on the said areas of land all the works
that may be necessary in connection with the effective protection of the
Canal. This gives no right to commercial exploitation or utilization of
the soil or subsoil, or of adjacent beaches and streams.

ARTICLE III. Military and naval aircraft of Panama shall be authorized to land at and take off from the airports established within the
areas referred to in Article I. Similarly, military and naval aircraft of
the United States shall be authorized to use military and naval airports
established by the Republic of Panama. The regulations covering such
reciprocal use shall be embodied in an agreement to be negotiated by
the appropriate authorities of the two countries.

ARTICLE IV. The Republic of Panama retains its sovereignty over
the areas of land and water mentioned in the Memorandum referred to
in Article I and the air space thereover, as well as complete jurisdiction
in civil matters, provided, however, that during the period of temporary

[1] *Documents, II, 1939-40*, p. 199.
[2] Not printed. Identification of the strategic areas involved is withheld for reasons
of military secrecy.

occupation contemplated by this Agreement, the Government of th
United States shall have complete use of such areas and exclusiv
jurisdiction in all respects over the civil and military personnel of th
United States situated therein, and their families, and shall be empow
ered, moreover, to exclude such persons as it sees fit without regard t
nationality, from these areas, without prejudice to the provisions of th
second paragraph of Article I of this Agreement, and to arrest, try an
punish all persons who, in such areas, maliciously commit any crim
against the safety of the military installations therein; provided, how
ever, that any Panamanian citizen arrested or detained on any charge
shall be delivered to the authorities of the Republic of Panama for tri
and punishment.

ARTICLE V. The Republic of Panama and the United States reiterat
their understanding of the temporary character of the occupation of th
defense sites covered by this Agreement. Consequently, the Unite
States, recognizing the importance of the cooperation given by Panam
in making these temporary defense sites available and also recognizin
the burden which the occupation of these sites imposes upon the Republi
of Panama, expressly undertakes the obligation to evacuate the lands t
which this contract refers and to terminate completely the use thereo
at the latest within one year after the date on which the definitive treat
of peace which brings about the cessation of the present war, shall hav
entered into effect. It is understood, as has been expressed in Article
that if within this period the two Governments believe that in spite
the cessation of hostilities, a state of international insecurity continu
to exist which makes vitally necessary the continuation of the use of an
of the said defense bases or sites, the two Governments shall again ent
into mutual consultation and shall conclude the new Agreement whic
the circumstances require.

ARTICLE VI. All buildings and structures which are erected by th
United States in the said areas shall be the property of the United State
and may be removed by it before the expiration of this Agreemen
Any other buildings or structures already existing in the areas at th
time of occupation shall be available for the use of the United State
There shall be no obligation on the part of the United States herein
the Republic of Panama to rebuild or repair any destruction or dama
inflicted from any cause whatsoever on any of the said buildings
structures owned or used by the United States in the said areas. Th
United States is not obliged to turn over to Panama the areas at th
expiration of this lease in the condition in which they were at the tin
of their occupation, nor is the Republic of Panama obliged to allow a

ompensation to the United States for the improvements made in the aid areas or for the buildings or structures left thereon, all of which hall become the property of the Republic of Panama upon the termination of the use by the United States of the areas where the structures ave been built.

ARTICLE VII. The areas of land referred to in Article I, the property f the United States situated therein, and the military and civilian ersonnel of the United States and families thereof who live in the said reas, shall be exempt from any tax, imposts or other charges of any kind y the Republic of Panama or its political subdivisions during the term f this Agreement.

ARTICLE VIII. The United States shall complete the construction at ts own expense of the highways described below, under the conditions nd with the materials specified:

Highway A–3. (Shall extend from Piña on the Atlantic side of the sthmus to the Canal Zone boundary at the Rio Providencia. It shall be t least ten feet in width and constructed of macadam.)

Extension of the Trans-Isthmian Highway following the line of the –8 road. (Specifications shall be the same as for the Trans-Isthmian Iighway. The extension shall start at Madrinal, by-passing Madden)am by a bridge over the Chagres River below the Dam to connect with ne P–8 road at Roque and shall extend the P–8 road from Pueblo uevo into Panama City. It is understood that the pavement of the ridge over the Chagres River will be located above the elevation stablished as the Canal Zone boundary.)

Upon the completion of these highways the Government of the United tates will assume the responsibility for any necessary post construction perations, that is, the performance of work necessary to protect the riginal construction until such time as the roads become stabilized.

The Government of Panama guarantees that the roads under its urisdiction used periodically or frequently by the armed forces of the nited States will be well and properly maintained at all times. The overnment of Panama will ask for the cooperation of the Government f the United States in the performance of repair and maintenance work n the said roads whenever it deems necessary such cooperation in order) fulfill the aforesaid guarantee, such as for example in the case of mergencies or situations which require prompt action.

The Government of the United States will bear one third of the total nnual maintenance cost of all Panamanian roads used periodically or equently by the armed forces of the United States, such cost to cover e expense of any wear or damage to roads caused by movements related

to defense activities. The amount payable by the United States will b
based upon accounts presented annually by the Republic of Panam
giving in detail the total annual expenditures made by it on each highwa
used periodically or frequently by the armed forces of the United States
and upon accounts similarly presented by the Government of th
United States giving in similar detail the expenditures made by tha
Government in response to requests from the Government of Panam
as set forth above. In the event that the Government of the Unite
States has rendered cooperation in the maintenance of the said road
the expenses incurred by that Government in so doing will be credite
toward the share of the United States in the total maintenance of th
roads under the jurisdiction of Panama.

In consideration of the above obligations and responsibilities of th
United States, the Government of the Republic of Panama grants th
right of transit for the routine movement of the members of the arme
forces of the United States, the civilian members of such forces and the
families, as well as animals, animal-drawn and motor vehicles employe
by the armed forces or by contractors employed by them for constructio
work or others whose activities are in any way related to the defens
program, on roads constructed by the United States in territory und
the jurisdiction of the Republic of Panama and on the other nation
highways which place the Canal Zone in communication with th
defense areas and of the latter with each other. It should be unde
stood that the United States will take at all times the precautior
necessary to avoid, if possible, interruptions of transit in the Republ
of Panama.

ARTICLE IX. All roads constructed by the United States in tl
territory under the jurisdiction of the Republic of Panama shall be und
the jurisdiction of Panama. As to those secondary roads constructe
by the United States for the purpose of giving access to any defense sit
Panama grants to the military authorities of the United States the rig
to restrict or prohibit public travel on such roads within a reasonab
distance from such sites if such restriction or prohibition is necessary
the military protection of such sites. It is understood that such restri
tion or prohibition is without prejudice to the free access of the inhabi
ants established within the restricted areas to their respective propertie
It is also understood that such restriction or prohibition is not to l
exercised on any part of any main highway.

ARTICLE X. The Government of the United States of America, wh
constructing the air bases and airports on any of the sites referred to
Article I, shall take into consideration, in addition to the requirements

technical order for the safety thereof, the regulations on the matter
s have been or may be promulgated by the joint Aviation Board.

The Republic of Panama shall not permit, without reaching an
greement with the United States, the erection or maintenance of any
erial lines or other obstructions which may constitute a danger for
ersons flying in the vicinity of the areas intended for air bases or air-
orts. If, in constructing the said air bases and airports, it should be
ecessary to remove lines of wire already strung because of their consti-
uting an obstacle thereto, the Government of the United States shall
ay the costs of the removal and new installation elsewhere which may
e occasioned.

ARTICLE XI. The Government of the United States agrees to take all
ppropriate measures to prevent articles imported for consumption
ithin the areas referred to in Article I from passing to any other terri-
ory of the rest of the Republic except upon compliance with Panamanian
scal laws. Whenever it is possible, the provisioning and equipping of
ne bases and their personnel will be done with products, articles and
oodstuffs coming from the Republic of Panama, provided they are
vailable at reasonable prices.

ARTICLE XII. The sites referred to in Article I consist both of lands
elonging to the Government of the Republic of Panama and of privately
wned lands.

In the case of the private lands, which the Government of Panama
nall acquire from the owners and the temporary use of which shall be
ranted by it to the Government of the United States, it is agreed that
ne Government of the United States will pay to the Government of
anama an annual rental of fifty balboas or dollars per hectare for all
ich lands covered by this Agreement, the Government of Panama
ssuming all costs of expropriation as well as indemnities and reim-
ursements for buildings, cultivations, installations or improvements
hich may exist within the sites chosen.

In the case of the public lands the Government of the United States
ill pay to the Government of Panama an annual rental of one balboa or
ollar for all such lands covered by this Agreement.

There are expressly excepted the lands situated in the Corregimiento
Rio Hato, designated by No. 12 in the attached Memorandum, it
eing understood that for this entire tract the United States Government
ill pay to the Government of Panama an annual rental of ten thousand
alboas or dollars.

The rentals set out in this Article shall be paid in balboas as defined
y the Agreement embodied in the exchange of notes dated March 2,

1936, referred to in Article VII of the Treaty of that date between th
United States of America and Panama, or the equivalent thereof :
dollars, and shall be payable from the date on which the use of the land
by the United States actually began, with the exception of the land
situated in the Corregimiento of Rio Hato designated by No. 12 in th
attached Memorandum, rental for which shall commence January 1,194

ARTICLE XIII. The provisions of this Agreement may be terminate
upon the mutual consent of the signatory parties even prior to the e:
piration thereof in conformity with Articles I and V above, it bein
understood also that any of the areas to which this Agreement refers ma
be evacuated by the United States and the use thereof by the Unite
States terminated prior to that date.

ARTICLE XIV. This Agreement will enter into effect when approve
by the National Executive Power of Panama and by the Nation
Assembly of Panama.

At the request of the Government of Panama, there was signed on July 7, 19
by Cordell Hull, Secretary of State, and Señor Don Ernesto Jaén Guardia, An
bassador of Panama at Washington, an agreement providing for the detail of ε
officer of the United States Army of the grade of colonel to serve as adviser to th
Minister of Foreign Affairs of Panama in relation to matters pertaining to th
defense of Panama. The agreement remains in force for one year from the da
of signature but may be extended at the request of the Government of Panam
The agreement contains provisions similar in general to provisions contained ι
agreements between the United States and certain other American Republi
providing for the detail of officers of the United States Army or Navy to advi
the armed forces of those countries.[1]

(3) *Agreement with Cuba for Use of Aviation Facilities. Department ¢ State Release, June 18, 1942* [2]

It has been announced that His Excellency José Manuel Cortina
Minister of State of Cuba, and the Honorable Spruille Braden, America
Ambassador to Cuba, have signed, at Havana, an agreement whereb
the Cuban Government offers facilities to the United States War Depar
ment for training aviation personnel and for operations against enem
underseacraft.

It is understood that after termination of the emergency the facilitie
will become a training center of the Cuban Air Force.

In offering these facilities the Cuban Government, an ally and cc
belligerent which was among the first of the American Republics t

---

[1] Department of State, *Bulletin*, VII, p. 624.   [2] *Ibid.*, VI, p. 553.

leclare war on the Axis, has taken a most important step in collaborating
n the joint war effort.

The training center will be located in the vicinity of Havana. By
pecial arrangement between the Cuban and United States Governments
nd between the British Royal Air Force and the United States War
Department, contingents of Royal Air Force personnel will be stationed
t this post, following their basic-training courses, to complete their
ombat training.

Work on the installations will begin at once.

6. JOINT MEXICAN–UNITED STATES DEFENSE COMMISSION

The Governments of Mexico and the United States, in identical statements
anded to the press on March 4, 1941, announced that conversations were being
eld in Washington between the military, naval, and aeronautical attachés
ssigned to the Mexican Embassy and representatives of the Government of the
nited States, to discuss the aid that the two countries would extend to each
ther in case of aggression against either of them. In view of the situation exist-
g after December 7, the two Governments "found it expedient to establish a
iixed defense commission to study the problems relating to the defense of the
vo countries and to propose to the respective governments the measures which
iould be adopted." [1] As finally organized, the Commission comprises Brig.
en. Miguel S. González Cadena and Brig. Gen. Tomás Sánchez Hernández, of
ie Mexican General Staff, as representatives of Mexico; Lt. Gen. Stanley
unbar Embick and Vice Admiral Alfred Wilkinson Johnson as representatives
f the United States.

Executive Order No. 9080 authorizes "on the part of the Government of the
nited States" the creation of the Commission.

l) *Executive Order No. 9080, February 27, 1942* [2]

By virtue of the authority vested in me by the Constitution and as
resident of the United States, and acting jointly and in full accord with
[is Excellency, the President of the Republic of Mexico, I hereby
uthorize, on the part of the Government of the United States, the
reation of a joint commission to be known as the Joint Mexican-United
tates Defense Commission.

The purposes of the Commission shall be to study problems relating
) the common defense of the United States and Mexico, to consider
road plans for the defense of Mexico and adjacent areas of the United
tates, and to propose to the respective Governments the cooperative
ieasures which, in its opinion, should be adopted.

As United States members of the Commission I hereby appoint the
ollowing: Lieutenant General Stanley D. Embick, United States Army,

[1] Department of State release, *ibid.*, p. 67.
[2] 7 *Fed. Reg.*, p. 1607.

Retired, Chairman, Vice Admiral Alfred W. Johnson, United States Navy, Retired.

The Commission will convene initially at a time and place agreeable to both Governments, and may thereafter proceed at any time with its professional and clerical assistants to such place or places in Mexico with the approval of the Government of Mexico, or in the United States as it may consider desirable or necessary to visit for the accomplishment of its purposes.

The United States members of the Commission, in agreement with their Mexican colleagues, may prescribe their own procedure. They are also empowered to employ such professional and clerical assistants as may be deemed necessary, and to incur such expenses for travel, services, supplies, and other purposes as may be required for the accomplishment of their mission.

Each of the United States members of the Commission and each of their professional assistants, including civilian advisers and any United States Army, Navy, or Marine Corps officers so employed, detailed, or assigned, shall receive, in lieu of subsistence while outside of the continental limits of the United States in connection with the business of the Commission, a per diem allowance of ten dollars.

All expenses incurred by the United States Section of the Commission shall be paid by Army disbursing officers from allocations to be made to the War Department for that purpose from the Emergency Fund for the President.

7. MILITARY, NAVAL AND AIR MISSIONS AND TRAINING OF PERSONNEL

(1) *List of Agreements Made by the United States*

[For a list of agreements made during the preceding year, see *Documents, III 1940–41*, p. 148.]

The Department of State *Bulletin* of July 19, 1941, listed agreements with the following countries as being in effect up to the time of the signing of the agreement with Costa Rica, which is included in the list for this year: Argentina, Brazil, Chile, Colombia, Ecuador, El Salvador, Guatemala, Haiti, Nicaragua, Peru, and Venezuela.

The list for the period June 30, 1941 to June 30, 1942 is as follows:

Agreement with Costa Rica. Signed July 14, 1941. Provides for the detail of United States Military Mission. Effective for a period of four years. Service of the Mission may be extended at request of the Government of Costa Rica. Executive Agreement Series 212.

Agreement with Nicaragua. Signed August 25, 1941. Provides for the continuation of the detail of an officer of the United States Army to serve as Director of the Military Academy of the National Guard of Nicaragua. In effect, a continuation of a similar agreement between the United States and Nicaragua, signed May 22, 1939 (Executive Agreement Series, 156). Executive Agreement Series 217.

Agreement with Colombia. Signed August 30, 1941. Makes certain modifications in the Naval Mission Agreement signed November 23, 1938 (Executive Agreement Series 140). Effective for the remainder of the original period of four years. Executive Agreement Series 218.

Agreement with Bolivia. Signed September 4, 1941. Provides for the detail of a United States Military Aviation Mission to Bolivia. Effective for a period of four years. Executive Agreement Series 219.

Agreement with Peru. Signed March 11, 1942. Provides for the detail of an officer of the United States Army of the grade of captain to serve as Assistant to the Adviser of the Remount Service of the Peruvian Army. In effect a revision of the Agreement of April 15, 1941 [1] (Executive Agreement Series 205). In force for a period of three years. Executive Agreement Series 240.

Agreement with Brazil. Signed on May 7, 1942. Provides for the detail of a United States Naval Mission to Brazil. In effect replaces the Agreement of May 27, 1936 (Executive Agreement Series 94). In force for a period of four years subject to right of Brazilian Government to extend it by request made six months before expiration of the agreement. Executive Agreement Series 247.

Agreement with Colombia. Signed on May 29, 1942. Provides for the detail of a United States Military Mission to Colombia. Effective for a period of four years, subject to right of Government of Colombia to extend period by request. Executive Agreement Series 250.

(2) *An Act to Authorize the Course of Instruction at the United States Naval Academy to Be Given to Not Exceeding Twenty Persons at a Time from the American Republics, Other than the United States, Approved July 14, 1941* [2]

Be it enacted by the Senate and House of Representatives of the United States of America in Congress assembled, That the Secretary of the Navy is hereby authorized to permit, upon designation of the President of the United States, not exceeding twenty persons at a time from the American Republics (other than the United States) to receive instruction at the United States Naval Academy at Annapolis, Maryland. Not more than three persons from any of such Republics shall receive instruction under authority of this Act at the same time. The persons receiving instruction under authority of this Act shall receive the same pay, allowances, and emoluments, to be paid from the same appropriations, and, subject to such exceptions as may be determined by the Secretary of the Navy, shall be subject to the same rules and regulations governing admission,

[1] *Documents, III, 1940–41,* p. 148.
[2] Public Law 168, 77th Cong.; originating as S. 207; Senate Report No. 313; House Report No. 874.

attendance, discipline, resignation, discharge, dismissal, and graduation, as midshipmen at the Naval Academy appointed from the United States; but such persons shall not be entitled to appointment to any office or position in the United States Navy by reason of their graduation from the Naval Academy.

(3) *Aviation Training for Citizens of Other American Republics. Department of State Release, October 18, 1941* [1]

A plan for increased cooperation with the other American Republics which will bring young men from those countries to be trained in the United States as pilots and aviation technicians will be put into operation early in 1942, under the sponsorship of the Interdepartmental Committee on Technical Aviation Training for Citizens of the Latin American Republics.

The program, which calls for the training of around 500 pilots, aeronautical administrative engineers, instructor mechanics, and airplane-service mechanics, will offer courses varying in length from six months to two years and will be under the supervision of the Army Air Corps and the Civil Aeronautics Administration.

Applicants are to be apportioned among the 20 other American Republics, taking into consideration the need of each for trained personnel, and selection boards will be set up in each country to consider applicants and award scholarships on a competitive basis.

Members of the Interdepartmental Committee are as follows: Thomas Burke, Chief, Division of International Communications, Department of State; William Barclay Harding, Vice President, Defense Supplies Corporation, representing the Coordinator of Inter-American Affairs; Maj. Eugene E. Gillespie, Air Corps, War Department, also representing Navy Department; G. Grant Mason, Member, Civil Aeronautics Board, and Brig. Gen. Donald H. Connolly, Administrator of Civil Aeronautics.

C. Economic and Financial Collaboration

1. INDUSTRIAL DEVELOPMENT OF LATIN AMERICAN COUNTRIES

(1) *Priority for Steel Mill Construction in Brazil. Department of State Release, July 9, 1941* [2]

This announcement was the outgrowth of conversations held in Washington in February and March, 1939, between the Secretary of State (Hull) and the

[1] Department of State, *Bulletin*, V, p. 296.   [2] *Ibid.*, p. 19.

Foreign Minister of Brazil (Dr. Oswaldo Aranha).[1] At this time the Brazilian Foreign Minister expressed the desire of his Government to obtain long-term credits to finance the purchase of industrial goods "with particular view to the systematic economic development" of Brazil. Secretary of State Hull, in his reply, noted this statement of purpose and stated to the Brazilian Foreign Minister that he was "informed that the Export-Import Bank, with a view to cooperation, in the facilitation of trade between the United States and Brazil and in the development of Brazilian natural resources, has agreed to consider the arrangement of suitable longer term credits to finance Brazilian purchases of economic equipment in the United States."[2] With the establishment of a system of priorities under the Act of June 28, 1940,[3] as amended by the Act of May 31, 1942,[4] the Brazilian Government was faced with the necessity of getting favorable priority action for the goods in question in addition to making necessary financial arrangements.

Priority aid for the construction of a $45,000,000 steel mill in Brazil has been assured by the Office of Production Management, acting on recommendations of the Department of State.

The decision to aid Brazil through priorities is in accordance with this Government's policy of assisting the other American Republics to obtain essential materials in this country, so far as this is compatible with our own defense requirements.

The National Steel Company of Brazil has already started ground-breaking operations. The priority aid, permitting the company to obtain steel, machinery, and many other kinds of equipment promptly, is designed to make possible the completion of this mill within two and one-half to three years.

Of the total cost of $45,000,000, the sum of $20,000,000 is being supplied through a loan from the Export-Import Bank. The rest is being supplied by the Brazilian Government and Brazilian financial institutions. The $20,000,000 supplied by this country is to be spent in the United States, through contracts with from 250 to 300 different manufacturers and suppliers.

The contracts and orders involved will be given priority ratings sufficiently high to secure adequate deliveries, without delaying deliveries of our own defense contracts.

As a result of the conversations held at Washington in the early part of 1939 between Dr. Oswaldo Aranha, the Foreign Minister of Brazil, and officials of this Government, a commitment was made on the part of the United States to assist Brazil in the development of its economic resources and of its industries.

The steel-mill project was thereafter presented by the Brazilian Government as the most important single item in this program. Such a

[1] *Documents, I, 1938–39*, p. 129–42. [2] *Ibid.*, p. 138–9.
[3] *Ibid., II, 1939–40*, p. 802. [4] *Ibid., III, 1940–41*, p. 748.

mill is of major importance to Brazil and also is of considerable interest to the United States. Not only will it provide for the utilization of a portion of Brazil's vast natural resources but it will also tend to improve the general standard of living of the country and thereby increase the market for products of the United States.

The output of the Brazilian steel mill will to that extent relieve the pressure on American industries in the prosecution of the Brazilian rearmament program.

In consideration of the foregoing factors and in the light of the demands on the American defense program, the Office of Production Management, acting upon the recommendations of the Department of State, which were concurred in by the Army and Navy Munitions Board, the Office of Price Administration and Civilian Supply, and the Coordinator of Commercial and Cultural Relations Between the American Republics, agreed to give the project the consideration which it deserves with a view to granting the necessary priorities for the equipment destined for the mill. The OPM's Priorities, Production, and Purchases Divisions, and the Army and Navy Munitions Board have accordingly worked out a program which will permit construction of the mill according to schedule and without interference with the defense program.

2. COMPREHENSIVE ARRANGEMENTS FOR THE PROMOTION OF ECONOMIC SOLIDARITY

(1) Proposals from Venezuelan Economic Mission. Statement of the Chairman of the Economic Defense Board (Wallace), October 29, 1941 [1]

The Venezuelan Economic Mission, supplementing the valuable co operation of the Venezuelan Embassy, has successfully carried out its task of presenting to officials of this government a detailed exposition of Venezuela's essential import needs. The Government of the United States is keenly appreciative of the necessity of maintaining exports of materials essential to Venezuela, and will take every step commensurate with the requirements of the defense program in order to do so. Official of this Government have consequently studied with the greatest care the statement of needs so ably presented by Messrs. Herrera Mendoza and Boulton, and are prepared to accept it in principle as the basis for allocation of materials for export to Venezuela.

The presentation of needs by the Venezuelan Economic Mission, the first comprehensive exposition made to this Government, will now be

[1] Department of State, Bulletin, V, p. 346.

presented to the Supply Priorities and Allocations Board for action.   It is expected that specific allocations will be made in the immediate future.

It is essential that similar studies of requirements be presented by all of the other American Republics.

In the course of their work in the United States Messrs. Herrera Mendoza and Boulton have evidenced an understanding of the serious problems confronting the United States, and on returning to Venezuela will be able to explain to their government and people the strain which the gigantic defense effort is placing on normal productive facilities in this country.

———

Announcement was made on December 5, 1941,[1] that a mission composed of four soil-conservation experts, headed by Dr. Hugh H. Bennett, Chief of the Soil Conservation Service of the United States Department of Agriculture, had sailed for Venezuela to assist the government of that country in connection with soil erosion and related land-use problems. The assignment was effected by the President at the request of the Venezuelan Government under the provisions of the Act of May 3, 1939 (Public No. 63, 76th Cong.) which authorizes the Chief Executive to detail employees of the Federal Government having special scientific or other technical or professional qualifications to the American Republics in agreement with the governments concerned.

(2) Agreements with Mexico, November 19, 1941 and April 8, 1942

Following the inauguration of President Manuel Avila Camacho on December 1, 1940, the attitude of the Mexican Government toward important issues involved in relations with the United States assumed a more conciliatory tone. This made possible the initiation of negotiations between the two governments with a view to a settlement of outstanding differences, notably, compensation for the expropriated petroleum properties,[2] and the advancement of the mutual economic and financial interests of the two countries. The agreements of November 19, 1941 were followed on April 8, 1942 by another comprehensive set of arrangements especially intended to develop the economic life of Mexico and facilitate the war effort of the United States.

(a) Statement by the Secretary of State (Hull), November 19, 1941 [3]

[Excerpt]

The agreements which Mexico and the United States have reached today are of outstanding importance in the relations between the two countries. Not only do they concern most of the principal mutual prob-

[1] *Ibid.*, p. 452.   [2] See p. 420.   [3] Department of State, *Bulletin*, V, p. 399.

lems which have long been pending between the two sister republics but they mark a new milestone of great importance in the cause of increasingly closer collaboration and solidarity between the countries of the New World. These agreements constitute a further concrete proof of the fact that problems existing between nations are capable of mutually satisfactory settlement when approached in a reciprocal spirit of good will, tolerance, and a desire to understand each other's points of view.

These agreements have been reached only after months of discussion and negotiation. Some of the questions involved, such as those coming under the heading of General Claims, have defied solution for generations Others, such as those growing out of the expropriation of petroleum properties owned by nationals of the United States, while of comparatively recent origin, have presented very difficult and complicated issues.

The scope of these agreements is evident from their mention. They cover an adjustment of property claims including the so-called General Claims and the agrarian claims, an agreement covering the expropriation of United States petroleum properties; an agreement in principle to negotiate a reciprocal trade agreement; an arrangement between the United States Treasury Department and the Mexican Government and the Banco de Mexico for the stabilization of the Mexican peso; an agreement for purchase by the United States Treasury Department of newly mined Mexican silver directly from the Mexican Government; and an agreement between the Export-Import Bank and the Mexican Government for the extension of credits to facilitate the completion of the Inter American Highway through Mexico. A separate statement regarding the broad outlines of the several agreements has been made available by the Department.

(b) *Summary of the Agreements of November 19, 1941. Department of State Release, November 19, 1941* [1]

I. EXPROPRIATION OF PETROLEUM PROPERTIES [2]

.   .   .   .

II. CLAIMS

The two Governments have found a means, so long lacking, of adjusting other outstanding property claims, including the so-called General Claims and the agrarian claims.

Under a claims convention signed on November 19, 1941, Mexico agrees to pay to the United States the sum of $40,000,000 in full settle

---

[1] Department of State, *Bulletin*, V, p. 400.   [2] See p. 420.

ment of these property claims. Mexico will make a payment of $3,000,-
000 on account at the time of exchange of ratifications of the convention.
Mexico has already made payments amounting to $3,000,000 on account
of agrarian claims arising between August 30, 1927 and October 7, 1940.

The balance remaining due to the United States amounting to
$34,000,000, after the $3,000,000 payment when ratifications are exchanged, will be liquidated over a period of years through the annual
payment by Mexico of $2,500,000, beginning in 1942.

III. TRADE AGREEMENT

The two Governments have decided in principle to negotiate a reciprocal trade agreement. Formal announcement of intention to negotiate will be made in due course, in accordance with the pertinent provisions of law.[1]

IV. STABILIZATION OF THE MEXICAN PESO–U. S. DOLLAR RATE OF EXCHANGE

The Treasury Department has entered into an agreement for monetary
and financial cooperation with the Mexican Government and the Banco
de Mexico, which will provide, among other things, for the purchase of
Mexican pesos with United States dollars. The U. S. dollars thus acquired by the Mexican authorities will greatly assist them in stabilizing
the exchange value of the peso in terms of the dollar, to the mutual
benefit and advantage of the two countries.

V. MEXICAN SILVER

The Treasury Department has also indicated its willingness to purchase newly mined Mexican silver direct from the Mexican Government
on a basis similar to that under which such purchases were made prior
to 1938.

VI. FINANCING OF MEXICAN PROJECTS

The Mexican Government has engaged for a number of years in an
important highway-construction program. It has financed a large part
of this construction through the issuance of highway bonds which have
been consistently serviced without any delays or difficulties. In order
that the Mexican Government may expedite this highway-construction
program, it has requested the Export-Import Bank to accept certain of

[1] Formal notice of intention to negotiate was given on April 4, 1942; *Ibid.*, VI, p.
78.

these highway bonds as security for credits. The Export-Import Bank has acceded to this request and has opened a credit on this account.

It will be recalled that the Mexican highway system is a most important part of the Inter-American Highway and that construction work is well advanced in Mexico and a number of the other American Republics

The Export-Import Bank is disposed to consider sympathetically other requests for credits for developments in Mexico, whether they are to be executed by the Mexican Government or are private enterprises guaranteed by that Government, or one of its official agencies.

VII. Other Problems

The two Governments are actively continuing to study all other problems of interest to them.

(i) Joint Statement by the Secretaries of the Treasury of the United States (Morgenthau) and of Mexico (Suarez), November 19, 1941

The two Governments, as a part of the over-all arrangements between Mexico and the United States, have today entered into a stabilization agreement and a silver purchase agreement. These arrangements are practical evidence of the Good Neighbor Policy. These agreements are based upon the principle that the welfare of the two countries is mutual and that common monetary and economic problems can be settled in a spirit of friendly cooperation. The two Treasuries are happy to affirm by these agreements their belief in neighborly cooperation, at a time when force rules so large a part of the world's economy.

The Stabilization Agreement, signed today by the Secretary of the Treasury of the United States, the Secretary of the Treasury of Mexico and Mr. Antonio Espinosa de los Monteros, the representative of the Bank of Mexico, proposes to stabilize the United States dollar-Mexican peso rate of exchange. The agreement provides that up to $40 million of the United States Stabilization Fund will be used for this purpose. The agreement also provides for periodic conferences among representatives of the two Treasuries and the Bank of Mexico to discuss monetary, financial, and economic problems of mutual interest.

The silver purchase agreement is a month to month arrangement between the United States and Mexico, whereby the United States Treasury undertakes to purchase monthly up to six million ounces of newly-mined Mexican silver. The silver will be purchased directly from the Bank of Mexico on a basis similar to the arrangements which were

[1] Treasury Department, Press Service No. 28–56.

n effect prior to 1938. The silver purchases are made pursuant to the
provisions of the Silver Purchase Act of 1934.

(c) *Joint Statement by the Under Secretary of State (Welles) and the
Foreign Minister of Mexico (Padilla), April 8, 1942* [1]

It has been not only a pleasure for us to renew our friendship formed at
the meeting of Foreign Ministers at Rio de Janeiro but also a very real
opportunity for exchanging views and reaching agreements regarding
matters of the first magnitude to the two countries.

In the short space of a few days we have agreed on a number of arrangements that not only will develop the economic life of Mexico and
the United States but will greatly speed the war effort of the United
States.

(1) Trade agreement.

Last fall our two Governments agreed to study the possibilities of
negotiating a trade agreement to expand commerce between the two
countries. The preliminary studies having indicated that a satisfactory
basis for a trade agreement exists, our two Governments made formal
announcement on April 4 of their intention to negotiate a trade agreement. Negotiations will begin immediately after the completion of the
public hearings required by United States procedure, which will be held
beginning May 18.

(2) Industrial enterprises.

Continuing the program of cooperation in the development of industries in Mexico which was undertaken last fall, we have agreed that
our two Governments shall collaborate in the establishment in Mexico
of a series of basic industries to meet Mexican consumption needs and to
supply goods required by the war effort of the United States. These
industries will be established in Mexico through cooperation between
private investors and the Mexican Government, and the Export-Import
Bank will give careful consideration to the possibility of providing
through the Nacional Financiera, S.A., credits for the acquisition in
individual cases in the United States of materials and equipment that
cannot be provided in Mexico. The obligations thus acquired by the
Export-Import Bank will bear the guaranty of the Mexican Government.

Several important specific projects are under consideration, including
steel- and tin-plate rolling mill. In the granting of priority rating for
the machinery, equipment, or other material produced in the United
States, the paramount criterion will be the degree to which each specific

[1] Department of State, *Bulletin*, VI, p. 325.

project contributes to the war effort of the United States and the security of the hemisphere.

(3) Priorities and allocations.

We have had mutually beneficial conversations regarding the organiza- tion and procedure for handling priorities and allocations matters, and arrangements have been concluded for the Mexican Under Secretary o: Finance, Licenciado Ramon Beteta, to establish a special office and organization in Washington for purposes of insuring the closest collabo- ration with the appropriate authorities of the United States. The alloca tion for the second quarter of 1942 by the Government of the United States of specific quantities of 45 major export articles, which was an nounced on April 4,[1] provides a definite working basis for export com merce between the United States and Mexico based on careful examina tion of Mexico's needs in relation to the war production effort of the United States.

(4) Mexican railways.

We have agreed that an immediate survey of the needs of the Mexican railway-transportation system is highly desirable in order to determine the materials that are required to enable this system to function properly in the support of Mexico's economy in order to permit it to transport to the United States the strategic war materials being produced in ever increasing quantities in Mexico. A United States expert has been sen to Mexico to make this study jointly with an expert appointed by the Mexican Government. They have been requested to present their repor within 30 days. In anticipation of the report of these experts, the Wa Production Board is taking into consideration Mexico's needs of rolling stock in formulating the United States manufacturing program of such *matériel* for the coming year.

(5) Shipyards.

In view of the urgent need for cargo vessels and of the existence c certain shipbuilding facilities in Mexico, we have agreed that expert from our two Governments should immediately determine what con struction of small cargo vessels in Mexico is feasible. On the basis of thi study the United States Government will endeavor, taking into accoun the demand in the United States for shipbuilding, to make available t Mexico the *matériel* and the tools required.

(6) High-octane gasoline plant.

In view of the desirability of establishing a high-octane gasoline plan in Mexico, we have agreed that a plant should be constructed as soon a the necessary equipment can be spared.

[1] See p. 389.

(3) *United States Economic Mission to Bolivia. Department of State Release, December 17, 1941* [1]

At the request of the Bolivian Government, the Government of the United States has now completed arrangements for the detail to Bolivia of an Economic Mission. The Economic Mission entered officially upon its duties on December 17, 1941, when the Chief of the Economic Mission and all the other experts except one had arrived in La Paz. It is made up of eight qualified experts of the Government of the United States who will study various aspects of the Bolivian national economy in order to prepare specific projects which may be considered by the Bolivian authorities for further economic development of the country. It is expected that the Economic Mission will complete its work in June 1942.

The economic survey work in Bolivia will include: A study of the needs for development in Bolivian communications, which it is expected will be principally highway needs; a study of the possibilities of expansion and diversification of agricultural production in Bolivia, involving both an increased degree of self-sufficiency in foodstuffs and the development of certain tropical or semi-tropical products; a study of the most practicable methods for stimulating production of tin, tungsten, and certain other minerals in Bolivia, particularly by small miners; and a consideration of the practicability of measures of financial cooperation between the Government of Bolivia and the Government of the United States.

The members of the United States Economic Mission to Bolivia are as follows:

Mr. Merwin L. Bohan, Chief
Mr. Rex A. Pixley, Assistant Chief
Mr. B. H. Thibodeaux, expert of the Department of Agriculture
Mr. Wilbur A. Harlan, expert of the Department of Agriculture
Mr. Harry P. Hart, expert of the Public Roads Administration of the Federal Works Agency
Mr. Clarence E. Mershon, expert of the Public Roads Administration of the Federal Works Agency
Mr. John Worcester, expert of the Bureau of Mines of the Department of the Interior
Mr. Ernest Oberbillig, expert of the Bureau of Mines of the Department of the Interior

These experts have been chosen for their special qualifications for carrying out the survey work, and they have all had extensive experience in their special fields of activity. Mr. Merwin L. Bohan, Chief of the Economic Mission, directing and coordinating the work of the other

[1] Department of State, *Bulletin*, V, p. 563.

experts, is a Foreign Service officer of the United States who has had 15 years of experience in the study and analysis of the economic problems of the other American Republics. As an officer in the foreign service of the Department of Commerce, he served at Havana, Guatemala City, Tegucigalpa, San Salvador, Lima, Quito, and Santiago, and he made a detailed economic study of Bolivia in 1937 on a special assignment for that purpose. Since the amalgamation of the foreign service of the Department of Commerce into the present single Foreign Service of the United States, Mr. Bohan has served at Santiago and Bogotá.

It is hoped that this contribution on the part of the United States to the development of a program of economic cooperation with Bolivia will promote the strengthening of the Bolivian national economy and the increased production of strategic materials vital to hemisphere defense.

(4) *Agreement with Brazil, March 3, 1942* [1]

To implement the resolutions of the meeting of the foreign ministers in Rio de Janeiro, His Excellency Dr. Arthur de Souza Costa, Minister of Finance of Brazil and officials of the Government of the United States concluded a series of important agreements designed to fortify the security of the American Republics These agreements were as follows:

1. The Finance Minister of Brazil and the Acting Secretary of State signed an exchange of notes providing for a program for the mobilization of the productive resources of Brazil, and for a line of credit of $100,000,000 to be made available through the Export-Import Bank.

2. Officials of the Export-Import Bank and the Metals Reserve Company signed agreements with the Minister of Finance of Brazil and the British Ambassador for the development of the Itabira mining properties and the Victoria Minas Railroad, with accompanying arrangements for the procurement by the United States and Great Britain of the high-grade iron ores to be produced in these properties.

3. The Ambassador of Brazil and the Acting Secretary of State signed an agreement providing for expanded assistance to Brazil under the provisions of the Lend-Lease Act of March 11, 1941.

4. The Brazilian Minister of Finance and the Acting Secretary of State signed and exchanged notes providing for the establishment of a $5,000,000 fund by the Rubber Reserve Company to be used in collaboration with the Brazilian Government in developing the raw-rubber production of the Amazon Valley and adjacent regions. The notes were accompanied by an agreement whereby the Rubber Reserve Company agreed to purchase Brazilian raw rubber for a period of five years.

(a) *The Brazilian Minister of Finance (Souza Costa) to the Acting Secretary of State (Welles), March 3, 1942*

In Resolution II of the Third Meeting of the Ministers of Foreign Affairs of the American Republics at Rio de Janeiro the Government of

---

[1] Department of State, *Bulletin*, VI, p. 205–7. The headnote is based on the statement accompanying the texts. For statements of the negotiators, see *ibid.*, p. 207–8

Brazil undertook to cooperate with the other American Republics to the utmost possible degree in the mobilization of its economic resources with the special objective of increasing the production of those strategic materials essential for the defense of the hemisphere and for the maintenance of the economies of Brazil and the other American Republics.

The Government of Brazil, through the Brazilian Economic Mission which I have the honor to head, proposes at once to take measures effectively to carry out this undertaking and to further the program of developing the production of such materials, upon which it has been engaged for some time.

The Government of Brazil believes that the most effective manner to carry out its broad purposes will be the establishment of a new government organization to investigate and promote the development of strategic materials and other natural resources of Brazil. The new organization, which might be a new department of the Brazilian Government or a government-controlled corporation, would examine all feasible projects for such development and would see that those recommended be effected, either by existing enterprises in Brazil, or, where suitable entities do not already exist, by new departments, independent organizations or private enterprises which would be established for the purpose.

In either case the new organization would function as a dependency of the Government of Brazil not primarily for profit, but rather for carrying out to the fullest degree possible in the interests of Brazil and the other American Republics, the development of the country's natural resources.

The new Brazilian organization would be aided in its work if it were able to rely to a very considerable degree on United States expert assistance. Moreover, to carry out its program the Brazilian Government would require, in addition to funds for local expenditures to be supplied by Brazil, a line of dollar credits, in an amount of about $100,000,000, to be drawn against as needed for dollar expenditures in connection with specific projects.

Such credits would be utilized in projects undertaken directly by the Brazilian Government or by private individuals approved by it.

On behalf of the Government of Brazil and in accordance with understandings which the Brazilian Economic Mission, which I have the honor to head, has had with officials of the Government of the United States, I should greatly appreciate it if Your Excellency's Government studied sympathetically the present program of financial and expert cooperation.

It is my firm conviction that a cooperative program such as that outlined above can be of the greatest value to both of our nations in carrying out the intent of the resolutions of Rio de Janeiro to mobilize the eco-

nomic potentialities of the hemisphere in our common defense. I avai]
[etc.]

(b) The Acting Secretary of State (Welles) to the Brazilian Minister of Finance (Souza Costa), March 3, 1942

I acknowledge the receipt of your note of March 3, 1942, outlining a
program for further economic cooperation between the United States and
Brazil in furtherance of Resolution II of the Third Meeting of the Ministers of Foreign Affairs of the American Republics at Rio de Janeiro,
calling for the mobilization of the productive resources of the American
Republics.

I have the honor to inform you that the appropriate agencies of the
Government of the United States have considered carefully this program
and are prepared to extend the financial and expert cooperation essential
to its success. I have been informed by the Secretary of Commerce that
he is agreeable to the opening of a line of credit of up to $100,000,000 for
the purpose of financing dollar expenditures in connection with specific
projects to be undertaken by the Brazilian Government through the
agency of the proposed new organization. It is contemplated that such
projects shall be undertaken after agreement between the Brazilian
Government, acting through the new organization, and the Government
of the United States, acting through the Department of Commerce, and
that appropriate United States technical and expert assistance shall be
made available as necessary and desirable. The Secretary of Commerce
will consider and act upon such projects within the period in which the
Export-Import Bank of Washington is in a position to provide these
credits, and to the extent that its funds may be available for this purpose
Details of the arrangements may be worked out between representatives
of the Government of Brazil and the Secretary of Commerce.

It is of course understood that although the United States is desirous
of cooperating to the fullest extent in the general development of the
Brazilian economy, the carrying out of specific projects which require
important amounts of machinery, equipment or other materials produced
in the United States must be conditioned upon careful investigation and
determination that the particular project will contribute in an important
manner to the progress of our war effort and to the security of the hemi
sphere, and has accordingly been granted the appropriate priority ratings

I believe that the cooperative program which the Governments of
Brazil and the United States of America are undertaking will constitute a
further great step forward in mutually beneficial economic relationship

between our two countries and in the mobilization of the economic resources of the Western Hemisphere.

Accept [etc.]

(5) Omnibus Memorandum covering Agreements between Haiti and the United States, Washington, April 6, 1942 [1]

Upon the occasion of the visit of His Excellency President Elie Lescot of the Republic of Haiti to Washington, a series of conferences was held with representatives of several agencies of the United States Government. These meetings were held with a view to strengthening and implementing the resolutions adopted at the recent meeting of the foreign ministers of the American Republics held at Rio de Janeiro and to making more effective, under present international conditions, the Declaration of the United Nations signed at Washington on January 2, 1942, and the Lend-Lease agreement between the United States of America and the Republic of Haiti signed at Washington September 16, 1941.

As a consequence of these meetings, which were also attended by His Excellency M. Maurice Dartigue, the Haitian Minister of Agriculture, and by His Excellency Fernand Dennis, Minister of Haiti at Washington, several agreements were reached.

Furthermore, communications were exchanged on April 7, 1942, by President Lescot and the Acting Secretary of State, providing for the active collaboration of the two Governments in carrying out a number of health and sanitation projects within the Republic of Haiti, to be undertaken in accordance with Resolution XXX regarding health and sanitary conditions adopted at the recent conference at Rio de Janeiro. The United States Government will send a small group of experts to Haiti to cooperate in the development of the specific program which will be decided upon in agreement with the appropriate Haitian officials.

I. There will be an exchange of notes whereby the two Governments will give their formal approval to a Memorandum of Understanding signed on March 28, 1942, by the Haitian and United States Secretaries of Agriculture, regarding the purchase by the Commodity Credit Corporation of the United States of the surplus cotton production of Haiti. According to the understanding the Commodity Credit Corporation will take over, at an agreed price, the carry-over of cotton from last year's crop as well as all of the surplus of the crop of 1942. The United States Government agrees to purchase, subject to an agreed price and within specified limitations of amount, the 1943 cotton crop and all subsequent cotton crops produced in Haiti during the present war. The Haitian Government on its part will take steps to restrict the production of cotton and to bring about an improvement in quality and an increase in the staple length of cotton produced in future years. The United States Department of Agriculture will be pleased to lend its assistance in the carrying out of the cotton improvement program.

[1] The memorandum was initialed by President Elie Lescot of Haiti and Sumner Welles, Acting Secretary of State; Department of State, *Bulletin*, VI, p. 353. The headnote is from that source.

II. The Export-Import Bank of Washington has extended a line of credit to the National Bank of the Republic of Haiti in amounts which may be agreed upon as necessary for the purpose of strengthening the Haitian Gourde–United States dollar exchange relationship which is peculiarly affected by the influence of shipping availability on exports and imports into the Republic. The Government of Haiti has agreed, on its part, to take all feasible measures to improve its budgetary position.

The two Governments will continue to explore the possibilities of extending assistance to the Republic of Haiti in handling the surpluses of its agricultural products.

III. In view of the pledge of the two Governments to employ their full resources against the common enemy, and the need for an immediate increase in the production of sisal in order to prosecute the common war effort, the two Governments agreed in principle to arrangements providing for the planting of approximately 24,000 additional acres of sisal in Haiti.

As much land as can be planted within one year's time from the present date, up to a maximum of 12,000 acres will be undertaken through the Société Haïtiano-Américaine de Développement Agricole; and as much additional acreage as practicable will be planted by private interests within one year's time from today's date, up to a maximum of 12,000 acres. The details of the financial arrangements necessary for the planting of the additional acreage are to be worked out with the appropriate agencies of the two Governments.

The Haitian Government agrees to grant every facility to the Société Haïtiano-Américaine de Développement Agricole and to the private interests concerned in order that they may obtain possession of the necessary lands, whether government or privately owned, and to facilitate the employment of such United States technical personnel as may be necessary. In so far as practicable, the areas operated by the Société Haïtiano-Américaine de Développement Agricole will be developed through a system of small holdings within short transportation distance of the decorticating machinery of the Société Haïtiano-Américaine de Développement Agricole.

If the planting of any additional acreage appears to be necessary to the successful prosecution of the joint war effort, the two Governments will consult together as to the method to be followed in any further sisal development.

IV. In order to assist the Government of Haiti to defend its own territory and to participate in the defense of the hemisphere, the Government of the United States, through its appropriate military and naval agencies, is taking steps:

a. To grant assistance in the construction of a marine railway at Port-au-Prince.

b. To station vessels suitable for coast guard and patrol purposes in Haitian waters. Provision will be made to train Haitian cadets on these vessels.

c. To make available a number of units of artillery for coast defense and other purposes.

d. To make available a number of military aircraft with mechanics and instructors who will give training to members of the Garde d'Haiti.

e. To construct a new patrol boat to be used in the defense of Haitian coastal waters.

f. To undertake the overhaul and repair of additional shipping of Haitian registry to be used for coastal and patrol duties.

) **Exchange of Notes between the Peruvian Minister of Finance and Commerce (*Dasso*) and the Secretary of State (*Hull*), April 23, 1942**

The visit of His Excellency Señor David Dasso, Minister of Finance and Commerce of Peru, to Washington resulted in the exchange with the Secretary of State of notes incorporating a series of decisions on collaboration giving effect to a number of the objectives of the resolutions of the Third Meeting of Ministers of Foreign Affairs, Rio de Janeiro, January 1942. In addition to the matters covered in the exchange of notes, other matters of mutual interest were discussed, including details of arrangements under the Lend-Lease agreement signed on March 11, 1942, and questions of export control, priorities and allocations. Following the above conversations, President Manuel Prado of Peru arrived in this country on May 6 and was a guest in Washington, May 7–11.

) **The Peruvian Minister of Finance and Commerce (*Dasso*) to the Secretary of State (*Hull*)** [1]

MR. SECRETARY:

I wish to express my sincere appreciation for the courtesies which have been extended to me and to my companions during our visit to Your Excellency's country. During my stay, I have had the opportunity to discuss with officials of a number of agencies of Your Excellency's Government a program of close collaboration to attain many of the objectives of the Resolutions of the Third Meeting of the Ministers of Foreign Affairs of the American Republics at Rio de Janeiro, and a series of important decisions have been reached on several points of this program. In order to carry out its undertaking in accordance with Resolution II on the Production of Strategic Materials,[2] the Government of Peru is establishing a Peruvian Amazon Corporation to develop the production

[1] Department of State, *Bulletin*, VI, p. 366.   [2] See p. 305.

and encourage the collection of wild rubber and other tropical product
Moreover, I have today transmitted to Your Excellency a note [1] cor
taining a proposal of the Government of Peru, in furtherance of the pr
visions relating to the production of strategic materials in Resolution
of the Third Meeting of the Ministers of Foreign Affairs of the America
Republics at Rio de Janeiro, for developing the production of rubber
Peru and for making available to the United States all rubber produce
in Peru other than a specified amount required for essential uses in Per
This proposal provides for the purchase of such rubber by Rubb
Reserve Company over a five-year period. The proposal also conter
plates the establishment of a fund of $1,125,000 to be made available
Peru for the purpose of increasing the production of wild rubber in Per

I have taken up with the Export-Import Bank of Washington t
question of obtaining an appropriate credit to assist in financing pu
chases in the United States of materials and equipment required in co
nection with the construction and development in Peru of useful publ
works and of agricultural, mining and industrial projects.

In order to provide the fullest technical facilities and cooperatic
necessary to the successful development in Peru of production of rubb
and other important and strategic tropical products, discussions we
begun with members of the United States Delegation at the Rio
Janeiro Meeting looking towards the establishment of an agricultur
experiment station in the Amazon region of Peru. These discussions ha
culminated in an agreement with the Secretary of Agriculture of t
United States, a copy of which is enclosed,[1] for the immediate establis
ment of such an experiment station at Tingo María. During my visit
Washington I have also taken up with appropriate officials of Yo
Excellency's Government the desire of the Government of Peru to obta
the services of experts in highway engineering, erosion control, coal mi
ing, and tea processing.

Discussions have also taken place with the Secretary of Agricultu
and officials of the Commodity Credit Corporation regarding propos:
for the purchase through the latter Corporation, for the duration of t
war, of that portion of the Peruvian cotton production which is in exce
of sales for Peruvian consumption and for export to other purchase
These discussions have resulted in the conclusion with the Secretary
Agriculture of an agreement, a copy of which is attached,[1] which shou
contribute in large measure to the maintenance of the Peruvian ag
cultural economy and the orderly handling of cotton crops in the face
dislocations of trade occasioned by the war.

[1] Not printed.

As Your Excellency is aware, the Government of Peru has just adopted
easures implementing further the recommendations contained in
esolution V on Severance of Commercial and Financial Relations [1]
opted at the Third Meeting of the Ministers of Foreign Affairs at Rio
Janeiro. By these measures the Government of Peru will control the
mmercial and financial operations of firms and persons whose activities
e deemed inimical to the security of the hemisphere. In this connec-
on, the Government of Peru will consult with the Government of the
ited States regarding any measures which may be necessary to prevent
ch persons and firms from benefiting from the agreements which have
en reached between our two Governments.

The Peruvian Government wishes to inform Your Excellency's Gov-
nment that it has entered into discussions with the Foreign Bond-
lders Protective Council, Incorporated, looking toward the early
sumption of payments on the Peruvian dollar debt. These discussions
th regard to the scale and amount of payments will be continued after
y return to Lima and subsequent announcement will be made by my
vernment.

In conclusion I wish to express to Your Excellency my firm conviction
at the program of further collaboration between our Governments
veloped during my visit will contribute greatly to the realization of
r common aim of hemisphere security.

I avail myself [etc.]

) *The Secretary of State (Hull) to the Peruvian Minister of Finance
and Commerce (Dasso)* [2]

xCELLENCY:

I have received with deep gratification Your Excellency's cordial note
April 23, 1942, with reference to the matters which I and other officials
the Government of the United States have had the privilege of dis-
ssing with you during your visit to Washington. I need not assure you
the personal satisfaction which it has been for me to collaborate with
u in the establishment of a program to attain certain of the objectives
the Resolutions of the Third Meeting of Ministers of Foreign Affairs
the American Republics at Rio de Janeiro, and I am convinced that
e decisions taken will contribute in important degree to the security of
e hemisphere.

My Government is pleased to note that, in furtherance of Resolution
on the Production of Strategic Materials, Your Excellency's Govern-

[1] See p. 310.   [2] Department of State, *Bulletin*, VI, p. 367.

ment is creating a Peruvian Amazon Corporation to undertake an stimulate the production of strategic tropical products. In this conne tion I have today transmitted to Your Excellency a note accepting t proposal of the Government of Peru with respect to the acquisition the Rubber Reserve Company over a period of five years of all rubb produced in Peru other than the specified amount required for essenti uses in Peru. This agreement marks an important step in the carryi out of the broad program for the mobilization of strategic materi resources for the security of the hemisphere which was undertaken the recent Rio de Janeiro Meeting.

I am informed by the Secretary of Commerce that the Export-Impc Bank finds itself heartily in sympathy with the objectives of the progra of the Government of Peru and is prepared to establish a credit in fav of Banco Central de Reserva del Peru in the sum of $25,000,000 to assi in financing purchases in the United States of materials and equipme required in connection with the construction and development in Peru useful public works, and of agricultural, mining and industrial projec It is recognized that the United States cannot undertake to furni machinery and equipment in short supply due to the exigencies of wa and that priorities necessary to acquire such items in the United Stat will be granted only after careful study and determination that the esta lishment of the industry for which they are needed will contribute direct in important measure to the war effort of the United States and t security of the hemisphere.

I have noted with satisfaction and interest the agreements entered in by Your Excellency with the Secretary of Agriculture for the establis ment of an agricultural experiment station at Tingo María and for t purchase through the Commodity Credit Corporation of that portion the Peruvian cotton production which is in excess of sales for Peruvi consumption and for export to other purchasers. I also take pleasure informing you that my Government has found it possible to arrange make available to Your Excellency's Government the services of cor petent experts in highway engineering, erosion control, coal mining, a tea processing.

My Government has noted with great satisfaction the measur adopted by the Peruvian Government to control the commercial ar financial operations of persons whose activities are deemed inimical the security of the hemisphere, which are referred to in Your Excellency note, as well as Your Excellency's statement that the Government Peru will consult with the Government of the United States regardi any measures which may be necessary to prevent such persons from ben

ing from the agreements reached between our two Governments. It is
understood that the two Governments will consult particularly with
respect to the policies and procedures to be adopted for dealing with
cotton which may be produced by persons or firms on the United States
Proclaimed List of Certain Blocked Nationals.

I likewise welcome the information that the Government of Peru is
carrying on discussions with the Foreign Bondholders Protective Council,
Incorporated, looking towards an early resumption of payments on the
Peruvian dollar debt.

Accept [etc.]

) Arrangements with Nicaragua. Department of State Release, April 25, 1942 [1]

The Nicaraguan Minister of Foreign Affairs, Dr. Mariano Arguello,
and the President of the National Bank of Nicaragua, Dr. Jesús Sanchez,
have concluded their visit in Washington, during the course of which
negotiations were undertaken relating to the construction of the Nicaraguan section of the Inter-American Highway, an extension of credit by
the Export-Import Bank, the availability of supplies and equipment for
the maintenance of certain industries vital to the economy of Nicaragua,
defense measures of mutual interest, and the development of rubber
production for purchase by the United States.

1. Notes were exchanged on April 8, 1942, providing for the cooperation of the United States in the construction of the Inter-American
Highway in Nicaragua, in accordance with the Inter-American Highway Act signed by the President of the United States on December 26,
1941.[2] This exchange of notes provides for the completion of the Inter-
American Highway in Nicaragua on the basis that Nicaragua will assume
one third of the cost of the construction of the Highway in Nicaragua;
the remaining two thirds will be borne by the United States under the
above-mentioned Act.

The section of the Inter-American Highway from Managua, the
capital of Nicaragua, north 65 miles to Sebaco and south 29 miles to
Diriamba, has been largely completed by the Nicaraguan Government.
The exchange of notes effected on April 8 will permit the completion of
this part of the Highway, and its extension to the Honduran and Costa
Rican frontiers, involving about 175 miles of construction.

2. Negotiations were concluded relating to the extension of a line of
credit, not to exceed $500,000, in favor of the Banco Nacional de Nica-
ragua by the Export-Import Bank of Washington.

[1] *Ibid.*, p. 368.   [2] See p. 407.

3. Expression was given by Dr. Arguello to the vital importance
certain industries in the internal economy of Nicaragua and to t
requirements of those industries for supplies and equipment essential
their continued operation. The Government of the United States h
assured the Nicaraguan Government that, so far as the materials a
available in the United States under present conditions, every effort w
be made to assist those industries essential to the national economy
Nicaragua to obtain supplies and equipment for the maintenance
production at normal levels.

4. Dr. Arguello also discussed, while in Washington, a number
matters of interest to the two Governments in relation to continent
defense. Agreement was reached regarding the cooperation of t
United States in the construction of a highway which will join t
Atlantic and Pacific sections of Nicaragua and will at the same time ha
an important bearing upon the defense of this highly important are

5. An agreement in principle has been reached whereby the Nicar
guan Government, acting through the Banco Nacional de Nicaragu
will make available for purchase by the Rubber Reserve Company :
crude rubber produced in Nicaragua which is available for export.

6. The Government of the United States, acting through the Depa▸
ment of Agriculture, has agreed to assist the Nicaraguan Government
the establishment of an agricultural-demonstration station with a vi◄
to increasing Nicaraguan agricultural production, particularly with ▸
spect to the development of rubber and abaca, and to that end will se▸
a group of competent experts to Nicaragua.

3. MODIFICATION OF AGREEMENTS IN FORCE TO TAKE ACCOUNT OF SPECIAL CIRCUMSTANCES

(1) *Exchange of Notes between the Governments of the United Stat*
   and Haiti, February 16 and 19, 1942

(a) *The Minister of Foreign Affairs of Haiti (Fombrun) to the Minist*▸
   of the United States (White), February 16, 1942 [1]

I have the honor to refer to the trade agreement entered into betwe
Haiti and the United States of March 28, 1935, and particularly to t
provisions thereof setting forth the principle of unconditional mo:
favored-nation treatment as the basis of commercial relations betwe
our two countries.[2]

[1] Department of State, *Bulletin*, VI, p. 174; Executive Agreement Series 238.
[2] The most-favored-nation provisions of the agreement (Executive Agreeme◄
Series 78) are set forth in Articles VII and XI.

The Government of Haiti adheres firmly to the principle of promoting
e multilateral development of international trade on the unconditional
ost-favored-nation basis. However, as the Government of the United
ates is aware, there are special and unusual conditions affecting trade
tween Haiti and the Dominican Republic which arise out of their ex-
ptional geographic situation. With a view to fostering closer economic
lations between these two contiguous countries, a Treaty of Commerce
tween Haiti and the Dominican Republic was signed on August 26,
41.[1] This treaty provides among other things for reductions in
aitian customs duties on a specified list of products imported from the
ominican Republic, which reductions are intended to be applicable
clusively to the latter country.[2]

In this connection, I have the honor to refer to the contractual formula
r tariff preferences to contiguous countries recommended by the Inter-
nerican Financial and Economic Advisory Committee. On September
, 1941, the Committee recommended that any such tariff preferences,
order to be an instrument for sound promotion of trade, should be
ade effective through trade agreements embodying tariff reductions or
emptions; that the parties to such agreements should reserve the right
reduce or eliminate the customs duties on like imports from other
untries; and that any such regional tariff preferences should not be
rmitted to stand in the way of any broad program of economic re-
nstruction involving the reduction of tariffs and the scaling down or
mination of tariff and other trade preferences with a view to the
llest possible development of international trade on a multilateral,
conditional most-favored-nation basis.

I have the honor to inquire whether the Government of the United
ates, in the light of the foregoing considerations, will agree not to in-
ke the provisions of the first paragraph of Article VII of the trade
reement of March 28, 1935 for the purpose of claiming the benefit of
e tariff preferences to the Dominican Republic specifically provided
r in the Treaty of Commerce signed on August 26, 1941, which tariff
eferences are considered by my Government to meet the requirements

[1] In force March 23, 1942.
[2] The products concerned are as follows: Leaf tobacco and cigars; live cattle, horses,
d mules; animals for slaughter; corn; toilet and laundry soap; perfumery and toilet
icles; lard; peanuts and peanut oil; butter; cheese; rice, up to 3,000 quintals (300,-
) pounds) annually; straw hats; preserved and refrigerated meats; matches; beer;
ginned cotton; fighting cocks; skins; and curried hides. Imports of these products
o Haiti from the United States accounted in the year 1939–40 (October 1–Septem-
r 30) for only about 8 per cent of Haiti's total imports from the United States in
at year.

of the aforementioned formula recommended by the Inter-America
Financial and Economic Advisory Committee.

Accept [etc.]

(b) The Minister of the United States (White) to the Minister of Forei₁ Affairs of Haiti (Fombrun), February 19, 1942 [1]

I have the honor to acknowledge the receipt of Your Excellency
note of today's date in which you reiterate the adherence of your Go
ernment to the principle of promoting the multilateral development
international trade on the unconditional most-favored-nation basis a₁
refer to the exclusive tariff reductions to the Dominican Republic speci
cally provided for in the Treaty of Commerce between Haiti and th
country signed on August 26, 1941. In this connection you mention t
contractual formula for tariff preferences to contiguous countries reco₁
mended on September 18, 1941 by the Inter-American Financial a₁
Economic Advisory Committee, and inquire whether, in view of t
Committee's recommendation and considering the special and unusu
conditions affecting trade between Haiti and the Dominican Republi
my Government would be willing to refrain from claiming, under t
provisions of the trade agreement between our two countries of Mar
28, 1935, the benefit of the tariff preferences to the Dominican Repub₁
specifically provided for in the Treaty of Commerce.

I have the honor to inform Your Excellency that my Government,
view of the considerations set forth, agrees not to invoke the pertine₁
provisions of the trade agreement for the purpose of claiming the bene
of such tariff preferences.

Accept [etc.]

(2) Exchange of Notes between the Governments of the United Stat and Ecuador. The Ecuadoran Minister of Foreign Affairs (D noso) to the United States Minister at Quito (Long), March 1942 [2]

EXCELLENCY:

I have the honor to refer to recent conversations which have tak
place with regard to the financial emergency with which the Governme
of the Republic of Ecuador is confronted and, in that connection,
certain provisions of the trade agreement between the Republic of Ecu
dor and the United States of America signed at Quito on August 6, 193

---

[1] Department of State, *Bulletin*, VI, p. 175.
[2] *Ibid.*, p. 221. The confirmatory note is omitted.

s amended by notes exchanged at Quito on August 6, 1938, September , 1938, and September 13, 1938.

In the course of these conversations, it has been pointed out that the iovernment of the Republic of Ecuador finds it necessary, as a fiscal neasure designed solely to meet the existing financial emergency, to ugment customs revenues, which make up such a large percentage of otal revenues, to an extent deemed necessary to safeguard vital interests f the nation.

Consideration was given to the possibility of terminating both sched-les of the trade agreement as a way out of the difficulty; but neither iovernment desired to adopt this course if it could be avoided. There-ore, the conversations to which I have referred have disclosed a mutual nderstanding which is as follows:

In view of the existing circumstances, the Government of the United tates of America will not invoke the provisions of Article I of the trade greement in respect of the application of the proposed increase in ustoms charges to articles imported into Ecuador from the United tates which are included in Schedule I of the agreement. It is under-tood that such increase will be applied generally to all dutiable imports om all foreign countries, and will not become effective, with regard to nports from the United States, prior to the expiration of thirty days om the date of this note. It is understood, further, that such increase ill be reduced and ultimately removed as soon as Ecuador's fiscal tuation improves sufficiently to warrant such action.

I also desire to take this occasion to confirm the understanding which as been reached between the Government of the Republic of Ecuador nd the Government of the United States of America that, notwithstand-ig the provisions of Article X of the trade agreement, concerning the ontrol of foreign exchange transactions relating to trade between the wo countries, the Governments of the two countries agree to apply and dminister any such control as follows:

1. If the Government of either country establishes or maintains any orm of control of the means of international payment, it shall accord nconditional most-favored-nation treatment to the commerce of the ther country with respect to all aspects of such control.

2. The Government establishing or maintaining such control shall npose no prohibition, restriction or delay on the transfer of payment for ny article the growth, produce or manufacture of the other country hich is not imposed on the transfer of payment for the like article the rowth, produce or manufacture of any third country. With respect to ates of exchange and with respect to taxes or charges on exchange trans-

actions, articles the growth, produce or manufacture of the other countr;
shall be accorded unconditionally treatment no less favorable than tha
accorded to the like articles the growth, produce or manufacture of an;
third country. The foregoing provisions shall also extend to the applica
tion of such control to payments necessary for or incidental to the impor
tation of articles the growth, produce or manufacture of the othe
country. In general, the control shall be administered so as not to ir
fluence to the disadvantage of the other country the competitive rela
tionships between articles the growth, produce or manufacture of tha
country and like articles the growth, produce or manufacture of thir
countries.

It is further understood that nothing in the provisions of paragraph
1 or 2, above, or in the trade agreement of August 6, 1938, as amendec
shall prevent the adoption or enforcement by either country of measure
relating to public security, or imposed for the protection of the country
essential interests in time of war or other national emergency.

I avail [etc.]

4. PRODUCTION AND PROCUREMENT OF RUBBER

(1) *Agreement with Costa Rica, signed June 16, 1942. Department*
State Release, June 16, 1942 [1]

The outbreak of war between the United States and Japan, followed by tł
Japanese military occupation of rubber-producing areas in British Malaya an
the Dutch East Indies, produced a critical situation for the United States ;
regards certain raw materials indispensable to the war effort. Of these rubber w;
perhaps the most important. The comprehensive arrangements with Brazi'
Peru,[3] and Nicaragua [4] already listed made special provision for the acquisitic
by the United States of available rubber and the development of potential r
sources. The agreement with Costa Rica is the first dealing exclusively wi
rubber. On July 3, 1942, the Department of State announced the signing of
similar agreement with Colombia,[5] and it was then stated that negotiations fe
similar agreements with a number of other American rubber-producing countrie
were in process.[6]

The Rubber Reserve Company, the Department of State, and tł
Board of Economic Warfare announced on June 16 the signing of ε
agreement with the Republic of Costa Rica, under the terms of which tł
Rubber Reserve Company will purchase within the next five years a
rubber produced in Costa Rica which is not required for essential neec
there.

[1] Department of State, *Bulletin*, VI, p. 554.   [2] See p. 364.   [3] See p. 369.
[4] See p. 373.   [5] Department of State, *Bulletin*, VII, p. 595.
[6] Bolivian agreement announced July 15, *ibid.*, p. 633.

While Costa Rica has in the past produced only a small amount of ubber, the country has considerable potential resources of that product, oth wild and cultivated. The Rubber Reserve Company, acting with he Board of Economic Warfare, will aid in the development of these esources and expend the necessary funds for that purpose.

The signing of the contract is another step in the program of the Jnited States to assure to the united war effort the maximum effective se of the rubber produced in the Western Hemisphere.

2) *An Act to Provide for the Planting of Guayule and Other Rubber-bearing Plants and to Make Available a Source of Crude Rubber for Emergency and Defense Uses, Approved March 5, 1942* [1]

[Excerpt]

The Senate Committee on Military Affairs began holding hearings on December 10, 1941, with a view to securing a domestic source of rubber by planting uayule as a substitute for the supplies cut off by the war in the Southeast 'acific. The guayule shrub, which can produce in two years after planting, rows in California, Arizona, New Mexico, Texas and other southern states, in Iexico and other Latin American states. The crude rubber derived from it, after eresination, is essentially the same as that from the Para rubber tree, which akes some 6 years or more to yield rubber.

The original bill was reported as S. 2152, which was much amended and re-ommitted for a second hearing, before being passed on Feburary 9, 1942. The 'resident vetoed that act on February 17 on the following grounds:

"On January 28, 1942, at the Third Meeting of the Ministers of Foreign ffairs of the American Republics in Rio de Janeiro, Brazil, there was passed nanimously by the 21 American Republics a resolution that continental olidarity be translated into positive and efficient action in the obtaining of trategic materials. Rubber, of course, is one of the most important of these aaterials, and this bill provides that guayule shall be a source of crude rubber or emergency and defense uses.

"The bill as it was amended by the House to limit the promotion of guayule ultivation to the United States would contradict the spirit of the resolution nd seriously handicap our joint war effort."

Public Law 473 met that objection.

Be it enacted by the Senate and House of Representatives of the United tates of America in Congress assembled, That the Secretary of Agriculture ereinafter called the "Secretary") is authorized —

(1) To acquire by purchase, license, or other agreement, the right) operate under processes or patents relating to the growing and har-esting of guayule or the extraction of rubber therefrom, and such roperties, processes, records, and data as are necessary to such oper-

[1] Public Law 473, 77th Cong.; originated as S. 2282; Senate Report No. 1099; ouse Report No. 1839. See also House of Representatives, Committee on Agri-ilture, *Guayule Rubber; Hearings* . . . 77th Cong., 2d sess., on H. R. 6299 . . , January 7, 8, and 13, 1942.

ation, including but not limited to any such rights owned or controlled by the Intercontinental Rubber Company, or any of its subsidiaries and all equipment, materials, structures, factories, real property, seed seedlings, growing shrub, and other facilities, patents and processes of the Intercontinental Rubber Company, or any of its subsidiaries located in California, and for such rights, properties, and facilities of the Intercontinental Rubber Company or any of its subsidiaries, the Secretary is authorized to pay not to exceed $2,000,000;

(2) To plant, or contract for the planting of, not in excess of seventy five thousand acres of guayule in areas in the Western Hemisphere where the best growth and yields may be expected in order to maintain a nucleus planting of guayule to serve as a domestic source of crud rubber as well as of planting material for use in further expanding guayule planting to meet emergency needs of the United States for crude rubber; to establish and maintain nurseries to provide seedling for field plants; and to purchase necessary equipment, facilities, and land for nurseries;

(3) To acquire by lease, or other agreement, for not exceeding ten years, rights to land for the purpose of making plantings of guayule to make surveys, directly or through appropriate Government agencies of areas in the Western Hemisphere where guayule might be grown and to establish and maintain records indicating areas to which guayule cultivation could be extended for emergency production;

. . . .

(8) To sell guayule or rubber processed from guayule and to use fund so obtained in replanting and maintaining an area of seventy-five thousand acres of guayule inside the Western Hemisphere; and

(9) To exercise with respect to rubber-bearing plants other than guayule the same powers as are granted in the foregoing provisions of this section with respect to guayule.

5. COFFEE MARKETING AGREEMENT

[For background and text of the Inter-American Coffee Agreement of November 28, 1940, see *Documents, III, 1940–41*, p. 97.]

By Article XX of the Inter-American Coffee Agreement, if, within ninety days from the date of signature, the instruments of ratification or approval of all the signatory Governments had not been deposited, the Governments which had deposited said instruments could put the agreement into force among themselves by means of a protocol.[1] With the deposit by the Cuban Government of it

[1] This was done by Protocol of April 15, 1941. *Documents, III, 1940–41*, p. 98.

nstrument of ratification, signed November 28, 1940, on December 31, 1941,[1] ll the signatory Governments had deposited their instruments of ratification or pproval with the Pan American Union. By proclamation dated February 27, 942,[2] supplementing his earlier proclamation of April 15, 1941, the President eclared this to be a fact, and that "in accordance with the provisions of Article XX of the said agreement the agreement entered into full force among all he signatory countries on December 31, 1941."

1) Inter-American Coffee Board. Statement and Resolutions, October 23, 1941

[For the initial activities of the Inter-American Coffee Board, see *Documents, III, 940–41*, p. 108.]

a) Statement of the Board [3]

The Inter-American Coffee Board has carefully studied the operation of the nter-American Coffee Agreement, and as a result of this study has arrived at ertain conclusions which, it is believed, will contribute materially to the suc-essful operation of the Agreement in the future. Specifically, the Board ex-resses the unanimous opinion of all the delegates to the effect that the future uccess of the Inter-American Coffee Agreement is assured by the understanding /hich has been reached on the following points.

Certain producing countries have deemed it necessary or desirable, as a meas-re of internal administration, to establish or maintain minimum prices in order o secure for coffee producers the full benefits of the Inter-American Coffee greement. The Board believes that, as a matter of policy which will facilitate he smooth operation and administration of the Agreement, any such minimum rices which exist or which may be established in the future should not be main-ained or fixed at levels exceeding the market prices for coffee which would exist nder the normal operation of the quota system in the absence of such minimum rices, nor should they prevent normal price fluctuations, nor disturb the normal nd usual operation of the coffee trade.

The Inter-American Coffee Board likewise considers that those countries aving adequate warehousing facilities in their respective ports of shipment nould maintain in those ports stocks of coffee in quantities sufficient to satisfy he requirements of the market, in order to facilitate the normal and usual opera-ion of the coffee trade.

In view of the unanimous agreement which has been reached on the foregoing oints, the Inter-American Coffee Board believes that the successful operation f the Inter-American Coffee Agreement is assured, and that there will be a nor-al and regular movement of coffee to the United States on terms fair to pro-ucers and consumers alike.

[1] Department of State, *Bulletin*, VI, p. 71.
[2] United States, *Treaty Series*, No. 979 (Supplementary to *Treaty Series* No. 970).
[3] Department of State, *Bulletin*, V, p. 324.

(b) Resolutions of the Board [1]

United States Quota

WHEREAS:

For the purposes of the Inter-American Coffee Agreement it is necessary t
adjust the quotas for the United States market because of the special circum
stances now existing;

THE INTER-AMERICAN COFFEE BOARD

Resolves:

1. To adjust the quotas for the United States market, effective October 2₄
1941, so that the quotas for the said market from that date shall be 110% ₍
the basic quotas.

2. To communicate this resolution to the Governments participating in th
Inter-American Coffee Agreement.

Warehousing of Shipments

WHEREAS:

It is necessary to take advantage of all available shipping facilities during tl
current quota year in order to avoid the fear of future shortage of coffee due t
shipping difficulties;

THE INTER-AMERICAN COFFEE BOARD

Resolves:

1. To authorize the participating producing countries, once they have e:
ported the total amount of their respective quotas for the current quota year, t
export to the United States before next September 30, to be charged to the
respective quotas for the next quota year, an amount of coffee not to excee
15 per cent of their respective basic quotas, on condition that the coffee ₅
exported be warehoused under the supervision of the United States custon
authorities so that it is not entered for consumption before October 1, 1942.

2. To communicate this resolution to the Governments of the countries part
cipating in the Inter-American Coffee Agreement.

(2) Allocation of Quota for Countries Not Signatories of the Agreemen Executive Order No. 8863, August 22, 1941 [2]

The quotas are expressed as percentages of the total quota for the countri
which are not signatories of the agreement, rather than in actual quantities :
bags, to obviate the necessity of issuing a new Executive Order in the eve
the import quotas are modified pursuant to the procedure set forth in the agre
ment. The percentages correspond to the proportion of coffee imports into tl
United States from countries which are not signatories of the agreement supplie
during the 4-year period 1937–40 by each of the groups of countries to whic
allocations are made by the Executive Order.

[1] *Ibid.*, p. 325.
[2] 6 *Fed. Reg.*, p. 4319; Department of State, *Bulletin*, V, p. 149. The headnote is ₍
exact quotation from a Department of State Release of the same date. *Ibid.*, p. 14

The allocations established by the Executive Order are designed to afford each
non-signatory country an opportunity to supply a fair share of the total quota for
such countries and, at the same time, to insure adequate supplies of certain
special types of coffee needed in this country for blending purposes. Termination
of the allocation order one month prior to the end of the quota year provides a
certain amount of flexibility which is deemed desirable. It means that during
the month of September 1942 the only restriction on the importation into the
United States of coffee from countries which are not signatories of the Inter-
American Coffee Agreement will be the total quota established for all such
countries pursuant to the terms of that agreement.

WHEREAS I find that it is necessary to allocate the quota established under
the Inter-American Coffee Agreement, signed on November 28, 1940, for countries which are not signatories of the said agreement in order to afford such countries an opportunity to supply a fair share of the quota:

Now, THEREFORE, by virtue of the authority vested in me by section 2 of the
joint resolution of Congress approved April 11, 1941 (Public Law 33, 77th Cong.,
1st sess.), it is hereby ordered as follows:

1. For the quota year beginning October 1, 1941, the quota limiting entries
or consumption of coffee produced in countries which are not signatories of the
Inter-American Coffee Agreement shall be allocated as follows:

British Empire, except Aden and Canada	33.04 percent
Kingdom of the Netherlands and its possessions	36.77 percent
Aden, Yemen, and Saudi Arabia	7.24 percent
Other countries not signatories of the Inter-American Coffee Agreement	22.95 percent

2. During the effective period of this order, no coffee produced in the countries
specified in paragraph 1 may be entered for consumption in excess of the respective quotas calculated by applying the percentages specified in paragraph 1 to
the total quota for countries not signatories of the Inter-American Coffee Agreement.

3. This order shall cease to be effective on September 1, 1942.[1]

3) *Entry of Coffee into the United States. Executive Order No. 8902,
September 17, 1941* [2]

The proper functioning of an international commodity agreement requires
careful and coordinated administration taking account of commercial practices.
The following order was designed to prevent the diversion to the United States
of coffee shipped from the producing countries under their quotas for exports
to the market outside the United States. Such diversion of coffee shipments may
result in the filling of the United States import quotas before the producing coun

---

[1] It has been decided not to allocate the non-signatory quota for the year beginning
October 1, 1942. Department of State, *Bulletin*, VII, p. 635.

[2] 6 *Fed. Reg.*, p. 4809; Department of State, *Bulletin*, V, p. 222.

tries' export quotas for the United States market are exhausted. This situation would interfere with the normal operations of the coffee trade and, in certain instances, would make it impossible for the traders to make deliveries in fulfill ment of contracts. The order establishes a procedure for coordinating control of coffee exports by the producing countries with control of coffee imports by the United States.

By virtue of the authority vested in me by section 2 of the joint resolution of Congress approved April 11, 1941 (Public Law 33, 77th Cong., 1st sess.) it i hereby ordered as follows:

1. No invoice of coffee produced in a country which is a signatory of the Inter-American Coffee Agreement shall be certified hereafter by a United State consular officer unless there shall be produced to the certifying officer a official document, required by Article VI of the Agreement, showing that the coffee is within the producing country's quota for exportation to United State customs territory.

2. Beginning October 1, 1941, coffee produced in a country which is a signa tory of the Inter-American Coffee Agreement shall not be admitted to entry fc consumption in the customs territory of the United States unless there shall b produced for each shipment of such coffee an invoice bearing a certificate of United States consular officer that there has been presented to him an officia document required by Article VI of the Agreement showing that such shipment i within the producing country's quota for exportation to United States custom territory; except that any such shipment may be so entered without the produc tion of such an invoice if the shipment is valued at less than $100, or if there i given a bond conditioned for the production of such an invoice within six month from the date of entry, or if the coffee was shipped from the producing countr under a through bill of lading to the United States prior to the date of this order

6. CONTROL OF EXPORTS TO THE AMERICAN REPUBLICS

The development of a general program of export control, under authority the Act of July 2, 1940, to promote the interests of our national defense, inevita bly affected our trade relations with the Latin American Republics and emba rassed our efforts to develop the economic solidarity of the countries of th Western Hemisphere. It became necessary to strike a balance between th demands of essentially conflicting programs. On details of the general progra of export control, see *Documents, II, 1939–40*, p. 786–801; *III, 1940–41*, p. 473 98; this volume, p. 718.

(1) *Exports Control. Statement of the Under Secretary of State (Welles to the Inter-American Financial and Economic Advisory Com mittee, July 17, 1941* [1]

On June 19, 1941,[2] I made a statement to the Inter-American Financia and Economic Advisory Committee with reference to organization fc

[1] Mr. Sumner Welles is the delegate of the United States Government on th committee. Department of State, *Bulletin*, V, p. 57.   [2] See p. 719.

considering and handling export control and related policies. In that statement I summarized the objectives of the United States system of export control, and pointed out that these objectives are of interest and importance to all of the American Republics. I indicated at that time that the response among the American Republics in individual conversations with the United States had been most gratifying. Since that time this Committee has adopted a resolution embodying a report of Subcommittee II recommending that the Governments of all of the American Republics establish parallel systems of export control, and several additional American Republics have taken legislative or executive action to establish such systems.

The report of Subcommittee II referred to touched on, but did not elaborate on, another important aspect of the general problem — that is, the procedures and organization required to carry out effectively such a policy of export control. I wish today to indicate the arrangements determined by the Government of the United States for handling export licensing and priorities questions relating to exports to the other American Republics.

The Government of the United States is establishing two parallel procedures for handling all export licensing and priorities matters, depending on whether the import requirements in question are those, on the one hand, of a Government of an American Republic or relate to needs which a Government wishes to sponsor, or those, on the other hand, of any other persons or concerns in the other American Republics.

The several American Governments are requested to take up all matters relating to government and government-sponsored needs directly with the Department of State. The various Governments are requested to submit to the Department of State lists of materials and products covering one or more quarters and broken down as far as possible into projects — such as governmental demands, governmental corporations and utilities, and other particular projects which they wish directly to sponsor.

The Governments of the American Republics are requested to designate a single representative or agency which will present these lists of materials and products required, which will indicate on behalf of the particular government the relative order of preference of the various requests listed, and which will be in a position to discuss the lists and any particular items required with the Department of State.

To the extent that it is agreed to be desirable, certain of the listed items will be procured by the Government of the United States directly for the account of the other American Government in question. Other items on the lists, subject to the approval of the Department of State will be transmitted to the Administrator of Export Control for prefer-ential processing, as necessary, through the Office of Production Manage-ment, the Army and Navy Munitions Board, and other appropriate agencies.

The Administrator of Export Control will undertake to furnish infor-mation to, and to service United States manufacturers and exporters and likewise importers in the other American Republics, in all aspects of the problem including priorities questions and shipping availabilities He will undertake to furnish regular and complete information regarding such matters and to take every appropriate step to facilitate a maximum of free movement within the Western Hemisphere which is compatible with the requirements of national and continental defense.

The Department of State and the Administrator of Export Control will thus, in their respective spheres, furnish to the Governments of the other American Republics and to businessmen of the Western Hemi-sphere full assistance in carrying out to the greatest extent possible during this period of emergency, trade in the essential imports of the other American nations. This procedure will make it unnecessary for governmental organizations, business concerns, and individuals to ap-proach a number of agencies of the United States Government in arranging for a particular export transaction.

Applications for specific export licenses will continue to be received by the Division of Controls of the Department of State.

(2) *Export Licensing and Priorities Control. Statement of the Under Secretary of State (Welles) to the Inter-American Financial and Economic Advisory Committee, December 5, 1941* [1]

On previous occasions I have discussed with you the policy and procedure of the Government of the United States with respect to export licensing and priorities controls imposed in the interests of the national and continental defense and in furtherance of the policy of my Government of material aid to those countries which are resisting the aggression of nations bent on world-dominance. The policy of the United States remains firm — to make every effort consistent with the defense program, to maintain a flow to the other American Republics of materials to satisfy the minimum essential import requirements of your countries. This policy is being interpreted by all of the appropriate agencies of the United States as calling for recognition of and provision

[1] Department of State, *Bulletin*, VI, p. 449.

for the essential needs of the other American Republics equal to the treatment accorded to United States civilian needs.

The Government of the United States is bending every effort to fashion administrative mechanism and procedure which will effectively translate into action this broad policy. Since I last discussed these matters with you, the President has created the Supply Priorities and Allocations Board, whose function it is to allocate materials and the means of production to the several main categories of use. This includes the provision of materials to meet the essential needs of the other American nations. Moreover, the President has transferred the functions of export licensing and control to the Economic Defense Board, which is charged with the responsibility of presenting to the Supply Priorities and Allocations Board the requirements of the other American Republics and of maintaining a clearance system for priorities and allocations applications. In order to carry out its own role in these matters, the Department of State has recently reorganized its economic-defense work. I am therefore able to state confidently that the agencies of the Government of the United States directly concerned with the problem of meeting the essential import requirements of the other American Republics are rapidly being geared for an efficient handling of the necessary details.

I believe that in general discussion of the problem some confusion may have arisen from the terminology employed. The export license is, properly speaking, a permission to pass merchandise through the customshouse at the port of exit. Before merchandise may actually be exported from the United States it must be manufactured and purchased. With the rapid growth of the programs of national and continental defense and aid to Britain and the other nations resisting aggression, the industrial organization of the United States is becoming more and more subject to rigid priorities and allocations control. As you are aware from the press, every day the Supply Priorities and Allocations Board and the Office of Production Management are curtailing radically various sectors of civilian production and consumption within the United States. There is no doubt that as the defense effort continues such restrictions will increase in severity.

As a result, the emphasis has already shifted from the simple export license to the preference rating or the general allocation as the important procedural step required in the exportation of merchandise to the other American Republics. And with the increasing severity of priority control it has become obvious that it is not desirable that export licenses be granted freely in cases where the priority restriction would prevent the actual purchase for export of the material involved. This has been

the experience of the Government of the United States with many o
the general export licenses which have been issued. Many of these ar
for iron and steel products and other articles now subject to the mos
rigid control by the Office of Production Management. Nevertheless, th
existence of a general license has given rise to an impression that th
countries to which such licenses have been extended are able to acquir
the materials in question in unlimited amounts and with complet
freedom from procedural forms and regulations. We all know that thi
is not the case. Nevertheless, it is easy to argue that some discriminatio
exists when certain countries are issued general licenses and others ar
not, even though it is now clear that the issuance of such genera
licenses to the remaining countries would not be a step towards facili
tating the basic trade which is the real problem. Consequently th
Government of the United States proposes to rescind all such genera
licenses now outstanding and to issue general licenses to all of th
American Republics for a limited list of goods in which the existenc
of such general licenses is of real value to the purchaser. Because of th
broad extension of priorities control, the list is necessarily short. Studie
continue of the possibility of adding certain additional items in the cas
of which general licenses would be of real importance. As condition
change in the future it may be necessary to withdraw certain of thes
general licenses. In every case the criterion will be whether or not th
general licenses are of real significance.

Turning to the more fundamental problem, that of priorities contro
the Government of the United States has during the last several months
through its own agencies and with the cooperation of this Committee an
of the Governments of the other American Republics, been carrying ou
a broad survey of the essential needs of the other American Republic
in order that these may be properly considered in relation to the require
ments of our own program and of other friendly nations. The results o
these studies, although still in very preliminary form, are now sufficientl
advanced so that my Government is enabled to work towards specifi
allocation of materials for export to the other American Republics.

The Supply Priorities and Allocations Board has already made a
allocation for the year beginning December 15, 1941, of 218,600 metri
tons of tin plate to the 20 other American Republics. The Office c
Production Management and the Supply Priorities and Allocation
Board are carefully considering a factual presentation relating to
number of other important commodities, and it is proposed to exten
the procedure to as many other articles as is practicable.

These allocations do not represent the final stage which we hope t attain in procedure but do provide a necessary basis for the more efficient handling of important commodity situations.

My Government sets great store on the development of this new allocations technique. It is not merely a passive permission to export; it constitutes positive action to insure, so far as is possible in the face of the tremendous demands of the national- and continental-defense program on the industrial production of the United States, the availability for export of those amounts of materials most essentially required or the maintenance of the economies of the other American Republics.

(3) *Certificate of Necessity and Allocation Program. Announcement of Board of Economic Warfare, Office of Export Control, February 25, 1942* [1]

[Excerpt]

The Board of Economic Warfare, Office of Export Control will give special consideration to applications for export licenses which are accompanied by Certificates of Necessity. Such Certificates are issued by agencies of other American Republics selected by their respective Governments.

Certificates of Necessity will apply only to those commodities which have been allocated for export from the United States. [2]

In order to assure the issuance of licenses for imports considered most vital to the Republics of South America each of these countries have designated an essential needs agency. [3] These agencies are authorized to issue Certificates of Necessity which in effect request the Government of the United States to grant licenses for the export of the commodity described. Each agency is notified periodically of the total allocation of each commodity for the country it represents and should issue Certificates of Necessity only up to the total amount of each allocation.

(4) *List of Commodities Allocated to the Other American Republics. Announcements of April 4 and May 4, 1942*

A list of commodities "allocated to the other American Republics" for the second quarter of 1942 was contained in an announcement made jointly by the Department of State, the War Production Board, and the Board of Economic

---

[1] Board of Economic Warfare, Office of Export Control, *Current Controls Bulletin* No. 8, par. 1. In this connection, see Resolution V, Third Meeting of the Ministers of Foreign Affairs of the American Republics, this volume, p. 310.

[2] See (4) below.

[3] The list of agencies is printed in *Comprehensive Export Control Schedule*.

Warfare on April 4.[1] It was stated that machinery had been established in the interested government agencies to carry out the allocations program, and that announcements dealing with special procedures to be followed in connection with particular commodities would be made later. On May 4, an announcement containing a supplementary list was issued.[2] It was also stated that in order to avoid congestion of export shipments at ports and railway terminals and to insure that the commodities most urgently needed by our neighboring republics are given preference over less essential materials, consideration was being given to a plan to coordinate the issuance of export licenses with the availability of ocean freight.

Acetic acid, acetone, aconite, ammonium sulphate, anhydrous ammonia, aniline, camphor, carbon tetrachloride, castor oil, caustic soda, chlorine, copper, cotton linters, dibutyl phthalate, electrodes, farm equipment, formaldehyde, glycerin, leather, ferro-manganese, methanol, molybdenum, neat's-foot oil, phenol, phosphorus, phthalic anhydride, plastics, potash salts, potassium permanganate, rayon, red squill, household electric refrigerators, soda ash, strontium chemicals, sulphuric acid, superphosphate, tanning materials, toluol, tricresyl phosphate, light trucks, tungsten and ferro-tungsten, ferro-vanadium, and wood pulp

---

Iron and steel; lead; natural amorphous graphite; fluorspar; uranium salts and compounds; ascorbic acid; thiamine hydrochloride; sulfanilamide; sulfaguanidine; cranes, hoists, and derricks; and mechanical household refrigerators.

(5) *Shipping Priorities. Release of Board of Economic Warfare, Office of Exports, May 6, 1942* [3]

A system of shipping priorities designed to expedite the production in the other American Republics of materials required for the war program, as well as providing shipping facilities to take care of essential needs of our neighboring republics was jointly announced today by the Board of Economic Warfare, State Department and the Coordinator of Inter-American Affairs. The plan was made public after consultation between these agencies and War Shipping Administration and the Office of Defense Transportation.

Beginning May 7, licenses covering goods moving by water to other American Republics will bear shipping priority ratings. These rating will become effective with steamship lines at a date to be announced

[1] Department of State, *Bulletin*, VI, p. 274. The list of allocated materials is frequently revised and extended. See latest *Comprehensive Export Control Schedule*
[2] Department of State, *Bulletin*, VI, p. 393.
[3] Press Release No. 53; *Current Controls Bulletin* No. 22.

n the near future. Steamship operators will be directed by the War Shipping Administration to book cargo in accordance with these ratings, as fixed by the Office of Exports.

Shipping priority ratings will be assigned entirely on the basis of the 'use" of the goods. Highest ratings will be given materials contributing directly to the United States war program, to hemispheric military defense, and to materials essential to the maintenance of industrial, economic, and civilian life of the country of destination. Data as to those materials essential to the other American Republics has been obtained from these republics through the Department of State and the Coordinator of Inter-American Affairs and in deciding into which categories the proposed shipments will fall, there will be taken into account expressions of need as furnished by the governments of the other republics. Lower ratings will be assigned materials which, while important to industrial and civilian life, are not vital to the economic stability of the country of destination.

These ratings were defined by the Office of Exports as follows: Rating A will be assigned to licenses authorizing the exportation of articles and material contributing directly to the war program of the United States or to hemispheric military defense. Rating B will be assigned to licenses for articles and materials essential to the maintenance of industrial, economic, and civilian life of the country of destination. Rating C will be assigned to licenses for commodities deemed important to the industrial and civilian life of the country of destination, but for which there is no immediate urgency, and the lack of which would not cause economic dislocation. Rating D will be assigned to licenses for non-essential articles and commodities which, while desirable, appear unnecessary in war-time, and for which there are substitutes, or without which the economic and civilian life of the country of destination would not be seriously harmed. Rating AA is a special rating held in reserve to be applied in cases which are considered of the utmost importance and urgency.

6) Distribution of Oil to the Other American Republics
a) Statement of the Secretary of State (Hull), June 8, 1942 [1]

The United States, with respect to oil as with other vital supplies, is adhering to the principle of equal and proportionate treatment for consumer needs in the other American Republics. This principle has been applied to the sharing of various essential and critical materials.

[1] Department of State, *Bulletin*, VII, p. 621. Release dated July 6, 1942.

The problem of maintaining a flow of petroleum products to various areas in this hemisphere is similar to that of supplying the Atlantic and Pacific coasts in the United States. It is mainly an ocean-transportation problem.

Today millions of automobile users in areas of the United States dependent upon water-borne transportation for fuel have reduced their gasoline consumption to an average of three gallons a week under a rationing system. Pleasure driving in rationed areas has been largely eliminated so that shipping may be concentrated on the primary tasks of supplying the fighting forces, strategic industries, and essential civilian needs.

Hemispheric application of the principle of equal treatment of consumers implies use of tankers for the most essential needs in the assignment of vessels on inter-American routes too.

Steps have been taken in cooperation with the other American Republics to maintain the flow of petroleum supplies to those countries on as favorable a basis as that prescribed within rationed areas of the United States.

In addition, the United States has undertaken to meet oil needs of certain operations in the other American Republics contributing directly and vitally to the war effort. It is essential that these operations be maintained.

Examples of these vital operations are the military forces of countries fighting the Axis nations, merchant ships trading in the interest of the United Nations and friendly neutrals, airlines, and the mining and transportation of strategic materials.

In determining how tankers should be employed, the total supplies available to each of the American Republics in relation to its own essential needs must be taken into account and the tankers sent where the unsatisfied need is greatest.

This view of the oil problem has been communicated to the governments of the other American Republics.

(b) Statement of the Secretary of State (Hull), July 6, 1942 [1]

Scarcity of available tanker tonnage is becoming increasingly acute and much more severe rationing and stricter conservation measures should be instituted without delay in those areas dependent on tanker-born supplies.

[1] Ibid.

7. INTER-AMERICAN CONFERENCE ON SYSTEMS OF ECONOMIC AND FINANCIAL CONTROL, WASHINGTON, JUNE 30–JULY 10, 1942

Resolutions V [1] and VI [2] adopted at the Third Meeting of the Ministers of Foreign Affairs of the American Republics at Rio de Janeiro recommended respectively the severance of commercial and financial relations with the nations signatory to the Tripartite Pact and the convoking of "a conference of representatives of the central banks or equivalent or analogous institutions of the American Republics for the purpose of drafting standards of procedure for the uniform handling of bank credits, collections, contracts of lease and consignments of merchandise, involving real or juridical persons who are nationals of a State which has committed an act of aggression against the American continent."

The Inter-American Financial and Economic Advisory Committee, on April 16, 1942, recommended that "allowing for a sufficient time to make adequate preparation" the Conference be held "prior to July 1st of the present year in the City of Washington." [3] The Committee, meeting in plenary session on May 22, 1942, set June 30 as the date for a conference of banking and financial representatives "to give effect to the purposes of the Conference as set forth in Resolutions V and VI." [4]

(1) *Address by the Under Secretary of State* (*Welles*), *June 30, 1942* [5]

DELEGATES TO THE INTER-AMERICAN CONFERENCE ON SYSTEMS OF ECONOMIC AND FINANCIAL CONTROL, YOUR EXCELLENCIES, LADIES AND GENTLEMEN:

It is a source of great pleasure to me to extend to all of you on behalf of the Inter-American Financial and Economic Advisory Committee a cordial welcome to this Inter-American Conference on Systems of Economic and Financial Control.

Once again the 21 American Republics are meeting in conference in order still further to fortify their solidarity, still further to strengthen their common purpose to maintain this hemisphere forever free from any encroachment upon the independence of the peoples of the Americas, and as a citadel of human liberty.

We are confronting an attack upon the New World which is being waged by the Axis Powers on every front upon which they can muster their forces of treachery and of deceit.

For this war is not being fought today on the military front alone. We, the free nations of America, are today faced with the supreme and historic mission of repelling a total assault on our freedom and our integrity,

---

[1] See p. 310.

[2] See p. 313.

[3] Department of State, *Bulletin*, VI, p. 383.

[4] Pan American Union, *Bulletin*, August 1942, p. 469.

[5] Delivered by Mr. Welles at the Pan American Union, June 30, 1942; Department of State, *Bulletin*, VII, p. 580.

an assault that is being carried on not only by pirate submarines and military arms but also by the colonies of subversive agents on the sovereign soil of each one of our countries. These human termites, carrying out the will of their Axis masters, have been gnawing for a long time, not only at the foundations of our inter-American system but also at the foundations of the economic structure that maintains us whole. It is for the purpose of completing and integrating controls that have already been established to thwart and to stamp out their activities that this meeting of technical experts from our 21 American Republics is convened in Washington today.

Even by the time that the Ministers of Foreign Affairs met at Rio de Janeiro to consult on measures for the common defense of our nations some measures had already been adopted by the American Republics to control the exportation or reexportation of merchandise, to restrict and control financial and commercial transactions with the nations signatory to the Tripartite Pact and the territories dominated by them, and to curb other alien economic activities prejudicial to the welfare of the Western Hemisphere.

At that meeting the representatives of the American Governments laid down, in Resolution V, an outline of the general nature and objective of commercial and financial controls that they were unanimous in believing should be established in order to defend the hemisphere against the encroachments of the sinister fifth columns that were operating in advance of the Axis military forces. At that time they recommended for immediate adoption "any additional measures necessary to cut off for the duration of the present hemispheric emergency all commercial and financial intercourse, direct or indirect, between the Western Hemisphere and the nations signatory to the Tripartite Pact and the territories dominated by them;" and also "measures to eliminate all other financial and commercial activities prejudicial to the welfare and security of the American Republics . . ."

The Ministers of Foreign Affairs at their meeting in Rio de Janeiro recognized, however, that in order to make such controls as they recommended effective against the Axis fifth column in the Western Hemisphere it would be necessary that the financial authorities charged with the administration of such controls in each of the American Republics should meet together to consult with each other, in order to exchange information and to pool their experience. It would be necessary to work out the details of joint procedures that would altogether eliminate the financial and commercial maneuvers by which the tools of the German and Italian and Japanese warlords, operating in this hemisphere seek to reduce our defenses and endeavor to prepare the way for our subjugation. It was with this in view that the Meeting in Rio de Janeiro recommended the convocation of this present Inter-American Conference on Systems of Economic and Financial Control.

The historic task that now confronts the peoples of America, the task of defending the traditional freedom of the American continent against attack from abroad, cannot be accomplished by military means alone. We must be no less resolute in measures to counter the economic assault than in the measures we are taking to meet the military threat. The soil of our own continent is one of the great battlefields of this war. On it we are fighting — and fighting with increasing success — the enemy who has insinuated himself in our midst.

Delegates to this conference, the decisions that are made by you here at this conference and the actions of our Governments in carrying out those decisions are of the utmost consequence in assisting in the creation of the assurance that the American continent shall continue to maintain its liberties and its independence. It is a solemn mission with which this conference is charged. I have faith that that mission will be fulfilled in a manner worthy of the spirit that has nurtured and defended the freedom of the Americas throughout the term of our independent life.

Upon you rests a responsibility to provide implements for the willing hands that are fighting today the economic battles to preserve our solidarity. I voice the hope of millions when I express the firm conviction that in this critical moment your vision, your leadership, and your high devotion will not be found wanting.

(2) *Recommendations of the Conference, July 10, 1942* [1]

[Excerpt]

The Final Act, from which the Recommendations are taken, contains the names of representatives in attendance at the Conference, a brief description of the organization of the Conference, the texts of eight recommendations and one resolution adopted, and the signatures of the representatives. Only the texts of the eight recommendations are given here.[2] The Argentine representative signed subject to the following understanding: [3]

" The approval of these recommendations by the Delegation of the Central Bank of the Argentine Republic must be considered subject to the terms of

[1] Pan American Union, *Final Act of the Inter-American Conference on Systems of Economic and Financial Control, Washington, D. C., June 30–July 10, 1942.* Washington, 1942, Congress and Conference Series No. 39, 24 p. mimeo. *Proceedings of the Inter-American Conference . . . ,* Pan American Union, Congress and Conference Series, No. 40, 160 p. mimeo.

[2] The resolution (numbered IX) provided for a vote of thanks to the personnel of the Pan American Union.   [3] See p. 312.

Recommendation V of the Meeting of Ministers of Foreign Affairs of the American Republics, held at Rio de Janeiro, as that Recommendation was accepted by the Argentine Delegation."

The Chilean representative signed with the following understanding:[1]

"I sign as the delegate of the Central Bank of Chile, with the understanding that these recommendations do not alter the obligations devolving upon my country as a result of Recommendation V of the Third Meeting of the Ministers of Foreign Affairs of the American Republics, held at Rio de Janeiro."

I. FINANCIAL AND COMMERCIAL TRANSACTIONS WITH AGGRESSOR NATIONS AND NATIONS DOMINATED BY THEM

The Inter-American Conference on Systems of Economic and Financial Control

Recommends:

That the Governments of the American Republics, pursuant to Resolution V of the Third Meeting of the Ministers of Foreign Affairs of the American Republics, held at Rio de Janeiro, adopt and put into effect as soon as possible, effective measures to achieve the following purposes:

(a) To block effectively the use, transmission or transfer of funds, securities and property within the American Republics now held by nations which have committed acts of aggression against the American Continent, or subsequently acquired for their account, as well as the funds, securities and property now held by a real or juridical person within such aggressor nations or in the territories dominated by them, or subsequently acquired for the account of such persons.

(b) To prevent any real or juridical person within the jurisdiction of an American Republic from engaging in any financial or commercial transaction which involves the exportation of any property of any nature whatsoever, the remittance of any funds, or orders or instructions to persons under the jurisdiction of aggressor nations or those dominated by them, whether such exportation or remittance be made, or such orders or instructions be given, directly or indirectly.

There shall be excepted remittances (i) for living expenses of citizens of such American Republic residing within the aggressor nations or in the territories dominated by them, and (ii) for the expenses of representing the governmental interests of such American Republics in the aggressor nations or in the territories dominated by them including the care and safeguarding of the property of the Governments of such American Republics. The said payments can only be made directly by the Government of the respective American Repub-

[1] See p. 310.

lic, or through the Government representing its interests in such aggressor nations, or in the territories dominated by them.

(c) To prevent any real or juridical person within the jurisdiction of an American Republic from engaging in any financial or commercial transaction which involves the importation of any property of any nature whatsoever or the receipt of any funds, or the acting upon any order or instruction from any person within the jurisdiction of the aggressor nations or nations dominated by them, whether such importation, receipt of funds, or compliance with such order or instruction be made directly or indirectly.

There shall be excepted the remittances which each Government in its discretion may authorize (i) for living expenses of citizens of such aggressor nations or nations dominated by them, residing within the American Republics, and (ii) for expenses of representing the governmental interests of the aggressor nations or nations dominated by them, in the American Republics, including the care and safeguarding of the property of the governments of said aggressor nations or the nations dominated by them.

Except in cases of effective reciprocity, the exceptional payments referred to in the preceding paragraph shall in no case be made out of blocked funds or other assets which the aggressor nations or the nations dominated by them may have in the American Republics, but shall only be made out of unblocked funds of foreign ownership originating in territory outside the American Republics. Remittances for said payments shall be received only directly by the Government of the respective American Republic, or through the intermediary of the Government which represents in such American Republic the interests of said aggressor nations or of nations dominated by them.

I. FINANCIAL AND COMMERCIAL TRANSACTIONS WITH COUNTRIES OUTSIDE THE WESTERN HEMISPHERE

The Inter-American Conference on Systems of Financial and Economic Control

Recommends:

That the Governments of the American Republics, in addition to cutting off all financial and commercial transactions with the aggressor nations and the nations dominated by them, adopt as soon as possible, endeavoring not to cause unnecessary damage to neutral nations, appropriate measures with respect to their financial and commercial relationships with all of the other nations outside the Western Hemisphere, in order to:

(*a*) Supervise adequately the funds and property within their respective jurisdictions now held or hereafter acquired by or for such other nations outside the Western Hemisphere or real or juridical persons within such nations, except those nations which have cut off commercial and financial transactions with the aggressor nations.

(*b*) Prevent any real or juridical person within the jurisdiction of such American Republic from engaging in any commercial or financial transaction which involves the exportation or importation of any property of any nature whatsoever to or from nations outside the Western Hemisphere, or the remittance of funds to or from any person in such other nations outside the Western Hemisphere, when such exportation, importation or remittance is of benefit to the aggressor nations or to nations dominated by them.

(*c*) Prevent all transactions between the American Republics and nations outside the Western Hemisphere involving any real or juridical person within any nation outside the Western Hemisphere whose activities are deemed by the respective American Republic concerned to be inimical to the security of the Western Hemisphere.

III. Transactions among the American Republics

The Inter-American Conference on Systems of Economic and Financial Control

Recommends:

That, to prevent financial and commercial transactions which are of benefit to any of the nations which have committed acts of aggression against the American Continent, and transactions undertaken by any real or juridical person within the American Republics whose activities are inimical to the security of the Western Hemisphere, the Governments of the American Republics adopt, as soon as possible, measures to:

(*a*) Establish between the American Republics an interchange of information with respect to commercial and financial transactions undertaken with real or juridical persons within other American Republics so that each nation, within its jurisdiction and in the exercise of its own authority, may prevent any transaction which would benefit the aggressor nations, the nations dominated by them, or persons whose activities are inimical to the security of the American Continent.

(*b*) Prevent any transaction, subject to the jurisdiction of an American Republic, undertaken by real or juridical persons within nations outside the Western Hemisphere which have not cut off commercial and financial transactions with the aggressor nations, involving th monetary unit of another American Republic; except a transaction which, together with the report necessary to establish its nature, is undertaken through a bank of the American Republic whose monetary unit is involved in the transaction.

(c) Prevent any transaction, subject to the jurisdiction of an American Republic, involving real or juridical persons within nations outside the Western Hemisphere which have not cut off commercial and financial relations with the aggressor nations, and real or juridical persons within another American Republic, unless such transactions are performed with the approval of the latter Republic.

V. CONTROL OF MOVEMENT AND TRANSFER OF SECURITIES

The Inter-American Conference on Systems of Economic and Financial Control

Recommends:

That the Governments of the American Republics, in order to prevent transactions in securities for the benefit of the aggressor nations, adopt appropriate measures to:

(a) Establish a precautionary blocking of securities which directly or indirectly are imported into the American Republics from countries outside the Western Hemisphere, as well as their coupons, interests, and dividends, until it is determined that the aggressor nations, or the nations dominated by them, or persons within such nations, have not or have not had any interest in them since the beginning of the present emergency.

Non-bearer securities imported into American nations from countries outside the Western Hemisphere after the beginning of the present emergency, likewise may be subjected to precautionary blocking.

(b) To supervise transactions of any nature whatsoever by persons within an American Republic in securities, or interests therein, which are located outside the Western Hemisphere, so as to prevent transactions in which persons in aggressor nations or nations dominated by them have an interest or have had an interest since the beginning of the present emergency; or those from which they may derive some benefit direct or indirect.

(c) Require registration, or adopt any other appropriate measures, in order to determine if any person within the aggressor nations or the nations dominated by them, has any interest in securities issued or payable in any of the American Republics.

V. Standards for the Application of Financial and Economic Controls within the American Republics

The Inter-American Conference on Systems of Economic and Financial Control

Recommends:

1. That the application of the economic and financial controls of the Governments of the American Republics, during the present emergency, should have as one of its objectives the control of the property and transactions of all persons, real or juridical, residing or situated within their respective jurisdictions, regardless of nationality, who by their conduct are known to be, or to have been, engaging in activities inimical to the security of the Western Hemisphere.

2. That each of the Governments of the American Republics, through the application of its economic and financial controls, eliminate from the economic life of the respective country all undesirable influence and activity of those persons, real or juridical, residing or situated within the American Republics, who are known to be, or to have been, engaging in activities inimical to the security of the Western Hemisphere.

VI. Standards of Effective Blocking

The Inter-American Conference on Systems of Economic and Financial Control

Recommends:

1. That the Governments of the American Republics that have not already done so adopt, in accordance with their constitutional principles, measures to carry out the effective blocking of assets belonging to real or juridical persons, whatever may be their nationality, when these persons are deemed by the respective Government to act in a manner contrary to the security or the national economies of the American Republics; these measures shall not exclude other measures which may be taken by the Governments with regard to commercial, industrial, agricultural, financial or other enterprises, which measures are recommended elsewhere.

2. That blocking shall include all cash, securities, income or other assets of any other kind, including the proceeds of the sale or liquidation of assets or firms.

3. That blocked assets may not be disposed of without the authorization of the respective Government or agencies. Any transaction contrary to these provisions shall be null and void.

4. That all blocked cash or securities shall be deposited in the central bank or in approved banks, or in appropriate organizations, subject to provisions adopted by the respective Government.

5. That the Governments shall not permit disposal of blocked assets if such action benefits, directly or indirectly, the interests of the aggressor nations or the nations dominated by them, whether such disposal takes place in the country in which the transaction originates or in any other country affected by the operation; or if such action is contrary to the fundamental purpose expressed in the first paragraph of this recommendation.

6. That the Governments may authorize the disposal of blocked funds when the applicant proves that such funds are essential to his subsistence and that of his family; but such authorization shall not exceed the maximum periodical amount fixed by the respective Government.

VII. Control of Business Enterprises

The Inter-American Conference on Systems of Economic and Financial Control

Recommends:

1. That, in accordance with the constitutional procedure of each country, all necessary measures be adopted as soon as possible, in order to eliminate from the commercial, agricultural, industrial and financial life of the American Republics, all influence of governments, nations, and persons within such nations who, through natural or juridical persons or by any other means are, in the opinion of the respective Government, acting against the political and economic independence or security of such Republics, and that to this end the following measures be adopted:

(a) The business, properties and rights of any real or juridical person included within the terms of the foregoing paragraph, whatever their nationality, shall be the object of forced transfer or total liquidation; and, if this should not be desirable in the opinion of the Government of each country, they shall be the object of blocking, occupation or intervention in order to give effect to the purposes of this recommendation.

(b) The officers and employees of any real or juridical persons, whose actions may be contrary to the purposes set forth in paragraph 1 of this recommendation, shall be removed from their positions and the severance payments to which they may be entitled shall be blocked; and the salaries and other remuneration of those who temporarily continue in service shall be limited and supervised, in order to comply with the aforementioned purposes.

(c) The contracts of such real or juridical persons which may be directly or indirectly contrary to the purposes set forth in the first paragraph of this recommendation, shall be rescinded; and in applying the measures set forth in paragraph (a), the contracts entered into by them and the concessions granted to them for the exploitation of natural resources and public services, such as land, mines, water rights, transportation and other similar activities, may also be considered rescinded and without effect.

(d) The following shall be effectively blocked in accordance with the regulations pertaining to blocking: the proceeds of the sale of transferred properties and rights; the profits accruing from intervened or supervised businesses; and the funds derived from total liquidations

(e) The alienation, in any form, of the said properties and rights in accordance with paragraph (a), can only be made to nationals of the respective country or to juridical persons formed by them. In the establishment of the conditions of these acquisitions or in the selection of the buyers, the Government of the country in which the transaction takes place shall not permit any direct or indirect participation by any real or juridical person whose activities are deemed contrary to the principles set forth in the first paragraph of this recommendation.

2. Each country shall designate one or more organizations to be in charge of the administration of the aforementioned measures.

3. The American Republics shall maintain an exchange of information on the measures adopted pursuant to this recommendation.

VIII. Reciprocal Cooperation among the American Republics

The Inter-American Conference on Systems of Economic and Financial Control

Recommends:

That the Governments of the American Republics lend each other the greatest measure of cooperation in the formulation and application of systems and procedures which will facilitate placing in effect, within their jurisdictions and in the exercise of their authority, Recommendations V and VI adopted by the Third Meeting of the Ministers of Foreign Affairs of the American Republics, the consequent recommendations adopted by this Conference, and measures which have been or may be taken by the Governments of the American Republics.

That in consequence the aforesaid Governments endeavor to establish an interchange of information and consultation which will afford knowledge of the experience acquired by each one of them.

8. INTER-AMERICAN DEVELOPMENT COMMISSION AND THE NATIONAL COUNCILS

[For the establishment of the Commission and the organization of National Councils in the 10 South American Republics, see *Documents, III, 1940–41*, p. 112.]

1) *Function of Inter-American Development Commission. Department of State Release, January 17, 1942* [1]

The Inter-American Development Commission, organized by the Inter-American Financial and Economic Advisory Committee, is seeking to stimulate the importation of non-competitive goods from the other American Republics to the United States, increase trade among the other Americas, and encourage the development of industry in Central and South America and the Caribbean area, with particular regard to the production of consumer goods. Members of the Inter-American Development Commission are as follows:

Nelson A. Rockefeller, *Chairman;* J. Rafael Oreamuno, *Vice Chairman;* Renato de Azevedo; G. W. Magalhaes; Anibal Jara; John C. McClintock, 417 Department of Commerce Building, Washington, D. C., *Executive Secretary;* William F. Machold, 7203 Department of Commerce Building, Washington, D. C., *Projects Director.*

The Coordinator of Inter-American Affairs and Chairman of the Inter-American Development Commission announced on November 29, 1941, and January 7, 1942, that 10 more National Councils had been formed as follows: Costa Rica, Cuba, Dominican Republic, El Salvador, Guatemala, Haiti, Honduras, Mexico, Nicaragua and Panama.

D. Shipping and Communications

1. USE OF FOREIGN–FLAG MERCHANT VESSELS IN AMERICAN PORTS

1) *Plan Adopted by the Inter-American Financial and Economic Advisory Committee, August 28, 1941* [2]

(1) The basic principle of the plan is that the vessels now lying in American ports shall be utilized in accordance with the resolution of April 26, 1941,[3] in such a manner as to promote the defense of the economies of the American Republics as well as the peace and security of the continent.

---

[1] Department of State, *Bulletin*, V, p. 439, and VI, p. 68, where the full membership of each council is given.
[2] *Ibid.*, V, p. 165. The plan was placed into effect on adoption, with the approval of all of the American Republics.
[3] *Documents, III, 1940–41*, p. 116.

(2) To this end there should be an immediate transfer of such vessel to active service. Just and adequate compensation for such vessels shal be made.

(3) In order to attain the maximum efficiency in the operation c available shipping, there must be the closest cooperation among th maritime authorities of the ship-operating nations of the Western Hemi sphere in planning the most effective use of all available vessels. Thi cooperation must extend to the allocation of particular vessels to th several trade routes; to efficient scheduling where more than one ship ping line serves an individual port or nation; to the diversion of at leas minimum shipping facilities to those nations not reasonably adequatel served and in which there lie no or not sufficient inactive vessels t alleviate at least partially the situation; and to the exchange or inter change among the ship-operating nations of vessels of various types i order that each may operate the type of vessels which it is in a positio to handle and which are appropriate to the type of commerce to be borne.

(4) It is recognized that several of the American nations operate mer chant marines and are in a position to handle efficiently the operation c some or all of the inactive vessels lying in their ports. Other America Republics may not have the appropriate organization to operate ship or may not desire to undertake to do so. In such cases, the Governmen of the United States and United States shipping companies are preparec in the closest cooperation and coordination with services provided b other ship-operating nations of the Western Hemisphere, to operate fc their account or in any other appropriate way those vessels other Amer can Republics do not operate themselves. The Government of th United States is also prepared to make appropriate arrangements to tak over and operate any such vessels in general services.

(5) The Government of the United States has been informed that th British Government agrees to recognize the transfers of vessels resultin from this plan of operation and to waive its belligerent rights so long a the following conditions are met:

(a) The vessels transferred are operated in accordance with th plan.

(b) The vessels are operated under the flag of any American republ in inter-American trade, or by the Government of the United States i general services in accordance with paragraph (4).

(c) Such service of the vessels now inactive shall not result in th diversion of any other vessels owned or controlled by Governments c nationals of an American republic to services inimical to the interes of Great Britain.

(*d*) Any funds or proceeds from such vessels shall not be made available to the governments or nationals of the countries whose flags they flew until the present war is terminated.

(*e*) Crews of the vessels shall be nationals of the countries whose flag the vessels fly or shall be comprised of officers and personnel satisfactory to the Inter-American Financial and Economic Advisory Committee.

(6) The Government of the United States is prepared to render through the Maritime Commission every possible technical assistance and cooperation to the Governments of the other American Republics.

a) *Note of the United Kingdom Government to the Argentine, Colombian, Costa Rican, Cuban, Chilean, Ecuadoran, Mexican, Uruguayan Governments, October 30, 1941* [1]

In consideration of the benefit which will accrue directly or indirectly to the war effort of His Majesty's Government in the United Kingdom by the adoption by the Governments concerned of the plan approved by the Inter-American Financial and Economic Advisory Committee on August 28, 1941, His Majesty's Government are prepared to waive their belligerent rights to intercept and place in prize those foreign vessels which have been immobilized in American ports, provided that they are operated in accordance with this plan and are notified to His Majesty's Government as such.

2) *Inter-American Maritime Commission. Resolution of the Inter-American Financial and Economic Advisory Committee, November 14, 1941* [2]

WHEREAS:

I

There was placed in effect on August 28, 1941, a plan for the effective use in the interest of inter-American commerce of the ships to which the Resolution of the Inter-American Financial and Economic Advisory Committee of April 26, 1941,[3] refers:

II

The principles in paragraphs 1 and 3 of the Inter-American plan to which the same Resolution refers are the following:

[Omitted here; see above, p. 403–4.]

[1] *The Times* (London), October 31, 1941, p. 3.
[2] Department of State, *Bulletin*, V, p. 403.
[3] *Documents, III, 1940–41*, p. 116.

III

The Inter-American Financial and Economic Advisory Committee on August 7, 1941, adopted a report of the Special Subcommittee on Immobilized Ships, that contains the following:

"6. The Subcommittee has noted that three of the Governments — Argentine, Chile and Mexico — have raised some questions with regard to paragraph 3 of the plan, which is intended to provide for the closest cooperation in the utilization of all available vessels in the Western Hemisphere. Such cooperation will be that of sovereign nations, however, and it is intended that the Inter-American Financial and Economic Advisory Committee shall have no more than an advisory status in the matter."

Resolves:

1. To recommend the organization of a Commission that will be a dependency of the Inter-American Financial and Economic Advisory Committee, and that will consist of one representative of the aforementioned Committee, who will act as Chairman of the Commission, and also of experts representing the respective Maritime Authorities, each one to be designated by each of the Governments of the American Republics that have taken, or are in a position to take over, the immobilized ships referred to by the inter-American plan approved August 28 1941. The representative of the Inter-American Financial and Economic Advisory Committee will be chosen by the Chairman from among those Delegates to the Committee that do not represent any of the countries appointing the other members of the Commission.

2. The Commission will carry out the aims contained in paragraphs 1 and 3 of the aforementioned inter-American plan, and to this effect, will meet regularly in its place of residence, which will be in the United States of America, in order to formulate plans for the efficient use of all the merchant vessels available for service between the American Republics and to recommend to the Maritime Authorities the allocation of such vessels to particular routes or to the carrying of articles of a specific nature. The Commission will communicate its recommendations to the Maritime Authorities through the Inter-American Financial and Economic Advisory Committee.

3. In order to avoid any delay in the functioning of the Commission, it will be considered as constituted as soon as four of its members have been designated.

2. INTER-AMERICAN HIGHWAY

(1) *An Act to Provide for Cooperation with Central American Republics in the Construction of the Inter-American Highway, Approved December 26, 1941* [1]

A connecting series of national highways throughout North and South America has for many years been part of the program of the Inter-American Conferences. The Pan American Railway Committee was established in 1890 and much railroad mileage has been built in accordance with the projects evolved under its initiative. The advent of the automobile brought inter-continental roads to attention. The Second Pan American Highway Congress, Rio de Janeiro, August 1929, and the Inter-American Highway Congress, Panama, October 1929, called for a reconnaissance survey of a road from Laredo, Texas, to Panama through Mexico, Costa Rica, El Salvador, Guatemala, Honduras, Nicaragua and Panama. The United States had on May 4, 1928, and on March 4, 1929, enacted legislation favoring the proposal and authorizing an appropriation.[2]

The survey, which cost $50,000,[3] showed that the project was feasible and on June 19, 1934,[4] an appropriation of $1,000,000 to contribute to cooperative construction of what is known as the Inter-American Highway was made. Other United States legislation made small appropriations for the administrative expenses.[5] Cooperative road construction with Panama was begun with appropriations of $3,000,000 by Acts of July 20 and August 9, 1939.[6]

The road surveyed from Laredo to Panama is 3,252 miles long. In 1941 it was completed from Laredo to beyond Mexico City and Mexico was building to the Guatemalan border, about half the total length, and 310 miles were complete from Panama City to David.

An all-weather highway has already been completed across Guatemala. During the year 1941 substantial progress was made in El Salvador, where a surfaced highway was completed over a large part of the route; in Nicaragua, where the route from Sebaco to Diriamba *via* Managua was nearing completion; in Costa Rica; and in Panama, where the Rio Hato road was expected to be finished in the summer of 1942.[7]

On April 28, 1941, the President in a message to Congress [8] proposed an appropriation to cooperate with the Central American countries in completing the road. Hearings were held by the Senate Committee on Foreign Relations and

---

[1] Public Law 375, 77th Cong.; originating as S. 1544 from the Committee on Foreign Relations, May 23, 1941; Senate Report No. 354; House Report No. 750. The Senate Committee on Foreign Relations held hearings on S. 1461, the draft submitted by message of the President, April 28, 1941. The House Committee on Foreign Affairs held hearings on S. 1544.

[2] 45 Stat. 490, 1697.

[3] Act of March 26, 1930, 46 Stat. 115.

[4] 48 Stat. 1032.

[5] June 18, 1934, 48 Stat. 996; March 5 and June 25, 1938, 52 Stat. 88 and 1146; August 9, 1939, 53 Stat. 1305; April 18, 1940, Public 459, 76th Cong.; April 5, 1941, Public Law 28, 77th Cong.

[6] 53 Stat. 1071, 1305.

[7] Department of State, *Bulletin*, VI, p. 73.

[8] House Doc. 197, 77th Cong., 1st sess.

the House Committee on Foreign Affairs and the act given was approved December 26, 1941.[1]

Be it enacted by the Senate and House of Representatives of the United States of America in Congress assembled, That there is hereby authorized to be appropriated the sum not to exceed $20,000,000 to enable the United States to cooperate with the Governments of the American Republics situated in Central America — that is, with the Governments of the Republics of Costa Rica, El Salvador, Guatemala, Honduras, Nicaragua, and Panama — in the survey and construction of the proposed Inter-American Highway within the borders of the aforesaid republics. Expenditures of such sums in any such country shall be subject to the receipt of a request therefor and of satisfactory assurance from the government of that country that appropriate commitments have been made by such government to assume at least one third of the expenditures proposed to be incurred henceforth by that country and by the United States in the survey and construction of such highway within the borders of such country. In no such country shall the expenditures of this Government from the appropriations herein authorized exceed two thirds of the total expenses henceforth incurred for said survey and construction in that country. No expenditures shall be made hereunder for the construction of said highway until the government of each of the above-named countries shall have given satisfactory assurance to the United States that it will assume at least one third of the expenditures proposed to be incurred henceforth by that government and by the United States in the survey and construction of such highway within the borders of such country, or has given other assurance satisfactory to the President that it has made appropriate arrangement to complete such survey and construction within a reasonable period. All expenditures by the United States under the provisions of this Act for material, equipment, and supplies shall, whenever practicable, be made for products of the United States or of the country in which such survey or construction work is being carried on.

SEC. 2. The survey and construction work authorized by this Act shall be under the administration of the Public Roads Administration, Federal Works Agency, which shall consult with the appropriate official of the Department of State with respect to matters involving the foreign relations of this Government, and such negotiations with the govern-

---

[1] For the draft convention on the regulation of international automotive traffic as revised January 24, 1941, which would define the use of the completed road, see U. S. Congress, House of Representatives, Committee on Foreign Affairs, *Inter American Highway; Hearings . . . 77th Cong., 1st sess., on S. 1544*, p. 17.

nents of the American Republics named in section 1 as may be required o carry out the purposes of this Act shall be conducted through, or as authorized by, the Department of State.

SEC. 3. The provisions of this Act shall not create or authorize the creation of any obligations on the part of the Government of the United States with respect to any expenditures for highway construction or urvey heretofore or hereafter undertaken in any of the countries numerated in section 1, other than the expenditures authorized by the provisions of this Act.

a) Department of State Release, July 28, 1942 [1]

[Excerpt]

Arrangements have been concluded with Guatemala, El Salvador, Honduras, Nicaragua, Costa Rica, and Panama for the immediate linking by a pioneer road f the already-constructed segments of the Inter-American Highway between the Mexican-Guatemalan border and Panama City. This will permit road raffic at an early date from the end of the existing standard-gauge railway in Mexico to the Canal Zone. The necessary surveying is already under way, and onstruction work will shortly be started, at the expense of the United States Government.

. . . .

The plan to complete the Inter-American Highway as a pioneer road will not modify the plan to construct a permanent Inter-American Highway conemplated by the Act of December 26, 1941. . . . The present plan will, howver, permit through traffic at a much earlier date than originally contemplated nd will facilitate the construction of the permanent highway, on the line of hich the pioneer road is to be built.[1]

2) Exchange of Notes with Costa Rica Regarding the Inter-American Highway, January 16, 1942 [2]

a) The Costa Rican Minister of Public Works and Agriculture (Volio) to the Secretary of State (Hull)

MY DEAR MR. SECRETARY:

In accordance with the provisions of Public Law 375 of December 26, 941, which provides for the cooperation of the United States with the Central American Republics in the construction of the Inter-American Highway, I hereby, fully authorized by my Government, beg to make ormal request to participate in the cooperative plan of said construction. n this connection I wish on behalf of my Government to offer the assurnces required by the Law that, with a view to receiving the cooperation

[1] Department of State, *Bulletin*, VII, p. 661.   [2] *Ibid.*, VI, p. 73.

envisaged in the Law, it has made commitments to assume at least one third of the expenditures to be incurred henceforth by it and by the United States in the survey and construction of the Highway within the borders of Costa Rica. To this end it has already concluded arrangements with the Export-Import Bank of Washington by which it has received a credit now amounting to $2,200,000 which, under its contract with the Bank, may not be expended, without the Bank's assent, for any purpose other than the construction of the Inter-American Highway. In addition, my Government owns road building equipment valued at several hundred thousand dollars which is being made available for the construction of the Inter-American Highway and which will substantially increase the contribution of my Government to the construction of the Highway. I trust that these facts will constitute ample assurance that my Government has made the commitments envisaged in the law to assume at least one third of the expenditures which are proposed to be incurred henceforth by Costa Rica and by the United States in the completion of the survey and construction of the Inter-American Highway in Costa Rica in accordance with present proposals.

I take pleasure in enclosing herewith the proper credentials.

With my highest regard, I beg [etc.]

(b) The Secretary of State (Hull) to the Costa Rican Minister of Public Works and Agriculture (Volio)

My Dear Mr. Minister:

I wish to acknowledge receipt of your kind note of January 16, 1942 in which, duly authorized by your Government, you request the cooperation of the Government of the United States in the construction of the Inter-American Highway in Costa Rica, and in which you offer the assurances required by Public Law 375 of December 26, 1941, in connection with such cooperation.

I take pleasure in informing you that the assurances which you offer are satisfactory to this Government. It is consequently the intention of this Government to extend to the Costa Rican Government the cooperation envisaged in the Law, subject to the appropriation of the necessary funds by the Congress of the United States and to the receipt of the necessary assurances from the other Republics mentioned in the Law

You are, of course, aware that by the terms of the Law the survey and construction work it authorizes shall be under the administration of the Public Roads Administration, Federal Works Agency. It is understood that you are now making a subsidiary agreement with the Administration to carry out this provision of the Law.

I wish to thank you for your courtesy in forwarding your credentials to me.

I am [etc.]

By an exchange of notes, dated April 8, 1942, between the Governments of Nicaragua and the United States, provision was made for the completion of the Inter-American Highway in Nicaragua on the basis that Nicaragua would assume one third and the United States two thirds of the cost of construction. See p. 373.

E. Cultural Relations

[See *Documents, III, 1940–41*, p. 149–55.]

For a detailed description of the work of the Department of State in the Inter-American field, as well as generally, see *The Program of the Department of State in Cultural Relations* (A Report to the Committee on Appropriations, House of Representatives, 77th Cong., 2d sess., January 1942), Department of State Publication 1702, Inter-American Series 21.

(1) *Duties Transferred to the Division of Cultural Relations, Department of State, Departmental Order 1047, April 15, 1942* [1]

[Excerpt]

In order to provide maximum concentration of responsibility and administration in matters involving cultural cooperative relations with the other American Republics, there is hereby transferred from the Division of the American Republics to the Division of Cultural Relations responsibility for the conduct of the Department's participation in the work of the Interdepartmental Committee on Cooperation with the American Republics, which was established at the instance of the President in May 1938,[2] and under the provisions of Public No. 355, 76th Congress, entitled "An Act to authorize the President to render closer and more effective the relationship between the American Republics," approved August 9, 1939;[3] and responsibility for matters involved in the administration of Public No. 63, 76th Congress, approved May 3, 1939,[4] and entitled "An Act to amend the Act entitled 'An Act authorizing the temporary detail of United States employees, possessing special qualifications, to governments of American Republics and the Philippines, and for other purposes,' approved May 25, 1938," in so far as the administration of that Act is vested in the Department of State.

In carrying out these functions, the Division of Cultural Relations shall have responsibility for enlisting the approval of the Division of the

[1] *Ibid.*, VI, p. 357. [2] *Documents, I, 1938–39*, p. 55.
[3] *Ibid.*, p. 58. [4] *Ibid.*, p. 61.

American Republics of all cooperative projects and personnel assign ments, and for enlisting the collaboration of other interested division and offices of the Department, and it shall maintain effective liaison with other interested departments and agencies of the Government.

Committees to Advise the Department of State.[1] On July 31, 1941, the President appointed four committees to advise the Department of State, through the Division of Cultural Relations, on certain phases of the program. This action was taken pursuant to section 2 of the Act of August 9, 1939, "An Act to Authorize the President to Render Closer and More Effective the Relationship between the American Republics." These committees, which were authorized to serve until June 30, 1942, are as follows:

The General Advisory Committee, to advise on general policy in the planning and execution of the program and to serve as a coordinating body for the other advisory committees; the Advisory Committee on Inter-American Cooperation in Agricultural Education, to advise particularly in connection with the Department's work with land-grant colleges of the United States in inter-America studies and exchange students, and in the proposed Institute of Tropical Agriculture; the Advisory Committee on the Adjustment of Foreign Students in the United States to advise on plans for more effective guidance and hospitality the Advisory Committee on Exchange Fellowships and Professorships, to advise on general matters and specifically on selection of graduate students and professors.

The committee membership is made up of persons from different sections of the country and of persons active in the work of the Office of the Coordinator of Inter-American Affairs.

F. Special Relations with Individual Countries

1. BOLIVIA — EXPROPRIATION OF PETROLEUM PROPERTIES

The Government of Bolivia and the Standard Oil Company of New Jersey on July 27, 1922, executed a contract which confirmed the company's prior acquisition of concessions and defined the terms for exploration and exploitation of oil properties. On March 13, 1937, the Government of Bolivia by executive decree canceled the concession-contract, which would normally run until 1979, and at the same time seized all of the properties, assets and papers of the Standard Oil Company of Bolivia, the subsidiary which operated the concession. The physical property consisted of 28 wells, two small refineries and the accessory constructions required for efficient operation in a remote area. The company claimed that some $17,000,000 had been invested in Bolivia. The Government of Bolivia alleged that some crude oil had been clandestinely exported in 1925 and that surface taxes had not been fully paid. The company's suits for recovery of the properties from the Government of Bolivia and Yacimientos Petroliferos Fiscales Bolivianos were declared "contrary to law and inadmissible" by a sentence of the Supreme Court of Justice of Bolivia on March 8, 1939.[2]

[1] Summary of statement in Department of State, *Bulletin*, V, p. 154–5.

[2] For the company's statements see Standard Oil Company of Bolivia, *Confiscation A History of the Oil Industry in Bolivia* (New York, 1939); Standard Oil Company (New Jersey), *Bolivia Takes What It Wants* (New York, 1941).

The agreement of January 27, 1942, which was negotiated with the full cog-
izance of the United States Government, was signed by Ante Matienzo, Bo-
vian Minister of Foreign Relations, and H. A. Metzger, president of Standard
)il Company of Bolivia and representative of the Standard Oil Company of New
ersey. The payment was effected as stipulated.

1) Agreement between the Government of Bolivia and the Standard Oil Company of New Jersey, January 27, 1942 [1]

The Government of Bolivia will pay to the Standard Oil Company
New Jersey) the sum of $1,500,000, United States Currency, at the
tate Department in Washington, for the sale of all of its rights, interests
nd properties in Bolivia and those of its subsidiary, Standard Oil Com-
any of Bolivia, as they existed immediately prior to March 13, 1937, and
ikewise for the sale of its existing maps and geological studies which are
he result of its explorations in Bolivia. This payment will be made
vith interest at the rate of three percent per annum, from March 13,
937, within ninety days from the date of the Supreme Resolution of the
Republic of Bolivia putting this Agreement into effect.

The Government of Bolivia, the Standard Oil Company (New Jersey),
nd the Standard Oil Company of Bolivia declare that upon the pay-
nent of the amounts referred to immediately above, no issue will remain
ending between them and that there will be no occasion for any claims
r counter-claims of whatsoever character, since the fulfillment of the
resent agreement, which has been freely entered into, shall be regarded
s having terminated satisfactorily and amicably all the differences
etween the Bolivian Government and the companies.

Signed in duplicate in Spanish and English at Rio de Janeiro, Brazil, on
anuary 27, 1942.

———

On April 22 the Department of State announced [2] that the Bolivian Govern-
ent had paid the Standard Oil Company (New Jersey) the sum of $1,729,375.
his amount represented the principal of $1,500,000 with interest at the rate of
iree percent per annum from March 13, 1937, and was in payment for all the
ghts, interest, and properties in Bolivia of the Standard Oil Company (New
ersey) and of its subsidiary, the Standard Oil Company of Bolivia, as they
xisted immediately prior to March 13, 1937, and for the sale of the existing maps
nd geological studies which are the result of their explorations in Bolivia.

[1] Department of State, *Bulletin*, VI, p. 172.
[2] *Ibid.*, p. 372.

2. CUBA — EXPORT OF ARMS FROM THE UNITED STATES

(1) *Proclamation Revoking Certain Restrictions on Exportation of Arms to Cuba, September 22, 1941* [1]

The United States Congress empowered the President to prohibit the export of arms or munitions at three different times before the enactment of the Neutrality Resolution of 1935. The earlier enactments were joint resolutions approved April 22, 1898 (30 Stat. 739), March 14, 1912 (37 Stat. 630), and superseding the earlier resolutions, January 31, 1922 (42 Stat. 361, U. S. Code, title 22, sec. 236). Under the last-named law a proclamation was issued January 29, 1934, by reason of the disturbed conditions in Cuba and was continued in force after the Munitions Control Board was established in November 1935. The control exercised by that board and under the "Export Control Act" (sec. 6 of the Act approved July 2, 1940, *Documents, III, 1940–41*, p. 474) superseded the control under the revoked proclamation.

BY THE PRESIDENT OF THE UNITED STATES

A Proclamation [No. 2511]

WHEREAS, by a proclamation of the President issued on June 29, 1934, under a joint resolution of Congress approved by the President on January 31, 1922, it was declared that there existed in Cuba conditions of domestic violence which were or which might be promoted by the use of arms or munitions of war procured from the United States; and

WHEREAS, by virtue of the joint resolution and proclamation above-mentioned it became unlawful to export arms or munitions of war to Cuba except under such limitations and exceptions as should be prescribed:

Now, THEREFORE, I, FRANKLIN D. ROOSEVELT, President of the United States of America, do hereby declare and proclaim that, as the conditions in Cuba which prompted the issuance of the proclamation of June 29, 1934, have ceased to exist, the said proclamation is hereby revoked.

IN WITNESS WHEREOF, I have hereunto set my hand and caused the seal of the United States of America to be affixed.

DONE at the city of Washington this 22nd day of September, in the year of our Lord nineteen hundred and forty-one, and of the [SEAL] Independence of the United States of America the one hundred and sixty-sixth.

FRANKLIN D. ROOSEVELT

By the President:
    CORDELL HULL
        Secretary of State

[1] 6 *Fed. Reg.*, p. 4855.

3. HAITI — FINANCIAL ARRANGEMENTS

(1) *Agreement between the United States and Haiti to Replace the Agreement of August 7, 1933, Signed September 13, 1941* [1]

The framework of the agreement derived from the negotiations conducted in April 1941, by President Elie Lescot of Haiti, then President-elect, and the Under Secretary of State of the United States, Sumner Welles. The text of the agreement was developed in the course of conversations conducted in the Department of State during the following July with the Minister of Haiti to the United States, M. Fernand Dennis, and the Haitian Minister of Finance, M. Abel Lacroix. By an exchange of notes at the time of the signing of the agreement, the American members of the Board of Directors of the National Bank were designated. The agreement replaced the Agreement of August 7, 1933.[2] It became effective October 1, 1941. A supplementary financial agreement was signed September 30, 1941, dealing with certain matters involved in the transition from the old to the new arrangement.[3]

WHEREAS the Government of the United States of America and the Government of the Republic of Haiti are both desirous of maintaining the friendly relations existing between the two countries and to that end of concluding an agreement establishing those relations upon a firm basis of mutual understanding and cooperation, the undersigned Plenipotentiaries, duly authorized by their respective Governments, have agreed upon the following Articles:

ARTICLE I. On the date on which the present agreement enters into effect, the offices of Fiscal Representative and Deputy Fiscal Representative, as provided for in Article VII of the Accord of August 7, 1933, shall be abolished.

All property and funds belonging to or in the custody of the Fiscal Representative or Deputy Fiscal Representative shall on that day be transferred to the National Bank of the Republic of Haiti as depository for the Government of the Republic of Haiti.

No claims shall be advanced by either Government against the other Government on account of any act of the Fiscal Representative, the Deputy Fiscal Representative or any of their employees.

ARTICLE II. The National Bank of the Republic of Haiti shall have fiscal functions as defined in this agreement, as well as the usual commercial operations of a national bank, and shall be the sole depository of all revenues and public funds of whatsoever nature of the Government of Haiti. These funds shall consist of revenues, customs, duties, excises, fees, fines, imposts, charges, levies or any other kind of income,

---

[1] Department of State, *Bulletin*, V, p. 214. Executive Agreement Series 220.

[2] Executive Agreement Series 46, modified by Executive Agreement Series 117, 128, 150, 183 and 201.

[3] Executive Agreement Series 224.

receipts or funds which belong to and are under the control of the national Government of the Republic of Haiti. It is understood that these
revenues and public funds will include funds under the control of the
Government of Haiti, which, under existing laws, and those which may
be made in future, are collected or expended on behalf of the Haitian
communes; a separate account of revenues and expenditures shall be
kept for each commune by the National Bank of the Republic of Haiti

The assets of the National Bank of the Republic of Haiti shall not be
alienated nor shall its investments be disposed of except with the ap
proval of the Board of Directors.

The Bank shall have all administrative powers necessary to carry
out its functions under this agreement.

ARTICLE III. The National Bank of the Republic of Haiti shall be
reorganized with a Board of Directors consisting of an Honarary Presi
dent and six voting members. The Haitian Minister of Finance or, in
his absence, the Acting Minister of Finance, shall be ex officio the Hon
orary President. Three of the voting members are always to be citizen
of the Republic of Haiti. The other three voting members are always
to be citizens of the United States of America. Decisions of the Board
of Directors shall require a majority vote of the voting members of the
Board. The President of the Republic of Haiti shall appoint the Haitian
members of the Board of Directors; the citizens of the United States of
America who are members of the Board shall be chosen by mutual agree
ment of the two Governments. All of the voting members of the Board
shall hold office for a period of five years and shall not be removed except
for cause. Vacancies on the Board of Directors shall be filled in the same
manner as the original appointments.

There shall be two Co-Presidents of the Board of Directors of the
Bank. One of these, the Haitian Minister of Finance, shall act as
Honorary President, as indicated above, and shall preside over the
meetings of the Board of Directors, and may be one of the three Haitian
voting members. The other Co-President shall be one of the three
citizens of the United States of America. It shall be his duty to represent
the holders of the bonds of 1922 and 1923 and to coordinate and direct
the functions and activities of the two Vice Presidents, who shall be
elected by the Board of Directors of the Bank, and who may be member
of the Board. One of the Vice Presidents shall be charged with super
vising and carrying out the commercial operations of the Bank, and the
other shall be charged with supervising and carrying out the fiscal
functions of the Bank, under the immediate direction of the President
who shall be responsible for such work.

Any voting member of the Board of Directors of the Bank who is unable to attend a meeting of the Board may give a proxy to any other member of the Board of Directors.

The Board of Directors shall exercise with respect to the fiscal functions of the Bank the powers hereinafter set forth. The fiscal functions of the Bank shall be undertaken by a Fiscal Department to be operated in accordance with the regulations issued by the Board of Directors pursuant to such powers.

The Board of Directors shall continue to exercise with respect to all other functions of the Bank the powers set forth in the charter and by-laws of the Bank.

ARTICLE IV. The Board of Directors of the National Bank of the Republic of Haiti shall be charged with the responsibility for:

(a) the formulation of the Haitian budget in the manner described in Article V of this agreement, and in accordance with the existing budgetary laws of the Republic of Haiti, which are to remain in effect except so far as they are modified to conform with this agreement;

(b) the accounting for and disbursing of the funds of the Government of Haiti;

(c) the collection of all customs revenues;

(d) the supervision and inspection of the collection of all revenues as defined in Article II, other than customs revenues;

(e) establishing the regulations and the administration, under such legislation as may be necessary, for the handling of the revenues of the various communes. These regulations or laws shall authorize the collection of communal revenues by the regular internal revenue collectors; disbursements on behalf of the communes shall be made by the National Bank of the Republic of Haiti; the budgets of revenues and expenditures of the communes shall be prepared and approved by the Government of the Republic of Haiti in agreement with the National Bank of the Republic of Haiti; the municipal services performed by, or in behalf of the communes, shall be paid, so far as it is possible, from the communal revenues.

ARTICLE V. Each year, as soon after January 1 as may be practicable but not later than March 1, the Haitian budget of income and expenditures shall be presented to the Legislature of the Republic by the Government of the Republic. Such budget shall be prepared cooperatively by the Government of the Republic and by the National Bank of the Republic of Haiti as follows:

(a) the Board of Directors of the National Bank shall estimate the expected revenues; shall estimate the global expenditures which can be

anticipated to be made within the revenues available; shall suggest limi
within which the various ministries, including the Garde d'Haiti, sha
operate, and shall fix by agreement with the Government of Haiti th
expenditures which are necessary for the operation of the Bank in i
fiscal functions; and

(b) the Government of the Republic shall estimate in detail the e
penditures envisaged for each of the various ministries, including th
Garde d'Haiti, within the limits suggested by the Board of Directors (
the National Bank.

ARTICLE VI. The National Bank of the Republic of Haiti, as the so
depository of all revenues as defined in Article II, shall have the pow
and duty of receiving in the first instance all the receipts of the Gover
ment and all payments made in favor thereof, and to set aside in prefe
ence to any other expenses the sums necessary for the service of the 192
and 1923 bonds, and, as the duly constituted agent of the Governmen
to make all the payments required by the loan contracts.

During the first ten days of each calendar month the representative (
the holders of the bonds of 1922 and 1923 who shall be, in accordanc
with Article III, a member of the Board of Directors of the Nation
Bank of the Republic of Haiti, shall receive from the said Bank the sun
necessary to cover monthly payments as follows:

(1) The payment of $\frac{1}{12}$ of the annual interest charges of all the ou
standing bonds of the external debt of 1922 and 1923;

(2) The payment of $\frac{1}{12}$ of the annual amounts designated for th
amortization of said bonds, including the interest of all the bonds whic
are or may be retained in the sinking fund.

The annual interest charges and the amounts of amortization sha
be computed and effected in accordance with the loan contracts date
October 6, 1922, and May 26, 1925, with the National City Compan
and the National City Bank of New York, authorized by the Haitia
Law of June 26, 1922, as modified by the Accord signed at Port-au-Prin
by the representatives of the Governments of the United States of Ame
ica and the Republic of Haiti on August 7, 1933, and as further modifi
by the agreements signed on January 13, 1938, July 1, 1938, July 8, 193
September 27, 1940, and February 13, 1941.

No disbursement of funds of the Government of Haiti shall be ma
by the National Bank of the Republic of Haiti until an allotment h
been made to satisfy the above provisions and, in addition, to make th
payment of $\frac{1}{12}$ of the annual amount agreed upon between the Gover
ment of Haiti and the National Bank of the Republic of Haiti as con
pensation for the services of the said Bank, or in the absence of any suc

greement, $\frac{1}{12}$ of the annual amount last agreed upon. After setting aside hose funds which are considered necessary by the Board of Directors of he National Bank of the Republic of Haiti to establish appropriate reerves during a given fiscal year in anticipation of seasonal variations in evenues and expenditures, to make the payments envisaged in Articles I and VIII hereof, and for other similar purposes, any surplus funds ill be held at the disposal of the Government of Haiti for necessary ublic expenditures in accordance with the approved budget.

ARTICLE VII. The Government of the Republic of Haiti declares that he interest and amortization service of the bonds of the external debt of 922 and 1923 constitute an irrevocable first lien upon àll its revenues as efined in Article II. It is understood that the communal revenues pecified in Article II shall not be included in the provision of this lause.

Until the complete amortization of the whole amount of the bonds of he external debt of 1922 and 1923 of the Government of Haiti, the public ebt of the Republic of Haiti shall not be increased except by previous greement between the Governments of the United States of America nd the Republic of Haiti.

ARTICLE VIII. In case the total collections of all the revenues as dened in Article II, exclusive of communal revenues, should in any fiscal ear exceed the equivalent of $7,000,000 in currency of the United States f America, there shall be applied to the sinking fund for the redemption f bonds of the external debt of 1922 and 1923, 10 per cent of the excess oove $7,000,000 but less than $8,000,000 and in addition 5 per cent of ll sums exceeding $8,000,000.

ARTICLE IX. The system of deposit and disbursing of all revenues, as efined in Article II, of the Government of Haiti shall be carried out in ccordance with Haitian laws relating to accounting methods and finanal regulations now governing such matters which shall not be modified uring the life of this agreement without the previous consent of both overnments.

The Government of Haiti agrees to enact and to maintain in effect he legislation and executive and administrative regulations necessary to ut this and other articles of the present agreement into effect.

ARTICLE X. Any controversy which may arise between the Governent of the United States of America and the Government of Haiti in lation to the interpretation or execution of the provisions of the present greement shall, if possible, be settled through diplomatic channels. pon notification by either the Government of the United States of merica or the Government of Haiti that, in its opinion, possibilities of settlement by this means have been exhausted, such controversies shal be settled in accordance with the procedure stipulated in the Inter-American Arbitration Convention signed at Washington January 5 1929, notwithstanding the provisions of Article 2 (*a*) thereof.

ARTICLE XI. The Accord signed by representatives of the Governments of the United States of America and the Republic of Haiti on August 7, 1933, shall cease to have effect when the present agreement shall enter into force, provided, however, that the Accord of August 7 1933, shall continue in full force and effect until the two Governments agree that there have been adopted and put into operation the measures necessary for the execution of the present agreement.

The present agreement shall continue in full force and effect during the existence of the outstanding external bonds of 1922 and 1923. After the redemption of the said bonds, the provisions of this agreement shal automatically cease to have effect.

IN WITNESS WHEREOF the respective Plenipotentiaries have signed at Port-au-Prince the present agreement in duplicate in the English and French languages, both texts being equally authoritative, and have hereunto affixed their seals.

DONE in the City of Port-au-Prince the 13th day of September nineteen hundred and forty-one.

[For the Government of the United States of America:

[SEAL]   J. C. WHITE
    Envoy Extraordinary and Minister Plenipotentiary of the
    United States of America to the Republic of Haiti

For the Government of the Republic of Haiti

[SEAL]   FOMBRUN
    Minister of Foreign Relations of the Republic of Haiti.] [1]

4. MEXICO — EXPROPRIATION OF PETROLEUM PROPERTIES

The decree of the President of Mexico of May 18, 1938, expropriating the properties of foreign oil companies in Mexico led to a serious diplomatic controversy between the United States and Mexico and put to a severe test the patience and understanding of the United States Government which has characterized the "Good Neighbor" policy. For the prior history of this controversy see *Documents, I, 1938–39*, p. 121–26; and *II, 1939–40*, p. 216–38. The inauguration of President Manuel Avila Camacho on December 1, 1940, resulted in the adoption of a more conciliatory attitude on the part of the Mexican Government which made possible the negotiation of a final settlement on November 19, 1941.

---

[1] Translation from French. In original form, the English and French texts appear in parallel columns with the signature and seal of the Haitian Minister of Foreign Affairs at the end of the French text.

1) *Statement by the Secretary of State (Hull), November 19, 1941* [1]

The agreement covering the petroleum expropriations deserves special mention. The petroleum properties were expropriated three and one half years ago. Since that time negotiations have been repeatedly undertaken by the Mexican Government and the affected United States interests. Unfortunately, the negotiations involving the largest United States interests were fruitless. Although this Government was not a direct participant in these negotiations it did what it could to facilitate solution of the problem through both formal and informal representations to the Mexican Government.

In view of the total absence of any negotiations between the American interests and the Mexican Government during the present calendar year, and because of the importance of advancing the petroleum dispute to a prompt settlement, this Government undertook to canvass the problem with the Mexican Government in the hope that a fair and equitable arrangement might be reached.

This Government believes that the arrangement signed today embodies a practical, efficient, and equitable procedure for promoting a solution of this question. Its central feature is provision for the determination of the value of the expropriated properties, rights, and interests. This information obviously is essential in connection with any settlement. The American interests involved will retain full liberty of action in determining the course they will pursue before, during, and after the valuation proceedings.

2) *Exchange of Notes Effected at Washington, November 19, 1941* [2]

a) *The Secretary of State (Hull) to the Mexican Ambassador (Castillo Nájera)*

EXCELLENCY:

I have the honor to acknowledge the receipt of Your Excellency's note of today's date, reading as follows:

"I have the honor to refer to recent conversations I have had with Your Excellency with reference to compensating the nationals of the United States of America whose properties, rights or interests in the

[1] Department of State, *Bulletin*, V, p. 399.
[2] *Ibid.*, p. 401. Only the confirming note, which embodies the proposing note, is printed here. The texts of the two notes are printed as Executive Agreement Series 234.

petroleum industry in the United Mexican States were affected by act of expropriation or otherwise by the Government of Mexico subsequent to March 17, 1938.

"It is my understanding that the following has been agreed upon:

"1. Each of the Governments will appoint, within the thirty day following the date of this note, an expert whose duty it shall be to determine the just compensation to be paid the nationals of the United State of America whose properties, rights or interests in the petroleum in dustry in the United Mexican States were affected to their detriment by acts of the Government of Mexico subsequent to March 17, 1938. Nevertheless, the provisions of this note do not apply to properties, right or interests which may have been included in any arrangement with respect to their purchase, transfer or indemnification concluded between their owners or possessors and the Government of the United Mexican States and, in consequence, the experts will exclude from their evaluation proceedings and reports said rights, interests and properties.

"2. The designated experts will hold their first meeting in Mexico City within 15 days following the appointment last made by either Government. The later meetings and other activities of the experts will take place on the dates and at the places which the experts themselves determine within the periods contemplated by this agreement and they shall be held on Mexican territory.

"3. Each Government shall designate such assistants as the respective experts may require to facilitate their labors.

"4. The expenses of salaries, maintenance, transportation and other incidental expenditures of the experts and their assistants, will be met by the Government naming them. The joint expenses incurred during the proceedings of the experts shall be shared equally by the two Governments.

"5. The experts shall at all times closely collaborate and cooperate in their evaluation proceedings. They may obtain directly such data and evidence as they may consider pertinent to forming their opinion, or receive them from the interested persons and institutions and from the Governments of Mexico and of the United States of America.

"6. The experts shall have free access to all records in the possession of the Mexican Government, as well as to the oil fields, lands, installations, offices, buildings and any other properties whatsoever involved directly or indirectly in the evaluation. The United States expert, on the request of the Mexican expert, will ask the interested persons and institutions for pertinent evidence; when such request relates to evidence already submitted by such persons or institutions their refusal to comply

ith the request will bring into operation the applicable provision of
aragraph 9.

"7. As soon as one expert obtains or learns of any pertinent data,
port, or evidence, he will inform the other. Either expert may request
om the other the furnishing of any data, report or evidence which for
ly reason are available only to the other.

"8. Within a period of two months, from the date of their first meet-
g, the experts shall obtain and receive all data, reports, and evidence;
xcept that a further period of one month shall be allowed for the pres-
ntation by either expert of additional data, reports and evidence com-
ementing, clarifying or rectifying the material obtained or received in
le said period of two months.

"9. The experts are required to examine and appraise all the proofs
tained directly or that may be submitted to them. They shall not
ke into account any specific evidence submitted *ex parte* when the
rson or institution submitting it refuses in connection with it to furnish
rtinent complementary evidence requested by the United States ex-
rt, in accordance with the provisions of paragraph 6. The experts shall
ot take into account reasons of a technical nature in formulating their
cisions — be these joint or those submitted in disagreement — but will
x adequate indemnities on the basis of common rules of justice and
uity and will be guided by the value of the properties, rights or in-
rests at the time they were affected by acts of the Government of
exico provided that these properties, rights or interests had been
quired by nationals of the United States of America prior to March
3, 1938.

"10. The experts shall complete their work within five months from
le date of this note. If they are in accord regarding the amount of the
mpensation due to the affected United States nationals, they shall
bmit a joint report to the two Governments fixing exactly the indem-
ties upon which they agree. The experts shall formulate recommenda-
ons as to the manner and conditions of payment of the compensation.

"11. The experts shall fix equitable interest upon the indemnity com-
nsation they find due; this interest will apply from the date fixed by
lese experts up to the time of payment.

"12. Both Governments agree to consider unappealable the joint
port resulting from the agreement of the experts, and, in consequence,
definitive, the compensation and interest fixed in such report.

"13. If, within the period indicated in paragraph 10, the experts are
lable to reach agreement regarding the amount of just compensation,
ch one, within an additional period of one month, shall submit to his

own Government a separate report specifying the compensations whic'
he considers due.

"14. In the event that the two experts fail to agree, and upon th
expiration of the period specified in paragraph 13, the two Government
shall, within a period of one month, initiate diplomatic negotiation
with a view to establishing the amount of the compensations to be paic

"15. If, within a period of five months from the date of initiation c
diplomatic negotiations, as provided in paragraph 14, the two Govern
ments do not agree upon the amount of compensation to be paid, th
present agreement shall be without effect, and there shall be returned t
the United Mexican States, at the request of the Government thereo'
the amount deposited in accordance with the pertinent stipulation c
the following paragraph.

"16. The two Governments shall agree upon the manner and cond
tions of payment of the compensation found to be due to the affecte
United States nationals under either of the two aforementioned pro
cedures. Such payment shall, however, be completed within a period c
not more than seven years.

"The Government of Mexico will deliver today, as a deposit, to th
Government of the United States of America, the sum of $9,000,0C
(NINE MILLION DOLLARS), United States currency, which sum shall k
applied immediately on account of the compensation determined to k
due.

"17. The Government of the United States will facilitate negotiatior
between the Government of Mexico and representatives of such o
companies as may be interested in an agreement for the marketing c
exports of Mexican petroleum products.

"18. Nothing contained in this note shall be regarded as a preceder
or be invoked by either of the two Governments in the settlement, b
tween them, of any future difficulty, conflict, controversy or arbitratior
The action herein provided for is considered as singular and exceptiona
appropriate solely to this case, and motivated by the character of tl
problem itself."

In reply, I have the honor to confirm the understanding we ha
reached as set forth in Your Excellency's note under reference.

Accept [etc.]

3) *Agreement of Experts on Compensation for Petroleum Properties Expropriated by Mexico, April 17, 1942* [1]

FRANKLIN DELANO ROOSEVELT

President of the United States of America

MANUEL AVILA CAMACHO

President of the United Mexican States

SIRS:

As provided in the exchange of notes dated November 19, 1941,[2] between His Excellency Cordell Hull, Secretary of State of the United States, and His Excellency Francisco Castillo Nájera, Mexican Ambassador to the United States, the undersigned were appointed by our respective Governments as experts authorized to determine according to "equity and justice" for purposes of indemnification the compensation to be paid the nationals of the United States of America whose properties, rights or interests in the petroleum industry were affected to their detriment by acts of the Government of Mexico subsequent to March 17, 1938, and in respect of which no settlement has heretofore been effected.

Expropriation, and the exercise of the right of eminent domain, under the respective constitutions and laws of Mexico and the United States, are a recognized feature of the sovereignty of all modern States.

We have surveyed the works and lands involved and studied the records of the properties, rights and interests appertaining thereto and have mutually agreed that their value, as of March 18, 1938, should be fixed, in the sum of $23,995,991, covering all elements of tangible and intangible value, allocated as follows:

Standard Oil of New Jersey group, $18,391,641:
1. Huasteca Petroleum Company;
2. Mexican Petroleum Company;
3. Tuxpam Petroleum Company;
4. Pamiahua Petroleum Company;
5. Compañia Petrolera Ulises S. A.;
6. Compañia Transcontinental de Petroleo S. A.;
7. Compañia Petrolera Minerva S. A.
Standard Oil of California group, $3,589,158:
1. California Standard Oil Company of Mexico S. A.;
2. Richmond Petroleum Company.

[1] Department of State, *Bulletin*, VI, p. 351.
[2] See p. 357.

Consolidated Oil Company, $630,151:
1. Consolidated Oil Company of Mexico S. A.;
2. Compañia Franco Española S. A.;
3. Compania Petrolera Aldamas y Brava S. A.

Sabalo group, $897,671:
1. Sabalo Transportation Company;
2. Compañia Petrolera "Claripa" S. A.;
3. Compañia Petrolera Cacalilao S. A.

Seaboard group, $487,370:
1. International Petroleum Company;
2. Compañia International de Petroleo y Oleo Ductos S. A.

Therefore, according to the said Oil Agreement of November 19, 194
it is our joint judgment that:

1. The Government of the United Mexican States shall pay to th
Government of the United States of America, on behalf of the above
mentioned claimants, the amount of $23,995,991, in accordance wit
schedule of payments finally approved by the two Governments.

2. Before any payment is made on account of these awards the cor
porations affected shall deposit in escrow and, when final payment ha
been made, shall deliver to the Government of Mexico all documents an
instruments of title pertaining to the expropriated properties.

3. The Government of Mexico and each of the said claimants sha
release each other respectively of all reciprocal claims that may still b
pending against one another, with the exception of those of the Mexica
Government against the companies for unpaid taxes and duties, as we
as those based on payments legally made by the Mexican Governmer
for the account of the said companies.

The Mexican Government will assume liability for all private clain
which may be instituted after this date by private individuals again
these companies as a result of expropriation, but not for the priva
claims against these companies now pending before the Mexican court

4. Recommendation is hereby made that the amount determined l
paid as follows: One-third on July 1, 1942, and the balance in five (
equal annual installments, payable on July 1 of each subsequent year

5. All balances as shown to be due these said claimants on the sever
dates prescribed shall bear interest at the rate of 3% per year datir
from March 18, 1938.

DONE in duplicate, in both Spanish and English, on this date Ap
17, 1942.

MORRIS L. COOKE
Representing the United States of America
MANUEL J. ZEVADA
Representing the Republic of Mexico

4) *The President of Mexico (Avila Camacho) to the President of the United States (Roosevelt), April 18, 1942* [1]

[Translation]

XCELLENCY:

In accord with the bases established between our respective Govern-ents, engineers Manuel J. Zevada and M. L. Cooke, State experts to etermine the compensation of Mexico to nationals of the United States fected by the measures of expropriations made by my country as of arch 18, 1938, have been able to achieve the formulation of a joint greement which carries with it a definite settlement of the so-called petroleum question."

On this pleasing occasion, I wish to express to Your Excellency that is a positive satisfaction for my Government and for the people of exico and for me personally that through a loyal endeavor of reciprocal d effective comprehension, it has been possible to arrive at the solu-n of a problem, which is not sufficient ever to separate our two nations r could be considered at any certain moment as a motive of doubt or controversy.

I have the certainty that so significant an act must be considered, be-use of the spirit of conciliation which it shows, as a confirmation of e attitude of my Government in its desire to grant ample guarantees the participation of private capital, national or foreign, in the exploita-n and development of the material resources of this Republic.

Such a policy, clearly defined and properly supported, has already en made felt with useful results in various fields of activity, among iich may be cited as an example that of the mineral industry, which is lled upon to reach given necessities of the actual epoch, development thout precedent.

Having been happily settled, this question of the compensation which exico is disposed to pay, within the general terms fixed in the Conven-n of November 19, 1941, the path remains open, so that in close col-oration we may go forward, redoubling our effort in the struggle for e common cause which we have embraced, the triumph of democracy d the defense of continental solidarity.

I reiterate to Your Excellency, with the greatest cordiality, the assur-ces of my highest consideration.

[1] Department of State, *Bulletin*, VI, p. 352.

(5) *The President of the United States (Roosevelt) to the President c Mexico (Avila Camacho), April 18, 1942* [1]

EXCELLENCY:

I wish to acknowledge the gracious message of Your Excellency wit regard to the agreement reached by the experts representing our tw Governments with respect to the amount of compensation to be pai to the citizens of the United States in compensation for certain o properties expropriated by Mexico subsequent to March 17, 1938.

From the moment that our two Governments agreed upon a procedur for settling the so-called "petroleum question" I have had every cor fidence that a settlement would be reached and I was happy therefor to learn that this confidence has been justified by the agreement arrive at as the outcome of the joint deliberations of our two experts. Mexic and the United States once again have given a demonstration to th world that the most difficult international problems can be satisfactoril solved when approached with good-will and in a spirit of fair play.

I welcome this opportunity to express to you and to the people c Mexico the very deep appreciation of my country for the active an constructive collaboration and assistance of Mexico in the cause freedom and democracy. Our two nations are joined together in unit of purpose, determination, and effective cooperation, and the triump of our cause is certain.

I extend to Your Excellency my deep appreciation for your friendl communication and I send my warm personal greetings and the assu ance of my highest regard.

5. PANAMA — NON-INTERVENTION IN INTERNAL AFFAIRS

Arnulfo Arias, a medical doctor, became president of Panama October 1, 194 after an election in which strong-arm methods were allegedly employed to elim nate other contestants. A new constitution extending the presidential term office from four to six years and giving additional powers to the President we into effect January 2, 1941. Policies cultivating nationalist emotions and chara teristic of totalitarian regimes irritated citizens and bred opposition to the Pre dent. On October 7, 1941, he left the country under an assumed name. Repor circulated in the press that he had been forced to leave as the result of the inte vention of the Government of the United States. By accepting Resolution XXV of the Buenos Aires Conference of 1936, the United States had agreed to t principle that "intervention by one state in the internal or external affairs another state is condemned." [2]

[1] *Ibid.*, p. 353.
[2] *Report of the Delegation of the United States of America to the Inter-Americ Conference for the Maintenance of Peace, Buenos Aires, Argentina, December 1–2 1936.* Department of State Publication 1088, Conference Series 33, p. 227–8.

1) *Statement by the Secretary of State (Hull), October 16, 1941* [1]

My attention has been called to an article which appeared in one of the local newspapers this morning [2] regarding recent events in the Republic of Panama. I am profoundly shocked by the glaring inaccuracies and wilful misrepresentations set forth in that article. Without any attempt to verify the facts or even to consult with the competent officials of this Government, the writer of this article presumes to place in question the good faith of the United States Government. It is deplorable that untrue statements of this character should appear in print, particularly when they are of a character to undermine our national reputation and give aid and comfort to forces inimical to the United States. The matters touched upon in this case are so important and affect so vitally the faith and integrity of the United States, that I do not feel that I can properly let them pass unnoticed.

I refer, of course, to the attempt which is being made to make political capital out of the recent events in Panama. Lest any individual be misled by such unfair tactics, I state clearly and categorically for the record that the United States Government has had no connection, direct or indirect, with the recent governmental changes in the Republic of Panama. This statement is borne out by the official telegraphic reports from our Embassy at Panamá during recent days, a summary of which I shall lay before you freely and frankly.

On October 7 a brief message was received from Ambassador Wilson indicating that he had received information from reliable sources for the first time indicating disaffection among Panamanian officials and the possibility of a movement against the Government. On the same day later information was received to the effect that a passenger by the name of A. Madrid taking the Pan American plane for Havana that morning was in fact President Arnulfo Arias. The Ambassador commented that this information did not necessarily bear any relation to the rumor reported earlier in the day, and that the President may merely have wished to make a brief visit to Cuba for personal reasons.

The same evening the Department informed our Embassy at Havana of President Arias' trip, stating that it might be merely a brief vacation trip, although there had been some reports of political unrest in Panama.

On October 9 Ambassador Wilson reported that he had received a call at 8:30 a.m. that day from high officials of the Panamanian Government,

[1] Department of State, *Bulletin*, V, p. 293.
[2] Under the heading "Probes Sought of U. S. Part in *Coup* That Ousted Arias."

who informed him that because of the Government of Panama's bein
without a head and because of popular demand for a change, the leader
of the Government had decided to take over the power in order t
maintain public order. They inquired as to how this movement woul
be regarded in the United States. The Ambassador called the attentio
of these officials to the well-known policy of the United States to refrai
from interfering in the internal affairs of other countries, emphasizin
that our desire was to cooperate loyally with all the American Republic
on a basis of complete equality and respect for each other's rights. Th
Ambassador went so far as to state that he would not depart an inch fror
this basic policy, irrespective of what apparent inducements of gain c
advantage might be offered the United States.

Further developments in the appointment of new officials wer
reported by the Ambassador later that day, October 9.

That same night Ambassador Wilson referred to the pertinent const
tutional provisions, specifically Article III of the Panamanian Const
tution of January 2, 1941. He reported the position taken by th
Panamanian officials to the effect that the President, having left th
country without permission of the National Assembly and withou
permission of the Supreme Court during the present recess of th
National Assembly, had effectively separated himself from the exerci:
of his functions; and that, accordingly, under Article 114 of the Const
tution, the power fell to the Second Designate, Mr. Jaén Guardia.

Mr. Jaén Guardia, having been sworn in as President and havin
appointed his Cabinet, resigned his post, and the Cabinet thereupc
elected one of its members, Ricardo Adolfo de la Guardia, to exerci:
the presidency, in accordance with the procedure established in Artic
116 of the Constitution.

Inasmuch as the procedure followed appeared at all stages to be i
conformity with Panamanian constitutional requirements, our Embass
and the Department felt that the only proper position to take was th:
of merely continuing normal relations with the Government of Panam
Any other action would have lent itself to undesirable interpretations
interference with internal political affairs.

From the foregoing summary of events it will be quite apparent to ar
fair and unbiased observer that the United States Government has in r
way deviated from its basic and fundamental policy of non-interferen
in the internal political affairs of the other American Republics. Or
can only speculate on the motives of uninformed people who deliberate
choose to express a different interpretation.

In this connection I believe it of interest to quote an excerpt from

port appearing in the Berlin *Deutsches Nachrichten Büro* of October 10
llowing the recent events in Panama:

"It is clear and beyond doubt that the United States used a temporary
sence of the President of Panama, who was inconvenient to it, to
age a *putsch* in this small Central American Republic."

6. ECUADOR–PERU BOUNDARY DISPUTE

[See *Documents, III, 1940–41,* p. 156–60.]

) *Appeal by the Minister of Foreign Affairs of Argentina (Ruiz-*
Guiñazú) to the Governments of Ecuador and Peru, July 23, 1941 [1]

Press news which unfortunately seems to be confirmed reports further
cidents occurring on the Peruvian-Ecuadoran border, in spite of the
peals made by all America to those two countries coupled with
aternal desires for peace which both Governments accepted with
rds of noble adherence.

At a time when in response to this common aspiration, we are pre-
ring to study the bases for conciliation which have been offered, the
newed aggravation of the conflict, the responsibility for which is not
rs to determine, delays a purpose which it is the duty of all, at this
ur, to maintain and to strengthen both for the sake of continental
ity and for the spirit of solidarity with which we have, from all our
ses made a common cause.

The Argentine Government therefore addresses a supreme appeal to
e Government of Peru (Ecuador) so that, conscious of its responsi-
ity, and so far as is in its power, the activities reported in the press be
spended, with the view at least to permit an effective start of the
nciliation proceedings which, with such justified and necessary hopes,
re to be initiated in Buenos Aires.

) *Supporting Telegram by the Acting Secretary of State (Welles) to*
the Ministers of Foreign Affairs of Ecuador (Donoso) and Peru
(Solf y Muro), July 24, 1941 [2]

I desire to express to Your Excellency the wholehearted support by
e Government of the United States of the appeal which has been
dressed to you and to His Excellency the Minister of Foreign Affairs
Peru (Ecuador) by His Excellency the Minister of Foreign Affairs of
e Argentine Republic in relation to recent developments on the
ntier between Peru and Ecuador.

[1] Department of State, *Bulletin,* V, p. 73.   [2] *Ibid.,* p. 73.

I am sure that Your Excellency will agree with me that it would l
impossible for the three powers which have offered their good offic
to assist in relieving the situation unless immediate measures are take
to restore quiet in the frontier region. I venture to express the hope th
Your Excellency will be able to announce to the three Governmen
tendering their good offices that such measures either have been take
or may immediately be taken.

I have had the honor of addressing an identic message to the Minist
of Foreign Affairs of Peru (Ecuador).

(2) Agreement for the Cessation of Hostilities. Message from tr President of the United States (Roosevelt) to the Presidents (Ecuador and Peru, August 1, 1941

(a) The President (Roosevelt) to the President of Ecuador (Arroyo d Río) [1]

I have just been informed of the agreement which has been reach
by the Governments of Ecuador and Peru to take measures which w
prevent the recurrence of the recent hostilities in the frontier regi
between the two countries. This agreement constitutes a notab
triumph for those principles of peace and continental solidarity to whi
all of the American Republics adhere. It therefore gives me pleasure
congratulate Your Excellency both on my behalf and on that of t
people of the United States on the taking of a step which will ensure t
continuing discussion of the frontier question between Ecuador a
Peru and its eventual solution in an atmosphere of harmony and go
will.

(b) The President (Roosevelt) to the President of Peru (Prado) [2]

The announcement that Peru and Ecuador have agreed upon
cessation of hostilities justifies the confidence which is shared by
of the American Republics that differences between the nations of t
continent will never again be reconciled except through the peace
processes which have been devised for the purpose and to which we
adhere. I take this opportunity of congratulating Your Excellency up
this auspicious occasion and of expressing my very best wishes for yo
personal welfare and that of the Peruvian people.

[1] Ibid., p. 93. A similar note was sent by the Acting Secretary of State (Well
to the Minister of Foreign Affairs of Ecuador (Donoso) under same date. Ibid.
[2] Ibid. A similar note was sent by the Acting Secretary of State (Welles) to
Minister of Foreign Affairs (Solf y Muro) under same date. Ibid.

3) *Protocol of Peace, Friendship and Boundaries between Ecuador and Peru, Rio de Janeiro, January 29, 1942* [1]

[Translation]

Ratified by the Congress of Peru, February 26 and by the Congress of Ecuador, February 28, 1942.

The Governments of Ecuador and Peru, desiring to find a solution to the question of boundaries which for a long period of time has separated them, and taking into consideration the offer which was made to them by the Governments of the United States of America, of the Argentine Republic, of the United States of Brazil, and of Chile, of their friendly services to find a prompt and honorable solution to the problem, and moved by the American spirit which prevails in the Third Consultative Meeting of the Ministers of Foreign Affairs of the American Republics, have resolved to celebrate a Protocol of peace, friendship and boundaries in the presence of the representatives of these four friendly Governments. To this end the following plenipotentiaries intervene:

For the Republic of Ecuador, Doctor JULIO TOBAR DONOSO, *Minister of Foreign Affairs*; and

For the Republic of Peru, Doctor ALFREDO SOLF Y MURO, *Minister of Foreign Affairs.*

Who, after having exhibited their full and respective powers on this subject and having found them in good and due form, agree to the signing of the following protocol;

ARTICLE 1. The Governments of Ecuador and Peru solemnly affirm their decided proposal to maintain between the two peoples relations of peace and friendship, of understanding and of good faith and to abstain the one with respect to the other from any action capable of disturbing these relations.

ARTICLE 2. The Government of Peru will retire within a period of fifteen days from this date its military forces to the line described in Article Eight of this Protocol.

ARTICLE 3. The United States of America, Argentina, Brazil and Chile will cooperate, by means of military observers, in adjusting the circumstances of this occupation, the retirement of troops, according to terms of the preceding Article.

ARTICLE 4. The military forces of the two countries will remain in their new positions until the definitive demarcation of the frontier line. In the interim, Ecuador will have only civil jurisdiction in the zones

[1] *Ibid.,* VI, p. 195.

disoccupied by Peru which will be in the same condition as the demilitarized zone of Act Talara.[1]

ARTICLE 5. The activity of the United States, Argentina, Brazil and Chile will continue until the definitive demarcation of frontiers between Ecuador and Peru has been completed. This Protocol and its execution will be under the guarantee of the four countries mentioned at the beginning of this Article.

ARTICLE 6. Ecuador will enjoy for the purposes of navigation on the Amazon and its northern tributaries the same concessions which Brazil and Colombia enjoy, in addition to those which were agreed upon in the Treaty of Commerce and Navigation designed to facilitate free and gratuitous navigation on the rivers referred to.

ARTICLE 7. Any doubt or disagreement which shall arise in the execution of this Protocol shall be resolved by the parties concerned with the assistance of the representatives of the United States, Argentina, Brazil and Chile in as short a period of time as may be possible.[2]

ARTICLE 8. The boundary line shall be marked by the following points

(A) In the west sector:

(1) Boca de Capones to the Pacific Ocean;
(2) The Zarumilla River and the Quebrada Balsamal or Lajas;
(3) The Puyango River or Tumbes to the Quebrada de Cazaderos
(4) The Cazaderos;
(5) The Quebrada de Pilares and the Alamor to the Chira River
(6) The Chira River upstream;
(7) The Macará, Calvas and Espíndola Rivers upstream to the sources of the last mentioned in the Nudo de Sabanillas
(8) From the Nudo de Sabanillas to the Canchis River;
(9) Along the Canchis downstream;
(10) The Chinchipe River, downstream to the point at which it receives the San Francisco River.

(B) In the Oriente:

(1) From the Quebrada de San Francisco, the "divertium aquarum" between the Zamora and Santiago Rivers, confluence of the Santiago with the Yaupi.

[1] Signed October 2, 1941, to assure the cessation of hostilities and to establish a demilitarized zone by the withdrawal of troops of both countries to specified lines.

[2] In order to carry out its share of the responsibility under these two articles, the United States through the Department of State appointed Dr. George M. McBride, professor of geography at the University of California, Los Angeles, as technical adviser to the boundary experts of the two countries, Department of State, *Bulletin* VI, p. 496.

(2) A line to the mouth of the Bobonaza at the Pastaza. The confluence of the Cunambo River with the Pintoyacu on the Tigre River.

(3) Mouth of the Cononaco on the Curaray, downstream to Bellavista.

(4) A line to the mouth of the Yasuni on the Napo River. Along the Napo downstream to the mouth of the Aguarico.

(5) Along this upstream to the confluence of the Lagartococha or Zancudo with the Aguarico.

(6) The Lagartococha River or Zancudo, upstream to its sources and from there a straight line which will meet the Guepi River and along this river to its mouth on the Putumayo, and along the Putumayo upstream to the boundary of Ecuador and Colombia.

ARTICLE 9. It is understood that the line previously described will be accepted by Ecuador and Peru for the demarcation of the frontier between the two countries by technical experts on the grounds. The parties can, however, in tracing the line on the ground, consent to reciprocal concessions which they may consider convenient in order to adjust the line to geographical realities. These rectifications shall be effectuated with the collaboration of the representatives of the United States of America, the Argentine Republic, Brazil and Chile.

The Governments of Ecuador and Peru will submit this Protocol to their respective Congresses and should obtain approval thereof within a period of not more than thirty days.

In witness whereof, the plenipotentiaries above-mentioned sign and seal, in two copies, in Spanish in the city of Rio de Janeiro at one a.m. on the twenty-ninth day of January, for the year nineteen hundred and forty-two, the present Protocol, under the auspices of His Excellency the President of Brazil and in the presence of the Ministers of Foreign Affairs of the Argentine Republic, Brazil and Chile and the Under Secretary of State of the United States of America.

J. TOBAR DONOSO	E. RUIZ GUIÑAZÚ
ALFREDO SOLF Y MURO	JUAN B. ROSSETTI
SUMNER WELLES	OSWALDO ARANHA

4) *Statement by the Acting Secretary of State (Welles), February 28, 1942* [1]

This Government has now been informed officially by the Government of Ecuador that the Congress of Ecuador has ratified the protocol of

[1] *Ibid.*, p. 194.

Rio de Janeiro which provides for the definitive settlement of the boundary controversy between Ecuador and Peru. As is known, the protocol of Rio de Janeiro was ratified by the Congress of Peru on February 26, 1942.

The final solution of this long-pending controversy is a matter of the deepest satisfaction to the Government of the United States. It affords a further proof of the ability and determination of the American Republics to settle all disputes between them by pacific methods. It has been a privilege for this Government to have been able, in association with the Governments of Argentina, Brazil, and Chile, to participate in the extension of its good offices in furthering this final settlement.

2. CANADIAN–AMERICAN RELATIONS

A. Mutual Defense: Military and Economic

[See *Documents, III, 1940–41*, p. 160–9.]

The joint committee has been found a very useful device of United States Canadian cooperation, especially during the present war emergency. In the Joint Statement of President Roosevelt and Prime Minister Mackenzie King o: August 18, 1940, announcement was made of the creation of the Permanent Join Board on Defense.[1] In order to implement the general principle of the "Hyde Park Declaration"[2] of April 20, 1941, "that in mobilizing the resources of this continent, each country should provide the other with the defense articles which it is best able to produce," the Joint Materials Coordinating Committee was set up.[3] Specifically, the primary purpose of this Committee was stated to be to make possible the free exchange of vital information relating to supplies o strategic raw materials between responsible officials of the two Governments The membership of the Committee as announced at the time was: William L Batt and E. R. Stettinius, Jr. (United States members); and G. C. Bateman and H. J. Symington (Canadian members). On June 17, 1941, announcement wa made of the creation of the Joint Economic Committees.[4]

(1) Establishment of Joint Defense Production Committee. Resolution of the Joint Economic Committees, September 19, 1941 [5]

Announcement was made on November 5, 1941, that the President and the Prime Minister of Canada had set up a Joint Defense Production Committee to coordinate the capacities of the two countries for the production of defense *matériel*. This action put into effect a recommendation of the Joint Economi Committees contained in the resolution of September 19, 1941.

WHEREAS: (A) At Hyde Park on April 20, 1941, the Prime Ministe of Canada and the President of the United States agreed "as a genera

---

[1] *Documents, III, 1940–41*, p. 160.　　[2] *Ibid.*, p. 161.

[3] Announced on May 14, 1941, by William S. Knudsen, Director General of th Office of Production Management. *United States Government Manual*, Spring, 1942 p. 99–100; *New York Times*, May 15, 1941, p. 10.

[4] *Documents, III, 1940–41*, p. 168; Executive Agreement Series 228.

[5] From the Office of the Secretary to the President; Department of State, *Bulletir* V, p. 360.

principle that in mobilizing the resources of this continent each country should provide the other with the defense articles which it is best able to produce, and above all, produce quickly, and that production programs should be coordinated to this end"; and

(B) The two Governments have established joint bodies in the field of military strategy (the Permanent Joint Board on Defense), in the field of primary materials (the Joint Materials Coordinating Committee), and in the field of general economic relations (the Joint Economic Committees); but

(C) No machinery has been established for the specific purpose of most effectively coordinating capacities of the two countries for the production of defense *matériel;*

THEREFORE, The Joint Economic Committees

RECOMMEND: (1) That the Governments of Canada and of the United States establish a joint committee on defense production to survey the capacity and potential capacity for the production of defense *matériel* in each country to the end that in mobilizing the resources of the two countries each country should provide for the common defense effort the defense articles which it is best able to produce, taking into consideration the desirability of so arranging production for defense purposes as to minimize, as far as possible and consistent with the maximum defense effort, maladjustments in the post-defense period;

(2) That the said joint committee be directed to report from time to time to the Prime Minister of Canada and to the President of the United States, with such recommendations as are found to be necessary to secure the purposes set forth above, as well as reports on progress made under their recommendations.

(3) That the said joint committee be furnished with such studies as have already been initiated in this field by the Joint Economic Committees and the Joint Materials Coordinating Committee; that the said joint committee be directed currently to furnish to the Joint Economic Committees copies of its surveys, findings and recommendations and reports, and to take appropriate steps to insure a continuing liaison between its secretariat and members and the secretariat and members of the Joint Economic Committees; and that the said joint committee be invited to consult with the Joint Economic Committees through joint meetings or otherwise, as occasion may indicate to be desirable, particularly with regard to the objective of minimizing post-defense economic maladjustments.

W. A. MACKINTOSH	ALVIN H. HANSEN
Canadian Chairman	*United States Chairman*

As the personnel of the committee is made up entirely of officials of the two Governments, its composition is significant. It was announced on November 5, 1941, that the President and the Prime Minister respectively had appointed the following members of the newly created joint committee:[1]

United States members
   Milo Perkins, Executive Director, Economic Defense Board, *Chairman*
   J. V. Forrestal, Under Secretary of the Navy
   W. H. Harrison, Director, Production Division, Office of Production Management
   R. P. Patterson, Under Secretary of War
   E. R. Stettinius, Jr., Administrator, Office of Lend-Lease Administration
   H. L. Vickery, Vice Chairman, United States Maritime Commission

Canadian members
   G. K. Sheils, Deputy Minister, Department of Munitions and Supply, *Chairman*
   J. R. Donald, Director General, Chemicals & Explosives Branch, Department of Munitions and Supply
   H. J. Carmichael, Director General, Munitions Production Branch, Department of Munitions and Supply
   R. P. Bell, Director General, Aircraft Production Branch, Department of Munitions and Supply
   H. R. MacMillan, President, War-Time Merchant Shipping, Ltd.
   Walter Gordon, Department of Finance

(2) *Statement of Joint War Production Committees of Canada and the United States, December 23, 1941* [2]

Having regard to the fact that Canada and the United States are engaged in a war with common enemies, the Joint War Production Committee of Canada and the United States recommends to the President of the United States and the Prime Minister of Canada the following statement of policy for the war production of the two countries:

1. Victory will require the maximum war production in both countries in the shortest possible time; speed and volume of war output, rather than monetary cost, are the primary objectives.

2. An all-out war production effort in both countries requires the maximum use of the labor, raw materials, and facilities in each country.

3. Achievement of maximum volume and speed of war output requires that the production and resources of both countries should be effectively integrated and directed toward a common program of requirements for the total war effort.

4. Each country should produce those articles in an integrated program of requirements which will result in maximum joint output of war goods in the minimum time.

[1] *Ibid.*   [2] *Ibid.* p. 578.

5. Scarce raw materials and goods which one country requires from
he other in order to carry out the joint program of war production
hould be so allocated between the two countries that such materials
nd goods will make the maximum contribution toward the output of
he most necessary articles in the shortest period of time.

6. Legislative and administrative barriers, including tariffs, import
uties, customs, and other regulations or restrictions of any character
vhich prohibit, prevent, delay, or otherwise impede the free flow of
ecessary munitions and war supplies between the two countries should
e suspended or otherwise eliminated for the duration of the war.

7. The two Governments should take all measures necessary for the
ullest implementation of the foregoing principles.

[Here follow signatures.]

a) *Statement of Approval by the President (Roosevelt), December 23,
1941* [1]

The Joint War Production Committees of Canada and the United States
ave unanimously adopted a declaration of policy calling for a combined all-
ut war production effort and the removal of any barriers standing in the way
f such a combined effort. This declaration has met the approval of the Canadian
Var Cabinet. It has my full approval. To further its implementation, I have
sked the affected departments and agencies in our Government to abide by its
tter and spirit so far as lies within their power. I have further requested
Ir. Milo Perkins, the Chairman of the American Committee, to investigate,
ith the aid of the Tariff Commission and other interested agencies, the extent
o which legislative changes will be necessary to give full effect to the declaration.

Through brute force and enslavement, Hitler has secured a measure of inte-
ration and coordination of the productive resources of a large part of the con-
inent of Europe. We must demonstrate that integration and coordination of
he productive resources of the continent of America is possible through demo-
ratic processes and free consent.

3) *Recommendations of the Joint Economic Committees, February 27,
1942* [2]

a) *Arrangement Respecting Increased Production of Oil-Bearing
Crops and Feed Grains*

Without changing the existing tariff structure, the arrangement provided for
ore effective utilization of the joint agricultural resources of the two countries
or the production of certain farm products needed in the war effort. Both Na-

[1] *Ibid.*
[2] *Ibid.*, VI, p. 313–4. The instrument is in form a series of recommendations of the
oint Economic Committees, Canada-United States, which became an arrangement
y the approval of the Prime Minister of Canada and the approval on April 10,
942, of the President of the United States.

tions were confronted by a shortage of fats and oils due to the loss of imported supplies, increased wartime requirements, and the necessity of supplying substantial quantities of these products to our allies. The increase in the acreage of oats and barley in Canada would not only provide more adequate feed supplies for the expanding livestock program of Canada but would make possible a greater expansion of soybean production in the corn belt by permitting crop acreage that would otherwise be used for feed-grain production to be shifted without impairing feed resources. In order to bring about the desired increase in production, the Canadian Government has adopted a definite program to encourage wheat growers to shift surplus wheat land into oats, barley, and flax The arrangement further strengthened the oil-crop-production-goal program already set up in the United States.

WHEREAS, The United States and Canada are confronted by a serious shortage of fats and oils due to inability to obtain customary imports owing to war operations and the shortage of shipping, increased wartime requirements, and the necessity of supplying substantial quantities of these products to the United Nations, chiefly the United Kingdom and the Union of Soviet Socialist Republics; and

WHEREAS, The United States and Canada, in addition to meeting their own expanded requirements, have each undertaken to supply the United Kingdom with extensive quantities of livestock products involving the necessity of increasing the supplies of feed grains; and

WHEREAS, An increased supply of oil can be obtained by expanding the acreage of soybeans in the United States and of flaxseed in Canada and

WHEREAS, A material increase in feed supplies can be obtained by expanding the acreage of oats and barley in Canada; and

WHEREAS, The facilitating of such a program of expansion would contribute to the joint war effort of the two countries, and at the same time encourage a more effective use of their respective resources;

THEREFORE, The Joint Economic Committees of Canada and the United States recommend:

A. That the Governments of the two countries, through their appropriate departments or agencies, undertake the following:

(1) The United States to increase its acreage of oil-producing crop with the object of alleviating the impending shortage of oils in both the United States and Canada.

(2) Canada to increase its acreage of flaxseed to provide as large a volume as possible for domestic needs and an excess to offset in part the reduction in North American imports of vegetable oil and oil seeds.

(3) Canada to increase its acreage of oats and barley with the object of obtaining adequate supplies of feed grains for the expanded

livestock program of Canada and supplementary supplies for the United States.

B. That in order to encourage such a program, while at the same time providing necessary assurances in the matter of market outlets, the respective Governments agree, effective from next autumn, that:

(1) Canada shall facilitate the delivery in the United States, at the then current United States prices, of whatever quantity of flaxseed, oats, and barley Canada may be in a position to supply;

(2) The United States shall not impose additional restrictions on the importation of flaxseed, oats and barley moving from Canada to the United States;

(3) The United States shall facilitate the sale to Canada, at the then current United States prices, of whatever quantity of vegetable oils or vegetable oil seeds the United States may be in a position to supply;

(4) Canada shall not impose additional restrictions on the importation of vegetable oils or vegetable oil seeds moving from the United States to Canada.

W. A. MACKINTOSH
Chairman, Canadian Committee
ALVIN H. HANSEN
Chairman, United States Committee

b) Arrangement Respecting Seasonal Movement of Farm Labor and Machinery

The Joint Economic Committees of Canada and the United States recommend that the Governments of the two countries take suitable action:

(1) To permit used agricultural machines and their operators or normal crews, to move across the border without payment of duty, with a minimum of restrictions, and with such regulations as either country may consider necessary to insure that the machines or members of the crews return within a specified time to the country from which they came.

(2) To facilitate the seasonal movement of farm labor across the common boundary under such rules and regulations as will further the efficient distribution of labor for peak requirements.

The reasons for these recommendations are:

Shortages of agricultural machines and of farm labor skilled in their use impede the wartime agricultural programs both in Canada and in the United States; and scarcities of steel and other metals limit the current output of labor-saving machinery. The movement of machines within each country has contributed to economies in the use of machines and labor and achieved greater efficiency of agricultural output. The removal of such regulations and restrictions as now impede the movements across the common boundary of both farm machines and the labor associated with them, would further increase their efficient use thereby contributing to the common war effort.

Seasonal requirements for farm labor especially in adjacent areas of Canada and the United States ordinarily occur in a time sequence that gives opportunity for the movement of such labor, especially at planting and harvest time when labor shortage caused by the war might have serious effects on farm production in many localities on both sides of the border.

W. A. MACKINTOSH
Chairman, Canadian Committee
ALVIN H. HANSEN
Chairman, United States Committee

B. Limitation of Naval Vessels on the Great Lakes

[See *Documents*, III, 1940–41, p. 169–78.]

(1) *The United States Minister to Canada (Moffat) to the Secretary of State for External Affairs (Mackenzie King), February 26, 1942*

(*No. 611*)

SIR:

May I refer to Dr. Skelton's note of October 30, 1940, and my reply of November 2, 1940,[2] interpreting the Rush-Bagot Agreement in the light of existing conditions and in conformity with the intent of the Agreement. I am now in receipt of instructions from my Government to suggest that in order to permit naval vessels being constructed on the Great Lakes to combat enemy action upon their arrival in the open sea, they may be permitted to have their armament placed in complete readiness for action and that all essential tests and trials of machinery and armament, including the submerged operations of submarines and test firing of torpedoes and guns be effected in Great Lakes waters. My Government in hopes that the Canadian Government will approve the suggestion

---

[1] Canada, *Treaty Series*, 1942, No. 3.
[2] *Documents, III, 1940–41*, p. 177.

t being understood that the proposed procedure is to be effective only
or the duration of the present hostilities.

Accept, Sir, the renewed assurances of my highest consideration.

2) *The Secretary of State for External Affairs (Mackenzie King) to
the United States Minister to Canada (Moffat), March 9, 1942* [1]

No. 21)

SIR:

I have the honor to refer to your Note No. 611 dated 26th February,
942, with regard to the further interpretation of the Rush-Bagot Agreement in the light of existing conditions and in conformity with the
ntent of the Agreement.

Consideration has been given to your suggestion, and I am now author-
zed to inform you that the Canadian Government agrees to a further
nterpretation of the Rush-Bagot Agreement based upon it. Accord-
ngly, in order to permit naval vessels being constructed on the Great
Lakes to combat enemy action upon their arrival in the open sea, they
vill be permitted to have their armament placed in complete readiness
or action and all essential tests and trials of machinery and armament
ncluding the submerged operations of submarines and test firing of
orpedoes and guns may be effected in Great Lakes waters.

The Canadian Government also concurs in your suggestion that this
procedure should be effective only for the duration of the present hos-
ilities.

Accept, Sir, the renewed assurances of my highest consideration.

C. Military Highway to Alaska

1) *Exchange of Notes between Canada and the United States, March
17, 18, 1942. The Secretary of State for External Affairs (Mackenzie King) to the United States Minister to Canada (Moffat),
March 18, 1942* [2]

The proposed construction of this military highway was taken up with the
Canadian Government on February 13, 1942. The Canadian Government

[1] Canada, *Treaty Series*, 1942, No. 3. The agreement entered into force March 9,
942.

[2] Department of State, *Bulletin*, VI, p. 237. The proposing note is not reprinted.
The Alaska International Highway Commission was created by Act of May 31, 1938
52 Stat. 590), and its scope was extended by Public Law 585, approved June 11, 1940

acquiesced immediately in the proposed surveys by the United States Army Engineers, and the first United States Army Engineers' officer arrived in Ottawa to discuss the detailed arrangements for these surveys on February 16.

The Canadian Government suggested that the question of the construction of this military highway be referred to the Permanent Joint Board on Defense United States and Canada, and that Board submitted a recommendation to the two Governments on February 26. On March 6 the Canadian Government announced its approval of the recommendation of the Permanent Joint Board on Defense and its acceptance of the offer of the Government of the United States to construct this military highway.

Detailed surveys were conducted by the United States Army Engineers troops.

SIR:

1. I have the honor to acknowledge the receipt of your note of March 17, 1942, in which you referred to the recommendation approved by the Permanent Joint Board on Defense, as a result of which the two Sections of the Board proposed to their respective Governments:

"The construction of a highway along the route that follows the general line of airports, Fort St. John — Fort Nelson — Watson Lake — Whitehorse — Boundary — Big Delta, the respective termini connecting with existing roads in Canada and Alaska."

2. As announced on March 6, 1942, the Canadian Government has approved this recommendation and has accepted the offer of the United States Government to undertake the building and war-time maintenance of the highway which will connect the airports already constructed by Canada.

3. It is understood that the United States Government will:

(A) carry out the necessary surveys for which preliminary arrangements have already been made, and construct a pioneer road by the use of United States Engineer troops for surveys and initial construction.

(B) arrange for the highway's completion under contracts made by the United States Public Roads Administration and awarded with a view to insuring the execution of all contracts in the shortest possible time without regard to whether the contractors are Canadian or American

(C) maintain the highway until the termination of the present war and for six months thereafter unless the Government of Canada prefer to assume responsibility at an earlier date for the maintenance of so much of it as lies in Canada;

(D) agree that at the conclusion of the war that part of the highway which lies in Canada shall become in all respects an integral part of the Canadian highway system, subject to the understanding that there shall at no time be imposed any discriminatory conditions in relation to the use of the road as between Canadian and United States civilian traffic.

4. The Canadian Government agrees:

(A) to acquire rights-of-way for the road in Canada (including the settlement of all local claims in this connection), the title to remain in the Crown in the right of Canada or of the Province of British Columbia as appears more convenient;

(B) to waive import duties, transit or similar charges on shipments originating in the United States and to be transported over the highway to Alaska, or originating in Alaska and to be transported over the highway to the United States;

(C) to waive import duties, sales taxes, license fees or other similar charges on all equipment and supplies to be used in the construction or maintenance of the road by the United States and on personal effects of the construction personnel;

(D) to remit income tax on the income of persons (including corporations) resident in the United States who are employed on the construction or maintenance of the highway;

(E) to take the necessary steps to facilitate the admission into Canada of such United States citizens as may be employed on the construction or maintenance of the highway, it being understood that the United States will undertake to repatriate at its expense any such persons if the contractors fail to do so;

(F) to permit those in charge of the construction of the road to obtain timber, gravel and rock where such occurs on Crown lands in the neighborhood of the right-of-way, providing that the timber required shall be cut in accordance with the directions of the appropriate Department of the Government of the Province in which it is located, or, in the case of Dominion lands, in accordance with the directions of the appropriate Department of the Canadian Government.

5. The Canadian Government agrees to the suggestion that the practical details of the arrangement be worked out by direct contact between the appropriate Governmental agencies subject, when desirable, to confirmation by subsequent exchange of notes.

Accept [etc.]

D. Military Service

(1) *Agreement for the Exchange of Personnel between the Armed Forces of the Two Countries. The United States Minister to Canada (Moffat) to the Secretary of State for External Affairs of Canada (Mackenzie King), March 18, 1942* [1]

From the outbreak of war in September 1939, United States citizens joined the Canadian armed forces in increasing numbers. A waiver of taking of the oath of allegiance made it possible to do this without loss of citizenship, but many did take that oath. With the entry of the United States into the war reciprocal arrangements for the return of nationals of one country to service in the forces of that country became desirable.

SIR:

With reference to conversations that have recently taken place among the competent officials of the United States and Canadian Governments concerning the proposed transfer to the armed forces of the United States of certain American citizens now serving in the naval, military or air forces of Canada, I have the honor to propose that an agreement be entered into between the two Governments as follows:

I. FORCES WITHIN CANADA

1. The appropriate Canadian and United States authorities shall prepare a statement of the conditions of transfer and thereafter, as soon as possible, but not later than April 6, 1942, the appropriate Canadian authorities shall inform all United States citizens and former United States citizens who have lost their citizenship as a result of having taken an oath of allegiance on enlistment in the Naval, Military or Air Forces of Canada, and who are now serving in these forces in Canada, that they have an opportunity prior to and not after April 20, 1942, to apply for appointment or enlistment in the United States Armed Forces. Personnel making such applications may withdraw them at any time prior to appointment or enlistment in the United States armed forces.

2. The United States War and Navy Departments shall furnish National Defense Headquarters, Ottawa, information governing the conditions of service in the United States armed forces, which information shall be communicated by National Defense Headquarters to all concerned.

3. National Defense Headquarters, Ottawa, shall send nominal rolls of the applicants to the War or Navy Departments of the United States.

4. The United States War and Navy Departments shall appoint

---

[1] Department of State, *Bulletin*, VI, p. 244. The confirming note of March 20, 1942, is not reprinted here. Both are issued as Canada, *Treaty Series*, 1942, No. 5.

Boards to come to Canada to interview applicants, with full power to appoint or to enlist them in the United States Forces.

5. The Naval, Military and Air Forces of Canada shall set up Boards empowered to authorize resignations and discharge of the applicants accepted by the United States Forces.

6. The Canadian Board shall be empowered to postpone transfers, if in their opinion immediate transfer would prejudicially affect the common war effort.

7. Medical examinations, resignations and discharges from the Naval, Military or Air Forces of Canada, and immediate appointment or enlistment in the United States forces, shall take place at joint meetings of the United States and Canadian Boards.

8. The United States Board will issue the necessary travel and meal vouchers to the appropriate assembly points in the United States to the accepted applicants. Accepted applicants shall be permitted to wear Canadian badges and uniform until such time as they arrive at the assembly point in the United States and are equipped with United States uniform. The United States armed forces will return all Public clothing, arms and equipment of such accepted applicants to points in Canada to be designated.

9. Sentences of detention of selected applicants will be remitted at the request of the United States board.

10. Except with the authority of National Defense Headquarters applicants for appointment or enlistment in the United States armed forces shall not be discharged from the Naval, Military, or Air Forces of Canada until their application has been heard by the United States Board in accordance with the proposed plan.

II. Forces Outside Canada

1. The rules which apply to the above mentioned persons serving within Canada will apply without change to those serving in the Canadian forces in Newfoundland and Jamaica. If despite all efforts notifications to United States citizens and former United States citizens serving in Newfoundland or Jamaica are not deliverable before April 6, 1942, the option to apply for transfer will be exercisable for 15 days after the receipt of the notification.

2. The rules which apply to the above mentioned persons serving within Canada will apply without change to those serving outside of Canada, Newfoundland, and Jamaica except that:

(a) The transfer will not ordinarily be made until the individual can be transferred to a United States unit serving in the area in which he is located, and (*b*) The option to apply for transfer will be exercisable within fifteer (15) days after notice of the right to exercise it has appeared in the orders of the unit with which he is serving.

3. Representatives of Canada and of the United States will discuss with the authorities of Great Britain the transfer to the United States forces of Royal Canadian Air Force personnel now serving in the Roya Air Force whose transfer might affect the efficiency of the Royal Air Force.

III. UNITED STATES FORCES

The United States will accord the same right of transfer to Canadian citizens now serving in the United States forces as is accorded United States citizens serving in Canadian forces.

In submitting the foregoing proposal I may add that if an agreement in this sense is acceptable to the Canadian Government, this note and your reply thereto accepting the terms outlined shall be regarded as placing on record the understanding arrived at between the two Gov ernments concerning this matter.

Accept [etc.]

(2) *Exchange of Notes in Regard to the Application of the United State. Selective Training and Service Act of 1940, as Amended, te Canadian Nationals Residing in the United States* [1]

(a) *The Acting Secretary of State (Welles) to the Canadian Ministe (McCarthy), March 30, 1942*

SIR:

I have the honor to refer to conversations which have taken place be tween officers of the Canadian Legation and of the Department with respect to the application of the United States Selective Training and Service Act of 1940, as amended, to Canadian nationals residing in the United States.

As you are aware the Act provides that with certain exceptions ever male citizen of the United States and every other male person residing in the United States between the ages of 18 and 65 shall register. Th Act further provides that, with certain exceptions, registrants within specified age limits are liable for active military service in the United States armed forces.

This Government recognizes that from the standpoint of morale o the individuals concerned and the over-all military effort of the countrie

[1] Department of State, *Bulletin*, VI, p. 315–18.

at war with the Axis Powers, it would be desirable to permit certain classes of individuals who have registered or who may register under the Selective Training and Service Act of 1940, as amended, to enlist in the armed forces of a co-belligerent country, should they desire to do so. It will be recalled that during the World War this Government signed conventions with certain associated powers on this subject. The United States Government believes, however, that under existing circumstances the same ends may now be accomplished through administrative action, thus obviating the delays incident to the signing and ratification of conventions.

This Government is prepared, therefore, to initiate a procedure which will permit aliens who have registered under the Selective Training and Service Act of 1940, as amended, who are nationals of co-belligerent countries and who have not declared their intention of becoming American citizens to elect to serve in the forces of their respective countries, in lieu of service in the armed forces of the United States, at any time prior to their induction into the armed forces of this country. Individuals who so elect will be physically examined by the armed forces of the United States, and if found physically qualified, the results of such examinations will be forwarded to the proper authorities of the co-belligerent nation for determination of acceptability. Upon receipt of notification that an individual is acceptable and also receipt of the necessary travel and meal vouchers from the co-belligerent government involved, the appropriate State Director of the Selective Service System will direct the local Selective Service Board having jurisdiction in the case to send the individual to a designated reception point for induction into active service in the armed forces of the co-belligerent country. If upon arrival it is found that the individual is not acceptable to the armed forces of the co-belligerent country, he shall be liable for immediate induction into the armed forces of the United States.

Before the above-mentioned procedure will be made effective with respect to a co-belligerent country, this Department wishes to receive from the diplomatic representative in Washington of that country a note stating that his government desires to avail itself of the procedure and in so doing agrees that:

(a) No threat or compulsion of any nature will be exercised by his government to induce any person in the United States to enlist in the forces of any foreign government;

(b) Reciprocal treatment will be granted to American citizens by his government; that is, prior to induction in the armed forces of his government they will be granted the opportunity of electing to serve in the armed forces of the United States in substantially the same manner as outlined above.

(c) No enlistments will be accepted in the United States by the government of American citizens subject to registration or of aliens of any nationality who have declared their intention of becoming American citizens and are subject to registration.

This Government is prepared to make the proposed regime effective immediately with respect to Canada upon the receipt from you of a note stating that your government desires to participate in it and agrees to the stipulations set forth in lettered paragraphs (a), (b), and (c) above

Accept [etc.]

(b) The Canadian Chargé d'Affaires ad interim (Wrong) to the Acting Secretary of State (Welles), April 6, 1942

SIR:

I have the honor to refer to your Note of March 30, 1942, concerning the application of the United States Selective Training and Service Act of 1940, as amended, to Canadian nationals residing in the United States.

2. In your note you make certain proposals which, so far as they affect Canada, may be set forth as follows: —

(1) The Government of the United States is prepared to initiate procedure which will permit non-declarant Canadian nationals who register under the United States Selective Training and Service Act of 1940, as amended, to elect, at any time prior to their induction into the Armed Forces of the United States, to serve in the Naval, Military or Air Forces of Canada in lieu of service in the Armed Forces of the United States. Individuals who elect for service with the Canadian Forces will be physically examined by the Armed Forces of the United States; if they are found to be physically qualified, the results of the examinations will be forwarded to the proper authorities of Canada. On receipt from the Canadian Government of notification that an individual is acceptable and also receipt of the necessary travel and meal vouchers, the appropriate State Director of the Selective Service System will direct the local Selective Service Board concerned to send the individual to a designated reception point for induction into the Naval, Military or Air Forces of Canada. If, on arrival at the reception point, the individual is found to be not acceptable to the Naval, Military or Air Forces of Canada, he shall be liable for immediate induction into the Armed Forces of the United States.

(2) The Government of the United States is prepared to make the proposed regime effective immediately with respect to Canada on receipt of a note stating that the Canadian Government desires to participate in the regime and agrees to the following stipulations: —

(a) The Canadian Government shall not exercise any threat or compulsion of any nature to induce any person in the United States to enlist in the Naval, Military or Air Forces of Canada or of any other foreign Government;

(b) The Canadian Government shall grant reciprocal treatment to United States citizens, that is, United States citizens subject to compulsory military service in Canada shall, prior to induction into the Naval, Military or Air Forces of Canada, be granted the opportunity of electing to serve in the Armed Forces of the United States in substantially the same manner as that outlined above;

(c) The Canadian Government shall not accept enlistments in the United States from United States citizens subject to registration or from aliens of any nationality who have declared their intention of becoming United States citizens and are subject to registration.

3. The policy of the Canadian Government and Canadian legislation have been based on the assumption that measures applying compulsory military service to aliens should be founded upon agreement with the interested Governments. The Canadian Government is of the opinion that difficulties might arise if there were general recognition of a right to conscript aliens, implying corresponding rights in other countries to conscript Canadian nationals. The Canadian Government, however, does not wish to raise a legal objection at the present time. In view of the close cooperation between Canada and the United States in the prosecution of the war, and in view of the time that will be saved and of the other undoubted, practical advantages to be derived from the acceptance of these United States proposals, the Canadian Government is prepared to cooperate with the Government of the United States by participating in the regime set forth above, full reciprocity on all points being assured by the United States Government.

4. The Canadian Government agrees to stipulation (a) on the understanding that the United States Government is willing, if requested, to make a reciprocal promise. It is understood, of course, that the engagement set out in stipulation (a) is limited to the present case and, furthermore, that it is not intended to prevent the Canadian Government from declaring the legal liability of Canadians everywhere, including the United States, to serve in the Canadian Forces, so long as nothing is said or done by the Canadian Government in the United States by way

of threat or compulsion. The reason for this reservation is that Canada may decide in the future to create a general legal liability of Canadian abroad to serve in the Canadian Forces similar to the existing provisio in the United States Selective Training and Service Act imposing liability on United States citizens everywhere. If Canada creates such a liability, the Canadian Government would not wish to exclude any part of the globe.

5. The Canadian Government agrees to stipulation (*b*) on the under standing, firstly, that the United States Government is agreeable to the Canadian Government imposing a liability to compulsory military serv ice on United States citizens residing in Canada, and secondly, tha declarant United States citizens in Canada, like declarant Canadian nationals in the United States, will not be granted an opportunity o electing to serve in the armed forces of the country of which they ar nationals.

6. The Canadian Government agrees to stipulation (*c*) on a basis c reciprocity, that is, that the United States will not accept enlistments i Canada from Canadian nationals or from declarant aliens of any natior ality who may be subject to liability to compulsory military servic under Canadian law.

7. The Canadian Government assumes that the words "active servic in the armed forces of the co-belligerent country" in paragraph four c your Note mean, so far as Canada is concerned, full time duty in th Naval, Military or Air Forces of Canada.

8. The Canadian Government understands that nothing in this ex change of notes will be construed as imposing any obligation on th Canadian Government to return to the United States Canadian national who may be deemed to be draft delinquents under United State law.

9. In order that non-declarant Canadian nationals in the Unite States may be informed of the conditions of service in the Naval, Mil tary and Air Forces of Canada, National Defense Headquarters i Ottawa will give the Selective Service System of the United State copies of a pamphlet setting forth the conditions of service, on th understanding that the Selective Service System will make the pam phlets available to non-declarant Canadian nationals who are called u for induction into the Armed Forces of the United States.

10. The Canadian Government trusts that Canadian nationals wh are permanent residents of the United States and who elect for servic in the Naval, Military or Air Forces of Canada and are accepted b one of those Forces will be permitted to return to the United States a

ny time within six months after the termination of their service with
he Canadian Forces.

I have [etc.]

c) The Acting Secretary of State (Welles) to the Canadian Chargé d'Affaires ad interim (Wrong), April 8, 1942

SIR:

I have the honor to acknowledge the receipt of your note No. 222 of
April 6, 1942, referring to my note of March 30 concerning the application of the United States Selective Training and Service Act of 1940,
as amended, to Canadian nationals residing in the United States and
stating that the Canadian Government is prepared to cooperate with
the Government of the United States by participating in the regime
outlined in my note of March 30, on the understanding that full reciprocity on all points contained therein will be accorded by the Government of the United States.

I am pleased to inform you that the Government of the United
States hereby assures the Government of Canada full reciprocity with
respect to the regime in question and likewise agrees to the understandings, limitations, and assumptions set forth in numbered paragraphs 4
through 9 inclusive of your note under acknowledgement.

With respect to numbered paragraph 10 of your note relating to the
return to the United States of Canadian nationals who elect to serve
in the Naval, Military or Air Forces of Canada and are accepted by
one of those forces, you are informed that the Department of State is
requesting the Department of Justice to recommend to the Congress of
the United States the adoption of appropriate legislation with a view
to simplifying to the fullest extent possible the reentry to the United
States of the individuals in question at any time within six months
after the termination of their service with the Canadian forces.

Accept [etc.]

3. ICELAND

A. Defense of Iceland by United States Forces

The sending of United States forces to Iceland for the protection of that island
raised the interesting question whether Iceland was to be regarded as within the
Western Hemisphere" as that term had been used in statements of American
policy such as the Monroe Doctrine [1] and in statutes such as the Selective Training and Service Act of 1940. The geographer of the Department of State in his

[1] President Monroe used the words " this hemisphere " in his message, but the
meaning was obviously the same.

letter to Representative Rogers, June 8, 1940,[1] suggested that it was better "to regard this hemisphere in which we live, in relation to the land area of the world as comprising North America (including Central America and the West Indies and also Greenland) and South America, together with all islands appertaining to the two continents." President Roosevelt, in his radio address of May 27 1941,[2] said that Nazi occupation of Iceland would "bring the war close to our continental shores" and stated that we would actively resist every attempt by Hitler "to extend his Nazi domination to the Western Hemisphere," emphasizing all the time the stupidity of waiting until the enemy had "gained a foothold from which to attack." At his press conference of July 8, when a reporter recalled that the President at a previous conference had marked the area of the Western Hemisphere in such a manner as to leave most of Iceland outside it, the President repeated an earlier reply that it all depended on what geographer one talked to last.[3] His attitude seemed to be that the line of demarcation should depend upon the defense needs of the United States. It is significant that in his message to Congress of July 7, the President referred to Iceland as a strategic outpost which might be used as a base for eventual attack against the Western Hemisphere and announced the use of "forces of the United States Navy" for its occupation thereby avoiding any charge of having violated the provisions of statutes preventing the use of draftees and national guard units outside the Western Hemisphere except in American possessions.

(1) *Exchange of Notes with Iceland, July 1, 1941* [4]

(a) *Message of the Prime Minister of Iceland (Jónasson) to the President of the United States (Roosevelt)*

In a conversation of June 24, the British Minister explained that British forces in Iceland are required elsewhere. At the same time he stressed the immense importance of adequate defense of Iceland. He also called my attention to the declaration of the President of the United States to the effect that he must take all necessary measures to ensure the safety of the Western Hemisphere — one of the President's measures is to assist in the defense of Iceland — and that the President is therefore prepared to send here immediately United States troops to supplement and eventually to replace the British force here. But that he does not consider that he can take this course except at the invitation of the Iceland Government.

After careful consideration of all the circumstances the Iceland Government, in view of the present state of affairs, admit that this measure is in accordance with the interest of Iceland, and therefore are ready to entrust the protection of Iceland to United States on the following conditions:

[1] *Documents, II, 1939–40*, p. 95.
[2] *Ibid., III, 1940–41*, p. 48.
[3] *New York Times*, July 9, 1941.
[4] House Doc. 307, 77th Cong., 1st sess.; Department of State, *Bulletin*, V, p. 16.

1. United States promise to withdraw all their military forces land, ir and sea from Iceland immediately on conclusion of present war.

2. United States further promise to recognize the absolute independence and sovereignty of Iceland and to exercise their best efforts with nose powers which will negotiate the peace treaty at the conclusion of ne present war in order that such treaty shall likewise recognize the bsolute independence and sovereignty of Iceland.

3. United States promise not to interfere with Government of Iceland either while their armed forces remain in this country nor afterwards.

4. United States promise to organize the defense of the country in uch a way as to ensure the greatest possible safety for the inhabitants nemselves and assure that they suffer minimum disturbance from uilitary activities; these activities being carried out in consultation ith Iceland authorities as far as possible. Also because of small population of Iceland and consequent danger to nation from presence of a umerous army, great care must be taken that only picked troops are ent here. Military authorities should be also instructed to keep in uind that Icelanders have been unarmed for centuries and are entirely naccustomed to military discipline and conduct of troops towards the nhabitants of the country should be ordered accordingly.

5. United States undertake defense of the country without expense) Iceland and promise compensation for all damage occasioned to the nhabitants by their military activities.

6. United States promise to further interests of Iceland in every way a their power, including that of supplying the country with sufficient ecessities, of securing necessary shipping to and from the country and f making in other respects favorable commercial and trade agreements ith it.

7. Iceland Government expects that declaration made by President a this connection will be in agreement with these promises on the part f Iceland, and Government would much appreciate its being given the pportunity of being cognizant with wording of this declaration before is published.

8. On the part of Iceland it is considered obvious that if United tates undertake defense of the country it must be strong enough to neet every eventuality and particularly in the beginning it is expected nat as far as possible effort will be made to prevent any special danger a connection with change-over. Iceland Government lays special stress n there being sufficient airplanes for defensive purposes wherever they re required and they can be used as soon as decision is made for United tates to undertake the defense of the country.

This decision is made on the part of Iceland as an absolutely free and sovereign state and it is considered as a matter of course that United States will from the beginning recognize this legal status of the country both states immediately exchanging diplomatic representatives.

(b) Message of the President of the United States (Roosevelt) to th Prime Minister of Iceland (Jónasson)

I have received your message in which you have informed me tha after careful consideration of all the circumstances, the Iceland Govern ment, in view of the present state of affairs, admits that the sending t Iceland of United States troops to supplement and eventually to replac the present British forces there would be in accordance with the inter ests of Iceland and that, therefore, the Iceland Government is ready t entrust the protection of Iceland to the United States on the followin considerations:

[Here are set forth the 8 conditions in the Message given above.]

You further state that this decision is made on the part of Iceland a an absolutely free and sovereign state and that it is considered as matter of course that the United States will from the beginning recog nize the legal status of Iceland, both states immediately exchangin diplomatic representatives.

I take pleasure in confirming to you hereby that the conditions se forth in your communication now under acknowledgment are full acceptable to the Government of the United States and that these con ditions will be observed in the relations between the United States an Iceland. I may further say that it will give me pleasure to request c the Congress its agreement in order that diplomatic representative may be exchanged between our two countries.

It is the announced policy of the Government of the United State to undertake to join with the other nations of the Western Hemispher in the defense of the New World against any attempt at aggression. I the opinion of this Government, it is imperative that the integrity an independence of Iceland should be preserved because of the fact tha any occupation of Iceland by a power whose only too clearly apparen plans for world conquest include the domination of the peoples of th New World would at once directly menace the security of the entir Western Hemisphere.

It is for that reason that in response to your message, the Govern ment of the United States will send immediately troops to supplemen and eventually to replace the British forces now there.

The steps so taken by the Government of the United States are taken
full recognition of the sovereignty and independence of Iceland and
ith the clear understanding that American military or naval forces
nt to Iceland will in no wise interfere in the slightest degree with the
ternal and domestic affairs of the Icelandic people; and with the
rther understanding that immediately upon the termination of the
resent international emergency, all such military and naval forces will
e at once withdrawn leaving the people of Iceland and their Govern-
ent in full sovereign control of their own territory.

The people of Iceland hold a proud position among the democracies
the world, with a historic tradition of freedom and of individual
berty which is more than a thousand years old. It is, therefore, all
e more appropriate that in response to your message, the Govern-
ent of the United States, while undertaking this defensive measure for
e preservation of the independence and security of the democracies
the New World should at the same time be afforded the privilege of
ooperating in this manner with your Government in the defense of the
storic democracy of Iceland.

I am communicating this message, for their information, to the Gov-
nments of all of the other nations of the Western Hemisphere.

) *Message of the President (Roosevelt) to the Congress, July 7, 1941* [1]

To the Congress of the United States:

I am transmitting herewith for the information of the Congress a
essage I received from the Prime Minister of Iceland on July first and
e reply I addressed on the same day to the Prime Minister of Iceland
response to this message.

In accordance with the understanding so reached, forces of the United
ates Navy have today arrived in Iceland in order to supplement, and
entually to replace, the British forces which have until now been
ationed in Iceland in order to insure the adequate defense of that
untry.

As I stated in my message to the Congress of September third last [2]
garding the acquisition of certain naval and air bases from Great
ritain in exchange for certain over-age destroyers, considerations of
fety from overseas attack are fundamental.

The United States cannot permit the occupation by Germany of
rategic outposts in the Atlantic to be used as air or naval bases for

[1] House Doc. 307, 77th Cong., 1st sess.; Department of State, *Bulletin*, V, p. 15.
[2] *Documents, III, 1940–41*, p. 206.

eventual attack against the Western Hemisphere. We have no desire t
see any change in the present sovereignty of those regions. Assuranc
that such outposts in our defense-frontier remain in friendly hands is th
very foundation of our national security and of the national security
every one of the independent nations of the New World.

For the same reason substantial forces of the United States have no
been sent to the bases acquired last year from Great Britain in Trinida
and in British Guiana in the south in order to forestall any pince
movement undertaken by Germany against the Western Hemispher
It is essential that Germany should not be able successfully to empl
such tactics through sudden seizure of strategic points in the sou
Atlantic and in the north Atlantic.

The occupation of Iceland by Germany would constitute a serio
threat in three dimensions:

The threat against Greenland and the northern portion of the Nor
American Continent, including the Islands which lie off it.

The threat against all shipping in the north Atlantic.

The threat against the steady flow of munitions to Britain — which
a matter of broad policy clearly approved by the Congress.

It is, therefore, imperative that the approaches between the Americ
and those strategic outposts, the safety of which this country regards
essential to its national security, and which it must therefore defen
shall remain open and free from all hostile activity or threat there

As Commander-in-Chief I have consequently issued orders to t
Navy that all necessary steps be taken to insure the safety of co
munications in the approaches between Iceland and the United Stat
as well as on the seas between the United States and all other strateg
outposts.

This Government will insure the adequate defense of Iceland wi
full recognition of the independence of Iceland as a sovereign sta

In my message to the Prime Minister of Iceland I have given t
people of Iceland the assurance that the American forces sent the
would in no way interfere with the internal and domestic affairs of th
country, and that immediately upon the termination of the prese
international emergency all American forces will be at once withdraw
leaving the people of Iceland and their Government in full and soverei
control of their own territory.

FRANKLIN D. ROOSEVELT

On the status of Iceland, see *Documents, II, 1939–40*, p. 143. The Sen
confirmed the nomination of Lincoln MacVeagh as Minister to Iceland

gust 7, 1941, and on September 30 he presented his credentials to the
gent of Iceland (Bjornsson).[1] On August 13, 1942, the nomination of Leland
Morris, formerly Chargé of the American Embassy at Berlin, to the post to
ke the place of Mr. MacVeagh was confirmed by the Senate.[2] On November 21,
41, Mr. Thor Thors was received by the President as the newly appointed
inister of Iceland.[3]

B. Exchange Stabilization

) *Exchange Stabilization Agreement. Treasury Department Announcement, May 5, 1942* [4]

As a further link in the closer relations which have developed between
e Governments of the United States and of Iceland during the last
ar, Secretary of the Treasury Henry Morgenthau, Jr., and Icelandic
inister Thor Thors signed an Exchange Stabilization Agreement today.
This agreement between the Government of the United States, the
overnment of Iceland and the National Bank of Iceland, provides
at up to $2,000,000 of the United States Stabilization Fund will be
ed for the purpose of stabilizing the United States dollar-Icelandic
ona rate of exchange.
The agreement also provides for periodic conferences among repre-
atatives of the parties to the agreement to discuss monetary, financial
d economic problems of mutual interest.

EUROPEAN POSSESSIONS IN THE WESTERN HEMISPHERE

A. British Caribbean Possessions

*Joint Communiqué Announcing the Establishment of Anglo-Ameri-
can Caribbean Commission, London and Washington, March
9, 1942* [5]

For the purpose of encouraging and strengthening social and economic
operation between the United States of America and its possessions
d bases in the area known geographically and politically as the
ribbean, and the United Kingdom and the British colonies in the

For remarks on this occasion, and the reply of the Regent, see Department of
te, *Bulletin*, V, p. 315.
Ibid., VII, p. 703.
For remarks made by Mr. Thors on the occasion of the presentation of his cre-
tials and the President's reply, see *ibid.*, V, p. 409.
Treasury Department, Press Service No. 31–42.
From the Office of the Secretary to the President; Department of State, *Bulletin*,
p. 229. The communiqué was released simultaneously in London and in
shington.

same area, and to avoid unnecessary duplication of research in these fields, a commission, to be known as the Anglo-American Caribbean Commission, has been jointly created by the two Governments. The Commission will consist of six members, three from each country, to be appointed respectively by the President of the United States and His Majesty's Government in the United Kingdom — who will designate one member from each country as a co-chairman.

Members of the Commission will concern themselves primarily with matters pertaining to labor, agriculture, housing, health, education, social welfare, finance, economics, and related subjects in the territories under the British and United States flags within this territory, and on these matters will advise their respective Governments.

The Anglo-American Caribbean Commission in its studies and in the formulation of its recommendations will necessarily bear in mind the desirability of close cooperation in social and economic matters between all regions adjacent to the Caribbean.

The following appointments of co-chairmen have been made:

For Great Britain:

Sir Frank Stockdale

For the United States:

Charles W. Taussig

The remaining members of the Commission will be named later by the Governments concerned.

In addition to naming Mr. Charles W. Taussig, of New York, as co-chairman for the United States of the Anglo-American Caribbean Commission, the President selected as the other two American members of the Commission the Honorable Rexford G. Tugwell, Governor of Puerto Rico, and Mr. Coert du Bois, Chief of the Caribbean Office of the Department of State.

He also named as a Caribbean Advisory Committee, to serve in an advisory capacity to the President, Governor Tugwell and the Honorable Martin Travieso, Justice of the Supreme Court of Puerto Rico; Judge William H. Hastie, Civilian Aide to the Secretary of War; and Mr. Carl Robins, of California, former President of the Commodity Credit Corporation, together with Mr. Charles W. Taussig, who was also chairman of this Committee.

B. French West Indies

(1) *Dispatch of Negotiating Mission to Martinique, May 9, 1942* [1]

The President has directed a visit by Admiral John H. Hoover, Commander of the Caribbean Sea Front, accompanied by a repr

[1] Department of State, *Bulletin*, VI, p. 391.

ntative of the Department of State, to Martinique for the purpose of
eking with the French High Commissioner there an understanding
ith respect to the local problem presented by the French possessions in
e Caribbean area arising out of the collaboration policy of Monsieur
aval.

Admiral Hoover and Mr. Samuel Reber, Assistant Chief of the
ivision of European Affairs, Department of State, arrived at Mar-
nique the morning of May 9.

Admiral Hoover is authorized to propose an arrangement whereby
e French flag may continue to fly over the French Caribbean pos-
ssions and French sovereignty there will remain unchanged, and
hereby Admiral Robert will continue to be recognized as the ultimate
verning authority of French Caribbean possessions.

Should mutually satisfactory arrangements be reached with Admiral
obert as High Commissioner, assuring that the French authorities in
e French Caribbean-Atlantic Coast area will not furnish aid or
mfort to Axis forces, the United States is prepared to safeguard the
terests of France in these areas, to maintain their economic life, and
assure that all assets of the French Government in the French Car-
bean possessions be held for the ultimate use of the French people.

) *The United States Government to the French High Commissioner
in the West Indies (Robert), May 9, 1942 (version of Vichy
Government)* [1]

The negotiations with Admiral Georges Robert, French Commissioner in the
est Indies, begun in December, 1941, were resumed by the United States Gov-
nment through Rear Admiral John H. Hoover and Samuel Reber of the
partment of State. The Vichy Government, under its pro-Axis Chief of Gov-
nment, Pierre Laval, desired to intervene in these negotiations. On the night
May 16, following a Cabinet meeting, Laval read to a press conference what
said was the text of a United States note making six demands and his reply.
pies were sent by the official Vichy agency to the United States Embassy at
chy and to the French Ambassador at Washington. The following is a transla-
n of what was released in Vichy:

The present French Chief of Government in Vichy having announced
at he intends to follow a policy of wider collaboration with Germany,
is no longer possible for the United States Government to maintain
e agreements concluded by Admirals Greenslade and Horne regard-
g French possessions in the Western Hemisphere. This agreement had
eviously been considered satisfactory.

Under these agreements, the French possessions might become bases
r aggression on the part of the Axis, either on word given by the High

Commissioner or through the arrival of a new High Commissioner.
is to be expected that Germany will exercise pressure to this effect.

These possessions are subject to the orders of M. Laval, which ca
not be considered as representing the free will of the French. If certa
conditions are fulfilled, the Government of the United States is prepar
to treat the High Commissioner in the West Indies and Guiana as t
supreme authority in these possessions on behalf of France and und
the French flag but acting independently of Vichy. The conditio
follow:

1. Effective measures under American control for the immobilizati
of French warships and airplanes at present in the West Indies.

2. Effective control by American authorities of wireless and te
graphic communications and also of censorship of mail.

3. American control of commercial traffic and of travelers, both
arrival and departure.

4. Limitation to policing needs of all activities of French military a
naval forces.

5. French freighters at present immobilized in the West Indies to
placed at the disposal of the United States under equitable conditio

6. The gold and governmental funds now in French possessions w
be frozen to be utilized ultimately by the French people.

On its part the United States is prepared to accept the followi
points:

1. French crews to be left aboard warships. These ships will contin
to fly the French flag and remain French property. The United Sta
will take the necessary dispositions for the return to France of milita
and naval personnel as well as civilians desiring to be repatriated.

2. Admiral Robert to be recognized as the supreme governmen
commander of French possessions in the Caribbean Sea on behalf
France. French courts and civil authorities to be maintained.

3. An economic accord to be concluded in order to insure necess
supplies to these colonies. This accord will extend to exchanges betwe
French possessions and neighboring territories.

4. Purchase of the principal exports of French possessions, there
helping to maintain their economic life.

It is essential that a clear reply should be made rapidly to the fi
of these conditions, namely that relating to the immobilization of w
ships and airplanes. An early reply would be appreciated as rega
the other propositions, which could be made the object of frienc
negotiations.

The High Commissioner alone is in a position to conclude a peace

cord safeguarding French interests and preserving to the French
ople its possessions.

It is recognized that if the High Commissioner ceased to have control
the situation, the status of these possessions might be modified and
e United States could no longer guarantee their possession by the
ench people.

) *Note of the French Government at Vichy in Reply to United States*
Note to the French High Commissioner (Robert), May 13, 1942 [1]

[Translation]

1. In October 1940, at a time when the United States was not at
r, an accord was concluded between the French Government and
it of the United States to fix, in function of events, the particular
tus of our American possessions — that is to say, St. Pierre and
iquelon, the West Indies and Guiana.

2. On May 9, 1942, the American Admiral Hoover, accompanied by
r. Reber of the State Department, presented to Admiral Robert,
gh Commissioner of France in the West Indies, demands tending to
dify this status.

3. These demands gravely threatened French sovereignty over the
est Indies. Admiral Hoover declared that if they were not accepted
American Government no longer guaranteed this sovereignty.

4. The status obtaining since 1940 answered the essential interests of
two countries. It was reaffirmed and clarified last March by the
o governments.[2]

5. The French Government always respected its engagements, and
change in the constitution of the new government can lead it to
dify this attitude.

6. Recent declarations made to Admiral Leahy established the fact
it the chief of Government not only never envisaged repudiating the
gagements undertaken vis-á-vis the United States but, on the con-
ry, he affirmed in the clearest manner his wish to do nothing that
ild affect Franco-American relations.

7. The French Government protests this interference by the American
vernment in French internal politics. By casting doubt on official
rmations made in the name of the French Government the Depart-
nt of State adopted an offensive attitude toward our country, which
ends to maintain its liberty and the choice of its government.

8. The Federal Government [of the United States], in acting as it

has, commits toward the French people a grave error in psycholog arising no doubt from the maneuvers of French émigrés and Frenc rebels against their country, who are continuing in foreign lands tho partisan struggles from which France has already suffered so much.

9. The Federal Government has just transmitted propositions tha if they were accepted, would have the effect of removing from t French Government, sole repository of national sovereignty, the exe cise of its essential rights in colonies that have been French territory f three centuries.

10. The Federal Government, by refusing to Admiral Robert, t High Commissioner, the right to report on his administration to t only French authorities to which he is responsible, and by virtue which he holds power, formulated demands that the French Gover ment feels it is its duty to reject.

11. The Federal Government, moreover, also demanded the delive of merchant vessels at present immobilized in West Indian ports. cannot be unaware that such a cession is formally prohibited by t terms of the armistice. If the French submitted to the Americ demand, it would violate the armistice convention. This hypothes by reason of the consequences it would entail, cannot be envisaged the French Government.

12. The Federal Government, in demanding the immobilization warships at present in West Indian waters, seems to fear the utilizati of those forces against American interests. The Federal Governme cannot invoke any argument of a military nature that would justi such pretensions.

13. The French Government, which has never failed its word, re firms, in order to dissipate any equivocation in this connection, determination strictly to respect the undertakings it has already mac

14. The French Government reaffirms today, solemnly, that it v never assume responsibility for an act that might jeopardize relatic with the American people. It can say this much: While remaini faithful to the obligations arising from the armistice convention, it p serves its independence and its liberty of action.

15. The French Government is disposed to envisage and to negotia through the intermediary of Admiral Robert, all proposals that mig be made to it — while respecting French sovereignty and neutrality tending to settle the status of possessions in the Western Hemisph and which would give every guarantee to the Federal Governme regarding the immobilization of warships and merchant vessels, it bei stipulated that in no event these could be used by the United States.

16. The Federal Government, which is aware that France is suffering under misfortune and is doing all she can to assure her reconstruction in line with her noble national traditions, would assume heavy responsibility before history by breaking with unjustified violence the bonds of friendship that have always united our two peoples.

C. St. Pierre and Miquelon

After the Franco-German armistice,[1] administration of St. Pierre and Miquelon, the French islands off the coast of Labrador and near the outlet of the St. Lawrence into the Atlantic, remained under control of officials obedient to the Vichy regime. On December 24, 1941, Vice Admiral Emile Muselier, having sailed from Canada and having been in touch with both the Canadian and United States Governments, arrived at the islands and raised the Free French flag with the authorization of General Charles de Gaulle. A plebiscite showed 98% of the voters in favor of the Free French regime.

The Canadian and United States Governments, not being at war with the Vichy Government, were desirous of not appearing to have instigated the *coup*.[2] Some discussion occurred of the question whether a change of control from one French regime to another brought the matter within the scope of the Convention on the Provisional Administration of European Colonies and Possessions in the Americas, signed at Havana, July 30, 1940 (*Documents, III, 1940–41,* p. 85), which relates to the replacement of one non-American State by another in the control of territory in the Americas.

1) *Free French Proclamation to Inhabitants of St. Pierre and Miquelon, December 24, 1941* [3]

[Translation]

INHABITANTS OF THE FRENCH ISLANDS OF ST. PIERRE AND MIQUELON:
Conforming to General de Gaulle's orders, I have come to let you take part freely and in due order in a plebiscite, for which you have begged for so long.

You may now choose between the course of the Free French and the course of collaboration with the Axis Powers, who starve, humiliate and martyrize our country.

There is no doubt in my mind that the oldest French territory overseas will side with Great Britain, the United States, Canada and our other Allies and will show en masse its loyalty to the traditions of honor and liberty, which have always been the pride of France. Long live France! Long live the Allies!

[1] *Documents, II, 1939–40*, p. 427.
[2] See *New York Times*, January 18, 1942, p. 31, for account of American correspondent who accompanied naval expedition of Free French forces.
[3] *New York Times*, December 25, 1941, p. 1.

(2) *Statement of the Department of State, December 25, 1941* [1]

Our preliminary reports show that the action taken by three so-called
Free French ships at St. Pierre-Miquelon was an arbitrary action con
trary to the agreement of all parties concerned and certainly withou
the prior knowledge or consent in any sense of the United States Govern
ment.

This Government has inquired of the Canadian Government as to th
steps that Government is prepared to take to restore the *status quo* o
these islands.

(3) *Verbal Statement of the French Ambassador (Henry-Haye), Decem ber 27, 1941* [2]

There is no reason to doubt restoration of the *status quo.*

All the conversations are based on that principle, and I believe
solution can be reached satisfactory to all parties concerned.

As far as the wireless station is concerned, that has been used only fo
fishermen, but I think that matters can be arranged so that there wil
not be any shadow of doubt that nothing dangerous is transmitted ove
the station.

———

The apparent disapproval by the Government of the United States of th
action of the Free French which no doubt in part prompted the optimistic state
ment of the French Ambassador (Henry-Haye) was not followed by action o
our part to restore the *status quo.* In fact, faced with a critical public opinion i
the United States and the apparent unwillingness of the Vichy regime to revers
its policy of collaboration with Nazi Germany, the authorities in Washingto
apparently welcomed the opportunity to allow the new situation to remain un
disturbed. At his press conference on February 13, Under Secretary of Stat
Welles stated that, in his judgment, the Act of Havana did not apply to th
islands of St. Pierre and Miquelon.[3]

[1] Department of State, *Bulletin*, V, p. 580.

[2] *New York Times*, December 28, 1941, p. 15.

[3] *New York Times*, February 14, 1942, p. 1. Reference apparently is to the *Conven
tion on the Provisional Administration of European Colonies and Possessions in th
Americas* (*Documents, III, 1940–41*, p. 85). Sec. 6 of the Preamble of that Conventio
provides "that by virtue of a principle of American international law, recognize
by various conferences, the acquisition of territory by force cannot be permitted.
It was this provision which the *Times* report quoted Secretary Hull as having in
voked earlier. For statement of Under Secretary of State Welles on United State
policy regarding territory under Free French control, see p. 635.

D. Netherlands Possessions

1) *Protection of Bauxite Mines in Surinam (Netherlands Guiana).*
   Release from the Office of the Secretary to the President,
   November 24, 1941 [1]

The bauxite mines in Surinam furnish upwards of 60% of the requirements of the United States aluminum industry, which is vital to the
defense of the United States, the Western Hemisphere, and the nations
actively resisting aggression.

It is therefore necessary that the safety of these mines should be as
completely assured as present conditions demand.

In normal circumstances the Government of the Netherlands would,
for the purpose of strengthening further the defenses of Surinam, draw
on the armed forces of the Netherlands Indies. In view, however, of the
present situation in the southwestern Pacific, it is thought inadvisable to
follow that course.

For this reason the Governments of the Netherlands and of the United
States of America have entered into consultation. As a result, the latter
has agreed to send a contingent of the United States Army to Surinam
to cooperate with the Netherlands forces in assuring the protection of
the bauxite mines in that territory. This contingent will, of course, be
withdrawn as soon as the present danger to the mines is removed and at
the latest at the conclusion of hostilities.

Simultaneously the Government of the Netherlands has invited the
Government of the United States of Brazil to participate in this defense
measure. It is understood that Brazil will contribute to the common
aim by exercising an especial measure of military vigilance in the frontier
zone adjacent to Surinam and by sending a mission to Paramaribo to
exchange information and concert all other steps on the basis indicated
to assure maximum efficiency of the safety measures thus being jointly
undertaken by the Brazilian, United States, and Netherlands forces.

The Government of Brazil has indicated its wholehearted approval
of the emergency measures.

At the same time, the Government of the United States has notified
the Governments of the American Republics of the foregoing arrangements, which have been reached in the interests of all.

[1] Department of State, *Bulletin*, V, p. 425. The release was given out simultaneously with the landing of the military contingent.

(2) *Defense of Curaçao and Aruba. Department of State Release February 7, 1942* [1]

Enemy submarines, prior to the dispatch of troops, had been attacking Unite States shipping in coastwise and Caribbean trade and had attacked the petroleur plant on Aruba.

The United States Government at the request of the Netherland Government has sent a contingent of the United States Army to Curaça and Aruba to assist the Dutch armed forces in the defense of thes islands and the oil refineries thereon, which are vital to the war effort o the United Nations and to the defense of the Western Hemisphere.

The United States forces will operate under the general supervisio of the Governor of Curaçao and will be withdrawn upon the terminatio of the emergency.

It is understood furthermore that the Venezuelan and the Nether lands Governments have reached an agreement whereby the former wi cooperate in this defense measure in a manner similar to that agree upon between the Governments of Brazil and the Netherlands in th case of Surinam.

The Government of Venezuela has indicated its wholehearte approval of these emergency measures.

The governments of the American Republics are being notified of th foregoing arrangements, which have been reached in the interests of al

[1] *Ibid.*, VI, p. 153.

CHAPTER VI

EASTERN ASIA AND THE PACIFIC AREA

1. RELATIONS WITH JAPAN

A. General Review

1) Summary of Past Policy, and of More Immediate Events, in Relation to the Pacific Area. Message of the President (Roosevelt) to the Congress, December 15, 1941 [1]

Following the Japanese attack on American forces on December 7 and the declaration of war by the United States against Japan on December 8, the President prepared and submitted to Congress this historical summary dealing particularly with our relations with Japan. Attached to the message were various documents which were printed as Annexes 1 to 16 and to which the President refers in his message. Some of these appear later in this chapter. The others are listed by title only in footnotes explaining textual references.

To THE CONGRESS OF THE UNITED STATES OF AMERICA:

On December 8, 1941, I presented to the Congress a message in person asking for a declaration of war as an answer to the treacherous attack made by Japan the previous day upon the United States. For the information of the Congress, and as a public record of the facts, I am transmitting this historical summary of the past policy of this country in relation to the Pacific area and of the more immediate events leading up to this Japanese onslaught upon our forces and territory. Attached hereto are the various documents and correspondence implementing this history.

I

A little over a hundred years ago, in 1833, the United States entered into its first Far Eastern treaty, a treaty with Siam. It was a treaty providing for peace and for dependable relationships.

Ten years later Caleb Cushing was sent to negotiate and in 1844 there was concluded our first treaty with China.

In 1853, Commodore Perry knocked on Japan's doors. In the next few years those doors began to open; and Japan, which had kept itself aloof from the world, began to adopt what we call Western civilization.

---

[1] House Doc. 458, 77th Cong., 1st sess.; Department of State, *Bulletin*, V, p. 529–41.

During those early years, the United States used every influence it coul⸱ exert to protect Japan in her transition stage.

With respect to the entire Pacific area, the United States has con sistently urged, as it has for all other parts of the globe, the fundamenta importance to world peace of fair and equal treatment among nation: Accordingly whenever there has been a tendency on the part of an other nation to encroach upon the independence and sovereignty o countries of the Far East, the United States has tried to discourage suc tendency wherever possible.

There was a period when this American attitude was especiall important to Japan. At all times it has been important to China and t other countries of the Far East.

At the end of the nineteenth century, the sovereignty of the Philippin Islands passed from Spain to this country. The United States pledge itself to a policy toward the Philippines designed to equip them to becom a free and independent nation. That pledge and that policy we hav consistently carried out.

At that time there was going on in China what has been called th "scramble for concessions." There was even talk about a possibl partitioning of China. It was then that the principle of the "open door in China was laid down. In 1900, the American Government declare that its policy was to "seek a solution which may bring about permaner safety and peace to China ... protect all rights guaranteed to friendl powers by treaty and international law and safeguard for the world th principle of equal and impartial trade with all parts of the Chines Empire."

Ever since that day, we have consistently and unfailingly advocate the principles of the open-door policy throughout the Far East.

In the year 1908 the Government of the United States and the Goverr ment of Japan concluded an agreement by an exchange of notes. I that agreement, the two Governments jointly declared that they wer determined to support "by all pacific means at their disposal the ind⸱ pendence and integrity of China and the principle of equal opportunit for commerce and industry of all nations in that Empire"; that it wɛ "the wish of the two Governments to encourage the free and peacefi development of their commerce on the Pacific Ocean"; and that "th policy of both Governments" was "directed to the maintenance of th existing *status quo*" in that region.

The United States has consistently practiced the principles enunciate in that agreement.

In 1921, following the close of the first World War, nine powei having interests in the western Pacific met in conference in Washington. China, Japan, and the United States were there. One great objective of this conference was the maintenance of peace in the Pacific. This was to be achieved by reduction of armament and by regulation of competition in the Pacific and Far Eastern areas. Several treaties and agreements were concluded at that conference.

One of these was the Nine Power Treaty (see Annex 1).[1] It contained pledges to respect the sovereignty of China and the principle of equal opportunity for the commerce and industry of all nations throughout China.

Another was a treaty between the United States, the British Empire, France, Italy, and Japan providing for limitation of naval armament.[2] (See Annex 1.)

The course of events which have led directly to the present crisis began ten years ago. For it was then — in 1931 — that Japan undertook on a large scale its present policy of conquest in China. It began by the invasion of Manchuria, which was part of China. The Council and the Assembly of the League of Nations, at once and during many months of continuous effort thereafter, tried to persuade Japan to stop. The United States supported that effort. For example, the Government of the United States on January 7, 1932, specifically stated in notes sent to the Japanese and the Chinese Governments that it would not recognize any situation, treaty, or agreement brought about by violation of treaties. (See Annex 2.)[3]

This barbaric aggression of Japan in Manchuria set the example and the pattern for the course soon to be pursued by Italy and Germany in Africa and in Europe. In 1933 Hitler assumed power in Germany. It was evident that, once re-armed, Germany would embark upon a policy of conquest in Europe. Italy — then still under the domination of Mussolini — also had resolved upon a policy of conquest in Africa and in the Mediterranean.

Through the years which followed, Germany, Italy, and Japan reached an understanding to time their acts of aggression to their common advantage — and to bring about the ultimate enslavement of the rest of the world.

[1] *Treaties, Conventions*, etc., 1923–1927, III, p. 3120. Annex 1 reprints Sen. Doc. 124, 67th Cong., 2d sess. which contains the treaties and resolutions of the Conference on the Limitation of Armaments, Washington, November 12, 1921–February 6, 1922, which also are printed in *Treaties, Conventions*, etc., 1923–1927, III, p. 3094–3140.
[2] *Ibid.*, p. 3100.
[3] Identic Notes to the Japanese and Chinese Governments, January 7, 1932. House Doc. No. 458, 77th Cong., 1st sess., p. 49.

In 1934, the Japanese Minister for Foreign Affairs sent a friendly not
to the United States, stating that he firmly believed that no question
existed between the two Governments that was "fundamentally incapa
ble of amicable solution." He added that Japan had "no intention
whatever to provoke and· make trouble with any other Power." (Se
Annex 3.) [1] Our Secretary of State, Cordell Hull, replied in kind. (Se
Annex 4.) [2]

But in spite of this exchange of friendly sentiments, and almost imme
diately thereafter, the acts and utterances of the Japanese Governmen
began to belie these assurances — at least so far as the rights and inter
ests of other nations in China were concerned.

Our Government thereupon expressed to Japan the view of the Ameri
can people, and of the American Government, that no nation has th
right thus to override the rights and legitimate interests of other sov
ereign states. (See Annex 5.) [3]

The structure of peace which had been founded upon the Washington
Conference treaties began to be discarded by Japan. Indeed, in Decem
ber of 1934, the Japanese Government gave notice of its intention t
terminate the Naval Treaty of February 6, 1922, which had limited
competition in naval armament. She thereafter intensified and multi
plied her rearmament program.

In 1936 the Government of Japan openly associated itself with Ger
many by entering the Anti-Comintern Pact.[4]

This Pact, as we all know, was nominally directed against the Sovie
Union; but its real purpose was to form a league of fascism against th
free world, particularly against Great Britain, France, and the United
States.

Following this association of Germany, Italy, and Japan, the stag
was now set for an unlimited campaign of conquest. In July 1937
feeling themselves ready, the armed forces of Japan opened new large
scale military operations against China. Presently, her leaders, dropping
the mask of hypocrisy, publicly declared their intention to seize and
maintain for Japan a dominant position in the entire region of eastern
Asia, the western Pacific, and the southern Pacific.

[1] Note from the Japanese Minister for Foreign Affairs (Hirota) handed to th
Secretary of State (Hull) by the Japanese Ambassador (Saito), February 21, 1934
ibid., p. 50.
[2] Reply thereto, handed to the Japanese Ambassador (Saito) by the Secretary o
State (Hull) on March 3, 1934, *ibid.*, p. 51.
[3] Statement by the American Ambassador to Japan (Grew) to the Japanese Min
ister for Foreign Affairs (Hirota), April 29, 1934, *ibid.*, p. 52.
[4] See p. 199.

They thus accepted the German thesis that seventy or eighty million Germans were by race, training, ability, and might superior in every way to any other race in Europe — superior to about four hundred million other human beings in that area. And Japan, following suit, announced that the seventy or eighty million Japanese people were also superior to the seven or eight hundred million other inhabitants of the Orient — nearly all of whom were infinitely older and more developed in culture and civilization than themselves. Their conceit would make them masters of a region containing almost one-half the population of the earth. It would give them complete control of vast sea lanes and trade routes of importance to the entire world.

The military operations which followed in China flagrantly disregarded American rights. Japanese armed forces killed Americans. They wounded or abused American men, women, and children. They sank American vessels — including a naval vessel, the *Panay*. They bombed American hospitals, churches, schools, and missions. They destroyed American property. They obstructed, and in some cases, drove out American commerce.

In the meantime, they were inflicting incalculable damage upon China, and ghastly suffering upon the Chinese people. They were inflicting wholesale injuries upon other nations — flouting all the principles of peace and good-will among men.

There are attached hereto (see, respectively, Annexes 6, 7, 8, and 9)[1] lists of American nationals killed or wounded by Japanese forces in China since July 7, 1937; of American property in China reported to have been damaged, destroyed, or seriously endangered by Japanese air bombing or air machine-gunning; of American nationals reported to have been assaulted, arbitrarily detained, or subjected to indignities; of interferences with American nationals, rights, and interests. These lists are not complete. However, they are ample evidence of the flagrant Japanese disregard of American rights and civilized standards.

[1] The first three lists are stated specifically to cover the period since July 7, 1937. The fourth list (Annex 9) appears to cover the same period. The four Annexes are printed, House Doc. No. 458, 77th Cong., 1st sess., p. 53–102.

Annex 6 lists 18 cases of American nationals killed or wounded by Japanese forces.

Annex 7 lists 298 cases of American property reported damaged, destroyed or seriously endangered by Japanese air bombing or air machine-gunning, distributed by years as follows: 35 in 1937; 86 in 1938; 75 in 1939; 43 in 1940 and 59 in 1941.

Annex 8 lists 101 incidents, occurring in China (99) and French Indo-China (2), where American nationals were assaulted, arbitrarily detained, subjected to indignities, et cetera, by Japanese authorities or agents.

Annex 9 summarized in 30 pages details with regard to Japanese interferences with American trade and enterprise in China.

II

Meanwhile, brute conquest was on the rampage in Europe and the Mediterranean.

Hitler and Mussolini embarked upon a scheme of unlimited conquest. Since 1935, without provocation or excuse they have attacked, conquered, and reduced to economic and political slavery some 16 independent nations. The machinery set up for their unlimited conquest included, and still includes, not only enormous armed forces but also huge organizations for carrying on plots, intrigue, intimidation, propaganda, and sabotage. This machine — unprecedented in size — has world-wide ramifications; and into them the Japanese plans and operations have been steadily interlocked.

As the forces of Germany, Italy, and Japan increasingly combined their efforts over these years, I was convinced that this combination would ultimately attack the United States and the Western Hemisphere — if it were successful in the other continents. The very existence of the United States as a great free people, and the free existence of the American family of nations in the New World, would be a standing challenge to the Axis. The Axis dictators would choose their own time to make it clear that the United States and the New World were included in their scheme of destruction.

This they did last year, in 1940, when Hitler and Mussolini concluded a treaty of alliance with Japan deliberately aimed at the United States.

The strategy of Japan in the Pacific area was a faithful counterpart of that used by Hitler in Europe. Through infiltration, encirclement intimidation, and finally armed attack, control was extended over neighboring peoples. Each such acquisition was a new starting point for new aggression.

III

Pursuing this policy of conquest, Japan had first worked her way into and finally seized Manchuria. Next she had invaded China; and has sought for the past four and one-half years to subjugate her.

Passing through the China Sea close to the Philippine Islands, she then invaded and took possession of Indo-China. Today the Japanese are extending this conquest throughout Thailand — and seeking the occupation of Malaya and Burma. The Philippines, Borneo, Sumatra Java come next on the Japanese timetable; and it is probable that further down the Japanese page, are the names of Australia, New Zealand, and all the other islands of the Pacific — including Hawaii and the great chain of the Aleutian Islands.

To the eastward of the Philippines, Japan violated the mandate under which she had received the custody of the Caroline, Marshall, and Mariana Islands after the World War, by fortifying them, and not only losing them to all commerce but her own but forbidding any foreigner even to visit them.

Japanese spokesmen, after their custom, cloaked these conquests with innocent-sounding names. They talked of the "New Order in Eastern Asia"; and then of the "co-prosperity sphere in Greater East Asia." What they really intended was the enslavement of every nation which they could bring within their power, and the enrichment — not of all Asia, not even of the common people of Japan — but of the warlords who had seized control of the Japanese State. Here too they were following the Nazi pattern.

By this course of aggression, Japan made it necessary for various countries, including our own, to keep in the Pacific in self-defense large armed forces and a vast amount of material which might otherwise have been used against Hitler. That, of course, is exactly what Hitler wanted them to do. The diversion thus created by Hitler's Japanese ally forced the peace-loving nations to establish and maintain a huge front in the Pacific.

IV

Throughout this course and program of Japanese aggression, the Government of the United States consistently endeavored to persuade the Government of Japan that Japan's best interests would lie in maintaining and cultivating friendly relations with the United States and with all other countries that believe in orderly and peaceful processes. Following the outbreak of hostilities between Japan and China in 1937, this Government made known to the Japanese Government and to the Chinese Government that whenever both those Governments considered it desirable we stood ready to exercise our good offices. During the following years of conflict that attitude on our part remained unchanged.

In October 1937, upon invitation by which the Belgian Government made itself the host, 19 countries which have interests in the Far East, including the United States, sent representatives to Brussels to consider the situation in the Far East in conformity with the Nine-Power Treaty and to endeavor to bring about an adjustment of the difficulties between Japan and China by peaceful means. Japan and Germany only of all the powers invited declined to attend. Japan was itself an original signatory of the treaty. China, one of the signatories, and the Soviet Union, not a signatory, attended. After the Conference opened, the countries in attendance made further attempts to persuade Japan to participate in the Conference. Japan again declined.

On November 24, 1937 the Conference adopted a declaration, urging that "hostilities be suspended and resort be had to peaceful processes."

Japan scorned the Conference and ignored the recommendation

It became clear that, unless this course of affairs in the Far East was halted, the Pacific area was doomed to experience the same horrors which have devastated Europe.

Therefore, in this year of 1941, in an endeavor to end this process by peaceful means while there seemed still to be a chance, the United States entered into discussions with Japan.

For nine months these conversations were carried on, for the purpose of arriving at some understanding acceptable to both countries.

Throughout all of these conversations, this Government took into account not only the legitimate interests of the United States but also those of Japan and other countries. When questions relating to the legitimate rights and interests of other countries came up, this Government kept in appropriate contact with the representatives of those countries.

In the course of these negotiations, the United States steadfastly advocated certain basic principles which should govern international relations. These were:

The principle of inviolability of territorial integrity and sovereignty of all nations.

The principle of non-interference in the internal affairs of other countries.

The principle of equality — including equality of commercial opportunity and treatment.

The principle of reliance upon international cooperation and conciliation for the prevention, and pacific settlement, of controversies.

The Japanese Government, it is true, repeatedly offered qualified statements of peaceful intention. But it became clear, as each proposal was explored, that Japan did not intend to modify in any way her greedy designs upon the whole Pacific world. Although she continually maintained that she was promoting only the peace and greater prosperity of East Asia, she continued her brutal assault upon the Chinese people

Nor did Japan show any inclination to renounce her unholy alliance with Hitlerism.

In July of this year the Japanese Government connived with Hitler to force from the Vichy Government of France permission to place

Japanese armed forces in southern Indo-China; and began sending her troops and equipment into that area.

The conversations between this Government and the Japanese Government were thereupon suspended.

But during the following month, at the urgent and insistent request of the Japanese Government, which again made emphatic profession of peaceful intent, the conversations were resumed.

At that time the Japanese Government made the suggestion that the responsible heads of the Japanese Government and of the Government of the United States meet personally to discuss means for bringing about an adjustment of relations between the two countries. I should have been happy to travel thousands of miles to meet the Premier of Japan for that purpose. But I felt it desirable, before so doing, to obtain some assurance that there could be some agreement on basic principles. This Government tried hard — but without success — to obtain such assurance from the Japanese Government.

The various proposals of the Japanese Government and the attitude taken by this Government are set forth in a document which the Secretary of State handed to the Japanese Ambassador on October 2, 1941 (see Annex 10).[1]

Thereafter, several formulas were offered and discussed. But the Japanese Government continued upon its course of war and conquest.

Finally, on November 20, 1941, the Japanese Government presented a new and narrow proposal (see Annex 11)[2] which called for supplying by the United States to Japan of as much oil as Japan might require, for suspension of freezing measures, and for discontinuance by the United States of aid to China. It contained however no provision for abandonment by Japan of her war-like operations or aims.

Such a proposal obviously offered no basis for a peaceful settlement or even for a temporary adjustment. The American Government, in order to clarify the issues, presented to the Japanese Government on November 26, a clear-cut plan for a broad but simple settlement. (See Annex 12.)[3]

The outline of the proposed plan for agreement between the United States and Japan was divided into two parts:

In section one there was outlined a mutual declaration of policy containing affirmations that the national policies of the two countries were directed toward peace throughout the Pacific area, that the two countries had no territorial designs or aggressive intentions in that area, and that they would give active support to certain fundamental principles of

[1] See p. 513.   [2] See p. 518.   [3] See p. 519.

peace upon which their relations with each other and all other nations
would be based. There was provision for mutual pledges to support and
apply in their economic relations with each other and with other nations
and peoples liberal economic principles, which were enumerated, based
upon the general principle of equality of commercial opportunity and
treatment.

In section two there were outlined proposed steps to be taken by the
two Governments. These steps envisaged a situation in which there
would be no Japanese or other foreign armed forces in French Indo-
China or in China. Mutual commitments were suggested along lines as
follows: (a) to endeavor to conclude a multilateral non-aggression pact
among the governments principally concerned in the Pacific area; (b) to
endeavor to conclude among the principally interested governments an
agreement to respect the territorial integrity of Indo-China and not to
seek or accept preferential economic treatment therein; (c) not to support
any government in China other than the National Government of the
Republic of China with capital temporarily at Chungking; (d) to relinquish extraterritorial and related rights in China and to endeavor to
obtain the agreement of other governments now possessing such rights
to give up those rights; (e) to negotiate a trade agreement based upon
reciprocal most-favored-nation treatment; (f) to remove freezing
restrictions imposed by each country on the funds of the other; (g) to
agree upon a plan for the stabilization of the dollar-yen rate; (h) to agree
that no agreement which either had concluded with any third power or
powers shall be interpreted by it in a way to conflict with the fundamental purpose of this agreement; and (i) to use their influence to cause
other governments to adhere to the basic political and economic principles provided for in this suggested agreement.

In the midst of these conversations, we learned that new contingents
of Japanese armed forces and new masses of equipment were moving
into Indo-China. Toward the end of November these movements were
intensified. During the first week of December new movements of
Japanese forces made it clear that, under cover of the negotiations
attacks on unspecified objectives were being prepared.

I promptly asked the Japanese Government for a frank statement of
the reasons for increasing its forces in Indo-China. (See Annex 13.)
I was given an evasive and specious reply (see Annex 14.) [2] Simultaneously, the Japanese operations went forward with increased tempo

We did not know then, as we know now, that they had ordered and
were even then carrying out their plan for a treacherous attack upon us

[1] See p. 523.   [2] See p. 524.

I was determined, however, to exhaust every conceivable effort for peace. With this in mind, on the evening of December sixth last, I addressed a personal message to the Emperor of Japan. (See Annex 15.) [1]

To this Government's proposal of November twenty-sixth the Japanese Government made no reply until December seventh. On that day the Japanese Ambassador here and the Special Representative whom the Japanese Government had sent to the United States to assist in peaceful negotiations, delivered a lengthy document to our Secretary of State, one hour after the Japanese had launched a vicious attack upon American territory and American citizens in the Pacific.

That document (see Annex 16) [2] was a few minutes after its receipt aptly characterized by the Secretary of State as follows:

"I must say that in all my conversations with you [the Japanese Ambassador] during the last nine months I have never uttered one word of untruth. This is borne out absolutely by the record. In all my fifty years of public service I have never seen a document that was more crowded with infamous falsehoods and distortions — infamous falsehoods and distortions on a scale so huge that I never imagined until today that any government on this planet was capable of uttering them."

I concur emphatically in every word of that statement.

For the record of history, it is essential in reading this part of my Message always to bear in mind that the actual air and submarine attack on the Hawaiian Islands commenced on Sunday, December 7, at 1 : 20 P.M., Washington time — 7 : 50 A.M.,[3] Honolulu time of same day — Monday, December 8, 3 : 20 A.M., Tokyo time.

To my message of December 6 (9 P.M. Washington time — December 7, 11 A.M., Tokyo time) to the Emperor of Japan, invoking his cooperation with me in further effort to preserve peace, there has finally come to me on December 10 (6 : 23 A.M., Washington time — December 10, 8 : 23 P.M., Tokyo time) a reply, conveyed in a telegraphic report by the American Ambassador at Tokyo dated December 8, 1 P.M. (December 7, 11 P.M., Washington time).

The Ambassador reported that at 7 o'clock on the morning of the eighth (December 7, 5 P.M., Washington time) the Japanese Minister for Foreign Affairs asked him to call at his official residence; that the Foreign Minister handed the Ambassador a memorandum dated December 8 (December 7, Washington time) the text of which had been transmitted to the Japanese Ambassador in Washington to be presented to

[1] See p. 525.
[2] See p. 527.
[3] In the Roberts Commission report the time is given as 7 : 55 A.M. Honolulu time.

the American Government (this was the memorandum which was delivered by the Japanese Ambassador to the Secretary of State at 2 : 20 P.M. on Sunday, December 7 — Monday, December 8, 4 : 20 A.M., Tokyo time); that the Foreign Minister had been in touch with the Emperor; and that the Emperor desired that the memorandum be regarded as the Emperor's reply to my message.

Further, the Ambassador reports, the Foreign Minister made an oral statement. Textually, the oral statement began, "His Majesty has expressed his gratefulness and appreciation for the cordial message of the President." The message further continued to the effect that, in regard to our inquiries on the subject of increase of Japanese forces in French Indo-China, His Majesty had commanded his Government to state its views to the American Government. The message concluded, textually, with the statement:

"Establishment of peace in the Pacific, and consequently of the world, has been the cherished desire of His Majesty for the realization of which he has hitherto made his Government to continue its earnest endeavors. His Majesty trusts that the President is fully aware of this fact."

Japan's real reply, however, made by Japan's warlords and evidently formulated many days before, took the form of the attack which had already been made without warning upon our territories at various points in the Pacific.

There is the record, for all history to read in amazement, in sorrow, in horror, and in disgust!

We are now at war. We are fighting in self-defense. We are fighting in defense of our national existence, of our right to be secure, of our right to enjoy the blessings of peace. We are fighting in defense of principles of law and order and justice, against an effort of unprecedented ferocity to overthrow those principles and to impose upon humanity a regime of ruthless domination by unrestricted and arbitrary force.

Other countries, too — a host of them — have declared war on Japan. Some of them were first attacked by Japan, as we have been. China has already been valiantly resisting Japan in an undeclared war forced upon her by Japan. After four and one-half years of stubborn resistance, the Chinese now and henceforth will fight with renewed confidence and confirmed assurance of victory.

All members of the great British Commonwealth, themselves fighting heroically on many fronts against Germany and her Allies, have joined with us in the Battle of the Pacific as we have joined with them in the Battle of the Atlantic.

All but three of the governments of nations overrun by German armies ave declared war on Japan. The other three are severing relations.

In our own hemisphere many of our sister republics have declared war n Japan and the others have given firm expression of their solidarity vith the United States.

The following are the countries which have to date declared war gainst Japan: Australia, Canada, China, Costa Rica, Cuba, Dominican Republic, Guatemala, Haiti, Honduras, the Netherlands, Nicaragua, Tew Zealand, Panama, El Salvador, South Africa, United Kingdom, Poland.

These and other peace-loving countries will be fighting as are we, rst, to put an end to Japan's program of aggression and, second, to lake good the right of nations and of mankind to live in peace under onditions of security and justice.

The people of this country are totally united in their determination to onsecrate our national strength and manpower to bring conclusively to n end the pestilence of aggression and force which has long menaced the orld and which now has struck deliberately and directly at the safety f the United States.

B. Statements of Japanese Policy

[For earlier pronouncements of Japanese foreign policy, see *Documents, I, 1938–*, p. 227; *II, 1939–40,*p. 273; *III, 1940–41,* p. 249.]

1) *Statement on "The World's Grave State of Emergency" by the Japanese Foreign Minister (Matsuoka), July 2, 1941* [1]

A "conference in the Imperial presence" was held July 2, 1941, being attended y the premier, the foreign minister, the home, finance, war and navy ministers, ie presidents of the Planning Board and Privy Council, the chiefs and vice-iefs of the army and navy general staffs. The conference determined an "im-ortant national policy" which is the subject of this statement.

Such conferences are infrequent in Japanese affairs and mark important turns f events. At the outbreak of the Sino-Japanese war one was held September 17 nd 20, 1894; for discussion of peace terms, January 27, 1895; to determine olicy toward Russia, June 23, 1903; on declaration of war, February 4, 1904; 1 peace terms, August 28, 1905; relations with Germany, August 15, 1914; eclaration of war on Germany, August 23, 1914; basic policy toward China, anuary 11, 1938; on the Three-Power Pact, September 19, 1940; recognition of Tang Ching-wei, November 13, 1940.

As announced by the Government today, an important national olicy has been decided upon at a council held in the Imperial presence. t goes without saying that the situation arising from the German-

Soviet War cannot be dealt with on the basis of the mere fact that a wa
has broken out between Germany and the Soviet Union. We, therefore
intend to keep a close watch over the development of the situation witl
the utmost caution and dependable preparedness as well as with a firn
determination, paying a constant attention not only to the development
directly attendant upon the war but also to the trend of individua
powers and the mutual relations among them in the light of the worl
situation in general.

I feel that a really grave state of super-emergency is developing befor
our eyes the world over as well as in East Asia, with the affairs of whicl
our nation is directly concerned. The more serious the situation, th
more calm and composed must our nation be, and with a nationwid
unity we must, in response to the august will of His Imperial Majesty
endeavor not to make even the slightest deviation from the path alon,
which our nation is to march forward.

(2) *Address of the Japanese Premier (Konoe) at the Organization c the Greater Japan and Asia Development League, July 6, 1941*

I have been deeply moved by this occasion on which you have gathere
to form a united federation through which to assist the East Asiati
movement. The current uncertain international situation is taking suc
turns that it may affect the progress of our country. This has added t
the need for the concentration of all the peoples of the Far East on th
movement to further the progress and objectives of their respectiv
countries. The spirit of Universal Brotherhood has been passed dow
to us through the ages. It aims at the security and peaceful cooperatio
of all peoples. The propagation of this spirit in the Far East has cause
us to call the Orient an East Asia Mutual Co-prosperity Sphere. Th
creation of such a sphere is the responsibility of our country, so that w
must cooperate and concentrate our undivided efforts on its creatior
I believe that the work undertaken by our nation during the past tw
thousand-odd years was in preparation for this great task.

The East Asia Development Federation has been created in order t
place the movement under unified control and guidance. By forgettir
your personal aims and uniting your efforts, all you members of Ea
Asia development organizations can serve the State and the Far Ea
toward the realization of their objectives. Our movement must nc
stop at the creation of a mutual co-prosperity sphere in East Asia alon
We must prosecute the movement for all time and so realize peace an

[1] *The Japan Weekly Chronicle*, July 10, 1941, p. 50.

ecurity for the whole world which is now being torn by a violent and
ll-sweeping conflagration. The movement is based on the spirit of the
mperial Way. In short, the basic objective for which the movement is
eing conducted is for assistance to the Throne.

I believe that this epoch-making creation of the federation, which will
nfluence the entire world, is being watched by every country in the
world. It is my sincere desire and hope that all members of this federa-
ion will discipline yourselves and strive to achieve the objective for
which it is being created.

On September 2, a delegation from the Greater Japan and Asia Development
League submitted to Prince Konoe, President of the League, the following pro-
ram: [1]
1. Adherence to the guiding spirit of Italian-German-Japanese Axis diplomacy;
2. Firm enforcement of the "new order" in "greater East Asia";
3. Intensified attack on all aid to Generalissimo Chiang Kai-shek;
4. Invocation of the right of self-defense in Japan's territorial waters.
Prince Konoe replied as follows:
"I fully understand the purpose of the recommendations. I shall consult
ne various quarters concerned in regard to them and make them contribute to
ne execution of the country's policies."

3) *Statement of the Japanese Premier* (*General Tojo*), *October 18, 1941* [2]

On October 16 the Konoe Cabinet resigned *en bloc*. On October 17, General
ideki Tojo was appointed Premier and Mr. Shigenori Togo became Foreign
linister. General Tojo's background and record placed him among those
voring a policy of aggressive continental expansion. He had ardently wel-
med the Three-Power Pact of September 27, 1941. Contrary to precedent,
ne new Premier, who had just been elevated to the rank of general, remained in
ctive service. Hardly less unusual and significant was his action in taking the
ortfolios of War and Home Affairs. Mr. Togo was Ambassador to Moscow,
938–40, and Ambassador to Berlin, 1937–38.

Having suddenly received the Imperial command in the face of an
nprecedentedly grave situation, I am filled with profound awe and
motion. I am convinced we can break through the current difficulties
nly by means of iron will and precise performance of duty under the
ngust virtue of His Majesty.
I am firmly determined to dispose of national affairs in this conviction
nd to take a courageous lead with unremitting spirit, thereby assisting
ne Imperial policies. The national policy calls for a successful settle-

[1] Wireless dispatch of Otto D. Tolischus, *New York Times*, September 3, 1941.
[2] Condensation for the press of a statement broadcast to the nation. Wireless dis-
atch, *New York Times*, October 19, 1941.

ment of the China incident and the establishment of the Greater Eas
Asia co-prosperity sphere as a contribution toward world peace.

If the whole country goes forward in unity and with firm conviction
am certain that these aims will be attained. Given the trust and cooper
ation of the entire nation I hope to promote the prosperity and welfare (
the nation and glorify the empire's 3,000-year history.

(4) *Address of the Japanese Premier (Tojo) before the Imperi«
Rule Assistance Association and the Greater Japan and Asi
Development League, October 30, 1941* [1]

[Summary]

Japan unquestionably has come to a crossroads in the history of th
modern empire. The question is whether the empire shall continue t
expand and develop or shall drift backward toward a status as a second
rate power. The Government is determined there shall be no retrea

In the field of domestic policy the Government's determination is t
create a total defense State. The Imperial Rule Assistance Associatio
must be one of the chief pillars supporting that State as a liaison agen
between the Government, the Throne and the people. Financial, ecc
nomic and military preparedness must be completed at once to cop
with the "unprecedented crisis" confronting the nation.

The Government intends to take the people fully into its confidenc
and will be as ready to listen to the viewpoint of public organizatior
as it is to expound its own viewpoint.

The creation of the proposed "greater East Asia co-prosperity sphere
is the hub around which Japanese policy revolves. The plan is for
union of East Asian nations on a basis of "independence, equality an
cooperation," so that the land of East Asia may be developed for th
welfare of their own peoples.

"At a time when the world is in an upheaval that seems to have n
end," the Premier said, "and when much of mankind is engaged in
most ruthless struggle, the Japanese Government fully appreciates i«
role in history and is ready to shoulder the task of establishing the pr«
jected greater East Asia co-prosperity sphere on a basis of lofty idea.
that will enable all nations to have their proper place in a movemer
designed to establish the solidarity of all races."

Without mentioning Britain or the United States the Premier said th
road of realization of Japan's ideal "is not strewn with roses and, as
matter of fact we now are being confronted with pressure and obstacl«
thrown in our way by countries of a hostile nature."

[1] United Press dispatch, *New York Times*, October 31, 1941.

"And it is as clear as the sun that we will be faced with a multitude of ifficulties in the future," he added. "Accordingly, we must first of all nite firmly together with an iron resolve to overcome any and all ifficulties that may be in our way. At the same time we must, with the ollaboration of all other East Asian nations, ward off any situation that night lead to new horrors similar to the present world catastrophe."

5) *Address of the Japanese Foreign Minister (Togo) to the Diet, November 17, 1941* [1]

With heavy responsibilities for the conduct of foreign affairs having nexpectedly devolved upon me, it is a great pleasure for me to avail yself of this opportunity today of speaking on the foreign policy of the nperial Government.

Japan, engaged for the past four years in military operations for the onstruction of a new order in East Asia, is now marching forward to irmount current difficulties with the unity of the entire nation. First i all, I wish good fortune and success to officers and men of our gallant ghting services who are distinguishing themselves on the front under ie august virtue of His Imperial Majesty, paying at the same time my umble and sincere tribute to the honored spirits of those who have .llen.

It needs no reiteration that the fundamental principle of Japan's reign policy aims at establishment of peace in East Asia based on stice, thereby contributing toward promotion of the general welfare of .ankind. It is by nothing other than the fruit of constant efforts exerted the espousal of this great principle that our country has witnessed ie unceasing development of her national fortune since the Meiji estoration.

It may be recalled that in the past seventy-odd years Japan has, on .ore than one occasion, successfully overcome national crises. Espe- ally noteworthy is the Russian-Japanese War, in which Japan staked r national existence in order to eliminate an obstacle to the peace of .ast Asia. She has since been advancing her position as a stabilizing rce in East Asia and is now endeavoring with unflinching courage to complish the great task of inaugurating a new order in East Asia on e basis of justice as a contribution toward the peace of the world.

Fortunately, Germany and Italy having similar views with Japan, ie Three-Power Pact [2] was brought into being. In little more than a ar of its existence, as is well known, the pact has made, as intended, a

---

[1] Associated Press dispatch, *New York Times*, November 17, 1941.
[2] *Documents, III, 1940–41*, p. 304.

great contribution toward the construction of a new order in East Asi
and Europe as well as toward the prevention of the spread of war.

The Empire of Manchukuo has become increasingly strong in he
foundation since her establishment. No less than thirteen countrie
have already recognized Manchukuo, and her international statu
together with her national prosperity, is being enhanced.

In China, Japan is conducting military operations to subjugate th
Chungking regime. The basic policy of Japan toward the China affa
consists in establishing cooperation between Japan and China, thereb
securing the stability of East Asia and the advancement of commc
prosperity in this region.

A basic treaty [has been entered into] regulating relations betwee
Japan and the national government [the Wang Ching-Wei pupp
regime] of China.[1] It is the determination of the Imperial Governmer
to extend their cooperation toward further strengthening of the nation:
government of China.

Along with successful conclusion of the China affair, Japan takes
great interest in the region of the north, and also in the South Sea
Following the outbreak of the European war Japan has exerted ever
effort to prevent the conflict from spreading to the east from the stanc
point of maintaining the peace of East Asia in general.

The Japanese-Soviet neutrality pact, concluded in April this year,[2]
also intended to secure safety in the north in conformity with the sai
policy. Although hostilities subsequently broke out between German
and the Soviet Union, our Government have steadfastly maintaine
this policy of preserving security in the north.

It is, in a word, Japan's determination to prevent by all means nc
only the causation of factors likely to disturb peace in the north, but al:
the development of such a situation as will menace the rights an
interests of Japan.

As regards the South Seas region, the Imperial Government succes
fully mediated in the settlement of a border dispute between Thailan
and French Indo-China, and also established close political and ec
nomic relations with French Indo-China. They further concluded wit
France a protocol for the joint defense of French Indo-China [3] to me
the international situation confronting the latter when it began
threaten seriously the security of French Indo-China and consequent
the tranquillity of East Asia and the security of Japan.

[1] *Documents, III, 1940–41*, p. 282.
[2] *Ibid.*, p. 291.
[3] See p. 494.

They have dispatched Mr. Yoshizawa as special Ambassador to rench Indo-China to draw still closer the bonds of friendship between apan and that country. They have also strengthened economic relations ith Thailand and are endeavoring to promote cooperation between the vo countries by exchanging Ambassadors.

It is extremely deplorable, however, that malicious propaganda should e let loose by some third powers representing Japan as harboring ggressive designs toward those regions. I have not the slightest doubt at the peoples of East Asia, understanding the real intentions of apan, will cooperate with our country for the establishment of a new der in East Asia.

Japan is thus concentrating her sincere and utmost efforts on success- l termination of the China affair and initiation of the new order in ast Asia. But when our troops entered the southern part of French do-China this summer in accordance with the protocol for joint fense referred to above, Great Britain and the United States chose to gard it as a menace to their territories and froze Japan's assets in their untries,[1] which constitutes a measure tantamount to rupturing onomic relations.

The British Dominions and colonies have all followed suit and the etherlands East Indies, too, has joined in similar steps. Great Britain d the United States have even gone to the length of establishing circling positions against Japan by inducing Australia, the Netherlands ast Indies and the Chungking regime to join in.

The international situation confronting Japan has thus become creasingly tense day after day, and pressure of the kind above referred from Great Britain and the United States toward our country consti- tes a really serious question, affecting as it deeply does the very istence of our empire.

In this connection I should like to call the attention of every one here d abroad to the fact that despite such developments the Imperial overnment, prompted by the high motive to preserve peace in the rld and particularly in the Pacific, and also to avert the worst eventu- ty, have hitherto devoted their utmost efforts in order to overcome e difficult situation.

Since the outbreak of the China affair Japanese-American relations ve progressively deteriorated, steadily gathering force, so that if they re left to drift without timely check there was no knowing whether the uation would not ultimately end in catastrophe.

Should such an eventuality occur it would entail great suffering

[1] See p. 499.

not only in countries in the Pacific basin, but on all of mankin as well.

Solicitous for peace as ever, the Japanese Government have, sine April last, carried on conversations with the Government of the Unite States, with a view to bringing about a fundamental adjustment Japanese-American relations. The former Cabinet endeavored earnest to reach a successful conclusion of negotiations, in view particularly the tension in the situation which had been accentuated since summe this year, but agreement of views was not reached between the tw countries.

The present Cabinet, in order to avert an international crisis ar preserve the peace of the Pacific, decided also to continue negotiation which are still in progress. I regret to say that I have not the liberty revealing, at this juncture, the details of the negotiations.

But I think an amicable conclusion is by no means impossible if th Government of the United States are, on the one hand, as genuine solicitous for world peace as are the Imperial Government, and on th other understand Japan's natural requirements and her position in Ea Asia and consider the situation as it exists there in the light of realiti

Moreover, the views of the two countries have generally been ma clear through conversations which have now lasted more than six month and consequently I believe it must be evident to the United Stat Government that, viewed even from the technical angle, there is necessity of spending much time on negotiations hereafter.

Such being the circumstances, the Japanese Government are bendi their best efforts to a successful conclusion of the negotiations, but the is naturally a limit to our conciliatory attitude. Should an occasion ar such as might menace the very existence of the empire or compromi the prestige of Japan as a great power, it goes without saying that Jap must face it with a firm and resolute attitude.

For my part, I am taking charge of negotiations with a firm resol regarding this point.

Japan is now confronted with an unprecedentedly difficult situati and it is necessary that the entire nation should unite and join forces overcome it. National defense and diplomacy are inseparable wh internal politics and external policy are a counterpart of each oth

At no time is the need for mobilization of the nation's total strengt with the Government and the people uniting, felt more acutely than the present juncture. In concluding the frank statement of my vie and opinions, I earnestly hope that the 100,000,000 of my fellow-countr men will extend their full support and cooperation.

6) *Statement of the Japanese Premier (Tojo), November 29, 1941* [1]

[Excerpt]

Chiang Kai-shek is dancing to the tune of American and British communism because the United States and Britain desire to fish in troubled waters, throwing the Asiatic peoples against each other.

This is the stock in trade of Britain and the United States and therefore we must purge this sort of action with a vengeance.

There are many countries engaged in actions hostile toward our co-rosperity sphere and they are trying to throw obstacles in our path and exploit Asia at the expense of the Asiatic peoples and thereby satisfy their greed for possessions.

. . . .

Nothing can be permitted to interfere with this sphere, because this sphere was decreed by Providence.

You are witnessing communism's cruelties and dastardly destruction. You are trying your best to eliminate British and other Western exploitations.

7) *Statement of the Japanese Foreign Minister (Togo), December 1, 1941* [2]

The world is confronted with unprecedented disturbances. In Greater East Asia, however, close relations of Japan, Manchoukuo and China must be further cemented. Japan, Manchoukuo and China must go forward toward the construction of a new order in East Asia on the basis of their co-existence and co-prosperity.

In our negotiations with the United States we have consistently upheld this principle. However, the United States does not understand the real situation in East Asia. It is trying forcibly to apply to East Asiatic countries fantastic principles and rules not adapted to the actual situation in the world and thereby tending to obstruct the construction of the new order. This is extremely regrettable.

---

[1] United Press version, *New York Times*, November 30, 1941, p. 1. The occasion of the statement was the anniversary of the signing of the Japan-Manchoukuo-Wang agreement, November 30, 1940 (*Documents, III, 1940–41*, p. 282).

[2] Version from special dispatch, *New York Times*, December 1, 1941, p. 1.

C. The Wang Ching-wei Regime at Nanking

[See *Documents, II, 1939–40*, p. 298–304; *III, 1940–41*, p. 282–88.]

(1) *Joint Statement of the Japanese Premier (Konoe) and the Pres dent of the Nanking Government (Wang Ching-wei), June 2. 1941* [1]

With a view to speedily settling the present Affair and, with this as turning point, to establishing a permanent relationship between Japa and China and marching forward toward the common goal of co-existen and co-prosperity as well as the reconstruction of East Asia, we respe tively made declarations some time ago concerning the establishment the new order in East Asia consisting of good neighborly and amicab relations, a common defense against communism and economic cooper tion. The purposes of the Basic Treaty [2] concluded between Japa and China on November 30, last year, and the Declaration of Japa Manchoukuo and China issued on the same day are not other tha this.

The significance of the establishment of the new order in East As lies in the eradication of the evils of aggression and of communism exis ing in East Asia and the establishment of States characterized by mutu cooperation, co-existence and co-prosperity on the basis of morality i herent in East Asia. There seem to be not a few among the people China who, though being desirous of the reconstruction of East As through the collaboration of Japan and China, lack confidence in t actual realization of such an undertaking and persist in an attitude hesitation and irresolution. But, the great task of reconstructing Ea Asia can only be accomplished by revealing as much as possible, ev at the present stage, the first light of the dawn of this new era, there winning the confidence of the majority of the people, and also by res lutely striving for the realization of general peace.

As the result of our conversation, the Governments of Japan and Chi have pledged their word to put forth increasing efforts toward the abov mentioned common goal. The National Government of China w endeavor to make their people understand that the collaboration l tween Japan and China and the reconstruction of East Asia are t common missions of the peoples of our two countries, by presenti concrete facts regarding the cooperation of Japan and China in politic military, economic and cultural spheres; and the Japanese Governme

---

[1] *Tokyo Gazette*, V, p. 77. Made public by the Japanese Board of Information.
[2] *Documents, III, 1940–41*, p. 282.

lso will exert themselves, by extending increasing assistance therefor,
o enable the National Government fully to demonstrate their inde-
endent and free authority and power, so that they may share the
esponsibility of constructing the new order of East Asia.

The 23rd of June, the 16th year of Showa (1941)

FUMIMARO KONOE
WANG CHING-WEI

2) *Statement of the Japanese President of the Board of Information
(Ito) on Recognition of the Nanking "Government of China"
by Certain States, July 1, 1941* [1]

It is a source of profound gratification for the Japanese Government
hat the Governments of Germany, Italy, Rumania, Slovakia and
roatia have now accorded recognition to the National Government of
he Republic of China. Since their establishment on March 30 of last
ear, the new National Government have steadily grown in strength,
nd through the Basic Treaty [2] concluded between Japan and China on
ovember 30 of last year, Japan took the initiative in recognizing that
overnment and has since been extending the greatest possible assist-
nce to that Government which are endeavoring to forge ahead toward
he objective of co-existence, co-prosperity and reconstruction of East
sia.

The fact that the German, Italian, Rumanian, Slovakian and Croatian
overnments have recognized the National Government is a telling
low to those who, still failing to be awakened to the great ideal of the
stablishment of a new order in East Asia, persist in their foolish efforts
o oppose Japan. We are convinced, without the slightest doubt, that,
ith this action of recognition as a turning point, a great stride will be
ken toward the establishment of a new world order.

D. French Indo-China

[See *Documents, III, 1940-41*, p. 274-78.]

By agreement of September 22, 1940 between French and Japanese authorities
a the spot, the French agreed to accord to the Japanese Army and Navy special
cilities which were necessary for the execution of the latter's military opera-
ons.[3] In obtaining French consent to this arrangement, advantage had been

[1] *Tokyo Gazette*, V, p. 108. Spain and Bulgaria subsequently recognized the Wang
vernment.
[2] *Documents, III, 1940-41*, p. 282.
[3] *Ibid.*, p. 277.

taken of the European situation, notably the military defeat of France, whic!
made it impossible for that country to offer any substantial resistance to Japan'
demands.

That Japan had other than purely military objectives in view became clea
with the signing on May 6, 1941 of an economic agreement between Japan an
French Indo-China, ratifications of which were exchanged on July 5. This agree
ment, while not including all of Japan's original demands, went a long wa;
toward incorporating French Indo-China economically in Japan's Greater Ea:
Asia scheme.[1] Appearing as an annex to this agreement was an agreement be
tween the Yokohama Specie Bank and the Banque de l'Indo-Chine providin
for certain banking arrangements to facilitate the general purposes of th
economic agreement.[2]

The German attack upon the Soviet Union on June 22, 1941 was apparentl
an important development in the world situation from the point of view of th
Japanese leaders. A council was "held in the Imperial presence"[3] on July 2 t
consider the new situation and a decision was apparently taken to complete th
military occupation of French Indo-China in line with what appears to hav
been the Japanese considered policy of southward expansion. The first ove.
tures to Vichy were made on July 16, according to a Rome report. The Toky
press featured charges of a de Gaullist plot to take over the colony with Britis
and Chinese help, for which the Cabinet spokesman, however, admitted the:
was no confirmation. The Vichy Government offered no resistance, and a
agreement in principle was announced on July 23. Japanese warships appeare
off Saigon, and General Sumita arrived to take command. On July 29 a protoc
was signed at Vichy.[4]

(1) Statement by the Acting Secretary of State (Welles), July 24, 1941

It will be recalled that in 1940 the Japanese Government gave expre
sion on several occasions to its desire that conditions of disturban
should not spread to the region of the Pacific, with special references
the Netherlands East Indies and French Indo-China. This desire w:
expressly concurred in by many other governments, including the Go
ernment of the United States. In statements by this Government,
was made clear that any alteration in the existing status of such are.
by other than peaceful processes could not but be prejudicial to t
security and peace of the entire Pacific area and that this conclusion w.
based on a doctrine which has universal application.

On September 23, 1940, referring to the events then rapidly happenii
in the Indo-China situation, the Secretary of State stated [5] that

[1] For discussion of terms, see *Far Eastern Survey*, X, June 2, 1941, p. 116.

[2] *The Oriental Economist*, VIII, p. 395.

[3] See p. 481.

[4] Based on account in *Far Eastern Survey*, X, August 11, 1941, p. 169.

[5] Department of State, *Bulletin*, V, p. 71; the statement was made in response
inquiries by press correspondents.

[6] *Documents, III, 1940–41*, p. 277.

eemed obvious that the existing situation was being upset and that the
hanges were being achieved under duress. Present developments relat-
ng to Indo-China provide clear indication that further changes are
ow being effected under duress.

The present unfortunate situation in which the French Government
f Vichy and the French Government of Indo-China find themselves is,
f course, well known. It is only too clear that they are in no position
o resist the pressure exercised upon them.

There is no doubt as to the attitude of the Government and people
f the United States toward acts of aggression carried out by use
r threat of armed force. That attitude has been made abundantly
lear.

By the course which it has followed and is following in regard to
ndo-China, the Japanese Government is giving clear indication that it
: determined to pursue an objective of expansion by force or threat of
orce.

There is not apparent to the Government of the United States any
alid ground upon which the Japanese Government would be warranted
a occupying Indo-China or establishing bases in that area as measures
f self-defense.

There is not the slightest ground for belief on the part of even the
ost credulous that the Governments of the United States, of Great
ritain, or of the Netherlands have any territorial ambitions in Indo-
hina or have been planning any moves which could have been regarded
s threats to Japan. This Government can, therefore, only conclude
at the action of Japan is undertaken because of the estimated value
Japan of bases in that region primarily for purposes of further and
ore obvious movements of conquest in adjacent areas.

In the light of previous developments, steps such as are now being
ken by the Government of Japan endanger the peaceful use by peace-
l nations of the Pacific. They tend to jeopardize the procurement by
e United States of essential materials such as tin and rubber which are
cessary for the normal economy of this country and the consummation
our defense program. The purchase of tin, rubber, oil, or other raw
aterials in the Pacific area on equal terms with other nations requiring
ese materials has never been denied to Japan. The steps which the
panese Government has taken also endanger the safety of other areas
the Pacific, including the Philippine Islands.

The Government and people of this country fully realize that such
velopments bear directly upon the vital problem of our national
curity.

(2) *Protocol between Japan and France regarding the Joint Defens*
of French Indo-China, Vichy, July 29, 1941 [1]

[Translation]

The Imperial Japanese Government and the French Government

Taking into consideration the present international situation;

Recognizing in consequence that should the security of French Indo-
China be menaced, Japan would have reason to consider the genera
tranquillity in East Asia and its own security endangered;

Renewing on this occasion the engagements undertaken, on the par
of Japan to respect the rights and interests of France in East Asia, i
particular, the territorial integrity of French Indo-China, and th
sovereign rights of France in all parts of the Union of Indo-China, an
on the part of France to conclude in regard to Indo-China no agreemen
or understanding with a third power which envisages political, economic
or military cooperation of a character directly or indirectly opposed t
Japan;

Have agreed upon the following dispositions:

1. The two Governments promise to cooperate in military matters fo
the defense of French Indo-China.

2. The measures to be taken for the purposes of the aforesaid cooper
ation shall constitute the object of special arrangements.

3. The foregoing dispositions shall remain in effect only so long as th
circumstances motivating their adoption continue to exist.

In witness whereof the undersigned, duly authorized by their respectiv
Governments, have signed the present protocol, which enters into effec
from this day, and have affixed their seals thereto.

Executed in duplicate, in the Japanese and French languages, a
Vichy, July 29 of the 16th year of Showa, corresponding to July 29, 194

SOTOMATSU KATO   [SEAL]

F. DARLAN   [SEAL]

(a) *Statement of the Japanese Foreign Office, July 26, 1941* [2]

French Indo-China and Japan have from olden times been closely bound
cultural, historical and economic relations. Prior to the closing of Japan
foreign intercourse by the Tokugawa Shogunate, there were two Japanese tow
each in Annam and Cambodia and very prosperous trade was carried on wi
Japan.

[1] Department of State, *Bulletin*, V, p. 286. The protocol was stated to form "t
political basis of measures of a technical character which will be taken." Milita
arrangements made at the same time were not published.

[2] Associated Press text, *New York Times*, July 27, 1941, p. 12.

However, these relations were interrupted when the Shogunate prohibited the
panese from going abroad. In recent times Indo-China has re-established her
l relations with Japan in a new sense as a source of materials for the industries
Japan.
Relations of late steadily have become closer and more cordial, with Indo-
iina constituting an important link in the sphere of common prosperity in
reater East Asia which Japan is endeavoring to establish.
Fully appreciating such close relationship, France definitely recognized the
e-eminent position of Japan in Indo-China through an exchange of documents
tween Yosuke Matsuoka [former Foreign Minister] and Charles Arsène Henry
rench Ambassador to Tokyo] in August of last year.[1]
Then, in May this year, she concluded with Japan the economic agreement [2]
d signed the protocol concerning political understanding, striving thereby to
lidify their good neighborly and amicable relations between Japan and Indo-
iina. France has thus consistently continued her friendly cooperation with
pan.
However, internal conditions in Indo-China recently have been greatly af-
ted by changes of the situations in Europe and East Asia, with increasing
ns that even the security of Indo-China would be threatened if such develop-
nts were left alone.
If, by any chance, the situation so developed that Indo-China was thrown
o a chaotic condition, it could not in self-defense be overlooked by Japan,
t to mention France herself.
It has been keenly felt, therefore, by both Japan and France that they are
und together by a very close relationship as well as common interest with
;ard to the position of Indo-China.
From such a point of view the Government carried on negotiations through
ibassador Kato at Vichy. These negotiations progressed smoothly, in an ex-
mely friendly atmosphere, and on July 21 a complete agreement of views was
.ched concerning their joint defense of Indo-China.
Japan and France thus have been ushered into more intimate relations, with
lo-China serving as a connecting link. Needless to say this will contribute
verfully toward stabilization, co-existence and co-prosperity of Greater East
ia.
it scarcely needs to be reiterated that the Government intends strictly to
serve various existing agreements between Japan and France concerning
lo-China and to respect the territorial integrity and sovereignty of Indo-China.
Japan will put forth increasing efforts for promotion of Japanese-French
ndly relations, thereby realizing the common prosperity of the two countries.

Explanation of the Vichy Government, August 4, 1941 [3]

. In Syria we had to do with plain aggression by England without an ulti-
tum and without forewarning. We had an army which we could hope to
ply with reinforcements and materials and which, in fact, resisted thirty-one
's.

[1] Documents, III, 1940–41, p. 274.
[2] Far Eastern Survey, X, June 2, 1941, p. 116.
[3] Associated Press version, New York Times, August 5, 1941, p. 1.

2. In Indo-China on August 30, 1940, we had to recognize the prepondera॑ position of Japan in the Far East and on that account gave it military faciliti॑ America did not react at that moment.

3. Now Japan tells us enemy [this was clarified orally to mean "Chinese," T᚞ Associated Press reported] concentrations were threatening Indo-China. At t᚞ moment Indo-China is cut off from the homeland. We could not send reinforc᚞ ments there. Hence we accepted Japanese military precautions through the Ka᚞ agreement [concluded with Japanese Ambassador Sotomatsu Kato].

This situation is not found in any other part of what is left of the Fren᚞ Empire and particularly in Africa.

(3) Statement in the House of Commons of the Secretary of State f᚞ Foreign Affairs of the United Kingdom (Eden), July 30, 1941 [1]

The occupation by Japan of bases in south Indo-China is the continu᚞ tion of a process which began last September, when the Japanese we᚞ granted certain military and air facilities in north Indo-China, ostensib᚞ for the purpose of their military campaign against China. There follow᚞ an agreement in May which assured to Japan a substantial portion᚞ the products of Indo-China, including the major part of the rubb᚞ and rice and the entire output of iron, manganese, tungsten, tin, an᚞ mony, and chrome.

Meanwhile Japan imposed her own mediation in a territorial dispu᚞ between Indo-China and Thailand, and exacted, as the price of h᚞ guarantee of the settlement, certain vague undertakings which could᚞ used as a pretext for further encroachments on the freedom of action᚞ both countries at any moment.

The ratification early in July of this settlement and of the commerc᚞ agreement between Japan and Indo-China synchronized with a rep᚞ that Japan contemplated the acquisition of naval and air bases in sou᚞ Indo-China and Thailand. His Majesty's Ambassador at Tokyo was᚞ once instructed to inquire whether there was any truth in this rep᚞ and to emphasize the seriousness of the situation which would in th᚞ case arise. Sir Robert Craigie received a categorical denial of its accura᚞ on July 5 from the Vice Minister for Foreign Affairs.

The report persisted, however, and there followed a concerted Jaǂ nese press campaign designed to show that Indo-China was threaten᚞ by Great Britain. The House will be familiar with what follow᚞ Demands, accompanied by threats, were made on the Vichy Gove᚞ ment about the middle of July and the reorganization of the Japan᚞ Cabinet merely had the effect of postponing their fulfilment.

On July 25 the new Japanese Minister for Foreign Affairs inform᚞

[1] Parliamentary Debates, House of Commons, 5th series, vol. 373, col. 1414.

is Majesty's Ambassador at Tokyo of the agreement which had been
ached and attempted to justify it on the ground of the alarming
ports which had been circulating that the existence and security of
do-China were endangered. The Minister for Foreign Affairs stated
at the agreement with the Vichy Government was strictly of a defen-
ve nature and not aimed at any third country and that the Japanese
overnment intended to observe strictly Japan's obligations regarding
spect for the territorial integrity and sovereignty of Indo-China. If
is step were misunderstood and measures were taken to oppose it, the
atter would naturally be of concern to the relations between Japan and
itain, a development which the Japanese Government ardently
shed to avoid.

Sir Robert Craigie at once pointed out in reply that the action of the
panese Government was in direct conflict with the categorical denial
iich the Vice-Minister for Foreign Affairs had given on July 5 and must
oduce the worst impression on the mind of His Majesty's Government.
hile the occupation of north Indo-China might be explained, though
t justified, as part of the military campaign against China, this reason
uld not be given in the case of southern Indo-China.

Sir Robert Craigie referred to the frequent warnings which he had
ven to Admiral Toyoda's predecessor that the occupation of naval and
: bases in Indo-China must necessarily constitute a potential threat
ainst British territory, and also to his various declarations to
r. Matsuoka that reports appearing in the Japanese press of aggressive
tentions by Great Britain, or by Great Britain and China jointly, in
gard to Indo-China or Thailand were entirely groundless. He then
mmunicated to the Minister for Foreign Affairs the categorical denial
these allegations, which I myself gave in this House on July 23, and
ited that so far as any British action was concerned our policy had been
erely to maintain trade relations with Indo-China and our normal
endly relations with Thailand.

The Japanese Government on July 26 issued an official statement
otesting the friendly nature of their agreement with the Vichy Govern-
nt. By way of comment I would only say that it is true that the
chy Government have made a virtue of necessity, but even they must
te with some disquiet the reiterated references in the official statement
the Greater East Asia sphere of co-prosperity — that latest euphe-
sm for economic exploitation in the interests of Japan. The document
o proclaims once more the intention of Japan to respect the territorial
egrity and sovereignty of French Indo-China. On this point let the
ure speak for itself.

___

In his broadcast of August 24, 1941,[1] Prime Minister Churchill referred to tʰ Japanese action as menacing Singapore, the British link with Australia. I said that the United States was laboring "with infinite patience to arrive at fair and amicable settlement" and expressed the hope that these negotiatioⁿ would succeed. But he asserted "that if these hopes should fail, we shall, course, range ourselves unhesitatingly at the side of the United States."

(4) *Statement of the Acting Secretary of State (Welles), August 2, 1941*

The French Government at Vichy has given repeated assurances ⁺ the Government of the United States that it would not cooperate wiᵗ the Axis Powers beyond the obligations imposed on it by the armisticᵉ and that it would defend the territory under its control against aⁿ aggressive action on the part of third powers.

This Government has now received information of the terms of tʰ agreement between the French and Japanese Governments covering tʰ so-called "common defense" of French Indo-China. In effect, tʰ agreement virtually turns over to Japan an important part of the Frenᶜ Empire.

Effort has been made to justify this agreement on the ground thᵃ Japanese "assistance" is needed because of some menace to the terˢ torial integrity of French Indo-China by other powers. The Governmeⁿ of the United States is unable to accept this explanation. As I stated ᵉ July 24, there is no question of any threat to French Indo-China, unlᵉ it lies in the expansionist aims of the Japanese Government.

The turning over of bases for military operations and of territoriˢ rights under pretext of "common defense" to a power whose territoriᵃ aspirations are apparent, here presents a situation which has a dire bearing upon the vital problem of American security. For reasons whiᶜ are beyond the scope of any known agreement, France has now decidᵉ to permit foreign troops to enter an integral part of its Empire, to occuᵖ bases therein, and to prepare operations within French territory whiᶜ may be directed against other peoples friendly to the people of Franᶜ

The French Government at Vichy has repeatedly declared its deterᵐ nation to resist all encroachments upon the sovereignty of its territoriᵉ However, when German and Italian forces availed themselves of certᵃ facilities in Syria to carry on operations directed against the British, tʰ French Government, although this was a plain encroachment on terˢ tory under French control, did not resist. But when the British undᵉ

[1] *New York Times*, August 25, 1941, p. 4.
[2] Department of State, *Bulletin*, V. p. 87. The statement was made in reply inquiries from the press.

ok defense operations in the territory of Syria,[1] the French Government
d resist.

Under these circumstances, this Government is impelled to question
hether the French Government at Vichy in fact proposes to maintain
s declared policy to preserve for the French people the territories both
home and abroad which have long been under French sovereignty.
This Government, mindful of its traditional friendship for France, has
eply sympathized with the desire of the French people to maintain
eir territories and to preserve them intact. In its relations with the
ench Government at Vichy and with the local French authorities in
ench territories, the United States will be governed by the manifest
ectiveness with which those authorities endeavor to protect these
rritories from domination and control by those powers which are
eking to extend their rule by force and conquest, or by the threat
ereof.

E. Freezing of Japanese Assets

From the point of view of the Government of the United States the Japanese
litary occupation of southern French Indo-China marked a turning point in
e development of American policy. Down to this time the Government had
parently been unwilling, in the application of economic and financial measures,
go beyond the threat implied in the termination of the 1911 Treaty of Com-
rce [2] and the application to Japan of measures of export control provided for
der the Act of July 2, 1940.[3] The President's Executive Order (No. 8785) of
ne 14, 1941 [4] regulating transactions in foreign exchange and foreign-owned
operty, and, in effect, freezing foreign assets in the United States which might
used to support European aggression, was not made applicable at the time to
pan.

This failure to apply strong economic and financial measures to Japan, ac-
mpanied as it was by the free flow to Japan of certain materials vitally needed
her military aggression against China, led to strong criticism in this country
ere from the beginning there had been widespread sympathy with the Chinese.
iticism became stronger when there was talk of a serious shortage, in certain
tions, at least, of materials which were still being allowed to go to Japan.
soline was a case in point.

In his talk to the men and women engaged in voluntary civilian defense
tivities on July 24, 1941 the President sought to explain this apparent attempt
"appease" the Japanese.

The reaction of the Government of the United States to the Japanese military
upation of southern French Indo-China was immediate. In addition to the
ezing of Japanese assets, conversations between the two Governments with a
w to reaching a comprehensive settlement were immediately suspended.

---

[1] See p. 667; also *Documents, III, 1940–41*, p. 334.

[2] *Ibid., II, 1939–40*, p. 242.

[3] *Ibid., II, 1939–40*, p. 795; *III, 1940–41*, p. 473.

[4] *Ibid., III, 1940–41*, p. 537. This order amended Executive Order No. 8389 of
ril 10, 1940, as amended. See *ibid., II, 1939–40*, p. 540.

(1) *Sale of Oil to Japan. Informal Talk of the President (Roosevel* to Men and Women Engaged in Voluntary Defense Activitie White House, July 24, 1941* [1]

[Excerpt]

Here on the East Coast, you have been reading that the Secreta of the Interior, as Oil Administrator, is faced with the problem of n enough gasoline to go around in the East Coast, and how he is aski everybody to curtail their consumption of gasoline. All right. Now am — I might be called an American citizen, living in Hyde Park, N. and I say: "That's a funny thing. Why am I asked to curtail my co sumption of gasoline when I read in the papers that thousands of tons gasoline are going out from Los Angeles — West Coast — to Japa and we are helping Japan in what looks like an act of aggression?"

All right. Now the answer is a very simple one. There is a Wo War going on, and has been for some time — nearly two years. One our efforts, from the very beginning, was to prevent the spread of th World War in certain areas where it hadn't started. One of those are is a place called the Pacific Ocean — one of the largest areas of the ear There happened to be a place in the South Pacific where we had to ge lot of things — rubber — tin — and so forth, and so on — down in t Dutch Indies, the Straits Settlements, and Indo-China. And we had help get the Australian surplus of meat and wheat, and corn, for Englar

It was very essential from our own selfish point of view of defense prevent a war from starting in the South Pacific. So our foreign poli was — trying to stop a war from breaking out down there. At the sa time, from the point of view of even France at that time — of cou France still had her head above water — we wanted to keep that line supplies from Australia and New Zealand going to the Near East — their troops, all their supplies that they have maintained in Syria, No Africa, and Palestine. So it was essential for Great Britain that we to keep the peace down there in the South Pacific.

All right. And now here is a Nation called Japan. Whether they h at that time aggressive purposes to enlarge their Empire southwa they didn't have any oil of their own in the north. Now, if we cut oil off, they probably would have gone down to the Dutch East Indie year ago, and you would have had war.

Therefore, there was — you might call — a method in letting t oil go to Japan, with the hope — and it has worked for two years — keeping war out of the South Pacific for our own good, for the good of t defense of Great Britain, and the freedom of the seas.

[1] Department of State, *Bulletin*, V, p. 72.

) *Freezing of Japanese and Chinese Assets in the United States. Press Release from the Office of the President (Roosevelt), July 25, 1941* [1]

Chinese assets were included in the order, at the request of China, as a means assisting that country. Japan had attempted to set up a "yen bloc" of cur-ncies which included several kinds of *yuan* issued in Chinese areas occupied by pan or which were under administration by the Wang Ching-wei regime. anipulation of such currencies [2] had been used both to destroy the trade of n-Japanese in China and to undermine the Chinese currency itself. The ssibility of those acting in the interest of Japan piling up negotiable assets in ;itimate Chinese currency was obviated by the extension of the freezing order Chinese funds.

In view of the unlimited national emergency declared by the President, issued, on July 25, an Executive Order freezing Japanese assets in the nited States in the same manner in which assets of various European untries were frozen on June 14, 1941.[3] This measure, in effect, brings financial and import and export trade transactions in which Japanese terests are involved under the control of the Government and imposes iminal penalties for violation of the order.

This Executive Order, just as the order of June 14, 1941, is designed 1ong other things to prevent the use of the financial facilities of the nited States and trade between Japan and the United States in ways rmful to national defense and American interests, to prevent the uidation in the United States of assets obtained by duress or conquest, d to curb subversive activities in the United States.

At the specific request of Generalissimo Chiang Kai-shek, and for the rpose of helping the Chinese Government, the President has, at the me time, extended the freezing control to Chinese assets in the United ates. The administration of the licensing system with respect to inese assets will be conducted with a view to strengthening the foreign de and exchange position of the Chinese Government. The inclusion China in the Executive Order, in accordance with the wishes of the inese Government, is a continuation of this Government's policy of sisting China.

---

[1] Department of State, *Bulletin*, V, p. 73.
[2] *Documents, I, 1938–39*, p. 238. See also "Federal Reserve Bank of China — An trument of Japanese Economic Policy," *Foreign Commerce Weekly*, August 16, 1, IV, No. 7, p. 4.
[3] Executive Order No. 8832, July 25, 1941 (6 *Fed. Reg.*, p. 3715), simply added na and Japan to the list of states in the Executive Order of June 14, 1941 (*Docu-nts, III, 1940–41*, p. 537).

(3) *Broadcast by President of Japanese Information Board (Ito), Ju*
　　26, 1941 [1]

[Excerpt]

. . . I wish to point out two aspects involved in the United Stat
decision to apply to Japan an executive order for the freezing of forei;
assets. First, the United States Government misunderstands the re
intentions of Japan, and second, our country is prepared to take steps
meet the situation.

With reference to the first point, the step taken by the United Stat
has probably been prompted by the arrangement for the joint defense
French Indo-China just concluded between Japan and France. If so
wish to rectify the United States misunderstanding. The Japan-F.I.
joint defense agreement was brought about peaceably and its purpose
defensive. It is not provocative, nor was it forced upon France. T'
two countries carried on conversations regarding joint defense in
peaceful atmosphere with a view to forestalling any untoward develo
ment within the Greater East Asia Co-prosperity Sphere. It is expect
that thanks to this joint defense arrangement no such undesirat
developments will arise in future in this area. Considered from t'
standpoint, the accord is of a more peaceful character than the landi;
of United States troops in Iceland. I shall not enlarge upon the issue b
Japan's real intentions have been made quite clear by the statements
the Government, as well as the Foreign Office statement issued at noc
The United States should calmly consider the actual situation in order
understand it clearly.

Regarding the second point, if the United States does not, or refu:
to, understand Japan's real intentions and is bent upon taking measur
to bring pressure to bear upon this country, it must be said that Washir
ton is the one that disturbs the peace and must bear the responsibili
for such disturbances.

The step taken by the United States will have no serious effect on c
country from the economic standpoint. But I believe that necessa
measures to cope with the situation must be adopted.

The Government authorities have fully considered such measures, ar
therefore, I believe our people can rest assured that no stone will be l
unturned in this connection.

I want to reiterate that the fact that Japan has no intention to distu
the peace of the Pacific is clearly known both at home and abroad.

In conclusion I want again to urge the United States to reconsider l

[1] *The Japan Weekly Chronicle*, July 31, 1941, p. 151.

titude and at the same time to express my earnest hope that the Japa-
se nation will continue to maintain its calm attitude and place their
nfidence in the measures to be taken by the Government.

) Retaliatory Measures of Japan. Statement of Japanese Department of Finance, August 1941 [1]

Upon receiving the report of the American Government freezing Japanese
sets held in the United States, which was effected by the Executive Order on
ly 25,[2] the Japanese Government immediately decided to take retaliatory
easures. The Foreigners Transactions Control Regulations [3] were accordingly
acted on the basis of the Foreign Exchange Law [4] recently revised and pro-
ulgated on July 28 as Ordinance No. 46 of the Department of Finance, whereby
 assets and transactions of Americans in this country will be controlled.

Thus, all economic transactions conducted by American interests are placed
der restriction and made subject to the permission of the Minister of Finance.
 this connection, a word of explanation may be necessary respecting the term
Americans" or "American interests" used in this article. Although no mention
made of "American" or "any other nationals" except "a national of a desig-
ted country" in the text of the regulations, the above-mentioned terms are
dely used herein for convenience, signifying nationals of the United States,
ristic persons whose head offices are in the United States, juristic persons estab-
hed under the laws of the United States, Japanese or any other juristic persons
hich are managed by nationals or juristic persons of the United States, Japanese
 any other nationals resident in the United States, or branch offices of Japanese
 any other juristic persons in the United States.

When an American in Japan acquires or disposes of any property listed below
e permission of the Minister of Finance must be obtained (Article 9):

1. Immovables or perpetual leases.
2. Movables valued at 100 yen or more.
3. Superficies, easements or the right of repurchasing immovables.
4. Pledges or mortgages.
5. Mining, placer mining, fishing or lumbering concessions.
6. Ownership of industrial property, copyrights or rights corresponding
   thereto.
7. Enterprises, business or investment therein.
8. Securities, other than domestic money orders, valued at 20 yen or more.
9. Domestic money orders.
10. Foreign currencies.

Any act of an American creditor or debtor specified below may not be per-
rmed in Japan unless with the permission of the Minister of Finance (Article
):

---

[1] *Tokyo Gazette*, V, p. 139–43.
[2] See p. 749; sec. 3(*k*), added by Executive Order No. 8963.
[3] For text of Articles 9 to 23, see *Japan Weekly Chronicle*, Commercial Supplement,
gust 7, 1941, p. 41.
[4] See for reference an article entitled "Tightening Exchange Control" in the August
41 issue of *Tokyo Gazette*.

1. Disposal of the right to a debt in terms of a foreign or Japanese currenc including set-off.
2. Assignment of the right to a debt in terms of Japanese currency.
3. Undertaking of a debt.
4. Guaranteeing of a debt.

Placing or receiving assets in trust by an American should be performed wi the permission of the Minister of Finance as specified below (Article 11):

1. To place or to receive in trust immovables, Japanese currency, forei currency, movables valued at 100 yen or more or securities valued at : yen or more.
2. To receive back any of the foregoing assets placed in trust, or to give ba any of the foregoing assets received in trust.

An American may not let, lease, sublet or sublease immovables, movab valued at 100 yen or more or securities valued at 20 yen or more; or acquire dispose of the right to lend or borrow any of the said assets in this country unle with the permission of the Minister of Finance (Article 12).

Any of the acts of an American, in connection with the transactions throu banking organs, specified below shall be performed with the permission of t Minister of Finance (Article 13):

1. Advancing or collecting a loan.
2. Contracting or redeeming a loan.
3. Placing or drawing out a deposit.
4. Receiving or paying out a deposit.

The acquisition or disposal of Japanese currency by an American is controll by the provisions of Article 14 as follows:

An American in Japan may not acquire or dispose of Japanese curren amounting to 500 yen (500 yen for each household in the case of a pers other than a corporation) or more in the course of one month unless with t permission of the Minister of Finance, except where permission has alrea been obtained in regard to acts likely to affect such acquisition or dispo under Articles 9–13 or under the provisions of the Foreign Exchange Cont Law Enforcement Regulations. A check drawn within Japan on a bank Japan and payable in Japan, insofar as it is used as a means of payment Japan, shall be considered as Japanese currency.

The control regulations on the transactions mentioned in the foregoing a applied not only to Americans (in the broader sense of the term as explain above) but also to Japanese when they perform these acts with Americans as their agents. Any Japanese individual or corporation may come under t control regulations in any transaction with an American.

The Foreign Exchange Control Law Enforcement Regulations contain ma mitigating clauses in order to modify the application of the original law, t they shall not govern the case of Americans, or nationals of designated countri thus discriminating them from other nationals.

With regard to designation by the Minister of Finance as those foreign coming within the purview of the present Regulations, the nationals and juris persons of the United States of America and her territories, the Philippin

England, Canada, Hong Kong, the Netherlands, the Netherlands East Indies, Burma, Australia, British Malaya and British India had been listed as of August 2. Those of the Union of South Africa and other members of the British Commonwealth of Nations may sooner or later become included in the list.

In the operation of the Regulations covering so wide a range of transactions it is expected that various difficulties will be encountered. The Government, therefore, will give much elasticity in the actual application by means of the general permit system, similar to the American general license system, by which certain economic activities in the designated cases may be performed without obtaining the Ministerial permission.

In principle, the Government is empowered to strictly apply the provisions of the Regulations to any transaction of the designated foreigners so as to prohibit entirely their economic activities in the country. The sole intention of the Japanese Government, however, is to take counter-measures against the unfriendly action by the countries which took the initiative in freezing Japanese assets, and the actual application of the Regulations to the Americans, for example, will be made as flexible as possible, corresponding to the manner of applying the American order, by means of the general permit system or others, thereby minimizing the effects on the economic relations between Japan and America.

Since the application of the Control Regulations covers a wide sphere of international and national economy, requiring the coordinated working of various government agencies for a smooth operation of the provisions of the Ordinance, a liaison committee composed of the representatives of the Board of Planning, the China Affairs Board, the Manchurian Affairs Board, the Departments of Foreign Affairs, War, the Navy, Commerce and Industry, Agriculture and Forestry, Communications, and Overseas Affairs, has been organized. At the committee meeting proper actions to be performed for coping with the international economic warfare are to be scrupulously studied on the basis of reports and information brought in by the members, and immediate retaliatory measures will be decided upon.

Simultaneously with the freezing of all Japanese assets, the American Government also froze all Chinese assets in the United States. According to the American Government's statement, Chinese assets were also included in the freezing order at Chiang Kai-shek's special request, apparently intended to prevent Chinese funds in the United States from being utilized by the National Government at Nanking.

When the Japanese Government effected, on July 28, retaliatory measures against the United States, Great Britain and the Dutch East Indies, the Governments of Manchoukuo and China also joined Japan in effecting the freezing of the assets of those countries.

On the same day the authorities in the Chinese territory occupied by the Japanese army issued an order freezing the holdings of nationals and juristic persons of the United States and Great Britain in that area.

Since the economic relations of Manchoukuo and China with the United States or Great Britain are different from those relating to Japan, the counter measures taken by these countries may differ accordingly. But the measures taken by the three countries, however, are essentially in common; their Governments will keep in close touch with each other in effecting reprisals against the unfriendly economic actions of the United States and other countries, all necessary communications being constantly exchanged between them.

Japan's present retaliation is not merely that of a tooth for a tooth, but that for causing the United States and other countries to reconsider their unfriendly economic actions against her. It is sincerely hoped that peace between Japan and these countries may be maintained and economic and commercial relations between them may be promoted even under numerous difficulties arising out of the present world conflict. It is believed that the true intention of the Japanese Government will be appreciated and recognized by the other party in the course of the operation of the Control Regulations.

F. The "Encirclement" of Japan

The freezing of Japanese funds by the United States was followed by other acts on the part of the American and other Governments which had the net effect of subjecting Japan to considerable economic and financial pressure. The notice of the British Ambassador to Tokyo, given below, was followed on July 28 by an announcement from the Netherlands East Indies that the existing licensing system for exports to Japan was being extended to all exports to that country. It was also announced that the Central Bank had suspended the quotation of the yen and that the currency authorities had suspended all foreign exchange transactions with Japan, following the abrogation on July 27 of the agreement concluded in December 1940, between the Yokohama Specie Bank and the Java Bank.[2] On July 31, President Roosevelt announced the setting up of the Economic Defense Board,[3] a harbinger of more vigorous use of economic and financial measures in our foreign relations. On August 1, President Roosevelt announced the prohibition of export from the United States of petroleum products suitable for aviation use to destinations outside the Americas except the British Empire and unoccupied territories of countries resisting aggression. Obviously, not unrelated to this policy of increasing economic pressure on Japan was the President's action on August 22 in proclaiming a fifty percent increase in the duty on imported crabmeat.

These measures, whether actually representing concerted action or not, taken together with diplomatic consultations and other acts of the so-called A B C D powers, gave the excuse to the Japanese to play up from about the middle of August on the idea of "A B C D encirclement."

(1) *Notice of Abrogation by the United Kingdom, India and Burma of Commercial Treaties with Japan, July 26, 1941* [5]

Economic relations of the United Kingdom and Japan were controlled by the treaty of commerce and navigation signed at London April 3, 1911 [6] and in force July 17, 1911 for an initial period of 12 years and thereafter subject to denunciation on 1-year's notice. Article 8 and the tariff schedule of the treaty were ter

---

[1] *The Bulletin of International News*, XVIII, August 9, 1941, p. 1053.
[2] *Tokyo Gazette*, V, p. 127.
[3] See p. 180.
[4] American — British — Chinese — Dutch.
[5] *The Japan Weekly Chronicle*, July 31, 1941, p. 151.
[6] *British and Foreign State Papers*, 104, p. 159.

ninated March 10, 1925, as a result of denunciation by Japan. A supplementary convention, signed at London July 30, 1925,[1] entered into force July 29, 1927 for an initial period of 5 years and thereafter until 1 year after denunciation by either party. This convention modified the treaty of April 3, 1911 in several respects and continued its remaining provisions in force until the expiration of the convention. As from August 9, 1928, the Dominion of New Zealand acceded to the instruments, subject to denunciation on 3-months' notice.[2]

Following the enactment of the United States tariff law of 1930, tariff increases and other restrictive measures affecting Japanese export trade multiplied. At the beginning of 1932 over 20 countries had taken such action. Japan entered into negotiations with various countries particularly in the interest of its cotton textile trade. The convention regarding commercial relations between India and Japan signed at London July 12, 1934,[3] was one result of such negotiations. A conference at London early in 1934 between representatives of the textile industries of the United Kingdom and Japan, held with the approval and assistance of the two governments, was broken off without agreement on March 14, 1934. On May 3, 1934, the United Kingdom Government informed the Japanese Government of action to be taken that resulted in a quota system in certain British colonies and a revision of the United Kingdom tariff on silk.[4]

The Indo-Japanese convention, with a protocol relating to cotton textiles, was extended at its initial expiration March 31, 1937[5] until March 31, 1940, subject to denunciation on 6-months' notice. Burma, under the Government of India Act of 1935, had ceased to be a province of India and had become a separate government. In consequence a convention was concluded between Burma and Japan on June 7, 1937,[6] and entered into force October 12, 1937, subject to denunciation on 6-months' notice after March 31, 1940.

The denunciation of July 26, 1941 put the treaty of 1911 and the convention of 1925 out of force between Japan and part of the British Empire[7] on July 25, 1942; a separate denunciation by New Zealand dated July 27, 1941 took effect October 26, 1942. The Indian and Burmese conventions ceased to be in force January 26, 1942.

Sir Robert Craigie, British Ambassador, called on Foreign Minister Admiral Teijiro Toyoda at his official residence at 2 : 30 P.M., under the instructions of his home Government and notified in written language under today's date its intention to abrogate the Treaty of Commerce and Navigation of April 3rd, 1934 [i.e. 1911], the treaty concluded between Japan and India on June 12, 1934, and the treaty concluded on June 7, 1937, regarding trade relations between Japan and Burma, on the ground

[1] *Ibid.*, 121, p. 812.

[2] Exchange of notes dated July 24, 1928, United Kingdom, *Treaty Series* No. 6 (1929), Cmd. 3287.

[3] League of Nations, *Treaty Series*, CLV, p. 31.

[4] *Economic Conditions in Japan, 1933–1934;* Report by G. B. Sansom and H. A. Macrae, p. 96–98 (United Kingdom, Department of Overseas Trade, No. 604).

[5] By exchange of notes, October 12, 1937, League of Nations, *Treaty Series*, LXXXV, p. 419.

[6] United Kingdom, *Treaty Series* No. 1 (1938), Cmd. 5636.

[7] For the extent of application, see United Kingdom, Foreign Office, *Handbook of Commercial Treaties, etc., with Foreign Powers*, 4th ed. (1931), p. 381, 398. The 1911 treaty was applicable to Canada and the Irish Free State.

that the British, Indian and Burmese Governments have reached the conclusion that the objectives they had at the time these treaties were signed can no longer be satisfied.

(2) *"Encirclement of Japan in the Making." Statement of Japanese Board of Information, August 1941* [1]

Among other factors seriously affecting the safety of French Indo China are, firstly, the move to encircle Japan by Great Britain, the United States, the Netherlands, Australia and the Chiang Kai-shek regime; and secondly, the machinations of the de Gaullists in French Indo-China.

This move has not been altogether unexpected, for there have been gradual indications of such a possibility noticeable since January this year. For some time past in the United States, Secretary of State Cordell Hull, British Ambassador Viscount Halifax and Australian Minister Richard Gardiner Casey have been holding frequent conferences reportedly for the purpose of bringing about a closer British, American and Australian cooperation in the South Pacific. Meanwhile in February this year, the United States appointed a military attaché to the United States Legation in Australia, sending, at the same time, a naval adviser to the port of Darwin, which is a naval and air base on the northern coast of Australia. These steps were followed in March by the sending of a squadron each to New Zealand and Australia, apparently as a demonstration of the United States' readiness to extend assistance in case of emergency. Furthermore, M. E. N. van Kleffens, the Foreign Minister of the Netherlands Government in London, calling at Washing ton, D.C., in March this year, on his way to the Netherlands East Indies conferred with President Roosevelt and later visited Manila, holding conferences with Mr. Francis B. Sayre, the United States High Com missioner for the Philippine Islands, Air Chief Marshal Sir Robert Brooke-Popham, commander-in-chief of the British forces in the Far East, and several other British and American officials concerned report edly on measures to be taken *vis-à-vis* Japan jointly by Great Britain the United States and the Netherlands. This common front of Britain the United States and the Netherlands is naturally expected to incorpo rate the Chiang Kai-shek regime, as indicated by the visits of the Chinese military mission to Singapore and of the British and American expert to Chungking. The recommendation by the American Government of Mr. Owen Lattimore, a foremost American student of Far Eastern affairs, widely known also for his anti-Japanese leanings, to a high

[1] *Tokyo Gazette* V, p. 125.

advisory post in the Chungking Government, may have an important bearing upon the consolidation of an anti-Japanese common front by these powers. Nor can the report of growing American aid to Chungking in the reconstruction of its air force be made light of, in view of our basic national policy for the speedy settlement of the China Affair.

The British and American maneuverings against Japan were not confined to what have been described above. They have also brought an increasing pressure upon Thailand. The British and American influences, and the former in particular, are deep-rooted in Thailand. Recently the British have been busy reinforcing their garrisons in Burma and British Malaya especially strongly near their Thai borders. They have tried to entice her with alluring offers of supplying her much needed oil and of assistance in other forms, unmistakably in an attempt to alienate Thailand from Japan and win her over to the Anglo-American camp. An instance of such efforts was the invitation of a military mission from Thailand to Singapore, where the Thai officers were made eye-witnesses to the prowess of the British Far Eastern forces.

Moreover, the anti-Japanese encirclement policy in Southern Asia has come to make its influence keenly felt in French Indo-China as a result of the machinations on the part of the de Gaulle regime in this part of the world. The de Gaullists have cooperated with the British and American interests in French Indo-China in such a way as to undermine the cause of France and to obstruct Japan's policy, these maneuverings obviously running counter to the sovereignty of France and also to the provisions of the Matsuoka-Arsène-Henry Agreement of August 1940.

In fact, the situation in French Indo-China came to such a pass that, if left alone, it would seriously impede and jeopardize the proposed establishment of the co-prosperity sphere of East Asia. It was feared, even, that it might cause in French Indo-China such a crisis as the one which recently befell Syria in the Near East. Japan and France, therefore, realizing their close relationships and common interests in French Indo-China, have decided to arrange for the aforesaid joint defense of the French colony.

3) *"A B C D Encirclement." Broadcast of the Chief of Army Press Bureau (Mabuchi), Japanese Imperial Headquarters, September 8, 1941* [1]

[Excerpt]

The German-Soviet conflict occurred suddenly at a time when we thought that the China affair which had begun to assume the character of

[1] *The Japan Weekly Chronicle*, September 11, 1941, p. 331.

a protracted campaign was near a settlement. One effect of the development was the acceleration of the completion of the movement of America, Britain, Chungking, and the Netherlands East Indies to encircle Japan. It goes without saying that the encirclement movement against Japan which is led by America and Britain constitutes as great an obstacle in the way of the disposal of the China affair as the assistance which is rendered to Chungking by countries which are opposed to Japanese policy. We are now confronted with the necessity of breaking this A B C D encirclement movement. Breaking this encirclement movement means engaging the countries included in this movement, notably America and Britain, in a long drawn-out armed conflict. The situation with which our country is faced is a crisis in the literal sense of the term. It would be the height of folly to look on with folded arms while forces bent on defeating this country are at work. The situation surrounding our country is developing in a manner which will compel us to stake all to strive to save ourselves as a nation. Any course open to us will present us with a question of life and death. I say with all emphasis that unless the defense resources we have are linked with those of the Greater East Asia Mutual Prosperity Sphere the future of the Japanese empire will be in danger. This is why I say that the firm establishment of the Greater East Asia Mutual Prosperity Sphere is a vital condition of the continued existence of our empire.

The policy of Britain and the United States in the southern area has been to strengthen the ties of the countries which are in the encirclement movement against this country. We, people of a country where production is in danger of lagging behind consumption, have to give serious thought to the question of how to break this encirclement movement against our country. In delaying action to break this encirclement movement we will be inviting a danger to our country. If the feared war does not come about, it will not make any great difference in the situation which finds us consuming lots of important materials. With sources of materials in foreign countries closed to us, that day will come when we will be at the end of our domestic resources. Countries which are opposed to Japanese policy are putting increased economic pressure against us, while using every care to avoid an armed conflict with our country. The action of Britain, America and other countries hostile toward us in freezing Japanese funds and assets was in line with a carefully mapped out policy to drive our country into a corner economically. They were telling a lie when they told the world that their economic measures against our country were in retaliation against the advance of Japanese armed forces into south French Indo-China, a move which they said, menaced the safety of the Philippines and Singapore. Both Britain and the United States have been guilty of unpardonable crimes. Britain has infringed the sovereignty of Iran. The United States has without reason placed peaceful Iceland under her military control. Now these countries are committing a crime against humanity by forcing their overseas territories, the Netherlands East Indies, Thailand, and other third countries to stop shipments to this country.

As has been suggested, the way to save our country from slow death is by breaking the encirclement movement of Britain, America, and other countries against Japan. We can hope to achieve this by resort to arms. Now arms are death-dealing devices, and we must see that they are used only when other means have failed to solve our national difficulties. The authorities have left nothing undone to find a peaceful settlement, and I am sure that they will continue their efforts to settle the situation by negotiation. If a peaceful way out of the difficulty can be found, nothing will be a matter of greater congratulation not only to Japan but also the world. Needless to say, a peace effort will not preclude the making of preparations for the situation to arise from its failure. This is why I stress the need of taking steps to establish the Greater East Asia Mutual Prosperity Sphere on a firm basis even though efforts are made by the authorities concerned to avoid war.

British Prime Minister Churchill in his recent radio speech [1] called Japan an aggressor and a disturber of peace. This is an inexcusable insult against Japanese fighting officers and soldiers who have faith in the object of the sacred war and are devoting their lives toward its accomplishment. The outrageous words cannot be tolerated.

There is nobody among the Japanese nation who accepts Churchill's words and doubts the significance of our sacred war. They must believe that Japan should not change its objective by calculation.

A matter of great moment to Japan should not be determined by calculation of immediate interests.

There is no doubt that Japan should aid the National Government of China and that the National Government should bolster efforts for the increase of Japan's national power.

In case Japan cannot reach a peaceful settlement through diplomatic negotiations, Japan must break through encirclement fronts by force to reach the solution of the matter.

In such a case, the Japanese nation should fight to the last man to defend the glorious national polity and history in the face of the enemy's fire no matter how long the war may be.

[1] See p. 498.

The defensive power and productive capacity of Japan is completing in four years what it attained in peace time in 20 years. The production in Manchoukuo and China is contributing much toward the completion of Japan's national defense.

The sphere of Japan's national defense now extends from the Manchoukuo-Soviet frontier to French Indo-China, covering a distance of more than 10,000 kilometres. The position of Japan in the world is based on this sphere. This is favorable for Japan's future progress.

The Japanese nation should eliminate individualism and liberalism and establish a new structure as strong as iron under which the nation can overcome any difficulty.

G. Termination of the Fur Seal Convention

(1) Statement of the Director of the Japanese Bureau of Fisheries October 23, 1941 [1]

The Fur Seals Convention concluded in 1911 among Japan, United States, Great Britain and Russia, comes to an end as of today. In connection with the termination of that convention, the competent authorities are carefully examining the question of canceling or revising law number 21 of 1912, prohibiting the hunting of fur seals, policy concerning the taking of seals, and other relevant matters. Until decision shall have been reached with regard to these matters, for internal purposes there will be no change and therefore as heretofore Japanese nationals will not be permitted to violate the law [2] and other measures taken by the government. As already stated, no decision has been reached with regard to the future cancellation or revision of the law, but the competent authorities will absolutely forbid any plan partaking of the character of a free enterprise. They wish to make it perfectly clear that operations hereafter will be carried on strictly in line with national policies.

H. Final Attempt at Comprehensive Settlement of Differences between Japanese and American Governments

Following the sending of Japanese armed forces into southern French Indo China and the announcement of the agreement between the Vichy French and Japanese Governments of July 29 [3] permitting the same, conversations which

---

[1] Department of State, Bulletin, V, p. 336; see also *Documents, III, 1940–41*, p. 28? The statement was reported by the Embassy at Tokyo.

[2] The Japanese authorities indicated informally that it was not the intention of the Japanese Government to abandon the possibility of the regulation of the taking of fur seals by international agreement, and that there was no possibility of an enactment before April 1942 of new Japanese legislation under which Japanese nationals might engage in pelagic sealing.

[3] See p. 494.

ere being carried on between the American and Japanese Governments with a
iew to reaching a comprehensive settlement of outstanding differences were
uspended. Early in August "at the urgent and insistent request of the Jap-
nese Government," [1] the conversations were renewed. The proposals and
ounter-proposal made are reviewed in the document handed to the Japanese
Ambassador (Nomura) by Secretary of State (Hull) on October 2, 1941.

1) Oral Document Handed by the Secretary of State (Hull) to the Japanese Ambassador (Nomura), October 2, 1941 [2]

Reference is made to the proposals of the Japanese Government
ommunicated on September 6, 1941, by the Japanese Ambassador to
he Secretary of State, and to statements relating thereto subsequently
ommunicated to this Government by the Japanese Government.

Thoughtful study has been given to the communications to which
eference is made, and in connection with that study careful review has
een made of other communications previously received from the Japa-
ese Government on the same subject. On the basis of this study obser-
ations are offered as follows:

The Government of the United States welcomed, as affording a possi-
le opportunity for furthering the broad-gauge objectives and principles
f a program of peace, the Japanese Government's suggestions made
hrough its Ambassador here in the early part of August that there be
eld a meeting of the responsible heads of the Japanese Government and
f the Government of the United States to discuss means for bringing
bout an adjustment of relations between the United States and Japan
nd that there be resumed the informal conversations which had been in
rogress between the two countries to ascertain whether there existed a
asis for negotiations relative to a peaceful settlement covering the
ntire Pacific situation.

Accordingly, in the reply made by the President on August 17, 1941,
o the Japanese Ambassador the view was expressed that such informal
onversations would naturally envisage the working out of a progressive
rogram attainable by peaceful means; that such a program would
volve the application in the entire Pacific area of the principle of
quality of commercial opportunity and treatment, thus making possible
ccess by all countries to raw materials and to all other essential com-
odities, and there were described the advantages which would flow to
ll countries, including Japan, from the adoption of such a program. In

[1] Summary of Past Policy . . . Message from the President, December 15, 1941,
e this volume, p. 469.
[2] Annex 10, House Doc. 458, 77th Cong., 1st sess., p. 102; Department of State,
ulletin, V, p. 537; marked "strictly confidential."

conclusion, it was stated that if the Japanese Government were i
position to embark upon a peaceful program for the Pacific along th
lines of the program and principles to which the United States is con
mitted, this Government would be prepared to consider resumption c
the informal exploratory discussions and would be glad to endeavor t
arrange a suitable time and place to exchange views.

In the light of the broad purposes and fundamental principles whic
this Government holds, it was gratifying to the President and th
Government of the United States to receive the message of the Prim
Minister and the statement of the Government of Japan on August 2&
1941, containing statements expressing Japan's desire and intent t
pursue courses of peace in harmony with the fundamental principles t
which the people and Government of the United States are committee
In its statement the Japanese Government gave, with some qualifice
tions, broad assurances of its peaceful intent, including a comprehensiv
assurance that the Japanese Government has no intention of usin
without provocation military force against any neighboring nation. Th
Japanese Government declared that it supported the program an
principles which had been briefly outlined by the President not onl
as applicable to the Pacific area but also as a program for the entir
world.

The Government of the United States, while desiring to proceed &
rapidly as possible with consideration of arrangements for a meetin
between the heads of state, felt it desirable, in order to assure that the
meeting would accomplish the objectives in view, to clarify the inte:
pretation of certain principles and the practical application thereof t
concrete problems in the Pacific area. It has not been the purpose of th
Government to enter into a discussion of details; this Government he
felt, however, that the clarification sought would afford a means c
expediting our effort to arrive at a meeting of minds.

On September 3, 1941, the President in giving reply to the Japane:
Ambassador expressed the earnest desire of the Government of th
United States to collaborate in efforts to make effective in practice th
principles to which the Japanese Government made reference. Th
President reiterated the four principles regarded by this Government a
the foundation upon which relations between nations should proper
rest. Those principles are:

1. Respect for the territorial integrity and the sovereignty of each ar
all nations.

2. Support of the principle of non-interference in the internal affairs c
other countries.

3. Support of the principle of equality, including equality of commercial opportunity.

4. Non-disturbance of the *status quo* in the Pacific except as the *status quo* may be altered by peaceful means.

The President pointed out that in order to bring about any satisfactory settlement of Pacific questions it was highly important to reach a community of view and a clear agreement upon certain points with respect to which fundamental differences of opinion between our two Governments had developed in the informal conversations; and the President requested an indication of the present attitude of the Japanese Government with regard to those fundamental questions.

On September 6, the Prime Minister of Japan in a conversation with the American Ambassador at Tokyo stated that he subscribed fully to the four principles above mentioned.

The foregoing developments and assurances, together with other statements made by the Japanese Government, seemed to justify this Government in concluding that the Japanese Government might be expected to adhere to and to give practical application to a broad progressive program covering the entire Pacific area. It was therefore a source of disappointment to the Government of the United States that the proposals of the Japanese Government presented by the Japanese Ambassador on September 6, 1941, which the Japanese Government apparently intended should constitute a concrete basis for discussions, appeared to disclose divergence in the concepts of the two Governments. That is to say, those proposals and the subsequent explanatory statements made in regard thereto serve, in the opinion of this Government, to narrow and restrict not only the application of the principles upon which our informal conversations already referred to had been based but also the various assurances given by the Japanese Government of its desire to move along with the United States in putting into operation a broad program looking to the establishment and maintenance of peace and stability in the entire Pacific area.

As has already been said, the various broad assurances given by the Japanese Premier and the Japanese Government are highly gratifying. In putting forward its attitude of peaceful intent toward other nations, the Japanese Government qualified its assurances with certain phrases the need for which is not easily understood. It is difficult to conceive of there developing under present circumstances in any of the territories neighboring French Indo-China, in Thailand or in the Soviet Union any aggressive threat or provocation to Japan. The inalienable right of self-defense is of course well recognized by all nations and there could arise

in some minds a question as to just what the Japanese Government ha
in view in circumscribing its assurances of peaceful intent with wha
would seem to be unnecessary qualifying phrases.

In the informal conversations there was tentatively arrived at
formula in regard to economic policy (Section V of the draft under
standing), which provided that Japanese activity and American activit
in the Pacific area shall be carried on by peaceful means and in con
formity with the principle of non-discrimination in international com
mercial relations. In the Japanese Government's proposals of Septembe
6 and in subsequent communications from the Japanese Government th
commitments contained in that formula were restricted to the countrie
of the Southwest Pacific area (not the Pacific area as a whole). I
reference to China, the Japanese Government states that it will respec
the principle of non-discrimination, but the explanation given in regar
to this point would seem to be open to the implication that the Japanes
Government has in mind some limitation upon the application of thi
principle occasioned by reasons of Japan's geographical propinquity t
China.

Obviously, it would not be likely to serve the purposes affirmed by th
Japanese Government or by this Government if either the United State
or Japan were to pursue one course or policy in certain areas while at th
same time pursuing an opposite course or policy in other areas.

This Government has noted the views of the Japanese Governmen
in support of its desire to station troops for an indeterminate period i
certain areas of China. Entirely apart from the question of the reason
for such a proposal, the inclusion of such a provision in the propose
terms of a peaceful settlement between Japan and China at a time whe
Japan is in military occupation of large areas in China is open to certai
objections. For example, when a country in military occupation c
territory of another country proposes to the second country the con
tinued stationing of troops of the first country in certain areas as
condition for a peaceful settlement and thus for the withdrawal of th
occupationary forces from other areas, such procedure would seem to b
out of keeping with the progressive and enlightened courses and princi
ples which were discussed in the informal conversations and thus woul
not, in the opinion of this Government, make for peace or offer prospect
of stability.

It is believed that a clear-cut manifestation of Japan's intention i
regard to the withdrawal of Japanese troops from China and Frenc
Indo-China would be most helpful in making known — in particular t
those who might be inclined to be critical — Japan's peaceful intention

nd Japan's desire to follow courses calculated to establish a sound basis
or future stability and progress in the Pacific area.

With reference to the attitude of each country toward the European
ar, this Government has noted with appreciation the further step taken
y the Japanese Government to meet the difficulties inherent in this
spect of the relations between the two countries. It is believed that
would be helpful if the Japanese Government could give further study
o the question of possible additional clarification of its position.

In the exchanges of views which have taken place between the two
overnments in an effort to reach an agreement in principle upon funda-
nental questions in order to prepare the ground for the proposed meeting
f the responsible chiefs of government, this Government has endeavored
o make clear that what it envisages is a comprehensive program calling
or the application uniformly to the entire Pacific area of liberal and
rogressive principles. From what the Japanese Government has so far
ndicated in regard to its purposes this Government derives the impres-
ion that the Japanese Government has in mind a program which would
e circumscribed by the imposition of qualifications and exceptions to
he actual application of those principles.

If this impression is correct, can the Japanese Government feel that
meeting between the responsible heads of government under such
ircumstances would be likely to contribute to the advancement of the
igh purposes which we have mutually had in mind?

As already stated, this Government welcomed the assurances con-
ained in the statement of the Japanese Government which accompanied
ne Japanese Prime Minister's message to the President of the United
tates that the Japanese Government subscribed to the principles which
ave long been advocated by this Government as the only sound basis
or stable international relations. This Government believes that
newed consideration of these fundamental principles may be helpful
our effort to seek a meeting of minds in regard to the essential ques-
ons on which we seek agreement and thus lay a firm foundation for a
eeting between the responsible heads of the two Governments. The
bject of the meeting proposed by the Prime Minister and the objectives
ught have engaged, and continue to engage, the close and active
terest of the President of the United States, and it is the President's
rnest hope that discussion of the fundamental questions may be so
eveloped that such a meeting can be held. It is also the President's
ope that the Japanese Government shares the conviction of this Gov-
nment that, if the Governments of Japan and of the United States are
solved to give those principles practical and comprehensive application,

the two Governments can work out a fundamental rehabilitation of th
relations between the United States and Japan and contribute to, th
bringing about of a lasting peace with justice, equity and order in th
whole Pacific area.

(2) *The Japanese Ambassador (Nomura) to the Secretary of Stat (Hull), November 20, 1941* [1]

Following the suggestion contained in Secretary Hull's oral document (
October 2 that an agreement on fundamental principles be reached as a prelud
to any personal meeting between President Roosevelt and Premier Kono
several formulas were offered and discussed. On November 5 it was announce
in Tokyo that Mr. Saburo Kurusu, former Japanese Ambassador to Berlin an
Brussels, was being sent to Washington to assist Ambassador Nomura in th
current negotiations. Mr. Kurusu arrived in Washington on November 1.
On November 18, Foreign Minister Togo declared in Tokyo that Mr. Kurus
had been sent to the United States only to assist Ambassador Nomura an
"carried no new instructions," thus implying that Japan's position had change
in no fundamental respect since the original opening of conversations seve
months before.[2] The proposal submitted by Ambassador Nomura on Novembe
20 certainly evidenced no substantial change in Japan's position.

1. Both the Governments of Japan and the United States undertak
not to make any armed advancement into any of the regions in the South
eastern Asia and the Southern Pacific area excepting the part of Frenc
Indo-China where the Japanese troops are stationed at present.

2. The Japanese Government undertakes to withdraw its troops no
stationed in French Indo-China upon either the restoration of peac
between Japan and China or the establishment of an equitable peac
in the Pacific area.

In the meantime the Government of Japan declares that it is prepare
to remove its troops now stationed in the southern part of French Ind
China to the northern part of the said territory upon the conclusion (
the present arrangement which shall later be embodied in the final agre
ment.

3. The Government of Japan and the United States shall cooperat
with a view to securing the acquisition of those goods and commoditi
which the two countries need in Netherlands East Indies.

4. The Governments of Japan and the United States mutually unde
take to restore their commercial relations to those prevailing prior to th
freezing of the assets.

[1] Annex 11, House Doc. 458, 77th Cong., 1st sess., p. 106; Department of Stat
Bulletin, V, p. 540; marked "strictly confidential."
[2] *New York Times,* November 19, 1941.

The Government of the United States shall supply Japan a required
quantity of oil.

5. The Government of the United States undertakes to refrain from
such measures and actions as will be prejudicial to the endeavors for
the restoration of general peace between Japan and China.

) *The Secretary of State (Hull) to the Japanese Ambassador (Nomura), November 26, 1941* [1]

ORAL

Strictly confidential

The representatives of the Government of the United States and of
the Government of Japan have been carrying on during the past several
months informal and exploratory conversations for the purpose of arriving
at a settlement if possible of questions relating to the entire Pacific
area based upon the principles of peace, law and order and fair dealing
among nations. These principles include the principle of inviolability
territorial integrity and sovereignty of each and all nations; the principle
of non-interference in the internal affairs of other countries; the
principle of equality, including equality of commercial opportunity and
treatment; and the principle of reliance upon international cooperation
and conciliation for the prevention and pacific settlement of controversies
and for improvement of international conditions by peaceful methods
and processes.

It is believed that in our discussions some progress has been made in
reference to the general principles which constitute the basis of a peaceful
settlement covering the entire Pacific area. Recently the Japanese
Ambassador has stated that the Japanese Government is desirous of
continuing the conversations directed toward a comprehensive and
peaceful settlement in the Pacific area; that it would be helpful toward
creating an atmosphere favorable to the successful outcome of the conversations
if a temporary *modus vivendi* could be agreed upon to be in
effect while the conversations looking to a peaceful settlement in the
Pacific were continuing. On November 20 the Japanese Ambassador
communicated to the Secretary of State proposals in regard to temporary
measures to be taken respectively by the Government of Japan and by
the Government of the United States, which measures are understood
have been designed to accomplish the purposes above indicated.

The Government of the United States most earnestly desires to con-

[1] Annex 12, House Doc. 458, 77th Cong., 1st sess., p. 107; Department of State,
Bulletin, V, p. 461. This note consists of two parts, an oral statement and an outline
a proposed basis for agreement between the United States and Japan.

tribute to the promotion and maintenance of peace and stability in th Pacific area, and to afford every opportunity for the continuance o discussions with the Japanese Government directed toward working ou a broad-gauge program of peace throughout the Pacific area. The prc posals which were presented by the Japanese Ambassador on Novembe 20 contain some features which, in the opinion of this Government, con flict with the fundamental principles which form a part of the genera settlement under consideration and to which each Government ha declared that it is committed. The Government of the United State believes that the adoption of such proposals would not be likely to cor tribute to the ultimate objectives of ensuring peace under law, orde and justice in the Pacific area, and it suggests that further effort b made to resolve our divergences of views in regard to the practical appl cation of the fundamental principles already mentioned.

With this object in view the Government of the United States offer for the consideration of the Japanese Government a plan of a broad bu simple settlement covering the entire Pacific area as one practical exen plification of a program which this Government envisages as somethin to be worked out during our further conversations.

The plan therein suggested represents an effort to bridge the gap be tween our draft of June 21, 1941 [1] and the Japanese draft of Septembe 25 [1] by making a new approach to the essential problems underlying comprehensive Pacific settlement. This plan contains provisions dealin with the practical application of the fundamental principles which w have agreed in our conversations constitute the only sound basis fc worthwhile international relations. We hope that in this way progre toward reaching a meeting of minds between our two Governments ma be expedited.

Strictly confidential, tentative and without commitment

NOVEMBER 26, 194

OUTLINE OF PROPOSED BASIS FOR AGREEMENT BETWEEN THE
UNITED STATES AND JAPAN

Section I

Draft Mutual Declaration of Policy

The Government of the United States and the Government of Japa both being solicitous for the peace of the Pacific affirm that their nation; policies are directed toward lasting and extensive peace throughout tl Pacific area, that they have no territorial designs in that area, that the

[1] Not printed.

have no intention of threatening other countries or of using military force aggressively against any neighboring nation, and that, accordingly, in their national policies they will actively support and give practical application to the following fundamental principles upon which their relations with each other and with all other governments are based:

(1) The principle of inviolability of territorial integrity and sovereignty of each and all nations.

(2) The principle of non-interference in the internal affairs of other countries.

(3) The principle of equality, including equality of commercial opportunity and treatment.

(4) The principle of reliance upon international cooperation and conciliation for the prevention and pacific settlement of controversies and for improvement of international conditions by peaceful methods and processes.

The Government of Japan and the Government of the United States have agreed that toward eliminating chronic political instability, preventing recurrent economic collapse, and providing a basis for peace, they will actively support and practically apply the following principles in their economic relations with each other and with other nations and peoples:

(1) The principle of non-discrimination in international commercial relations.

(2) The principle of international economic cooperation and abolition of of extreme nationalism as expressed in excessive trade restrictions.

(3) The principle of non-discriminatory access by all nations to raw material supplies.

(4) The principle of full protection of the interests of consuming countries and populations as regards the operation of international commodity agreements.

(5) The principle of establishment of such institutions and arrangements of international finance as may lend aid to the essential enterprises and the continuous development of all countries and may permit payments through processes of trade consonant with the welfare of all countries.

Section II

Steps To Be Taken by the Government of the United States and by the Government of Japan

The Government of the United States and the Government of Japan propose to take steps as follows:

1. The Government of the United States and the Government of Japan will endeavor to conclude a multilateral non-aggression pact among the British Empire, China, Japan, the Netherlands, the Soviet Union, Thailand and the United States.

2. Both Governments will endeavor to conclude among the American British, Chinese, Japanese, the Netherland and Thai Governments an agreement whereunder each of the Governments would pledge itself to respect the territorial integrity of French Indo-China and, in the event that there should develop a threat to the territorial integrity of Indo-China, to enter into immediate consultation with a view to taking such measures as may be deemed necessary and advisable to meet the threat in question. Such agreement would provide also that each of the Governments party to the agreement would not seek or accept preferential treatment in its trade or economic relations with Indo-China and would use its influence to obtain for each of the signatories equality of treatment in trade and commerce with French Indo-China.

3. The Government of Japan will withdraw all military, naval, air and police forces from China and from Indo-China.

4. The Government of the United States and the Government of Japan will not support — militarily, politically, economically — any government or regime in China other than the National Government of the Republic of China with capital temporarily at Chungking.

5. Both Governments will give up all extraterritorial rights in China including rights and interests in and with regard to international settlements and concessions, and rights under the Boxer Protocol of 1901

Both Governments will endeavor to obtain the agreement of the British and other governments to give up extraterritorial rights in China, including rights in international settlements and in concession and under the Boxer Protocol of 1901.

6. The Government of the United States and the Government of Japan will enter into negotiations for the conclusion between the United States and Japan of a trade agreement, based upon reciprocal most favored-nation treatment and reduction of trade barriers by both countries, including an undertaking by the United States to bind raw silk on the free list.

7. The Government of the United States and the Government of Japan will, respectively, remove the freezing restrictions on Japanese funds in the United States and on American funds in Japan.

8. Both Governments will agree upon a plan for the stabilization of the dollar-yen rate, with the allocation of funds adequate for this purpose, half to be supplied by Japan and half by the United States.

9. Both Governments will agree that no agreement which either has concluded with any third power or powers shall be interpreted by it in such a way as to conflict with the fundamental purpose of this agreement, the establishment and preservation of peace throughout the Pacific area.

10. Both Governments will use their influence to cause other governments to adhere to and to give practical application to the basic political and economic principles set forth in this agreement.

(4) *Memorandum Addressed by the President (Roosevelt) to the Secretary of State and the Under Secretary of State, Read and Handed by the Under Secretary of State (Welles) under Authorization of the President to the Japanese Ambassador (Nomura), December 2, 1941* [1]

In the midst of these conversations, the Government of the United States learned that new contingents of Japanese armed forces and additional supplies of war material were being moved into French Indo-China. Toward the end of November these movements were intensified. It became clear to the authorities in Washington that under cover of negotiations preparations were being made for attacks on unspecified points. [2] On November 24, 1941, acting on the basis of information received by the Navy Department from the Secretary of State, the Chief of Naval Operations sent a message to Admiral Husband Kimmel, Commander-in-Chief of the Pacific Fleet, stating that a surprise aggressive movement by Japan in any direction was now considered possible and that this opinion was supported by the uncertainty as to the favorable outcome of pending negotiations, the statements of the Japanese Government and the movements of Japanese army and naval forces. [3] Under these tense circumstances, President Roosevelt directed that inquiry be made regarding Japanese troop movements in French Indo-China and the purposes back of them.

I have received reports during the past days of continuing Japanese troop movements to southern Indo-China. These reports indicate a very rapid and material increase in the forces of all kinds stationed by Japan in Indo-China.

It was my clear understanding that by the terms of the agreement — and there is no present need to discuss the nature of that agreement — between Japan and the French Government at Vichy that the total number of Japanese forces permitted by the terms of that agreement to be stationed in Indo-China was very considerably less than the total amount of the forces already there.

[1] Annex 13, House Doc. 458, 77th Congress, 1st sess., p. 110; Department of State, *Bulletin*, V, p. 540. The President discussed his action in sending this inquiry at his press conference, *New York Times*, December 3, 1941, p. 1.

[2] See *Summary of Past Policy . . . Message from the President*, p. 473.

[3] *Report of the Commission Appointed by the President of the United States to Investigate and Report the Facts relating to the Attack Made by Japanese Armed Forces*, Senate Doc. No. 159, 77th Cong., 2d sess. [Roberts Commission Report.]

The stationing of these increased Japanese forces in Indo-China would seem to imply the utilization of these forces by Japan for purposes of further aggression, since no such number of forces could possibly be required for the policing of that region. Such aggression could conceivably be against the Philippine Islands; against the many islands of the East Indies; against Burma; against Malaya or either through coercion or through the actual use of force for the purpose of undertaking the occupation of Thailand. Such new aggression would, of course, be additional to the acts of aggression already undertaken against China, our attitude towards which is well known, and has been repeatedly stated to the Japanese Government.

Please be good enough to request the Japanese Ambassador and Ambassador Kurusu to inquire at once of the Japanese Government what the actual reasons may be for the steps already taken, and what I am to consider is the policy of the Japanese Government as demonstrated by this recent and rapid concentration of troops in Indo-China. This Government has seen in the last few years in Europe a policy on the part of the German Government which has involved a constant and steady encroachment upon the territory and rights of free and independent peoples through the utilization of military steps of the same character. It is for that reason and because of the broad problem of American defense that I should like to know the intention of the Japanese Government.

(5) Statement of the Japanese Ambassador (Nomura) to the Secretary of State (Hull), December 5, 1941 [1]

Reference is made to your inquiry about the intention of the Japanese Government with regard to the reported movements of Japanese troops in French Indo-China. Under instructions from Tokyo, I wish to inform you as follows:

As Chinese troops have recently shown frequent signs of movements along the northern frontier of French Indo-China bordering on China, Japanese troops, with the object of mainly taking precautionary measures, have been reinforced to a certain extent in the northern part of French Indo-China. As a natural sequence of this step, certain movements have been made among the troops stationed in the southern part of the said territory. It seems that an exaggerated report has been made of these movements. It should be added that no measure has been taken

[1] Annex 14, House Doc. 458, 77th Cong., 1st sess., p. 111; Department of State *Bulletin*, V, p. 464. The statement was transmitted by the Secretary of State to the President, who released the text through the Office of the Secretary to the President

on the part of the Japanese Government that may transgress the stipulations of the Protocol of Joint Defense between Japan and France.[1]

(6) *Message of the President of the United States (Roosevelt) to the Emperor of Japan (Hirohito), December 6, 1941* [2]

Almost a century ago the President of the United States addressed
to the Emperor of Japan a message extending an offer of friendship of
the people of the United States to the people of Japan. That offer was
accepted, and in the long period of unbroken peace and friendship which
has followed, our respective nations, through the virtues of their peoples
and the wisdom of their rulers have prospered and have substantially
helped humanity.

Only in situations of extraordinary importance to our two countries
need I address to Your Majesty messages on matters of state. I feel I
should now so address you because of the deep and far-reaching emergency which appears to be in formation.

Developments are occurring in the Pacific area which threaten to
deprive each of our nations and all humanity of the beneficial influence
of the long peace between our two countries. Those developments
contain tragic possibilities.

The people of the United States, believing in peace and in the right of
nations to live and let live, have eagerly watched the conversations
between our two Governments during these past months. We have
hoped for a termination of the present conflict between Japan and China.
We have hoped that a peace of the Pacific could be consummated in such
a way that nationalities of many diverse peoples could exist side by side
without fear of invasion; that unbearable burdens of armaments could
be lifted for them all; and that all peoples would resume commerce
without discrimination against or in favor of any nation.

I am certain that it will be clear to Your Majesty, as it is to me, that
in seeking these great objectives both Japan and the United States
should agree to eliminate any form of military threat. This seemed
essential to the attainment of the high objectives.

More than a year ago Your Majesty's Government concluded an
agreement with the Vichy Government by which five or six thousand
Japanese troops were permitted to enter into Northern French Indo-
China for the protection of Japanese troops which were operating against
China further north. And this Spring and Summer the Vichy Govern-

---

[1] See p. 494.
[2] Annex 15, House Doc. 458, 77th Cong., 1st sess., p. 111; Department of State,
Bulletin, V, p. 464; released from the Office of the Secretary to the President.

ment permitted further Japanese military forces to enter into Southern French Indo-China for the common defense of French Indo-China. I think I am correct in saying that no attack has been made upon Indo-China, nor that any has been contemplated.

During the past few weeks it has become clear to the world that Japanese military, naval and air forces have been sent to Southern Indo-China in such large numbers as to create a reasonable doubt on the part of other nations that this continuing concentration in Indo-China is not defensive in its character.

Because these continuing concentrations in Indo-China have reached such large proportions and because they extend now to the southeast and the southwest corners of that Peninsula, it is only reasonable that the people of the Philippines, of the hundreds of Islands of the East Indies, of Malaya and of Thailand itself are asking themselves whether these forces of Japan are preparing or intending to make attack in one or more of these many directions.

I am sure that Your Majesty will understand that the fear of all these peoples is a legitimate fear inasmuch as it involves their peace and their national existence. I am sure that Your Majesty will understand why the people of the United States in such large numbers look askance at the establishment of military, naval and air bases manned and equipped so greatly as to constitute armed forces capable of measures of offense

It is clear that a continuance of such a situation is unthinkable

None of the peoples whom I have spoken of above can sit either indefinitely or permanently on a keg of dynamite.

There is absolutely no thought on the part of the United States of invading Indo-China if every Japanese soldier or sailor were to be withdrawn therefrom.

I think that we can obtain the same assurance from the Governments of the East Indies, the Governments of Malaya and the Government of Thailand. I would even undertake to ask for the same assurance on the part of the Government of China. Thus a withdrawal of the Japanese forces from Indo-China would result in the assurance of peace throughout the whole of the South Pacific area.

I address myself to Your Majesty at this moment in the fervent hope that Your Majesty may, as I am doing, give thought in this definite emergency to ways of dispelling the dark clouds. I am confident that both of us, for the sake of the peoples not only of our own great countries but for the sake of humanity in neighboring territories, have a sacred duty to restore traditional amity and prevent further death and destruction in the world.

7) *Statement of the Secretary of State (Hull), December 7, 1941* [1]

Japan has made a treacherous and utterly unprovoked attack upon he United States.[2]

At the very moment when representatives of the Japanese Government vere discussing with representatives of this Government, at the request »f the former, principles and courses of peace, the armed forces of Japan vere preparing and assembling at various strategic points to launch new ttacks and new aggressions upon nations and peoples with which Japan vas professedly at peace including the United States.

I am now releasing for the information of the American people the tatement of principles governing the policies of the Government of the Jnited States and setting out suggestions for a comprehensive peaceful ettlement covering the entire Pacific area, which I handed to the apanese Ambassador on November 26, 1941.

I am likewise releasing the text of a Japanese reply thereto which was anded to me by the Japanese Ambassador today. Before the Japanese Ambassador delivered this final statement from his Government the reacherous attack upon the United States had taken place.

This Government has stood for all the principles that underlie fair-ealing, peace, law and order, and justice between nations and has teadfastly striven to promote and maintain that state of relations be-ween itself and all other nations.

It is now apparent to the whole world that Japan in its recent profes-ions of a desire for peace has been infamously false and fraudulent.

8) *Memorandum of the Japanese Government, Presented by the Japanese Ambassador (Nomura) to the Secretary of State (Hull), 2:20 P.M., December 7, 1941* [3]

At 1 P.M. December 7 the Japanese Ambassador asked for an appointment »r the Japanese representatives to see the Secretary of State. The appoint-ient was made for 1 : 45 P.M. The Japanese representatives arrived at the office f the Secretary of State at 2 : 05 P.M. They were received by the Secretary at : 20 P.M. The Japanese Ambassador handed to the Secretary of State what was nderstood to be a reply to the document handed to him by the Secretary of tate on November 26. At 1:25 P.M. Japanese forces had attacked American »rces in the Hawaiian Islands. See p. 116.

[1] Department of State, *Bulletin*, V, p. 461.

[2] The time of the attack was 1 : 20 P.M. (Washington time) according to the Presi-ent's message (see p. 479); 1 : 25 P.M. (Washington time), according to the report of he Roberts Commission (Senate Doc. No. 159, 77th Cong., 2d sess.)

[3] Annex 16, House Doc. 458, 77th Cong., 1st sess., p. 113; Department of State, *Bulletin*, V, p. 466.

Secretary Hull carefully read the statement presented by the Japanese representatives and immediately turned to the Japanese Ambassador and with the
greatest indignation said:

"I must say that in all my conversations with you [the Japanese Ambassador
during the last nine months I have never uttered one word of untruth. This is
borne out absolutely by the record. In all my 50 years of public service I have
never seen a document that was more crowded with infamous falsehoods and
distortions — infamous falsehoods and distortions on a scale so huge that I never
imagined until today that any Government on this planet was capable of uttering them." [1]

1. The Government of Japan, prompted by a genuine desire to come
to an amicable understanding with the Government of the United States
in order that the two countries by their joint efforts may secure the peace
of the Pacific Area and thereby contribute toward the realization of world
peace, has continued negotiations with the utmost sincerity since April
last with the Government of the United States regarding the adjustment
and advancement of Japanese-American relations and the stabilization
of the Pacific Area.

The Japanese Government has the honor to state frankly its views
concerning the claims the American Government has persistently maintained as well as the measures the United States and Great Britain have
taken toward Japan during these eight months.

2. It is the immutable policy of the Japanese Government to insure
the stability of East Asia and to promote world peace and thereby to
enable all nations to find each its proper place in the world.

Ever since China Affair broke out owing to the failure on the part of
China to comprehend Japan's true intentions, the Japanese Government
has striven for the restoration of peace and it has consistently exerted
its best efforts to prevent the extension of warlike disturbances. It
was also to that end that in September last year Japan concluded the
Tripartite Pact with Germany and Italy.

However, both the United States and Great Britain have resorted to
every possible measure to assist the Chungking regime so as to obstruc
the establishment of a general peace between Japan and China, inter
fering with Japan's constructive endeavors toward the stabilization of
East Asia. Exerting pressure on the Netherlands East Indies, or menac
ing French Indo-China, they have attempted to frustrate Japan'
aspiration to the ideal of common prosperity in cooperation with these
regions. Furthermore, when Japan in accordance with its protocol with
France took measures of joint defense of French Indo-China, both Ameri

---

[1] Statement issued by the Department of State concerning the circumstances at
tending the delivery of the Memorandum, *ibid.*

an and British Governments, willfully misinterpreting it as a threat
o their own possessions, and inducing the Netherlands Government to
ollow suit, they enforced the assets freezing order, thus severing economic
elations with Japan. While manifesting thus an obviously hostile atti-
ude, these countries have strengthened their military preparations
erfecting an encirclement of Japan, and have brought about a situation
hich endangers the very existence of the Empire.

Nevertheless, to facilitate a speedy settlement, the Premier of Japan
roposed, in August last, to meet the President of the United States for a
iscussion of important problems between the two countries covering
he entire Pacific area. However, the American Government, while
ccepting in principle the Japanese proposal, insisted that the meeting
hould take place after an agreement of view had been reached on funda-
ental and essential questions.

3. Subsequently, on September 25 the Japanese Government sub-
itted a proposal based on the formula proposed by the American
overnment, taking fully into consideration past American claims and
lso incorporating Japanese views. Repeated discussions proved of no
vail in producing readily an agreement of view. The present cabinet,
erefore, submitted a revised proposal, moderating still further the
apanese claims regarding the principal points of difficulty in the nego-
ation and endeavored strenuously to reach a settlement. But the
merican Government, adhering steadfastly to its original assertions,
iled to display in the slightest degree a spirit of conciliation. The
gotiation made no progress.

Therefore, the Japanese Government, with a view to doing its utmost
r averting a crisis in Japanese-American relations, submitted on No-
ember 20 still another proposal in order to arrive at an equitable solu-
on of the more essential and urgent questions which, simplifying its
revious proposal, stipulated the following points:

) The Governments of Japan and the United States undertake not to
dispatch armed forces into any of the regions, excepting French
Indo-China, in the Southeastern Asia and the Southern Pacific
area.

) Both Governments shall cooperate with the view to securing the
acquisition in the Netherlands East Indies of those goods and commodities of which the two countries are in need.

) Both Governments mutually undertake to restore commercial relations to those prevailing prior to the freezing of assets.

The Government of the United States shall supply Japan the required quantity of oil.

(4) The Government of the United States undertakes not to resort to measures and actions prejudicial to the endeavors for the restoration of general peace between Japan and China.

(5) The Japanese Government undertakes to withdraw troops now stationed in French Indo-China upon either the restoration of peace between Japan and China or the establishment of an equitable peace in the Pacific Area; and it is prepared to remove the Japanese troops in the southern part of French Indo-China to the northern part upon the conclusion of the present agreement.

As regards China, the Japanese Government, while expressing its readiness to accept the offer of the President of the United States to act as "introducer" of peace between Japan and China as was previously suggested, asked for an undertaking on the part of the United States to do nothing prejudicial to the restoration of Sino-Japanese peace when the two parties have commenced direct negotiations.

The American Government not only rejected the above-mentioned new proposal, but made known its intention to continue its aid to Chiang Kai-shek; and in spite of its suggestion mentioned above, withdrew the offer of the President to act as so-called "introducer" of peace between Japan and China, pleading that time was not yet ripe for it. Finally on November 26, in an attitude to impose upon the Japanese Government those principles it has persistently maintained the American Government made a proposal totally ignoring Japanese claims, which is a source of profound regret to the Japanese Government.

4. From the beginning of the present negotiation the Japanese Government has always maintained an attitude of fairness and moderation and did its best to reach a settlement, for which it made all possible concessions often in spite of great difficulties. As for the China question which constitutes an important subject of the negotiation, the Japanese Government showed a most conciliatory attitude. As for the principle of non-discrimination in international commerce, advocated by the American Government, the Japanese Government expressed its desire to see the said principle applied throughout the world, and declared that along with the actual practice of this principle in the world, the Japanese Government would endeavor to apply the same in the Pacific area including China, and made it clear that Japan had no intention of excluding from China economic activities of third powers pursued on an equitable basis. Furthermore, as regards the question of withdrawing troops from French Indo-China, the Japanese Government even volunteered, as mentioned above, to carry out an immediate evacuation of

roops from Southern French Indo-China as a measure of easing the
situation.

It is presumed that the spirit of conciliation exhibited to the utmost
degree by the Japanese Government in all these matters is fully appreci-
ted by the American Government.

On the other hand, the American Government, always holding fast to
heories in disregard of realities, and refusing to yield an inch on its
mpractical principles, caused undue delay in the negotiation. It is
ifficult to understand this attitude of the American Government and the
apanese Government desires to call the attention of the American
iovernment especially to the following points:

1. The American Government advocates in the name of world peace
hose principles favorable to it and urges upon the Japanese Government
he acceptance thereof. The peace of the world may be brought about
nly by discovering a mutually acceptable formula through recognition
f the reality of the situation and mutual appreciation of one another's
osition. An attitude such as ignores realities and imposes one's selfish
iews upon others will scarcely serve the purpose of facilitating the
onsummation of negotiations.

Of the various principles put forward by the American Government as
basis of the Japanese-American Agreement, there are some which the
apanese Government is ready to accept in principle, but in view of the
orld's actual condition it seems only a utopian ideal on the part of the
merican Government to attempt to force their immediate adoption.

Again, the proposal to conclude a multilateral non-aggression pact
etween Japan, United States, Great Britain, China, the Soviet Union,
he Netherlands and Thailand, which is patterned after the old concept
f collective security, is far removed from the realities of East Asia.

2. The American proposal contained a stipulation which states —
Both Governments will agree that no agreement, which either has
oncluded with any third power or powers, shall be interpreted by it in
ich a way as to conflict with the fundamental purpose of this agreement,
he establishment and preservation of peace throughout the Pacific
rea." It is presumed that the above provision has been proposed with
view to restrain Japan from fulfilling its obligations under the Tri-
artite Pact when the United States participates in the war in Europe,
nd, as such, it cannot be accepted by the Japanese Government.

The American Government, obsessed with its own views and opinions,
ay be said to be scheming for the extension of the war. While it seeks,
n the one hand, to secure its rear by stabilizing the Pacific Area, it is
ngaged, on the other hand, in aiding Great Britain and preparing to

attack, in the name of self-defense, Germany and Italy, two powers tha
are striving to establish a new order in Europe. Such a policy is totall
at variance with the many principles upon which the American Govern
ment proposes to found the stability of the Pacific Area through peacefu
means.

3. Whereas the American Government, under the principles it rigidl
upholds, objects to settle international issues through military pressure
it is exercising in conjunction with Great Britain and other nation
pressure by economic power. Recourse to such pressure as a means c
dealing with international relations should be condemned as it is a
times more inhumane than military pressure.

4. It is impossible not to reach the conclusion that the America
Government desires to maintain and strengthen, in coalition with Grea
Britain and other Powers, its dominant position it has hitherto occupie
not only in China but in other areas of East Asia. It is a fact of histor
that the countries of East Asia for the past hundred years or more hav
been compelled to observe the *status quo* under the Anglo-America
policy of imperialistic exploitation and to sacrifice themselves to th
prosperity of the two nations. The Japanese Government cann
tolerate the perpetuation of such a situation since it directly runs count
to Japan's fundamental policy to enable all nations to enjoy each i
proper place in the world.

The stipulation proposed by the American Government relative t
French Indo-China is a good exemplification of the above-mentione
American policy. Thus the six countries, — Japan, the United State
Great Britain, the Netherlands, China, and Thailand, — exceptir
France, should undertake among themselves to respect the territori
integrity and sovereignty of French Indo-China and equality of trea
ment in trade and commerce would be tantamount to placing th
territory under the joint guaranty of the Governments of those s
countries. Apart from the fact that such a proposal totally ignores tl
position of France, it is unacceptable to the Japanese Government i
that such an arrangement cannot but be considered as an extension
French Indo-China of a system similar to the Nine-Power Trea
structure which is the chief factor responsible for the present predicame
of East Asia.

5. All the items demanded of Japan by the American Governme
regarding China such as wholesale evacuation of troops or uncondition
application of the principle of non-discrimination in international cor
merce ignored the actual conditions of China, and are calculated
destroy Japan's position as the stabilizing factor of East Asia. Tl

ttitude of the American Government in demanding Japan not to support militarily, politically or economically any regime other than the
egime at Chungking, disregarding thereby the existence of the Nanking
Government, shatters the very basis of the present negotiation. This
demand of the American Government falling, as it does, in line with its
above-mentioned refusal to cease from aiding the Chungking regime,
demonstrates clearly the intention of the American Government to
obstruct the restoration of normal relations between Japan and China
and the return of peace to East Asia.

5. In brief, the American proposal contains certain acceptable items
such as those concerning commerce, including the conclusion of a trade
agreement, mutual removal of the freezing restrictions, and stabilization
of yen and dollar exchange, or the abolition of extraterritorial rights in
China. On the other hand, however, the proposal in question ignores
Japan's sacrifices in the four years of the China affair, menaces the
Empire's existence itself and disparages its honor and prestige. Therefore, viewed in its entirety, the Japanese Government regrets that it
cannot accept the proposal as a basis of negotiation.

6. The Japanese Government, in its desire for an early conclusion of
the negotiation, proposed simultaneously with the conclusion of the
Japanese-American negotiation, agreements to be signed with Great
Britain and other interested countries. The proposal was accepted by
the American Government. However, since the American Government
has made the proposal of November 26 as a result of frequent consultation with Great Britain, Australia, the Netherlands and Chungking,
and presumably by catering to the wishes of the Chungking regime in
the questions of China, it must be concluded that all these countries are
at one with the United States in ignoring Japan's position.

7. Obviously it is the intention of the American Government to conspire with Great Britain and other countries to obstruct Japan's efforts
toward the establishment of peace through the creation of a new order
in East Asia, and especially to preserve Anglo-American rights and
interests by keeping Japan and China at war. This intention has been
revealed clearly during the course of the present negotiation. Thus, the
earnest hope of the Japanese Government to adjust Japanese-American
relations and to preserve and promote the peace of the Pacific through
cooperation with the American Government has finally been lost.

The Japanese Government regrets to have to notify hereby the American Government that in view of the attitude of the American Government it cannot but consider that it is impossible to reach an agreement
through further negotiations.

I. Respect for the Laws of War

(1) *Statement of the Spokesman of the Japanese Cabinet Information Board (Hori), December 8, 1941* [1]

This is a war between States, not between individual nationals of Japan and enemy countries. Therefore, the Japanese Government will follow a policy of every possible precautionary measure to insure the safety of nationals of the United States and the British Empire residing in Japan.

The Government has notified the embassies of the United States and Britain and the Legation of Canada to cease their functions assuring them protection according to international usage. At the same time it stated that special attention would be paid to protection of their nationals.

(2) *Japanese Allegations regarding Killing of Nationals. Statement of the Department of State, December 29, 1941* [2]

The Department of State has received through the Swiss Legation representing Japanese interests in the Philippines, a communication from the Japanese Government in which it protests the alleged killing of 10 Japanese nationals at the time of the assault by the Japanese forces against the city of Davao on the Island of Mindanao.

This Government had not previously heard of the alleged incident and has no reports whatsoever which would substantiate in the slightest degree the incident complained of by the Japanese Government.

For days previous to the delivery of this note, the Japanese not only had been continuing their unprovoked aggression against the Philippine Islands but they had also ruthlessly, wantonly, and with a complete lack of humanity bombed the defenseless civilian population of a declared open city, killed scores of civilians, and wounded hundreds more.

While the United States would not condone the acts of any of its officials or of any persons under its authority which contravene accepted rules of international law, and will always investigate complaints and take such proper steps as may be warranted under the facts, the record established by Japan over a number of years and in her recent activities in the Philippines clearly shows a wholly wanton disregard by Japan of international law and of principles of humanity and even of the elementary rules of decency designed to avoid needless injury to defenseless civilian populations. The objective of the Japanese in making this protest is

[1] Associated Press version, *New York Times*, December 9, 1941, p. 15.
[2] Department of State, *Bulletin*, VI, p. 5.

clear, that is, to attempt to divert attention from their iniquities by making accusations against others.

(3) Statement of the President (Roosevelt) on Use of Poison Gas, June 5, 1942 [1]

Authoritative reports are reaching this Government of the use by Japanese armed forces in various localities of China of poisonous or noxious gases. I desire to make it unmistakably clear that, if Japan persists in this inhuman form of warfare against China or against any other of the United Nations, such action will be regarded by this Government as though taken against the United States, and retaliation in kind and in full measure will be meted out. We shall be prepared to enforce complete retribution. Upon Japan will rest the responsibility.

2. RELATIONS WITH CHINA

A. Aid to China under the Lend-Lease Act of March 11, 1941

[For other material on Lend-Lease aid, see Chapter III, p. 169.]

1) Military Mission to China. Announcement of the President (Roosevelt), August 26, 1941 [2]

This Government is preparing to send a military mission to China. The mission will be sent for the purpose of assisting in carrying out the purposes of the Lend-Lease Act. It is being organized and it will operate under the direction of the Secretary of War. Its chief will be Brig. Gen. John Magruder.

The function of the mission will be to study, in collaboration with Chinese and other authorities, the military situation in China, the need of the Chinese Government for *matériel* and materials; to formulate recommendations regarding types and quantities of items needed; to assist in procurement in this country and in delivery in China of such *matériel* and materials; to instruct in the use and maintenance of articles thus provided; and to give advice and suggestions of appropriate character toward making lend-lease assistance to China as effective as possible in the interest of the United States, of China, and of the world effort in resistance to movements of conquest by force.

The sending of this mission is in keeping with and is on parallel lines to the sending of a similar mission to the Soviet Union. The purposes of the two missions are identical.

[1] *Ibid.*, p. 506, released by the Office of the Secretary to the President.
[2] Reprinted in *ibid.*, V, p. 166.

General Magruder has had long experience in China, where he twic
served as military attaché. He, therefore, will be working on familia
ground, among people he knows well and to whom he is well known. A
adequate staff of thoroughly qualified officers will accompany Genera
Magruder.

(2) *Statement of the Department of State on Lend-Lease Aid, Octobe
25, 1941* [1]

[Excerpt]

Lend-lease aid is also being extended to China, and progress is bein
made toward the completion of an agreement with China. Cargo vessel
have been supplied to carry needed goods to Rangoon, Burma, th
principal remaining port of entry into Free China; materials are bein
supplied for the repair and upkeep of China's lifeline, the Burma Roac
medicine and technical assistance are being furnished to fight the ravage
of malaria; and contracts have been concluded to deliver fighter plane
to reinforce the Chinese Air Force. A military mission to advise ar
consult with the Chinese authorities concerning the use of these defens
articles has proceeded to China.

B. Financial Assistance to China

[For record of loans and credits to the Chinese Government since 1938, see *Document*
I, 1938–39, p. 271; *II, 1939–40*, p. 554; *III, 1940–41*, p. 241.]

1. STABILIZATION OF CURRENCY

(1) *Joint American-British Support of the Stabilization Board. Ar
nouncement of Secretary of Treasury* (*Morgenthau*), *Septembe
6, 1941* [2]

The Secretary of the Treasury today announced that the United Stat
Government had requested banks in the Far East to give their full co
operation to the newly created Stabilization Board of China. The Britis
Government is taking similar action. Included among the banks whos
cooperation was asked were those named in General License No. &
issued under the freezing orders.

This measure, the Secretary stated, was in harmony with previou
measures taken by the American and British Treasuries in the field o
monetary cooperation with China. Both the United States and Gre&

[1] *Ibid.*, p. 313.
[2] U. S. Treasury Department, Press Service No. 27–38. On creation of Stabiliz
tion Board, see *Documents, III, 1940–41*, p. 241.

ritain have previously entered into stabilization agreements with
hina whereby dollar and sterling exchange have been made available
o the Stabilization Board of China. Such Board was established recently
y China and consists of three Chinese, an American appointed by China
n the recommendation of the Secretary of the Treasury, and a British
ational appointed on the recommendation of the British Treasury.

2. LOAN TO CHINA

1) *Joint Resolution to Authorize the President of the United States to
Render Financial Aid to China, and for Other Purposes, Approved
February 7, 1942* [1]

Vhereas China has for more than four years valiantly resisted the forces
of Japanese aggression; and

Vhereas financial and economic aid to China will increase her ability
to oppose the forces of aggression; and

Vhereas the defense of China is of the greatest possible importance:
Therefore be it

*Resolved by the Senate and House of Representatives of the United States
f America in Congress assembled,* That the Secretary of the Treasury,
ith the approval of the President, is hereby authorized, on behalf of
he United States, to loan or extend credit or give other financial aid to
hina in an amount not to exceed in the aggregate $500,000,000 at such
me or times and upon such terms and conditions as the Secretary of
he Treasury with the approval of the President shall deem in the interest
f the United States.

Sec. 2. The authority herein granted shall be in addition to any other
uthority provided by law.

Sec. 3. There is hereby authorized to be appropriated, out of any
money in the Treasury not otherwise appropriated, such sum or sums
ot to exceed $500,000,000 as may be necessary to carry out the provi-
ons of this joint resolution.

2) *The President (Roosevelt) to the President of the Executive Yuan
and Chairman of the Military Affairs Committee (Chiang),
February 7, 1942* [2]

It is a source of great gratification to me and to the Government and
eople of the United States that the proposal which I made to the Con-

---

[1] Public Law 442, 77th Cong., originated as H. J. Res. 276 from Committee on
oreign Affairs; House Report No. 1739; Senate Report No. 1016.

[2] From the Office of the Secretary to the President; Department of State, *Bulletin*,
I, p. 142.

gress that there be authorized for the purpose of rendering financi
aid to China in the sum of $500,000,000 was passed unanimousl
by both the Senate and the House of Representatives and has no
become law.

The unusual speed and unanimity with which this measure was acte
upon by the Congress and the enthusiastic support which it receive
throughout the United States testify to the wholehearted respect an
admiration which the Government and people of this country have f
China. They testify also to our earnest desire and determination to b
concretely helpful to our partners in the great battle for freedom. Th
gallant resistance of the Chinese armies against the ruthless invade
of your country has called forth the highest praise from the America
and all other freedom-loving peoples. The tenacity of the Chinese peopl
both armed and unarmed, in the face of tremendous odds in carrying o
for almost five years a resolute defense against an enemy far superior i
equipment is an inspiration to the fighting men and all the peoples of th
other United Nations. The great sacrifices of the Chinese people i
destroying the fruits of their toil so that they could not be used by th
predatory armies of Japan exemplify in high degree the spirit of sacrifi
which is necessary on the part of all to gain the victory toward whic
we are confidently striving. It is my hope and belief that use which wi
be made of the funds now authorized by the Congress of the Unite
States will contribute substantially toward facilitating the efforts of th
Chinese Government and people to meet the economic and financia
burdens which have been thrust upon them by an armed invasion an
toward solution of problems of production and procurement which ar
essential for the success of their armed resistance to what are now ou
common enemies.

I send you my personal greetings and best wishes. I extend to yo
across land and sea the hand of comradeship for the common good, th
common goal, the common victory that shall be ours.

(b) Joint Resolution Making an Appropriation to Provide Financi Aid to China, Approved February 12, 1942 [1]

*Resolved by the Senate and House of Representatives of the United Stat
of America in Congress assembled,* That the sum of $500,000,000 is hereb
appropriated, out of any money in the Treasury not otherwise appro

[1] Public Law 452, 77th Cong., originated as H. J. Res. 278 from Appropriatio
Committee; House Report No. 1759.

riated, to enable the Secretary of the Treasury to carry out the provisions of the joint resolution entitled "Joint resolution to authorize the
President of the United States to render financial aid to China, and for
other purposes," approved February 7, 1942, and to remain available
until June 30, 1943.

2) Agreement between the United States and China Giving Effect to Public Law 442, February 7, 1942, Signed at Washington, March 21, 1942 [1]

In force March 21, 1942

WHEREAS, The Governments of the United States of America and of
the Republic of China are engaged, together with other nations and
peoples of like mind, in a cooperative undertaking against common
enemies, to the end of laying the bases of a just and enduring world
peace securing order under law to themselves and all nations, and

WHEREAS, The United States and China are signatories to the Declaration of United Nations of January 1, 1942, which declares that "Each
government pledges itself to employ its full resources, military or economic, against those members of the Tripartite Pact and its adherents
with which such government is at war"; and

WHEREAS, the Congress of the United States, in unanimously passing
Public Law No. 442, approved February 7, 1942, has declared that
financial and economic aid to China will increase China's ability to
oppose the forces of aggression and that the defense of China is of the
greatest possible importance, and has authorized the Secretary of the ·
Treasury of the United States, with the approval of the President, to
give financial aid to China, and

WHEREAS, such financial aid will enable China to strengthen greatly
its war efforts against the common enemies by helping China to

(1) strengthen its currency, monetary, banking and economic system;
(2) finance and promote increased production, acquisition and dis-
     tribution of necessary goods;
(3) retard the rise of prices, promote stability of economic relation-
     ships, and otherwise check inflation;
(4) prevent hoarding of foods and other materials;
(5) improve means of transportation and communication;
(6) effect further social and economic measures which promote the
     welfare of the Chinese people; and

[1] Treasury Department, Press Service No. 30–42; Department of State, *Bulletin*,
I, p. 263.

(7) meet military needs other than those supplied under the Lend
Lease Act and take other appropriate measures in its war effor

In order to achieve these purposes, the undersigned, being duly au
thorized by their respective Governments for that purpose, have agree
as follows:

ARTICLE I. The Secretary of the Treasury of the United States agree
to establish forthwith on the books of the United States Treasury
credit in the name of the Government of the Republic of China in th
amount of 500,000,000 U. S. dollars. The Secretary of the Treasur
shall make transfers from this credit, in such amounts and at such time
as the Government of the Republic of China shall request, through th
Minister of Finance, to an account or accounts in the Federal Reserv
Bank of New York in the name of the Government of the Republic c
China or any agencies designated by the Minister of Finance. Suc
transfers may be requested by and such accounts at the Federal Reserv
Bank of New York may be drawn upon by the Government of the Re
public of China either directly or through such persons or agencies as th
Minister of Finance shall authorize.

ARTICLE II. The final determination of the terms upon which th
financial aid is given, including the benefits to be rendered the Unite
States in return, is deferred by the two contracting parties until th
progress of events after the war makes clearer the final terms and benefi
which will be in the mutual interest of the United States and Chin
and will promote the establishment of lasting world peace and securit
In determining the final terms and benefits full cognizance shall be give
to the desirability of maintaining a healthy and stable economic an
financial situation in China in the post-war period as well as during th
war and to the desirability of promoting mutually advantageous eco
nomic and financial relations between the United States and Chin
and the betterment of world-wide economic and financial relations.

ARTICLE III. This Agreement shall take effect as from this day
date.

Signed and sealed at Washington, District of Columbia, in duplica
this 21st day of March, 1942.

On behalf of the United States of America
(Signed) HENRY MORGENTHAU, JR.
Secretary of the Treasury

On behalf of the Republic of China
(Signed) T. V. SOONG
Minister for Foreign Affairs

C. United Nations Collaboration

1. DECLARATION OF WAR AGAINST JAPAN, GERMANY AND ITALY

1) *Declaration of War by the National Government of China against Japan, Effective December 9, 1941* [1]

Japan's national policy has always aimed at the domination of Asia and the mastery of the Pacific. For more than four years, China has resolutely resisted Japan's aggression regardless of suffering and sacrifice in order not only to maintain her national independence and freedom, but also to uphold international law and justice and to promote world peace and human happiness.

China is a peace-loving nation. In taking up arms in self-defense, China entertained the hope that Japan might yet realize the futility of her plan of conquest. Throughout the struggle all other powers have shown utmost forbearance likewise in the hope that Japan might one day repent and mend her ways in the interest of peace in the entire Pacific region.

Unfortunately Japan's aggressive propensities have proven to be incorrigible. After a long and fruitless attempt to conquer China, Japan, far from showing any sign of penitence, has treacherously launched an attack on China's friends, the United States of America and Great Britain, thus extending the theatre of aggressive activities and making herself an arch enemy of Justice and World Peace. This latest act of aggression on the part of Japan lays bare her insatiable ambition and has created a situation which no nation that believes in international good faith and human decency can tolerate.

The Chinese Government hereby formally declares war on Japan. The Chinese Government further declares that all treaties, conventions, agreements and contracts concerning the relations between China and Japan are and remain null and void.

2) *Declaration of War by the National Government of China against Germany and Italy, Effective December 9, 1941* [2]

Since the conclusion of the Tripartite Pact in September 1940, Germany, Italy, and Japan have unmistakably banded themselves into a bloc of aggressor states working closely together to carry out their common program of world conquest and domination. To demonstrate their solidarity Germany and Italy successively accorded recognition to

[1] Department of State, *Bulletin*, V, p. 506.
[2] *Ibid.*

Japan's puppet regimes in northeast China and Nanking. As a conse quence, China severed diplomatic relations with Germany and Italy las July.

Now the Axis Powers have extended the theatre of aggressive activitie and have thrown the whole Pacific region into turmoil making themselve the enemies of international justice and world civilization. This stat of affairs can no longer be tolerated by the Chinese Government an people.

The Chinese Government hereby declares that as from midnight c December 9, 1941, a state of war exists between China and Germany an between China and Italy. The Chinese Government further declare that all treaties, conventions, agreements, and contracts concernin; relations between China and Germany and between China and Ital are and remain null and void.

2. ADHERENCE TO PRINCIPLES

(1) *Signature of the Declaration of United Nations, January 1, 194*

[See p. 203.]

(2) *Text of Generalissimo Chiang Kai-shek's Message to the India. People, February 22, 1942*

[See p. 217.]

3. IMPLEMENTATION

(1) *Agreement for Mutual Aid Pursuant to the Lend-Lease Act o March 11, 1941 between the United States and China, Signe June 2, 1942*

[See p. 237.]

(2) *The Pacific War Council. Announcement of the President (Roose- velt), March 30, 1942*

[See p. 244.]

(3) *The Assignment of Joint Commands in the Southwest Pacific Area, January 3, 1942*

[See p. 244.]

3. INDIA

A. Exchange of Diplomatic Representatives

1) *Announcement of the Department of State, July 21, 1941* [1]

The British Government has on many occasions made it clear that its objective is dominion status for India. One of the prerogatives of dominion status is
the independent conduct of foreign relations. India was an original Member of
the League of Nations. The importance of India in the fight against aggression
and the acceptance by our Government of the principle of political self-determination for all peoples made it appropriate and timely that there should be an
exchange of diplomatic representatives with India.

The Government of the United States and the British Government,
in consultation with the Government of India, have agreed to an exchange
of representatives on a reciprocal basis between the United States and
India.

It is expected that an American Foreign Service officer will be designated to represent the United States in the capacity of Commissioner at
Delhi, the capital of India.

The representative of the Government of India in the United States
appointed by the Governor General is Sir Girja Shankar Bajbai, who
will bear the designation of Agent General for India in the United States
and who, it is understood, will assume his duties in Washington in the
early autumn.

The nomination of Thomas M. Wilson, a Foreign Service officer of class I, to
act as Commissioner of the United States of America to India, with rank of
Minister, was confirmed by the Senate on July 24, 1941.

B. United Nations Collaboration

[See Chapter IV, p. 198.]

1) *Technical Advisory Mission. Department of State Release, March 6, 1942* [2]

The military situation in southeastern Asia emphasizes the need
to develop fully, and as rapidly as feasible, the industrial resources of
India as a supply base for the armed forces of the United Nations in the
Near East and the Far East. The Government of the United States,

---

[1] *Ibid.*, p. 74.
[2] *Ibid.*, VI, p. 209, 230. For some account of the Eastern Supply Group and the
Central Provision Office, see "The Indian Supply Centre," *The Times* (London),
September 23, 1941, p. 5.

accordingly, inquired whether the Government of India would agre
to the despatch to India of a technical mission which could examine an
report on the possibilities of American assistance in such developmen
The Government of India has expressed its readiness to receive such
mission and has invited it to be its guests during the mission's stay i
India. Accordingly, it has been decided that the mission should procee
to India as soon as possible.

It is hoped that the personnel of the mission may be announced shortl
The Government of the United States and the Government of Indi
earnestly hope that this step in American-Indian collaboration ma
serve to make an effective contribution to the success of the Unite
Nations in the war against aggression.

The Department of State announced on March 9 the personnel of the Advisor
Mission of the United States to assist the war effort in India. The personnel c
the Mission follows:

Col. Louis Johnson, former Assistant Secretary of War, *chairman*

Honorable Henry F. Grady, former Assistant Secretary of State — gener
economic surveys

Honorable Arthur W. Herrington, President, Society of Automotive Engineers -
production of armored vehicles and automotive equipment

Honorable Harry E. Beyster, President, Beyster Engineering Company -
organization of plants for production

Honorable Dirk Dekker, Director of Personnel and Training, Illinois Steel Co
poration — specialist in training unskilled workers into semi-skilled an
skilled workers

It is understood that, should it appear advantageous, additional membe
may be added to the Mission to assist in solving specific technical problems.

C. The Cripps Mission

Under the Atlantic Charter the Governments of Great Britain and the Unite
States committed themselves to the principle that all peoples had "the right . .
to choose the form of government under which they will live." [1] Prime Minist
Churchill, in his House of Commons statement of September 9, 1941 [2] asserte
that the joint declaration did not qualify in any way various statements
policy which had been made from time to time about the development of co
stitutional government in India, notably the declaration of August 1940,[3] an
that he and President Roosevelt had primarily in mind the restoration
sovereignty to the peoples of Europe under Nazi yoke. The formal extension
the war to the Far East and the general acceptance by the nations engaged
fighting the Axis Powers of the Declaration by United Nations made the

[1] See p. 209.   [2] See p. 213.

[3] For full text of declaration of the Viceroy, August 8, 1940, see *Indian Informatio*
VII, August 15, 1940, p. 101. An important statement was made by the Secreta
of State for India in the House of Commons, August 1, 1941. Text was publishe
by the British Library of Information.

qualifications highly anomalous. This fact was implicit in the expression of hope by Generalissimo Chiang Kai-shek, in his farewell message to the Indian people, February 22, 1942,[1] that Great Britain would speedily and without waiting for any demands on their part give to the Indian people real political power. Speaking for moderate Indian opinion Sir Tej Bahedur Sapru in his presidential address to a non-party conference in New Delhi on February 21, argued that a people's war could not be conducted with an immobile bureaucracy at the top, that Indian faith in British good intentions had been greatly weakened and that Great Britain must lose no time in taking a bold courageous step.[2] The action of the British Government in arranging for the representation of the Government of India in the War Cabinet and the Pacific War Council in London [3] did not apparently greatly impress Indian opinion. The weakness of United Nations resistance in Burma, due in large part to the support given by dissatisfied Burmese to the Japanese, no doubt strengthened the pressure for a fresh initiative on the part of Great Britain. On March 11, Prime Minister Churchill announced in the House of Commons that the War Cabinet had agreed unitedly on conclusions for present and future action in India and that Sir Stafford Cripps would go to India to lay the Cabinet proposals before the different groups. He arrived at New Delhi March 23. Long conferences were held with the representatives of these groups, especially the Congress Party and the Moslem League. On April 10, the Congress Working Committee and the Moslem League rejected the British proposals,[4] and on the following day, April 11, Sir Stafford informed the press that the British Government's offer to India had been withdrawn, as the replies received had resulted in his regretfully advising the Government "that there is not such measure of acceptance of their proposals as to justify their making a declaration in the form of the draft." [5]

While the Cripps Mission might be regarded as primarily a matter concerning the British and Indian peoples and therefore not properly to be covered in a volume of documents on American foreign relations, the interest which we have in a fair settlement of the Indian question, both from the point of view of winning the war and from the point of view of winning the peace after the war, would seem to justify the inclusion in this volume of the basic documents bearing upon the negotiations.

1) *Statement by the British Prime Minister (Churchill) in the House of Commons, March 11, 1942* [6]

The crisis in the affairs of India arising out of the Japanese advance has made us wish to rally all the forces of Indian life, to guard their land from the menace of the invader.

[1] See p. 217.

[2] *The Bulletin of International News*, XIX, March 21, 1942, p. 253.

[3] See p. 243.

[4] For summary of correspondence between Sir Stafford Cripps and Maulana Abul Kalam Azad, President of the All-India Congress and Mr. Jinnah representing the Moslem League, the resolution of the India States Delegation, and resolutions and statements by representative bodies in British India, see United Kingdom, Parliamentary Papers, *India (Lord Privy Seal's Mission)*, Cmd. 6350, p. 5–15; also reprinted in *International Conciliation*, No. 381, June 1942, p. 316–30.

[5] *The Bulletin of International News*, XIX, April 18, 1942, p. 352; *International Conciliation*, No. 381, June 1942, p. 330.

[6] United Kingdom, Parliamentary Papers, *India (Lord Privy Seal's Mission)*, Cmd. 6350, p. 3.

In August 1940, a full statement was made about the aims and policy we are pursuing in India. This amounted, in short, to a promise that as soon as possible after the war, India should attain dominion status in full freedom and equality with this country and the other Dominions under a Constitution to be framed by Indians, by agreement amongst themselves and acceptable to the main elements in Indian national life This was, of course, subject to the fulfillment of our obligations for the protection of minorities, including the depressed classes, and of ou treaty obligations to the Indian States and to settlement of certain lesser matters arising out of our long association with the fortunes of the Indian subcontinent.

However, Sir, in order to clothe these general declarations with pre cision and to convince all classes, races and creeds in India of our sincer resolve, the War Cabinet have agreed unitedly upon conclusions fo present and future action which, if accepted by India as a whole, would avoid the alternative dangers either that resistance of a powerful minority might impose an indefinite veto upon the wishes of the majority or tha a majority decision might be taken which would be resisted to a point destructive of internal harmony and fatal to the setting up of a new constitution.

We had thought of setting forth immediately the terms of this attempt by a constructive British contribution, to aid India in the realization of full self-government; we are, however, apprehensive that to make public announcement at such a moment as this might do more harm than good.

We must first assure ourselves that our scheme would win a reasonable and practical measure of acceptance, and thus promote the concentratio of all Indian thought and energies upon the defense of the native soi We should ill serve the common cause if we made a declaration whic would be rejected by essential elements in the Indian world and whic provoked fierce constitutional and communal disputes at the momen when the enemy is at the gates of India.

Accordingly, we propose to send a member of the War Cabinet t India, to satisfy himself upon the spot, by personal consultation, that th conclusions upon which we are agreed, and which we believe represen a just and final solution, will achieve their purpose. My right honorabl and learned Friend the Lord Privy Seal and leader of the House [S Stafford Cripps], has volunteered to undertake this task. He carrie with him the full confidence of His Majesty's Government, and he wi strive in their name to procure the necessary measure of assent, no only from the Hindu majority, but also from those great minoritie amongst which the Moslems are the most numerous and on many grounds pre-eminent.

The Lord Privy Seal will, at the same time consult with the Viceroy and the Commander-in-Chief upon the military situation, bearing always in mind the paramount responsibility of His Majesty's Government by every means in their power to shield the peoples of India from the perils which now beset them. We must remember that India has a great part to play in the world's struggle for freedom and that her helping hand must be extended in loyal comradeship to the valiant Chinese people, who have fought alone so long. We must remember also that India is one of the bases from which the strongest counter-blows must be struck at the advance of tyranny and aggression.

My right honorable Friend will set out as soon as convenient and suitable arrangements can be made. I am sure he will command in his task the heartfelt good wishes of all parts of the House and that meanwhile, no words will be spoken or Debates be held, here or in India, which would add to the burden he has assumed in his mission or lessen the prospects of a good result.

During my right honorable and learned Friend's absence from this House his duties as Leader will be discharged by my right honorable Friend, the Foreign Secretary.

(2) *Draft Declaration for Discussion with Indian Leaders, Taken to India by Sir Stafford Cripps, and Published March 30, 1942* [1]

The conclusions of the British War Cabinet as set out below are those which Sir Stafford Cripps has taken with him for discussion with the Indian Leaders and the question as to whether they will be implemented will depend upon the outcome of these discussions which are now taking place.

His Majesty's Government, having considered the anxieties expressed in this country and in India as to the fulfilment of the promises made in regard to the future of India, have decided to lay down in precise and clear terms the steps which they propose shall be taken for the earliest possible realization of self-government in India. The object is the creation of a new Indian Union which shall constitute a Dominion, associated with the United Kingdom and the other Dominions by a common allegiance to the Crown, but equal to them in every respect, in no way subordinate in any aspect of its domestic or external affairs.

[1] *Ibid.*, p. 4.

His Majesty's Government therefore make the following declaration:

(a) Immediately upon the cessation of hostilities, steps shall be taken to set up in India, in the manner described hereafter, an elected body charged with the task of framing a new Constitution for India.

(b) Provision shall be made as set out below for the participation of the Indian States in the constitution-making body.

(c) His Majesty's Government undertake to accept and implement forthwith the Constitution so framed subject only to:

(i) the right of any Province of British India that is not prepared to accept the new Constitution to retain its present constitutional position, provision being made for its subsequent accession if it so decides.

With such nonacceding Provinces, should they so desire, His Majesty's Government will be prepared to agree upon a new Constitution, giving them the same full status as Indian Union, and arrived at by a procedure analogous to that here laid down.

(ii) the signing of a Treaty which shall be negotiated between His Majesty's Government and the constitution-making body. This Treaty will cover all necessary matters arising out of the complete transfer of responsibility from British to Indian hands; it will make provision, in accordance with the undertakings given by His Majesty's Government, for the protection of racial and religious minorities but will not impose any restriction on the power of the Indian Union to decide in the future its relationship to the other Member States of the British Commonwealth.

Whether or not an Indian State elects to adhere to the Constitution, it will be necessary to negotiate a revision of its Treaty arrangements, so far as this may be required in the new situation.

(d) the constitution-making body shall be composed as follows, unless the leaders of Indian opinion in the principal communities agree upon some other form before the end of hostilities:

Immediately upon the result being known of the provincial elections which will be necessary at the end of hostilities, the entire membership of the Lower Houses of the Provincial Legislatures shall, as a single electoral college, proceed to the election of the constitution-making body by the system of proportional representation. This new body shall be in number about one tenth of the number of the electoral college.

Indian States shall be invited to appoint representatives in the same proportion to their total population as in the case of the representatives of British India as a whole, and with the same powers as the British Indian members.

(*e*) During the critical period which now faces India and until the new Constitution can be framed His Majesty's Government must inevitably bear the responsibility for and retain control and direction of the defense of India as part of their world war effort, but the task of organizing to the full the military, moral, and material resources of India must be the responsibility of the Government of India with the cooperation of the peoples of India. His Majesty's Government desire and invite the immediate and effective participation of the leaders of the principal sections of the Indian people in the counsels of their country, of the Commonwealth, and of the United Nations. Thus they will be enabled to give their active and constructive help in the discharge of a task which is vital and essential for the future freedom of India.

3) *Statement Broadcast by Sir Stafford Cripps, New Delhi, March 30, 1942* [1]

[Excerpt]

So much for the general framework of the proposals. But, as we all know, the most vital and difficult question is that which concerns the interests of the various communities among the Indian people. I'll not attempt to go into any of the historical origins of these difficulties. Let us instead face them as a present fact.

In the great sub-continent of India there is more than one people — there are many peoples and races — as there are in the great sub-continent of Russia. Our object is to give to the Indian peoples full self-government, with complete freedom as to how they will devise and organize their own constitution.

There are those who claim that India should form a single united country; there are others who say it should be divided up into two, three or more separated countries. There are those who claim that provincial autonomy should be very wide, with a few centrally controlled federal services. Others stress the need for centralization, in view of the growing complexity of economic development.

These and many other various ideas are worthy to be explored and debated. But it is for the Indian people, and not any outside authority, to decide under which of these forms India will in the future govern herself.

If the Indian people ask our help it will, of course, be gladly given. But it is for you, the Indian people, to discuss and decide upon your future constitution. We shall look on with deep interest and hope that your wisdom will guide you truly in this great adventure.

[1] *New York Times*, March 31, 1942, p. 15.

We ask you, therefore, to come together, all religions and races, in a constitution-making body, as soon as hostilities are over, to form your own constitution. We have specified the form which that body will take unless — and this is an important point — the leaders of the principal factions of the Indian people agree between themselves before the end of hostilities upon some other and better form.

That constitution-making body will have as its object the framing of a single constitution for the whole of India — that is, of British India together with such of the Indian States as may decide to join in.

But we realize this very simple fact — if you want to persuade a number of people who are inclined to be antagonistic to enter the same room, it's unwise to tell them that once they go in there is no way out. They might fear being locked in together.

It's much wiser to tell them they can go in, and if they find they cannot come to a common decision, then there is nothing to prevent those who wish from leaving again by another door. They are much more likely all to go in if they have knowledge that they can, by their free will, go out again if they cannot agree.

Well, that's what we say to the Provinces of India. Come together to frame a common constitution. If you find after all your discussion and all the give-and-take of a constitution-making assembly that you cannot overcome your differences, and that some Provinces are still not satisfied with the constitution, then such Provinces can go out and remain out if they wish, and just the same degree of self-government and freedom will be available for them as for the Union itself — that is to say, complete self-government.

We hope and expect to see an Indian Union, strong and united because it is founded upon the free consent of all its people. But it is not for us Britishers to dictate to you, the Indian people. You will work out and decide your problem for yourselves. So we provide the means and the road by which you can attain that form of the absolute and united self-government which you desire at the earliest possible moment.

In the past we have waited for different Indian communities to come to a common decision as to how a new constitution for a self-government of India should be framed. And because there has been no agreement among the Indian leaders the British Government has been accused by some of using this fact to delay the granting of freedom to India. We are now giving the lead that has been asked for, and it is in the hands of the Indians, and the Indians only, whether they will accept that lead and so attain their own freedom. If they fail to accept this opportunity the responsibility for that failure must rest with them. We ask you to ccept this fulfilment of our pledges in the past, and it is that request hat I have put before your leaders in the document which you have now een.

In regard to the position of minority communities within the new ndian Union, I am confident that the constitution-making body will nake just provisions for their protection. But in view of the undertaking iven to those minorities by His Majesty's Government in the past, 'e propose that in the treaty, which under the Draft Declaration will e concluded between His Majesty's Government and the constitution-naking body, the new Indian Union should undertake to protect the ights of these minorities.

If there should be any nonacceding Provinces, a similar treaty pro-ision would be made in respect to minority communities within their orders.

I have already indicated to you the position as to the immediate future. know that His Excellency the Viceroy has the greatest hope that the cceptance in principle of this document by the leaders of Indian opinion ill make it possible for him to start forthwith on the consultations which ill enable him to implement the principle laid down in the last para-raph of the document which I have already read over to you.

It contains one essential reservation; that in respect of the responsi-ility for the war. This reservation does not mean that the Governor-eneral and the Executive Council will, or indeed could be, excluded om taking an effective share in the council for the defense of India. a this wide-flung war defense cannot be localized in a single country nd its preparation must permeate the activities of every department government and must demand from every department the fullest ooperation.

If His Majesty's Government are to take full responsibility for the onduct of the naval, military and air defense of India, as it is their duty o do, then the defense of India must be dealt with by them as part of the orld war effort on which they are now engaged, with the direction of at defense directly in the hands of the Commander-in-Chief under the ar Cabinet and their highest staff officers.

But, as I have already pointed out, the Government of India must also ave an effective share in the defense councils. And so we have decided at the Commander-in-Chief should retain his position as a member of e Executive Council.

In order, however, that India will have her full voice in this central ntrol of strategy — defensive and offensive — not only in India herself, it in all the interrelated theaters of war, we have invited the appointment of a representative Indian to the War Cabinet and to the Pacific Council of the United Nations.

That is one of the ways in which India will have her full say in the councils of the Commonwealth and of the United Nations as an equal partner. And when it comes to the making of the peace, India will appoint her own representatives to the peace conference, side by side with those of the other free nations, and so make her contribution to the building of a new world order.

(4) Resolution of the All-India Congress Working Committee, Issued on April 11, 1942 [1]

The Working Committee have given full and earnest consideration to the proposals made by the British War Cabinet with regard to India and the elucidation of them by Sir Stafford Cripps.

These proposals, which have been made at the very last hour because of the compulsion of events, have to be considered not only in relation to India's demand for independence but more especially, in the present grave war crisis, with a view to meeting effectively the perils and danger that confront India and envelop the world.

Congress has repeatedly stated, ever since the commencement of the war in September 1939, that the people of India would line themselves with the progressive forces of the world and assume full responsibility to face the new problems and shoulder the new burdens that had arisen and it asked for the necessary conditions to enable them to do so to be created. The essential condition was the freedom of India, for only the realization of present freedom could light the flame which would illuminate millions of hearts and move them to action.

At the last meeting of the All-India Congress Committee, after the commencement of the war in the Pacific, it was stated that: "Only a free and independent India can be in a position to undertake the defense of the country on a national basis and be able to help in the furtherance of the larger causes that are emerging from the form of war."

The British War Cabinet's new proposals relate principally to the future, upon the cessation of hostilities. The Committee, while recognizing that self-determination for the people of India is accepted in principle in that uncertain future, regret that this is fettered and circumscribed and that certain provisions have been introduced which gravely imperil the development of a free and united national government and

[1] United Kingdom, Parliamentary Papers, India (Lord Privy Seal's Mission) Cmd. 6350, p. 16.

he establishment of a democratic State. Even the constitution-making
ody is so constituted that the people's right of self-determination is
nitiated by the introduction of nonrepresentative elements.

The people of India have, as a whole, clearly demanded full independ-
nce, and Congress has repeatedly declared that no other status except
hat of independence for the whole of India could be agreed to or could
neet the essential requirements of the present situation.

The Committee recognize that future independence may be implicit
n the proposals, but the accompanying provisions and restrictions are
uch that real freedom may well become an illusion.

The complete ignoring of ninety millions of people in the Indian States,
nd their treatment as commodities at the disposal of their Rulers, is a
egation both of democracy and self-determination. While the repre-
entation of an Indian State in the constitution-making body is fixed
n a population basis, the people of the State have no voice in choosing
hose representatives, nor are they to be consulted at any stage while
ecisions vitally affecting them are being taken. Such States may in
nany ways become barriers to the growth of Indian freedom, enclaves
here foreign authority still prevails, and where the possibility of main-
aining foreign-armed forces has been stated to be a likely contingency
nd a perpetual menace to the freedom of the people of the States as
ell as of the rest of India.

The acceptance beforehand of the novel principle of nonaccession for a
rovince is also a severe blow to the conception of Indian unity and an
pple of discord likely to generate growing trouble in the Provinces, and
hich may well lead to further difficulties in the way of the Indian States
nerging themselves into an Indian Union. Congress has been wedded to
ndian freedom and unity and any break of that unity especially in the
nodern world when peoples' minds inevitably think in terms of ever
arger federations would be injurious to all concerned and exceedingly
ainful to contemplate. Nevertheless the Committee cannot think in
erms of compelling the people of any territorial unit to remain in an
ndian Union against their declared and established will. While recog-
izing this principle, the Committee feel that every effort should be made
o create conditions which would help the different units in developing
 common and cooperative national life. Acceptance of this principle
nevitably involves that no changes should be made which would result
n fresh problems being created and compulsion being exercised on other
bstantial groups within that area. Each territorial unit should have
ne fullest possible autonomy within the Union consistent with a strong
National State.

The proposal now made on the part of the British War Cabinet encou ages and will lead to attempts at separation at the very inception of th Union and thus create great friction just when the utmost cooperatio and good will are most needed. This proposal has been presumably mad to meet the communal demand, but it will have other consequences als and lead politically reactionary and obscurantist groups among th different communities to create trouble and divert public attention from the vital issues before the country.

Any proposal concerning the future of India must demand attentio and scrutiny, but in today's grave crisis it is the present that counts an even the proposals for the future in so far as they affect the present. Th Committee necessarily attached the greatest importance to this aspe of the question and on this ultimately depends what advice they shoul give to those who look to them for guidance. For this the present Britis War Cabinet's proposals are vague and altogether incomplete, and the would appear to be no vital changes in the present structure conten plated. It has been made clear that the defense of India will in an event remain under British control. At any time Defense is a vit subject; during war time it is all-important and covers almost ever sphere of life and administration. To take away Defense from th sphere of responsibility at this stage is to reduce that responsibilit to a farce and nullity, and to make it perfectly clear that India is n going to be free in any way and her Government is not going function as a free and independent Government during the pendenc of the war.

The Committee would repeat that the essential fundamental pr requisite for the assumption of responsibility by the Indian people the present is their realization as a fact that they are free and are charge of maintaining and defending their freedom. What is most want is the enthusiastic response of the people, which cannot be evoked wit out the fullest trust in them and the devolution of responsibility on the in the matter of Defense. It is only thus that even in this grave elevent hour it may be possible to galvanize the people of India to rise to th height of the occasion. It is manifest that the present Government India, as well as its Provincial agencies, are lacking in competence an are incapable of shouldering the burden of India's defense. It is on the people of India, through their popular representatives, who m shoulder this burden worthily. But that can only be done by prese freedom and full responsibility being cast upon them. The Committ are, therefore, unable to accept the proposals put forward on behalf the British War Cabinet.

) *Resolution of the All-India Moslem League Working Committee, Issued on April 11, 1942* [1]

The Working Committee of the All-India Moslem League have given heir most earnest and careful consideration to the announcement made y Mr. Churchill, the British Prime Minister, in the House of Commons 1 March 11, 1942, and the Draft Declaration of the War Cabinet of is Majesty's Government regarding the future of India, and also the terim proposals during the critical period which now faces India for le immediate participation of the Leaders of the principal sections of le Indian People in the counsels of their country.

The Committee appreciate that the British Prime Minister in his conouncement made it clear that the Draft Declaration embodied only le proposals of His Majesty's Government and not their decision, and lat they are subject to agreement between the main elements in India; lus maintaining the validity of the Declaration of August 8, 1940, hich had promised to the Moslems that neither the machinery for le framing of the Constitution should be set up, nor the Constitution self should be enforced, without the approval and consent of Moslem ldia.

The Committee, while expressing their gratification that the possi- lity of Pakistan is recognized by implication by providing for the itablishment of two or more independent Unions in India, regret that le proposals of His Majesty's Government embodying the fundamentals e not open to any modification and therefore no alternative proposals e invited. In view of the rigidity of the attitude of His Majesty's overnment with regard to the fundamentals not being open to any odification, the Committee have no alternative but to say that the oposals in their present form are unacceptable to them for the following asons:

(1) The Mussulmans, after twenty-five years of genuine efforts for the conciliation of the two major communities and the bitter experience of le failure of such efforts, are convinced that it is neither just nor possible, the interests of peace and the happiness of the two peoples, to compel constitute one Indian Union composed of the two principal nations — indus and Moslems: but this appears to be the main object of His ajesty's Government as adumbrated in the preamble of the Draft eclaration, the creation of more than one Union being relegated only the realm of remote possibility, and is purely illusory.

[1] *Ibid.*, p. 18.

(2) In the Draft Declaration a constitution-making body has been proposed with the primary object of creating one Indian Union. So far as the Moslem League is concerned, it has finally decided that the only solution of India's constitutional problem is the partition of India into independent zones: and it will therefore be unfair to the Moslems to compel them to enter such a constitution-making body whose main object is the creation of a new Indian Union. With conditions as they are it will be not only futile but on the contrary may exacerbate bitterness and animosity among the various elements in the country.

The machinery which has been proposed for the creation of the constitution-making body, namely that it will consist of members elected by the newly elected Lower Houses of the eleven Provinces upon the cessation of hostilities as a single electoral College by the system of proportional representation, is a fundamental departure from the right of the Mussulmans hitherto enjoyed by them to elect their representatives by means of separate electorates, which is the only sure way in which true representatives of the Mussulmans can be chosen.

The constitution-making body will take decisions by a bare majority on all questions of the most vital and paramount character involved in the framing of the Constitution, which is a departure from the fundamental principles of justice and contrary to constitutional practice so far followed in the various countries and Dominions; and the Mussulmans by agreeing to this will instead of exercising their right and judgment as a constituent factor, be at the entire mercy of the constitution making body in which they will be a minority of about 25 per cent.

(3) The right of nonaccession to the Union as contemplated in the Draft Declaration has been conceded presumably in response to the insistent demands by the Mussulmans for the partition of India : but the method and procedure laid down are such as to negative the professed object; for in the draft proposals the right of nonaccession has been given to the existing Provinces which have been formed from time to time for administrative convenience and on no logical basis.

The Mussulmans cannot be satisfied by such a Declaration on a vital question affecting their future destiny, and demand a clear and precise pronouncement on the subject. Any attempt to solve the future problem of India by the process of evading the real issue is to court disaster.

In the draft proposals no procedure has been laid down as to how the verdict of the Province is to be obtained in favor of or against accession to the one Union, but in the letter dated April second from the Secretary of Sir Stafford Cripps addressed to the President of the All-India Moslem League it is stated that "a Province should reach the decision whether or

ot to stand out of the Union by a vote in the Legislative Assembly on a
esolution to stand in." [1]

If the majority for accession to the Union is less than 60 per cent the
inority will have the right to demand a plebiscite of the adult male
opulation. In this connection it must be emphasized that in the Prov-
ices where the Mussulmans are in a majority, as in the case of the major
rovinces of Bengal and the Punjab, they are in a minority in the Legisla-
ve Assemblies, and in the Assemblies of Sind and the Northwest
rontier Province the total number (namely 60 and 50 respectively) is
) small and the weightage given to the non-Moslems so heavy that it
an be easily manipulated, and a decision under such conditions cannot
e the true criterion of ascertaining the real opinion of the Mussulmans
f those Provinces.

As regards the suggested plebiscite in the Provinces in which the
Iussulmans are in a majority, in the event of the requisite majority not
eing available in the Legislative Assemblies, the procedure laid down
 that reference shall be made to the whole adult population of the
rovinces and not to the Mussulmans alone; which is to deny them the
iherent right to self-determination.

(4) With regard to the Indian States, it is the considered opinion of
ie Committee that it is a matter for them to decide whether to join or
ot to join or form a Union.

(5) With regard to the Treaties to be negotiated between the Crown
nd the Indian Union or Unions, the proposals do not indicate as to what
ould happen in case of disagreement on the terms between the contract-
ig parties; nor is there any provision made as to what would be the
rocedure when there is a difference of opinion in negotiating a revision
f treaty arrangements with the Indian States in the new situation.

(6) With regard to the interim arrangement there is no definite pro-
osal except the bare statement that His Majesty's Government desire
nd invite the effective and immediate participation of the leaders of
ie principal sections of the Indian people in the counsels of their country,
 the Commonwealth, and of the United Nations. The Committee are
ierefore unable to express their opinion until a complete picture is
vailable. Another reason why the Committee are unable to express
ieir opinion on the interim arrangements for participation in the
ounsels of the country is that Sir Stafford Cripps has made it clear that
ie scheme goes through as a whole or is rejected as a whole, and that it
ould not be possible to retain only the part relating to the immediate
rrangements at the center and discard the rest of the draft scheme; and

[1] *Ibid.*, p. 6.

as the Committee has come to the conclusion that the proposals for th
future are unacceptable, it will serve no useful purpose to deal furth
with the question of the immediate arrangements.

(6) *Address by Sir Stafford Cripps to the House of Commons, Ap 28, 1942* [1]

The Lord Privy Seal (Sir Stafford Cripps): When it was announce
by the Prime Minister that I was to go to India with the Cabinet
proposals, this House was good enough to express its hopes that th
Mission might have a successful conclusion. That hope was, I kno
shared by a great mass of the British people, by the Dominions and by
multitude of the friends of Great Britain and of India both in the Unite
States of America and elsewhere. Unfortunately events have broug
disappointment to these hopes, but I do not think that anyone in th
country need feel regretful that the proposals were put forward or ne
blame His Majesty's Government or the British people for the unfc
tunate fact of failure to reach an agreement. Moreover, I should like
emphasize at the outset of what may, I fear, prove a rather long accou
of my Mission that, in my view, nothing but good will result both fro
the fact that the proposals were made and from the almost equal
important fact that the War Cabinet sent one of its own number
discuss them in India with the leaders of Indian opinion. This method
presentation of the proposals has, I believe, demonstrated our sinceri
of purpose.

BACKGROUND

Let me first say a word or two as to the background of my vis
Undoubtedly the moment was a difficult one, and a number of peoj
have made the comment that it is a pity that something on the same lin
was not done earlier. There is much in the relationships of this country
India that could be criticized, analyzed and argued about, but I do n
propose to embark upon any such argument, as it is far more profitab
to spend the time available in an examination of the present and t
future rather than in an attempt to allot blame for the past — that is
task which we can very well leave to the historians.

The moment was a difficult one, for three main reasons. First, becau
of the imminent approach of the enemy to the shores of India. The Jaj
nese forces by land, sea and air were almost at the gates of India, and
such circumstances many things that might have been usefully discuss

[1] British Information Services, New York.

id negotiated in more peaceful times could not be dealt with because
ere was an overriding need to do everything in our power to carry out
ir duty to defend India from the foreign invader. Second, owing to
ents in the Far Eastern theater of war, accompanied by a highly
illed though grossly misleading propaganda from Axis sources, an
mosphere of defeatism and of anti-British sentiment was showing itself
certain sections of Indian opinion. The Indians were, too, uncertain of
ie future and of His Majesty's Government's view as to what that
ture would be. Third, with the approach of self-government or Domin-
n status as a reality, communal differences of view as to the form of
vernment which would be suitable for the future India had tended to
come more definitely crystallized, and especially the idea of two
parate Indias, which, even two years ago, was little more than a vague
sion of certain extremists, had come to be the definite and accepted pro-
am of the most powerful Moslem political organization.

There were, of course, other factors in the situation, but these were the
incipal ones which increased the difficulties of obtaining any general
iderstanding among the Indian peoples. It was the need for clarifica-
on of the situation and for the consolidation of Indian opinion in a
vorable direction that impelled His Majesty's Government to decide
at some positive step must be taken, and taken quickly. The objective
id the hope of His Majesty's Government were that we might use these
iry difficulties of the occasion to bring together all the main leaders of
idian opinion for the double purpose of solving India's future and of
inforcing her defense against the invader that was threatening her
ores. In order to accomplish this, two things were necessary: first, to
ve a clear and unequivocal promise as regards the future, and, second,
address an invitation to the various communal and political sections
Indian opinion to come together on the Viceroy's Executive Council
r the immediate prosecution of the war in India. This invitation would
ve to be made upon the basis of the offer as to the future status of
dia.

FUTURE INTENTIONS

In the circumstances of the communal situation in India at the present
ne, it must be borne in mind that the future is inevitably linked with the
esent, and I personally am quite confident that no mere temporary
rangement could have been come to without some exposition of our
ture intentions. Had we attempted to deal only with the present, we
ould immediately have been met with a demand for clarification as
the future.

The difficulty of that communal situation has recently been emphasize by Mr. Gandhi in an article in "Harijan" of 19th April, where he make the following statement:

Attainment of independence is an impossibility till we have solved the com munal tangle. We will never tackle this problem so long as either or both parti think that independence will or can come without any solution of the tang There are two ways of solving what has almost become insoluble, the royal wa of non-violence or violence.

His Majesty's Government also had to deal with certain definite - and often conflicting — demands which had been voiced by the variou leaders of important sections of Indian opinion. The Congress was know to have demanded repeatedly independence for India and a Constituei Assembly which should devise a new Constitution for the Indian peop and, perhaps most important of all, a single Indian Government for th whole of India — British India and the Indian States together. Th Moslem League, on the other hand, had adopted as the main plank of i program the demand for Pakistan — a territory made up of the rath vague congeries of areas in which Moslems are in a majority. The mo dispersed but still important minority of the depressed classes desir specific protection against the adverse effect of the caste system; whi the Sikhs, that brave fighting race who have done and are doing so muc to help Great Britain and the defense of India, desired some form protection against the majority rule of another community. There we many other minorities, religious, racial or social, who equally asked f special treatment, either along the lines of that already accorded to the under the Act of 1935 or upon a more generous scale. Then, outsi British India, were the Princes and their peoples, some of the Princ having special Treaty rights, arising in many cases over a century a but the whole under the paramountcy of the King-Emperor.

Among those conflicting claims it was necessary for His Majesty Government to act with the mind of an arbitrator and attempt to l down some method by which the Indian peoples could determine the own future, a method that would be acceptable to as many shades opinion as possible. It was, of course, wholly consistent with the trer of earlier declarations that if all sections of Indian opinion could agr upon some alternative method of self-determination, there would be difficulty as to its acceptance by His Majesty's Government. In th past when it had been left to the Indian communities to agree upon son manner of deciding the future the British Government had been accuse of relying upon the impossibility of agreement in order to perpetua their own domination over India. It was, therefore, necessary, to devise

heme whereby the refusal of a large minority to cooperate would not
ld up the majority in their attainment of self-government.

WHITE PAPER

So much for the considerations upon which that part of the draft
eclaration dealing with the future Constitution of India was based and
iich resulted in the form in which it was laid before the Indian leaders
d in which it appears on page 4 of the White Paper.[1] The second part
the draft Declaration — paragraph (e) — was to deal with the im-
ediate period before the new Constitution could come into being. It
is left in vague and general terms but was subject to one vital and pre-
e reservation. The reason for this form was that it was desired to leave
en for discussion the way in which participation by the Indian leaders
n the counsels of their country, of the Commonwealth and of the United
ations" — to use the words of the document — could be made most
ective and immediate. The single express reservation was as to defense,
d I will return to that point in detail, since it was one of the difficulties
iich arose in the course of the discussions in Delhi.

Let me now say a word about the manner of conducting these discus-
ns. I was most anxious that there should be no suspicion whatever
at His Majesty's Government were handpicking those whom I saw,
d, consequently, I asked the main organizations themselves to appoint
ose whom they wished to meet me. This they did, and they mostly
pressed the wish that I should not interview any other members of
eir Working Committees. Certain individuals I saw, such as Mr.
ndhi, Sir Taj Bahadur Sapru, Mr. Joshi and Mr. Jayakar, the present
past Prime Ministers of all the Provincial Governments, the Governors
the Provinces and, lastly, but by no means least, the members of the
ceroy's Executive Council. It was to this latter body that I first dis-
sed the details of the draft Declaration, immediately upon my arrival
India, and after seeing them each one individually, it was to the same
dy that I first announced the failure of agreement. His Majesty's
vernment are fully aware of the service that has been done by the
mbers of the Viceroy's Executive and especially by those Indians
o have represented the interests of their peoples in that body, and it
s for that reason that I considered it necessary to go first and last to
em. As the House will know, I kept the draft Declaration from publica-
n for the first week of my stay in Delhi, during which time I sub-
tted it to all the principal Indian representative leaders personally.

United Kingdom, Parliamentary Papers, *India* (*Lord Privy Seal's Mission*),
d. 5380, London, 1942.

It then became clear that its contents were becoming generally know
and it was considered better that it should be published, and this w
done. The Indian Press were both helpful and fair, in that they gave t
fullest publicity to all that I said to them at the Press conferences whi
I held every other day, while of course, at the same time, expressing th
own views, often very forcibly.

SELF-GOVERNMENT

It is worthy of note that the skilful and analytical minds of the India
sometimes lead them to seek out and emphasize every point as to whi
there might be doubt, or disagreement, while they are apt to pass ov
the more uninteresting points as to which there is agreement. Th
sometimes gives the appearance of a much more keen and concentrat
opposition than in fact exists. Upon the fundamental and vital poi
of their self-government and self-determination there was, I believe,
single case of disagreement, not excluding the representatives of t
European community, whom I saw twice. Disagreement came upon t
way in which that self-determination should be exercised and upon t
transitory provisions for the government of India until the new Constit
tion could come into force. It must always be remembered that o
legacy of the past is the unwillingness of any considerable section
Indian opinion to accept any British offer unless it is also accepted
at least one of the two principal bodies — Congress and the Mosle
League. The state of internal opinion is such that unless there is to b
large measure of acceptance of an offer, no minority cares to lay its
open to the accusation of being the creature of British imperialis
It was therefore to be anticipated, and we did anticipate, that there wou
either be a general acceptance or a general rejection of the draft Declar
tion.

Before I pass to the particular matters around which the discussio
developed, I must make clear one other matter in relation to the negot
tions. When I was sent to India by the War Cabinet I was given f
authority to arrive at a settlement within the terms of the draft Decla
tion. That is to say, its essentials had to be maintained, a matter whi
I myself regarded as of importance, as it was the one and only way
which a general discursive and endless discussion could be avoide
But I alone was responsible for what was put forward to Indian leaders
way of explanation or amplification of details in the draft Declaratio
I naturally maintained the closest contact with the Viceroy. We met,
fact, every night during my stay and discussed the progress of even
I also maintained the closest contact with the Commander-in-Chief, a

•th of them were most helpful, but the responsibility for what was done
is mine and was not theirs. There was a tendency in some Indian
quarters to suggest that they were responsible for the difficulties over
fense. Nothing could be further from the truth.

COLONEL LOUIS JOHNSON

There is, perhaps, one other person to whom I should make reference
as to avoid any misunderstanding, since his name has been somewhat
ndied about in the Press. It so happened by coincidence that while I
was in New Delhi an Economic Mission arrived from the United States
America, headed by Colonel Louis Johnson, representing directly in
at matter the President. He was entertained by the Viceroy at his
use on his first arrival, and while he was there one of the Congress
ders asked to see him. After consulting with the Viceroy and in
cordance with the latter's advice he saw Pandit Nehru and in a most
lpful conversation ascertained what at that time seemed to be the
ficulty in the way of a settlement. I also called upon Colonel Louis
hnson by way of courtesy on his arrival and gave him as accurate a
ture of the situation as I could. Thereafter, on my suggestion, and
accordance with his own personal desire to be of any assistance that
could, he had other interviews which were of great help in clarifying
e situation. At no time did he act otherwise than in a purely personal
pacity, and he, like two or three of my good Indian friends, merely
l his best to give what help he could to the parties. I am personally
st grateful to him, and I am sure the leaders of Congress are similarly
   But I wish to make it abundantly clear that there was no question
any American intervention but only the personal help of a very able
nerican citizen.
Let me now come to the difficulties that arose. These were mostly con-
ntrated into my discussions and correspondence with Congress leaders.
e Moslem League did not deliver to me their objections until after they
ew the results of my negotiations with Congress. The questions out-
e the Congress objections which were raised by other sections of
nion I will deal with separately. The difficulties fell under three heads,
will be observed from a perusal of the final resolution of Congress [1]
l the letter from the Congress President of 10th April which appear
pectively on pages 16 and 9 of the White Paper. First were those
ating to the method of determining the new Constitution; second were
se relating to defense; and third were those relating to the general
m of the interim Government.

[1] See p. 552.

So far as the first cartegory was concerned, there were three objection First, to the use of the word "Dominion" and its definition in the openi paragraph of the draft Declaration. This was not a matter of prime im portance. The claim of Congress had been, as we know, for independen and they were afraid that their followers would attach undue importan to the apparent limitations included in the definition, though I think t leaders themselves appreciated that with the added words in Clause II) of the draft Declaration —

will not impose any restriction on the power of the Indian Union to dec in the future its relationship to the other Member States of the British Co monwealth —

it was made perfectly clear that India could, in fact, leave the Brit Commonwealth of Nations should the Indian Government under the n Constitution so decide. I pass, therefore, from that objection.

NON-ACCESSION

The second objection was a most substantial one. That was as to t right of non-accession of the Provinces after the new Constitution h been decided upon. In this relation I would ask hon. Members to stu the two resolutions of Congress and the Moslem League and then to lo at the draft Declaration. They will, I think, come to the conclusion tl the draft Declaration does no more than Mr. Gandhi and other Congr leaders have constantly stated that they were prepared to do, that is, keep open the issue of Pakistan, and they will also, I am sure, realize tl the scheme of the draft Declaration is as fair a compromise as possi between the two extreme views. It was the duty of His Majest Government to find that agreement by compromise and not to give eit party all of what they wanted and then force it upon the other. I do personally believe that it is possible to find under existing circumstan a fairer solution of the problem, a solution which aims at and provi for a single united India but which admits that if in the last resort parties cannot agree upon a form of Constitution which will enable th to work together, then the Moslems must be allowed in those Provin where they can get a majority of the whole electorate to vote th Provinces out of the Union.

I should add one word of explanation as to the proposal which made for effecting this non-accession and which does not appear in document itself. The only ultimate test must be the wish of the act majority of the adult male population in the Provinces — that is to s a plebiscite. But it is not necessary to go to the trouble of a plebisc

ere the result is a foregone conclusion. It was, therefore, suggested that
ery Province should pass in its Lower House a formal vote of accession
 the new Union, but if there was a minority of 40 % or more against
at accession, then the minority should have the right to challenge a
ebiscite, which should then determine the matter by a simple majority.
lesire to emphasize once again that this whole scheme was no rigid and
changing plan, since it was expressly to be open to the Indian com-
unities to agree among themselves as to a better alternative.
The third and last objection under this head was as regards the posi-
n of the Indian States. Congress has for many years now interested
elf in the lot of the people in the Indian States and has declared that
 any new Constitution these people, as distinct from their autocratic
ers, must have a say. They therefore protested, not against the
dian States coming into the Constitution-making authority, but against
eir representatives being nominated by the rulers and not elected by
e people. Unfortunately, in my view, representative institutions have
t yet developed in the great majority of the Indian States, which
ust be dealt with as they are if they are to be brought into the Constitu-
n-making authority. That participation, I believe, almost everyone
sires, including indeed most of the States' rulers themselves.

RAPID DEVELOPMENT WELCOME

His Majesty's Government would be only too glad to see as rapid a
velopment of suitable representative institutions as is possible in all the
dian States, and if by the time a Constitution-making body came to be
osen there was machinery in the States by which popular representa-
es could be chosen, His Majesty's Government would be only too
ased. Already, as some hon. Members may know, a small beginning
s been made in some States by more enlightened rulers and their
wans, and I am certain this House would wish the British Administra-
n in India to do all it can to encourage and expedite that development.
t for the moment we can only deal with the situation as it exists his-
ically. I need not trouble the House with all the complexities of the
esent constitutional position so far as the Indian States are concerned,
ce, under the draft Declaration, that position would have been altered
ly so far as alteration was necessary to adjust economic relationships
th the new Indian Union or was caused by the action of the Indian
ates themselves in joining the new Union.
However, none of these three differences with Congress Working Com-
ttee would have been decisive of a negative result. For though object-
; and registering their protest, both Congress, the Moslem League and

other bodies such as the Hindu Mahasabha, would have been prepare
to cooperate upon the immediate situation despite the making of t
Declaration of His Majesty's Government, and that is probably t
most that one could expect in the circumstances. It would, in fact, ha
meant that the solution for self-determination laid down in the docume
would have then held the field with finality subject only to the vario
communities and bodies in India arriving at some alternative method l
agreement.

There is one other matter with regard to the future that I must ref
to, and that is the position of the minorities, such as the depressed classe
the Sikhs, the Indian Christians and others. Each one wished, and n
unnaturally, to have some special and specific measure of protectic
included to cover its own case. But once self-determination had be
promised to India as was proposed in the draft Declaration, it would
impossible for His Majesty's Government to impose terms in the ne
Indian Constitution. To do so would be the negation of self-determin
tion. We have, however, in the past given undertakings to these mino
ties, but in none of the cases other than that of the Moslems could the
promises be dealt with by such a device as non-accession. The minoriti
are not sufficiently localized or self-contained, even in the case of t
Sikhs, to make that possible, assuming upon other grounds that it w
desirable.

Some other solution, therefore, had to be found. I have not the sligh
est doubt that these minorities, all of whom would have been represente
in the Constitution-making body, in accordance with their streng
under the communal award, would have obtained ample protection und
the Constitution from the majority. Indeed, the forces operating with
that Constitution-making body would have tended very much in favor
the minorities. But in view of our pledges we could not leave the mino
ties to rely upon this alone. We, therefore, inserted the express clause
to a treaty covering minority protection which will be found in par
graph (c, II) of the draft Declaration. I should like to record here th
neither Congress nor the Moslem League expressed the slightest obje
tion to this method of treatment of the subject. The minorities the
selves were, of course, unable to say at this stage what form of protecti
they wished for, since till the form of the new Constitution is known
one can state how within that form minorities can best be protecte
That would have had to have been a matter for negotiation when t
main lines of the Constitution had been decided upon. The minoriti
were all of them, I think, anxious to come into the temporary governme
had it been formed under the terms of the draft Declaration, despi

heir criticism of the scheme as a whole, as lacking more specific protec-
on for their own interests.

DEFENSE

I now pass to the second category of objection, that relating to defense.
his is a matter which is far more complicated than might appear on the
ce of it, and one as to which there was a distinct division of opinion
mong Indians themselves. Upon one thing there was, I think, practical
nanimity, and that was that the actual technical conduct of the war in
dia — the control of the Armed Forces for fighting purposes — must re-
ain under the British Commander-in-Chief. Everyone realized that that
as mere common sense, and so there was no difficulty with regard to it.
he difference of opinion came when the responsibilities of the Govern-
ent of India — as apart from those of His Majesty's Government —
ere considered. These latter — that is the direct responsibilities of
is Majesty's Government — would have been quite satisfactorily
alt with by having a representative Indian on the War Cabinet and
the Pacific Council, both of which posts were offered to the Indian
aders. It was first sought to clarify the position as between His
ajesty's Government's direct responsibilities and those of the Govern-
ent of India by a rewording of the final draft of clause (e) in the form
which it now appears in the White Paper on page 5. The document
ys:

During the critical period which now faces India and until the new Constitu-
n can be framed His Majesty's Government must inevitably bear the re-
nsibility for and retain control and direction of the defense of India as part
their world war effort, but the task of organizing to the full the military,
ral and material resources of India must be the responsibility of the Gov-
ment of India with the cooperation of the peoples of India.

was sought by those words to define as clearly as possible the division
responsibilities direct of His Majesty's Government and those of the
vernment of India. But there is another cross division of responsi-
ities which is much more difficult to define and separate out. The
use will appreciate that since the last war the Commander-in-Chief
India has also held the post of Defense Member on the Viceroy's
ecutive Council, and his actual functions and activities are divided
tween the two posts that he holds. In fact, the Defense Secretariat, the
efense Department and the Staff are, from the mere fact that they have
common chief — a single individual — all interlinked and interde-
ndent in such a way as to make anything like a complete and detailed
paration of the functions of the Commander-in-Chief from those of the

Defense Minister a very long and complicated matter, and one which, it were to be attempted at such a critical moment as this, would thro into chaos the whole defense organization of India. Nevertheless took the view — and in this the Viceroy and Commander-in-Chief agree — that it would be difficult for the representative Indians on the Vic roy's Executive to rouse the people of India to their defense, unless th could say with justice that at least some part of that defense was t responsibility of a representative Indian, and so of the Indian peopl That was the point that was stressed by practically everyone whom interviewed, including the Europeans.

NEW DELHI

It was in the attempt to get over this very real difficulty that I spen good deal of my time at New Delhi. Various suggestions were made, a several formulae were tried, until eventually that one was worked o which became the final suggestion, and that is the only one with which need now deal. It will be found on page 8 of the White Paper, Docume No. (8). Its object was quite simple: to allocate to the Commander-i Chief, as War Member of the Viceroy's Executive, all those administ tive functions under the Government of India that were vital to I efficient carrying on of the war — that is, the governmental relations all his Staffs, his General Staff, his Naval Staff and his Air Staff — wh at the same time leaving to a representative Indian other functions of t Defense Member roughly corresponding to the list on page 8 of the Wh Paper under the heading, Annex (I), together with a number of other ve important functions, examples of which are given under Annex (II) the same page, and which would, in fact, have made the new Defer Department one of the largest of all Departments in India. The Hou will, of course, realize that numerous other aspects of defense, such civil defense, communications, labor and so on, are already in the han of Indian Members of the Viceroy's Council and would, of course, ha so continued, although the personages might have been changed.

It was impossible for His Majesty's Government to go further w safety — and no risk could be taken at such a moment as the present on vital and immediate a matter as the defense of India. Moreover, I do i myself believe that the minorities who contain some of the finest fighti elements in India — such as the Punjaubi Moslems and Sikhs — wou have been prepared to consent at this stage to any further devolution defense responsibilities. The question did not actually arise, as I Majesty's Government were not able to go any further, but from attitude of those minorities I am confident they would not have consen

ɔ any further transfer in this field. I believe that this latest formula
ɹight have gained acceptance, and at one moment, as the House is aware,
ɪe Indian people seemed to think a satisfactory solution had been found.
myself feel pretty sure that had Congress leaders been able to accept
nally the draft Declaration and enter the new Government they would,
pon the question of defense, have been able to rally their Indian followers
ehind them.

THE FINAL BREAK

But it was not upon this issue that the final break came, although it
as no doubt to some undefined extent involved in the breakdown. The
nal question which was raised at my last and long meeting with the
resident of Congress and Pandit Nehru was as to the form of the tem-
orary Government that should be in power until the end of the war and
ɪe coming into operation of the new Constitution. I had from the outset
ɪade it clear to all those whom I saw that it was not possible to make any
ɔnstitutional changes except of the most insignificant kind prior to the
ew Constitution which would come into operation as a result of the
bors of the Constitution-making Assembly. This fact had been accepted
y everyone without discussion, and it was obvious that it was a practical
npossibility to start upon the discussion and framing of a new Constitu-
on at this present time, and that if such a discussion had been prac-
cable and had been embarked upon, it would have occupied many
ɪonths, during which nothing could have been done by way of forming a
ew Government. Not only so, but any such alteration now made would
ave been thought to prejudge the situation under the new Constitution,
ɪd that would no doubt have met with opposition for that reason.
herefore, any such step as recasting the Constitution at the present
ɪme was admittedly out of the question. This was made quite clear in
ɪy letter to the President of Congress, dated 17th April, where I stated:

As the Working Committee have fully understood, it is impossible to make
ɪy change in the existing Constitution during the period of hostilities.

t the same time His Majesty's Government were most anxious to make a
ɹality of the offer under Clause (e) of the draft Declaration in any way
ɪat was practicable consistently with the existing Constitution. It
always possible in such circumstances by mutual understanding and
ɪth the cooperation of both sides to do much, especially when all are
ɪtent upon a common object so vital and all-embracing as the defense of
ɪdia. The question as to the formation of a new Government, how the
embers of the Viceroy's Executive should be treated and how the

business therein should be conducted, were, of course, essential matter
for the Viceroy, who had to carry on the Government of India, and no
for me as a member of the War Cabinet on a visit to India. I therefor
told the Congress leaders that the general principle of participation of
cooperation was laid down in Clause (e) of the Declaration, which stated

His Majesty's Government desire and invite the immediate and effecti
participation of the leaders of the principal sections of the Indian people in th
counsels of their country.

but that the exact nature of its operation could only be decided as th
result of discussions with the Viceroy, once Indian leaders had made u
their minds that they could accept the draft Declaration upon othe
points. I stated that I was prepared to remain in India in such an ever
until the new Government was formed, so that I could, if necessary, giv
any help that was required, but that I was not prepared to bind th
Viceroy to accept any particular arrangement for the conduct of h
Executive. I informed them, after discussion with the Viceroy, that in
mediately they decided to accept he would call the principal leaders int
consultation as to the formation of his new Government and that th
only British members upon whom the scheme insisted were the Vicerc
himself and the Commander-in-Chief. I also pointed out to them tha
if the conditions offered by the Viceroy were such that they could ne
see their way to accept them, they would, of course, be free, as woul
any other individuals, to refuse to take office or, if they found they cou.
not work in the Government, they would be free to resign, though nat
rally I hoped that such a situation would never in fact arise.

IMPOSSIBLE SITUATION

I see no other way myself in which the matter could have been a
ranged, but the Congress leaders, as is shown by their final letter, ap
parently felt that they would not have the wide powers which the
thought necessary for their successful participation in the Governmen
As I pointed out in my broadcast on this subject from New Delhi,[1] th
position of complete power asked for by Congress — which was n
demanded by any other section of opinion in India — would leave th
matter in an impossible situation. The Executive Council, once chose
by the Viceroy, would not have been responsible to anyone but ther
selves, or, in a somewhat loose way perhaps, to their political or con
munal organizations, and there would have been no protection therefo

[1] Farewell broadcast to the People of India, April 11, 1942, *International Concili
tion*, No. 381, June 1942, p. 332.

or any of the minorities. I am quite confident that none of the minori-
ies would have accepted such a position, and least of all the Moslems.
t was on this issue that the final break came, followed, as I had expected,
y a rejection by the Moslem League, for reasons the precise opposite of
hose stated by Congress, but all of them concerned with the future
ather than with the present.

I regret, and His Majesty's Government regret, most profoundly that
ur efforts have failed. But do not let the House or the people of this
ountry imagine that all the results of the War Cabinet's action and of my
Mission are on the debit side. There is much, I think, on the credit side
s well. First there is the advantage which accrues from the methods
which have been adopted in this case. Instead of a somewhat vague
eclaration put out without previous consultation with leaders of
ndian opinion, a precise and clear statement of a suggested solution has
een discussed in India with all the Indian leaders by a member of the
War Cabinet sent there for that particular purpose. And the fact that a
member of the Cabinet was sent in the stressed circumstances of today
as indicated the depth and genuineness of our desire to reach a settlement of our outstanding difficulties. Second, the content of the scheme
as put beyond all possibility of doubt or question that we desire to give
ndia self-government at the earliest practicable moment and that we
ish her to determine for herself the form which that Government shall
ake. However great the criticism of detail may have been, no respon-
ble Indian leader has challenged our sincerity upon that point. I think
would be accurate to say that this is the first time that such an assertion
ould be truly made, and it is a most important and significant fact for our
uture relationships. Third, the whole of the discussions have proceeded
pon a basis of frank and mutual understanding and in an atmosphere
f friendliness. Though the past is still perhaps too strong for complete
onfidence to have been established, I have the feeling that we have taken
 step forward, especially so far as the younger elements in India are
oncerned, who are perhaps less influenced by the struggles and bitterness
f the past than some of their older colleagues who still retain their
eadership.

DETERMINATION

And, finally, the whole discussion upon the issue of defense has served
o bring to the front the determination of the Indian peoples to defend
heir own country. Such statements as that made by Pandit Nehru, a
man of great courage and determination, or the more recent attitude of
Ir. Rajagopalachari must do much to influence Indian opinion. The

representative of the Moslem League, Mr. Jinnah, and the leaders c other parties and communities, such as the Sikhs and the Mahratta: have all of them expressed to me personally their readiness to stand wit us in the defense of their country and to do their utmost to help in ever way. It is unfortunate that they do not find themselves in a positio to give that help as members of the Viceroy's Executive Council, bu it is good to know that each in his own way is prepared to assist. W have been brought closer, I believe, to our Indian friends as fellow d fenders of their country, but we are not yet so close as we would wish c even as is necessary for the most effective defense of India.

Looking back at this historical incident, an important incident in th history of both our countries, I feel no regret at the decisions taken b His Majesty's Government. I am convinced that they were just and tha we have done all that we could in an admittedly difficult situation t bring about an agreement and a better understanding between th peoples of the two countries. It is, in fact, the past exercising its influenc upon all parties that has proved too strong for us, and we must no leave the leaven of better understanding to work quietly towards a ultimate and satisfactory solution of the political problem. If we ar to do this, let us at all costs forego the transient satisfaction of blamin others and of encouraging those very antagonisms which have been major part of our difficulty.

Door Not Closed

I stated when I left India that, in default of acceptance, the dra: Declaration must be considered as being withdrawn. But this does nc and cannot close the door to that closer cooperation which we desi to see in the defense of India or to the solution of the problem of sel government after the war. It means that His Majesty's Governmer have done their best to make their contribution to the solution of th problem both in the substance of the draft Declaration and in the methc of its presentation to the Indian people. For the time being there nothing further we can do. We must be patient and open-minded, willin to consider any proposals upon which the Indian leaders can agre But we must concentrate upon our duty to do our utmost for the defen: of India, a task in which our great American Allies have generously con forward to offer their help, a help which we and the Indians alike welcon and appreciate. Many of the Indian leaders, too, will do their best arouse the Indian peoples in their own defense, and I hope that by c operation in defense we may move a step nearer to the solution of ou problem.

Of this I am certain, that the Members of this House, the British
eople and all well-wishers of democracy the world over will continue
i the hope that through a successful resistance to the brutal aggression
f Japan the Indian peoples will reach their goal of self-government and
elf-determination without internal strife and bitterness, and that thus
ndia will emerge as a great equal of the free nations of the world able
o make her full contribution to the future of a new civilization after
he victory of the Allied cause.

4. THE NETHERLANDS EAST INDIES

1) *Declaration of the Netherlands Government to the People's Council, Netherlands East Indies, Batavia, November 13, 1941* [1]

The 28 native members of the Volksraad (People's Council) of the
Tetherlands East Indies on August 26 asked the Netherlands Govern-
ient in London to explain the consequences of the Atlantic Charter
r the Indonesian population. The reply was this declaration to the
olksraad, which is the representative advisory body of the Governor-
eneral.

The Netherlands Government at the recent Inter-Allied Conference in
ondon approved the Atlantic Charter, thereby expressing confidence
iat the Charter's principles — if duly executed — will promote a
etter international order which can bring to all countries national and
iternational security and prosperity.

The Charter lays down general rules of conduct for the establishment
f good international relationships. Although it does not concern itself
irectly with the internal relations in the individual states, every Gov-
rnment accepting the Charter should also be willing to accept the prin-
ples as far as rules of conduct inside the State are concerned.

As these principles were already adopted long ago by the Netherlands
overnment and, as far as appropriate thereto, executed within the
ingdom, adherence to the Charter does not represent a special reason
r new consideration regarding the aims of its policy, more especially
s far as the Indonesian population is concerned.

It may be considered as generally known how much the Netherlands
overnment pursues a policy of ordered, free collaboration for all groups
f the population and interests within the Kingdom, and how, through
ractical statesmanship, it tries to bring about the quickest possible
evelopment toward this aim.

[1] *Netherlands News*, Vol. 2, No. 2, p. 63.

A post-war investigation of constitutional relations, for which purpos
a conference of prominent persons from all parts of the Kingdom is t
be held, will give the Government, as well as those governed, an oppor
tunity to form a clear idea of the stage of development which has bee
reached, and to plan reforms.

(2) *Statement of the Netherlands Government Relating to the Hos*
tilities between the Netherlands East Indies and Japan, Londor
March 9, 1942 [1]

With reference to messages from enemy sources alleging that th
Japanese have conferred with the Governor-General of the Netherland
East Indies with a fixed view to reaching an agreement on cessation c
hostilities, the Netherlands Government points out —

1. No communication exists between the Netherlands Governmen
and the Netherlands East Indies. The enemy is therefore free to ci
culate any stories which they may think useful.

2. The actual military position on the islands is not known. Th
military commanders, including those having to operate singly, hav
been instructed to fight to the last. They have freedom of action wher
resistance would no longer serve any useful purpose.

3. The Governor-General of the Netherlands East Indies was relieve
of military responsibility when he handed over his command to Lieu
Gen. ter Poorten and Acting Rear-Admiral van Staveren.

4. Whatever the outcome of the military operations in the Nethe
lands East Indies, the powers of the Netherlands Authorities, whethe
military or civil, do not extend beyond arrangements regarding cessatio
of local military operations.

5. Preparation of any other arrangements with Japan would in theor
be a matter for the Royal Netherlands Government in London, but :
can be stated without reserve that in practice any such arrangemen
are out of the question.

5. THE PHILIPPINES

(1) *The President of the Philippine Commonwealth* (*Quezon*) *to th*
President (*Roosevelt*), *December 9, 1941* [2]

I have just arrived from Baguio the summer capital of the Philippine
where I was when the war between the United States and Japan w:
declared. I have covered the country by automobile and I am happ

[1] *The Inter-Allied Review*, II, No. 3, March 15, 1942, p. 56.
[2] Department of State, *Bulletin*, V, p. 511.

o report that everywhere the people are loyal to America and deter-
ained to stand by her in testimony of their gratitude to you, to the
iovernment of the United States and to the American people and be-
ause of their devotion to the cause of Democracy and freedom. I am
roud therefore that the reiterated assurance I have given to you to the
ffect that you can count upon us was no empty word.

2) *The President (Roosevelt) to the President of the Philippine Commonwealth (Quezon), December 11, 1941* [1]

Your renewed assurances of the devotion and loyalty of the Philippine
eople to the United States and to democracy are particularly appre-
iated in this grave hour. The hearts of all Americans are deeply touched
y the fortitude and gallantry being shown by your people in this
resent ordeal. We are at one with you in our faith in the ultimate
riumph of our common ideals.

3) *Message of the President (Roosevelt) to the People of the Philippines, December 28, 1941* [2]

THE PEOPLE OF THE PHILIPPINES:
News of your gallant struggle against the Japanese aggressor has
licited the profound admiration of every American. As President of
ie United States, I know that I speak for all our people on this solemn
ccasion.
The resources of the United States, of the British Empire, of the
Netherlands East Indies, and of the Chinese Republic have been dedi-
ated by their people to the utter and complete defeat of the Japanese
arlords. In this great struggle of the Pacific the loyal Americans of the
hilippine Islands are called upon to play a crucial role.
They have played, and they are playing tonight, their part with the
reatest gallantry.
As President I wish to express to them my feeling of sincere admira-
on for the fight they are now making.
The people of the United States will never forget what the people of
ie Philippine Islands are doing this day and will do in the days to come.

[1] *Ibid.*, p. 512.
[2] From the Office of the Secretary to the President; *ibid.*, VI, p. 5. The message was
nt by the President by short-wave broadcast to Manila and distributed by radio and
ie press.

I give to the people of the Philippines my solemn pledge that their free
dom will be redeemed and their independence established and protected
The entire resources, in men and in material, of the United States stan
behind that pledge.

It is not for me or for the people of this country to tell you wher
your duty lies. We are engaged in a great and common cause. I coun
on every Philippine man, woman, and child to do his duty. We wi
do ours.

6. AUSTRALIA AND NEW ZEALAND

A. Direct Wireless Service between Australia and New Zealand and the United States

**(1) *The President (Roosevelt) to the Prime Minister of Australi
(Curtin), December 25, 1941* [1]**

MY DEAR MR. PRIME MINISTER:

The opening of a direct radiotelegraph circuit between Australia an
the United States normally would be an event of great interest to ou
respective peoples. Today, however, the event which we celebrat
assumes proportions that extend far beyond its peacetime significance
The deep-rooted and sturdy friendship which has existed between u
has survived the years because it has been nurtured in the principles c
democracy. In my opinion this new link will serve not only to facilitat
the more rapid exchange of communications between the United State
and Australia but to serve notice on the Axis Powers that the free people
of the world are leaving nothing undone effectively to guarantee throug
spiritual and physical unification the ultimate victory which lies ahea
of us.

I extend my greetings to you personally and to you as the represent:
tive of the people of Australia.

Mr. Churchill, who is staying with me, joins in these greetings an
we give you our assurance that we consider the safety of your grea
Commonwealth as a definite essential in every plan of defense and i
every plan of offensive action against our common foes.

The reply of Prime Minister Curtin is not given.[2]

On February 23, 1942 there was a similar exchange between President Roos
velt and Prime Minister Fraser of New Zealand on the occasion of the opening
direct radio communication between the United States and New Zealand.[3]

[1] *Ibid.*, V, p. 599.   [2] *Ibid.*, p. 600.   [3] *Ibid.*, VI, p. 196.

B. Diplomatic Representation

(1) *Address of Walter Nash upon Presentation of Credentials as First Minister of New Zealand, February 16, 1942* [1]

The fact that the Government of New Zealand saw fit to exercise the right of direct diplomatic representation in Washington was striking evidence of the increased importance attached to relations with the United States by what has been considered the most British of the British Dominions. Australia had been represented for two years before by a minister,[2] but hitherto the interests of the New Zealand Government had been represented by the British Ambassador.

MR. PRESIDENT:

I have the honor in presenting to you today letters by which the King, my Sovereign, accredits me to be His Majesty's Envoy Extraordinary and Minister Plenipotentiary with the special object of representing in the United States the interests of the Dominion of New Zealand. In doing so, I am commanded by His Majesty to convey to you his hope that the appointment of a Minister especially charged with representing New Zealand affairs, will result in strengthening the friendly relations between the United States, the Dominion of New Zealand, and the British Commonwealth of Nations.

On behalf of His Majesty's Government in the Dominion of New Zealand and of the people of New Zealand, I desire to convey to you their fraternal greetings for your personal happiness and for the prosperity and well-being of the nation over whose destinies you preside.

We are grateful to you and your people for the splendid assistance and cooperation which has been and is being given in the fight for the freedom of the democracies.

The New Zealand Government also feels that the establishment of a Legation in Washington will tend towards the strengthening of the goodwill which already exists between our two countries, and no effort on my part will be spared in fostering this objective — and I may assure you that the Government and the people of New Zealand, who so enthusiastically welcomed the appointment of a Minister in the Dominion, are looking forward to his safe arrival and sojourn in New Zealand which we feel will not only be a happy one but of immense value and help in these critical days.

I look forward to meeting your people in the United States and the establishment of friendly and cordial relations to the mutual benefit of our two countries and the Commonwealth of Nations as a whole.

[1] *Ibid.*, p. 173.
[2] Richard Gardiner Casey, succeeded June 10, 1942 by Sir Owen Dixon, *ibid.*, p. 537.

(2) *Reply of the President (Roosevelt), February 16, 1942* [1]

MR. MINISTER:

I am very happy to welcome you to Washington and to accept from your hands the letters which accredit you as His Majesty's Envoy Extraordinary and Minister Plenipotentiary with the special object of representing in the United States the interests of the Dominion of New Zealand.

I greatly appreciate the friendly personal greetings and the expression of good wishes for the people of the United States which you have just conveyed to me from your Government. May I in turn take this occasion to reaffirm the warm friendly feeling of myself and the American people for the people of New Zealand and of the whole British Commonwealth of Nations. I share to the utmost your confident hope that your presence in the United States and the presence of an American Minister in New Zealand will further strengthen the good-will which already exists between our two countries and between the United States and the British Commonwealth as a whole.

Both the United States and New Zealand are Pacific Powers and the interests of our two countries are inextricably woven together. The spread of wanton Axis aggression has only drawn our countries closer together and made us more conscious of our interdependence. Our countries have pledged themselves, along with all other United Nations to employ our full resources in the defeat of Axis aggressors. We shall not falter until the task is complete and our freedom made secure.

You are no stranger in Washington and I welcome this opportunity of renewing our acquaintance. Let me assure you that in all your work here you may always count upon my full cooperation and the cooperation of the State Department and other agencies of this Government.

C. Australia and United Nations Collaboration

During the early months of the War, the Australian Government under Prime Minister Menzies was inclined to accept the political and strategic leadership of Great Britain. When Mr. John Curtin, the leader of the Labor Party, became Prime Minister on October 6, 1941, a marked change in the general orientation of Australian policy occurred. Particularly after the Japanese attack, the new Labor government became increasingly insistent that Australia be accepted as an equal partner in war planning. Furthermore, with the fall of Singapore, referred to as Australia's Dunkirk, the Australian Government looked, almost frantically to the United States for aid and an orientation in policy towards close cooperation with the United States was apparent. This was based on the realistic view that the paramount obligation of Great Britain under the circumstances was

[1] *Ibid.*, p. 173.

to give all possible aid to the Soviet Union and that only the United States was able to come to the assistance of Australia in case of threatened invasion. The establishment of the Pacific War Council at Washington [1] and the setting-up of a unified command for the United Nations forces in the Southwest Pacific were to a considerable extent the product of Australian pressure and initiative. This development of Australian dependence on the United States during the emergency has important immediate and long-time significance from the point of view of American relations with the members of the British Commonwealth of Nations as well as from the point of view of our Far Eastern policy. Some of the striking expressions of this attitude by Australian leaders are given here. See Chapter IV, The United Nations for documents implementing in part the collaboration which the Australians have been demanding.

(1) *Statement of the Australian Prime Minister (Curtin), February 14, 1942* [2]

When I said that Australia looks to America I meant that America was the major Allied power in the Pacific. Whatever America does in the Pacific war is America's affair, but I do point out that the battle for America may very well be won or lost by the way the battle for Australia goes.

Americans can and will save America if Australia is saved.

Now, after ten years' fighting for air power, I have come to the head of the Australian Government and I find myself with an alarmingly low air strength at my command.

I fully realize the magnitude of America's difficulties, and no Australian would dare to presume to tell America what she should do anywhere in the whole world. What she has done has earned the undying gratitude of democratic people of the whole world. What she will do in the future will be the overweighting factor in the war.

Anzac-American air power can save Australia and, by that, immensely strengthen America's position, not only in the Pacific but the Atlantic, too.

You Americans know about our Anzacs. There is no need for me to praise them, for what they have done speaks for itself.

(2) *Statement of the Australian Minister for External Affairs (Evatt) at the Opening Session of the Federal Parliament, February 25, 1942* [3]

[Excerpt]

The Japanese having fully exploited the advantage of surprise, have overrun Malaya and reduced the supposedly impregnable Singapore in

[1] See p. 244.

[2] United Press report of statement made in course of an interview, *New York Times*, February 15, 1942, p. 6.

[3] Release of the Australian News and Information Bureau, February 27, 1942.

rapid time. As a result, their surface vessels have gained access to the Indian Ocean. They have separated the Pacific Allies into two land areas, the northern and western area is in India and Burma, and the southern and eastern is partly in the Indies and mainly in Australia and New Zealand. I have not forgotten one magnificent outpost of resistance. In the Philippines, with unconquerable will, the United States' forces under General MacArthur are still rivalling the defenders of Tobruk and of Leningrad. On the other hand, we should not underestimate the titanic strength of our American partner in the war against the Axis. The whole of the manpower and industrial resources of that great nation of 130 million people are dedicated to an Allies' victory. In his Message to Congress on January 7,[1] President Roosevelt announced a war program for the coming year, equivalent to £17,500,000,000 (Australian) and foreshadowed the production of 60,000 airplanes, including 10,000 combat types this year, and 125,000 airplanes next year; the production of 45,000 tanks this year and 75,000 next year; the building of 8 million tons of shipping this year, and 10 million tons next year. In China also, we have gained as an Ally a great and courageous people who for more than four years have shown the greatest tenacity against a skillful enemy possessing far greater mechanical resources.

By adding up population and industrial output of the Allied nations particularly the British Commonwealth, the United States, the Soviet Union and China it could be made to appear that Allied strength far outweighs Axis strength. This is a paper argument and the danger is that the comforting simplicity may help to create yet another imaginary Maginot Line behind which we can remain on the defensive and wait for victory. Men and resources are only effective if they are used in the right way, in the right places, and at the right time. All three are essential conditions of victory. In practical terms the coordination of Allied effort includes at least:

(1) machinery for the higher direction of the war so that while decisions can be made with speed and firmness, due weight is given to all phases of the conflict and to the special situation of the various Allies;

(2) the setting up of a unified command or commands to wage war against the enemy;

(3) machinery to handle reinforcements and supplies in accordance with the decisions of the higher authority.

Thereupon, the Commonwealth Government tried hard to secure the establishment in Washington of an inter-allied body for the higher direction of the war in the Pacific. We preferred Washington as a venue

[1] Compare Message of the President to the Congress, January 6, 1942, p. 49.

but we desired above all that the Commonwealth should have the opportunity of conferring as an Ally with the United States and China at the same council table and on a common footing. On neither point was our proposal acceptable, although as we subsequently ascertained, it was favored, in part at least, by New Zealand, China and the Netherlands which are also directly affected by the Pacific war. Eventually, in view of the urgency of the position, the Government accepted on February 6, a proposal made by Prime Minister Churchill for a Far Eastern Pacific Council to sit in London and to be composed of representatives of the United Kingdom, Australia, New Zealand and the Netherlands.

We expressed the hope then, and we hope still, that the question of Allied machinery will be reviewed in the light of our recent military experiences. The subject of unified commands in the Pacific is one that is difficult to discuss with frankness in a public statement, as actual problems of strategy must arise. One thing is plain enough. In dealing with an enemy whose movements are not dictated by degrees of latitude and longitude, an over-strict delimitation either of strategical areas or of the jurisdiction of commanders, may be dangerous. The Commonwealth Government has tried to secure action based upon this postulate.

The third of the general problems of coordination is that of reinforcement and supply. A Raw Materials Board [1] and Munitions Assignment Boards [2] are now functioning in the United States with parallel bodies in London. The Commonwealth Government has appointed its accredited representative in London and the Australian Director-General of War Supplies Procurement in Washington as its representatives for consultation by the bodies. Again, however, the only countries directly represented on the Boards themselves are the United Kingdom and the United States. We are associated with these authorities which hold the keys to the essential supplies and munitions. We are not members.

For reasons which are obvious, the deciding question of priority for the despatch of troops and instruments of war, and for their transport to widely separated fronts is one of the major problems now facing us. It is common knowledge that we lost Malaya and Singapore largely because of the inadequacy and insufficiency of aircraft. There were special difficulties in the way of rapid reinforcement with effective implements, and these are well understood. None the less, it is suggested that the function of planning for the effective and timely reinforcement of key positions in Allied plans will best be performed by an authority, which can dispose of divergent, conflicting and competitive claims or

[1] See p. 248.   [2] See p. 249.

arguments on the body where the advice of all Allies can be given unde
consultation. The establishment of such an authority will help to en
retreatism and to open the way to the ultimate offensive.

The war has happily brought about very close contact betwee
Australia and the United States, now become a powerful leader of th
nations fighting aggression. Before war came to the Pacific, the Unite
States had already given considerable material aid against the Axi
Powers. Up to the end of November last, the United States Congres
had appropriated a total of $9,000,000,000 which had been allocated t
a variety of purposes which included the production of aircraft, tank
ordnance, ships and general equipment, repairing of ships, and th
provision of foodstuffs. As American war production got under way
the actual delivery of aid to the belligerent countries was being acceler
ated and the Allies had already received the direct benefit of ove
$100,000,000 worth of the Lend-Lease aid. An agreement had bee
made to provide $1,000,000,000 worth of Lend-Lease aid to Russia b
next June, in addition to earlier exports of Russian purchases. Th
acceleration in production and delivery which had already becom
marked, will no doubt assist the much greater effort that has bee
promised now that the United States has entered the war.

The recognition of the immense strength of our new Ally does no
mean that we hope to creep into safety behind her. The Australia
Commonwealth will maintain a front line spirit and will continue t
make a front line fight. We have done and shall continue to do every
thing we can to facilitate American plans. We shall contribute all tha
we can from our necessarily smaller resources towards the commo
cause. After preparing a review of the international situation generall
one is acutely aware that today there is in reality only a war situatio

. . . .

(3) Statement of the Australian Prime Minister (Curtin) in the Aus tralian House of Representatives, March 25, 1942 [1]

[Excerpt]

In referring to events since the last sitting of the House, I give firs
and outstanding place to the achievement of unified Allied Comman
in the Pacific war area. The United Kingdom and the United States (
America have given ready cooperation with the Commonwealth Goverr
ment in this matter, and have shown a cordial understanding of or
wishes. This Government, Parliament and the whole country gree

[1] Release of the Australian News and Information Bureau, March 25, 1942.

with pride and intense satisfaction the appointment to the Supreme Command of General Douglas MacArthur.

Since Japan entered the war the Commonwealth Government has concentrated its efforts in two main directions; first to secure the rapid disposition of men and supplies in maximum possible strength to the points where they could be used most effectively; and second to secure speed and efficiency in the higher Allied war direction.

Under the second head I am satisfied that the appointment of General MacArthur represents a very considerable advance. Unified command in the person of one who enjoys authority of the highest order, both here and in America, is a vital condition for the defense of Australia and for the gradual organization of offensive action against Japan, which we are now undertaking with the powerful aid of the United States armed forces.

I wish to record here that General MacArthur may count to the limit on the cooperation of the Australian Government and people and all Australian wartime authorities in the great task assigned to him by President Roosevelt.

Close discussions have been held with General MacArthur since his arrival, with a view to defining without delay the new arrangements in the Commonwealth, which his appointment entails.

Meanwhile Minister for External Affairs, Dr. Herbert V. Evatt, is actively pursuing in Washington the further plans which the Government has in mind for the better adaptation of the machinery of Allied war direction to the present needs of the Australian-New Zealand-Pacific area.[1]

There can be no dispute that the developments of the past month have far outrun the arrangements concluded last February for the division of control in the Pacific Area between London and Washington.

The Commonwealth Government has now become a much more active partner in the operational direction of the war. Previously this was a matter for the United Kingdom Government and the Commanders-in-Chief in the Middle East and Far East, acting under the direction of the United Kingdom Government.

With the visit of Mr. Menzies to London, he participated in the decisions of War Cabinet relating to the Middle East campaign. He was later followed by Sir Earle Page who was recently admitted to the United Kingdom War Cabinet as the accredited representative of the Australian Government, and is also its representative on the Pacific War Council in London.

[1] Announcement of the establishment of a Pacific War Council at Washington was made on March 30, 1942, see p. 243.

When a council is established in Washington there will also be an accredited representative of the Commonwealth Government there Major questions of policy will necessarily be referred back to the War Cabinet by the Australian representative in London and Washington.

The Australian service advisory machinery will be the Chiefs-of-Staff Committee in Australia, as the general advisers to War Cabinet, except where, on the highest strategical questions, the supreme or the local commanders may be consulted.

There will also be the service representatives in London and Washington, who will assist the Government representatives on the respective councils, and who will maintain liaison with the United Kingdom Chiefs-of-Staff in London and the United States Chiefs-of-Staff in Washington

The conduct of operations in the Anzac area will be vested in the supreme commander. There will be local commanders of the Australian forces for the Navy and the Army. For the Air Force General Brett has that office.

Australia has, and has had from the beginning, two major requirements to press in this connection: the first that whatever machinery is set up should be uncomplicated, and such as to help and not hinder quick decision; and second that at the final stage of decision the Commonwealth Government should have a direct voice on equal terms with the other principals.

The weight and authority which that voice might command are for ourselves to ensure. They will bear a direct relation to the resolution we bring to our own defense, and to exertions we apply to the common cause of the United Nations.

I affirm that in neither respect will the force of Australia's representation in war councils abroad ever find cause for impairment or hesitation

Simultaneously with the news of General MacArthur's arrival in Australia, announcement was made of the presence in this country of substantial numbers of American armed forces, together with general war equipment. That announcement was received in a way which laid before the whole world the cordiality of our association in arms with the United States.

We have all known that when the danger of violent assault on Australian independence, democratic institutions and ways of life moved nearer this continent, no spur would be needed to inspire Australian patriotism to the extremity of effort and resistance. If we had had to stand alone Australians would have fought in the only way consonant with the traditions of the British race and our own spirit. That in passing can serve as our answer to General Tojo's suggestion to Australia to consider a separate peace. Yet if there is one thing more that could encourage in us a greater resilience and a stronger determination it is the knowledge that powerful support is already with us.

Australia is of cardinal importance in the Allied conduct of the war. This Government has never wavered in the view that on the grounds of highest strategy, as well as by reason of all that Australia and New Zealand represent on the side of human values for which the Allies are fighting, the Anzac area is a vital area to the world war. The calamitous trend of events since the invasion of Malaya has reinforced that view which is now generally accepted and may well indicate a turning point in the war.

I should make this proviso — a turning point, provided it is followed by swift and resolute action. The support that has now reached us imposes a high obligation on Australians to spare nothing in their own efforts. As we envisage our role in the major strategy of the war our necessities in manpower and equipment become more, and not less, exacting. There have been forecasts of Australia's function as an offensive base in the ultimate process of driving back Japan from the southwestern Pacific. That is in fact our goal, but let us not exaggerate the speed with which we can reach it. We must first ensure that Australia is held, and to that end accumulate all the resources open to us.

Both here and in Washington, the many questions arising out of the direct provision of war materials by the United States, as well as the supply needs of the American forces in Australia, are now being closely examined with a view to setting up the simplest possible machinery, and reducing delays and unnecessary procedure. This work also is part of the activity of the Minister for External Affairs on his mission. The despatch of Dr. Evatt abroad is a step which was taken after the House last met. The Government regards it as a most important step, for the special and highly urgent questions which the present phase of the war has forced on Australia.

No representation abroad and at a great distance can entirely take the place of direct contact with the authorities concerned of a Minister of State fully conversant with the mind of the Government at home, and with the priority of needs as seen from the Australian angle. Dr. Evatt's instructions are in wide terms. He is to deal with all matters in which the Commonwealth and the countries he visits have mutual interest, and he is to collaborate with the appropriate authorities so as to secure the fullest possible achievement advantageous to the war effort of Australia and of the Allied cause. The range of questions on which we are in constant touch with other Governments and administrations has been enlarged during this month by the most valuable discussions, held shortly after the House adjourned, with Mr. Joseph Gordon Coates and Mr. Daniel Giles Sullivan, members of the New Zealand War Council. These conversations gave us a thorough insight into the preoccupations which the New Zealand Government, in common with ourselves, holds in face of the imminent Japanese threat to the Anzac area. A full and satisfactory agreement of views is now firmly established between the two Governments as to the place and role of each Dominion in the defensive and offensive strategy of the Anzac area. It is intended that these consultations shall be continued.

* * * * * * *

(4) Address of the Australian Prime Minister (Curtin) before the Roya Empire Society, Sydney, May 18, 1942 [1]

[Excerpts]

The Prime Minister had come in for considerable criticism because of his appeal to the United States for protection and his seeming inclination to attach greater importance to consultation with the United States than to consultation with Great Britain.

Let it be clearly and definitely understood that the relationship between Australia and the United States, between Australia and Canada and between Australia and New Zealand is covered by one supreme purpose — retaining Australia as an integral part of the British Commonwealth of Nations.

* * * * * * *

Strategically Australia is vital to the whole structure of Empire in this war. We in the South are what the Motherland is in the North. The two together are complementary. When Japan struck she struck at the points she chose. Ships could not be sent from the Atlantic nor troops from Britain. With Malaya going and Russia asking for planes and other supplies Britain, however keenly she may have desired to do so, was incapable of sending help to Australia. Therefore, I do not make any apologies or recant a single word of the statements I have made to the United States in regard to the Pacific zone being of vital importance, not only to us but also for the safety of the United States.

[1] Release of the Australian News and Information Bureau, May 18, 1942.

CHAPTER VII

EUROPE, AFRICA AND WESTERN ASIA

The entrance of the United States into World War II has given to our foreign relations a different orientation from that which existed previously. While to an increasing extent we were aligning ourselves with those nations engaged in resisting aggression, our position was still strictly speaking that of a non-participant in the war and our relations with different countries of the world were determined to a large extent by geographical factors. In 1942 the dominant fact in our foreign relations is our being engaged in a common struggle with the other United Nations for the defeat of the Axis Powers. That has meant that winning the war has become our primary objective and close collaboration with the other United Nations has become the means by which we seek to attain that goal. In view of this it has seemed advisable to include in the chapters on "From Neutrality to Belligerency," "Defense and the War Effort" and "The United Nations" many documents that bear upon our relations with particular European countries. Cross references are given in most cases to facilitate their use.

1. RELATIONS WITH PARTICULAR EUROPEAN COUNTRIES

A. Great Britain and Northern Ireland

1. WAR AIMS

1) *Address of the Secretary of State for Foreign Affairs (Eden) before the Foreign Press Association, London, July 29, 1941* [1]

We are met in the midst of big-scale events, and their development is by no means wholly unfavorable to us.

Four great communities are moving ever closer together in their determination to withstand the common menace of Hitler and of any who work for him.

The U.S.S.R., China, the United States of America and the British Empire are surely pretty formidable obstacles to aggression.

It may be this sense of events to come which is causing a new note to creep into Hitler propaganda, covertly for the present, but, we may be sure, more openly later on.

Hitler has broken countless promises. He has betrayed in turn every nation to which he has given pledges. There are in this room Allied statesmen who are living witnesses to his perfidy.

But now, for the first time, there is a change. Now he is trying desperately to keep a promise. It is a promise that he has made to the Ger-

[1] Text furnished by British Library of Information, New York.

man people; a promise that the war shall end this year in a victorious German peace. In an attempt to fulfil it Hitler has embarked upon his Russian campaign.

He seeks two objectives in these vast Russian spaces. First, to smash speedily Russia's military power; second, in the pose of the champion of anti-Communism, to offer a German peace to the world.

Hitler's time-table for the first objective is plainly already out of joint. The Russians are putting up a magnificent resistance, which clearly exceeds the German calculations and many other calculations also.

This does not mean that his second objective has been abandoned. Another kind of German blitz will soon be hurled at us — a peace blitz, by means of which Hitler hopes to keep his promise to the German people. For if Hitler cannot secure a German peace this year — and he cannot — he will offer a compromise peace, and plan to try again later. Others, he hopes, will be less watchful and less ready to take up arms again.

I have recently made it plain, on behalf of His Majesty's Government, in a speech at Leeds only a few weeks ago, that we are not prepared to negotiate with Hitler at any time on any subject.

Let me now explain our position a little further.

A peace with Hitler is a contradiction in terms. There can be no peace with such a man, there can only be a truce, an uneasy truce which will give him time to overhaul and oil his war machine, a truce which will give the German people a breathing-space before he and they resume the war.

Hitler will never abandon war, he will only interrupt it as a matter of tactics, or of military necessity.

Of course all this will be carefully disguised from the world and from the German people.

We must not underrate the attractions of the mirage which will dazzle our eyes. The business will be cleverly staged.

The offer of a compromise peace will be a monument of moderation and sweet reasonableness — and hypocrisy.

It will promise many things to many peoples, perhaps even liberation to some of the occupied countries, maybe restoration of France to her place as a great power, recognition — indeed perhaps a guaranty — of the British Empire.

Such an offer in itself should suffice to warn us, for few indeed are the nations that have survived a Hitler guaranty of their integrity. His enmity is less dangerous than his friendship.

Germany, we shall be told, will be ready as a good neighbor and a good European to cooperate in the restoration of trade.

This is a man who conducts his diplomacy with two sets of weapons, guns and olive branches. The olive branches served for years to mask the guns when it suited Hitler's purpose. They deceived many and they brought us to deadly danger. They will soon be in evidence again.

But what would be the value of any promises given by such a man? Would Norway believe him? Would Holland? Would Belgium? Would Poland? Would Yugoslavia? Would Greece? Would Czechoslovakia? Would Russia? Each and all of them have had a taste of Hitler's promises and broken faith.

Above all, would this country believe him, knowing as she does that she always and inevitably stands in his way, barring the road to world domination?

The stark truth is that any peace or truce with Hitler would last just as long as Hitler chose for the execution of his own plans. Such a truce would bring no security to the world, no return of confidence, no opportunity of reconstruction. It would be a denial of everything that we have fought and striven for for nearly two years. Just consider the conditions that would exist under a Hitler truce.

Every nation would have to remain at its war stations so as not to be caught unawares by a sudden attack launched without warning. We could never demobilize, we could never relax our war preparations and our war restrictions, the fortifications round our coasts could not be removed, our factories would have to continue to manufacture munitions of war to keep up with those which Hitler would be piling up in secret for his next war — his next bid for world domination.

Our Air Force would have to go on patrolling the skies by day and by night; our Navy would have to remain cleared for action.

So long as Hitler and his men rule in Germany, so long as Germany's military power is unbroken, we and Europe, and indeed the world, can only expect lies, deceit and plots, culminating inevitably in another and more terrible war than the present one. For Hitler is the embodiment of war. The only peace he can endure is a peace of annihilation, a peace of universal conquest, in fact a victorious German peace, a peace that is death for freedom everywhere.

Let us recall this.

Hitler is not a rare and transient phenomenon in German history. He is a symptom. He is the expression of the present German will and temper which has shown itself over and over again in German history. It is his mission in life to give the German people war. It is all he has to give them.

And so long as he is in power the German people will continue to expect war. They will begin again to prepare for war. They will wish and work for war. You cannot get figs from thistles and you cannot get peace from one of the greatest war-makers the world has seen.

If we are to have peace in our life-time the German people must learn to unlearn all that they have been taught, not only by Hitler but by his predecessors, for the last 100 years by so many of their philosophers and teachers, the disciples of blood and iron. They can never even start to do this until Hitler, the great war-maker, has been exposed as a fraud and deposed as a failure.

Therefore we state in advance: we are not interested in any peace terms that Hitler and his Government may put forward.

We are determined upon the destruction of Hitler, his regime and all it stands for. For we know that until this is achieved no foundation will exist upon which lasting peace can be built.

How then do we conceive the future of Germany?

It seems to me that, when this war is won, the nations will have a two-fold task with which to deal.

In the military sphere it is our bounden duty to ensure that Germany is not again in another twenty years in a position to plunge the world into the misery and horror of total war. It would be criminal to neglect any precaution to ensure this. It would be unforgivable to run risks in this sphere after the lessons that we have been taught with so much pain and so much suffering. Our conditions of peace for Germany will therefore be designed to prevent a repetition of Germany's misdeeds.

But while these military measures must be taken, it is not part of our purpose to cause Germany, or any other country, to collapse economically. I say that not out of any love of Germany, but because a starving and a bankrupt Germany in the midst of Europe would poison all of us who are her neighbors. That is not sentiment, it is common sense.

Let us look for a moment at the future that is beginning to shape itself before our eyes.

Germany will be defeated. Yes. But what then?

Europe, after this war, will be in a state of exhaustion, short of materials necessary for reconstruction, torn by hatreds, confused and doubtful of the road to follow.

Then there will be a great task to be undertaken. And as we believe the United States of America will help us — is indeed helping us — to defeat Germany, so we hope that they will work with us in keeping through the generations, the peace we shall have won.

We have suffered bitter disillusionment between the two wars. We had believed perhaps too easily that a peace system that would recom-

nend itself to the good sense of all peoples could be planned and debated
n the Council Room without other effort and without harder sacrifice
on our part.

We have learnt that that is not so: That the price of peace is constant
vigilance, readiness, courage; and we must never forget that lesson.

The sacrifices of peacetime, necessary to guard against the ever-recur-
ing danger of war, are hard, but they may be hardening and salutary.
They will, for some time to come, be inevitable.

But while keeping watch and ward, it will be our duty to start at once
upon the fashioning of the world in such a shape that the causes of
rivalry and nature may be gradually removed and, we pray, eventually
eradicated. Only in proportion as we can be sure that this healing
influence is having its effect shall we be able to relax our vigilance.

We are already beginning to formulate our own ideas on the shape of
things to come. And in one sense we are truly fortunate. Here in
London are the Governments of many Allied Powers.

They form an invaluable nucleus for the work we have to do. We are
already meeting and discussing our problems, though not always publicly. We have had one public meeting at St. James' to register our
united purpose. I hope that we may shortly be able to hold another in
which we can begin our examination of the problems that the "Cease
Fire" will bring in its train.

If we can look forward, in all this work, to the sympathy and cooper-
tion of the United States of America and indeed the American continent
as a whole, then we can feel that we are building on a solid foundation,
and we can go ahead in the firm faith that, however dark the outlook,
ur task can and will one day be achieved.

2) *Declaration of Principles, Known as the Atlantic Charter, by the*
   President of the United States of America (Roosevelt) and the
   Prime Minister of the United Kingdom (Churchill), August 14,
   1941

[For official comment on the interpretation given to these principles by the British
Government, see excerpts from Prime Minister Churchill's broadcast of August 24,
1941 (p. 210) and from his statement in the House of Commons, September 9, 1941
p. 213).]

[See p. 209.]

2. LEND-LEASE AID

[For additional documents, see Chapter III, p. 169, and IV, p. 235.]

(1) *United Kingdom Memorandum on Distribution of Lend-Lease Material. The United Kingdom Secretary of State for Foreign Affairs (Eden) to the American Ambassador at London (Winant), September 10, 1941* [1]

Before the Lend-Lease Act became operative, the British found it necessary to promote vigorously their export trade in order that they might have the exchange with which to make their foreign purchases, all of which in the United States had to be on a cash basis. After Lend-Lease went into effect, there were common complaints that the British were now using Lend-Lease materials in their export trade or were obtaining materials from us under Lend-Lease in order that they might export comparable British materials, thus, it was alleged, using this assistance to promote exclusively national purposes.

MY DEAR AMBASSADOR:

With reference to the conversations about Lend-Lease material which have recently taken place in London and in which you have participated I enclose a memorandum on the policy of His Majesty's Government in the United Kingdom with regard to exports from this country and with regard to the distribution here of Lend-Lease material. I shall be glad if you will transmit it to your Government.

Yours sincerely,
ANTHONY EDEN

[Enclosure]

MEMORANDUM

1. All materials which we obtain under the Lend-Lease Act are required for the prosecution of the war effort. This principle governs all questions of the distribution and use of such goods and His Majesty's Government have taken and will continue to take action to secure that these goods are not in any case diverted to the furtherance of private interests.

Export Policy.

2. Lend-Lease materials sent to this country have not been used for export and every effort will be made in the future to ensure that they are not used for export, subject to the principle that where complete physical segregation of Lend-Lease materials is impracticable domesti-

---

[1] Department of State, *Bulletin*, V, p. 204. The memorandum was published by the United Kingdom as *Correspondence respecting the Government in the United Kingdom in Connection with the Use of Materials received under the Lend-Lease Act, London, September 10, 1941* (United States No. 2 (1941), Cmd. 6311).

onsumption of the material in question shall be at least equal to the
mounts received under Lend-Lease.

3. His Majesty's Government have not applied and will not apply any
materials similar to those supplied under Lend-Lease in such a way as to
nable their exporters to enter new markets or to extend their export
rade at the expense of United States exporters. Owing to the need to
evote all available capacity and manpower to war production, the
Jnited Kingdom export trade is restricted to the irreducible minimum
ecessary to supply or obtain materials essential to the war effort.

4. For some time past, exports from the United Kingdom have been
more and more confined to those essential (I) for the supply of vital
equirements of overseas countries, particularly in the sterling empire;
II) for the acquisition of foreign exchange, particularly in the Western
Iemisphere. His Majesty's Government have adopted the policy
ummarized below:

(I) No materials of a type the use of which is being restricted in the
Jnited States on the grounds of short supply and of which we obtain
upplies from the United States either by payment or on Lend-Lease
erms will be used in exports with the exception of the following special
ases:

(a) Material which is needed overseas in connection with supplies
ssential to the war effort for ourselves and our Allies, and which cannot
e obtained from the United States.

(b) Small quantities of such materials needed as minor though essential
omponents of exports which otherwise are composed of materials not in
iort supply in the United States.

(c) Repair parts for British machinery and plant now in use, and
achinery and plant needed to complete installations now under con-
ruction, so long as they have already been contracted for.

Steps have been taken to prevent the export (except to Empire and
llied territories) of such goods which do not come within the exceptions
ferred to in (a), (b) and (c) above.

(II) Materials similar to those being provided under Lend-Lease
hich are not in short supply in the United States will not be used for
port in quantities greater than those which we ourselves produce or
iy from any source.

istribution in the United Kingdom of Lend-Lease goods.

5. The general principle followed in this matter is that the remuner-
ion received by the distributors, whatever the method of distribution,
controlled and will be no more than a fair return for the services

rendered in the work of distribution. The arrangements rigorousl;
exclude any opportunity for a speculative profit by private interest
from dealing in Lend-Lease goods. In most cases, Lend-Lease supplie
will be distributed through organizations acting as agents of His Majes
ty's Government in the strict sense of the term and not as principals
Where for strong practical reasons this cannot be done a full explanatio
will be supplied to the United States Administration and their concu
rence sought beforehand in any alternative arrangements proposed. Th
justification for retaining existing channels of distribution operatin,
under strict Government control, is that the creation of elaborate ne
organizations in their place would inevitably result in loss of efficienc
and the wasteful use of manpower, and retard the war effort. In th
distribution of Lend-Lease goods there will be no discrimination agains
United States firms.

6. Food is a special case. Only some 5 or 6 % in tonnage of the tot;
British food supply is coming from the United States and without grea
practical complications it would be impossible to have a separate syste
for the distribution of Lend-Lease food. Food distribution is carrie
out in the United Kingdom by wholesalers, to whom the Governmen
sells food as principals. In fact, the Ministry of Food has established
close control over all distributive margins so that neither the whol
salers nor the retailers receive any greater remuneration than is adequa
to cover the cost of the services performed. No food obtained on Len
Lease terms is or will be sold at uncontrolled prices. Thus the gener
arrangements as regards the issue of Lend-Lease food fit into His Ma
esty's Government's policy of stabilizing the whole price level of foo
stuffs, a policy to which the Government contributes £100 millions a yea

7. In some cases direct free distribution is practicable and will l
adopted. For example, some milk products (including Lend-Lea;
supplies from the United States) are distributed direct and free of char;
to children and others in need through schools, clinics and hospitals. T
distribution is undertaken by State agencies and the cost of the dist
bution is borne by the Government.

*(a) The American Ambassador at London (Winant) to the United Kin
dom Secretary of State for Foreign Affairs (Eden), Septemb
10, 1941* [1]

DEAR MR. EDEN:

Thank you for your letter of September 10, enclosing a memorandum
United Kingdom export policy and on the distribution of Lend-Lease materi
I have caused the memorandum to be transmitted immediately to Washingt
for the information of my Government.

[1] Department of State, *Bulletin*, V, p. 206.

b) **Statement Sent by the Department of State to Representative Malcolm C. Tarver of Maryland, published November 15, 1941** [1]

[Excerpt]

Since the issuance of the White Paper,[2] machinery has been set up both in Washington and in London for following up in detail all of the administrative and policy problems arising in connection with the White Paper. The fact of the matter is that the British have been leaning over backward in their desire to avoid doing anything to justify a charge that they are not complying with the obligations which they have assumed. Not a single instance has been encountered in which they have violated their pledge. They are going out of their way, in case of doubt with regard to any particular export shipment, to ascertain whether this Government would regard such shipment as in violation of the letter or spirit of British pledges. In fact, an orderly process has been set up for clearing all such doubtful cases in advance.

2) **Procedure under the Memorandum. Statement of the Department of State, January 24, 1942** [3]

On September 10, 1941 Mr. Anthony Eden, British Secretary of State for Foreign Affairs, communicated to the Department, through the American Ambassador, Mr. John G. Winant, a memorandum with respect to "the policy of His Majesty's Government in the United Kingdom in connection with the use of materials received under the Lend-Lease Act." This memorandum was issued as the British White Paper of September 10, 1941, and is sometimes informally referred to as "the Eden Memorandum." [4]

It was clear from the outset that many problems would arise in the course of the administrative application of the White Paper which would involve either questions of interpretation of its provisions or the recognition, in particular cases, of exceptional circumstances warranting deviation from the principles incorporated in it. After informal discussion by officials of both Governments, it was agreed that a regular procedure should be established for consultation on questions of interpretation and for clearing with the Government of the United States requests for export licenses in the United Kingdom involving possible deviation from or exception to the terms of the White Paper where necessary for the war effort or otherwise essential for United States interests. It was likewise agreed that such requests should be directed

[1] *Ibid.*, p. 385–6.
[2] See p. 592 for United Kingdom Memorandum, etc.
[3] Department of State, *Bulletin*, VI, p. 81.
[4] United Kingdom, Parliamentary Papers, United States No. 2 (1941), Cmd. 6311.

to and handled by the Office of Lend-Lease Administration as the agency directly responsible for the administration of the Lend-Lease Act, and not to other agencies of the Government.

In order, however, to assist the Office of Lend-Lease Administration in passing on such requests, particularly with respect to their broader implications from the standpoint of foreign trade and commercial policy informal arrangements were established for furnishing to the Office of Lend-Lease Administration, in an orderly manner, advice and assistance from other interested agencies of the Government. It was recognized in this connection that the application of the terms of the White Paper would have policy implications extending beyond the immediate range of the Lend-Lease Act as such. Accordingly, there was set up, quite informally, a committee known as the Interdepartmental Advisory Committee on the Eden Memorandum, under the chairmanship of Mr. Lynn R. Edminster, of the Department of State; and this committee has been functioning in this informal way for a considerable number of weeks.

A particularly pressing problem arising out of the application of the White Paper, involving, in turn, a further problem of administrative procedure, arose in connection with the application of paragraph, section (I), of the White Paper. This provision relates to the use of exports from the United Kingdom of materials similar to those provided under lend-lease which are in short supply in the United States. The British Government needed from the United States Government a list of materials "the use of which is being restricted in the United States on grounds of short supply." This list, which has from time to time been subject of discussion by the Interdepartmental Committee, has been furnished to the British Government by the Office of Lend-Lease Administration. It is, of course, subject to change at the instance of the Office of Lend-Lease Administration.

As an outgrowth of this arrangement, it became necessary to establish a method whereby, in exceptional circumstances, this provision of the White Paper can be waived with respect to particular exports containing materials similar to an item on the list, and this has been done.

The essential feature of this procedure is the maintenance of a routine by which the British Board of Trade is apprised of the fact that the United States Government does not object to — perhaps even desires — the approval by the Board of an export permit for the goods in question. The actual initiation and routing of the process may vary. If the desired permit is for shipment to the United States, the American importer may have communicated his desires directly to the United Kingdom supplier

r his agent, who then makes application to the Board of Trade, in which
ase the Board requests the British Embassy to ascertain from the
)ffice of Lend-Lease Administration whether there is objection to the
;ranting of the permit.

In a great many cases, however, the process is just the reverse. That
s to say, the United States firm which desires to import the particular
;oods in question communicates directly either with the Office of Lend-
.ease Administration or with another agency of the Government, which
)romptly refers the matter to the Lend-Lease Office. If, after careful
onsideration of the matter, including consultation with other Govern-
nent agencies concerned (including the Department of State), the Office
»f Lend-Lease Administration decides that such importation is desirable
r even essential to the national interest, it takes the matter up with the
3ritish Embassy, stating that it has no objection to the granting of an
xport waiver for the goods in question. This advance approval given
»y the Office of Lend-Lease Administration does not necessarily imply,
.owever, that the Board of Trade will in fact be able to grant the export
.cense, since there may be other reasons why this cannot be done.

If the proposed shipment is to a country other than the United States,
he basis upon which the British Board of Trade decides to initiate a
equest will presumably be more or less similar to the foregoing.

By agreement, a copy of each communication addressed by the British
mbassy to the Office of Lend-Lease Administration is sent by the Com-
nercial Counselor of the Embassy to Mr. Lynn R. Edminster, of the
tate Department, who, as Special Assistant to the Secretary of State,
s assigned to this and related tasks by Departmental Order 1006.[1] The
urpose of this is to give the State Department an opportunity at the
nception of each case to consider whether any international aspects of
iirect interest to the Department are involved. Whenever, in the prem-
ses, any such aspect appears to be involved, Mr. Edminster clears the
natter with appropriate officials within the Department and informally
ommunicates to the Office of Lend-Lease Administration whatever
bservations may be pertinent from the point of view of the Department.
imilarly, with respect to requests communicated directly to the Office
f Lend-Lease Administration by United States importers or other
omestic interests, it is understood that any of these which involve, or
ppear to involve, international aspects of concern to the State Depart-
nent will be brought to the attention of the Department for further
rocessing, as indicated.

[1] See p. 850.

(3) *Agreement between the United States and the United Kingdom for Mutual Aid Pursuant to the Lend-Lease Act of March 11, 1941 Signed February 23, 1942*

[See p. 235.]

3. THE WASHINGTON CONFERENCES BETWEEN PRESIDENT ROOSEVELT AND PRIME MINISTER CHURCHILL

[See p. 239.]

4. THE PACIFIC WAR COUNCIL

[See p. 243.]

5. COMBINED WAR STAFFS AND JOINT COMMANDS

[See p. 244.]

6. COMBINED ECONOMIC BOARDS AND COMMITTEES

[See p. 248.]

B. Ireland (Eire)

(1) *Entrance of United States into the War. Statement by the Premier of Ireland (De Valera), December 14, 1941* [1]

[Excerpt]

With the entry of the United States of America into the war, stranger who do not understand our conditions have begun to ask how America' entry into the war will affect our State policy here. We answer tha question in advance. The policy of the State remains unchanged. W can only be a friendly neutral. From the moment this war began ther was for this State only one policy possible — neutrality.

Our circumstances and history and the incompleteness of our nationa freedom through the partition of our country made any other polic impracticable. Any other policy would have divided our people and fo a divided nation to fling itself into this war would be to commit suicide

We are fully aware that in a world at war each set of belligerents hav every right to regard those who are not with them as against them bu we have followed a just course.

[1] *New York Times*, December 15, 1941, p. 3.

(2) *Landing of American Troops in Northern Ireland. Statement by the Premier of Ireland (De Valera), January 27, 1942* [1]

The Irish Government has not been consulted either by the British Government or the American Government with regard to the coming of American troops to the six counties.

Every one knows that Ireland twenty years ago was partitioned and the six counties cut off from the rest of the country by act of the British Parliament despite the expressed will of the Irish people.

They knew when the United States entered the last war that President Wilson declared Americans meant to fight for democracy and for the rights of peoples to national self-determination. The Irish people took him at his word and in the general election of 1918, by the overwhelming vote of more than three to one, declared for national independence and for the establishment of a republic.

This decision was reaffirmed after two years of conflict with Britain in the general election of 1921 when the partition candidates returned were less than a fourth of the total representation.

Nevertheless, the British Government set up a separate Parliament for six of the thirty-two counties. These counties formed no historical or geographical entity. They were chosen fully with the view of securing a majority for it.

In one-half of the area, including the city of Derry, and in the whole area on the boundary of the twenty-six counties a majority of candidates were against partition.

Partition of the territory of an ancient nation was one of the cruelest wrongs that could be committed against a people. The partition of Ireland was no different in essence from the former partition of Poland.

Nor were the evils that flow from it less than those Abraham Lincoln foresaw from the projection of the partition of the United States when he determined to prevent it, even at the cost of fighting one of the bitterest civil wars in history.

Ireland has no hostility toward nor any desire in any way to be brought into conflict with the United States for reasons to which I referred a few weeks ago. The contrary is the truth.

It is our duty to make it clearly understood that no matter what troops occupy the six counties, the Irish people's claim to union of national territory and for supreme jurisdiction will remain unabated.

Four years ago the British Government and Parliament recognized fully the sovereignty of the Irish nation over that part of the nation's

[1] *Ibid.*, January 28, 1942.

territory included in the twenty-six counties and the bargain has been honorably kept in that regard.

But maintenance of the partition of Ireland is as indefensible a aggression against all nations, which it is the avowed purpose of Britain and the United States in this war to bring to an end.

C. Union of Soviet Socialist Republics

1. AMERICAN AID IN RESISTANCE TO GERMAN AGGRESSION

(1) *Economic Assistance to the Soviet Union.   Exchange of Notes August 2, 1941* [1]

(a) *The Acting Secretary of State (Welles) to the Ambassador of the Soviet Union at Washington (Oumansky)*

MY DEAR MR. AMBASSADOR:

I am pleased to inform you that the Government of the United States has decided to give all economic assistance practicable for the purpose of strengthening the Soviet Union in its struggle against armed aggression. This decision has been prompted by the conviction of the Government of the United States that the strengthening of the armed resistance of the Soviet Union to the predatory attack of an aggressor who i threatening the security and independence not only of the Soviet Union but also of all other nations is in the interest of the national defense of the United States.

In accordance with this decision of the Government of the United States and in order to implement the policy enunciated above, the Government of the United States is giving the most friendly consideration to requests from the Government, institutions, or agencies of the Soviet Union relative to the placing in this country of orders for article and materials urgently required for the needs of the national defense of the Soviet Union and, for the purpose of promoting the speedy completion and delivery of such articles and materials, is extending to these orders priority assistance upon the principles applicable to the orders of countries struggling against aggression.

In order to facilitate the extension of economic assistance to the Soviet Union, the Department of State is also issuing unlimited license permitting the export to the Soviet Union of a wide variety of article and materials needed for the strengthening of the defense of that country in accordance with the principles applicable to the furnishing of such

[1] Department of State, *Bulletin*, V, p. 109; Executive Agreement Series 215.

rticles and materials as are needed for the same purpose by other
ountries resisting aggression.

The appropriate authorities of the Government of the United States,
n pursuance of the decision to which I have above referred, are also
;iving their favorable consideration to requests for the extension of
,vailable American shipping facilities for the purpose of expediting the
hipment to the Soviet Union of articles and materials needed for the
1ational defense of that country.

I am [etc.]

b) The Ambassador of the Soviet Union at Washington (Oumansky) to the Acting Secretary of State (Welles)

My DEAR MR. ACTING SECRETARY:

I am pleased to take notice of the contents of your communication of
his date in which you informed me that the Government of the United
States has decided to give all economic assistance practicable for the
urpose of strengthening the Soviet Union in its struggle against armed
ggression. You add that this decision has been prompted by the con-
iction of the Government of the United States that the strengthening
f the armed resistance of the Soviet Union to the predatory attack of an
ggressor who is threatening the security and independence not only of
he Soviet Union but also of all other nations is in the interest of the
1ational defense of the United States.

On behalf of my Government, I wish to emphasize the correctness of
he view that the aggressor who has treacherously invaded my country
; threatening the security and independence of all freedom-loving nations
nd that this threat naturally creates a community of interest of national
efense of those nations. My Government has directed me to express to
he Government of the United States its gratitude for the friendly
ecision of the Government of the United States and its confidence that
he economic assistance you refer to in your note will be of such scope
nd carried out with such expedition as to correspond to the magnitude
f the military operations in which the Soviet Union is engaging, in
ffering armed resistance to the aggressor — a resistance which, as you
o justly observed, is also in the interest of the national defense of the
Jnited States.

I am also pleased to note your statement that:

[Here is textually repeated the 2d–4th paragraphs of the note of the
Acting Secretary of State.]

I am [etc.]

(2) *Joint Message from the President (Roosevelt) and the Prime Minister of the United Kingdom (Churchill) to the President of the Soviet of People's Commissars of the U.S.S.R. (Stalin), August 15, 1941* [1]

We have taken the opportunity afforded by the consideration of the report of Mr. Harry Hopkins [2] on his return from Moscow to consult together as to how best our two countries can help your country in the splendid defense that you are making against the Nazi attack. We are at the moment cooperating to provide you with the very maximum of supplies that you most urgently need. Already many shiploads have left our shores and more will leave in the immediate future.

We must now turn our minds to the consideration of a more long term policy, since there is still a long and hard path to be traversed before there can be won that complete victory without which our efforts and sacrifices would be wasted.

The war goes on upon many fronts and before it is over there may be further fighting fronts that will be developed. Our resources though immense are limited, and it must become a question as to where and when those resources can best be used to further [to] the greatest extent our common effort. This applies equally to manufactured war supplies and to raw materials.

The needs and demands of your and our armed services can only be determined in the light of the full knowledge of the many factors which must be taken into consideration in the decisions that we make. In order that all of us may be in a position to arrive at speedy decisions as to the apportionment of our joint resources, we suggest that we prepare for a meeting to be held at Moscow, to which we would send high representatives who could discuss these matters directly with you. If this conference appeals to you, we want you to know that pending the decisions of that conference we shall continue to send supplies and material as rapidly as possible.

We realize fully how vitally important to the defeat of Hitlerism is the brave and steadfast resistance of the Soviet Union and we feel therefor that we must not in any circumstances fail to act quickly and immediately in this matter on planning the program for the future allocation of our joint resources.

[1] Department of State, *Bulletin*, V, p. 134. The message was delivered personally by the United States and United Kingdom Ambassadors at Moscow. The question of aid to the Soviet Union was one of the topics discussed by President Roosevelt and Prime Minister Churchill at their Atlantic meeting in August 1941.

[2] Mr. Hopkins was formally designated by the President on April 14, 1941 to supervise purchasing operations under the Lend-Lease Act (*Documents, III, 1940–4* p. 729, 730). Following a visit to the United Kingdom in July he spent several days beginning August 1 in Moscow to learn the requirements of the Soviet Government

3) *Conference at Moscow, September 29–October 1, 1941*

1) *Announcement Concerning United States Mission to the Soviet Union, September 3, 1941* [1]

Announcement was made on September 3 of appointment by the President of the members of the mission to the Union of Soviet Socialist Republics as follows:

W. Averell Harriman, now serving as the President's Special Representative in London on Material Aid to the British Empire, *chairman*.

Maj. Gen. James H. Burns, Executive Officer, Division of Defense Aid Reports associated with Harry L. Hopkins. General Burns has served with distinction in the Ordnance Department of the Army

Maj. Gen. George H. Brett, Chief of Air Corps, at present on a special mission to Great Britain and the Middle East in connection with deliveries of American aircraft

Admiral William Harrison Standley, U. S. Navy, former Chief of Naval Operations, 1933–37. Admiral Standley was a member of the Delegation of the United States to the General Disarmament Conference held in London, 1934; also a delegate on the part of the United States to the London Naval Conference of 1935

William L. Batt, Deputy Director, Production Division, Office of Production Management; Chairman, Business Advisory Council for the Department of Commerce. Mr. Batt is President of S. K. F. Industries, Inc., and Chairman of the Board, American Management Association

The mission will join with a similarly constituted British mission under the chairmanship of Lord Beaverbrook for a conference in Moscow with the Government of the Soviet Union regarding the supplying to the Soviet Union by the United States and Great Britain of munitions, raw materials, and other supplies needed by the Soviet Union for her defense against German aggression.

The holding of this conference was agreed to between the President and the Prime Minister at their recent meeting at sea.

2) *The President (Roosevelt) to the President of the Soviet of People's Commissars of the Soviet Union (Stalin)* [2]

My Dear Mr. Stalin:

This note will be presented to you by my friend Averell Harriman, whom I have asked to be head of our delegation to Moscow.

[1] Office of the Secretary to the President; Department of State, *Bulletin*, V, p. 180.
[2] Released by the Office of the Secretary to the President on October 8, 1941, in view of the publication in Berlin of a garbled English version. The released text was prefaced with this comment:
"Careful comparison of the language of the German announcement made in Berlin October 8, 1941, by DNB, official German news agency, and that actually contained the President's letter of introduction of Mr. Harriman to Mr. Stalin, is invited. When such a comparison is made, the propaganda objectives of the Nazi action become very clear." (*Ibid.*, p. 276.)
According to the DNB text, the letter began "My Dear Friend Stalin" and concluded "Yours in cordial friendship," *New York Times*, October 9, 1941, p. 2.

Mr. Harriman is well aware of the strategic importance of your fron
and will, I know, do everything that he can to bring the negotiations i
Moscow to a successful conclusion.

Harry Hopkins has told me in great detail of his encouraging an
satisfactory visits with you. I can't tell you how thrilled all of us ar
because of the gallant defense of the Soviet armies.

I am confident that ways will be found to provide the material an
supplies necessary to fight Hitler on all fronts, including your own

I want particularly to take this occasion to express my great conf
dence that your armies will ultimately prevail over Hitler and to assu
you of our great determination to be of every possible material assistanc

Yours very sincerely,

FRANKLIN D. ROOSEVELT

(c) Closing Address by the United States Delegate (Harriman) on beha of the United States and the United Kingdom, October 1, 1941

The Moscow conference of the representatives of the Governments (
the Union of Soviet Socialist Republics, the United States of Americ
and Great Britain has ended.

The delegates to the conference were sent here in order to examine th
question of the needs of the Soviet Union, which is fighting against th
Axis Powers, for supplies which the United States and Great Britai
must deliver.

The conference, which has taken place under the chairmanship
Mr. Molotov, the People's Commissar for Foreign Affairs, carried on i
work since Monday without interruption. The conference examined th
question of the resources of the Soviet Government in connection wi
the production possibilities of the United States and Great Britai

The conference decided to place at the disposal of the Soviet Gover
ment practically everything which was requested by the Soviet milita
and civil authorities. The Soviet Government is supplying Gre
Britain and the United States with large quantities of raw materia
which are urgently needed by those countries.

The question of transport possibilities has been examined in deta
and plans have been worked out for increasing the flow of freight in a
directions.

Mr. Stalin has instructed me and Lord Beaverbrook to transmit h
thanks to the United States and Great Britain for the generous deliveri
of raw materials, machine tools, and armaments with which the Sovi

[1] Department of State, *Bulletin*, V, p. 365.

orces will be in a position immediately to strengthen their defense and
o develop vigorous attacks against the invading armies.

Lord Beaverbrook and I, on behalf of our Governments, confirm the
eceipt from the Soviet Government of large deliveries of Russian raw
naterials, which will considerably assist armaments production in our
ountries.

We note the cordiality with which the conference was imbued and
vhich made it possible to conclude an agreement in record short time.
Ve particularly note the completely sympathetic cooperation and under-
tanding on the part of Mr. Stalin. We express our thanks to Mr. Molo-
ov for his excellent management of the conference in his capacity as
hairman, and to all the Soviet representatives for their assistance.

In completing its work, the conference declares that it is the determi-
ation of the three Governments to establish, after the final destruction
f Nazi tyranny, a peace which will give all countries an opportunity to
ve in security on their own territory without knowing either fear or
vant.

**4) *Assistance to the Soviet Union. Announcement of the President
(Roosevelt), October 13, 1941*** [1]

The President announced on October 13 that within the few days
rior to that date large amounts of supplies had been sent to Russia.
Ie further stated that all of the munitions, including tanks, airplanes,
nd trucks, promised at the Moscow conference for delivery in October,
ill be sent to Russia before the end of the month. These supplies are
aving United States ports constantly.

The staffs of the Army and the Maritime Commission have worked
ver the past weekend rushing supplies to the seaboard, and everything
ossible is being done to send material to Russia to help the brave defense
hich continues to be made.

5) *Arrangements Concerning Aid to the Soviet Union*

**1) *The President of the United States (Roosevelt) to the President of
the Soviet of People's Commissars of the Soviet Union (Stalin),
October 30, 1941*** [2]

[Paraphrase]

I have examined the record of the Moscow Conference and the mem-
ers of the mission have discussed the details with me. All of the military

---

[1] From the Office of the Secretary to the President; *ibid.*, p. 296.
[2] *Ibid.*, p. 365.

equipment and munitions items have been approved and I have ordered that as far as possible the delivery of raw materials be expedited. Deliveries have been directed to commence immediately and to be fulfilled in the largest possible amounts. In an effort to obviate any financial difficulties immediate arrangements are to be made so that supplies up to one billion dollars in value may be effected under the Lend-Lease Act. If approved by the Government of the U.S.S.R. I propose that the indebtedness thus incurred be subject to no interest and that the payments by the Government of the U.S.S.R. do not commence until five years after the war's conclusion and be completed over a ten-year period thereafter.

I hope that special efforts will be arranged by your Government to sell us the available raw materials and commodities which the United States may need urgently under the arrangement that the proceeds thereof be credited to the Soviet Government's account.

At this opportunity I want to tell you of the appreciation of the United States Government for the expeditious handling by you and your associates of the Moscow supply conference, and to send you assurance that we will carry out to the limit all the implications thereof. I hope that you will communicate with me directly without hesitation if you should so wish.

(b) The President of the Soviet of People's Commissars of the Soviet Union (Stalin) to the President of the United States (Roosevelt) November 4, 1941 [1]

[Paraphrase]

The American Ambassador, Mr. Steinhardt, through Mr. Vyshinski, presented to me on November 2, 1941 an *aide-mémoire* containing the contents of your message, the exact text of which I have not yet received.

First of all I would like to express my sincere thanks for your appreciative remarks regarding the expeditious manner in which the conference was handled. Your assurance that the decisions of the conference will be carried out to the limit is deeply appreciated by the Soviet Government.

Your decision, Mr. President, to grant to the Soviet Union a loan in the amount of one billion dollars subject to no interest charges and for the purpose of paying for armaments and raw materials for the Soviet Union is accepted with sincere gratitude by the Soviet Government as unusually substantial aid in its difficult and great struggle against our common enemy, bloodthirsty Hitlerism.

[1] *Ibid.*, p. 366.

I agree completely, on behalf of the Government of the Soviet Union, with the conditions which you outlined for this loan to the Soviet Union, namely that payments on the loan shall begin five years after the end of the war and shall be completed during the following ten-year period.

The Government of the U.S.S.R. stands ready to expedite in every possible way the supplying of available raw materials and goods required by the United States.

I am heartily in accord with your proposal, Mr. President, that we establish direct personal contact whenever circumstances warrant.

6) Directive of the President (Roosevelt) to the Lend-Lease Administrator (Stettinius), November 7, 1941 [1]

On November 7, 1941, I addressed a letter [2] to His Excellency President Kalinin in which I congratulated him upon the national anniversary of the Union of Soviet Socialist Republics and expressed the admiration of the people of the United States for the "valiant and determined resistance of the army and people of the Soviet Union" and the determination of the United States that the "sacrifices and sufferings of those who have the courage to struggle against aggression will not have been in vain."

In that letter I assured President Kalinin "of the desire of the Government and people of the United States to do everything possible to assist your country in this critical hour."

In accordance with that pledge and pursuant to the power conferred upon me by the Lend-Lease Act, I have today found that the defense of the Union of Soviet Socialist Republics is vital to the defense of the United States. I therefore authorize and direct you to take immediate action to transfer defense supplies to the Union of Soviet Socialist Republics under the Lend-Lease Act and to carry out the terms of my letter of October 30, 1941 to Premier Stalin.

I should appreciate it if you would work out as quickly as possible details of this program with representatives of the Union of Soviet Socialist Republics.

7) Agreement between the United States and the Union of Soviet Socialist Republics for Mutual Aid Pursuant to the Lend-Lease Act of March 11, 1941, signed June 11, 1942

[See p. 238.]

[1] *Ibid.*, p. 366.   [2] *Ibid.*

2. RECEPTION OF NEW SOVIET AMBASSADOR AT WASHINGTON

(1) *Remarks of Maxim Litvinov on Presentation of Credentials a Ambassador, December 8, 1941* [1]

MR. PRESIDENT:

I have the honor to present you with the letters of credence accreditin; me Ambassador Extraordinary and Plenipotentiary of the Union o Soviet Socialist Republics to you and also with the letters of recall c my predecessor.

I consider it my pleasing duty at the same time to reiterate and t emphasize my predecessors' expressions of the friendship and hig] esteem which the peoples of the Soviet Union entertain for the America> people and the unswerving desire of my Government for the maintenanc of the friendliest possible relations and closest cooperation with th Government of the United States of America. I am proud and happ; that the honor of being the interpreter of these feelings and desires belongs to me.

The Soviet Union has, like other countries, in its turn, been subjecte< to a treacherous attack by Nazi imperialist Germany and has, for ove five months, been waging a determined struggle against the aggressoi

The peoples of the Soviet Union are happy in the realization that the are receiving from the American people not only their sympathy in thi struggle, but also substantial material support, and it affords me kee> pleasure to express to you, Mr. President, and to your people, the warm gratitude of my Government and my country, for this generous support

The fact that this aid is proffered and being increasingly extende< testifies to the growing recognition by the American people of the terribl danger to all nations created by the fulfillment by Nazi Germany of th criminal program drawn up in advance by Hitler for the destruction c the political and economic independence of all countries, and the enslave ment of their peoples.

The struggle against the aggression of Hitler and his imitators an< against his voluntary and involuntary allies — a struggle in which a the liberties, all the spiritual, moral, cultural and political values, gaine< by humanity in the course of many centuries, are at stake, is becomin more and more the cause of all honest, liberty-loving, peace-lovin> people. While the heaviest blows and sacrifices in this struggle hav fallen to the lot of the Soviet Union, the part played in it by the Unite< States is becoming more and more prominent and active.

The successful outcome of this struggle in the shortest possible tim

[1] *Ibid.*, p. 504.

will to a great extent depend on the coordination of the activities of its more energetic and powerful participants, on the timely and rational use of their resources, and last but not least on the maintenance among themselves of the utmost mutual understanding and confidence, which will be necessary not merely during the struggle itself, but also during the subsequent period.

I shall consider the extent to which I may be able to contribute to the creation of these conditions in the relations between our countries as the measure of the success of my mission. I feel confident, Mr. President, that I may rely upon your support and that of your Government in the fulfillment of this mission.

My arrival in Washington coincided precisely with the moment in which American territory and American armed forces were subjected to attack from another state — an attack no less unexpected than that to which, five and a half months ago, the Soviet Union was subjected. This event, arising from the present international situation, was brought about by the same forces and the same ideology which let loose sanguinary war in Europe and other continents. I must limit myself, at the present moment, Mr. President, to the assurance of the best wishes and warm sympathy of the people of the Soviet Union towards the American people in these days of their ordeal. I am convinced that the similar trial of the Soviet and American peoples will rivet still more strongly the bonds of friendship between them.

(2) *Reply of the President (Roosevelt), December 8, 1941* [1]

EXCELLENCY:

It is with pleasure that I receive from you the letters of credence accrediting you as Ambassador Extraordinary and Plenipotentiary of the Union of Soviet Socialist Republics. I deem it most fortunate in these tragic days when the maintenance between our two countries of mutual understanding and confidence is of such vital importance not only to them but to the very future of humanity that the Soviet Government should have deemed it advisable to send as its representative in the United States a statesman who has already held such distinguished office in his own country.

I accept the letters of recall of your predecessor, who for more than two years has occupied and so ably performed the duties of the office which you are now assuming.

I deeply appreciate the expressions of friendship and esteem which the peoples of the Soviet Union entertain for the people of the United

[1] *Ibid.*, p. 505.

States. That these feelings are fully reciprocated it is hardly necessary for me to affirm since I am sure that you are encountering spontaneous expressions of them from many directions.

I thank you also for conveying the gratitude of your Government and country for the support and sympathy which they are receiving from the Government and people of the United States in the struggle which the peoples of the Soviet Union are so heroically and effectively making against the forces of aggression and assure you that it is the firm intention of the Government of the United States to continue to carry out its program of aid to the Soviet Union in the conduct of the struggle.

You are taking up your duties here upon a day of great historic import. As you have pointed out, coincident with your arrival yesterday in Washington American territory and American armed forces were subjected to an attack from another State. This attack, as you quite correctly state, has been brought about by the same forces and the same ideology which have unleashed war in Europe and other continents. In response to this attack, at this very moment Congress is voting upon a declaration of war with Japan, which is guilty of deliberate and unprovoked aggression against the United States. I am grateful for your assurances of the best wishes and warm sympathy of the people of the Soviet Union for the American people during these trying days.

There can be no doubt that the struggle in which the United States is being forced to engage is closely connected with, if not a component part of, a gigantic struggle on a world scale which has been brought about by kindred forces of aggression inflamed with ambitions for world conquest and world domination. I agree with you that the successful and speedy outcome of this struggle will depend largely upon the extent to which the countries opposing aggression are willing to coordinate their activities, to use their resources in a timely and rational manner, and to maintain among themselves full understanding and confidence; and can assure you that your efforts to create conditions in the relation between the United States and the Soviet Union most favorable fo bringing about a successful outcome of this struggle will be met by similar efforts on the part of the American Government.

3. PROSECUTION OF THE WAR

(1) Statement of the Soviet Ambassador at Washington (Litvinov) t the Press, December 13, 1941 [1]

[Excerpts]

. . . Thus, for five-and-a-half months, the Red Army has had to endure without outside aid, the full pressure of the powerful military machine o

[1] Information Bulletin of the Embassy of the Union of Soviet Socialist Republics December 15, 1941.

Hitler's Germany, with its mighty reserves and resources, for during this period Hitler did not have to fight anywhere else. His dream of war on only one front had come true.

We, naturally, would have welcomed the creation, somewhere in Europe, of a second front, which would have drawn away some of Hitler's forces and given us a moment's respite, enabling us to do a certain amount of regrouping of our own forces in order to pass to the offensive. We never complained, however, never made any demands upon our ally, England, that she should create such a front, but took into consideration her assurances as to the impossibility, difficulty or prematureness of invasion of the Continent.

When I left Moscow a month ago the enemy was at its very gates, subjecting the capital to hourly bombardments, by day and by night. According, however, to Hitler's solemn promise to his people, his hordes should have been marching through the Red Square six weeks before that, and the Red Army should have been completely washed out. Instead of this, not only have the Germans been held up almost all along the front, but they have been forced to retreat while the three great centers which have always been their most coveted objects — Leningrad, Moscow and Rostov — are all in our hands.

It would, in my opinion, be wrong to give all the credit of this to the Winter season, though it has undoubtedly played its part. The truth is rather that a favorable combination of circumstances has come into being. There can be no doubt that the Germans, in their scramble for territory, their hasty grasping at fortified towns, have lost their best military units, and have had to fill up the breaches with those of inferior quality. The determined defense of the Red Army caused an atmosphere of hopelessness and apathy among the attackers, breaking down their belief in a rapid victory. This atmosphere was in its turn thickened by the German Army's reaction to Hitler's boastful and unfulfilled promises. Here we are confronted, beyond all doubt, by a considerable lowering of the morale of Hitler's armies, if not by their complete demoralization. I am not inclined to believe that Hitler has during the last week or two transferred any troops from the Russian to any other front (existing or newly created).

As a matter of fact there exists only one other land front which has lately become active, and this is Libya. And, important as this front is both in itself and potentially, Hitler is, after all, not sufficiently interested in the preservation of Libya for Italy, or the salvaging of the Italian Army there, to risk failure on the Eastern Front. Hitler could easily recover from any defeat in Libya, for it will not settle his hash. Defeat on the Eastern Front, on the contrary, would mean the shipwreck of all his hopes and plans, and would seal his fate forever. Hitler would get over the defeat of his satellites, or at any rate could keep his head above water without their help for some time, but Hitler's "allies" without Hitler would no longer constitute a grave danger and could be polished off without much trouble. After all, it is Hitler who is the chief culprit in all the present wars, the inspirer and moving spirit of the whole gang and the destruction of Hitler would mean the end of them all.

. . . .

In this struggle against the international gangsters the heavy end has fallen to the Soviet Union, Great Britain and the United States. We are proud and happy to count ourselves the allies of your great country. I am quite sure that complete understanding exists or will be arrived at among these three allies as to which of them should concentrate its greatest efforts and energy on which sector, and that they will be ruled in this by the interests of the common cause. We are all in the same boat now, and will either perish together or together triumph over the greatest evil of our times, over the spirit of aggression, of international infamy and barbarity. And triumph we will!

(2) Conference of the President of the United States (Roosevelt) with the People's Commissar of Foreign Affairs of the U.S.S.R (Molotov), Washington, May 29–June –, 1942

[See p. 242.]

(3) Address of the Soviet Ambassador at Washington (Litvinov) at Madison Square Garden, New York City, June 22, 1942 [1]

[Excerpt]

In concluding a pact of non-aggression with the Soviet Union in 1939 Hitler was moved by the sole aim of avoiding war on two fronts, which he always feared. When he could sum up the position in the west as practically a state of truce, from which he could anticipate no disturbances, he attacked the Soviet Union.

. . . .

At the same time, while bringing to a halt the onslaught of the Nazi hordes, the Red Army hurled them back in some places, compelling them in others to mark time for long months, and to go over to the defensive

[1] *Ibid.*, June 23, 1942.

his forced Hitler to mobilize all the remnants of his forces and resources, oth in Germany and in the countries of his satellites, and once more uild up that front which he is bound to consider decisive for himself, preparations for a fresh offensive. By pinning Hitler's forces to the astern Front, the Soviet Union enabled its ally, England — and after s entry into the war, the United States — to prepare and accumulate rces for future operations. These forces, unfortunately, have had to be attered over separate fronts, while even forces not in use, and inactive, re not available to counterbalance Hitler's new and very considerable forts on the Eastern Front.

Valuable as is the material aid received from the United States and reat Britain, it has not, so far, come into scale with the scope of oper- tions. There is now, however, every ground for hoping that this tuation will be changed in the near future, and that Hitler will have to elinquish his pet idea of war on one front only. But in the meantime e has been able to take the initiative on certain sections of the Eastern 'ront and, passing again to the offensive, to gain several new positions. Iaturally, the more such positions he gains, the greater will be the perations required on a new front to equalize the changing situation. 'here can be no sort of doubt that if the German forces had been diverted om the Eastern Front at the moment when the initiative was in the ands of the Red Army, when the German troops were weakened and emoralized, the whole military situation might have been changed, nd it would certainly have been possible to inflict considerable, if not nal defeat on the main Hitler army. This moment was allowed to slip. et us hope the lesson has not been in vain.

Hitler has now embarked upon a fresh offensive on the Soviet front, inging upon it all his forces and resources. This is his final throw of the ice, on which he is staking his all. The Soviet troops are meeting his ew assault with the same unexampled heroism, tenacity and fearlessness hich they displayed all through the past year, enriched by the experi- nce of war and the study of the enemy's insidious military tricks. No mporary setbacks and retreats can break down their fighting spirit. 'hey know that the United States and their ally Great Britain not only ill not leave them without considerable material aid, but will increase his aid from week to week, from month to month. They know that the yes of all the United Nations, the hopes of all humanity not caught in he Nazi and Fascist toils, are upon them and upon their duel with the Iitler monster. The warm sympathy and good wishes reaching out to hem from all over the world are no slight moral support in their struggle. 'hey know of the generous aid extended both to their wounded and to

civilian war victims by the American people. I should like to take th
opportunity to express on their behalf gratitude to Russian War Relie
the American Red Cross and all contributors for their splendid help.
know what American generosity is and have not the slightest doul
that Americans will not soon be weary of well doing.

In the recently concluded agreements the Soviet, British and America
Governments have again, and in no uncertain tones, given mutu
pledges not to lay down their arms or cease from the struggle till th
international terrorist Hitler, together with his henchmen, have bee
swept from the face of the earth, till the ideological and material foun
dations for their criminal aggressive intentions have been destroyec

The inexhaustible resources of the three most powerful states — th
U.S.S.R., the British Empire, and the United States of America — wi
enable them to endure any temporary setbacks or military failure
whatsoever. This is where they differ from Hitler's Germany, whos
endurance is strictly limited both as to time and resources. It woulc
however, be wrong to suppose that superiority of resources is boun
mechanically and in all circumstances to ensure victory. Much depenc
on the rational and timely use of resources. Their dispersal in space an
time might neutralize their superiority and lead to disastrous consc
quences. The foe cannot be beaten if his forces of today, mobilized an
developed as they are to the utmost, are opposed by forces of tomorrow

(4) *Message of Congratulation of the Secretary of State (Hull) to th
People's Commissar of Foreign Affairs of the Soviet Union (Mc
lotov) on the Successful Resistance to the Nazi Aggressior
June 22, 1942* [1]

I extend through you to the Government and people of the Sovie
Union on behalf of the Government and people of the United States
congratulations upon the success with which you have resisted the bruta
aggression of Nazi Germany and have thus frustrated the plans for worl
conquest so over-confidently laid by our common enemy. For one yea
the peoples of the Soviet Union have been engaging the armies not onl
of Nazi Germany but also of those other European countries the govern
ments of which have accepted Nazi dictation. In this struggle the arme
forces of the Soviet Union, with the heroic support of the entire popu
lation, have so acquitted themselves as to win the admiration of th
liberty-loving peoples of the world and to earn a place in history besid
those Russian Armies which over a century and a quarter ago did s
much to ruin the plans of another aspirant to world conquest.

[1] Department of State, *Bulletin*, VI, p. 562.

During the past year the American people, although themselves threatened by aggression from several directions, have gladly shared their arms and supplies with the Soviet Union. It is planned that during the coming year these arms and supplies will pour forth from our factories and countryside in an ever widening stream until final victory has been achieved.

We are confident that before the end of another year the instigators of this war will have been given to understand how seriously they have underestimated the determination and the ability for effective action of the peace-loving nations and will have learned that in an aroused world aggressors can no longer escape the consequences of acts resulting in human suffering and destruction.

4. WAR AIMS

[In addition to document given below, see Address of the Ambassador of the Soviet Union at London (Maisky) to the Inter-Allied Meeting, London, September 24, 1941, p. 214; Declaration by United Nations, signed January 1, 1942, p. 203; Treaty of Alliance . . . between the Union of Soviet Socialist Republics and the United Kingdom, signed May 26, 1942, p. 254; and Agreement for Mutual Aid pursuant to the Lend-Lease Act, signed June 11, 1942, p. 238.]

1) *Address of the President of the Soviet of People's Commissars of the Soviet Union (Stalin) before the Supreme Soviet, Moscow, November 6, 1941* [1]
[Excerpt]

. . Unlike Hitlerite Germany, the Soviet Union and its Allies are waging a war for liberation — a just war for the liberation of the enslaved peoples of Europe and the U.S.S.R. from Hitler's tyranny. Therefore, all honest people must support the armies of the U.S.S.R., Great Britain and the other Allies as armies of liberation.

We have not nor can we have such war aims as the seizure of foreign territories or the conquest of other peoples, irrespective of whether European peoples and territories or Asiatic peoples and territories, including Iran, are concerned. Our first aim is to liberate our territories and our peoples from the German Nazi yoke.

We have not nor can we have such war aims as the imposition of our will and our regime on the Slavic and other enslaved peoples of Europe who are waiting for our help. Our aim is to help these peoples in their struggle for liberation from Hitler's tyranny, and then to accord them the possibility of arranging their lives on their own land as they

[1] Received from the Embassy of the U.S.S.R., Washington, D. C.

think fit, with absolute freedom. No interference of any kind with the domestic affairs of other nations!

But to realize these aims it is necessary to crush the military might of the German invaders. It is necessary to exterminate to the last man all the German invaders who have penetrated our native land to enslave it. . . .

This is our task. Now we can and must fulfill this task. Only by fulfilling this task and routing the German invaders can we achieve a lasting and just peace.

For the complete destruction of the German invaders!

For the liberation of all oppressed peoples groaning under the yok of Hitlerite tyranny! . . .

D. Germany

[See Chapter II, From Neutrality to Belligerency.]

1. GERMAN THREAT TO SECURITY OF THE UNITED STATES

(1) *Statement Issued from Headquarters of the German Führer (Hitler) November 1, 1941* [1]

In his Navy Day address of October 27, 1941,[2] President Roosevelt informed the American people that "America has been attacked." He announced the attack upon the destroyer *Kearny*, following upon the attack on the *Greer* referred to in his address of September 11,[3] and then described a map which he had in his possession which made clear the nature of the Nazi design on Latin America. The statement given below purports to answer these charges.

The Reich Government makes the following official announcement

I. The President of the United States of America made the following statements in a speech October 28:

"The Government of the United States is in possession of a secret map which was prepared in Germany by the Reich Government. It is a map of Middle South America as the Führer wants to reorganize it in that he wants to make five subject states out of fourteen countries in this area and thereby bring the entire South American continent under his control. One of these five states allegedly should include the Republic of Panama as well as the Panama Canal.

"II. The American Government is in possession of a second document which was composed by the Reich Government. This document contains a plan eliminating all existing religions in the world after the war is won by Germany. Catholic, Protestant, Mohammedan, Hindu, Buddhist and Jewish religions are to be removed in the same way, church property confiscated, the crucifix and all other religious symbols

[1] Associated Press version, *New York Times*, November 2, 1941, p. 13; circulated to the diplomatic corps at Berlin.
[2] See p. 27.   [3] See p. 27.

rbidden, the clergy brought to silence under the penalty of the con-
entration camp.

"In place of the churches an international National Socialist church is
> be established in which the speakers sent out by the National Socialist
overnment would perform offices. In place of the Bible, words out of
ne Führer's book, 'Mein Kampf,' would be imposed by force and
nforced as Holy Writ. The crucifix is to be replaced by the swastika
nd the naked sword and finally the Führer is to take the place of God."

In answer the Reich Government declares:

1. There exists neither map prepared in Germany by the Reich Gov-
rnment regarding the dividing up of Central South America nor
ocument pronounced by the Reich Government regarding the dissolu-
on of religions in the world. Therefore both are forgeries of the clumsi-
st, grossest type.

2. Assertions of the conquest of South America by Germany and
imination of the religions of the churches in the world and their
placement by the National Socialist church are so nonsensical and
osurd that it is superfluous for the Reich Government to discuss them.

The Reich Government has notified through diplomatic channels all
eutral governments, including the Central South American govern-
ents, of the above.

II. The President of the United States of America declared in his
eech of October 28 that an American destroyer was attacked by
erman naval forces on September 4 and another American destroyer
1 October 17. The American Government was willing to avoid shoot-
g. But the shooting has begun and history has established who fired
ie first shot. America has been attacked.

Reports of German U-boat commanders and published official decla-
tion of the American Navy authorities actually show the following
rcumstances:

The American destroyer *Greer* was involved in an incident September
the American destroyer *Kearny* in an incident October 17. The
stroyer *Greer* pursued a German U-boat for hours in close military
operation with English naval forces. In the course of this pursuit this
erman U-boat, which was under water, was attacked with depth bombs.
Only after this attack did the German U-boat use its weapons. The
stroyer continued its pursuit with depth bombs for a number of hours.

The destroyer *Kearny* was sailing as protector of one convoy as it
ceived a call for help from a second convoy which was in battle action
th German naval forces in another part of the Atlantic Ocean. The
earny thereupon changed course, went to the scene of the battle and
tacked the German U-boat with depth bombs.

2. DECLARATION OF WAR AGAINST THE UNITED STATES

[For notification, see p. 118.]

(1) Speech of the Reichsführer (Hitler) in the Reichstag, Decembe 11, 1941 [1]

[Excerpt]

A difference of regime and form of government between Germany an America was always present.

That difference, therefore, could not have been a sufficient reason. One of the two nations interfered in the other's affairs.

An ocean always has been between them and whether the differen has been that of a country ruled by a president and that of a count ruled in the form of a monarchy, or the present difference between authoritarian President and the Führer, these differences could not ha served as sufficient pretext for enmity.

In fact, differences existing between the United States and the Sovi Union at present should by rights be much greater than those that ha existed between Germany and the U. S. A.

Two men only were responsible for this enmity between the Unite States and Germany — Woodrow Wilson and Franklin Delano Roos velt.

It was a broken pledge, as history since has proved; a pledge brok by Woodrow Wilson that in its consequences led to untold misery bo for the victors and the vanquished in the last World War. And it w this broken pledge that made Versailles possible.

At that time German people certainly paid dearly for being credulo and believing in President Wilson's assurances, and today we have mc or less the same picture of an American President inciting the world to to war against Germany.

I can well understand that there is a world-wide gulf between t outlook of President Roosevelt and myself.

Roosevelt, of course, comes from a wealthy family and has had all a vantages of upbringing in that circle.

I, myself, come from a small, very poor family and have always had work for myself.

During the first World War Roosevelt was able to go into politics a to see to it that he made money. I, of course, became a soldier a simply took orders for four years. I tried to do nothing but my du

[1] As recorded by Reuter and the Associated Press. New York Times, December 1941, p. 4.

In fact, I shared my fate with millions and Roosevelt shared his fate
ith the upper 10,000.

During inflation Roosevelt went on earning money, whereas I remained
ι hospitals.

Then we both developed in politics. Roosevelt became boss of a City
ouncil, a position to which he had risen by his money, and I became
hancellor because I was leader of a popular movement. One thing,
f course, we both have in common. Our coming into power was closely
onnected with democracy — that is, with the failure of States which
ad relied on democracy.

In both countries there was ruin and nobody had any work. While in
ermany, during the next years an immense regeneration of labor,
ade and art took place, Roosevelt did not succeed in altering anything
ι spite of the fact that in America there were only 18 people to the
quare kilometer compared to 145 in Germany.

This can only be due to total incompetence. In five years it has been
ossible in Germany to find work for every one. During the same period
ι America Roosevelt has succeeded in undermining American economy,
ι devaluating the dollar and in keeping up the figure of unemployed.
ews, of course, have flourished.

In fact, in Europe it seems inconceivable that Roosevelt should not
ave ended up before a State court. In fact, he would presumably —
efore a civil court — have received a term of imprisonment for sharp
ractice in business.

For what possible reason could such enmity against the German
eople have arisen?

First — Germany practically is the only country in Europe which
ever possessed any colonies whatsoever on the soil of the North Ameri-
ιn Continent. Apart from German emigrants to the United States,
ermany has never interfered in the affairs of America. . . .

Second — Germany has never adopted any antagonistic attitude
ιward the United States, but, in fact, the Germans who emigrated gave
ιeir blood fighting for the liberty of the United States.

Third — Germany never has taken part in any war waged against the
nited States.

Fourth — In 1917 the United States on their part entered the war
ιainst Germany for reasons which since have been proved to be entirely
ιurious. They have been proved to be such by an investigation com-
ιittee set up by none other than President Roosevelt himself. This
ιmmittee has proved that only vested interests of a small capitalistic
ιique were benefited.

There have been no territorial claims or any other differences of opinion standing in the way of any understanding between the United States and Germany.

Under various influences Roosevelt has tried to create conflicts every where, to deepen existing conflicts and to prevent a peaceful settlemen of existing conflicts.

For years he wished there might arise in Europe a conflict in whic by taking sides he might engage American industry.

From 1937 onward he took all the opportunities which he coul possibly seize to act against the Reich. In his speech of October 5, 1937 he began his campaign of hatred against us by talking of a quarantin which he would establish against the dictatorships.

Then he recalled his Ambassador, so from that moment onward th two countries were only represented by chargés d'affaires in thei respective capitals.

In November 1938, he checked every possibility of peaceful settlemen by giving the impression that he himself was in favor of peace, but at th same time threatening all those countries who were trying to settle thei own affairs peacefully with economic reprisals, financial measures an other acts.

About that also we have very clear reports from the Polish embassie in Washington, London and Paris.

In 1939 he went on with his work of hatred and warmongering. H interfered in internal European affairs which were none of his busines which were just as little his business as the affairs of one of the America States are of the head of the German State.

He did not recognize certain governments which had establishe themselves in Europe. He failed to recognize the new order. On th contrary, he recognized and upheld puppet governments . . . and wit the representative of one of these governments even made treaty t secure a foothold in territory which was not American.

President Roosevelt addressed an appeal to me and to the Duce o April 5, 1939, which was a mixture of arrogance and ignorance of th geographic conditions of our continent.

When I had given President Roosevelt a very polite but firm answer, h ceased to talk for the time, but, instead, Mrs. Roosevelt began a campaig She and her son refused to live in the world as we National Socialis understand it, . . . a world of work and not a world of falsehood.

Then, on April 11, 1939, President Roosevelt obtained an amendme to the Neutrality Act by repealing the arms exportation embarg unilaterally. . .

Roosevelt froze Norwegian and Danish assets, though it was well
known that they were not subject to German control or interference.
Then the Norwegian, Dutch and Belgian puppet governments were
recognized by Roosevelt, and finally, on June 15, Roosevelt sent a
telegram to the then Prime Minister of France, M. Reynaud, promising
to double American aid to France if France only continued her resistance
against Germany.

He also assured France he would not recognize in the name of the
United States any territorial changes such as return of Alsace-Lorraine
to Germany. It goes without saying that such recognition from America
is of no consequence whatever to Germany and the German Government.

These examples I have only cited in order to show up the activities of
this warmonger in their proper light.

Roosevelt was afraid even then of a European peace because it might
interfere with his plans. He was afraid that Europe might realize peace,
after all, was possible and in her best interests.

He froze French assets, but only in order to get hold of gold which had
been transported from Casablanca to the United States on board a
United States cruiser.

Then, in August 1940, Roosevelt made a further step toward war,
announcing a joint military program between the United States and
Canada. He continually invented crises and interrupted journeys on
week-ends, rapidly returning to Washington to make these crises more
credible.

Finally, he drew still closer to war in November 1940, lending fifty
destroyers to England, although he received in return British bases of
considerable value. It is not quite certain whether it was hate or a desire
to take over the British Empire which was the primary driving force in
this act.

Then, when British assets in the United States had become exhausted,
he concluded the Lease-Lend agreement, and in the meantime a whole
series of incidents had been directed by Roosevelt against Germany.

Then Roosevelt declared the Red Sea open to American shipping.
He had shortly before that confiscated German ships in the United
States and German subjects had been interned and treated contrary to
international law in a most despicable manner.

Of all such incidents the fate meted out to two escaped German prisoners who reached the United States territory from Canada was particularly despicable — they were handcuffed and handed back to Canadian
authorities contrary to all international agreement and custom.

Roosevelt also interfered in the Balkans. He sent the notoriou
Colonel Donovan to incite a revolt there.

He gave Yugoslavia and Greece guarantees, he recognized the exile
governments and froze their assets.

On April 26, America delivered twenty motor speed boats to Eng
land; on April 6, American troops landed in Greenland for the firs
time, and soon after a German submarine was attacked with dept
charges.

On June 17, all German Consulates, the German Library of Infor
mation and other official German bureaus were closed at the demand c
the American Government, while on June 20, American troops landed i
Iceland, a move by which Roosevelt hoped to render ineffective th
operations of German submarines.

On July 10, American Secretary of State for Navy Knox ordered th
American Navy to fire on Axis ships.

As a result, a great number of incidents occurred, such as when, o
September 26, depth charges were fired on a German submarine, a fee
which was repeated on October 6 in the case of the American destroye
Kearny.

A few weeks later the American Navy even went so far as to seize th
harmless German merchant ship *Odenwald*, which was crossing to a
American port. The crew was imprisoned.

It does not impress me very much if Roosevelt sees fit to call me
gangster. After all, one would do well to remember that "gangster"
an American term, and apparently gangsters prevail in that countr
On the other hand, I cannot feel insulted by Roosevelt because, just
with President Wilson, I consider Roosevelt to be insane.

Against Japan, Roosevelt resorted to similar methods, making hyp
critical demands. The world must have been relieved to see at last
State rise up to tell Roosevelt to mind his own business, and he cann
very well complain this was not called for. That Japan took this ste
and decided to defend her freedom must fill all decent people wit
profound satisfaction.

We know, of course, that the eternal Jew is behind all this. Rooseve
himself may not realize it, but then that only shows his own limitation

Indeed, we all know the intention of the Jews to rule all civilize
States in Europe and America. We know this is a time when for natio
it is the question of "to be or not to be."

When President Roosevelt sees fit to give me good advice, he is lik
the bald hairdresser recommending a famous hair tonic to his client

Economically, countries like the United States and Great Britain a

backward that we will not accept gifts from them; we merely demand
r rights.

These countries have done everything to prevent both Germany and
aly from creating conditions essential to their existence . . . I have
erefore given to the American Chargé d'Affaires his passports to-
y.

In pursuing a policy of world dictatorship President Roosevelt has
rained from no step to prevent Germany and Italy from creating
nditions that could secure their existence.

Both he and England have opposed every revision, and, in flagrant
ntradiction of international law, America has attacked our ships,
terned the crews and, in the end, went even so far as to give its Navy,
ntrary to all international law, the order to attack and sink German
d Italian ships.

Since then a plan prepared by President Roosevelt has been revealed
the United States, according to which his intention was to attack
rmany by 1943 with all the resources at the disposal of the United
ates. Thus our patience has come to the breaking point.

An agreement has been made by the three countries concerned. It is
follows:

[For text of German-Italian-Japanese joint declaration, see p. 202.]

E. France

1. STATEMENTS OF MARSHAL PÉTAIN

[See *Documents, III, 1940–41*, p. 389.]

) *Address of the French Chief of State (Pétain), August 12, 1941* [1]

[Excerpts]

Frenchmen!

I have grave things to tell you!

For the last several weeks I have felt an ill wind rising in many regions
France. Disquiet is overtaking minds; doubt is gaining control of
irits. The authority of my government is made the subject of discus-
n; orders are often being ill executed.

In an atmosphere of false rumors and intrigues, the forces of recon-
ruction are growing discouraged. Others are trying to take their place
thout their nobleness or disinterestedness. My sponsorship is too
ten invoked, even against the government, to justify self-styled under-

[1] Associated Press version, *New York Times*, August 13, 1941, p. 4.

takings of salvation which, in fact, amount to nothing more than appea
for indiscipline.

A real uneasiness inflicts the French nation. The reasons for th
uneasiness are easy to understand. Cruel hours are always followed b
difficult times.

While at the frontiers of the nation — which defeat has put out
action but whose empire leaves her vulnerable — the war goes o
ravaging new continents every day; everybody wonders with anguis
about the future of our country.

Some feel themselves betrayed; others think they are abandone
Some wonder where their duty lies; others first seek their own interes

The London radio and certain French newspapers add to this confusic
of minds. The sense of national interest in the end loses in justice ar
vigor. From this disorder of ideas springs disorder of affairs. Is thi
indeed, the fate France has deserved after thirteen months of calm,
work, of incontestable revival?

Frenchmen, I put this question to you. I ask you to measure i
scope and answer it in the confines of your consciences.

Our relations with Germany have been defined by an armistice co
vention the character of which could only be provisional. Dragging o
this situation makes it that much harder to support in so far as it gover
relations between two great nations.

As for collaboration — offered in the month of October 1940, by t
Chancellor of the Reich under conditions that made me appreciate the
deference — it was a long-term labor and has not yet been able to be
all its fruits.

We must be able to overcome a heavy heritage of distrust hande
down by centuries of dissensions and quarrels and to turn ourselv
toward broad perspectives that can open up a reconciled continent
our activity.

That is the goal toward which we are heading; but it is an immen
labor, which requires on our part as much will as it does patience. Oth
tasks absorb the German Government, gigantic tasks in developmen
to the east in defense of a civilization and which can change the map
the world.

As regards Italy, our relations likewise are controlled by an armisti
convention. Here again our desires are to escape from these provision
relations to create more stable ties without which the European ord
cannot be constructed.

I would also recall to the great American republic the reasons why
has no cause to fear a decline of French ideals. Certainly our parliame

ury democracy is dead, but it never had more than a few traits in
ommon with the democracy of the United States. As for the instinct
: liberty, it still lives within us, proud and strong.

The American press has often misjudged us. Let it now make an
ffort to comprehend the quality of our souls and the destiny of a nation
hose soil, through the course of history has been periodically ravaged,
hose youth has been decimated, whose well being has been troubled by
he fragility of a Europe in whose reconstruction France intends today
• participate.

Our domestic difficulties have sprung above all from troubled minds,
om lack of men and from scarcity of products.

Troubled minds do not have as their sole origin the vicissitudes of our
reign policy. They come especially from our slowness in building a
ew order or, more correctly, in imposing one. The National Revolution,
hich I outlined in my message last October 11, has not yet taken its
ace among accomplished facts.

It has not yet forced its way through because between the people and
e — who understand one another so well — there has risen a double
reen of partisans of the old regime and those serving the trusts.

.   .   .   .

And yet, in spite of these difficulties the future of our country is
eing built with a precision that becomes more assured every day.
The family, communities, trades, provinces will be pillars of the
nstitution at which the best workers for our reconstruction are laboring
·elessly. Its preamble will open up clear perspectives for the future of
·ance.

Our most recent reforms are being made the object of methodical
vision, the outline of which will appear clearer as soon as legislative
xts have been simplified and codified.

But lawmaking and building are not enough. Governing is needed.
is both the necessity and the will of the whole people.

France cannot really be governed except from Paris. I cannot yet
:urn there, and I shall not return there until certain facilities are
·ered me.

France cannot be governed except without the assent of public
inion — an assent more necessary than ever in the authoritarian
;ime.

This public opinion is today divided. France cannot be governed
·less the initiative of her chief finds corresponding exactness and
·thfulness in the bodies transmitting it. This exactness and faithful-
ss are still lacking.

France, however, cannot wait. A nation like ours, forged in the cruc
ble of races and passions, proud and courageous, as ready for sacrifice a
for violence and ever bristling when its honor is at stake, needs certai
ties, space and discipline.

The Government's problem thus goes far beyond the framework of
simple ministerial change. It demands above all the unqualified maint
nance of certain principles.

Authority no longer emanates from below. The only authority
that which I entrust or delegate.

I delegated it in the first place to Admiral Darlan, to whom publ
opinion has not always been favorable or fair, but who has ever help
me with loyalty and courage.

I have given him the Ministry of National Defense in order that
may exercise more direct control on all our land, sea and air force

To my Government I shall leave the necessary initiative, but in vario
fields I intend to trace for it a very clear line. This is what I ha
decided:

1. Activity of political parties and groups of political origin is su
pended until further notice in the unoccupied zone. These parties m
no longer hold either public or private meetings. They must cease a
distribution of tracts or notices. Those that fail to conform to the
decisions will be dissolved.

2. Payment of Members of Parliament is suppressed as of Septemb
30.

3. The first disciplinary sanctions against State officials guilty
false declarations regarding membership in secret societies has be
ordered. The names of officials have been published this morning in t
Journal Officiel. Holders of high Masonic degrees — of which the fi
list has just been published — may no longer exercise any public fu
tion.

4. The Legion of War Veterans remains the best instrument in t
free zone of the National Revolution. But it is able to carry out its ci
task only by remaining in all ranks subordinate to the Governme

5. I will double the means of police action, whose discipline a
loyalty should guarantee public order.

6. A group of Commissars of Public Power is created. These hi
officials will be charged with studying the spirit in which the la
decrees, orders and instructions of the central power will be carried o
They will have the mission of ferreting out and destroying obstac
which abuse of the rules of administrative routine or activity of sec
societies can oppose to the work of National Revolution.

7. Powers of regional prefects, the first units of those who will be
overnors of provinces in the France of tomorrow, will be reenforced.
heir power, so far as the central administration is concerned, is in-
·eased. Their authority over all heads of local services is direct and
omplete.

8. The labor charter designed to regulate, according to the principles
' my St. Etienne speech, relations among workers, artisans, technicians
id employers in an agreement reached with mutual understanding,
is resulted in a solemn accord. It will be published shortly.

9. The provisional statute of economic organization will be revamped
a basis of reorganization of committees with larger representation of
nall industry and artisans, with revision of their financial administra-
on and their relations with provincial arbitration organisms.

10. The powers, role and organization of the National Food Supply
ureau will be modified according to means which, safeguarding the
terests of consumers, permit the authority of the State to make itself
lt at the same time on a national and regional basis.

11. I have decided to use the powers given me by Constitutional Act
o. 7 to judge those responsible for our disaster. A Council of Justice is
eated to that effect. It will submit its reports before October 15.

12. In the application of this same Constitutional Act, all Ministers
id high officials must swear an oath of fealty to me and engage them-
lves to carry out duties in their charge for the well-being of the State
·cording to the rules of honor and propriety.

This first series of measures will reassure the French who think only of
ell-being of the fatherland.

Prisoners who still are waiting in camps and who are preparing your-
lves in silence for the work of national restoration, peasants of France
10 are gathering harvest in particularly difficult conditions, people of
e reserved [occupied] zone who place all your confidence in the unity of
·ance, workmen of our suburbs, deprived of meat and wine and of
bacco and yet so brave, you are the ones I think of. You are the ones
whom I address these French words.

I know by my calling what victory is; I see today what defeat is. I
ve received the heritage of a wounded France. It is my duty to defend
at heritage by maintaining your aspirations and your rights.

In 1917 I put an end to mutiny. In 1940 I put an end to rout. Today
wish to save you from yourselves.

When a man of my age dedicates his person to his country there is no
crifice that he can evade. His only concern is the public salvation.
emember this:

If a beaten country is divided against itself it dies. If a beate
country can unite it is reborn. Vive la France!

(2) *Letter of the French Chief of State (Pétain) to the Commander*
the Legion of French Volunteers Against Bolshevism (La Bonne
November 6, 1941 [1]

After the German invasion of the Soviet Union German authorities in ter
tories under their control exerted themselves to secure French participatio
The Legion of French Volunteers Against Bolshevism was organized and train
in occupied France, where this letter was released with the comment that it w
an "act of political importance" that "completes and strengthens the gestu
of Montoire." [2]

The message of fidelity which you have sent me in your own name a
that of your men before going to the front line has deeply touched in r
both the soldier and the Chief of State.

On the eve of your coming fight I am happy to learn that you do n
forget that part of our military honor rests in your hands. There
perhaps no more useful task at the present moment than to restore
our country confidence in its own virtue. But you will serve France a
in a more direct manner.

By participating in that crusade of which Germany has taken t
lead, thus acquiring rightful title to the gratitude of the world, you w
contribute to warding off from us the Bolshevist peril; thereby you w
be protecting your country while at the same time saving the hope o
reconciled Europe.

For these reasons Admiral Darlan, Minister of National Defense, a
myself wish you good luck in the accomplishment of the noble du
which you have chosen.

For my part I shall follow you in your trials with all my solicitu
until the glorious day of your return to your homeland.

2. VICHY COLLABORATION WITH AXIS POWERS IN
THE MEDITERRANEAN AREA

(1) *Summary of Report of the Vice Premier (Darlan), November*
1941 [3]

The appointment of General Maxime Weygand as Delegate General of
French Government in French Africa by the Chief of State September 6, 1
was regarded in occupied France and elsewhere as evidence of an intention
maintain autonomy in that part of French territory. Weygand, who was

[1] English version, *New York Times*, November 7, 1941, p. 7.
[2] *Documents, III, 1940–41*, p. 396.
[3] English version of *New York Times*, November 21, 1941, p. 6.

st Commander-in-Chief of the French Army, enjoyed the full confidence of the
rench people, and was credited with having saved the French African posses-
ons from becoming German bases for Mediterranean operations. He received
ders, if at all, only from the Chief of State until Admiral Darlan as vice premier
cured the signing of a decree in September 1940 subordinating the Delegate
eneral to his orders on the ground of "facilitating collaboration" with Ger-
any. Confidence in Weygand was a factor in the relaxation of the United States
port control restrictions.

The report to the Marshal [Henri Philippe Pétain] of the law suppres-
ng the office of Delegate General of the Government in French Africa
dicates notably that at the time it was created [September 6, 1940] it
as a question of guaranteeing by an active liaison the security of the
rritories which were most directly threatened — Morocco, Tunisia
d Senegal — and of improving the economic regime of the different
ossessions in such a way as to protect the populations, both colonial
d native, from the effects of the blockade, to accomplish in a coherent
anner the changes or adaptations required by the spirit of the National
evolution and finally to distribute our much-reduced military forces
hile taking account of a plan for general defense.

The work accomplished during the past year by General Weygand as
elegate General of the Government in French Africa has been suffi-
ently established now so that, without weakening the organs of political
d administrative liaison which are of permanent character, the excep-
onal function of Delegate General may be suppressed. His task having
en accomplished, this function threatened to encumber on the one
nd the initiative of the authorities in the different possessions and on
e other hand the relations of these authorities with the central power
they are defined in the existing statutes.

) *Message of the Delegate General (Weygand) to the High Commissioners, Residents and Governors General in French Africa,
November 20, 1941* [1]

At the moment, when the mission as Delegate General ends, I address
u my farewell and ask you to convey it to your collaborators and the
pulations of French Africa.
Your efforts and your confidence have always sustained me in my
sk. I wish to express my profound gratitude for this.
There never shall be effaced from my memory and heart the recollec-
on of the honor which fell to me to coordinate your activities, which
re entirely consecrated to French prosperity and unity with that of
e empire.

[1] *Ibid.*

Thanks to you, the union behind the Marshal, Chief of State, is dail
consolidating. It is the safeguard of our future.

See that all remain zealously faithful in their loyalty and their disc
pline. Vive la France!

(3) *Suspension of Economic Assistance to French North Africa. De partment of State Release, November 20, 1941* [1]

According to reports reaching the Department the French Governmen
has acquiesced to the express demand of Hitler to remove Genera
Weygand from his post as Delegate General of France in Africa, thu
permitting a German control over French authority entirely outside o
the provisions of the Armistice.[2] As a result of these reports America
policy toward France is being reviewed, and all plans for economi
assistance to French North Africa are suspended. It remains to be see
to what further extent Hitler will attempt to take over by force or threa
of force the sovereignty and control of the French Empire.

(4) *Relations with the French Government at Vichy. Statement of th Acting Secretary of State (Welles), February 27, 1942* [3]

The relations between the Government of the United States and th
French Government of Vichy have been predicated upon the forma
assurances given to this Government by the French Government upo
repeated occasions that the French Government in its relations wit
the Axis powers will not exceed the terms of its armistice agreemen
with those powers, and in particular, that the French Government will i
no wise relinquish to those powers any control over or use of Frenc
territorial possessions nor any control over nor use of the French flee
The assurances received by the United States Government in this regar
likewise include the assurance that the French Government will gi
no military assistance to the Axis Powers.

On February 10 the President sent a personal message to Marsh
Pétain informing him that the Government of the United States had bee
advised that supplies had been shipped from Metropolitan France
North Africa for the use of the Axis forces in Libya. The Preside
made it clear that the position of France and the limitations placed upo
France through the armistice agreements which had been signed wi
Germany and Italy are fully recognized and understood by the Gover
ment and the people of the United States. He stated further, howeve

---

[1] Department of State, *Bulletin*, V, p. 407.
[2] *Documents, II, 1939–40*, p. 427.
[3] Department of State, *Bulletin*, VI, p. 189.

1at in the opinion of the Government of the United States, if France
'ere to ship war materials or supplies to the Axis Powers and to render
ssistance to these powers, or to take any action in that regard which
'rance was not obligated to take under the terms of her armistice agree-
1ents, the French Government would place itself in the category of
overnments which are directly assisting the declared enemies of the
eople of the United States. The President further stated that he was
onfident that any such action would be contrary to the wishes of the
eople of France and disastrous to their aspirations and to their final
estiny.

Since that time several additional communications have been ex-
hanged between the two Governments.

On February 24 the American Ambassador in Vichy received in
riting a communication from the French Government.

In the course of this communication the French Government stated
1at it affirmed once again its will to abstain from any action, under
eservation of the obligations resulting to it from the armistice agree-
1ents, which would not be in conformity with the position of neutrality
1 which it had been placed since June 1940 and which it intended to
1aintain. The French Government further stated that it would not,
1erefore, lend any military aid to one of the belligerents in any place in
1e theater of operations, particularly the use of French vessels for the
1rposes of war, nor all the more, adopt a policy of assistance to the
xis Powers beyond the terms of the armistice agreements.

The British Government has been kept fully informed of the exchange
' communications which has taken place between the French Govern-
1ent and the Government of the United States.

While this statement of French policy as above set forth is of value
. estimating the relations between this Government and the French
overnment at Vichy, further clarifications with regard to other impor-
1nt questions are awaited by this Government before it will be enabled
• complete its examination of the present situation.

) *Economic Assistance to French North Africa. Department of State
Release, April 7, 1942* [1]

As a result of conversations with the French Government relating to
resumption of the program of economic assistance under the North
frican agreement, satisfactory assurances with regard to the issues
1volved have been received from the French Government, which will

[1] *Ibid.*, p. 318.

permit the agreed departure of two French vessels now in New Yor
with cargoes of limited supplies for North Africa.

Conditions governing previous shipments with the undertaking tha
the supplies thus received or their equivalent shall not in any way serv
to further Axis ends will likewise regulate these shipments and the
distribution to the local populations under the direct supervision (
American control officers. No military supplies of any character are t
be included in the shipments.

It is also agreed that a simultaneous departure of two ships carryin
materials from North Africa to the United States will take place.

———

Following the admission of Pierre Laval to the reorganized Vichy Goverr
ment as "Chief of Government" on April 17, Acting Secretary of State Welle
announced that the two French vessels had not sailed and that the plans whic
the State Department had been carrying out were once more held in abeyance

3. ORGANIZATION OF THE FREE FRENCH NATIONAL COMMITTEE

(1) *Text of the Decree of September 24, 1941* [2]

In furtherance to the ordinance of September 24, 1941, and decre
being taken thereon, the management of public affairs (*les pouvoi.
publics*) of Free France has been, until such a date when the Frenc
nation may freely elect its representatives, provisionally organized ɛ
follows:

A National Committee has been thus constituted:

President: General de Gaulle, of the Free French; René Plevei
National Commissioner for Economy, Finance and Colonies, Coordinate
of the Civil Commissariats; Hervé Alphand, Director of Econom
Affairs; Maurice Dejean, National Commissioner for Foreign Affair
General LeGentilhomme, National Commissioner for War; Admir
Muselier, National Commissioner for the Navy and the Merchai
Marine; René Cassin, National Commissioner for Justice and Publ
Education; Colonel Valin, National Commissioner for Aviation; And.
Diethelm, National Commissioner for Labor and Information; Heni
Hauck, Director of Labor; Commander Georges Thierry D'Argenlie
National Commissioner without department.

Legislative powers are to be exercised by General de Gaulle, Presidei
of the Committee, by way of ordinances and upon deliberation by tl

[1] *Ibid.*, p. 337.
[2] *The Inter-Allied Review*, I, No. 10, November 15, 1941, p. 9. For an account
the Free French Movement see "The Rise of Free France," *The Times* (Londor
August 20, 1941, p. 5; also *La France Libre* (15 Queensberry Place, London).

National Committee. Decrees taken in execution of these ordinances will be signed by General de Gaulle and countersigned by one or several National Commissioners.

The representatives of Foreign Powers will be accredited to General de Gaulle, President of the Committee.

The representatives of Free France to Foreign Powers will be appointed by decree and will receive their credentials from General de Gaulle, President of the Committee.

The Council for the Defense of the French Empire will continue to give advice upon matters concerning the defense of the territories of the Empire and the participation of these territories in any activities or in war.

A Military High Committee is to be entrusted with the task of giving advice concerning the general conduct of the war, and with the coordination of the activities of the land, sea and air forces.

An advisory National Council, entrusted with the task of furnishing the National Committee with as complete an expression of the wishes and opinions of the French as possible, is to be constituted by a forthcoming ordinance.

2) *Free French Movement. Statement of the United Kingdom Secretary of State for Foreign Affairs (Eden), House of Commons, November 26, 1941* [1]

His Majesty's Government have informed General de Gaulle that they are prepared to regard the Free French National Committee as representing all Free Frenchmen wherever they may be who rally to the Free French Movement in support of the Allied cause, and that they will treat with the National Committee on all questions involving their collaboration with the Free French Movement and with the French oversea territories which place themselves under its authority. This seems to his Majesty's Government to be the appropriate character in which to regard the executive organ of a movement which, under the fighting leadership of General de Gaulle, embodies the hopes of Frenchmen of free mind, wherever they may be.

4. RECOGNITION FOR CERTAIN PURPOSES BY THE UNITED STATES OF THE FRENCH NATIONAL COMMITTEE

While the Government of the United States has not been willing to accord recognition to the French National Committee as the Government of France, it has been willing to deal with French authorities responsible to the Committee, when those authorities are in effective control of certain French territories, on a

[1] United Kingdom, Parliamentary Debates, 5th Series, vol. 376, p. 727.

de facto basis. In addition, according to a statement of Secretary Hull at hi press conference on May 21, 1942, the United States Government gives suppor to the French National Committee as the organization representing French re sistance in the war situation. In line with this policy, Free France has been de clared eligible to receive Lend-Lease assistance.[1]

(1) *The Vice Consul at Nouméa (MacVitty) to the High Commissione of New Caledonia (Thierry d'Argenlieu), February 28, 1942* [2]

The policy of the Government of the United States as regards Franc and French territory has been based upon the maintenance of th integrity of France and of the French Empire and of the eventua restoration of the complete independence of all French territorie Mindful of its traditional friendship for France, this Government deepl sympathizes not only with the desire of the French people to maintai their territories intact but with the efforts of the French people to cor tinue to resist the forces of aggression. In its relations with the loca French authorities in French territories the United States has been an will continue to be governed by the manifest effectiveness with whic those authorities endeavor to protect their territories from dominatio and control by the common enemy.

With the French authorities in effective control of French territori in the Pacific this Government has treated and will continue to treat o the basis of their actual administration of the territories involved. Th Government recognizes, in particular, that French island possessions i that area are under the effective control of the French National Con mittee established in London, and the United States authorities a cooperating for the defense of these islands with the authorities estal lished by the French National Committee and with no other Frenc authority. This Government appreciates the importance of Ne Caledonia in the defense of the Pacific area.

(2) *African Territories under French National Committee. Departme of State Release, April 4, 1942* [3]

In view of the importance of French Equatorial Africa in the unite war effort, the decision has been taken to establish an American Co sulate General at Brazzaville, the capital of French Equatorial Afric Arrangements are under way with the appropriate authorities looki to the establishment of this office and to the appointment of Mr. Mayna

[1] See p. 178, n. 1.
[2] Department of State, *Bulletin*, VI, p. 208.
[3] *Ibid.*, p. 273.

arnes, American Foreign Service officer, as Consul General.[1] Mr. Barnes
ill proceed to Brazzaville at the expiration of leave of absence in the
nited States. In the meanwhile, Mr. Laurence Taylor, who has
cently returned from French Equatorial Africa, will proceed to
razzaville to establish the office.

As has been previously stated, this Government has treated with the
rench authorities in effective control of French territories in Africa
d will continue to treat with them on the basis of their actual admin-
tration of the territories involved. The French territories of Equatorial
frica and the French Cameroons are under the effective control of the
rench National Committee established in London, and the United
tates authorities are cooperating on matters relating to these territories
ith the authorities established by the French National Committee.

) The Acting Secretary of State (Welles) to the Ambassador of the French Government at Vichy (Henry-Haye), April 13, 1942 [2]

XCELLENCY:

I have received Your Excellency's communication of April 9, 1942,
ntaining certain observations of the French Government at Vichy
ith regard to the announcement of the establishment of a Consulate
eneral of the United States at Brazzaville.

In this connection Your Excellency informs me that your Government
usts that the Government of the United States will make it known
blicly that this step on the part of the United States should not be
terpreted as having any political implications, and that it should like-
ise not be interpreted as being a step in derogation of the "exclusive
ghts of the French Government over the territory in question."

The considerations advanced in the communication addressed to me
y Your Excellency provide an appropriate and welcome opportunity
r the Government of the United States to reiterate with the utmost
arity its policy with regard to France and with regard to the French
ople.

From the earliest days of the independence of the United States of
merica the relations between the people of France and the people of
e United States have been founded upon ties of more than ordinary
iendship and confidence. The Government of France, and many citi-
ns of France, assisted the people of the United States in achieving
eir freedom. The great principles of liberty, equality and fraternity

[1] Confirmed by the Senate as consul general, May 1, 1942.
[2] Department of State, *Bulletin*, VI, p. 335.

proclaimed by the French Revolution have been an inspiration to th
American people throughout their national existence, and the tradition
understanding between our two nations has in no small part been du
to their common faith in democratic institutions and in their like devotio
to the cause of human freedom.

Only twenty-five years ago the armies of France and of the Unite
States were fighting side by side against the same ruthless aggresse
who has now once more invaded France.

As this Government has informed Your Excellency's Governmer
upon several occasions, the Government of the United States recogniz(
the sovereign jurisdiction of the people of France over the territory
France and over French possessions overseas.

The Government of the United States fervently hopes that it may s(
the reestablishment of the independence of France and of the integrit
of French territory.

But only by the total destruction of the present criminal regime i
Germany, and by the complete defeat of the armies of Germany an
of the dictatorships which have aligned themselves with Germany, ca
that hope be realized. That is a fact well known to all of the people
France, including even that handful of Frenchmen who, in contempt f
the high tradition of liberty and individual freedom which has mac
France great, have sordidly and abjectly, under the guise of "collobor:
tion," attempted to prostitute their country to that very regime i
Germany which is bent upon nothing less than the permanent enslav
ment of France.

At the present moment continental France is in great part occupi(
by German armies. Your Excellency's Government is bound by th
terms of the armistice agreement into which it entered with Germar
in June 1940.

Marshal Pétain has had occasion to appreciate the full understandir
of the Government of the United States of the difficulties under whic
he and his Government have been suffering because of these reason
and the sympathy of the Government and people of the United Stat
for the people of France in the tragic situation in which they have be(
placed.

A part of France's territories overseas remains under the effecti
jurisdiction of Your Excellency's Government. Still other territori
of France are under the effective control of French authorities who (
not recognize the jurisdiction of the French Government at Vichy, b
who are fighting actively on the side of the forces of freedom.

This latter situation is the case in French Equatorial Africa and t

̓ameroons where the Government of the United States has recently
ppointed a Consul General at Brazzaville. This is the step to which
̓our Excellency's communication under acknowledgment refers.

Were the French Government at Vichy in effective control of the
̓rritory in question, the Government of the United States would neces-
̔rily have communicated with Your Excellency's Government prior
̓ the establishment of this Consulate General of the United States, in
̓ccordance with the convention between our two countries of February
̓3, 1853[1] to which reference is made in Your Excellency's communication.
̓The French Government at Vichy, however, is not in control of that
̓rritory.

Consequently, until the final victory of the United Nations is won, and
̓e people of France are once more in full and soveriegn control of their
̓wn destinies, the Government of the United States, in accordance with
̓e policy above set forth, will continue, with regard to French territories
̓ Africa or in the Pacific areas, to maintain, or to enter into, relations
̓ith those French citizens who are in actual control of such territories.

The German invaders by deceit, and by their habitual propaganda of
̓lsehood, are daily seeking to sow doubt and mistrust of their traditional
̓d proven friends among the minds of the French people. That effort
̔s failed, and will continue to fail. The people of France have never
̓ubted the sincerity of the friendship of the people of the United States.

The French people may rest assured that the Government and people
̓ the United States will continue to maintain unimpaired their full
̓spect for the sovereign rights of the people of France. They may
̓ntinue to be confident that by the victory of the United Nations those
̓ghts will be restored intact to them.

Accept [etc.]

F. Finland

Following the German attack on the Soviet Union, war between Finland and
̓e Soviet Union was quickly renewed. (See *Documents, III, 1940–41*, p. 365.)
̓nce the British Government treated the Soviet Union as an ally from the begin-
̓ng it was naturally to its interest to restore peace between the two countries
̓ soon as possible. The interest of the United States was identical. In both
̓untries there was considerable embarrassment experienced since in the earlier
̔r between the two countries (1939–40) public sympathy in both Great Britain
̔d the United States had been overwhelmingly with Finland. The British
̓overnment and people were in the position in the summer and fall of 1941
̓here they could not allow their acts to be governed by past sympathies to the
̓tent that the Americans still could. Furthermore, Finland's continued parti-
̓pation in the war assumed an aggressive character once her forces invaded
̓rritory not forming part of Finland before the Soviet attack in 1939.

[1] *Treaties, Conventions, etc.*, 1776–1909, I, p. 528.

1. ADHERENCE TO ANTI-COMINTERN PACT

(1) *Statement of the Finnish Legation at Washington, November 2.*
    1941 [1]

The adherence of Finland to the Anti-Comintern Pact is in conformit
with the attitude Finland always has taken with regard to Communism
As one of the first countries Finland became aware of the danger th
Communist Internationale constitutes to the whole civilized worl
striving by illegal and violent means to overthrow and destroy the socia
order, the national unanimity and the independence of individual state
As a next-door neighbor of the Soviet Union and as a victim of it
attacks already in 1918, a few weeks after the Soviet Union had recog
nized Finland's independence, Finland has in the course of twenty yea
had ample experience of the international character of the Communis
subversive activities which are led from the high quarters in Russia.

As the governments in other democratic countries, the Governmer
of Finland has all the time by rigorous measures, approved by th
Finnish Parliament and by the Finnish courts, combated the illega
machinations of the Comintern without infringing upon the civil righ
granted in the Constitution. Legal proceedings having been take
against the subversive elements guilty of high treason, the Finnis
courts have declared illegal the Communistic organizations affiliate
with the Comintern. Since 1930 the Communists, subservient to th
Third International have been outlawed by act of Parliament. A seri
of laws protecting the country against the Red peril and other subversiv
movements were enacted and the Social-Democrat party (the labo
party) and the labor organizations have been in constant fight again
the subversive elements which inspired and led from Moscow hav
attempted, although without success, to gain a foothold in the
organizations.

According to the Pact the High Contracting Parties agree to mutual
inform each other of the activities of the Communist International
to consult with each other concerning measures to combat these activiti
and to execute these measures in close cooperation with each othe
As far as is known this collaboration has always been interpreted
consist of police and judicial measures to defend existing order and leg
institutions of the countries concerned.

Under these circumstances it is only natural that Finland shou
avail herself of the advantages presented by collaboration with oth
countries to resist the Communist evil, says one of the leading Finni

[1] Release of the Legation.

newspapers, even if Finland's relations with the Soviet Union previously
imposed upon her great caution. But since the Soviet threw off its
mask and forced Finland to armed resistance against the Communist
aggression from outside, there is no reason for Finland to hesitate any-
more, the newspaper concludes. It goes without saying that during the
troubled conditions of war-time it is doubly necessary to ward off Communist machinations as the leaders of the Communist Internationale
in such times are particularly eager to bring about dissension and
destruction in other countries.

The joining of the Anti-Comintern Pact does not imply any change
of Finland's general political attitude. The Pact is not a war-pact; it
was in force between the signatories also while the Russo-German Non-
aggression Agreement was in force.

Says the above mentioned Finnish newspaper: "Our attitude to the
war of the great powers has not changed through our signing the pact.
Public opinion would be almost unanimous against any such trend.
The Soviet Union is our only adversary and the Anti-Comintern Pact
will, we hope, effectively contribute to the frustration of the designs
which the agents of the Comintern are directing against us now as they
did in peace-time."

Suomen Sosiaalidemokraatti, the leading paper of the Finnish Social
Democrat party (labor party), the biggest in Parliament, in stating that
the pact constitutes public recognition of the evil nature of Communism
and of the necessity of combating it, writes: "the pact does not, as its
contents show, limit Finland's independent freedom of action; it does
not alter our relations to other powers nor does it in general bind us to
any alien ideology, as it does not commit us politically any further than
its stipulations go. The statements our Government have made to
Britain and America are in no way affected and the character of our war
remains unchanged."

Finland feels that in adopting the idea of combating Communistic
Internationale as contained in the pact she emphasizes her wish to repel
foreign interference in her own national life.

2. BRITISH DECLARATION OF WAR ON FINLAND

1) *The United Kingdom Government to the Finnish Government,
September 22, 1941* [1]

So long as Finland, in alliance with Germany, is carrying on an aggressive war against and on the territory of the ally of Great Britain, His

[1] *The Times* (London), September 29, 1941, p. 3. This warning was transmitted to
the Finnish Government through the Norwegian Minister at Helsinki.

Majesty's Government are bound to consider Finland to be a membe
of the Axis, since it is impossible to separate the war which Finland i
waging against Russia from the general European war.

If, therefore, the Finnish Government persist in invading purel
Russian territory, a situation will arise in which Great Britain will b
forced to treat Finland as an open enemy, not only while the war last
but also when peace comes to be made.

His Majesty's Government would greatly regret such a developmen
in view of the friendship which has always existed between Great Britai
and Finland. Although the Finnish Government have expelled th
British Minister from Helsingfors, His Majesty's Government are read
to overlook this act of discourtesy, and would welcome an early restora
tion of normal diplomatic intercourse between the two countries. Bu
the Finnish Government will realize that for this to be possible the firs
essential is that Finland should terminate her war against Russia an
evacuate all territories beyond her frontiers of 1939. As soon as thi
had been accomplished His Majesty's Government would be ready, fo
their part, to study sympathetically any proposals for the improvemen
of relations between Great Britain and Finland, even though the con
tinued presence of German armies on Finnish soil might render impossibl
at first the restoration of full diplomatic relations and the resumptio
of oversea trade on the same basis as existed so long as Finland was sti
neutral.

(2) *The Government of the United Kingdom to the Government o Finland, November 28, 1941* [1]

On September 22 the Norwegian Government in behalf of Hi
Majesty's Government in the United Kingdom sent a message to th
effect that if the Finnish Government persisted in invading purel
Russian territory a situation would arise in which Great Britain woul
be forced to treat Finland as an open enemy, not only while the wa
lasts but also when peace comes to be made; but that if Finland shoul
terminate her war against Russia and evacuate all territories beyon
her frontier of 1939 His Majesty's Government would be ready to stud
proposals for improvement in relations between Great Britain an
Finland.

The Finnish Government's reply [2] showed no disposition to respon

[1] Communication transmitted by the American Minister at Helsinki. Associate
Press dispatch, *New York Times*, December 7, 1941, p. 19.

 [2] In its reply, dated October 7, the Finnish Government declared that it was con
ducting a purely defensive war. (*Bulletin of International News*, XVIII, Octobe
18, 1941, p. 1773.)

to this overture nor have they ceased to pursue aggressive military operations on territory of the Union of Soviet Socialist Republics, an ally of Great Britain, in the closest collaboration with Germany.

The Finnish Government have sought to contend that their war against Soviet Russia does not involve participation in the general European war. This contention His Majesty's Government find it impossible to accept.

His Majesty's Government in the United Kingdom in these circumstances find it necessary to inform the Finnish Government that unless by December 5 the Finnish Government cease military operations and in practice withdraw from all active participation in hostilities, His Majesty's Government will have no choice but to declare the existence of a state of war between the two countries.[1]

(3) *The Finnish Foreign Office to the Government of the United Kingdom, December 7, 1941* [2]

The Finnish Government has received on November 28, 1941, through the Minister of the United States in Helsinki a communication to the effect that, unless by December 5 the Finnish Government cease military operations and withdraw from all active participation in hostilities, His Britannic Majesty's Government will have no choice but to declare the existence of a state of war between the two countries.

In reply to the previous communication of the British Government received August [September] 22 the Finnish Government showed that Finland's military operations are defensive warfare dictated by a vital consideration of her own relating to her existence and security. With reference to this definition of their attitude and to the memorandum they handed the Government of the United States November 11, a note with which the British Government is doubtless acquainted. The Finnish Government repeat their statement that the struggle Finland is waging has no other aim than safeguarding the existence and security of the Finnish nation which have been threatened with total destruction.

The Finnish people possess a sense of reality and are aware of their limitations and do not strive any further in their pursuit of the war than is essentially demanded by their own aims.

[1] War was declared, effective December 7, 1941, 1 : 01 A.M., Department of State, *Bulletin*, V, p. 557.
[2] Associated Press version, *New York Times*, December 8, 1941, p, 20. The note was transmitted through the Legation of the United States at Helsinki. For a statement by the Minister of Finland at Washington, see *New York Times*, December 8, 1941, p. 20.

On this basis there is a cause in the present situation to establish that the Finnish Army is not far from the achievement of its strategic aims namely: the liberation of parts of Finland's State territory lost under terms of the Peace of Moscow and rendering harmless areas from where the enemy has been preparing to destroy Finland.

The Finnish Government find it difficult to conceive that there is anything in their attitude which could give the British Government cause to declare and extend a state of war between the two countries It would be to Finland's deep regret if that were to happen.

3. ATTITUDE OF THE UNITED STATES GOVERNMENT TOWARD CONTINUED FINNISH PARTICIPATION IN THE WAR

(1) *Memorandum of Conversation between the Under Secretary of State (Welles) and the Minister of Finland (Procopé), August 18, 1941* [1]

The Minister of Finland called to see me this afternoon at my request

I told the Minister that I wished to inform him in the utmost confidence that this Government had received information to the effect that should the Government of Finland be so disposed, the Soviet Government was prepared to negotiate a new treaty of peace with Finland which would involve the making of territorial concessions by the Soviet Union to Finland.

I said that I was communicating this information as a transmitting agent and that at the moment I was expressing no official opinion with regard thereto. I said that I wished to make it, however, completely clear that the information I was giving the Minister implied in no sense whatever any weakening on the part of the Soviet Government. I said that, from the official statements made to us by the Soviet Union and from every other evidence available to this Government, the Soviet Government is not only resisting magnificently German aggression against Russia but is likewise prepared to fight indefinitely against Germany, and that from our knowledge of the military situation there seemed every reason to suppose that Russia may do so successfully and for a protracted period. I said that this information referred solely to Finland and should consequently be viewed solely in that light.

The Minister at once raised certain obvious questions. First, in view of the experience Finland had had with the Soviet Union in 1939, what guarantees would Great Britain and the United States offer Finland that any peace treaty which the Soviet Union might now be disposed

[1] Department of State, *Bulletin*, V, p. 362. The memorandum was prepared by the Under Secretary of State.

to negotiate would be maintained? Second, what assurance would Finland be given that, in the event that Germany was defeated and the Soviet Union were to become the predominant military power, Russia would respect any promises which Great Britain or the United States might have made and would not again undertake to seize Finland and deprive the Finnish people of their independence?

I replied that these questions were questions which I was not prepared to discuss. I said it seemed to me, first of all, that it was necessary to determine what the attitude of Finland might be with regard to the possibilities which I had communicated to the Minister and that consequently the questions which he had raised were questions which need only come up for discussion in the event that the Government of Finland desired to explore these possibilities.

I said further that it appeared to me that the question was a momentous one for the Finnish Government to determine. I added that in view of the considerations the Minister had advanced I wondered what guarantees or assurances Finland thought she would have of retaining her own independence and autonomy if Germany succeeded in winning and were then the overlord of all of Europe. I said that in such event Finland could look to no one for assistance whereas if Germany were defeated she would have many extremely powerful friends on her side.

(2) *Memorandum of Conversation between the Secretary of State (Hull) and the Minister of Finland (Procopé), October 3, 1941* [1]

[Excerpt]

The Minister of Finland called at my request. I proceeded at once to say that it was unnecessary to go over the pros and cons of the situation as the war relates to Finland and to the United States, or to the likes and dislikes of either Government with respect to Stalin and Hitler or their respective countries. I said that as heretofore stated by me to the Minister, I am glad to see Finland recover her lost territory. My Government and country and I have been loyal friends of Finland and would like very much to see our fine relations continue, but even this consideration was beside the governing question just now. That question, which is of the greatest importance to my country without contemplating the slightest injustice to Finland and her best interests, relates to the future safety of the United States and of all peaceful countries in the world; that this Government, profoundly convinced as it is, that Hitler, practicing loathsome barbaric methods, is under-

[1] *Ibid.*, p. 363. The memorandum was prepared by the Secretary of State.

taking to conquer the earth; that in these circumstances my country is expending and is ready to expend 15 or 25 or 40 or 75 billions of dollars to aid in resisting and suppressing Hitler and Hitlerism; therefore, the one question uppermost in the mind of my Government with respect to Finland is whether Finland is going to be content to regain her lost territory and stop there, or whether she will undertake to go further, if she has not already done so, so that the logical effect of her course and action would be to project her on the side of Hitler into the general war between Germany and Russia and the other countries involved.

(3) Memorandum Presented by the Finnish Ministry of Foreign Affairs to the American Minister at Helsinki (Schoenfeld), November 11, 1941 [1]

The Finnish Government was slow to reply to the communication of August 18. At his regular press conference on November 3, Secretary of State Hull emphasized the belief of the American Government that the continued association of Finland with Germany in pursuit of the war against the Soviet Union would lead to the complete subjugation of Finland to the whims of Adolph Hitler. In addition, he raised the question whether this association might not also force abandonment by the United States of its friendly attitude toward Finland.[2] On November 7 texts of the Welles and Hull Memoranda were released to prove that Finland had been notified as far back as August 18 of the Soviet willingness to discuss peace.

With reference to the memoranda of the Legation of the United States of America presented on October 27 and 30, 1941,[3] the Ministry for Foreign Affairs has the honor to state the following:

I

In its memoranda the Government of the United States calls on Finland to terminate hostilities and withdraw troops to a line corresponding to the border of 1939 between Finland and the Soviet Union. They contain no mention of cessation of hostilities on the part of the Soviet Union nor do they say whether compliance with the request presented to Finland would entail withdrawal also of Soviet troops from the areas within the 1939 frontiers of Finland which they still continue to occupy. These areas are: the Finnish part of the Fisher Peninsula which enables enemy artillery to threaten Petsamo, Finland's sole ocean harbor, further outer islands in the Gulf of Finland, and Cape Hanko which dominates the maritime routes in the Gulf of Finland.

[1] From the Finnish Legation in Washington.
[2] *New York Times*, November 4, 1941.
[3] Not reprinted.

The character of the struggle between Finland and the Soviet Union is known to the Government of the United States. The Ministry for Foreign Affairs wishes to refer in this respect to the recent exchange of *aide mémoires* between the Governments of Great Britain and Finland, and to the publication of the Finnish Government concerning the Finno-Soviet relations.[1] These show, point by point, retracing the development of the events from November 30, 1939 onward, how the position of Finland as a neighbor of the Soviet Union has been one of incessant self-defense against imperialistic strivings on the part of the Soviet Union. The first attack by the Soviet Union ended in the dictated Peace of Moscow. A feature of this peace was the occupation of such areas from which attack could be resumed in the most favorable circumstances. In addition, the Soviet Government compelled Finland, *inter alia*, to construct, as a continuation of the railway laid from the Murmansk railway to the Finnish frontier, and linking up with the Finnish railways, a railway to provide the Soviet Union with convenient access to northern Finland and onward to the Atlantic Ocean. The peace terms also included occupation of Hanko which was to serve the Soviet Union as a naval base but where, immediately after the conclusion of the peace, a strong garrison with tanks and other equipment was stationed. From Hanko air attacks are still being launched on cities and the civilian population of Southern Finland. Hardly had the Peace of Moscow been concluded before the Soviet Union presented new and unjustified demands, *inter alia*, compelling Finland to permit transit traffic on her railways to Cape Hanko at the rate of two pairs of Russian trains per day. The Finnish authorities had not the right to inspect these trains. The Soviet Union also interfered in unscrupulous fashion with Finnish domestic affairs and attempted to organize street demonstrations. The Soviet Union established her Legation in Helsinki with a staff of 150 persons, a large proportion of whom were active in purely espionage work. The Soviet Union forbade the fortification of the Aaland Islands and compelled Finland to submit to the opening in a city in these Islands of a Consular Office with a staff of 40 persons. A corresponding Consular Office was founded for purposes of espionage also in Petsamo.

The Peace of Moscow thus denoted for the Soviet Union merely an armistice for preparations for a final conquest. This phase then terminated in a new military attack by the Soviet Union which compelled Finland to resume her self-defense by the use of arms. The character and purpose of this attack is reflected in the proclamation by the leading

[1] *Finland Reveals Her Secret Documents on Soviet Policy, March 1940–June 1941.* New York, Funk, 1941. 109 p.

Moscow newspaper, Pravda, in its issue of June 23, 1941, that "Finns are to be exterminated off the surface of the earth."

In these attacks areas beyond the old Finnish frontier have been systematically utilized as advanced bases against Finland. The Soviet Union has equipped both these areas and those acquired by the Peace of Moscow in the most complete manner possible for attacks westward It has now been possible to establish this *ipso loco*. Branch lines from the Murmansk railway, leading in the direction of the Finnish frontier of which six have been discovered up to the present, as well as new highways constructed solely for offensive purposes and numerous air fields reveal beyond any doubt the aggressive plans of the Soviet Union and the untenable strategic position in which Finland had been placed by these preparations. An effective defense of Finland's right which none can deny is possible to Finland only by transferring her defense into these very areas, and in this respect no distinction can be made between the areas ceded under the terms of the Peace of Moscow and other areas now occupied by Finland.

No documents can give a lifelike picture of the wretched state to which these areas — both those beyond the 1939 frontier and those ceded under the peace treaty — had been brought. It has been possible however, for members of the staff of the United States Legation in Helsinki and several American journalists to acquaint themselves on the spot with conditions in the areas occupied during the present military phase by Finnish troops. This is indeed the only method by which an accurate idea can be gained of conditions in these areas. Neglected cultivations and buildings allowed to fall into ruins or destroyed desecrated churches and graveyards and a population living in bottom less misery, ravaged by murders and mass deportations reveal to what a pitiable state the Finnish people would have been condemned under Soviet rule insofar as they had not, in conformity with the fate that befell Estonia and other states annexed by the Bolsheviks, been partly or wholly physically liquidated. All this serves to show the fate that would befall Finland if she neglected proper care of her security. It is for this reason that the men of Finland elect rather to fall in defensive war than passively to await execution of their families and themselves

It is understandable that it has been extremely difficult for the United States to conceive the situation Finland is in, especially as the United States have never directly experienced the danger which Bolshevism constitutes to a community built up on Western principles.

The character of Finland's struggle is not altered by circumstance that, on the grounds of her natural views of her own security, Finland

s striving to render innocuous and to occupy the enemy's offensive
ositions also beyond the 1939 frontier. Precisely the same considera-
ions would have made it urgently necessary for Finland, in the interests
f the effectiveness of her defense, to undertake such measures already
n 1939–40, during the first phase of the war, if only her strength had
hen been equal to the task. On that occasion there would hardly have
een any doubt as to the justification of these Finnish military operations.

For the appreciable material aid Finland received from America
uring the winter war the Finnish people feel the greatest gratitude,
ut this is still more the case in regard to the understanding and moral
upport which the American people lent Finland in her struggle against
he Bolshevist invasion. On that occasion the unjustified attack on
'inland by the Soviet Union aroused great indignation in the United
tates.

Finland notes with satisfaction that the Government of the United
tates had intimated its willingness to continue to lend its support to
he vital interests of Finland. The Finnish Government fails, however,
o see how the said noble principle actuating the Government of the
Jnited States could be reconciled with the demand that the Finnish
rmy should withdraw from areas it has, for reasons of security, occupied
eyond the 1939 frontier and which the Soviet Union would then imme-
iately be in a position to utilize again for an aggression on Finland.
)n the contrary Finland is compelled to establish that the measures
ecommended by the Government of the United States would be fateful
o the security of Finland and accordingly in conflict with the vital
nterests of Finland.

The attitude of the Finnish Government in regard to the war begun
y the Soviet Union has been and is that Finland is desirous of terminat-
ng the struggle as soon as the danger threatening her existence has been
verted and guarantees created for continuous security. If it is being
ssumed that Finland has any wider aims than these then Finland's
onception of her own resources is being exaggerated.

II

During the military phase in 1939–40, proposals for mediation of
eace made by the United States did not any more than those from
ther neutral sources prevent the Soviet Union from pursuing her attack
n Finland. The Soviet Union replied to these proposals that she had
lready concluded a treaty of assistance and friendship with a government alleged to represent Finland, a puppet government which the
oviet Government had itself appointed, in which connection the areas

settled by Finns beyond the 1939 frontier — areas which Finnish troops have now occupied — were amalgamated, as being Finnish, with Finland.

The population of the areas beyond the 1939 frontier now occupied by Finnish troops, areas which have been under Bolshevist administration for 23 years, has been and is, for by far the most part, Finnish Depending on historical circumstances a part of the Finnish nation has been left to live outside the frontiers of Finland and the areas in question belong to the dwelling-areas of just this part of the nation. In connection with the Peace of Tartu, 1920, the Soviet Government promised to guarantee this Finnish population considerably wider rights of national self-determination. These promises she has meanwhile left unfulfilled

To what a pitiable state the measures recommended by the Government of the United States would reduce the civilian population that has remained behind in these areas the history of the Bolshevist regime provides frightful examples. This consideration too supports the view that there is cause to keep the areas in question occupied by Finnish troops in order that freedom and security can be guaranteed to this population. Taking into account the national composition of the population of these areas this would be in conformity with the principles enunciated in the declaration given by the President of the United States and the Prime Minister of Great Britain on the Atlantic Ocean August 14, 1941.

III

The Government of the United States had intimated that it must hold Finland responsible for not even having attempted to explore the possibilities of peace held out by the information given by Mr. Sumner Welles on August 18, 1941,[1] to the Finnish Minister in Washington.

According to the information in possession of the Finnish Government Mr. Welles stated, in the conversation that took place between him and M. Procopé on said date, that he had been asked to convey to the knowledge of the Finnish Government that the Soviet Government would be disposed to make territorial concessions and negotiate a new peace treaty. On M. Procopé's asking whether the Soviet Government had requested the Government of the United States to transmit this information the answer was in the negative, Mr. Welles amending his statement as follows: "I know the Soviet Government would be disposed to discuss a new peace treaty with Finland through which territorial concessions would be made." He added that his statement was not a recommenda-

[1] See p. 642.

ion on the part of the United States but an information. To M. Procopé's question as to what territorial concessions might possibly be
intended, Mr. Welles was unable to reply. Equally unclear remained the
views of the Government of the United States as to what guarantees
would exist that the Soviet Union would not again attack Finland.
Mr. Welles stated, however, in this connection that at the end of the
war the Soviet Union would be the preponderant power in Eastern
Europe. When in this same connection M. Procopé asked whether the
clause relating to disarmament in the well-known declaration by President Roosevelt and Prime Minister Churchill referred also to the Soviet
Union, Mr. Welles stated that this question was a hypothetical one
and that up to 1939 the Soviet Union had been a state striving for peace
and international order.

In the early days of September M. Procopé, acting on instructions
received by him, explained in the Department of State of the United
States the attitude of his Government in regard to Finland's defensive
war. In ensuing conversations, grave doubts of Finland, based on many
bitter experiences, regarding the trust that can be reposed in promises
given by the Soviet Union, were explained to the Government of the
United States on behalf of the Finnish Government. To observations
made by Finland regarding the essential premises for an eventual peace,
no elucidation has been forthcoming from the Government of the United
States, in particular no guarantees of security have even been offered
Finland as a pledge of a new peace between Finland and the Soviet
Union.

In the view of the Finnish Government, Mr. Welles' statement
to M. Procopé on August 18, 1941, was not intended as an offer of peace
by the Soviet Union or as an offer of mediation, or even as a recommendation on the part of the United States, but merely as a piece of information on the basis of which Finland was to sue for peace. In these circumstances the Finnish Government at that stage of military operations,
when even Viipuri had not yet been taken, continued to await the
development of events.

While these conversations were in progress unfounded rumors began
to be apparent in the press abroad to the effect that Finland intended
to conclude a separate peace with the Soviet Union, and that certain
prominent Finns had been conducting negotiations to that end with
governments of third powers. On the 5th of November the British
Broadcasting Corporation circulated reports of peace terms in detail,
alleged to have been brought to the knowledge of the Finnish Government in the aforesaid conversation of August 18, 1941. Neither these nor

other offers of peace terms were made through the Government of the United States on August 18 or later, nor have such peace terms been proposed to the Finnish Government from any other quarters.

IV

The Government of the United States, in its memorandum of October 30, 1941, has intimated that it regards recent military operations on the part of Finland as a direct threat to the security of the United States. Finnish troops cannot threaten the United States, which constitute a mighty power, protected by two oceans and secured by numerous bases of which some are situated thousands of miles beyond the frontiers of the United States. Neither can the Finnish Government see that the occupation by Finnish troops of certain areas from which the security of Finland is permanently threatened, could conflict with American interests in regard to security. Nevertheless the anxiety felt by the United States for her own security gives Finland the right to expect from the Government and the people of the United States understanding for Finland's striving to protect her existence and to secure her future and to defend her ancient democratic freedom after being subjected on two separate occasions, within the space of less than two years, to unjustified armed attacks on the part of the mighty Bolshevist terrorist state, neither the United States nor any other country being able either to prevent them or to provide guarantees that such attacks would not be renewed. Finland hopes that the great American nation will recognize the right also of a small nation to live and to defend itself. During the course of centuries Finland has indeed been compelled to make abundant use of the right of self-defense in shedding her blood in defensive war on her eastern flank, the aggregate term of which in Finnish history exceeds one hundred years.

It is probably difficult for a nation of 130 millions, living on the other side of the globe, whose resources of money and industrial capacity are illimitable, to understand from a military point of view the position of a nation of 3.8 millions with a coastline 1500 kilometers long, exposed to attack, and a 1000-kilometers long land frontier against a neighbor of 200 millions strong, regarding whose inimical intentions there is not the slightest doubt.

It is almost inconceivable that the great American democracy can demand of a small nation which has again been attacked by its fifty times bigger neighbor and is fighting for its existence that it should, while hostilities are in progress, withdraw to await a new attack within frontiers the defense of which, if the advantages gained are given up for the benefit of the enemy, may easily, in view of resources on each side, become an overwhelming task.

In the memorandum of October 27 and in other connections, assumption has been made by the Government of the United States that Finland's freedom of action and even her independence are imperilled by Germany. Finland herself has no reason to assume that she is in any such danger. Finland is desirous of conducting her own affairs in the shelter of that national unity based on a centuries old farmer-citizen democracy, which especially in the war periods of recent years has proved to be a dependable force also in the defense of the nation.

The significance to Finland of the circumstance now that she has been drawn into a resumed war of defense against the Soviet Union, that Germany is simultaneously at war with this enemy of Finland, is obvious. When offensive preparations, directed against Finland by the Soviet Union, to which that country again resorted after the Peace of Moscow, carrying them out at ever accelerating speed, are taken into account and also the fact that the enormous industries of the Soviet Union had been directed almost entirely to the production of war material, there can be no doubt but that a new war, if Finland had again had to stand alone, would have denoted the doom of Finland and the entire North.

The President of the Republic of Finland stated to the Minister of the United States on October 23, 1941, that the Finnish nation which has not asked for more than to be allowed to live and work in peace, will continue her war with the Soviet Union only until her security and working peace have been achieved. The President added: that the Finnish Government hoped it would be possible before long to release on leave a certain number of men from the army for work on the home front.

This is indeed the case, but Finland in her fight for existence cannot enter into any engagements that would denote an imperilling of her national security by artificial suspension or annulment of fully justified military operations.

Viewing the immense trials and sufferings mankind now has to endure, and then observing in the prevailing situation the Government of the United States, fixing its attention on individual fateful problems of a small nation, the thought arises that the supreme task which Providence at the present juncture has assigned the United States for the remedying of prevailing conditions and ensuring the existence of millions of human beings, would be achievement of a permanent state of law between nations that would enable also a small nation to feel its existence secure.

(4) *Statement of the Secretary of War (Stimson), November 25, 1941*

A situation exists along the present Russo-German battle line from Leningrad north which indicates that the Finnish Army has been placed in an unenviable position tactically in that area. Information at hand shows that the troops opposing the Russians in that area are disposed approximately as follows:

In the north, in the vicinity of Murmansk, we find the German concentration of two German front line divisions with one Finnish regiment. As we move south along the frontier, we encounter another German corps of three divisions, showing a concentration of German troops in that northern area opposite the Murmansk supply line almost solidly German and designed very evidently with one purpose in view — to close the Murmansk-Moscow supply line against any supply reinforcements from the democracies.

By far the major portion of the Finnish Army is concentrated east, north and west of Lake Ladoga, and the greater part of these forces is actively engaged against the Russians. While on the Karelian Isthmus (to the north of Leningrad) these Finnish forces have not advanced beyond their old 1939 frontier, they are fighting east of Lake Ladoga along the River Svir (to Lake Onega), as partners in the German scheme of opposing Russia in Russian territory.

Regardless of the laudable ambition of the Finnish nation to recover ground lost to the Russians in the last war between these nations, it is evident that the Finns are now being used by the Germans to further the German efforts to defeat the Russian forces in the Leningrad-Lake Onega theatre.

It is regrettable that the Finnish Army should allow this condition to continue. It is not only inimical to the final interests of Finland, but it enables Germany to concentrate her efforts on a line harmful to the interests of the United States.

(5) *Finnish Cooperation with Germany. Department of State Release November 28, 1941* [2]

In response to inquiries as to developments in the Finnish situation the Secretary of State stated on November 28 that the Finnish note had been given careful consideration but that it had thrown no light upon the question uppermost in the mind of this Government, that is

---

[1] *New York Times,* November 26, 1941.
[2] Department of State, *Bulletin,* V, p. 434.

how far and to what extent the Finnish military policy is one of combined operations of the Germans and Finns vitally to injure Great Britain and her associates and to threaten the northern supply lines over which Russia is now receiving supplies and assistance from Great Britain and the United States to aid Russia in resisting the Hitler forces of invasion and conquest, and to what extent that Finnish policy is a menace to all America's aims for self-defense. The recent journey of the Finnish Foreign Minister to Berlin to join with Hitler's puppet governments over Europe in signing the "Anti-Comintern Pact," used by Hitler solely as an instrument to wage a war of conquest and domination against free peoples, is highly significant and cannot be camouflaged or explained away by propaganda attacks on nations engaged in defending themselves.

The Secretary went on to say that the Department was giving careful attention to all the reports and information which might furnish a definite answer to this question. The concern of this Government, which has been emphasized by the studies made by the War Department and the statement of the Secretary of War on November 25, as to Finnish policy in this regard, has been made abundantly clear to the Finnish Government, the Secretary said.

The Secretary concluded by saying that every act of the Finnish Government since the delivery of its note has confirmed our apprehensions that it is fully cooperating with the Hitler forces.

6) Statement of the Secretary of State (Hull) concerning Hitler's Visit to Finland, June 6, 1942 [1]

It is evident that the visit is a deliberate ruse on the part of the Germans to compromise Finland further in the eyes of the anti-Axis world and a cover for the desperate attempts of Hitler to induce Finland to make further contributions to Axis military campaigns. A reported statement yesterday of a Finnish spokesman in Helsinki may be interpreted to mean that Finland is balking at the German pressure. [2]

We are watching the situation most closely to see whether this visit of Hitler results in any greater degree of cooperation with Hitler against the United Nations.

[1] *Ibid.*, VI, p. 522. This statement was made in reply to inquiries from the press. Hitler had flown to Finland on June 4 to present personal congratulations to Field Marshal Carl Gustav Mannerheim on his 75th birthday. Mannerheim's reference to German-Finnish "brotherhood in arms" in his reply evoked the statement given below. (*New York Times*, June 5, 1942, p. 7.)

[2] *Ibid.*, June 7, 1942, p. 1.

2. THE OCCUPIED TERRITORIES

A. Status of Governments-in-Exile

(1) *The American Ambassador at London (Winant) to the Foreign Minister of the Provisional Government of Czechoslovakia (Masaryk), July 30, 1941* [1]

The Secretary of State has directed me to inform Your Excellency that the Government of the United States, mindful of the traditional friendship and special interest, which has existed between the peoples of the United States and Czechoslovakia since the foundation of the Czechoslovak Republic, has watched with admiration the efforts of the people of Czechoslovakia to maintain their national existence, notwithstanding the suppression of the institutions of free government in their country.

The American Government has not acknowledged that the temporary extinguishment of their liberties has taken from the people of Czechoslovakia their rights and privileges in international affairs, and it has continued to recognize the diplomatic and consular representatives of Czechoslovakia in the United States in the full exercise of their functions.

In furtherance of its support of the national aspirations of the people of Czechoslovakia the Government of the United States is now prepared to enter into formal relations with the Provisional Government established at London for the prosecution of the war and the restoration of the freedom of the Czechoslovak people, under the Presidency of Dr. Beneš, and while continuing its relations with the Czechoslovak Legation at Washington, would be pleased to accredit to the Provisional Government an Envoy Extraordinary and Minister Plenipotentiary to reside in London, for the conduct of relations pending the reestablishment of the Government in Czechoslovakia.

I shall later communicate with Your Excellency regarding the diplomatic representative whom my Government would like to designate.

––––––––

On September 17, 1941 the United States Senate confirmed the Ambassador Extraordinary and Plenipotentiary of the United States to Poland, Anthony J. Drexel Biddle, Jr., to be concurrently Envoy Extraordinary and Minister Plenipotentiary near the Provisional Government of Czechoslovakia, established in London. The incumbent Envoy Extraordinary and Minister Plenipotentiary of Czechoslovakia to the United States, Vladimir Hurban, began his service at Washington December 30, 1936, since which date his tenure was uninterrupted by events in Europe. *Documents, I, 1938–39,* p. 299–305.

[1] Department of State, *Bulletin,* V, p. 88.

2) *Exchange of Ambassadors with the Government of the Netherlands*

The decision to raise the rank of diplomatic representation between the United tates and the Netherlands to that of an embassy was put into effect three days efore the second anniversary of the invasion of Netherlands territory by German rmies on May 10, 1940 as a tribute to the heroic defense of their liberties by the)utch people throughout the world.

a) *The Queen of the Netherlands (Wilhelmina) to the President of the United States (Roosevelt), May 7, 1942* [1]

With you I feel, Mr. President, that it is fitting to give adequate xpression to the ties of especially close friendship which have come ito being between our countries through their joint sacrifices in our ommon endeavor to uphold, together with the other United Nations, a roper balance between the rights and the duties of human beings and f states against those who, in order to satisfy ambition and greed, are ut to enslave others. I share your conviction that this purpose can be erved by resolving that the diplomatic envoys we exchange should enceforth have the status of Ambassador Extraordinary and Plenipoten- iary, and it gives me great pleasure to know that you agree when I ereby accredit Dr. Alexander Loudon in that capacity to the United tates.

I trust that he will continue to prove himself worthy of this new mark f my confidence and to merit your approbation.

b) *The President of the United States (Roosevelt) to the Queen of the Netherlands (Wilhelmina), May 7, 1942* [2]

'OUR MAJESTY:

The stouthearted courage and gallant spirit which Hollanders have hown on every front in their determined resistance to wanton aggression y Germany and by Japan have stirred the imagination of the American eople.

We are proud that the men of our armed forces have in recent months)ught side by side with the brave soldiers, sailors and airmen of the Jetherlands forces in the Indies and in the Caribbean.

It seems fitting therefore that the United States and the Netherlands hould as a mark of their united efforts against their common enemies

[1] *Ibid.*, VI, p. 402. The Senate on May 12, 1942 confirmed the nomination of nthony J. Drexel Biddle, Jr., as Ambassador. The headnote is quoted from the re- ase of the Department of State.
[2] *Ibid.*

henceforth exchange diplomatic representatives with the rank of Ambas
sador. I have been very pleased to learn that you have agreed to receiv
the Honorable Anthony J. D. Biddle as Ambassador Extraordinary anc
Plenipotentiary of the United States of America near Your Majesty'
Government, and I trust that you will give full faith to any action whicl
he may take on behalf of his Government.

(3) *Exchange of Ambassadors with the Government of Norway*

In like recognition of the courageous struggle of the Norwegian people t
preserve their liberties by unrelenting resistance to the German invaders who ha
occupied their country for over two years, the Government of the United State
decided to raise the rank of diplomatic representation between the United State
and Norway to that of an embassy.[1]

Challenging the right of the Norwegian Government-in-Exile to represent th
Norwegian people, the so-called Nasjonal Samling, constituted by certain follow
ers of Vidkun Quisling acting in concert with the German authorities, electe
Quisling "minister-president" of Norway on February 1, 1942. The Norwegia:
Government-in-Exile announced on the same date that "Vidkun Quisling has n
position or authority other than that given him by the occupying power, and an
settlement made with him is a settlement with Germany's own representative.
(Royal Norwegian Government's Press Representative in the United State
News of Norway, II, No. 3, p. 1.)

(a) *The King of Norway (Haakon) to the President of the United State (Roosevelt), May 13, 1942* [2]

I greatly appreciate your proposal that the representatives of ou
respective countries should be given the rank of Ambassador in recog
nition of the special ties of friendship and collaboration which unite ou
peoples in their common fight against the enemies of all free nation:

In consequence I hereby accredit Mr. Wilhelm von Munthe a
Morgenstierne to you as my Ambassador Extraordinary and Plenipo
tentiary and I am convinced that he will continue to merit your fu.
confidence in his new capacity.

[1] *Ibid.*, p. 438.

[2] *Ibid.* On May 12, 1942 the Senate confirmed the nomination of Anthony .
Drexel Biddle, Jr., of Pennsylvania, as Ambassador Extraordinary and Plenipotent
ary of the United States of America near the Governments of the Netherlands an
Norway now established in London. Mr. Biddle will continue to serve concurrentl
and without additional compensation as Ambassador Extraordinary and Plenipc
tentiary to Poland and Belgium and as Envoy Extraordinary and Minister Plen
potentiary to Czechoslovakia, Yugoslavia, and Greece, the Governments of whic
are now established in London.

b) *The President of the United States (Roosevelt) to the King of Norway (Haakon), May 13, 1942* [1]

YOUR MAJESTY:

It is with great satisfaction that I have learned of your agreement to receive the Honorable Anthony J. Drexel Biddle, Jr., as first Ambassador Extraordinary and Plenipotentiary of the United States of America near the Government of Norway.

In peace, and now in war, unique ties link the destinies of the peoples of Norway and of the United States. Norwegian-born men and women by the hundreds of thousands have found in the New World a warm welcome among kindred people and have made immeasurable contributions to the spiritual and material development of their adopted land.

Intrepid Norwegian sailors on every sea face daily dangers alongside their comrades in arms of the United States to the end that the horror of war brought on both our nations by a ruthless enemy shall give way to a peaceful world dedicated to the uninterrupted advancement of the principles of freedom.

It is peculiarly fitting, therefore, that the United States and Norway should exchange Ambassadors as a symbol to our friends and to our enemies of the unity of purpose of two nations equally determined to maintain their freedom against the assault of evil forces.

I trust that Mr. Biddle will continue to enjoy Your Majesty's confidence and that you will give full credence to what he shall say on the part of the United States.

B. Attitude of United States Government Toward Acts of Territorial Invasion and Dismemberment

1) *The Yugoslav Minister (Fotitch) to the Under Secretary of State (Welles), November 4, 1941* [2]

SIR:

I have the honor to refer to your Notes of May 28,[3] and September 25, 1941 in which you have made reference to the indignation of the American Government and of the American people in regard to the invasion and dismemberment of Yugoslavia by the various states adhering

[1] *Ibid.*
[2] *Ibid.*, V, p. 511.
[3] *Documents, III, 1940–41*, p. 333.

to the Tripartite Pact. I desire again to express to Your Excellency th
deep sense of gratitude with which the Royal Yugoslav Governmer
received this declaration.

I have now been instructed by my Government to register an emphat:
protest against the incorporating of national Yugoslav territory by th
Kingdom of Bulgaria. Following the German attack on Yugoslavi
and the subsequent military occupation of its territory, the Germa
military authorities have allowed the Bulgarian army to take possessio
of certain southern and eastern parts of Yugoslav national territor;
Bulgarian military cooperation with Germany on that occasion ha
caused the Royal Yugoslav Government to declare war on Bulgaria -
a fact of which Your Excellency has been apprised.

It appears to be clear that the Bulgarian Government consider thes
territories as definitely and permanently included within Bulgaria
national boundaries. This view is borne out by the various Bulgaria
declarations which have been made by responsible officials, and mo
particularly by the actions of the Bulgarian Government which, b
changing the legal status of the occupied Yugoslav areas, patent)
exceed the limits of their rights as the authority of occupation.

There have been published by the Bulgarian Government in the
official gazette (No. 166 of July 31 of this year) three decrees of which tl
first, under No. 2620, concerns the creation of the new Bulgarian distri
of Skoplje; the second, under No. 2618, creating the district of Bitol
and the third, under No. 2619, joining four Yugoslav counties to tl
existing district of Sofia. Moreover, the Bulgarian Government
carrying on military recruitment in these Yugoslav territories.

The Royal Yugoslav Government have the honor to draw Yo
Excellency's attention to the facts referred to above which constitute
flagrant violation of international law and usage and desires to regist
with Your Excellency a most emphatic protest against this new attem;
at dismemberment of the Yugoslav State, this time by Bulgaria.

Accept, Sir, the assurances of my highest consideration.

(2) *The Under Secretary of State (Welles) to the Yugoslav Minist*
    (Fotitch), December 3, 1941 [1]

SIR:

I have the honor to acknowledge the receipt of your note of Novem
ber 4, 1941, informing me that you have been instructed by your Gover
ment to register the emphatic protest of the Royal Yugoslav Gover
ment against the action of the Kingdom of Bulgaria in its incorporatic

---

[1] Department of State, *Bulletin*, V, p. 510.

f national territory of the Kingdom of Yugoslavia. You refer to the
leclaration of war on the part of the Royal Yugoslav Government
gainst Bulgaria as a result of Bulgarian military cooperation with
iermany at the time of the German attack on Yugoslavia, and in
articular to certain acts of the Bulgarian Government since that time
s indicating that the Bulgarian Government considers the territories
a occupation as definitely and permanently included within Bulgarian
ational boundaries.

In my notes of May 28 and September 25 I made reference to the
ndignation of the Government of the United States and of the American
eople in regard to the invasion and dismemberment of Yugoslavia by
ertain neighboring states. I wish to assure you that this Government
iews with the same sentiments the acts of the Bulgarian Government
a extending its control over those parts of Yugoslavia occupied by
3ulgarian forces.

Accept, Sir, the renewed assurances of my highest consideration.

C. Relief to Occupied Countries

1) *The Secretary of State (Hull) to the Chairman, Senate Committee on Foreign Relations (George), June 19, 1941* [1]

IY DEAR SENATOR GEORGE:

I have received your letter of June 3, 1941, enclosing a copy of S. Res.
24 relating to a proposal for the supplying of relief to occupied countries
a Europe.

This Government has a deeply sympathetic attitude toward all
hases of distress, suffering and needs for relief alike in every part of the
orld, from China to Finland, and the Department of State is constantly
bserving developments in these respects and is assembling facts and
ircumstances relating to suffering and the problem of its possible relief.
o these ends the Government, in particular this Department, is
onstantly conferring with individuals, groups and other governments.
n pursuance of its broad general policy in these respects and the appli-
ation of this policy to practical relief purposes, this Department follows
general policy rather than one of advocating or opposing individual or
roup plans or proposals for relief. Its conclusions with respect to par-
icular aspects of this problem may either support in part or may oppose
a part such individual or group projects.

Proposals similar to that contained in S. Res. 124 have repeatedly been

[1] Released September 25, 1941, by the Chairman of the Senate Committee on
oreign Relations (Connally), *ibid.*, p. 233.

brought to the Department's attention during the past months. After having given the most careful and thorough consideration to them from the humanitarian point of view the Department has replied in the following sense.

It is clear that the responsibility and manifest duty to supply relief rests with the occupying authorities as it is well known that the German authorities have removed from the countries under occupation vast quantities of foodstuffs belonging to the peoples of those countries and within those countries have diverted food supplies from children to persons working in behalf of the German military effort. The removal of such foodstuffs is in the primary sense responsible for the lack of stock of food in those countries at the present time.

The Department has no knowledge of the terms under which the German Government may have agreed to the proposal described in the resolution; but, in any event, it is extremely difficult to understand why in the light of the direct responsibility for the German Government to replace the stocks of food removed from the occupied countries, and it direct responsibility for the feeding of the populations of the occupied territories, no effort has been made to have the German Government carry out the duty which it assumed when it undertook to take over by force the countries concerned. It is all the more difficult to understand why no demand has been made upon Germany to fulfill its obligation in this regard when the German Government has never put forth any claim to poverty of food for its own people and its huge armies which are striking at the roots of freedom and civilization wherever they can

I cannot consistently elaborate in writing on the difficult and highly complicated military and other closely allied considerations involved in this Resolution.

Under the circumstances no further comment with regard to the proposed legislation seems appropriate.

(2) Joint British-American Relief to Greece. Statements of United Kingdom and United States Governments

The occupation of Greece following the surrender of the German sympathizer General Tsolakoglou on April 23, 1941 (Documents, III, 1940–41, p. 319) did not end Greek resistance nor did the forced evacuation of Crete in May. The Greek Government reestablished itself in London on September 22 and the Greek people at home remained unreconciled to the Tsolakoglou regime set up at Athens under German protection in a country assigned to Italian troops for occupation. Food supplies within their reach were seized by the Germans and exported to Germany, leaving the people in Greece in a real state of famine. The conditions became so serious that relief measures were undertaken on the initiative of private associations.

a) Statement of the United Kingdom Minister of Economic Warfare (Dalton), House of Commons, January 27, 1942 [1]

The United Kingdom and United States Governments have viewed with increasing dismay the appalling conditions obtaining in Greece. Despite their undoubted ability to do so, the German Government have done practically nothing to meet the situation created by the pillage and extortion of their Armies in the spring of 1941. They have indeed shown themselves quite indifferent to the fate of the Greek population, no doubt because the industrial resources of Greece are too small to be of any value to the German war machine.

His Majesty's Government and the United States Government have accordingly authorized a single shipment of eight thousand tons of wheat to Greece to be applied under the auspices of the International Red Cross in relief of the present emergency. This is an addition to the existing relief schemes, namely shipments of foodstuff from Turkey which is inside the blockade area), and the proposed evacuation of Greek children and nursing mothers.

The two Governments, nevertheless, continue to maintain in the most categorical manner that it is incumbent upon the enemy to feed the countries occupied by him and their policy in this respect remains unaffected by the exception which it has been found necessary to make in the special circumstances obtaining in Greece.

b) Department of State Release, March 6, 1942 [2]

The United States and British Governments have agreed to a request by the Greek War Relief Association of New York for permission immediately to charter a vessel to transport 2,300 long tons of flour from the United States to Greece, provided adequate guaranties are obtained from the Axis Governments and satisfactory arrangements can be made for the distribution of the flour to the suffering Greek population.

The program of aid to Greece through shipments from Turkey is also going forward to the extent that food is available. Permission, furthermore, has recently been granted to the Greek Government to transfer to Switzerland the equivalent of one million Swiss francs from funds of the Greek Government in the United States, to purchase condensed milk in Switzerland for the relief of children in Greece.

---

[1] *Ibid.*, VI, p. 93. The statement of the joint program was made with the approval of the United States Government.
[2] *Ibid.*, p. 208.

In considering plans for the relief of Greece, particular attention i
paid to the provisions for the distribution of the food to the Gree
peoples themselves and for preventing the Axis Powers, who have create
the appalling conditions of famine which exist in that country, fron
being aided by the relief measures employed. It is realized that n
measures for the adequate relief of Greece will be possible until th
final defeat of the Axis. The necessity, however, for the prompt use o
any feasible means for assisting Greece is fully realized.

D. Execution of Hostages and Other
Acts of Cruelty

(1) *Execution of Hostages by the Nazis. Statement of the Presiden (Roosevelt), October 25, 1941* [1]

The practice of executing scores of innocent hostages in reprisal fo
isolated attacks on Germans in countries temporarily under the Na
heel revolts a world already inured to suffering and brutality. Civilize
peoples long ago adopted the basic principle that no man should b
punished for the deed of another. Unable to apprehend the person
involved in these attacks the Nazis characteristically slaughter fifty o
a hundred innocent persons. Those who would "collaborate" wit
Hitler or try to appease him cannot ignore this ghastly warning.

The Nazis might have learned from the last war the impossibility c
breaking men's spirit by terrorism. Instead they develop their *lebens
raum* and "new order" by depths of frightfulness which even they hav
never approached before. These are the acts of desperate men who kno
in their hearts that they cannot win. Frightfulness can never bring peac
to Europe. It only sows the seeds of hatred which will one day brin
fearful retribution.

(a) *Statement of the British Prime Minister (Churchill), October 25 1941* [2]

His Majesty's Government associate themselves fully with the sentiments c
horror and condemnation expressed by the President of the United States upo
the Nazi butcheries in France.

These cold-blooded executions of innocent people will only recoil upon th
savages who order and execute them.

The butcheries in France are an example of what Hitler's Nazis are doing i
many other countries under their yoke.

[1] From the Office of the Secretary to the President; Department of State, *Bulleti* V, p. 317.

[2] *New York Times*, October 26, 1941, p. 13.

The atrocities in Poland, in Yugoslavia, in Norway, in Holland, in Belgium nd above all behind the German fronts in Russia surpass anything that has •een known since the darkest and most bestial ages of mankind.

They are but a foretaste of what Hitler would inflict upon the British and American peoples if only he could get the power.

Retribution for these crimes must henceforward take its place among the major •urposes of the war.

2) *Allied Declaration on German War Crimes, Adopted at London, January 13, 1942, by Representatives of Nine Occupied Countries* [1]

WHEREAS Germany since the beginning of the present conflict, which rose out of her policy of aggression, has instituted in occupied countries regime of terror characterized in particular by imprisonments, mass xpulsions, execution of hostages and massacres,

AND WHEREAS these acts of violence are being similarly perpetrated •y Allies and associates of the Reich and in certain countries by accom- •lices of the occupying power,

AND WHEREAS international solidarity is necessary in order to avoid epression of these acts of violence simply by acts of vengeance on the •art of the general public and in order to satisfy the sense of justice of he civilized world,

Recalling that international law and, in particular, the convention igned at The Hague in 1907 regarding laws and customs of land warfare lo not permit belligerents in occupied countries to perpetrate acts of iolence against civilians, to bring into disrepute laws in force or to verthrow national institutions,

The undersigned representatives of the Government of Belgium, the iovernment of Czechoslovakia, the Free French National Committee, he Government of Greece, the Government of Luxemburg, the Govern- 1ent of The Netherlands, the Government of Norway, the Government f Poland and the Government of Yugoslavia.

1. Affirm that acts of violence thus perpetrated against civilian popula- ions are at variance with accepted ideas concerning acts of war and •olitical offenses as these are understood by civilized nations;

2. Take note of the declaration made in this respect on October 25, 941, by the President of the United States of America and the British 'rime Minister;

3. Place amongst their principal war aims punishment through the hannel of organized justice of those guilty and responsible for these

[1] *The Inter-Allied Review*, II, No. 1, January 15, 1942, p. 2.

crimes, whether they have ordered them, perpetrated them or in any
way participated in them;

4. Determine in the spirit of international solidarity to see to it tha⸱
(a) those guilty and responsible, whatever their nationality, are sough⸱
for, handed over to justice and judged; (b) that sentences pronounced
are carried out.

In faith whereof the signatories duly authorized have signed the
present declaration.

[Here follow signatures.]

(3) *Message of the President (Roosevelt) to the People of Belgium January 1942* [1]

During the month of January 1942, the President addressed a message to the
people of Belgium, Czechoslovakia, Denmark, Occupied France, Greece, Yugoslavia, the Netherlands, Norway and Poland. This message was broadcast to
each of these countries in its own language by the Office of the Coordinator o⸱
Information.

People of Belgium! The President of the United States is deeply
concerned by the atrocities visited upon you by the brutal Nazis.

The President will not forget the terrible sufferings inflicted by the
Germans on the innocent men, women and children of Belgium. He
will always remember what this once free country is going through unde⸱
oppression. The United States pledges its entire resources to destroy
the conqueror and to restore self-government to Belgium. Only by ⸱
complete destruction of Hitlerism can the occupation be ended.

The annihilation of Hitlerism has already begun with a vengeance
Its armies are being soundly defeated for the first time, on several fronts
The United States is engaged in a mighty effort of production for war
It is such an effort that no combination of enemy countries can possibly
match it. The President said that this year the United States will
produce 60 thousand planes to be followed by 125 thousand next year
Tank production will reach 45 thousand this year; 75 thousand next
year. By the end of this year 8 million tons of new shipping will be
launched to help carry these weapons of war to the men in all nation
opposed to the Axis who are anxious to use them. Ten million tons o⸱
new ships will be added to this great fleet next year.

The Nazis have exacted a terrible price from Belgium, in blood and
torture, and starvation and cruelties without number. But the loyalty
and patriotism of the Belgians remain staunch. Death itself is still
preferable to them than slavery.

President Roosevelt has authorized the United States radio to say i⸱

[1] *Ibid.*, No. 2, February 15, 1942, p. 27.

iis name that the sacrifices of all people who love liberty shall not be in
vain. Belgium will emerge from her present struggle a better and a
tronger country.

Americans are appalled by the Nazi policy of reducing Belgium by
leliberate starvation. They understand thoroughly how that country
ias been plundered by the Germans. The horde of German troops and
;estapo agents saddled on once-prosperous Belgium are well fed, while
3elgian men, women and children hunger. The Nazis maintain huge
tocks of food for their soldiers — food rightfully belonging to Belgians.
)ther food supplies of all kinds are exported to Germany to help maintain
rder within that country.

Belgians are not deceived by German propaganda efforts to persuade
hem to believe that shortages are caused by the United Nations blockde. German looting has gone on under their very eyes. Belgians under-
tand that while food reserves exist in abundance in America, no help
an be forthcoming that would give comfort to the enemy. But that
ood is waiting, and one day it will be forthcoming.

America is sparing no resource to aid in the destruction of Nazism.
American might is pouring into the common battle. German defeat is
nevitable. It cannot be delayed long.

And after the war, the United Nations, including Belgium, are assured
f winning the peace. President Roosevelt said: "We are determined
ot only to win the war, but also to maintain the security of the peace
vhich will follow."

The President of the United States will always remember the sacrifices
f Belgium. Unprovoked murder, executions, imprisonments, tortures
nd starvation, have proved unavailing to the Nazis. The will to resist has
ever been so consolidated as in the face of these inhuman persecutions.

Belgium continues the fight. At home, increasing Nazi measures of
epression testify to the success of Belgian sabotage and slowing down in
vork. Abroad, loyal Belgians all over the world devote their every
vaking moment to the cause of a free Belgium. Thousands of Belgian
nen and young men are participating in actual combat with the armies
f the United Nations. Their cause is the just cause of freedom for
3elgium. Their victory is assured by the spiritual and physical might
f the peoples of the world who reject bondage.

At the second year of Nazi occupation of Belgium, hope is brighter
han ever for release. The might of the United Nations is now so great,
ts aims so clear, that only the time of defeat for Hitlerism remains
loubtful. President Roosevelt said: "We shall not fight isolated wars,
ach nation going its own way. Twenty-six nations are united, not in

spirit and determination alone, but in the broad conduct of war in al
its phases. . . . Gone forever are the days when the aggressors coul
attack and destroy their victims one by one without unity of resistance.

President Roosevelt pointed out that the militarists in Berlin and
Tokyo started this war. "But," he said, "the massed, angered forces o
common humanity will finish it."

The objectives in this war are clear, the President said: "The objectiv
of smashing the militarism imposed by war lords upon their enslave
peoples — the objective of liberating the subjugated nations — th
objective of establishing and securing freedom of speech, freedom o
religion, freedom from want and freedom from fear everywhere in th
world."

These aims are not new to Belgians — nor to Americans. The Unite
States and Belgium have worked for them shoulder to shoulder in th
community of nations. Belgium's contributions toward the bettermen
of humanity have been great in the past. In culture, in art, and in scienc
and industry, Belgium has ranked in the forefront of progressive nation:
That country is guiltless of aggression. She has suffered terribly by th
aggressive ambitions of Germany — twice, within the memory of mo:
of her people. These wrongs shall be righted. Germany shall not agai
be allowed to impose her tyranny on peace-loving Belgium. Belgium
cause is humanity's cause.

The hearts of the Belgians are with their free government in Londo
and with their brave King Leopold, now a prisoner of the hated Nazi
Nothing Germany has been able to do has altered this condition.

King Leopold asked the support of his army in May 1940. He sai
then: "Belgium expects you all to honor her flag. Officers, soldiers, wha
ever happens, my fate will be the same as yours. . . . Our cause is ju:
and unsullied. Providence will help us. Long live Belgium."

As more details are learned, Belgium's honor has indeed been great
augmented by the heroic resistance of the army that died in its track
opposing Hitler. Americans look forward to the day when soon Kin
Leopold may say again, "our cause is just and unsullied. Long li
Belgium."

(4) *The Secretary of State (Hull) to the Yugoslav Minister (Fotitch* April 22, 1942 [1]

SIR:

I have the honor to acknowledge the receipt of your note of April 1:
in which you place on record the protest of the Royal Yugoslav Gover:

---

[1] Department of State, *Bulletin*, VI, p. 364.   [2] Not reprinted.

ıent with respect to the order of the authorities now in control at
3elgrade, demanding the surrender of General Draza Mihajlovič and
is staff, and announcing, in the event of noncompliance, that their
amilies will be taken as hostages, and further that the families of other
ersons having contact with, or rendering assistance to the campaign
f General Mihajlovič will be held in reprisal, and their property held
ubject to confiscation.

The position of this Government with respect to the taking of hostages
as already been made known. This barbarous practice as a German
ıethod of warfare was stigmatized in a declaration made public by the
'resident of the United States on October 25, 1941,[1] which in turn was
ited, as your Government is aware, in the joint declaration recently
igned at London by the representatives of nations whose territory is
ow under German tyranny, proclaiming to the world the resolve of
utraged peoples that retribution would be exacted.

The Government and people of the United States have watched with
dmiration the resourceful and heroic operations of General Mihajlovič
nd his men and are proud to acknowledge the contribution of Yugoslav
atriots in the common struggle against the forces bent on the destruc-
ion of free nations throughout the world. The shocking proclamation
o which your note has reference is but another of a series of savage and
uthless measures whereby German terrorism has sought to break the
pirit of brave men.

Accept [etc.]

3. AFRICA AND WESTERN ASIA

A. Syria and Lebanon

[See *Documents, III, 1940–41*, p. 334.]

1) Convention between the Allied Forces in Palestine and Syria and the Commander-in-Chief of the Levant Ending Hostilities in Syria and the Lebanon, July 14, 1941 [2]

General Sir Henry Maitland Wilson, General Officer Commanding-in-
'hief of the Allied Forces in Palestine and Syria, acting in the name of
ʰe Commanders-in-Chief, Middle East, on the one hand, and General
e Verdillac, Commander of the Legion of Honor, Deputy Commander-

---

[1] See p. 662.
[2] *The Times* (London), July 16, 1941, p. 3. An alternative English version by the
ssociated Press from the French text as made public at Vichy is in *New York Times*,
ıly 15, 1941, p. 4.

in-Chief of the French troops in Syria, acting in the names of the French High Command, on the other hand, have agreed to a Convention which ends hostilities in Syria and the Lebanon, of which the following are the terms: —

1. Hostilities ceased on July 11, 1941, at 21.01 hours, G. M. T.

2. The Allied Forces will occupy Syro-Lebanese territory. The French forces will be concentrated in certain areas selected by a committee formed of representatives of both parties. This concentration will be completed by Tuesday, July 15, 1941, at 12.00 hours, at which hour Allied forces will move to occupy certain strategic points.

Up to the time of their repatriation the French troops will remain under French command with a restricted establishment, which will provide for their maintenance from existing stocks.

Special measures are foreseen for the Jebel Druze, where for security reasons the French troops will remain in garrison until relieved by British troops.

3. In order to ensure public security, the occupation of the principal ocalities in Syria and the Lebanon will be undertaken in accordance with the program which will allow immediate replacement of French by the occupying forces.

4. Minefields, whether on sea or on land, will be disclosed to the occupying authorities.

5. Full honors of war will be granted to the French Forces. The latter will retire to the selected areas with all arms, including guns, machine guns, tanks and armored cars, and their ammunition. All measures will be taken by the French Command to prevent arms and ammunition being left unguarded on the battlefield or elsewhere. French military authorities will give every assistance in recovering arms which may be in the hands of the population.

6. In consideration of the honors of war, French officers and non-commissioned officers and soldiers are permitted to retain their individual arms (rifles or carbines, revolvers, bayonets, swords, or sabres). However, the soldiers will not be allowed to carry ammunition. In each unit, for security reasons, a small quantity of ammunition will be retained. The gendarmerie will retain its arms and limited amount of ammunition. All other war material, including guns, coastal batteries, anti-aircraft guns, and military transport will be stocked under British control. The latter will inspect this material and will have the right to take over the material that may be required by them. The remainder will be destroyed by the French authorities under British control.

7. Prisoners of the Allied Forces will be forthwith set free, including

hose who have been transferred to France. As regards the latter, the British authorities reserve the right to hold as prisoners of war an equal number of French officers as far as possible of similar rank until those prisoners transferred to France have been released. The French prisoners will be released when the whole of the Syro-Lebanese territory has been occupied and the clauses of this convention have been fulfilled. They will then be enabled to join their units for repatriation.

8. The alternative of rallying to the Allied cause or of being repatriated will be left to the free choice of the individual whether military or civil. In the case of civilians who do not rally to the Allied cause individual applications to remain in Syria or Lebanon will be considered by the British authorities.

9. Executive officials, officials of the technical services and special service officers will remain at their posts so long as it is necessary to ensure the continuance of the administration of the country and until such time as they can be relieved. They can then be repatriated if they so wish. Their services may be dispensed with if their work or attitude is not satisfactory.

10. The British Authorities agree to the repatriation by French ships of French troops and of French subjects, with the reservation that this repatriation will be limited to those who have opted therefor. The British Authorities reserve the right to control all matters relative to the repatriation of these people.

11. Holdings of French subjects to be repatriated will be transferred in accordance with terms to be arranged. These people will receive treatment not less favorable than that accorded to British subjects who have lately left Syria.

12. French cultural institutions, including hospitals, schools, missions, etc., are assured that their rights will be respected. The rights of these institutions must not be allowed to conflict with Allied military interests.

13. All public services, including railways, tramways, public transport, electricity, and water, will be maintained in operation and handed over intact.

14. All means of communication, including telephones, telegraphs, wireless, and the submarine cable, will be handed over intact to the occupying authorities. The French Command will have the use of telegraph facilities with France on the same conditions as the general public.

15. Port installations, naval establishments, and all ships, including British, in Syrian and Lebanese territorial waters will be handed over intact to the occupying authorities.

16. All aircraft and air installations and equipment in Syria or the Lebanon will be handed over intact. On the signature of the presen agreement British aircraft are empowered to use any air base and alight ing area in the Lebanon and Syria.

17. Fuel stocks shall be handed over intact. The quantity necessary for military transport will be placed at the disposal of the Frencl Command.

18. Currency and other means of payment in circulation or in reserve in possession of banks or other public authorities will be safeguarded.

19. The British military authorities reserve the right to take into thei service "Troupes Spéciales du Levant" progressively as they are dis charged by the French authorities. The arms of these troops will be handed over to the British authorities.

20. The British authorities will not prosecute in any way native Syria and Lebanese who have been involved in the recent hostilities in military or official capacity.

21. The carrying into effect of the terms of this convention will b controlled and regulated by a "Commission of Control" which will si at Beirut and will be composed of five members. Three of the member including the President will be nominated by the British authorities the remaining two by the French authorities. This "Commission o Control" is empowered to appoint subcommissions and co-opt th services of such experts as may be necessary.

22. This convention is drawn up in English and in French. In cas of dispute the English text will be authoritative.

PROTOCOL

With reference to par. 9 of the Convention the following are considere to be executive officials: — The Chief Secretary of the High Commis sioner; the members of the Civil and Military Cabinets, and of th Direction of Political Affairs; the Financial Adviser; the Economi Adviser; the Legislative Adviser; the Delegates and Assistant Delegate of the High Commissioner; the Administrative Advisers; the Officers on the Active List, of the Commissariat (Supplies); Special Servic Officers, French Officials of the Sûreté (C. I. D.) and Police and Gendar merie. All other officials are considered to be officials of the technica services.

Signed H. MAITLAND WILSON, *General Officer Commanding in-Chief, Allied Forces in Palestine and Syria.*

Signed DE VERDILLAC, *Deputy Commander-in-Chief, the Frenc Troops in Syria.*

2) *Exchange of Notes between the United Kingdom Government and the Free French National Committee, London, August 15, 1941* [1]

a) *The Minister of State of the United Kingdom (Lyttelton) to the President of the Free French National Committee (de Gaulle)*

At the conclusion of our talk today I am happy to repeat to you the assurances that Great Britain has no interest in Syria or the Lebanon, except to win the war. We have no desire to encroach in any way upon the position of France. Both Free France and Great Britain are pledged to the independence of Syria and the Lebanon. When this essential step has been taken, and without prejudice to it, we freely admit that France should have the predominant position in Syria and the Lebanon over any other European power. It is in this spirit that we have always acted. You will have seen recent utterances of the Prime Minister in this sense. I am glad to reaffirm them now to our friends and allies, who have our full sympathy and support.

On our side, I am happy again to receive your assurances of the determination of Free France, as friend and ally of Great Britain and in accordance with the agreements and declarations which you have already made, to pursue relentlessly to the finish the war against the common enemy. I am happy that we should thus reaffirm our complete understanding and agreement.

b) *The President of the Free French National Committee (de Gaulle) to the Minister of State of the United Kingdom (Lyttelton)*

I have received the letter which you have been kind enough to send me following our interview of today. I am happy to take note of your renewed assurances regarding the disinterestedness of Great Britain in Syria and the Lebanon, and the fact that Great Britain admits as a basic principle the pre-eminent and privileged position of France when these shall have attained independence in conformity with the undertaking which Free France has taken with regard to them.

I take this opportunity of repeating that Free France, that is to say, France, is resolved to pursue the war at the side of Great Britain, her friend and ally, until the attainment of complete victory against our common enemies.

[1] *The Times* (London), August 16, 1941, p. 3.

(3) *Attitude of the United States. Department of State Release, November 29, 1941* [1]

The historic area of Syria and Lebanon, after ceasing to be Turkish territory was assigned by the Principal Allied and Associated Powers on May 5, 1919 to France and the terms of the "A" mandate were defined by the Council of the League of Nations on July 24, 1922. The United States, the "associated power" of the allocating group, on April 4, 1924 [2] concluded with France a convention by which it acquired rights without responsibility under the mandate. France on May 22, 1930 promulgated an organic statute [3] as a step in advancing the area toward the independence envisaged by the mandate, which dealt differently with the five sections, the Lebanese Republic, Syria, Alexandretta, Latakia and the Jebel Druse. The establishment of the independence of Iraq, a former "A" mandated territory, on October 3, 1932 accelerated the aspirations of its neighbors. In 1936 treaties of friendship and alliance were negotiated by France with Syria and the Lebanon for application when their independence was realized. These had not been approved by the French Senate at the time of the outbreak of war. Under an arrangement of June 23, 1939 between France and Turkey, which was submitted to the Council of the League of Nations,[4] Alexandretta was transferred to Turkey and in September 1939 became the Hatay Republic. Before and after the Franco-German armistice of June 1940 [5] the Syrians and Lebanese actively pushed for independence. For the Free French entry into and promise made upon the taking over of the territory, see *Documents, III, 1940–41*, p. 335–8.

At Beirut on November 26, 1941, in the name of Free France, General George Catroux read to the President and members of the Lebanese Cabinet and other dignitaries a charter declaring the Lebanon to be an independent sovereign state with power to appoint diplomatic representatives and to constitute its own national military forces. Free France promised the Lebanon help and guidance on the lines of the treaty of friendship and alliance, signed at Beirut November 13, 1936,[6] which was unanimously approved by the Lebanese Parliament. The Lebanon became an ally *de facto*, placing its facilities at the disposal of the Allied Command and entering the "sterling area." [7]

Under the encouragement of the Free French regime which assumed responsibility after the armistice of July 12, 1941, the Syrian authorities organized a government with a view to realizing the independence contemplated by the treaty of friendship and alliance with France signed at Damascus, December 22, 1936, as completed by the exchange of notes of December 11, 1937.[9] An exchange of letters on August 15, 1941 between Oliver Lyttelton, United Kingdom Minister

[1] Department of State, *Bulletin*, V, p. 440.

[2] *Treaties, Conventions, etc.*, 1923–1937, IV, p. 4169.

[3] League of Nations, *Official Journal*, Vol. 11 (1930), p. 1099.

[4] *Ibid.*, Vol. 20 (1939), p. 356.

[5] *Documents, II, 1939–40*, p. 423.

[6] France, Ministère des affaires étrangères, *Rapport à la Société des Nations sur la situation de la Syrie et du Liban (année 1936)*, p. 229–50; also *L'Europe nouvelle* November 28, 1936, documentaire no. 48, VII; *Documentation internationale*, 1937 p. 1.

[7] *The Times* (London), November 28, 1941, p. 3, 5.

[8] France, Ministère des affaires étrangères, *Rapport à la Société des Nations sur la situation de la Syrie et du Liban (année 1936)*, p. 201. A preliminary text, covered by procès-verbal signed at Paris September 9, 1936, is printed in *Documentation internationale*, 1936, p. 138, and *L'Europe nouvelle*, documentaire no. 48, p. 1.

[9] France, Ministère des affaires étrangères, *Rapport*, etc., année 1937, p. 215.

f State, after a visit to the scene, and General de Gaulle stated that "Great Britain
as no interest in Syria and Lebanon, except to win the war. We have no desire to
ncroach in any way upon the position of France. Both Free France and Great
3ritain are pledged to the independence of Syria and the Lebanon." Sheikh Taj
d-Din, the former Premier, was proclaimed first President of the Syrian Repub-
ic on September 20, 1941 and on September 26 the Free French commander-in-
hief proclaimed that the Syrian Republic would exercise the rights and prerog-
tives of an independent sovereign state, nominating diplomatic representatives
nd creating its own military forces. It became a *de facto* ally in closest collabora-
ion with France and the United Kingdom, which sought its recognition by other
overnments.

The organic statutes for the territories of the Jebel Druse promulgated De-
ember 2, 1936, and of the Aluite (Latakia) promulgated December 5, 1936[1]
ntered into force from the ratification, or its equivalent, of the 1936 treaty.

Inquiries have been received as to the attitude of this Government in
iew of the proclamation issued at Damascus on September 27, 1941
egarding the independence of Syria, and the proclamation issued at
3eirut on November 26, 1941 regarding the independence of Lebanon.

The American Government and people have always sympathized
vith the natural and legitimate aspirations of the peoples of Syria and
,ebanon. This Government therefore welcomes any steps toward the
ealization of these aspirations, chief among which is, of course, the full
njoyment of sovereign independence.

The convention between the United States and France, signed at Paris
n April 4, 1924, and the provisions of the mandate for Syria and
,ebanon included therein, clearly embody the idea of Syrian and
,ebanese independence. The American Government continues to
upport these provisions which it endorsed in 1924 and which are a
ornerstone of the mandate principle. The 1924 convention, which also
et forth the rights of the United States and its nationals in the areas
oncerned, was formally ratified by the American Government in
ccordance with the required constitutional procedure, and must be
egarded as continuing in effect until new instruments of a mutually
atisfactory nature can be similarly negotiated and ratified. This
overnment is hopeful that, as soon as international conditions permit,
uch negotiations may be undertaken, enabling this Government to
xtend formal recognition to Syria and Lebanon.

[1] *Ibid.*, année 1936, p. 214, 217.

B. Iran

(1) British and Soviet Statements of Decision to Send Military Forces into Iran, August 25, 1941

(a) Statement of the British Foreign Office, August 25, 1941 [1]

During the past months, His Majesty's Government have repeatedly warned the Iranian Government of the potential dangers arising from the presence in Iran of an excessively large German colony. Germans resident in Iran, as in other countries, have long been subjected to the organized discipline of the German Nazi Party. As in other neutral countries, the German authorities have endeavored to pursue in Iran a policy of infiltration by sending their agents to mingle with and to replace the resident German community. The attention of the Iranian Government has therefore frequently been called to the desirability in the interests of Iran herself, of taking effective steps to check this process of infiltration. It has been pointed out that the presence of large numbers of German technical experts and agents in various parts of Iran, employed in factories and public works, as well as on roads and railways, and in many other important posts, cannot fail to constitute a serious danger to the maintenance of Iranian neutrality. There can be no doubt that, as in other neutral countries, the German resident community would be employed, whenever it seemed to the German Government that the appropriate moment had arrived, to create disorders with a view to assist the execution of Germany's military plans. The fact that Germans occupy in Iran so many key positions in industry and communications gives them unique facilities for doing so.

It has also been made clear to the Iranian Government that His Majesty's Government regard this as a matter of grave concern to themselves. The underground measures taken by the German Government to spread German influence in Iran, and to establish eventually German control and domination in that country, obviously constitute a serious danger for the Iranian Government themselves, as well as for the British interests in Iran; but they are also a danger to neighboring countries. India clearly cannot disinterest herself from such developments in an adjacent territory. Iraq is also closely concerned, especially since the Germans in Iran are known to have played a part in the revolt of last April against the legal Government at Bagdad, and in the subsequent events when the rebels were induced to take up arms against Iraq's British allies. Soviet Russia also, when she was attacked by Germany

[1] Text furnished by British Information Services, New York; United Press dispatch, *New York Times*, August 26, 1941.

ook a serious view of the threat to Russian interests caused by German activities in Iran.

Towards the middle of July, His Majesty's Government, realizing that the representations made at Tehran for many months past had remained without effect, instructed His Majesty's Minister again to impress upon the Iranian Government as a matter of the utmost gravity and urgency the need for. taking immediate action. The German invasion of Soviet Russia, by extending the zone of hostilities to include one of the countries adjacent to Iran, had obviously greatly increased the necessity for an early settlement of this problem. Sir R. Bullard was accordingly instructed to press for a drastic reduction in the number of Germans who were permitted to remain in the country. Parallel action was taken by the Soviet Ambassador at Tehran on instructions from his Government.

In their reply to this strong recommendation, the Iranian authorities appeared to recognize in principle the wisdom of the advice offered to them by His Majesty's Government and the Soviet Government. They indicated that they were taking some steps to reduce the number of Germans in Iran, and admitted the obligation incumbent upon them to keep under strict control the activities of those Germans who remained.

No doubt, however, because they were reluctant to offend the German Government, even in the defense of their own vital interests, the proportion of Germans whom the Iranian authorities actually removed from the country was very small, and on August 16 Sir R. Bullard and the Soviet Ambassador accordingly repeated to the Iranian Government in the most formal and emphatic manner the view of their two Governments that the German community in Iran should be required to leave the country without further delay. The Iranian Government were told that His Majesty's Government and the Soviet Government accepted and endorsed the Iranian policy of neutrality, that they had no designs against Iran's political independence or territorial integrity, and that it was their sincere desire to maintain a policy of friendship and cooperation with Iran. This communication contained a proposal devised in order to meet Iran's special needs, by which a few German technicians engaged on specially important work might be retained temporarily; and His Majesty's Government and the Soviet Government offered to assist the Iranian Government by endeavoring to find suitably qualified experts to replace the departing German technicians, and also stated that they would gladly concert with the Iranian Government measures to alleviate any temporary hardships that might be caused by the simultaneous departure of large numbers of trained personnel.

The Iranian Government's reply to the communications addressed t‹ them on August 16 shows that they are not prepared to give adequat satisfaction to the recommendations of His Majesty's Government an‹ the Soviet Government in this important matter. It is now clear tha further friendly representations to the Iranian Government on the sam lines as hitherto would serve no useful purpose, and that His Majesty' Government and the Soviet Government must have recourse to othe measures to safeguard their essential interests. These measures will i‹ no way be directed against the Iranian people: His Majesty's Govern ment have no designs against the independence and territorial integrit; of Iran, and any measures they may take will be directed solely agains the attempts of the Axis Powers to establish their control of Iran.

(b) Note Submitted by the People's Commissariat for Foreign Affair of the U.S.S.R. to the Government of Iran, August 25, 1941 [1]

The People's Commissariat of Foreign Affairs has the honor on instruc tions of the Soviet Government to inform the Iranian Government c the following:

The Soviet Government, guided by its feeling of friendship for th Iranian people and respect for the sovereignty of Iran, has always an invariably pursued a policy of consolidating friendly relations betwee the U.S.S.R. and Iran, and of furthering to the utmost the prosperit of the Iranian state.

This friendly policy of the Soviet Union toward Iran has found expre‹ sion in such important documents as the notes of the Soviet Governmen of January 14, 1918, and June 26, 1919, concerning the basic principle of Soviet policy toward the Iranian people, and also in numerous treatie and agreements concluded between the Soviet Union and Iran. Th basis underlying all the treaties and agreements of the Soviet Goverr ment with the Iranian Government is the inviolable principle of respec for the independence and territorial integrity of Iran. In accordanc with this principle, the Soviet Government in its note of January 1‹ 1918, proclaimed null and void all agreements which limited or restricte in any respect the rights of the Iranian people to a free and independer existence.

The Soviet Government annulled all payments by Iran under oblig‹ tions to the Tsarist Government, put an end to all interference in th revenues of Iran, and completely abrogated the consular jurisdictio‹

---

[1] *Moscow News*, August 25, 1941, p. 3, received from Embassy of the U.S.S.R Washington, D.C.

xempting Russian citizens in Iran from the jurisdiction of Iranian
ourts, which was humiliating to Iran and incompatible with the principle
f its sovereignty as a state.

By the same act the Soviet Government undertook to transfer without
ompensation to the possession of the Iranian people, and subsequently
iid in fact so transfer, a number of enterprises established by Russia,
amely, the Meshad-Seistan telegraph line; the Astrabad district tele-
raph; the Enzeli-Tehran highway and all the highways built by the
Russians in 1914–18, together with all their structures; the Enzeli harbor
vorks, together with all their property, to wit, the power station, break-
vaters, buildings, equipment, and so on; the Julfa-Tabriz railway,
including its Safyan branch line, together with all its rolling stock,
uildings and equipment, and also all Russian postal institutions, tele-
hone and telegraph lines and the like. At the same time, by decision
f the Soviet Government, the Discount Bank with all its movable and
eal property was transferred to the possession of the Iranian people.

By its acts of January 14, 1918, and June 26, 1919, the Soviet Govern-
ent thus palpably and effectively proved its disinterested readiness to
irther the political and economic prosperity of Iran.

By the Soviet-Iranian treaty of February 26, 1921, the Soviet Govern-
ent annulled the treaties and agreements concluded between the
iovernment of Tsarist Russia and the Iranian Government, which
iolated the sovereignty of Iran, the Soviet Government relinquishing
ll claims to the use of the Ashur-Ada Islands and other islands off the
oast of the Astrabad (Gorgand) Province of Iran. The Soviet Govern-
ent at the same time waived all its rights to the loans granted to Iran
y the Tsarist Government as being loans designed to enslave Iran,
nd also its right to the state revenues of Iran guaranteeing these loans.
teaffirming the transfer without compensation to the sole possession
f the Iranian people of the enterprises enumerated in the note of 1919,
he Soviet Government in addition transferred to Iran the railway line
om Safyan to Lake Urmia, including its rolling stock and other
roperty, as well as the wharves, warehouses, steamers, barges and other
eans of transportation on Lake Urmia.

Thereafter the Soviet Government over a period of many years
ivariably assisted Iran in its economic development as well, as is
videnced in particular by the Trade Agreement between the U.S.S.R.
nd Iran of July 3, 1924, which afforded Iran numerous privileges in
ie import and export of Soviet and Iranian goods. The favorable and
iendly attitude of the Soviet Union toward Iran is also evidenced by
ie Water Convention of 1926, the Fishery Convention of 1927, the

Convention on Combating Agricultural Pests of 1935, the Convention on Combating Locusts of 1935, the Trade Agreement of 1940 and a number of other treaties and agreements.

Thanks to the cooperation of the Soviet Union, Iran has, by virtue of the aforementioned treaties and agreements, obtained the opportunity of organizing on a large scale such vital branches of its national economy as fishing, cotton-growing and others.

Recently the Soviet Government has undertaken a number of further steps to consolidate and develop its economic relations with Iran. In particular the Soviet Government has expressed its readiness to supply Iran at the present time with goods vitally necessary to the Iranian people.

However, already at the time of the conclusion of the principal Soviet Iranian Treaty of February 26, 1921, the Soviet Government, as also the Government of Iran, were fully alive to the peculiar difficulties which might be encountered on the way to the consolidation of friendly relations between the Soviet Union and Iran, foreseeing that the territory of Iran might be used by elements hostile both to the U.S.S.R. and to Iran itself, and that these elements might attempt to convert Iran into a base for an attack on the U.S.S.R.

In order to anticipate any danger of this order, Article 6 of the Soviet Iranian Treaty provided for the following:

"The two High Contracting Parties are agreed that, should any attempts be made on the part of a third party by means of armed intervention to pursue a policy of annexation on the territory of Persia, or to convert the territory of Persia into a base for military hostilities against Russia, should this endanger the borders of the Russian Socialist Federative Soviet Republic or its allied powers, and should the Persian Government, after receiving warning from the Russian Soviet Government, not prove capable of itself averting this danger, the Russian Soviet Government will be entitled to send its troops into the territory of Persia in order to take the necessary military measures in the interests of self defense. After elimination of the danger in question, the Soviet Government undertakes immediately to withdraw its troops from the confines of Persia."

The Soviet Government thus took upon itself, with the full consent of the Iranian Government, the defense of the interests of the U.S.S.R. in Iran in the contingency of the danger specified in the Treaty of 1921, at the same time affirming its undertaking immediately to withdraw its troops from the confines of Iran after this danger had passed. As is known, during the 20 years that the Treaty of 1921 has been in opera tion, the Soviet Government has not found it necessary for the defense of its interests to have recourse to Article 6 of the Treaty of 1921.

However, of late, and particularly since the beginning of the perfidious attack on the U.S.S.R. by Hitlerite Germany, a menacing character has been assumed by activities hostile to the U.S.S.R. and to Iran on the part of German Fascist conspiratorial groups on the territory of Iran. German agents who have wormed their way into important official posts in over 50 Iranian departments are making every manner of attempt to sow unrest and disorder in Iran, to upset the peaceful life of the Iranian people, to provoke Iran against the U.S.S.R. and to involve it in a war with the U.S.S.R.

Such agents of German Fascism as Von Radanovich, Gamotta, Meyer, Wilhelm Sapow, Gustav Bohr, Heinrich Kellinger, Trappe, and others, camouflaged by their employment in various German firms (the A.E.G., Ferrostahl, Garber, Ortel, Loehn, Schichau), have at present gone to extremes in their subversive activities of, on the one hand, organizing wrecking and terrorist groups to be smuggled into Soviet Azerbaijan — above all into the principal Soviet oil district of Baku — and into Soviet Turkmenistan, and, on the other, of preparing for a military coup in Iran.

These activities are at present conducted by recent arrivals from Iraq — a German named Ganotta, chief of the German intelligence service in Tehran, and his assistant, an employee of the Mercedes Company named Meyer. The group of German agents organized by them and directed by the German Embassy in Tehran is engaged in organizing at a number of Iranian border points armed groups to be smuggled into Baku and other important Soviet border points for the purpose of causing fires and explosions on the territory of the U.S.S.R. The German agents command stores of arms and ammunition at various points in Iran. In particular, they have laid in for their criminal ends over 50 tons of explosives in the environs of Miane, in North Iran. In the guise of hunting they conduct in the environs of Tehran military training of their criminal accomplices among the German citizens. Fifty-six German intelligence service agents have penetrated into Iranian military plants in the guise of engineers and technicians. Among these a part of particular importance is played by a spy named Artel, who is the representative of the German Friedrich Krupp firm in Iran, by the notorious German spy Von Radanovich, who is director of the branch of the German Siemens firm, by Kevkin, his assistant, and by a German named Wolf, an employee of the Iran Express Office in Pehlevi, who is at the same time chief of the German intelligence service in North Iran

and on the Caspian coast.   In their criminal activities these Germa
agents trample in the crudest and grossest manner on the elementary re
quirements of respect for the sovereignty of Iran and have converte
the territory of Iran into a scene of preparations for a military attack o
the Soviet Union.

The situation which has arisen in Iran in virtue of the above-enu
merated factors is fraught with great danger.   This requires from th
Soviet Government the immediate realization of all the measures whic
it is not only entitled but in duty bound to undertake for its self-defens
in strict accordance with Article 6 of the Treaty of 1921.

Since Germany's attack on the U.S.S.R., the Soviet Government ha
three times — on June 26, July 19 and August 16, 1941 — drawn th
attention of the Iranian Government to the danger offered by the sul
versive spying and wrecking activities of German agents in Iran.

On June 26, 1941, the Soviet Government informed the Shah of Ira
that it had in its possession serious evidence of a *coup d'état* being plotte
by the Germans in Iran.   On July 19, 1941, the Soviet Governmen
simultaneously with the Government of Great Britain, again raised wit
the Government of Iran the issue of terminating the hostile activiti
of the Germans and of the disorders they were plotting, which threatene
the interests both of Iran itself and of its neighboring states; both th
Soviet Government and the Government of Great Britain insisted o
the expulsion from Iran of the Germans whose sojourn in Iran w?
incompatible with the interests of Iran itself and also with the interes
of the Soviet Union and Great Britain.

Lastly, on August 16, 1941, for the third time, the Soviet Governmen
and likewise the Government of Great Britain, once more raised with th
Iranian Government the necessity of taking urgent measures to termina
these activities of the German agents in Iran directed against the interes
of Iran and also of the Soviet Union and Great Britain, and once mo?
insisted on the earliest expulsion of these Germans from the confines •
Iran.

Thus the Soviet Government on three occasions warned the Irania
Government of the danger threatening its interests and also the interes
of the U.S.S.R. and Great Britain, with a view to the adoption of tl
necessary measures.

The Government of Iran unfortunately refused to take the measur
which would put an end to the unrest and disorder being fomented l
German agents on the territory of Iran, thereby encouraging the
agents of Germany in their criminal activities.   The Soviet Governme
in consequence has found itself obliged to take the necessary measur

d immediately to exercise the right belonging to the Soviet Union
der Article 6 of the Treaty of 1921 of temporarily sending its troops
to Iranian territory in the interests of self-defense.

These measures are in no wise directed against the Iranian people.
ie Soviet Government has no designs on the territorial integrity and
ite independence of Iran. The military measures taken by the Soviet
)vernment are directed solely and exclusively against the danger
eated by the hostile activity of the Germans in Iran. As soon as this
nger threatening the interests of Iran and of the U.S.S.R. has been
moved, the Soviet Government, in discharge of its obligation under
e Soviet-Iranian Treaty of 1921, will at once withdraw the Soviet
)ops from the confines of Iran.

oscow, *August 25, 1941*

) *Treaty of Alliance between the United Kingdom, the Union of Soviet
Socialist Republics and Iran, Signed at Tehran January 29, 1942* [1]

In force January 29, 1942

On the morning of August 25, 1941, British and Russian troops crossed the
inian frontier. On August 27, the Iranian Government resigned and on the
lowing day a new ministry was formed by Ali Faroughli. On September 3, the
itish and Soviet Commanders met at Kazvin. On September 9 the Iranian
reign Minister accepted the terms put forward by the British and Soviet
)vernments, which included the closing of the German, Italian, Hungarian and
imanian Legations at Tehran and the handing over of German nationals,[2]
t the British and Soviet authorities were not as yet convinced of the good faith
the Iranian Government. Pressure continued, and on September 16, the Shah
nounced his abdication. The Crown Prince, Muhammed Riza Pahlevi suc-
eded, and it was subsequently announced that he would rule as a "completely
istitutional monarch." The Treaty of Alliance of January 29, 1942 undertook
define the relations between Iran, on the one hand, and the United Kingdom
d the Soviet Union, on the other. Both Great Britain and the Soviet Union
d already accepted the principles of the Atlantic Charter (p. 210, 214).

His Majesty the King of Great Britain, Ireland and the British
)minions beyond the Seas, Emperor of India, and the Union of Soviet
cialist Republics, on the one hand, and His Imperial Majesty the
ahinshah of Iran, on the other;
Having in view the principles of the Atlantic Charter [3] jointly agreed
on and announced to the world by the President of the United States

[1] Department of State, *Bulletin*, VI, p. 249; reprinted from United Kingdom,
rliamentary Papers, 1941–42, Persia No. 1, 1942, Cmd. 6335.
[2] *The Bulletin of International News*, XVIII, September 30, 1941, p. 1249.
[3] See p. 209.

of America and the Prime Minister of the United Kingdom on the 14
August, 1941, and endorsed by the Government of the Union of Sovi
Socialist Republics on the 24th September, 1941, with which H
Imperial Majesty the Shahinshah declares his complete agreement ar
from which he wishes to benefit on an equal basis with other nations
the world; and

Being anxious to strengthen the bonds of friendship and mutu
understanding between them; and

Considering that these objects will best be achieved by the conclusic
of a Treaty of Alliance:

Have agreed to conclude a treaty for this purpose and have appointe
as their plenipotentiaries;

His Majesty the King of Great Britain, Ireland and the Briti
Dominions beyond the Seas, Emperor of India,

For the United Kingdom of Great Britain and Northern Irelan
His Excellency Sir READER WILLIAM BULLARD, K.C.M.G., C.I.F
*His Majesty's Envoy Extraordinary and Minister Plenipotentia
in Iran.*

The Union of Soviet Socialist Republics,
His Excellency M. ANDRE ANDREEWICH SMIRNOV, *Ambassad
Extraordinary and Minister Plenipotentiary of the Union of Sov
Socialist Republics in Iran.*

His Imperial Majesty the Shahinshah of Iran,
His Excellency M. ALI SOHEILY, *Minister for Foreign Affair*
Who, having communicated their full powers, found in good and d
form, have agreed as follows:

ARTICLE 1. His Majesty the King of Great Britain, Ireland and t
British Dominions beyond the Seas, Emperor of India, and the Union
Soviet Socialist Republics (hereinafter referred to as the Allied Powei
jointly and severally undertake to respect the territorial integrit
sovereignty, and political independence of Iran.

ARTICLE 2. An alliance is established between the Allied Powers
the one hand and His Imperial Majesty the Shahinshah of Iran on t
other.

ARTICLE 3. (i) The Allied Powers jointly and severally undertake
defend Iran by all means at their command from all aggression on t
part of Germany or any other Power.

(ii) His Imperial Majesty the Shahinshah undertakes —

(a) to cooperate with the Allied Powers with all the means at l
command and in every way possible, in order that they may be al
to fulfil the above undertaking. The assistance of the Iranian forc

shall, however, be limited to the maintenance of internal security on Iranian territory;

(b) to secure to the Allied Powers, for the passage of troops or supplies from one Allied Power to the other or for other similar purposes, the unrestricted right to use, maintain, guard, and, in case of military necessity, control in any way that they may require all means of communication throughout Iran, including railways, roads, rivers, aerodromes, ports, pipelines and telephone, telegraph and wireless installations;

(c) to furnish all possible assistance and facilities in obtaining material and recruiting labor for the purpose of the maintenance and improvement of the means of communication referred to in paragraph (b);

(d) to establish and maintain, in collaboration with the Allied Powers, such measures of censorship control as they may require for all the means of communication referred to in paragraph (b).

(iii) It is clearly understood that in the application of paragraph (ii) (b), (c) and (d) of the present article the Allied Powers will give full consideration to the essential needs of Iran.

ARTICLE 4. (i) The Allied Powers may maintain in Iranian territory, land, sea, and air forces in such number as they consider necessary. The location of such forces shall be decided in agreement with the Iranian Government so long as the strategic situation allows. All questions concerning the relations between the forces of the Allied Powers and the Iranian authorities shall be settled so far as possible in cooperation with the Iranian authorities in such a way as to safeguard the security of the said forces. It is understood that the presence of these forces on Iranian territory does not constitute a military occupation and will disturb as little as possible the administration and the security forces of Iran, the economic life of the country, the normal movements of the population, and the application of Iranian laws and regulations.

(ii) A separate agreement or agreements shall be concluded as soon as possible after the entry into force of the present Treaty regarding any financial obligations to be borne by the Allied Powers under the provisions of the present article and of paragraphs (ii) (b), (c) and (d) of article 3 above in such matters as local purchases, the hiring of buildings and plant, the employment of labor, transport charges, etc. A special agreement shall be concluded between the Allied Governments and the Iranian Government defining the conditions for any transfers to the Iranian Government after the war of buildings and other improvements effected by the Allied Powers on Iranian territory. These agreements

shall also settle the immunities to be enjoyed by the forces of the Alli
Powers in Iran.

ARTICLE 5. The forces of the Allied Powers shall be withdrawn fro
Iranian territory not later than six months after all hostilities betwe
the Allied Powers and Germany and her associates have been suspend
by the conclusion of an armistice or armistices, or on the conclusion
peace between them, whichever date is the earlier. The expressi
"associates" of Germany means all other Powers which have engag
or may in the future engage in hostilities against either of the Alli
Powers.

ARTICLE 6. (i) The Allied Powers undertake in their relations wi
foreign countries not to adopt an attitude which is prejudicial to t
territorial integrity, sovereignty, or political independence of Iran, nor
conclude treaties inconsistent with the provisions of the present Trea
They undertake to consult the Government of His Imperial Majesty t
Shahinshah in all matters affecting the direct interests of Iran.

(ii) His Imperial Majesty the Shahinshah undertakes not to adopt
his relations with foreign countries an attitude which is inconsistent wi
the alliance, nor to conclude treaties inconsistent with the provisions
the present Treaty.

ARTICLE 7. The Allied Powers jointly undertake to use their best e
deavors to safeguard the economic existence of the Iranian peo
against the privations and difficulties arising as a result of the prese
war. On the entry into force of the present Treaty, discussions shall
opened between the Government of Iran and the Governments of t
Allied Powers as to the best possible methods of carrying out the abo
undertaking.

ARTICLE 8. The provisions of the present Treaty are equally bindi
as bilateral obligations between His Imperial Majesty the Shahinsh
and each of the two other High Contracting Parties.

ARTICLE 9. The present Treaty shall come into force on signatu
and shall remain in force until the date fixed for the withdrawal of t
forces of the Allied Powers from Iranian territory in accordance wi
Article 5.

IN WITNESS WHEREOF, the above-named plenipotentiaries have sign
the present Treaty and have affixed thereto their seals.

DONE AT Tehran in triplicate in English, Russian, and Persian,
being equally authentic, on the 29th day of January 1942.

[L.S.] R. W. BULLARD
[L.S.] A. A. SMIRNOV
[L.S.] ALI SOHEILY

) Identic Notes Addressed to the Iranian Minister for Foreign Affairs (Soheily) by His Majesty's Minister (Bullard) and the Soviet Ambassador (Smirnov), January 29, 1942 [1]

With reference to Article 6, paragraph (i), of the Treaty of Alliance gned today, I have the honor, on behalf of His Majesty's Government . the United Kingdom [the Government of the Union of Soviet Socialist epublics] to assure Your Excellency that my Government interpret ₁e provisions of this clause as being applicable to any peace conference or ₂nferences held at the conclusion of the present war, or other general ₃ternational conferences. Consequently they consider themselves bound ₃t to approve anything at any such conference which is prejudicial to ₁e territorial integrity, sovereignty, or political independence of Iran, ₁d not to discuss at any such conference anything affecting the direct terests of Iran without consultation with the Government of Iran.

His Majesty's Government [the Government of the Union of Soviet ₃cialist Republics] will further do their best to secure that Iran will be presented on a footing of equality in any peace negotiations directly fecting her interests.

•) Identic Notes Addressed to His Majesty's Minister (Bullard) and the Soviet Ambassador (Smirnov) by the Iranian Minister for Foreign Affairs (Soheily), January 29, 1942 [2]

With reference to Article 6, paragraph (ii), of the Treaty of Alliance ₃ned this day, I have the honor, on behalf of the Iranian Government, assure Your Excellency that the Iranian Government would consider contrary to their obligations under this clause to maintain diplomatic ₁ations with any State which is in diplomatic relations with neither of ₃e Allied Powers.

) Identic Notes Addressed to the Iranian Minister for Foreign Affairs (Soheily) by His Majesty's Minister (Bullard) and the Soviet Ambassador (Smirnov), January 29, 1942 [2]

I have the honor, on behalf of His Majesty's Government in the United ₁ngdom [the Government of the Union of Soviet Socialist Republics] convey to Your Excellency the following assurances: —

(1) With reference to Article 3 (ii) (*a*) of the Treaty of Alliance which ₃ been signed today, the Allied Powers will not require of Iran the ₃rticipation of her armed forces in any war or military operations ₃ainst any Foreign Power or Powers.

[1] Department of State, *Bulletin*, VI, p. 251.   [2] *Ibid.*, p. 252.

(2) With reference to Article 4 (ii), it is understood that there is n provision in the Treaty which requires that the Iranian Governmer shall bear the cost of any works which the Allied Powers carry out fc their own military ends and which are not necessary for the needs of Ira⟩

(3) It is understood that Annex 1[1] will remain in force even if tł Treaty ceases to be valid, in accordance with the provisions of Article ⁑ before peace has been concluded.

C. British-Soviet Démarche to Turkey

(1) *Oral Remarks of the Soviet Ambassador at Ankara* (*Vinogradov* August 10, 1941 [2]

As late as March 1941, that is to say, during the period of well-know treaty relations between the Soviet Union and Germany, the Sovi⟨ Government exchanged assurances with the Government of the Turkis Republic in connection with reports that were then being spread to tł effect that if Turkey were compelled to enter the war the Soviet Unic would take advantage of Turkey's difficulties to attack her.

It will be recalled that the Soviet Government for their part considere it necessary at that time to declare that such reports in no way corr sponded to the attitude of the Soviet Union and that if Turkey were ⟨ fact attacked and compelled to enter the war for the defense of h⟨ territories she could count on full understanding and neutrality of tⁱ Soviet Union on the basis of the non-aggression pact between the tv countries.

It is known that after the treacherous attack of Nazi Germany on tⁱ Soviet Union, the Germans conducted, and are still conducting, a ma cious propaganda against the Soviet Union, intended *inter alia* to bri⟩ about discord between the Soviet Union and Turkey.

In view of the fact that this propaganda, which is being intensive conducted by the German Government, has become even stronger present, and considering that in the present international situation it opportune that an exchange of views should take place between t Soviet Government and the Turkish Government on the subject relations between the Soviet Union, Turkey, and Great Britain, tⁱ Soviet Government have instructed me, M. le Ministre, to make to yo Excellency the Declarations.

[1] See (a) on p. 685, which was labelled as Annex 1 in Department of State, B letin, VI, p. 251.

[2] *Bulletin of International News*, XVIII, p. 1079; cf. *New York Times*, Aug⟨ 13, 1941, p. 3.

2) *Oral Remarks of the British Ambassador at Ankara (Knatchbull-Hugessen), August 10, 1941* [1]

In view of anti-Russian propaganda by the Germans, His Majesty's Government and the Soviet Government have considered it right to reaffirm categorically their attitude towards Turkey in order that the Turkish Government may be under no delusion in the formation of their own policies towards Great Britain and the Soviet Union.

In communicating to your Excellency my note of today containing the text of the declaration of His Majesty's Government in the United Kingdom and of the Union of Soviet Socialist Republics, I have the honor to explain, with the permission of my Government, that in so far as the British Government is concerned, this declaration is intended to be a simple reiteration of their engagements toward Turkey as contained in Article I of the Anglo-Turkish treaty of October 19, 1939. [2] The declaration in no way modifies that treaty and neither enlarges nor limits the obligations which derive from it.

3) *The British Ambassador (Knatchbull-Hugessen) and the Soviet Ambassador (Vinogradov) at Ankara to the Turkish Minister for Foreign Affairs (Saracoglu), August 10, 1941* [3]

His Majesty's Government in the United Kingdom confirm their fidelity to the Montreux Convention, [4] and assure the Turkish Government that they have no aggressive intentions or claims whatever with regard to the Straits.

His Majesty's Government, as also the Soviet Government, are prepared scrupulously to observe the territorial integrity of the Turkish Republic.

While fully appreciating the desire of the Turkish Government not to be involved in war, His Majesty's Government, as also the Soviet Government, would nevertheless be prepared to render Turkey every help and assistance in the event of her being attacked by a European power.

---

[1] *Bulletin of International News*, XVIII, p. 1079; the second paragraph from *New York Times*, August 13, 1941, p. 3.
[2] League of Nations, *Treaty Series*, CC, p. 167.
[3] *Bulletin of International News*, XVIII, p. 1079; cf. *New York Times*, August ?, 1941, p. 3.
[4] League of Nations, *Treaty Series*, CLXXIII, p. 213.

D. British Occupation of Madagascar

(1) *Approval by the Government of the United States. Department (
State Release, May 4, 1942* [1]

After Japanese occupation of the Netherlands East Indies and Burma,
became evident that the world-wide aggressive plans of Japan and German
envisaged Madagascar, the third largest island in the world, as a strategic bas
The island is 900 miles long and 250 miles wide, lies 570 nautical miles from M
zambique and 2000 nautical miles from Aden at the southern entrance to the Re
Sea. Along with German pressure for further "collaboration" upon the Vich
Government of Pierre Laval, a delegation of Japanese naval officers arrived
Vichy. United Nations authorities were unwilling to see a Japanese agreemer
for occupying the island effected under the German duress to which Laval w
notoriously open and subject. Since the local French regime had not declar
itself with the Free French National Committee, forestalling of the Japane
military intentions was undertaken by the British strategic landing at Die
Suarez on May 4, 1942, followed by the progressive occupation of the islan
The United States Government timed its declaration on the same day so as
make clear its complete association with the action. The statement was convey
to the Vichy regime by communication to its ambassador in Washington and I
instruction to the American chargé d'affaires at Vichy.

The President of the United States has been informed that Madagasc
has been occupied by British forces. This occupation has the full approv
and support of the Government of the United States. The island
Madagascar presents the definite danger to the United Nations of occ
pation or use by the Axis Powers, especially Japan. Such occupati
by the Axis Powers would constitute a definite and serious danger
the United Nations in their fight to maintain the kind of civilization
which France and to which the United Nations have been so lo.
accustomed.

The Government of the United States is at war with the Axis Powe
and if it becomes necessary or desirable for American troops or ships
use Madagascar in the common cause, the United States will not hesita
to do so at any time.

The United States and Great Britain are in accord that Madagasc
will, of course, be restored to France after the war or at any time th
the occupation of Madagascar is no longer essential to the common cau
of the United Nations.

In view of the fact that the island of Madagascar will be held in tru
for France, in order to protect it from attack by any one of the A
Powers, any warlike act permitted by the French Government agai
the Government of Great Britain or the Government of the Unit
States would, of necessity, have to be regarded by the Government
the United States as an attack upon the United Nations as a whole.

[1] Department of State, *Bulletin*, VI, p. 391.

E. Saudi Arabia

) *Agricultural Mission. Department of State Release, March 25, 1942* [1]

German efforts to use the Arabian peninsula for enlisting Moslem countries in bversive operations failed. King Ibn Saud, the most able and astute ruler of s period, refused to allow Fritz Grobba, the German provocateur for the liddle East, to remain in Saudi Arabia, to which he was "accredited" as inister. The tribal leaders met at Taif, near Mecca, in August 1941, where rince Feisal, viceroy of Hejaz and second son of Ibn Saud, gave them a message om his father in which they were counseled to maintain order and pursue their llings without bothering about international developments.

In response to an inquiry by the Government of Saudi Arabia as to hether the services of two American experts in irrigation and agri-ultural matters could be made available, this Government has organized n Agricultural Mission to Saudi Arabia. The Mission will examine and port to the Government of Saudi Arabia upon the water and agri-ultural resources of that country and the possibilities of their develop-ent. It will also conduct experimental plantings. The personnel of the lission, which has already departed, follows:

Ir. K. S. Twitchell, *Chief*
Ir. Albert L. Wathen, Acting Chief, Engineering Branch, Office of
    Indian Affairs, United States Department of the Interior
Ir. James G. Hamilton, Regional Agronomist at Albuquerque, N. Mex.,
    Soil Conservation Service, United States Department of Agriculture.

Mr. Twitchell has had extensive technical experience in Saudi Arabia. he other members of the Mission are, as indicated, government experts miliar with conditions in a section of this country which are similar to hose prevailing in Saudi Arabia.

This Government is pleased to have been able to respond in this way the inquiry of the Saudi Arabian Government.

[1] *Ibid.,* p. 261.

CHAPTER VIII

TRADE AND FINANCE

1. BASIC POLICY OF THE UNITED STATES

(1) *Address of the Under Secretary of State (Welles) at the World Trade Dinner of the 28th National Foreign Trade Convention, New York City, October 7, 1941* [1]

[Excerpt]

But the future no less than the present presses itself upon our atten tion. It seems to me that there is nothing more urgently demanded than that the people of the United States, the governments of the Western Hemisphere, and the governments of all of the nations which have been assailed or menaced by the Axis Powers should daily be considering and determining upon the policies and practices whose future enforcement could render the greatest measure of assurance that the tragedy which we now see being unfolded should not once more be brought to pass.

I can conceive of no greater misfortune than that the people of the United States and their Government should refrain from devoting them selves to the study of reconstruction until the end of the war; than that they should permit themselves to adopt the passive policy of "wait and see."

The period following the present war will be fully as critical for us as is the present crisis. Forces of aggression now menace us from without. But dangers of another nature here and elsewhere will threaten us even after the war has ended in the victory of Great Britain and her allies over the powers that are seeking to place the whole of the world under their own ignominious form of tyranny.

There exists the danger, despite the clear lessons of the past, that the nations of the world will once more be tempted to resort to the same misguided policies which have had such disastrous consequences. And in the economic field especially there is danger that special interests and pressure groups in this country and elsewhere will once again selfishly

[1] Department of State, *Bulletin*, V, at p. 269. Raymond H. Geist, Chief of the Division of Commercial Affairs, Department of State, also addressed the convention on "Assistance of the Department of State to Foreign Trade," *ibid.*, p. 271.

nd blindly seek preferences for themselves and discriminations against
thers.

The creation of an economic order in the post-war world which will
ive free play to individual enterprise, and at the same time render
ecurity to men and women, and provide for the progressive improvement of living standards, is almost as essential to the preservation of
ree institutions as is the actual winning of this war. And the preserva-
ion of our liberties — all-important in itself — is essential to the realiza-
ion of the other great objective of mankind — an enduring peace.
'here can be no peace in a Hitler-ridden world.

In brief, in my judgment, the creation of that kind of sound economic
rder which I have described is essential to the attainment of those three
reat demands of men and women everywhere — freedom, security and
eace.

The stakes are therefore tremendous in the task to which we must
arnestly set ourselves. All of the talent of such organizations as this
reat organization of yours, of research institutions, and of the agencies
f government, must be brought to bear upon the solution of the post-
var economic problems.

These problems are of two kinds: those which will present themselves
s the immediate aftermath of the war and those involved in the creation
f a more permanent economic order.

In the immediate post-war period the task will primarily be one of
econstruction. Food and material of all kinds will be sorely needed.
Both humanitarian considerations and self-interest require that we
ooperate to these ends to the fullest extent of our ability. So long as
ny important part of the world is economically sick, we cannot be well.

Plans for meeting these requirements are already being considered.
n planning commodity agreements for stabilizing prices of basic com-
nodities, such as the wheat agreement now under consideration by
everal of the producing countries directly concerned, these unusual
ost-war needs must be kept in mind in order that adequate supplies
nay be available to meet them.

Both from the standpoint of immediate post-war needs and in the
onger-range aspect, we must give serious attention to the problems of
nutrition. Here again humanitarian considerations and self-interest
ombine to make this subject one of outstanding importance to our
eople. If the dietary needs of the world's population could be satisfied
o the extent necessary to meet minimum standards for sustaining
ealth, the burdensome surpluses which normally trouble producers of
nany staple products would disappear. I am glad to be able to assure

you that this subject is being given preferential attention by agencie of this and other governments.

These are some of the problems with which we shall be faced imme diately after the war. But the basic problem in establishing a new an better world order is to obtain the application by the nations of th world of sound principles of commercial and economic policy.

The basic principles which, in my judgment, should guide the policie of nations in the post-war world have recently been enunciated in th eight-point joint declaration of the President and Mr. Churchill [1] at th historic meeting of the Atlantic.

This set of basic principles, appropriately called "The Atlanti Charter," deals with commercial policy in its fourth point which read "They will endeavor, with due respect for their existing obligations, t further the enjoyment by all states, great or small, victor or vanquishe of access, on equal terms, to the trade and to the raw materials of th world which are needed for their economic prosperity."

This categorical statement of the essentials of post-war commerci policy requires no interpretation. I should, however, like to emphasiz its meaning and significance.

The basic conception is that your Government is determined to mov towards the creation of conditions under which restrictive and unco scionable tariffs, preferences, and discriminations are things of the pas under which no nation should seek to benefit itself at the expense o another; and under which destructive trade warfare shall be replaced b cooperation for the welfare of all nations.

The Atlantic Declaration means that every nation has a right to expec that its legitimate trade will not be diverted and throttled by towerin tariffs, preferences, discriminations, or narrow bilateral practices. Mos fortunately we have already done much to put our own commercial polic in order. So long as we adhere and persistently implement the principl and policies which made possible the enactment of the Trade Agree ments Act, the United States will not furnish, as it did after the last wa an excuse for trade-destroying and trade-diverting practices.

The purpose so simply set forth in the Atlantic Declaration is t promote the economic prosperity of all nations "great or small, victc or vanquished." Given this purpose and the determination to act i accordance with it, the means of attaining this objective will alwa be found. It is a purpose which does not have its origin primarily i altruistic conceptions. It is inspired by the realization, so painfull forced on us by the experiences of the past and of the present, that in th

[1] See p. 209.

ing run no nation can prosper by itself or at the expense of others and
hat no nation can live unto itself alone.

No nation's peace can be assured in the disordered world in which we
ave lived since 1914.

It is the task and responsibility of every one of us, and like-minded
eople everywhere, to see that our objective is attained.

We cannot afford to repeat the tragic mistakes of the past.

2) *Statement of the Secretary of State (Hull), May 17, 1942*

[See p. 69.]

2. RECIPROCAL TRADE AGREEMENTS PROGRAM

[See *Documents, I, 1938–39*, p. 334; *II, 1939–40*, p. 448; *III, 1940–41*, p. 459.]

A. Status as of June 30, 1942

1) *Reciprocal Trade Agreements Entered into Under the Trade Agreements Act of 1934*

The authority of the President to enter into foreign-trade agreements in the
orm of executive agreements extends to June 12, 1943 by Public Resolution No.
1, 76th Cong., approved April 12, 1940 (*Documents, II, 1939–40*, p. 468). On
une 30, 1942 there were 27 agreements in effect with 23 states and negotiations
rere pending with 5 others. Of the agreements in effect 3 were supplementary
rith Canada and 2 supplementary with Cuba, all of these illustrating the flexible
pplication of the main principles in meeting unusual conditions.

During the period June 30, 1941 to June 30, 1942, new trade agreements were
igned with Argentina [1] and Peru [2] on October 14, 1941 and March 7, 1942
espectively. A supplemental trade agreement with Cuba was signed December
3, 1941.[3] By an exchange of notes with Ecuador, signed March 2, 1942, the
Jnited States agreed not to invoke the pertinent provisions of the Trade Agreement of August 6, 1938 in respect to increased charges on certain products
nported from the United States.[4] By an exchange of notes of April 25, 1942,
greement was reached between the Governments of the United States and
Iaiti regarding the interpretation of certain provisions of the trade agreement
f March 28, 1935.[5]

[1] See p. 695.

[2] The provisions of the Peruvian agreement are explained in an analysis prepared
or the Department of State and published in Department of State, *Bulletin*, VI,
. 410. The agreement was proclaimed by the President of the United States and
y the President of Peru on June 29, 1942, and, under the terms of the agreement,
ntered into force July 29, 1942, *ibid.*, p. 597.

[3] Its provisions are explained in an analysis published in Department of State,
Bulletin, V, p. 603.

[4] *Ibid.*, VI, p. 221; this volume p. 376.

[5] *Ibid.*, p. 384; this volume p. 367.

Country	Date Signed	Date Effective	Executive Agreement
Cuba	Aug. 24, 1934	Sept. 3, 1934	67
Belgium	Feb. 27, 1935	May 1, 1935	75
Haiti	Mar. 28, 1935	June 3, 1935	78
Sweden	May 25, 1935	Aug. 5, 1935	79
Brazil	Feb. 2, 1935	Jan. 1, 1936	82
Canada (see revised agreement below)	Nov. 15, 1935	Jan. 1, 1936	91
Kingdom of the Netherlands (Netherlands in Europe, Netherlands India, Surinam, and Curaçao)	Dec. 20, 1935	Feb. 1, 1936	100
Switzerland	Jan. 9, 1936	Feb. 15, 1936	90, 193
Honduras	Dec. 18, 1935	Mar. 2, 1936	86
Colombia	Sept. 13, 1935	May 20, 1936	89
Guatemala	Apr. 24, 1936	June 15, 1936	92
France and its colonies, dependencies, and protectorates other than Morocco. . . .	May 6, 1936	June 15, 1936	146
Nicaragua [1]	Mar. 11, 1936	Oct. 1, 1936	95, 120
Finland	May 18, 1936	Nov. 2, 1936	97
El Salvador	Feb. 19, 1937	May 31, 1937	101
Costa Rica	Nov. 28, 1936	Aug. 2, 1937	102
Czechoslovakia [2]	Mar. 7, 1938	Apr. 16, 1938	147
Ecuador	Aug. 6, 1938	Oct. 23, 1938	133
United Kingdom, including Newfoundland and the British Colonial Empire. . . .	Nov. 17, 1938	Jan. 1, 1939	164
Canada (revision of agreement of 1935)	Nov. 17, 1938	Jan. 1, 1939	149, 170
Turkey	Apr. 1, 1939	May 5, 1939	163
Venezuela	Nov. 6, 1939	Dec. 16, 1939	180
Cuba (supplementary agreement)	Dec. 18, 1939	Dec. 23, 1939	165
Canada (supplementary agreement)	Dec. 30, 1939	Jan. 1, 1940	184
Canada (supplementary agreement)	Dec. 13, 1940	Dec. 20, 1940	216
Argentina	Oct. 14, 1941	Nov. 15, 1941	—
Cuba (supplementary agreement)	Dec. 23, 1941	Jan. 5, 1942	229
Peru.	May 7, 1942	July 29, 1942	—

[1] Certain provisions of the trade agreement ceased to be in force as of March 1, 1938.

[2] The operation of this agreement was suspended as of April 22, 1939.

2) Countries With Which Intention to Negotiate Has Been Announced

COUNTRY	DATE OF ISSUANCE OF NOTICE	LATEST DATE FOR SUBMITTING WRITTEN STATEMENTS	DATE FOR ORAL PRESENTATION OF VIEWS
hile	Oct. 2, 1939	Nov. 11, 1939	Nov. 27, 1939
ruguay	May 13, 1941	June 12, 1941	June 23, 1941
eland [1]	Nov. 17, 1941	Dec. 8, 1941	Dec. 15, 1941
olivia [2]	April 4, 1942	May 4, 1942	May 18, 1942
Iexico [3]	April 4, 1942	May 4, 1942	May 18, 1942

B. Trade Agreement with the Argentine Republic

1) Trade Agreement between the United States of America and the Argentine Nation, October 14, 1941 [4]

Effective November 15, 1941

The treaty of friendship, commerce and navigation of July 27, 1853,[5] between 1e Argentine Confederation and the United States contained only a conditional 1ost-favored-nation clause. For many years trade relations with Argentina were 1ggravated by the circumstance that importation of Argentine beef was ham-1ered by United States customs rulings that Argentine cattle suffered from foot-1nd-mouth disease. Opposition of cattle-raisers accounted for the Senate's failure 1 advise and consent to ratification of a convention relating to sanitary regula-1ons concerning plant and animal products signed May 24, 1935 [6] and since 1en pending in the Senate.

Argentine export trade is principally in agricultural products and with the 1strictions due to the outbreak of war in Europe in 1939, Argentine economy 1as seriously affected. Tension resulted from the continued narrowness of the 1arket for Argentine products in the United States. Negotiations for a trade 1greement proposed August 23, 1939 were discontinued January 8, 1940 for 1easons given by both Governments in announcing their failure.[7] A fresh notice

[1] For full information, including list of products on which the United States will 1nsider granting concessions to Iceland, see Department of State, *Bulletin*, V, p. 411.

[2] For information as above, see *ibid.*, VI, p. 287.

[3] For information as above, see *ibid.*, p. 278, 327, 373. In the case of Mexico, two 1pplementary lists have been issued.

[4] Department of State Release No. 494; a full analysis of the general provisions and 1eciprocal benefits, together with detailed statistical data concerning the items 1ffected, trade experience therewith and tabulated reductions was published as 1epartment of State, *Bulletin*, V, No. 121 A (October 18, 1941, Supplement), 1ublication 1656. See also Macgowan, H. P., "The Trade Agreement with Argen-1ina," *Foreign Commerce Weekly*, V, No. 4 (October 25, 1941), p. 8. For the exchanges 1f messages between the Presidents and other officials of Argentina and the United 1tates at the signing of the agreement, see Department of State, *Bulletin*, V, p. 300.

[5] *Treaties, Conventions, etc.*, 1776–1909, I, p. 20.

[6] Executive O, 74th Cong., 1st sess.

[7] *Documents, II, 1939–40*, p. 471–81.

of intention to negotiate was issued May 13, 1941 [1] and the agreement wa concluded on October 14. Due to special conditions prevailing in Argentina an the requirements of our defense policy, the agreement contained certain uniqu provisions which are explained in the Department of State commentary.

The text of the agreement and two exchanges of notes are reprinted. Tw additional exchanges of notes dealing with the placement of sundry items in th Argentine tariffs for the purposes of Schedule I and with the marketing of Ar gentine fresh pears in the United States are not reprinted.

The President of the United States of America and the Vice Presiden of the Argentine Nation in the exercise of the Executive Power, bein, desirous of strengthening the traditional bonds of friendship existin, between the two countries through the maintenance of the principle c equal treatment in its unconditional and unlimited form as the basi of commercial relations and through the granting of mutual and recip rocal concessions for the promotion of trade, have resolved to conclud a Trade Agreement so providing and have appointed for this purpos as their Plenipotentiaries:

The President of the United States of America:

> Norman Armour, *Ambassador Extraordinary and Plenipoten tiary of the United States of America to the Argentine Republic* and

The Vice President of the Argentine Nation in the exercise of th Executive Power:

> His Excellency Señor Doctor Don Enrique Ruiz Guiñazú *Minister of Foreign Affairs and Worship;*

Who, after having exchanged their full powers, found to be in goo and due form, have agreed upon the following provisions:

ARTICLE I.[2] 1. The United States of America and the Argentin Republic will grant each other unconditional and unrestricted most favored-nation treatment in all matters concerning customs duties an subsidiary charges of every kind and in the method of levying duties and, further, in all matters concerning the rules, formalities and charge imposed in connection with the clearing of goods through the customs and with respect to all laws or regulations affecting the sale or use o imported goods within the country.

2. Accordingly, articles the growth, produce or manufacture of eithe country imported into the other shall in no case be subject, in regard t

---

[1] *Documents, III, 1940–41*, p. 459. The list of products under consideration may b consulted in Department of State, *Bulletin*, IV, p. 680.

[2] For agreement as to application of this article, see exchange of notes betwee the Argentine Minister of Foreign Affairs and the American Ambassador at tim of signature, this volume, p. 704.

the matters referred to above, to any duties, taxes or charges other or
higher, or to any rules or formalities other or more burdensome, than
those to which the like articles the growth, produce or manufacture
of any third country are or may hereafter be subject.

3. Similarly, articles exported from the territory of the United States
of America or the Argentine Republic and consigned to the territory of
the other country shall in no case be subject with respect to exportation
and in regard to the above-mentioned matters, to any duties, taxes or
charges other or higher, or to any rules or formalities other or more
burdensome, than those to which the like articles when consigned to the
territory of any third country are or may hereafter be subject.

4. Any advantage, favor, privilege or immunity which has been or
may hereafter be granted by the United States of America or the Argentine Republic in regard to the above-mentioned matters, to any article
originating in any third country or consigned to the territory of any third
country shall be accorded immediately and without compensation to
the like article originating in or consigned to the territory of the Argentine Republic or the United States of America, respectively.

ARTICLE II.[1] 1. Articles the growth, produce or manufacture of the
United States of America or the Argentine Republic, shall, after importation into the other country, be exempt from all internal taxes, fees,
charges or exactions other or higher than those payable on like articles
of national origin or of any other foreign origin.

2. The provisions of this Article relating to national treatment shall
not apply to taxes imposed by the Argentine Republic on alcohols,
alcoholic beverages, beers, natural mineral waters, and fabrics containing
40 per centum or more of silk or artificial silk.

ARTICLE III.[1] 1. No prohibition or restriction of any kind shall be
imposed by the Government of either country on the importation of any
article the growth, produce or manufacture of the other country or upon
the exportation of any article destined for the other country, unless the
importation of the like article the growth, produce or manufacture of
all third countries, or the exportation of the like article to all third
countries, respectively, is similarly prohibited or restricted.

2. No restriction of any kind shall be imposed by the Government of
either country on the importation from the other country of any article
in which that country has an interest, whether by means of import
licenses or permits or otherwise, unless the total quantity or value of
such article permitted to be imported during a specified period, or any

---

[1] See p. 696, n. 2.

change in such quantity or value, shall have been established and made public. If the Government of either country allots a share of such total quantity or value to any third country, it shall allot to the other country a share equivalent to the proportion of the total imports of such article supplied by that country during a previous representative period, and shall make such share available so as to facilitate its full utilization unless it is mutually agreed to dispense with such allotment. No limitation or restriction of any kind other than such an allotment shall be imposed, by means of import licenses or permits or otherwise, on the share of such total quantity or value which may be imported from the other country.

3. The provisions of the preceding paragraph shall apply in respect of the quantity or value of any article permitted to be imported at a specified rate of duty.

ARTICLE IV.[1] 1. If the Government of either country establishes or maintains any form of control of the means of international payment it shall accord unconditional most-favored-nation treatment to the commerce of the other country with respect to all aspects of such control.

2. The Government establishing or maintaining such control shall impose no prohibition, restriction or delay on the transfer of payment for any article the growth, produce or manufacture of the other country which is not imposed on the transfer of payment for the like article the growth, produce or manufacture of any third country. With respect to rates of exchange and with respect to taxes or charges on exchange transactions, articles the growth, produce or manufacture of the other country shall be accorded unconditionally treatment no less favorable than that accorded to the like articles the growth, produce or manufacture of any third country. The foregoing provisions shall also extend to the application of such control to payments necessary for or incidental to the importation of articles the growth, produce or manufacture of the other country. In general, the control shall be administered so as not to influence to the disadvantage of the other country the competitive relationships between articles the growth, produce or manufacture of the territories of that country and like articles the growth, produce or manufacture of third countries.

3. Notwithstanding any of the provisions of paragraphs 1 and 2 of this Article, the Government of each country may adopt such measures as it may deem necessary for the protection of its essential interests in time of war or other national emergency.

[1] See p. 696, n. 2.

ARTICLE V. 1. In the event that the Government of the United States of America or the Government of the Argentine Republic establishes or maintains a monopoly for the importation, production or sale of a particular article or grants exclusive privileges, formally or in effect, to one or more agencies to import, produce or sell a particular article, the commerce of the other country shall receive fair and equitable treatment in respect of the foreign purchases of such monopoly or agency. To this end such monopoly or agency will, in making its foreign purchases of any article, be influenced solely by considerations, such as those of price, quality, marketability and terms of sale, which would ordinarily be taken into account by a private commercial enterprise interested solely in purchasing on the most favorable terms.

2. The Government of each country, in the awarding of contracts for public works and generally in the purchase of supplies, shall accord fair and equitable treatment to the commerce of the other country as compared with the treatment accorded to the commerce of other foreign countries.

ARTICLE VI. 1. Laws, regulations of administrative authorities and decisions of administrative or judicial authorities of the United States of America or the Argentine Republic, respectively, pertaining to the classification of articles for customs purposes or to rates of duty shall be published promptly in such manner as to enable traders to become acquainted with them.

2. No administrative ruling by the United States of America or the Argentine Republic effecting advances in rates of duties or in charges applicable under an established and uniform practice to imports originating in the territory of the other country, or imposing any new requirement with respect to such importations, shall be effective retroactively or with respect to articles either entered for consumption or withdrawn for consumption prior to the date of publication of notice of such ruling in the usual official manner. The provisions of this paragraph do not apply to administrative orders imposing antidumping duties, or relating to regulations for the protection of human, animal or plant life or health, or relating to public safety, or giving effect to judicial decisions.

ARTICLE VII. 1. Articles the growth, produce or manufacture of the United States of America, enumerated and described in Schedule I annexed [1] to this Agreement and made an integral part thereof, on their importation into the Argentine Republic, if now exempt from ordinary customs duties, shall continue to be so exempt or, if now dutiable, shall

[1] Not here reprinted.

be exempt from ordinary customs duties in excess of those set forth and provided for in the said Schedule, subject to the conditions therein set out.

2. The said articles shall also be exempt from all other duties, taxes, fees, charges or exactions, imposed on or in connection with importation, in excess of those imposed on the day of the signature of this Agreement or required to be imposed thereafter under the laws of the Argentine Republic in force on that day.

ARTICLE VIII. 1. Articles the growth, produce or manufacture of the Argentine Republic, enumerated and described in Schedules II and III [1] annexed to this Agreement and made an integral part thereof, on their importation into the United States of America, if now exempt from ordinary customs duties, shall continue to be so exempt or, if now dutiable, shall be exempt from ordinary customs duties in excess of those set forth and provided for in the said Schedules, subject to the conditions therein set out.

2. The said articles shall also be exempt from all other duties, taxes, fees, charges or exactions, imposed on or in connection with importation, in excess of those imposed on the day of the signature of this Agreement or required to be imposed thereafter under the laws of the United States of America in force on that day.

3. The Government of the United States of America reserves the right to withdraw or to modify the concession granted on any article enumerated and described in Schedule III at any time after the termination of hostilities between the Governments of the United Kingdom and Germany, on giving six months' written notice to the Government of the Argentine Republic.

ARTICLE IX. The provisions of Articles VII and VIII of this Agreement shall not prevent the Government of either country from imposing at any time on the importation of any article a charge equivalent to an internal tax imposed in respect of a like domestic article or in respect of a commodity from which the imported article has been manufactured or produced in whole or in part.

ARTICLE X. In respect of articles the growth, produce or manufacture of the United States of America or the Argentine Republic enumerated and described in Schedule I or in Schedules II or III, respectively, imported into the other country, on which ad valorem rates of duty, or duties based upon or regulated in any manner by value, are or may be assessed, it is understood and agreed that the bases and methods of determining dutiable value and of converting currencies shall be no less

[1] Not here reprinted.

favorable to importers than the bases and methods prescribed under laws and regulations of the Argentine Republic and the United States of America, respectively, in force on the day of the signature of this Agreement.

ARTICLE XI. 1. No prohibition, restriction or any form of quantitative regulation, whether or not operated in connection with any agency of centralized control, shall be imposed by the Argentine Republic on the importation or sale of any article the growth, produce or manufacture of the United States of America enumerated and described in Schedule I, or by the United States of America on the importation or sale of any article the growth, produce or manufacture of the Argentine Republic enumerated and described in Schedules II or III.

2. The foregoing provisions shall not apply to quantitative regulations in whatever form imposed by the United States of America or the Argentine Republic on the importation or sale of any article the growth, produce or manufacture of the other country, in conjunction with governmental measures or measures under governmental authority operating to regulate or control the production, market supply or prices of like domestic articles, or tending to increase the labor costs or production of such articles, or to maintain the exchange value of the currency of the country.

ARTICLE XII. 1. If the Government of either country should consider that any circumstance, or any measure adopted by the other Government, even though it does not conflict with the terms of this Agreement, has the effect of nullifying or impairing any object of the Agreement or of prejudicing an industry or the commerce of that country, such other Government shall give sympathetic consideration to such representations or proposals as may be made with a view to effecting a mutually satisfactory adjustment of the matter. If no agreement is reached with respect to such representations or proposals, the Government making them shall be free to suspend or terminate this Agreement in whole or in part on thirty days' written notice.

2. The Governments of the two countries agree to consult together to the fullest possible extent in regard to all matters affecting the operation of the present Agreement. In order to facilitate such consultation, a Commission consisting of representatives of each Government [1] shall

[1] Establishment of the commission was announced April 22, 1942 (Department of State, *Bulletin*, VI, p. 373). The representatives of the Government of the United States are members of the staff of the American Embassy at Buenos Aires who participated in the negotiation of the agreement; those of the Government of Argentina are members of the Inter-Ministerial Committee. The commission functions as a

be established to study the operation of the Agreement, to make recommendations regarding the fulfillment of the provisions of the Agreement
and to consider such other matters as may be submitted to it by the two
Governments.

ARTICLE XIII. The provisions of this Agreement relating to the
treatment to be accorded by the United States of America and the
Argentine Republic, respectively, to the commerce of the other country
shall apply, on the part of the United States of America, to the continental territory of the United States of America and such of its territories
and possessions as are included in its customs territory. The provisions
of this Agreement relating to most-favored-nation treatment shall apply
furthermore, to all articles the growth, produce or manufacture of any
territory under the sovereignty or authority of the United States of
America or the Argentine Republic, imported from or exported to any
territory under the sovereignty or authority of the other country. The
provisions of this Article shall not apply to the Panama Canal Zone.

ARTICLE XIV. 1. The advantages now accorded or which may hereafter be accorded by the United States of America or the Argentine
Republic to adjacent countries in order to facilitate frontier traffic, and
advantages accorded in virtue of a customs union to which either country
may become a party, shall be excepted from the operation of this
Agreement.

2. The advantages now accorded or which may hereafter be accorded
by the United States of America, its territories or possessions or the
Panama Canal Zone to one another or to the Republic of Cuba shall be
excepted from the operation of this Agreement. The provisions of this
paragraph shall continue to apply in respect of any advantages now or
hereafter accorded by the United States of America, its territories or
possessions or the Panama Canal Zone to one another, irrespective of
any change in the political status of any of the territories or possessions
of the United States of America.

ARTICLE XV. 1. Subject to the requirement that, under like circumstances and conditions, there shall be no arbitrary discrimination by
either country against the other country in favor of any third country

convenient agency for informal discussion of trade-agreement matters of interest to
one or both Governments. It does not supersede in any way the usual diplomatic
channels of communication between the two Governments; nor does it, either as a
joint commission or as separate United States and Argentine commissions, supersede established channels in either country for communication between private individuals or firms and the Government concerned in regard to matters affecting the
trade agreement, or the established organization and procedure for reaching decisions
relating to such matters.

and without prejudice to the provisions of paragraphs 1 and 2 of Article XVI, the provisions of this Agreement shall not extend to prohibitions or restrictions

(a) relative to public security;

(b) imposed for the protection of public health or on moral or humanitarian grounds;

(c) imposed for the protection of plants or animals, including measures for protection against disease, degeneration or extinction as well as measures taken against harmful seeds, plants, or animals;

(d) relating to prison-made goods;

(e) relating to the enforcement of police or revenue laws and regulations; and

(f) imposed for the protection of national treasures of artistic, historic or archaeological value.

2. Nothing in this Agreement shall be construed to prevent the adoption or enforcement of such measures as the Government of either country may see fit (a) relating to the importation or exportation of gold or silver; (b) relating to the control of the export or sale for export of arms, ammunition, or implements of war, and, in exceptional circumstances, all other military supplies; (c) relating to neutrality.

3. It is understood that the provisions of this Agreement relating to laws and regulations affecting the sale, taxation or use of imported articles within the United States of America and the Argentine Republic are subject to the constitutional limitations on the authority of the Governments of the respective countries.

ARTICLE XVI. 1. The Government of each country will accord sympathetic consideration to, and when requested will afford adequate opportunity for consultation regarding such representations as the other Government may make with respect to the operation of customs regulations, quantitative regulations or the administration thereof, the observance of customs formalities, and the application of sanitary laws and regulations for the protection of human, animal or plant life or health.

2. In the event that the Government of either country makes representations to the other Government in respect of the application of any sanitary law or regulation for the protection of human, animal or plant life or health, and if there is disagreement with respect thereto, a committee of technical experts on which each Government shall be represented shall, on the request of either Government, be established to consider the matter and to submit recommendations to the two Governments.

ARTICLE XVII. This Agreement shall be proclaimed by the President of the United States of America and shall be ratified by the Government of the Argentine Republic. It shall enter definitively into force thirty days after the exchange of the instrument of ratification and the proclamation, which shall take place in Washington as soon as possible.

ARTICLE XVIII. Pending the definitive coming into force of this Agreement as provided in Article XVII, the provisions thereof shall be applied provisionally on and after November 15, 1941, subject to a right to terminate the provisional application of the Agreement pursuant to the provisions of paragraph 1 of Article XII or upon six months' written notice.

ARTICLE XIX. Subject to the provisions of paragraph 1 of Article XII, and of Article XVIII, this Agreement shall remain in force until November 15, 1944, and, unless at least six months before November 15, 1944, the Government of either country shall have given notice in writing to the other Government of intention to terminate the Agreement on that date, it shall remain in force thereafter until the expiration of six months from the date on which such notice shall have been given.

IN WITNESS WHEREOF the respective Plenipotentiaries have signed this Agreement and have affixed hereto their seals.

DONE in duplicate, in the English and Spanish languages, both authentic, at the City of Buenos Aires, this 14th day of October, 1941.

For the President of the United States of America:

NORMAN ARMOUR

For the Vice President of the Argentine Republic in the exercise of the Executive Power:

E. RUIZ GUIÑAZÚ

[Schedules I, II and III omitted.]

(a) *The Minister of Foreign Affairs of Argentina (Ruiz Guiñazú) to the American Ambassador at Buenos Aires (Armour), October 14, 1941* [1]

[Translation]

MR. AMBASSADOR:

I have the honor to refer to the conversations between representatives of the Argentine Government and the Government of the United States of America, in connection with the Trade Agreement signed this day in regard to trade relations between Argentina and contiguous countries

---

[1] The confirmatory note of the exchange is not here reprinted.

During the course of these conversations the Argentine representatives ave indicated that their Government intends to promote the development of reciprocal trade between the countries of this hemisphere, specially the neighboring countries, and to improve the internal economic conditions through the encouragement of domestic and foreign investments in new industries well adapted to the resources and possibilities of the country and have referred to the purpose of the Argentine Government in pursuance of the above to promote tariff reductions between Argentina and contiguous countries with a view to the gradual and ultimate achievement of a customs union among such countries.

The Argentine and Brazilian Ministers of Finance have recently agreed on the bases of such arrangements and have submitted them to the consideration of their respective Governments. Moreover, pursuant to Resolution LXXX of the Seventh Conference of the American States at Montevideo approved December 24, 1933, the Argentine and Brazilian representatives on the Inter-American Financial and Economic Advisory Committee submitted jointly to that Committee for consideration a contractual formula for tariff preferences to contiguous countries, and on September 18, 1941, the Committee recommended that any such tariff preferences, in order to be an instrument for sound promotion of trade, should be made effective through trade agreements embodying tariff reductions or exemptions; that the parties to such agreements should reserve the right to reduce or eliminate the customs duties on like imports from other countries; and that any such regional tariff preferences should not be permitted to stand in the way of any broad program of economic reconstruction involving the reduction of tariffs and the scaling down or elimination of tariff and other trade preferences with a view to the fullest possible development of international trade on a multilateral unconditional most-favored-nation basis.

The representatives of the Argentine Government have also referred to the special facilities other than tariff preferences which have been accorded to the commerce of contiguous countries and Peru in an effort to mitigate the serious effects of the curtailment of overseas markets as a result of the European conflict, and have pointed out that until such time as the present hostilities between the Governments of the United Kingdom and Germany are terminated, such special facilities must be continued.

The conversations to which I have referred have disclosed a mutual understanding which is as follows:

(1) The Government of the United States will not invoke the provisions of Article I of the Trade Agreement signed this day for the

purpose of obtaining the benefit of tariff preferences meeting the require
ments of the aforementioned formula recommended by the Inter-Amer
can Financial and Economic Advisory Committee which Argentin
may accord to a contiguous country, it being understood that if an
such preference should be extended by Argentina to any noncontiguou
country it would be extended immediately and unconditionally to th
United States; (2) the Government of the United States will not invok
the provisions of Articles III and IV of the Trade Agreement for th
purpose of obtaining the benefit of any exchange or quota preferenc(
accorded by Argentina to contiguous countries and Peru on the unde:
standing that such preferences shall cease when the present hostiliti(
between the Governments of the United Kingdom and Germany sha
have terminated, except as may be otherwise agreed upon by the Goverr
ments of the United States and the Argentine Republic upon the recon
mendation of the mixed commission provided for in the second paragrap
of Article XII of the Trade Agreement.

Accept, Mr. Ambassador, the renewed assurances of my highe:
consideration.

(b) *The Minister of Foreign Affairs of Argentina (Ruiz Guiñazú) to th
American Ambassador at Buenos Aires (Armour), Octob(
14, 1941* [1]

[Translation]

Mr. Ambassador:

I have the honor to refer to the discussions during the course of tł
negotiations of the Trade Agreement between our two Governmen
signed this day regarding the provisions of the Agreement which provic
for nondiscriminatory treatment by each country of the trade of tł
other.

During the negotiation of the Agreement, the representatives of tł
United States Government have emphasized the great importance whic
that Government attaches to these provisions. The representatives (
the Argentine Government have stated, on their part, that their Gover
ment likewise attaches great importance to these provisions and to tł
principle of unconditional most-favored-nation treatment which unde
lies them. They have pointed out that this principle is the basis (
Argentine commercial policy, which has for its objective the develo)
ment of Argentine foreign trade on a multilateral basis.

The representatives of the Argentine Government have also point(
out that the ability of Argentina to give full effect to these principl(

[1] The exchanged letter taking note of the assurance given is not here reprinted.

dependent on circumstances beyond the control of Argentina.
Recently, the Argentine trade and payments position has been aggra-
ated to a very important extent by the trade and financial controls
which have been adopted by the belligerents in the present European
onflict, notably the United Kingdom, one of the principal markets for
Argentine export products. In particular, the inability of Argentina
o convert freely into dollars the proceeds of sales to the United Kingdom
makes it impossible for the Argentine Government to extend full non-
iscriminatory treatment to the trade of the United States of America.

The representatives of the Argentine Government have accordingly
tated in the negotiations that the acceptance by the Argentine Govern-
ent of the provisions of the Trade Agreement relating to nondis-
riminatory treatment must be qualified by the practical limitations
which are imposed on the Argentine Government's freedom of action
y the circumstances to which I have referred. However, they have
ssured the representatives of the United States Government that,
ubject to the practical limitations imposed by the existing payments
rrangement in effect between Argentina and the United Kingdom,
he Argentine Government will at all times give the fullest possible
ffect to the provisions under reference. They have further assured
he representatives of the United States Government that, as soon as
becomes possible for Argentina to convert its sterling balances into
ree currencies, the Argentine Government will give full effect to those
rovisions.

The representatives of the Argentine Government expressed the hope
hat the reconstruction of world economy after the war would create
avorable conditions that would enable Argentina to participate in an
ctive interchange with other nations within a liberal system in which
he barriers, which in recent times handicapped its normal development,
ave been eliminated.

Accept, Mr. Ambassador, the renewed assurances of my highest
onsideration.

) **Release of the Department of State, October 14, 1941** [1]

[Excerpt]

A reciprocal trade agreement between the United States and Argentina
as signed October 14, 1941 at Buenos Aires by Norman Armour,
mbassador Extraordinary and Plenipotentiary of the United States
America to the Argentine Republic, and His Excellency Señor Dr. Don

[1] Department of State, *Bulletin*, V, p. 297.

Enrique Ruiz-Guiñazú, Minister of Foreign Affairs and Worship of th
Argentine Nation.

This agreement, which is designed to improve trade relations betwee
the two countries during the present emergency and after the wa
represents a significant forward step in the carrying out of the broa
program of cooperation between the democracies of the Western Hem
sphere.

As a result of the agreement, American exporters of many product
will benefit from the duty reductions, and assurances against dut
increases, specifically provided for in Schedule I and a related not
Furthermore, exchange will be made available, at least in limite
amounts in accordance with Argentina's exchange availabilities, fc
every product listed in Schedule I of the agreement as well as man
products not listed in that schedule.

American exporters to Argentina will benefit generally from impo:
tant assurances contained in the general provisions of the agreemen
Prominent among these is the general assurance against discriminator
tariff, exchange, or quota treatment; in other words, the general assu
ance of unconditional most-favored-nation treatment. The only speci:
exceptions to this assurance are dealt with in two exchanges of note
one of which provides in substance that during the present emergenc
and so long as the proceeds of Argentine exports to the United Kingdo:
are blocked by that country, the Government of the United State
will not invoke the most-favored-nation provisions of the agreement i
respect of Argentine exchange or quota treatment of imports from tl
sterling area; and the other of which relates to Argentina's special trac
relations with contiguous countries and Peru.

To the extent that the agreement facilitates an increase in Argentir
exports to the United States, Argentina's purchasing power for man
products needed from the United States, including some things n
now obtainable from Europe, will be increased. Such increased pu
chasing power will benefit American exporters, and at the same tin
increased supplies from Argentina will benefit American consumers an
American industries dependent upon imported materials. Nevertheles
if, as a result of the concession granted, imports of a particular produ
should enter in such quantities and under such conditions as to threate
serious injury to domestic producers, appropriate action could be take
to remedy the situation.

· · · · · · · ·

The tariff concessions obtained include benefits for United State
exports in the form of reductions in, or bindings against increase c

rgentine customs duties on a list of 127 tariff items covering products hich in 1940 accounted for about 30% of total United States exports Argentina, or 32 out of 106 million dollars. Among these conces- ons are those benefiting American exports to Argentina of fresh oples, pears, grapes, raisins, prunes, tobacco, motor vehicles and parts, itomatic refrigerators, certain items of electrical machinery and oparatus, agricultural and industrial machinery, office appliances, and rest products.

In return, Argentina is granted reductions in duties or assurances of ie continuance of existing tariff treatment on a list of 84 tariff items overing products which in 1938 and 1939 accounted for about 93% of tal United States imports from Argentina and in 1940 accounted for out 75% of such imports. The principal concessions include tariff ductions on flaxseed, canned corned beef, coarse wools, quebracho :tract, casein, tallow, oleo oil and oleo stearin, cattle hides, Italian-type ieeses, and binding on the free list of a considerable number of products, cluding furs and skins and various animal by-products.

In part because of existing abnormal conditions affecting international ade, the agreement contains certain special provisions not previously cluded in trade agreements negotiated under the authority of the rade Agreements Act. Among these are the following:

(1) Provision for consultation regarding all matters affecting the oeration of the agreement through the medium of a mixed commission onsisting of representatives of each Government;

(2) A separate schedule of concessions (Schedule III) granted by the nited States to Argentina on a list of products (principally wines and queurs, Italian-type cheeses, macaroni and similar products, and nflower oil) in respect of which previous principal sources of supply e curtailed because of the war and which accordingly are made subject modification or termination by the United States on six months' tice at any time after the termination of hostilities between the nited Kingdom and Germany; and

(3) Provision that a specified proportion of the full tariff reductions anted by Argentina to the United States (Schedule I) shall not become fective until Argentine customs revenue from imports again equals, a calendar year, at least 270 million paper pesos, which amount proximates the annual average customs revenue in the 10-year period 31–40 and is about 40 million pesos higher than the receipts in 1940.

The United States and Argentina are important markets for each her's products, and the concessions made by the two countries in the reement cover a substantial proportion of that trade. The volume and

value of the trade have fluctuated widely, largely with changes i
tariffs and other trade restrictions and, since many products importe
from Argentina are raw materials used by United States industrie
with the level of industrial activity in the United States.

A high level of trade between the two countries was reached in tł
1920's, with 1929 the peak year. The value declined abruptly after tł
enactment of·our Tariff Act of 1930 and during the depression of tł
early 1930's. It recovered somewhat, with industrial recovery in tł
United States, from a low point in 1932 to almost pre-depression leve
in 1937, but suffered another check in 1938 with the industrial recessic
in this country. Since 1938 the value of the trade has risen each yea
in 1940 and 1941 partly because of the effects of the European war.

The annual average combined value of United States exports to Arge
tina and imports from that country during the five-year period 1925–
was 265 million dollars, with a high of 328 million dollars in 1929. I
the period 1930–34 the annual average was only 96 million dollars, ar
a low of 47 million was reached in 1932. During the next five years, 193
39, the annual average was 146 million dollars, and in 1940 the figu
was 190 million dollars. In the first six months of 1941 total trade betwe
the two countries amounted to more than 119 million dollars.

United States exports to Argentina

United States exports to Argentina have fluctuated somewhat le
widely than have imports from that country, yet they have ranged fro
a value of 31.1 million dollars in 1932 to a high of 210.3 million in 192
In the past decade they have not reached the levels attained in 1925–2
when they averaged 169 million dollars a year. In 1930–34 the annu
average was 58.7 million dollars, and in 1935–39 it moved upward to 71
million. In 1940 United States exports to Argentina were valued
107 million dollars, and in the first six months of 1941, 37 million dolla

United States imports from Argentina

Imports into the United States from Argentina have ranged in val
from a low of 15.8 million dollars in 1932 to a high of 138.9 million
1937, when imports of Argentine agricultural products to replace
part the crops destroyed by drought in the United States were unusua
large. The annual average value of United States imports in 1925–
was 96.5 million dollars. This average declined to 37.4 million doll
in 1930–34 and rose to 74.6 million in 1935–39. The value of Unit
States imports from Argentina was 83.3 million dollars in 1940 a
82.4 million dollars in the first six months of 1941.

eneral excess of exports over imports in trade with Argentina

Except in three years of the period 1925–40, the value of United States xports to Argentina has exceeded the value of imports from that coun- ry. The three exceptional years were 1935, 1936, and 1937, when the nited States imported unusually large quantities of agricultural prod- cts because of the droughts in this country. In the period 1925–29 the nnual average export balance of the United States in its trade with rgentina was 72.5 million dollars. In the five years 1930–34 the balance eclined to an annual average of 21.3 million dollars as the total trade olume reached low levels. In 1935–39, very largely because of the ree exceptional years of import balances, there was an average annual nport balance of 2.9 million dollars.

In 1940 the value of United States exports to Argentina exceeded the alue of imports from that country by 23.6 million dollars, but for the rst six months of 1941 the United States had an import balance of 5 million dollars.

nited States share of Argentine exports and imports

In 1929 and 1930 the United States supplied a greater share of imports to Argentina than did any other country, the United Kingdom being econd. But from 1931 through 1939 the United States took second lace and the United Kingdom first. In 1940 this country again exceeded l other countries as a source of imports into Argentina. Throughout the eriod 1929–40 the United Kingdom and other European countries took e major part of the exports of Argentina. However, the United States nked second in six of these years. In the first six months of 1941, the nited States took first place as a market for Argentine products.

3. TRADE AGREEMENT WITH THE SOVIET UNION

The commercial agreement between the United States and the Soviet Union hich became effective on a year-to-year basis on August 6, 1937(*Documents, I,* 38–39, p. 383; *II, 1939–40,* p. 492; *III, 1940–41,* p. 469) was renewed for other year August 2, 1941, under conditions entirely different from those hich had existed. The German attack launched on June 22, 1941, made the oviet Union eligible for aid under the Lend-Lease Act and the character and mount of total trade with the Soviet Union were governed during the agree- ent year largely by the defense needs of the United States, the Soviet Union d other countries struggling against the forces of armed aggression, rather than y the usual commercial considerations. The exchange of notes was designed to sure the continuance during the emergency period of established commercial lations with the Soviet Union on the basis of the 1937 commercial agreement.

The following table [1] gives the value in dollars of exports to and imports fro: the Soviet Union in the agreement years:

Agreement Year (Beginning August)	U. S. Domestic Exports to U.S.S.R. (In Thousands of U. S. Dollars)	U. S. Imports for Con sumption from U.S.S.F (In Thousands of U. S Dollars)
1935–36	33,286	21,200
1936–37	30,987	23,240
1937–38	64,338	22,874
1938–39	50,160	24,739
1939–40	73,636	24,773
1940–41 (10 months) [2]	57,481	22,710

(1) *Exchange of Notes between the Acting Secretary of State (Welle:
and the Soviet Ambassador at Washington (Oumansky), Augu
2, 1941* [3]

Excellency:

In accordance with the conversations which have taken place, I hav the honor to confirm on behalf of my Government the agreement whic has been reached between the Governments of our respective countri that the agreement regarding commercial relations between the Unite States of America and the Union of Soviet Socialist Republics recorde in the exchange of notes of August 4, 1937,[4] between the Ambassador the United States of America at Moscow and the People's Commissar fo Foreign Affairs of the Union of Soviet Socialist Republics, which can into force on August 6, 1937, on the date of proclamation thereof by th President of the United States of America and approval thereof by th Council of People's Commissars of the Union of Soviet Socialist Repul lics and which was renewed on August 5, 1938, August 2, 1939, ar August 6, 1940, shall continue in force until August 6, 1942.

The present agreement shall be proclaimed by the President of th United States of America and approved by the Council of People Commissars of the Union of Soviet Socialist Republics.

Accept [etc.]

[1] Source: Official records of the United States Department of Commerce.
[2] Preliminary data for the 10 months, August 1940 through May 1941.
[3] Department of State, *Bulletin*, V, p. 116. The proposing note is printed ther This is the confirming note.
[4] Executive Agreement Series 105; *Documents, I, 1938–39*, p. 384.

4. REGULATION BY INTERNATIONAL AGREEMENT OF THE PRODUCTION AND MARKETING OF WHEAT

The existence for several years of large wheat surpluses, the threat of disorganization and confusion at the end of the war, and the necessity of facing up to the problem of feeding large undernourished populations in the war areas once the fighting is over have combined to make the wheat problem one transcending purely national lines. The Washington meeting was an important step toward the conclusion, as soon as circumstances permit, of a comprehensive wheat agreement.

The Washington Wheat Meeting comprised officials of five of the ten countries which participated in the work of the Preparatory Committee established by the International Wheat Advisory Committee at London in January 1939. The work of the Preparatory Committee was near completion when war broke out in September 1939. The war aggravated in several important respects the world wheat problem, and, following an exchange of views between their Governments, officials of Argentina, Australia, Canada, the United Kingdom, and the United States met in Washington on July 10, 1941,[1] to resume the discussions which were interrupted by the outbreak of war. They submitted to their Governments preliminary report in August 1941,[2] reconvened in October, and have met at frequent intervals since then to carry on their discussions.[3]

The Memorandum of Agreement now concluded provides for the convening by the United States, when the time is deemed propitious, of a conference of all the nations having a substantial interest in wheat, whether as consumers or producers; and there is attached to it for consideration at that conference a Draft Convention prepared by the Washington Wheat Meeting. In the meantime the Memorandum of Agreement requires the adoption and maintenance on the part of the four exporting countries of positive measures to control production with the object of minimizing the accumulation of excessive stocks during the war.

The approval of the five Governments was notified by the Government of the United States to the other four Governments on June 27, 1942, and, in accordance with the minutes of the final session of the Washington Wheat Meeting, the provisions of the Memorandum of Agreement came into effect on that date.

a) Final Communiqué of the International Wheat Meeting, Washington, August 4, 1941 [4]

The representatives of Argentina, Australia, Canada, the United Kingdom and the United States of America who have been considering world wheat problems in Washington since the tenth of July recessed on the third of August to meet again on the eighteenth of August. A provisional draft agreement is being submitted to the Governments forthwith, together with a request for instructions which will enable the delegates to prepare a definitive text when they reconvene.

The range of the wheat discussions has been considerably wider than hitherto. The problems of furnishing post-war relief to countries which

[1] Department of State, *Bulletin*, V, p. 23.
[2] See the final communiqué given below.
[3] Department of State, *Bulletin*, V, p. 302.
[4] *Ibid.*, p. 116.

have suffered from the devastation of war occupied a prominent place
in the agenda. The need for an equitable sharing of world markets to
avoid cut-throat competition was fully considered as a new phase of an
old problem. Stocks available for export at the end of July 1941
amounted to about two years' normal requirements of imported wheat
and, in consequence, the representatives of the exporting countries
have been compelled to face the necessity of controlling production in
order to prevent stocks from continuing to rise above their present
record high level.

The representatives have recognized that when the war is over
European agriculture will be distorted, livestock herds will be severely
reduced by the acute shortage of feed grains, farm equipment will be
dilapidated, and, in consequence, there will be urgent need and oppor
tunity for reconstruction.

The advance of knowledge about the relationship of food to health
suggests that this reconstruction should result in the provision for each
country of diets more adequate for health and happiness, thus improving
upon pre-war conditions.

Much progress has been made in the consideration of all these prob
lems in the hope that by the establishment of an ever-normal granary
and of a large pool of relief wheat, the consumers of the world may be
guaranteed abundant post-war supplies at prices reasonable both to
them and to producers and free of charge to those in need of relief

(2) *Memorandum of Agreement, approved by the Governments of
Argentina, Australia, Canada, the United Kingdom and the United
States, Washington, April 22, 1942* [1]

1. Officials of Argentina, Australia, Canada and the United States
wheat exporting countries, and of the United Kingdom, a wheat import
ing country, met in Washington on July 10, 1941 to resume the wheat
discussions which were interrupted in London by the outbreak of war
in September 1939 and to consider what steps might be taken toward
a solution of the international wheat problem.

2. The discussions at Washington, which extended over a period of
many months, have made it clear that a satisfactory solution of the prob
lem requires an international wheat agreement and that such an agree
ment requires a conference of the nations willing to participate which
have a substantial interest in international trade in wheat. It was also
recognized that pending the holding of such a conference the situation
should not be allowed to deteriorate. The Washington Wheat Meeting

[1] *Ibid.*, VII, p. 582.

1as recorded the results of its deliberations in the attached Draft Convention [1] in order to facilitate further international consideration of the subject at such time as may be possible and to provide a basis for such nterim measures as may be found necessary.

3. The Washington Wheat Meeting has recognized that it is impracticable to convene at the present time the international wheat conference eferred to above. Accordingly, the five countries present at that Meeting have agreed that the United States, so soon as after consulation with other countries it deems the time propitious, should convene wheat conference of the nations having a substantial interest in interational trade in wheat which are willing to participate, and that the Draft Convention above mentioned should be submitted to that conerence for consideration.

4. In the meantime there should be no delay in the provision of wheat for relief in war-stricken and other necessitous areas so soon as in he view of the five countries circumstances permit. Likewise it is mperative that the absence of control measures over the accumulation f stocks in the four countries now producing large quantities of wheat or markets no longer available should not create insoluble problems for future conference. Accordingly, the five countries have agreed to egard as in effect among themselves, pending the conclusions of the onference referred to above, those arrangements described in the ttached Draft Convention [1] which are necessary to the administration nd distribution of the relief pool of wheat and to the control of producion of wheat other than those involving the control of exports.

5. If the conference contemplated above shall have met and concluded n agreement prior to the cessation of hostilities, no further action will e needed by the countries represented at the Washington Meeting. owever, if this is not the case, it will be necessary, in order to prevent sorganization and confusion in international trade in wheat, to institute mporary controls pending the conclusions of the conference. Accordgly the five countries agree that in the period following the cessation hostilities and pending the conclusion of a wheat agreement at the onference referred to the arrangements described in the attached raft Convention [1] which relate to the control of production, stocks and ports of wheat and to the administration thereof will be brought into fect among themselves. Those arrangements will come into effect such date as may be unanimously agreed. Announcement of that te will be made within six months after the cessation of hostilities.

[1] The text of the Draft Convention, because of its tentative character and length, not reprinted; see *ibid.*, p. 584.

6. Pending the conclusions of the conference contemplated above, the five countries, on the cessation of hostilities or such earlier date as they may agree, will regard as in effect among themselves the arrangements described in the attached Draft Convention [1] for the control of the price of wheat. The determination of prices required to be made in accordance with those arrangements will be made by unanimous consent. If no determination of prices has been made in the cessation of hostilities, the five countries will, pending such determination but for a period not exceeding six months, maintain as the export price of wheat the last price negotiated by the United Kingdom for a bulk purchase of wheat from the principal country of supply; equivalent f.o.b. prices will be calculated for wheats of the other exporting countries and will be adjusted from time to time to meet substantial changes in freight and exchange rates.

7. In taking any decisions under this Memorandum and the arrangements of the Draft Convention which it brings into operation each of the five countries will have one vote and a two-thirds majority will be required for decision except as otherwise provided herein.

8. The provisions of this Memorandum will be superseded by an agreement reached at the proposed wheat conference or by any arrangements which the five countries and other interested countries may make to deal with the period pending such a conference. In any event they are to terminate two years from the cessation of hostilities.

<table>
<tr><td>A. M. V.</td><td>H. F. C.</td></tr>
<tr><td>For Argentina</td><td>For the United Kingdom</td></tr>
<tr><td>E. McC.</td><td>L. A. W.</td></tr>
<tr><td>For Australia</td><td>For the United States</td></tr>
<tr><td>C. F. W.</td><td></td></tr>
<tr><td>For Canada</td><td></td></tr>
</table>

(a) *Minutes of the Final Session of the Washington Wheat Meeting April 22, 1942* [2]

The officials of the five countries participating in the Washington Wheat Meeting record as follows their understanding regarding certain provisions of the Memorandum of Agreement entered into pursuant that Meeting:

1. The arrangements referred to in paragraph 4 of the Memorandum relating to the relief pool of wheat and to the control of production

[1] *Ibid.*   [2] *Ibid.*, p. 594.

mean the following provisions of the Draft Convention attached thereto: paragraph 3 of Article II (Production Control), Articles VI (Relief Pool), VII (The Council) except paragraph 6, X (Finance), XVII Definitions) and, should the Council at any time so decide, Article VIII The Executive Committee).

2. The arrangements referred to in paragraph 5 of the Memorandum, relating to the control of production, stocks and exports and to the administration thereof, mean the following provisions of the Draft Convention, in addition to Articles VII (except paragraph 6), VIII, X and XVII referred to above: paragraphs 1 and 2 of Article II (Production Control), Article III (Stocks), Article IV (Export Control) except the provisions of paragraphs 10 and 12 relating to the obligations of importing countries since those provisions are not regarded as essential to the interim measures contemplated in the Memorandum, Article IX Reports to the Council) and Article XVI (Territories).

3. The words "cessation of hostilities" in the Memorandum mean the earliest date at which none of the five countries is engaged in substantial belligerent operations.

4. The words "arrangements described in the attached Draft Convention" in paragraph 6 of the Memorandum mean the provisions of Article V of the Draft Convention.

5. The words "equivalent f.o.b. prices" which will be calculated for wheats of the other exporting countries under paragraph 6 of the Memorandum mean the prices of Argentine, Australian and United States wheats which will be ascertained by the unanimous vote of the Council as equivalent to the last price negotiated by the United Kingdom for a bulk purchase of wheat from Canada.

6. The seat of the Council will be in Washington during the period which the Memorandum of Agreement is in force, unless the Council would otherwise determine.

7. The Minutes of the Washington Wheat Meeting, together with the reports of its Committees, will be available for the information of the Council during the period in which the Memorandum of Agreement is in force.

8. The English texts of the Memorandum of Agreement and of the present Minutes have been initialled by Anselmo M. Viacava, Edwin McCarthy, Charles F. Wilson, Harold F. Carlill, and Leslie A. Wheeler, officials of Argentina, Australia, Canada, the United Kingdom and the United States respectively, as competent experts in a position to reflect the views of their respective Governments. The Memorandum, the Draft Convention and the present Minutes will be transmitted in English

and Spanish by the Government of the United States to the other fou
Governments for their approval. So soon as the approval of the fiv
Governments has been notified to each of them the provisions of th
Memorandum of Agreement will be deemed to come into effect and th
Memorandum of Agreement together with the Draft Conventio
attached thereto and the present Minutes will be made public.

[Initialled as above.]

5. EXPORT CONTROL

[See *Documents, II, 1939–40*, p. 786–801, and *III, 1940–41*, p. 473–98, for th
establishment and evolution until July 1, 1941 of the system of export control unde
sec. 6 of the Act of July 2, 1940.]

Since July 1, 1941 the system of export control has been expanded and con
solidated to keep pace with rapidly changing conditions. It has become mor
important from month to month. The original effect of the legislation was t
rescind the rule of impartiality in neutral trade with belligerents. The syster
has since been employed to supervise the commodities, quantity and directio
of external trade to accommodate the countries at war with the Axis Power
It has been supplemented by the identification of hostile nationals resident i
friendly countries and the prohibition of intercourse with those "blocked na
tionals."[1] The system has facilitated the Lend-Lease program by the requis
tioning procedure of the Act of October 10, 1940 (*Documents, III, 1940–4*
p. 744) and operates in conjunction with the program of importing critical an
strategic materials. With the entrance of the United States into war, it becam
a means of utilizing materials to the best advantage for the war effort.

The Administrator of Export Control was designated to exercise the authorit
vested in the President on July 2, 1940. By Executive Order No. 8900 and A
ministrative Order No. 1, September 15, 1941 all delegations of authority to th
Administrator of Export Control were transferred to the Economic Defens
Board (*6 Fed. Reg.*, p. 4795, 4818). That Board was renamed the Board of Ec
nomic Warfare on December 17, 1941 (Executive Order No. 8982, 6 *Fed. Reg
p. 6530). In April 1942 the expanding functions of that Board caused it
organize the Office of Exports in which the Export Control Branch continued i
specialized work.

From July 2, 1940 until August 27, 1941 commodities subject to export licen
were designated by proclamation and by Executive Order No. 8712, March 1
1941,[2] the Administrator was authorized to determine the forms, conversions ar
derivatives of the articles and materials subject to control. Export Contr
Schedules — 27 in number — making those determinations were issued fro
March 15, 1941 until January 3, 1942. The great number of items affected ha
to be announced in this piecemeal way while the scope of the system was bei
developed. In August 1941 *Comprehensive Export Control Schedule* No. 1 w
issued as a single alphabetized list of some 7000 commodities subject to licens
The list, issued bimonthly since November-December 1941, was apparent
stabilized in content by March-April 1942.

[1] See p. 752.
[2] *Documents, III, 1940–41*, p. 481; 6 *Fed. Reg.*, p. 1501.

The *Comprehensive Export Control Schedule* in its successive issues contains regulations which explain the procedures to which exporters are then subject. Additions, special rulings and changes in the procedure or the requirements are published in a series of *Current Control Bulletins,* No. 1 of which was issued November 22 and effective December 8, 1941.

The exhibits presented below show the status of essential features of the export license system as of June 30, 1942. Documentary items are given in their first form in order to indicate when each feature became effective, changes of importance being edited in by various devices. Part II, Regulations concerning Export of Commodities, of the latest issue of the *Comprehensive Export Control Schedule* summarizes authentically the material on each subject with all relevant details.

A. Basic Policies

1) *Export Licensing and Priorities. Statement of the Under Secretary of State (Welles) to the Inter-American Financial and Economic Advisory Committee, June 19, 1941* [1]

The broad program in which the United States is engaged of production of materials and equipment essential to national and continental defense has led to a situation of scarcity with respect to many commodities and the establishment by the United States of a system of control of the export and, in many cases, the domestic consumption of such items. At the present time some 60%, by value, of the articles exported from the United States are subject to export licensing and/or priorities.

It is the objective of this policy on the one hand to restrict the exportation, and in some cases domestic consumption, of goods produced in the United States to amounts consistent with the demands of the defense program, while on the other hand to facilitate in so far as is feasible the exportation to the other American nations of at least their essential import requirements, and in general as large amounts of particular United States products as are consistent with the exigencies of defense.

A separate but related phase of policy concerns the acquisition abroad of strategic materials essential to the defense program, and, in general, the utilization of the materials of the hemisphere in the continental defense.

It is the view of the United States that these objectives are of interest and importance to all of the American Republics, and that they may best be realized by the creation of an inter-American system of export control involving strict restriction and control of the exportation of products outside of the Western Hemisphere with a maximum of free commerce within the hemisphere which is compatible with defense requirements. To this end the United States has been seeking in individual conver-

[1] Department of State, *Bulletin,* V, p. 54.

sations the fullest cooperation of all of the American Republics, and i is the opinion of the Government of the United States that such cooper ation could most advantageously take the form of the establishmen by each of the American Republics of a system of export control over

1. Materials subject to export control by the United States which ar exported to the other American Republics by the United States or whic are produced in the other American Republics.

(a) The United States will continue to permit exports to the othe American Republics in all cases unless United States stocks of th commodity in question are dangerously small and are essential to th defense program. In the cases of products the supply of which is nc affected by such considerations an attempt will be made to issue licens freely for use within the American Republics or at least in amounts u to the recent import requirements of the nations in question.

It has been found possible to issue general licenses for the export certain of such products to all of the other American Republics. Mor over, it is possible to issue general licenses to products in this categor for export to American Republics which also control the exportatic and re-exportation of such products, whether imported from the Unite States or elsewhere or produced domestically. Such general licens greatly facilitate trade among the American Republics.

(b) In the case of articles of the greatest stringency and importan to the defense program, it has been and it will continue to be necessa to impose a system of priorities as between the demands of the defen program, the requirements of the other American Republics, and civili consumption in the United States. In these cases it will at best possible to grant priorities for only the most urgent requirements of t other American Republics, and, in view of the control thus obtaine it will be possible to simplify the administrative procedure by issui general licenses for the exportation of articles for which such prioriti have been granted.

(c) In the case of all other articles the United States supply of whi is less than the several demands, it will be necessary to impose sor quantitative restriction on exports, and, in many cases, on domes consumption. In all of these cases an effort will be made, if it is at possible, to fulfil the most urgent requirements of the other Americ Republics, deferring fulfilment of less urgent requirements until t supply situation improves. In these cases exportations must be in vidually licensed, and it will be necessary that the Government of t United States be assured that the materials so exported reach th specific destinations.

2. Strategic materials and materials important in the national and continental defense, which are produced in the American Republics.

(a) This is an essentially separate though closely related phase of policy involved in the defense program. As a result of the great expansion in production, there exist in the United States strong commercial markets for most, if not all, strategic and critical materials produced in the Western Hemisphere. Moreover, the appropriate agencies of the Government of the United States stand ready to give consideration to purchasing supplies of such commodities as a regular part of its program or building up its own defense reserves and stock-piles.

This approach on the part of the United States for cooperative action among the American Republics has met with a most gratifying general response, and, indeed, many of the other American Republics had already embarked on similar and related courses of action. At the present time all of the American Republics have established, or are actively considering, some form of export control directed to ends similar to those set forth above. As a result, the United States has been in a position already to issue general licenses for the export to Argentina, Brazil, Cuba, and the Dominican Republic, respectively, of lists of commodities in category (a) mentioned above, as well as of certain commodities which are subject to priority approval. Arrangements for the issuance of similar general licenses for the export of commodities in these categories to a number of additional American Republics are also being completed.

With respect to the related policy of acquisition of strategic materials, appropriate agencies of the United States have entered into arrangements for the purchase of many commodities from individual producers, groups of producers, or the Governments of a number of the American Republics.

As is inevitable, the several systems of export control already imposed or in contemplation, although they point toward the same end, differ considerably in scope and form. There arise as a result a number of practical problems such as, for example, the question of the control only of the re-exportation of articles imported from one particular country as contrasted with control over all exports of the particular articles, whether imported from any source or produced domestically. Another problem which gives rise to extensive and complex administrative difficulties lies in application by the several republics of controls to varying lists or groups of commodities. As a result, the United States, and other nations, have been compelled to limit the issuance of general licenses and to restrict the exportation and re-exportation of the goods therein covered to such other American Republics as happen to control the particular item.

Commerce among the American nations can obviously be made most free under present world conditions which have occasioned the imposition of all of these types of export control, if all of the American Republics adopt parallel systems of export control thus establishing an inter-American system. To this end, the Government of the United States suggests:

1. That the Inter-American Financial and Economic Advisory Committee undertake the consideration of problems of export control and the formulation of a plan for an inter-American control system.

2. That the matter appropriately be referred to Subcommittee II on Commercial Problems.

3. That Subcommittee II elicit information from the several delegates and governments regarding the essential import requirements of the individual American Republics, and concerning the various systems of export control already established by a number of them.

4. That Subcommittee II consider the steps towards a broad hemisphere program of control already taken by a number of the republics and formulate detailed recommendations for an inter-American system which would permit a maximum of freedom of interchange among the American Republics.

If this suggestion meets with general approval, the Government of the United States is prepared to place at the disposal of the Advisory Committee and Subcommittee II information regarding the policies and administrative procedures with respect to export licensing and priorities controls established by it; special arrangements entered into with and general licenses issued for exports to particular American Republics which have adopted some form of export control; data available to it regarding the systems of control in effect in other American nations; and such information as it has collected with regard to the import requirements for certain materials of some of the American Republics.

(2) *Export Control. Statement of the Under Secretary of State (Welles) to the Inter-American Financial and Economic Advisory Committee, July 17, 1941*

[See p. 384.]

(3) *Export Licensing and Priorities Control. Statement of the Under Secretary of State (Welles) to the Inter-American Financial and Economic Advisory Committee, December 5, 1941*

[See p. 386.]

4) *Basic Export Control Policies. Statement of Board of Economic Warfare, Office of Export Control, April 8, 1942* [1]

[Excerpt]

1. Unless absolute necessity can be shown, exporters should not submit applications for license to export *commodities in the supply of which there is known to be a critical shortage* and which are needed for war purposes by the United States. Export trade publications and the daily press provide the means for exporters to keep posted on matters of this character.

2. Limited supplies of essential war materials dictate the need for the consideration of export license applications strictly from the point of view of "vital needs" in the country of destination. Examples of "vital needs" are:

(a) Requirements of national defense.
(b) Requirements of producers abroad contributing materials for United States war industries.
(c) Replacement parts for repairs and maintenance of equipment essential to the defense activity or national economy.
(d) Requirements for essential public utilities.
(e) Requirements of industries essential to the national economy and for which adequate substitutes cannot be obtained locally in the country of destination.

3. Shortages of *shipping space* in respect to exports to certain countries necessitate the limitation of licenses to authorize the exportation of strictly essential materials only. Frequent contacts with traffic managers, freight forwarders, and steamship officials will serve to enable exporters to keep abreast of the situation with regard to shipping accommodations.

4. Applications should contain *sufficient assurances* that the materials described therein will be used for the purposes stated. In their own interests, as well as those of their customers abroad, exporters should require their foreign customers to be as specific as possible in providing this information. In the event that sufficient information in regard to the ultimate use of the materials described in a shipment is not available, is suggested that the exporter furnish with his application for an export license a comprehensive statement relative to the consignee's purchaser's business and affiliations, together with a statement concerning the urgency of the need for the materials in question.

5. Procedures have been established in the Office of Exports for the

[1] *Current Controls Bulletin*, No. 15.

expeditious review of applications for export licenses to insure that th
prices stated therein are in accordance with schedules established by th
Office of Price Administration. It will help further to expedite the cor
sideration of applications if exporters will include in their applications
statement to the effect that they have complied with applicable pric
schedules if such is the case. If price ceilings have not been establishe
in respect to the commodity named in the application, the exporte
should indicate that the quoted prices conform to current market quc
tations. Applications which state excessive prices without an adequat
explanation may be delayed for further investigation of the factor
involved.

6. Exporters should avoid misleading or obscure statements in th
description of the commodity named in their applications and in statin
the proposed use of the commodity.

B. Administration

[See Chapter III, p. 163.]

C. Use of Licenses

Trading under the export control system is by license originally issued by th
Department of State and subsequently by the Board of Economic Warfare, Offi
of Exports. Licenses are as follows:

General licenses (G–1, etc.) extended to all exporters authorizing the shipmer
of designated commodities to designated countries. General licenses exist fo
practically all commodities for groups of designated destinations which a
indicated in the commodity list published in the *Comprehensive Export Contr
Schedule*. A general license (GUS) permits exportation for the United Stat
Government and its armed forces.

General intransit licenses (GIT) are general licenses permitting shipments
foreign origin to pass through the jurisdictional area of the United States
transit to a foreign destination. The system was put into effect in May 19
(*Documents, III, 1940–41*, p. 492) with respect to the British Empire and th
Western Hemisphere and has since been extended to other areas. It operat
in conjunction with the Canadian Export Permit and the British Imperial E
port License where those are applicable.

Unlimited licenses have been granted to several foreign purchasing agenci
to cover certain commodities to specific destinations; they may be used on
with the approval of the holders. The commodities covered by them are list
in the *Comprehensive Export Control Schedule*. Unlimited licenses are held
Amtorg Trading Corporation (for the Soviet Union), Belgian Congo Purchasi
Commission, British Purchasing Commission and Universal Trading Corpor
tion (for Free China).

Individual licenses [1] are obtained by application for the shipment of speci

---

[1] Effective January 5, 1942, the numbers previously used on individual licens
were discontinued and applications for licenses were given a "case number" whi
appeared on licenses for identification purposes (Board of Economic Warfare, Offi
of Exports, *Current Controls Bulletin* No. 6, par. 2). This facilitated the tracing of a
particular transaction on which questions might arise.

ommodities to specific destinations. Detailed conditions applicable to them as
well as special provisions [1] for certain commodities are given in the *Comprehensive Export Control Schedule.*
Technical data licenses are issued in general, blanket or special form.

1) *Executive Order No. 8889 Amending Regulations Governing the Exportation of Articles and Materials Designated in Proclamations Issued Pursuant to the Provisions of Section 6 of the Act of Congress Approved July 2, 1940, September 2, 1941* [2]

By virtue of and pursuant to the authority vested in me by section 6
of the act of Congress approved July 2, 1940, entitled "An Act to
expedite the strengthening of the national defense," 54 Stat. 712, 714,
as amended, I hereby prescribe that sections 7 and 8 of Executive
Order 8712,[3] dated March 15, 1941, shall be amended to read as follows:

7. Export licenses shall not be transferred except by written authorization of the Secretary of State. All export licenses are subject to
revocation without notice. If not revoked, licenses are valid for one year
from the date of issuance.[4]

8. No article or material, the exportation of which is prohibited or
curtailed pursuant to the said section 6, shall be loaded or carried onto
an exporting carrier for export by water or by air or presented to such
an exporting carrier for loading or presented to the collector of customs
for inspection and clearance for exportation until an original license
therefor, or such other document as the Secretary of State shall prescribe,
has been presented to the collector of customs at the port at which the
article or material is to be so loaded, carried, or presented. No such
article or material shall be mailed for exportation until an original license,
or such other document as the Secretary of State shall prescribe, has
been presented to the postmaster at the post office where the article
or material is to be mailed. If the article or material is to be exported

---

[1] Export Schedule No. 25, effective December 23, 1941, revoked the provision of
Export Schedule No. 10, effective June 20, 1941 (6 *Fed. Reg.*, p. 3059) which permitted without license individual shipments valued at $25 or less (*Documents, III, 1940–41*, p. 484). They were placed under general license to all friendly destinations.
For the commodities affected see *Comprehensive Export Control Schedule*, Regulations,
General Licenses, D.

[2] 6 *Fed. Reg.*, p. 4601; Department of State, *Bulletin*, V, p. 179.

[3] *Documents, III, 1940–41*, p. 481.

[4] Individual export licenses were limited in validity to a period of six months after
April 10, 1942. Exports were already subject to preference ratings and lack of shipping space was an added factor which resulted in a census of orders already licensed
and awaiting shipment. By learning of the freight space required up to April 30,
1942 (*Current Controls Bulletin* No. 14) it was possible to plan relief of the congestion
by the more accurate allocation of shipping.

by any means of export other than by water, air, or mail, such license or other document need not be presented to the collector of customs prior to loading, carrying onto, or presentation to, the exporting carrier but must be presented to the collector of customs at the port of exit prior to inspection by the customs inspectors or other export inspection officials at that port, and at all events prior to exportation. Upon specific authorization to collector of customs or postmaster by the Secretary of State, the presentation of a license may be waived.

D. Articles and Materials Subject to Export Control

(1) *List of Proclamations and Schedules*

[See *Documents, III, 1940–41*, p. 474.]

Proclamation No. 2496, issued July 5, 1941; effective July 23, 1941
  6 *Fed. Reg.*, p. 3263.

  No. 2503, issued August 19, 1941; effective September 10, 1941
  6 *Fed. Reg.*, p. 4231.

  No. 2506, issued and effective August 27, 1941, 6 *Fed Reg.*, p. 4469
Export Control Schedule No. 14, July 22, 1941, effective August 1, 1941
  6 *Fed. Reg.*, p. 3672.

  No. 15, issued and effective August 2, 1941, 6 *Fed. Reg.*, p. 3888

  No. 16, August 8, 1941, effective August 27, 1941, 6 *Fed. Reg.*, p. 4004

  No. 17, August 15, 1941, effective August 29, 1941, 6 *Fed. Reg.*, p. 4136

  No. 18, August 20, 1941, effective September 10, 1941, 6 *Fed. Reg.*
  p. 4664.

  No. 19, issued and effective August 27, 1941, 6 *Fed. Reg.*, p. 4470

  No. 20, issued and effective August 30, 1941, 6 *Fed. Reg.*, p. 4535

  No. 21, issued and effective October 1, 1941, 6 *Fed. Reg.*, p. 5006.

  No. 22, October 13, 1941, effective October 29, 1941, 6 *Fed. Reg.*
  p. 5216.

  No. 23, October 24, 1941, effective November 11, 1941, 6 *Fed. Reg.*
  p. 5468.

  No. 24, December 6, 1941, effective December 23, 1941, 6 *Fed. Reg.*
  p. 6306.

  No. 25, December 9, 1941, effective December 23, 1941, 6 *Fed. Reg*
  p. 6329.

  No. 26, issued and effective December 10, 1941, 6 *Fed. Reg.*, p. 6373

  No. 27, January 3, 1942, effective January 2, 1942, 7 *Fed. Reg.*, p. 113

Applicable to Proclaimed List of Blocked Nationals

The following two Export Schedules covering "the forms, conversions and derivatives of other military equipment or munitions, or component parts thereof, or machinery, tools, or materials or supplies necessary for the manufacture, servicing or operation thereof" were issued to apply specifically to the persons included in the Proclaimed List of Blocked Nationals:

Z, July 19, 1941, effective July 21, 1941, 6 *Fed. Reg.*, p. 3584.

Y (supplementing Z), August 14, 1941, 6 *Fed. Reg.*, p. 4073.

(2) *Petroleum Products. Announcement of the President (Roosevelt), August 1, 1941* [1]

It was announced today that the President has directed the Administrator of Export Control to initiate further regulation in respect to the export of petroleum products in the interest of the national defense.

The action will have two immediate effects. It will prohibit the exportation of motor fuels and oils suitable for use in aircraft and of certain raw stocks from which such products are derived to destinations other than the Western Hemisphere, the British Empire and the unoccupied territories of other countries engaged in resisting aggression. It will also limit the exportation of other petroleum products, except to the destinations referred to above, to usual or pre-war quantities and provide for the pro rata issuance of licenses on that basis.

(3) *Technical Data. Export Control Schedule B, September 15, 1941* [2]

[See *Documents, III, 1940–41*, p. 486.]

Export control of technical data, first brought under the system by Proclamation No. 2465, March 4, 1941, became an important part of the scheme. It does not extend to patent applications. A control list for technical data licensing is published in *Comprehensive Export Control Schedule*, where full details as to general, blanket and special licenses are given.

The Export Control Schedules for technical data were designated by letters and were as follows:

A, issued April 1, 1941; effective April 15, 1941; 6 *Fed. Reg.*, p. 1814, 2392;

B, issued September 15, 1941; effective September 20, 1941, 6 *Fed. Reg.*, p. 4730;

C, issued February 20, 1942, effective March 1, 1942, 7 *Fed. Reg.*, p. 1492.

By virtue of the Military Order of July 2, 1940,[3] and Executive Order No. 8713 [4] of March 15, 1941, I, RUSSELL L. MAXWELL, Administrator of Export Control, have determined that effective September 20,

---

[1] From the Office of the Secretary to the President. This statement covered the issuance of Export Control Schedule No. 15, August 2, 1941 (6 *Fed. Reg.*, p. 3888).

[2] 6 *Fed. Reg.*, p. 4730.   [3] *Documents, III, 1940–41*, p. 473.   [4] *Ibid.*, p. 487.

1941, the articles and materials designated in Proclamation No. 2465 [1] of March 4, 1941, issued pursuant to Section 6 of the Act of July 2, 1940 [2] (54 Stat. 714, 50 U.S.C.A. Supp. Sec. 99), shall not include: Any application for patent or for the registration of a utility model, industrial design or model in respect of any invention made in the United States, for which a license is required from the Commissioner of Patents under the authority of Public Law 239, 77th Congress, c. 393, 1st Sess., approved August 21, 1941.

By direction of the President:

(Signed) RUSSELL L. MAXWELL,
Brigadier General, U. S. Army
Administrator of Export Control

(4) Rubber. *Release of Economic Defense Board, Office of Export Control, December 11, 1941* [3]

The Economic Defense Board, Office of Export Control, today advised collectors of customs at all ports of entry not to clear, until further notice, the exportation of rubber tires or tubes of any kind, crude rubber, or crepe rubber. These commodities may not be shipped to any destination whatever, unless consigned to the military or naval forces of the United States Government, or the shipment is to be made under provisions of the Lend-Lease Act.[4]

Customs collectors were warned that this prohibition must be considered effective immediately. It applies to all shipments of the character referred to whether or not laden aboard the exporting carrier, whether or not a license authorizing such exportation has been issued, and regardless of any other circumstance which may be involved.

The prohibition of such exportations does not apply to tires which are being exported as component parts of either new or used vehicles.

(5) *Placement of All Commodities of Use in War under License. Export Control Schedule No. 25, December 9, 1941, Effective December 23, 1941* [5]

By virtue of Executive Order No. 8712, of March 15, 1941, Executive Order No. 8900, of September 15, 1941, and Order No. 1, of the Economic

---

[1] *Ibid.*, p. 486.
[2] *Ibid.*, p. 474.
[3] Press Release No. 20.
[4] Rubber and rubber manufactures could be shipped under general license to Canada from April 10, 1942 (*Current Controls Bulletin* No. 17).
[5] 6 *Fed. Reg.*, p. 6329.

Defense Board, of September 15, 1941, I, Milo Perkins, Executive Director, Economic Defense Board, have determined that:

1. In addition to items previously listed in the several Export Control Schedules, effective December 23, 1941, all other articles and materials of any character or description whatsoever are determined to be forms, conversions, and derivatives of military equipment, or munitions, or component parts thereof, or machinery, tools, or materials, or supplies necessary for the manufacture, servicing, or operation thereof, the exportation of which has been prohibited pursuant to the provisions of the several Proclamations issued pursuant to Section 6 of the Act of July 2, 1940.

2. Nothing in this order shall be construed to include articles or materials the exportation of which is governed by rules and regulations prescribed pursuant to Section 5b of the "Trading with the Enemy Act" approved October 6, 1917 (40 Stat. 415), as amended, or the "Narcotic Drugs Import and Export Act" approved February 9, 1909, as amended (21 U.S.C. sec. 182).

(Signed) MILO PERKINS
Executive Director, Economic Defense Board

(6) *War Project Licenses. Announcement of the Board of Economic Warfare, April 30, 1942* [1]

The Board of Economic Warfare has issued from time to time, and will issue in certain instances, War Project Licenses authorizing the exportation of all articles and materials required for a specific project in a foreign country. Such licenses *originate in the Board of Economic Warfare* and are not generally available. They are limited to a few special projects of direct interest to the military authorities of this country and endorsed by the Army and Navy Munitions Board for licensing as war projects.

Projects will be given consideration for licensing as War Projects only if they have the following characteristics:

(*a*) The project is directly involved in, and considered essential to, the prosecution of the war effort;

(*b*) The project is advocated by the Army and Navy Munitions Board as necessary to a military effort;

(*c*) The project is of such importance that it bears or will bear, upon consideration and approval by the Board of Economic Warfare and the War Production Board, a preference rating of A–1–A, A–1–B, or A–1–C to insure supply.

[1] Current Controls Bulletin No. 19, par. 8.

E. Countries and Destinations

(1) *List of Countries with Numbers, Used in Issuance of General Licenses, as Prepared by the Department of State and Revised by the Board of Economic Warfare, as of June 30, 1942* [1]

[See *Documents, III, 1940–41,* p. 488.]

As the export control system expanded, the issuance of licenses for single shipments became onerous and general licenses for particular commodities or particular destinations were authorized by Executive Order No. 8640, January 15, 1941. In order to accommodate exporters general licenses with respect to various commodities were issued for destinations by groups as well as specific country destinations. Group C includes Canada, Great Britain and Northern Ireland, Greenland, Iceland, Labrador, Newfoundland and the U.S.S.R. Group J embraces the Western Hemisphere, and the other surviving groups (K and P) other areas with which communication is longer, more difficult or less desirable. The countries were designated by numerals when general licenses were consolidated for trade with a single country instead of trade in specific articles with a country. This originally facilitated the issuance of licenses and became available to direct trade conveniently into desirable quarters. The list developed by the Department of State is here printed as revised to June 30, 1942 by the Board of Economic Warfare, Office of Exports, Export Control Branch. The revision shows from No. 74 on.

The Secretary of State announced on September 8 that a revision has been made in the Department's system of numbering export licenses, and that all general licenses issued by the Department are being replaced by a single general license for each country.

This consolidation of numerous licenses under one number does not alter the list of articles and materials which may be exported to the respective countries under general license.

General licenses will be designed hereafter by the letter "G" followed by the number assigned to the respective country of destination. As an example, general license number "G–1" authorizes the exportation to Canada of all those commodities previously authorized by numerous separate general licenses. When any additional commodities are added to the list of those authorized to be exported to Canada under general license, they will be included under license number "G–1."

1. Canada
2. Great Britain and Northern Ireland
3. Cuba
4. Argentina
5. Bolivia
6. Brazil
7. Chile
8. Colombia
9. Costa Rica
10. Curaçao (including the islands of Curaçao; Aruba; Bonaire; Saba; St. Eustatius; and St. Martin, southern part)
11. Dominican Republic

[1] Department of State, *Bulletin,* V, p. 200.

12. Ecuador
13. El Salvador
14. Guatemala
15. Haiti
16. Honduras
17. Mexico
18. Nicaragua
19. Panama
20. Paraguay
21. Peru
22. Surinam
23. Uruguay
24. Venezuela
25. Aden
26. Australia (except Papua and the Territory of New Guinea under mandate) including Nauru, mandated territory
27. Bahamas
28. Barbados
29. Bermuda
30. British East Africa (including Kenya; Uganda; Nyasaland; Zanzibar; and Tanganyika, mandated territory)
31. British Guiana
32. British Honduras
33. British Malaya (including British North Borneo; Brunei; Federated Malay States; Sarawak; Straits Settlements; Unfederated Malay States; Christmas Island, Indian Ocean; Cocos (Keeling) Islands)]
34. British West Africa (including Nigeria; British Cameroons, mandated territory; Gambia; Sierra Leone; Gold Coast, including Ashanti and Northern Territory; and British Togoland, mandated territory)
35. Burma
36. Ceylon
37. Cyprus
38. Ireland (Eire) until April 1, 1942]
39. Falkland Islands (including South Georgia)
40. Kuweit
41. Gibraltar
42. Hong Kong
43. India
44. Jamaica
45. Leeward Islands (including Antigua, Barbuda, Redonda, St. Christopher (St. Kitts) Island, Nevis Island, Anguilla Island, Montserrat, Sombrero, and British Virgin Islands)
46. Mauritius (including Rodrigues Island and Diego Garcia Island)
47. Newfoundland
48. New Zealand
49. New Guinea, British (comprising Papua or British New Guinea; and Territory of New Guinea, mandated territory)
50. Northern Rhodesia
51. Palestine and Trans-Jordan
52. St. Helena (including Ascension Island, Gough Island, Inaccessible Island, Nightingale Island, and Tristan da Cunha Island)
53. Seychelles and Dependencies
54. Oceania, British (including British Solomon Islands; Fiji Islands; Gilbert and Ellice Islands; New Hebrides Islands; Pitcairn Island; Tonga or Friendly Islands; Santa Cruz Islands; Cook Islands; and Western Samoa, mandated territory)
55. Southern Rhodesia
56. Trinidad and Tobago
57. Union of South Africa (including South-West Africa)
58. Windward Islands (including Grenada, Grenadines, St. Lucia, St. Vincent, and Dominica)
59. Egypt
60. Anglo-Egyptian Sudan
61. Greenland
62. Iceland
[63. Philippine Islands]
64. Netherlands Indies
65. China (Free)
66. Belgian Congo
67. Bahrein Islands
68. French West Indies (including Désirade; Guadeloupe; Les Saintes; Martinique; Marie Galante; St. Martin, northern part; and St. Bartholomew)
69. French Guiana
70. Miquelon and St. Pierre
71. French Oceania (all French possessions in the Pacific)
72. French Cameroons
73. French Equatorial Africa
74. Iraq, until April 1, 1942, then 89
75. Liberia, until April 1, 1942, then 91
76. Union of Soviet Socialist Republics

77. Turkey, until April 1, 1942, then 99
78. Syria, until April 1, 1942, then 96
79. Reserved [1]; Afghanistan in Group K from June 25, 1942
80. Iran, until April 1, 1942, then 88
81. Saudi Arabia
82. Spain and Possessions
83. Portugal and Possessions
84. Sweden and Possessions
85. Switzerland and Possessions
86. French West Africa (Mauritania, Senegal, French Guinea, Ivory Coast, Togoland, Dahomey, French Sudan and Niger)
87. French North Africa (Algeria, French Morocco and Tunisia)
88. Iran
89. Iraq
90. Ireland
91. Liberia
92. Madagascar
93. Portuguese Atlantic Islands
94. Portuguese Guinea
95. Réunion
96. Lebanon (Syria)
97. Spanish Atlantic Islands
98. Spanish Morocco and Tangier
99. Turkey

(2) General Intransit Licenses for British Licensed Trade, Effective April 2, 1942 [2]

In order to permit trade from certain foreign sources of origin to certain foreign destinations by shipment through the United States, general intransit licenses were inaugurated by the Secretary of State on May 9, 1941 (*Documents, III 1940–41*, p. 492). Groups of territories were set up between which intransit trade was permitted. The first two groups were the territories of the British Commonwealth of Nations (A) and the American Republics with the Netherlands West Indies (B). The scheme was developed by the Office of Export Control in connection with the system of general licenses, under which countries having common characteristics were assigned to lettered groups and, for the convenience of shippers, these letters were attached to the commodity list in the Comprehensive Export Control Schedule. Group trade in the commodities available to the countries within a given group by intransit shipments was thus made possible without further requirements. A need arose in British trade to distinguish between shipments of British and those of Lend-Lease origin. For this purpose British trade was covered by British Imperial Export Licenses, and shipments were facilitated by issuance in the United States of the following general intransit licenses.

General Intransit License GIT—C/D [Y/Z] authorizes the exportation of all articles and materials subject to export control when being shipped from the List C [Y] destinations listed below to the List D [Z] destinations listed below subject to the following provisions:

(1) Each shipment must be accompanied by a Canadian Export Permit or by a British Imperial Export License (British Imperial Export Licenses may be distinguished from other British licenses by the letter prefix IEL to the reference number of the license issued by the country of origin), specifying the nature of the shipment and naming the ultimate consignee in the country of destination which must agree with the other shipping documents.

(2) If the shipment is not accompanied by an export license or permit, as provided in paragraph 1 above, an individual yellow export license from the Board of Economic Warfare must be secured.

[1] On December 3, 1941 "79. All other destinations" was stricken from the Country Designation Number list (Economic Defense Board, Office of Exports, *Current Controls Bulletin* No. 3, pars. 2–4).

[2] Board of Economic Warfare, Office of Export Control, *Current Controls Bulletin* No. 16, April 11, 1942.

GENERAL INTRANSIT LICENSES GIT, ISSUED TO MAY 1, 1942[1]

FROM	TO	GENERAL LICENSE DESIGNATIONS
Western Hemisphere . . .	British Empire	GIT — B/A [2]
British Empire	Western Hemisphere	GIT — A/B
British Empire	British Empire	GIT — A/A
Western Hemisphere . . .	Western Hemisphere	GIT — B/B
Netherlands Indies . . .	Western Hemisphere	GIT — N/B
Western Hemisphere . . .	Netherlands Indies	GIT — B/N
Western Hemisphere . . .	Belgian Congo	GIT — B/BC
Belgian Congo	Western Hemisphere	GIT — BC/B
British Empire	Belgian Congo	GIT — A/BC
Belgian Congo	British Empire	GIT — BC/A
Western Hemisphere . . .	U.S.S.R.	GIT — B/R
British Empire	U.S.S.R.	GIT — A/R
U.S.S.R.	Western Hemisphere	GIT — R/B
U.S.S.R.	British Empire	GIT — R/A
Portugal	Western Hemisphere	GIT — P/B
Portugal	British Empire	GIT — P/A
Spain	Western Hemisphere	GIT — S/B
Spain	British Empire	GIT — S/A
Switzerland	Western Hemisphere	GIT — SW/B
Switzerland	British Empire	GIT — SW/A
Sweden	Western Hemisphere	GIT — SD/B
Sweden	British Empire	GIT — SD/A
Netherlands Indies . . .	British Empire	GIT — N/A
British Empire	Netherlands Indies	GIT — A/N
Y Countries	Z Countries	GIT — Y/Z

(3) IEL licenses (British Imperial Export Licenses) and Canadian Export Permits shall be surrendered to Collectors of Customs at the last port of exit from the United States, who forward all such licenses and permits to the Board of Economic Warfare, Washington, D. C.

LIST C [Y]

India	Bermuda
Burma	Sierra Leone
Dominion of Canada	Nigeria
British Colonies including only:	Seychelles Islands
British Guiana	Kenya
Jamaica	Northern Rhodesia
Windward Islands	Uganda
Bahamas	Cyprus

[1] Board of Economic Warfare, Office of Exports, Export Control Branch, Comprehensive Export Control Schedule No. 7, p. 78.

[2] For the countries included in Groups A and B, see *Documents, III, 1940–41*, p. 493. The "Western Hemisphere" included countries designated by Nos. 3 through 54, 61 and 62.

LIST C [Y] — *Continued*

Fiji	Ceylon
British Honduras	Aden
Trinidad	Tanganyika
Leeward Islands	Nyasaland
Barbados	Zanzibar
Gambia	Palestine and Transjordania
Gold Coast	Western Pacific Islands

LIST D [Z]

French West Africa	Iran
French North Africa	Iraq
Eire	Spain
Liberia	Syria
Madagascar	Spanish Atlantic Islands
Portugal	Spanish Morocco and Tangier
Portuguese Atlantic Islands	Sweden
Portuguese Guinea	Switzerland
Réunion	Turkey

F. Control of Export Prices

(1) *Maximum Export Price Regulation. Office of Price Administration, Regulation 1375, April 25, 1942* [1]

[Excerpt]

1375.1 *Maximum export price*

On and after April 30, 1942, the effective date of this Maximum Export Price Regulation, regardless of the terms of any contract of sale or purchase, or of any export license thereafter issued by the Board of Economic Warfare, no person shall export any commodity at a price in excess of the following maximum export prices:

(*a*) In the case of a person other than the manufacturer or producer of the commodity the maximum export price shall be the price at which such commodity was acquired for export, plus the additions thereto authorized by paragraphs (*a*) and (*b*) of section 1375.2 hereof, and

(*b*) In the case of the manufacturer or producer the maximum export price shall be his maximum domestic price for the commodity, or, in case there is no such price, shall be his maximum domestic price for the most nearly similar commodity of equal or lower quality or grade or,

[1] 7 *Fed. Reg.*, p. 3096; *Foreign Commerce Weekly*, VII, No. 5, p. 36; issued under authority of Public Law 421, 77th Cong., as Code of Federal Regulations, Title 32, National Defense, Chap. XI, Office of Price Administration, Part 1375, Export Prices.

in the absence of both of the foregoing, the price at which the commodity to be exported is customarily sold in the domestic market, plus the additions thereto authorized by paragraphs (*a*) and (*b*) of section 1375.2 hereof.

1375.2 *Additions to cost or domestic price*

(*a*) An amount not in excess of the average premium charged in the export trade for the particular services or functions performed during either the period July 1–December 31, 1940 or March 1–April 15, 1942, whichever average premium is the lower,[1] may be added by the exporter to his cost of acquisition, maximum domestic price or other base price, as provided in section 1375.1 of this Maximum Export Price Regulation. In determining the applicable premium, due recognition should be given to existing differentials in the export premiums charged by different types of exporters, differences in premium resulting from variations in the size or value of exports or from variations in the volume of business done by various exporters, as well as to differentials in premium between exports to the Territories and possessions of the United States, Canada and the various foreign nations, provided, that in no event shall more than one such premium be added by the exporter with respect to a particular export.

(*b*) An amount, in addition to the foregoing premium, may be added by the exporter to his cost of acquisition, maximum domestic price or

[1] The selection of the periods is explained by the Administrator in an accompanying statement of the considerations involved in the issuance of the regulation as follows:

"The periods to be used in determining the average margins were chosen in order that the margins established would reflect as closely as possible normal conditions. Since the outbreak of the present war, the prices in the export field have been increasingly affected by many highly speculative influences. The effect of these influences had progressed to such a degree by October 1, 1941 that the period of October 1 to October 15 would not, in and of itself, supply an adequate basis for freezing export margins. Further, because of the seasonal nature of many of our exports, it was necessary to choose a base period covering a larger period of time. In order to avoid freezing into the current structure these abnormalities and to allow for seasonal variations it was determined that a more representative base period must be selected.

"Accordingly two base periods were determined upon. During the first, July 1–December 31, 1940, the average unit value of exports was approximately the same as the 1937–1939 average. Other statistical evidence indicates that during that period the abnormal tendencies had not seriously distorted normal export conditions. The second period March 1–April 15, 1942 was chosen because during that period with respect to certain commodities, the Office of Export Control was scrutinizing export prices and margins in an effort to eliminate speculative increases. By fixing as the applicable premium the lower of the two base period average margins, normal export profits should be approximated. At the same time, the limitation to domestic ceiling prices plus such normal margin and expenses should provide foreign purchasers adequate protection against excessive prices."

other base price as provided in section 1375.1 of this Maximum Export Price Regulation, to compensate for expenses, such as war risk insurance, consular fees, demurrage charges and shipping charges, incident to the export and absorbed or to be absorbed by the exporter.

G. Coordination of British and American Procedures

(1) *Coordination of British and American Export Procedures. Announcement of Arrangements as of April 1, 1942* [1]

Arrangements have been made between the Governments of the United States and the United Kingdom for the coordination and simplification of their respective economic warfare procedures.

Heretofore it has been necessary for exporters sending goods from the United States to certain countries in Europe, Africa, and the Near East, or to their colonial possessions, to obtain two documents — an American export license and a British navicert.[2] On April 1, 1942 a new arrangement will come into effect under which only one document, the American export license, need be obtained. British consuls in the United States will not issue navicerts for exports to be shipped from this country after April 1.

Export licenses issued by the Board of Economic Warfare before March 1 will be invalid after April 10, whether shipment is by freight, parcel post, or mail, to the following destinations: French West Africa, French North Africa, Iran, Iraq, Eire, Liberia, Madagascar, Portugal, Portuguese Atlantic islands, Portuguese Guinea, Réunion, Spain, Syria, Spanish Atlantic islands, Spanish Morocco and Tangier, Sweden, Switzerland, and Turkey.

Applications for export licenses for goods to be exported to these destinations after April 1 will be received by the Board of Economic Warfare on and after March 1. Under the new procedure export licenses for these destinations will be issued on a quarterly basis. Detailed regulations are being issued by the Board of Economic Warfare to which all inquiries should be addressed.

Beginning April 1 certificates fulfilling the purpose now fulfilled by ship navicerts will be issued by United States collectors of customs to vessels leaving United States ports. Issuance of ship navicerts by British consular officers will accordingly be discontinued as of that date.

[1] Press release of February 13, 1942, Department of State, *Bulletin*, VI, p. 153.
[2] For the form of the navicert, see *Documents, III, 1940–41*, p. 501.

2) *Discontinuance of Navicert, Mailcert and Aircert from April 1, 1942. Announcement of Board of Economic Warfare, Office of Export Control, March 3, 1942* [1]

The use by the United Kingdom of navicerts [2] was designed to keep the blockde of the enemy effective. As a nonparticipant in the war the United States cquiesced in its application to export shipments. With the United States a elligerent the objective of the navicert and the export license became sub-tantially identical and the British system was no longer necessary with respect) many shipments from the United States. Blockade control permits (prior learance) were made a required condition for granting licenses to export certain rticles and materials to Eire, Portugal, Spain, Spanish Atlantic islands, Spanish Iorocco and Switzerland.

Export Control procedures are now greatly simplified as the result of recent agreement between the Governments of the United States and Ireat Britain. For articles and materials to be exported after March 31, american exporters need no longer apply for navicerts, mailcerts, or ircerts, but have only to obtain export licenses from the Board of Iconomic Warfare. There will be no change in the procedure for btaining export licenses for gold or narcotics required by the Treasury Iepartment or for arms, ammunition, implements of war, helium, and in-plate scrap required by the State Department, with the exception hat the navicerts will be eliminated.

I. Export of Arms, Ammunition and Implements of War under Joint Resolution of November 4, 1939

1) *Proclamation Listing Articles to Be Considered Arms, Ammunition and Implements of War, Dated April 9, 1942* [3]

'or the previous enumeration see Proclamation No. 2237, May 1, 1937, *Documents, II, 1939–40*, p. 693.]

BY THE PRESIDENT OF THE UNITED STATES OF AMERICA

A Proclamation [*No. 2549*]

WHEREAS section 12 (i) of the joint resolution of Congress approved Iovember 4, 1939, entitled "Joint resolution to preserve the neutrality

---

[1] Board of Economic Warfare, Office of Export Control, *Current Controls Bulletin* Io. 9, par. 1.

[2] *Documents, III, 1940–41*, p. 501.

[3] 7 *Fed. Reg.*, p. 2769; Department of State, *Bulletin*, VI, p. 323. New regulations ere issued June 2, 1942 (7 *Fed. Reg.*, p. 4216) as Code of Federal Regulations, Title 2, Foreign Relations; Chap. I, Department of State, Subchap. D, Munitions Control, art 201, International Traffic in Arms, Ammunition and Implements of War. arts 202, 203, 204, issued in revised form June 2, 1942 (7 *Fed. Reg.*, p. 4220, 4221) ealt with exportation of helium gas, tin-plate scrap and articles involving military ecrets. For earlier regulations see 4 *Fed. Reg.*, p. 4512.

and the peace of the United States and to secure the safety of its citizen and their interests," provides in part as follows (54 Stat. 11; 22 U. S C. 452 (i)):

"The President is hereby authorized to proclaim upon recommenda tion of the Board from time to time a list of articles which shall b considered arms, ammunition, and implements of war for the purpose of this section . . ."

Now, THEREFORE, I, FRANKLIN D. ROOSEVELT, President of th United States of America, acting under and by virtue of the authorit; conferred upon me by the said joint resolution of Congress, and pursuan to the recommendation of the National Munitions Control Board declare and proclaim that the articles listed below shall, on and afte April 15, 1942, be considered arms, ammunition, and implements o war for the purposes of section 12 (i) of the said joint resolution o Congress:

Category I
(1) Rifles and carbines using amunition in excess of caliber .22, and barrels fo those weapons;
(2) Machine guns, automatic or autoloading rifles, and machine pistols usin ammunition in excess of caliber .22, and barrels for those weapons; machine-gu mounts;
(3) Guns, howitzers, and mortars of all calibers, their mountings and barrel:
(4) Ammunition in excess of caliber .22 for the arms enumerated under (1 (2), and (3) above, and cartridge cases or bullets for such ammunition; shells an projectiles, filled or unfilled, for the arms enumerated under (3) above;
(5) Grenades, bombs, torpedoes, mines and depth charges, filled or unfillec and apparatus for their use or discharge;
(6) Tanks, military armored vehicles, and armored trains; armor plate an turrets for such vehicles.

Category II
Vessels of war of all kinds, including aircraft carriers and submarines, an armor plate and turrets for such vessels.

Category III
(1) Aircraft, unassembled, assembled, or dismantled, both heavier and light than air, which are designed, adapted, and intended for aerial combat by the u: of machine guns or of artillery or for the carrying and dropping of bombs, which are equipped with, or which by reason of design or construction are pr pared for, any of the appliances referred to in paragraph (2) below;
(2) Aerial gun mounts and frames, bomb racks, torpedo carriers, and bom release or torpedo-release mechanisms; armor plate and turrets for military ai craft.

Category IV
(1) Revolvers and automatic pistols using ammunition in excess of caliber .22;
(2) Ammunition in excess of caliber .22 for the arms enumerated under (1) above, and cartridge cases or bullets for such ammunition.

Category V
(1) Aircraft, unassembled, assembled or dismantled, both heavier and lighter than air, other than those included in category III;
(2) Propellers or air-screws, fuselages, hulls, wings, tail units, and under-carriage units;
(3) Aircraft engines, unassembled, assembled, or dismantled.

Category VI
(1) Livens projectors, flame throwers, and fire-barrage projectors;
(2) *a.* Mustard gas (dichlorethyl sulphide);
    b. Lewisite (chlorvinyldichlorarsine and dichlordivinylchlorarsine);
    c. Methyldichlorarsine;
    d. Diphenylchlorarsine;
    e. Diphenylcyanarsine;
    f. Diphenylaminechlorarsine;
    g. Phenyldichlorarsine;
    h. Ethyldichlorarsine;
    i. Phenyldibromarsine;
    j. Ethyldibromarsine;
    k. Phosgene;
    l. Monochlormethylchlorformate;
    m. Trichlormethylchlorformate (diphosgene);
    n. Dichlordimethyl ether;
    o. Dibromdimethyl ether;
    p. Cyanogen chloride;
    q. Ethylbromacetate;
    r. Ethyliodoacetate;
    s. Brombenzylcyanide;
    t. Bromacetone;
    u. Brommethylethyl ketone.

Category VII
(1) Propellant powders;
(2) High explosives as follows:
    a. Nitrocellulose having a nitrogen content of more than 12%;
    b. Trinitrotoluene;
    c. Trinitroxylene;
    d. Tetryl (trinitrophenol methyl nitramine or "tetranitro methylaniline");
    e. Picric acid;
    f. Ammonium picrate;
    g. Trinitroanisol;
    h. Trinitronaphthalene;
    i. Tetranitronaphthalene;
    j. Hexanitrodiphenylamine;
    k. Pentaerythritetetranitrate (penthrite or pentrite);
    l. Trimethylenetrinitramine (hexogen or T_4);
    m. Potassium nitrate powders (black saltpeter powder);
    n. Sodium nitrate powders (black soda powder);
    o. Amatol (mixture of ammonium nitrate and trinitrotoluene);
    p. Ammonal (mixture of ammonium nitrate, trinitrotoluene, and powdered aluminum, with or without other ingredients);
    q. Schneiderite (mixture of ammonium nitrate and dinitronaphthalene, with or without other ingredients).

Effective April 15, 1942, this proclamation shall supersede Proclamation 2237, dated May 1, 1937, entitled "Enumeration of Arms, Ammunition, and Implements of War."

. . . .

6. FOREIGN FUNDS CONTROL

[See *Documents, III, 1940–41*, p. 533–43.]

The objectives of the foreign funds control since its inception under Executive Order No. 8389, April 10, 1940, have changed as the policy of the United State developed from theoretical aloofness to full participation in the war. The issuance of Executive Order No. 8785, June 14, 1941 (*Documents, III, 1940–41* p. 537) was an important landmark in the evolution of the system and has remained the basis of the system under war conditions. Amendments to the order extended its operation territorially as conditions required. In the exercise of it authority under Section 2B of the Order, the Treasury Department has, by mean of "regulations, rulings, instructions, licenses or otherwise" determined th application of the general prohibitions of the Order to concrete circumstances.

The first important geographical extension of foreign funds control after Jun 14, 1941 came with the freezing of Japanese and Chinese funds by Executiv Order No. 8832 of July 26, 1941.[1] Parallel action was taken by the Unite Kingdom and made known by announcement of the British Treasury on Jul; 26, 1941.[2] Corresponding action was taken by other parts of the British Com monwealth and by the Netherlands Government at London. The Japanes Government retaliated by applying the Foreign Transactions Control Regula tions.[3] The control was extended by the United States to Chinese assets at th specific request of Generalissimo Chiang Kai-shek and announcement was mad at the time that the administration of the licensing system with respect t Chinese assets would be conducted with a view to strengthening the foreig trade and exchange position of the Chinese Government.[4]

In the actual administration of the system the Treasury Department ha been successful in steadily improving the effectiveness of the control. Som examples are here given. Clearance certificates were required to be attached t blocked foreign bonds as a further step to prevent the sale of looted securitie in the United States.[5] After September 15, owners of such securities which di not bear a clearance certificate were required to trace their ownership since Apr 8, 1940. Remittances to nationals of a blocked country within any foreig country were curtailed by amendment of General Licenses 32 and 72 so as t prevent free dollars or valuable foreign currency from being available to Gei many, Italy or Japan, remittances being permitted only if the transaction re sulted in blocked dollars [6] Blocked nationals were eliminated from transactior in commodity future contracts on October 25, 1941.[7] The importation of postag

[1] 6 *Fed. Reg.*, p. 3715. See statement of the Department of State, this volume p. 501.

[2] *The Times* (London), July 29, 1941, p. 4.

[3] *Japan Weekly Chronicle*, September 25, 1941, p. 416.

[4] See p. 501.

[5] Public Circular No. 6, September 13, 1941.

[6] 6 *Fed. Reg.*, p. 5467, 5468.

[7] General License 9, as amended.

tamps from enemy or enemy-occupied countries was prohibited on January 16,
942, thereby halting a considerable traffic in artificially created issues of stamps
rom which dollar exchange was derived.[1]

The whole system, which was originally based on sec. 5(b) of the Trading with
he Enemy Act of 1917, became intermingled with other applications of that
ct after the declaration of war. Title III, sec. 301 of the First War Powers Act,
pproved December 16, 1941 [2] broadened the basis of authority. The setting up
f the Office of Alien Property Custodian [3] resulted in the transfer from the
Treasury Department to the Alien Property Custodian of all power and au-
hority conferred on the President by secs. 3(a) and 5(b) of the Trading with the
Enemy Act of 1917, as amended, and by Sections 301 and 302 of Title III of the
First War Powers Act, 1941, except such powers and authority as had been
delegated to the Secretary of the Treasury by Executive Orders issued prior to
February 12, 1942 and to the Board of Governors of the Federal Reserve System
y Executive Order No. 8843 of August 9, 1941.

The foreign funds control provided the machinery for a census of "all property
ubject to the jurisdiction of the United States on the opening of business on
June 1, 1940, and . . . on June 14, 1941, in which on the respective dates any
oreign country or any national thereof had any interest of any nature whatso-
ver direct or indirect." [4] The initial census report on Form TFR–300 was due
n October 31, 1941. The data thus obtained provided the most complete infor-
nation of the kind ever collected. It provided the basis for the operations of the
Alien Property Custodian.

The foreign funds control cuts athwart the normal conduct of financial and
conomic transactions to such an extent that attention has been given in the
ulings, licenses and circulars to almost every technical phase of the international
ransfer of valuables. The Treasury Department compiled the texts of all relevant executive orders, regulations, general rulings, general licenses and public
irculars under the title *Documents Pertaining to Foreign Funds Control* up to
August 16, 1941; subsequent editions are issued from time to time.

1) *General Licenses Covering Use of Chinese Funds, November 12, 1941*

General Licenses Nos. 58 and 59, issued July 26, 1941, defined the terms and
onditions applicable to import and export transactions between the United
States and China, and designated the generally licensed banks. The policy at
hat time was to place such restrictions on China as would leave its trade as
nhampered as possible and would not permit it to inure to the benefit of Japan.
On November 12, 1941, after further exchange experience under the Stabiliza-
ion Agreements with China,[5] a new program was made effective. General Li-
ense No. 58 was broadened and General License No. 75 authorized remittances
n any amount to any part of China except Manchuria provided the dollar ex-
hange arising from them was made available to the Stabilization Board of
China. Other general licenses were amended to conform with this policy,[6] as was
Philippine practice.

[1] Treasury Department, Press Service No. 29–66.
[2] See p. 764.
[3] See p. 830.
[4] Regulations under Executive Order No. 8389 as amended, June 14, 1941, sec.
30. 4.
[5] *Documents, III, 1940–41*, p. 243.
[6] Particularly Nos. 59 and 61.

(a) General License No. 58, as amended, November 12, 1941 [1]

[Excerpt]

(1) A general license is hereby granted licensing all transactions ordinarily incident to the importing and exporting of goods, wares and merchandise between the United States and any part of China other than Manchuria, *provided* the following terms and conditions are complied with:

(a) Such transaction shall not involve property in which any one of the following has at any time on or since the effective date of the Order had any interest and shall not be by, or on behalf of, or pursuant to the direction of any one of the following:

(i) any blocked country other than China, or

(ii) any person within Manchuria, or

(iii) any national of any blocked country other than China unless such national is within China;

(b) Exports from the United States to China having a value in excess of $100 shall be effected only provided *both* of the following conditions are satisfied:

(i) payment therefore has been or will be made through a domestic bank and such domestic bank has been notified by an appointed bank that the importer within China has paid or has completed arrangements to pay therefor with United States dollars acquired from such appointed bank, or in lieu of the foregoing a domestic bank has been notified by an appointed bank that the shipment has been otherwise approved by the Stabilization Board of China; and

(ii) on each shipment the domestic bank referred to in (1) shall execute Form TFR–158 in quadruplicate. The original of such executed form shall be transmitted by the domestic bank directly to the collector of customs at the port of exportation and shall be received by such collector of customs prior to the exportation of the shipment. The duplicate of such executed form shall be delivered by the domestic bank to the exporter or his agent who shall present and, if requested deliver such copy to the collector of customs at the port of exportation at the time the Shipper's Export Declaration is filed. The remaining two copies of such executed form shall be filed promptly by the domestic bank with the appropriate Federal Reserve Bank.

[1] 6 *Fed. Reg.*, p. 5802.

(*c*) Imports into the United States from China having a value in excess of $100 shall be effected only provided *both* of the following conditions are satisfied:

  (*i*) payment therefor in United States dollars has been or will be made through a domestic bank and the exporter within China has sold or has completed arrangements for selling such United States dollars to an appointed bank, or in lieu of the foregoing, the shipment has been otherwise approved by the Stabilization Board of China; and

  (*ii*) prior to the release of any such shipment from customs custody the collector of customs of the port of entry through which the shipment is imported shall have received a consular invoice covering such shipment and such consular invoice shall bear the certification of a United States consul in China that an appointed bank has duly notified the consul that the exporter within China has sold or has completed arrangements for selling the United States dollar proceeds from such shipment to such appointed bank or that the shipment has been otherwise approved by the Stabilization Board of China.

[(*d*) Specifying certain exceptions, is omitted.]

(*e*) Any domestic bank prior to issuing, confirming or advising letters of credit, or accepting or paying drafts drawn, or reimbursing themselves for payments made, under letters of credit, or making any other payment or transfer of credit, in connection with any importation or exportation pursuant to this general license, or engaging in any other transaction herein authorized, shall satisfy itself (from the shipping documents or otherwise) that:

  (*i*) any such transaction is incident to a bona fide importation or exportation and is customary in the normal course of business, and that the value of such importation or exportation reasonably corresponds with the sums of money involved in financing such transaction; and

  (*ii*) such importation or exportation is or will be made pursuant to all the terms and conditions of this license.

(2) As used in this general license:

(*a*) The term "appointed bank" shall mean any of those banks cooperating with the Stabilization Board of China and buying and selling foreign exchange with the permission of, and subject to the conditions prescribed by, such Board, the names of which appear on

Schedule A [1] of this general license at the time the transaction i effected.

(b) A person shall not be deemed to be "within China" unless suc person was situated within and doing business within China on an since June 14, 1941.

E. H. FOLEY, JR.
Acting Secretary of the Treasury.

(b) General License No. 75, November 12, 1941 [2]

(1) A general license is hereby granted authorizing remittances in an amount by any person through any domestic bank to any person in an part of China except Manchuria, and any domestic bank is authorize to effect such remittances, provided the following terms and conditior are complied with:

(a) Such remittances may be made from any account other than blocked account and, subject to item (b) hereof, such remittanc may be made from the blocked account of any national of China.

(b) Such remittances may not be made from any blocked accoun if any of the following has an interest in such account:

(i) Any national of any blocked country other than China;

(ii) Any person within Manchuria; or

(iii) Any blocked country other than China; and

(c) Such remittances shall be effected by a domestic bank payin the dollar amount of the remittance to a designated agent of th Central Bank of China for the account of an appointed bank.

(2) All domestic banks effecting such remittances shall satisfy the selves that the foregoing terms and conditions are complied with.

(3) With respect to each remittance made pursuant to this gener license reports on Form TFR–132 shall be executed and filed in t manner and form and under the conditions prescribed in Gener License No. 32. Domestic banks through which any such remittanc originate shall note on the reverse side of such form the nature of t transaction for which the remittance is being made but need not furni the information called for in item 6 of such form.

(4) All dollars accruing to any appointed bank pursuant to th general license shall, if so required by the Stabilization Board of Chin be made available to the Board by payment to the Central Bank China against delivery of an equivalent amount of Chinese nation currency.

---

[1] Not reprinted here.   [2] 6 *Fed. Reg.*, p. 5804.

(5) This general license shall not be deemed to authorize any transaction incidental to imports and exports between the United States and China.

(6) As used in this general license:

(a) The term "appointed bank" shall have the same meaning as that prescribed in General License No. 58.

(b) The term "designated agent of the Central Bank of China" shall mean either the Bank of China or the Philippine Bank of Communications.

E. H. FOLEY, JR.
Acting Secretary of the Treasury.

) *Japanese Nationals Continually Residing in the United States. General License No. 68A, December 15, 1941* [1]

[Excerpt]

All licenses and authorizations for Japanese funds were revoked December 7, 941 by Public Circular No. 8 [2] and Treasury agents took custody of the premises Japanese banking and business enterprises in the United States.[3] The Treasry Department on December 8, 1941 [4] stated the following to be the significant mmediate effects of Public Circular No. 8:

" (1) No Japanese national now has the status of a generally licensed national. this connection, attention is called to the following:

(a) Japanese nationals resident in this country are blocked under the freezing order, irrespective of the length of their residence in this country;

(b) No Japanese bank, business enterprise or other organization now has the status of a generally licensed national, including the Yokohama Specie Bank, Ltd. and all its branches, the Bank of Taiwan, the Sumitomo Bank of Hawaii, the Sumitomo Bank of California, the Sumitomo Bank of Seattle, and the Pacific Bank, Honolulu.

" (2) No withdrawals whatsoever are allowed from any account in any anking institution, if Japan or any national of Japan, has any interest in such ccount. This includes withdrawals for living expenses as well as for any other urpose.[5]

" (3) No withdrawals whatsoever are allowed from any safe deposit box by pan or any national of Japan; access is not allowed to any safe deposit box in e contents of which Japan or any national of Japan has any interest.

---

[1] 6 *Fed. Reg.*, p. 6454.

[2] 6 *Fed. Reg.*, p. 6304, Public Circular No. 8A, December 20, 1941 (6 *Fed. Reg.*, 6679) by specifying the general licenses revoked authorized payment of taxes and es and the deposit of funds in blocked accounts.

[3] Treasury Department, Press Service No. 28–82.

[4] Press Service No. 28–80.

[5] General License No. 11-A and 77, December 11, 1941, allowed withdrawals for ving expenses and transactions by Japanese nationals engaged in the business of oducing, marketing and distributing food within the continental United States.

"(4) No remittances in any amounts whatsoever may be made to Japa or any national of Japan, wheresoever located, including remittances to Unite States citizens resident in Japan.

"(5) No trade transaction with any part of the world, including trade wit Latin America, in which Japan or any national of Japan has any interest ma be effected."

Relaxation of this complete blocking was granted to Japanese nationa resident in the United States since June 17, 1940 by General License No. 68. issued December 15, 1941, reports on accounts being filed by February 15, 194

(a) A general license is hereby granted:

(1) Licensing as a generally licensed national any individual wh is a national of Japan and who has been residing only in the co tinental United States at all times on and since June 17, 194 and

(2) Licensing as a generally licensed national any partnershi association, corporation or other organization within the cont nental United States which is a national of Japan solely l reason of the interest therein of a person or persons licensed generally licensed nationals pursuant to this general license.

(b) This general license shall not be deemed to license as a general licensed national:

(1) Any individual, partnership, association, corporation of oth organization on the premises of which the Treasury Departmer maintains a representative or guard or on the premises of whi there is posted an official Treasury Department notice that t premises are under the control of the United States Gover ment, or

(2) Any bank, trust company, shipping concern, steamship agenc or insurance company, or

(3) Any person who, on or since the effective date of the Orde has represented or acted as agent for any person located outsi the continental United States or for any person owned controlled by persons located outside the continental Unit States, or

(4) Any person who on or since the effective date of the Order h acted or purported to act directly or indirectly for the bene or on behalf of any blocked country, including the governme thereof, or any person who is a national of Japan by reas of any fact other than that such person has been domiciled i or a subject or citizen of, Japan at any time on or since t effective date of the Order.

3) *Restrictions with Respect to Resident Aliens, including Refugees. Amendment of General License 42, February 23, 1942* [1]

Original General License 42, June 14, 1941 (6 *Fed. Reg.*, p. 2907) related o individuals who had been both domiciled and residing in the United States ince June 17, 1940 and freed the accounts of *bona fide* refugees who qualified. ;eneral License 68, July 26, 1941 (6 *Fed. Reg.*, p. 3726) applied similarly to ıationals of China and Japan. Study of the census reports filed on Form TFR–;00 made it possible to liberalize those licenses for refugees who could not meet he domicile requirement; General License 42 A, November 27, 1941 (6 *Fed. ?eg.*, p. 6104) granted this relaxation to those who had made the census report •n Form TFR–300. A further liberalization occurred February 23, 1942 when ;eneral Licenses 42 A and 68 were revoked and an amended General License -2 issued. This change accorded refugees arriving in the United States after une 17, 1940 the same treatment extended to other refugees. Nationals of)hina were consolidated with other resident aliens. Experience had enabled he Treasury Department to be more liberal to *bona fide* immigrants and refugees ınd also to tighten controls in their application to individual cases singled out ɔr close supervision.

(1) A general license is hereby granted:

(*a*) Licensing as a generally licensed national any individual residing in the United States on February 23, 1942, and

(*b*) Licensing as a generally licensed national any partnership, association, corporation or other organization which is a national of a foreign country designated in the Order solely by reason of the interest therein of a person or persons licensed as generally licensed nationals pursuant to this general license.

(2) The following provisions shall govern the filing of reports under his general license:

(*a*) Before effecting any transaction pursuant to this general license, the following persons licensed herein as generally licensed nationals shall file a report in triplicate on Form TFR–42 with the appropriate Federal Reserve Bank:

(*i*) Every individual who was not residing in the United States on June 17, 1940; and

(*ii*) Every partnership, association, corporation or other organization which prior to February 23, 1942, was not a generally licensed national solely by reason of the interest of an individual or individuals referred to in (*i*) above.

Any person failing to comply with this reporting requirement is not authorized to engage in any transaction pursuant to this general license.

[1] 7 *Fed. Reg.*, p. 1492.

(b) Individuals and other persons licensed herein as generally licensed nationals and not falling within classes referred to in 2(a need not file reports on Form TFR–42.

(c) This general license shall not be deemed to suspend, cancel or otherwise modify in any way the requirements of the Order and regulations relating to reports on Form TFR–300 with respect to the property interests of certain persons licensed herein as generally licensed nationals; *provided, however*, that if reports on TFR–300 were not, prior to February 23, 1942, required to be filed in any case o class of cases, such reports are not required to be filed pursuant to thi general license.

(3) This general license shall not be deemed to license as a generally licensed national:

(a) Any individual who on or since the effective date of the Orde has acted or purported to act directly or indirectly for the benefit o on behalf of any blocked country, including the government thereof

(b) Any individual who is a national of a blocked country b reason of any fact other than that such individual has been domicile in, or a subject, citizen, or resident of a blocked country at any tim on or since the effective date of the Order;

(c) Any individual who enters a blocked country after February 2ℨ 1942; or

(d) Any national of Japan. Nationals of Japan shall continue t be governed by the provisions of General License No. 68A in so fa as General License No. 68A may be applicable.

E. H. FOLEY, JR.
Acting Secretary of the Treasury.

(4) Regulation of Transactions in Foreign Exchange and Foreign-Owne Property, and Provision for the Reporting of All Foreign-Owne Property, and Related Matters. Executive Order No. 8785, Jun 14, 1941,[1] as amended by Executive Order No. 8998, Decembe 26, 1941 [2]

[Excerpt]

As the amendments in this Executive Order affected only the "foreign cou tries" named in sec. 3 and the stipulations of sec. 5, the preamble of the amend ing Executive Order No. 8998, December 26, 1941 basing the authority upo the new Trading with the Enemy Act, and the two amended sections are give: Sec. 3 specifies the countries to which the foreign funds control applies.

By virtue of the authority vested in me by Sections 3(a) and 5(b) the Trading with the Enemy Act of October 6, 1917 (40 Stat. 415),

---

[1] *Documents, III, 1940–41*, p. 537.　　　　[2] 6 *Fed. Reg.*, p. 6785.

...mended by Title III of the First War Powers Act, 1941 (Public No. 354,
'7th Congress), and by virtue of all other authority vested in me, I,
'RANKLIN D. ROOSEVELT, PRESIDENT of the UNITED STATES OF
AMERICA, do hereby amend Executive Order No. 8389 of April 10, 1940,
.s amended, in the following respects:

. . . .

SEC. 3. The term "foreign country designated in this order" means a
oreign country included in the following schedule, and the term "effec-
ive date of this Order" means with respect to any such foreign country,
.r any national thereof, the date specified in the following schedule:
  (a) April 8, 1940 — Norway and Denmark;
  (b) May 10, 1940 — The Netherlands, Belgium and Luxemburg;
  (c) June 17, 1940 — France (including Monaco);
  (d) July 10, 1940 — Latvia, Estonia and Lithuania;
  (e) October 9, 1940 — Rumania;
  (f) March 4, 1941 — Bulgaria;
  (g) March 13, 1941 — Hungary;
  (h) March 24, 1941 — Yugoslavia;
  (i) April 28, 1941 — Greece;
  (j) June 14, 1941 — Albania, Andorra, Austria, Czechoslovakia,
)anzig, Finland, Germany, Italy, Liechtenstein, Poland, Portugal,[1]
;an Marino, Spain,[2] Sweden,[3] Switzerland,[3] and Union of Soviet Socialist
\Republics;
  (k) [4] June 14, 1941 — China and Japan;
  (l) [5] June 14, 1941 — Thailand;
  (m) [6] June 14, 1941 — Hong Kong.

The "effective date of this Order" with respect to any foreign country
.ot designated in this order shall be deemed to be June 14, 1941.

. . . .

SEC. 5. A. As used in the first paragraph of Section 1 of this Order
'transactions [which] involve property in which any foreign country

[1] General License 70, August 11, 1941, authorized transactions by the Government
f Portugal and Banco de Portugal for themselves and for the account of Portuguese
.ationals.
[2] General License 52, July 11, 1941, authorized transactions by the Spanish Insti-
\ute of Foreign Exchange for the account of Spanish nationals.
[3] See *Documents, III, 1940–41*, p. 542.
[4] Amendment by Executive Order No. 8832, July 26, 1941 (6 *Fed. Reg.*, p. 3715).
[5] Amendment by Executive Order No. 8963, December 9, 1941 (6 *Fed. Reg.*,
\. 6348); General License 76 (*ibid.*, p. 6350).
[6] Amendment by Executive Order No. 8998 of December 26, 1941 (6 *Fed. Reg.*,
\. 6785).

designated in this Order, or any national thereof, has . . . any interest of any nature whatsoever, direct or indirect," shall include, but not by way of limitation (1) any payment or transfer to any such foreign country or national thereof, (2) any export or withdrawal from the United States to such foreign country, and (3) any transfer of credit or payment of an obligation, expressed in terms of the currency of such foreign country.

B. [1] The term "United States" means the United States and any place subject to the jurisdiction thereof, and the term "continental United States" means the states of the United States, the District of Columbia, and the Territory of Alaska; *provided, however*, that for the purposes of this Order the term "United States" shall not be deemed to include any territory included within the term "foreign country" as defined in paragraph D of this section.

C. The term "person" means an individual, partnership, association, corporation or other organization.

D. The term "foreign country" shall include, but not by way of limitation:

(*i*) The State and the government thereof on the effective date of this order as well as any political subdivision, agency, or instrumentality thereof or any territory, dependency, colony, protectorate, mandate, dominion, possession or place subject to the jurisdiction thereof,

(*ii*) Any other government (including any political subdivision, agency, or instrumentality thereof) to the extent and only to the extent that such government exercises or claims to exercise de jure or de facto sovereignty over the area which on such effective date constituted such foreign country, and

(*iii*) [2] Any territory which on or since the effective date of this Order is controlled or occupied by the military, naval or police forces or other authority of such foreign country;

(*iv*) [3] Any person to the extent that such person is, or has been or to the extent that there is reasonable cause to believe that such person is, or has been, since such effective date, acting or purporting to act directly or indirectly for the benefit or on behalf of any of the foregoing.

---

[1] Amendment by sec. (3) of Executive Order No. 8998, December 26, 1941 (*Fed. Reg.*, p. 6785); the amendment consists of the proviso.

[2] Amendment by sec. (3) of Executive Order No. 8998, December 26, 1941 (*Fed. Reg.*, p. 6785); the subparagraph is an addition. The section specifies the "Hong Kong shall be deemed to be a foreign country within the meaning of the subdivision."

[3] Subparagraph (*iii*) before the preceding amendment.

E. The term "national" shall include,

(1) Any person who has been domiciled in, or a subject, citizen or
sident of, a foreign country at any time on or since the effective date
this order,[1]

(2) Any partnership, association, corporation or other organization,
ganized under the laws of, or which on or since the effective date of
is order had or has had its principal place of business in such foreign
untry, or which on or since such effective date was or has been con-
olled by, or a substantial part of the stock, shares, bonds, debentures,
tes, drafts, or other securities or obligations of which, was or has been
ned or controlled by, directly or indirectly, such foreign country and
r one or more nationals thereof as herein defined,

(3) Any person to the extent that such person is, or has been, since
ch effective date, acting or purporting to act directly or indirectly
the benefit or on behalf of any national of such foreign country, and

(4) Any other person who, there is reasonable cause to believe, is a
national" as herein defined.[2]

In any case in which by virtue of the foregoing definition a person is a
tional of more than one foreign country, such person shall be deemed
be a national of each such foreign country. In any case in which the
mbined interests of two or more foreign countries designated in this
ler and/or nationals thereof are sufficient in the aggregate to con-
tute, within the meaning of the foregoing, control of 25 per centum
more of the stock, shares, bonds, debentures, notes, drafts, or other
urities or obligations of a partnership, association, corporation or
her organization, but such control or a substantial part of such stock,
ares, bonds, debentures, notes, drafts, or other securities or obligations
not held by any one such foreign country and/or national thereof,
ch partnership, association, corporation or other organization, shall
deemed to be a national of each of such foreign countries. . . .

F. The term "banking institution" as used in this order shall include
y person engaged primarily or incidentally in the business of banking,
granting or transferring credits, or of purchasing or selling foreign
change or procuring purchasers and sellers thereof, as principal or
ent, or any person holding credits for others as a direct or incidental
rt of his business, or brokers; and, each principal, agent, home office,
anch or correspondent of any person so engaged shall be regarded as
eparate "banking institution."

[1] General License No. 42 of June 14, 1941 (6 *Fed. Reg.*, p. 2907) applies to such indi-
uals.
[2] The Roman Curia of the Vatican City State is a generally licensed national by
neral License No. 44 (6 *Fed. Reg.*, p. 2907).

G. The term "this Order," as used herein, shall mean Executiv Order No. 8389 of April 10, 1940, as amended.[1]

(5) *Property Frozen under Foreign Funds Control, as of March 13, 1942*

BY TYPE

Short-term funds, including earmarked gold	$4,000,000,00
Securities	2,000,000,00
Direct investments and miscellaneous	1,000,000,00
Blocked nationals resident in the United States . . .	500,000,00

BY COUNTRY

Netherlands, including Netherland East Indies . . .	$1,800,000,00
Switzerland	1,500,000,00
France and Monaco	1,300,000,00
Belgium	500,000,00
Sweden	400,000,00
China	200,000,00
Norway	200,000,00
Japan	150,000,00
Germany	100,000,00
Italy	50,000,00
All others	800,000,00
Nationals resident in the United States (other than business enterprises owned abroad)	500,000,00
TOTAL	7,500,000,00

7. PROCLAIMED LIST OF CERTAIN BLOCKED NATIONALS[3]

In World War I it was found advisable by the United Kingdom and lat by the United States to prevent trade by their nationals with firms situated : foreign countries which purchased for enemy account or which in devious wa acted as agents for the enemy. These so-called "black lists" included chief the names of firms in the American Republics. With the outbreak of war wi Germany on September 1, 1939 the United Kingdom followed a similar pract and issued statutory rules and orders under the title of "Trading with t Enemy. Specified Persons."

Quite unconnected with that action at the outset was an investigation of t representation of American business in the American Republics which w undertaken by the Coordinator of Commercial and Cultural Relations Betwe

[1] *Documents, II, 1939–40,* p. 543.

[2] United States Congress, House of Representatives, Committee on Appropriation Sixth Supplemental National Defense Appropriation Bill for 1942; *Hearings befc Subcommittees* . . . 77th Cong., 2d sess., Part I, p. 295.

[3] Department of State, *Bulletin,* V, p. 20.

he American Republics, who reported on January 8, 1941.[1] That report and
ubsequent information showed that German-controlled firms were undermining
he American firms they represented and in many instances were using the funds
f their principals for subversive purposes. The Coordinator made a formal
tatement on July 11 and on July 17 the President issued a proclamation direct-
ng the publication of the "proclaimed list of certain blocked nationals." That
st contained the names of 1800 firms in the 20 other American Republics.
upplements containing deletions from and amendments and additions to the
st were issued frequently, the list being successively consolidated in Revision I
ssued February 7, 1942 and in Revision II issued May 12, 1942. These Revi-
ions, prepared after the United States was engaged in war, were divided into
wo parts, Part I containing the "black list" of the Western Hemisphere and
'art II that of the rest of the world. Revision II contained 8241 names, 5972 in
'art I and 2269 in Part II.

The Proclaimed List is published by the Department of State, Division
f World Trade Intelligence.

Collaboration with the American Republics with respect to the Proclaimed
ist was close. Under Secretary of State Sumner Welles in his capacity as
resident of the Inter-American Financial and Economic Advisory Committee
nnounced the action taken by the United States at the committee's meeting
n July 17, 1941[2] and on motion his statement was "referred to Subcommittee I
n order that this Subcommittee may request the presence of officials and author-
ies of the Government of the United States so that they may explain in detail
nything concerning this declaration and any amendments or suggestions
hich delegates may wish to formulate may be taken into account."

1) Proclamation Authorizing a Proclaimed List of Certain Blocked Nationals and Controlling Certain Exports, July 17, 1941 [3]

As a further step in view of the unlimited national emergency declared by the
resident on May 27, 1941, this proclamation was issued. It was stated that
e list[4] would consist of certain persons deemed to be acting for the benefit
f Germany or Italy or nationals of those countries and persons to whom the
xportation, directly or indirectly, of various articles or materials was deemed
be detrimental to the interest of national defense. The President gave
arning that anyone serving as a cloak for a person on the list will have his
ame added forthwith to the list.

The list was stated as having two principal functions: (1) to prevent the
xportation of any article covered by the Export Control Act of July 2, 1940
persons named in the list except under special circumstances; (2) to extend
persons on the list the same treatment as if they were nationals of Germany
Italy within the meaning of Executive Order No. 8389, as amended, under
hich, on June 14, 1941, the freezing control was extended to all of the countries
the continent of Europe and nationals thereof.[5]

---

[1] *Documents, III, 1940–41*, p. 111.
[2] See p. 384.
[3] 6 *Fed. Reg.*, p. 3555; Department of State, *Bulletin*, V, p. 42.
[4] 6 *Fed. Reg.*, p. 3557; the list, with current supplements, is published separately
d obtainable from the offices mentioned in sec. 1 of the proclamation. In the Code
Federal Regulations, the list is Title 32, National Defense, Chap. VIII, Export
ontrol, Subchap. B.
[5] *Documents, III, 1940–41*, p. 537.

At the time of the issuance of the proclamation, it was also announced that ir attaining the objectives of Executive Order No. 8389, as amended, all effort were being made to cause the least possible interference with legitimate inter American trade. With that end in view the Treasury Department issued : general license with respect to inter-American trade transactions and the financia transactions incidental thereto involving persons in the other American Re publics who might be nationals of a European country designated in the Order This general license would permit such classes of transactions without the necessity of applying for specific licenses.

The general license, however, would not apply to persons so long as their name appeared on the proclaimed list. In addition, exporters and importers in the United States might from time to time be advised by their banks, or otherwise that instructions had been issued by the Secretary of the Treasury requirin, specific-license applications for trade transactions involving certain persons ii the other American Republics who were not named on the proclaimed list.

Furthermore, financial transactions which were not incidental to license trade transactions were not covered by the general license. With respect to such purely financial transactions, appropriate specific licenses would have to be obtained from the Treasury Department.

The proclaimed list would also serve as a guide to United States firms in the selection of agents and representatives in the other American Republics.

BY THE PRESIDENT OF THE UNITED STATES OF AMERICA

A Proclamation [No. 2497]

I, FRANKLIN D. ROOSEVELT, President of the United States o America, acting under and by virtue of the authority vested in me b Section 5(b) of the Act of October 6, 1917 (40 Stat. 415) as amende and Section 6 of the Act of July 2, 1940 (54 Stat. 714) as amended an by virtue of all other authority vested in me, and by virtue of the exist ence of a period of unlimited national emergency and finding that th Proclamation is necessary in the interest of national defense, do hereb order and proclaim the following:

SECTION 1. The Secretary of State, acting in conjunction with th Secretary of the Treasury, the Attorney General, the Secretary (Commerce, the Administrator of Export Control, and the Coordinat of Commercial and Cultural Relations Between the American Republic shall from time to time cause to be prepared an appropriate list of

(a) certain persons deemed to be, or to have been acting or purpor ing to act, directly or indirectly, for the benefit of, or under th direction of, or under the jurisdiction of, or on behalf of, or in collabor tion with Germany or Italy or a national thereof; and

(b) certain persons to whom, or on whose behalf, or for who account, the exportation directly or indirectly of any article (material exported from the United States, is deemed to be detriment to the interest of national defense.

In similar manner and in the interest of national defense, additions and deletions from such list shall be made from time to time. Such list and any additions thereto or deletions therefrom shall be filed pursuant to the provisions of the Federal Register Act and such list shall be known as "The Proclaimed List of Certain Blocked Nationals."

SECTION 2. Any person, so long as his name appears in such list, shall, for the purpose of Section 5(b) of the Act of October 6, 1917, as amended, and for the purpose of this Proclamation, be deemed to be a national of a foreign country, and shall be treated for all purposes under Executive Order No. 8389, as amended,[1] as though he were a national of Germany or Italy. All the terms and provisions of Executive Order No. 8389, as amended, shall be applicable to any such person so long as his name appears in such list, and to any property in which any such person has or has had an interest, to the same extent that such terms and provisions are applicable to nationals of Germany or Italy, and to property in which nationals of Germany or Italy have or have had an interest.

SECTION 3. The exportation from the United States directly or indirectly to, or on behalf of, or for the account of any person, so long as his name appears on such list, of any article or material the exportation of which is prohibited or curtailed by any proclamation heretofore or hereafter issued under the authority of Section 6 of the Act of July 2, 1940, as amended, or of any other military equipment or munitions, or component parts thereof, or machinery, tools, or material, or supplies necessary for the manufacture, servicing, or operation thereof, is hereby prohibited under Section 6 of the Act of July 2, 1940, as amended, except (1) when authorized in each case by a license as provided for in Proclamation No. 2413 of July 2, 1940,[2] or in Proclamation No. 2465 of March 4, 1941,[3] as the case may be, and (2) when the Administrator of Export Control under my direction has determined that such prohibition of exportation would work an unusual hardship on American interests.

SECTION 4. The term "person" as used herein means an individual, partnership, association, corporation or other organization.

The term "United States" as used herein means the United States and any place subject to the jurisdiction thereof, including the Philippine Islands, the Canal Zone, and the District of Columbia and any other territory, dependency or possession of the United States.

SECTION 5. Nothing herein contained shall be deemed in any manner to limit or restrict the provisions of the said Executive Order No. 8389, as amended, or the authority vested thereby in the Secretary of the

[1] *Documents, III, 1940–41,* p. 537.   [2] *Ibid.,* p. 474.   [3] *Ibid.,* p. 486.

Treasury and the Attorney General. So far as the said Executive Orde
No. 8389, as amended, is concerned, "The Proclaimed List of Certai
Blocked Nationals," authorized by this Proclamation, is merely a li:
of certain persons with respect to whom and with respect to whos
property interests the public is specifically put on notice that the pro
visions of such Executive Order are applicable; and the fact that an
person is not named in such list shall in no wise be deemed to mean tha
such person is not a national of a foreign country designated in suc
order, within the meaning thereof, or to affect in any manner the applica
tion of such order to such person or to the property interests of suc
person.

IN WITNESS WHEREOF, I have hereunto set my hand and caused th
seal of the United States of America to be affixed.

DONE at the city of Washington this 17th day of July, in the year •
our Lord nineteen hundred and forty-one, and of the Ind•
[SEAL]   pendence of the United States of America the one hundred an
sixty-sixth.

FRANKLIN D. ROOSEVELT

By the President:
    SUMNER WELLES
        Acting Secretary of State

(2) *"The Generally Licensed Trade Area" and Transactions Therei. General License No. 53, as amended, July 17, 1941* [1]

Simultaneously with the issuance of the Proclaimed List of Certain Block•
Nationals, this general license of the Foreign Funds Control Division defin•
the conditions of trade with the American Republics. It was amended August
and October 9, 1941 in sec. 3(a) so as to embrace the generally licensed tra
area. In the amended form as given, the territories included comprised t
countries outside of the influence of Germany, Italy and Japan.

(1) A general license is hereby granted licensing all transactio
ordinarily incident to the importing and exporting of goods, wares a•
merchandise between the United States and any of the members of t
generally licensed trade area [2] or between the members of the general
licensed trade area if (*i*) such transaction is by, or on behalf of,
pursuant to the direction of any national of a blocked country with
he generally licensed trade area, or (*ii*) such transaction involves pro•

---

[1] 6 *Fed. Reg.*, p. 3556; amended August 5, 1941, 6 *Fed. Reg.*, p. 3946; October
1941, 6 *Fed. Reg.*, p. 5180; December 26, 1941, 6 *Fed. Reg.*, p. 6792; March
1942, 7 *Fed. Reg.*, p. 2083.

[2] The original of July 17, 1941 applied only to the American Republics.

rty in which any such national has at any time on or since the effective ate of the Order had any interest, *provided* the following terms and onditions are complied with:

(*a*) Such transaction is not by, or in behalf of, or pursuant to the direction of (*i*) any person whose name appears on "The Proclaimed List of Certain Blocked Nationals," or (*ii*) any blocked country or national thereof not within the generally licensed trade area;

(*b*) Such transaction does not involve property in which (*i*) any person whose name appears on "The Proclaimed List of Certain Blocked Nationals," or (*ii*) any blocked country or national thereof not within the generally licensed trade area, has at any time on or since the effective date of the Order had any interest; and

(*c*) Any banking institution within the United States, prior to issuing, confirming or advising letters of credit, or accepting or paying drafts drawn, or reimbursing themselves for payments made, under letters of credit, or making any other payment or transfer of credit, in connection with any importation or exportation pursuant to this general license, or engaging in any other transaction herein authorized, shall satisfy itself (from the shipping documents or otherwise) that: (*i*) any such transaction is incident to a bona fide importation or exportation and is customary in the normal course of business, and that the value of such importation or exportation reasonably corresponds with the sums of money involved in financing such transactions; and (*ii*) such importation or exportation is or will be made pursuant to all the terms and conditions of this license.

(2) Subject to all other terms and conditions of this general license ny national of a blocked country doing business within the United tates pursuant to a license is also hereby authorized, while so licensed,) engage in any transaction referred to in paragraph (1) to the same ctent that such national is licensed to engage in such transaction involv- g persons within the generally licensed trade area who are not nationals f a blocked country.

(3) As used in this general license:

(*a*) The term "generally licensed trade area" shall mean the following:

    (*i*) the American Republics, i.e., (1) Argentina, (2) Bolivia, (3) Brazil, (4) Chile, (5) Colombia, (6) Costa Rica, (7) Cuba, (8) the Dominican Republic, (9) Ecuador, (10) El Salvador, (11) Guatemala, (12) Haiti, (13) Honduras, (14) Mexico, (15) Nicaragua, (16) Panama, (17) Paraguay, (18) Peru, (19) Uruguay, and (20) Venezuela;

 (*ii*) [1] the British Commonwealth of Nations, i.e., (1) the United Kingdom (England, Wales, Scotland and Northern Ireland, (2) The British Dominions (Canada, Australia, New Zealand, the Union of South Africa and Newfoundland), (3) Eire (4) The Isle of Man, (5) India, (6) Egypt, (7) Anglo-Egyptian Soudan, (8) Iraq, (9) all colonies and protectorates under the British Crown, and (10) all mandated territories administered by the United Kingdom or by any British Dominion;

 (*iii*) the Union of Soviet Socialist Republics;

 (*iv*) the Netherlands West Indies;

 (*v*) the Belgian Congo and Ruanda-Urundi;

 (*vi*) Greenland;

 (*vii*) Iceland;

 (*viii*) [2] Syria and Lebanon; and

 (*ix*) (1) French Equatorial Africa, including the Cameroons (2) New Caledonia; (3) Tahiti; (4) the French Establishments in India.

Provided, however, that the term "generally licensed trade area" shall not include any territory which is controlled or occupied by the military, naval or police forces or other authority of Japan, Germany or Italy, or allies thereof.

 (*b*) The term "member" of the generally licensed trade area shall mean any of the foreign countries or political subdivisions comprising the generally licensed trade area.

 (*c*) The term "any national of a blocked country within the generally licensed trade area" shall mean any national of a blocked country who was situated within and doing business within such area on and since June 14, 1941.

 (*d*) The term "The Proclaimed List of Certain Blocked Nationals" shall mean "The Proclaimed List of Certain Blocked Nationals" as amended and supplemented promulgated pursuant to the proclamation of July 17, 1941.

(3) *Statement of the Acting Secretary of State* (*Welles*), *July 29, 1941*

The chief effect of the publication of the list of blocked nationals is to deny the benefits of inter-American trade to persons who have hitherto

[1] Sec. (3) (*a*) was amended to read as it stands, with the addition of subparagraph (*ii–viii*), on August 5, 1941. The Netherlands East Indies was included until March 13, 1942.

[2] The following subparagraphs added by amendment October 9, 1941.

[3] Department of State, *Bulletin*, V, p. 99. The statement was made in response to inquiries at the press conference.

)een using large profits to finance subversive activities aimed at under-
nining the peace and independence of the Western Hemisphere. Trade
hat had previously been usurped by such anti-American interests is
now being transferred into the hands of persons, largely citizens of the
other republics, who are devoted to the best interests of the countries
n which they reside, all of which are committed to the solidarity of the
Americas in the face of threats from abroad.

Recent events have emphasized the correctness of the charge that
he totalitarian powers are striving to disturb the peace of this hemi-
phere and to extend their disruptive control over the affairs of American
Republics. Swift action by the governments affected has nipped dangerous plans of the totalitarians in the bud and indicates the determination
f the American Republics to defend their integrity and peace. The
ssuance of the proclaimed list, marking persons who are contributing
o these anti-American activities, is but another step in blocking the
fforts of those who have sinister designs on the Americas.

A great many American firms have for several months been voluntarily
hanging their trade connections when it became evident that their
ousiness was in the hands of groups unfriendly to inter-American interests.
Publication of the list of blocked nationals is a clarifying step in marking
hose who under present conditions should not participate in vital inter-
American transactions. Such a step is of the utmost importance in view
f the steady increase in trade between the United States and the other
American Republics, and at a time when the United States is making
very effort to see that essential materials are made available to the other
epublics for use in their defense efforts.

The list as first published is of course not final. Changes have already
een announced;[1] and other deletions, as well as additions, will be made
n order that the list may reflect accurately the results of continuing
tudy of the firms and persons involved. This Government will show
he greatest zeal in removing names whenever altered situations with
espect to individual firms warrant such action.

*4) Extension to Japanese Interests. Comment by the Department of
State on Supplement 5, issued December 9, 1941*[2]

This supplement, which is devoted exclusively to Japanese firms and
ersons in the American Republics, contains 470 additions to the Pro-
laimed List. Several non-Japanese individuals are included because

[1] Supplement No. 1 containing both deletions and amendments was issued July
3, 1941.
[2] Department of State, *Bulletin*, V, p. 521.

of their important affiliation with Japanese enterprises. A further supplement containing additional Japanese cases will be issued shortly

The attention of the public is again called to the fact that the Treasury Department has revoked all outstanding general and specific licenses so far as they authorize any transactions by, or on behalf of, or for the benefit of Japan and her nationals wherever situated. Supplement 3 merely contains the names of certain Japanese firms and persons in the American Republics, and the fact that the name of a particular concern or individual is omitted from the Proclaimed List should not be taken to mean that such firm or person is not a Japanese national or to authorize transactions in which any Japanese national not on the list may have an interest. Individuals and concerns subject to the jurisdiction of the United States, including all branches, subsidiaries, agents, and affiliates of such concerns in the American Republics, may not have any financial, business, or commercial dealings of any nature whatsoever in which Japan or her nationals have an interest.

8. TRADING WITH THE ENEMY

Secs. 2, 3 and 5 of the Trading with the Enemy Act of October 6, 1917 (40 Stat. 411) were put into effect immediately upon the attack of the Japanese at Pearl Harbor. The Secretary of the Treasury on the night of December 7, 1941 ordered all collectors of customs and customs personnel to enforce immediately sec. 3 and instructed them that the words "ally" or "ally of enemy" under sec. 2 of the act applied to Japan.[1] On December 18, 1941 the approval of the "First War Powers Act" amended sec. 5(b) of the Act, upon which the foreign funds control was based, so as to provide for flexible administration of the control of alien property. On March 18, 1942 the Secretary of the Treasury and the Director of Censorship by General Ruling No. 11 and Communication Ruling No. 1 adapted the restrictions of the 1917 act on trade and communication to the requirements of the war. The new concept of "enemy national" for both trade and communication was substituted for that of "enemy" and "ally of enemy," the prohibition of trade and communication was made definite in its application to those listed on the Proclaimed List of Certain Blocked Nationals, and the ruling was so phrased as to apply to all General Licenses of the Foreign Funds Control system unless specifically excepted. The standard of conduct which United States concerns doing business within Latin America are required to follow to avoid commerce with blacklisted firms was laid down by Public Circular No. 18, March 30, 1942.[2]

(1) Secs. 2 and 3 of the Trading with the Enemy Act, October 6, 1917[3]

SEC. 2. That the word "enemy," as used herein, shall be deemed to mean, for the purpose of such trading and of this Act —

[1] Treasury Press Service No. 28–79.

[2] For decisions relevant to this control, see Resolution VI, Third Meeting of the Ministers of Foreign Affairs of the American Republics, p. 313.

[3] 40 Stat. 411; reprinted from United States, House of Representatives, Legislative Counsel, *Trading with the Enemy Act as Amended* (*together with the original act and*

(a) Any individual, partnership, or other body of individuals, of any ationality, resident within the territory (including that occupied by ɪe military and naval forces) of any nation with which the United tates is at war, or resident outside the United States and doing business ithin such territory, and any corporation incorporated within such ɪrritory of any nation with which the United States is at war or incorɔrated within any country other than the United States and doing usiness within such territory.

(b) The government of any nation with which the United States is ɪ war, or any political or municipal subdivision thereof, or any officer, ficial, agent, or agency thereof.

(c) Such other individuals, or body or class of individuals, as may be atives, citizens, or subjects of any nation with which the United States at war, other than citizens of the United States, wherever resident ː wherever doing business, as the President, if he shall find the safety ː the United States or the successful prosecution of the war shall so ɪquire, may, by proclamation, include within the term "enemy."

The words "ally of enemy," as used herein, shall be deemed to ɪean —

(a) Any individual, partnership, or other body of individuals, of any ationality, resident within the territory (including that occupied by ɪilitary and naval forces) of any nation which is an ally of a nation ith which the United States is at war, or resident outside the United tates and doing business within such territory, and any corporation corporated within such territory of such ally nation, or incorporated ithin any country other than the United States and doing business ithin such territory.

(b) The government of any nation which is an ally of a nation with hich the United States is at war, or any political or municipal subvision of such ally nation, or any officer, official, agent, or agency ɪereof.

(c) Such other individuals, or body or class of individuals, as may be atives, citizens, or subjects of any nation which is an ally of a nation ith which the United States is at war, other than citizens of the United ːates, wherever resident or wherever doing business, as the President, he shall find the safety of the United States or the successful prosecuon of the war shall so require, may, by proclamation, include within ɪe term "ally of enemy."

ɪendments thereto) and the Settlement of War Claims Act of 1928 as Amended (to-
ɪher with amendments thereto); prepared for the use of the Committee on Ways and
ʾeans, Washington, 1941. 118 p.

The word "person," as used herein, shall be deemed to mean a individual, partnership, association, company, or other unincorporate body of individuals, or corporation or body politic.

The words "United States," as used herein, shall be deemed to mea all land and water, continental or insular, in any way within the juri diction of the United States or occupied by the military or naval force thereof.

The words "the beginning of the war," as used herein, shall be deeme to mean midnight ending the day on which Congress has declared shall declare war or the existence of a state of war.

The words "end of the war," as used herein, shall be deemed to mea the date of proclamation of exchange of ratifications of the treaty peace, unless the President shall, by proclamation, declare a prior dat in which case the date so proclaimed shall be deemed to be the "en of the war" within the meaning of this Act.

The words "bank or banks," as used herein, shall be deemed to mea and include national banks, State banks, trust companies, or other bank or banking associations doing business under the laws of the Unite States, or of any State of the United States.

The words "to trade," as used herein, shall be deemed to mean —

(a) Pay, satisfy, compromise, or give security for the payment c satisfaction of any debt or obligation.

(b) Draw, accept, pay, present for acceptance or payment, or indors any negotiable instrument or chose in action.

(c) Enter into, carry on, complete, or perform any contract, agree ment, or obligation.

(d) Buy or sell, loan or extend credit, trade in, deal with, exchang transmit, transfer, assign, or otherwise dispose of, or receive any form c property.

(e) To have any form of business or commercial communication c intercourse with.

Sec. 3. That it shall be unlawful

(a) for any person in the United States, except with the license of th President, granted to such person, or to the enemy, or ally of enemy as provided in this act, to trade, or attempt to trade, either directly c indirectly, with, to, or from, or for, or on account of, or on behalf o or for the benefit of, any other person, with knowledge or reasonabl cause to believe that such other person is an enemy or ally of enem or is conducting or taking part in such trade, directly or indirectly, fo or on account of, or on behalf of, or for the benefit of, an enemy or all of enemy.

(*b*) For any person, except with the license of the President, to trans-
ort or attempt to transport into or from the United States, or for any
vner, master, or other person in charge of a vessel of American registry
o transport or attempt to transport from any place to any other place,
ny subject or citizen of an enemy or ally of enemy nation, with knowl-
lge or reasonable cause to believe that the person transported or
tempted to be transported is such subject or citizen.

(*c*) For any person (other than a person in the service of the United
tates Government or of the Government of any nation, except that of
ny enemy or ally of enemy nation, and other than such persons or
asses of persons as may be exempted hereunder by the President or
y such person as he may direct), to send, or take out of, or bring into,
r attempt to send, or take out of, or bring into the United States, any
tter or other writing or tangible form of communication, except in the
gular course of the mail; and it shall be unlawful for any person to
nd, take, or transmit, or attempt to send, take, or transmit out of the
nited States, any letter or other writing, book, map, plan, or other
per, picture, or any telegram, cablegram, or wireless message, or
her form of communication intended for or to be delivered, directly
indirectly, to an enemy or ally of enemy; provided, however, that
y person may send, take or transmit out of the United States anything
rein forbidden if he shall first submit the same to the President, or to
ch officer as the President may direct, and shall obtain the license or
nsent of the President, under such rules and regulations, and with such
emptions, as shall be prescribed by the President.[1]

) *"First War Powers Act, 1941," Title III, Trading with the Enemy,*
    Approved December 18, 1941 [2]

[Title I, Coordination of Executive Bureaus in the Interest of the More Efficient
ncentration of the Government, printed at p. 126.]

The original Trading with the Enemy Act became law on October 6, 1917
0 Stat. 411). Some sections of the act were still in effect, some had terminated
d doubt existed as to the effectiveness of others.[3] The present sec. 303, dealing

[1] Sec. 3(*d*) was reenacted as sec. 303 of the "First War Powers Act," Title III.
low, p. 766.
[2] Public Law 354, 77th Cong., An Act to Expedite the Prosecution of the War
fort; originated as H. R. 6233, from the Committee on the Judiciary, December
, 1941; House Report No. 1567.
[3] The legislation centering in the Act embodied important precedents and therefore,
of October 1, 1941, it was compiled separately: United States, House of Represent-
ives, Legislative Counsel, *Trading with the Enemy Act as Amended (together with the
iginal act and amendments thereto) and the Settlement of War Claims Act of 1928 as
nended (together with amendments thereto); prepared for the use of the Committee
Ways and Means.* Washington, 1941. 118 p.

with the censorship of international communications, is identical with t
provisions of sec. 3(d) and the penalty provision of sec. 16 of the 1917 act. T
present sec. 301 is a further amendment of sec. 5(b) of the 1917 act which, a
amended May 7, 1940 [1] (Documents, II, 1939-40, p. 541), gives authority t
prohibit and to license transactions in foreign property. The present sec. 30
provides a system which can affirmatively compel the use and application
foreign property in the best interests of the United States. The report of th
House Committee on the Judiciary stated: " The provisions of section 301 wou
permit the establishment of a complete system of alien property treatment.
vests flexible powers in the President, operating through such agency or agenci
as he might choose, to deal with the problems that surround alien property or i
ownership or control in the manner deemed most effective in each particular cas
In this respect the bill avoids the rigidity and inflexibility which characterize
the alien property custodian law enacted during the last war. The necessit
for flexibility in legislation on this subject is accentuated by the vastness of th
alien property problem confronting the Government today. At the peak of h
activity, the Alien Property Custodian of the last war administered propert
valued at something over $500,000,000. Today there is over $7,000,000,00
worth of property already subject to the existing control.

"This provision of the bill to a considerable extent follows the pattern
existing law and is a logical extension of the present foreign property contr
system, which has been operating very satisfactorily for almost 2 years. Th
extension could be put into immediate operation with a minimum amount
trouble or dislocation of legitimate activities."

SEC. 301. The first sentence of subdivision (b) of section 5 of th
Trading with the Enemy Act of October 6, 1917 (40 Stat. 411), a
amended, is hereby amended to read as follows:

"(1) During the time of war or during any other period of nation
emergency declared by the President, the President may, through ar
agency that he may designate, or otherwise, and under such rules ar
regulations as he may prescribe, by means of instructions, licenses,
otherwise —

"(A) investigate, regulate, or prohibit, any transactions in foreig
exchange, transfers of credit or payments between, by, through,
to any banking institution, and the importing, exporting, hoardin
melting, or earmarking of gold or silver coin or bullion, currency
securities, and

"(B) investigate, regulate, direct and compel, nullify, void, prevei
or prohibit, any acquisition holding, withholding, use, transfer, wit
drawal, transportation, importation or exportation of, or dealing i
or exercising any right, power, or privilege with respect to, or tran
actions involving, any property in which any foreign country or
national thereof has any interest,

[1] The provision was previously amended by sec. 5 of the Act of Approval Septer
ber 24, 1918 (40 Stat. 966) and by sec. 2 of the Act approved March 9, 19:
(48 Stat. 1).

y any person, or with respect to any property, subject to the juris-
iction of the United States; and any property or interest of any foreign
ountry or national thereof shall vest, when, as, and upon the terms,
irected by the President, in such agency or person as may be designated
om time to time by the President, and upon such terms and conditions
s the President may prescribe such interest or property shall be held,
sed, administered, liquidated, sold, or otherwise dealt with in the
nterest of and for the benefit of the United States, and such designated
gency or person may perform any and all acts incident to the accom-
lishment or furtherance of these purposes; and the President shall, in
he manner hereinabove provided, require any person to keep a full
ecord of, and to furnish under oath, in the form of reports or otherwise,
omplete information relative to any act or transaction referred to in
his subdivision either before, during, or after the completion thereof,
r relative to any interest in foreign property, or relative to any property
n which any foreign country or any national thereof has or has had
ny interest, or as may be otherwise necessary to enforce the provisions
f this subdivision, and in any case in which a report could be required,
he President may, in the manner hereinabove provided, require the
roduction, or if necessary to the national security or defense, the seizure,
f any books of account, records, contracts, letters, memoranda, or other
apers, in the custody or control of such person; and the President may,
n the manner hereinabove provided, take other and further measures
ot inconsistent herewith for the enforcement of this subdivision.

"(2) Any payment, conveyance, transfer, assignment, or delivery
f property or interest therein, made to or for the account of the United
tates, or as otherwise directed, pursuant to this subdivision or any
le, regulation, instruction, or direction issued hereunder shall to
he extent thereof be a full acquittance and discharge for all purposes
: the obligation of the person making the same; and no person shall
e held liable in any court for or in respect to anything done or omitted
n good faith in connection with the administration of, or in pursuance
f and in reliance on, this subdivision, or any rule, regulation, instruction,
r direction issued hereunder.

"(3) As used in this subdivision the term 'United States' means the
nited States and any place subject to the jurisdiction thereof, including
he Philippine Islands, and the several courts of first instance of the
ommonwealth of the Philippine Islands shall have jurisdiction in all
ases, civil or criminal, arising under this subdivision in the Philippine
slands and concurrent jurisdiction with the district courts of the United
tates of all cases, civil or criminal, arising upon the high seas: *Provided,*

however, That the foregoing shall not be construed as a limitation upon the power of the President, which is hereby conferred, to prescribe from time to time, definitions, not inconsistent with the purposes of this subdivision, for any or all of the terms used in this subdivision." [1]

SEC. 302. All acts, actions, regulations, rules, orders, and proclamations heretofore taken, promulgated, made, or issued by, or pursuant to the direction of, the President or the Secretary of the Treasury under the Trading with the Enemy Act of October 6, 1917 (40 Stat. 411), as amended, which would have been authorized if the provisions of this Act and the amendments made by it had been in effect, are hereby approved, ratified, and confirmed.

SEC. 303.[2] Whenever, during the present war, the President shall deem that the public safety demands it, he may cause to be censored under such rules and regulations as he may from time to time establish communications by mail, cable, radio, or other means of transmission passing between the United States and any foreign country he may from time to time specify, or which may be carried by any vessel or other means of transportation touching at any port, place, or Territory of the United States and bound to or from any foreign country. Any person who willfully evades or attempts to evade the submission of any such communication to such censorship or willfully uses or attempts to use any code or other device for the purpose of concealing from such censorship the intended meaning of such communication shall, upon conviction be fined not more than $10,000, or, if a natural person, imprisoned for not more than ten years, or both; and the officer, director, or agent of any corporation who knowingly participates in such violation shall be punished by a like fine, imprisonment, or both, and any property, funds, securities, papers, or other articles or documents, or any vessel, together with her tackle, apparel, furniture, and equipment, concerned in such violation shall be forfeited to the United States.

---

[1] The penalty clause completing this section reads: "Whoever willfully violates any of the provisions of this subdivision or of any license, order, rule, or regulation issued thereunder, shall, upon conviction, be fined not more than $10,000, or, if a natural person, may be imprisoned for not more than ten years, or both; and any officer, director, or agent of any corporation who knowingly participates in such violation may be punished by a like fine, imprisonment, or both. As used in this subdivision the term "person" means an individual, partnership, association, or corporation."

[2] For establishment of Office of Censorship, see p. 186.

3) *"Enemy National" and "Enemy Territory." General Ruling No. 11 of the Treasury Department, March 18, 1942* [1]

(1) No license or other authorization now outstanding or hereafter issued, unless expressly referring to this general ruling, shall be deemed to authorize any transaction which, directly or indirectly, involves any trade or communication with an enemy national.

(2) As used in this general ruling and in any other rulings, licenses, instructions, etc.:

(*a*) The term "enemy national" shall mean the following:

(*i*) The Government of any country against which the United States has declared war (Germany, Italy and Japan) and the Governments of Bulgaria, Hungary and Rumania and any agent, instrumentality or representative of the foregoing Governments, or other person acting therefor, wherever situated (including the accredited representatives of other Governments to the extent, and only to the extent, that they are actually representing the interests of the Governments of Germany, Italy and Japan and Bulgaria, Hungary and Rumania); and

(*ii*) The government of any other blocked country having its seat within enemy territory, and any agent, instrumentality, or representative thereof, or other person acting therefor, actually situated within enemy territory; and

(*iii*) Any individual within enemy territory and any partnership, association, corporation or other organization to the extent that it is actually situated within enemy territory; and

(*iv*) Any person whose name appears on The Proclaimed List of Certain Blocked Nationals and any other person acting therefor.

(*b*) The term "enemy territory" shall mean the following:

(*i*) The territory of Germany, Italy and Japan; and

(*ii*) The territory controlled or occupied by the military, naval or police forces or other authority of Germany, Italy or Japan.

The territory so controlled or occupied shall be deemed to be the territory of Albania; Austria; that portion of Belgium within continental Europe; Bulgaria; that portion of Burma occupied by Japan; that portion of China occupied by Japan; Czechoslovakia; Danzig; that portion of Denmark within continental Europe; Estonia; that portion of France within

[1] *7 Fed. Reg.*, p. 2168.

continental Europe occupied by Germany or Italy; Frenc
Indo-China; Greece; Hong Kong; Hungary; Latvia; Lith
uania; Luxemburg; British Malaya; that portion of th
Netherlands within continental Europe; that portion of th
Netherlands East Indies occupied by Japan; Norway; tha
portion of the Philippine Islands occupied by Japan; Poland
Rumania; San Marino; Thailand; that portion of the Unio
of Soviet Socialist Republics occupied by Germany; Yugc
slavia; and any other territory controlled or occupied b
Germany, Italy or Japan.

(c) The term "The Proclaimed List of Certain Blocked Nationals
shall mean "The Proclaimed List of Certain Blocked Nationals" a
amended and supplemented, promulgated pursuant to the President'
Proclamation of July 17, 1941.

(d) The term "trade or communication with an enemy national
shall mean the sending, taking, bringing, transportation, importatior
exportation, or transmission of, or the attempt to send, take, brinɡ
transport, import, export or transmit

(i) any letter, writing, paper, telegram, cablegram, wireless mes
sage, telephone message or other communication of any natur
whatsoever, or

(ii) any property of any nature whatsoever, including any good:
wares, merchandise, securities, currency, stamps, coin, bullioı
money, checks, drafts, proxies, powers of attorney, evidence
of ownership, evidences of indebtedness, evidences of property
or contracts

directly or indirectly to or from an enemy national after March 18
1942.

(3) This general ruling shall not be deemed to affect any outstandin
specific license in so far as such license expressly authorizes any tran:
action which involves trade or communication with any person whos
name appears on The Proclaimed List of Certain Blocked Nationals.

(4) Any transaction prohibited by section 3(a) of the Trading wit
the Enemy Act, as amended, is licensed thereunder unless such tran:
action is prohibited pursuant to section 5(b) of that Act and not license
by the Secretary of the Treasury. In this connection, attention i
directed to the General License under section 3(a) of the Trading wit
the Enemy Act, issued by the President on December 13, 1941.[1]

E. H. FOLEY, JR.
Acting Secretary of the Treasury

[1] 6 *ibid.*, p. 6420.

(a) Public Circular No. 18 under Executive Order No. 8389, as amended, Relating to Foreign Funds Control, March 30, 1942 [1]

(1) Reference is made to General Ruling No. 11, relating to transactions involving trade or communication with an enemy national. Inquiry has been made as to the standard of conduct which United State concerns doing business within Latin America are required to follow with respect to transactions involving enemy nationals.

(2) Any person within the Western Hemisphere who is subject to the jurisdiction of the United States shall not engage in any financial, business, trade or other commercial transaction which is directly or indirectly with, by, on behalf of, or for the benefit of an enemy national, except as specifically authorized by the Secretary of the Treasury, by means of regulations, rulings, instructions. licenses or otherwise.

(3) As used herein, the term "person subject to the jurisdiction of the United States" shall include:

(a) any citizen of the United States whether within the United States or within any foreign country;

(b) any person within the United States;

(c) any partnership, association, corporation, or other organization

(i) which is organized under the laws of the United States; or

(ii) which has its principal place of business within the United States; or

(iii) which is owned or controlled by, directly or indirectly, one or more persons subject to the jurisdiction of the United States as herein defined; and

(d) any agent, subsidiary, affiliate or other person owned or controlled, directly or indirectly, by any person subject to the jurisdiction of the United States as herein defined.

(4) In appropriate cases, United States diplomatic and consular officers in the other American Republics should be consulted with respect to the matters referred to herein and applications for licenses to engage in transactions referred to herein may be filed with such officers in lieu of filing such applications in the United States. The Treasury Department has delegated authority to such officers through the State Department, and accordingly such officers are in a position to take action on applications in certain cases without first referring such applications to the Treasury Department.

E. H. FOLEY, JR.
Acting Secretary of the Treasury

[1] 7 *ibid.*, p. 2503.

CHAPTER IX

SHIPPING AND COMMUNICATIONS

1. SHIPPING CONSTRUCTION

The general shipping situation became more critical during the period under review than it had been in the previous year. This resulted not only from the loss of merchant ship tonnage by sinkings, but also from the diversion of ships from ordinary and direct routes to longer routes, the need for the increased carriage of strategic and critical materials and the changing sources of supply of them and other materials. This situation imperilled the success of our Lend-Lease program, threatened the stability of our domestic economy and endangered the success of our national defense and war effort.

The construction of new ships was one obvious way to meet the situation. Consequently, the program of new ship construction, proposed in the President's message of January 16, 1941 (*Documents, III, 1940–41*, p. 616) was continued and greatly amplified. The "First Supplemental National Defense Appropriation Act, 1942," approved August 25, 1941 (Public Law 247, 77th Cong.[1]) carried an appropriation of $698,650,000 for new construction and related purposes. The "Fifth Supplemental National Defense Appropriation Act, 1942," approved March 5, 1942 (Public Law 474, 77th Cong.[2]) carried an appropriation of $1,502,000,000 for new construction, and, in addition, authorized contracts to the amount of $2,350,000,000. In his annual message to Congress, January 6, 1942 (see p. 49), President Roosevelt stated that he had sent a letter of directive to the United States Maritime Commission to increase our production rate of merchant ships so that "in this year, 1942, we shall build 8,000,000 deadweight tons as compared with a 1941 production of 1,100,000 tons."

2. ACQUISITION AND USE OF FOREIGN MERCHANT SHIPS

(1) *Executive Order No. 8771, June 6, 1941, Authorizing the United States Maritime Commission to Take Over Certain Foreign Merchant Vessels, as amended September 2, 1941 and January 28, 1942*

[For text of Executive Order No. 8771, see *Documents, III, 1940–41*, p. 634.]

Executive Order No. 8881, September 2, 1941,[3] made the provisions of Executive Order No. 8771 applicable to "any or all foreign merchant vessels, including all appurtenances thereto as described in said order, lying idle in waters within

[1] Public Law 247, 77th Cong.; originating after hearings by the Committee on Appropriations as H. R. 5412; House Report No. 988; Senate Report No. 632; House (conference) Report No. 1187.

[2] Public Law 474, 77th Cong.; originating after hearings by the Committee on Appropriations as H. R. 6611; House Report No. 1790; Senate Report No. 1113.

[3] 6 *Fed. Reg.*, p. 4551.

the jurisdiction of the United States, including the Philippine Islands and the Canal Zone, at any time after June 6, 1941 and up to and including June 30, 1942." [1]

By Executive Order No. 9046, January 28, 1942,[2] sec. 2, par (c) of Executive Order No. 8771 was amended to refer to "any other country in the Western Hemisphere" instead of "any neutral country of the Western Hemisphere."

Acting under the authority of Executive Order No. 8771, as amended, the Maritime Commission formally took over on December 27, 1941 sixteen Finnish-owned merchant vessels laid up in American ports. These vessels had been under the protective custody of the Coast Guard since they came into United States ports following the British declaration of war on Finland (see p. 639). The ships had a total tonnage of 51,878 tons.[3]

Announcement was made on December 12, 1941 that arrangements had been completed to remove the French crews on all French vessels in United States ports.[4] On December 16, it was announced that the Maritime Commission was taking over the *Normandie* under an arrangement calling for fair and adequate compensation to the owners.[5] Similar action had been announced in the case of the Swedish motorship *Kungsholm* on December 13.[6] In this instance it was specifically stated that the right of angary was being exercised. But on January 2, 1942, the announcement was made that the American Government had arranged to acquire the *Kungsholm* by purchase from its private owners instead of through the exercise of the right of angary.[7]

(2) Use of Danish Ships by United States. Statement of United Kingdom Embassy, July 7, 1941 [8]

Following conversations between the British and United States authorities in Washington on the question of the enemy ships now sheltering in United States, the British Embassy has been authorized to issue the following statement:

"His Majesty's Government in the United Kingdom announce in connection with the recent agreement for the employment of the Danish ships in United States ports that they have consented in respect of these ships to waive their rights as a belligerent to refuse recognition of the transfer of an enemy merchant ship to a neutral flag unless they have first satisfied themselves as to the validity of the transfer.

"The principal reason hitherto for the immobilization of these ships has been the fact that His Majesty's Government have felt unable to

[1] Department of State, *Bulletin*, V, p. 108.
[2] 7 *Fed. Reg.*, p. 595.
[3] *New York Times*, December 28, 1941, p. 24.
[4] Department of State, *Bulletin*, V, p. 518.
[5] *Ibid.*, p. 544.   [6] *Ibid.*, p. 519.   [7] *Ibid.*, VI, p. 7.
[8] *New York Times*, July 8, 1941, p. 37.

waive these rights, to the maintenance of which they attach the greatest importance.

"They are, however, now satisfied and gratefully recognize that the use to which these ships are to be put will contribute directly or indirectly to the war effort of the democracies. Accordingly they have waived the exercise of their belligerent rights so far as these vessels are concerned."

(3) *Plan Adopted by the Inter-American Financial and Economic Advisory Committee, August 28, 1941*

[See p. 403; for text of resolution adopted by the Inter-American and Economic Advisory Committee, November 14, 1941, providing for the creation of an Inter-American Maritime Commission to carry out the above plan, see p. 405.]

3. FULLER AND MORE EFFICIENT USE OF AVAILABLE SHIPPING FACILITIES

(1) *An Act to Provide for Priorities in Transportation by Merchant Vessels in the Interests of National Defense, and for Other Purposes, Approved July 14, 1941* [1]

Be it enacted by the Senate and House of Representatives of the United States of America in Congress assembled, That during the emergency declared by the President on May 27, 1941, to exist but not after June 30, 1943, the President may, notwithstanding any other provisions of law, whenever he deems it in the interest of national defense, including the maintenance of essential supplies and services, authorize the United States Maritime Commission to issue warrants [2] as hereinafter provided with respect to any vessel documented under the laws of the United States or any vessel not so documented but owned by a citizen of the United States. Such warrants may also be issued to foreign-flag vessels not owned by citizens of the United States upon application therefor by the owner of said vessel or the charterer thereof on behalf of such owner. Such application shall be in such form as the United States Maritime Commission may prescribe. All warrants shall be issued and may be revoked pursuant to regulations issued by the United States Maritime Commission with the approval of the President.

[1] Public Law 173, 77th Cong.; introduced as H. R. 4700 from the Committee on Merchant Marine and Fisheries; House Report No. 526; Senate Report No. 484; House (conference) Report No. 895.

U. S. Congress, House of Representatives, Committee on Merchant Marine and Fisheries, *Priorities for Vessels Holding Warrants;* Executive Hearing . . . 77th Cong., 1st sess., on H. R. 4583 . . . May 7 and 8, 1941.

[2] The authority was authorized by Executive Order No. 8871, August 26, 1941 (6 *Fed. Reg.*, p. 4469).

SEC. 2. The warrants to be issued pursuant to this Act shall be in such form as the Maritime Commission shall prescribe, and shall set forth the conditions to be complied with by the affected vessel as a condition to receiving the priorities and other advantages provided in this Act, by reference to an undertaking of the owner or charterer with respect to the trades in which such vessel shall be employed, the voyages which it shall undertake, the class or classes of cargo or passengers to be carried, the fair and reasonable maximum rate of charter-hire or equivalent, and such incidental and supplementary matters as appear to the United States Maritime Commission to be necessary or expedient for the purposes of the warrant. Nothing in this Act shall authorize the United States Maritime Commission to require the owner or charterer to relinquish the manning, storing, victualing, supplying, fueling, maintaining, or repairing of his vessel to any other person or persons. Nothing in this Act shall be deemed to alter, amend, or repeal any of the coastwise laws of the United States.

SEC. 3. Vessels holding warrants issued pursuant to this Act shall be entitled to priority over merchant vessels not holding such warrants, with respect to the use of facilities for loading, discharging, lighterage or storage of cargoes, the procurement of bunker fuel or coal, and the towing, overhauling, drydocking or repair of such vessels. Vessels holding warrants shall have such priority as among themselves, as the United States Maritime Commission shall determine to be necessary and advisable in the interests of national defense, or as may be specified in the warrants. Persons in the United States, including the Philippine Islands and the Canal Zone, furnishing any of the above-mentioned facilities shall be authorized, and under rules and regulations prescribed by the United States Maritime Commission with the approval of the President may be required, to grant such priorities, anything in any contract whether heretofore or hereafter made to the contrary notwithstanding.

SEC. 4. In the administration of this Act it shall be the policy of the Commission to make fair and reasonable provision for priorities with respect to (1) the importation of substantial quantities of strategic and critical materials, (2) the transportation of substantial quantities of materials when such transportation is requested by any defense agency, and (3) the transportation in the foreign or domestic commerce of the United States of substantial quantities of materials deemed by the Commission to be essential to the defense of the United States: *Provided*, That there shall be no unjust discrimination between ports of the United States. Nothing in this Act shall authorize the exaction of any sum from the holder of a warrant solely for the privilege of carrying cargo on any route. Vessels that on January 1, 1941, were engaged primarily in the coastwise transportation of coal for national defense and domestic consumption shall be granted warrants only so long as they continue in the same service as of said date, except that in case any such vessel ceased, before June 15, 1941, to engage in such transportation of coal and before such date became principally engaged in the transportation of defense materials, the Commission may grant such vessel a warrant for such service as it deems suitable pursuant to section 2.

SEC. 5. The term "citizen of the United States" as used in this Act includes corporations, partnerships, and associations existing, authorized, or organized under the laws of the United States or any State, district, Territory, or possession thereof.

SEC. 6. Whoever willfully violates any rule, regulation, or order issued under the authority conferred herein shall be punished by a fine of not more than $5,000, or by imprisonment for not more than two years or both: *Provided,* That the District Court of the Canal Zone and the several courts of first instance of the Commonwealth of the Philippine Islands shall have jurisdiction over offenses committed against the provisions of this Act within the Canal Zone and the Philippine Islands, respectively.

(2) Suspension of International Load Line Convention. Proclamation by the President (Roosevelt), August 9, 1941 [1]

The International Load Line Convention was signed at London, July 5, 1930.[2] It contained provisions with respect to the placing of load lines on ships engaged in international voyages other than ships of war, ships solely engaged in fishing, pleasure yachts, ships not carrying cargo or passengers, and those of less than 150 tons.

The suspension of the Convention was prompted by the pressing need for tonnage. In view of the bearing of the action on hemispheric defense, the Department of State conferred with the American Republics that were parties to the Convention. All agreed to the suspension.

The proclamation was based upon an opinion of the Attorney-General dated July 28, 1941 [3] in which he concluded that peacetime commerce and voyages were assumed as the basis of the Convention; that the then existing situation with respect to shipping was wholly different from that obtaining at the time the Convention was signed; and that the conditions essential to the operation of the Convention and assumed as the basis of it were in almost complete abeyance. He pointed out that of the 36 countries which became parties to the Convention, 10 were at war and 16 were under military occupation and that in these cir-

[1] 6 *Fed. Reg.*, p. 3999; Department of State, *Bulletin*, V, p. 114.
[2] *Treaties, Conventions,* etc., 1923–1937, IV, p. 5287.
[3] 40 Op. Att. Gen., No. 24.

cumstances the Government of the United States was free to declare the Convention inoperative or suspended.

It was announced that during the period of suspension load lines would be fixed by the Secretary of Commerce under the Act of Congress of March 2, 1929.[1]

BY THE PRESIDENT OF THE UNITED STATES OF AMERICA

A Proclamation [No. 2500]

WHEREAS a convention establishing uniform principles and rules with regard to the limits to which ships on international voyages may be loaded, entitled "International Load Lines Convention," was signed by the respective plenipotentiaries of the United States of America and certain other countries at London on July 5, 1930; and

WHEREAS, following ratification by the United States of America and certain other countries, the Convention, in accordance with Article 24 thereof, came into force with respect to the United States of America and certain other countries on January 1, 1933; and

WHEREAS the provisions of the Convention were carefully formulated "to promote safety of life and property at sea" in time of peace by regulating the competitive loading of merchant ships employed in the customary channels of international trade; and

WHEREAS the conditions envisaged by the Convention have been, for the time being, almost wholly destroyed, and the partial and imperfect enforcement of the Convention can operate only to prejudice the victims of aggression, whom it is the avowed purpose of the United States of America to aid; and

WHEREAS it is an implicit condition to the binding effect of the Convention that those conditions envisaged by it should continue without such material change as has in fact occurred; and

WHEREAS under approved principles of international law it has become, by reason of such changed conditions, the right of the United States of America to declare the Convention suspended and inoperative:

NOW, THEREFORE, I, FRANKLIN D. ROOSEVELT, President of the United States of America, exercising in behalf of the United States of America an unquestioned right and privilege under approved principles of international law, do proclaim and declare the aforesaid International Load Line Convention suspended and inoperative in the ports and waters of the United States of America, and in so far as the United States of America is concerned, for the duration of the present emergency.

IN WITNESS WHEREOF, I have hereunto set my hand and caused the seal of the United States of America to be affixed.

[1] 45 Stat. 1492.

DONE at the City of Washington this 9th day of August, in the year of our Lord nineteen hundred and forty-one, and of the [SEAL]   Independence of the United States of America the one hundred and sixty-sixth.

FRANKLIN D. ROOSEVELT

By the President:
CORDELL HULL
Secretary of State

(3) *Executive Order No. 9054 Establishing a War Shipping Administration in the Executive Office of the President and Defining Its Functions and Duties, February 7, 1942* [1]

The losses of merchant shipping due to mines, submarine and air attacks and the activities of surface raiders before the entrance of the United States into the war had made necessary adoption of special measures by the United States to make available more seagoing ships (see *Documents, III, 1940–41*, p. 615–35) and had also led to our active participation in the work of protection, first through patrol activities, and then through actual shooting (see p. 88 ff.).

Following the entrance of the United States into the war, the situation momentarily at least became more serious than it had hitherto been, partly because of increased American demand for shipping, but more particularly because of the success of German submarine attacks upon shipping off our Eastern Coast, in the Gulf of Mexico and in the Caribbean. To meet this critical situation it was necessary not only to increase the number of ships available and to increase the effectiveness of protection but also to make more efficient use of the ships in service. Executive Order No. 9054 provided for unified administration of American shipping and laid the basis for closer British-American cooperation (see p. 174). Precedents for efficient use of United Nations shipping resources existed in the very successful Allied Shipping Control of World War I.[2]

By virtue of the authority vested in me by the Constitution and Statutes of the United States, including the First War Powers Act, 1941, approved December 18, 1941,[3] as President of the United States and Commander-in-Chief of the Army and Navy, and in order to assure the most effective utilization of the shipping of the United States for the successful prosecution of the war, it is hereby ordered:

1. There is established within the Office for Emergency Management of the Executive Office of the President a War Shipping Administration under the direction of an Administrator [4] who shall be appointed by and responsible to the President.

[1] *7 Fed. Reg.*, p. 837. For regulations affecting maritime carriers, see 7 *Fed. Reg.*, p. 1505, 1548.
[2] For excellent account, see Sir Arthur Salter, *Allied Shipping Control: An Experiment in International Administration* (New York, 1921).
[3] See p. 126.
[4] Rear Admiral Emory S. Land (U.S.N. retired), Chairman of the United States Maritime Commission, was appointed Administrator.

2. The Administrator shall perform the following functions and duties:

    a. Control the operation, purchase, charter, requisition, and use of all ocean vessels under the flag or control of the United States, except (1) combatant vessels of the Army, Navy, and Coast Guard; fleet auxiliaries of the Navy; and transports owned by the Army and Navy; and (2) vessels engaged in coastwise, intercoastal, and inland transportation under the control of the Director of the Office of Defense Transportation.

    b. Allocate vessels under the flag or control of the United States for use by the Army, Navy, other Federal departments and agencies, and the governments of the United Nations.

    c. Provide marine insurance and reinsurance against loss or damage by the risks of war as authorized by Title II of the Merchant Marine Act, 1936, as amended.

    d. Establish the conditions to be complied with as a condition to receiving priorities and other advantages as provided in Public Law 173, Seventy-Seventh Congress, approved July 14, 1941.

    e. Represent the United States Government in dealing with the British Ministry of War Transport and with similar shipping agencies of nations allied with the United States in the prosecution of the war, in matters related to the use of shipping.

    f. Maintain current data on the availability of shipping in being and under construction and furnish such data on request to the Departments of War and the Navy, and other Federal departments and agencies concerned with the import or export of war materials and commodities.

    g. Keep the President informed with regard to the progress made in carrying out this Order and perform such related duties as the President shall from time to time assign or delegate to him.

3. The functions, duties, and powers conferred by law upon the United States Maritime Commission with respect to the operation, purchase, charter, insurance, repair, maintenance, and requisition of vessels, and the issuance of warrants with respect thereto, under the Merchant Marine Act of 1936 as amended, 49 Stat. 1985, Public Law 101 Seventy-Seventh Congress, approved June 6, 1941, and Executive Order 8771 issued pursuant thereto, Public Law 173, Seventy-Seventh Congress, approved July 14, 1941, are hereby transferred to the Administrator; and such part of existing personnel of the United States Maritime Commission together with such records and public property as the Administrator may deem necessary to the full exercise of his functions and duties

prescribed by this Order are hereby assigned to the War Shipping Administration.

4. Vessels under the control of the War Shipping Administration shall constitute a pool to be allocated by the Administrator for use by the Army, Navy, other Federal departments and agencies, and the governments of the United Nations. In allocating the use of such vessels, the Administrator shall comply with strategic military requirements.

5. For the purpose of carrying out the provisions of this Order, the Administrator is authorized to utilize the services of available and appropriate personnel of the United States Maritime Commission, the War and Navy Departments, the Bureau of Marine Inspection and Navigation of the Department of Commerce, and other government departments and agencies which are engaged in activities related to the operation of shipping.

6. In the discharge of his responsibilities the Administrator shall collaborate with existing military, naval, and civil departments and agencies of the government which perform wartime functions connected with transportation overseas, in order to secure the most effective utilization of shipping in the prosecution of the war. The Administrator particularly shall maintain close liaison with the Departments of War and the Navy through the Assistant Chief of Staff for Transportation and Supply and the Director, Naval Transportation Service, respectively, with respect to the movement of military and naval personnel and supplies; and with the Director of the Office of Defense Transportation with respect to the relation of overseas transportation to coast-wise and intercoastal shipping and inland transportation. With respect to the overseas transportation of cargoes essential to the war production effort and the civilian economy the Administrator shall be guided by schedule transmitted to him by the Chairman of the War Production Board prescribing the priority of movement of such commodities and materials.

7. The Administrator may establish committees or groups of advisor representing two or more departments of the Federal government, or agencies or missions of governments allied with the United States in the prosecution of the war, as the case may require to carry out the purpose of this Order. Further, he may appoint representatives to such join missions or boards dealing with matters within the scope of this Order a may be established with governments associated with the United State in the prosecution of the war.

8. Within the purposes of this Order, the Administrator is authorized to issue such directives concerning shipping operations as he may deem necessary or appropriate, and his decisions shall be final with respect to

the functions and authorities so vested in him. The Administrator may exercise the powers, authority and discretion conferred upon him by this Order through such officials or agencies and in such manner as he may determine.

9. The Administrator is further authorized within the limits of such funds as may be allocated, transferred, or appropriated to the War Shipping Administration to employ necessary personnel and make provisions for necessary supplies, facilities, and services. So much of the unexpended balances of appropriations, allocations, or other funds available (including funds and contract authority available for the fiscal year ending June 30, 1942) for the use of the United States Maritime Commission in the exercise of the functions transferred to the Administrator and the War Shipping Administration, as the Director of the Bureau of the Budget with the approval of the President shall determine, shall be transferred to the War Shipping Administration for use in carrying out the functions and authority transferred to the Administrator and the War Shipping Administration pursuant to the provisions of this Order. In determining the amounts to be transferred from the United States Maritime Commission, the Director of the Bureau of the Budget may include amounts necessary to provide for the liquidation of obligations previously incurred by the United States Maritime Commission against such appropriations, allocations or other funds prior to the transfer; *Provided*, that the use of the unexpended appropriations, allocations or other funds transferred by this Section shall be subject to the provisions of Section 3 of the First War Powers Act, 1941.

(4) *An Act to Amend the Merchant Marine Act, 1936, as amended, to Provide for the Coordination of the Forwarding and Similar Servicing of Water-borne Export and Import Foreign Commerce of the United States, Approved March 14, 1942* [1]

[Excerpt]

Be it enacted by the Senate and House of Representatives of the United States of America in Congress assembled, That title II of the Merchant Marine Act, 1936,[2] as amended, is hereby amended by adding at the end thereof a new section to read as follows:

"SEC. 217. (a) The Commission is hereby authorized and directed, through such administrative measures, agreements with other Federal

[1] Public Law 498, 77th Cong.; originating as H. R. 6291, after hearings under H. Res. 281 and 297, 77th Cong., 1st sess., and on H. R. 6001 and H. R. 6002; House Report No. 1682; Senate Report No. 1117.
[2] U. S. Code, title 46, sec. 1111 *ff*.

departments and agencies, contracts with individuals or private business concerns, or other arrangements, as it may deem to be necessary or appropriate in the public interest, to coordinate the functions and facilities of public and private agencies engaged in the forwarding and similar servicing of water-borne export and import foreign commerce of the United States, for the efficient prosecution of the war, the maintenance and development of present and post-war foreign trade, and the preservation of forwarding facilities and services for the post-war restoration of foreign commerce. As used herein the term 'water-borne export and import foreign commerce of the United States' shall be deemed to include export shipments from the Government of the United States to the governments of nations whose defense is deemed by the President to be vital to the defense of the United States under the authority of the Act of March 11, 1941 (Public Law 11, Seventy-seventh Congress).

"(b) Other Federal departments and agencies are hereby authorized and directed to cooperate with the Commission by entering into and carrying out such agreements as may be necessary to effectuate the purposes of this section: . . . "

4. RULES GOVERNING SEAMEN

(1) *Rules Governing Employment of Seamen. Department of State Release, April 9, 1942* [1]

The Special Interdepartmental Committee on Maritime Labor set up by the Department of State, the Department of Justice, and the War Shipping Administrator on February 14, 1942 reported on April 9 to the Acting Secretary of State, the Attorney General, and the War Shipping Administrator.

Its report dealt with the problems resulting from the fact that seamen on United Nations ships, under American law, could freely leave their ships and transfer to other United Nations ships. The practice of "floating" from ships of one flag to ships of other flags has occasioned delay in prompt turn-around of vessels engaged in the war effort.

The Committee reported that it had secured adoption by the War Shipping Administrator of rules having the following results: [2]

(1) Employment on Panamanian and Honduran ships has in substance been closed to all United Nations sailors (other than Americans, Hondurans, and Panamanians) not heretofore or presently employed on such ships. The Panamanian and Honduran fleets are thus eliminated as competitors for United Nations seamen.

[1] Department of State, *Bulletin*, VI, p. 321.   [2] *7 Fed. Reg.*, p. 2761.

(2) That ships flying the United States flag be permitted to employ no seamen of the United Nations (other than Americans) except:

(a) Alien seamen employed on American ships on or prior to April 8, 1942;

(b) Alien seamen of the United Nations, other than Canada, situated in the Western Hemisphere;

(c) Alien seamen presently in the United States who have not been at sea or on ships (other than American) subsequent to September 1, 1939.

In addition to the foregoing:

(1) The Committee has recommended, and the Department of Justice has instituted, enforcement of the laws against inducing illegal entries of seamen into the United States.

(2) Through the Immigration Service and with the assistance of the Bureau of Marine Inspection and Navigation, the Committee has instituted an informal spot conciliation and inspection service so that disputes which can be settled on the ship can be heard and disposed of immediately and without delay, and so that in respect of conditions such remedial action as is practicable can, where required, be promptly secured.

(3) On recommendation of the Committee, the Department of Justice has made certain variations in its immigration practice. Shore leave has been substituted for the presumption that a seaman has a right to enter the United States seeking other maritime employment. The rule with regard to holding on board *mala-fide* seamen has been strengthened.

(4) With the cooperation of the Federal Security Administration and of the Coast Guard, the Committee is presently working on measures which it is hoped will improve the morale of seamen. Included in this program are: (a) a better patrolling of port areas; (b) better provisions for sailors ashore; (c) provision for clubs and facilities for sailors who are either on furlough or awaiting ships.

The results of the measures taken have already substantially reduced the difficulty. More United Nations seamen have presented themselves as willing to ship out, and the number of seamen who have been "floating" has been materially reduced.

The measures taken were made possible through the cooperation of Admiral E. S. Land, War Shipping Administrator; Attorney General Francis Biddle; the Federal Security Administration; and the Coast Guard.

The Committee is composed of A. A. Berle, Jr., Assistant Secretary of State, *Chairman;* Marshall E. Dimock, Associate Commissioner, Immigration and Naturalization Service; and Commissioner Edward Macauley and Robert G. Hooker, Jr., representing the War Shipping Administrator.

(2) *Passport Requirements for American Seamen. Department of State Release, June 23, 1942* [1]

On November 25, 1941, the Department of State, by Departmental Order 1003,[2] laid down rules governing the departure from and entry into the United States of American citizens. Under this order, American nationals following the vocation of seaman were required to be in possession of valid passports in order to depart from the United States on or after January 15, 1942. In view of the acute shipping situation and the importance of avoiding any unnecessary interference with the full use of shipping facilities, as well as for other reasons, the date was subsequently indefinitely extended.[3] On April 2, 1942, it was announced that the date had been set at July 1, 1942.[4]

Under the amendment of April 2, 1942 to the rules and regulations prescribed by the Secretary of State on November 25, 1941 relating to the supervision and control over the departure from and entry into the United States or the outlying possessions thereof of American nationals, a seaman when traveling in the pursuit of his vocation between any territory under the jurisdiction of the United States and any foreign country or territory for which a valid passport is required under the regulations of November 25, 1941, as amended, is not required, prior to 6 o'clock in the forenoon of July 1, 1942, to be in possession of a valid passport.

Notwithstanding the inconvenience and difficulties which are sometimes involved in obtaining the evidence of American nationality required as a condition to the issuance of passports, a large majority of American nationals who pursue the vocation of seamen have applied for and obtained American passports. However, because of the exigencies of the present situation due to the conditions growing out of the war, the lack of knowledge on the part of many seamen who have been at sea for long periods of the application to them of the rules and regulations of November 25, 1941, as amended, and the short periods of time in which seamen now remain in American ports before again going to sea, a number of seamen have not yet applied for and obtained passports.

While it has not been deemed advisable to extend beyond 6 o'clock in the forenoon of July 1, 1942 the period when American seamen traveling between territory under the jurisdiction of the United States and any foreign country or territory will be exempted as a class from the

[1] Department of State, *Bulletin*, VI, p. 563.   [2] *Ibid.*, V, p. 431.
[3] *Ibid.*, VI, p. 231.   [4] *Ibid.*, p. 292.

ecessity of bearing passports, the Secretary of State has taken cogni-
ance of the valid reasons which have existed in the cases of many Amer-
:an seamen who have not yet applied for passports and is consequently
uthorizing the collectors of customs and immigration officials at the
arious ports in territory under the jurisdiction of the United States to
ermit until further notice any American seaman to depart from or enter
merican territory if he has in his possession a continuous discharge
ook, a certificate of identity, or a license or other document qualifying
im to serve as an officer or seaman on vessels of the United States and
pon the understanding that he will at the earliest opportunity apply
or a passport. The exercise of such authority is permitted by section
8.3(g) of the rules and regulations issued on November 25, 1941, which
eads as follows:

"No valid passport shall be required of a citizen of the United States
r a person who owes allegiance to the United States:

. . . .

"(g) When specifically authorized by the Secretary of State, through
he appropriate official channels, to depart from or enter into the conti-
ental United States, the Canal Zone, the Commonwealth of the
'hilippines, and all territories, continental or insular, subject to the
urisdiction of the United States."

5. COMMUNICATIONS

1) *An Act . . . Granting to the President, in Time of War or Threat
   of War, Certain Powers with respect to Communication by Wire,
   Approved January 26, 1942* [1]

Special war-time control of wire facilities was effected during World War I
y Public Resolution No. 38, 65th Cong., approved July 16, 1918, and
'roclamations Nos. 1466 and 1492-A of July 22 and November 2, 1918. The
resent legislation follows that precedent and was favored by the Defense
'ommunications Board. In form it amends the Communications Act of 1934,
J. S. Code, title 47, sec. 606, by inserting subsections (d), (f) and (g) as given
elow.

SEC. 606. (a) During the continuance of a war in which the United
states is engaged, the President is authorized, if he finds it necessary for
he national defense and security, to direct that such communications
s in his judgment may be essential to the national defense and security
hall have preference or priority with any carrier subject to this Act.

[1] Public Law 413, 77th Cong.; originated as H. R. 6263; House Report No. 1546.

He may give these directions at and for such times as he may determine and may modify, change, suspend, or annul them and for any such pur pose he is hereby authorized to issue orders directly, or through suc person or persons as he designates for the purpose, or through the Com mission. Any carrier complying with any such order or direction fo preference or priority herein authorized shall be exempt from any and a provisions in existing law imposing civil or criminal penalties, obligations or liabilities upon carriers by reason of giving preference or priority i compliance with such order or direction.

(b) It shall be unlawful for any person during any war in which th United States is engaged to knowingly or willfully, by physical force o intimidation by threats of physical force, obstruct or retard or aid i obstructing or retarding interstate or foreign communication by radi or wire. The President is hereby authorized, whenever in his judgmen the public interest requires, to employ the armed forces of the Unite States to prevent any such obstruction or retardation of communication *Provided*, That nothing in this section shall be construed to repea modify, or affect either section 6 or section 20 of an Act entitled "A Act to supplement existing laws against unlawful restraints and monopo lies, and for other purposes," approved October 15, 1914.

(c) Upon proclamation by the President that there exists war or : threat of war or a state of public peril or disaster or other nationa emergency, or in order to preserve the neutrality of the United States the President may suspend or amend, for such time as he may see fit, th rules and regulations applicable to any or all stations within the juris diction of the United States as prescribed by the Commission, and ma cause the closing of any station for radio communication and the remova therefrom of its apparatus and equipment, or he may authorize the us or control of any such station and/or its apparatus and equipment b any department of the Government under such regulations as he ma prescribe, upon just compensation to the owners.

(d) Upon proclamation by the President that there exists a state o threat of war involving the United States, the President, if he deems i necessary in the interest of the national security and defense, may during a period ending not later than six months after the terminatio of such state or threat of war and not later than such earlier date as th Congress by concurrent resolution may designate, (1) suspend or amen the rules and regulations applicable to any or all facilities or stations fo wire communication within the jurisdiction of the United States a prescribed by the Commission, (2) cause the closing of any facility o station for wire communication and removal therefrom of its apparatu and equipment, or (3) authorize the use or control of any such facility or station and its apparatus and equipment by any department of the Government under such regulations as he may prescribe, upon just compensation to the owners.

(e) The President shall ascertain the just compensation for such use or control and certify the amount ascertained to Congress for appropriation and payment to the person entitled thereto. If the amount so certified is unsatisfactory to the person entitled thereto, such person shall be paid only 75 per centum of the amount and shall be entitled to sue the United States to recover such further sum as added to such payment of 75 per centum will make such amount as will be just compensation for the use and control. Such suit shall be brought in the manner provided by paragraph 20 of section 24, or by section 145, of the Judicial Code, as amended.

(f) Nothing in subsection (c) or (d) shall be construed to amend, repeal, impair, or affect existing laws or powers of the States in relation to taxation or the lawful police regulations of the several States, except wherein such laws, powers, or regulations may affect the transmission of Government communications, or the issue of stocks and bonds by any communication system or systems.

(g) Nothing in subsection (c) or (d) shall be construed to authorize the President to make any amendment to the rules and regulations of the Commission which the Commission would not be authorized by law to make; and nothing in subsection (d) shall be construed to authorize the President to take any action the force and effect of which shall continue beyond the date after which taking of such action would not have been authorized.

———

By Executive Order No. 9089, March 6, 1942, the President gave to the Defense Communications Board,[1] James L. Fly, Chairman, the powers with regard to the use, control and closing of stations and facilities for wire communication conferred upon him by the Act of January 26, 1942. Earlier, December 10, 1941, the President had by Executive Order No. 8964 [2] delegated to the Defense Communications Board the power and authority over radio facilities vested in the President under the provisions of sec. 606 of the Communications Act of 1934.[3]

[1] 7 *Fed. Reg.*, p. 1777.
[2] 6 *ibid.*, p. 6367.
[3] 48 Stat. 1104; U.S.C. title 47, sec. 606.

CHAPTER X

TREATMENT OF PERSONS AND PROPERTY

1. THE NATIONALITY ACT OF 1940

[For original text see *Documents, III, 1940–41*, p. 562.]

A. Amendments

(1) *An Act to Amend the Nationality Act of 1940 to Preserve the Nationality of Citizens Residing Abroad, Approved October 16, 1941* [1]

Sec. 409 of the Nationality Act of 1940 provided that nationality would not be lost under secs. 404 or 407 until the expiration of one year following the date of approval of the Act. World conditions, and particularly the resultant travel conditions, made it seem reasonable to extend this period to two years.

Be it enacted by the Senate and House of Representatives of the United States of America in Congress assembled, That chapter IV of the Nationality Act of 1940, section 409, is amended to read as follows:

"SEC. 409. Nationality shall not be lost under the provisions of section 404 or 407 of this Act until the expiration of two years following the date of the approval of this Act: *Provided, however*, That a naturalized person who shall have become subject to the presumption that he has ceased to be an American citizen as provided for in the second paragraph of section 2 of the Act of March 2, 1907 (34 Stat. 1228), and who shall not have overcome it under the rules in effect immediately preceding the date of the approval of this Act, shall continue to be subject to such presumption for the period of two years following the date of the approval of this Act unless it is overcome during such period."

(2) *An Act to Provide for the Expeditious Naturalization of Former Citizens of the United States Who Have Lost United States Citizenship Through Service with the Allied Forces of the United States During the First or Second World War, Approved April 2, 1942* [2]

Be it enacted by the Senate and House of Representatives of the United States of America in Congress assembled, That section 323 of the Act of

---

[1] Public Law 275, 77th Cong.

[2] Public Law 513, 77th Congress; passed as S. 2339.

October 14, 1940 (54 Stat. 1149), entitled "An Act to revise and codify the nationality laws of the United States into a comprehensive nationality code," is hereby amended to read as follows:

"Sec. 323. A person who, while a citizen of the United States and during the first or second World War, entered the military or naval service of any country at war with a country with which the United States was or is at war, who has lost citizenship of the United States by reason of any oath or obligation taken for the purpose of entering such service, or by reason of entering or serving in such armed forces, and who intends to reside permanently in the United States, may be naturalized by taking before any naturalization court specified in subsection (a) of section 301, the oaths prescribed by section 335. Any such person who has lost citizenship of the United States during the second World War may, if he so desires, be naturalized by taking, before any diplomatic or consular officer of the United States abroad, the oaths prescribed by section 335. For the purposes of this section, the second World War shall be deemed to have commenced on September 1, 1939, and shall continue until such time as the United States shall cease to be in a state of war. Certified copies of such oath shall be sent by such diplomatic or consular officer or such court to the Department of State and to the Department of Justice."

B. Administration

(1) *Review of Nationality Cases. Departmental Order No. 994 of the Department of State, November 4, 1941* [1]

There is hereby created in the Passport Division, as of November 1, 1941, a Board of Review consisting of three persons, two of whom shall be senior attorneys having experience in citizenship and related matters. The third shall be a Foreign Service Officer, whenever one is available for such assignment; otherwise, an officer similarly qualified in citizenship work. The Assistant Chief of the Passport Division is designated as adviser to the Board.

The Board will review all cases involving the loss of nationality under the nationality laws of the United States and will conduct, in appropriate instances, formal or informal hearings. It will also handle such other matters as may be assigned to it by the Chief of the Passport Division.

The findings of the Board of Review will be subject to the approval of the Technical Adviser and Assistant Chief of the Passport Division, Mr. John J. Scanlan.

[1] Department of State, *Bulletin*, V, p. 371.

The Board will provide a forum for hearings and discussions in order to obviate as far as may be practicable hardships and inequities in the application of the new Nationality Act of 1940 [1] and will make in every case reviewed by it a formal record for the files of the Department with respect to the pertinent facts and laws involving the possible loss of nationality or other matter assigned to the Board.

The Chief of the Passport Division is hereby authorized to make such regulations as may be necessary to carry out the purpose of the establishment of the Board of Review.

2. PERSONS ENTERING AND LEAVING THE UNITED STATES

(1) *Proclamation Establishing Control of Persons Entering and Leaving the United States, November 14, 1941* [2]

The proclamation establishes the basis for checking all human movement across the borders, whether by citizens, nationals or aliens. The extension of control to citizens and nationals subjected the utilization of passports to the rules and regulations issued under the proclamation as Code of Federal Regulations, title 22, chap. 1, part 58.

BY THE PRESIDENT OF THE UNITED STATES

A Proclamation [No. 2523] [2]

WHEREAS the act of Congress approved on May 22, 1918 (40 Stat. 559) as amended by the act of Congress approved on June 21, 1941 (Public Law 114, 77th Cong., chap. 210, 1st sess., 55 Stat. 252) [3] vests authority in me to impose restrictions and prohibitions in addition to those otherwise provided by law upon the departure of persons from and their entry into the United States when the United States is at war, or during the existence of the national emergency proclaimed by the President on May 27, 1941,[4] or, as to aliens, whenever there exists a state of war between or among two or more states, and when I find that the interest of the United States so require; and

WHEREAS the national emergency proclaimed by me on May 27, 1941 is still existing; and

WHEREAS there unhappily exists a state of war between or among two or more states and open hostilities engage a large part of the Eastern Hemisphere; and

[1] *Documents, III, 1940–41*, p. 562.
[2] 6 *Fed. Reg.*, p. 5821, 5869; Department of State, *Bulletin*, V, p. 381.
[3] *Documents, III, 1940–41*, p. 607.
[4] *Ibid.*, p. 754.

WHEREAS the exigencies of the present international situation and of the national defense require that restrictions and prohibitions, in addition to those otherwise provided by law, be imposed upon the departure of persons from and their entry into the United States, including the Panama Canal Zone, the Commonwealth of the Philippines, and all territory and waters, continental or insular, subject to the jurisdiction of the United States:

Now, THEREFORE, I, FRANKLIN D. ROOSEVELT, President of the United States of America, acting under and by virtue of the authority vested in me as set forth above, do hereby find and publicly proclaim and declare that the interests of the United States require that restrictions and prohibitions, in addition to those otherwise provided by law, shall be imposed upon the departure of persons from and their entry into the United States, including the Panama Canal Zone, the Commonwealth of the Philippines, and all territory and waters, continental or insular, subject to the jurisdiction of the United States; and I make the following rules, regulations, and orders which shall remain in force and effect until otherwise ordered by me:

(1) After the effective date of the rules and regulations hereinafter authorized, no citizen of the United States or person who owes allegiance to the United States shall depart from or enter, or attempt to depart from or enter, the United States, including the Panama Canal Zone, the Commonwealth of the Philippines, and all territory and waters, continental or insular, subject to the jurisdiction of the United States, unless he bears a valid passport issued by the Secretary of State or, under his authority, by a diplomatic or consular officer of the United States, or the United States High Commissioner to the Philippine Islands, or the chief executive of Hawaii, of Puerto Rico, of the Virgin Islands, of American Samoa, or of Guam, or unless he comes within the provisions of such exceptions or fulfils such conditions as may be prescribed in rules and regulations which the Secretary of State is hereby authorized to prescribe in execution of the rules, regulations, and orders herein prescribed. Seamen are included in the classes of persons to whom this paragraph applies.

(2) No alien shall depart from or attempt to depart from the United States unless he is in possession of a valid permit to depart issued by the Secretary of State or by an officer designated by the Secretary of State for such purpose, or unless he is exempted from obtaining a permit, in accordance with rules and regulations which the Secretary of State, with the concurrence of the Attorney General, is hereby authorized to prescribe in execution of the rules, regulations, and orders herein

prescribed; nor shall any alien depart from or attempt to depart from the United States at any place other than a port of departure designated by the Attorney General or by the Commissioner of Immigration and Naturalization or by an appropriate permit-issuing authority designated by the Secretary of State.

No alien shall be permitted to depart from the United States if it appears to the satisfaction of the Secretary of State that such departure would be prejudicial to the interests of the United States as provided in the rules and regulations hereinbefore authorized to be prescribed by the Secretary of State, with the concurrence of the Attorney General.

(3) After the effective date of the rules and regulations hereinafter authorized, no alien shall enter or attempt to enter the United States unless he is in possession of a valid unexpired permit to enter issued by the Secretary of State, or by an appropriate officer designated by the Secretary of State, or is exempted from obtaining a permit to enter in accordance with the rules and regulations which the Secretary of State, with the concurrence of the Attorney General, is hereby authorized to prescribe in execution of these rules, regulations, and orders.

No alien shall be permitted to enter the United States if it appears to the satisfaction of the Secretary of State that such entry would be prejudicial to the interests of the United States as provided in the rules and regulations hereinbefore authorized to be prescribed by the Secretary of State, with the concurrence of the Attorney General.

(4) No person shall depart from or enter, or attempt to depart from or enter, the United States without submitting for inspection, if required to do so, all documents, articles, or other things which are being removed from or brought into the United States upon or in connection with such person's departure or entry, which are hereby made subject to official inspection under rules and regulations which the Secretary of State in the cases of citizens, and the Secretary of State with the concurrence of the Attorney General in the cases of aliens, is hereby authorized to prescribe.

(5) A permit to enter issued to an alien seaman employed on a vessel arriving at a port in the United States from a foreign port shall be conditional and shall entitle him to enter only in a case of reasonable necessity in which the immigration authorities are satisfied that such entry would not be contrary to the interests of the United States; but this shall not be deemed to supersede the provisions of Executive Order 8429, dated June 5, 1940 concerning the documentation of seamen.

(6) The period of validity of a permit to enter or a permit to depart, issued to an alien, may be terminated by the permit-issuing authority

or by the Secretary of State at any time prior to the entry or departure of the alien, provided the permit-issuing authority or the Secretary of State is satisfied that the entry or departure of the alien would be prejudicial to the interests of the United States which it was the purpose of the above-mentioned acts to safeguard.

(7) Except as provided herein or by rules and regulations prescribed hereunder, the provisions of this proclamation and the rules and regulations issued in pursuance hereof shall be in addition to, and shall not be held to repeal, modify, suspend, or supersede any proclamation, rule, regulation, or order heretofore issued and now in effect under the general statutes relating to the immigration of aliens into the United States; and compliance with the provisions of this proclamation or of any rule or regulation which may hereafter be issued in pursuance of the act of May 22, 1918, as amended by the act of June 21, 1941, shall not be considered as exempting any individual from the duty of complying with the provisions of any statute, proclamation, rule, regulation, or order heretofore issued and now in effect.

(8) I direct all departments and agencies of the Government to cooperate with the Secretary of State in the execution of his authority under this proclamation and any subsequent proclamation, rule, regulation, or order promulgated in pursuance hereof. They shall upon request make available to the Secretary of State for that purpose the services of their respective officials and agents. I enjoin upon all officers of the United States charged with the execution of the laws thereof the utmost diligence in preventing violations of the act of May 22, 1918, as amended by the act of June 21, 1941, and in bringing to trial and punishment any persons who shall have violated any provisions of such acts.

(9) Paragraph 6, part I, of Executive Order 8766, issued June 3, 1941, is hereby superseded by the provisions of this proclamation and such regulations as may be prescribed hereunder.

IN WITNESS WHEREOF, I have hereunto set my hand and caused the seal of the United States of America to be affixed.

DONE at the city of Washington this 14th day of November, in the year of our Lord nineteen hundred and forty-one, and of the Independence of the United States of America the one hundred and sixty-sixth.

FRANKLIN D. ROOSEVELT

The Secretary of State has prescribed, with the concurrence of the Attorney General, regulations governing the entry and departure of aliens in accordance with the above proclamation. These regulations are published in the *Federal Register*.[1]

[1] 6 *Fed. Reg.*, p. 5911–8.

Under the proclamation and the regulations aliens desirous of departing from the United States are required to obtain exit permits from the Secretary of State unless they fall within one or more of the classes which are exempt from the exit-permit requirement. Permits to depart are sent to the departure-control officers of the Immigration and Naturalization Service at the ports of departure designated in the applications. Such permits are issued subject to the condition that the applicant shall have complied with all other laws and regulations of the United States, particularly to laws relating to public safety, prior to the date of contemplated departure.[1]

The regulations [2] governing the entry of aliens under the act and the proclamation issued thereunder construe and adopt visas and other present documentation as permits to enter within the meaning of the act, subject to certain additional restrictions which have been placed upon the issuance of such documents for the purpose of protecting the interests of the United States.

The new procedure for the issuance of visas, which became effective on July 1, 1941, has been laid down in formal regulations, which, with certain specified exceptions, provide for the issuance of advisory opinions by the Secretary of State to American diplomatic and consular officers before visas are issued. Advisory opinions are to be formulated through the various Interdepartmental Committees which are now functioning and sifting the great mass of information in possession of Government agencies concerning visa applicants.

Sponsors of visa applicants, attorneys, agents, and other intermediaries are permitted to appear before an Interdepartmental Committee of Review in the Department of State and make appropriate statements concerning their knowledge of, and interest in, visa applicants. The written record of cases not finally disposed of by the Committees may be reviewed by a Board of Appeals composed of two members appointed by the President from persons outside of the Government. As this Board will confine its consideration of cases to the record received from the Interdepartmental Committees there will be no hearings by the Board. Cases requiring further hearing of interested persons may be returned by the Board to the Committee of Review.

In case the opinion of the Board of Appeals is not acceptable to the Secretary of State, or if the members of the Appeals Board are unable to agree, the Secretary of State substitutes his own opinion, which decision is transmitted to the appropriate consular or diplomatic officials as the advisory opinion of the Department of State.

The departure from and entry into the United States of American citizens is governed by Departmental Order 1003, issued by the Secretary of State on November 25, 1941.[3] Under the regulations contained therein, all citizens of the United States or persons who owe allegiance to the United States are required, after six o'clock in the forenoon of January 15, 1942, to bear valid passports in order to depart from or enter the continental United States (territory of the several states and Alaska), the Canal Zone, the Commonwealth of the Philippines, and all territories, continental or insular, subject to the jurisdiction of the United States, except that, effective immediately (November 25, 1941), "no such

[1] Department of State, *Bulletin*, V, p. 383.
[2] The summary of the regulations as given is taken practically verbatim from the Department of State, *Bulletin*, V, p. 384.
[3] *Ibid.*, p. 431; 6 *Fed. Reg.*, p. 6069.

)erson shall depart from or attempt to depart from any such territory for any
oreign country or territory in the Eastern Hemisphere, or any foreign country or
erritory in the Western Hemisphere under the jurisdiction of Great Britain in
vhich the United States maintains defense bases or in which such bases are being
:onstructed by or under contract with the Government of the United States,
inless he bears a valid passport for such travel issued by or under the authority
»f the Secretary of State or is otherwise authorized by the Secretary of State."

The regulations provide that passports shall not be required of any such person
vhen travelling between the continental United States and the territories of
Iawaii, Puerto Rico, and the Virgin Islands, or between any such places; when
ravelling between points in the continental United States and points in Canada
ind Mexico; when travelling between the continental United States or Puerto
Rico or the Virgin Islands and islands adjacent to Canada or the United States or
he islands of the West Indies, including the Bahamas, except any such island as
s subject to the jurisdiction of a non-American country other than Great
3ritian and such island subject to British jurisdiction in which a United States
lefense base is maintained or being constructed; when travelling as a member of
he armed forces of the United States or a civil employee of the War or Navy
Departments if he is in possession of a document of identification issued by one
»f the departments in question; and when travelling under specific authoriza-
.ion from the Secretary of State.

The regulations also apply to seamen, though the date when the requirement
»f the possession of a passport was to take effect was put ahead for such persons
o February 15, 1942.[1] Furthermore, a seaman when travelling as such is ex-
»mpted from the necessity of complying with the requirement that a passport
nust be verified by an American diplomatic or consular officer before entering
»r attempting to enter any territory of the United States.

a) Passport Verification. Regulations Applicable to Citizens, May 7, 1942 [2]

Verification of passports is provided for by the Act of May 22, 1918, as
imended, U. S. Code, title 22, secs. 223–26.

No verification of passport shall be required of a citizen of the United
States, or a person who owes allegiance to the United States:

(a) When returning to the United States from a foreign country
vhere he had gone in pursuance of the provisions of a contract with
he War or Navy Departments on a matter vital to the war effort if
ie is in possession of evidence of having been so engaged and has a
'alid passport; or

(b) When returning to the United States from a foreign country as a
nember of the flying staff, operating personnel, or crew on board an
:rriving aircraft which is under lease to or contract with the Govern-

---

[1] The date was subsequently further advanced. See p. 780.

[2] Department of State, *Bulletin*, VI, p. 480.

ment of the United States or on board an American aircraft which is
engaged in commercial air-transport service for the carriage of goods
passengers, or mail between the territory of the United States and a
foreign country.

3. PERSONS ENGAGED IN POLITICAL ACTIVITIES FOR FOREIGN GOVERNMENTS AND ORGANIZATIONS

(1) *Registration of Foreign Agents. An Act to Amend the Act of June 8 1938, as amended, Approved April 29, 1942* [1]

Experience with administering the Foreign Agents Registration Act (*Documents, I, 1938–39*, p. 559) caused the Department of State to suggest certain amendments in July 1941. Legislative proposals were considered in Congress in November and December 1941 to revise the act by transferring its administration to the Attorney General and to incorporate four major changes: [2]

"1. A new provision has been added to require the labeling of all political propaganda disseminated in this country by registrable foreign agents. This requires a statement on every piece of political propaganda which such persons disseminate in the mails or in interstate or foreign commerce to the effect that it is sent by a registered foreign agent, his name and address, and that his registration statement, as well as copies of his political propaganda, are on file for public inspection.

"2. The administration of the act is transferred from the Department of State, where it has been lodged since the original act was passed to the Department of Justice, and all registrants are required to file copies of all political propaganda distributed by them with the Department of Justice and with the Library of Congress.

"3. The application of the statute is extended to include the use of the United States by foreign agents as a base for propaganda activities in Central and South America.

"4. The enforcement provisions of the act are strengthened and clarified through various detailed changes in language."

The President vetoed H. R. 6269 on February 9, 1942 [3] on the general ground that it was a bill "drafted in peacetime to protect a nation at peace" and "was not drafted with a view to the situation created by the Axis assault upon our country and our entry into the war in fighting partnership with 25 United Nations." "To achieve victory," the President pointed out, "we must be certain that there is a minimum of interference with the strengthening and perfecting of joint action." "It is far from clear," the President concluded "that the requirements of this legislation would not in many instances be unnecessary, inappropriate, and onerous in respect to the representatives of friendly nations." The Act of April 29, 1942 met this objection.

[1] Public Law 532, 77th Cong.; originating as S. 2399 from Committee on the Judiciary; Senate Report No. 1227; House Report No. 2038. Subcommittee No. 4 of the House Committee on the Judiciary held hearings on H. R. 6045, which was reported out in a revised form as H. R. 6269 on December 18, 1941; House Report No. 1547. Senate Report No. 913 on S. 2060; House (conference) Report No. 1662. The President vetoed the proposal February 9, 1942 and S. 2399 was a revision to meet this objection.

[2] Senate Report No. 913, 77th Cong., 1st sess., p. 9.

[3] For text of the President's message, see H. R. Doc. No. 611, 77th Cong., 2d sess.

Be it enacted by the Senate and House of Representatives of the United States of America in Congress assembled, That the Act of June 8, 1938 [1] 52 Stat. 631, U. S. C., title 22, sec. 233 (*a*) to sec. 233(*g*)), entitled. "An Act to require the registration of certain persons employed by agencies to disseminate propaganda in the United States, and for other purposes," as amended, is hereby amended to read as follows:

POLICY AND PURPOSE

It is hereby declared to be the policy and purpose of this Act to protect the national defense, internal security, and foreign relations of the United States by requiring public disclosure by persons engaging in propaganda activities and other activities for or on behalf of foreign governments, foreign political parties, and other foreign principals so that the Government and the people of the United States may be informed of the identity of such persons and may appraise their statements and actions in the light of their associations and activities.

DEFINITIONS

SECTION 1. As used in and for the purposes of this Act —

(*a*) The term "person" includes an individual, partnership, association, corporation, organization, or any other combination of individuals;

(*b*) The term "foreign principal" includes —

(1) a government of a foreign country and a foreign political party;

(2) an individual affiliated or associated with, or supervised, directed, controlled, financed, or subsidized, in whole or in part, by any foreign principal defined in clause (1) of this section 1 (*b*);

(3) a person outside of the United States, unless it is established that such person is an individual and is a citizen of and domiciled within the United States or that such person is not an individual, is organized under or created by the laws of the United States or of any State or other place subject to the jurisdiction of the United States, and has its principal place of business within the United States. Nothing in this clause (3) shall limit the operation of clause (5) of this section 1 (*b*);

(4) a partnership, association, corporation, organization, or other combination of individuals organized under the laws of, or having its principal place of business in, a foreign country;

(5) a domestic partnership, association, corporation, organization, or other combination of individuals, subsidized directly or indirectly, in whole or in part, by any foreign principal defined in clause (1), (3), or (4) of this section 1 (*b*);

(*c*) Except as provided in section 1 (*d*) hereof, the term "agent of a foreign principal" includes —

(1) any person who acts or agrees to act, within the United States, as, or who is or holds himself out to be whether or not pursuant to contractual relationship, a public-relations counsel, publicity agent, information-service employee, servant, agent, representative, or attorney for a foreign principal;

[1] *Documents, I, 1938–39*, p. 559.

(2) any person who within the United States collects information for o
reports information to a foreign principal; who within the United States soli
cits or accepts compensation, contributions, or loans, directly or indirectly
from a foreign principal; who within the United States solicits, disburses
dispenses, or collects compensation, contributions, loans, money, or anythin
of value, directly or indirectly, for a foreign principal; who within the Unite
States acts at the order, request, or under the direction, of a foreign prin
cipal;

(3) any person who assumes or purports to act within the United States a
an agent of a foreign principal in any of the respects set forth in clauses (1
and (2) of this section 1 (c); and

(4) any person who is an officer or member of the active or reserve military
naval, or other armed forces of any foreign principal defined in clause (1) o
section 1 (b) hereof, or who is an officer of or employed by any such foreig
principal; and proof of any affiliation or employment, specified in this claus
(4), of any person within a period of five years previous to the effective dat
of this Act shall create a rebuttable presumption that such person is an agen
of a foreign principal;

(d) The term "agent of a foreign principal" does not include any news or pres
service or association organized under the laws of the United States or of an
State or other place subject to the jurisdiction of the United States, or any news
paper, magazine, periodical, or other publication for which there is on file wit
the Postmaster General a sworn statement in compliance with section 2 of th
Act of August 24, 1912 (37 Stat. 553), as amended, published in the Unite
States, solely by virtue of any bona fide news or journalistic activities, includin
the solicitation or acceptance of advertisements, subscriptions, or other compen
sation therefor, so long as it is at least 80 per centum beneficially owned by, an
its officers and directors if any, are citizens of the United States, and such new
or press service or association, newspaper, magazine, periodical, or other publica
tion, is not owned, directed, supervised, controlled, subsidized, or financed, an
none of its policies are determined by any foreign principal defined in clause (1)
(2), or (4) of section 1 (b) hereof, or by any agent of a foreign principal require
to register under this Act;

(e) The term "government of a foreign country" includes any person or grou
of persons exercising sovereign de facto or de jure political jurisdiction over an
country, other than the United States, or over any part of such country, an
includes any subdivision of any such group and any group or agency to whic
such sovereign de facto or de jure authority or functions are directly or indirectl
delegated. Such term shall include any faction or body of insurgents within
country assuming to exercise governmental authority whether such faction o
body of insurgents has or has not been recognized by the United States;

(f) The term "foreign political party" includes any organization or any othe
combination of individuals in a country other than the United States, or an
unit or branch thereof, having for an aim or purpose, or which is engaged in an
activity devoted in whole or in part to, the establishment, administration, cor
trol, or acquisition of administration or control, of a government of a foreig
country or a subdivision thereof, or the furtherance or influencing of the politic
or public interests, policies, or relations of a government of a foreign country or
subdivision thereof;

(g) The term "public-relations counsel" includes any person who engages directly or indirectly in informing, advising, or in any way representing a principal in any matter pertaining to political or public interests, policies, or relations;

(h) The term "publicity agent" includes any person who engages directly or indirectly in the publication or dissemination of oral, visual, graphic, written, or pictorial information or matter of any kind, including publication by means of advertising, books, periodicals, newspapers, lectures, broadcasts, motion pictures, or otherwise;

(i) The term "information-service employee" includes any person who is engaged in furnishing, disseminating, or publishing accounts, descriptions, information, or data with respect to the political, industrial, employment, economic, social, cultural, or other benefits, advantages, facts, or conditions of any country other than the United States or of any government of a foreign country or of a foreign political party or of a partnership, association, corporation, organization, or other combination of individuals organized under the laws of, or having its principal place of business in, a foreign country;

(j) The term "political propaganda" includes any oral, visual, graphic, written, pictorial, or other communication or expression by any person (1) which is reasonably adapted to, or which the person disseminating the same believes will, or which he intends to, prevail upon, indoctrinate, convert, induce, or in any other way influence a recipient or any section of the public within the United States with reference to the political or public interests, policies, or relations of a government of a foreign country or a foreign political party or with reference to the foreign policies of the United States or promote in the United States racial, religious, or social dissensions, or (2) which advocates, advises, instigates, or promotes any racial, social, political, or religious disorder, civil riot, or other conflict involving the use of force or violence in any other American Republic or the overthrow of any government or political subdivision of any other American Republic by any means involving the use of force or violence. As used in this section 1 (j) the term "disseminating" includes transmitting or causing to be transmitted in the United States mails or by any means or instrumentality of interstate or foreign commerce or offering or causing to be offered in the United States mails;

(k) The term "registration statement" means the registration statement required to be filed with the Attorney General under section 2 (a) hereof, and any supplements thereto required to be filed under section 2 (b) hereof, and includes all documents and papers required to be filed therewith or amendatory thereof or supplemental thereto, whether attached thereto or incorporated therein by reference;

(l) The term "American Republic" includes any of the states which were signatory to the Final Act of the Second Meeting of the Ministers of Foreign Affairs of the American Republics at Havana, Cuba, July 30, 1940;

(m) The term "United States," when used in a geographical sense, includes the several States, the District of Columbia, the Territories, the Canal Zone, the insular possessions, including the Philippine Islands, and all other places now or hereafter subject to the civil or military jurisdiction of the United States;

(n) The term "prints" means newspapers and periodicals, books, pamphlets, sheet music, visiting cards, address cards, printing proofs, engravings, photographs, pictures, drawings, plans, maps, patterns to be cut out, catalogs, prospectuses, advertisements, and printed, engraved, lithographed, or autographed notices of various kinds, and, in general, all impressions or reproductions obtained on paper or other material assimilable to paper, on parchment or on cardboard, by means of printing, engraving, lithography, autography, or any other easily recognizable mechanical process, with the exception of the copying press stamps with movable or immovable type, and the typewriter.

REGISTRATION

SEC. 2. (a) No person shall act as an agent of a foreign principal unless he has filed with the Attorney General a true and complete registration statement and supplements thereto as required by this section 2 (a) and section 2 (b) hereof or unless he is exempt from registration under the provisions of this Act. Except a hereinafter provided, every person who is an agent of a foreign principal on the effective date of this Act shall, within ten days thereafter and every person who becomes an agent of a foreign principal after the effective date of this Act shall within ten days thereafter, file with the Attorney General, in duplicate, a registration statement, under oath, on a form prescribed by the Attorney General of which one copy shall be transmitted promptly by the Attorney General to the Secretary of State for such comment, if any, as the Secretary of State may desire to make from the point of view of the foreign relations of the United States Failure of the Attorney General so to transmit such copy shall not be a bar to prosecution under this Act. The registration statement shall include the following, which shall be regarded as material for the purposes of this Act:

(1) Registrant's name, principal business address, and all other business addresses in the United States or elsewhere, and all residence addresses, if any

(2) Status of the registrant; if an individual, nationality; if a partnership name, residence addresses, and nationality of each partner and a true and complete copy of its articles of copartnership; if an association, corporation organization, or any other combination of individuals, the name, residenc addresses, and nationality of each director and officer and of each person per forming the functions of a director or officer and a true and complete cop of its charter, articles of incorporation, association, constitution, and bylaw and amendments thereto; a copy of every other instrument or document and statement of the terms and conditions of every oral agreement relating to it organization, powers, and purposes; and a statement of its ownership an control;

(3) A comprehensive statement of the nature of registrant's business; complete list of registrant's employees and a statement of the nature of the work of each, unless, and to the extent, this requirement is waived in writin by the Attorney General; the name and address of every foreign principal fo whom the registrant is acting, assuming or purporting to act or has agreed t act; the character of the business or other activities of every such foreign prin cipal, and, if any such foreign principal be other than a natural person, statement of the ownership and control of each; and the extent, if any, t which each such foreign principal is supervised, directed, owned, controlled financed, or subsidized, in whole or in part, by any government of a foreig country or foreign political party;

(4) Copies of each written agreement and the terms and conditions of eac oral agreement, including all modifications of such agreements, or, where n

contract exists, a full statement of all the circumstances, by reason of which the registrant is an agent of a foreign principal; a comprehensive statement of the nature and method of performance of each such contract, and of the existing and proposed activity or activities engaged in or to be engaged in by the registrant as agent of a foreign principal for each such foreign principal;

(5) The nature and amount of contributions, income, money, or thing of value, if any, that the registrant has received within the preceding sixty days from each such foreign principal, either as compensation or for disbursement or otherwise, and the form and time of each such payment and from whom received;

(6) A detailed statement of every activity which the registrant is performing or is assuming or purporting or has agreed to perform for himself or any other person other than a foreign principal and which requires his registration hereunder;

(7) The name, business, and residence addresses, and, if an individual, the nationality, of any person who has within the preceding sixty days contributed or paid money or anything of value to the registrant in connection with any of the activities referred to in clause (6) of this section 2 (a) and the amount or value of the same;

(8) A detailed statement of the money and other things of value spent or disposed of by the registrant during the preceding sixty days in furtherance of or in any way in connection with activities which require his registration hereunder and which have been undertaken by him either as an agent of a foreign principal or for himself or any other person;

(9) Copies of each written agreement and the terms and conditions of each oral agreement, including all modifications of such agreements, or, where no contract exists, a full statement of all the circumstances, by reason of which the registrant is performing or assuming or purporting or has agreed to perform for himself or for a foreign principal or for any person other than a foreign principal any activities which require his registration hereunder;

(10) Such other statements, information, or documents pertinent to the purposes of this Act as the Attorney General, having due regard for the national security and the public interest, may from time to time require;

(11) Such further statements and such further copies of documents as are necessary to make the statements made in the registration statement and supplements thereto, and the copies of documents furnished therewith, not misleading.

(b) Every agent of a foreign principal who has filed a registration statement required by section 2 (a) hereof shall, within thirty days after the expiration of each period of six months succeeding such filing, file with the Attorney General a supplement thereto under oath, on a form prescribed by the Attorney General, which shall set forth with respect to such preceding six months' period such facts as the Attorney General, having due regard for the national security and the public interest, may deem necessary to make the information required under section 2 hereof accurate, complete, and current with respect to such period. In connection with the information furnished under clauses (3), (4), (6), and (9) of section 2 (a) hereof, the registrant shall give notice to the Attorney General of any changes therein within ten days after such changes occur. If the Attorney General, having due regard for the national security and the public interest, determines that it is necessary to carry out the purposes of this Act, he may, in any particular case, require supplements to the registration statement to be filed at more frequent intervals in respect to all or particular items of information to be furnished.

(c) The registration statement and supplements thereto shall be executed under oath as follows: If the registrant is an individual, by him; if the registrant is a partnership, by the majority of the members thereof; if the registrant is a person other than an individual or a partnership, by a majority of the officers thereof or persons performing the functions of officers or by a majority of the board of directors thereof or persons performing the functions of directors, if any

(d) The fact that a registration statement or supplement thereto has been filed shall not necessarily be deemed a full compliance with this Act and the regulations thereunder on the part of the registrant; nor shall it indicate that the Attorney General has in any way passed upon the merits of such registration statement or supplement thereto; nor shall it preclude prosecution, as provided for in this Act, for willful failure to file a registration statement or supplement thereto when due or for a willful false statement of a material fact therein or the willful omission of a material fact required to be stated therein or the willful omission of a material fact or copy of a material document necessary to make the statements made in a registration statement and supplements thereto, and the copies of documents furnished therewith, not misleading.

(e) If any agent of a foreign principal, required to register under the provisions of this Act, has previously thereto registered with the Attorney General under the provisions of the Act of October 17, 1940 (54 Stat. 1201), the Attorney General, in order to eliminate inappropriate duplication, may permit the incorporation by reference in the registration statement or supplements thereto filed hereunder of any information or documents previously filed by such agent of a foreign principal under the provisions of the Act of October 17, 1940 (54 Stat. 1201).

EXEMPTIONS

SEC. 3. The requirements of section 2 (a) hereof shall not apply to the following agents of foreign principals:

(a) A duly accredited diplomatic or consular officer of a foreign government who is so recognized by the Department of State, while said officer is engaged exclusively in activities which are recognized by the Department of State as being within the scope of the functions of such officer;

(b) Any official of a foreign government, if such government is recognized by the United States, who is not a public-relations counsel, publicity agent, information-service employee, or a citizen of the United States, whose name and status and the character of whose duties as such official are of public record in the Department of State, while said official is engaged exclusively in activities which are recognized by the Department of State as being within the scope of the functions of such official;

(c) Any member of the staff of, or any person employed by, a duly accredited diplomatic or consular officer of a foreign government who is so recognized by the Department of State, other than a public-relations counsel, publicity agent or information-service employee, whose name and status and the character of whose duties as such member or employee are of public record in the Department

of State, while said member or employee is engaged exclusively in the performance of activities which are recognized by the Department of State as being
within the scope of the functions of such member or employee;

(d) Any person engaging or agreeing to engage only in private, nonpolitical,
financial, mercantile, or other activities in furtherance of the bona fide trade or
commerce of such foreign principal or in the soliciting or collecting of funds and
contributions within the United States to be used only for medical aid and assistance, or for food and clothing to relieve human suffering, if such solicitation or
collection of funds and contributions is in accordance with and subject to the
provisions of the Act of November 4, 1939, as amended (54 Stat. 48), and such
rules and regulations as may be prescribed thereunder;

(e) Any person engaging or agreeing to engage only in activities in furtherance of bona fide religious, scholastic, academic, or scientific pursuits or of the
fine arts;

(f) Any person, or employee of such person, whose foreign principal is a government of a foreign country the defense of which the President deems vital to
the defense of the United States while, (1) such person or employee engages only
in activities which are in furtherance of the policies, public interest, or national
defense both of such government and of the Government of the United States,
and are not intended to conflict with any of the domestic or foreign policies of
the Government of the United States, (2) each communication or expression by
such person or employee which he intends to, or has reason to believe will, be
published, disseminated, or circulated among any section of the public, or portion
thereof, within the United States, is a part of such activities and is believed by
such person to be truthful and accurate and the identity of such person as an
agent of such foreign principal is disclosed therein, and (3) such government of a
foreign country furnishes to the Secretary of State for transmittal to, and reten-
tion for the duration of this Act by, the Attorney General such information as to
the identity and activities of such person or employee at such times as the Attorney General may require. Upon notice to the Government of which such person
is an agent or to such person or employee, the Attorney General, having due
regard for the public interest and national defense, may, with the approval of
the Secretary of State, and shall, at the request of the Secretary of State,
terminate in whole or in part the exemption herein of any such person or
employee.

FILING AND LABELING OF POLITICAL PROPAGANDA

SEC. 4. (a) Every person within the United States who is an agent of a foreign
principal and required to register under the provisions of this Act and who trans-
mits or causes to be transmitted in the United States mails or by any means or
instrumentality of interstate or foreign commerce any political propaganda (i) in
the form of prints, or (ii) in any other form which is reasonably adapted to being,
or which he believes will be, or which he intends to be, disseminated or circulated
among two or more persons shall, not later than forty-eight hours after the beginning of the transmittal thereof, send to the Librarian of Congress two copies
thereof and file with the Attorney General one copy thereof and a statement,
duly signed by or on behalf of such agent, setting forth full information as to the
places, times, and extent of such transmittal.

(*b*) It shall be unlawful for any person within the United States who is an agent of a foreign principal and required to register under the provisions of this Act to transmit or cause to be transmitted in the United States mails or by any means or instrumentality of interstate or foreign commerce any political propaganda (*i*) in the form of prints, or (*ii*) in any other form which is reasonably adapted to being, or which he believes will be, or which he intends to be, disseminated or circulated among two or more persons, unless such political propaganda is conspicuously marked at its beginning with, or prefaced or accompanied by, a true and accurate statement, in the language or languages used in such political propaganda, setting forth that the person transmitting such political propaganda or causing it to be transmitted is registered under this Act with the Department of Justice, Washington, District of Columbia, as an agent of a foreign principal, together with the name and address of such agent of a foreign principal and of each of his foreign principals; that, as required by this Act, his registration statement is available for inspection at and copies of such political propaganda are being filed with the Department of Justice; and that registration of agents of foreign principals required by the Act does not indicate approval by the United States Government of the contents of their political propaganda. The Attorney General, having due regard for the national security and the public interest, may by regulation prescribe the language or languages and the manner and form in which such statement shall be made and require the inclusion of such other information contained in the registration statement identifying such agent of a foreign principal and such political propaganda and its sources as may be appropriate.

(*c*) The copies of political propaganda required by this Act to be sent to the Librarian of Congress shall be available for public inspection under such regulations as he may prescribe.

(*d*) For purposes of the Library of Congress, other than for public distribution, the Secretary of the Treasury and the Postmaster General are authorized, upon the request of the Librarian of Congress, to forward to the Library of Congress fifty copies, or as many fewer thereof as are available, of all foreign prints determined to be prohibited entry under the provisions of section 305 of title III of the Act of June 17, 1930 (46 Stat. 688), and of all foreign prints excluded from the mails under authority of section 1 of title XII of the Act of June 15, 1917 (40 Stat. 230).

Notwithstanding the provisions of section 305 of title III of the Act of June 17, 1930 (46 Stat. 688), and of section 1 of title XII of the Act of June 15, 1917 (40 Stat. 230), the Secretary of the Treasury is authorized to permit the entry and the Postmaster General is authorized to permit the transmittal in the mails of foreign prints imported for governmental purposes by authority or for the use of the United States or for the use of the Library of Congress.

BOOKS AND RECORDS

SEC. 5. Every agent of a foreign principal registered under this Act shall keep and preserve while he is an agent of a foreign principal such books of account and other records with respect to all his activities, the disclosure of which is required under the provisions of this Act, as the Attorney General, having due regard for the national security and the public interest, may by regulation prescribe as necessary or appropriate for the enforcement of the provisions of this Act and shall preserve the same for a period of three years following the termination of such status. Until regulations are in effect under this section every agent of a foreign principal shall keep books of account and shall preserve all written records with respect to his activities. Such books and records shall be open at all reasonable times to the inspection of any official charged with the enforcement of this Act. It shall be unlawful for any person willfully to conceal, destroy, obliterate, mutilate, or falsify, or to attempt to conceal, destroy, obliterate, mutilate, or falsify, or to cause to be concealed, destroyed, obliterated, mutilated, or falsified, any books or records required to be kept under the provisions of this section.

PUBLIC EXAMINATION OF OFFICIAL RECORDS

Sec. 6. The Attorney General shall retain in permanent form one copy of all registration statements and all statements concerning the distribution of political propaganda furnished under this Act, and the same shall be public records and open to public examination and inspection at such reasonable hours, under such regulations, as the Attorney General may prescribe, and copies of the same shall be furnished to every applicant at such reasonable fee as the Attorney General may prescribe. The Attorney General may withdraw from public examination the registration statement and other statements of any agent of a foreign principal whose activities have ceased to be of a character which requires registration under the provisions of this Act.

LIABILITY OF OFFICERS

Sec. 7. Each officer, or person performing the functions of an officer, and each director, or person performing the functions of a director, of an agent of a foreign principal which is not an individual shall be under obligation to cause such agent to execute and file a registration statement and supplements thereto as and when such filing is required under sections 2 (a) and 2 (b) hereof and shall also be under obligation to cause such agent to comply with all the requirements of sections 4 (a), 4 (b), and 5 and all other requirements of this Act. In case of failure of any such agent of a foreign principal to comply with any of the requirements of this Act, each of its officers, or persons performing the functions of officers, and each of its directors, or persons performing the functions of directors, shall be subject to prosecution therefor.

ENFORCEMENT AND PENALTIES

Sec. 8. (a) Any person who —
  (1) willfully violates any provision of this Act or any regulation thereunder, or
  (2) in any registration statement or supplement thereto or in any statement under section 4 (a) hereof concerning the distribution of political propaganda or in any other document filed with or furnished to the Attorney General under the provisions of this Act willfully makes a false statement of a material fact or willfully omits any material fact required to be stated therein or willfully omits a material fact or a copy of a material document necessary to

make the statements therein and the copies of documents furnished therewith not misleading, shall, upon conviction thereof, be punished by a fine of not more than $10,000 or by imprisonment for not more than five years, or both.

(b) In any proceeding under this Act in which it is charged that a person is an agent of a foreign principal with respect to a foreign principal outside of the United States, proof of the specific identity of the foreign principal shall be permissible but not necessary.

(c) Any alien who shall be convicted of a violation of, or a conspiracy to violate, any provision of this Act or any regulation thereunder shall be subject to deportation in the manner provided by sections 19 and 20 of the Immigration Act of 1917 (39 Stat. 889, 890), as amended.

(d) The Postmaster General may declare to be nonmailable any communication or expression falling within clause (2) of section 1 (j) hereof in the form of prints or in any other form reasonably adapted to, or reasonably appearing to be intended for, dissemination or circulation among two or more persons, which is offered or caused to be offered for transmittal in the United States mails to any person or persons in any other American Republic by any agent of a foreign principal, if the Postmaster General is informed in writing by the Secretary of State that the duly accredited diplomatic representative of such American Republic has made written representation to the Department of State that the admission or circulation of such communication or expression in such American Republic is prohibited by the laws thereof and has requested in writing that its transmittal thereto be stopped.

APPLICABILITY OF ACT

SEC. 9. This Act shall be applicable in the several States, the District of Columbia, the Territories, the Canal Zone, the insular possessions, including the Philippine Islands, and all other places now or hereafter subject to the civil or military jurisdiction of the United States.

RULES AND REGULATIONS

SEC. 10. The Attorney General may at any time make, prescribe, amend, and rescind such rules, regulations, and forms as he may deem necessary to carry out the provisions of this Act.

REPORTS TO THE CONGRESS

SEC. 11. The Attorney General shall, from time to time, make a report to the Congress concerning the administration of this Act, including the nature, sources, and content of political propaganda disseminated or distributed.

SEPARABILITY OF PROVISIONS

SEC. 12. If any provision of this Act, or the application thereof to any person or circumstances, is held invalid, the remainder of the Act, and the application of such provisions to other persons or circumstances, shall not be affected thereby.

SEC. 13. This Act is in addition to and not in substitution for any other existing statute.

SHORT TITLE

SEC. 14. This Act may be cited as the Foreign Agents Registration Act of 1938, as amended.

TRANSFER OF ADMINISTRATION

SEC. 2. Upon the effective date of this Act, all powers, duties, and functions of the Secretary of State under the Act of June 8, 1938 (52 Stat. 631), as amended, shall be transferred to and become vested in the Attorney General, together with all property, books, records, and unexpended balances of appropriations used by or available to the Secretary of State for carrying out the functions devolving on him under the above-cited Act. All rules, regulations, and forms which have been issued by the Secretary of State pursuant to the provisions of said Act, and which are in effect, shall continue in effect until modified, superseded, revoked, or repealed.

EFFECTIVE DATE

SEC. 3. This Act shall take effect on the sixtieth day after the date of its approval, except that prior to such sixtieth day the Attorney General may make, prescribe, amend, and rescind such rules, regulations, and forms as may be necessary to carry out the provisions of this Act.

(a) *Executive Order No. 9176 Transferring the Administration of the Act of June 8, 1938, as amended, Requiring the Registration of Agents of Foreign Principals, from the Secretary of State to the Attorney General, May 29, 1942* [1]

By virtue of the authority vested in me by Title I of the First War Powers Act, 1941, approved December 18, 1941 (Public Law No. 354, 77th Congress), and as President of the United States, it is hereby ordered as follows:

1. All functions, powers and duties of the Secretary of State under the act of June 8, 1938 (52 Stat. 631), as amended by the act of August 7, 1939 (53 Stat. 1244), requiring the registration of agents of foreign principals, are hereby transferred to and vested in the Attorney General.

2. All property, books and records heretofore maintained by the Secretary of State with respect to his administration of said act of June 8, 1938, as amended, are hereby transferred to and vested in the Attorney General.

[1] 7 *Fed. Reg.*, p. 4127.

3. The Attorney General shall furnish to the Secretary of State for such comment, if any, as the Secretary of State may desire to make from the point of view of the foreign relations of the United States, one copy of each registration statement that is hereafter filed with the Attorney General in accordance with the provisions of this Executive Order.

4. All rules, regulations and forms which have been issued by the Secretary of State pursuant to the provisions of said act of June 8, 1938, as amended, and which are in effect shall continue in effect until modified, superseded, revoked or repealed by the Attorney General.

5. This order shall become effective as of June 1, 1942.

(2) Policy Regarding "Free Movements" in the United States. Statement of the Department of State, December 10, 1941 [1]

The United States has traditionally been a haven and land of opportunity for peoples of different nationalities and cultural origins. As a result, in addition to the many aliens resident in the country, there are a large number of people who, while owing allegiance to the United States, have an interest in and sympathy with political developments in foreign countries. In view of the nature of American ideals and the reasons that have brought alien peoples to American shores, it is but natural that there should be present among us people of a strong faith in freedom and a firm opposition to oppression and persecution.

Traditionally peoples seeking political freedom have counted on sympathy for their aspirations or movements from Americans, and instances of self-determination enunciated or initiated on American soil dot United States history. A familiar example is the Philadelphia declaration of independence of the Mid-European Union, October 26, 1918,[2] on behalf of Czecho-Slovaks, Poles, Jugoslavs, Ukrainians, Ukro-Russians, Lithuanians, Rumanians, Italian Irredentists, Unredeemed Greeks, Albanians and Zionists. Political leaders from foreign countries have, from headquarters established here, planned campaigns to gain control of their home governments. The occupation of areas and countries by Germany, Italy and Japan has resulted in the continuation of governments-in-exile, which have sometimes been supplanted at home by regimes supported, organized or controlled by the occupying forces; in the emergence of irredentist organizations previously quiescent or active in national affairs through the customary channels of their country; and in movements originating abroad for the support of resistance to the forces in control of the homeland. The statement of December 10 was issued during a state of war as a cautionary guide to citizens of the United States.

The military occupation by Axis Powers of many areas and countries in Europe has led to the destruction of a number of governments and to domination by the Axis over a number of other governments.

---

[1] Department of State, *Bulletin*, V, p. 519.
An officer of the Department, Mr. Harold B. Hoskins, has been assigned to keep informed on the activities of these movements.

[2] *International Conciliation*, January 1919, Special Bulletin, p. 23.

As a result, political leaders assuming to represent the peoples of such countries, or various groups in them, have been coming to the United States in increasing numbers. It seems advisable to make clear the attitude of this Government toward them and toward their political activities in the United States.

The United States is composed of citizens from many national backgrounds. Despite a natural interest in their country of origin, all American citizens of whatever background owe, and have, an undivided allegiance to the United States. This is in no way inconsistent with the pride which they naturally take in the cultural, artistic and spiritual contributions made to American life by citizens of their national background, and made to civilization by the countries from which they or their ancestors may have come. The Government of the United States does not look with favor on any activities designed to divide the allegiance of any group of American residents between the United States and any foreign government, in existence or in prospect. The first concern of the United States must always be the unity of the country, based on the American way of life and the ideal of liberty many times invoked since its first statement in our Declaration of Independence.

In harmony with the basic principles of liberty, the people of the United States do have a sympathetic interest in movements by aliens in this country who desire to liberate their countries from Axis domination.

The Department of State is glad to be informed of the plans and proposed activities of such "free movements" and of organizations representing such movements. It will be realized that agents of foreign principals, including agents of foreign governments or committees, are required to register with the State Department under existing law. Such registration does not indicate either approval or disapproval of the organization so registered.

In general the Government of the United States does not favor "free movements" or groups representing such movements which carry on activities contrary to the established policies, domestic or foreign, of the Government of the United States; and prefers that the governing committees of such movements shall be composed of citizens of the foreign country, rather than of American sympathizers. It disapproves of any attempt to enlist the support of American citizens of like racial background on the theory that they are "fellow nationals," though it recognizes that because of a common race background American citizens acting as Americans and with full allegiance to the United States may nevertheless be sympathetic to the national aspirations of their country of racial origin, and may organize in sympathetic and friendly support of such aspirations.

The Department has taken cognizance of the existence of a number of committees representing free movements but has not extended any form of recognition to them, formal or informal. The Department has not sought to influence any resident alien or any American citizen in determining whether or not it is desirable for him to associate himself with the support of any such free movement or any organization designed for that end.

4. PROTECTION OF AMERICAN NATIONALS AND THEIR PROPERTY ABROAD

In time of peace, an important function of the national government in the field of foreign relations is the protection of American nationals and their property abroad. The performance of this function often involves the government in complicated and even critical negotiations with the governments of foreign countries, as in the case of the Mexican petroleum controversy.[1] In time of war or threat of war, special demands are placed upon the government to make every reasonable provision for the safety of its nationals in enemy or potentially enemy countries.

During the period of stress and strain preceding the Japanese attack upon the United States, American nationals in certain areas of the Far East were urged to return to the United States as soon as practicable and arrangements were made to place special facilities at their disposal for that purpose.[2] Similar action was taken by the Department of State in the case of American nationals living in European areas threatened by or directly involved in war.[3]

With the outbreak of war in December 1941, the liberty of movement of American nationals abroad became severely restricted. Those living in countries now at war with the United States were subject to treatment as alien enemies. They were denied permission to leave the country except by special arrangement. Furthermore, because of the impossibility of direct diplomatic dealings with the enemy country, the American Government found itself in the position of being able to do relatively little immediately for the aid of these people. In general our position was that American nationals as enemy aliens were subject to restrictions but that if taken into custody they should be treated at least as favorably as prisoners of war.[4]

The property of American nationals in countries with which the United States was at war became immediately, as from the time of the commencement of war, liable to treatment as enemy property. The Government of the United States was not in a position immediately to take any action in protection of such

[1] See p. 420.
[2] *Documents, III, 1940–41*, p. 582; Department of State, *Bulletin*, V, p. 135, 276. Embassy circular, issued on Department of State orders, Tokyo, November 27, 1941 as printed in *New York Times*, November 27, 1941, p. 6.
[3] *Documents, III, 1940–41*, p. 580–2; Department of State, *Bulletin*, V, p. 221.
[4] Under the Geneva Prisoners of War Convention signed July 27, 1929, se *Treaties, Conventions, etc.*, 1923–1937, IV, p. 5224. For text of Department of State statement of May 23, 1942, see p. 812.

roperty. However, on January 31, 1942, the Department of State announced [1] lat it was prepared to receive "for its information" statements in regard to ıch properties, covering nature, value, location, manner and date of acquisition, ɛtails as to ownership and details as to treatment.

The following exhibits are Department of State announcements regarding ıe limited assistance the American Government is prepared to give to American ıtionals and property of American nationals situated in enemy-controlled ʔ threatened territory.

l) *Aid to Citizens Stranded Abroad. Statement of the Department of State, January 20, 1942* [2]

In line with the Department's efforts ever since international condi- ʔns became disturbed to assist, as far as possible, Americans stranded ʔroad in dangerous areas to return to the United States, the Depart- ıent has recently arranged with the Department of Commerce and the ʔnited States Maritime Commission for an extension of the arrange- ıents by which American-flag vessels, wherever available in the Far ıd Middle East, may carry from dangerous areas there as many assengers as possible within the limits of safety beyond the normal ırrying capacity of such vessels. The Department has also made ınds available to this Government's representatives at dangerous places ı those areas from which advances may be made as loans to needy ımericans unable to finance their return transportation to the United tates, or where such return transportation is not immediately available, ʔ places of greater safety than the dangerous areas in which they find ıemselves stranded.

The Department has also been giving careful consideration to the ʔoblem of providing some form of financial assistance to those Amer- ans who, due to the war, have been unable to return to the United tates from enemy and enemy-occupied countries and who find them- ʔlves stranded without financial resources.

Sometime ago the Department requested the Swiss Government, ʔhich is representing American interests in enemy areas, to furnish the ʔepartment, as soon as possible, a statement of the financial situation ʔ Americans in the various areas where this Government's interests ʔe under the protection of Switzerland and an estimate of the amount f funds immediately needed to relieve their situation. The Swiss ʔovernment was likewise requested to furnish the Department, in ʔhalf of Americans in enemy areas having resources in the United tates upon which they can draw, the names and addresses of persons

---

[1] Department of State, *Bulletin*, VI, p. 93.
[2] *Ibid.*, p. 80.

in this country to be approached, the amount needed, and purposes fo which desired. Upon receipt of this information the Department hope to put into effect a satisfactory procedure for transmitting funds fro private sources in the United States to needy Americans in enemy o enemy-occupied areas, as well as for providing temporary financi assistance to needy Americans in those areas who may be withot private resources. In the meantime, the Swiss Government has bee requested to authorize its representatives in enemy territory whereve the need is determined to be urgent to make small relief payments t those Americans having need of immediate financial assistance.

(2) *Financial Aid to Nationals in Enemy and Enemy-Occupied Territor Announcement of the Department of State, March 12, 1942* [1]

Arrangements have been completed to advance small amounts o United States Government funds to American nationals remaining i enemy and enemy-occupied territories except the Philippine Island sufficient to meet the ordinary needs of existence.

It is expected that sums advanced will be repaid either by the recip ents or by relatives, friends, business associates, or other representative in the United States.

Private deposits to reimburse the Government for sums advance should be made with the Department of State. Persons wishing t make such deposits should indicate the names of the beneficiaries an should remit by postal money orders or certified checks payable to tl "Secretary of State of the United States." In the event it should I necessary, it is expected that small additional advances for medic and other necessary expenses will be made.

Aliens, including alien spouses and alien children of American natio als, cannot qualify for payments from funds of the United States Gover ment.

However, in the cases of prisoners of war and interned civilians wl are supported by the detaining power, it is expected that paymen made to them will generally not exceed a small sum sufficient to provic spending money for miscellaneous personal needs not supplied by tl detaining power. No payments will be made to officers or to persons equivalent status held as prisoners of war, who receive pay under tl convention relating to the treatment of prisoners of war, signed . Geneva on July 27, 1929.

Sums advanced will in all cases be limited as far as possible in ord to prevent foreign exchange becoming available to the enemy.

[1] *Ibid.*, p. 230.

5. TREATMENT OF ALIEN ENEMIES

A. General Policy

The principles governing the treatment of enemy aliens in time of war have
een evolved over a period of time through practice and international agreement.
he treatment of civilian enemy aliens, both as to their persons and property,[1]
as been less clearly defined than that to be accorded to prisoners of war. The
eatment of prisoners of war is prescribed, so far as states which have ratified it
re concerned, by the terms of the Prisoners of War Convention, signed at
eneva, July 27, 1929.[2] This Convention was ratified by the United States,
anuary 16, 1932, and became effective so far as the United States was conerned on August 4, 1932, six months following the date of deposit at Berne,
witzerland, of the instrument of ratification.[3]
Generally speaking, the United States Government has been guided in its
ction regarding enemy nationals in the United States by the rules of interational law and the principle of reciprocity.[4]

1) *Measures Taken with Respect to Japanese Nationals. Announcement of the Department of State, December 9, 1941* [5]

Because of the state of war that exists between this Government and
he Government of Japan, the following measures have been taken with
spect to Japanese nationals in this country:

1. A protective cordon of police has been thrown around the Japanese
mbassy. The movement of the staff of the Embassy has been restricted
) the building and grounds. The police are for the purpose of protecting
e staff of the Embassy and its property. The Embassy is permitted
) send out an officer, a clerk, or household personnel to procure what-
ver may be needed of food, clothing, fuel, etc. Any such person leaving
e Embassy is accompanied on his trip by a representative of the police
) afford him protection. There is no officer of any character of this
overnment within the Embassy.

2. Each Japanese consulate in the United States has received police
rotection. This protection is in the interest of the protection of the
nsul and the consular property. There is no other restriction on the
ovement of the consul. He is free to move about, to make whatever
urchases may be required.

[1] See James W. Garner, *International Law and the World War*, I, chaps. 3–5, for
scussion of treatment of civilian enemy aliens in World War I.
[2] Sen. Doc. No. 134, 75th Cong., 3d sess; *Treaties, Conventions, etc.*, 1923–1937, IV,
5224.
[3] *Ibid.*, p. 5249.
[4] See statement of the Department of State regarding attitude towards representa-
ves of enemy powers, Department of State, *Bulletin*, V, p. 544.
[5] *Ibid.*, p. 512.

3. Japanese civilians in this country have not been subjected to special restriction other than that of transportation and communication. If an individual is suspected of activities inimical to the interests of this country, he is taken into custody for questioning. If he is found incriminated, he is held. If nothing is discovered against him, he is set free. Japanese civilians here are free to continue at their abodes and to go about their normal activities. They cannot engage in movement which would necessitate the use of airplane, train, vessel, or bus. They are not permitted to make use of international communications.

(2) Treatment of Civilian Alien Enemies and Prisoners of War. Statement of the Department of State, May 23, 1942 [1]

Upon the outbreak of war in Europe the Government of the United States, actuated by humanitarian motives, expressed the earnest hope to the British, French, and German Governments that they could give thought to avoiding harsh treatment of enemy aliens. It was pointed out that there had grown gradually among civilized states the conviction that there should be no retaliation against prisoners of war for acts of their governments. This conviction received international sanction in the Prisoners of War Convention which was signed at Geneva in 1929.[2] It was suggested that the same reasoning should apply to civilian enemy aliens unfortunate enough to be caught under enemy jurisdiction and that just as the nations had abandoned the idea that prisoners of war are hostages for the good behavior of the enemy so the same idea in respect to civilians might be held. It was recognized that belligerents might feel it essential to maintain surveillance and some restriction upon the acts of civilian enemy aliens. These ideas were in general accepted and applied by the three belligerents to whom the American Government addressed its communication.

Upon the entry of the United States into the war the Government of the United States with reference to its declaration to the British, French, and German Governments informed the German, Italian, and Japanese Governments that it intended on its part to apply the principles set forth in its declaration and in line therewith to apply to civilian enemy aliens as liberal a regime as was consistent with the safety of the United States. This Government declared that enemy aliens whom it might be found necessary to intern would be treated at least as favorably as prisoners of war. To that end this Government informed

[1] *Ibid.*, VI, p. 445.
[2] *Treaties, Conventions, etc.*, 1923–1937, IV, p. 5224.

he German, Italian, and Japanese Governments that it intended to pply to civilian enemy aliens taken into custody by it the provisions f the Geneva Prisoners of War Convention, so far as those provisions ight be adaptable to civilians, and that it expected the enemy governents to extend like treatment to American citizens taken into cusody by them. The Italian Government replied that it would be glad eciprocally to apply the Geneva Prisoners of War Convention to merican civilians interned by it. The Japanese Government replied hat it would extend the provisions of the Convention reciprocally to merican civilian internees provided that the American Government id not make use of the provisions of the Convention to compel Japanese ivilians in its hands to work against their will — to which this Government agreed. The German Government stated that pending the completion of negotiations which were going on between the German and merican Governments for the mutual repatriation of each other's ationals, it preferred not to undertake additional international obliations, especially since it hoped that it would be possible to substitute epatriation for internment. This Government replied that, as it had tated at the outbreak of the war, it did not desire to effect general nternment of German nationals and preferred that citizens of the other ountry whose presence in either country appears prejudicial to the ational safety should be repatriated. It added that pending the repatriation of German nationals held in custody in the United States the iovernment of the United States would in accordance with its previous eclaration to the German Government apply to them the provisions f the Geneva Prisoners of War Convention and that it had taken ote from reports received by it from official neutral sources that the ierman Government was apparently applying the provisions of this Convention to American civilians held in custody by it.

Upon the declaration of war between the United States and Germany nd the United States and Italy, the Geneva Prisoners of War Convention, to which all three countries are parties, was put into effect as egards prisoners of war. Japan, which is not a party to the Prisoners f War Convention, has agreed to apply it reciprocally to American risoners of war.

The Geneva Prisoners of War Convention lays down in general terms he rights and duties of prisoners of war. The prisoners may be interned n towns, fortresses, or enclosed camps but they may not be imprisoned xcept as an indispensable measure of safety nor held in unhealthful egions. They must be lodged in buildings or in barracks affording all ossible guaranties of hygiene and healthfulness and given generally

the same accommodations and food as the depot troops of the holdin
power. They must receive medical treatment and be given liberty i
the exercise of their religion. Sports and intellectual recreational dive
sions organized by them are to be encouraged by the holding powers. Off
cer prisoners must receive from the holding power the same pay as office
of corresponding rank in the armies of that power, provided this pa
does not exceed that to which they are entitled in their own arm
The labor of private soldiers may be utilized by the holding power wit
payment of wages in accordance with the rates in force for soldiers i
the national army doing the same work or, if no such rates exist, accor
ing to rates in harmony with the work performed.

The Convention also provides that prisoners of war may be allowe
to correspond with friends and relatives and that their correspondenc
shall enjoy the postal frank. They may receive parcels containin
foods, books, and other items. They may deal with the authoritie
through men of confidence or agents appointed by them from amon
themselves. The Convention specifies the procedure to be followed i
imposing disciplinary punishments on prisoners of war and in the
trial and punishment for crimes. Sick and wounded prisoners are t
be repatriated.

The Convention further provides for the establishment of offici
information bureaus to exchange lists of prisoners among the belligerer
powers and for work by relief societies in the prisoner-of-war camp
It also provides that representatives of the protecting powers sha
visit camps to insure compliance with the provisions of the Conventio
and permits the carrying out by the International Red Cross Committe
with the consent of the interested belligerents, of its recognized humai
itarian work.

The German, Italian, and Japanese Governments are apparentl
abiding by their undertakings to apply to prisoners of war the Genev
Prisoners of War Convention and, so far as they are adaptable, t
extend the application of the provisions of that Convention to America
civilians.

The Japanese have permitted official neutral observers to visit Ame
ican prisoners of war in Japan and American civilians interned in Japa
and in a number of places which were in Japanese hands at the ou
break of the war between the United States and Japan. The Japane
have permitted these official neutral observers in some cases to spea
alone with the Americans and in other cases to speak with them in tl
presence of Japanese officials. American prisoners of war and civilia
internees so interviewed have made no serious complaints of infractior

the Convention. The prisoners are reported to be receiving standard
apanese Army rations. The private soldiers at the camp at Zentsuji
e being given employment in agriculture for which they receive pay.
ivilians are in part interned under similar conditions in camps, in part
ader forced residence in their own houses, and in part at large under
arole.

The Government of the United States, however, still remains without
formation from official neutral sources regarding the condition of
mericans in the Philippines, in parts of occupied China, in Hong Kong,
 Malaya, and in the Netherlands East Indies, to which the Japanese
overnment has not yet admitted official neutral observers. Efforts
ave been made and are currently being continued to obtain Japanese
ansent to admit to these places also official neutral observers for the
arpose of investigating the condition of American citizens, both interned
ad not interned.

Americans interned in Germany are accommodated in heated build-
gs and are reported to receive the rations of German depot troops.
hey are permitted to receive visits from their relatives and are allowed
) exchange mail with friends and relatives and to receive parcels and
applementary food and clothing. They receive good medical attention,
ad in most cases the aged and sick are reliably reported to have been
deased. Their general health is stated to be good.

Americans interned in Italy are reliably reported not to be confined
 camps but to be under orders to remain in certain towns and districts.

This Government is endeavoring to fulfil its undertakings with regard
) the Geneva Conference and at the same time is insisting that the
ll benefits of the Convention be reciprocally granted by the enemy
auntries to American citizens in their hands.

————

According to an announcement of the American Red Cross on January 30,
942,[1] the Japanese Government accepted appointment of a delegate from the
.ternational Red Cross and agreed to "transmit through the Central Agency,
eneva, information concerning prisoners of war on the basis of reciprocity."
ae Japanese Government also stated that it was ready to exchange information
ancerning interned non-combatants "as far as possible." By decree of Decem-
ar 27, 1941, a Prisoners of War Information Bureau was established in Tokyo.
r. Paravicini, a Swiss citizen, was appointed as the International Red Cross
alegate in Tokyo. Mr. Marc Peters, former Swiss Minister to the United States,
acupies a similar position in Washington. Chairman Norman H. Davis of the
merican Red Cross stated that the first action under the agreement would be

[1] Department of State, *Bulletin*, VI, p. 92.

an exchange between the United States and Japan of names of prisoners of wa and interned nationals.

In addition to the exchange of diplomatic and consular personnel arranged b tween the United States and enemy states,[1] arrangements have been made f the exchange of a limited number of other nationals not possessing official statu The vessels engaged in carrying such persons proceed under safe conducts issue by the belligerent governments. As an example, the motorship *Gripsholm* sail from New York on June 18,[2] with approximately 495 Japanese and Thai officia and 602 Japanese with no official character. The ship called at Rio de Janei where it took on approximately 403 additional Japanese and Thais, making total of about 1500. These persons were carried by the *Gripsholm* to Louren Marques, Mozambique, Africa, where the vessel took on for its return voyage similar number of official and non-official nationals of the United States ar other countries in the Western Hemisphere whose transportation to Louren Marques was arranged by the Japanese Government.

B. Naturalization of Alien Enemies

(1) *Executive Order No. 9106 Permitting Certain Persons Excepte from the Classification of "Alien Enemy" to Apply for Naturaliz tion, March 20, 1942* [3]

WHEREAS section 326 of the Nationality Act of 1940, approve October 14, 1940 (54 Stat. 1150; U. S. C., title 8, sec. 726),[4] reads follows:

SEC. 326. (*a*) An alien who is a native, citizen, subject, or denizen of a country, state, or sovereignty with which the United States is at war may naturalized as a citizen of the United States if such alien's declaration of inte tion was made not less than two years prior to the beginning of the state of wa or such alien was at the beginning of the state of war entitled to become a citiz of the United States without making a declaration of intention, or his petiti for naturalization shall at the beginning of the state of war be pending and t petitioner is otherwise entitled to admission, notwithstanding such petition shall be an alien enemy at the time and in the manner prescribed by the la passed upon that subject.

(*b*) An alien embraced within this section shall not have such alien's petiti for naturalization called for a hearing, or heard, except after ninety days' noti given by the clerk of the court to the Commissioner to be represented at the hea ing, and the Commissioner's objection to such final hearing shall cause the pe tion to be continued from time to time for so long as the Commissioner m require.

(*c*) Nothing herein contained shall be taken or construed to interfere with prevent the apprehension and removal, agreeably to law, of any alien enemy any time previous to the actual naturalization of such alien.

[1] See p. 865.
[2] Department of State, *Bulletin*, VI, p. 553.
[3] 7 *Fed. Reg.*, p. 2199.
[4] *Documents, III, 1940–41*, p. 575.

(*d*) The President of the United States may, in his discretion, upon investigation and report by the Department of Justice fully establishing the loyalty of
any alien enemy not included in the foregoing exemption, except such alien enemy
from the classification of alien enemy, and thereupon such alien shall have the
privilege of applying for naturalization.

Now, THEREFORE, by virtue of the authority vested in me by the
foregoing statutory provisions, and in order to carry out the purposes
thereof, I hereby except from the classification "alien enemy" all
persons whom the Attorney General of the United States shall, after
investigation fully establishing their loyalty, certify as persons loyal
to the United States.

This order supersedes Executive Order No. 3008 of November 26,
1918, entitled "Excepting Certain Persons from the Classification of
' Alien Enemy' for the Purpose of Permitting Them to Apply for Naturalization."

C. Restrictions on the Freedom of Action of Alien Enemies

(1) *Proclamation Designating Japanese Subjects as Enemy Aliens and Prescribing Regulations Governing the Conduct of the Same, December 7, 1941* [1]

BY THE PRESIDENT OF THE UNITED STATES OF AMERICA

A Proclamation [No. 2525]

WHEREAS it is provided by Section 21 of Title 50 of the United
States Code as follows:

" Whenever there is a declared war between the United States and any
foreign nation or government, or any invasion or predatory incursion
is perpetrated, attempted, or threatened against the territory of the
United States by any foreign nation or government, and the President
makes public proclamation of the event, all natives, citizens, denizens,
or subjects of the hostile nation or government, being of the age of
fourteen years and upward, who shall be within the United States and
not actually naturalized, shall be liable to be apprehended, restrained,
secured, and removed as alien enemies. The President is authorized in
any such event, by his proclamation thereof, or other public act, to
direct the conduct to be observed, on the part of the United States,
toward the aliens who become so liable; the manner and degree of the
restraint to which they shall be subject and in what cases, and upon

[1] 6 *Fed. Reg.*, p. 6321.

what security their residence shall be permitted, and to provide for the removal of those who, not being permitted to reside within the United States, refuse or neglect to depart therefrom; and to establish any other regulations which are found necessary in the premises and for the public safety."

AND WHEREAS by Sections 22, 23 and 24 of Title 50 of the United States Code further provision is made relative to alien enemies:

NOW, THEREFORE, I, FRANKLIN D. ROOSEVELT, as PRESIDENT of the United States, and as Commander in Chief of the Army and Navy of the United States, do hereby make public proclamation to all whom it may concern that an invasion has been perpetrated upon the territory of the United States by the Empire of Japan.

And, acting under and by virtue of the authority vested in me by the Constitution of the United States and the said sections of the United States Code, I do hereby further proclaim and direct that the conduct to be observed on the part of the United States toward all natives citizens, denizens or subjects of the Empire of Japan being of the age of fourteen years and upwards who shall be within the United States or within any territories in any way subject to the jurisdiction of the United States and not actually naturalized, who for the purpose of this Proclamation and under such sections of the United States Code are termed alien enemies, shall be as follows:

All alien enemies are enjoined to preserve the peace towards the United States and to refrain from crime against the public safety, and from violating the laws of the United States and of the States and Territories thereof; and to refrain from actual hostility or giving information, aid or comfort to the enemies of the United States or interfering by word or deed with the defense of the United States or the political processes and public opinions thereof; and to comply strictly with the regulations which are hereby or which may be from time to time promulgated by the President.

All alien enemies shall be liable to restraint, or to give security, or to remove and depart from the United States in the manner prescribed by Sections 23 and 24 of Title 50 of the United States Code, and as prescribed in the regulations duly promulgated by the President.

And, pursuant to the authority vested in me, I hereby charge the Attorney General with the duty of executing all the regulations hereinafter contained regarding the conduct of alien enemies within continental United States, Puerto Rico, the Virgin Islands and Alaska, and the Secretary of War with the duty of executing the regulations which are hereinafter set forth and which may be hereafter adopted regarding the conduct of alien enemies in the Canal Zone, the Hawaiian Islands and the Philippine Islands. Each of them is specifically directed to cause the apprehension of such alien enemies as in the judgment of each are subject to apprehension or deportation under such regulations. In carrying out such regulations within the continental United States, Puerto Rico, the Virgin Islands and Alaska, the Attorney General is authorized to utilize such agents, agencies, officers and departments of the United States and of the several states, territories, dependencies and municipalities thereof and of the District of Columbia as he may select for the purpose. Similarly the Secretary of War in carrying out such regulations in the Canal Zone, the Hawaiian Islands and the Philippine Islands is authorized to use such agents, agencies, officers and departments of the United States and of the territories, dependencies and municipalities thereof as he may select for the purpose. All such agents, agencies, officers and departments are hereby granted full authority for all acts done by them in the execution of such regulations when acting by direction of the Attorney General or the Secretary of War, as the case may be.

And, pursuant to the authority vested in me, I hereby declare and establish the following regulations which I find necessary in the premises and for the public safety:

(1) No alien enemy shall enter or be found within the Canal Zone and no alien enemy shall enter or leave the Hawaiian Islands or the Philippine Islands except under such regulations as the Secretary of War shall from time to time prescribe. Any alien enemy found in the Canal Zone, the Hawaiian Islands, or the Philippine Islands in violation of any such regulations and any alien enemy who enters or is found within any restricted area to be hereafter prescribed by the Military Commanders of each such territory in the Canal Zone, the Hawaiian Islands, and the Philippine Islands, may be immediately apprehended by authority of the Military Governors in each such territory, or if there be no Military Governor, then by authority of the Secretary of War, and detained until it is determined, under the regulations to be prescribed by the Secretary of War, whether any such alien enemy should be permanently interned following which such alien enemy shall either be released, released on bond, or permanently interned, as the case may be.

(2) The exercise of the power to prescribe restricted areas and the power of arrest, detention and internment of alien enemies in the Canal Zone, the Hawaiian Islands or the Philippine Islands shall be under the jurisdiction of the Military Commanders of each such territory,

each acting under such regulations as the Secretary of War shall hereafter prescribe.

(3) No alien enemy shall enter or leave Alaska, Puerto Rico or the Virgin Islands except under such regulations as the Attorney General shall from time to time prescribe. Any alien enemy found in Alaska, Puerto Rico or the Virgin Islands in violation of any such regulations and any alien enemy who enters or is found within any restricted area to be hereafter prescribed by the Military Commanders of each such territory in Alaska, Puerto Rico and by the Naval Commander in the Virgin Islands, shall be immediately apprehended by the authority of the Attorney General acting through the United States Attorney in each such territory and detained until it is determined, under the regulations to be prescribed by the Attorney General, whether any such alien enemy shall either be released, released on bond, or permanently interned, as the case may be.

(4) The Military Commanders in Alaska and Puerto Rico and the Naval Commander in the Virgin Islands shall have the power to prescribe restricted areas.

(5) No alien enemy shall have in his possession, custody or control at any time or place or use or operate any of the following enumerated articles:

    a. Firearms.

    b. Weapons or implements of war or component parts thereof.

    c. Ammunition.

    d. Bombs.

    e. Explosives or material used in the manufacture of explosives.

    f. Short-wave radio receiving sets.

    g. Transmitting sets.

    h. Signal devices.

    i. Codes or ciphers.

    j. Cameras.

    k. Papers, documents or books in which there may be invisible writing; photograph, sketch, picture, drawing, map or graphical representation of any military or naval installations or equipment or of any arms, ammunition, implements of war, device or thing used or intended to be used in the combat equipment of the land or naval forces of the United States or of any military or naval post, camp or station.

All such property found in the possession of any alien enemy in violation of the foregoing regulations shall be subject to seizure and forfeiture.

(6) No alien enemy shall undertake any air flight or ascend into the air in any airplane, aircraft or balloon of any sort whether owned governmentally, commercially or privately, except that travel by an alien enemy in an airplane or aircraft may be authorized by the Attorney General, or his representative, or the Secretary of War, or his representative, in their respective jurisdictions, under such regulations as they shall prescribe.

(7) Alien enemies deemed dangerous to the public peace or safety of the United States by the Attorney General or the Secretary of War, as the case may be, are subject to summary apprehension. Such apprehension shall be made in the continental United States, Alaska, Puerto Rico and the Virgin Islands by such duly authorized officer of the Department of Justice as the Attorney General may determine. In the Canal Zone, the Hawaiian Islands and the Philippine Islands, such arrests shall be made by the Military Commanders in each such territory by authority of the respective Military Governors thereof, and if there be no Military Governor, then by authority of the Secretary of War. Alien enemies arrested shall be subject to confinement in such place of detention as may be directed by the officers responsible for the execution of these regulations and for the arrest, detention and internment of alien enemies in each case, or in such other places of detention as may be directed from time to time by the Attorney General, with respect to continental United States, Alaska, Puerto Rico and the Virgin Islands, and by the Secretary of War with respect to the Canal Zone, the Hawaiian Islands and the Philippine Islands, and there confined until he shall have received such permit as the Attorney General or the Secretary of War with respect to the Canal Zone, the Hawaiian Islands and the Philippine Islands shall prescribe.

(8) No alien enemy shall land in, enter or leave or attempt to land in, enter or leave the United States, except under the regulations prescribed by the President in his Proclamation dated November 14, 1941 [1] and the regulations promulgated thereunder or any proclamation or regulation promulgated hereafter.

(9) Whenever the Attorney General of the United States, with respect to the continental United States, Alaska, Puerto Rico and the Virgin Islands, or the Secretary of War, with respect to the Canal Zone, the Hawaiian Islands, and the Philippine Islands, deems it to be necessary, for the public safety and protection, to exclude alien enemies from a designated area, surrounding any fort, camp, arsenal, airport, landing field, aircraft station, electric or other power plant, hydroelectric dam,

[1] 6 *Fed. Reg.*, p. 5821.

government naval vessel, navy yard, pier, dock, dry dock, or any factory, foundry, plant, workshop, storage yard, or warehouse for the manufacture of munitions or implements of war or any thing of any kind, nature or description for the use of the Army, the Navy or any country allied or associated with the United States, or in any wise connected with the national defense of the United States, or from any locality in which residence by an alien enemy shall be found to constitute a danger to the public peace and safety of the United States or from a designated area surrounding any canal or any wharf, pier, dock or dry dock used by ships or vessels of any designated tonnage engaged in foreign or domestic trade, or of any warehouse, shed, elevator, railroad terminal, depot or yard or other terminal, storage or transfer facility, then no alien enemy shall be found within such area or the immediate vicinity thereof. Any alien enemy found within any such area or the immediate vicinity thereof prescribed by the Attorney General or the Secretary of War, as the case may be, pursuant to these regulations, shall be subject to summary apprehension and to be dealt with as herein above prescribed.

(10) With respect to the continental United States, Alaska, Puerto Rico, and the Virgin Islands, an alien enemy shall not change his place of abode or occupation or otherwise travel or move from place to place without full compliance with any such regulations as the Attorney General of the United States may, from time to time, make and declare; and the Attorney General is hereby authorized to make and declare, from time to time, such regulations concerning the movements of alien enemies within the continental United States, Alaska, Puerto Rico and the Virgin Islands, as he may deem necessary in the premises and for the public safety.

(11) With respect to the Canal Zone, the Hawaiian Islands and the Philippine Islands, an alien enemy shall not change his place or abode or occupation or otherwise travel or move from place to place without full compliance with any such regulations as the Secretary of War may, from time to time, make and declare; and the Secretary of War is hereby authorized to make and declare, from time to time, such regulations concerning the movements of alien enemies within the Canal Zone, the Hawaiian Islands, and the Philippine Islands as he may deem necessary in the premises and for the public safety.

(12) No alien enemy shall enter or be found in or upon any highway, waterway, airway, railway, railroad, subway, public utility, building, place or thing not open and accessible to the public generally, and not generally used by the public.

(13) No alien enemy shall be a member or an officer of, or affiliated

with, any organization, group or assembly hereafter designated by the Attorney General, nor shall any alien enemy advocate, defend or subscribe to the acts, principles or policies thereof, attend any meetings, conventions or gatherings thereof or possess or distribute any literature, propaganda or other writings or productions thereof.

This proclamation and the regulations herein contained shall extend and apply to all land and water, continental or insular, in any way within the jurisdiction of the United States.

IN WITNESS WHEREOF, I have hereunto set my hand and caused the seal of the United States of America to be affixed.

DONE at the City of Washington this 7th day of December, in the year of our Lord nineteen hundred and forty-one, and of [SEAL] the Independence of the United States of America the one hundred and sixty-sixth.

FRANKLIN D. ROOSEVELT

By the President:
CORDELL HULL
    Secretary of State

By proclamations Nos. 2526 [1] and 2527 [2] issued on December 8, 1941, the President extended the designation "alien enemies" to all "nationals, citizens, denizens, or subjects" of Germany and Italy, respectively, and prescribed identical regulations for their conduct.

Regulations governing travel and other conduct of aliens of enemy nationalities were prepared and issued by the Attorney General under date of February 5, 1942. [3] For subsequent amendments see 7 *Fed. Reg.*, p. 1084, 1474.

As of March 9, 1942 the Department of Justice, Immigration and Naturalization Service, [4] had taken into custody 5,182 alien enemies, of whom 4,023 remained in custody as follows:

	MALE	FEMALE	TOTAL
Japanese	2,755	36	2,791
German	773	119	892
Italian	289	9	298
Others	35	7	42
	3,852	171	4,023

[1] 6 *Fed. Reg.*, p. 6323.
[2] *Ibid.*, p. 6324.
[3] 7 *ibid.*, p. 844.
[4] Compiled from United States Congress, House of Representatives, Committee on Appropriations, *Sixth Supplemental National Defense Appropriation Bill for 1942, Hearings before Subcommittees* . . . 77th Cong., 2d sess., Part I, p. 233.

(2) *Proclamation Prescribing Regulations Pertaining to Alien Enemies, January 14, 1942* [1]

BY THE PRESIDENT OF THE UNITED STATES OF AMERICA

A Proclamation [No. 2537]

[Excerpt]

WHEREAS section 21 of title 50 of the United States Code provides as follows: [2]

.   .   .   .

WHEREAS by sections 22, 23, and 24 of title 50 of the United States Code further provision is made relative to alien enemies;

WHEREAS by Proclamation No. 2525 [3] of December 7, 1941, and Proclamations Nos. 2526 [4] and 2527 [5] of December 8, 1941, I prescribed and proclaimed certain regulations governing the conduct of alien enemies; and

WHEREAS I find it necessary in the interest of national defense to prescribe regulations additional and supplemental to such regulations:

NOW, THEREFORE, I, FRANKLIN D. ROOSEVELT, President of the United States of America, acting under and by virtue of the authority vested in me by the Constitution of the United States and the aforesaid sections of the United States Code, do hereby prescribe and proclaim the following regulations, additional and supplemental to those prescribed by the aforesaid proclamations of December 7, 1941, and December 8, 1941:

All alien enemies within the continental United States, Puerto Rico, and the Virgin Islands are hereby required, at such times and places and in such manner as may be fixed by the Attorney General of the United States, [6] to apply for and acquire certificates of identification; and the Attorney General is hereby authorized and directed to provide, as speedily as may be practicable, for the receiving of such applications and for the issuance of appropriate identification certificates, and to make such rules and regulations as he may deem necessary for effecting such identifications; and all alien enemies and all other persons are hereby required to comply with such rules and regulations. The Attorney General in carrying out such identification procedure, is hereby authorized to utilize such agents, agencies, officers, and depart-

---

[1] 7 *Fed. Reg.*, p. 329.   [2] See p. 817.
[3] *Ibid.*   [4] 6 *Fed. Reg.*, p. 6323.   [5] *Ibid.*, p. 6324.
[6] Regulations were prepared and issued under this authority, under date of January 22, 1942, 7 *ibid.*, p. 1477.

ments of the United States and of the several states, territories, dependencies, and municipalities thereof and of the District of Columbia as he may select for the purpose, and all such agents, agencies, officers, and departments are hereby granted full authority for all acts done by them in the execution of this regulation when acting by the direction of the Attorney General. After the date or dates fixed by the Attorney General for completion of such identification procedure, every alien enemy within the limits of the continental United States, Puerto Rico, or the Virgin Islands shall at all times have his identification card on his person.

IN WITNESS WHEREOF, I have hereunto set my hand and caused the seal of the United States to be affixed.

DONE at the City of Washington this 14th day of January in the year of our Lord nineteen hundred and forty-two, and of the Independence of the United States of America the one hundred [SEAL] and sixty-sixth.

FRANKLIN D. ROOSEVELT

By the President:
  CORDELL HULL
    The Secretary of State

(3) *Executive Order No. 9066 Authorizing the Secretary of War to Prescribe Military Areas, February 19, 1942* [1]

The authorization to create military areas was granted by the President in the exercise of his constitutional powers. The action was not directed against enemy aliens as such but rather against "any or all persons." It was obvious, however, that the restriction of alien enemies was particularly intended, and, in addition, the restriction of those persons of American nationality who because of race or national origin or political belief could not be fully trusted to conduct themselves with proper regard to the national security. As Lieut. General H. A. Drum, Commander of the Eastern Defense Command and First Army, stated, "the object of prescribing a military area is to facilitate control so as to prevent subversive activities and aid being given the enemy, such as by lighting along our coasts. . . . The fundamental policy embodied in the plan is not to interfere in any manner whatever with the lives of the great mass of loyal Americans in the states included in the military area, or with the economic life of the area." [2]

WHEREAS the successful prosecution of the war requires every possible protection against espionage and against sabotage to national-defense material, national-defense premises, and national-defense utilities as defined in Section 4, Act of April 20, 1918, 40 Stat. 533, as amended by

---

[1] 7 *ibid.*, p. 1407.
[2] *New York Times*, April 27, 1942, p. 3.

the Act of November 30, 1940, 54 Stat. 1220, and the Act of August 21 1941, 55 Stat. 655 (U. S. C., Title 50, Sec. 104):

Now, THEREFORE, by virtue of the authority vested in me as President of the United States, and Commander-in-Chief of the Army and Navy I hereby authorize and direct the Secretary of War, and the Military Commanders whom he may from time to time designate, whenever he or any designated Commander deems such action necessary or desirable, to prescribe military areas in such places and of such extent as he or the appropriate Military Commander may determine, from which any or all persons may be excluded, and with respect to which, the right of any person to enter, remain in, or leave shall be subject to whatever restrictions the Secretary of War or the appropriate Military Commander may impose in his discretion. The Secretary of War is hereby authorized to provide for residents of any such area who are excluded therefrom, such transportation, food, shelter, and other accommodations as may be necessary, in the judgment of the Secretary of War or the said Military Commander, and until other arrangements are made, to accomplish the purpose of this order. The designation of military areas in any region or locality shall supersede designations of prohibited and restricted areas by the Attorney General under the Proclamations of December 7 and 8 1941, and shall supersede the responsibility and authority of the Attorney General under the said Proclamations in respect of such prohibited and restricted areas.

I hereby further authorize and direct the Secretary of War and the said Military Commanders to take such other steps as he or the appropriate Military Commander may deem advisable to enforce compliance with the restrictions applicable to each Military area hereinabove authorized to be designated, including the use of Federal troops and other Federal Agencies, with authority to accept assistance of state and local agencies.

I hereby further authorize and direct all Executive Departments independent establishments and other Federal Agencies, to assist the Secretary of War or the said Military Commanders in carrying out this Executive Order, including the furnishing of medical aid, hospitalization food, clothing, transportation, use of land, shelter, and other supplies equipment, utilities, facilities, and services.

This order shall not be construed as modifying or limiting in any way the authority heretofore granted under Executive Order No. 8972, dated December 12, 1941, nor shall it be construed as limiting or modifying the duty and responsibility of the Federal Bureau of Investigation

[1] 6 *Fed. Reg.*, p. 6420.

with respect to the investigation of alleged acts of sabotage or the duty and responsibility of the Attorney General and the Department of Justice under the Proclamations of December 7 and 8, 1941, prescribing regulations for the conduct and control of alien enemies, except as such duty and responsibility is superseded by the designation of military areas hereunder.

Acting under the authority conferred by Executive Order No. 9066 defense areas have been proclaimed extending the length of the Atlantic and Pacific coastlines. By Public Proclamation No. 1 of the Commanding Officer (Lieut. Gen. H. A. Drum) of the Eastern Defense Command and First Army, Governors Island, N. Y., dated May 16, 1942, an area along the Atlantic seaboard embracing fifteen states, part of another state and the District of Columbia was declared a Military Area. Special restrictions were put in force, and wilful violation of such restrictions, by any person, or repeated careless violations, were declared to be cause for expulsion or prosecution, or, in the case of an alien enemy, for internment.

By Public Proclamation No. 1 of the Commanding Officer (Lieut. Gen. J. L. DeWitt) of the Western Defense Command and Fourth Army, Presidio of San Francisco, California, dated March 2, 1942, as amended by Public Proclamation No. 2, similar Military Areas and Zones were established along the Pacific seaboard, embracing the states of Arizona, California, Idaho, Montana, Nevada, Oregon, Utah and Washington.

(4) Executive Order No. 9102 Establishing the War Relocation Authority in the Executive Office of the President and Defining Its Functions and Duties, March 18, 1942 [1]

Lack of confidence in the loyalty of Japanese persons, whether citizens or aliens, the fact of the high degree of concentration of this group along the Pacific seaboard and the sense of insecurity which prevailed among the people along the west coast following the attack on Pearl Harbor and isolated coastal raids were primarily responsible for the adoption of the relatively drastic procedure of mass transfer or relocation. It is to be noted that the persons affected were not alone alien enemies but included citizens under suspicion as well.

Of the 126,947 Japanese, citizens and aliens, living in the United States on April 1, 1940, 117,364, or 92%, were living in the military areas and zones proclaimed March 2, 1942 by the Commanding Officer of the Western Defense Command and Fourth Army. Of the total 71,000 were United States citizens and 41,000 aliens. In the three west coast states there were 57,878 Italian nationals and 22,000 German nationals. All these persons were made subject to evacuation from places of residence and to detention in camps. The origin and progress of this procedure are described in the reports of a Select Committee of the U. S. House of Representatives set up pursuant to H. Res. 113 to investigate national defense migration (House Report No. 1911, 77th Cong., 2d sess., p. 21; No. 2124, 77th Cong., 2d sess., p. 96).

[1] 7 *ibid.*, p. 2165.

By virtue of the authority vested in me by the Constitution and statutes of the United States, as President of the United States and Commander-in-Chief of the Army and Navy, and in order to provide for the removal from designated areas of persons whose removal is necessary in the interests of national security, it is ordered as follows:

1. There is established in the Office for Emergency Management of the Executive Office of the President the War Relocation Authority, at the head of which shall be a Director appointed by and responsible to the President.

2. The Director of the War Relocation Authority is authorized and directed to formulate and effectuate a program for the removal, from the areas designated from time to time by the Secretary of War or appropriate military commander under the authority of Executive Order No. 9066 of February 19, 1942,[1] of the persons or classes of persons designated under such Executive Order, and for their relocation, maintenance, and supervision.

3. In effectuating such program the Director shall have authority to —

(*a*) Accomplish all necessary evacuation not undertaken by the Secretary of War or appropriate military commander, provide for the relocation of such persons in appropriate places, provide for their needs in such manner as may be appropriate, and supervise their activities.

(*b*) Provide, insofar as feasible and desirable, for the employment of such persons at useful work in industry, commerce, agriculture, or public projects, prescribe the terms and conditions of such public employment, and safeguard the public interest in the private employment of such persons.

(*c*) Secure the cooperation, assistance, or services of any governmental agency.

(*d*) Prescribe regulations necessary or desirable to promote effective execution of such program, and, as a means of coordinating evacuation and relocation activities, consult with the Secretary of War with respect to regulations issued and measures taken by him.

(*e*) Make such delegations of authority as he may deem necessary.

(*f*) Employ necessary personnel, and make such expenditures, including the making of loans and grants and the purchase of real property, as may be necessary, within the limits of such funds as may be made available to the Authority.

4. The Director shall consult with the United States Employment

[1] See p. 825.

Service and other agencies on employment and other problems incident to activities under this order.

5. The Director shall cooperate with the Alien Property Custodian appointed pursuant to Executive Order No. 9095 of March 11, 1942,[1] in formulating policies to govern the custody, management, and disposal by the Alien Property Custodian of property belonging to foreign nationals removed under this order or under Executive Order No. 9066 of February 19, 1942;[2] and may assist all other persons removed under either of such Executive Orders in the management and disposal of their property.

6. Departments and agencies of the United States are directed to cooperate with and assist the Director in his activities hereunder. The Departments of War and Justice, under the direction of the Secretary of War and the Attorney General, respectively, shall insofar as consistent with the national interest provide such protective, police and investigational services as the Director shall find necessary in connection with activities under this order.

7. There is established within the War Relocation Authority the War Relocation Work Corps. The Director shall provide, by general regulations, for the enlistment in such Corps, for the duration of the present war, of persons removed under this order or under Executive Order No. 9066 of February 19, 1942, and shall prescribe the terms and conditions of the work to be performed by such Corps, and the compensation to be paid.

8. There is established within the War Relocation Authority a Liaison Committee on War Relocation, which shall consist of the Secretary of War, the Secretary of the Treasury, the Attorney General, the Secretary of Agriculture, the Secretary of Labor, the Federal Security Administrator, the Director of Civilian Defense, and the Alien Property Custodian, or their deputies, and such other persons or agencies as the Director may designate. The Liaison Committee shall meet at the call of the Director and shall assist him in his duties.

9. The Director shall keep the President informed with regard to the progress made in carrying out this order, and perform such related duties as the President may from time to time assign to him.

10. In order to avoid duplication of evacuation activities under this order and Executive Order No. 9066 of February 19, 1942, the Director shall not undertake any evacuation activities within military areas designated under said Executive Order No. 9066, without the prior approval of the Secretary of War or the appropriate military commander.

[1] See p. 830.   [2] See p. 825.

11. This order does not limit the authority granted in Executive Order No. 8972 of December 12, 1941;[1] Executive Order No. 9066 of February 19, 1942;[2] Executive Order No. 9095 of March 11, 1942;[3] Executive Proclamation No. 2525 of December 7, 1941;[4] Executive Proclamation No. 2526 of December 8, 1941;[5] Executive Proclamation No. 2527 of December 8, 1941;[6] Executive Proclamation No. 2533 of December 29, 1941;[7] or Executive Proclamation No. 2537 of January 14, 1942;[8] nor does it limit the functions of the Federal Bureau of Investigation.

———

By proclamation [9] of August 18, 1942, Secretary of War Stimson declared all territory within the boundaries of War Relocation Centers near Cody, Wyoming; Rohwer and Jerome, Arkansas; and Granada, Colorado to be Military Areas under the provisions of the President's proclamation of February 19, 1942.

D. Treatment of Enemy Property. Alien Property Custodian

While the practice of World War I was highly equivocal, the generally favored principle of international law has been that private enemy property is not liable to confiscation in time of war though it is liable to such restrictions as to its use as will give assurance that it will not be made to serve the interest of the enemy state. The action of the President in establishing an Alien Property Custodian was in line with the action taken in World War I and in fact was based on the Trading with the Enemy Act of October 6, 1917, as amended by the First War Powers Act, 1941.[10]

(1) *Executive Order No. 9095 Establishing the Office of Alien Property Custodian and Defining Its Functions and Duties, March 11, 1942* [11]

By virtue of the authority vested in me by the Constitution, by the Trading with the Enemy Act of October 6, 1917, as amended, by the First War Powers Act, 1941, and as President of the United States, it is hereby ordered as follows:

1. There is hereby established in the Office for Emergency Management of the Executive Office of the President the Office of Alien Property Custodian, at the head of which shall be an Alien Property Custodian appointed by the President. The Alien Property Custodian shall receive compensation at such rate as the President shall approve and in addition shall be entitled to actual and necessary transportation, subsistence, and other expenses incidental to the performance of his duties.

[1] 6 *Fed. Reg.*, p. 6420.   [2] 7 *ibid.*, p. 1407.   [3] *Ibid.*, p. 1971.   [4] 6 *ibid.*, p. 6321.
[5] *Ibid.*, p. 6323.   [6] *Ibid.*, p. 6324.   [7] 7 *ibid.*, p. 55.   [8] *Ibid.*, p. 329.
[9] Public Proclamation No. WD 1, War Department Release, August 18, 1942.
[10] See p. 126.   [11] 7 *Fed. Reg.*, p. 1971.

Within the limitation of such funds as may be made available for that purpose, the Alien Property Custodian may appoint assistants and other personnel and delegate to them such functions as he may deem necessary to carry out the provisions of this Order.

2. All power and authority conferred on the President by Sections 3(a) and 5(b) of the Trading with the Enemy Act of October 6, 1917, as amended, and by Sections 301 and 302 of Title III of the First War Powers Act, 1941, approved December 18, 1941,[1] except such powers and authority as were delegated to the Secretary of the Treasury by Executive Orders issued prior to February 12, 1942, and to the Board of Governors of the Federal Reserve System by Executive Order No. 8843 of August 9, 1941 [2] (which powers and authority shall continue to be vested in and exercised by the Secretary of the Treasury and the Board of Governors respectively), are hereby delegated to and vested in the Alien Property Custodian. The memorandum of February 12, 1942, delegating to the Secretary of the Treasury certain powers and authority under said sections, is hereby revoked and canceled.[3] Any and all action heretofore taken by the Board of Governors of the Federal Reserve System after February 11, 1942, in pursuance of Executive Order No. 8843 of August 9, 1941, is hereby confirmed and ratified. In the exercise of the authority herein delegated, the Alien Property Custodian shall be subject to the provisions of Executive Order No. 8839 of July 30, 1941,[4] and shall designate a representative to the Board of Economic Warfare in accordance with section 6 thereof.

3. Any property, or interest therein, of any foreign country or a national thereof shall vest in the Alien Property Custodian whenever the Alien Property Custodian shall so direct;[5] and, in the case of any property, or interest therein, subject to the control of the Secretary of the Treasury, when the Alien Property Custodian shall notify the Secretary of the Treasury in writing that he has so directed, the Secretary of the Treasury shall release all control of any such property, or interest therein, to the Alien Property Custodian.

[1] See p. 764–6.

[2] Regulation of consumer credit.   6 *Fed. Reg.*, p. 4035.

[3] 7 *ibid.*, p. 1409.

[4] See p. 180.

[5] Vesting orders are issued with respect to specific corporations or properties. For the ones relating to the Schering Corporation, April 18, 1942, see 7 *Fed. Reg.*, p. 2922, and to the General Aniline and Film Corporation, April 24, 1942, *ibid.*, p. 3148.

The Secretary of the Treasury by regulations issued February 16, 1942 (7 *Fed. Reg.*, p. 1021) had set up the Vested Property Claims Committee "to hear claims respecting property vested in the Secretary pursuant to sec. 5(b) of the Trading with the Enemy Act."

4. Any outstanding order, proclamation, regulation, ruling, license, or instruction issued pursuant to, or relating to the administration of, any power or authority vested in the Alien Property Custodian by this Order shall remain in effect unless and until amended or revoked by the Alien Property Custodian.

(2) *Executive Order No. 9142 Transferring Certain Functions, Property, and Personnel from the Department of Justice to the Alien Property Custodian, April 21, 1942* [1]

[Excerpt]

By virtue of the authority vested in me as President of the United States, under the Constitution and laws of the United States, and in particular by Title I of the First War Powers Act, 1941, approved December 18, 1941 (Public Law No. 354, 77th Congress), it is hereby ordered as follows:

1. All authority, rights, privileges, powers, duties, and functions transferred or delegated to the Department of Justice, to be administered under the supervision of the Attorney General, by Executive Order No. 6694 of May 1, 1934, or vested in, transferred or delegated to, the Attorney General or the Assistant Attorney General in charge of the Claims Division of the Department of Justice, by Executive Order No. 8136 of May 15, 1939, are hereby transferred to the Alien Property Custodian provided for by Executive Order No. 9095, dated March 11, 1942.[2]

2. Subject to the provisions of paragraph 5 hereof, all property of the Alien Property Division of the Department of Justice, including records, files, supplies, furniture, and equipment, and all funds, securities, choses in action, real estate, patents, trade marks, copyrights, and all other property of whatsoever kind, held or administered by the Attorney General under and pursuant to the Trading with the Enemy Act, as amended, are hereby transferred to the Alien Property Custodian, to be administered and disposed of under his supervision and direction.

.   .   .   .

5. All litigation in which the Alien Property Custodian or the Office of the Alien Property Custodian is interested shall be conducted under the supervision of the Attorney General. The Department of Justice and the Attorney General shall from time to time render such advice on legal matters to the Alien Property Custodian and the Office of the Alien Property Custodian as the Attorney General and the Alien Property

[1] 7 *Fed. Reg.*, p. 2985.   [2] See p. 830.

Custodian may from time to time agree upon. For the purpose of defraying such expenses as may be incurred by the Department of Justice or the Attorney General in the rendering of advice as aforesaid or in the conduct of litigation in which the Alien Property Custodian or the Office of Alien Property Custodian is interested, including expenses for salaries of personnel and all other charges, the Alien Property Custodian may from time to time make available out of the funds or other property in his possession or control such funds as the Attorney General and the Alien Property Custodian may from time to time agree to be necessary therefor. Nothing in this order shall be construed to require the Department of Justice to surrender possession of any files and records relating to any litigation heretofore or hereafter conducted by it.

6. This order shall not be construed as modifying or limiting in any way the authority heretofore granted to the Federal Bureau of Investigation.

7. This order shall remain in force during the continuance of the present war and for six months after the termination thereof.

8. All prior Executive Orders insofar as they are in conflict herewith are hereby superseded.

_____

The War Relocation Authority in the Executive Office of the President, established by Executive Order No. 9102, March 18, 1942 (7 *Fed. Reg.*, p. 2165),[1] which handles the classes of persons designated by Executive Order No. 9066, February 19, 1942 (7 *Fed. Reg.*, p. 1407),[2] cooperates with the Alien Property Custodian in formulating policies to govern the custody, management and disposal of the property of foreign nationals affected.

6. COORDINATION OF RELIEF

[See *Documents, III, 1940–41*, p. 609.]

(1) Statement of the President's Committee on War Relief Agencies, January 22, 1942 [3]

The Committee has already suggested to foreign war-relief agencies in the United States the desirability of continuing their efforts for urgent foreign-relief needs, for morale as well as material considerations but to slow down and give the right-of-way to the Red Cross and other domestic agencies since the United States is now in the war. The Committee has, moreover, definitely recommended to all that these foreign relief agencies do not embark as such in the domestic field and that they

[1] See p. 827.   [2] See p. 825.
[3] Department of State, *Bulletin*, VI, p. 80.

do not undertake any new activities without first clearing through the Committee in order to assure that there is no duplication with already existing agencies. For all of these various foreign agencies to enter the domestic field would, in the Committee's opinion, only make confusion worse confounded.

It is recalled that the purposes of the Committee, as recommended by the Secretary of State to the President and approved by him, are to suggest the appropriate steps which might be taken to preserve local and essential welfare services and to maintain a balance between the facilities and resources available for foreign war relief, with particular regard to the financing of new welfare activities in connection with national-defense measures and so avoid the danger that all of these efforts, while inspired by the finest human instincts, might be frustrated if conducted without regard to one another and without proper coordination.

While the earlier activities of the Committee have had to do primarily with the coordination of foreign relief, the United States declaration of war has changed the situation, and at present its main interests and responsibilities have to do with the coordination of those services to the armed forces of the United States toward which the American public has been asked to contribute and for which there will be further appeals to the public.

CHAPTER XI

INTERNATIONAL ORGANIZATIONS

1. GENERAL POLICY

(1) *Statement of Assistant Secretary of State (Shaw) to the Subcommittee, Committee on Appropriations, House of Representatives, January 28, 1942* [1]

[Excerpt]

On the basis of information available to it, the Department, by administrative action, has withheld the payment of contributions to international organizations domiciled in territories in Europe under military occupation of the Axis Powers. In many instances it was impossible to receive any reports whatever concerning the activities of such organizations and in any event, it was obvious that the restrictions of military occupation would preclude their operation as independent entities. Consequently, in deference to the realities of the situation, the Department did not include in its requests for appropriations for the fiscal year 1943 items covering quota payments to organizations in occupied territories. This has been done with the understanding that should the world situation improve, deficiency appropriations would be requested in order that these obligations may be discharged.

It is the consensus within the executive departments and agencies primarily responsible for activities represented in these fields that this Government should continue its support of the international agencies and organizations which are still in a position to function independently during the war, although in some instances to a reduced degree. These international organizations have been built up over a period of many years and constitute the normal and wholesome channels of intercourse between the governments and intellectual and professional leaders of the world. In fact, during the period immediately prior to the outbreak of hostilities in Europe and continuing into the actual war period, interrupted diplomatic intercourse left these organizations as the only practical means of continuing important relationships of a scientific, technical, and humanitarian nature.

---

[1] House of Representatives, Committee on Appropriations, *Department of State Appropriation Bill for 1943; Hearings before the Subcommittee* . . . 77th Cong., 2d sess., p. 222.

It is believed important that this Government do everything within its power to safeguard the effectiveness and in some instances the very existence of these valuable peacetime institutions. It is feared that the withdrawal of our support might in some cases result in complete collapse of the organizations with a seriously damaging effect to scientific progress and enlightenment.

The ability of these organizations to function during the present war will have an important effect upon their capacity to perform the role expected of them in the reconstruction period. Many of them are today actively engaged in drawing up plans for immediate large-scale operation as soon as peace is restored. Were they to cease to function simply with the expectation of resumption of activity at the end of the war, valuable time would be lost in reorganization and in planning and executing a comprehensive reconstruction program.

The Department feels very strongly that this Government's financial support of the organizations still operating as independent agencies should be maintained not only in recognition of a formal obligation, but with equal importance, in the interest of safeguarding and encouraging normal international collaboration in these important fields.

(a) Contributions Omitted for the Fiscal Year 1943 [1]

International Bureau of Weights and Measures.	$4,342.50
International Bureau for Publication of Customs Tariffs	1,318.77
International Bureau of Permanent Court of Arbitration	1,722.57
International Office of Public Health	3,015.63
International Statistical Bureau	2,000.00
International Technical Committee of Aerial Legal Experts	6,745.00
Convention Relating to Liquor Traffic in Africa	55.00
Permanent International Association of Road Congresses	588.00
International Labor Organization Quota (to round out total)	.24
International Council of Scientific Unions:	
International Union of Chemistry	675.00
International Union of Physics	62.73
International Geographical Union	125.44
International Union of Biological Sciences	154.40

2. THE LEAGUE OF NATIONS

Following the fall of France which had the effect of preventing Geneva from functioning as an international center, the work of the League of Nations was necessarily reduced to a skeleton basis. For a description of League activity

[1] From breakdown of the justification of the estimates, House of Representatives Committee on Appropriations, *Department of State Appropriation Bill for 1943; Hearings before the Subcommittee* . . . 77th Cong., 2d sess., p. 221.

or the period 1941–1942, see *Report on the Work of the League, 1941–1942*, submitted by the Acting Secretary-General in May 1942 (League of Nations Document. General. 1942. 1).

One of the important departments of the technical staff of the Secretariat — the Economic, Financial and Transit Organization — established itself at Princeton, New Jersey, on mission, by invitation of Princeton University, the Rockefeller Institute for Medical Research, and the Institute for Advanced Study.[1] Branch offices of the Permanent Central Opium Board and the Supervisory Board were opened in Washington.[2]

From the point of view of American relations with the League the important question at present is perhaps not so much that of the extent of United States support of or participation in the very limited activities of the League as that of the attitude of the Government toward revival of the League after the war. No reference to the League is to be found in the Atlantic Charter or in the Declaration by United Nations, nor has President Roosevelt in his public statements given any clear indication of his attitude. In an address delivered at the laying of the cornerstone of the new wing of the Norwegian Legation on July 22, 1941, Acting Secretary of State Welles made some direct references to the League which are given here for whatever light they may throw on Administration policy. In his Memorial Day address, May 30, 1942 Mr. Welles reiterated his belief in the necessity for a world organization. (See p. 71.)

1) *Address of the Acting Secretary of State (Welles) at the Norwegian Legation, Washington, July 22, 1941* [3]

[Excerpt]

At the end of the last war, a great President of the United States gave his life in the struggle to further the realization of the splendid vision which he had held up to the eyes of suffering humanity — the vision of an ordered world governed by law.

The League of Nations, as he conceived it, failed in part because of the blind selfishness of men here in the United States as well as in other parts of the world; it failed because of its utilization by certain powers primarily to advance their own political and commercial ambitions; but it failed chiefly because of the fact that it was forced to operate, by those who dominated its councils, as a means of maintaining the *status quo*. It was never enabled to operate as its chief spokesman had intended, as an elastic and impartial instrument in bringing about peaceful and equitable adjustments between nations as time and circumstance proved necessary.

Some adequate instrumentality must unquestionably be found to achieve such adjustments when the nations of the earth again undertake the task of restoring law and order to a disastrously shaken world.

[1] *Documents, III, 1940–41*, p. 640.
[2] *Ibid.*
[3] Department of State, *Bulletin*, V, p. 76.

3. INTERNATIONAL LABOR ORGANIZATION CONFERENCE

The Conference of the International Labor Organization has held session annually except in 1940, in which year the International Labor Organization was transferred from Geneva to Montreal. The Conference was convened at New York and Washington October 27–November 6, 1941 for an unnumbered session which considered the broad aspects of the Organization's present and future responsibilities.[1] Of the 34 state delegations, 22 had a full representation of Government, Employer and Worker delegates and 15 member states sent cabinet ministers. Unlike ordinary sessions of the Conference, no draft conventions or recommendations were considered; of the resolutions adopted, only those of widest significance are here given.

The states represented were Argentine Republic, Australia, Belgium, Bolivia, Brazil, British Empire, Canada, Chile, China, Colombia, Czechoslovakia, Dominican Republic, Ecuador, Egypt, France, Greece, India, Iran, Ireland, Luxemburg, Mexico, New Zealand, Norway, Panama, Peru, Poland, South Africa, Thailand, United States, Uruguay, Venezuela and Yugoslavia. Costa Rica sent an observer.

The importance which the Government of the United States attaches to the International Labor Organization is evidenced by the character of the delegation [2] which President Roosevelt appointed to represent this country at the conference, as well as by the fact that he addressed in person the final session of the Conference at the White House.[3] The delegates were as follows:

Representing the Government:
   The Honorable Frances Perkins, *Secretary of Labor*
   The Honorable Adolph A. Berle, Jr., *Assistant Secretary of State*

Representing the Employers:
   Mr. Henry I. Harriman, *Chairman of the Board, New England Power Association*

Representing the Workers:
   Mr. Robert J. Watt, *American Federation of Labor*

To carry further the work initiated by the New York-Washington Conference in the field of post-war reconstruction, a meeting of the Emergency Committee of the Governing Body of the I. L. O. was held in London, April 20, 1942. At this meeting, "financial arrangements necessary to permit of the effective development of the reconstruction work of the I. L. O. were approved. The machinery necessary to equip the Organization to handle more effectively some of the interactions of economic and social policy were established, in the form of the committee of economic statesmen which is to advise the Governing Body. New programs of study, relating in the first instance primarily to public works policy, migration, agriculture, and textiles, were sanctioned." [4]

[1] For a narrative account of the session see International Labour Office, *The I. L. O. at Work*, January 1942 (Montreal, 1942).
[2] For complete details as to delegation, see Department of State, *Bulletin*, V p. 333.
[3] See p. 32.
[4] International Labour Office, *International Labour Review*, XLVI (July 1942) p. 42. For a detailed account of this meeting, see *ibid.*, p. 1–43.

(1) *Resolution on Post-war Emergency and Reconstruction Measures,
November 5, 1941* [1]

WHEREAS the victory of the free peoples in the war against totalitarian aggression is an indispensable condition of the attainment of the ideals of the International Labor Organization; and

WHEREAS the close of the war must be followed by immediate action, previously planned and arranged, for the feeding of peoples in need, for the reconstruction of the devastated countries, for the provision and transportation of raw materials and capital equipment necessary for the restoration of economic activity, for the reopening of trade outlets, for the resettlement of workers and their families under circumstances in which they can work in freedom and security and hope, for the changing over of industry to the needs of peace, for the maintenance of employment, and for the raising of standards of living throughout the world; and

WHEREAS the accomplishment of these purposes will require the "fullest collaboration between all nations in the economic field"; and

WHEREAS such collaboration will set tasks of organization and administration calling for the highest ability and for the most sympathetic understanding of the needs of peoples; and

WHEREAS the International Labor Organization, which possesses the confidence of the free peoples and includes in its structure the representatives of workers and employers, is for these reasons peculiarly fitted to take part in this work in such a way as to minimize misunderstanding and unrest and to promote a stable and enduring peace:

The Conference of the International Labor Organization

Requests the Governing Body:

(*a*) To transmit this resolution forthwith to the Governments of all Member States, to call their attention to the desirability of associating the International Labor Organization with the planning and application of measures of reconstruction, and to ask that the International Labor Organization be represented in any Peace or Reconstruction Conference following the war;

(*b*) To suggest to the Governments of the Member States that they should, if they have not already done so, set up representative agencies for the study of the social and economic needs of the post-war world and that such agencies should consult with the appropriate organs of the International Labor Organization;

---

[1] *Ibid.*, XLV (January, 1942), p. 22: Conference of the International Labour Organisation, 1941, New York and Washington, D. C., *Record of Proceedings*, Montreal, 1941, .p. 163. See p. 166 for the Canadian, Polish, Belgian, Czechoslovak, United States, Netherlands and Uruguayan proposals on which the resolution was based.

(c) To set up from its own membership a small tripartite committee, instructed to study and prepare (i) measures of reconstruction and (ii) emergency measures to deal with unemployment, which should be empowered to enlist the assistance of technically qualified experts and authorized to cooperate with governmental, inter-governmental, and private agencies engaged in similar studies and with those agencies whose present activities in the social and economic field affect the conditions under which post-war programs will be carried out;

(d) To make full use of such existing organs of the International Labor Organization as the International Public Works Committee, the Permanent Agricultural Committee, the Permanent Committee on Migration for Settlement, and the Joint Maritime Commission, and from time to time to make such modifications in the composition of these agencies, and to set up such new agencies, as may be needed to meet the responsibilities implied in this resolution;

(e) To direct the program of work of the International Labor Office to fulfil the purposes of this resolution; and

(f) To report on the subject matter of this resolution to the next and subsequent meetings of the International Labor Conference so that the International Labor Organization shall be in a position to give authoritative expression to the social objectives confided to it, in the rebuilding of a peaceful world upon the basis of "improved labor standards, economic advancement and social security."

(2) *Resolution Endorsing the Atlantic Charter, November 5, 1941* [2]

WHEREAS by the Atlantic Charter the President of the United States of America and the Prime Minister of the United Kingdom have announced eight common principles in the national policies of their respective Governments on which they base their hopes for the better future of the world; and

WHEREAS these principles have been approved by all the Allied Governments; and

---

[1] The establishment of the committee was agreed to unanimously at the London meeting of the Emergency Committee, but it was agreed that the actual choice of members should be approved by that committee by telegraphic communication at a later date and that in constituting the committee due account should be taken of the need to secure "advice as regards economic and financial problems as they affect four or five great regions of the world." (*International Labour Review*, XLVI, July 1942, p. 18).

[2] Conference of the International Labour Organisation, 1941, New York and Washington, D. C., *Record of Proceedings*, p. 163; I. L. O., *International Labour Review*, XLV (January 1942), p. 22.

WHEREAS the Fourth, Fifth, and Sixth of these principles are as
ollows:

[Here follows the text of the principles cited.] [1]

nd

WHEREAS the Constitution of the International Labor Organization
roclaims that a lasting peace "can be established only if it is based on
ocial justice";

The Conference of the International Labor Organization endorses
ne aforementioned principles of the Atlantic Charter, requests that
ne fullest use be made of the machinery and experience of the Interational Labor Organization in giving effect to these principles, and
ledges the full cooperation of the International Labor Organization in
neir implementation.

3) *Resolution on the War and Peace, November 5, 1941* [2]

The Conference of the International Labor Organization meeting in
Vew York from 27 October to 5 November and attended by delegates
rom forty nations,

Having received the reports of the representatives from the countries
ccupied by the Axis armies,

Notes that in all the countries occupied by these armies freedom of
ssociation has been suppressed, as well as all other democratic rights
nd liberties;

Expresses its deepest sympathy with the millions of human beings in
China, Great Britain, Russia and on the continent of Europe on whom
he Axis war machine has inflicted indescribable sufferings and who are
ving at the present time in the most acute moral and material distress.

The Conference solemnly declares that it is only the victory of free
ations the world over, who are fighting for democracy and for the
naintenance of the inalienable rights of man, which can save the world
rom hopeless chaos.

The Conference expresses its warmest admiration and profound
ratitude to the brave peoples who are fighting against the most savage
arbarians that history has ever known, and thus saving mankind from
omplete defeat; by their heroic resistance these free men and women
ave not only saved the world from defeat but have also laid the foun-
lations for the victory of democracy which can alone guarantee social
rogress and freedom.

[1] See p. 210.
[2] Conference of the International Labour Organisation, 1941, New York and Wash-
ngton, D. C., *Report of Proceedings*, p. 164.

The Conference urges all free peoples to contribute to the uttermos limit of their power for the victory of China, Great Britain, Russia an their Allies by supplying all the arms which their industry can produce

The Conference insists that, after having made sure of victory, th most important task for the democracies will be to establish the princ ples of economic cooperation which should be laid down between a the nations of the world; it is important that a start should be mad immediately with the study of the economic conditions which will mak social progress possible, so that, when victory has been won, the fre nations will be ready to face the great task of reconstruction in orde that the blessings of peace on earth and goodwill among men may becom real and universal.

(4) *Resolutions on the Report of the Committee on Collaboratior Adopted November 4, 1941* [1]

I

The Conference

(1) Recognizes the universal and permanent importance for a nations of effective collaboration between the public authorities an workers' organizations and employers' organizations, which occupy place of increasing prominence in economic and social developmen

(2) Underlines the special importance of such collaboration

    (a) during the present war, because the success of the militar operations largely depends on the result of the battle c production which will be won by the democracies only b the complete collaboration between the workers and th employers in the work of national defense;

    (b) after victory, for the transition from war economy to peac economy and for the economic and social reconstruction c the world, which will be of interest to all countries, belligeren and neutral, and which will call for a gigantic and coord nated effort on the part of the public authorities, worker and employers;

(3) Declares that real collaboration is possibly only within the frame work of democratic political institutions which guarantee the freedor of association of workers and employers;

---

[1] Conference of the International Labour Organisation, 1941, New York and Wasl ington, D. C., *Report of Proceedings*, p. 166. The report of the Committee on Collal oration is printed at p. 170.

(4) Affirms that the application of the principle of collaboration requires that in law and in fact

    (a) the right of industrial organizations to represent workers and employers should be recognized by the State;

    (b) the workers' and employers' organizations should recognize each other's right to represent workers and employers respectively;

(5) Recognizes that methods of collaboration vary with place, social pattern, prior experience, temperament and custom, from country to country and within the experience of a single nation, as is illustrated by the variety and adaptability or practices in countries dealing with similar situations which have been reported in the discussions of the Conference, and that positive results can best be assured by development along the lines of national experience, always provided that collaboration is based on the principles enunciated above and subject to the fundamental necessity for full participation of employers' and workers' organizations through representatives of their own designation being fully assured.

II

WHEREAS it is the desire of this Conference to secure that the International Labor Organization render the greatest possible service in extending the practice of collaboration, both in emergency organization and in the field of permanent industrial and economic organization: The Conference

(1) Requests the Governing Body of the International Labor Office to take steps to ensure the fullest use of the resources of the Organization for

    (a) the exchange between Governments and organizations of workers and employers of information concerning both wartime and permanent machinery of collaboration so as to facilitate its widest developments, and

    (b) aiding interested countries to make use in their machinery for emergency industrial and economic organization of the most suitable methods of collaboration in the field under consideration;

(2) Urges the Governments to provide the Office not only with a record of structural developments, but with adequate information on the operation of the machinery of collaboration, both where it is successful and where it falls short of achieving its purpose, so as to permit comparative analysis.

III

WHEREAS the question of methods of collaboration between the publi authorities, workers' organizations and employers' organizations i very complex and it has been impossible in the present occasion, owin to shortness of time, to proceed to a detailed discussion of its man aspects:

The Conference requests the Governing Body of the Internation Labor Office to place the question on the agenda of the next Conferenc

CHAPTER XII

THE DEPARTMENT OF STATE AND THE
FOREIGN SERVICE

1. ORGANIZATION AND FUNCTIONS

A chart showing the organization of the Department of State, as of June 28, 1941, reproduced from the Department of State, *Bulletin*, IV, p. 754, is given in *Documents, III, 1940–41*, p. 760. A similar chart, showing the organization in November 24, 1941, is to be found in the *Bulletin*, V, p. 446.

A general survey of the historical development of the Department, its present organization and activities, and its relation to other branches of the governmental organization is to be found in "The Department of State of the United States" prepared by William Gerber, Division of Research and Publication (Department of State Publication 1744).

A. Economic Operations

The intensification of activities in the field of economic defense following the establishment of the Economic Defense Board, July 30, 1941 [1] resulted in an extensive reorganization of the Department of State with a view to the more effective performance of its duties in this connection. By a series of Departmental Orders effective October 8, 1941,[2] there were established a Board of Economic Operations and six Divisions relating thereto in order better to coordinate the functions of the Department with those of the Office for Emergency Management, the National Defense Board and other emergency offices of the Government.[3]

The former Division of Controls was abolished.[4] The Red, White and Blue License Unit was transferred to the newly created Division of Exports and Defense Aid. That portion of the Registration Unit concerned with registration of agents of alien principals was transferred to the Division of Foreign Activity Correlation, and that portion of the Registration Unit concerned with funds for relief was transferred to the Special Division. The Statistical Unit of the Division of Controls was transferred to the Division of Studies and Statistics.

Selections from the orders defining functions are given.

[1] See p. 180.
[2] Departmental Orders 973, 975, 976, 977, 978, 979, 980, Department of State, *Bulletin*, V, p. 278–80.
[3] For a description of the functioning of these agencies see the address of Dean Acheson, Assistant Secretary of State, to the Foreign Policy Association, New York, October 25, 1941, entitled "The Role of the Department of State in the Field of International Economic Operations," Department of State, *Bulletin*, V, p. 308.
[4] Departmental Order 981, *ibid.*, p. 281.

(1) *Board of Economic Operations. Departmental Order 973, October 1941* [1]

There is hereby created in the Department of State a Board of Economic Operations, the members of which shall be Assistant Secretaries of State Acheson and Berle, the Adviser on International Economic Affairs, Dr. Herbert Feis, the Special Assistant to the Secretary of State, Dr. Leo Pasvolsky, and the Chiefs, or in their absence, the Acting Chief of the following divisions: Commercial Policy and Agreements, Export and Defense Aid, Defense Materials, Studies and Statistics, World Trade Intelligence, and Foreign Funds and Financial Division.

Assistant Secretary of State Acheson shall be Chairman of the Board and Assistant Secretary of State Berle and the Adviser on International Economic Affairs shall be Vice Chairmen. The latter, in addition to his present duties, shall be Adviser to the Board; the Executive Secretary and the constituent Divisions of the Board shall keep him informed and shall appropriately seek his advice.

It shall be the duty of the Board, in order most effectively to carry out the Department's functions in connection with the economic defense of the United States, under the supervision of Assistant Secretary of State Acheson, to assist in formulating policies and to coordinate the activities of the various Divisions of which the Board is composed.

Mr. Emilio G. Collado [2] is hereby designated as Executive Secretary of the Board and Mr. Jack C. Corbett is designated as Assistant Executive Secretary. In their respective capacities these officers shall prepare agenda for meetings of the Board and shall maintain minutes of such meetings. Under the direction of the Chairman and in behalf of the Board, they shall assist in correlating the policies and activities of the Divisions represented in the Board and in assuring effective liaison with other interested departments and agencies of the Government, and may sign communications. Communications for the signature or consideration of the Chairman or Vice Chairmen of the Board shall pass through the secretariat.

(a) *Division of Commercial Policy and Agreements. Departmental Order 975, October 7, 1941* [3]

Henceforth the Division of Commercial Treaties and Agreements shall be known as the Division of Commercial Policy and Agreements.

[1] Department of State, *Bulletin*, V, p. 278.
[2] By Departmental Order 874, October 7, 1941, Mr. Collado was also designated Special Assistant to the Under Secretary of State to perform such duties as might be assigned to him. *Ibid.*, p. 279.   [3] *Ibid.*

/hich is hereby established to have general charge of the formulation, egotiation and administration of all commercial treaties and agreeaents having to do with the international commercial relations of the Jnited States, as well as matters of tariff, general trade and other quesions relating to the international commercial policy of the United States.

The new Division, under the general supervision of Assistant Secretary f State Acheson, shall operate as a component part of the Board of Economic Operations and shall have general responsibility for the Deartment's correspondence and contacts with the American exportnport interests, with our representatives abroad, and with representaives of foreign governments in this country in regard to the negotiation, nterpretation and enforcement of the terms of commercial treaties and greements and problems relating to American foreign commerce.

b) *Division of Exports and Defense Aid. Departmental Order 976, October 7, 1941* [1]

There is hereby created a Division of Exports and Defense Aid, which hall operate as a component part of the Board of Economic Operations f the Department under the general supervision of Assistant Secretary f State Acheson. This Division shall have responsibility for all matters f foreign policy involved in the administration of the Act of July 2, 940 (the Export Control Act), the Act of March 11, 1941 (the Lendease Act), the Acts of June 28, 1940 and May 31, 1941 (in so far as riorities or allocations for export are concerned), and for the administration of Sec. 12 of the Act of November 4, 1939 (the Neutrality Act), he Act of September 1, 1937 (the Helium Act), and the Act of February 5, 1936 (the Tin Plate Scrap Act). The Division of Exports and Deense Aid shall have responsibility in matters under its control for dealing vith the Department's correspondence and contacts with our representatives abroad and with representatives of foreign governments in this ountry, and through the Board of Economic Operations will collaborate vith the geographical and other Divisions concerning the formulation nd coordination of policy, and shall establish and maintain effective iaison with other Departments and agencies of the Government, conerned with the administration of the above-mentioned Acts.

c) *Division of Defense Materials. Departmental Order 977, October 7, 1941* [2]

In addition to such other duties as may be assigned to him as Special Assistant to the Secretary, Mr. Thomas K. Finletter is designated as

[1] *Ibid.*   [2] *Ibid.*, p. 280.

Acting Chief of the Division of Defense Materials, which is hereby estal lished effective October 8, 1941. This Division shall be a componer part of the Board of Economic Operations and operate under the ger eral supervision of Assistant Secretary of State Acheson. Mr. Finlette shall have responsibility in the formulation and execution of policies i the field of defense materials, in collaboration with the interested Div sions and Offices of the Department. Together with the Adviser o International Economic Affairs, he shall establish and maintain effectiv liaison with other interested departments and agencies of the Goverr ment concerned with these matters. The symbol of this Division sha be DM.

(d) Division of Studies and Statistics. Departmental Order 978, Octc ber 7, 1941 [1]

There is hereby established, as a component part of the Board o Economic Operations to operate under the joint supervision of Assistar Secretaries of State Berle and Acheson, a Division of Studies an Statistics, which shall have responsibility, in collaboration with the intei ested Divisions and Offices of the Department, for the preparation o current studies, analyses and statistical data needed in connection wit matters arising before the Board of Economic Operations or as may b required by any of the Divisions of which it is composed in connectio with policy considerations and national defense activities. Nothing i this Order shall be construed as modifying Departmental Order N 917–A of February 3, 1941.[2]

(e) Division of World Trade Intelligence

(i) Departmental Order 956, July 21, 1941 [3]

There is hereby established in the Department of State a Division o World Trade Intelligence, the routing symbol of which will be WT, t handle the activities and problems envisaged in the President's Procla mation of July 17, 1941,[4] relating to trade with aliens whose interest are inimical to the United States.

[1] *Ibid.* In addition to such other duties and responsibilities as might be assigned t him as Special Assistant to the Secretary, Mr. Lynn Edminster assumed responsibilit as Acting Chief of this Division.

[2] The Order established "a Division of Special Research charged with the conduc of special studies in the foreign relations field; the analysis and appraisal of develop ments and conditions arising out of present-day disturbed international relations collaboration in this field as necessary with other interested departments and agencie of the Government; and with such other duties as may be assigned by the Secretar of State."   [3] *Ibid.*, p. 78.   [4] See p. 753.

Mr. John S. Dickey is designated Acting Chief of the Division which will function in its present quarters in the Department of Commerce Building under the general administrative supervision of Assistant Secretary Dean Acheson in close collaboration with the Division of Commercial Affairs and the other divisions and offices of the Department concerned. . . .

The provisions of this Order shall be effective on July 21, 1941.

(ii) *Departmental Order 979, October 7, 1941* [1]

Departmental Order 956 . . . is hereby amended to provide that this Division operate as a component part of the Board of Economic Operations under the general supervision of Assistant Secretary of State Acheson.

The provisions of this Order shall be effective as of October 8, 1941 and shall supersede the provisions of any existing Order in conflict therewith.

(f) *Foreign Funds and Financial Division. Departmental Order 980, October 7, 1941* [2]

There is hereby created a Foreign Funds and Financial Division which shall serve as a component part of the Board of Economic Operations under the general supervision of Assistant Secretary of State Berle.

Mr. Frederick Livesey is designated Assistant and Acting Chief of the Foreign Funds and Financial Division. Mr. Adrian Fisher is designated Assistant Chief in charge of foreign funds control.

This Division shall have responsibility in all matters of foreign policy in foreign funds control and other financial matters, as well as responsibility for establishing and maintaining effective liaison with other interested departments and agencies of the Government concerned with these matters.

When problems of foreign funds control or other fiscal operational problems directly affect the fields of commerce or defense the Division shall report to Assistant Secretary of State Acheson.

The symbol of the Division shall be FF.

[1] Department of State, *Bulletin*, V, p. 280.
[2] *Ibid.*

The provisions of this Order shall supersede the provisions of any existing Order in conflict therewith and become effective October 8, 1941.

By Departmental Orders 1000 and 1001, effective November 24, 1941,[1] the Foreign Funds and Financial Division was separated into the Financial Division and the Foreign Funds Control Division. The former was to have responsibility "in all matters of foreign policy in financial matters other than foreign funds control"; the latter, "in all matters of foreign policy in foreign funds control matters, including the application of the Proclamation of the President dated July 17, 1941 to firms and individuals whose names are included in the Proclaimed List of Certain Blocked Nationals."

(2) *Distribution of Lend-Lease Articles. Departmental Order 1006, December 2, 1941* [2]

The duties and responsibilities conferred by Departmental Order 976 upon the Division of Exports and Defense Aid in so far as they concern the administration of the Act of Congress of March 11, 1941 (the Lend-Lease Act) are hereby modified as hereinafter provided.

As Special Assistant to the Secretary, Mr. Lynn R. Edminster shall, in addition to his other duties, have responsibility for coordinating with the activities of the Department in the general field of commercial policy such matters arising in connection with the administration of the Act of Congress of March 11, 1941, as involve questions of commercial policy, such as matters relating to the distribution of articles within the country receiving them under the Act or the commercial reexport thereof and related matters affecting the foreign commerce of the United States arising out of the operation of the Act. He shall collaborate with the geographical and other divisions, particularly the Division of Commercial Policy and Agreements, the Division of Exports and Defense Aid, and the Adviser on International Economic Affairs, in the formulation and coordination of policy, and shall establish and maintain effective liaison with other departments and agencies of the Government concerning the above-mentioned aspect of the administration of the Lend-Lease Act. In the execution of the foregoing activities Mr. Edminster shall act as a component part of the Board of Economic Operations of the Department.

The provisions of this Order shall be effective as of November 12, 1941.

(3) *Abolition of Division of Exports and Defense Aid and the Division of Studies and Statistics. Departmental Order 1061, June 18, 1942* [3]

The Division of Exports and Defense Aid and the Division of Studies and Statistics are hereby abolished.

[1] *Ibid.*, p. 441. [2] *Ibid.*, p. 454. [3] *Ibid.*, VI, p. 556.

The responsibility for administration of section 12 of the Act of November 4, 1939 (the Neutrality Act), the Act of September 1, 1937 (the Helium Act), and the Act of February 15, 1936 (the Tin Plate Scrap Act), which has heretofore been vested in the Division of Exports and Defense Aid, is hereby transferred to the Division of Commercial Affairs.

Matters of foreign policy involved in the Act of July 2, 1940 (the Export Control Act), and the Acts of June 28, 1940 and May 31, 1941 (in so far as priorities or allocations for export are concerned and in so far as they remain unaffected by the responsibilities vested in the American Hemisphere Exports Office, established by Departmental Order No. 1029, dated February 20, 1942) shall be the responsibility of the Division of Defense Materials in collaboration with the Economic Adviser and the affected political divisions.

The responsibility for all matters of foreign policy coming under the Act of March 11, 1941 (the Lend-Lease Act) is hereby transferred to the Division of Commercial Policy and Agreements.

In addition, there is hereby transferred to the Division of Commercial Policy and Agreements, the responsibility formerly vested in the Division of Studies and Statistics to collaborate with the interested divisions and offices of the Department and to prepare current studies, analyses and data of statistical value needed in connection with matters arising before the Board of Economic Operations, or as may be required by any of the divisions of which it is composed, in connection with policy considerations, the conduct of economic warfare and related activities.

Nothing in this Order shall be construed as modifying Departmental Order No. 917-A of February 3, 1941.

Mr. Charles Bunn, in addition to such other duties and responsibilities that may be assigned to him as Special Assistant to the Under Secretary, shall serve as consultant to the Division of Commercial Policy and Agreements.

The Division of Personnel Supervision and Management will take the necessary action to effect the transfer and classification of affected personnel and their equipment.

The provisions of this Order shall be effective immediately and shall supersede the provisions of any existing order in conflict therewith.

(4) *Clarification and Interpretation of Executive Order No. 9128 of April 13, 1942,*[1] *in Respect of Certain Functions of the Department of State and the Board of Economic Warfare, May 20, 1942*

[See p. 183]

B. Other Activities

(1) *Establishment of Office of the Geographer as an Independent Office. Departmental Order 972, October 7, 1941* [2]

[Excerpt]

As a result of the growth of its activities, particularly in the field of geographic research and mapping necessary in the proper appraisal of problems in the field of international relations, the Office of the Geographer is hereby established as an independent office and shall function under the supervision of the Assistant Secretary and Budget Officer. The office designation shall continue to be Ge.

(2) *Establishment of Caribbean Office. Departmental Order 984, October 9, 1941* [3]

For the purpose of encouraging and strengthening social and economic cooperation between the United States of America and its possessions and bases in the area known geographically or politically as the Caribbean, and other countries, colonies and possessions in this area, it is hereby ordered that there shall be established in the Department of State a Caribbean Office.

The Office will be subordinate to the Division of the American Republics and the Division of European Affairs with respect to all matters in which those Divisions are primarily responsible. With regard to such matters as are not of primary concern to those Divisions and which relate to the interplay between the countries, colonies and possessions in the Caribbean area of social and economic conditions, the Office will have original jurisdiction but its activities will be subject to the review of the two aforementioned geographical divisions. It will assist in the preparation and interpretation of treaties and agreements in this field. It will supervise the formulation of regulations and procedure necessary for the fulfillment of such treaties and agreements. It will draft or review correspondence with foreign governments, American diplomatic and con-

[1] See p. 182.
[2] Department of State, *Bulletin*, V, p. 282.
[3] *Ibid.*, p. 281.

sular offices and all other correspondence pertaining to these activities. It will collaborate with other departments and agencies, particularly those having jurisdiction in the fields of labor, agriculture, housing, health, education, finance, trade relations and tariffs. It will cooperate with other economic, educational and labor agencies and foreign missions in Washington.

(3) *Transfer of Certain Duties from the Division of American Republics to the Division of Cultural Relations. Departmental Order 1047, April 15, 1942* [1]

[See p. 411]

(4) *Liaison with the Office of War Information. Departmental Order 1064, June 25, 1942* [2]

By Departmental Order 985, October 9, 1941, the Division of Current Information was charged with the establishment and maintenance of effective liaison with all agencies of the Government concerned with the collection and dissemination of information in which the Department of State had an interest. The creation of the Office of War Information charged with over-all responsibility for the collection and dissemination of information pertaining to the war effort and the establishment within the Office of a Committee on War Information Policy of an advisory character led to the new order of June 25, 1942.

On June 13, 1942, the President of the United States signed Executive Order No. 9182 [3] establishing an Office of War Information and providing specifically in Article 3 that the Secretary of State shall be represented, together with the heads of other Departments and Agencies of the Government, on a Committee on War Information Policies.

The special section of the Division of Current Information responsible for maintaining liaison with the information agencies of the Government is hereby charged exclusively with the establishment and maintenance of liaison with the Office of War Information.

Mr. Michael J. McDermott, Chief of the Division of Current Information, is designated to represent the Secretary of State on the Committee on War Information Policies. In the event that Mr. McDermott is unable to be present personally at a meeting of the Committee on War Information Policies he may designate to represent him, depending upon the subject under discussion by the Committee at the time, the appropriate officer assigned to assist him by the respective geographical divisions of the Department or the Division of Cultural Relations. . . .

[1] *Ibid.*, VI, p. 357.
[2] *Ibid.*, p. 566.
[3] See p. 189.

C. Establishment of Foreign Service Auxiliary

(1) *Statement of the Department of State, October 11, 1941* [1]

[Excerpt]

Appointments totaling approximately 60 officers and 100 clerks have been made to positions in a branch of the Foreign Service referred to as the Foreign Service Auxiliary, which has been established to fill the need for additional help in American missions and consular establishments, principally in the other American Republics. This need arises both from a very considerable expansion of the regular activities of the Foreign Service and from the imposition upon it of certain additional duties of an emergency nature for which the Service is not normally sufficiently staffed. Appointees will be under the direction and supervision of the officer in charge of the American Foreign Service post at which they are stationed.

Appointments are of a temporary nature, for the period of the emergency only, funds being available from the President's emergency appropriation only up to and including June 30, 1942. Should the emergency which occasions the present action be prolonged beyond that date, it may be necessary to continue the services of these special assistants accordingly.

Part of this auxiliary personnel performs responsible and technical work in the field of economics, particularly economic problems growing out of wartime conditions, involving investigation of and reporting on such matters as the following: Movements of vessels and cargoes; problems relating to export control in the United States and the essential economic needs of the foreign country concerned; information relating to the determination of priorities; problems connected with the proclaimed list of certain blocked nationals; availability of strategic raw materials and terms and conditions for procuring them; development projects financed by the Export-Import Bank; and in general all problems of an economic character having direct bearing on the current emergency. A limited number of economic analysts have been appointed exclusively for agricultural reporting.

Another group of officers is primarily responsible for the development and maintenance of friendly relations with cultural leaders in the country in which they are stationed. They are concerned with such matters as the exchange of professors and students; the distribution and exhibition of motion-picture films; arrangements for visits of officials or distin-

[1] Department of State, *Bulletin*, V, p. 283. One paragraph regarding administrative details is omitted.

guished citizens between the United States and the foreign country in which the officer is stationed; the cultural activities of the Coordinator of Inter-American Affairs; and liaison with local cultural and scientific institutions. They are expected to report on all of these matters and to submit recommendations regarding ways and means for improving the program of cultural relations.

Included in the number of 60 officers is a group of non-career vice consuls, composed of younger men, whose duties are of a general nature.

The duties of any one of the officers will not necessarily be restricted to any one of the above descriptions; as they progress in experience and become more adapted to the work of the offices to which they are assigned, it is to be expected that they may be called upon to perform duties of other character for which they are qualified.

2. OFFICIAL RECORDS AND VIEWS OF THE DEPARTMENT OF STATE

(1) *Opening of Original Records. Departmental Order 955, July 18, 1941* [1]

The original records of the Department of State up to August 14, 1906 were opened to the unofficial use of properly qualified persons under the regulations set forth in Departmental Orders 309 dated August 11, 1924 and 377 dated June 15, 1926. Departmental Order 751 [2] governed the use of records later than August 14, 1906, after the records of earlier date were transferred to the National Archives, and Departmental Order 796 dated June 19, 1939 [3] prescribed conditions for use of confidential or unpublished records prior to December 31, 1918, or such subsequent date as might be fixed by the Department of State.

By Departmental Order 796 of June 19, 1939, the confidential or unpublished records of the Department prior to December 31, 1918 were made available for consultation by persons who are not officials of the United States Government, subject to conditions set forth in that order. The provisions of that order are hereby amended to make available to such persons the records of the Department up to January 1, 1921, with the exception of the Department's unpublished records concerning the Paris Peace Conference of 1919 and related subjects. After the publication of the Paris Peace Conference volumes of *Foreign Relations of the United States*, consideration will be given to the possibility of making the records on the Peace Conference and related subjects available to qualified persons.

[1] *Ibid.*, p. 78.
[2] Department of State, *Press Releases*, 19, p. 401.
[3] Department of State, *Bulletin*, I, p. 10.

(2) Representation of the Government's Views. Statement of the Secretary of State (Hull), January 21, 1942 [1]

Governments speak to one another through their foreign offices, in the United States through the Department of State as the executive agent of the President. In a free society public affairs are openly discussed by the citizenry and officials in other branches of the Government. The views expressed by officials concerning matters not responsibly before them at the time may easily be misunderstood or have a weight not intended. In order that no confusion should persist in a particular instance, the Secretary of State made it clear that Senator Tom Connally, Chairman of the Committee on Foreign Relations, was not speaking for the Secretary in a statement reported in the press as follows: [2] Regarding Argentina's failure at the Inter-American Conference to agree with other Latin American countries on breaking relations with the Axis Powers, Senator Connally said:

"We are trusting that before the meeting at Rio is over, Mr. Castillo [Acting President Ramón S. Castillo of Argentina] will change his mind or the Argentines will change their President."

Mr. Connally further remarked:

"If she persists in hanging out, this might result in the cutting off of all contact and communication between Argentina and other American nations. Some of them would not want to open their borders to Axis infiltration. Our information is that there is a very critical political situation there and that if the people could have a free election they would all vote to go along with us."

Asked if he expected an internal uprising to accomplish this, Mr. Connally said he did not mean to go that far.

"If you are negotiating with a fellow to go along with you," the Senator said, "you don't hit him in the nose. We have been friendly to Argentina, with the exception of our prohibitions against their shipments of fresh and some canned beef to us.

"Of course, they are mad and sore. They figure that this country is vulnerable because we have such long coastlines to defend and that Germany ultimately might win the war and that then they would be 'sitting pretty.'

"But Argentina is taking a long chance in adhering to any such position as that."

The Secretary of State was asked whether the questions taken up in Senator Connally's press conference on January 21 had been discussed with the Secretary by the Senator. He replied that they had not and added that members of the legislative department of the Government are accustomed to express their individual views relating to public questions. Their views and attitude so expressed, as in the present case, are, of course, not to be construed as representing the views of the executive branch of the Government and they are not the views of this Government.

[1] Department of State, *Bulletin*, VI, p. 79.
[2] *New York Times* dispatch, January 22, 1942.

3. DIPLOMATIC REPRESENTATION

(1) *Control of Special Missions Abroad. Letter of the Acting Secretary of State (Welles) to Executive Departments and Agencies despatched February 26–March 20, 1942* [1]

The conduct of the war has brought about a great increase in the dispatch of individuals and groups to foreign countries on a variety of missions. It is essential that orderly procedure be established to determine the propriety and scope of proposed missions in the light of all our relations with the country concerned, to facilitate necessary war work, to prevent duplication of effort, and to provide centralized control over Government representatives abroad and over our dealings with foreign governments. Only in this way can the Department of State discharge its responsibility under the President for the conduct of foreign relations, assure the full utilization of the existing and potential personnel of the Foreign Service and do its part to see that the combined efforts of all the executive agencies in the foreign field shall be unified and effective.

In order to discharge this responsibility the Department desires to clarify the procedure by which Government agencies wishing to send individuals or groups outside the United States may have their proposals promptly considered and acted upon and by which the status and duties of such persons while outside the United States and as representatives of the Government may be defined.

The Department has established a committee of three under the chairmanship of the Under Secretary of State to consider with the interested Government agencies — except the War and Navy Departments, as to which a regular procedure is already in effect — all plans and proposals which require the dispatch of personnel on official business outside the limits of the United States and its insular and territorial possessions. To consider the administrative aspects of these trips, Mr. G. Howland Shaw, Assistant Secretary of State, and to consider the economic aspects Mr. Dean Acheson, Assistant Secretary of State, will be members of the committee.

The interested Departments and agencies are asked to designate ranking officers to meet with the committee from time to time as the need arises. Wherever a proposal may concern Departments or agencies other than the one presenting it, their representatives will be notified and asked to present their views to and meet with the committee.

[1] Department of State, *Bulletin*, VI, p. 477.

The interested Departments and agencies are also asked in the future to submit to this Department in writing all plans and projects in as complete detail as possible. These letters should be addressed to the Secretary of State, attention of Mr. G. Howland Shaw, Assistant Secretary of State. Full information should be furnished as to

(a) the name of the project and country or countries to be visited,

(b) the names of the proposed representatives with a brief biographical sketch of each along with a statement as to what investigation has been made of the loyalty and responsibility of each,

(c) the complete itinerary,

(d) a description of operations and objectives of the project,

(e) the relation of the project to those in the same field carried on by other agencies of this Government,

(f) any expressions of interest on the part of the governments of the countries to be visited,

(g) the proposed instructions to be given to these representatives, and

(h) the manner in which it is proposed that salary, travel and contingent expenses of such representatives are to be paid.

To insure complete coordination and centralization of the activities of representatives of this Government in the countries in which they operate, instructions have gone forth to the chiefs of the appropriate diplomatic missions directing them to establish machinery fully adequate to assure thorough direction and supervision of all such representatives operating in the countries to which they are accredited. These instructions have made it abundantly clear that all official representatives of this country are responsible at all times to the chief of mission in the country in which they operate. The appropriate chiefs of mission have been further informed that in order to assure the adequate fulfillment of this responsibility, all correspondence of whatever nature between representatives abroad and the branch of this Government by which they are employed will be carried out through the diplomatic pouch and this Department's telegraphic service.

It is believed that the procedures described will eliminate duplication of effort by Government agencies, keep to a minimum difficulties and misunderstandings with the governments of the countries to which representatives are sent, and permit these representatives to perform abroad in an orderly and efficient manner the missions with which they have been entrusted.

The above letter was dispatched to the following departments and agencies under the dates indicated:

Board of Economic Warfare	Feb. 26, 1942
War Production Board	" " "
Coordinator of Inter-American Affairs	" " "
Coordinator of Information	" " "
Department of Commerce	" " "
Treasury Department	" " "
Department of Agriculture	" " "
Department of the Interior . . . . :	" " "
War Shipping Board	" " "
Lend-Lease Administration	" " "
Federal Security Agency	" " "
Federal Communications Commission	" " "
Office of Civilian Defense	
Department of Justice	Mar. 3, 1942
Post Office Department	" " "
Department of Labor	" " "
Maritime Commission	" " "
Smithsonian Institution	" " "
Tariff Commission	" " "
Tennessee Valley Authority	" " "
National Housing Agency	" 18 "
Office of Price Administration	" 20 "

a) Departmental Order 1052, Department of State, April 18, 1942 [1]

Attached is a copy of a letter addressed recently to the various executive Departments and Agencies which have had, or may have, occasion to send representatives on special missions abroad. It was written with a view to insuring complete coordination and centralization of the activities of this Government in foreign countries.

If the proposed procedure is to be effective, it is essential that individual officers of the Department not enter directly into agreements with officials of other Departments and Agencies concerning the dispatch of their representatives abroad prior to consideration of the matter by the Committee set up in the Department for that purpose. All informal proposals of this character should first be referred to Assistant Secretary Shaw who will see that they are given prompt attention.

The Committee will not act definitely upon any proposals without first conferring with the appropriate Geographic and other interested Divisions of the Department.

To provide a central, consolidated file of the representatives of other Departments and Agencies carrying on activities abroad, the Division

[1] *Ibid.*, p. 476. As originally published the letter of Acting Secretary of State Welles was attached to this order.

of Foreign Service Administration is hereby designated to maintain complete record of such representatives.

It will be noted from the attached letter that Army and Navy personnel are excepted from the prescribed procedure; in addition, modifications of the requirements will be made in the case of: (1) official of the United States Government sent abroad under the provisions of Public Law No. 63, 76th Congress;[1] (2) persons sent under the Department's program of cooperation with the other American Republics and (3) persons sent by the Coordinator of Inter-American Affair under projects which have been cleared with the Department in accordance with established procedure.

(2) *Representation of Interests of Belligerent Countries. Departmen of State Release, December 18, 1941* [2]

I

In view of the outbreak of hostilities between the United States and Japan, Germany, and Italy and the subsequent rupture of diplomati relations with Bulgaria, Rumania, and Hungary, the United States has relinquished the representation of foreign interests in the countrie indicated in the list printed below. The representation of such interest has been entrusted provisionally to the Government of Switzerland.

1. American Legation, Sofia: (*a*) Great Britain, including overseas possessions (*b*) Canada; (*c*) New Zealand; (*d*) Australia; (*e*) Union of South Africa (*f*) Belgium; (*g*) Netherlands; (*h*) Yugoslavia; (*i*) Greece; (*j*) Luxemburg
2. American Embassy, Berlin (covering Germany and German-occupied Po land; Bohemia; Moravia; Belgium; Netherlands; Norway; Luxemburg Paris, for occupied France; Salonika; Belgrade): (*a*) Great Britain, in cluding India, overseas possessions and mandated territories; (*b*) Australia (*c*) New Zealand; (*d*) Canada; (*e*) France; (*f*) Belgium; (*g*) Luxemburg (*h*) Union of South Africa; (*i*) Egypt; (*j*) Panama (at Brussels); (*k*) Haiti (*l*) Costa Rica.
3. American Legation, Budapest: (*a*) Great Britain; (*b*) Australia; (*c*) Canada (*d*) Union of South Aftica; (*e*) Belgium; (*f*) New Zealand; (*g*) Yugoslavia (*h*) Greece (custody of property only).
4. American Embassy at Rome (covering Athens): (*a*) Australia; (*b*) Belgium (*c*) Great Britain, including overseas possessions; (*d*) Canada; (*e*) Egypt (*f*) France; (*g*) New Zealand; (*h*) Union of South Africa; (*i*) Norway (*j*) Haiti; (*k*) Luxemburg.

[1] *Documents, I, 1938–39*, p. 69.
[2] Department of State, *Bulletin*, V, p. 541; cf. *Documents, II, 1939–40*, p. 815 *III, 1940–41*, p. 763.

5. American Legation, Bucharest: (*a*) Great Britain, including overseas possessions; (*b*) Canada; (*c*) New Zealand; (*d*) Australia; (*e*) Union of South Africa; (*f*) Belgium; (*g*) Yugoslavia; (*h*) Greece; (*i*) China (informal).
6. American Consulate, Saigon: (*a*) Belgium; (*b*) Yugoslavia; (*c*) China; (*d*) Cuba; (*e*) Portugal.
7. American Consulate, Hanoi: (*a*) Belgium; (*b*) Yugoslavia; (*c*) China.
8. American Legation, Bangkok: (*a*) Cuba.
9. American Consulate, Chefoo: (*a*) Panama.
0. American Consulate, Dairen: (*a*) Panama.
1. American Consulate General, Shanghai: (*a*) Panama.
2. American Consulate General, Tientsin: (*a*) Panama.

The representation of Italian interests in Lagos, Nigeria, has been discontinued and, pending contrary instructions from the Italian Government within two weeks, the protection of these interests will be turned over to the local authorities.

II

American diplomatic and consular officers continue to represent the interests of certain countries as indicated in the list printed below.

1. American Legation, Copenhagen: (*a*) Great Britain, including overseas possessions; (*b*) Australia; (*c*) Canada; (*d*) Union of South Africa; (*e*) France; (*f*) Belgium; (*g*) New Zealand.
2. American Embassy, Vichy, for occupied France and Monaco (see also paragraphs 14 to 19 inclusive): (*a*) Australia; (*b*) Great Britain, including overseas possessions; (*c*) Canada; (*d*) New Zealand; (*e*) Belgium; (*f*) Luxemburg; (*g*) Yugoslavia; (*h*) Haiti.
3. American Embassy, Moscow: (*a*) Great Britain (at Moscow).
4. American Legation, Helsinki: (*a*) Belgium; (*b*) Great Britain; (*c*) New Zealand; (*d*) Canada; (*e*) Australia; (*f*) South Africa; (*g*) Yugoslavia.
5. American consular offices in India: (*a*) France.
6. American Consulate, Georgetown, British Guiana: (*a*) France.
7. American Consulate, Barbados, British West Indies: (*a*) France.
8. American Consulate, Kingston, Jamaica, British West Indies: (*a*) France.
9. American Consulate, Nassau, Bahamas: (*a*) France.
10. American Consulate, Colombo, Ceylon: (*a*) France.
11. American Consulate, Trinidad: (*a*) France.
12. American Consulate General, Rangoon: (*a*) France.
13. American Consulate, Aden: (*a*) France; (*b*) Yugoslavia.
14. American Consulate General, Casablanca: (*a*) Great Britain, including overseas possessions; (*b*) Canada; (*c*) New Zealand; (*d*) Belgium; (*e*) Australia; (*f*) Luxemburg (limited); (*g*) Yugoslavia; (*h*) Egypt (passport services).
15. American Consulate, St. Pierre-Miquelon: (*a*) Yugoslavia.
16. American Consulate General, Algiers: (*a*) Great Britain, including overseas possessions; (*b*) Canada; (*c*) New Zealand; (*d*) Australia; (*e*) Belgium; (*f*) Luxemburg; (*g*) Yugoslavia; (*h*) Panama.

17. American Consulate, Tunis: (a) Great Britain, including overseas possessions (b) Canada; (c) New Zealand; (d) Australia; (e) Belgium; (f) Yugoslavia

18. American Consulate, Martinique: (a) Great Britain, including overseas possessions; (b) Canada; (c) New Zealand; (d) Australia; (e) Belgium (f) Yugoslavia.

19. American Consulate, Dakar: (a) Great Britain, including overseas possessions (b) Canada; (c) New Zealand; (d) Australia; (e) Belgium; (f) Yugoslavia

20. American Legation, Stockholm: (a) Costa Rica.

III

American interests in Bulgaria, Germany and German-occupied territories, Hungary, Italy and Italian-occupied territories, Japan, and Rumania have been entrusted to the Government of Switzerland.

With regard to representation of United States interests in territorie occupied by Japan, Switzerland has also been requested to undertake this representation. Switzerland has expressed its willingness to do so subject to Japanese assent. However, the Department has not yet been informed that the Japanese have accepted Swiss representation for American interests in Japanese-occupied territories.

IV

Bulgarian, German, Hungarian, Italian, Japanese, and Rumanian interests in the United States are being represented by the countries listed below.

Belligerents	Country representing interests of belligerents
Bulgaria	Switzerland
Germany	Switzerland
Hungary	Sweden
Italy	Switzerland
Japan (in the United States)	Spain
Japan (in the Commonwealth of the Philippines and the Samoan Islands)	Switzerland
Japan (in Hawaii)	Sweden
Rumania	Sweden

(3) *List of New Diplomatic and Consular Establishments, June 30, 1941–June 30, 1942* [1]

ESTABLISHMENT OF NEW LEGATIONS

Place of Establishment	Date of Establishment
Afghanistan	June 6, 1942
Iceland	October 1, 1941
New Zealand	April 1, 1942
Saudi Arabia	May 1, 1942

[1] Compiled by the Department of State.

ESTABLISHMENT OF OFFICE OF AMERICAN COMMISSIONER [1]

Place of Establishment	Date of Establishment
India	October 4, 1941

ELEVATION OF LEGATIONS TO RANK OF EMBASSY [2]

Name of Embassy	Date of Elevation
Bolivia	May 23, 1942
Ecuador	April 14, 1942
Netherlands	May 8, 1942
Norway	May 13, 1942
Paraguay	April 15, 1942
Uruguay	July 12, 1941

ESTABLISHMENT OF NEW CONSULAR OFFICES

Type of Post	Place of Establishment	Date of Establishment
CG [3]	Brazzaville, French Equatorial Africa	May 28, 1942
C [4]	Accra, Gold Coast, West Africa	May 1, 1942
C	Antigua, British West Indies	December 1, 1941
C	Asmara, Eritrea	June 17, 1942
C	Basra, Iraq	December 26, 1941
C	Cayenne, French Guiana	March 7, 1942
C	Cúcuta, Colombia	March 5, 1942
C	Foynes, Ireland	May 9, 1942
C	St. Lucia, British West Indies	January 15, 1942
C	Tabriz, Iran	April 15, 1942
VC [5]	Arequipa, Peru	May 21, 1942
VC	Aruba, West Indies	January 7, 1942
VC	Caripito, Venezuela	May 6, 1942
VC	Curitiba, Brazil	October 23, 1941
VC	Iquitos, Peru	April 27, 1942
VC	Puntarenas, Costa Rica	January 3, 1942
VC	Reynosa, Mexico	May 1, 1942
VC	Riohacha, Colombia	July 25, 1941
VC	Salina Cruz, Mexico	February 11, 1942

[1] The Commissioner has the rank of Minister; however, the Office is not formally designated as a Legation.

[2] The date selected (for the purpose of this table) as the effective date of elevation of a legation to the rank of embassy is the date upon which the representative of the United States presented his letter of credence to the head of the foreign state.

[3] CG — Consulate General

[4] C — Consulate

[5] VC — Vice Consulate

4. TREATMENT OF DIPLOMATIC AND CONSULAR OFFICERS FOLLOWING OUTBREAK OF WAR

The following releases of the Department of State give details of the treatmen accorded diplomatic and consular staffs after the commencement of war. Th United States Government has been guided in its action by the rules of inter national law and the principle of reciprocity.[1]

(1) Staff of German Embassy at Washington. Department of Stati Release, December 26, 1941 [2]

The State Department has requested the American Legation in Berr to inform the Swiss Government for transmission to the German Gov ernment that all members of the German Embassy at Washington anc their dependents have been assembled at the well-known Greenbrian Hotel at White Sulphur Springs, W. Va.

In particular the following conditions apply:

(1) The whole group is permitted freely to move about in an exten sive area of the park grounds outside the hotel. This arrangemen includes the Mineral Springs.

(2) The German Chargé d'Affaires with his wife can upon request also visit the town.

(3) The representative of the Swiss Legation is permitted free access to the German group at all times.

(4) There is unrestricted two-way telephone communication at all times between the German group and the Swiss Legation at Washington.

(5) Postal communication between the Swiss Legation and the German group is also permitted.

(2) Note of Japanese Government on Treatment of United States Diplomatic and Consular Officers in Japan. Department of State Release, December 23, 1941 [3]

American Embassy at Tokyo is hereby notified that it is the intention of the Japanese Government to accord a correct and liberal treatment, on condition of reciprocity, to the staff of the American Embassy and Consulates in Japan, Manchukuo, and China pending their departure.

[1] Department of State Release, December 17, 1941. *Bulletin*, V, p. 544.
[2] *Ibid.*, p. 582. German and United States consular officials had been deported in July 1941 from the respective countries (*Documents, III, 1940–41*, p. 414).
[3] Department of State, *Bulletin*, V, p. 582. Information transmitted from the Swiss Legation at Tokyo through the Swiss Foreign Office and the United States Legation at Bern, December 23, 1941, to the Department of State.

very effort shall be made to accord adequate protection to the staff f the Embassy and Consulates as well as their families. They will be ccorded every reasonable assistance and facilities in liquidating their ersonal affairs. The American Embassy staff will be given free and ontinuous access to the representatives of the diplomatic mission which ssumes the representation of American interests in Japan. The American diplomatic and consular staff will not be subjected to any form of nternment prior to their departure, provided naturally that they do othing inimical to Japanese interests while awaiting their departure. he American Embassy is also informed that the American diplomatic nd consular staff in Manchukuo and China are receiving a correct and ourteous treatment. American citizens in Japan, Manchukuo, and China are also enjoying a fair and courteous treatment.

3) Closing of Shanghai Consulate General. Report of the Consul General (Stanton), December 8, 1941 [1]

I have received a formal communication dated today [December 8] rom the Japanese Consul General, reading as follows:

"I have the honor to inform you that I have been instructed by his mperial Japanese Majesty's Government to request you that the functions of the American Consulate General at Shanghai will be henceforth uspended and that the office of the American Consulate General be losed as from today. All the officers of the American Consulate General will be treated in accordance with international law and on the rinciple of reciprocity."

The Consulate General was closed up at one P.M. and sealed by the Japanese authorities. All officers, the Judge of the United States Court or China, and the District Attorney required to live in Metropole Hotel. The Japanese Consulate General states this is a temporary measure for rotection of officers. Other members of staff permitted to continue to reside at their homes. All members of staff safe and well.

4) Exchange of Official Representatives of Countries at War. Department of State Release, February 2, 1942 [2]

The Department of State announces that the arrangements for the exchange of the official representatives of the United States for those of the governments with which we are at war have proceeded to the point where an agreement has been reached in principle and in man details.

The American representatives from Bulgaria have left that country The American representatives in Hungary and Rumania have bee allowed to depart and are now in Portugal waiting to be exchange from that point.

American representatives in Germany are all in Bad Nauheim, an the American representatives in Italy are all in Rome, awaiting transfe Conversely, the German and Italian representatives are at White Su phur Springs, W. Va., along with the representatives of Hungary Rumania, and Bulgaria.

The Japanese representatives in the United States are in Hot Springs Va. The American representatives in Japan, China, and occupied te ritories have not been assembled in any one place. They are understoo to be well and to be receiving sufficient food and adequate accommo dations.

Various important details remain to be agreed upon, and negotiation are being pushed as rapidly as possible under the circumstances. Thes circumstances include indirect communication with the government concerned through the intermediation of different protecting powers delays in transmission of messages, translations into and out of variou languages, and limitations which are placed upon the rapid conclusio of negotiations by wartime conditions.

Lisbon has been agreed upon as the point of exchange for the repre sentatives of European powers. Axis representatives will be transporte to Lisbon by a United States vessel which will return with our own rep resentatives. The vessel will travel both ways under a safe conduct o all belligerents. Portugal has been asked by the various powers t guarantee the exchange.

The exchange with the Japanese will take place at Lourenço Marque in Portuguese East Africa. The Portuguese Government is being aske to guarantee the exchange there. The representatives of Japan will b carried to Lourenço Marques on an American vessel, and the Unite States representatives will be brought from there to the United State on that vessel and will be transported to that point by Japan. Bot vessels will travel under a safe conduct by all belligerents.

Contemporaneously the representatives of the enemy government who were stationed in the American Republics may be assembled in th United States and exchanged at the same time for the representative in the Axis countries of the Central and South American republic which have declared war against or broken relations with those coun

ries. Some of the Axis representatives have arrived in the United
States and are assembled with their colleagues at White Sulphur Springs
r Hot Springs. Others are expected to arrive.

INTERNATIONAL CONFERENCES IN WHICH THE UNITED STATES GOVERNMENT PARTICIPATED, JULY 1, 1941–JUNE 30, 1942 [1]

[Continues lists in *Documents, I, 1938–39*, p. 471; *II, 1939–40*, p. 822; *III, 1940–41*, p. 761. See also *American Delegations to International Conferences, Congresses and Expositions and American Representation on International Institutions and Commissions, with Relevant Data. — Fiscal Year ended June 30, 1941*, 130 p. (Department of State, Conference Series 51, Publication 1718).]

International Wheat Meetings, Washington, D. C., July 10–August 3, October 14, 1941.[2] (Department of State, *Bulletin*, V, p. 23, 116, 302.)

International Assembly of Surgeons, Mexico City, Mexico, August 10–14, 1941. (*Bulletin*, V, p. 104.)

Fourth Pan American Highway Congress, Mexico City, Mexico, September 15–24, 1941. (*Bulletin*, V, p. 183.)

Second Inter-American Travel Congress, Mexico City, Mexico, September 15–24, 1941. (*Bulletin*, V, p. 184.)

The Ninetieth Session of the Governing Body of the International Labor Office, New York City, New York, October 25, 29, and November 5, 1941. (*International Labour Review*, XLV, No. 1, January 1942, p. 64.)

Conference of the International Labor Organization, New York City–Washington, October 27–November 6, 1941. (*Bulletin*, V, p. 173, 333, 357.)

Third Meeting of the Ministers of Foreign Affairs of the American Republics, Rio de Janeiro, Brazil, January 15–28, 1942. (*Bulletin*, V, p. 483, 584; VI, p. 12, 55, 77, 88, 117.)

First Pan American Congress of Mining Engineering and Geology, Santiago, Chile, January 14–23, 1942. (*Bulletin*, VI, p. 48.)

Meeting of the Emergency Committee of the Governing Body of the International Labor Office, London, England, April 20–24, 1942. (*International Labour Review*, XLVI, No. 1, July 1942, p. 1.)

Eighth Pan American Child Congress, Washington, D. C., May 2–9, 1942. (*Bulletin*, V, p. 277; VI, p. 222, 386, 405.)

[1] From Department of State, Division of International Conferences.
[2] Not official governmental conference in the usual sense.

Inter-American Conference of Police and Judicial Authorities, Buenos Aires, Argentina, May 27–June 9, 1942. (*Bulletin*, VI, p. 480.)

Inter-American Conference on Systems of Economic and Financial Control, Washington, D. C., June 30–July 10, 1942. (*Bulletin*, VII, p. 383, 474, 567.)

6. APPROPRIATIONS

(1) *Department of State Appropriations for Fiscal Year 1943 Compared with 1942* [1]

Appropriation Title	Appropriations for 1943	Appropriations for 1942	Increase (+), Decrease (−) for 1943
Department Proper . . .	$ 5,583,200	$ 3,168,440	+ $2,414,760
National Defense Activities	750,000	150,000	+ 600,000
Foreign Service (exclusive of Emergency Fund) . .	14,783,800	13,681,900	+ 1,101,900
Emergency Fund	1,500,000	500,000	+ 1,000,000
Foreign Service Buildings .	275,000	450,000	− 175,000
International Obligations .	4,164,700	3,548,000	+ 615,800
Grand Total	$27,056,700 [2]	$21,499,240 [2]	+ $5,557,460

[1] Department of State, *Bulletin*, VII, p. 671.

[2] Supplemental and deficiency appropriations to the extent of $9,932,601 were made for 1942. Supplemental appropriations for 1943 had not been made up to September 1, 1942, but a number were pending.

INDEX

C

members of conference, 290
resolutions:
  Atlantic Charter, support and adherence to principles of, 329
  aviation, civil and commercial, 321
  banking operations of nationals of aggressor countries, conf. to standardize procedure in, 313
  capital, investment of, 316
  commercial and financial relations, severance of, 310
    reservation of Argentine delegation, 312
  commercial facilities to inland countries, 317
  commercial interchange, development of, 313
    reservation of U.S. delegation, 313
  communications, 318
  conflicts, condemnation of, 302
  continental solidarity in observance of treaties, 300
  coordination of resolutions of meetings, 328
  diplomatic relations, breaking of, 293
  economic collaboration, 318
  economy, maintenance of internal, 308
  espionage, investigation of, 299
  Good Neighbor policy, 302
  health and sanitary conditions, 324
  humanitarian and health, 323
  inland countries, commercial facilities for, 317
  Inter-American Bank, 315
  Inter-American Defense Board, 305
  Inter-American Development Commission, 314
  Inter-American Juridical Committee, 326
    reservation of Peruvian delegation, 328
  Inter-American Statistical Institute, 316
  international stabilization fund, 317
  investments, 316
  Japanese aggression, condemnation of, 303

law, affirmation of traditional theory of, 328
"minorities," non-recognition of, 300
non-American countries, interests of, 304
occupied countries, relations with, 305
penal colonies of non-American nations on American territory, 304
police and judicial measures, Inter-American conf. on coordination of, 297
post-war problems, 325
raw materials, utilization of, 316
Red Cross, 323
reservations:
  Argentine delegation, 312
  Chilean delegation, 293
  Guatemalan delegation, 329
  Peruvian delegation, 301, 328
  U.S. delegation, 313
sabotage, investigation of, 299
severance of commercial and financial relations, 310
stabilization fund, international, 317
strategic materials, 305
subversive activities, 293
  memorandum on regulation of, 295
  systems of investigation, 299
telecommunications, 322
transportation facilities, mobilization of, 318
treaties, continental solidarity in observance of, 300
  reservation of Peruvian delegation, 301
war, humanization of, 324
Good Neighbor policy, resolution of Rio Conf. on, 302
Highway, Inter-American. See Inter-American Highway.
Inter-American Commission for Territorial Administration, 333
Inter-American Development Commission, 165, 314, 403
Inter-American Highway. See that title.
Inter-American Maritime Commission, resolution of Inter-American

war in:
message of Pres. Roosevelt to peo-
ple of Philippines, Dec. 28, 1941,
575
notes exchanged between Pres.
Roosevelt and Pres. Quezon,
Dec. 9 and 11, 1941, 574–5
Physics, Int. Union of, 836
Pink Star, S.S., sinking, 87
Poland:
Atlantic Charter, observations on, by
representative at Inter-Allied
Meeting, 219
Central and Eastern European Planning Board. *See that title.*
Czechoslovakia, relations with:
agreement for confederation, 273
joint communiqué, 275
joint declaration at Inter-Allied
Meeting, 221
German war crimes, declaration on,
663
message of Pres. Roosevelt to people
of, 664
U.S.S.R., re-establishment of rela-
tions with:
agreement, July 30, 1941, 260
joint declaration of friendship and
mutual aid, Dec. 4, 1941, 261
war, declarations, etc., table, 204–7
Police and Judicial Measures, Inter-
American Conf. on, 297, 868
Policy, American foreign, statements
on, 1–79 (*see also under subject head-
ings*)
Policy and principles, general state-
ments on, 1–79
Polish-Czechoslovak Confederation, 273
Postage stamps, importation blocked,
741
Post-war organization:
addresses:
Acting Secy. Welles:
July 22, 1941, 1
Oct. 7, 1941, 690
May 30, 1942, 71
British Secy. of State for Foreign
Affairs, July 29, 1941, 587
Pres. Roosevelt to Int. Labor
Conf., Nov. 6, 1941, 32
Soviet Ambassador at London be-
fore Inter-Allied Meeting, Sept.
24, 1941, 214
Vice Pres. Wallace to Free World
Assoc., May 8, 1942, 62

Atlantic Charter. *See that title.*
Central and Eastern European Plan-
ning Board. *See that title.*
Great Britain-U.S.S.R.:
conferences in Moscow, 253
Treaty of Alliance, 254
Inter-Allied Meetings, London. *See
that title.*
I.L.O. Conf., resolution of, Nov. 5,
1941, 839
International Wheat Meeting, Wash-
ington. *See that title.*
lend-lease agreements, role of, 233
Rio Conf., resolution, 325
statement by Secy. Hull on int.
trade, 69
Price Administration, Office of, 165, 723
export price regulation, 734
Prince of Wales, British warship, 147
Principles and policy, general statements on American, 1–79
Priorities. *See* Export control.
Prisoners of War. *See* Persons and
property, treatment of.
Proclaimed List of Certain Blocked
Nationals, 752
Proclamations:
alien enemies, prescribing regulations
for, Jan. 14, 1942, 817
arms, ammunition and implements
of war, export of, Apr. 9, 1942,
737
blocked nationals, proclaimed list of,
and control of certain exports,
July 17, 1941, 753
export control, list of, and schedules,
726
exports, control of certain, July 17,
1941, 753
Free French, to inhabitants of St.
Pierre and Miquelon, Dec. 24, 1941,
465
German nationals, citizens, denizens
or subjects designated as "alien
enemies," Dec. 8, 1941, 823
International Load Line Convention,
suspension of, Aug. 9, 1941, 774
Italian nationals, citizens, denizens or
subjects designated as "alien
enemies," Dec. 8, 1941, 823
Japanese subjects as enemy aliens,
and prescribing regulations governing conduct of same, Dec. 7, 1941,
817–23

U.S. Naval Academy, training given to citizens of American Republics, 353

Uruguay:
  Axis plot to seize govt., 18
  declaration of solidarity and non-belligerency, 339–40
  memorandum of Acting Secy. Welles to Minister Richling, 334
  memorandum of Alberto Guani on aggression and hemisphere defense, 333
  note of United Kingdom on foreign-flag vessels in American ports, 405
  severance of diplomatic relations with Axis Powers, 339–40
  trade agreement with U.S., notice of intention to negotiate, 695

V

Venezuela:
  declaration of solidarity and non-belligerency, 340
  economic mission, statement of chairman of the Economic Defense Board, 356
  severance of diplomatic relations with Axis Powers, 340
  soil conservation mission of U.S. experts, 357

Vinson-Trammell Act, Mar. 27, 1934, 147

W

W. C. Teagle, S.S., sinking, 87

Wake Island, 38, 47, 51

Wallace, Henry A.:
  statement on Venezuelan Economic Mission, 356
  The Price of Free World Victory, address, May 8, 1942, 62

Wang Ching-wei regime in China:
  adherence to Anti-Comintern Pact, 201
  joint statement of Japanese Premier and president of, 490
  statement of Japanese President of the Board of Information, 491

War:
  aims:
    Great Britain, 587
    occupied countries, 663
    U.S.S.R., 615
  American entrance into:
    Bulgaria:
      declaration of war by Bulgaria, 123
      war message of Pres. Roosevelt to Cong., 123
      joint resolution declaring war, 124
    Germany:
      declaration of war by Germany, 118–9
      war message of Pres. Roosevelt to Cong., 121
      joint resolution declaring war, 122
    Hungary:
      declaration of war by Hungary, 123
      war message of Pres. Roosevelt to Cong., 123
      joint resolution declaring war, 124
    Italy:
      inquiry of Italian Ambassador regarding status, 121
      notification of state of war by Italy, 120
      war message of Pres. Roosevelt to Cong., 121
      joint resolution declaring war, 122
    Japan (*see also that title*):
      message of Pres. to nation on attack by, Dec. 15, 1941, 113
      Pearl Harbor, attack on:
        Roberts Commission report, 152
      rescript of Emperor Hirohito, 115
      war message of Pres. Roosevelt to Cong., Dec. 8, 1941, 116
      joint resolution declaring war, 118
    Rumania:
      declaration of war by Rumania, 122
      war message of Pres. Roosevelt to Cong., 123
      joint resolution declaring war, 124
  appropriations. *See that title.*
  Combined Boards. *See that title.*
  coordination of war effort, in U.S., 239–62
  cost, estimated, U.S., 50